CALENDAR OF PAPAL REGISTERS

GENERAL EDITOR
LEONARD E. BOYLE OP
PREFECT OF THE VATICAN LIBRARY

Reg. Lat. 1078, fo 71ʳ (c. 75% of actual size); the hand is that of Giuliano Marasca of Mantua. See Calendar no. 394

COIMISIÚN LÁIMHSCRÍBHINNÍ NA hÉIREANN

CALENDAR OF ENTRIES IN THE

PAPAL REGISTERS

RELATING TO

GREAT BRITAIN AND IRELAND

PAPAL LETTERS, Vol. XVII, PART I
ALEXANDER VI (1492 - 1503)
LATERAN REGISTERS
PART TWO: 1495 - 1503

EDITED BY

ANNE P. FULLER

DUBLIN
IRISH MANUSCRIPTS COMMISSION
1994

Typeset by Tony Moreau and printed in the Republic of Ireland by
ColourBooks Limited, Baldoyle, Dublin 23.

ISBN 1 874280 04 5

CONTENTS

The Centenary of the Calendars
Leslie J. Macfarlane, Chairman, CPR New Series Project vii

Editor's Preface xi

Table of Abbreviations and Symbols xv

Chronological Table of Letters xix

Concordance lxiii

Calendar Text 1

Rubricellae of Lost Letters 641

Index of Persons and Places 657

Index of Subjects 881

THE CENTENARY OF THE CALENDARS

The publication of this volume, a century after the appearance of Vol I of the *Calendars*, provides a fitting opportunity not only to look briefly at the circumstances which led to the initiation and subsequent progress of the series, but also to reflect on its achievement as a whole. Long before 1894, of course, the Vatican Archives were known to contain a vast amount of source material which could supply evidence critical to the ecclesiastical history of most European nations, and to their political relations with the Holy See, and in fact the transcribing of a considerable number of papal documents containing such evidence had been permitted by the Vatican authorities at the request of the British government as early as 1825. It was not until 1881, however, when Leo XIII opened the Archives for public consultation, that scholars, supported by their governments, were at last freely able to extract, translate and publish the information they sought in order to augment the records already held in their own national, diocesan and monastic repositories at home. This being so, W.H.Bliss, following in the pioneer footsteps of Joseph Stevenson, was sent off to Rome in 1889 by Henry Maxwell Lyte, the Deputy Keeper of the Public Record Office, with the mandate "to provide an English Calendar of all the entries in the Papal Regesta of the Middle Ages which illustrate the history of Gt Britain and Ireland".

Thus it came about that between 1894 and 1960, fourteen volumes of the *Calendars*, drawn from the Vatican and Lateran Registers and covering the period between 1198 and 1492, were published by HMSO under the auspices of the PRO, Bliss editing Vols I and II alone, Vol III with C.A.Johnson, Vols IV and V with J.A.Twemlow, and Twemlow editing Vol VI to XIV alone, after which the PRO was no longer able to sustain the series, which the Irish Manuscripts Commission then generously undertook to continue. Accordingly, in 1970, Dr. Michael Haren was appointed by the IMC to edit Vol XV, and in 1972 the British Academy awarded Mrs. Anne Fuller a major grant to commence editing Vol XVI, thus allowing the series to continue anew on a double front under the General Editorship of the Rev. Professor L.E.Boyle OP, now Prefect of the Vatican Library. As work on the series progressed, however, it became clear that despite the considerable achievement of the earlier *Calendars*, Bliss's original editorial policy was in need of revision, in that although he quite properly examined successive registers page by page, and noticed entries in their due order, he gave only abstracts of, or extracts from all the enregistered letters, he omitted formal clauses of frequent occurrence, left the date of each entry in its Latin form, and given the inability of the scribes compiling the registers to grapple with English, Irish, Welsh and Scottish place names and surnames, he understandably left them in their original and frequently unrecognisable form. It was therefore imperative to devise a new editorial policy which would at least ensure that a full rendering of the historical information contained in each register entry would be given, and its previously omitted legal clauses accounted for, that the Latin dating of each entry would be given its English equivalent, and that the rendering of problematic personal and place names would be standardised and their variants given in full in the index. As the editors worked away on their volumes in the Vatican Archives, however, and became increasingly absorbed in the extensive historical and prosopographical literature which had been published on Chancery procedures and papal diplomatic since the days of Bliss and Twemlow, it also became clear that this information would not only help them to resolve a number of their own textual problems, but that they themselves would now be able to provide the basis for a new and authoritative study of the papal Chancery which English readers had long required since the works of R.L.Poole, Geoffrey Barraclough and Christopher Cheney had first appeared.

The editors of the new series, therefore, have not only rectified the textual shortcomings of the earlier *Calendars*, but they have also encompassed within the introductions to their volumes a wealth of entirely new information which considerably extends our present knowledge of the workings of the papal Chancery in the later Middle Ages and Renaissance period. In the introduction to Vol XV, for example, following Professor Boyle's account of the processes through which a supplication to the Chancery had to pass before it emerged as a letter of grace, Dr.Haren has included a classified table and discussion on the main types of business dealt with in the letters, a classification and explanation of those legal clauses which the Chancery employed either to restrict or amplify the contents of a letter, and a concluding schedule of these clauses as they appear *seriatim* in the Calendar, thus enabling readers to ensure that nothing of consequence has been omitted from any of the English texts. Likewise in the introduction to Vol XVI, Mrs. Fuller's close study of the scribes, abbreviators and masters working in the Chancery during the pontificate of Alexander VI, has enabled her not only to identify them and to explain the meaning of their tax marks, but also to demonstrate the real, as opposed to the supposed, role of these papal officials in the sequence of events between the engrossment of a letter and its enregistration. In this sense, therefore, given its attractive new layout, its revealing introductions, clear English texts, massively detailed indexes, and much other useful information like the inclusion of the tables of lost bulls however brief their information, it is not surprising that the new series has been widely acclaimed as a landmark in the hundred years history of the project, and one which augurs well for its final run up to the Reformation.

It is fitting in conclusion, then, as we reflect on the series published so far, that we should remember the debt we owe to those who have produced it over the years. Henry Maxwell Lyte may not have realised the magnitude of the task he had set W.H.Bliss when he sent him off to the Vatican Archives in 1889, but he undoubtedly recognised that the information they contained would greatly enlarge our understanding of the religious and political history of Gt. Britain and Ireland throughout the Middle Ages, the Renaissance and Reformation periods, and his having persuaded the British government of the day to sustain the work and inaugurate the publication of the *Calendars* has justly earned him the gratitude of historians ever since. Nor should we forget that the British and Irish governments, through the British Academy and Irish Manuscripts Commission, have generously continued to commit themselves to this project since the new series began. We also have reason to be grateful for the tireless support of Dr.Brian Trainor, the Chairman of the Irish Manuscripts Commission, and of his predecessor in office, Dr.Donal Cregan, who have steered Vols XV to XVIII through to their publication, and who have done so much to make the series more widely known. Again, the project has gained appreciably by the setting up of a consultative committee whose members have specialised knowledge on particular localities or subjects, upon which the editors may usefully draw. Recent welcome additions to it include Professors Patrick Collinson, Jane Sayers, Art Cosgrove, Drs. Brendan Bradshaw and Patrick Zutshi, although it is with keen regret that we have to record the early death, in December 1990, of Professor Ian Cowan, our very helpful representative on Scottish matters. Finally, when we recall that the value of purely archival publications like these Calendars depends entirely on the accuracy of the texts and the reliability of the ancillary information they are able to offer, it is fitting that we should remember with gratitude the palaeographical and translational skills, dedication and tenacity of Bliss, Twemlow and our present editors, and their editor in chief, who have made all this rich source material available to the world of scholars and historians. Our debt to them remains incalculable.

Department of History
University of Aberdeen

LESLIE J. MACFARLANE
Chairman, CPR New Series Project

EDITOR'S PREFACE

Far more registers have come down to us from the pontificate of Alexander VI (1492 - 1503) than from that of any of his predecessors. The present volume of the *Calendar* carries on from where the editor's previous volume (*CPL* XVI) left off and covers the remaining chancery registers of Alexander, namely *Reg. Lat.* 1027-1126, 1128, 1129, 1129A, 1275 and 1406, as well as the relevant section (7-11 Alexander) of *Reg. Lat.* 2463 (a modern made-up volume). A freak letter (of 1504) in *Reg. Lat.* 1150 — a register of Julius II — is also calendared. Altogether, one thousand and thirty-eight letters of British and Irish interest have been collected from the one hundred and seven registers. The selection brings to light several items of outstanding interest, including Richard Kidderminster's statutes for Winchcombe Abbey (no. 394) and a letter of Alexander III (1159 - 1181) (no. 174). Tudor specialists will also note that Wolsey makes his *début*. In addition to the extant letters, *rubricellae* or brief summaries of another three hundred and four letters from chancery registers now lost have been extracted from the remaining portion (*Anni VII-Anni XII*) of the *Index Bullarum Alexandri VI* (*Ind.* 341, 342 and 343). Alexander's Vatican Registers, which contain letters expedited by the camera, by the apostolic secretariate and by his domestic secretaries, will be calendared in volume XVII, Part II.

The CPR is a collaborative enterprise and the present instalment of the Calendar is, like the previous one, the outcome of Anglo-Irish cooperation. The editor is again grateful to the British Academy for the series of generous awards which enabled her to prepare the volume; and to the Irish Manuscripts Commission for publishing it. The project is fortunate in its sponsors.

And the editor in her colleagues. Throughout the volume's preparation she has enjoyed the constant support and encouragement of Professor L.E.Boyle,OP, Prefect of the Vatican Library and General Editor of the series. He has seen the entire Calendar Text in typescript; verified readings; made numerous helpful suggestions; and repeatedly saved the editor from error. Without his guidance, inspiration and scholarship the calendar would not have been completed. The editor is also greatly indebted to Dr. L.J. Macfarlane, Chairman of the Consultative Committee, for the business-like way in which he has administered the Academy's awards and for much kindness and consideration. Professor Jane E.Sayers, who takes over the Chairmanship on Dr. Macfarlane's retirement, inherits a model administration.

The present volume could not have been prepared without the goodwill of two great institutions. Special thanks are due to the authorities of the Archivio Segreto Vaticano for permission (readily given) to inspect the original registers; and to the National Library of Ireland for the loan of the microfilm selection which formed the basis of the calendar. Mons. Charles Burns, Senior Archivist at the Vatican, and Dr. Patricia Donlon, Director of the National Library, have both, in their different spheres, facilitated the editor's work. The resources of other libraries and archives have also been drawn upon. The editor thanks the staffs of the British Library; the

Institute of Historical Research; the Public Record Office, London; Worcester Cathedral Library; Hereford and Worcester Record Office; and (not least) Dr. Williams's Library, London.

The move from computerised volume to print was attended with unforeseen technical problems. The editor is grateful to Professor Gearóid MacNiocaill of University College, Galway, who skilfully contrived the conversion of her disks; to Mr. Tony Moreau of Dublin for his expert typesetting and unfailing good humour; and to Dr. Brian Trainor, Chairman of the Commission, for coordinating the printing process and some very helpful time-tabling.

A.P.F., London, 1994

CONSULTATIVE COMMITTEE

The Rev. Dr. Brendan Bradshaw
Queens' College, University of Cambridge

Mgr. Charles Burns
Senior Archivist, Vatican Archives, Vatican City, Rome

Patrick Collinson
Regius Professor of Modern History, Trinity College, University of Cambridge

Mgr. Patrick J. Corish
Professor Emeritus of Modern History, St Patrick's College, Maynooth

Art Cosgrove
Professor of Medieval History, University College, Dublin

A. Geoffrey Dickens
Professor Emeritus of History, University of London

Sir Geoffrey Elton
Regius Professor Emeritus, Clare College, University of Cambridge

† Denys Hay
Professor Emeritus of Medieval and Renaissance History, University of Edinburgh

James F. Lydon
Lecky Professor of History, Trinity College, Dublin

Leslie J. Macfarlane
Department of History, University of Aberdeen
Chairman

Gearóid MacNiocaill
Professor of History, University College, Galway

Francis X. Martin OSA
Professor Emeritus of Medieval History, University College, Dublin

Professor Jane Sayers
School of Library, Archive and Information Studies, University College, London

J. J. Scarisbrick
Professor of History, University of Warwick, Coventry

Brian Trainor
Chairman, Irish Manuscripts Commission, Dublin

Patrick Zutshi
Keeper of Manuscripts and University Archives, University of Cambridge

TABLE OF ABBREVIATIONS AND SYMBOLS

AH   *Archivium Hibernicum*

Annates, Ardfert   'Obligationes pro Annatis Diocesis Ardfertensis',
                                     ed. J. O'Connell, *AH*, XXI (1958), pp.1-51

Annates, Clonfert   'Obligationes pro Annatis Diocesis Clonfertensis',
                                     ed. P.K. Egan, *AH*, XXI (1958), pp.52-74

Annates, Cork   'Obligationes pro Annatis Diocesis Corcagiensis',
                                     ed.Sister M. Angela Bolster, *AH*, XXIX (1970), pp.1-32

Annates, Killaloe   'Obligationes pro Annatis Diocesis Laonensis, 1421-1535',
                                     ed.D.F.Gleeson, *AH*, X (1943), pp.1-103

Annates, Limerick   'Obligationes pro Annatis Diocesis Limiricensis, 1421-1519',
                                     ed. M.Moloney, *AH*, X (1943), pp. 104-162

Annates, Lismore   'Obligationes pro Annatis Diocesis Lismorensis, 1426-1529',
                                     ed. P.Power, *AH*, XII (1946), pp. 15-61

Annates, Ossory   'Obligationes pro Annatis Diocesis Ossoriensis, 1413-1531',
                                     ed. T.J.Clohosey, *AH*, XX (1957), pp. 1-37

Annates, Tuam Province   'Obligationes pro Annatis Provinciae Tuamensis',
                                     ed. J.F. O'Doherty, *AH*, XXVI (1963), pp. 56-117

Annates, Ulster   *De Annatis Hiberniae, I: Ulster*, ed. M.A.Costello, Dublin,
                                     1912

Annates, Waterford   'Obligationes pro Annatis Diocesis Waterfordnesis [!],
                                     1421-1507', ed. P.Power, *AH*, XII (1946), pp.1-14

ASV   Archivio Segreto Vaticano

BA   Bachelor of Arts

BDec   Bachelor of Canon Law

Brady, *Episcopal Succession*	W. Maziere Brady, *The Episcopal Succession in England Scotland and Ireland, A.D. 1400 to 1875*, I, II (Rome, 1876), III (Rome, 1877)
BTheol	Bachelor of Theology
CPL	*Calendar of Entries in the Papal Registers relating to Great Britain and Ireland : Papal Letters*, ed. W.H.Bliss, C.Johnson, J.A.Twemlow, M.J.Haren, and A.P.Fuller, 17 vv. to date, London and Dublin, 1893-1989
d.	in *or* of the diocese of
DDec	Doctor of Canon Law
ds.	in *or* of the dioceses of
DTheol	Doctor of Theology
Emden, *Oxford to 1500*	A.B.Emden, *A Biographical Register of the University of Oxford to A.D. 1500*, 3 vv, Oxford, 1957
HWRO	Hereford and Worcester Record Office
Ind.	ASV, *Indici*
Lic A	Licentiate in Arts
Lic UI	Licentiate in both Laws
LLB	Bachelor of Laws
LLD	Doctor of Laws
MA	Master of Arts
MMed	Master of Medicine
MTheol	Master of Theology
OCarm	Carmelite Order
OCist	Cistercian Order
OClun	Cluniac Order

OESA	Augustinian Order (Friars Hermits)
OFM	Franciscan Order
OP	Dominican Order
OPrem	Premonstratensian Order
OSA	Augustinian Order (canons regular)
OSB	Benedictine Order
OTrin	Trinitarian Order
PRO	Public Record Office (London)
Reg. Lat.	ASV, *Registra Lateranensia*
Regs. King & Castello	*The Registers of Oliver King Bishop of Bath and Wells 1496-1503 and Hadrian de Castello Bishop of Bath and Wells 1503-1518*, ed. H.Maxwell-Lyte, Somerset Record Society, v. LIV, 1939
Sayers	J.E.Sayers, *Original papal documents in Lambeth Palace Library*, Bulletin of the Institute of Historical Research, Special Supplement vi (1967)
UIB	Bachelor of both Laws
UID	Doctor of both Laws
[ ]	enclose words supplied by the editor
< >	enclose insertions by registry staff

in nos. 174 and 394:-

/	when it has a footnote reference number, represents a deleted word or letter

in no. 174 and in the *Rubricellae*:-

.	placed beneath a letter, indicates that the reading of that letter is doubtful

CHRONOLOGICAL TABLE OF LETTERS

Note. The letters,which are calendared below in register order, are here arranged in order of the dates under which they are drawn. Other particulars are included in the table so that the passage of a letter through the bureaucracy and the manner of its impetration can (in outline, at least) be read at a glance. (*See CPL* XVI, p.lxiv). 'E&W' means that the letter is of English and Welsh interest; 'S' of Scottish interest; 'I' of Irish. The diocese and (if any) order is that of the petitioner. *Consistoriales* and related letters are asterisked and the name then is that of the benefice concerned. Other information is self explanatory. Nos. 51, 73, 106, 115, 504, 860, 901, 902 , 999 and 1038 are undated.

DATE Rome, St. Peter's unless otherwise noted[1]	DATE OF EXPEDITION IN THE *BULLARIA*	*REG. LAT.*	COUNTRY, DIOCESE, ORDER, ETC.	CAL. ENTRY NO.
1495, 5 Sep.	————	1103, fos 287ʳ-288ʳ	E&W (York; OSA)	742
1496, 8 July	————	1087, fos 99ᵛ-100ᵛ	E&W (Salisbury)	503
1496, 23 Dec.	————	1093, fos 110ᵛ-111ʳ	E&W (Salisbury)	557
1497, 13 Feb.	————	1093, fos 211ᵛ-212ʳ	E&W (York)	566
1497, 14 Feb.	————	1093, fos 230ᵛ-231ᵛ	E&W (Exeter)	568
1497, 18 Feb.	————	1093, fos 167ᵛ-168ʳ	E&W (Lincoln; OSA)	563
1497, 7 Mar.	————	1093, fo 212ʳ⁻ᵛ	E&W (Coventry & Lichfield)	567
1497, 3 Apr.	————	1035, fos 180ʳ-181ᵛ	S (Lismore)*	55
"	————	1035, fo 182ʳ	S (Lismore)*	56
"	————	1035, fo 183ʳ⁻ᵛ	S (Lismore)*	58
1497, 4 Apr.	————	1035, fo 182ᵛ	S (Lismore)*	57
1497, 22 Apr.	————	1093, fos 316ʳ-317ʳ	S (Glasgow)	572
1497, 29 May	————	1093, fos 156ʳ-157ʳ	E&W (London)	559
1497, 30 May	————	1093, fos 153ᵛ-154ᵛ	S (Dunkeld)	558
1497, 20 June	————	1093, fos 93ʳ-94ᵛ	E&W (Coventry & Lichfield)	556
1497, 5 Aug.	————	1093, fo 166ʳ⁻ᵛ	E&W (Bath & Wells)	561
"	————	1093, fo 169ʳ⁻ᵛ	E&W (Lincoln)	565

[1] For Alexander's itinerary, *see CPL* XVI, pp.lvii-lxiii

DATE Rome, St. Peter's unless otherwise noted	DATE OF EXPEDITION IN THE *BULLARIA*	*REG. LAT.*	COUNTRY, DIOCESE, ORDER, ETC.	CAL. ENTRY NO.
1497, 11 Aug.	———————	1093, fos 168^v-169^r	E&W (London; OSA)	564
1497, 15 Aug.	———————	1093, fo 165^{r-v}	E&W (Lincoln)	560
"	———————	1093, fo 167^{r-v}	E&W (Lincoln)	562
1497, 5 Sep.	———————	1027, fos 191^v-192^r	E&W (Worcester)	10
1497, 23 Sep.	———————	1027, fos 131^v-132^r	E&W (Canterbury; OSA)	7
1497, 29 Sep.	———————	1027, fo 131^r	E&W (Bath & Wells; OSA)	6
1497, 2 Oct.	———————	1027, fos 193^v-194^r	E&W (Lincoln)	11
1497, 3 Oct.	———————	1027, fos 186^r-187^v	E&W (London)	8
1497, 6 Oct.	———————	1027, fos 189^v-190^r	E&W (Hereford)	9
1497, 7 Oct.	———————	1027, fos 194^v-195^r	E&W (Lincoln; OSA)	12
"	———————	1027, fo 195^{r-v}	E&W (Exeter; OCist)	13
1497, 20 Oct.[1]	———————	1093, fos 297^v-298^r	E&W (Lincoln; OSA)	571
1497, 16 Dec.	———————	1093, fo 296^{r-v}	E&W (Lincoln)	569
"	———————	1093, fos 296^v-297^v	E&W (Coventry & Lichfield)	570
1498, 8 Jan.	———————	1027, fo 70^{r-v}	E&W (Lincoln)	2
"	———————	1027, fo 71^{r-v}	E&W (Norwich)	3
"	———————	1027, fo 72^{r-v}	E&W (Bath & Wells)	4
"	———————	1031, fos 141^v-142^v	E&W (Worcester)	39
1498, 9 Jan.	———————	1027, fos 66^r-67^v	S (King of Scots)	1
1498, 29 Jan.	———————	1027, fos 73^v-74^v	S (St Andrews)	5
1498, 19 Feb.	———————	1093, fos 403^v-406^v	I (*dioc. wanting*)	576
1498, 20 Feb.	———————	1036, fos 92^r-93^r	S (king of Scots; Aberdeen)	64
1498, 26 Feb.	———————	1093, fos 372^r-374^r	I (Lismore; OSA)	573

[1] Ostia

DATE Rome, St. Peter's unless otherwise noted	DATE OF EXPEDITION IN THE *BULLARIA*	*REG. LAT.*	COUNTRY, DIOCESE, ORDER, ETC.	CAL. ENTRY NO.
1498, 3 Mar.	————	1093, fos 391^V-394^V	I (Ossory)	575
1498, 7 Mar.	————	1093, fos 387^r-391^V	I (Cashel)	574
1498, 14 Mar.	————	1096, fos 272^r-273^r	S (Ross)*	637
"	————	1096, fo 273^V	S (Ross)*	639
"	————	1096, fo 273^V	S (Ross)*	640
1498, 15 Mar.	————	1096, fo 273^r	S (Ross)*	638
1498, 10 Apr.	————	1031, fo 138^{r-V}	E&W (Coventry & Lichfield)	35
"	————	1031, fos 138^V-139^V	E&W (Norwich)	36
"	————	1031, fos 139^V-140^r	E&W (Exeter; OCist)	37
"	————	1031, fos 140^V-141^r	E&W (Coventry & Lichfield)	38
"	————	1031, fos 142^V-143^V	E&W (Exeter)	40
1498, 18 Apr.	————	1030, fos 2^V-3^r	E&W (York)	19
1498, 30 Apr.	————	1035, fo 3^{r-V}	I (Emly)*	52
"	————	1035, fo 4^r	I (Emly)*	53
"	————	1035, fo 4^V	I (Emly)*	54
1498, 2 May	————	1036, fos 244^V-245^V	S (Dunkeld)	65
1498, 22 May	————	1031, fos 43^r-44^r	E&W (Lincoln; Gilb)	30
1498, 29 May	1498, 16 June	1028, fos 202^r-204^V	I (Killaloe)	14
1498, 12 June	————	1029, fos 1^r-6^r	I (Clonfert)	16
"	————	1031, fo 127^{r-V}	E&W (Norwich)	31
"	————	1031, fo 128^r	E&W (Exeter; OCist)	32
"	————	1031, fos 128^V-129^r	E&W (Chichester)	33
"	————	1031, fos 129^r-130^r	E&W (Winchester)	34
1498, 15 June	————	1029, fo 222^{r-V}	E&W (Lincoln)	17
1498, 23 June	————	1028, fos 230^V-233^r	I (Cloyne)	15

DATE Rome, St. Peter's unless otherwise noted	DATE OF EXPEDITION IN THE *BULLARIA*	*REG. LAT.*	COUNTRY, DIOCESE, ORDER, ETC.	CAL. ENTRY NO.
1498, 14 July	——————	1036, fos 260^v-262^v	S (St Andrews)	66
1498, 20 July	——————	1036, fos 11^r-12^v	S (Paisley)*	61
"	——————	1036, fos 90^r-91^v	S (Paisley)*	63
1498, 25 July	——————	1031, fos 19^v-21^v	E&W (Winchester and Lincoln)	28
1498, 27 July	——————	1029, fo 252^{r-v}	I (Meath)	18
"	——————	1030, fo 69^{r-v}	E&W (Norwich)	25
"	——————	1030, fos 70^r-71^r	E&W (Salisbury)	26
"	——————	1031, fo 178^{r-v}	E&W (Exeter, Lincoln)	41
1498, 28 July	——————	1030, fo 50^{r-v}	E&W (Hereford; OSB)	20
"	——————	1030, fos 53^v-54^v	E&W (Bath & Wells)	21
1498, 1 Aug.	——————	1030, fos 54^v-55^r	I (Meath; OSA)	22
1498, 2 Aug.	——————	1031, fos 21^v-23^r	E&W (Worcester)	29
1498, 4 Aug.	——————	1036, fos 36^v-37^r	E&W (Lincoln)	62
1498, 9 Aug.	——————	1030, fo 103^r	S (Glasgow; OClun)	27
1498, 18 Aug.	——————	1030, fos 60^r-61^r	E&W (Bath & Wells)	23
"	——————	1030, fos 61^r-62^r	E&W (Chichester)	24
1498, 21 Aug.	——————	1039, fo 181^{r-v}	E&W (Winchester; OSA)	87
1498, 1 Sep.	——————	1039, fos 116^r-117^v	E&W (Exeter)	85
1498, 3 Sep.	——————	1039, fo 95^r	S (Brechin)	83
1498, 7 Sep.	——————	1033, fo 341^{r-v}	E&W (Lincoln; OSB)	49
1498, 13 Sep.	——————	1039, fos 62^r-63^v	S (Glasgow)	80
1498, 24 Sep.	1498, 2 Oct.	1034, fos 245^r-246^r	S (Aberdeen)	50
1498, 25 Sep.	——————	1039, fos 74^r-75^r	E&W (Ely)	81
1498, 29 Sep.	——————	1039, fos 75^r-76^r	E&W (Salisbury)	82
1498, 6 Oct.	——————	1039, fo 14^v	E&W (*dioc. wanting*)	76

DATE Rome, St. Peter's unless otherwise noted	DATE OF EXPEDITION IN THE *BULLARIA*	*REG. LAT.*	COUNTRY, DIOCESE, ORDER, ETC.	CAL. ENTRY NO.
1498, 10 Oct.	——————	1045, fos 127^r-128^v	S (Glasgow)	130
1498, 18 Oct.	——————	1053, fo 77^{r-v}	E&W (Lincoln)	194
1498, 3 Nov.	——————	1033, fos 309^v-310^v	E&W (Norwich)	47
1498, 10 Nov.	——————	1039, fos 210^v-211^v	E&W (Exeter)	90
"	——————	1048, fos 132^r-133^r	E&W (Canterbury)	168
1498, 13 Nov.	——————	1049, fos 90^r-91^r	E&W (Lincoln)	176
1498, 20 Nov.	——————	1039, fos 105^r-106^r	E&W (Winchester)	84
"	——————	1039, fos 310^v-311^v	E&W (Lincoln)	95
"	——————	1039, fos 312^r-313^r	E&W (Winchester)	96
"	——————	1042, fos 164^r-166^v	E&W (Bangor)	118
1498, 24 Nov.	——————	1033, fos 103^r-104^r	E&W (Coventry & Lichfield)	44
"	——————	1033, fos 104^r-105^r	E&W (Lincoln)	45
"	——————	1039, fos 313^v-314^r	E&W (*none*; OFM)	97
1498, 1 Dec.	——————	1039, fos 232^v-234^r	E&W (Salisbury, Lincoln)	91
1498, 3 Dec.	——————	1039, fos 173^v-174^v	S (Glasgow)	86
"	——————	1039, fos 314^v-315^v	E&W (Salisbury)	98
"	——————	1039, fos 315^v-316^v	E&W (London)	99
1498, 5 Dec.	——————	1039, fos 299^v-300^v	E&W (London)	93
1498, 6 Dec.	——————	1039, fos 246^r-247^r	E&W (York; OClun)	92
1498, 15 Dec.	——————	1033, fos 12^v-13^r	E&W (Norwich; OPrem)	42
"	——————	1053, fo 78^{r-v}	E&W (Canterbury)	195
1498, 18 Dec.	——————	1039, fos 319^r-320^r	E&W (York)	100
1498, 21 Dec.	——————	1039, fos 303^v-304^v	E&W (Durham; [OSB])	94
1498, 23 Dec.	——————	1039, fos 35^r-36^v	E&W (Bath & Wells)	77

DATE Rome, St. Peter's unless otherwise noted	DATE OF EXPEDITION IN THE *BULLARIA*	*REG. LAT.*	COUNTRY, DIOCESE, ORDER, ETC.	CAL. ENTRY NO.
"	———	1039, fos 42^r-43^r	E&W (Worcester)	78
"	———	1039, fos 43^r-44^r	E&W (Chichester)	79
1498, 24 Dec.	———	1035, fos 257^r-258^v	E&W (Worcester)*	59
"	———	1035, fos 258^v-259^r	E&W (Worcester)*	60
1498, 27 Dec.	———	1039, fos 192^r-193^r	E&W (Canterbury)	88
"	———	1039, fos 193^v-194^v	E&W (Exeter)	89
1498, 28 Dec.	1499, 5 March	1038, fos 231^v-234^v	I (Ardfert)	72
1499, 9 Jan.	1499, 19 Jan.	1038, fos 55^v-57^v	S (Aberdeen)	68
1499, 19 Jan.	———	1033, fos 13^v-14^v	E&W (London; OSA)	43
1499, 24 Jan.	———	1117, fos 207^v-209^r	E&W (London, York)	873
1499, 28 Jan.[1]	1499, 28 Feb.	1043, fos 39^v-41^v	I (Clonfert)	123
1499, 29 Jan.[1]	1499, 23 Feb.	1043, fos 25^r-27^r	I (Tuam)	122
" [1]	———	1043, fos 318^v-321^r	I (Tuam; OSA)	127
" [1]	———	1048, fos 90^r-93^r	I (Elphin)	164
1499, 30 Jan.[1]	1499, 5 March	1038, fos 260^v-264^v	I (Tuam)	75
" [1]	1499, 28 Feb.	1048, fos 94^v-97^r	I (Tuam)	165
" [1]	1499, 5 March	1048, fos 100^r-103^r	I (Tuam)	166
1499, 4 Feb.	1499, 6 March	1043, fos 46^v-48^r	I (Killala)	124
1499, 5 Feb.	1499, 5 March	1043, fos 50^r-51^v	I (Tuam)	126
1499, 14 Feb.	1499, 6 March	1038, fos 259^r-260^v	I (Cloyne)	74
1499, 15 Feb.	———	1094, fos 250^v-253^r	I (Cork & Cloyne)*	610
"	———	1094, fo 253^{r-v}	I (Cork & Cloyne)*	611
1499, 17 Feb.	———	1042, fos 197^r-198^r	I (Cork & Cloyne)*	121
1499, 20 Feb.	1499, 2 March	1043, fos 48^r-50^r	I (Ardfert)	125
1499, 22 Feb.	———	1049, fos 70^r-71^r	E&W (Winchester)	175
1499, 23 Feb.	———	1033, fos 258^v-259^v	E&W (Lincoln; OSB *for* OCist)	46

[1] Ostia

DATE Rome, St. Peter's unless otherwise noted	DATE OF EXPEDITION IN THE *BULLARIA*	*REG. LAT.*	COUNTRY, DIOCESE, ORDER, ETC.	CAL. ENTRY NO.
1499, 25 Feb.	1499, 27 March	1048, fos 104^r-107^r	I (Tuam, Clonfert)	167
1499, 26 Feb.	————	1048, fos 3^v-6^v	I ([Annaghdown, Tuam])	163
"	————	1050, fos 189^r-190^v	E&W (London)	189
1499, 28 Feb.	————	1041, fos 79^r-80^r	E&W (London)	107
1499, 1 March	————	1038, fos 92^r-93^v	I (Ross)	70
1499, 2 March	1499, 20 March	1037, fos 285^r-288^v	I (Cork)	67
"	1499, 20 March	1038, fos 94^r-96^v	I (Cork)	71
"	1499, 20 Apr.	1047, fos 92^r-94^v	I (Cloyne)	160
1499, 9 March	————	1038, fos 90^v-92^r	I (Tuam)	69
"	————	1041, fos 99^v-101^r	S (Dunkeld)	108
1499, 12 March	1499, 16 March	1045, fos 40^v-41^v	I (Cloyne)	128
1499, 15 March	————	1045, fos 45^r-46^r	I (Ross)	129
1499, 4 Apr.	1499, 30 Apr.	1047, fos 98^r-100^v	I (Killaloe)	162
1499, 7 Apr.	————	1053, fos 75^v-76^v	E&W (Salisbury)	193
1499, 12 Apr.	1499, 27 Apr.	1047, fos 96^v-98^r	I (Killaloe)	161
1499, 13 Apr.	1499, 14 May	1047, fos 71^r-73^v	I (Lismore)	158
1499, 16 Apr.	1499, 7 May	1047, fos 58^r-61^r	I (Ossory)	157
"	1499, 14 May	1047, fos 73^v-77^r	I (Lismore)	159
1499, 17 Apr.	————	1094, fos 142^r-143^r	I (Elphin)*	591
"	————	1094, fo 143^v	I (Elphin)*	592
"	————	1094, fo 144^r	I (Elphin)*	593
1499, 20 Apr.	————	1041, fos 131^r-132^r	E&W (Canterbury)	113
1499, 24 Apr.	————	1049, fos 237^v-238^v	E&W (Lincoln)	185
1499, 27 Apr.	————	1033, fos 332^r-333^r	E&W (Norwich; OSA)	48
1499, 29 Apr.	1500, 5 Jan.	1051, fos 159^r-160^v	S (Aberdeen)	190
1499, 30 Apr.	————	1053, fos 108^v-110^v	E&W (*foreign;* OSB)	196

DATE Rome, St. Peter's unless otherwise noted	DATE OF EXPEDITION IN THE *BULLARIA*	*REG. LAT.*	COUNTRY, DIOCESE, ORDER, ETC.	CAL. ENTRY NO.
1499, 15 May	———————	1049, fos 170^r-171^r	E&W (Chichester)	179
1499, 20 May	———————	1041, fos 135^r-136^v	E&W (Lincoln)	114
1499, 8 June	———————	1042, fos 124^v-125^r	E&W (York)	117
1499, 12 June	———————	1049, fos 12^v-13^v	E&W (Lincoln)	169
"	———————	1049, fos 14^v-15^v	E&W (Lincoln; OCist)	171
"	———————	1053, fos 191^r-192^v	E&W (York; OSA)	200
1499, 13 June	———————	1049, fos 13^v-14^v	E&W (Lincoln)	170
1499, 14 June	———————	1041, fos 40^v-42^r	E&W (Norwich)	102
"	———————	1041, fos 42^r-43^v	E&W (Lincoln)	103
"	———————	1041, fos 44^r-45^r	E&W (York)	104
"	———————	1041, fos 45^v-47^r	E&W (Winchester)	105
"	———————	1041, fos 103^r-104^v	E&W (Salisbury)	109
"	———————	1041, fos 104^v-106^v	E&W (Lincoln)	110
"	———————	1092, fos 389^v-391^v	E&W (Norwich)*	553
"	———————	1092, fos 392^v-393^r	E&W (Norwich)*	555
1499, 15 June	———————	1049, fos 191^v-193^r	S (Sodor)	181
"	———————	1092, fo 392^{r-v}	E&W (Norwich)*	554
1499, 16 June	———————	1049, fos 179^v-180^v	E&W (Norwich)	180
1499, 18 June	———————	1049, fos 59^v-67^v	E&W (Bath & Wells; OSA)	174
1499, 23 June	———————	1053, fos 74^r-75^v	I (Ferns)	192
1499, 26 June	———————	1094, fos 312^r-313^v	I (Cork & Cloyne)*	612
"	———————	1094, fos 314^v-315^r	I (Cork & Cloyne)*	614
"	———————	1094, fo 315^r	I (Cork & Cloyne)*	615
1499, 27 June	———————	1049, fos 223^v-224^v	E&W (York, Ely)	182
"	———————	1049, fos 225^r-226^r	E&W (Ely)	183

DATE Rome, St. Peter's unless otherwise noted	DATE OF EXPEDITION IN THE *BULLARIA*	*REG. LAT.*	COUNTRY, DIOCESE, ORDER, ETC.	CAL. ENTRY NO.
"	——————	1053, fos 10^r-11^r	E&W (Coventry & Lichfield)	191
"	——————	1094, fos 313^v-314^v	I (Cork & Cloyne)*	613
1499, 28 June	——————	1050, fo 32^{r-v}	E&W (Salisbury; OSA)	186
1499, 30 June	1499, 24 July	1041, fos 195^r-198^r	S (Sodor)	116
1499, 1 July	——————	1050, fos 69^v-70^r	S (Dunkeld)	187
1499, 6 July	——————	1041, fos 106^v-108^r	E&W (Exeter)	111
"	——————	1049, fos 226^r-227^r	E&W (Chichester)	184
1499, 8 July	——————	1053, fos 167^v-168^v	I (*foreign*)	199
1499, 3 Aug.	——————	1053, fos 153^r-154^v	E&W (Exeter)	198
1499, 13 Aug.	——————	1041, fos 119^v-120^v	E&W (Lincoln)	112
"	——————	1053, fos 143^v-144^v	E&W (Chichester)	197
1499, 16 Aug.	——————	1041, fos 1^r-2^v	E&W (Canterbury)	101
1499, 20 Aug.	——————	1050, fos 76^v-78^r	S (Dunkeld)	188
1499, 22 Aug.	——————	1049, fo 152^{r-v}	E&W (Norwich)	178
1499, 25 Aug.	——————	1049, fos 38^v-39^v	E&W (Chichester)	172
1499, 28 Aug.	——————	1046, fos 146^r-148^v	E&W (Exeter)	147
1499, 29 Aug.	——————	1054, fos 242^v-243^r	E&W (Lincoln)	223
1499, 30 Aug.	——————	1054, fos 171^r-172^r	I (Cashel)	221
1499, 31 Aug.	——————	1049, fos 135^v-136^v	E&W (Exeter)	177
1499, 6 Sep.	——————	1070, fos 164^r-165^r	E&W (*foreign*)	358
1499, 7 Sep.	——————	1046, fo 32^{r-v}	E&W (*none*; OFM)	136
"	——————	1046, fos 32^v-33^r	E&W (Salisbury)	137
"	——————	1046, fos 55^v-56^v	E&W (Salisbury; OSB)	139
"	——————	1049, fos 46^r-47^r	E&W (Lincoln)	173

DATE Rome, St. Peter's unless otherwise noted	DATE OF EXPEDITION IN THE *BULLARIA*	*REG. LAT.*	COUNTRY, DIOCESE, ORDER, ETC.	CAL. ENTRY NO.
1499, 12 Sep.	——————	1046, fo 157^{r-v}	E&W (Exeter; OCist)	148
1499, 21 Sep.	——————	1064, fos 335^r-336^r	E&W (Canterbury)	326
"	——————	1065, fos 34^v-37^v	I (Kilmacduagh)	330
1499, 26 Sep.[1]	——————	1062, fos 80^v-83^v	E&W (Coventry & Lichfield)	292
1499, 3 Oct.	——————	1054, fos 180^v-181^v	E&W (Salisbury)	222
1499, 4 Oct.	——————	1046, fos 29^r-30^r	S (Glasgow)	134
1499, 5 Oct.	——————	1046, fos 30^r-31^r	E&W (Lincoln)	135
"	——————	1054, fos 135^v-136^v	E&W (London)	215
"	——————	1054, fos 136^v-137^v	E&W (Exeter)	216
"	——————	1054, fos 137^v-138^v	E&W (Coventry & Lichfield)	217
"	——————	1054, fo 139^{r-v}	E&W (Exeter)	218
"	——————	1054, fo 140^{r-v}	E&W (Carlisle; OPrem)	219
"	——————	1061, fo 106^{r-v}	E&W (Winchester; OSB)	264
1499, 8 Oct.	——————	1059, fos 294^r-295^v	E&W (Lincoln)	246
1499, 10 Oct.	——————	1046, fos 202^r-203^v	E&W (Exeter)	149
"	——————	1046, fos 203^v-205^r	E&W (Coventry & Lichfield)	150
1499, 11 Oct.	——————	1046, fos 48^r-49^v	E&W (*none*; OESA)	138
"	——————	1046, fos 213^r-214^r	E&W (*none;* OESA)	151
1499, 12 Oct.	——————	1065, fos 91^r-92^v	E&W (Lincoln)	331
1499, 15 Oct.	1499, 7 Nov.	1056, fos 235^r-237^r	I (Clonmacnois)	228
1499, 19 Oct.	1499, 7 Nov.	1056, fos 237^r-239^v	I (Clonfert)	229
1499, 26 Oct.	——————	1054, fo 162^{r-v}	E&W (Salisbury)	220

[1] Nepi

DATE Rome, St. Peter's unless otherwise noted	DATE OF EXPEDITION IN THE *BULLARIA*	*REG. LAT.*	COUNTRY, DIOCESE, ORDER, ETC.	CAL. ENTRY NO.
1499, 29 Oct.	————	1046, fos 232^v-234^r	E&W (Salisbury, Lincoln)	154
1499, 5 Nov.	————	1068, 10^r-11^v	E&W (Lincoln, Norwich)	351
1499, 12 Nov.	1499, 21 Nov.	1056, fos 255^r-258^r	I (Killaloe)	230
1499, 16 Nov.	————	1046, fos 1^r-2^v	E&W (Lincoln, York)	131
"	————	1046, fos 13^v-14^v	E&W (Coventry; OSB)	133
"	————	1054, fos 131^v-132^v	E&W (Winchester)	213
"	————	1054, fos 132^v-133^v	E&W (Bath)	214
1499, 18 Nov.	————	1054, fos 128^v-129^v	E&W (Norwich)	211
1499, 19 Nov.	————	1046, fos 218^r-219^v	E&W (Lincoln)	152
"	————	1046, fos 219^v-221^r	E&W (Worcester)	153
"	————	1054, fos 129^v-130^r	E&W (York)	212
1499, 26 Nov.	————	1046, fos 142^r-144^r	I (Clonfert)	146
1499, 27 Nov.	1499, 19 Dec.	1056, fos 179^v-182^v	I (Clonmacnois)	226
1499, 30 Nov.	————	1046, fos 12^r-13^r	E&W (Bath & Wells)	132
1499, 3 Dec.	————	1056, fos 188^r-190^v	I (Ossory)	227
1499, 6 Dec.	————	1059, fos 131^r-132^r	S (Moray)	237
"	————	1062, fos 135^v-136^r	E&W (London)	296
"	————	1062, fos 136^v-137^v	E&W (Canterbury)	297
1499, 10 Dec.	————	1054, fos 81^v-82^r	E&W (London)	201
1499, 14 Dec.	————	1054, fos 84^r-85^r	E&W (Worcester, Lincoln)	202
"	————	1054, fos 88^r-89^r	E&W (Lincoln)	203
"	————	1054, fo 246^r	E&W (Salisbury)	224
"	————	1059, fos 299^v-301^r	E&W (Chichester)	247
"	————	1062, fos 119^r-120^v	E&W (Bath & Wells)	293

DATE Rome, St. Peter's unless otherwise noted	DATE OF EXPEDITION IN THE *BULLARIA*	*REG. LAT.*	COUNTRY, DIOCESE, ORDER, ETC.	CAL. ENTRY NO.
"	————	1062, fos 120^V-121^V	E&W (Worcester)	294
"	————	1068, fos 175^V-176^V	E&W (York, Coventry & Lichfield)	355
1499, 20 Dec.	————	1046, fos 106^V-107^V	E&W (Lincoln)	141
"	————	1046, fos 107^V-108^V	E&W (York)	142
"	————	1046, fos 108^V-110^V	E&W (York, Coventry & Lichfield)	143
1499, 27 Dec.	————	1062, fos 131^V-133^r	E&W (Wells)	295
1499, 29 Dec.	————	1054, fos 95^r-96^r	E&W (Salisbury)	204
"	————	1054, fos 96^r-97^r	E&W (London)	205
"	————	1054, fos 97^r-98^r	E&W (Salisbury)	206
1499, 31 Dec.	————	1065, fos 298^V-300^r	E&W (Norwich; OSA)	336
1500, 2 Jan.	————	1059, fos 237^V-238^r	I (Cloyne)	244
1500, 3 Jan.	————	1054, fo 99^{r-V}	E&W (Ely)	207
"	————	1054, fo 100^{r-V}	E&W (Salisbury)	208
1500, 6 Jan.	————	1054, fo 103^{r-V}	E&W (Coventry & Lichfield)	209
"	1500, 18 Jan.	1056, fos 137^r-140^r	I (Clonfert)	225
1500, 7 Jan.	————	1061, fos 170^V-171^V	E&W (St David's)	272
"	————	1062, fo 73^{r-V}	E&W (Winchester; OCist)	291
1500, 8 Jan.	————	1046, fos 75^r-76^r	E&W (Lincoln)	140
"	————	1066, fos 90^V-91^V	E&W (Salisbury)*	349
"	————	1094, fos 117^V-119^V	E&W (Salisbury)*	581
"	————	1094, fo 120^r	E&W (Salisbury)*	582
"	————	1094, fo 120^V	E&W (Salisbury)*	583

DATE Rome, St. Peter's unless otherwise noted	DATE OF EXPEDITION IN THE *BULLARIA*	*REG. LAT.*	COUNTRY, DIOCESE, ORDER, ETC.	CAL. ENTRY NO.
"	——————	1094, fos 151^r-153^r	E&W (St Asaph)*	594
"	——————	1094, fos 154^r-155^r	E&W (St Asaph)*	596
"	——————	1094, fo 155^v	E&W (St Asaph)*	597
"	——————	1094, fos 156^r-158^v	E&W (Llandaff)*	598
"	——————	1094, fos 159^v-160^r	E&W (Llandaff)*	600
"	——————	1094, fo 160^v	E&W (Llandaff)*	601
1500, 9 Jan.	——————	1094, fos 153^v-154^r	E&W (St Asaph)*	595
"	——————	1094, fos 158^v-159^r	E&W (Llandaff)*	599
1500, 11 Jan.	——————	1046, fos 125^v-128^v	S (St Andrews)	144
"	——————	1046, fos 131^v-132^v	S, E&W (St Andrews; OSB)	145
"	——————	1054, fos 114^r-115^r	E&W (London)	210
"	——————	1059, fos 238^r-239^r	I (Cloyne)	245
"	——————	1065, fos 302^r-303^r	E&W (Norwich; OPrem)	337
"	——————	1065, fo 329^{r-v}	E&W (Rome, Lincoln; OSA)	339
1500, 13 Jan.	——————	1046, fos 234^r-237^r	S (Moray; OCist)	155
1500, 15 Jan.	1500, 28 Jan.	1046, fos 249^r-250^v	I (Cloyne)	156
1500, 16 Jan.	——————	1065, fos 125^r-126^r	S (St Andrews)	332
1500, 18 Jan.	1500, 20 Feb.	1060, fos 114^v-117^v	I (Derry)	249
1500, 20 Jan.	——————	1061, fo 162^{r-v}	E&W (Exeter; OClun)	267
"	——————	1061, fos 162^v-163^r	E&W (Chichester; OSA)	268
"	——————	1061, fos 167^v-169^r	E&W ('York', Coventry & Lichfield)	270
1500, 25 Jan.	——————	1064, fos 336^r-337^r	E&W (Salisbury)	327
"	——————	1065, fos 131^v-132^v	E&W (Lincoln)	334

DATE Rome, St. Peter's unless otherwise noted	DATE OF EXPEDITION IN THE *BULLARIA*	*REG. LAT.*	COUNTRY, DIOCESE, ORDER, ETC.	CAL. ENTRY NO.
1500, 27 Jan.	————	1065, fos 133^r-134^r	E&W (Canterbury)	335
"	————	1065, fos 305^r-306^r	E&W (Salisbury)	338
1500, 28 Jan.	————	1061, fos 165^r-166^r	E&W (Norwich)	269
"	————	1065, fos 130^v-131^v	S (St Andrews)	333
1500, 30 Jan.	————	1059, fos 301^r-302^v	S (St Andrews)	248
1500, 31 Jan.	————	1061, fos 169^r-170^v	E&W (Rochester)	271
1500, 8 Feb.	1500, 17 March	1064, fos 21^v-24^r	I (Ardfert)	306
1500, 11 Feb.	————	1061, fo 89^{r-v}	E&W (Norwich)	263
"	————	1061, fo 122^{r-v}	E&W (Worcester)	265
1500, 20 Feb.	————	1060, fos 153^r-155^v	I (Derry)	253
1500, 21 Feb.	————	1066, fos 37^v-38^v	E&W (Lincoln)	345
1500, (?)25 Feb.	————	1066, fos 39^r-40^r	E&W (Winchester)	346
1500, 28 Feb.	1500, 11 March	1058, fos 51^v-53^r	I (Cork)	231
"	————	1063, fo 44^{r-v}	E&W (*none*; OFM)	302
"	————	1064, fo 2^{r-v}	E&W (Lincoln)	303
"	————	1064, fo 7^{r-v}	E&W (Worcester)	304
"	————	1064, fo 8^{r-v}	E&W (Norwich; OSB)	305
"	1500, 11 Apr.	1070, fos 203^v-205^r	I (Derry)	361
1500, 2 March	1500, 14 March	1091, fos 207^v-209^r	I (Ossory)	545
1500, 15 March	————	1060, fos 155^v-158^r	I (Cork)	254
"	1500, 4 Apr.	1060, fos 166^v-169^r	I (Ross)	256
"	————	1064, fos 80^r-81^r	E&W (London, Lincoln)	309
"	1500, 28 Apr.	1070, fos 201^r-203^r	I (Ardfert)	360
1500, 16 March	————	1061, fo 229^{r-v}	E&W (Lincoln)	275
"	————	1061, fos 234^r-235^v	E&W (Bath & Wells, Salisbury)	276

DATE Rome, St. Peter's unless otherwise noted	DATE OF EXPEDITION IN THE *BULLARIA*	*REG. LAT.*	COUNTRY, DIOCESE, ORDER, ETC.	CAL. ENTRY NO.
"	————	1061, fo 263^{r-v}	E&W (York)	278
1500, 17 March	————	1060, fos 158^{r}-161^{v}	I (Cork)	255
1500, 18 March	1500, 7 Apr.	1060, fos 140^{v}-143^{v}	I (Ross)	251
"	————	1064, fo 279^{r-v}	E&W (Norwich; OPrem)	321
1500, 19 March	————	1061, fo 1^{r-v}	E&W (Bath & Wells; OSA)	260
"	————	1061, fos 48^{v}-50^{r}	E&W (Exeter, Chichester)	262
"	————	1061, fos 153^{v}-154^{r}	E&W (Exeter)	266
"	————	1061, fo 268^{r-v}	E&W (Lincoln)	279
1500, 23 March	1500, 11 Apr.	1060, fos 137^{v}-140^{v}	I (Cloyne)	250
1500, 24 March	————	1060, fos 215^{r}-218^{r}	I (Cork)	257
"	————	1061, fo 204^{r-v}	E&W (*none*; OCarm)	273
"	————	1061, fos 269^{v}-270^{r}	E&W (Winchester; OClun)	280
"	————	1064, fos 257^{v}-259^{r}	E&W (St David's)	318
1500, 27 March	————	1064, fos 260^{v}-262^{r}	E&W (St David's)	320
1500, 28 March	————	1061, fos 254^{v}-256^{r}	E&W (Salisbury)	277
"	————	1064, fos 259^{v}-260^{r}	E&W (St David's; OCist)	319
1500, 2 Apr.	————	1064, fos 280^{r}-281^{r}	E&W (Salisbury, Norwich; OSB)	322
1500, 3 Apr.	————	1059, fos 61^{v}-62^{v}	I (Dromore)	235
"	————	1060, fos 143^{v}-147^{v}	I (Cork)	252
1500, 4 Apr.	1500, 14 Apr.	1060, fos 221^{r}-224^{v}	I (Cork)	258
"	————	1061, fo 214^{r-v}	E&W (*none*; OESA)	274
1500, 6 Apr.	————	1059, fo 63^{r-v}	I (Connor)	236

DATE Rome, St. Peter's unless otherwise noted	DATE OF EXPEDITION IN THE *BULLARIA*	*REG. LAT.*	COUNTRY, DIOCESE, ORDER, ETC.	CAL. ENTRY NO.
1500, 8 Apr.	———	1064, fos 284^v-285^r	E&W (Exeter)	323
"	1500, 24 Apr.	1070, fos 194^v-197^r	I (Ardfert)	359
1500, 12 Apr.	———	1064, fo 285^{r-v}	E&W (Exeter)	324
"	———	1064, fos 293^r-294^r	E&W (Worcester; OSB)	325
1500, 18 Apr.	———	1064, fos 227^v-228^v	E&W (York)	315
"	———	1064, fos 228^v-229^v	E&W (York)	316
"	———	1064, fos 231^r-232^r	E&W (Lincoln)	317
1500, 20 Apr.	———	1066, fos 5^v-7^v	E&W (Winchester; OSB)	341
1500, 22 Apr.	———	1062, fos 26^r-27^r	E&W (Coventry & Lichfield)	290
"	———	1064, fo 108^{r-v}	E&W (Bath & Wells)	310
"	———	1064, fo 109^{r-v}	E&W (Bath & Wells)	311
"	———	1064, fo 116^{r-v}	E&W (York)	312
"	———	1070, fos 310^r-312^r	E&W (*foreign*)	364
1500, 25 Apr.	1500, 9 May	1070, fos 221^r-222^r	I (Cork)	362
1500, 27 Apr.	———	1068, fos 17^r-18^r	E&W (Worcester)	352
1500, 28 Apr.	———	1064, fos 212^r-213^r	E&W (Norwich; OSB)	314
"	———	1068, fo 18^{r-v}	E&W (Bath & Wells)	353
1500, 1 May	———	1061, fos 272^r-273^r	E&W (London)	281
"	———	1061, fos 281^v-282^v	E&W (Lincoln, Worcester)	282
1500, 2 May	———	1061, fos 311^v-312^r	E&W (Norwich; OClun)	287
1500, 4 May	———	1065, fos 29^v-30^v	E&W (Norwich)	328
"	———	1065, fos 30^v-31^v	E&W (Lincoln)	329

DATE Rome, St. Peter's unless otherwise noted	DATE OF EXPEDITION IN THE *BULLARIA*	*REG. LAT.*	COUNTRY, DIOCESE, ORDER, ETC.	CAL. ENTRY NO.
"	———————	1094, fos 19ᵛ-21ᵛ	I (*foreign*)*	577
"	———————	1094, fos 21ᵛ-22ʳ	I (*foreign*)*	578
"	———————	1094, fos 164ʳ-165ᵛ	E&W (Bangor)*	602
"	———————	1094, fos 166ᵛ-167ʳ	E&W (Bangor)*	604
"	———————	1094, fos 167ʳ-168ʳ	E&W (Bangor)*	605
1500, 5 May	———————	1094, fo 166ʳ⁻ᵛ	E&W (Bangor)*	603
1500, 12 May	1500, 2 June	1070, fos 266ᵛ-268ᵛ	E&W (London; OSB)	363
1500, 13 May	———————	1061, fos 283ʳ-284ʳ	E&W (Salisbury; OSA)	283
1500, 20 May	———————	1061, fos 39ᵛ-40ʳ	E&W (London)	261
"	———————	1061, fos 332ᵛ-333ʳ	E&W (Hereford)	289
1500, 21 May	———————	1066, fos 174ᵛ-175ʳ	I (Cashel)	350
1500, 22 May	———————	1061, fo 322ʳ⁻ᵛ	E&W (Exeter)	288
1500, 24 May	———————	1064, fos 40ʳ-41ʳ	E&W (London)	307
1500, 25 May	———————	1066, fos 44ʳ-45ʳ	E&W (Norwich)	347
1500, 28 May	———————	1066, fos 45ᵛ-46ᵛ	E&W (Coventry & Lichfield)	348
1500, 1 June	———————	1061, fos 301ᵛ-302ᵛ	E&W (Norwich)	284
"	———————	1061, fos 308ʳ-309ʳ	E&W (Exeter)	285
1500, 3 June	———————	1094, fos 127ᵛ-130ʳ	S (Holyrood)*	584
"	———————	1094, fo 130ʳ⁻ᵛ	S (Dunfermline)*	585
"	———————	1094, fos 130ᵛ-131ʳ	S (Holyrood)*	586
"	———————	1094, fos 131ʳ⁻ᵛ	S (Holyrood)*	587
"	———————	1094, fos 131ᵛ-133ᵛ	S (Dunfermline)*	588
"	———————	1094, fo 133ᵛ	S (Dunfermline)*	589
"	———————	1094, fo 134ʳ	S (Dunfermline)*	590
"	———————	1094, fos 177ʳ-179ʳ	I (Killala)*	606

DATE Rome, St. Peter's unless otherwise noted	DATE OF EXPEDITION IN THE *BULLARIA*	*REG. LAT.*	COUNTRY, DIOCESE, ORDER, ETC.	CAL. ENTRY NO.
"	—————	1094, fos 180^r-181^r	I (Killala)*	608
"	—————	1094, fo 181^{r-v}	I (Killala)*	609
1500, 4 June	—————	1094, fos 179^v-180^r	I (Killala)*	607
1500, 9 June	—————	1062, fo 166^{r-v}	E&W (York; OSA)	299
1500, 10 June	—————	1061, fo 311^{r-v}	E&W (Salisbury)	286
1500, 15 June	—————	1064, fos 41^v-42^v	E&W (St Asaph)	308
1500, 16 June	—————	1069, fos 84^v-86^r	S (St Andrews; OSA)	356
1500, 18 June	—————	1095, fos 100^r-101^v	E&W (*foreign*)	616
1500, 20 June	—————	1058, fos 203^r-204^r	S (Glasgow)	232
1500, 22 June	—————	1068, fos 171^r-172^r	E&W (Bath & Wells)	354
1500, 29 June	1500, 20 July	1060, fos 279^v-282^r	I (Derry)	259
1500, 30 June	—————	1059, fos 194^v-195^r	S (St Andrews)	243
1500, 1 July	—————	1066, fos 20^v-21^v	E&W (Ely)	343
1500, 4 July	—————	1058, fos 213^r-214^v	E&W (Coventry & Lich- field, London / Canterbury)	233
1500, 10 July	—————	1092, fos 336^r-338^r	S (Orkney)*	549
"	—————	1092, fo 338^v	S (Orkney)*	550
"	—————	1092, fos 340^r-341^v	S (Orkney)*	552
1500, 11 July	—————	1092, fo 339^{r-v}	S (Orkney)*	551
1500, 15 July	—————	1062, fos 144^v-146^r	E&W (Worcester; OCist)	298
1500, 16 July	1500, 22 July	1064, fos 200^v-203^v	I (Killaloe)	313
1500, 31 July	—————	1059, fos 147^v-148^v	E&W (Exeter)	239
1500, 4 Aug.	—————	1062, fos 291^r-293^r	S (St Andrews)	301
1500, 7 Aug.	—————	1066, fos 10^v-11^v	E&W (Winchester)	342
1500, 8 Aug.	—————	1059, fos 141^v-142^v	E&W (Lincoln)	238
"	—————	1059, fos 161^r-162^r	E&W (York)	240

DATE Rome, St. Peter's unless otherwise noted	DATE OF EXPEDITION IN THE *BULLARIA*	*REG. LAT.*	COUNTRY, DIOCESE, ORDER, ETC.	CAL. ENTRY NO.
"	————	1059, fos 167^r-168^r	E&W (Norwich)	241
"	————	1066, fos 4^r-5^r	E&W (St David's)	340
"	————	1066, fos 22^r-23^r	E&W (Winchester)	344
1500, 10 Aug.	————	1062, fos 258^r-259^r	E&W (London, Coventry & Lichfield)	300
1500, 19 Aug.	————	1058, fos 217^r-219^v	I (Clonfert)	234
1500, 20 Aug.	————	1059, fos 169^r-170^r	E&W (Coventry & Lichfield)	242
1500, 21 Aug.	————	1094, fos 65^r-66^v	I (Glendalough)*	579
"	————	1094, fos 66^v-67^r	I (Glendalough)*	580
"	————	1106, fo 232^r	I (Glendalough)*	776
1500, 29 Aug.	————	1086, fos 87^r-88^r	E&W (Winchester)	466
"	————	1086, fos 88^v-89^v	E&W (London)	467
"	————	1086, fos 92^v-93^r	E&W (Coventry & Lichfield; OCist)	468
1500, 31 Aug.	————	1075, fos 147^v-149^r	I (Limerick; OCist)	383
1500, 1 Sep.	1500, 28 Sep.	1091, fos 183^r-184^r	I (Limerick; OSA)	542
1500, 2 Sep.	————	1071, fos 58^v-59^v	S (St Andrews)	366
1500, 3 Sep.	————	1077, fos 219^r-220^r	E&W (Bangor)	393
1500, 4 Sep.	————	1071, fos 48^r-49^r	E&W (London)	365
1500, 5 Sep.	————	1086, fos 264^r-265^r	I (Limerick)	485
1500, 7 Sep.	————	1074, fos 212^v-213^v	E&W (Worcester)	373
"	1500, 19 Sep.	1075, fos 151^r-152^r	I (Tuam)	384
1500, 11 Sep.	————	1086, fos 45^v-46^v	E&W (Coventry & Lichfield)	455
1500, 12 Sep.	————	1079, fos 160^r-164^r	I (Tuam)	402
"	————	1086, fos 47^r-48^r	E&W (Exeter)	456
1500, 21 Sep.	1500, 13 Oct.	1079, fos 136^r-138^v	I (Tuam)	401

DATE Rome, St. Peter's unless otherwise noted	DATE OF EXPEDITION IN THE *BULLARIA*	*REG. LAT.*	COUNTRY, DIOCESE, ORDER, ETC.	CAL. ENTRY NO.
1500, 26 Sep.	1500, 31 Oct.	1075, fos 8^r-9^v	I (Lismore)	381
1500, 28 Sep.	——————	1086, fos 268^r-269^r	I (Ardfert)	486
1500, 17 Oct.	1500, 14 Nov.	1091, fos 193^v-194^v	I (Ossory)	543
1500, 20 Oct.	——————	1075, fos 3^r-5^r	I (Killaloe)	380
1500, 24 Oct.	——————	1086, fos 61^r-62^v	E&W (Norwich)	457
"	——————	1086, fos 63^r-64^r	E&W (York)	458
1500, 26 Oct.	1500, 10 Nov.	1075, fos 167^v-169^v	I (Cashel)	385
1500, 29 Oct.	——————	1086, fos 270^v-271^r	E&W (Canterbury)	487
1500, 3 Nov.	——————	1086, fo 271^{r-v}	E&W (Norwich)	488
"	——————	1086, fo 301^{r-v}	E&W (Canterbury)	491
1500, 8 Nov.	——————	1087, fos 311^r-312^v	E&W ('Exeter')	508
1500, 10 Nov.	——————	1086, fo 37^{r-v}	E&W (*none*; OP)	454
1500, 17 Nov.	——————	1089, fos 1^r-3^r	E&W (*foreign*; OCist)	515
1500, 22 Nov.	——————	1091, fo 197^{r-v}	E&W (Norwich)	544
1500, 5 Dec.	——————	1074, fo 235^{r-v}	E&W (Ely)	376
"	——————	1074, fos 236^r-237^r	E&W (Worcester)	378
"	——————	1084, fo 240^{r-v}	E&W (Lincoln; OCist)	447
1500, 12 Dec.	——————	1074, fos 233^v-234^v	E&W (London)	375
1500, 19 Dec.	——————	1074, fos 232^v-233^r	E&W (London)	374
1500, 20 Dec.	——————	1074, fos 237^r-238^v	E&W (Lincoln)	379
1500, 23 Dec.	——————	1087, fos 23^r-24^v	E&W (Winchester, St David's)	495
1500, 24 Dec.	——————	1074, fo 236^r	E&W (Norwich)	377
1500, 30 Dec.	——————	1090, fos 10^v-11^v	E&W (Hereford)	517
1501, 4 Jan.	——————	1074, fos 28^v-29^v	E&W (Exeter)	372
1501, 9 Jan.	1501, 1 Feb.	1079, fos 176^v-180^r	I (Cashel)	404

DATE Rome, St. Peter's unless otherwise noted	DATE OF EXPEDITION IN THE *BULLARIA*	*REG. LAT.*	COUNTRY, DIOCESE, ORDER, ETC.	CAL. ENTRY NO.
"	————	1086, fos 186^r-187^r	E&W (Lincoln)	479
"	————	1090, fos 102^r-103^r	E&W (Winchester; OSA)	524
1501, 12 Jan.	————	1086, fos 185^r-186^r	E&W (Salisbury)	478
"	————	1086, fos 187^v-188^v	E&W (Chichester)	480
1501, 13 Jan.	1501, 1 Feb.	1079, fos 170^r-174^r	I (Killaloe)	403
1501, 16 Jan.	————	1071, fos 136^v-137^v	E&W (Hereford)	367
1501, 18 Jan.	————	1092, fos 254^r-256^r	E&W (York)*	546
"	————	1092, fos 256^{r-v}	E&W (York)*	547
"	————	1092, fos 256^v-257^r	E&W (York)*	548
1[501], 19 Jan.	————	1086, fos 201^v-203^r	E&W (Winchester; OSA)	484
1501, 23 Jan.	————	1075, fos 30^v-32^r	E&W (*foreign*)	382
"	————	1086, fos 192^r-193^r	E&W (Lincoln)	481
"	————	1086, fos 279^v-280^r	E&W (Canterbury)	489
1501, 24 Jan.	————	1086, fos 197^r-198^r	E&W (Lincoln)	482
"	————	1086, fo 280^{r-v}	E&W (Canterbury)	490
1501, 26 Jan.	————	1086, fos 200^r-201^v	E&W (St Asaph)	483
1501, 9 Feb.	————	1083, fos 177^r-178^v	E&W (*foreign*)	441
1501, 12 Feb.	————	1086, fo 141^{r-v}	E&W (Norwich)	471
1501, 13 Feb.	————	1071, fo 274^{r-v}	I (Armagh; OCist)	368
1501, 14 Feb.	————	1086, fo 142^{r-v}	E&W (Salisbury)	472
1501, 16 Feb.	————	1083, fos 205^v-207^r	E&W (Salisbury / Worcester; OSA)	442
1501, 19 Feb.	————	1069, fos 124^r-125^r	I (Killaloe)	357
"	————	1071, fos 277^r-278^v	S (Dunkeld)	369
1501, 26 Feb.	————	1096, fos 244^r-246^r	E&W (Norwich)*	634

DATE Rome, St. Peter's unless otherwise noted	DATE OF EXPEDITION IN THE *BULLARIA*	*REG. LAT.*	COUNTRY, DIOCESE, ORDER, ETC.	CAL. ENTRY NO.
"	————	1096, fo 246^v	E&W (Norwich)*	635
1501, 27 Feb.	————	1083, fo 319^{r-v}	S (St Andrews;OSA)	443
"	————	1096, fo 247^{r-v}	E&W (Norwich)*	636
1501, 2 March	————	1086, fos 333^v-334^r	S (Lismore)	493
"	————	1088, fos 174^v-177^r	I (Clonfert; OSA)	513
1501, 3 March	————	1086, fos 160^r-161^r	E&W (Wells)	473
1501, 4 March	————	1083, fo 123^{r-v}	E&W (Salisbury)	439
1501, 5 March	————	1042, fos 177^v-178^r	E&W (Worcester)	119
"	————	1042, fos 178^r-179^r	E&W (Exeter)	120
1501, 6 March	————	1080, fos 266^r-267^v	I (Meath; OSA)	416
"	————	1082, fos 224^r-225^r	E&W (Worcester, Lincoln)	424
"	————	1086, fos 71^r-72^r	E&W (Winchester)	459
"	————	1086, fos 72^r-73^r	E&W (St David's)	460
"	————	1086, fos 161^v-162^v	E&W (London)	474
"	————	1086, fos 162^v-164^r	E&W (Coventry & Lichfield)	475
1501, 8 March	1501, 27 March	1088, fos 167^r-172^r	I (Clonfert)	512
1501, 10 March	————	1080, fos 57^v-59^r	S (Glasgow)	407
1501, 12 March	————	1078, fo 157^{r-v}	S (Glasgow)	395
1501, 13 March	————	1071, fo 296^{r-v}	S (St Andrews)	370
"	————	1080, fo 64^{r-v}	S (St Andrews; OSB)	409
1501, 14 March	1501, 18 March	1088, fos 55^r-56^r	I (Ossory)	510
1501, 15 March	————	1084, fos 39^r-40^v	S (Aberdeen)	444
"	————	1086, fos 323^r-324^r	I (Clonfert)	492
1501, 16 March	————	1080, fo 66^{r-v}	S (Glasgow)	412
1501, 19 March	1501, 30 March	1088, fos 69^r-71^r	I (Killaloe)	511

DATE Rome, St. Peter's unless otherwise noted	DATE OF EXPEDITION IN THE *BULLARIA*	*REG. LAT.*	COUNTRY, DIOCESE, ORDER, ETC.	CAL. ENTRY NO.
1501, 21 March	——————	1086, fos 73^r-74^v	E&W (Bath & Wells)	461
"	——————	1086, fos 167^v-168^v	E&W (Salisbury)	476
"	——————	1086, fos 358^r-359^r	E&W (Rochester)	494
"	1501, 30 March	1091, fos 170^v-171^v	I (Ardfert)	540
1501, 23 March	——————	1071, fos 304^v-306^r	S (St Andrews)	371
"	——————	1080, fos 63^r-64^r	S (Glasgow)	408
"	——————	1080, fo 64^v-65^r	S (St Andrews; OCist)	410
"	——————	1080, fos 65^v-66^r	S (Aberdeen)	411
"	1501, 6 Apr.	1091, fo 167^{r-v}	I (Cork)	539
"	1501, 3 Apr.	1091, fos 175^v-176^v	I (Cloyne)	541
"	——————	1097, fos 73^r-74^v	E&W (Coventry & Lichfield)	641
1501, 24 March	——————	1090, fos 119^v-120^r	E&W (Norwich; OPrem)	525
1501, 27 March	——————	1086, fos 74^v-75^v	E&W (Lincoln)	462
"	——————	1090, fo 122^{r-v}	E&W (Chichester; OCist)	527
1501, 28 March	——————	1080, fos 240^r-241^r	E&W (Norwich)	414
"	——————	1086, fo 76^{r-v}	E&W (Coventry & Lichfield)	463
"	——————	1086, fo 78^{r-v}	E&W (London)	464
"	——————	1086, fo 79^{r-v}	E&W (Norwich; OSA)	465
1501, 29 March	1501, 7 Apr.	1077, fos 107^r-109^v	I (Down)	391
"	——————	1080, fo 225^{r-v}	E&W (Exeter)	413
1501, 30 March	——————	1080, fos 241^r-242^r	E&W (York)	415
1501, 1 Apr.	——————	1090, fos 121^r-122^r	E&W (Lincoln)	526

DATE Rome, St. Peter's unless otherwise noted	DATE OF EXPEDITION IN THE *BULLARIA*	*REG. LAT.*	COUNTRY, DIOCESE, ORDER, ETC.	CAL. ENTRY NO.
1501, 2 Apr.	1501, 7 Apr.	1077, fos 110^r-112^r	I (Cloyne)	392
"	1501, 7 Apr.	1088, fos 209^r-211^r	I (Cloyne)	514
1501, 7 Apr.	————	1087, fos 81^r-82^r	E&W (Salisbury)	499
"	————	1087, fos 82^r-83^r	E&W (York)	500
"	————	1087, fos 83^r-84^r	E&W (Lincoln)	501
"	————	1090, fo 86^{r-v}	E&W (Rochester)	522
"	————	1090, fo 87^{r-v}	E&W (Carlisle)	523
1501, 11 Apr.	————	1090, fos 6^v-7^v	E&W (Ely)	516
1501, 19 Apr.	1501, 3 Aug.	1076, fos 41^r-43^v	E&W (Ely, Lincoln)	386
1501, 20 Apr.	————	1083, fos 158^v-159^r	E&W (Lincoln)	440
1501, 21 Apr.	————	1090, fos 26^v-27^v	E&W (London)	518
1501, 23 Apr.	————	1086, fos 178^v-179^v	E&W (Lincoln)	477
"	————	1091, fos 81^r-82^v	I (Cork; OCist)	536
1501, 24 Apr.	————	1082, fos 283^r-284^r	E&W (London)	426
1501, 27 Apr.	————	1078, fos 164^v-165^v	E&W (Bath & Wells; OSA)	396
"	————	1082, fos 117^r-120^r	E&W (*foreign*)	417
1501, 4 May	————	1078, fos 308^r-309^r	E&W (Llandaff)	399
1501, 5 May	————	1084, fo 41^{r-v}	E&W (*none*; OFM)	445
"	————	1087, fo 154^{r-v}	E&W (Worcester; OSB)	505
"	1501, 13 May	1091, fos 127^v-128^v	I (Kilmore)	538
1501, 6 May	————	1090, fos 49^r-50^r	E&W (London)	519
"	————	1090, fo 56^{r-v}	E&W (York)	521
"	————	1090, fos 141^v-142^v	E&W (London)	528
1501, 11 May	1501, 6 June	1091, fos 89^v-90^v	I (Kilmore)	537
1501, 15 May	————	1082, fo 223^{r-v}	E&W (mother of king of England)	423

DATE Rome, St. Peter's unless otherwise noted	DATE OF EXPEDITION IN THE *BULLARIA*	*REG. LAT.*	COUNTRY, DIOCESE, ORDER, ETC.	CAL. ENTRY NO.
"	————	1083, fos 53^v-55^r	E&W (Exeter, Lichfield)	434
"	————	1109, fos 131^r-132^v	E&W (mother of king of England)	807
1501, 18 May	————	1083, fos 52^v-53^r	E&W (Worcester)	433
"	————	1090, fo 55^{r-v}	E&W (Bath & Wells)	520
1501, 19 May	————	1087, fos 158^v-159^v	E&W (Coventry & Lichfield)	506
"	————	1087, fos 159^v-160^v	E&W (Rochester)	507
1501, 26 May	————	1077, fos 35^r-36^r	S (Dunblane)	390
"	————	1096, fos 53^r-55^v	E&W (Ely)*	627
"	————	1096, fos 55^v-56^r	E&W (Ely)*	628
"	————	1096, fo 56^{r-v}	E&W (Ely)*	629
1501, 28 May	————	1076, fos 188^r-189^r	E&W (London)	387
1501, 5 June	————	1090, fo 225^{r-v}	E&W (Exeter)	531
1501, 9 June	————	1076, fos 189^r-190^r	E&W (Norwich)	388
1501, 10 June	————	1083, fos 74^r-75^r	S (Dunblane)	435
1501, 12 June	————	1083, fos 77^v-78^v	E&W (Exeter)	436
"	————	1083, fos 78^v-79^v	E&W (Canterbury)	437
"	————	1083, fo 92^{r-v}	E&W (Chichester; OSA)	438
"	————	1090, fo 229^{r-v}	E&W (Canterbury)	533
"	————	1090, fo 230^{r-v}	E&W (Coventry & Lichfield)	534
1501, 15 June	————	1087, fos 67^v-68^r	E&W (Lincoln)	498
1501, 22 June	————	1076, fos 190^r-191^r	E&W (Salisbury)	389
"	————	1078, fos 368^r-369^r	E&W (Canterbury; OSA)	400

DATE Rome, St. Peter's unless otherwise noted	DATE OF EXPEDITION IN THE *BULLARIA*	*REG. LAT.*	COUNTRY, DIOCESE, ORDER, ETC.	CAL. ENTRY NO.
1501, 25 June	———	1080, fo 37^{r-v}	E&W (Lincoln)	406
1501, 26 June	———	1082, fos 296^v-297^v	E&W (Lincoln)	427
"	———	1082, fos 315^v-317^r	E&W (Lichfield, Lincoln)	428
"	———	1086, fos 3^v-4^v	E&W (Lincoln)	450
"	———	1086, fo 5^{r-v}	E&W (York; OSA)	451
1501, 6 July	1501, 31 July	1088, fos 14^v-16^v	S (St Andrews; OSA)	509
1501, 7 July	———	1083, fos 32^v-33^r	E&W (Worcester)	431
"	———	1083, fos 38^v-39^v	E&W (Worcester)	432
"	———	1090, fo 226^{r-v}	E&W (Norwich)	532
1501, 8 July	———	1083, fos 8^v-9^v	E&W (Durham)	429
1501, 9 July	———	1083, fos 31^r-32^r	E&W (Bath & Wells)	430
1501, 14 July	———	1086, fos 11^v-13^r	E&W (Bath & Wells, Llandaff)	452
"	———	1086, fos 13^v-14^r	E&W (Bath & Wells, OSA)	453
"	———	1086, fos 119^v-120^v	E&W (Lincoln)	469
"	———	1086, fos 121^r-122^r	E&W (Lincoln)	470
"	———	1087, fos 98^v-99^v	E&W (Rochester, London)	502
1501, 15 July	———	1080, fos 34^r-35^r	E&W (*foreign*)	405
"	———	1082, fos 251^v-254^r	E&W (Lincoln; OSB)	425
1501, 19 July	———	1078, fos 242^v-243^v	E&W (London)	398
1501, 20 July	1501, 9 Aug.	1085, fo 298^{r-v}	I (Derry)	448
1501, 24 July	———	1090, fos 282^v-284^r	S (St Andrews;OSB)	535
1501, 7 Aug.	———	1090, fos 179^v-180^v	E&W (*foreign*)	530
1501, 20 Aug.	———	1096, fo 32^r	E&W (Winchester)*	624
"	———	1096, fo 32^v	E&W (Winchester)*	625

DATE Rome, St. Peter's unless otherwise noted	DATE OF EXPEDITION IN THE *BULLARIA*	*REG. LAT.*	COUNTRY, DIOCESE, ORDER, ETC.	CAL. ENTRY NO.
"	——————	1096, fos 33^r 35^r	E&W (Winchester)*	626
1501, 21 Aug.	——————	1078, fo 240^{r-v}	E&W (York; OClun)	397
"	——————	1082, fo 211^{r-v}	E&W (Salisbury)	418
"	——————	1082, fo 212^{r-v}	E&W (Norwich)	419
"	——————	1082, fos 215^v-216^r	E&W (Salisbury)	420
"	——————	1082, fos 217^v-218^v	E&W (Exeter)	421
"	——————	1082, fos 221^r-222^v	E&W (Worcester, Canterbury)	422
"	1502, 13 Sep.	1097, fos 133^v-135^r	S (Glasgow)	642
1501, 22 Aug.	——————	1090, fos 169^v-171^v	E&W (Coventry & Lichfield)	529
1501, 23 Aug.	1501, 24 Sep.	1085, fos 311^r-312^r	I (Kilfenora)	449
1501, 24 Aug.	——————	1078, fos 71^r-80^r	E&W (Worcester; OSB)	394
1501, 28 Aug.	——————	1103, fo 132^{r-v}	E&W (York)	718
"	——————	1103, fos 133^r-134^r	E&W (Salisbury)	719
"	——————	1103, fos 134^v-135^r	E&W (Lincoln)	720
"	——————	1103, fo 136^{r-v}	E&W (Salisbury)	722
"	——————	1103, fo 153^{r-v}	E&W (London)	727
"	——————	1103, fo 160^{r-v}	E&W (Lincoln; Gilb)	728
1501, 29 Aug.	——————	1087, fos 46^v-47^v	E&W (Coventry & Lichfield)	496
"	——————	1087, fo 48^{r-v}	E&W (Lincoln)	497
"	——————	1103, fos 99^v-100^v	E&W (Coventry & Lichfield)	715
"	——————	1103, fos 131^r-132^r	E&W (Exeter, Bath & Wells)	717
1501, 31 Aug.	——————	1109, fos 337^v-339^r	I (Limerick)	815

DATE Rome, St. Peter's unless otherwise noted	DATE OF EXPEDITION IN THE *BULLARIA*	*REG. LAT.*	COUNTRY, DIOCESE, ORDER, ETC.	CAL. ENTRY NO.
1501, 2 Sep.	————	1103, fo 135^{r-v}	E&W (Lincoln)	721
1501, 5 Sep.	1501, 20 Sep.	1111, fos 5^r-6^r	I (Killaloe)	818
1501, 6 Sep.	1501, 28 Sep.	1111, fos 10^v-11^r	I (Clonfert)	819
1501, 7 Sep.	————	1105, fos 245^v-246^r	E&W (Norwich)	771
1501, 10 Sep.	————	1100, fos 65^v-66^v	E&W (Exeter, Bath & Wells)	663
"	————	1100, fos 67^r-68^r	E&W (London, Norwich)	664
1501, 11 Sep.	————	1100, fos 72^v-73^v	E&W (London)	665
"	————	1100, fos 75^v-76^r	E&W (Norwich; OPrem)	668
"	————	1103, fos 64^r-65^r	E&W (Norwich)	704
1501, 14 Sep.	————	1100, fo 43^{r-v}	E&W (Norwich)	662
"	————	1103, fo 152^{r-v}	E&W (Norwich)	726
(?)1501, 18 Sep.	————	1100, fo 338^{r-v}	E&W (Durham)	696
1501, 21 Sep.	————	1099, fos 185^r-186^r	E&W (Salisbury)	654
"	————	1105, fos 252^v-253^r	E&W (Salisbury)	772
1501, 24 Sep.	————	1100, fos 73^v-74^v	E&W (Salisbury)	666
"	1501, 7 Oct.	1111, fos 16^v-17^v	I (Limerick)	820
1501, 25 Sep.	————	1100, fo 8^{r-v}	E&W (Chichester)	657
"	————	1100, fo 9^{r-v}	E&W (Norwich; OClun)	658
"	————	1100, fos 74^v-75^r	E&W (Canterbury)	667
1501, 28 Sep.[1]	————	1103, fos 139^v-140^r	E&W (Bath & Wells)	723
" [1]	————	1103, fos 140^v-141^v	E&W (Coventry & Lichfield)	724
" [1]	————	1103, fo 143^{r-v}	E&W (St David's)	725

[1] Civita Castellana

DATE Rome, St. Peter's unless otherwise noted	DATE OF EXPEDITION IN THE *BULLARIA*	*REG. LAT.*	COUNTRY, DIOCESE, ORDER, ETC.	CAL. ENTRY NO.
1501, 2 Oct.	————	1103, fos 21^v-22^r	E&W (Thérouanne)	699
"	————	1103, fos 22^v-23^r	E&W (Norwich)	700
"	————	1103, fo 31^{r-v}	E&W (Ely)	701
1501, 19 Oct.	————	1100, fos 234^v-235^v	E&W (Coventry & Lichfield; OSA)	686
1501, 20 Oct.	————	1096, fos 5^r-7^r	E&W (London)*	617
"	————	1096, fo 7^{r-v}	E&W (London)*	618
1501, 21 Oct.	————	1096, fos 7^v-8^r	E&W (London)*	619
1501, 23 Oct.	————	1100, fos 337^r-338^r	E&W (Worcester)	695
1501, 2 Nov.	————	1103, 265^v-267^v	E&W (St David's)	739
1501, 3 Nov.	————	1100, fos 189^r-190^r	E&W (London)	681
"	————	1100, fos 190^v-191^v	E&W (Bath & Wells)	682
1501, 4 Nov.	————	1100, fos 196^v-198^r	E&W (Exeter, Wells)	683
1501, 18 Nov.	1501, 11 Dec.	1111, fos 64^v-65^r	I (Kilmore)	831
"	1501, 14 Dec.	1111, fos 65^v-66^r	I (Kilmore)	832
1501, 20 Nov.	————	1109, fo 177^{r-v}	E&W (London)	810
1501, 21 Nov.	————	1109, fo 176^{r-v}	E&W (Rochester)	809
1501, 26 Nov.	————	1096, fos 16^v-18^v	S (Caithness)*	620
"	————	1096, fo 19^v	S (Caithness)*	622
"	————	1096, fo 20^{r-v}	S (Caithness)*	623
"	————	1096, fos 105^r-107^v	S (Moray)*	630
"	————	1096, fos 108^v-109^r	S, E&W (Moray)*	632
"	————	1096, fo 109^v	S (Moray)*	633
"	————	1103, fos 15^v-16^v	S, E&W (Moray)*	698
1501, 27 Nov.	————	1096, fos 18^v-19^r	S (Caithness)*	621
"	————	1096, fos 107^v-108^r	S (Moray)*	631
"	————	1103, fo 91^{r-v}	E&W (Ely; OSA)	712

DATE Rome, St. Peter's unless otherwise noted	DATE OF EXPEDITION IN THE *BULLARIA*	*REG. LAT.*	COUNTRY, DIOCESE, ORDER, ETC.	CAL. ENTRY NO.
"	——————	1103, fos 97^v-98^r	E&W (Lincoln)	714
"	1501, 2 Dec.	1111, fos 53^v-54^r	I (Elphin)	830
"	1501, 18 Dec.	1111, fos 68^r-69^r	I (Kilmore)	834
1501, 28 Nov.	——————	1111, fos 66^v-67^v	I (Tuam)	833
1501, 29 Nov.	1502, 11 Jan.	1111, fos 22^r-23^v	I (Kilmore)	821
1501, 1 Dec.	——————	1103, fos 96^v-97^r	E&W (Winchester)	713
1501, 4 Dec.	——————	1100, fos 91^v-92^v	E&W (Winchester)	669
"	——————	1100, fos 92^v-93^v	E&W (London)	670
"	——————	1100, fo 94^{r-v}	E&W (Worcester)	671
1501, 11 Dec.	——————	1100, fos 262^v-263^r	S (St Andrews)	687
"	1501, 22 Dec.	1111, fos 75^v-76^v	I (Ardagh; OSA)	836
"	——————	1114, fos 105^v-106^r	S (St Andrews)	842
"	——————	1114, fo 106^{r-v}	S (St Andrews)	843
"	——————	1115, fo 37^{r-v}	S (St Andrews)	851
1501, 14 Dec.	——————	1107, fos 127^r-129^v	S (St Andrews)	778
1501, 15 Dec.	——————	1111, fos 74^v-75^r	I (Tuam)	835
"	1502, 11 Jan.	1111, fos 80^r-81^r	I (Emly)	838
1501, 18 Dec.	1501, 30 Dec.	1111, fos 76^v-77^v	I (Ardagh; OSA)	837
1501, 26 Dec.	1502, 12 Feb.	1104, fos 183^v-184^v	I (Ardagh)	763
1501, 27 Dec.	1502, 16 Apr.	1108, fos 247^r-248^v	S (Glasgow)	791
1501, 31 Dec.	——————	1100 fo 23^{r-v}	E&W (Worcester)	659
"	——————	1100, fos 26^r-27^r	E&W (Norwich)	660
"	——————	1100, fo 282^{r-v}	E&W (London)	688
"	——————	1100, fos 282^v-283^r	E&W (London)	689
"	——————	1100, fos 283^r-284^r	E&W (Coventry & Lichfield)	690
1502, 8 Jan.	——————	1107, fos 80^r-81^r	E&W (Norwich)	777

DATE Rome, St. Peter's unless otherwise noted	DATE OF EXPEDITION IN THE *BULLARIA*	*REG. LAT.*	COUNTRY, DIOCESE, ORDER, ETC.	CAL. ENTRY NO.
"	1502, 4 Feb.	1111, fos 30^v-31^v	I (Cork)	823
1502, 10 Jan.	————	1128, fos 188^r-190^r	E&W (Salisbury)*	1021
"	————	1128, fos 190^{r-v}	E&W (Salisbury)*	1022
"	————	1128, fos 190^v-191^r	E&W (Salisbury)*	1023
1502, 11 Jan.	————	1103, fos 71^r-72^r	E&W (Winchester; OPrem)	707
1502, 13 Jan.	————	1100, fos 35^r-36^v	E&W (Chichester)	661
1502, 15 Jan.	————	1100, fos 120^v-121^r	E&W (London)*	672
"	————	1103, fos 61^r-62^r	E&W (Salisbury)	702
"	————	1103, fos 62^v-63^v	E&W (London, Lincoln)	703
"	————	1103, fos 65^r-66^r	E&W (Lincoln)	705
"	————	1103, fos 66^r-67^r	E&W (Lincoln)	706
"	————	1103, fos 72^v-73^v	E&W (Norwich)	708
"	————	1103, fos 73^v-74^v	E&W (Lincoln)	709
"	————	1103, fos 75^r-76^r	E&W (Salisbury)	710
"	————	1103, fos 76^r-77^r	E&W (Coventry & Lichfield)	711
"	1502, 29 Jan.	1111, fos 27^v-28^v	I (Cork)	822
"	1502, 15 Feb.	1111, fos 34^v-36^r	I (Limerick)	824
1502, 18 Jan.	————	1103, fos 288^v-289^r	E&W (Canterbury; OSB)	743
1502, 22 Jan.	1502, 22 Apr.	1098, fos 60^v-62^v	E&W (Worcester)	644
1502, 23 Jan.	————	1109, fos 209^v-210^v	I (Cloyne)	811
"	————	1109, fos 210^v-212^r	S (Glasgow)	812
1502, 27 Jan.[1]	————	1109, fo 212^{r-v}	E&W (Worcester)	813
1502, 31 Jan.	1502, 15 Feb.	1109, fos 355^v-356^r	I (Cork)	816

[1] Frascati

DATE Rome, St. Peter's unless otherwise noted	DATE OF EXPEDITION IN THE *BULLARIA*	*REG. LAT.*	COUNTRY, DIOCESE, ORDER, ETC.	CAL. ENTRY NO.
"	1502, 17 Feb.	1111, fos 36^r-37^v	I (Cork)	825
1502, 1 Feb.	——————	1099, fos 344^v-345^r	E&W (Norwich)	655
1502, 3 Feb.	1502, 21 Feb.	1111, fos 38^v-39^v	I (Tuam)	826
1502, 5 Feb.	——————	1103, fos 289^v-290^v	E&W (London)	744
"	——————	1103, fos 290^v-291^r	E&W (Winchester; OSB)	745
"	——————	1103, fos 291^v-292^r	E&W (Carlisle)	746
"	1502, 21 Feb.	1111, fos 40^r-41^v	I (Tuam)	827
1502, 12 Feb.	——————	1100, fos 214^r-215^r	E&W (Exeter)	684
"	——————	1109, fos 160^v-161^v	E&W (London)	808
1502, 16 Feb.	1502, 1 March	1111, fos 43^v-44^r	I (Tuam)	828
1502, 17 Feb.	——————	1100, fos 217^v-218^v	E&W (Lincoln, Ely)	685
1502, 20 Feb.[1]	——————	1107, fos 162^r-164^r	S (Moray, Glasgow)	780
1502, 22 Feb.[2]	——————	1105, fos 66^v-68^r	E&W (York)	764
1502, 24 Feb.[2]	——————	1107, fo 136^v-137^v	I (*foreign*)	779
" [2]	1502, 3 March	1111, fo 45^{r-v}	I (Annaghdown)	829
1502, 10 March[3]	——————	1099, fo 367^{r-v}	E&W (Lincoln)	656
1502, 15 March	——————	1100, fos 172^r-173^r	E&W (Winchester)	678
"	——————	1100, fos 173^r-174^r	E&W (Bath & Wells)	679
"	——————	1100, fos 174^r-175^r	E&W (Winchester)	680
"	——————	1105, fos 108^v-110^v	S (Glasgow)	769
1502, 18 March	——————	1105, fos 74^v-75^v	S (Glasgow)	766
1502, 19 March	——————	1105, fos 72^r-74^v	S (chapel royal, Stirling)	765
1502, 28 March	——————	1103, fos 113^v-114^v	E&W (Lincoln)	716

[1] Corneto
[2] Piombino
[3] Civitavecchia

DATE Rome, St. Peter's unless otherwise noted	DATE OF EXPEDITION IN THE *BULLARIA*	*REG. LAT.*	COUNTRY, DIOCESE, ORDER, ETC.	CAL. ENTRY NO.
1502, 1 Apr.	————	1109, fo 120^r	E&W (Norwich; OSA)	802
"	————	1109, fos 124^v-125^v	E&W (Exeter)	803
"	————	1109, fos 125^v-126^r	E&W (York)	804
"	————	1109, fos 126^v-127^r	E&W (Hereford)	805
"	————	1109, fos 127^v-128^r	E&W (Worcester)	806
1502, 5 Apr.	————	1099, fos 24^v-25^v	E&W (Exeter)	653
"	————	1114, fo 184^v	S (St Andrews)	848
1502, 16 Apr.	————	1105, fo 76^{r-v}	S (chapel royal, Stirling)	767
"	————	1105, fos 76^v-83^r	S (chapel royal, Stirling)	768
"	————	1107, fos 265^v-275^r	S (chapel royal, Stirling)	781
"	————	2463, fos 242^v-244^r	E&W (London)	1036
"	————	2463, fos 244^r-245^r	E&W (Hereford)	1037
1502, 19 Apr.	1502, 7 May	1108, fo 151^{r-v}	I (Elphin)	784
"	1502, 14 May	1108, fos 155^r-156^r	I (Cashel)	786
"	1502, 10 May	1108, fos 160^v-161^r	I (Elphin)	788
1502, 20 Apr.	1502, 12 May	1108, fos 153^v-154^v	I (Lismore)	785
"	————	1108, fos 161^v-162^v	I (Lismore)	789
"	1502, 18 May	1108, fos 162^v-164^r	I (Ardfert)	790
1502, 27 Apr.	————	1128, fos 72^r-74^v	S (Jedburgh)*	1009
"	————	1128, fos 74^v-75^r	S (Jedburgh)*	1010
"	————	1128, fos 75^v-76^r	S (Jedburgh)*	1011
1502, 30 Apr.	————	1101, fos 200^r-202^v	E&W (*foreign*)	697
1502, 4 May	1502, 10 June	1097, fos 401^r-403^v	S (Ross)	643
"	1502, 10 May	1108, fos 156^v-157^v	I (Ossory)	787

DATE Rome, St. Peter's unless otherwise noted	DATE OF EXPEDITION IN THE *BULLARIA*	*REG. LAT.*	COUNTRY, DIOCESE, ORDER, ETC.	CAL. ENTRY NO.
1502, 6 May	1502, 18 May	1108, fos 141^V-142^V	I (Cashel)	783
"	——————	1109, fos 73^r-74^r	E&W (Norwich, York)	797
1502, 7 May	——————	1109, fos 71^V-72^r	E&W (Bath & Wells)	795
"	——————	1109, fos 72^r-73^r	E&W (Exeter)	796
"	——————	1109, fo 76^{r-V}	E&W (Lincoln; OPrem)	798
"	——————	1110, fos 88^r-89^V	E&W (*none*; OP)	817
1502, 10 May	——————	1109, fo 44^{r-V}	E&W (London)	794
"	——————	1109, fos 78^r-79^r	E&W (York)	799
1502, 12 May	1502, 28 May	1098, fos 110^V-111^V	I (Annaghdown)	646
1502, 14 May	1502, 24 May	1098, fos 109^r-110^r	I (Ossory)	645
1502, 18 May	1502, 25 May	1098, fo 113^{r-V}	I (Killaloe)	647
1502, 19 May	——————	1103, fos 335^V-336^V	E&W (Worcester)	759
1502, 21 May	——————	1100, fo 292^{r-V}	E&W (Coventry & Lichfield)	692
"	——————	1100, fo 293^{r-V}	E&W (Lincoln)	693
1502, 26 May	——————	1103, fos 256^r-257^r	E&W (Salisbury)	734
"	——————	1103, fos 261^r-262^V	E&W (Salisbury)	736
1502, 27 May	——————	1114, fos 301^V-303^r	S (Glasgow)	850
1502, 30 May	——————	1103, fos 269^r-270^r	E&W (Carlisle; OESA)	741
1502, 31 May	1502, 26 June	1098, fos 127^r-129^r	I (Kilfenora)	648
"	——————	1098, fos 129^r-130^r	I (Killaloe)	649
1502, 1 June	——————	1100, fos 286^V-288^r	S (St Andrews)	691
1502, 2 June	——————	1103, fo 257^{r-V}	E&W (Chichester; OSA)	735
"	——————	1103, fos 304^V-305^V	E&W (London)	748

DATE Rome, St. Peter's unless otherwise noted	DATE OF EXPEDITION IN THE *BULLARIA*	*REG. LAT.*	COUNTRY, DIOCESE, ORDER, ETC.	CAL. ENTRY NO.
"	————	1105, fo 209^{r-v}	E&W (Norwich)	770
1502, 3 June	————	1103, fos 263^r-264^r	E&W (Norwich)	737
"	————	1103, fos 264^v-265^v	E&W (Hereford)	738
"	————	1103, fos 303^r-304^r	E&W (Exeter; OPrem)	747
1502, 4 June	————	1103, fos 267^v-268^v	E&W (London)	740
1502, 6 June	————	1100, fos 299^r-300^r	I (Meath)	694
1502, 7 June	————	1103, fos 332^v-333^v	E&W (Carlisle)	756
1502, 10 June	————	1107, fos 354^r-356^r	S (Aberdeen)	782
"	1502, 25 June	1111, fos 133^r-135^r	S (Ross)	839
1502, 11 June	————	1106, fos 129^r-130^r	E&W (London)	774
1502, 13 June	————	1103, fos 317^v-319^r	E&W (Lincoln)	749
1502, 14 June	————	1100, fo 135^{r-v}	E&W (Lincoln)	673
"	————	1100, fo 136^{r-v}	E&W (Chichester)	674
"	————	1100, fo 137^{r-v}	E&W (Winchester)	675
"	————	1100, fo 142^{r-v}	E&W (Exeter)	676
"	————	1100, fo 143^{r-v}	E&W (Norwich)	677
1502, 16 June	————	1103, fos 319^v-320^v	E&W (London)	750
"	————	1103, fos 321^r-322^r	E&W (York)	751
"	————	1103, fos 323^r-324^v	E&W (Lincoln, York)	752
"	————	1103, fos 325^r-326^v	E&W (Exeter)	753
"	————	1103, fos 326^v-327^v	E&W (Coventry & Lichfield; OCist)	754
"	————	1103, fos 328^r-329^r	E&W (Norwich)	755
"	————	1114, fos 25^r-26^r	S (Ross)	840
"	1502, 5 Nov.	1114, fos 27^r-29^r	S (Glasgow)	841
1502, 18 June	————	1106, fos 128^r-129^r	E&W (London)	773

DATE Rome, St. Peter's unless otherwise noted	DATE OF EXPEDITION IN THE *BULLARIA*	*REG. LAT.*	COUNTRY, DIOCESE, ORDER, ETC.	CAL. ENTRY NO.
"	——————	1106, fos 130^v-131^v	E&W (London)	775
1502, 21 June	——————	1103, fos 334^v-335^v	E&W (Chichester; OSA)	758
"	——————	1109, fos 260^v-262^r	E&W (Norwich)	814
1502, 25 June	——————	1103, fos 235^v-236^v	E&W (Lincoln)	731
"	——————	1103, fos 333^v-334^v	E&W (Lincoln)	757
1502, 27 June	——————	1128, fos 53^v-56^r	E&W (Durham)*	1006
"	——————	1128, fo 56^v	E&W (Durham)*	1007
"	——————	1128, fo 57^{r-v}	E&W (Durham)*	1008
1502, 28 June	——————	1098, fos 137^v-138^v	I (Kilfenora)	651
1502, 29 June	——————	1103, fos 251^r-252^v	E&W (Salisbury)	733
1502, 1 July	——————	1109, fos 85^r-86^r	E&W (London)	800
1502, 2 July	——————	1098, fos 133^v-135^r	I (Killaloe)	650
"	——————	1103, fos 249^v-250^v	E&W (Worcester)	732
1502, 6 July	——————	1109, fos 1^r-2^v	S (St Andrews)	792
"	——————	1109, fos 2^v-4^r	S (Brechin)	793
1502, 16 July	——————	1109, fos 93^v-94^v	E&W (Salisbury)	801
"	——————	1114, fos 299^r-300^r	S (St Andrews)	849
1502, 26 July	——————	1103, fo 381^{r-v}	E&W (Exeter)	762
1502, 27 July	1502, 22 Aug.	1098, fos 141^r-142^v	I (Killaloe)	652
1502, 30 July	——————	1103, fos 231^v-232^v	E&W (Lincoln, York; OSA)	730
1502, 5 Aug.	——————	1114, fos 113^v-114^v	S (St Andrews)	844
1502, 6 Aug.	——————	1084, fos 112^v-113^r	E&W (*none*; OFM)	446
"	——————	1103, fos 223^r-224^r	E&W (Lincoln)	729
"	——————	1103, fos 378^v-379^v	E&W (Canterbury)	760
"	——————	1103, fo 380^{r-v}	E&W (York)	761

DATE Rome, St. Peter's unless otherwise noted	DATE OF EXPEDITION IN THE *BULLARIA*	*REG. LAT.*	COUNTRY, DIOCESE, ORDER, ETC.	CAL. ENTRY NO.
1502, 27 Aug.	———	1118, fos 272^v-274^r	I (Meath)	927
1502, 28 Aug.	———	1122, fo 2^r	S (St Andrews)	979
1502, 3 Sep.	———	1118, fo 33^{r-v}	E&W (London)	897
1502, 5 Sep.	———	1121, fos 264^r-265^r	S (St Andrews)	971
1502, 7 Sep.	1502, 20 Dec.	1116, fo 88^{r-v}	I (Clonfert)	853
1502, 8 Sep.	———	1118, fo 38^{r-v}	E&W (Norwich)	898
1502, 9 Sep.[1]	———	1117, fos 120^v-121^v	E&W (Winchester)	866
" 1	———	1118, fo 135^{r-v}	E&W (Canterbury)	917
" 1	———	1121, fos 76^v-77^v	E&W (Lincoln)	957
" 1	———	1121, fos 276^v-277^r	E&W (Lincoln; OCist)	973
" 1	———	1121, fos 277^v-278^r	E&W (Chichester; OPrem)	974
1502, 10 Sep.[1]	———	1118, fo 42^{r-v}	E&W (Canterbury; OSA)	899
1502, 13 Sep.[2]	———	1121, fos 266^r-267^r	S (*foreign*; OSA)	972
1502, 15 Sep.[3]	———	1118, fos 13^v-14^r	E&W (Lincoln)	896
" 3	———	1118, fos 138^r-139^r	E&W (Norwich)	918
1502, 17 Sep.[3]	———	1122, fos 23^v-24^r	I (Kilmacduagh)	983
1502, 22 Sep.	———	1119, fos 119^r-121^r	S (Moray)	931
"	———	1121, fos 284^v-285^r	E&W (Chichester)	975
1502, 1 Oct.	———	1118, fos 143^v-144^r	E&W (Chichester)	919
1502, 4 Oct.[!]	1502, 24 Sep.[!]	1123, fos 166^r-167^r	E&W (*foreign*)	996
1502, 5 Oct.[!]	1502, 19 Sep.[!]	1123, fos 117^v-119^r	S (Aberdeen)	992
1502, 8 Oct.	———	1121, fos 150^r-151^v	I (Armagh & Meath)	964

[1] Nepi
[2] Gallese
[3] Civita Castellanas

DATE Rome, St. Peter's unless otherwise noted	DATE OF EXPEDITION IN THE *BULLARIA*	*REG. LAT.*	COUNTRY, DIOCESE, ORDER, ETC.	CAL. ENTRY NO.
1502, 15 Oct.	1502, 31 Oct.	1119, fos 154^v-156^r	I (Clonfert)	933
"	1502, 20 Oct.	1126, fos 122^v-124^r	E&W (*foreign*)	1002
1502, 18 Oct.	———	1117, fos 247^v-249^r	E&W (York)	879
"	———	1117, fos 249^v-250^v	E&W (Exeter)	880
1502, 24 Oct.	———	1122, fos 24^v-25^v	I (Killaloe)	984
1502, 1 Nov.	———	1121, fos 33^v-34^r	E&W (Norwich)	952
"	———	1121, fos 34^v-35^r	E&W (Norwich)	953
1502, 2 Nov.	1502, 17 Nov.	1119, fos 152^v-153^r	I (Leighlin)	932
"	———	1122, fo 12^{r-v}	I (Leighlin)	981
1502, 5 Nov.	———	1117, fos 253^r-254^r	E&W (Rochester; OSB)	882
"	———	1122, fo 10^{r-v}	I (Kilfenora)	980
1502, 8 Nov.	———	1122, fos 16^r-17^v	I (Leighlin)	982
1502, 12 Nov.	———	1117, fos 252^r-253^r	E&W (Exeter)	881
"	———	1118, fos 227^v-228^v	E&W (London)	924
1502, 13 Nov.	———	1118, fo 231^{r-v}	E&W (mother of king of England)	925
1502, 22 Nov.	———	1118, fos 243^v-244^r	E&W (Chichester; OCist)	926
1502, 23 Nov.	1502, 18 Dec.	1119, fos 164^r-165^r	I (Annaghdown)	935
1502, 26 Nov.	———	1117, fos 111^r-112^r	E&W (London)	865
"	———	1117, fos 206^r-207^v	E&W (Norwich, London)	872
"	———	1117, fos 224^v-225^v	E&W (Hereford)	875
"	———	1117, fos 225^v-226^v	E&W (Hereford)	876
"	———	1117, fos 230^r-231^r	E&W (Lincoln; OSA)	877
1502, 29 Nov.	———	1117, fos 234^v-235^r	E&W (Salisbury)	878

DATE Rome, St. Peter's unless otherwise noted	DATE OF EXPEDITION IN THE *BULLARIA*	*REG. LAT.*	COUNTRY, DIOCESE, ORDER, ETC.	CAL. ENTRY NO.
1502, 1 Dec.	——————	1118, fos 183^v-184^v	S (St Andrews or another)	921
1502, 3 Dec.	——————	1118, fo 186^{r-v}	E&W (Norwich)	922
"	——————	1118, fos 193^r-194^r	E&W (London, Worcester)	923
1502, 10 Dec.	1502, 18 Dec.	1119, fos 160^v-162^r	I (?Kildare)	934
1502, 17 Dec.[!]	1502, 3 Jan.[!]	1119, fos 165^v-167^v	I (Elphin)	936
1502, 20 Dec.	——————	1121, fos 74^v-75^r	E&W (Lincoln)	956
1502, 22 Dec.	1503, 5 Jan.	1125, fos 174^v-177^v	I (Cloyne)	1000
1502, 24 Dec.	——————	1118, fos 71^v-72^v	E&W (Lincoln; OSA)	904
"	——————	1118, fos 75^r-76^r	E&W (Lincoln)	906
"	——————	1118, fos 81^r-82^v	E&W (Salisbury)	908
"	——————	1118, fos 82^v-85^r	E&W (Exeter)	909
"	——————	1121, fos 69^v-70^r	E&W (Lincoln)	955
1502, 28 Dec.	——————	1118, fos 74^r-75^r	E&W (London)	905
1502, 30 Dec.	——————	1117, fo 145^{r-v}	E&W (Coventry & Lichfield; OSB)	867
1502, 31 Dec.	——————	1117, fos 301^v-302^v	E&W (Lincoln)	894
"	——————	1118, fos 76^v-77^r	E&W (Exeter)	907
1503, 1 Jan.	1503, 7 Jan.	1116, fos 85^r-86^r	I (Cloyne)	852
1503, 16 Jan.	——————	1117, fos 289^r-290^r	E&W (Exeter)	889
1503, 17 Jan.	——————	1117, fo 283^{r-v}	E&W (Bath & Wells)	883
"	——————	1117, fos 284^r-285^r	E&W (Exeter)	884
"	——————	1117, fos 285^r-286^r	E&W (Lincoln)	885
"	——————	1117, fos 286^r-287^r	E&W (Bath & Wells)	886
"	——————	1117, fos 287^v-288^r	E&W (York)	887

DATE Rome, St. Peter's unless otherwise noted	DATE OF EXPEDITION IN THE *BULLARIA*	*REG. LAT.*	COUNTRY, DIOCESE, ORDER, ETC.	CAL. ENTRY NO.
"	———	1117, fos 288^V-289^r	E&W (Lincoln; OSA)	888
1503, 18 Jan.	———	1117, fos 295^r-296^r	E&W (Salisbury)	891
1503, 19 Jan.	1503, 28 March	1119, fos 21^r-23^V	S (Glasgow)	929
1503, 20 Jan.	———	1117, fos 298^V-300^r	E&W (St David's)	892
"	———	1117, fos 300^r-301^V	E&W (St David's)	893
"	———	1117, fos 302^V-303^V	E&W (Canterbury)	895
1503, 1 Feb.	———	1117, fos 294^r-295^r	E&W (Exeter)	890
"	———	1128, fos 168^V-172^r	S (Melrose)*	1015
"	———	1128, fos 172^V-173^r	S (Melrose)*	1016
"	———	1128, fo 173^{r-V}	S (Melrose)*	1017
"	———	1128, fos 173^V-174^V	S (Melrose)*	1018
"	———	1128, fos 174^V-175^V	S (Melrose)*	1019
"	———	1128, fos 175^V-177^r	S (Melrose)*	1020
1503, 7 Feb.	———	1117, fos 35^V-36^V	E&W (Lincoln)	858
"	———	1118, fos 100^V-101^V	E&W (Norwich)	912
"	1503, 11 March	1119, fos 61^V-64^V	I (Ossory)	930
1503, 8 Feb.	———	1121, fos 104^r-105^r	E&W (Exeter)	958
1503, 11 Feb.	1503, 21 Feb.	1119, fos 171^V-172^r	S (St Andrews)	937
"	———	1124, fos 235^r-236^V	I (Cashel)	998
1503, 14 Feb.	1503, 6 March	1119, fos 176^r-177^V	I (Cashel)	938
"	———	1122, fo 38^r	E&W (Winchester)	985
1503, 18 Feb.	———	1118, fos 94^r-95^r	E&W (London)	910
"	———	1118, fos 95^r-96^V	E&W (Salisbury)	911
1503, 21 Feb.	1503, 6 Apr.	1119, fos 257^V-258^r	I (Elphin)	947
1503, 22 Feb.	1503, 1 June	1119, fo 189^{r-V}	I (Kilmore)	940
1503, 24 Feb.	———	1121, fo 120^{r-V}	E&W (Winchester)	959

DATE Rome, St. Peter's unless otherwise noted	DATE OF EXPEDITION IN THE *BULLARIA*	*REG. LAT.*	COUNTRY, DIOCESE, ORDER, ETC.	CAL. ENTRY NO.
1503, 1 March	———	1119, fos 202^r-203^v	I (Limerick)	942
1503, 3 March	1503, 12 July	1119, fos 321^v-322^r	I (Killaloe)	948
1503, 4 March	1503, 9 March	1119, fos 200^r-201^r	I (Cloyne)	941
1503, 8 March	———	1121, fos 124^v-126^v	E&W (Ascalon)*	963
1503, 11 March	———	1121, fos 122^r-123^r	E&W (Carlisle)	960
"	———	1121, fo 123^{r-v}	E&W (York; OCist)	961
"	———	1121, fo 123^v-124^r	E&W (Chichester; OCist)	962
1503, 19 March	———	1114, fos 127^v-128^v	I (Elphin; OPrem)	846
"	1503, 13 May	1123, fo 161^{r-v}	I (Elphin; OPrem)	995
1503, 21 March	———	1126, fos 307^v-308^v	E&W (Durham)	1004
1503, 25 March	1503, 8 April	1116, fos 276^r-277^v	E&W (*foreign*)	855
1503, 28 March	1503, 22 April	1125, fos 283^r-288^v	E&W (*foreign*)	1001
"	———	1126, fos 308^v-310^v	I (Meath)	1005
1503, 29 March	———	1128, fos 275^v-277^v	S (Cambuskenneth)*	1024
"	———	1128, fos 278^{r-v}	S (Cambuskenneth)*	1025
"	———	1128, fos 278^v-279^r	S (Cambuskenneth)*	1026
"	———	1128, fos 279^v-280^r	S (Cambuskenneth)*	1027
"	———	1128, fo 280^{r-v}	S (Cambuskenneth)*	1028
1503 1 Apr.	———	1117, fos 213^r-214^r	E&W (Lincoln; OSA)	874
1503, 8 Apr.	1503, 2 May	1120, fos 145^v-146^v	E&W (*foreign*)	951
"	———	1121, fo 291^{r-v}	E&W (Lincoln)	977
1503, 10 Apr.	———	1117, fo 44^{r-v}	E&W (Lincoln; OSA)	859
"	———	1121, fos 288^v-289^r	E&W (York)	976
1503, 15 Apr.	———	1117, fo 193^{r-v}	E&W (Rochester; OSA)	871

DATE Rome, St. Peter's unless otherwise noted	DATE OF EXPEDITION IN THE *BULLARIA*	*REG. LAT.*	COUNTRY, DIOCESE, ORDER, ETC.	CAL. ENTRY NO.
1503, 19 Apr.	————	1114, fos 146^v-147^r	E&W (Chichester)	847
"	————	1117, fos 13^v-14^v	E&W (London)	856
"	————	1117, fos 14^v-15^r	E&W (York; OSA)	857
"	————	1121, fo 306^{r-v}	E&W (Worcester)	978
1503, 22 Apr.	————	1119, fos 209^r-210^v	I (Raphoe; OCist)	943
1503, 24 Apr.	1503, 24 May	1120, fos 100^r-101^v	I (Lismore)	949
1503, 27 Apr.	1503, 5 May	1123, fos 143^v-144^v	I (Ardfert)	993
1503, 3 May	1503, 24 May	1119, fos 221^v-222^v	I (Ardfert)	945
1503, 5 May	————	1129A, fos 1^r-4^r	E&W (Coventry & Lichfield)*	1029
"	————	1129A, fo 4^{r-v}	E&W (Coventry & Lichfield)*	1030
"	————	1129A, fos 278^r-280^r	S (Newbattle)*	1032
"	————	1129A, fo 280^v	S (Newbattle)*	1033
"	————	1129A, fo 281^r	S (Newbattle)*	1034
1503, 13 May	————	1118, fos 121^r-122^r	E&W (Exeter)	915
"	————	1118, fos 122^r-123^r	E&W (Bath & Wells)	916
"	————	1118, fos 175^v-176^v	E&W (Salisbury)	920
1503, 14 May	————	1129A, fos 4^v-6^r	E&W (Coventry & Lichfield)*	1031
1503, 16 May	1503, 23 May	1116, fos 161^r-163^r	E&W (*foreign*)	854
"	————	1121, fo 223^{r-v}	E&W (London)	969
"	————	1121, fo 224^{r-v}	E&W (Winchester)	970
1503, 20 May	————	1122, fo 63^{r-v}	S (St Andrews)	986
1503, 21 May	————	1117, fos 169^r-170^r	E&W (Coventry & Lichfield)	868
"	————	1117, fos 170^v-171^v	E&W (Salisbury)	869
"	————	1117, fos 117^v-118^r	E&W (London)	913

DATE Rome, St. Peter's unless otherwise noted	DATE OF EXPEDITION IN THE *BULLARIA*	*REG. LAT.*	COUNTRY, DIOCESE, ORDER, ETC.	CAL. ENTRY NO.
"	——————	1118, fos 118^v-119^r	E&W (Winchester; OSB)	914
"	1503, 27 May	1119, fos 224^r-225^r	I (Lismore)	946
"	——————	1126, fos 277^r-278^v	E&W (Exeter, Wells)	1003
1503, 22 May[!]	——————	1128, fos 152^v-153^r	E&W (Carlisle)*	1013
1503, 23 May	1503, 1 June	1119, fos 187^r-189^r	I (Ardfert)	939
"	1503, 3 June	1119, fos 218^r-219^r	I (Limerick; OSA)	944
"	1503, 24 May	1120, fos 106^v-108^r	I (Raphoe; OCist)	950
1503, 25 May	——————	1117, fos 171^v-172^v	E&W (Chichester)	870
1503, 27 May	——————	1117, fos 70^r-71^v	E&W (Bath & Wells; OSA)	863
1503, 30 May	——————	1121, fos 218^v-219^r	E&W (Winchester)	968
"	1503, 14 June	1123, fos 145^r-146^r	I (Ardfert)	994
1503, 2 June	——————	1117, fos 68^v-70^r	E&W (Bangor, Coventry & Lichfield)	862
1503, 8 June	——————	1122, fos 96^r-97^v	I (Ferns; OSA)	989
1503, 9 June	——————	1124, fos 121^v-122^r	E&W (Lincoln; OSA)	997
1503, 10 June	——————	1122, fos 100^r-101^r	E&W (*dioc. wanting*)	990
1503, 11 June	——————	1117, fo 68^{r-v}	E&W (*none*) OFM	861
1503, 13 June	——————	1121, fo 60^{r-v}	E&W (Exeter)	954
"	——————	1121, fos 164^v-165^v	E&W (Salisbury)	965
1503, 14 June	——————	1114, fos 120^v-121^r	I (Annaghdown)	845
1503, 21 June	——————	1128, fos 150^r-152^v	E&W (Carlisle)*	1012
1503, 23 June	——————	1128, fo 153^r	E&W (Carlisle)*	1014
1503, 28 June	——————	1119, fos 17^r-20^r	S (Brechin)	928
1503, 1 July	——————	1118, fos 43^r-44^r	E&W (Exeter)	900
1503, 4 July	——————	1121, fos 178^r-179^r	E&W (Winchester)	966

DATE Rome, St. Peter's unless otherwise noted	DATE OF EXPEDITION IN THE *BULLARIA*	*REG. LAT.*	COUNTRY, DIOCESE, ORDER, ETC.	CAL. ENTRY NO.
"	————	1121, fos 179^r-180^r	E&W (Canterbury; OSB)	967
1503, 8 July	————	1118, fos 52^v-53^r	E&W (Worcester; OSB)	903
1503, 11 July	————	1122, fos 81^v-83^r	E&W (Bath & Wells)	987
1503, 15 July	————	1122, fos 85^r-86^v	E&W (Coventry & Lichfield)	988
1503, 22 July	————	1117, fos 91^v-92^v	E&W (London)	864
1503, 4 Aug.	————	1122, fos 138^v-139^v	E&W (Coventry & Lichfield)	991
1504, 1 Aug.	————	1150, fos 169^v-171^r	E&W (Lincoln)	1035

CONCORDANCE

CONCORDANCE BETWEEN THE CURRENT NUMERATION OF THE LATERAN REGISTERS COVERED BY THE PRESENT VOLUME AND THEIR ORIGINAL DESIGNATIONS

Note. Unless otherwise noted, the original designation is taken from the bottom cut. (*See CPL* XVI, p. cxiii). Contractions have been silently expanded.

Reg. Lat.	Original
1027	Quintus De Diversis Anno Sexto Alexandri pape VI.
1028	Sextus de Vacantibus Anno Sexto D.Alexandri pape VI
1029	Octavus de diversis Anno VI⁰ Alexandri
1030	X. De Diversis Anno VI Alexandri
1031	Sextus de Diversis Anno Sexto D. Alexandri pape VI
1032	Primus de Vacantibus Anno VII Alexandri
1033	IIII De Diversis Anno VII Alexandri
1034	Secundus De Vacantibus Anno VII⁰ Alexandri
1035	Mixtus de provisionibus prelatorum Annorum V et VI Alexandri VI
1036	Nonus de Diversis Anno VI Alexandri
1037	VII de vacantibus Anno VII Alexandri
1038	III de vacantibus anno VII Alexandri
1039	Secundus de Diversis anno VII⁰ Alexandri
1040	X. de Vacantibus VII. d. Alexandri
1041	Nonus de diversis.VII. Alexandri
1042	XVI De Diversis Anno Septimo Alexandri pape VI
1043	Nonus de Vacantibus Anno VII⁰ Alexandri
1044	Mixtus Vacantium et diversorum Anno VII⁰ d. Alexandri pape VI
1045	VI De Vacantibus Anno VII Alexandri
1046	Secundus De Diversis VIII Alexandri

Reg.Lat.	*Original*
1047	Quintus de vacantibus Anno VII Alexandri
1048	VIII de Vacantibus Anno VII Alexandri
1049	VIII de Diversis Anno Septimo d. Alexandri pape Sexti
1050	XV de diversis Anno Septimo Alexandri pape VI
1051	XVI De Vacantibus anno Septimo Alexandri pape VI
1052	XV de Vacantibus anno Septimo Alexandri pape VI
1053	X. De Diversis. VII⁰. D. Alexandri
1054	Primus de diversis Anno VII et VIII Alexandri
1055	Secundus de Vacantibus Anno VIII Alexandri
1056	III De Vacantibus VIII. Alexandri
1057	XI De Vacantibus Anno Octavo Alexandri pape VI
1058	Quintus de Vacantibus Anno octavo Alexandri pape VI
1059	Quintus de diversis Anno octavo Alexandri pape VI
1060	VII De Vacantibus anno octavo Alexandri pape VI
1061	VII de diversis anno octavo Alexandri pape VI
1062	VI de diversis anno octavo Alexandri pape VI
1063	Octavus de diversis Anno octavo Alexandri pape VI
1064	IX de diversis anno octavo Alexandri pape VI
1065	X de Diversis Anno octavo Alexandri pape VI
1066	XII de Diversis Anno Octavo Alexandri pape VI
1067	XII de Vacantibus Anno octavo Alexandri pape VI
1068	XIIII de diversis anno octavo Alexandri pape VI
1069	Mixtus de Vacantibus et diversis anno octavo Alexandri pape VI
1070	VI de Vacantibus anno octavo Alexandri pape VI
1071	IIII de diversis Anno Nono ALEXANDRI
1072	Quartus Vacantium Nono Alexandri pape VI
1073	Quintus De Vacantibus Nono Alexandri VI
1074	VI de diversis Nono ALEXANDRI

Reg. Lat.	Original
1075[1]	[Lib 7][2] [Vacantium Nono Alexandri .VI.][3]
1076	XIII Vacantium Anno IX Alexandri VI
1077	Secundus de diversis Nono ALEXANDRI
1078	Primus diversorum IX et Vacantium X⁰ Alexandri VI
1079	Secundus de Vacantibus IX Alexandri
1080	III diversorum Nono
1081	Tertius Vacantium Nono Alexandri pape VI
1082	Mixtus Vacantium et Diversorum Nono Alexandri pape VI
1083	Quintus de diversis Nono Alexandri VI
1084	XII Diversorum Nono Alexandri pape VI
1085	Nonus Vacantium Nono Alexandri pape VI
1086	Nonus de Diversis IX Alexandri
1087	X. de diversis Nono
1088	XI Vacantium Nono Alexandri pape VI
1089	XIIII. de Vacantibus Nono Alexandri VI [4]
1090	VII de Diversis Nono D Alexandri pape VI
1091	Decimus Diversorum et Vacantium Nono Alexandri
1092	Primus de Provisionibus Prelatorum Annorum V. VI. VII. VIII. et IX Alexandri
1093	Decimus de diversis anno Quinto Alexandri pape VI
1094	2ᵘˢ de provisionibus prelatorum Annorum V,VII et VIII Alexandri VI.
1095	Mixtus Diversorum et Vacantium annorum VII VIII.X. et XI Alexandri pape VI
1096	Tertius de Provisionibus prelatorum annorum IX et X Alexandri pape VI

[1] At some stage the *liber* was broken and the constituent *quinterni* re-assembled in reverse order. The original designations inscribed on the top and bottom cuts are consequently now illegible.

[2] This comes from the early nineteenth century title on the upper part of the spine and may well reflect the original number of the *liber*.

[3] thus the contemporary heading on fo 141ʳ -- the start of a *quinternus*

[4] from top cut; bottom blank

Reg. Lat.	Original
1097	Primus Mixtus diversorum et vacantium IX⁰ et X⁰ Alexandri VI
1098	VII Vacantium X Alexandri VI
1099	Primus de Diversis X⁰ Alexandri VI
1100	Tertius de diversis decimo Alexandri VI
1101	Tertius de Vacantibus X⁰. Alexandri [5]
1102	Quartus de Vacantibus X⁰ Alexandri [5]
1103	Quintus de diversis decimo Alexandri VI
1104	Quintus De Vacantibus X⁰ Alexandri VI
1105	Mixtus [6] vacantium et diversorum decimo Alexandri pape VI
1106	Sextus de Diversis.X⁰. Alexandri
1107	Septimus de Vacantibus et Diversis Decimo Alexandri VI
1108	Undecimus Vacantium X⁰. Alexandri VI
1109	Quartus de diversis X⁰. Alexandri
1110	Decimus Vacantium X. Alexandri VI
1111	XII Vacantium decimo Alexandri pape VI
1112	XIII. de Vacantibus Anno X⁰ Alexandri pape VI.
1113	XIIII. Vacantium X. Alexandri VI
1114	IX.ᵘˢ de diversis Anno X⁰ Alexandri VI.
1115	Primus Mixtus Diversorum et Vacantium X et XI Alexandri VI
1116	Nonus Vacantium XI⁰ Alexandri VI
1117	Primus de diversis XI Alexandri VI
1118	VIII de diversis XI. Alexandri VI.
1119	Tertius[7] Vacantium XI⁰ Alexandri VI
1120	VI. Vacantium XI Alexandri VI[8].
1121	Quartus de diversis XI. Alexandri VI.
1122	Quintus de diversis XI. Alexandri VI

[5] likewise top cut; but there deleted

[6] or *Quintus*

[7] uncertain

[8] see note to *Reg. Lat.* 1123 below

Reg. Lat.	Original
1123	Sextus [9] Vacantium XI. Alexandri VI.
1124	VII. de diversis XI. Alexandri VI
1125	VII. Vacantium XI. Alexandri VI.
1126	VIII Vacantium XI Alexandri VI [10] .
1128	Quartus de provisionibus prelatorum Annorum .X. et XI. Alexandri VI
1129	XIII. de diversis Anno primo d. Julii pape II
1129A	Primus Mixtus de provisionibus prelatorum Annorum XI d. Alexandri VI et Primi d. Julii .II.
1150	XV de diversis anno primo d. Julii pape II
1275	LIBER UNICUS DIVERSORUM PONTIFICUM ET ANNORUM VIDELICET INNOCENTII ALEXANDRI ET JULII
1406	LIBER UNICUS DIVERSORUM PONTIFICUM ET ANNORUM VIDELICET ALEXANDRI VI JULII II ET LEONIS X
2463	*modern made-up volume*

[9] apparently; but that exists (see *Reg. Lat.* 1120 above); *recte* 'Secundus' ?

[10] thus the top cut; the bottom has: *X Vacantium anno primo Julii pape 2*

CALENDAR TEXT

1   9 January 1498   *Reg. Lat.* 1027, fos 66^r-67^v

To James, king of Scots, licence as below. A recent petition on James's part stated that because of the singular devotion which he bears to the order of friars minor, called of the observance, living under vicars, and to their persons on account of their exemplary life and the abundant fruits which they are accustomed to bring to the inhabitants of the places where they live by assiduous and devout celebration of divine offices, preaching of God's word, and separate hearing of confessions, the king very much wants to cause, out of the goods conferred on him by God, a house to be constructed and built for their perpetual use and habitation in the town of Sternilyng in his dominion, d. St Andrews, if a licence is granted by the apostolic see : to him for causing the house to be constructed and built; to the friars for receiving it for their habitation and use. The pope — at his supplication — hereby grants to the king a licence for causing the said house, with a church, low bell-tower, bell, cemetery, cloister, refectory, dormitory, gardens, allotments (*ortalitiis*) and other necessary [outhouses][1], to be founded, constructed, and built in the said town for the friars' perpetual use and habitation, without prejudice to anyone; and to the friars a licence for receiving it for their perpetual use and habitation and for inhabiting it in perpetuity; the constitution of Boniface VIII prohibiting the friars minor or those professed of any other mendicant order from receiving new places, etc. , notwithstanding. The pope also grants and indulges that the said house (if it were to be constructed and built by the king by virtue of the presents) and its guardian and friars for the time being may use all the privileges, indults, immunities, exemptions, prerogatives and graces granted in general by the apostolic see to the order and its other houses and their guardians and friars for the time being which they are using or will be able to use in the future.

Dum inter nostre mentis archana . . . [2]
L putius / ~V· / V· xxxx De Phano:

[1] *officiis; recte:* 'officinis'
[2] L. Wadding, *Annales Minorum,* XV (Quaracchi, 1933), pp. 650-1 which prints *Ex lib. 156* [= the present register] an abridged and in part quite discrepant text of this letter — supplied in transcript by the *custos registri?* — gives the incipit of the proem as *Dum inter cetera.* Wadding's text is also reproduced (from an older edition of the *Annales*) by W. M. Bryce, *The Scottish Grey Friars,* II (Edinburgh and London, 1909), pp. 257-8.

2   8 January 1498   *Reg. Lat.* 1027, fo 70^{r-v}

To Robert Lounde *alias* Louude, perpetual vicar of the parish church of Glenth(a)m,[1] d. Lincoln. Dispensation — at his supplication — to receive and retain for life, together with the perpetual vicarage of the above parish church, one, or without them, any two other benefices, etc. [as below, no. 3].[2]

Vite ac morum honestas . . .
L patius³ / . L. / L. L^{ta}. Dulcius:-

¹ MS: *Glenthm'*
² save that 'ecclesiastical' does not occur
³ *sic*; for 'putius'

3   8 January 1498   *Reg. Lat.* 1027, fo 71^{r-v}

To John Clyff, rector of the parish church of St Mary, Reynham, d. Norwich. Dispensation — at his supplication — to receive and retain for life, together with the above parish church, one, and without them, any two other benefices, with cure or otherwise mutually incompatible, even if parish churches or their perpetual vicarages, or chantries, free chapels, hospitals or annual services, usually assigned to secular clerics in title of a perpetual ecclesiastical benefice, or dignities, *personatus*, administrations or offices in cathedral, even metropolitan, or collegiate churches, even if the dignities in question should be major *post pontificalem* in cathedral, even metropolitan, churches, or principal in collegiate churches, or a combination, and even if the dignities etc. should be customarily elective and have cure of souls, if he obtains them otherwise canonically, to resign them, at once or successively, simply or for exchange, as often as he pleases, and in their place receive up to two other, similar or dissimilar, incompatible benefices and retain them together for life, as above. Notwithstanding etc. With the proviso that the above church¹ and other incompatible benefices shall not, on this account, be defrauded of due services and the cure of souls in the church and (if any) the other incompatible benefices shall not be neglected.

Vite ac morum honestas . . .
L putius / . L. / . L. L^{ta}. Dulcius:-

¹ Other entries relating to England and Wales of this type are summarised in the present volume in an abridged form and refer to this entry as to the fully extended prototype. When necessary, a term appropriate to the previous content of the entry should be substituted here (e. g. in no. 2: read 'vicarage' for 'church'; and in no. 79 'chaplaincy').

4   8 January 1498   *Reg. Lat.* 1027, fo 72^{r-v}

To William Morys, LLD, rector of the parish church of St Dubritius, Pornoke, canonically mutually united dioceses of Bath and Wells. Dispensation — at his supplication — to receive and retain for life, together with the above parish church, one, and without them, any two other benefices, etc. [as above, no. 3].

Litterarum scientia, vite ac morum honestas . . .
L puteus / . L. / L. L^{ta}. Dulcius:-

5   29 January 1498   *Reg. Lat.* 1027, fos 73^v-74^v

To William Sandeland, rector of the parish church of Slamanan', d. St Andrews. Dispensation — at his supplication — to receive and retain for life, together with the above parish church, any other, or without it, any two other benefices, with cure or otherwise mutually incompatible, even if parish churches or their perpetual vicarages, or dignities, *personatus*, administrations or offices in cathedral, even metropolitan, or collegiate churches, even if the dignities in question should be major *post pontificalem* in cathedral, even metropolitan, churches, or principal in collegiate churches, or a combination, and even if the dignities etc. should be customarily elective and have cure of souls, if he obtains them otherwise canonically, to resign them, at once or successively, simply or for exchange, as often as he pleases and in their place receive up to two other, similar or dissimilar, incompatible benefices and retain them together for life, as above. Notwithstanding etc. With the proviso that the above church[1] and other incompatible benefices shall not, on this account, be defrauded of due services and the cure of souls in the church and (if any) the other incompatible benefices shall not be neglected.

Vite ac morum honestas . . .
F de Parma / . B. / . B. xxxx. - Bagarothus Proton'

[1] Other entries relating to Scotland of this type are summarised in the present volume in an abridged form and refer to this entry as to the fully extended prototype. When necessary, a term appropriate to the previous content of the entry should be substituted here (e. g. in no. 187: read 'vicarage' for 'church').

6   29 September 1497   *Reg. Lat.* 1027, fo 131^r

To John Harww, canon of the priory of St Peter, Tawnton', OSA, canonically mutually united dioceses of Bath and Wells. Dispensation — at his supplication — to him, who, as he asserts, is expressly professed of the above order,[1] to receive and retain for life any benefice, with or without cure, usually held by secular clerics, even if a parish church or its perpetual vicarage, or a chantry, free chapel, hospital or annual service, usually assigned to secular clerics in title of a perpetual ecclesiastical benefice, if he obtains it otherwise canonically, to resign it, simply or for exchange, when he pleases, and in its place receive and retain for life another, similar or dissimilar, benefice, with or without cure, defined as above. Notwithstanding etc.

Religionis zelus, vite ac morum honestas . . .
. S. de. Castello / . L. / . L. xxx. Dulcius:-

[1] This information comes from a notwithstanding clause.

7   23 September 1497   *Reg. Lat.* 1027, fos 131^v-132^r

To John Clerk, master of the hospital of Maison Dieu (*domus dei*), Dovor', OSA,
called of those marked with a Cross, d. Canterbury. Dispensation[1] to him — who, as
he asserts, holds the above hospital to which many pilgrims travelling to and from
the tombs of the Apostles Peter and Paul and the Roman curia and also St James in
Compostella resort and in which they are charitably received and given all necessary
hospitality; and because the hospital is close to the seashore it has, on account of the
impact of the sea, sustained such severe damage that it is reduced and rendered quite
slender in its fruits etc. so that unless the masters of the hospital for the time being
are provided with assistance from elsewhere hospitality and other charitable works
cannot be carried out there — as also to his successors, masters for the time being,
holding the hospital, to receive and retain *in commendam* for life, together with the
hospital, one benefice, with or without cure, usually held by secular clerics, even if a
parish church or its perpetual vicarage, or a chantry, free chapel, hospital or annual
service, usually assigned to secular clerics in title of a perpetual ecclesiastical
benefice, or an administration or office, even if pertaining — by reason of the
hospital — to the collation, provision, presentation or other disposition, of himself or
his successors, if he or they obtain it otherwise canonically through a vicar or other
person specially deputed by him or them at the time; and to resign it, as often as he
or they please, cede the commend and in its place receive and retain *in commendam*
for life another, similar or dissimilar, benefice, defined as above (he and his
successors may — due and customary burdens of the benefice having been
supported — make disposition of the rest of its fruits etc. just as those holding it *in
titulum* could and ought to do, alienation of immovable goods and movable
valuables being however forbidden). Notwithstanding etc. and [notwithstanding]
constitutions etc. of the above hospital and of the above order, of which, as John
asserts, he is expressly professed, etc. With the proviso that the benefice held *in
commendam* shall not, on this account, be defrauded of due services and the cure of
souls therein (if any) shall not be neglected; but that its customary burdens shall be
supported.

Religionis zelus, vite ac morum honestas . . .
S. de . Castello- / ~ [2] / . L. Lxxxxv. Dulcius:-

[1] 'at his supplication' does not occur
[2] a swung dash; but no initial (which in this case should be 'L')

8[1]   **3 October 1497**[2]   *Reg. Lat.* 1027, fos 186^r-187^v

To the abbot of the monastery of Myssenden', d. Lincoln, the archdeacon of the church of London and John Jurdan', canon of the church of York, mandate in favour of Josiana Leuues, woman, London. A recent petition to the pope on Josiana's part stated that, formerly, Joan Auubrey, woman, London — falsely asserting that Josiana had inflicted certain injuries and insults on her then expressed — sued Josiana (not by apostolic delegation) before the official of the court of the archdeacon of London (whom she said was a competent judge), praying that Josiana be condemned and compelled to make proper amends; that the official, proceeding duly, promulgated a definitive sentence, by which he acquitted Josiana from Joan's accusation; that Joan — falsely asserting that the sentence was unjust — appealed from it to John, cardinal priest of St Anastasia, legate of the apostolic see in those parts, and sued Josiana before Hugh Peyntwyn', archdeacon of the church of Canterbury, to whom the legate had committed the appeal; that Josiana, aggrieved by certain sufficient grievances, then expressed, successively inflicted on her by Hugh, successively appealed to the apostolic see, and impetrated apostolic letters over her appeals to the prior of the priory of St Botulph, d. London, (his own name not expressed), and certain colleagues, and by virtue of them sued Joan before John Stampe, prior of the said priory; that John Hill', canon of the church of London, to whom prior John had totally committed his powers after he had proceeded to several judicial acts short of a conclusion, proceeding lawfully, confirmed the earlier sentence by his own definitive sentence; that Joan — claiming untruthfully that she had appealed to the apostolic see from a certain grievance, then expressed, *de facto* inflicted on her, as she said, by prior John or John Hill' — impetrated apostolic letters over her appeal to the dean of the church of Hereford, (his own name not expressed), and certain colleagues, and by pretext of them, sued Josiana before, firstly, John Hervye, dean of the church of Hereford, and then, before Benedict Dodyn', canon of Hereford, to whom dean John had totally committed his powers after he had proceeded to several judicial acts short of a conclusion; and that appeal was made to the apostolic see on the part of Josiana (who was aggrieved by Benedict because he refused to examine, or cause to be examined, certain witnesses which she produced and other worthy witnesses whom she nominated for testifying to the truth and proving it; and because he improperly refused to admit certain lawful exceptions, declinatory or against his jurisdiction in the case, exhibited before him at a suitable time and place). At Josiana's supplication to the pope to commit to some upright men in those parts the cases of her later appeal; of everything perchance attempted and innovated after and against it; of everything done against her invalidly; and of the principal matter, the pope hereby commands that the above three (or two or one of them), having summoned Joan and others concerned, and having heard both sides, taking cognizance even of the principal matter, shall decree what is just, without appeal, causing by ecclesiastical censure what they have decreed to be strictly observed; [and moreover compel] witnesses etc. Notwithstanding etc.

Humilibus et cetera.

F de parma[3] / . *L.* / . *L. xij. Dulcius:-*

[1] Belongs to a series of six rescripts of justice enregistered by Resta and (ostensibly) signed by Dolci (*Reg. Lat.* 1027, fos 185^r-191^r). In every one key particulars have been added (presumably at a later stage) by another scribe, Galeatius de Petra. In all six he has entered the name of the abbreviator; and in all but the sixth letter he has completed the dating clause. See notes 2 and 3. No. 9 below also belongs to the series; the others are foreign to the Calendar.

[2] *Datum . . . millesimo quadringentesimo nonagesimo septimo quinto nonas Octobris anno sexto* where *Datum . . . septimo*] is in the hand of the enregistering scribe (Resta), *quinto . . . anno sexto*] of another scribe (Galeatius de Petra).

[3] In the hand of Galeatius de Petra. See note 1 above.

9[1]   **6 October 1497**[2]   *Reg. Lat.* 1027, fos 189^v-190^r

To the priors of the priories of St Wolstan, St <Guthlac>[3], and Wenloke, ds Worcester and Hereford, mandate in favour of Hugh Grene, cleric living in the city or diocese of Hereford. A recent petition to the pope on Hugh's part stated that, formerly — when it had, through common report, come to the notice of John Ervyc, dean of the church of Hereford, that Robert Spicer, John Backer,[4] and John Du(n)mow [also spelt *Du(n)mouu*],[5] laymen of the city and diocese of Hereford, living within the district of the deanery of the church of Hereford, had committed certain things and crimes then expressed, and Hugh (to whom the dean — to whom, by ancient, approved and hitherto peacefully observed custom, the inquisition, punishment, and correction of crimes and excesses committed from time to time by laymen living in the said district, pertains — had handed down (*descendisset*) the inquisition etc. of the crimes and excesses committed by the above laymen) proceeding duly, had promulgated sentence of excommunication against the laymen, (whom he had caused to be summoned to his presence for inquisition), and had ordered them to be published as excommunicates, because they had contumaciously refused to appear in a certain term fixed beforehand by Hugh for responding to certain articles or interrogatories — William Wiltan, who bore himself as a cleric living in the kingdom of England, falsely informed by the laymen that Hugh had rashly promulgated sentence of excommunication against them without reasonable cause, proceeding suddenly and *de facto*, at the laymens' instance, rashly excommunicated Hugh, although he had no ordinary or delegated jurisdiction over him, whence Hugh appealed to the apostolic see. At Hugh's supplication to the pope to command that he be absolved conditionally from the sentence of excommunication laid on him by William, and to commit to some upright men in those parts the cases of his appeal and of anything perchance attempted and innovated after and against it, and also the cases which Hugh intends to bring over the injuries done to him by the laymen and by William, the pope hereby commands that the above three (or two or one of them), having summoned Robert, the two Johns, William, and others concerned, shall, if and as it is just, for this once only, conditionally absolve Hugh, if he so requests, having first received suitable security from him that if they find that the excommunication was justly inflicted on him, he will obey their commands and those of the church; and, as regards the rest, having heard both sides, that they shall decree what is just, without appeal, causing by ecclesiastical censure what they have decreed to be strictly observed. Notwithstanding etc.

Humilibus et cetera.
N. Bregeon[6] / . *L.* / . *L. xiiij. Dulcius:-*

[1] Forms part of a series : see above, no. 8, note 1

[2] *Datum . . . millesimo quadringentesimo nonagesimo septimo pridie nonas Octobris anno sexto* where *Datum . . . septimo* is in the hand of the enregistering scribe (Resta), *pridie nonas Octobris anno sexto* of another scribe (Galeatius de Petra). See previous note.

[3] *Gutlaci* inserted in the margin by another scribe (Galeatius de Petra), initialled . *L.* ; *G. . l.* . deleted and initialled . *L.* , in the line

[4] in one instance changed (by deletion of the 'r') from *Bracker*

[5] MS : *Du'mow, Du'mouu*

[6] not in the hand of the enregistering scribe (Resta) but in that of another scribe (Galeatius de Petra)

10   5 September 1497   *Reg. Lat.* 1027, fos 191[v]-192[r]

To John Porter, perpetual vicar of the parish church of Trynley, d. Worcester. Dispensation — at his supplication — to receive and retain for life, together with the perpetual vicarage of the above parish church, any other, and having resigned them, any two other benefices, etc. [as above, no. 3].

Vite ac morum honestas . . .
· *P· de· Castello* / . *L.* / . *L. L[ta]. Dulcius:-*

11   2 October 1497   *Reg. Lat.* 1027, fos 193[v]-194[r]

To Thomas Thymylby, rector of the parish church of Tetford, d. Lincoln, dispensation. Some time ago, the pope by other letters of his dispensed him to receive and retain for life, together with the above parish church (which, as he asserted, he was holding), one, and having resigned it, any two other benefices, etc. [as below, no. 131, [1] to '. . . as is more fully contained in those letters'].[2] The pope — at his supplication — hereby further dispenses Thomas, who, as he asserts, is of noble birth, is a BA and still holds the above church, to receive and retain for life, together with the two incompatible benefices held by him at the time by the said dispensation, any third benefice, etc. [as below, no. 131].

Nobilitas generis, vite ac morum honestas . . .
· *S· de Castello /. L. /. L. Lx. Dulcius:-*

¹ save that in the present instance 'or a combination' does not occur
² summarised in *CPL*, XVI at no. 767

12   7 October 1497   *Reg. Lat.* 1027, fos 194ᵛ-195ʳ

To Thomas Garford *alias* Thomas Crouulandi, canon of the priory of B. Mary the
Virgin, Stoneley, OSA, d. Lincoln. Dispensation — at his supplication — to him, who,
as he asserts, is expressly professed of the above order, ¹ to receive and retain any
benefice, with or without cure, usually held by secular clerics, etc. [as below, no. 32].

Religionis zelus, vite ac morum honestas . . .
· *S· de Castello /. L. / L. xxx. Dulcius:-*

¹ This information comes from a notwithstanding clause.

13   7 October 1497   *Reg. Lat.* 1027, fo 195ʳ⁻ᵛ

To John Ffouuler, monk of the monastery¹ of B. Mary the Virgin, Dunxwy, OCist, d.
Exeter. Dispensation — at his supplication — to him, who, as he asserts, is expressly
professed of the above order,² to receive and retain any benefice, with or without
cure, usually held by secular clerics, etc. [as below, no. 32].³

Religionis zelus, vite ac morum honestas . . .
· *S· de Castello /. L. / L. xxx· Dulcius:-*

¹ *prioratus* in the line, deleted and initialled . *V.* ; *Monasterii* inserted in the margin; *Cassatum et
Correctum De Mandato R(everendissimi) D(omini) A(loysii) Regentis per me · V· De Phano.* against the
insertion. This correction is repeated below, in a notwithstanding clause: *prioratus* in the line, deleted
and initialled . *V.* ; *Monasterii* inserted in the margin, *Cassatum et Correctum ut Supra . V·*
² This informatiom comes from a notwithstanding clause.
³ save that 'ecclesiastical' does not occur

14   29 May 1498   *Reg. Lat.* 1028, fos 202ʳ-204ᵛ

To Donat Ohogayn, canon of the church of Killaloe, mandate in favour of John
Ymecayr, cleric, d. Killaloe (who, as he asserts, notwithstanding a defect of birth as

the son of a cleric and an unmarried woman, has been marked with clerical character, otherwise however duly). The pope has learned that a canonry of the church of Cashel and the rectory of the parish church of Chiller, d. Cashel, which is usually held as the prebend of the said canonry and is customarily given to a canon of this church as a prebend, and also the perpetual vicarages of the parish churches of Buorm *alias* Ogarryn and St Cronan (*Sancti Curonani*), Rostre, d. Killaloe, are vacant at present and have been for so long that by the Lateran statutes their collation has lawfully devolved on the apostolic see, although William Omecayr, cleric, has detained the canonry and prebend, the prior of the house of the monastery, usually governed by a prior, of B. Mary, *de Ynsulaviventium* [Monaincha], OSA, d. Killaloe, the first vicarage, and William Machillefoyl *alias* Ochalen, the second — bearing themselves as priests, d. Killaloe — without any title or support of law, temerariously and *de facto*, for a certain time, as they still do. A recent petition on John's [part] stated that if the vicarages were to be united etc. to the canonry and prebend, for as long as he holds the canonry and prebend, after he has acquired them, it would be to his benefit; and added, moreover, that a certain spot has unexpectedly developed on his left eye and although he is thereby deprived of the sight of that eye, no excessive deformity is apparent; and that he is eager to be promoted to all other sacred orders. Wherefore supplication has been made on the part of John — who, as he asserts, at another time with certain associates of his[1] took hold, forcibly and violently, of a certain cleric and bound his hands behind his back and led him, bound thus, to his[2] house, and did not release him until he swore not to meddle with a certain benefice over which John (or his father) was in litigation with a certain adversary of his, incurring excommunication — to the pope to absolve him from the sentence of excommunication and unite etc. the vicarages to the canonry and prebend, for as long as John holds the canonry and prebend. The pope, not having certain knowledge of the foregoing, hereby commands the above canon to absolve John, after he has made amends, if he so requests, from the sentence of excommunication incurred by occasion of the foregoing, in the customary form of the church, having enjoined a salutary penance on him etc. ; and, having brought John personally before him, diligently inspect the defect of sight; and if it seems to him that no excessive deformity is apparent from the loss of sight of that eye and that it will not create scandal among the people — concerning which the pope burdens the canon's conscience — dispense John to be promoted to all, even sacred, orders and to receive and retain the canonry and prebend, if conferred on him by virtue of the presents; notwithstanding the defect of eye and of birth, etc. ; and rehabilitate him on account of all disability and infamy arising therefrom; and, in that event, having summoned respectively William Omecayr, the prior of the monastery and William Machillefoyl and others concerned, [if] he finds the canonry and prebend, whose annual value does not exceed 8, the first vicarage, 12, and the second vicarage, 16, marks sterling, to be vacant (howsoever etc.) and, having summoned those interested in the union, the foregoing to be true, (even if the canonry and prebend and vicarages be specially reserved etc.) collate and assign the canonry and prebend to John, with plenitude of canon law; and unite etc. the vicarages to them, for his lifetime, with all their rights and appurtenances, inducting him etc. having removed William Omecayr from the canonry and prebend, the prior from the first vicarage and William Machillefoyl from the second and any other unlawful detainers and causing John (or his proctor) to be received as a canon of the church of Cashel, with plenitude of canon law, and the fruits etc., rights and obventions of the canonry and prebend and of the vicarages to be annexed thereto to be delivered to him. [Curbing] gainsayers by the pope's authority etc. Notwithstanding etc. With the proviso that the vicarages shall not, on account of this union etc., be defrauded of due services and the cure of souls therein shall not be neglected; but that their customary burdens shall be supported; and that on John's death or his resignation etc. of the canonry and prebend the union etc. shall be dissolved and the vicarages shall revert to their original condition and be deemed vacant automatically.

Apostolice sedis indefessa clementia lapsis ad eam post excessum cum humilitate recurrentibus personis libenter se propitiam exhibet et benignam . . .
· *S· de Castello / · V· / V. xxxx Sexto decimo kalendas Julii anno sexto* [16 June 1498], *De Phano:-*

1 *eis*; for 'eius'?
2 *suam*

15   23 June 1498   *Reg. Lat.* 1028, fos 230ᵛ-233ʳ

To the abbot of the monastery *de Antro Sancti Fimbarei*[1] [Gill Abbey], d. Cork, and Philip (?)Giulus and Eugene Ossullewayn, canons of the church of Cork, mandate in favour of Maurice Ilongayn, rector of the parish church of Athinach, d. Cloyne. At a recent petition on Maurice's part to the pope to erect and institute a canonry in the church of Cloyne and the said parish church, which is of lay patronage and which Maurice holds, into a simple prebend in the same, for his lifetime — asserting that the annual value of the parish church does not exceed 10 marks sterling — the pope, not having certain knowledge of the foregoing, hereby commands that the above three (or two or one of them), having summoned the bishop and chapter of the church of Cloyne and others concerned, shall inform themselves as to the foregoing and, if they find it to be thus, erect and institute a canonry in the church of Cloyne and the parish church into a simple prebend in the same, for Maurice's lifetime, without prejudice to anyone; and, in that event, collate and assign the newly erected canonry and prebend, being vacant, with plenitude of canon law and all rights and appurtenances, to Maurice, inducting him etc. having removed any unlawful detainer, and causing Maurice (or his proctor) to be received as a canon of the church of Cloyne, with plenitude of canon law, and the prebend's fruits etc., rights and obventions to be delivered to him. [Curbing] gainsayers by the pope's authority etc. Notwithstanding etc. His will is, however, that the parish church shall not, on account of this erection etc., be defrauded of due services and the cure of souls therein shall not be neglected, but that its customary burdens shall be supported; and that on Maurice's death or his resignation etc. of the canonry and prebend this erection and institution shall be extinguished and so deemed and the parish church deemed vacant automatically.

Apostolice sedis providentia circumspecta ad ea libenter intendit . . .
· *S· de· Castello· | · V· |· V· xv. De Phano:*

1 (?)*Fimbareyi' Fe*, deleted and initialled *V* twice, occurs here

16   12 June 1498   *Reg. Lat.* 1029, fos 1^r-6^r

To Thady Ofathy and Florence Ogernayn, canons of the church of Clonfert, and the official of Kilmacduagh, mandate in favour of Edmund de Burgo, cleric, d. Clonfert (who, as he asserts, notwithstanding a defect of birth as the son of an unmarried nobleman and a married woman, has been marked with clerical character otherwise however duly[1]). Some time ago — the pope having learned that the rectories of the parish churches of Fhynunc [also spelt *Fhynnuc*] and Thyrdaglas, d. Killaloe, were then vacant and had been vacant for so long that by the Lateran statutes their collation had lawfully devolved on the apostolic see, although John Olonayn [also spelt *Olonnayn*] had detained the first rectory and Dermot Olonayn the second (bearing themselves as clerics or priests) without any title or support of law, temerariously and *de facto*, for a certain time, as they were then doing — after representation was made on the part of Philip Yhanllyd, cleric, d. Killaloe, to the pope to erect and institute a canonry in the church of Killaloe and the first rectory into a simple prebend in the same, for his lifetime, and unite etc. the second rectory to them, after they should be erected, also for his lifetime, the pope by other letters of his charged the abbot of the monastery of Ogorlakane and the priors of the monasteries, usually governed by priors, *de insula viventium* [Monaincha] and *Font(is) Vivi*, Loro, their own names not expressed, that, having summoned John and Dermot and, as regards the erection and institution, the bishop and chapter of Killaloe and those interested in the union, if they found the foregoing to be true and the rectories to be vacant, they were to erect and institute a canonry in the church of Killaloe and the first rectory into a simple prebend in the same, for Philip's lifetime, and unite etc. the second rectory to them after they should be erected, as is more fully contained in those letters. However, a recent petition to the pope on Edmund's part stated that the rectories are of lay patronage, and no mention was made of this patronage in the said letters which have not yet been committed for execution. The pope therefore — considering that if it is thus the letters and whatever ensued by pretext of them do not hold good; and, as he has learned, the rectories are vacant still as above; and also the archdeaconry of the church of Clonfert and the perpetual vicarage[2] of the parish church of Locrerdh [also spelt *Locrecdh*], d. Clonfert, are vacant at present and have been for so long that by the Lateran statutes their collation has lawfully devolved on the apostolic see, although John Okelhyd [also spelt *Ohelhyd*] has detained the archdeaconry and William (?)Odimusia, the vicarage (bearing themselves as priests, d. Clonfert) without any title or support of law, temerariously and *de facto*, for a certain time, as they still do; and, at the same petition to him to erect and institute a canonry in the church of Clonfert and the vicarage into a simple prebend in the same, for Edmund's lifetime, and also unite etc. the archdeaconry and rectories to them after they should be erected, likewise for Edmund's lifetime — not having certain knowledge of the foregoing, hereby commands that the above three (or two or one of them), having summoned respectively John Okelhyd, William, John Olonayn, Dermot and Philip and, as regards the erection and institution, the bishop and chapter of Clonfert and those interested in the union and others concerned, shall inform themselves as to the foregoing and, if they find it to be true, decree and declare the aforesaid letters to be surreptitious and whatever ensued by pretext of them to be and have been null and invalid; and, in that event, if they find the archdeaconry (which is a non-major dignity *post pontificalem*) and the vicarage and rectories, whose annual value together does not exceed 52 marks sterling, to be vacant (howsoever etc.), even if they are specially reserved etc., erect and institute a canonry in the church of Clonfert and the vicarage into a simple prebend in the same, for Edmund's lifetime, without prejudice to anyone; and unite etc. to them after they should be erected the archdeaconry ((?)having first severed[3] from it the united and annexed vicarage of the parish church of Chyltoloch, d. Clonfert) and the said rectories, also for Edmund's lifetime; and, in the event of such erection etc. and union etc., collate and assign the newly erected canonry and prebend, with plenitude of canon law and all rights and appurtenances, to Edmund, inducting him etc. having removed John Okelhyd from the archdeaconry, William from the vicarage of Locrerdh, John Olonayn from the rectory of Fhynunc, Dermot from that of Thyrdaglas and any other [un]lawful[4] detainers and causing Edmund (or his proctor) to be received as a canon of the church of Clonfert, with plenitude of canon law, and their fruits etc., rights and obventions and those of the archdeaconry and rectories to be annexed to them to be delivered to him. [Curbing] gainsayers by the pope's authority etc. Notwithstanding etc. Also the pope dispenses Edmund to receive and retain the canonry and prebend, if conferred on him by virtue of the presents, notwithstanding the aforesaid defect etc. With the proviso that the vicarage to be erected into a prebend and the archdeaconry and rectories to be united shall not, on account of this erection, institution and union etc., be defrauded of due services and the cure of souls in the vicarage and rectories and (if any) the archdeaconry shall not be neglected, but that their customary burdens shall be supported; and that on Edmund's death or resignation etc. of the canonry and prebend this erection and institution shall be extinguished and union etc. dissolved and the vicarage, archdeaconry and rectories shall revert to their original condition and be deemed vacant automatically.

Apostolice sedi[5] providentia circumspecta ad ea libenter intendit . . .
S. de Castello / . V. [6] */ · V· xxxv*[7] *De Phano:-*

[1] *recte*; for 'rite'?

² *perpetue vicarie*; *recte*: 'perpetua vicaria'?
³ MS: (?)*deuta* [for devta (=devoluta)]; the doubtful letters are overwritten
⁴ MS: *licitis*; *recte*: 'illicitis'
⁵ *sic*; *recte*: 'sedis'
⁶ a dash to the left
⁷ wants expedition date?

17　15 June 1498　　　　　　　　　　　　　　　*Reg. Lat.* 1029, fo 222^{r-v}

To Thomas Chapman', MA, rector of the parish church of the Nativity of B. Mary the Virgin, Conyngton', d. Lincoln. Dispensation — at his supplication — to him, who is also a BDec and, as he asserts, holds a canonry and prebend of the church of B. Mary, Leicester (*Leicestrie*), d. Lincoln, new establishment (*novi operis*), and the above parish church, to receive and retain for life, together with the parish church, two, and without it, any three other benefices, with cure or otherwise mutually incompatible, even if dignities, *personatus,* administrations or offices in cathedral, even metropolitan, or collegiate churches, even if the dignities in question should be major *post pontificalem* in cathedral, even metropolitan, churches, or principal in collegiate churches, or chantries, free chapels, hospitals or annual services, usually assigned to secular clerics in title of a perpetual ecclesiastical benefice, or two of them be parish churches or their perpetual vicarages, or a combination, and even if the dignities etc. be customarily elective and have cure of souls, if he obtains them otherwise canonically, to resign them, at once or successively, simply or for exchange, as often as he pleases, and in their place receive up to three other, similar or dissimilar, incompatible benefices — provided that of three such benefices not more than two be parish churches or their perpetual vicarages — and retain them for life, as above. Notwithstanding etc. With the proviso that the above parish church and other incompatible benefices shall not, on this account, be defrauded of due services and the cure of souls in the church and (if any) the other incompatible benefices shall not be neglected.

Litterarum scientia, vite ac morum honestas . . .
· *A de Sancto severino* / · *V·* / *V· C· De Phano:*

18　27 July 1498　　　　　　　　　　　　　　　*Reg. Lat.* 1029, fo 252^{r-v}

To Robert Pluncket, scholar, d. Meath. Dispensation — at his supplication — to him, who, as he asserts, is below his nineteenth year of age and wishes to become a cleric, to receive and retain — after he is marked with clerical character and is in his nineteenth year — any benefice, with cure or otherwise incompatible, etc. [as below, no. 240].

Vite ac morum honestas . . .
· *A· de Sanctoseverino* / *F~* / *F · xx Sanctor(is)*

19　18 April 1498　　　　　　　　　　　　　*Reg. Lat.* 1030, fos 2ᵛ-3ʳ

To John Rerysby, subdeacon, d. York. Dispensation — at his supplication — to receive and retain — as soon as he reaches his twentieth year of age — any benefice, with cure or otherwise incompatible, etc. [as below, no. 240, to '. . . receive and retain'] — as soon as he reaches his said twentieth year — another, similar or dissimilar, benefice, with cure or otherwise incompatible, as above. Notwithstanding the above defect of age etc. With the proviso that the benefice in question shall not, on this account, be defrauded of due services and the cure of souls therein (if any) shall not be neglected.

Vite ac morum honestas . . .
· *P· de· Castello* / · *V·* / *V· · xx De Phano:*

20　28 July 1498　　　　　　　　　　　　　*Reg. Lat.* 1030, fo 50ʳ⁻ᵛ

To John Brent, monk of the monastery, usually governed by a prior, of B. Mary, Monomuth', OSB, d. Hereford. Dispensation and indult — at his supplication — to receive and retain any benefice, with or without cure, usually held by secular clerics, even if a parish church or its perpetual vicarage, or a chantry, free chapel, hospital or annual service, usually assigned to secular clerics in title of a perpetual ecclesiastical benefice, even if of lay patronage and of whatsoever tax or annual value, if he obtains it otherwise canonically, to resign it, simply or for exchange, as often as he pleases, and in its place receive and retain another, similar or dissimilar, benefice, with or without cure, usually held by secular clerics; and, after he has acquired the benefice, to receive as before the monacal portion he receives in the above monastery (of which he is a monk and, as he asserts, expressly professed of the above order), and to have a stall in the choir and a place and voice in the chapter of the monastery. Notwithstanding etc.

Religionis zelus, vite ac morum honestas. . .
. *P. de Planca* / . *V.* / . *V. L. De Phano:-*

21   28 July 1498   *Reg. Lat.* 1030, fos 53^V-54^V

To John Ffox, perpetual vicar of the parish church of Coston', d. Bath and Wells.
Dispensation and indult — at his supplication — to receive and retain for life,
together with the perpetual vicarage of the above parish church, one, and without it,
any two other benefices, etc. [as above, no. 3, to '. . . retain them together for life, as
above']; and, for life, while residing in the Roman curia or any one of his benefices
or attending a *studium generale*, not to be bound to reside in his other benefices, nor
to be liable to be compelled by anyone to do so against his will. Notwithstanding etc.
With the proviso that the above vicarage[1] and other incompatible benefices shall not,
on this account, be defrauded of due services and the cure of souls in the vicarage
and (if any) the other incompatible benefices shall not be neglected.[2]

Vite ac morum honestas . . .
. Jo. Ortega / · V· / V· Lx De Phano:

[1] Other such indults for non-residence (see note 2 below) are summarised in the present volume in an
abridged form and refer to this entry as to the fully extended prototype. When necessary, a term
appropriate to the previous content of the entry should be substituted here (e. g. in no. 204: read 'church'
for 'vicarage').
[2] There is, however, in this instance (and in those entries referring to this as the prototype) no clause
protecting benefices specifically in case of non-residence (such as in no. 238) or providing for vicars
(such as in no. 135).

22   1 August 1498   *Reg. Lat.* 1030, fos 54^V-55^r

To Martin Durham, canon of the priory of St Peter, Trym', in Ireland, OSA, d.
Meath. Dispensation — at his supplication — to him, who, as he asserts, is expressly
professed of the above order, [1] to receive and retain any benefice, with or without
cure, usually held by secular clerics, even if a parish church or its perpetual vicarage,
or a chantry, free chapel, hospital or annual service, usually assigned to secular
clerics in title of a perpetual ecclesiastical benefice, and of [?][2] patronage and of
whatsoever tax or annual value, if he obtains it otherwise canonically, to resign it,
simply or for exchange, when he pleases, and in its place receive and retain another,
similar or dissimilar, benefice, with or without cure, usually held by secular clerics.
Notwithstanding etc. and [notwithstanding] the constitutions of Otto and Ottobuono
formerly legates of the apostolic see in the kingdom of England[3] etc.

Religionis zelus, vite ac morum honestas . . .
A. de Sanctoseverino / : V· / . V. xxx. De Phano:

[1] This information comes from a notwithstanding clause.
[2] 'laicorum' wanting?
[3] The inclusion of these constitutions gives Durham the option of holding his secular benefice in
England.

23   18 August 1498   *Reg. Lat.* 1030, fos 60^r-61^r

To John Borde, rector of the parish church of Lymyngton, d. Bath and Wells. Dispensation and indult — at his supplication — to receive and retain for life, together with the above parish church, one, and without it, any two other benefices, etc. [as above, no. 3, to '. . . retain them together for life, as above']; and, also for life, while residing in the Roman curia or any one of his benefices or attending a *studium generale*, not to be bound to reside in his other benefices, etc. [as above, no. 21].

Vite ac morum honestas . . .
· *Jo· ortega / · V· / · V· · Lx· De Phano:*

24   18 August 1498   *Reg. Lat.* 1030, fos 61^r-62^r

To John Morys, rector of the parish church of Tetylscombe [also spelt *Tetilscombe*], d. Chichester. Dispensation — at his supplication — to receive and retain for life, together with the above parish church, one, and without it, any two other benefices, etc. [as above, no. 3].

Vite ac morum honestas . . .
Jo· ortega / · V· / · V· L· De Phano:

25   27 July 1498[1]   *Reg. Lat.* 1030, fo 69^{r-v}

To John Copping, perpetual vicar of the parish church of Tatington',[2] d. Norwich. Dispensation — at his supplication — to receive and retain for life, together with the perpetual vicarage of the above parish church, one, and without them, any two other benefices, etc. [as above, no. 3].

Vite ac morum honestas . . .
· *L· puccius / F / · F· L. Sanctor(is)*

[1] The writing and ink of *sexto kalendas Augusti anno sexto* suggests that this part of the date was added later — perhaps when the magistral signature was written.
[2] (?)*Tha. . . . . st*, deleted and (apparently) initialled *F*, occurs before the first occurrence

26   27 July 1498   *Reg. Lat.* 1030, fos 70^r-71^r

To John Hyde, BDec, perpetual vicar of the parish church of Tylehurst, d. Salisbury.

Dispensation — at his supplication — to receive and retain for life, together with the perpetual vicarage of the above parish church, one, and without it, any two other benefices, etc. [as above, no. 3].

Litterarum scientia, vite ac morum honestas . . .
· L· puccius / F / · F· L· Sanctor(is)

27   9 August 1498   *Reg. Lat.* 1030, fo 103^r

To Thomas Pannetter, monk of the monastery of Paisley (*de Pasleto*), OClun, d. Glasgow. Dispensation and indult — at his supplication — to him, who, as he asserts, suffers from a defect of birth as the son of an unmarried man and an unmarried woman, and is, as he also asserts, expressly professed of the above order,[1] to receive and retain any regular benefice, with or without cure, OClun, or secular benefice with cure, for which the presentation of a suitable person at a time of vacancy belongs to the abbot and convent of the above monastery, even if the [(?)regular][2] benefice should be a priory, *prepositura*, dignity, *personatus*, administration or office, and the priory or dignity be conventual or the office claustral, and the secular benefice should be a perpetual vicarage, and the priory etc. should be customarily elective and have cure of souls, if he obtains it otherwise canonically; and also to be chosen abbot of the above, or any other, monastery of the said order , and be appointed to and preside over it and rule and govern it in spiritualities and temporalities; and also to resign the said benefice, simply or for exchange, as often as he pleases and cede the rule and administration of the said monastery and in its place receive and retain likewise another, similar or dissimilar, regular benefice, with or without cure, of the said order, or a secular benefice with cure for which the presentation of a suitable person belongs to the above abbot and convent and to be appointed and preside as abbot of any other monastery of the said order and rule and govern it in spiritualities and temporalities; and — even after he has acquired the secular or regular benefice in question, if — by reason of it — he resides outside the said monastery of Paisley with the licence of his superior — to be able in every way in future to use, possess and enjoy all the privileges, immunities and graces and an active and a passive voice which the other monks of the monastery resident in it use, possess and enjoy or are able so to do. Notwithstanding the above defect etc. and [notwithstanding] constitutions etc. and also privileges and indults granted under whatsoever tenors to the said order. And the pope hereby derogates the said privileges, having their tenors as expressed, specially and expressly, for this once only.

Religionis zelus, vite ac morum honestas . . .
?3 / · V· / V· Lx De Phano:-

[1] The latter information comes from a notwithstanding clause.

2 *seculare*; *recte*: 'regulare'?
3 shaved away

28   25 July 1498   *Reg. Lat.* 1031, fos 19^v-21^v

To the bishops of Lincoln, Salisbury, and *Rossen.*,[1] mandate in favour of William Baylli, layman, d. Winchester, and Joan Rose, woman, d. Lincoln, married couple. A recent petition to the pope on William and Joan's part stated that, formerly, after they had lawfully contracted marriage *per verba de presenti*, Joan sued Robert Ardern', layman, d. Coventry and Lichfield, (who was, and had been for some time, putting it about publicly that Joan had contracted marriage with him *per verba de presenti* before she had so contracted it <with>[2] William), before Hugh Peyntwyn', LLD, archdeacon of the church of Canterbury, to whom John, cardinal priest of St Anastasia, (who is understood to preside over the church of Canterbury by apostolic concession and dispensation, is primate of the whole kingdom of England and legate of the apostolic see in those parts, and who had sufficient power from the apostolic see) had committed the case; that when Hugh had proceeded to several judicial acts in the case short of a conclusion and Robert had resummoned it before him, praying that Joan be adjudged his lawful wife, and William had, in his own interest, been duly admitted to the cause, Hugh refused to proceed summarily, after the couple had lawfully requested him to, and — claiming untruthfully that it had come to his notice that William had been in contact with Joan after he had inhibited him from contact under sentence of excommunication and other ecclesiastical sentences and censures then expressed — proceeding suddenly and *de facto*, excommunicated the couple when they had been neither summoned nor cited, while they were absent (but not through contumacy), from which (as soon as it came to their notice) and from the refusal, they appealed to the apostolic see, impetrated apostolic[3] letters over the appeal, things attempted and innovated after and against it, nullity of Hugh's process, and whole principal [matter][4], to the bishop of Salisbury, (his own name not expressed), and certain colleagues, and caused Robert to be summoned to trial, in the cause of the appeal, before the above John, bishop of Salisbury;[5] that after the above bishop of Salisbury[6] had proceeded to several judicial acts short of a conclusion and wholly committed his powers, *de facto*, to Richard Draper, LLD, and Richard had similarly proceeded to several judicial acts <also>[7] short of a conclusion, and after William — broken by the threats of certain powerful magnates who totally favoured Robert — had renounced his right, suit, case, and later appeal, and also the benefit, advantage, force, and authority to him of the delegation and sub-delegation, and it had been explained to the cardinal legate on William's part that his renunciation had been made under the above threats and otherwise in fear, the cardinal legate, with the express consent of the parties, by his letters charged the bishop of Durham and a certain colleague commanding them (or one of them) to take cognizance of the principal matter and the marriage case (and everything connected with it), and to decree what was canonical, without appeal, in accordance with the form of the cardinal's letters, as is said to be more fully contained in them; that the bishop of [Durham][8] and his colleague, having summoned the parties to trial before them, proceeding wrongly, by one definitive sentence, declared that Joan was Robert's lawful wife and Robert Joan's lawful husband, and by another definitive sentence, as they called them, absolved Joan from an accusation (*impetitione*) of Robert's as regards a certain article contained in a libel of William's exhibited in the case; and that the couple successively appealed from the above sentences to the apostolic see. At the supplication to the pope of William and Joan (who assert that Joan is imprisoned or kept strictly confined by Hugh's order)[9] to command that Joan be released, and that they be absolved conditionally from sentence of excommunication and other censures if any have been inflicted on them, and to commit to some upright men in those parts the cases of the two later appeals; of everything attempted and innovated after and against them; of the nullity and invalidity of the sentences, processes, and everything done wrongly and temerariously against them; and of the principal matter, the pope hereby commands that the above three (or two or one of them), [10] having summoned Robert and others concerned, and when, (if right), Joan has been released, shall, if and as it is just, for this once only, conditionally absolve William and Joan, if they so request, having first received suitable security from them that if they find that the sentences etc. were justly inflicted on them, they will obey their commands and those of the church; and, as regards the rest, having heard both sides, taking cognizance even of the principal matter, that they shall decree what is canonical, without appeal, causing by ecclesiastical censure what they have decreed to be strictly observed. Notwithstanding etc.

Humilibus et cetera.
S· de Castello[11] / · *V·* / · *V· xiiij· De Phano:*

[1] *recte:* 'Roffen.' (Rochester)?
[2] *quam cum* inserted in margin by enregistering scribe; not initialled; *cf.* note 11 below
[3] at the end of a line, well into margin : an insertion (though not initialled)?
[4] MS wants 'negotii'
[5] *coram te Johanne episcopo (?)coram* [deleted] *Saresbirien.*; as John is not named in the address clause the 'te' here is unexpected. *Cf.* next note
[6] *tu episcope*; *cf.* previous note; the use of the vocative is likewise unexpected
[7] *etiam* inserted above line by enregistering scribe; not initialled
[8] MS : *Dunelinien.*; the 'ne' being written over (?)'li'; *recte*: 'Dunelmen.'
[9] the allegation is defective : . . . *asserentes quod dicta Johanna de mandato dicti Joha* [deleted] *Hugonis* [fo 21[r]] *ip(su)mque et dictum Willelmum carceribus mancipita existit seu sub arcta custodia detinetur* . . . A passage was perhaps omitted when the new leaf was started
[10] MS : *discretioni vestre;* 'fraternitati vestre' required by the *stilus*: all the mandataries are bishops
[11] entered later ? : ink and pen the same as that of the marginal insertion noted above (note 2)

29   2 August 1498   *Reg. Lat.* 1031, fos 21[v]-23[r]

To the bishop of Hereford, the abbot of the monastery of Evyshin', d. Worcester, and the prior of the church of Worcester, mandate in favour of Thomas Porter [also spelt *Porteʒ*], layman, d. Worcester. A recent petition to the pope on Thomas's part stated that, formerly, he sued William Leicetre, layman, d. Worcester — who had inflicted serious damage on him and badly defamed him by saying that he had forged and falsified certain instruments or letters called evidences by the English — before John Borbol, UIB, to whom the late Robert, bishop of Worcester, (to whom cognizance of such cases arising between lay persons of the diocese of Worcester pertains by ancient, approved and hitherto peacefully observed custom) had committed the case, praying that he be condemned and compelled to make proper amends to him for the damage and defamation; that William, untruthfully claiming that he had been temerariously aggrieved by John Borbol, had recourse to John, cardinal priest of St Anastasia, (who is legate of the apostolic see in the kingdom of England, primate of the whole kingdom, and is understood to preside over the church of Canterbury by concession and dispensation of the apostolic see), and, in the case referred by him (as was said) to the cardinal legate, sued Thomas before Thomas Cooki and, on his death, before Hugh Peyntwyn, LLD, archdeacon of the church of Canterbury, to whom the cardinal had, successively, committed it; that the archdeacon, duly proceeding in the case, promulgated a definitive sentence in favour of Thomas and against William who, falsely asserting that the sentence was unjust, appealed to the apostolic see, and, in the case of the appeal, sued Thomas before William Mors, (who bore himself as a canon of the church of Annaghdown), whom he said was the judge deputed by apostolic authority; that William Mors, proceeding wrongly in the case, revoked the previous sentence by his unjust definitive sentence, condemning Thomas in costs (the taxation of which he reserved to himself for the future); that Thomas appealed to the apostolic see, but William Mors, contemptuous of this appeal (of which he was not ignorant) and while Thomas was still well within the time for prosecuting it, taxed the costs excessively and then, because Thomas did not pay William the taxed costs, excommunicated him and commanded that he be published excommunicate. At Thomas's supplication to the pope to command that he be absolved conditionally from the sentence of excommunication and other ecclesiastical sentences and censures perchance inflicted on him, and to commit to some upright men in those parts the cases of the later appeal; of everything attempted and innovated after and against [the appeal][1]; of the nullity of William's process and sentence; of everything done to Thomas's prejudice; and of the whole principal matter, the pope hereby commands that the above three (or two or one of them), having summoned William Leicetre and others concerned, shall, if and as it is just, for this once only, conditionally absolve Thomas, if he so requests, having first received suitable security from him that if they find the sentences etc. were justly inflicted on him, he will obey their commands and those of the church; and, as regards the rest, having heard both sides, taking cognizance even of the principal matter, shall decree what is just, without appeal, causing by ecclesiastical censure what they have decreed to be strictly observed. Notwithstanding etc.

Humilibus et cetera.
F de parma / · V· / · V· xiiij· De Phano: —

---

[1] MS wants 'eam'

30   22 May 1498   *Reg. Lat.* 1031, fos 43ʳ-44ʳ

To John Smyth, canon of the priory of St Mary, Watithon', order of St Gilbert of
Sempringham (*Semprynghm*), d. Lincoln.[1] Dispensation, at his supplication, to him
— who, as he asserts, was presented to the local ordinary for the perpetual vicarage
of the parish church of St Andrew, Ottwrby, d. Lincoln (which is customarily held by
canons of the above order) at another time when it was vacant *certo modo* by the
then prior of the priory of Ormsby, Lincoln,[2] of the said order, d. Lincoln (since the
presentation of a suitable person for the vicarage at a time of vacancy pertains by
ancient and approved custom hitherto peacefully observed to the prior of the said
priory) and at this presentation was instituted into the perpetual vicarage by ordinary
authority, and holds it; and who, as he also asserts, is expressly professed of the
above order[3] — to receive and retain, having resigned the vicarage, any other
benefice, with or without cure, usually held by secular clerics, even if a parish
church or its perpetual vicarage, or a chantry, free chapel, hospital or annual service,
usually assigned to secular clerics in title of a perpetual ecclesiastical benefice, even
if of clerical or lay patronage and of whatsoever tax or annual value, if he obtains it
otherwise canonically, to resign it, simply or for exchange, as often as he pleases,
and in its place to receive and retain another, similar or dissimilar, benefice, with or
without cure, usually held by secular clerics. Notwithstanding etc.

Religionis zelus, vite ac morum honestas . . .
F. de parma / V· [4] */ · V· xx De Phano:-*

[1] applicable only to Sempringham; Watton is d. York (not mentioned)
[2] MS: *Ormsby Lincolinen. dicti ordinis Lincolinen. diocesis* [!]
[3] This latter information comes from a notwithstanding clause.
[4] a swung dash before it

31   12 June 1498   *Reg. Lat.* 1031, fo 127ʳ⁻ᵛ

To Thomas Larbe,[1] rector of the parish church of Ffolsham [also spelt *Ffolham*], d.
Norwich. Dispensation — at his supplication — to receive [and retain for life], [2]
together with the above parish church, one, and without it, any two other benefices,
etc. [as above, no. 3].[3]

Vite ac morum honestas . . .
Jo· ortega / F· / F· Lᵗᵃ. Sanctor(is)

[1] or possibly *Lorbe* (the second letter is overwritten)
[2] 'et insimul quoadvixeris retinere' does not occur at this point, but does below
[3] save that 'ecclesiastical' does not occur

32   12 June 1498   *Reg. Lat.* 1031, fo 128^r

To William Wherre *alias* Excester, monk of the monastery of B. Mary, Fforde [also
spelt *Ffoder*], OCist, d. Exeter. Dispensation — at his supplication — to him, who,
as he asserts, is expressly professed of the above order,[1] to receive and retain any
benefice, with or without cure, usually held by secular clerics, even if a parish
church or its perpetual vicarage, or a chantry, free chapel, hospital or annual service,
usually assigned to secular clerics in title of a perpetual ecclesiastical benefice, and
of lay patronage and of whatsoever tax or annual value, if he obtains it otherwise
canonically, to resign it, simply or for exchange, when he pleases, and in its place
receive and retain another, similar or dissimilar, benefice, with or without cure,[2]
usually held by secular clerics. Notwithstanding etc.

Religionis zelus, vite ac morum honestas . . .
Jo· ortega / F· / F· xxx Sanctor(is)

[1] This information comes from a notwithstanding clause.
[2] Other entries of this type are summarised in the present volume in an abridged form and refer to this
entry as to a fully extended prototype. In this entry the phrase 'with or without cure' contained in the text
above happens to be repeated at this point — as it is in many — though not all — such entries.

33   12 June 1498   *Reg. Lat.* 1031, fos 128^v-129^r

To John <Edimundi>,[1] <BTheol>,[2] rector of the parish church of Patuorth', d.
Chichester. Dispensation — at his supplication — to receive and retain for life,
together with the above parish church, one, and without it, any two other benefices,
etc. [as above, no. 3].

Vite[3] *ac morum honestas . . .*
Jo· ortega / F· [4] */ F· L^{ta}. Sanctor(is)*

[1] marginal insertion, initialled *F.*; (?)*Edmundi*, deleted and initialled *F.*, in the line
[2] *Bacallario in theologia* inserted in the margin, initialled *F.*; *in Theologia Bacallario*, deleted and
initialled *F.*, in the line
[3] *sic*; 'Litterarum scientia, vite . . . ' would accord with the degree
[4] partially shaved

34   12 June 1498   *Reg. Lat.* 1031, fos 129^r-130^r

To Clement Bangchier', rector of the parish church of Assh', d. Winchester.
Dispensation — at his supplication — to receive and retain for life, together with the

above parish church, one, and without it, any two other benefices, etc. [as above, no. 3].[1]

Vite ac morum honestas . . .
Jo· ortega / F· / F· L. Sanctor(is)

[1] save that the present entry wants 'or collegiate'

35   10 April 1498   *Reg. Lat.* 1031, fo 138[r-v]

To Stephen de Surteys, BTheol, perpetual vicar of the parish church of Ashburne, d. Coventry and Lichfield. Dispensation — at his supplication — to him, (who, some time ago, was dispensed by apostolic authority, notwithstanding a defect of birth as the son of an unmarried man[1] and an unmarried woman, to be promoted to all, even sacred, orders and to hold a benefice, even if it should have cure of souls; and afterwards was duly marked with clerical character and holds the perpetual vicarage of the above parish church by this dispensation), to receive and retain for life, together with the above perpetual vicarage, one, and without it, any two other benefices, with cure or otherwise mutually incompatible, even if parish churches or their perpetual vicarages, or chantries, free chapels, hospitals or annual services, usually assigned to secular clerics in title of a perpetual ecclesiastical benefice, or dignities, *personatus*, administrations or offices in cathedral, even metropolitan, or collegiate churches, or a combination, even if the dignities etc. should be customarily elective and have cure of souls, if he obtains them otherwise canonically, to resign them, at once or successively, simply or for exchange, as often as he pleases, and in their place receive up to two other, similar or dissimilar, incompatible benefices — provided that such dignities be not major *post pontificalem* in cathedral, even metropolitan, churches or principal in collegiate churches — and retain them together for life, as above. Notwithstanding the above defect etc. With the proviso that the above vicarage and other incompatible benefices shall not, on this account, be defrauded of due services and the cure of souls in the vicarage and (if any) the other incompatible benefices shall not be neglected.

Litterarum scientia, vite ac morum honestas . . .
Jo· ortega / . L. / . L. L^{ta}. Dulcius:-

[1] *presbytero* in the line deleted and initialled . L.; *soluto* inserted in the margin; *Cassatum et Corectum de mandato Domini A[loysii] pisauren' .L.*

36   10 April 1498   *Reg. Lat.* 1031, fos 138[v]-139[v]

To Robert Honywoode,[1] archdeacon of the church[2] of Norwich. Dispensation — at his supplication — to receive and retain for life, together with the above archdeaconry, one, and without it, any two other benefices, etc. [as above, no. 3].

Vite ac morum honestas . . .
Jo ortega / L. / . L. L^{ta}. Dulcius:-

[1] changed (by overwriting) from (?) *Honywolde*
[2] *sic*

---

37   10 April 1498   *Reg. Lat.* 1031, fos 139^{v}-140^{r}

To Richard Garlond, monk of the monastery of Newham, OCist, d. Exeter. Dispensation — at his supplication — to him, who, as he asserts, is expressly professed of the above order, [1] to receive and retain any benefice, with or without cure, usually held by secular clerics, etc. [as above, no. 32].

Religionis zelus, viteque[2] ac morum honestas . . .
Jo ortega / . L.[3] / . L. xxx. Dulcius:-

[1] This information comes from a notwithstanding clause.
[2] *sic*
[3] a '2' before the point before the 'L'; a swung dash developed from the point after it *Cf.* nos. 38 and 39

---

38   10 April 1498   *Reg. Lat.* 1031, fos 140^{v}-141^{r}

To Robert Eliston', perpetual vicar of the parish church of Sondebach, d. Coventry and Lichfield. Dispensation — at his supplication — to receive and retain for life, together with the above perpetual vicarage, one, and without it, any two other benefices, etc. [as above, no. 3].

Vite ac morum honestas . . .
Jo ortega / . L. [1] / . L. L^{ta}. Dulcius:-

[1] a '2' above the point before the 'L'; a swung dash developed from the point after it *Cf.* nos. 37 and 39

---

39   8 January 1498   *Reg. Lat.* 1031, fos 141^{v}-142^{v}

To Walter Blownt, LLB, rector of the parish church of All Saints, Worcester. Dispensation and indult — at his supplication — to receive and retain for life, together with the above parish church, two, and without it, any three other benefices, etc. [as above, no. 17, to '. . . retain them for life, as above']; and, also for life, while residing in the Roman curia or any one of his benefices or attending a *studium generale*, not to be bound to reside in his other benefices etc. [as above, no. 21].

Litterarum scientia, vite ac morum honestas . . .
Jo. ortega / . *L.* [1] / . *L. C. Dulcius:-*

[1] a '2' above the point before the 'L'; a swung dash developed from the point after it (*Cf.* nos. 37 and 38)

40   10 April 1498   *Reg. Lat.* 1031, fos 142^V-143^V

To Thomas Gutfold', DDec, rector of the parish church of St George, Ham', d. Exeter. Dispensation — at his supplication — to receive and retain for life, together with the above parish church, one, and without it, any two other benefices, etc. [as above, no. 3].

Litterarum scientia, vite ac morum honestas . . .
Jo. ortega / . *L.* [1] / . *L. L^{ta}. Dulcius:-*

[1] a swung dash developed from the point after the 'L'

41   27 July 1498   *Reg. Lat.* 1031, fo 178^{r-v}

To Thomas Ruer, MA, rector of the parish church of St Thomas the Martyr, Dodbroke [also spelt *Drodbroke*], d. Exeter. Indult for life — at his supplication — to him, who, as he asserts, holds by apostolic dispensation the above parish church and the perpetual vicarage of the parish church of B. Mary, Klay, d. Lincoln, not to be bound, while residing in the Roman curia or the parish church or the perpetual vicarage aforesaid or the benefices he shall hold or attending a *studium generale*, to reside in the other benefices, with or without cure, in whatsoever churches or places, held by him now and at the time, nor to be liable to be compelled by anyone to do so against his will. Notwithstanding etc. With the proviso that the benefices in question shall not, on this account, be defrauded of due services and the cure of souls therein shall not be neglected; but that their customary burdens shall be supported.

Litterarum scientia, vite ac morum honestas . . .
F de parma / · *V·* / · *V· xx De Phano:-*

42   15 December 1498   *Reg. Lat.* 1033, fos 12^v-13^r

To Thomas Doget, abbot of the monastery of B. Mary the Virgin, Leyston', OPrem, d. Norwich. Dispensation — at his supplication — to receive and retain *in commendam* for life, together with the above monastery, or without it, any benefice, with or without cure, usually held by secular clerics, even if a parish church or its perpetual vicarage, or a chantry, free chapel, hospital or annual service, usually assigned to secular clerics in title of a perpetual ecclesiastical benefice, and of lay patronage and of whatsoever tax or annual value, if he obtains it otherwise canonically, to resign it when he pleases and cede the commend and in its place receive a similar or dissimilar benefice, with or without cure, usually held by secular clerics, and retain it *in commendam* for life, with or without the said monastery; (he may — due and customary burdens of the benefice having been supported — make disposition of the rest of its fruits etc. just as those holding it *in titulum* could and ought to do, alienation of immovable goods and precious movables being however forbidden). Notwithstanding etc.[1] With the proviso that the benefice shall not, on this account, be defrauded of due services and the cure of souls therein (if any) shall not be neglected; but that its aforesaid burdens shall be supported.

Personam tuam nobis et apostolice sedi devotam tuis exigentibus meritis paterna benivolentia prosequentes illa tibi favorabiliter concedimus . . .
Jo ortega / V· / . V· L^{ta}. De Phano:

[1] no mention of his being expressly professed of the order

43   19 January 1499   *Reg. Lat.* 1033, fos 13^v-14^v

To Simon Sponar, canon of the priory of St John the Evangelist, Lyesp(er)na,[1] OSA, d. London. Dispensation — at his supplication — to him, who, as he asserts, is expressly professed of the above order,[2] to receive any two regular benefices, with or without cure, of any order, or with one of them, or without them, one secular benefice, with cure, even if the regular benefices should be priories, *prepositure*, *prepositatus*, dignities, *personatus*, administrations or offices and the secular benefice should be a parish church or its perpetual vicarage, or a chantry, free chapel, hospital or annual service, usually assigned to secular clerics in title of a perpetual ecclesiastical benefice, even if the priories etc. should be customarily elective and have cure of souls, if he obtains them otherwise canonically, and to retain whichever one of the regular benefices he chooses, even if it should be a priory, *prepositura*, or other conventual dignity or a claustral office, *in titulum*, and the other regular benefice, which may not be suchlike, or the secular benefice, *in commendam*, together for life, to resign them, at once or successively, simply or for exchange, as often as he pleases, and cede the commend, and in their place receive up to two other, similar or dissimilar, regular benefices, with or without cure, of any order, or with one of them, or without them, one secular benefice with cure, and retain whichever one of the regular benefices he chooses, even if it be conventual or claustral, *in titulum*, and the other regular benefice, which may not be suchlike, or the secular benefice, *in commendam*, together for life, as above; (he may — due and customary burdens of the regular or secular benefice held *in commendam* having been supported — make disposition of the rest of its fruits etc. just as those holding it *in titulum* could and ought to do, alienation of immovable goods and precious movables being however forbidden). Notwithstanding etc. With the proviso that the benefice held *in commendam* shall not, on this account, be defrauded of due services and the cure of souls therein (if any) shall not be neglected; but that its aforesaid burdens shall be supported.

Religionis zelus, vite ac morum honestas . . .
A de Sancto Severino / V· / · V· L· De Phano:

[1] MS: *Lyesp'na oris'* [i. e. 'Lyesp(er)na ordinis'] in the margin, against the end of the line: an insertion? (?)*Lyesp(er)naoris'* in the line at the end, deleted and initialled . *V.* twice, with a vertical stroke between *Lyesp(er)na* and *oris'* The name recurs later in MS spelt *Lyesp'na* or, possibly, *Lyesp'ita* — the p' here being differently formed to represent 'pro' not 'per') i. e. 'Lyesp(ro)na' etc.
[2] This information comes from a notwithstanding clause.

44   24 November 1498   *Reg. Lat.* 1033, fos 103^r-104^r

To John Meynoryng, rector of the parish church of Wermyngeham [also spelt *Wermyngheam*], d. Coventry and Lichfield. Dispensation — at his supplication — to receive and retain for life, together with the above parish church, one, and without it, any two other benefices, etc. [as above, no. 3].

Vite ac morum honestas . . .
. L. puccius / · V· / V· L. De Phano:

45   24 November 1498   *Reg. Lat.* 1033, fos 104^r-105^r

To John Mandevyl, rector of the parish church of the Holy Trinity, Onyrtonlongevyle, d. Lincoln. Dispensation — at his supplication — to receive and retain, together with the above parish church, one, and without it, any two other benefices, etc. [as above, no. 3].

Vite ac morum honestas . . .
. L. Puccius / · V· [1] */ · V· L· De Phano:*

[1] the point to the right is actually on the stroke of the 'V'

46   23 February 1499   *Reg. Lat.* 1033, fos 258^{V}-259^{V}

To the abbots of the monasteries of Croxton' and Oselveston', and the prior of the priory of Launde (*de Lauda*), d. Lincoln, mandate in favour of the abbot and convent of the monastery of Thame, OSB or other order, d. Lincoln. A recent petition to the pope on the abbot and convent's part stated that, formerly, after Thomas Hutten', cleric then living in the city or diocese of Lincoln — proceeding duly in a cause which had arisen between the abbot and convent and Robert,[1] rector of the parish church of Cʒakenden, d. Lincoln, over certain matters then expressed, and which the then bishop of Lincoln had committed to him — had promulgated a definitive sentence, (which, in the absence of an appeal, had become a final judgement), in their favour and against Robert, and after John Vesy, (who had been duly appointed by commission of John Vallos, administrator of the church of Lincoln while the episcopal see was vacant), had, at the abbot and convent's instance, duly ordered the execution of the sentence, Robert — untruthfully claiming that the sentence was null and invalid and that he was unduly aggrieved by it and the execution — sued the abbot and convent before Hugh Peyntwyn', archdeacon of the church of Canterbury, to whom John, cardinal priest of St Anastasia, (who is archbishop of Canterbury by apostolic dispensation, primate of the whole kingdom of England, and legate of the apostolic see in those parts) committed the case, praying that it be declared that the sentence and execution were null and invalid and that they ought to be revoked; and that Hugh, proceeding wrongly and lawlessly, promulgated an unjust definitive sentence, by which he declared that the sentence and [execution][2] were null and invalid and revoked them, condemning the abbot and convent in costs, from which they appealed to the apostolic see. At the abbot and convent's supplication to the pope to commit to some upright men in those parts the cases of their appeal; of anything perchance attempted and innovated after and against it; of the nullity of the later sentence and of Hugh's process; and of the principal matter, the pope hereby commands that the above three (or two or one of them), having summoned Robert and others concerned, and having heard both sides, taking cognizance even of the principal matter, shall decree what is just, without appeal, causing by ecclesiastical censure what they have decreed to be strictly observed; [and moreover compel] witnesses etc. Notwithstanding etc.

Humilibus et cetera.
· *L· puccius /· V /· V· xij· De Phano:-*

[1] surname not mentioned

[2] MS : *excommunicationem*; *recte* 'executionem'

47   3 November 1498   *Reg. Lat.* 1033, fos 309ᵛ-310ᵛ

To Thomas Gerard, BDec, rector of the parish church of St Andrew, Stokysby, d.
Norwich. Dispensation — at his supplication — to receive and retain for life,
together with the above parish church, one, and having resigned it, any two other
benefices, etc. [as above, no. 3].

Litterarum scientia, vite ac morum honestas . . .
· S· de castello /· V· / · V· L· De Phano:[1]

[1] changed (by overwriting) from *Fan*

48   27 April 1499   *Reg. Lat.* 1033, fos 332ʳ-333ʳ

To Henry Myleh(a)m,[1] prior of the monastery, usually governed by a prior, of B.
Mary, Cokefford, OSA, d. Norwich. Dispensation — at his supplication — to him,
who, as he asserts, is expressly professed of the above order,[2] to receive, together
with the priory of the above monastery, one, and without it, any two other regular
benefices, with or without cure, of the aforesaid or any other order, or with one of
them, or without them, one benefice, with or without cure, usually held by secular
clerics, even if the regular benefices should be priories, *prepositure, prepositatus,*
dignities, *personatus,* administrations or offices and the secular benefice should be a
parish church or its perpetual vicarage, or a chantry, free chapel, hospital or annual
service, usually assigned to secular clerics in title of a perpetual ecclesiastical
benefice, even if the priories etc. should be customarily elective and have cure of
souls, if he obtains them otherwise canonically, and to retain for life whichever one
of the regular benefices he chooses, even if it should be a priory or other conventual
dignity or a claustral office, *in titulum,* and with it the other regular benefice, which
may not be suchlike, or the secular benefice, *in commendam,* to resign them, at once
or successively, simply or for exchange, as often as he pleases, and to cede the
commend, and in their place receive up to two other, similar or dissimilar, regular
benefices, of the aforesaid or any other order, or with one of them, or without them,
one secular benefice, with or without cure, usually assigned to secular clerics, and
retain for life whichever one of the regular benefices he chooses *in titulum,* and the
other regular benefice, which however may not be a conventual priory or other
conventual dignity or a claustral office, or the secular benefice, *in commendam,* as

above; (he may — due and customary burdens of the benefice held *in commendam* having been supported — make disposition of the rest of its fruits etc. just as those holding it *in titulum* could and ought to do, alienation of immovable goods and precious movables being however forbidden). Notwithstanding etc. With the proviso that the priory and other regular and secular benefices in question shall not, on this account, be defrauded of due services and the cure of souls therein ([if] any) shall not be neglected; but that the aforesaid burdens of the benefice retained *in commendam* shall be supported.

Religionis zelus, vite ac morum honestas . . .
F de parma / F / F L^{*ta*}. *Sanctor(is)*

[1] MS: *Mylehm'*; the 'y' written over another letter (now illegible but without ascenders or descenders)
[2] This information comes from a notwithstanding clause.

49   7 September 1498   *Reg. Lat.* 1033, fo 341^{r-v}

To John Wytheley, monk of the monastery of St Alban, OSB, d. Lincoln. Dispensation — at his supplication — to him, who, as he asserts, is living in the cell of Walyngfordi, immediately subject to the above monastery, and is expressly professed of the above order,[1] to receive and retain any benefice, with or without cure, usually held by secular clerics, even if a parish church or its perpetual vicarage, or a chantry, prebend,[2] free chapel, etc. [as above, no. 32].

Religionis zelus, vite ac morum honestas . . .
? . . .[3] */ . L. / L. xxx. Dulcius:-*

[1] This latter information comes from a notwithstanding clause.
[2] *sic*, though 'prebend' is unexpected in the context
[3] shaved horizontally; largely lost

50   24 September 1498   *Reg. Lat.* 1034, fos 245^r-246^r

To the bishops of Modena and Moray and the official of Moray, mandate in favour of James Steluart, priest, d. Aberdeen. A recent petition to the pope on James's part stated that at another time when the rectory of the parish church of Slanis, d. Aberdeen, which is of lay patronage and which Gilbert Ottirburn, its late rector, held while he lived, was vacant by his death outside the Roman curia, the patron of the rectory being in peaceful possession or almost of the right of patronage or of presenting a suitable person for it at a time of vacancy presented James for it, vacant as above, to the then bishop of Aberdeen or his vicar general, within the lawful time; but the bishop or his vicar, unjustly refused to institute James at the presentation. Moreover, as the same petition added, James fears that for certain reasons the presentation does not hold good; and, as the pope has learned, the rectory is known to be still vacant as above. The pope — wishing to give a special grace to James who asserts that he has appealed to the apostolic see against the above refusal — hereby commands that the above three, or two or one of them, in person or by proxy, shall collate and assign the rectory, whose annual value does not exceed 9 pounds sterling, (vacant as above or howsoever etc.; even if it has been vacant for so long that by the Lateran statutes its collation has lawfully devolved on the apostolic see, etc.), to James, with all rights and appurtenances, inducting him etc., having removed any unlawful detainer and causing James (or his proctor) to be admitted to the rectory and its fruits etc., rights and obventions to be delivered to him. [Curbing] gainsayers etc. Notwithstanding etc.

Vite ac morum honestas . . .
. *L. puccius* / *F.* / *F . xx . Sexto Non. ' Octobr. ' Anno Septimo* [2 October 1498], *Sanctor(is)*

51 — ¹   *Reg. Lat.* 1034, fo 270ʳ

Beginning of a letter addressed: 'to John Dey, perpetual chaplain, [called] custodian or provost, of the [perpetual] chantry [ends];' *nuncupato*, deleted, after *preposito*; no abbreviator's name; no magistral initial.

Occupies two lines at top of otherwise blank page; not deleted; no explanatory note.

Considerations of date suggest that the fragment is an abortive enregistration of a letter now lost, namely the dispensation for plurality rubricated at no. 1056 below. The present register is a *liber* of the seventh year (1498, 26. viii - 1499, 25. viii); so, probably, was the lost one (*cf.* its *signatura*: *I Anni VII*).

Ordinarily, dispensations and the like were enregistered in *libri de diversis. Reg. Lat.* 1034 is a *liber de vacantibus*, the lost register was evidently a *liber de diversis*. The scribe saw his mistake and corrected it.

¹ dating clause wanting

52   30 April 1498   *Reg. Lat.* 1035, fo 3ʳ⁻ᵛ

To Charles Macbrien, elect of Emly. Consistorial provision of him — canon of the church of Emly — to the church of Emly, vacant by the death, outside the Roman curia, of the late bishop Philip, during whose rule the pope specially reserved the said church to his own disposition; and appointment of Charles as bishop, committing to him the care and administration of the church in spiritualities and temporalities.

Conclusions to (i) the chapter of the church of Emly; (ii) the people of the city and diocese; (iii) the clergy of the city and diocese, (iv) the archbishop of Cashel.

Apostolatus officium quamquam insufficientibus meritis nobis ex alto commissum . . .
The conclusions begin: *(i) Hodie ecclesie . . . (ii), (iii) Hodie et cetera. (iv) Ad cumulum et cetera.*
F de parma; A de brinis[1] */ F / F xx. . x. x. x. x. Sanctor(is)*

[1] The writing and ink of the abbreviators' names suggest they were entered later.

53   30 April 1498   *Reg. Lat.* 1035, fo 4[r]

To Charles Macbreyn, canon of Emly. Since the pope, on the advice of the cardinals, intends this day to make provision of Charles to the church of Emly, vacant *certo modo,* and to appoint him bishop, he hereby absolves him from any sentences of excommunication, suspension and interdict and other ecclesiastical sentences, censures and pains under which he may perchance lie, so far only as regards the taking effect of the said provision and appointment and each of the relevant letters. Notwithstanding etc.

Apostolice sedis indefessa clementia ad ea libenter intendit. . .
F de parma[1] */ F / F. xx. Sanctor(is)*

[1] probably entered later; *cf.* no. 52

54   30 April 1498[1]   *Reg. Lat.* 1035, fo 4[v]

To Charles Macbreyn, canon of Emly. Since the pope, on the advice of the cardinals, intends this day to make provision of Charles to the church of Emly, vacant *certo modo,* and to appoint him bishop, he — *motu proprio* — hereby dispenses him (who, some time ago, as the pope has learned, was dispensed by apostolic authority, notwithstanding a defect of birth as the son of an unmarried man and an unmarried woman, having been duly marked with clerical character, to be promoted to all even sacred orders) to receive the care and administration of the said church, preside over it, rule and govern it in spiritualities and temporalities, and receive and use [consecration].[2] Notwithstanding the said defect etc.

Divina supereminens[3] *largitas . . .*
F de parma[4] / *F* / *F xxx. Sanctor(is)*

[1] Though unquestionably written by the same scribe the script of the dating clause is noticeably less cursive than that of the rest of the letter. Written later?

[2] MS: *benedictionis*; *recte*: 'consecrationis'?

[3] *sic*; *cf.* 'superveniens'

[4] probably entered later; *cf.* no. 52

55   3 April 1497   *Reg. Lat.* 1035, fos 180[r]-181[v]

To David Hamulton, elect of Lismore. Consistorial provision of him — cleric, d. Glasgow, MA, marked with clerical character only — to the church of Lismore, vacant by the death, outside the Roman curia, of the late bishop Robert, during whose rule the pope specially reserved the said church to his own ordinance; and appointment of David as bishop, committing to him the care and administration of the church in spiritualities and temporalities.
    Conclusions to (i) the clergy of the city and diocese of Lismore; (ii) the chapter of the church of Lismore; (iii) the people of the said city and diocese; (iv) the vassals of the said church; (v) the archbishop of Glasgow; (vi) James, king of Scots.

Apostolatus officium quamquam insufficientibus meritis nobis ex alto commissum . . .
The conclusions begin: *(i), (iii), (iv) Hodie ecclesie Lismoren. . . . (ii) Hodie ecclesie vestre . . . (v) Ad cumulum et cetera. (vi) Gratie divine premium et cetera.*
. N. Bregeon / . L. / . L. xx. x. x. x. x. x. x. Dulcius:

56   3 April 1497   *Reg. Lat.* 1035, fo 182[r]

To David Hamulton, MA, cleric, d. Glasgow. Since the pope, on the advice of the cardinals, intends this day to make provision of David to the church of Lismore, vacant *certo modo*, and to appoint him bishop, he hereby absolves him from any sentences of excommunication, etc. [as above, no. 53].

Apostolice sedis circumspecta benignitas ad ea libenter intendit . . .
· N· Bregeon / . L. / L. xx. Dulcius:-

57   4 April 1497   *Reg. Lat.* 1035, fo 182[v]

To David, elect of Lismore. Since the pope has recently made provision of David to the church of Lismore, as is more fully contained in his letters drawn up in that regard,[1] he hereby grants faculty to David (who is marked with clerical character only) — at his supplication — to receive consecration from any catholic bishop of his choice in communion with the apostolic see, assisted by two or three catholic bishops similarly in communion; and to the bishop concerned to consecrate him, having first received from him in the name of the pope and the Roman church the usual oath of fealty in accordance with the form noted in the presents. The pope decrees, however, that if the bishop consecrates David without receiving the said oath and David receives consecration they shall both be suspended automatically. Moreover it is the pope's will that David shall send him, at once, by his own messenger, the form of oath taken by him, verbatim, by his letters patent, marked with his seal; and that the above shall not be to the prejudice of the archbishop of Glasgow, to whom the aforesaid church is understood to be subject by metropolitical law. With the form of oath appended.[2]

Cum nos pridem . . .
· *N· Bregeon* / . *L.* / *L. xL. Dulcius:-*

[1] above, no. 55

[2] not cited in full (the first nine words only, then *et cetera*)

---

58   3 April 1497   *Reg. Lat.* 1035, fo 183[r-v]

To David Hamilton', MA, cleric, d. Glasgow. Since the pope, on the advice of the cardinals, intends this day to make provision of David to the church of Lismore, vacant *certo modo*, and to appoint him bishop, and, as the pope has learned, David is in his twenty-sixth year of age and suffers from a defect of birth as the son of an unmarried man of noble birth and an unmarried woman, the pope — *motu proprio* — hereby dispenses him (who, some time ago, was dispensed by apostolic authority, the said defect of birth notwithstanding, to be promoted to all even sacred orders and receive and retain a benefice, even if it should have cure of souls; and afterwards was duly marked with clerical character) to receive the care and administration of the said church, preside over it, rule and govern it in spiritualities and temporalities and receive and use consecration. Notwithstanding the said defects of age and birth etc.

Divina superveniens largitas . . .
· *N· Bregeon* / . *L.* / *L. Lx. Dulcius:-*

---

59   24 December 1498   *Reg. Lat.* 1035, fos 257[r]-258[v]

To Silvester, elect of Worcester. Consistorial provision of him — archpriest and canon of the church of Lucca — to the church of Worcester, OSB, vacant by the death, at the apostolic see, of the late bishop John, and reserved to the pope's disposition under his reservation of provisions to all churches vacated then and in the future at the said see; and appointment of Silvester as bishop, committing to him the care and administration of the church of Worcester in spiritualities and temporalities.

Conclusions to: (i) the chapter of the church of Worcester; (ii) the clergy of the city and diocese; (iii) the people of the city and diocese; (iv) the vassals of the church; (v) the archbishop of Canterbury; (vi) Henry, king of England.

Apostolatus officium quamquam insufficientibus meritis nobis ex alto commissum . . .
The conclusions begin: *(i) Hodie ecclesie vestre . . . (ii), (iii), (iv) Hodie ecclesie . . .*
(v) Ad cumulum et cetera. (vi) Gratie divine premium . . .
. P. de. Castello. / · V· / · V· xx. x. x. x. x. x. x. De Phano:-

60   24 December 1498   *Reg. Lat. 1035, fos 258ᵛ-259ʳ*

To Silvester de Giglis, archpriest of the church of Lucca. Since the pope, on the advice of the cardinals, intends this day to make provision of Silvester to the church of Worcester, OSB, vacant *certo modo,* and to appoint him bishop, he hereby absolves him from any sentences of excommunication, etc. [as above, no. 53].

Apostolice sedis indefessa clementia ad ea libenter intendit . . .
. P. de. Castello. / · V· / V· xx De Phano:-

61   20 July 1498   *Reg. Lat. 1036, fos 11ʳ-12ᵛ*

To George Schaw, monk, recently abbot of the monastery of B. Mirren, Paisley (*de Pasleto*), OClun, d. Glasgow, immediately subject to the Roman church, concession and indult, as below. This day George has, spontaneously and freely, ceded into the pope's hands the rule and administration of the above monastery, over which he was presiding at the time, and the pope, admitting the cession, has, on the advice of the cardinals, commended the monastery, thus vacant, to Robert Schaw, perpetual vicar of the parish church of Mukton', d. Glasgow, to hold, rule and govern for six months reckoned thenceforth; and, on the advice of the cardinals, made provision of Robert and appointed him abbot as from when he is received as a monk of the monastery, has the regular habit bestowed on him and makes his regular profession, as is more fully contained in the pope's letters drawn up in that regard. Lest George should suffer excessive loss from this cession, the pope, on the advice of the cardinals, hereby grants and indulges George that — on Robert's death or resignation etc., or the monastery falling vacant in any way, even at the apostolic see — he may have free re-entry to the monastery and the rule and administration, without having to be provided to the monastery anew; and he may, on his own authority, in person or by proxy, take corporal possession of its rule and administration and goods; and, by virtue of his earlier title, preside over the monastery, just as before; and rule and govern it in spiritualities and temporalities in and for all things, just as if he had not ceded the said rule and administration. Notwithstanding etc.

Executory to the bishop of Penne, the abbot of the monastery of Dunfermiling, (d. St Andrews),[1] and the prior of the church of Whithorn,[2] or two or one of them, acting in person or by proxy.

Religionis zelus, vite ac morum honestas . . . The executory begins: *Hodie cum dilectus filius Georgius Schaw* . . .
F de parma; A de sanctoseverino / *F.* / *F. xxxx. xx. Sanctor(is)*

[1] *Sancti Andree diocesis* inserted in the margin (in a different script); *Cassatum et Correctum De Man(da)to R(everendissimi) D(omini) A(loysii) pisaurien' per me . V. de Phano:* (in a third script) after the insertion

[2] Originally, the address clause read: *venerabili fratri episcopo Pennen. et dilectis filiis abbati monasterii de Dunfermiling ac priori priori* [the latter 'priori' deleted and initialled *F.*] *prioratus Candide Case Sancti Andree diocesis salutem et cetera. .* It was then changed by V. de Phano by order of the regent of the chancery to: *venerabili fratri episcopo Pennen. et dilectis filiis abbati monasterii de Dunfermiling Sancti Andree diocesis ac priori ecclesie Candide Case salutem et cetera.* Cf. below, no. 63, note 9.

62   4 August 1498   *Reg. Lat.* 1036, fos 36^v-37^r

To Laurence Dotson', perpetual vicar of the parish church of Pen, d. Lincoln. Dispensation — at his supplication — to him, who is a BA, to receive and retain for life, together with the perpetual vicarage of the above parish church, any other, and without it, any two other benefices, etc. [as above, no. 3].

Vite ac morum honestas . . .
F de parma / *F·* / *F L^{ta}. Sanctor(is)*

63   20 July[1] 1498   *Reg. Lat.* 1036, fos 90^r-91^v

To George Schaw, monk, recently abbot of the monastery of B. Mirren, Paisley (*de Pasleto*), OClun, d. Glasgow, immediately subject to the Roman church, reservation, grant and assignment, as below. This day George has, spontaneously and freely, ceded into the pope's hands the rule and administration of the above monastery, over which he was presiding at the time, and the pope, admitting the cession, has, on the advice of the cardinals, commended the monastery, thus vacant, to Robert Schaw, perpetual vicar of the parish church of Mu'kton', d. Glasgow, to hold, rule and govern for six months reckoned thenceforth; and, on the advice of the cardinals, made provision of Robert as from when he is received as a monk of the said monastery, has the regular habit bestowed on him and makes his regular profession, as is more fully contained in the pope's letters drawn up in that regard. Lest George should suffer excessive loss from this cession, the pope — *motu proprio* — hereby reserves, grants and assigns the lands, mills and annual revenues, together with fisheries, in the lordship or territory of the places of Mukton' Dalmilling[2] within the county[3] of Air [also spelt *Ayr*], d. Glasgow, and all the fruits etc. of the churches of Dundonald, Ricardton', Cragyn', Mukton', St Kennocha (*Sancte Kenoce*), Prestwik, Althinelek[4] (with its annual revenue), and of Largis and Cumray within the aforesaid [county] of Air, and of Lotwinʒok[5] , and (the lands)[6] of Glen' within[7] the county of Renfrow, d. Glasgow, pertaining to the said monastery and which, as the pope has learned, do not exceed a third part of the monastery's fruits, for him to possess, have the usufruct of and receive for life, in place of an annual pension; decreeing that, for life, George cannot be and ought not to be molested by Robert or anyone else over the possession and usufruct of the lands and mills and over the receipt of the above fruits etc.[8] Notwithstanding etc.

Executory to the bishop of Penne, the abbot of the monastery of Dunfermiling and the prior of the priory of Whithorn (*Candide Case*), d. St Andrews.[9]

Religionis zelus, vite ac morum honestas . . . The executory begins: *Hodie cum dilectus filius Georgius Schaw* . . .
F de parma; A de sanctoseverino / · *V·* / · *V· xx . x. De Phano:-*

[1] . . . *Augustini; recte*: '. . . *Augusti*'

[2] spelt *Dalmillyng* in the executory

[3] *vicecom(itatum)* deleted in the line (not initialled); yet *[vi]cecomitatum* (shaved), inserted, initialled .*V.*, in the margin.

[4] spelt *Athinlek* in the executory

[5] spelt *Lothwynʒ ok* in the executory

[6] *terrarum* inserted in the margin initialled . *V*.; (?)*Therrarum* deleted and initialled . *V*. , in the line

[7] *in/fra*; the 'fra' changed (by deletion) from (?)*Ayr*, initialled . *V*.; *Air*, deleted and initialled . *V*. , against it in the margin

[8] *de eorundem fratrum consilio concedimus pariter et indulgemus* occurs at the end of the *dispositiva*, but there is no matching concession and indult. The occurrence is suggestive of omission; but as 'induli' does not occur in the *sanctio* it could be gratuitous.

[9] MS: . . . *abbati monasterii de Dunfermiling ac priori prioratus Candide Case Sancti Andree diocesis* Cf. above, no. 61.

64   20 February 1498   *Reg. Lat.* 1036, fos 92[r]-93[r]

To the bishop of Aberdeen, mandate. A recent petition to the pope on the part of

James, king of Scots, and the residents and inhabitants of the new vill within the
boundary of the parish church of St Machar, outside and near the city of Aberdeen,
stated that from a certain time onwards in the new vill, in which once there were
only three or four dwellings, the number of those living there has, by the industry of
the inhabitants, grown and multiplied and is expected to multiply daily; and that if in
the new vill, where king James — to induce people to live there all the more — has
proposed to set up a public market in which merchandise and other necessities for
the people's use could be bought and sold once a week — a parish church where
those living in the said vill now and at the time could hear mass and other divine
offices were to be erected, it would be to the welfare of their souls with increase of
divine worship. At the supplication of king James and the residents and inhabitants
as well as of William Strachakin, cleric, d. Aberdeen, to the pope to erect in the new
vill a parish church with a bell-tower, bell, cemetery, sacristy, baptismal font and
other distinguishing marks of a parish church; to assign, apply and appropriate to it,
in perpetuity, as its parish and parish boundary, the said place or vill, with its
territory and boundary; and, for its true endowment, the tithes, first-fruits, and other
obventions, falling to it; and to make provision of the newly erected church, whose
annual value does not exceed 4 pounds sterling, to William, the pope — not having
certain knowledge of the foregoing — hereby commands the above bishop to do,
personally, in the foregoing, as seems to him ought to be done, without however
prejudice to anyone. Notwithstanding etc.

Honestis petentium presertim catholicorum principum votis libenter annuimus . . .
F de parma / F / F . xxx. Sanctor(is)

65   2 May 1498   *Reg. Lat.* 1036, fos 244^V-245^V

To Robert Betonen', MA, rector of the parish church of Ludie, d. Dunkeld.
Dispensation — at his supplication — to receive and retain for life, together with the
above parish church, one, and without it, any two other benefices, etc. [as above, no. 5].

Litterarum scientia, vite ac morum honestas . . .
. F. de parma / · V· / · V· xxxx. De Phano:

66   14 July 1498   *Reg. Lat.* 1036, fos 260^V-262^V

To Alexander Colvil, cleric, d. St Andrews. Dispensation and indult — at his
supplication — to him (who, some time ago, as he asserts, was dispensed by
apostolic authority notwithstanding a defect of birth as the son of an unmarried man
and an unmarried woman to be promoted to all, even sacred, orders and to hold two
mutually compatible benefices, even if one of them should have cure of souls; and

who afterwards was marked with clerical character otherwise duly; and is in his fifteenth year of age or thereabouts) to receive — as soon as he has reached his eighteenth year — one, and — at the lawful age — with it, one other, or without them, any two other benefices, with cure or otherwise mutually incompatible, and also — henceforth — any number of benefices without cure, and — at the lawful age — with and without cure, compatible mutually and with the said two incompatible benefices, even if the compatible benefices should be canonries and prebends and they as well as the incompatible benefices should be parish churches or their perpetual vicarages, or dignities, *personatus*, administrations or offices in cathedral, even metropolitan, or collegiate churches, and the dignities should be major *post pontificalem* in cathedral, even metropolitan, churches, or principal in collegiate churches, or a combination, and even if the benefices without cure, even those to be held henceforth, should be sacerdotal or requiring other sacred orders by their foundation, statute or custom, if he obtains them otherwise canonically, and to retain even the incompatible benefices together for life, to resign them all, at once or successively, simply or for exchange, as often as he pleases and in their place receive other, similar or dissimilar, benefices, viz.: — as soon as he has reached his eighteenth year — one, and — at the lawful age — with it, one other, or [without them] up to two other benefices, with cure or otherwise mutually incompatible, and — henceforth — any number of benefices without cure, even sacerdotal or requiring other sacred orders, and — at the said [lawful] age — with and without cure, compatible mutually and with the said two incompatible benefices[1] and to retain even the incompatible benefices for life, as above. Notwithstanding the aforesaid defects of birth and age etc., and foundations etc. of the said benefices requiring sacred, even priest's, orders, and that he is not (or shall not be at the time) in priest's, or other, orders. The pope hereby specially and expressly derogates the said foundations for this once only. With the proviso that the incompatible and sacerdotal benefices in question shall not, on this account, be defrauded of due services and the cure of souls in the compatible benefices (if any) shall not be neglected; but that the customary burdens of these benefices, sacerdotal or requiring other sacred orders, shall be supported.

Vite ac morum honestas . . .
. F. de parma· / · V· / V· Lx. De Phano:

[1] hereabouts in MS there is repetition of a previous passage occasioned by confusion of *quecunque* and *qualiacunque*, the repeated passage is of a length of line of an appropriate bull

67   2 March 1499   *Reg. Lat.* 1037, fos 285^r-288^v

To Edmund Omurchu, canon [of the church] of Cork, mandate in favour of John Barrus, cleric, d. Cork (who, as he asserts, wishes to enter the monastery of B. Mary, Tracton (*de Albotractu*), OCist, under the regular habit, is of noble birth by both parents and of the progeny of its founder). The pope has learned that the above

monastery and the perpetual vicarage of the parish church of Breyny, d. Cork, which
is of lay patronage, are vacant *certo modo* at present and have been vacant for so
long that by canonical sanctions the provision of the monastery and by the Lateran
statutes the collation of the vicarage have lawfully devolved on the apostolic see,
although William Roche, who bears himself as abbot of the monastery, and Dermot
Olacgacy, as a priest or cleric, have detained the monastery and vicarage
respectively, without any title or support of law, temerariously and *de facto*, for a
certain time, as they still do. At a recent petition on John's part to the pope to unite
etc. the vicarage to the monastery, after he should be provided to it, for his lifetime,
the pope, wishing to encourage John in his purpose and to make provision of a
capable and suitable person to the monastery to rule and direct it, but not having
certain knowledge of John's merits and suitability, hereby commands the above
canon, if, having summoned respectively William and Dermot and others concerned
and those interested in the union, he finds the monastery, whose annual value does
not exceed 100, and the vicarage, 10, marks sterling, to be vacant (howsoever etc.)
and the foregoing regarding the union to be true and (for whatever reason the
disposition of the monastery belongs specially or generally to the apostolic see and
even if the vicarage be specially reserved, etc.) to unite etc. the vicarage, with all
rights and appurtenances, to the monastery, for as long as John presides over the
monastery; and, in that event, receive John — if he is suitable and there is no
canonical obstacle — as a monk in the monastery, bestow the regular habit on him in
accordance with the custom of the monastery, cause him to be given charitable
treatment therein, and also, if John spontaneously wishes to make before him the
usual regular profession made by the monks, receive and admit it; and inform
himself as to John's merits and suitability and, if he finds John to be capable and
suitable for the rule and administration of the monastery — concerning which the
pope burdens the canon's conscience — make provision of John to the monastery
and appoint him abbot, committing the care, rule and administration of the
monastery to him in spiritualities and temporalities and inducting him etc. having
removed William from the monastery and Dermot from the vicarage and any other
unlawful detainers and causing John (or his proctor) to be admitted to the vicarage
and its fruits etc., rights and obventions to be delivered to him and obedience and
reverence to be given him by the convent and customary services and rights by the
vassals and other subjects of the monastery. [Curbing] gainsayers by the pope's
authority etc. Notwithstanding etc. Also the pope grants that John (if he should be
provided to the monastery by virtue of the presents and preside over it as abbot) may
receive benediction from any catholic bishop of his choice in communion with the
apostolic see; and that the bishop concerned may impart it to him; without prejudice
to the bishop of Cork to whom the monastery is understood to be subject by ordinary
law. The pope's will is, however, that the vicarage shall not, on account of this union
etc., be defrauded of due services and the cure of souls therein shall not be neglected,
but that its customary burdens shall be supported; and that on John's death or
resignation etc. of the monastery this union etc. shall be dissolved and so deemed
and the vicarage shall revert to its original condition and be deemed vacant
automatically. Also the pope indulges John — even while he is a secular cleric not

having taken the regular habit and made his profession — to preside over the rule and administration of the monastery for a month after he has acquired peaceful possession, or almost, of its rule [and] administration and of its goods or the greater part of them and to rule and govern it; notwithstanding etc. The pope's will is, however, that John shall be bound — before the said month has elapsed — to take the habit and make his profession; failing which, he decrees, the monastery is to be vacant henceforth.

Apostolice sedis <et>[1] *circumspecta benignitas cupientibus vitam ducere regularem . . .* · *S· de· Castello· / V / · V· . xxxx. Tertio decimo Kl' aprilis Anno Septimo* [20 March 1499], *De Phano:-*

[1] marginal insertion, initialled . V.

68   9 January 1499   *Reg. Lat.* 1038, fos 55^V-57^V

To the bishop of Moray, the dean of the church of Moray and the archpriest of the church of St Prosper, Colliculo, d. Parma, mandate in favour of Patrick Bog, priest, d. Aberdeen. A recent [petition][1] to the pope on Patrick's part stated that at another time — when the canonry and prebend of Ryerin' and Forbes of the church of Aberdeen, which[2] are of the patronage of the temporal [lord] of Forbes for the time being and which the late John Forbes, canon of this church, held while he lived, were vacant by his death outside the Roman curia — although the present temporal lord (who was in peaceful possession or almost of the right of presenting a suitable person for the canonry and prebend at a time of vacancy) had presented Patrick for them, thus vacant,[3] to the present bishop of Aberdeen or his vicar general within the lawful time, nevertheless the bishop or his vicar unjustly refused to institute Patrick as a canon of the said church. Moreover, as the same petition[4] added, Patrick fears that for certain reasons the said presentation does not hold good; and, as the pope has learned, the canonry and prebend are known to be still vacant as above. The pope hereby commands that the above three, or two or one of them, in person or by proxy, shall collate and assign the canonry and prebend, whose annual value does not exceed 15 pounds sterling (vacant as above or howsoever or by the deaths, outside the Roman curia, of the late Alexander Forbes or Alexander ʒung who, as is asserted, once held the said canonry and prebend, or by the free resignation of John or Alexander Forbes or Alexander ʒung or anyone else etc., even if they have been vacant for so long that by the Lateran statutes their collation has lawfully devolved on the apostolic see etc.), with plenitude of canon law and all rights and appurtenances, to Patrick, inducting him etc. having removed any unlawful detainer and causing Patrick (or his proctor) to be received as a canon of the said church, with plenitude of canon law, and the fruits etc., rights and obventions of the canonry and prebend to be delivered to him. [Curbing] gainsayers by the pope's authority etc. Notwithstanding etc.

Vite ac morum honestas . . .
F. de. parma / · V· / · V· xx Quarto decimo kl' Februarii Anno Sep. ^mo [19 January
1499], *De Phano:*

[1] (?)*petitio* or *Patritio* deleted here, initialled . *V.*; 'petitio' wanting

[2] *quod*; apparently changed (by deletion) from 'qui'

[3] (?)*vivent(es); recte:* 'vacantes'?

[4] *cf.* note 1 above

69   9 March 1499   *Reg. Lat.* 1038, fos 90^v-92^r

To William Oconcenndynd,[1] Charles Omulcaryll and Cristinus Ospelayn, canons of
the church of Tuam, mandate in favour of John Ycellayd,[2] canon of the church of
Tuam (who, as he asserts, holds the monastery of B. Mary, Knockmoy
(*Collisvictorie*), OCist, d. Tuam, *in commendam*, by apostolic concession and
dispensation). Some time ago — after the pope had learned that the deanery of the
church of Tuam and the perpetual vicarage of the parish church of Kilelonne, d.
Tuam, were vacant *certo modo* and had been vacant for so long that by the Lateran
statutes their collation had lawfully devolved on the apostolic see, although the late
Walter[3] Bremichian, who was bearing himself as dean of the said church of Tuam,
had detained the deanery and vicarage, without any title or support of law,
temerariously and *de facto*, for a certain time, as he was detaining them then —
representation was made on John's part to the pope to unite etc. the said vicarage and
a canonry of the church of Tuam and the prebend of Teachsassan *alias* Templegaile
(*de Templo Albo*) in the same, which John was holding (with the rectory of the parish
church of Kylareyrud *alias* Monteray, which is of lay patronage, canonically
annexed to them, and the appurtenances of Achyarta, d. Tuam, and other annexes),
to the deanery, for his lifetime. At that time the pope — at John's supplication — by
other letters of his charged the above three that they (or two or one of them), if,
having summoned Walter and other interested parties, they found the deanery and
vicarage to be vacant (howsoever and by whatsoever person) were to collate and
assign the deanery to John, and unite etc. the vicarage and also the canonry and
prebend with the rectory and other annexes and with all their rights and
appurtenances, to the deanery, for John's lifetime, as is more fully contained in the
said letters drawn up in that regard[4] in which it was expressed that Walter was
detaining the deanery and vicarage without any title, as above. Moreover since, as a
recent petition to the pope on John's part stated, by the time of the said letters Walter
had died outside the Roman curia, and while he lived he was holding the deanery
and vicarage not without title but, on the contrary, with canonical title, and no
mention was made of this in the said letters which have not yet been committed for
execution; and, on this account, John fears that the said letters could be surreptitious
and their effect be frustrated with the passage of time. Therefore the pope hereby

commands that the above three (or two or one of them) shall decree the said letters, with each and every clause contained therein, to be valid from the date of the presents and to have full force and to be of support to John; and shall proceed to the execution of them otherwise in accordance with their form and content, in and for all things, just as if it had been expressed in the said letters that the deanery and vicarage [were vacant][5] not *certo modo* but by the death of Walter who died as above, and that while he lived Walter had detained, or was then detaining, them, not without title, but with canonical title. Notwithstanding etc.

Apostolice sedis providentia circumspecta ad ea libenter intendit . . .
S. de. *castello*[6] / · V· / · V· *xv De Phano:*-

[1] uncertain reading: the 'nnd' is blotched

[2] the 'Y' changed from 'I'?

[3] variously: *Vacherus, Vaterus, Vatherus*

[4] below, no. 75

[5] *valebant*; *recte*: 'vacabant'?

[6] *. Jo. ortega*, deleted but not initialled, above it

70   1 March 1499   *Reg. Lat.* 1038, fos 92[r]-93[v]

To John Ohederscoyll and Lewis (?)Ochvygh,[1] canons of the church of Ross, and Edmund Omurchu, canon of the church of Cork, mandate in favour of Bernard Yhhederscoyll, canon of Ross. A petition[2] to the pope on Bernard's part stated that formerly, when the perpetual vicarage of the parish church of Cribach, d. Ross, was vacant *certo modo*, the then bishop of Ross by ordinary authority collated and made provision of it, thus vacant, to Bernard and he acquired possession by virtue of this collation and provision. Moreover, as the said petition added, Bernard fears that for certain reasons the said collation and provision do not hold good; and, as the pope has learned, the vicarage is known to be vacant still, as above. At the supplication on Bernard's part to the pope to unite etc. the vicarage to the canonry and the prebend of (?)Kyllmuna[3] of the church of Ross, which Bernard holds, for as long as he does so — asserting that the annual value of the canonry and prebend does not exceed 2, and of the vicarage, 20, marks sterling — the pope, not having certain knowledge of the foregoing, hereby commands that the above three (or two or one of them), having summoned those interested, shall inform themselves as to each and every one of the aforesaid matters and if they find it to be thus, unite etc. the vicarage (vacant howsoever etc.; even if vacant for so long that by the Lateran statutes its collation has lawfully devolved on the apostolic see, etc.), with all rights and appurtenances, to the canonry and prebend, for as long as Bernard holds the canonry and prebend, to the effect that he may, on his own authority, in person or by proxy, take corporal possession of the vicarage and the said rights and appurtenances, and convert its fruits etc. to his own uses and those of the canonry and prebend and the vicarage without the licence of the local diocesan or of anyone else. Notwithstanding etc. With the proviso that the vicarage shall not, on account of this union etc., be defrauded of due services and the cure of souls therein shall not be neglected; but that its customary burdens shall be supported. The pope's will is, however, that on Bernard's death or resignation etc. of the canonry and prebend the union etc. shall be dissolved and so deemed and the vicarage shall revert to its original condition and be deemed vacant automatically.

Romanum decet pontificem votis illis gratum prestare assensum . . .
. S. de Castello / · V· / · V· xx De Phano:-

[1] the 'v' blotched and uncertain

[2] 'nuper' does not occur

[3] the three letters before the last doubtful: a succession of seven minims capable of various readings

71   2 March 1499   *Reg. Lat.* 1038, fos 94[r]-96[v]

To the abbots of the monasteries of Tracton (*de Albotractu*) and *de Antro Sancti Phymbarrii* [Gill Abbey], d. Cork, and Edmund Omurchu, canon of the church of Cork, mandate in favour of Nicholas Ykayllis, cleric, d. Cork (who, as he asserts, notwithstanding a defect of birth as the son of a cleric and an unmarried woman, has been marked with clerical character otherwise however duly). The pope has learned that the rectory of the parish church of Ryncorrain and the perpetual vicarage of the parish church of (?)Ynyseonan,[1] d. Cork, which are of lay patronage, are vacant at present and have been for so long that by the Lateran statutes their collation has lawfully devolved on the apostolic see, although John Barry has detained the rectory and Matthew Olaegarii the vicarage — bearing themselves as clerics or priests of the said diocese — without any title or support of law, temerariously and *de facto*, for a certain time, as they still do. At a recent petition on Nicholas's part to the pope to erect and institute a canonry in the church of Cork and the said rectory into a simple prebend in the same, for his lifetime, and unite etc. the vicarage to the erected canonry and prebend, also for his lifetime, the pope, not having certain knowledge of the foregoing, hereby commands that the above three (or two or one of them), if, having summoned respectively John and Matthew and the bishop and chapter of Cork and others concerned, they find the rectory and vicarage to be vacant (howsoever etc.) and having summoned those interested in the union, the foregoing to be true, shall erect and institute a canonry in the church of Cork and the rectory into a simple prebend in the same, for Nicholas's lifetime, without prejudice to anyone, (even if the rectory be specially reserved etc.), and collate and assign the newly erected canonry and prebend, being vacant, annual value not exceeding 8 marks sterling, to Nicholas, and unite etc. the vicarage, annual value not exceeding 7 marks sterling, to the erected canonry and prebend, with plenitude of canon law and all rights and appurtenances, inducting Nicholas etc. having removed John from the rectory and Matthew from the vicarage and any other unlawful detainers and causing Nicholas (or his proctor) to be received as a canon of the church of Cork, with plenitude of canon law, and the fruits etc., rights and obventions of the canonry and prebend and of the vicarage to be annexed thereto to be delivered to him. [Curbing] gainsayers by the pope's authority etc. Notwithstanding etc. Also the pope dispenses Nicholas to receive and retain the canonry and prebend, if conferred on him by virtue of the presents, notwithstanding the defect of birth etc. With the proviso that the rectory and vicarage shall not, on account of this erection and institution and union etc., be defrauded of due services and the cure of souls therein shall not be neglected, but that their customary burdens shall be supported; and that on Nicholas's death or resignation etc. of the canonry and prebend this erection and institution shall be extinguished and union etc. dissolved and so deemed and the rectory and vicarage shall revert to their original condition and be deemed vacant automatically.

Apostolice sedis providentia circumspecta ad ea libenter intendit . . .
. S. de castello / · V· / · V· xxx. Tertio decimo kalendas aprilis Anno Septimo. [20 March 1499], *De Phano:-*

[1] the 'n' blotched

72   28 December 1498   *Reg. Lat.* 1038, fos 231[v]-234[v]

To the prior of the monastery, usually governed by a prior, of St Michael, *de Rupe* [Ballinskelligs], d. Ardfert, mandate in favour of Galfrigidus Ochonyll, cleric, d. Ardfert (who, as he asserts, is in his ninth year of age or thereabouts and is studying arts). The pope has learned that the perpetual vicarage of the parish church of Kylldacu(m)[1] *alias* Turere, d. Ardfert, is vacant *certo modo* at present and has been vacant for so long that by the Lateran statutes its collation has lawfully devolved on the apostolic see, although Edmund Ohullachayn, who bears himself as a priest, d. Ardfert, has detained it with no title and no support of law, temerariously and *de facto*, for a certain time, as he still does. At a recent petition on the part of Galfrigidus to the pope to erect and institute the vicarage into a simple prebend in the church of Ardfert, the pope (who has willed that provisions or grants or mandates of provision to canonries and prebends of cathedral churches to persons who have not completed their fourteenth year of age shall have no force except by consent of the apostolic see) hereby commands that the above prior, if, having summoned respectively Edmund and the bishop and chapter of Ardfert and others concerned, he finds the vicarage [to be vacant][2] (howsoever etc.) shall erect and institute it into a simple prebend in the said church of Ardfert, (even if specially reserved etc.), for the lifetime of Galfrigidus, without prejudice to anyone, and if, having taken his age into account — concerning which the pope burdens the prior's conscience — he finds

Galfrigidus to be suitable, collate and assign a canonry of the said church of Ardfert and the newly erected prebend, being vacant, whose annual value does not exceed 6 marks sterling, to him, with plenitude of canon law and all rights and appurtenances, inducting him etc. having removed Edmund and any other unlawful detainer and causing Galfrigidus (or his proctor) to be received as a canon of Ardfert, with plenitude of canon law, and the fruits etc., rights and obventions to be delivered to him. [Curbing] gainsayers by the pope's authority etc. Notwithstanding etc. Also the pope hereby indulges Galfrigidus to receive and retain the said canonry and prebend, if conferred on him by virtue of the presents, notwithstanding etc. With the proviso that the erected vicarage shall not, on account of this erection and institution, be defrauded of due services and the cure of souls therein shall not be neglected; but that its customary burdens and those of the canonry and prebend shall be supported. The pope's will is, however, that on Galfrigidus's death or resignation etc. of the canonry and prebend this erection and institution shall be extinguished and so deemed and the vicarage shall revert to its original condition and be deemed vacant automatically. And he has commanded that — if Galfrigidus be found suitable — provision of the said canonry and prebend be made to him from the date of the presents.

Apostolice sedis circumspecta providentia votis fidelium . . .
S de Castello / F / . F. xxx. *Tertio Non' martii Anno Septimo* [5 March 1499], *Sanctor(is)*

1 MS: *Kyllda cu'*
2 *vacaria*; *recte*: 'vacare'

73 — 1   *Reg. Lat.* 1038, fo 258[r]

Start of a mandate, (evidently provisory), addressed 'to William Oconceanind, Cristinus Ospelayn, and Charles Omulcaryl, canons of the church of Tuam'. Does not extend beyond the proem: *Apostolice sedis providentia circumspecta ad ea libenter intendit per que decori et venustati ecclesiarum quarumlibet presertim cathedralium et divino cultu ac personarum ecclesiasticarum commoditatibus oportune consuli possit* [ends]. (Though grammatically sufficient as it stands, the proem could well have continued). Abbreviator: S de Castello. No magistral initial.

Occupies 5 1/5 lines at top of otherwise blank page; next blank too; deleted; no explanatory note.

Belongs, almost certainly, to the seventh year: *V[acantibus]* 7 at the top of the left margin; cf. year of the *liber* and of the adjacent letters.

Identical, so far as it goes, with the mandate, dated 29 January 1499 (i. e. in the seventh year), in favour of Donat OKelly, entered at fos 90[r]-93[r] of *Reg. Lat.* 1048 (= no. 164 below) and enregistered by the same scribe. Probably, an abortive enregistration of it.

[1] dating clause wanting

74 14 February 1499 *Reg. Lat.* 1038, fos 259[r]-260[v]

To the abbot of the monastery of B. Mary, Fermoy (*de Castrodei*) and the prior of the monastery, usually governed by a prior, of St Thomas the Martyr, near Buttevant (*iuxta Botaniam*), d. Cloyne, and Edmund (?)Mageier,[1] canon of the church of Cloyne, mandate in favour of Donat Oflin, priest, d. Cloyne. The pope has learned that the perpetual vicarage of the parish[2] of Chilsane, d. Cloyne, is vacant *certo modo* at present and has been vacant for so long that by the Lateran statutes its collation has lawfully devolved on the apostolic see, although Dermot Osicham, who bears himself as a cleric or priest, has detained it without any title or support of law, temerariously and *de facto*, for a certain time, as he still does. He hereby commands that the above three (or two or one of them), if, having summoned Dermot and others concerned, they find the vicarage, whose annual value does not exceed 10 marks sterling, to be vacant (howsoever etc.), shall collate and assign it, (even if specially reserved etc.), with all rights and appurtenances, to Donat, inducting him etc. having removed Dermot and any other unlawful detainer and causing Donat (or his proctor) to be admitted to the vicarage and its fruits etc., rights and obventions to be delivered to him. [Curbing] gainsayers by the pope's authority etc. Notwithstanding etc.

Vite ac morum honestas . . .
. S. de Castello / · V· / · V· x pridie nonas Martii anno septimo. [6 March 1499], *De Phano:-*

[1] the 'i' is doubtful
[2] *ecclesi*e, deleted and initialled . *V.,* occurs here

75 30 January 1499 *Reg. Lat.* 1038, fos 260[v]-264[v]

To William Oconcenind,[1] Charles Omulcaryl and Cristinus Ospellayn, canons of the church of Tuam, mandate in favour of John Ycellayd, canon of Tuam (who, as he asserts, is in his twentieth year of age, and holds the monastery of B. Mary, Knockmoy (*Collisvictorie'*), OCist, d. Tuam, *in commendam*, by apostolic concession and dispensation, and is of noble birth by both parents). The pope has learned that the deanery of the church of Tuam and the perpetual vicarage of the parish church of Kylclomee,[2] d. Tuam, are vacant *certo modo* at present and have been vacant for so long that by the Lateran statutes their collation has lawfully devolved on the apostolic see, although Walter[3] Bremichiam, who bears himself as a deacon,[4] has detained the deanery and vicarage, without any title or support of law, temerariously and [*de facto*],[5] for a certain time, as he still does. At a recent petition to the pope on John's part to unite etc. the vicarage and the canonry of the church of Tuam and the prebend of Teachsasari *alias* Templegaile (*de Templo Albo*) in the same (to which is canonically annexed the rectory of the parish church of Kylarerynd *alias* Monterahy, which is of lay patronage, with the appurtenances of Achyarta, d. Tuam, and other annexes), which John holds, to the deanery, for his lifetime — asserting that the annual value of the deanery does not exceed 30, and of the vicarage, 2, and of the canonry and prebend, rectory and other annexes, 12, marks sterling — the pope, not having certain knowledge of the foregoing, hereby commands that the above three (or two or one of them), if, having summoned Walter and others concerned, they find the deanery, which is a dignity major *post pontificalem*, and vicarage, to be vacant (howsoever etc.), and, having summoned those interested in the union etc., the foregoing to be true, shall collate and assign the deanery to John, and also unite etc. the vicarage and the canonry and prebend (even if the deanery be generally reserved as a major dignity, as above, or it and the vicarage be specially reserved etc.), with the rectory and other annexes and all rights and appurtenances, to the deanery, for John's lifetime, inducting him etc. into corporal possession of the deanery, vicarage, canonry and prebend, rectory and other annexes and rights and appurtenances aforesaid, having removed Walter and any other unlawful detainers from the deanery and vicarage and causing John (or his proctor) to be admitted to them and their fruits etc., rights and obventions to be delivered to him. [Curbing] gainsayers by the pope's authority etc. Notwithstanding etc. Also the pope hereby dispenses John to receive and retain the above deanery, if conferred on him by virtue of the presents, notwithstanding the above defect of age etc. With the proviso that the deanery, meanwhile, and the vicarage, canonry and prebend, on account of the union etc., shall not be defrauded of due services and the cure of souls in the deanery (if any) shall not be neglected; but that the customary burdens of it and the vicarage, other annexes and canonry and prebend aforesaid shall be supported. The pope's will is, however, that on John's death or his resignation etc. of the deanery this union etc. shall be dissolved and so deemed and the vicarage, canonry and prebend shall revert to their original condition and be deemed vacant automatically. Given at Ostia.

Ex iniuncto nobis desuper apostolice servitutis officio ad ea libenter intendimus . . . · *S· de Castello* / · *V·* / · *V· xxxvi Tertio non' martii Anno Sep.* [mo] [5 March 1499], *De Phano:-*

[1] (?)*Oco. . . . . . o* has been deleted and initialled . *V.*

[2] the 'mee' blotched and doubtful

[3] *Vaterus, Waterus*

[4] MS: *pro diacono; recte*: 'pro decano'? *Cf.* above, no. 69.

[5] *defecto; recte*: 'de facto'

76[1]   **6 October 1498**   *Reg. Lat.* 1039, fo 14[v]

To [the (arch)bishop] . . .,[2] commission and mandate. A recent petition presented to the pope on the part of John Stanley and Ann Ardion', woman, of his diocese, stated that to preserve and increase the friendship between their kinsmen and friends and for other reasonable causes, they desire to be joined together in marriage, but because they are related in the second and third degrees of affinity through one line doubly and in the third and fourth through another they cannot fulfil their desire in this matter without an apostolic dispensation. The pope therefore,[3] for the aforesaid and certain other reasons represented to him — at this supplication — hereby commissions and commands the above bishop — if it is so and Ann has not been ravished on this account — to dispense John and Ann to contract marriage together and remain therein notwithstanding the said impediments, declaring the offspring of the marriage legitimate.

Oblate nobis nuper pro parte [. . .] petitionis series continebat . . .
[-][4] */ [-]*[5] */ [-]*[6]

[1] register entry struck through; no explanation

[2] MS begins: *Alexander et cetera venerabili fratri (?)nr* (or *(?)m*; start of word only; 'nostro' (inappropriate here)?; 'moderno'?); thereafter there is a space of approx. 2/3 of a line left in MS for rest of address clause: '(archi)episcopo N salutem et cetera'

[3] no mention of absolution

[4] no abbreviator's name

[5] no magistral initial

[6] no magistral signature

77   **23 December 1498**   *Reg. Lat.* 1039, fos 35[r]-36[v]

To William Andrew, rector of the parish church of St Martin, Westcoker, d. Bath and Wells. Dispensation — at his supplication — to receive and retain for life, together with the above parish church, one, and without it, any two other benefices, etc. [as above, no. 3].

Vite ac morum honestas . . .
· L· puccius / · V· / · V· L· De Phano·

78   **23 December 1498**   *Reg. Lat.* 1039, fos 42[r]-43[r]

To John Paynter, BDec, perpetual vicar of the parish church of Sodburi, d. Worcester. Dispensation — at his supplication — to receive and retain for life, together with the perpetual vicarage of the above parish church, one, and without it, any two other benefices, etc. [as above, no.3].

Litterarum scientia, vite ac morum honestas . . .
· L puccius / · V· / V· L· De Phano:

79   23 December 1498   *Reg. Lat.* 1039, fos 43^r-44^r

To John Goodwyn', perpetual chaplain, called cantor, in the parish church of St Clement, Astingg', d. Chichester. Dispensation — at his supplication — to receive and retain for life, together with the chaplaincy of the above parish church, which is incompatible with another benefice, one, and without it, any two other benefices, etc. [as above, no. 3]. [1]

Vite ac morum honestas . . .
· L· puccius /· V· / · V· L· De Phano:

[1] save that the present entry has *similiter* [*recte*: 'simpliciter'] *vel ex causa permutationis*

80   13 September 1498[1]   *Reg. Lat.* 1039, fos 62^r-63^v

To the bishop of Lismore, the prior of the monastery, usually governed by a prior, of Coldingham (*de Coldinghamo*), d. St Andrews, and William Wauvri, canon of the church of Aberdeen, mandate in favour of Robert, archbishop of Glasgow. A recent petition to the pope on Robert's part stated that, formerly, after he had, by ordinary authority, collated and made provision of the precentorship (*cantoriam*) of the church of Glasgow (which is a non-major dignity *post pontificalem* and was then vacant *certo modo*) to Robert Forman', cleric, and had ordered that he be inducted into actual possession of it, John Aurifabri, who bore himself as a priest, d. Glasgow — falsely asserting that the precentorship rightfully belonged to him by pretext of certain apostolic letters of expectative grace and of the processes had over them, and supported by a large force of the noblemen Hugh, lord of Mungmuri, John Mungmuri, knight, Robert Mungmuri, Alexander Mungmuri of Bravidestare, James of Carmechet, John Scot, and other followers, armed men, and accomplices, d. Glasgow — in a daring act of sacrilege, invaded the [cathedral] church of Glasgow on the vigil of Palm Sunday, entered its choir in a hostile manner, and spent the night there with his accomplices and supporters in drunkenness and shameful games, committing many offences and irregularities in the church; that through certain persons, (whom he said were executors or sub-executors of the letters and processes), he caused the processes to be published, and the archbishop to be warned, irregularly, rashly, and *de facto*, under certain censures and pains then expressed, not to impede him over possession of the precentorship; that the archbishop appealed to the apostolic see; and that afterwards, because John, Hugh, Robert, Alexander, James, John, and the other followers and accomplices did not, when they had been properly warned by the archbishop, desist from their attacks and offensive conduct and leave the church, the archbishop, proceeding duly, *ex officio*, [excommunicated][2] John, Hugh, Robert, Alexander, James, and the other accomplices and followers. At archbishop Robert's supplication to the pope — made [because John, Hugh, Robert, Alexander, James][2] and the other accomplices and followers are not afraid, to the grave scandal of all, to hold the said excommunication in contempt — to command that he be absolved conditionally from any sentence of excommunication, and other censures and pains, by which, perchance, he is deemed bound, and to commit to some upright men in those parts the cases of his aforesaid appeal and of any others lodged by him; of everything attempted and innovated after and against them; of the nullity of the warning, censures, executors and sub-executors' whole process, and of everything else done in contempt of the archbishop and his censures by the executors and sub-executors, John, Hugh, Robert, Alexander, James, John, the other accomplices and followers, and any others, in connection with the foregoing; and of the principal matter; also, to command that the sentence of excommunication imposed by the archbishop be observed, the pope hereby commands that the above three (or two or one of them), having summoned John, Hugh, Robert, Alexander, James, John, and the other accomplices and followers, and others concerned, shall, if and as it is just, for this once only, conditionally absolve archbishop Robert, if he so requests, having first received suitable security from him that if they find that the sentence of excommunication etc. were justly inflicted on him, he will obey their commands and those of the church; and, as regards the rest, having heard both sides, taking cognizance even of the principal matter, that they shall decree what is just, short of capital punishment, without appeal, causing by ecclesiastical censure what they have decreed to be strictly observed; and that, insofar as it was issued with reason, they shall cause the sentence of excommunication imposed by the archbishop on John, Hugh, Robert, James, Alexander, John, and the other accomplices and followers, to be inviolably observed until they have made proper amends. Notwithstanding etc.

Humilibus et cetera.
S de Castello / · V· / · V· xiiij De Phano:

[1] the pontifical year corrected: originally . . . *anno octavo*; *octavo* deleted and *septimo* written after it, in the line

[2] supplied tentatively as follows: *Et deinde quia Johannes Hugo Robertus Alexander Jacobus Johannes et alii satellites et complices predicti per eundem archiepiscopum debite moniti ab invasionibus et scand* [del.] *scandalis huiusmodi desistere ecclesiamque predictam exire non curarunt ex suo offitio super hiis rite procedens eosdem Johannem Hugonem Robertum Alexandrum Jacobum et alios* [*complices et satellites excommunicavit; et quia Johannes Hugo Robertus Alexander Jacobus et alii*] *complices et satellites predicti excommunicationis* [changed from (?)*excommunicati*] *sententiam huiusmodi contempnere implurimorum grave scandalum non vereantur pro parte dicti archiepiscopi nobis fuit humiliter supplicatum* . . . The omission could well be more extensive than here conjectured.

81[1]　**25 September 1498**　　　　*Reg. Lat.* 1039, fos 74^r-75^r

To Nicholas Clayton', BDec, perpetual vicar of the parish church of Bassingbron' [also spelt *Bassyngbron'*], d. Ely. Dispensation — at his supplication — to receive and retain for life, together with the perpetual vicarage of the above parish church, one, and without it, any two other benefices, etc. [as above, no. 3].

Litterarum scientia, vite ac morum honestas . . .
L puccius / · V· / · V· L· De Phano:-

[1] *Nicolaus Claiton'* occurs in the index to the gathering on fo. 73^r

82[1]　**29 September 1498**　　　　*Reg. Lat.* 1039, fos 75^r-76^r

To Thomas Thilde, perpetual vicar of the parish church of Deuuleyse, d. Salisbury. Dispensation — at his supplication — to receive and retain for life, together with the perpetual vicarage of the above parish church, one, and without it, any two other benefices, etc. [as above, no. 3]. [2]

Vite ac morum honestas . . .
P de Castello / · V· / · V· L· De Phano:

[1] *Thomas Thilde* occurs in the index to the gathering on fo. 73^r
[2] save that in the present instance 'or a combination' does not occur

83　**3 September 1498**　　　　*Reg. Lat.* 1039, fo 95^r

To James Scrungeour, scholar, d. Brechin. Dispensation — at his supplication — to him, who, as he asserts, suffers from a defect of birth as the son of an unmarried man and an unmarried woman and wishes to become a cleric, to be promoted — after he has been duly marked with clerical character — to all, even sacred, orders and receive and retain any benefice, with or without cure, even if a parish church or its perpetual vicarage, and, with or without it, a canonry and prebend in a cathedral, even metropolitan, or collegiate church, even if the canonry and prebend should be customarily elective, if he obtains them otherwise canonically, to resign them, simply or for exchange, as often as he pleases, and in their place receive and retain another, similar or dissimilar, benefice, and, with or without it, another canonry and prebend. Notwithstanding the above defect etc.

Vite ac morum honestas . . .

A de Sancto Severino / F· / F· xx Sanctor(is)

84[1]   **20 November 1498**   *Reg. Lat.* 1039, fos 105[r]-106[r]

To John Smyth', LLB, perpetual vicar of the parish church of Hekfelde, d. Winchester. Dispensation — at his supplication — to receive and retain for life, together with the perpetual vicarage of the above parish church, one, and without it, any two other benefices, etc. [as above, no. 3].

Litterarum scientia, avite[2] *ac morum honestas . . .*
L Puccius / . L. / L. L^{ta}. Dulcius:-

[1] A cancelled enregistration of this letter occurs below (no. 96).

[2] *sic*

85   1 September 1498   *Reg. Lat.* 1039, fos 116[r]-117[v]

To John Nans, UID, provost of the church of St Thomas the Martyr, Glasney (*de Glasnaya*), d. Exeter, dispensation. Some time ago, Innocent VIII dispensed him, by certain letters of his, to receive and retain for life, together with the parish church of Gwennap (*Sancte Veneppe*), d. Exeter, (which, he asserted, he was holding), any other, or having resigned it, any two other benefices, etc. [as below, no. 131,[1] to '. . . as is more fully contained in those letters']. [2] The pope therefore — at his supplication — hereby dispenses him, who, as he asserts, holds, by the said dispensation, the provostship of the above church and the perpetual vicarage of the church of St Gluvias (*Sancti Cluniati*), d. Exeter, to receive and retain for life, together with the provostship and vicarage, or any two other incompatible benefices held by him at the time by the said dispensation, any third benefice, etc. [as below, no. 131].

Litterarum scientia, vite ac morum honestas . . .
. Jo. Orte[ga][3] */ · V· /* [4]*V. Lxx. De phano:*[5]

[1] save that in the present instance 'or a combination' does not occur

[2] summarised in *CPL*, XV at no. 54

[3] shaved

[4] unusually, a flourish before the initial (*Cf.* below, note 5)

[5] *sic*; as a rule 'De Phano:' (*Cf.* above, note 4)

86   3 December 1498   *Reg. Lat.* 1039, fos 173^V-174^V

To the provost of the church of Dumbertane', d. Glasgow, and the chancellor and
John Gibson', canon, of the church of Glasgow, mandate in favour of Margaret
Simpill, woman, d. Glasgow. A recent petition to the pope on Margaret's part stated
that the late James Creithonen, knight, lawfully contracted marriage with her *per
verba de presenti*, connection followed, and they were dispensed by apostolic
authority to remain married, notwithstanding a certain degree of consanguinity or
affinity by which they were related; that on James's death, his son, James Creithone'
of Carnis, nobleman, knight, d. Dunkeld — falsely asserting that the marriage was
null and invalid — sued Margaret (not by apostolic delegation) before James Konx,
commissary or deputy of David Cuunyglan', official of Glasgow, praying that the
marriage be declared null and that Margaret be therefore condemned to give up
vacant and free possession to him of certain goods then expressed; that James the
commissary, proceeding duly, promulgated a definitive sentence in Margaret's
favour and against James, from which the latter — falsely asserting that the sentence
was unjust — appealed to the apostolic see, and impetrated apostolic letters to the
archdeacon, precentor, and subdean of the church of Dunkeld,[1] their own names
[not][2] expressed, and by virtue of these letters sued Margaret before the <then>[3]
archdeacon, precentor, and subdean; and that they, proceeding wrongly, promulgated
an unjust definitive sentence by which they revoked the above sentence and
condemned Margaret to restore the goods to James, condemning her in costs, (the
taxation of which was reserved to them in the future), from which Margaret appealed
to the apostolic see. At her supplication to the pope to commit to some upright men
in those parts the cases of her appeal; of anything perchance attempted and
innovated after and against it; of the nullity of the process and sentence of the
archdeacon, precentor, and subdean, and of everything done rashly against her in the
case; and of the whole principal matter, the pope hereby commands that the above
three (or two or one of them), having summoned James the son and others
concerned, and having heard both sides, shall decree what is just, without appeal,
causing by ecclesiastical censure what they have decreed to be strictly observed.
Notwithstanding etc.

Humilibus et cetera.
· *N· Bregeon* / · *V·* / · *V. xij· De Phano:* —

[1] *cf. CPL* XVI, no. 518
[2] MS wants 'non'
[3] marginal insertion by enregistering scribe, initialled . *V.*

87   21 August 1498   *Reg. Lat.* 1039, fo 181^{r-v}

To James Herbert *alias* Newlond, canon of the priory of B. Mary, Merton', OSA, d.

Winchester. Dispensation — at his supplication — to him, who, as he asserts, is expressly professed of the above order,[1] to receive and retain any benefice, with or without cure, usually held by secular priests,[2] even if a parish church or its perpetual vicarage, or a chantry, free chapel, hospital or annual service, usually assigned to secular clerics[3] in title of a perpetual ecclesiastical benefice, if he obtains it otherwise canonically, to resign it, simply or for exchange, as often as he pleases, and in its place receive and retain another, similar or dissimilar, benefice, defined as above. Notwithstanding etc.

Religionis zelus, vite ac morum honestas . . .
F de parma / · V· / · V· xxx De Phano:

[1] This information comes from a notwithstanding clause.

[2] MS: *presbyteros seculares; rectius*: 'clericos seculares'? (*cf.* note 3)

[3] MS: *eisdem clericis*

88   27 December 1498   *Reg. Lat.* 1039, fos 192ʳ-193ʳ

To David Byford, MA, perpetual vicar of the parish church of Monkton' in the Isle of Thanet (*insula de Taneto*), d. Canterbury. Dispensation — at his supplication — to receive and retain for life, together with the perpetual vicarage of the above parish church, one, and having resigned it, any two other benefices, etc. [as above, no. 3].

Litterarum scientia, vite ac morum honestas . . .
S de Castello / F / F Lᵗᵃ. Sanctor(is)

89   27 December 1498   *Reg. Lat.* 1039, fos 193ᵛ-194ᵛ

To Peter Androw, rector of the parish church of Rouaborugh', d. Exeter. Dispensation — at his supplication — to him, who is a priest, to receive and retain for life, together with the above parish church, one, and without it, any two other benefices, etc. [as above, no. 3].

Vite ac morum honestas . . .
S de Castello / F / F Lᵗᵃ. Sanctor(is)

90   10 November 1498   *Reg. Lat.* 1039, fos 210ᵛ-211ᵛ

To Nicholas Morton', rector of the parish church of Ministre *alias* Talkaryn' or

Terkaryn', d. Exeter. Dispensation — at his supplication — to receive and retain for
life, together with the above parish church, one, and without it, any two other
benefices, etc. [as above, no. 3].

Vite ac morum honestas . . .
A. De sancto severino / · V· / · V· L· De Phano:-

91   1 December 1498   *Reg. Lat.* 1039, fos 232[v]-234[r]

Union etc. At a recent petition on the part of Thomas Davy[1], perpetual beneficed
cleric (*clerici perpetui beneficiati*), called prebendary, in the parish church of Sarum,
d. Salisbury, the pope hereby unites etc. the parish church of Sutton' near Pattoy, d.
Lincoln, (whose annual value does not exceed 18 pounds[2] sterling, equivalent to 80
gold ducats of the camera or thereabouts), to a certain perpetual simple ecclesiastical
benefice, called the prebend of Blebery, in the said church of Sarum, which he holds
together with the above church of Sutton', for as long as he holds the benefice, to the
effect that Thomas[3] may, on his own authority, take [and] retain corporal possession
of the church of Sutton' and of its rights and appurtenances, for as long as he holds
the benefice, and convert its fruits etc. to his own uses and those of the church of
Sutton' and the benefice without licence of the local diocesan or of anyone else.
Notwithstanding etc. The pope's will is, however, that the church of Sutton' shall
not, on account of this union etc., be defrauded of due services and the cure of souls
therein shall not be neglected, but that its customary burdens shall be supported, and
that on Thomas's death or resignation etc. of the benefice the union etc. shall be
dissolved and the church of Sutton' shall revert to its original condition and be
deemed vacant automatically.

Ad[4] futuram rei memoriam. Ex iniuncto nobis desuper . . .
Jo. ortega / · V· / · V· xxxx De Phano:

[1] *Dabi* in the line, deleted and initialled *F.*; *Davy* inserted in the margin; *Cassatum et correctum de
mandato R(everendissimi) p(atris) domini A(loysii) pisauren' F. Sanctor(is)* in the margin against the
correction. The script of 'Davy' differs from that of both the scribe and the master.

[2] *marcharum* in the line deleted and initialled *F.*; *librarum* inserted in the margin; *Ca[ssatum et]
corectum [ut supra]* in the margin (shaved) against the correction.

[3] 'per se vel alium seu alios' does not occur

[4] *perpetuam* deleted and initialled *. V.*

92   6 December 1498   *Reg. Lat.* 1039, fos 246[r]-247[r]

To John Flint, prior of the monastery, usually governed by a prior, of St John the

Evangelist, Pontefract (*de Pontefracto*), OClun, d. York. Dispensation — at his supplication — to receive and retain for life, together with the priory of the above monastery, or another priory or monastery, of the aforesaid or another order held by him at the time, or without it, any benefice, with or without cure, usually held by secular clerics, even if a parish church or its perpetual vicarage, or a chantry, free chapel, hospital or annual service, usually assigned to secular clerics in title of a perpetual ecclesiastical benefice, and of lay patronage and of whatsoever tax or annual value, if he obtains it otherwise canonically, to resign it, simply or for exchange, as often as he pleases, and in its place receive another, similar or dissimilar, benefice, usually held by secular clerics, and retain it for life, together with the priory or monastery held by him at the time as above. Notwithstanding etc.[1] With the proviso that the priory or monastery and other benefice shall not, on this account, be defrauded of due services and the cure of souls therein (if any) shall not be neglected.

Religionis zelus, vite ac morum honestas . . .
Jo· ortega / F· / F L^{ta}. Sanctor(is)

[1] no mention of his being expressly professed of the order

93   5 December 1498   *Reg. Lat.* 1039, fos 299^{v}-300^{v}

To Richard Synyer, perpetual vicar of the parish church of Pelh(a)mffurneux,[1] d. London. Dispensation — at his supplication — to receive and retain for life, together with the perpetual vicarage of the above parish church, one, and without it, any two other benefices, etc. [as above, no. 3].

Vite ac morum honestas . . .
· Jo· ortega / F / F L^{ta}. Sanctor(is)

[1] MS: *Pelhm'ffurneux*

94   21 December 1498   *Reg. Lat.* 1039, fos 303^{v}-304^{v}

To the abbots of the monasteries of Alnewik and Newminster (*de Novo Monasterio*), d. Durham, and the treasurer of the church of Lichfield, mandate in favour of the prior and chapter of the church of Durham. A recent petition to the pope on the prior and chapter's part stated that although the parish church of Brantynghn', d. York, together with the chapels of Elberkat and (?)Blalitoff annexed perpetually to it, with all their rights and appurtenances, was (and still is) united in perpetuity to the capitular *mensa* of the church of Durham, and the prior and chapter have held and possessed the parish church, together with its chapels and all the rights and appurtenances, from the time of the union and have themselves, or through their factors, peacefully and quietly received and levied the tithes, both of the fruits arising within the boundaries of the parish of the parish church and of the chapels, as also of the wool and lambs, called two year old sheep,[1] grazing on the pastures and other possessions and lands within the parish boundaries, as well as the oblations, obventions, and emoluments falling to the church and chapels, William Stewardi of Howeden', priest, d. York had nevertheless presumed (and was then presuming), unjustly, to receive, levy, and convert to his own uses all the tithes of the wool and lambs from the sheep, called two year olds,[2] grazing, treading, and giving birth, in certain places and fields or enclosures, then expressed, within the parish boundaries, as well as other tithes of fruits arising within the borders of places in which the receipt of the tithes lawfully pertains to the prior and chapter, despoiling them *de facto* of the right of receiving them; that the prior and chapter sued William before Martin Colyns, DDec, official and commissary general of Thomas, archbishop of York, primate of England, and legate of the apostolic see in those parts, on the strength of this legation, praying that he be condemned and compelled to restore the tithes or reach a settlement with them; and that after the official had proceeded to several judicial [acts] short of the conclusion between the parties, and had kept the case in suspense for a long time, and had committed it to Thomas Metralff, who bears himself as a cleric, to be resumed in due state, heard further, and duly determined, Thomas, by pretext of this commission, having resumed the case in due state, proceeding wrongly to the more advanced stages, promulgated an unjust definitive sentence in favour of William and against the prior and chapter, condemning them in costs (the taxation of which he reserved to himself for the future), from which the prior and chapter appealed to the apostolic see. At their supplication to the pope to commit to some upright men in those parts the causes of their appeal; of everything perchance attempted and innovated after and against the appeal; of the nullity of the processes of the official and Thomas; of everything done temerariously against them in the case; and of the principal matter, the pope hereby commands that the above three (or two or one of them), having summoned William and others concerned, and having heard both sides, taking cognizance even of the principal matter, shall decree what is just, without appeal, causing by ecclesiastical censure what they have decreed to be strictly observed; [and moreover compel] witnesses etc. Notwithstanding etc.

Humilibus et cetera.
Jo· Ortega / · V· / · V· xij· De Phano:

[1] *lambs . . . sheep*] MS: *agnorum oviuum*[!] *bidentium nuncupatorum*: age expressed by dentition; but see next note

[2] *lambs . . . olds*] MS: *agnorum ex ovibus bidentibus nuncupatis*: here the nuncupative statement relates to the sheep and not (as before) to the lambs (see previous note); but the sense must be the same

95   20 November 1498   *Reg. Lat.* 1039, fos 310^v-311^v

To Thomas Bexwike, perpetual vicar of the parish church of Hareodon', d. Lincoln. Dispensation — at his supplication — to receive and retain for life, together with the perpetual vicarage of the above parish church, one, and without it, any two other benefices, etc. [as above, no. 3].

Vite ac morum honestas . . .
· *L· puccius / [F]*^{1} */ F. L^{ta}. Sanctor(is)*

^{1} shaved

96^1 20 November 1498   *Reg. Lat.* 1039, fos 312^r-313^r

To John Smyth', LLB, perpetual vicar of the parish church of Helifelde [also spelt *Hekfelde*], d. Winchester. Dispensation etc. [as above, no. 84].

Litterarum scientia, vite ac morum honestas . . .
· *L· puccius / F· / F· L^{ta}. Sanctor(is)*

^{1} Cancelled entry; each page struck through; . *L. Scripta ante, folio . cv. Dulcius.* — i. e. at fo 105^r of the present register — at the base of the first page (fo 312^r). *Cf.* above, no. 84.

97   24 November 1498   *Reg. Lat.* 1039, fos 313^v-314^r

To Francis of Sassello (*de Saxello*), professor OFM and of theology. Dispensation and indult — at his supplication — to receive and retain any benefice with cure, usually held by secular clerics, even if a parish church or its perpetual vicarage, and of lay patronage, if he obtains it otherwise canonically; and — even after he has acquired the benefice — to have an active and a passive voice in any acts, even capitular, OFM. Notwithstanding <the constitutions of Otto and Ottobuono formerly legates of the apostolic see in the kingdom of England>^{1}, etc. <and apostolic privileges and indults>^{2} granted to the said order, in particular those in which it is said to be provided that no professor of the order holding a secular benefice at the time may have an active and a passive voice in the said capitular acts etc., the which privileges and indults (which otherwise remain in force) the pope, for this once only, specially and expressly derogates, even if they and their whole tenors should be mentioned verbatim — and not by general clauses implying such mention — or any other recherché form should be observed.

Religionis zelus, litterarum scientia, vite ac morum honestas . . .
L· puccius / L. / . L. L^{ta}. Dulcius:-

1 The inclusion of these constitutions gives Francis the option of holding his secular benefice in England. MS has several deletions in the line, with marginal insertions ordered by the regent of the chancery. Here, in the margin: *apostolicis necnon bone memorie Octonis et Octoboni olim in regno Anglie apostolice sedis legatorum ac in provincialibus et sinodalibus conciliis editis generalibus vel specialibus constitutionibus et ordinationibus ac dicti ordinis*; beneath which, is: *Cassat(um) et Corectu(m) de man(da)to ut sup(ra). L.* (see below, note 2).

2 Marginal insertion: *privilegiis quoque et indultis apostolicis*; beneath which, is: *Cassat(um) et Corectu(m) de man(da)to D(omini) Jo(hannis) Regen(tis) e(pisco)pi mutinen' . L*

98   3 December 1498   *Reg. Lat.* 1039, fos 314^V-315^V

To Thomas Cowley, rector of the parish church of Pollesholt, d. Salisbury. Dispensation — at his supplication — to receive and retain for life, together with the above parish church, one, and without it, any two other benefices, etc. [as above, no. 3].

Vite ac morum honestas . . .
· L· puccius. / . L. / . L. L^{ta}. Dulcius;-

99   3 December 1498   *Reg. Lat.* 1039, fos 315^V-316^V

To Thomas Wetton, perpetual vicar of the parish church of Cheswyk [also spelt *Cheswik*], d. London. Dispensation — at his supplication — to receive and retain for life, together with the perpetual vicarage of the above parish church, one, and without it, any two other benefices, etc. [as above, no. 3].

Vite ac morum honestas . . .
· L· puccius / L. / . L. L^{ta}. Dulcius:-

100   18 December 1498   *Reg. Lat.* 1039, fos 319^r-320^r

To Humphrey Gaysconye, LLB, rector of the parish church of Newton' Kyme, d. York. Dispensation — at his supplication — to receive and retain for life, together with the above parish church, one, and without it, any two other benefices, etc. [as above, no. 3].[1]

Litterarum scientia, vite ac morum honestas . . .
· *L· puccius / L / . L. L^{ta}. Dulcius:-*

[1] save that in the present instance MS wants the line 'vel collegiatis et dignitates ipse in cathedralibus etiam metropolitanis' (probably merely an oversight occasioned by the repetition of 'etiam metropolitanis' when the scribe turned over the page)

101   16 August 1499   *Reg. Lat.* 1041, fos 1^r-2^v

To Thomas Watrer, BTheol, rector, called master, of the hospital called of poor priests, in the city of Canterbury, d. Canterbury. Dispensation — at his supplication — to him, who, as he asserts, holds the above hospital, usually assigned to secular clerics in title of a perpetual ecclesiastical benefice, to receive and retain for life, together with the hospital, which is incompatible with another benefice, one, and without it, any two other benefices, etc. [as above, no. 3].

Litterarum scientia, vite ac morum honestas . . .
. *L. pulccius*[1] / *V* / . *V. L De Phano:-*

[1] *sic*

102   14 June 1499[1]   *Reg. Lat.* 1041, fos 40^v-42^r

To James Bradshawe,[2] rector of the parish church of Ktylbore *alias* Ketilbergh', d. Norwich. Dispensation — at his supplication — to receive and retain for life, together with the above parish church, one, and without it, any two other benefices, etc. [as above, no. 3].

Vite ac morum honestas . . .
. *L. puccius*[3] / *F* / *F. L. Sanctor(is)*

[1] *Julii* inserted in the margin, initialled *F·* ; *Junii* deleted and initialled *F* in the line; both alterations made in a darker ink similar to that of the magistral initial and signature : all entered at the same time? *Cf.* below, no. 103, note 1.

[2] a large 'S' has been written over the 'sh' (in darker ink : *cf.* above, note 1)

[3] the surname seemingly altered

103   14 June 1499[1]   *Reg. Lat.* 1041, fos 42^r-43^v

To Hugh Harrison', rector of the parish church of Evedon', d. Lincoln. Dispensation

— at his supplication — to receive and retain for life, together with the above parish church, one, and without it, any two benefices, etc. [as above, no. 3].

Vite ac morum honestas . . .
. L. puccius / F / F L Sanctor(is)

[1] *Julii* changed from *Junii* (by overwriting in a darker ink similar to that of the magistral initial and signature). *Cf.* above, no. 102, note 1.

104   14 June 1499   *Reg. Lat.* 1041, fos 44^r-45^r

To Edward Staynclyff, priest, d. York. Dispensation — at his supplication — to receive and retain for life any two benefices, with cure or otherwise mutually incompatible, etc. [as above, no. 3, to '. . . Notwithstanding etc. '] With the proviso that the incompatible benefices in question shall not, on this account, be defrauded of due services and the cure of souls therein shall not be neglected.

Vite ac morum honestas . . .
. L. puccius / F / F. L. Sanctor(is)

105   14 June 1499   *Reg. Lat.* 1041, fos 45^v-47^r

To Thomas Hungersord' *alias* Doderoffe,[1] rector of the parish church of St Mary Magdalen near Barmondesey, d. Winchester. Dispensation — at his supplication — to receive and retain for life, together with the above parish church, one, and without it, any two other benefices, etc. [as above, no. 3].

Vite ac morum honestas . . .
. L. puccius / F / F L . Sanctor(is)

[1] or *Boderoffe*

106   ?[1]   *Reg. Lat.* 1041, fos 47^r-48^v

To John Thome, BDec, perpetual vicar of the parish church of All Saints, Bristott,[2] d. Worcester. Dispensation — at his supplication — to receive and retain for life, together with the perpetual vicarage of the above parish church, one, and without it, any two other benefices, etc. [as above, no. 3].

Litterarum scientia, vite ac morum honestas . . .
. L. puccius / F / [-][3]

[1] Date wanting. The letter ends: *Nulli ergo et cetera nostre absolutionis et dispensationis,* wanting an ending — i. e. the rest of the 'sanctio poenalis' (from 'infringere' onwards) and the date clause — on fo 48[v] and a new, unrelated, entry begins at the top of the next page (fo 49[r]). However, all the evidence points to its having been mutilated rather than abandoned. It bears the magistral initial, which as a rule was not added until the letter was finished, at the beginning. And it ends abruptly at the bottom of the page (fo 48[v]), and at the end of the line. As the register has evidently been re-constituted — it has visibly been refoliated — the leaf (the last of the gathering (and otherwise blank)?) which must have born the end of the letter was presumably removed at some stage, perhaps in rebinding, and is now lost.

[2] *sic*; the 'tt' arguably a corruption of 'll' with a bar through it

[3] Magistral signature ['F L. Sanctor(is)'?] wanting; see above, note 1

107   28 February 1499   *Reg. Lat.* 1041, fos 79[r]-80[r]

To Roger Leversege,[1] perpetual vicar of the parish church of Elyng, d. London. Dispensation — at his supplication — to receive and retain for life, together with the perpetual vicarage of the above parish church, one, or having resigned them, any two other benefices, etc. [as above, no. 3].

Vite ac morum honestas . . .
(?). L. [2] *Pulccius*[3] */ · V· / · V· L· De Phano:-*

[1] or *Leversegt*
[2] strangely formed and partially shaved away
[3] *sic*

108   9 March 1499   *Reg. Lat.* 1041, fos 99[v]-101[r]

Letters of protection, as below. A recent petition on the part of the abbot and convent of the monastery of Inchcolm (*Insule Sancti Columbe*), OSA, d. Dunkeld, stated that since the monastery is situated on the said island which is surrounded on all sides by the sea and to which, as often happens, many pirates and corsairs resort from whose minds the fear of God has departed and who do not hesitate to devastate, rob, plunder, and carry off the monastery's possesions and goods, on the island and off it; and because the pirates and other corsairs are not only from the kingdom of Scotland (within whose borders the island is) but rather from sundry other parts of the world the abbot and convent — to their and the monastery's grave damage — are unable to sue some of the robbers, especially the pirates, for the recovery of the removed goods before any judge, ordinary or delegate, and obtain justice; and, as the petition added, unless the abbot, convent and monastery are provided with a remedy and help against the pirates, robbers, and pillagers, especially the help of ecclesiastical censures, more serious damage will be inflicted on the monastery as time goes on. At the supplication of the abbot and convent — who assert that the island of St Columba is a mile in circumference or thereabouts and that besides the monastery (in which there are about nineteen religious) no other habitations exist — to be protected like the other islands, called the 'baptized islands' (*insularum baptizatarum*), near to the island of St Columba, the pope takes the island, the monastery, the abbot and convent, and the monastery's goods and possessions, both on the island and off it, under his protection and that of the apostolic see, in perpetuity, after the manner of the 'baptized islands' and he hereby excommunicates, as of now and as of then, all pirates, robbers, pillagers, violators, and any others who plunder, rob, or remove against the abbot and convent's will, any of the monastery's goods, on the island and off it, or who injure the said things, goods, or possessions, or their inhabitants; and he grants indult[1] that after his letters have been published on the island and in public places, they will not, except on the point of death, be able to obtain absolution unless they have previously made satisfaction; and he grants, without prejudice to the local ordinary, licence and faculty to the abbot for the time being to aggravate and re-aggravate the sentence of excommunication, as often as necessary. Notwithstanding, etc.

Ad perpetuam rei memoriam. Iniunctum nobis desuper apostolice servitutis officium . . .
S. de Castello / V· / V· xxxx De Phano: —

[1] MS: *indulgemus*; by reason of *statuere* the narrative contemplates 'statuimus' here.

109   14 June 1499   *Reg. Lat.* 1041, fos 103ʳ-104ᵛ

To John Elys, rector of the parish church of Sylton', d. Salisbury. Dispensation — at his supplication — to receive and retain for life, together with the above parish church, one, and without it, any two other benefices, etc. [as above, no. 3].

Vite ac morum honestas . . .
. L. puccius / F / F· Lᵗᵃ. Sanctor(is)

110   14 June 14[9]9[1]   *Reg. Lat.* 1041, fos 104ᵛ-l06ᵛ

To George Turtom',[2] rector of the parish church of Broxhome [also spelt *Broxhonie*],
d. Lincoln. Dispensation — at his supplication — to receive and retain for life,
together with the above parish church, one, and without it, any two other benefices,
etc. [as above, no. 3].

Vite ac morum honestas . . .
. *L. puccius / F / F. L^{ta}. Sanctor(is)*

[1] MS wants 'nonagesimo'
[2] final letter altered, possibly '-n'

111   6 July 1499   *Reg. Lat.* 1041, fos 106ᵛ-108ʳ

To Richard More, rector of the parish church of St Mary,[1] Bonleghe, d. Exeter.[2]
Dispensation — at his supplication — to receive and retain for life, together with the
above parish church, one, and without them, any two other benefices, etc. [as above,
no. 3].

Vite ac morum honestas . . .
. *L. puccius / · V· / . V· L· De Phano:-*

[1] 'Marthe' deleted and initialled *A*; *Marie* inserted in the margin; the insertion preceded by *A* and
followed by *Cassatum et Correctum de mandato R(everendissimi) p(atris) d(omini) Regentis Colotius.* .
Below, in the body of the letter, 'Marthe' is deleted and initialled *A*; *Marie*, initialled *A*, against it in the
margin. The script of the corrections differs from that of the letter.
[2] *Oxonien.* deleted and initialled *A*; *Exonien.* inserted in the margin and initialled *A*; below *Oxonien.*
changed (by overwriting) to *Exonien.* and initialled *A*. Other deletions in the line bear the magistral
initial (. *V.*)

112   13 August 1499   *Reg. Lat.* 1041, fos 119ᵛ-120ᵛ

To Robert Hawlay, MA, rector of the parish church of Conesgrave, d. Lincoln.
Dispensation — at his supplication — to receive and retain for life, together with the
above parish church, one, and without it, any two other benefices, etc. [as above, no. 3].

Litterarum scientia, vite ac morum honestas . . .
. *A. de Sanctoseverino / · V· / · V· L· De Phano:-*

113   20 April 1499   *Reg. Lat.* 1041, fos 131^r-132^r

To John Pykton', cleric, d. Canterbury. Dispensation — at his supplication — to him, who, as he asserts, is in his sixteenth year of age, to receive and retain any benefice, with cure or otherwise[1] incompatible, even if a parish church or its perpetual vicarage, or a dignity, etc. [as below, no. 240].

Vite ac morum honestas . . .
. *L. puccius*[2] / · *V·* / · *V· xxx De Phano:-*

[1] MS: *alias invicem . . . incompatibile*; but *invicem* is evidently inappropriate here and was, perhaps, overlooked when the word after it was being deleted

[2] or *pulccius*

114   20 May 1499   *Reg. Lat.* 1041, fos 135^r-136^v

To Richard Nicholl', rector of the parish church of Holcote, d. Lincoln. Dispensation — at his supplication — to receive and retain for life, together with the above parish church, one, and without it, any two other benefices, etc. [as above, no. 3].

Vite ac morum honestas . . .
· *L. puccius* / *F* / . *F L^{ta}. Sanctor(is)*

115   —[1]   *Reg. Lat.* 1041, fo 172^v

Incomplete (and apparently unfinished) entry, as follows:

To Roger Magonghail, canon of Raphoe. Collation and provision, *motu proprio*, as if granted *sub data kalendis Marcii pontificatus nostri anno quarto* [1 March 1496], to him who is a priest and, as the pope has learned, has not had another expectative grace, of a canonry of the church of Raphoe and a canonry of the church of Killala, with plenitude of canon law, and [reservation] of prebends of the same churches, and of a dignity, (provided it be not major *post pontificalem*), *personatus*, administration, or office, of one or other of the churches, even if customarily elective and with cure of souls, such as are vacant now or shall, at once or successively, fall vacant, which he, in person or by proxy . . . [ends: . . . *procuratorem tuum ad hoc*]

Vite ac morum honestas . . .
S. de Castello; a. de sanctoseverino[2] / —/ —[3]

The fragment occupies an entire page, extending to end of last line; one passage corrected in margin; deleted; marked *non signata nec finita* in a contemporary hand (but not the enregistering scribe's); perhaps once continued on another leaf; but that leaf never bound : fo 172 (modern mechanical foliation) = fo Lxxxvij (original), fo 173 (the *recto* of which occupied by start of wholly unconnected letter) = fo Lxxxviij Belongs, probably, to the seventh year (26. viii. 1498-25. viii. 1499) : thus the *liber* and thus the surrounding letters.

Cannot be matched with any other letter in an extant chancery register; or with an entry in the *rubricellae* of registers now lost; perhaps never expedited (at least by the chancery)

[1] dating clause wanting

[2] abbreviator of the executory (otherwise lost)

[3] no magistral signature

116   30 June 1499   *Reg. Lat.* 1041, fos 195[r]-198[r]

To the prior of the priory of Ardkathan', d. Lismore, mandate in favour of John (?)Nacleobi,[1] priest, d. Sodor. A recent petition to the pope on John's part stated that at one time — after he had been dispensed by apostolic authority notwithstanding a defect of birth as the son of a priest and an unmarried woman to be promoted to all, even sacred, orders, and to hold a benefice even if it should have cure of souls; and had been promoted to the said orders and had acquired by the said dispensation a certain benefice with cure, which was canonically collated to him while vacant *certo modo*, and had resigned it — when the rectory of the parish church of Li in Leowas, d. Sodor, which is of lay patronage, and which the late Rynardus,[2] its last rector, held while he lived, became vacant by his death, outside the Roman curia, John had himself presented for the rectory, thus vacant, by its true patrons, (who were in peaceful possession or almost of the right of patronage and of presenting a suitable person for it at a time of vacancy), without having obtained any other dispensation, to the local ordinary within the lawful time, albeit *de facto*, and instituted as its rector at the presentation by the said ordinary by ordinary authority, also *de facto* and, taking possession of the rectory by pretext of this presentation and institution, then detained it for a certain time, as he does at present, likewise *de facto*, receiving no fruits from it. Moreover since, [according to][3] the foregoing, the said presentation and institution do not hold good; and, as the pope has learned, the rectory is known to be vacant still as above, the pope hereby commands the above prior, if by diligent examination he finds John to be suitable — concerning which the pope burdens the prior's conscience — to collate and assign the rectory, whose annual value does not exceed 3 pounds sterling, (vacant as above or in any other way, etc. ; even if it has been vacant for so long that by the Lateran statutes its collation has lawfully devolved on the apostolic see, etc.), with all rights and appurtenances, to John, inducting him etc. having removed any unlawful detainer and causing[4] the rectory's fruits etc., rights and obventions to be delivered to him. [Curbing] gainsayers by the pope's authority etc. Notwithstanding etc. Also the pope dispenses John to receive and retain the rectory, if conferred on him by virtue of the presents, to resign it, simply or for exchange, as often as he pleases, and in its place receive and retain another, notwithstanding the above defect etc. The pope has commanded that — if John is found suitable — provision of the rectory be made to him from the date of the presents.

Dignum arbritramur[5] *et cetera.*
A. de sancto severino / · *V·* / · *V· xxx. Nono Kalendas Augusti Anno Septimo* [24 July 1499], *De Phano:-*

[1] or *Macleobi*; the 'cl' doubtful, apparently altered from 'ch'

[2] only this one name occurs

[3] *secum*; *recte*: 'secundum'?

[4] there is no mention of his being admitted

[5] *sic*

117   8 June 1499   *Reg. Lat.* 1042, fos 124ᵛ-125ʳ

To Martin Colyns, DDec, cleric, d. York. Dispensation — at his supplication — to him, who, as he asserts, is a counsellor of Henry, king of England, to receive and retain for life, any three benefices, etc. [as above, no. 17, to '. . . Notwithstanding etc. ']¹ With the proviso that the incompatible benefices in question shall not, on this account, be defrauded of due services and the cure of souls therein shall not be neglected.

Litterarum scientia, vite ac morum honestas . . .
S de Castello / *F* / *F· Cᵗᵘᵐ. Sanctor(is)*

[1] as to content; though the order of words is not identical

118   20 November 1498   *Reg. Lat.* 1042, fos 164ʳ-166ᵛ

To the official of Worcester, mandate in favour of Henry, bishop of Bangor. A recent petition to the pope on bishop Henry's part stated that in a general synod celebrated in the church of Bangor in 1497 he — mindful that formerly, under a synodal constitution published in this regard by Anian, bishop of Bangor, the rectors or vicars for the time being of the parish churches of the city and diocese of Bangor were due to have one third of all the tithes of the said churches, and Bangor cathedral and sundry other churches, monasteries, and persons were due to have the remaining two thirds, called *gologoith*[1]; and that, while those who received two thirds had no burdens, the rectors and vicars were unable out of their one third to discharge the burdens incumbent on them by reason of their parish churches, and as a result the churches were abandoned and defrauded of due services and the cure of souls neglected, serious inconvenience and scandal arising daily; and desiring to provide for the indemnity of the parish churches and for the welfare of the souls under him and also to remedy the inconvenience and scandal — established and ordained by ordinary authority, in perpetuity, with the express consent of the dean and chapter and of the clergy of the city and diocese (who compromised <in>[2] the bishop over this matter and swore to observe his ordinance and decree), that after the following feast of St Michael the Archangel, no prelate, canon, or prebendary of the church of Bangor or of any collegiate church or convent or priory, or anyone else, whatever their dignity, status, or condition, was to seek, exact, or claim, by any title or colour, any predial, personal, lactual[3], or liberal tithes, or anything else, in the name of the right of *gologoith*, within the city and diocese of Bangor, even by pretext of any custom, prescription, or synodal constitution, of bishop Anian or any other bishop of Bangor, or of any other right or title; that all rectors and vicars were to receive from their parishioners the predial, lactual, and liberal tithes in their entirety, and any other ecclesiastical rights, without diminution; that any rector, vicar, prebendary, portioner, or anyone else wanting to seek, exact, or collect tithes in the name of *gologoith* before the feast of St Michael was to do so only in accordance with the tenor of bishop Anian's constitution; and, lest any rights or tithes of *gologoith* be sought etc. after the feast, he expressly commanded and decreed that after it the constitutions of Anian and any other bishop of Bangor, as well as customary and prescriptive rights, assigning or granting any tithes (or parts thereof) in the name of *gologoith*, to prelates, canons, and prebendaries, to cathedral or collegiate churches, to places, within the diocese and without,[4] whose revenue is shared by portioners, or to any other churches or places, within the diocese and without, were utterly invalid and he revoked, made void, and annulled them as of then, quashed and condemned them in perpetuity, and declared them to be revoked, quashed, and null after the feast; and thereafter, he commanded the constitution published by him to be inviolably observed by everyone in perpetuity, binding those who sought, exacted, and collected, (or attempted to exact and collect), tithes or anything else in the name of *gologoith* and — unless they did so through fear of death or torture — those who paid them to the same, after the said [feast][5], by sentence of greater excommunication, decreeing them to be so bound automatically as often as they opposed his constitution or violated any part of it, and only able to be absolved from the sentence by him or succeeding bishops of Bangor or their vicars or commisssaries general; as is said to be more fully contained in an instrument drawn up in this regard. At bishop Henry's supplication, the pope, not having certain knowledge of the foregoing, hereby commands the above official, if, after the dean and chapter and others concerned have been summoned, it appears to him to be lawful, to approve and confirm, by the pope's authority, the constitution, statute, ordinance, decree, revocations, quashings, makings void, makings null, declarations, mandate and compromise aforesaid, and, everything else of relevance in the said instrument, supplying any defects; to decree that it must be inviolably observed in perpetuity, under pain of excommunication, adding the force of perpetual strength; and, as a further precaution, to establish, ordain, and decree anew everything done and ordained by bishop Henry. Notwithstanding the statutes and customs of Bangor and the other churches, monasteries, and priories aforesaid, etc.

Ea que pro ecclesiarum omnium . . .
L. puccius / Jo. / Jo· Lxxxx. de Galves

[1] *cf.* Welsh *colegaidd,* collegiate

[2] marginal insertion by enregistering scribe, initialled *Jo.*

[3] MS *lactuales;* see J. Ekton, *Thesaurus Rerum Ecclesiasticarum* (London, 1742), p. 635

[4] *within . . . without*] occurs again below; perhaps written in error

[5] MS wants 'festum' here

119   5 March 1501   *Reg. Lat.* 1042, fos 177ᵛ-178ʳ

To John Brown, MA, perpetual chaplain, called cantor, in the parish church of St Laurence, Lechelade, d. Worcester. Dispensation — at his supplication — to him (who, as he asserts, holds the perpetual chaplaincy, called a chantry, dedicated to B. Mary, in the above parish church, which, according to its foundation <or otherwise>[1] cannot be held with another benefice) to receive and retain for life, together with the above chaplaincy, one, and without it, any two other benefices, etc. [as above, no. 3].

Litterarum scientia, vite ac morum . . .
Jo ortega / F / F· Lᵗᵃ Sanctor(is)

[1] marginal insertion (in darker ink, no initial)

120   5 March 1501   *Reg. Lat.* 1042, fos 178ʳ-179ʳ

To Christopher Speke, LLB, rector of the parish church of Moneton' Hampsted, d. Exeter. Dispensation — at his supplication — to receive and retain for life, together with the above parish church, one, and without them, any two other benefices, etc. [as above, no. 3].

Litterarum scientia, vite ac morum honestas . . .
Jo ortega / F / F· xxxx[1] Sanctor(is)

[1] *sic*; *recte*: 'L'?

121   17 February 1499   *Reg. Lat.* 1042, fos 197^r-198^r

To Patrick, elect of Cork and Cloyne, whom the pope has this day provided to the canonically mutually united churches of Cork and Cloyne and appointed bishop, as is more fully contained in his letters drawn up in that regard.[1] Since, at the time of the said provision and appointment, Patrick was presiding, as he still does, over the monastery of B. Mary, Fermoy (*de Castro Dei*), OCist, d. Cloyne, the pope — *motu proprio* — hereby dispenses him to retain the monastery, whose fruits etc. do not exceed 32 marks sterling, *in commendam* — after he has received consecration and, on the strength of the said provision and appointment, acquired peaceful possession, or almost, of the rule and administration and of the goods of the said churches or of the greater part of them — together with the said churches, for as long as he presides over them; (he may — due and customary burdens of the monastery and its convent having been supported — make disposition of the rest of its fruits etc. just as abbots could and ought to do, alienation of immovable goods and precious movables being however forbidden). Notwithstanding etc. and [notwithstanding] privileges, indults and apostolic letters granted to the Cistercian order by the pope or the apostolic see, especially those in which it is expressly laid down that the order's monasteries cannot be commended to anyone save cardinals of the holy Roman church and with the consent of the abbot for the time being and convent of the monastery of Cîteaux, d. Chalon-sur-Saône, and commends made otherwise, even by the said see, are void and commendataries for the time being are bound to cede the said commends within a certain time and that the order's privileges and indults cannot be derogated, (and if they are derogated they are deemed not to be derogated in any way), except under a certain way, form and formulation of words expressed therein, and with their insertion, and the derogation must first be communicated by sundry letters to the order's superiors, at certain intervals, the which privileges, indults and letters the pope — likewise *motu proprio* — hereby derogates, specially and expressly, for this once only, decreeing that the above monastery shall not be made vacant on this account. With the proviso that divine worship and the usual number of monks and ministers in the monastery shall not, on account of this commend, be diminished; but that the aforesaid burdens of the monastery and convent shall be supported.

Personam tuam nobis et apostolice sedi devotam . . .
· *S· de castello / Jo / Jo. xxxx. Electus Terracinen'*

122   29 January 1499   *Reg. Lat.* 1043, fos 25^r-27^r

To Magonius Omullayd, canon of the church of Clonfert, and Charles Omullcaryl
and Thomas Meranayn, canons of the church of Tuam, mandate in favour of
Cristinus Ospelan, perpetual vicar of the parish church of the Great Gate (*Porte
Magne*) at the monastery of Knockmoy (*Collis Victorie*), d. Tuam. The pope has
learned that a perpetual vicarage, called a stipend, of the church of Tuam, is vacant
at present and has been for so long that by the Lateran statutes its collation has
lawfully devolved on the apostolic see, although Magonius Omuynayn has detained
it without any title or support of law, temerariously and *de facto*, for a certain time,
as he still does. He hereby commands that the above three (or two or one of them),
if, having summoned Magonius and others concerned, they find the said vicarage of
the church of Tuam, which has cure of souls and whose annual value does not
exceed 5 marks sterling, to be vacant (howsoever etc.), shall collate and assign it,
(even if specially reserved etc.), with all rights and appurtenances, to Cristinus,
inducting him etc. having removed Magonius and any other unlawful detainer and
causing Cristinus (or his proctor) to be admitted to this vicarage and its fruits etc.,
rights and obventions to be delivered to him. [Curbing] gainsayers by the pope's
authority etc. Notwithstanding etc. Also the pope dispenses Cristinus to receive and
retain for life the vicarage of the church of Tuam, if it is conferred on him by virtue
of the presents and he acquires it peacefully, together with the vicarage of the above
parish church of the Great Gate, to resign them, at once or successively, simply or
for exchange, as often as he pleases, and in their place receive other, similar or
dissimilar, perpetual vicarages and retain them for life, as above. Notwithstanding
etc. With the proviso that the vicarages of the church of Tuam and of the parish
church of the Great Gate and the other vicarages in question shall not, on this
account, be defrauded of due services and the cure of souls in any of them shall not
be neglected. Given at Ostia.

Vite ac morum honestas . . .
. *S. de Castello* / · *V·* / · *V· xxiiij Septimo Kalendas Martii Anno Septimo* [23
February 1499], *De Phano:-*

123   28 January 1499   *Reg. Lat.* 1043, fos 39^v-41^v

To Cristinus Ospelayn, Malachy Omanin and John Omogri, canons of the church of
Tuam, mandate in favour of Charles Omulcaryll, priest, d. Clonfert (who, some time

ago, as he asserts, was dispensed by apostolic authority, notwithstanding a defect of birth as the son of a priest, professed of the third order of [friars] minor,[1] and a married woman, to be promoted to all, even sacred, orders, and to hold a benefice, even if it should have cure of souls, and afterwards was promoted to all, even sacred, orders, and the priesthood). The pope has learned that a certain perpetual vicarage, called a stipend, in the church of Tuam, which John Oberynd, its late perpetual vicar, called stipendiary, held while he lived, has become vacant by his death outside the Roman curia and is vacant at present, although Malachy Ohugynd, who bears himself as a deacon or subdeacon, has detained it without any title or support of law, temerariously and *de facto*, for a certain time, as he still does. He hereby commands that the above three (or two or one of them), if, having summoned Malachy and others concerned, they find the vicarage, which has cure of souls and whose annual value does not exceed 5 marks sterling, to be vacant (as above or howsoever etc.), shall collate and assign it (even if it has been vacant for so long that by the Lateran statutes its collation has lawfully devolved on the apostolic see etc.), with all rights and appurtenances, to Charles, inducting him etc. having removed Malachy and any other unlawful detainer and causing Charles (or his proctor) to be admitted to the vicarage and its fruits etc., rights and obventions to be delivered to him. [Curbing] gainsayers by the pope's authority etc. Notwithstanding etc. Given at Ostia.

Vite ac morum honestas . . .
. *S. de Castello / · V / · V· Gratis pro deo Pridie kalendas Martii Anno Septimo* [28 February 1499], *De Phano:*

[1] *minorum*; i. e. friars minor though 'fratrum' does not occur

124   4 February 1499   *Reg. Lat.* 1043, fos 46ᵛ-48ʳ

To the archdeacon and Richard de Burgo and Thomas Obruchan, canons, of the church of Killala, mandate in favour of Eugene Macdonall, cleric, d. Killala (who, as he asserts, notwithstanding a defect of birth as the son of an unmarried man and an unmarried woman, has had himself dispensed first by ordinary authority to be marked with clerical character, otherwise however duly, and then by apostolic authority to be promoted to all, even sacred, orders and hold a benefice, even if it should have cure of souls). The pope has learned that the perpetual vicarage of the parish church of Castleconor (*de Castro Co(n)cubare*), d. Killala, is vacant *certo modo* at present and has been vacant for so long that by the Lateran statutes its collation has lawfully devolved on the apostolic see, although John Odunnegan, who bears himself as a priest, has detained it, without any title or support of law, temerariously and *de facto*, for a certain time, as he does. He hereby commands that the above three (or two or one of them), if, having summoned John and others concerned, they find the vicarage, whose annual value does not exceed 8 marks sterling, to be vacant (howsoever etc.) shall collate and assign it, (even if specially reserved etc.), with all rights and appurtenances, to Eugene, inducting him etc. having removed John and any other unlawful detainer and causing Eugene (or his proctor) to be admitted to the vicarage and its fruits etc., rights and obventions to be delivered to him. [Curbing] gainsayers by the pope's authority etc. Notwithstanding etc.

Vite ac morum honestas . . .
. *S de*[1] *Castello* / · *V·* / · *V Gratis pro deo Pridie nonas Martii Anno Septimo* [6 March 1499], *De Phano:-*

[1] heavily blotched

125   20 February 1499   *Reg. Lat.* 1043, fos 48[r]-50[r]

To Donat Oconayll' and Edmund Magniell' and Felmicus Makaryg, canons of the churches of Ardfert and Cloyne,[1] mandate in favour of Florence Osulenayn, priest, d. Ardfert. The pope has learned that the perpetual vicarage of the parish church of Drumtaryf, d. Ardfert, is vacant *certo modo* at present and has been vacant for so long that by the Lateran statutes its collation has lawfully devolved on the apostolic see, although Dermot Oscolayn, who bears himself as a priest, d. Ardfert, has detained it, without any title or support of law, temerariously and *de facto*, for some years, as he still does. He hereby commands that the above three (or two or one of them), if, having summoned Dermot and others concerned, they find the vicarage, whose annual value does not exceed 12 marks sterling, to be vacant (howsoever etc.), shall collate and assign it, (even if specially reserved etc.), with all rights and appurtenances, to Florence, inducting him etc. having removed Dermot and any other unlawful detainer and causing Florence (or his proctor) to be admitted to the vicarage and its fruits etc., rights and obventions to be delivered to him. [Curbing] gainsayers by the pope's authority etc. Notwithstanding etc.

Vite ac morum honestas . . .
. *S. de. Castello* / · *V·* / *V xij· Sexto nonas Martii Anno Septimo* [2 March 1499], *De Phano:-*

[1] drawn thus, undifferentiatable, outside *stilus*; MS has *Elonen.* for 'Clonen'

126   5 February 1499   *Reg. Lat.* 1043, fos 50[r]-51[v]

To the archdeacon and William[1] de Burgo and David Ocherim,[2] canons, of the church of Tuam, mandate in favour of Fracha Macnrocnallyd, cleric, d. Tuam. The pope has learned that the perpetual vicarage of the parish church of <Omy>,[3] d. Tuam, is vacant *certo modo* at present and has been vacant for so long that by the

Lateran statutes its collation has lawfully devolved on the apostolic see, although Robert[4] de Stantona, who bears himself as a priest, d. Tuam, has detained it, without any title or support of law, temerariously and *de facto*, for a certain time, as he still does. He hereby commands that the above three (or two or one of them), if, having summoned Robert and others concerned, they find the vicarage, whose annual value does not exceed 2 marks sterling, to be vacant (howsoever etc.), shall collate and assign it, (even if specially reserved etc.), with all rights and appurtenances, to Fracha, inducting him etc. having removed Robert and any other unlawful detainer and causing Fracha (or his proctor) to be admitted to the vicarage and its fruits etc., rights and obventions to be delivered to him. [Curbing] gainsayers by the pope's authority etc. Notwithstanding etc.

Vite ac morum honestas . . .
. S. de Castello | · V· | · V· Gratis pro deo Tertio Nonas Martii Anno Septimo [5 March 1499], *De Phano:-*

[1] *Guillermo*

[2] or *Ocherrm*

[3] marginal insertion initialled . V. ; (?) . . . . heavily deleted and initialled . V. twice in the line; the name, apparently much longer than the one inserted, extended into the margin

[4] *Robertus* once; otherwise *Obertus*

127   29 January 1499   *Reg. Lat.* 1043, fos 318[v]-321[r]

To William[1] de Burgo, canon of Annaghdown, commission and mandate in favour of Thomas de Burgo, canon of the monastery of B. Mary, Cong (*de Comga*), OSA, d. Tuam (who, as he asserts, is expressly professed of the said order, holds *in commendam* the perpetual vicarages of the parish churches of Ropba in Concnecule Obeara and also of Anachdrilin, d. Tuam, by apostolic concession and dispensation, and — notwithstanding a defect of birth as the son of an unmarried man and an unmarried woman, related in the second and third degrees of consanguinity and also the second and third of affinity, and in the third and third of consanguinity and affinity, of comital birth by both parents — has been marked with clerical character, otherwise however duly). It has been referred to the pope's audience by Thomas that Richard[2] de Burgo, abbot of the said monastery, has dared to alienate, or rather strip (*dispare*), several immovable goods lawfully pertaining to the monastery, to convert the price fetched by them to his own uses and to be present at several conflicts some of which he was the author of and at some of which men were slaughtered. And, as a recent petition to the pope on Thomas's part stated, although Thomas himself at another time — in defence of his things and his friends[3] — was present at various and divers conflicts, of which he was not the author, in which several men were fatally wounded, some had their hands mutilated and some were killed, contracting irregularity, nevertheless he has not wounded, mutilated or killed anyone with his own hands. At his supplication to the pope to dispense him for irregularity contracted by occasion of the foregoing and rehabilitate him on account of all disability and infamy arising therefrom, the pope — considering that if the foregoing is true, Richard has rendered himself unworthy of the rule and administration of the said monastery — not having certain knowledge, hereby commissions and commands the above canon William to absolve Thomas from the excess, if he so requests, for this once only, in the customary form of the church, having enjoined a salutary penance on him etc., dispense him for the irregularity contracted by him by occasion of the foregoing and to use the orders taken by him so that he may be promoted to all other, even sacred and priest's, orders and minister in them all, even in the ministry of the altar, and preside over the rule and administration of the monastery, if he is provided thereto, and rule and govern it in spiritualities and temporalities, and retain the vicarages *in commendam*, together with the monastery, as before, and rehabilitate him on account of all disability and infamy arising by occasion of the foregoing; and, in the event of such dispensation and rehabilitation and if Thomas will accuse Richard over the foregoing before the above canon and proceed in form of law, thereafter, having summoned Richard and others concerned, to make inquiry into these matters and, if he finds the truth of them to be substantiated, deprive Richard of the said rule and administration and remove him from them; and, in that event, inform himself as to Thomas's merits and suitability, and if he finds him to be suitable for the rule and administration — concerning which the pope burdens the canon's conscience — make provision of Thomas to the monastery, whose annual value does not exceed 50 marks sterling, (if vacant by the above deprivation and removal or in any other way etc.), and appoint him abbot, committing to him the care, rule and administration of the monastery in spiritualities and temporalities and causing obedience and reverence to be given him by the convent of the monastery and customary services and rights by the vassals and other subjects of the monastery. [Curbing] gainsayers etc. Notwithstanding etc. And, if provision of Thomas to the monastery be made by virtue of the presents and he be appointed abbot, the pope grants by the presents that he may receive benediction from any catholic bishop of his choice in communion with the apostolic see and that the bishop concerned may impart it to him; and that this shall not be to the prejudice of the archbishop of Tuam to whom the aforesaid monastery is understood to be subject by ordinary law. Given at Ostia.

Sasedes[4] *apostolica, pia mater, recurrentibus ad (?)illam cum humilitate. . .*
S de Castello / F / F L[ta] *Sanctor(is)*

[1] *Guillelmo*

[2] *Resterdus*

[3] reading *amicorum*

[4] *sic; recte:* 'Sedes'

128   12 March 1499   *Reg. Lat.* 1045, fos 40ᵛ-41ᵛ

To the abbot of the monastery of B. Mary, *de Castrodei* [Fermoy], d. Cloyne, Edmund Omurcha, canon of the church of Cloyne, and Donat Ocomyll, canon of the church of Ardfert, mandate in favour of David Maginell, cleric, d. Cloyne. The pope has learned that the priorship of the monastery, usually governed by a prior, of the house of St Thomas the Martyr, Ballybeg (*iuxta Betomam*), OSA, d. Cloyne, is vacant *certo modo* at present and has been vacant for so long that by the Lateran statutes its collation[1] has lawfully devolved on the apostolic see, although Thomas Barri, who bears himself as prior, has detained it without any title or support of law, temerariously and *de facto*, for a certain time, as he still does; and, furthermore, that David wishes to enter the monastery under the regular habit. Therefore, he hereby commands that the above three (or two or one of them) shall receive David, if he is suitable and there is no canonical obstacle, as a canon in the said monastery and bestow the regular habit on him in accordance with the custom of the monastery and cause him to be given charitable treatment therein and also receive and admit from David the profession usually made by the canons if he spontaneously wishes to make it into their hands, or the hands of anyone of them; and, in that event, if, having summoned Thomas and others concerned, they find the priorship, which is conventual and whose annual value does not exceed 300 marks sterling, to be vacant (howsoever etc.), collate and assign it, (even if specially reserved to apostolic disposition or generally reserved as a conventual dignity etc.), with all rights and appurtenances, to David, inducting him etc., having removed Thomas and any other unlawful detainer, and causing David (or his proctor) to be admitted to the priorship and its fruits etc., rights and obventions to be delivered to him. [Curbing] gainsayers by the pope's authority. Notwithstanding etc.

Apostolice sedis circumspecta benignitas cupientibus vitam ducere regularem . . .
P de Castello / F / F xxx. Decimo septimo Kl' Aprilis Anno Septimo [16 March 1499], *Sanctor(is)*[2]

[1] unexpected; *recte* : 'provisio iuxta canonicas sanctiones'?

[2] *Anno Septimo Sanctor'* in darker ink : entered later?

129   15 March 1499   *Reg. Lat.* 1045, fos 45ʳ-46ʳ

To John Makterrelaigh, canon of the church of Cork, mandate in favour of Odo Yhedrscoyll, cleric, d. Ross. The pope has learned that the perpetual vicarage of the parish church of Clery and its rectory and also the rectory of the parish church of Crybach and Gornaclohy, d. Ross, are vacant at present and have been for so long that by the Lateran statutes their collation has lawfully devolved on the apostolic see, although Dermot Ochedrscoyll, who bears himself as a priest, has detained the vicarage, the prior and convent of the monastery, usually governed by a prior, of B. Mary, Ross (*de Rosso*), OSB, d. Ross, have detained the first rectory, and Donald Ohedrscoyll,[1] who bears himself as a cleric, the second rectory, without any title or support of law, temerariously and *de facto*, for a certain time, as they still do. At a recent petition on Odo's part to the pope to erect and institute a canonry in the church of Ross and the vicarage into a simple prebend in the same, for his lifetime; and unite etc. the rectories to them, after their erection, likewise for his lifetime; and — it being asserted on Odo's part that he had promised Dermot on oath not to impetrate the said vicarage, and had incurred perjury on account of the impetration — to absolve him from the perjury and rehabilitate him on account of all disability and infamy arising therefrom, the pope, not having certain knowledge of the foregoing, hereby commands the above canon to absolve Odo, if he so requests, from the perjury, for this once only, in the customary form of the church, having enjoined a salutary penance on him etc., and also rehabilitate him on account of all disability and infamy arising therefrom; and, in that event, if, having summoned respectively Dermot, the prior and convent, Donald and the bishop and chapter of Ross and others concerned, he finds the rectories and vicarage to be vacant (howsoever etc.) and, having summoned those interested in the union, the foregoing to be true, to erect and institute a canonry in the church of Ross and the vicarage into a simple prebend in the same, for Odo's lifetime, and collate and assign the newly erected canonry and prebend, whose annual value does not exceed 8 marks sterling, being vacant, to Odo, with plenitude of canon law, and unite etc. the rectories, whose annual value together does not exceed 10 marks sterling, (even if specially reserved etc.), to the canonry and prebend, with all rights and appurtenances, inducting Odo etc. having removed Dermot from the vicarage, the prior and convent from the first rectory and Donald from the second rectory and any other unlawful detainers, and causing Odo (or his proctor) to be received as a canon of the church of Ross, with plenitude of canon law, and causing the fruits etc., rights and obventions of the canonry and prebend and rectories to be annexed to be delivered to him. [Curbing] gainsayers by the pope's authority etc. Notwithstanding etc. With the proviso that the vicarage and rectories shall not, on account of this erection, institution and union etc., be defrauded of due services and the cure of souls therein shall not be neglected, but that their customary burdens shall be supported; and that on Odo's death or resignation etc. of the canonry and prebend this erection and institution shall be extinguished, union etc. shall be dissolved and so deemed and the vicarage and rectories shall revert to their original condition and be deemed vacant automatically.

Apostolice sedis indefessa clementia recurrentibus ad eam cum humilitate. . .
S[2] *de Castello* / *F*[3] / *F xxx.* [4] *Sanctor(is)*

[1] the surname occurs at the end of a line and enters the margin; it has not been changed; the magistral initial *F* nevertheless above it (in error?)

[2] blotched

[3] fuzziness characteristic of enregistering scribe (Boccapaduli)

[4] wants expedition date?

130   10 October 1498   *Reg. Lat.* 1045, fos 127^r-128^v

To the bishop of Nepi, mandate. The hospital of the poor of Drons, d. St Andrews, which is of lay patronage and which Edward Cokburn', its late rector, held while he lived, has become vacant by his death, in the Roman curia, and is vacant at present. Therefore, the pope — wishing that provision of a capable and suitable governor be made to the said hospital and having considered the foregoing and the merits of John Barbour, cleric, d. Glasgow (who, as he asserts, is a continual commensal member of the household of Ascanius Maria, cardinal deacon of S. Vitus in Macello Martirum) — hereby derogates the right of lay patronage to the above bishop for this once only; and commands him to commit the said hospital, which is customarily ruled by secular clerics and whose annual value and that of the parish church of Ellam, said diocese, annexed to it, do not exceed 8 pounds sterling (vacant in the above [way] or at another time in any other etc. ; even if its provision be specially reserved etc.), with the said annex and all rights and appurtenances, to John, if he is suitable and there is no canonical obstacle, to be held, ruled and governed by him even for life, in accordance with the constitutions of Clement V regarding this published in the Council of Vienne, in person or by proxy, inducting John (or his proctor) into corporal possession of the hospital, annex and rights and appurtenances aforesaid etc. having removed any unlawful detainer and causing John (or his proctor) to be admitted to the hospital and its universal fruits etc., rights and obventions (which in accordance with the said constitution are to be laid out and deployed in the support of the poor and infirm and otherwise to the utility of the hospital) to be delivered to him. [Curbing] gainsayers etc. Notwithstanding etc.

Gerentes in desideriis cordis nostri ut hospitalia et alia pia loca sub bono et felici regimine gubernentur . . . [1]
. L. puccius / F· / F· gratis pro familiari R(everendissi)mi d(omini) Vicecancellarii Sanctor(is)

[1] proem defective; wants statement about provisees

131   16 November 1499   *Reg. Lat.* 1046, fos 1^r-2^v

To Thomas [S]vyst,[1] rector of the parish church of Newton' [also spelt *Newtn'*], d. Lincoln, dispensation. Some time ago, Innocent Vlll by his letters dispensed him to receive and retain for life, together with the parish church of Brokelsby [also spelt *Brokelesdy*], d. Lincoln, (which, he asserted, he was then holding), one, and without it, any two other benefices, with cure or otherwise mutually incompatible, even if parish churches or their perpetual vicarages, or chantries, free chapels, hospitals or annual services, usually assigned to secular clerics in title of a perpetual ecclesiastical benefice, or dignities, *personatus*, administrations or offices in cathedral, even metropolitan, or collegiate, churches, even if the dignities in question should be major *post pontificalem* in cathedral, even metropolitan, churches, or principal in collegiate churches, or a combination, and even if the dignities etc. should be customarily elective and have cure of souls, if he obtained them otherwise canonically; to resign them, at once or successively, simply or for exchange, as often as he pleased, and in their place receive up to two other, similar or dissimilar, incompatible benefices, and retain them together for life, as is more fully contained in those letters.[2] The pope therefore — at his supplication — hereby dispenses Thomas, who, as he asserts, having resigned the church of Brokelsby, holds, by the said dispensation, the parish churches of Newton', d. Lincoln, and Wikerslere [also spelt *Wikersleye*], d. York, (having acquired them at another time when they were canonically collated to him, being successively vacant *certo modo*), to receive and retain for life, together with the churches of Newton' and Wikerslere, or any two other incompatible benefices held by him at the time by the said dispensation, any third benefice, with cure or otherwise incompatible, even if a parish church or its perpetual vicarage, or a chantry, free chapel, hospital or annual service, usually assigned to secular clerics in title of a perpetual ecclesiastical benefice, or a dignity, *personatus*, administration or office in a cathedral, even metropolitan, or a collegiate church, even if the dignity in question should be major *post pontificalem* in a cathedral, even metropolitan, church, or principal in a collegiate church, and even if the dignity etc. should be customarily elective and have cure of souls, if he obtains it otherwise canonically, to resign it, simply or for exchange, as often as he pleases, and in its place receive another, similar or dissimilar, benefice — provided that of three such benefices not more than two be parish churches or their perpetual vicarages — and retain it for life, as above. Notwithstanding etc. With the proviso that this third incompatible benefice shall not, on this account, be defrauded of due services and the cure of souls therein (if any) shall not be neglected.

Vite ac morum honestas . . .
L. puccius / L / . L. Lxx. Dulcius:-

[1] first letter deleted or overwritten; supplied; see next note
[2] summarised in *CPL* XV at no. 444 (where his surname is spelt *Suuis*t)

132　　30 November 1499　　　　　　　　　*Reg. Lat.* 1046, fos 12[r]-13[r]

To William Lynton', rector of the parish church of Spaxton', d. Bath and Wells. Dispensation — at his supplication — to receive and retain for life, together with the above parish church, one, and without it, any two other benefices, etc. [as above, no. 3].

Vite ac morum honestas . . .
. L. puccius / · V· / · V· L· De Phano:

133   16 November 1499   *Reg. Lat.* 1046, fos 13^v-14^v

To Robert Colman, monk of the monastery of St Mary, Coventry, OSB, dispensation. Some time ago, the pope by other letters of his dispensed him to receive and retain any benefice, with and without cure, usually held by secular clerics, even if a parish church or its perpetual vicarage, or a chantry, free chapel, hospital or annual service, usually assigned to secular clerics in title of a perpetual ecclesiastical benefice, if he obtained it otherwise canonically, to resign it, simply or for exchange, when he pleased, and in its place receive and retain another, similar or dissimilar, benefice, with or without cure, defined as above, as is more fully contained in those letters.[1] The pope, therefore — at his supplication — hereby further dispenses him, who, as he asserts, holds a place and monacal portion of the above monastery and is expressly professed of the order,[2] to retain for life, together with the benefice he may acquire by the said dispensation, his place and monacal portion; and also have, for life, a stall in the choir and an active and a passive voice in the chapter and any acts of the monastery just as if he had not acquired the benefice. Notwithstanding etc. With the proviso that the benefice and portion shall not, on this account, be defrauded of due services and the cure of souls in the benefice (if any) shall not be neglected; but that its customary burdens and those of the portion shall be supported.

Religionis zelus, vite ac morum honestas . . .
. L. puccius / · V· / . V. xxx. De Phano:

[1] Summarised in *CPL*, XVI at no. 541. 'Quoadviveres' ('for life'), which occurs in that entry, does not, however, occur here.

[2] The latter information comes from a notwithstanding clause.

134   4 October 1499   *Reg. Lat.* 1046, fos 29^r-30^r

To Robert[1] Elphinstonen', scholar, d. Glasgow.[2] Dispensation — at his supplication — to him, who, as he asserts, suffers from a defect of birth as the son of a priest and an unmarried woman and wishes to become a cleric — after he has been duly marked with clerical character — to be promoted to all, even sacred, orders and also receive and retain any number of mutually compatible benefices, with and without cure, even if canonries and prebends, dignities, *personatus*, administrations or offices, in cathedral, even metropolitan, or collegiate churches, even if the dignities etc. should be customarily elective and have cure of souls, if he obtains them otherwise canonically, to resign them, at once or successively, simply or for exchange, as often as he pleases, and in their place receive and retain any number of mutually compatible benefices, as above — provided that such dignities be not major *post pontificalem* in cathedral, even metropolitan, churches or principal in collegiate churches. Notwithstanding etc.

Vite ac morum honestas . . .
. *L. puccius* / . *V.* / . *V. xxxv. De Phano:*

[1] *Johanni* in the line has been deleted, initialled . *V.* ; with *Roberto* (in a different script) inserted in the margin; *Cassatum et Correctum de Mandato R(everendissimi) D(omini) Jo(hannis) Ragusini Regentis* . *V. De Phano*: (in a different hand) beneath it

[2] *Glasenen.* ; for Glasgow?

135   5 October 1499   *Reg. Lat.* 1046, fos 30[r]-31[r]

To Henry Tybardi, MA, perpetual vicar of the parish church of Bledlow [also spelt *Bledelow*], d. Lincoln. Dispensation and indult — at his supplication — to receive and retain for life, together with the perpetual vicarage of the above parish church, one, and without it, any two other benefices, etc. [as above, no. 3, to '. . . retain them together for life, as above']; and, also for life, while residing in the Roman curia or any one of his benefices or attending a *studium generale*, not to be bound to reside personally in his other benefices, nor to be liable to be compelled by anyone to do so against his will. Notwithstanding etc. With the proviso that the above perpetual vicarage and other incompatible benefices shall not, on this account, be defrauded of due services and the cure of souls in the perpetual vicarage and (if any) the other incompatible benefices shall not be neglected; but that the cure shall be exercised and things divine served by good and sufficient vicars maintained from the proceeds of these benefices.[1]

Litterarum scientia, vite ac morum honestas . . .
L· puccius / *V* / . *V Lx. De Phano:-*

[1] MS has numerous small deletions (five of which are initialled . *V.*) and various textual oddities (in particular, 'tibique pariter' (or suchlike) does not occur in the body of the letter; and 'indulti' or 'concessionis' (or suchlike) does not occur in the *Nulli ergo* clause).

136   7 September 1499   *Reg. Lat.* 1046, fo 32[r-v]

To James Ryman', professor OFM. Dispensation — at his supplication — to receive and retain any benefice, with or without cure, usually held by secular clerics, etc. [as above, no. 32, to '. . . Notwithstanding etc. '] and [notwithstanding] the constitutions of Otto and Ottobuono formerly legates of the apostolic see in the kingdom of England etc.[1]

Religionis zelus, vite ac morum honestas . . .
. *p. de Castello* / · *V·* / · *V· xxxx. De Phano:-*

1 The inclusion of these constitutions gives Ryman the option of holding his secular benefice in England.

137   7 September 1499   *Reg. Lat.* 1046, fos 32^v-33^r

To the bishop of Salisbury, commission and mandate. A petition presented to the pope on the part of Richard Weston', layman, and Agnes Recte, woman, d. Salisbury, stated that they desire to be joined together in marriage, but because they are related in the third degree of consanguinity they cannot fulfil their desire in this matter without an apostolic dispensation. The pope therefore — at their supplication — hereby commissions and commands the above bishop — if it is so and Agnes has not been ravished on this account — to dispense Richard and Agnes to contract marriage together and remain therein, (declaring)[1] the offspring of the marriage legitimate. Notwithstanding the above impediment etc.

Oblate nobis pro parte [. . .] petitionis series continebat . . .
. p. de Castello / · V· / · V· xx. De Phano:-

1 *nuntiando* inserted in the margin, initialled . V. ; (?)*decernendo*, deleted and initialled . V., in the line

138   11 October 1499   *Reg. Lat.* 1046, fos 48^r-49^v

To Thomas Ellbardi, BTheol, professor OESA. Dispensation — at his supplication — to receive any secular benefice, with or without cure, or regular benefice of any order, even Cluniac, even if the secular benefice should be a parish church or its perpetual vicarage, or a chantry, free chapel, hospital or annual service, usually assigned to secular clerics in title of a perpetual ecclesiastical benefice, even of lay patronage, and the regular should be a priory, *prepositura, prepositatus*, dignity (even conventual), *personatus*, administration or office, and even if the dignity, *personatus*, etc. should be customarily elective and have cure of souls, if he obtains it otherwise canonically, and to retain the secular benefice *in titulum* and the regular *in commendam*, for life, to resign it, simply or for exchange, as often as he pleases, and cede the commend, and in its place receive one other, similar or dissimilar, benefice, secular or regular of any order, even Cluniac, and to retain the secular benefice *in titulum* or the regular benefice — which may not be a claustral office — *in commendam*, for life, as above; (he may — due and customary burdens of the regular benefice having been supported — make disposition of the rest of its fruits etc. just as those holding it at the time could and ought to do, alienation of immovable goods and precious movables being however forbidden); and also — even after he has acquired such a benefice — to use, possess and enjoy all the prerogatives, exemptions, privileges, graces and indults, granted and to be granted to the OESA, (of which, as he asserts, he is expressly professed), under any forms of words and clauses; and to have an active and a passive voice in the chapter of the said order of St Augustine. Notwithstanding etc. and [notwithstanding] privileges, indults and apostolic letters granted to the orders of Cluny and of St Augustine and also to the general and minister of the province of England for the time being of the said order of St Augustine, especially those in which it is said to be expressly laid down that no professed member of the said order of St Augustine who holds a benefice may have an active and a passive voice in the [daily][1] chapter acts; that the general or minister are not bound, until they are commanded twice, to obey any apostolic letters specially granted to professed members of the said order of St Augustine which seem to them in any way scandalous; and that benefices of the Cluniac order cannot, without the consent of the abbot for the time being and convent of the monastery of Cluny, d. Mâcon, be commended to anyone save cardinals of the Holy Roman Church or expressly professed members of the Cluniac order, and commends of them made otherwise, even by the apostolic see, are void. The pope specially and expressly derogates these privileges and indults, for this once only, even if they and their whole tenors ought to be specially, specifically, expressly and individually mentioned, or otherwise expressed, word for word, (and not by general clauses implying full mention), or other recherché form ought to be observed. With the proviso that the regular benefice in question shall not, on this account, be defrauded of due services and the cure of souls therein (if any) shall not be neglected; but that its aforesaid burdens shall be supported.

Religionis zelus, litterarum scientia, vite ac morum honestas ...
· L· puccius· / · L· / . L. Lxx. Dulcius:-

[1] uncertain reading : written *dieb(us)b(us)*; the first 'bus' apparently deleted

139   7 September 1499   *Reg. Lat.* 1046, fos 55ᵛ-56ᵛ

To John Trebel, monk of the monastery of Serne, OSB, d. Salisbury. Dispensation — at his supplication — to him, (who, as he asserts, holds a place and monacal portion of the above monastery and is expressly professed of the above order[1]), to receive and retain for life, together with the above place and monacal portion, any benefice, with or without cure, usually held by secular clerics, even if a parish church or its perpetual (vicarage),[2] or a chantry, free chapel, hospital, or annual service, usually assigned [to secular clerics] in title of a perpetual ecclesiastical benefice, and of lay patronage and of whatsoever tax or annual value, if he obtains it otherwise canonically, to resign it, simply or for exchange, as often as he pleases, and in its place receive another, similar or dissimilar, benefice, usually held by secular clerics, and retain it for life, as above; and also — even after he has acquired the above benefice — to have as before, also for life, a stall in the choir and a place and an active and a passive voice in the chapter of the monastery, just as if he had not acquired the benefice. Notwithstanding etc. With the proviso that the benefice and portion shall not, on this account, be defrauded of due services and the cure of souls in the benefice (if any) shall not be neglected; but that its customary burdens and those of the portion shall be supported.

Religionis zelus, vite ac morum honestas . . .
. L. puccius / · V· / · V· · xxxx. De Phano:-

[1] The latter information comes from a notwithstanding clause.

[2] *vicaria* inserted in the margin, initialled . *V.* ; several words hereafter have been altered from plural to singular, and there are various other minor oddities and alterations in the text hereabouts

140   8 January 1500   *Reg. Lat.* 1046, fos 75^r-76^r

To Robert Gilbert,[1] MA, rector of the parish church of All Saints, Saltflmbr,[2] d. Lincoln. Dispensation — at his supplication — to receive and retain for life, together with the above parish church, one, and, without it, any two other benefices, etc. [as above, no. 3].[3]

Litterarum scientia, vite ac morum honestas . . .
. L. puccius /· V· / V· · L· De Phano:

[1] changed (by overwriting) from (?)*GilberR*; the (?)'R' written in anticipation of *Rectori*?

[2] the second occurrence changed (by deletion of the second 'r') from *Saltflmbrr*; no magistral initial

[3] save that 'or a combination' does not occur

141   20 December 1499   *Reg. Lat.* 1046, fos 106^v-107^v

To Richard Helwys, rector of one of two portions of the parish church of Grymolbe, d. Lincoln. Dispensation to him (who, as he asserts, holds [one of two portions][1] of the above parish church usually ruled by two rectors) — at his supplication — to receive and retain for life, together with the above portion, one, and without it, any two other benefices, etc. [as above, no. 3].

Vite ac morum honestas . . .
. L. puccius / · V· / · V· L· De Phano:-

[1] MS wants 'alteram portionem' (or suchlike)

142   20 December 1499   *Reg. Lat.* 1046, fos 107^V-108^V

To John Valle, BDec, perpetual vicar in the church[1] of Maschin' [also spelt
Maschin], d. York. Dispensation — at his supplication — to him (who, as he asserts,
holds a perpetual vicarage in the above church) to receive and retain together for life
any two benefices, with cure or otherwise mutually incompatible, etc. [as above, no.
3, to '. . . Notwithstanding etc']. With the proviso that the <incompatible>[2] benefices
in question shall not, on this account, be defrauded of due services and the cure of
souls therein shall not be neglected.

Vite ac morum honestas . . . [3]
· *L· puccius* / · *V·* / . *V. L. De Phano:*

[1] *sic*; (i. e. does *not* say '*parish* church')

[2] *incompatibilia* inserted in the margin initialled . *V.* ; 'vicaria obtenta et alia' (or suchlike) does not
occur

[3] *sic*; yet an address clause, where the recipient of the grace is designated by a degree, calls for a proem
in the form 'Litterarum scientia, vite . . . '

143   20 December 1499   *Reg. Lat.* 1046, fos 108^V-110^V

To George Strangways, MA, rector of the parish church of All Saints, vill of Riplay,
d. York. Some time ago, Paul II by his letters dispensed him to receive and retain for
life, together with the parish church of Bulin' [also spelt *Bulin*], d. York, (which, as
he asserted, he was then holding), one, and without it, any two other benefices, etc.
[as above, no. 131, to '. . . as is more fully contained in those letters']. The pope
therefore — at his supplication — hereby further dispenses George (who, as he
asserts, <is of noble and of knightly birth; and>,[1] having resigned the church of
Bulin', holds by the said dispensation the parish church of All Saints, d. York, and
the archdeaconry of (?)Conventre,[2] d. Lichfield and Coventry, having acquired them
at another time when they were canonically collated to him, being successively
vacant *certo modo*), to receive and retain for life, together with the church of All
Saints and the archdeaconry, or any two other incompatible benefices held by him at
the time by the said dispensation, any third benefice, etc. [as above, no. 131].[3]

<*Nobilitas generis*>,[4] *litterarum scientia, vite ac morum honestas . . .*
. *L puccius* / *V* / . *V. Lxx. De Phano:-*

[1] marginal insertion, initialled . *V.*

[2] final letter changed (by overwriting) from (?) 'i'; not initialled

[3] save that in the present instance MS wants 'vel collegiata [ecclesia]'

[4] marginal insertion, initialled . *V.*

144   11 January 1500   *Reg. Lat.* 1046, fos 125^V-128^V

Exemplification in full from the register of Innocent VIII at a recent petition to the pope on the part of Hugh Martini, cleric, d. St Andrews, of the letter *Vite ac morum honestas . . .* (dated 7 November 1491) and its executory *Hodie cum dilectus filius Hugo Martini . . .*, as follows: This day Hugh — of whom at another time provision had been made by apostolic authority *sub certis modo et forma* to the monastery of Kinloss, OCist, d. Moray, then vacant *certo modo* — has, spontaneously and freely, ceded into the pope's hands all right belonging to him in or to the rule and administration of the monastery, not having had possession of them; and the pope, admitting the cession, has approved and confirmed the election made canonically at one time by the convent of the monastery of William Culross as abbot of the monastery, then vacant *certo modo*, and the ensuing confirmation made canonically in accordance with the privileges and indults granted to the said order by the apostolic see; and the pope has appointed William abbot, committing the care, rule and administration of the monastery to him in spiritualities and temporalities, as is more fully contained in his letters drawn up in that regard. Lest Hugh should suffer excessive loss on this account, the pope — *motu proprio* — hereby reserves, constitutes and assigns to him an annual pension of 100 marks Scots on the fruits etc. of the parish church of Elone, d. Aberdeen, canonically united in perpetuity to the said monastery, especially for the 100 marks the <tithes of>[1] corn, pertaining to the parish church, of the places of Alathan', <Petmedan>,[2] Eraghed,[3] Vodlande,[4] Tulimaod,[5] Torci,[6] Esil<mund>[7] with the annexes Dumbred also with the annexes <and Argrane, Utherellon and Valtertoun>,[8] for life or until provision be made to him of benefices whose fruits etc. are annually worth 100 pounds Scots (after deduction of expenses), payable in full to him (or to his specially mandated proctor), by William and his successors as abbots of the monastery for the time being, each year, one half of the said pension on the feast of St Martin in the winter and the other on that of Pentecost, with the express consent of abbot William and the convent.[9] With decree that if abbot William (or any one of his successors) fails to make payment on the said feasts or at least within the thirty days immediately following, he shall, after this time has elapsed, incur sentence of excommunication, from which he cannot be absolved, except on the point of death, until he shall have made satisfaction in full or reached agreement in respect of it with Hugh (or his proctor) and, if he remains obdurate under that sentence for a further six months, he shall thereupon be deprived in perpetuity of the rule and administration of the monastery which shall be deemed vacant automatically. Notwithstanding etc.

Executory to the deans of the churches of Moray and of St Germain, Monten', d. Cambrai, and the official of Moray, or two or one of them, acting in person or by proxy.

The pope hereby decrees that this exemplification shall everywhere have the same force as the original.

Ad futuram rei memoriam. Provisionis nostre debet provenire subsidio . . .
F: de parma / . L. / . L. xviiij. Dulcius:-

---

[1] in the line: *garbas locorum* with a reference mark in between; in the margin: a corresponding mark

then *B decimales Corectu(m) ut sup(ra). B Bolis.* (in a different hand); a like correction: *. B. decimales Corectu(m) ut sup(ra) . B. Bolis* occurs in the margin of the executory

2 in the line: (?)*Pennedan* deleted and initialled *B*; in the margin: *B Petmedan Cassatum et corectu(m) de Man(da)to R(everendissimi) p(atris) d(omini) Jo(hannis) ragusin(i) rege(n)t(is) . B. Bolis* (in the different hand)

3 the 'd' written over a 't'; not initialled

4 changed (by deletion and overwriting) from (?)*Voldlande*; not intialled

5 the 'T' written over a 'J'; not initialled

6 or *Torri*

7 *mund* inserted in the margin; *. B* before the insertion; *ut supra . B.* after it

8 in the line: *Garbam (?)Biherellen' et (?)Bonchan'* deleted; in the margin: *. B,* then the insertion, then *Casatu(m) et corectu(m) ut sup(ra) B. Bolis;*

9 further corrections of detail hereabouts, including: *id expresso accedente consensu* deleted initialled *. B. ;* in the margin: *. B. hoc expressus accedat assensus Cassatu(m) et corectu(m) de Man(da)to R(everendissimi) p(atris) d(omini) Jo(hannis) ragusin(i) rege(n)t(is) p(er) me . B. Bolis* (in the different hand)

---

145   11 January 1500   *Reg. Lat.* 1046, fos 131^V-132^V

To Robert Swynton, monk of the monastery of Du(n)fermlyn',[1] OSB, d. St Andrews. Dispensation — at his supplication — to him, who is a priest and, as he asserts, expressly professed of the above order,[2] to receive and retain any benefice, with or without cure, usually held by secular clerics, even if a parish church or its perpetual vicarage, or a chantry, free chapel, hospital or annual service, usually assigned to secular clerics in title of a perpetual ecclesiastical benefice, even if of lay patronage, if he obtains it otherwise canonically, to resign it, simply or for exchange, as often as he pleases, and in its place receive and retain another, similar or dissimilar, benefice, with or without cure, usually assigned to secular clerics. Notwithstanding etc. and [notwithstanding] the constitutions of Otto and Ottobuono formerly legates of the apostolic see in the kingdom of England etc.[3]

Religionis zelus, vite ac morum honestas . . .
. F. de. parma. / L. / L. xxx. Dulcius:-

1 MS: *Du'fermlyn'*

2 The latter information comes from a notwithstanding clause.

3 The form of the entry (particularly the inclusion of 'chantry . . . annual service' and of the constitutions of Otto and Ottobuono) is suggestive of a benefice in England.

146   26 November 1499   *Reg. Lat.* 1046, fos 142^r-144^r

To the prior of the monastery, usually governed by a prior, of B. Mary, Gabine, d. *Clonen.*,[1] and the dean of the church of *Clonen.*,[2] mandate in favour of William Jacobi viventis and Odo de Obroch, clerics of Clonfert. Some time ago, representation was made to Eugenius IV on the part of the late James of the clan (*nationis*) of Obrog, cleric of Clonfert, that Gregory, the late bishop of Clonfert, had, for certain reasons then expressed, given and granted James and his successors certain ecclesiastical lands lawfully belonging to the episcopal *mensa* of the church of Clonfert, namely (?)Goven Glochmor and Gortuaglothbg' by the walls of Clonfert, lengthwise from the square upto Gortnuybg'[3] and Bearnduamlegynd, sideways [from] Arodmuneach upto the lands of Montere Kenayd' and [from] two parts of the gorge which is called Bruachtalach at Syliam, in a perpetual tenancy (*emphiteosim*), under a certain annual payment payable by James and his successors every year to the bishop of Clonfert for the time being, in evident utility of the said *mensa*; and thereafter — at James's supplication — Eugenius confirmed and approved the said gift and concession, as is more fully contained in his letters drawn up in this regard. Then Paul II issued letters of the tenor: *Paulus episcopus servus servorum dei ad perpetuam rei memoriam. Cum in omnibus iudiciis...* And, as a recent petition to the pope on the part of the above William and Odo, (successors of the late James), stated, Thomas, bishop of Clonfert (Gregory's successor in the church of Clonfert) — after Eugenius's confirmation and approval and before the issue of Paul's letters — gave and granted anew, with the consent of the then dean and chapter of the church of Clonfert, Eugenius's confirmation and approval, (insofar as it was correct and acceptable), and the lands in question, (the total of whose fruits etc. does not exceed annually 2 marks sterling or thereabouts, payable under the said annual payment by the predecessors of William and Odo, as above), as is said to be more fully contained in certain letters patent drawn up by bishop Thomas in this regard. At the supplication of William[4] and Odo as well as of other successors of the late James, to the pope to give the force of apostolic approval and confirmation anew to all the foregoing, he — not having certain knowledge of the foregoing — hereby commands the above two, having observed the tenor and form of Paul's letters and summoned the present bishop of Clonfert and the chapter and others concerned, to inform themselves jointly as to each and every one of the foregoing matters and also all the circumstances of them and if — the lands in question having been previously specified and designated before them — they find it to be thus and all the above to be and have been ceded in evident utility of the said episcopal *mensa*, to approve and confirm all those things and decree that this approval and confirmation has force in perpetuity; and in that event the above two (or one of them) shall thereafter cause the above William, Odo and the successors of James to enjoy peaceful possession of the lands, not permitting them to be molested unlawfully by the bishops of Clonfert for the time being and the chapter and anyone else. [Curbing] gainsayers by the pope's authority etc., having also called in the aid of the secular arm if necessary. Notwithstanding etc.

*Hiis que p(ro) ecclesiarum presertim cathedralium utilitate provide processisse
comperimus . . .*
. S. de Castello / · V / · V· xv De Phano:

1 *recte*: 'Cluanen.' (Clonmacnois)

2 *recte*: 'Cluanen.' (Clonmacnois)? (See previous note.)

3 uncertain reading: the 'G' heavily blotched

4 *Willelmi ac Jacobi viventis*; for 'Willelmi Jacobi viventis'. There is similar confusion below where the
text has *Willelmum ac Jacobum* for 'Willelmum Jacobi'

147   28 August 1499   *Reg. Lat.* 1046, fos 146ʳ-148ᵛ

To Thomas Bodley, perpetual vicar of the parish church of St Neot in Cornwall (*in
Cornevallia*), d. Exeter. Dispensation and indult — at his supplication — to receive
and retain for life, together with the perpetual vicarage of the above parish church,
one, and without it, any two other benefices, etc. [as above, no. 3, to '. . . retain them
together for life, as above']; and, while [residing]1 in the Roman curia or any one of
his benefices, or attending a *studium generale*,2 to receive for life the fruits etc. of
the said vicarage as well as of all the other benefices, with and without cure, which
he holds and shall hold in any churches or places, even if they should be canonries
and prebends, dignities, *personatus*, administrations or offices in cathedral, even
metropolitan, or collegiate churches, even if the dignities should be major *post
pontificalem* in cathedral, even metropolitan, churches, or principal in collegiate
churches and otherwise defined, as above, the daily distributions alone excepted, as
if he were resident personally, and not to be bound to reside personally, nor to be
liable to be compelled by anyone to do so against his will. Notwithstanding that he
may not have made the customary first residence in the said churches or places
personally and the constitutions of Boniface VIII prohibiting grants of this type
[?without a limit set on their duration]3; and [notwithstanding] constitutions etc. ;
even if he or his proctor has perchance taken or shall take an oath to observe them
and not to impetrate apostolic letters contrary to them or make use of such letters
even if impetrated by another or others or granted in any other way, etc. With the
proviso that the above vicarage and the incompatible and other benefices in question
shall not, on this account, be defrauded of due services and the cure of souls in the
vicarage and (if any) in the other benefices aforesaid shall not be neglected; but that
the cure shall be exercised and things divine served by good and sufficient vicars
maintained from the proceeds of these benefices.

Executory to the bishops of Capaccio and Modena and the official of Exeter, or
two or one of them, acting in person or by proxy.

Vite ac morum honestas . . .
. N Bregeon; . P. de castello / V / · V Lxxx · xx De Phano:

[1] *resignando*; *recte*: 'residendo'; in the executory *resig(endo)* has been corrected (by overwriting) to *residendo*

[2] MS: *generali*

[3] *sine presumptione temporis* . . . ; *recte*: 'sine prefinitione temporis . . . '? Many other oddities exist in the text, but have not been specially noted here.

148   12 September 1499   *Reg. Lat.* 1046, fo 157[r-v]

To Richard Hoper *alias* Pittemyster, monk, recently abbot, of the monastery of Dunkeswell',[1] OCist, d. Exeter.[2] Dispensation — at his supplication — to him, (who, as he asserts, receives annually a certain annual pension reserved, established and assigned by apostolic authority to him some time ago on the fruits etc. of the above monastery of which he is a monk; and is, as he asserts, expressly professed of the above order), to receive and retain for life, even together with the above pension, any benefice, with or without cure, usually held by secular clerics, even if a parish church or its perpetual vicarage, or a chantry, free chapel, hospital or annual service, usually assigned to secular clerics in title of a perpetual ecclesiastical benefice, if he obtains it otherwise canonically, to resign it, simply or for exchange, when he pleases, and in its place receive another, similar or dissimilar, benefice, usually held by secular clerics, and retain it <even together with the pension, for life, as above>.[3] Notwithstanding etc.[4]

Religionis zelus, vite ac morum honestas . . .
Jo ortega / · V· / V. xxxx De Phano:-

[1] the first occurrence is a marginal insertion initialled *V·*, (?)*Dwkesuell'* in the line has been deleted, initialled . *V.*

[2] in the second instance, MS has *Eduen.* ; *recte*: 'Exonien.'

[3] marginal insertion initialled . *V.* (having been deleted earlier in the text)

[4] the usual clause safeguarding due services and the cure of souls in the benefice has been deleted, initialled . *V.*

149   10 October 1499   *Reg. Lat.* 1046, fos 202[r]-203[v]

To Robert Freste, rector of the parish church of St Peter, Shogbroke,[1] d. Exeter. Dispensation — at his supplication — to receive and retain for life, together with the above parish church, one, and without it, any two other benefices, etc. [as above, no. 3].

Vite ac morum honestas . . .

. *L. puccius* / *V* / · *V· L· De Phano:-*

[1] MS: *Vocat* [for 'vocate'] *Shogbroke*

150   10 October 1499

To Henry Fydkoc, perpetual vicar of the parish church of St Cedd[1], vill of Abbots Bromley (*Ville Abbatis Bromley*), d. Coventry and Lichfield. Dispensation — at his supplication — to receive and retain for life, together with the perpetual vicarage of the above parish church, one, and, without it[2], any two other benefices, etc. [as above, no. 3].

Vite ac morum honestas...
. *L. puccius* / *V* /· *V·· L· De Phano:-*

[1] or possibly St Chad: MS: *Sancti Cedde*
[2] MS: *alia*; *recte*: 'illa'; *cf.* nos. 152 and 153

151   11 October 1499

To <Robert>[1] Stokys,[2] professor OESA and of theology. Dispensation and indult — at his supplication — to receive and retain any benefice, with or without cure, usually held by secular clerics, even if a parish church or its perpetual vicarage, of lay patronage and of whatsoever annual value, if he obtains it otherwise canonically, to resign it, simply or for exchange, as often as he pleases, and in its place receive another, similar or dissimilar, benefice, usually held by secular clerics; and also — after he has acquired the benefice — to use, possess and enjoy any privileges, liberties, exemptions and indults granted (and to be granted in the future) to friars, of the said order and living in its houses; and[3] to have an active and a passive voice in any capitular acts of the order. Notwithstanding etc. and [notwithstanding] any apostolic privileges and indults of the order and granted perchance to its general for the time being, especially those in which it is said to be expressly laid down that they are not bound, up to[4] the second command, to obey apostolic letters granted specifically to professors of the said order which in some way seem scandalous to them, and that no-one professed of the order may have an active and a passive voice in the said capitular acts while holding a secular benefice. The pope hereby derogates these privileges and indults, specially and expressly, for this once only.

Religionis zelus, licterarum[5] scientia, vite ac morum honestas...
. *L. puccius* / *F* / *F. Lx. Sanctor(is)*

[1] marginal insertion (in different hand) initialled *F.*

[2] fourth letter overwritten

[3] *ore*; for 'ac'?

[4] *eisque ad secundam iussionem*; *recte*: 'usque ad... '?

[5] *sic*

152   19 November 1499   *Reg. Lat.* 1046, fos 218[r]-219[v]

To Thomas Wygston', MA, rector of the parish church of Honghton' on the Hill (*super Hill*), d. Lincoln. Dispensation — at his supplication — to receive and retain for life, together with the above parish church, one, and without it,[1] any two other benefices, etc. [as above, no. 3].

Litterarum scientia, vite ac morum honestas...
. L. puccius[2] */ V. /. V. L. De Phano:*

[1] MS: *alia*; *recte*: 'illa'; *cf.* nos. 150 and 153

[2] the first 'c' written over an 'l'

153   19 November 1499   *Reg. Lat.* 1046, fos 219[v]-221[r]

To Richard Varter, rector of the parish church of Boxuuel (?) Leyghtterten' [also spelt *Boxwel (?)Leyghtterten'*][1], d. Worcester. Dispensation — at his supplication — to receive and retain for life, together with the above parish church, one, and without it,[2] any two other benefices, etc. [as above, no. 3].

Vita[3] *ac morum honestas. . .*
. L. puccius /· V· /· V· L. De Phano:

[1] in both instances the penultimate letter is overwritten

[2] corrected (by overwriting) from *alia*; no initial; *cf.* nos. 150 and 152

[3] *sic*; *recte*; 'Vite'

154   29 October 1499   *Reg. Lat.* 1046, fos 232[v]-234[r]

Union etc. At a petition on the part of Henry Hornby, MTheol, canon of the church of Lincoln, to the pope[1] to unite etc. the parish church of Birton', d. Salisbury, which he holds, to the canonry and prebend of Nassyngton',[2] of the church of Lincoln, which he holds, for as long as he holds the canonry and prebend — asserting that the annual value of the parish church does not exceed 16 marks sterling, equivalent to 48 gold ducats of the camera or thereabouts — the pope hereby unites etc. the parish church, with all rights and appurtenances, to the canonry and prebend, for as long as Henry holds the latter; to the effect that he may, on his own authority, in person or by proxy, take corporal possession of the parish church and the rights and appurtenances aforesaid, retain it for as long as he holds the canonry and prebend, and convert its fruits etc. to his own uses and those of the parish church and the canonry and prebend, without licence of the local diocesan or of anyone else. Notwithstanding etc. The pope's will is, however, that the said parish [church][3] shall not, on account of this union etc., be defrauded of due services and the cure of souls therein shall not be neglected, but that its customary burdens shall be supported; and that on Henry's death or resignation etc. of the canonry and prebend this union etc. shall be dissolved and the parish church shall revert to its original condition and be deemed vacant automatically.

Ad futuram rei memoriam. Decet romanum pontificem votis illis gratum prestare assensum . . .
Jo ortega / L. /. L. xxxv. Dulcius:-

[1] *At... pope*] originally: *Sane pro parte dilecti filii Henrici Hornby canonici ecclesie de Nassington' Lincolinen. diocesis magistri in theologia nobis nuper...*; then: *de Nassington', diocesis,* and *nuper* deleted (the rest left standing); in the margin opposite: *cassatu(m) de ma(nda)to R(everendissimi) p(atris) d(omini) Jo(hannis) archiepi(scopi) Ragusin' Regent(is).* The marginal note is not in the hand of the enregistering scribe; and neither it nor the deletions is initialled; but the note is in the same hand as the next marginal note (below, note 2) which is initialled *Jo.*

[2] *nuncupatis* in margin, initialled *Jo.*; insertion and initial, as well as *cass* (deleted) which occurs beneath *nuncupatis*, are all in the same hand. See note 1 above.

[3] 'ecclesia' wanting: a cross (signalling error?) in the margin at the end of the line

155   13 January 1500   *Reg. Lat.* 1046, fos 234[r]-237[r]

To William Culross, monk, recently abbot of the monastery of B. Mary, Ry'nlos [also spelt *Kynlos*][1], OCist, d. Moray, *motu proprio* reservation, constitution and assignment of a pension, as below. This day William has, spontaneously and freely, ceded the rule and administration of the above monastery, over which [he was presiding][2] at the time, into the pope's hands, and the pope, admitting the cession, made provision of abbot Thomas, as is more fully contained in his letters drawn up in that regard. Lest William should suffer excessive loss from this cession, the pope — *motu proprio* — hereby reserves, constitutes, grants and assigns to him an annual pension of 100 pounds of the money of those parts on the fruits etc. of the abbatial *mensa* of the monastery payable in full to William, for life (or to his specially appointed proctor) by Thomas and his succesors as abbots for the time being, each year, one half on the Nativity of Jesus Christ and the other on that of St John the Baptist, and also the vill of Haltowm',[3] lawfully pertaining to the monastery whose fruits etc. together with the said 100 pounds, do not, as the pope has learned, exceed a third part of the annual value of the monastery's fruits etc.) with all rights and appurtenances, to William, also for life, to hold, inhabit, possess and have the usufruct of (in person or by proxy, on his own authority) in place of an annual pension; decreeing that abbot Thomas and his successors be obliged to make payment in full of the said pension to William in accordance with the reservation, constitution and assignment aforesaid; and willing and establishing that if abbot Thomas, or any one of his successors, fails to make payment on the said feasts, or within the thirty days immediately following, he shall, after this time has elapsed, incur sentence of excommunication, from which he cannot be absolved, except on the point of death, until he shall have made satisfaction in full or reached agreement in respect of it with William (or his proctor) and, if he remains obdurate under that sentence for a further six months, he shall thereupon be deprived in perpetuity of the rule and administration of the monastery which shall be deemed vacant automatically. Notwithstanding etc.

Executory to the bishop of Sovana and the treasurer and William Wawan', canon, of the church of Aberdeen, or two or one of them, acting in person or by proxy.

Religionis zelus, vite ac morum honestas . . . The executory begins: *Hodie dilecto filio Willelmo Culross* . . .
A de sancto severino; G[4] de Castello / V /· V· xx· x· De Phano:

[1] spelt *Rinlos* in the executory

[2] *per eas*; *recte*: 'preeras' (as in the executory)

[3] spelt *Haltavm* in the executory

[4] *sic*; for 'S' (rather than 'N' or 'P')?

156   15 January 1500   *Reg. Lat.* 1046, fos 249[r]-250[v]

To the abbot of the monastery of B. Mary, Midleton (*de Choro Benedicti*) and [the prior][1] of the monastery, usually governed by a prior, of St Thomas the Martyr, near Buttevant (*iuxta Butttomam*), d. Cloyne, and the treasurer of the church of Cloyne, mandate in favour of John Ohynwayn', cleric, d. Cloyne. The pope has learned that the perpetual vicarage of the parish church of Tullales, d. Cloyne, is vacant at present and has been vacant for so long that by the Lateran statutes its collation has lawfully devolved on the apostolic see, although Thady Ohynwayn', who bears himself as a priest, has detained it, without any title or support of law, temerariously and *de facto*, for a certain time, as he still does. He hereby commands that the above three (or two or one of them), if, having summoned Thady and others concerned, they find the vicarage, whose annual value does not exceed 6 marks sterling, to be vacant (howsoever etc.), shall collate and assign it, even if specially reserved etc., with all rights and appurtenances, to John, inducting him etc. having removed Thady and any other unlawful detainer and causing John (or his proctor) to be admitted to the vicarage, and its fruits etc., rights and obventions to be delivered to him. [Curbing] gainsayers etc. Notwithstanding etc.

Vite ac morum honestas...
S. de Castello /· V· /· V· x. Quinto kalendas Februarii Anno Octavo [28 January 1500], *De Phano:*

1 'priori' wanting

157   16 April 1499   *Reg. Lat.* 1047, fos 58ʳ-61ʳ

To the priors of the monasteries, usually governed by priors, of B. Mary, *de Insula Viventium* [Monaincha], d. Killaloe, of B. Mary, Killis, d. Ossory, and of St Catherine, d. Waterford, mandate in favour of Hoellus Brenache, priest, d. Ossory (who asserts that he is of noble birth by both parents). A recent petition to the pope on the part of Hoellus stated that formerly when the perpetual vicarage of the parish church of Polruan, d. Ossory, was vacant *certo modo*, the present bishop of Ossory, or his vicar general, having a special faculty from him by his letters, by virtue of this faculty, by ordinary authority collated and made provision of the vicarage, vacant as above, to Hoellus, and he acquired it by virtue of the said collation and provision. Moreover since, as the said petition added, Hoellus fears that for certain reasons the collation and provision do not hold good; and, as the pope has learned, the vicarage is vacant still as above; and also the chancellorship of [the church of] Ossory and the perpetual vicarage of the parish church of Dunket¹ [also spelt *Dubiliret, Dubiket, Dunuket, Dubuket*] and the rectory (which is of lay patronage) of the parish church of Kiltochichan, d. Ossory, are vacant *certo modo* at present and the chancellorship, the vicarage of the church of Dunket and the rectory have been vacant for so long that by the Lateran statutes their collation has lawfully devolved on the apostolic see, although William Clinchon has detained the chancellorship and John Brant' the vicarage of Dunket and the rectory — bearing themselves as priests — with no title and no support of law, of their own temerity and *de facto*, for a certain time, as they do; and if the vicarages and rectory were to be united etc. to the chancellorship, for as long as Hoellus holds the latter, if conferred on him by virtue of the presents, it would be to the benefit of Hoellus, who asserts that the annual value of the chancellorship does not exceed 12, and of the vicarages and rectory together, 24, marks sterling. The pope, therefore, hereby commands that the above three (or two or one of them), if, having summoned William and John and others concerned and those interested in the union, they find the chancellorship (which is a non-major dignity *post pontificalem*) the rectory and the vicarage of Dunket to be vacant (howsoever etc.) and the foregoing to be true, and the vicarage of Polruan to be vacant, (even if it has been for so long that by the Lateran statutes its collation has lawfully devolved on the apostolic see, and the vicarages, chancellorship and rectory be specially reserved etc.), shall unite etc. the vicarages and rectory to the chancellorship, for as long as Hoellus holds the latter, if conferred on him by virtue of the presents; and also collate and assign the chancellorship to Hoellus, with annexes and all rights and appurtenances, inducting him etc. into corporal possession of the chancellorship and vicarages[2] and rights and appurtenances aforesaid, having removed William from the chancellorship, John from the vicarage of Dunket and the rectory and any other unlawful detainers, and causing Hoellus (or his proctor) to be admitted to the chancellorship, vicarage and rectory, and their fruits etc., rights and obventions to be delivered to him. [Curbing] gainsayers by the pope's authority etc. Notwithstanding etc. The pope's will is, however, that the vicarages and rectory shall not, on account of this union etc., be defrauded of due services and the cure of souls therein shall not be neglected, but that their customary burdens shall be supported; and that on Hoellus's death or resignation etc. of the chancellorship this union etc. shall be dissolved and so deemed and the vicarages and rectory shall revert to their original condition automatically.

Nobilitas generis, vite ac morum honestas . . .
· *Jo ortega.* /· *V·* /· *V· xxx. Non' Maii Anno Sep.*[mo] [7 May 1499], *De Phano*:

[1] the second and third letters uncertain: reworked

[2] the rectory is not mentioned here

158   13 April 1499   *Reg. Lat.* 1047, fos 71[r]-73[v]

To the abbot of the monastery of Mylanochv, d. Lismore, mandate in favour of Gerald Johannis de Geraldinis, cleric, d. Lismore (who, as he asserts, is in his fourteenth year of age or thereabouts and, notwithstanding a defect of birth as the son of an unmarried man and an unmarried woman of noble birth, has been duly marked with clerical character). The pope has learned that the [precentorship][1] of the church of Lismore is vacant *certo modo* at present and has been vacant for so long that by the Lateran statutes its collation has lawfully devolved on the apostolic[2] see, although Walter Mandyllyll', who bears himself as a priest of Lismore, has detained it, with no title and no support of law, of his own temerity and *de facto,* for a certain time, as he does. He hereby commands the above abbot, if, having summoned Walter and others concerned, he finds the precentorship, which is a non-major dignity *post pontificalem* and whose annual value does not exceed 32 marks sterling, to be vacant (howsoever etc.), to commend it, (even if specially reserved etc.), with all rights and appurtenances, to Gerald until he has reached his eighteenth year to hold, rule and govern; during which time he may — due and customary burdens of the precentorship having been supported — make disposition of the rest of its fruits etc. just as those holding it *in titulum* could and ought to do, alienation of immovable goods and precious movables being however forbidden; and then, if through diligent examination — concerning which the pope burdens the abbot's conscience — he finds Gerald to be suitable in other respects, to collate and assign the precentorship to him, with all rights and appurtenances, inducting him etc. having removed Walter and any other unlawful detainer and causing Gerald (or his proctor) to be admitted to the precentorship and its fruits etc., rights and obventions to be delivered to him. [Curbing] gainsayers by the pope's authority etc. Notwithstanding etc. Also the pope dispenses Gerald to receive the precentorship, if commended to and conferred on him by virtue of the presents, and retain it *in commendam* until he has reached his eighteenth year and then *in titulum*, notwithstanding the above defects of age and birth. With the proviso that the precentorship shall not, on this account, be defrauded of due services and the cure of souls therein (if any) shall not be neglected; but that the aforesaid burdens shall be supported, even during the commend. And the pope has commanded that — if Gerald be found suitable — provision of the precentorship after he has reached his eighteenth year shall be made as from this day.

Dignum et cetera. .
S. de castello /· V· /· V· xxxx Pridie Id' Maii Anno Sep.^{mo} [14 May 1499], *De Phano:*

1 here *preceptoria*; *recte*: 'precentoria'; the error recurs once; thereafter *precentoria* is deployed correctly

2 *sedem predictam*; 'sedes apostolica' occurs in the proem (here abridged)

159   16 April 1499   *Reg. Lat.* 1047, fos 73^v-77^r

To Donat Omurchu, William Hanlan and Edmund Omurchu, canons of the church of Cloyne, mandate in favour of John Philippi de Geraldinis, canon of the church of Lismore (who, as he asserts, is of noble birth by both parents). The pope has learned that the deanery of the church of Lismore is vacant *certo modo* at present and has been vacant for so long that by the Lateran statutes its collation has lawfully devolved on the apostolic see, although William Boteller *alias* Okynala, who bears himself as a cleric or priest of Lismore, has detained it, with no title and no support of law, temerariously and *de facto*, for a certain time, as he still does. At a recent petition on John's part to the pope to unite etc. a canonry of the church of Lismore and the prebend of Clasmor in the same (with the perpetual vicarage of the parish church of Kikonan, d. Lismore, annexed to them, which John holds), to the deanery, after provision of it is made to him and he peacefully acquires it, for as long as he holds it — asserting that the annual value of the canonry and prebend and the vicarage annexed to them does not exceed 12 marks sterling — the pope, not having certain knowledge of the foregoing, hereby commands that the above three (or two or one of them), if, having summoned William and others concerned, they find the deanery (which is a major dignity *post pontificalem*, has cure of souls, whose annual value and of annexes thereto does not exceed 40 like marks) to be vacant in any way or still by the death, outside the Roman curia, of the late Gillasius Ytreyth', or Gerald de Geraldinis or Thomas Russell' or James de Geraldinis successively deans of that church while they lived, or of anyone else, or by the resignation of Gillasius, Gerald, Thomas or James, etc., and, having summoned those interested in the union etc., the foregoing to be true, shall unite etc. the canonry and prebend with the annexed vicarage, to the deanery, for as long as John holds the latter; and also collate and assign the deanery, with the annexes aforesaid and with all rights and appurtenances, (even if it is specially or — because it is a major dignity as above — generally reserved to apostolic disposition, etc.), to John, inducting him etc. into corporal possession of the deanery, canonry and prebend, vicarage and other annexes and the rights and appurtenances aforesaid, having removed William[1] and any other unlawful detainer from the deanery and causing John (or his proctor) to be admitted to the deanery and its fruits etc., rights and obventions and those of the canonry and prebend, vicarage and other annexes aforesaid to be delivered to him. [Curbing] gainsayers by the pope's authority etc. Notwithstanding etc. Also the pope dispenses John not to be bound, by reason of the deanery, if conferred on him by virtue of the presents, and of any other benefices, with cure or otherwise requiring sacred, even priest's, orders by law, custom, foundation, statute or otherwise in any way, held by him at the time, to have himself promoted for a period of up to seven years, calculated from the end of the year prefixed by law, to any of the higher orders, provided that he shall be duly promoted to the subdiaconate within two years, nor to be liable to be compelled to do so by anyone against his will. Notwithstanding etc. With the proviso that the deanery and other benefices held at the time and the canonry and prebend and annexed vicarage shall not, on account of this union etc., be defrauded of due services and the cure of souls in the deanery, vicarage and other benefices aforesaid shall not be neglected; but that the customary burdens of the canonry and prebend shall be supported. The pope's will is, however, that on John's death or resignation etc. of the deanery this union etc. shall be dissolved and so deemed and the canonry and prebend shall revert to their original condition and be deemed vacant automatically.

Ex iniuncto nobis desuper apostolice servitutis officio ad ea libenter intendimus . . . .
S. de Castello. / *F*[2] / *F xxxx. Pridie Id' maii Anno Septimo* [14 May 1499], *Sanctor(is)*

[1] here: *prefato Guillermo*; previously: *Willelmus*
[2] written over *.V.*

160   2 March 1499   *Reg. Lat.* 1047, fos 92ʳ-94ᵛ

To Edmund Omurcha and William Hanlan', canons of the church of Cloyne, and John Philippi de Gerarldinis,[1] canon of the church of Lismore, mandate in favour of Philip Ymirechu, cleric, d. Cloyne (who, as he asserts, notwithstanding a defect of birth as the son of a cleric and an unmarried woman has been duly marked with clerical character). The pope has learned that the perpetual vicarage of the parish church of Belach, d. Cloyne, which Thady Omurchu, its late perpetual vicar, held while he lived, has become vacant by his death, outside the Roman curia, and is vacant at present. At a recent petition on Philip's part to the pope to erect and institute the said vicarage into a simple prebend of the church of Cloyne, the pope hereby commands that the above three, or two or one of them, in person or by proxy, shall erect and institute the vicarage, whose annual value does not exceed 3 marks sterling, (vacant as above or howsoever etc., even if it has been vacant for so long that by the Lateran statutes its collation has lawfully devolved on the apostolic see etc.), into a simple prebend of the church of Cloyne, for as long as Philip holds it, without prejudice to anyone and having summoned the bishop and chapter of Cloyne and others concerned; and collate and assign a canonry of the church of Cloyne and the newly erected prebend, being vacant, with plenitude of canon law and all rights and appurtenances, to Philip, inducting him etc. having removed any unlawful detainer and causing Philip (or his proctor) to be received as a canon of the church of Cloyne, with plenitude of canon law, and the fruits etc., rights and obventions of the canonry and prebend to be delivered to him. [Curbing] gainsayers by the pope's authority etc. Notwithstanding etc. Also the pope dispenses Philip to be promoted to all, even sacred, orders and the priesthood and to receive and retain for life the said canonry and prebend, if conferred on him by virtue of the presents, notwithstanding the said defect etc. With the proviso that the vicarage to be erected into a prebend shall not, on this account, be defrauded of due services and the cure of souls therein shall not be neglected; but that its customary burdens shall be supported. The pope's will is, however, that on Philip's death or resignation etc. of the canonry and prebend this erection and institution shall be extinguished and so deemed and the vicarage then erected into a prebend shall revert to its original condition and be deemed vacant automatically.

In suprema militantis ecclesie specula constitutus Romanus pontifex . . .
· S· de castello /. L. /. L. xxv. Duodecimo kl' Maii Anno Septimo [20 April 1499], *Dulcius:-*

[1] *sic*

161   12 April[1] 1499   *Reg. Lat.* 1047, fos 96ᵛ-98ʳ

To the prior of the monastery, usually governed by a prior, of B. Mary, *de Insula Viventium* [Monaincha], d. Killaloe, and William Odnyguyn and Dermot Omachar, canons of the church of Killaloe, mandate in favour of William Machclofol, priest, d. Killaloe. A recent petition to the pope on William's part stated that at one time when the perpetual vicarage of the parish church of Roch, d. Killaloe, was vacant *certo modo* the then bishop of Killaloe by ordinary authority collated and made provision of it, thus vacant — after its devolution to the apostolic see — to William, albeit *de facto,* and he took possession of it by pretext of the said collation and provision, receiving fruits from it. Moreover since, according to the foregoing, the aforesaid collation and provision and whatsoever ensued therefrom do not hold good; and, as the pope has learned, the vicarage is known to be still vacant as above, the pope, rehabilitating William on account of all disability and infamy arising from the foregoing, hereby commands that the above three, or two or one of them, in person or by proxy, shall collate and assign the said vicarage, whose annual value does not exceed 16 marks sterling, (vacant howsoever etc., even if it has been vacant for so long that by the Lateran statutes its collation has lawfully devolved on the apostolic see etc.), with all rights and appurtenances, to William, inducting him etc. having removed any unlawful detainer and causing William (or his proctor) to be admitted to the vicarage and its fruits etc., rights and obventions to be delivered to him. [Curbing] gainsayers by the pope's authority etc. Notwithstanding etc. The pope's will is, however, that before the above three shall proceed to the [execution][2] of the presents in any way William shall be bound to resign the vicarage genuinely and completely.

Apostolice sedis indefessa clementia recurrentibus ad illam cum humilitate . . .
· *P· de castello* /· *V·* /· *V xv. Quinto Kl' maii Anno Sep.*[mo] [27 April 1499], *De Phano:*

[1] *... pridie idus Aprilis...*; after *idus*, *(?)Aprllis* has been deleted, initialled . *V.*

[2] *assecutionem*; *recte*: 'executionem'?

162   4 April 1499   *Reg. Lat.* 1047, fos 98[r]-100[v]

To the priors of the monasteries, usually governed by priors, of B. Mary, *Insula Viventium*[1] [Monaincha] and *Fontisvivi*, Lopa, d. Killaloe, and the chancellor of the church of Killaloe, mandate in favour of John Ychernolii [also spelt *Ochenolii, Ochernolii, Ychernolica*], [(?)cleric, d. Killaloe][2] (who, as he asserts, is of noble birth by both parents). The pope has learned that the rectories of Chinallarga (situate in a lay fief), d. Killaloe, and of Linguiaila[3] [also spelt *Linguiana*], d. Meath, which are of lay patronage, and the perpetual vicarages of the parish churches of Thilcorim [also spelt *Chilcomiqonnis*] and of Locquyn, d. Killaloe, are vacant *certo modo* at present and have been vacant for so long that by the Lateran statutes their collation has lawfully devolved on the apostolic see, although John Okellayll[4] [also spelt *Okelbayl*] and Cornelius Okellayll, who bears himself as a cleric, have detained the first rectory, dividing its [(?)fruits] between themselves,[5] the prior and convent of the monastery, usually governed by a prior, of B. Mary, Connayl, OSA, d. Kildare, have detained the second rectory, and David Ohaynayn, the first vicarage, and Pilapus[6] Geddac *alias* Ocoggobayn, the second — bearing themselves as priests — without any title or support of law, temerariously and *de facto*, for a certain time, as they still do. At a recent [petition][7] on the part of the above John Ychernolii to the pope [to erect and institute a canonry in the church of Killaloe and the first rectory into a simple prebend in the same, for his lifetime, and after] provision of [the said canonry and prebend] be made [to him], unite etc. the other rectory and the vicarages [to the said canonry and prebend], also for his lifetime, the pope, not having certain knowledge of the foregoing, hereby commands that the above three (or two or one of them), if, having summoned respectively the bishop and chapter of Killaloe and John Okellayll, Cornelius, the prior and convent, David and Pilapus aforesaid and others concerned, they find the rectories of Chinallarga, whose annual value does not exceed 15, and Linguiaila, 60, and the vicarages of Thilcorim, 8, and Loquyn, 10, marks sterling, to be vacant (howsoever etc.), and, having summoned those interested in the union, the foregoing to be true, shall erect and institute a canonry in the church of Killaloe and the first rectory into a simple prebend in the same, for the lifetime of John Ychernolii, without prejudice to anyone; collate and assign the newly erected canonry and prebend, being vacant, with plenitude of canon law, to John Ychernolii; and unite etc. the second rectory and the vicarages (even if they and the first rectory be specially reserved etc.), to the erected canonry and prebend, with all rights and appurtenances, for the lifetime of John Ychernolii, inducting him etc. having removed John Okellayll and Cornelius from the first rectory, the prior and convent from the second rectory, David from the first vicarage and Pilapus from the second vicarage and any other unlawful detainers and causing John Ychernolii to be received as a canon of the church of Killaloe, with plenitude of canon law, and the fruits etc., rights and obventions of the canonry and prebend, last rectory and the vicarages aforesaid to be delivered to him. [Curbing] gainsayers by the pope's authority etc. Notwithstanding etc. With the proviso that the rectories and vicarages shall not, on account of this [erection][8] and institution and union etc., be defrauded of due services and the cure of souls therein shall not be neglected; but that their customary burdens shall be supported. The pope's will is, however, that on John Ychernolii's death or resignation etc. of the canonry and prebend the said erection and institution shall be extinguished and union etc. shall be dissolved and so deemed and the rectories and vicarages shall revert to their original condition and be deemed vacant automatically.

Piis fidelium votis per que divini cultus augumentum . . .
· *S· de. castello /· V· /· V· xxxv.. Pridie kl' Maii Anno Sep.^{mo}* [30 April 1499], *De Phano:*

[1] *de* does not occur

[2] see below, note 7

[3] uncertain reading

[4] in the first instance a bar through the final 'll' has been deleted; this and other instances are possibly readable as *Okelbayll*

[5] *... pro clerico illius inter se dividendo...*

[6] repeatedly thus; but also once *Priapus*

[7] There is an evident omission in MS which may be supplied conjecturally as follows: 'clericus Laonen. diocesis petitio continebat si in ecclesia Laonen. unus canonicatus et prima in simplicem prebendam in eadem ad vitam dicti Johannis Ychernolii erigerentur et instituerentur et (eisdem canonicatui et prebende postquam de illis dicto Johanni Ychernolii)'. The passage in parentheses is highly conjectural. The omission as conjectured — occasioned by the occurrence in proximate positions of *Johannis Ychernolii* and [Johanni Ychernolii] — approximates the length of a line of writing in an engrossment. In the present summary the words supplied are enclosed within brackets.

8 *institutionem et institutionem*; *recte*: 'erectionem et institutionem'

163   26 February 1499   *Reg. Lat.* 1048, fos 3^V-6^V

To Cristinus Ospellayn, Charles Omullcaryl and Thomas Macravayn, canons of the church of Tuam, mandate in favour of Thomas [de Burgo].[1] The pope has learned that the monastery of B. Mary, *de Portu Patrum* [Annaghdown], OSA, and the church, called a prebend, of Lechacolay, d. Annaghdown, and also the perpetual vicarage of the parish church of Serin [also spelt *(?)Scrm*][2] *alias* the custodianship of the relics of St Jarlath (*Sancti Ylartey*) just outside the walls of Tuam, and also the perpetual vicarages of the parish church of Chilenanna [also spelt *Chilevanna*, *Chilevan'a*], d. Annaghdown, and of the cathedral church of Annaghdown (*maioris Enachdunen. ecclesiarum*) are vacant *certo modo* at present and have been vacant for so long that by the canonical sanctions the provision of the monastery and by the Lateran statutes the collation of the vicarages have lawfully devolved on the apostolic see, although William de Burgo, who bears himself as abbot, has detained the monastery and the church, called a prebend, and Thomas de Burgo the vicarages of the church of Serin and of the cathedral church of Annaghdown (but receiving no fruits from them) and Aulanus Maicha the vicarage of the church of Chilenanna - bearing themselves as clerics or priests — without any title or support of law, temerariously and *de facto*, for a certain time, as they still do. At a recent petition on the part of the said Thomas to the pope to erect and institute a canonry in the church of Annaghdown and the church, called a prebend, into a simple prebend in the same, for his lifetime, and unite etc. the vicarages to the canonry and prebend, after their erection, also for his lifetime — asserting that the annual value of the monastery does not exceed 30, of the church, called a prebend, 1, of the vicarages of Serin, 5, of Chilenanna, 3, and of that of the church of Annaghdown (which has cure of souls), also 5, marks sterling — the pope, not having certain knowledge of the foregoing, hereby commands that the above three (or two or one of them), if, having summoned respectively William and Aulanus and the bishop and chapter of Annaghdown and others concerned, they find the monastery and the church, called a prebend, and the vicarages to be vacant (howsoever etc.) and the foregoing regarding the union to be true, shall commend the monastery to Thomas for life to be held, ruled and governed by him together with every benefice he holds and shall hold (he may — due and customary burdens of the monastery and its convent having been supported — make disposition of the rest of its fruits etc. just as abbots could and ought to do, alienation of immovable goods and precious movables being however forbidden) and commit to him the care, rule and administration of the monastery in spiritualities and temporalities; erect and institute a canonry in the church of Annaghdown and out of the said church, called a prebend, which is without cure, a simple prebend in the same, for Thomas's lifetime, without prejudice to anyone; and collate and assign the newly erected canonry and prebend, being vacant, to Thomas; and unite etc. the vicarages (even if they and the church, called a prebend, be specially reserved etc.) with plenitude of canon law and all rights and appurtenances, for Thomas's lifetime, [to the erected canonry and prebend], inducting him etc. having removed William from the monastery and Aulanus from the vicarage of Chilenanna and any other unlawful detainers and causing Thomas (or his proctor) to be received as a canon of the church of Annaghdown, with plenitude of canon law, and the fruits etc., rights and obventions of the canonry and prebend and of the vicarages to be annexed to them to be delivered to him; and [causing] due obedience and reverence to be given him by the convent and customary services and rights by the vassals and other subjects of the monastery. [Curbing] gainsayers by the pope's authority etc. Notwithstanding etc. With the proviso that the church, called a prebend, shall not, on account of the erection, and the vicarages, on account of the union etc., be defrauded of due services and the cure of souls in the vicarages shall not be neglected, and divine worship and the usual number of ministers in the monastery shall not, on account of the commend, be diminished, but that the monastery and convent's customary burdens and those of the church, called a prebend, and of the vicarages shall be supported; and that on Thomas's death or resignation etc. of the canonry and prebend the erection shall be extinguished, union etc. dissolved and the church, called a prebend, and the vicarages shall revert to their original condition and be deemed vacant automatically.

Romani pontificis providentia circumspecta ecclesiis et monasteriis singulis [...] prospicit diligenter . . .
· *S· de Castello* /· *V·* /· *V·· L·* [3] *De Phano:-*

[1] MS: *dicti Thome*, with reference to Thomas de Burgo mentioned in the text above as a detainer. It is decidedly unusual for a petitioner to be a detainer and so introduced. The petitioner's identity is, however, confirmed by the relevant annate (*Obligationes Pro Annatis Provinciae Tuamensis*, no. 320 in *Archivium Hibernicum*, XXVI,1963).

[2] in the first instance: *Dscrm*; for 'de Scrm'?

[3] wants expedition date?

164[1]   **29 January 1499**   *Reg. Lat.* 1048, fos 90[r]-93[r]

To William Oconceanind, Cristinus Ospelayn and Charles Omulcaryl, canons of the church of Tuam, mandate in favour of Donat Ycellard, canon of the church of Elphin (who, as he asserts, is of noble birth by both parents). The pope has learned that the perpetual vicarage of the church[2] of Kyllosailam and the rectory of it and of the parish church of Hathasecuth, d. Elphin, are vacant *certo modo* at present and have been vacant for so long that by the Lateran statutes their collation has lawfully devolved on the apostolic see, although Cornelius Ocellayd, who [bears himself] as a cleric, has detained the vicarage, and the prior and convent of the monastery, usually governed by a prior, of Bs. Peter and Paul the Apostles, OSB, near Hathluam, d.

Elphin, the rectories, without any title or support of law, temerariously and *de facto*, for a certain time, as they still do. At a recent petition on Donat's part to the pope to erect and institute the vicarage into a simple prebend in the said church of Elphin, for the canonry which he, Donat, holds in the same, for his lifetime, and unite etc. the rectories to them, after the prebend should be erected, also for his lifetime, the pope, not having certain knowledge of the foregoing, hereby commands that the above three (or two or one of them), if, having summoned respectively Cornelius and the prior and convent and, as regards the erection, the bishop and chapter of Elphin, and others rightfully concerned, they find the vicarage, whose annual value does not exceed 8, and the rectories, together 32, marks sterling, to be vacant (howsoever etc.) and, having summoned those interested in the union, the foregoing to be true, shall erect and institute out of the said vicarage a simple prebend in the church of Elphin, for Donat's lifetime, without prejudice to anyone, for the said canonry; collate and assign the newly erected prebend, being vacant, to Donat; and unite etc., with all rights and appurtenances, the rectories (even if they and the vicarage be specially reserved etc.) to the canonry and erected prebend, for Donat's lifetime, inducting him etc. having removed Cornelius from the vicarage and the prior and convent from the rectories and any other unlawful detainers and causing Donat to be admitted to the prebend, and its fruits etc., rights and obventions and those of the canonry and of the rectories to be annexed to be delivered to him. [Curbing] gainsayers by the pope's authority. Notwithstanding etc. With the proviso that the vicarage and rectories shall not, on account of this erection, institution and union etc., be defrauded of due services and the cure of souls therein shall not be neglected, but that their customary burdens shall be supported; and that on Donat's death or resignation of the canonry and prebend the erection and institution shall be extinguished, the union etc. shall be dissolved and so deemed, and the vicarage and rectories shall revert to their original condition and be deemed vacant automatically. Given at Ostia.

Apostolice sedis providentia circumspecta ad ea libenter intendit . . .
· *S· de· Castello· |· V· |· V. xxx.* [3] *De Phano:-*

[1] *Cp.* no. 73 above (an incomplete and probably abortive entry which, so far as it goes, matches this one).

[2] *sic*; (i. e. does *not* say 'parish church')

[3] wants expedition date?

165   30 January 1499   *Reg. Lat.* 1048, fos 94ᵛ-97ʳ

To John Oculay, John de Burgo and Rory[1] Amalle, canons of the church of Tuam, mandate in favour of Cormac Ymaylle,[2] cleric, d. Tuam (who, as he asserts, notwithstanding a defect of birth as the son of a priest, an expressly professed monk, OCist, and an unmarried woman, related in the double fourth degrees of consanguinity, has been marked with clerical character, otherwise however duly). The pope has learned that the church, called a prebend, of the place of Tilmadim, Wmallyacd and Vacdachr and the perpetual vicarage of the parish church of Vachamayll, d. Tuam, are vacant *certo modo* at present and have been vacant for so long that by the Lateran statutes their collation has lawfully devolved on the apostolic see, although John de Burgo, who bears himself as a cleric, has detained the church, called a prebend, without any title or support of law, temerariously and *de facto*, for a certain time, as he still does. At a recent petition on Cormac's part to the pope to unite etc. the said vicarage to the church, called a prebend — after provision of the latter is made to him and he acquires it — for his lifetime, the pope, not having certain knowledge of the foregoing, hereby commands that the above three (or two or one of them), if, having summoned John and others concerned, they find the church, called a prebend, which is without cure, annual value not exceeding 3, and the vicarage, also 3, marks sterling, to be vacant howsoever etc., and, having summoned those interested in the union etc., the foregoing to be true, shall collate and assign the church, called a prebend, to Cormac, and unite etc., with all rights and appurtenances, the vicarage to the church, called a prebend, even if they are specially reserved etc., for Cormac's lifetime, inducting Cormac (or his proctor) into corporal possession of the church, called a prebend, and the vicarage to be annexed thereto, and the rights and appurtenances aforesaid, having removed John from the church, called a prebend, and any other unlawful detainers from it and the said vicarage, and causing Cormac (or his proctor) to be admitted to the vicarage and its fruits etc., rights and obventions and those of the church, called a prebend, to be delivered to him. [Curbing] gainsayers by the pope's authority etc. Notwithstanding etc. Also the pope dispenses Cormac to be promoted to all, even sacred, orders and the priesthood and receive and retain the church, called a prebend, if conferred on him by virtue of the presents, notwithstanding the said defect of birth etc. With the proviso that the vicarage shall not, on account of this union etc., be defrauded of due services and the cure of souls therein shall not be neglected; but that its customary burdens shall be supported. The pope's will is, however, that on Cormac's death or resignation etc. of the church, called a prebend, this union etc. shall be dissolved and so deemed and the vicarage shall revert to its original condition and be deemed vacant automatically. Given at Ostia.

Iniunctum[3] *nobis desuper apostolice servitutis officium mentem nostram excitat et inducit* . . .
· *S· de Castello /· V· /· V xxv Pridie Kl' Martii Anno Sep.*[mo] [28 February 1499], *De Phano:*

[1] *Rurico* or possibly *Runco*

[2] the 'Y' strangely formed

[3] changed (by overwriting) from (?)*inductis*

166   30 January 1499   *Reg. Lat.* 1048, fos 100^r-103^r

To Magonius Omullalyd, Malachy Omanuyn and John Omullalyd, canons of the church of Clonfert, mandate in favour of Odo Ycellayd, canon of the church of Tuam (who, as he asserts, is of noble birth by both parents). The pope has learned that a perpetual chaplaincy, called a stipend, in the church of Tuam and the monastery of the Holy Trinity, just outside the walls of Tuam, OPrem, are vacant *certo modo* at present and have been vacant for so long that by the Lateran statutes the collation of the vicarage[1] and by canonical sanctions the provision of the monastery have lawfully devolved on the apostolic see, although William Premichiam, who bears himself as a priest and as the archdeacon of the church of Tuam, has detained the monastery and vicarage without any title or support of law, temerariously and *de facto*, for a certain time, as he still does. At a recent petition on Odo's part to the pope to erect and institute the vicarage into a simple prebend in the church[2] of Tuam for the canonry, which Odo holds in the same and which is without a prebend, for his lifetime, the pope, not having certain knowledge of the foregoing, hereby commands that the above three (or two or one of them), if, having summoned respectively William and the archbishop and chapter of Tuam regarding the erection and institution and others concerned, he finds the vicarage, which has cure of souls, and the monastery to be vacant (howsoever etc.), and the foregoing regarding the erection and institution to be thus, shall (even if provision of the monastery belongs specially or generally to the apostolic see and the vicarage is specially reserved etc.) erect and institute the vicarage into a simple prebend in the church of Tuam, for the said canonry, for Odo's lifetime and without prejudice to anyone, and collate and assign the vicarage thus newly erected [into a prebend], whose annual value does not exceed 5 marks sterling, being vacant, to Odo; and also commend the monastery, the annual value of which and of the annexed chapel of B. Mary, *Templi Collis* at Galway (*iuxta Galviam*), d. Annaghdown, does not exceed 12 marks sterling, with the annexed chapel and all rights and appurtenances, to Odo to be held, ruled and governed by him for life; (he may — due and customary burdens of the monastery having been supported — make disposition of the rest of its fruits etc., just as those holding the monastery *in titulum* could and ought to do, alienation of immovable goods and precious movables being however forbidden), committing the care, rule and administration of the monastery to him in spiritualities and temporalities; inducting Odo etc. having removed William from the vicarage and monastery and any other unlawful detainers and causing Odo (or his proctor) to be admitted to the prebend and its fruits etc., rights and obventions and those of the annexed chapel to be delivered to him and due obedience and reverence to be given him by the convent and customary services and rights by the vassals and other subjects of the monastery. [Curbing] gainsayers by the pope's authority etc. Notwithstanding etc. With the proviso that the vicarage shall not, on account of this erection and institution, be defrauded of due services and divine worship and the usual number of canons and ministers in the monastery be diminished and the cure of souls in the vicarage be neglected; but that the aforesaid burdens of the monastery and convent shall be supported. The pope's will is, however, that on Odo's death or resignation etc. of the canonry and prebend this erection and institution shall be extinguished and so deemed and the vicarage shall revert to its original condition and be deemed vacant automatically. Given at Ostia.

Admonet nos subscepti[3] *circa*[4] . . .
. *S de Castello /· V· / V xxxvi Tertio Non' Martii Anno Sep.*[mo] [5 March 1499], *De Phano:-*

[1] *sic*; (previously *perpetua cape(llani)a*)
[2] *ecclesiarum*; *recte*: 'ecclesia'
[3] *sic*
[4] *sic*; for 'cura'?

167[1]   **25 February 1499**[2]   *Reg. Lat.* 1048, fos 104[r]-107[r]

To the dean of the church of Tuam, commission and mandate in favour of Malachy Ymarryn, cleric, d. Tuam. Some time ago — following the renewal and approbation by Paul II of all papal sentences of excommunication, suspension, interdict and deprivation, and other ecclesiastical sentences, censures and pains against simoniacs (his will being that every simoniac, manifest or occult, should incur them automatically) and his reservation of their absolution to himself and his successors alone — representation having been made to Innocent VIII that if a canonry in the church of Clonfert and a simple prebend in the same (out of the tithes of Ycluelin, d. Clonfert, lawfully belonging to the capitular *mensa* of the said church) were to be erected and instituted, for Malachy's lifetime, it would be to the decorum and beauty of that church with the increase of divine worship, Innocent — at his supplication in this behalf — by other letters of his charged Cornelius Ochoncenayn, canon of Tuam, having summoned the bishop and chapter of Clonfert and others concerned, to erect and institute a canonry in the said church and a simple prebend in the same out of the aforesaid tithes, for Malachy's lifetime, and assign the newly erected canonry and prebend, being vacant, to Malachy, with plenitude of canon law, as is more fully contained in those letters. Next, as a recent petition to the pope on Malachy's part stated, since the said judge Cornelius died outside the Roman curia before the letters in question had been presented to him, Charles Omulkaryll', priest, d. Clonfert, asserting untruthfully that he was the subdelegate of Cornelius, erected and instituted by virtue of the said letters a canonry in the church of Clonfert and a simple prebend in the same out of the tithes, albeit *de facto*; collated and made provision of the newly erected canonry and prebend, being vacant, to Malachy, also *de facto*; and by pretext of the aforesaid collation and provision Malachy took possession of the canonry and prebend, receiving fruits from them, for a certain time, *de facto*; and, as the same petition added, several of Malachy's relatives (by affinity and consanguinity) caused Thomas Machranayn, of the parish church of Kyllosala,[3] d. Tuam, perpetual vicar of that church, to resign the perpetual vicarage, which he was then holding, into the hands of the local ordinary, outside the Roman curia, by force and fear and also by a certain amount of money given to and received by him; and the ordinary admitted his resignation outside the said curia by ordinary authority, and, a certain amount of money having then been received also from Malachy, united etc. the vicarage, thus vacant, to the canonry and prebend, for Malachy's lifetime, also *de facto*, incurring simony and the other sentences, censures and pains aforesaid. Moreover since, according to the foregoing, the aforesaid erection, institution, concession, assignment, union etc. and whatever ensued therefrom do not hold good; and, as the pope has learned, the vicarage is known to be still vacant as above; and, as the same petition added, if a canonry in the church of Clonfert and a simple prebend (out of the said tithes) in the same were to be erected and instituted anew, for Malachy's lifetime, it would be to the decorum and beauty of the church of Clonfert and the benefit of Malachy. At Malachy's supplication to the pope to absolve him from simony and from the sentences, censures and pains arising therefrom, dispense him on account of irregularity if he contracted it while bound by the censures by celebrating mass and other divine offices or otherwise taking part in them, rehabilitate him on account of all disability and infamy arising from the foregoing, and also erect and institute a canonry in the church of Clonfert and a [simple]⁴ prebend (out of the said tithes) in the same, for his lifetime, and unite etc. the vicarage to the erected canonry and prebend, also for his lifetime, the pope, not having certain knowledge regarding the union, hereby commits and commands [the above dean]⁵ to absolve Malachy, if he so requests, from simony and the aforesaid sentences, censures and pains, for this once only, in the customary form of the church, having enjoined a salutary penance on him etc., dispense him on account of irregularity if he contracted it by occasion of the foregoing and rehabilitate him on account of all disability and infamy contracted by occasion of the foregoing; and, in that event and if the above dean finds the foregoing regarding the union to be true, erect and institute, without prejudice to anyone, a canonry in the church of Clonfert and a simple prebend (out of the said tithes) in the same, for Malachy's lifetime, having summoned the bishop of Clonfert and the dean and chapter and others concerned; and collate and assign the newly erected canonry and prebend, whose annual value does not exceed 4 marks sterling, being vacant, to Malachy, with plenitude of canon law; and also, having summoned interested parties, unite etc. the vicarage, whose annual value does not exceed 5 marks sterling (whether vacant as above, or howsoever etc.;even if vacant for so long that by the Lateran statutes its collation has lawfully devolved on the apostolic see, etc.) to the canonry and prebend, for Malachy's lifetime, with all rights and appurtenances, inducting him etc., having removed any unlawful detainers and causing Malachy (or his proctor) to be received as a canon of Clonfert, with plenitude of canon law, and the fruits etc., rights and obventions of the [canonry and prebend]⁶ and annexed vicarage to be delivered to him. [Curbing] gainsayers by the pope's authority etc. Notwithstanding etc. With the proviso that the vicarage shall not, on account of this union etc., be defrauded of due services and the cure of souls shall not be neglected; but that its customary burdens shall be supported. The pope's will is, however, that on Malachy's death or resignation etc. of the canonry and prebend the union etc. shall be dissolved, the canonry and prebend be extinguished and so deemed and the vicarage and tithes revert to their original condition and the vicarage be deemed vacant automatically; [and that][7] before the above dean shall proceed to the execution of the presents in any way Malachy shall resign the canonry and prebend and vicarage into [his][8] hands genuinely and completely.

Solet sedis apostolice indefessa clementia recurrentibus ad eam cum humilitate . . .
S. de Castello / F / F. xxx. Sexto Kl' Aprilis Anno Septimo [27 March 1499], *Sanctor(is)*

[1] In this connection, *cf. CPL*, XV, no. 604, and XVI, no. 27, in favour of the same petitioner. But it would appear from the narrative here summarised e. g. the *de facto* nature of the actions of Charles Omulkaryll and the question of simony — that at least one other petition must have been made to Alexander on Malachy's part.

[2] (?)*quinto* (or *quarto*) *quinto* (or *quarto*) deleted and initialled *F.*, occurs directly after *nonagesimo* and before *octavo*

[3] the penultimate letter uncertain; possibly changed from a 'b'

[4] *silem'* (for *similem*); *recte*: 'simplicem'?

[5] *discretioni vestre; recte*: 'discretioni tue'? *Cf.* note 8.

[6] *canonicatibus et prebendis; recte*: 'canonicatus et prebende'?

[7] *volumus autem*, deleted and initialled *F*, occurs here

[8] *nostris* or *vestris; recte*: 'tuis'? *Cf.* note 5.

168   10 November 1498   *Reg. Lat.* 1048, fos 132^r-133^r

To Richard Gardener, rector of the parish church of Chedyngstone, d. Canterbury. Dispensation — at his supplication — to receive and retain for life, together with the above parish church, one, and without it, any two other benefices, etc. [as above, no. 3].

Vite ac morum honestas . . .
· A· de Sanctoseverin[o][1] */· V· / V· L· De Phano:*

[1] shaved

169   12 June 1499   *Reg. Lat.* 1049, fos 12^v-13^v

To Edward Lane, LLB, rector of the parish church of Werketon, d. Lincoln. Dispensation — at his supplication — to receive and retain for life, together with the above parish church, one, and without them, any two other benefices, etc. [as above, no. 3].

Litterarum scientia, vite ac morum honestas . . .

· *S· de Castello.* / *F* / *F. L. Sanctor(is)*

170   13 June 1499   *Reg. Lat.* 1049, fos 13^V-14^V

To Thomas Husse, perpetual vicar of the parish church of Okeley, d. Lincoln. Dispensation — at his supplication — [to receive and retain for life],[1] together with the perpetual vicarage of the above parish church, one, and without them, any two other benefices, etc. [as above, no. 3]. [2]

Vite ac morum honestas . . .
· *S· de castello* / *F* / *F. L. Sanctor(is)*

[1] following *instituaris*, MS wants: 'in eis recipere et insimul quoadvixeris retinere illaque simul vel successive simpliciter vel ex causa permutationis quotiens tibi placuerit dimittere et loco dimissi vel dimissorum aliud vel alia simile vel dissimile aut similia vel dissimilia beneficium seu beneficia ecclesiasticum vel ecclesiastica duo duntaxat invicem incompatibilia similiter' (or suchlike)

[2] save that the above passage (note 1) is wanting

171   12 June[1] 1499   *Reg. Lat.* 1049, fos 14^V-15^V

To Henry Helmesley, monk of the monastery of B. Mary, Revesbi [also spelt *Revesby*], OCist, d. Lincoln. Dispensation — at his supplication — to him, who, as he asserts, is expressly professed of the above order,[2] to receive and retain any benefice, with or without cure, usually held by secular clerics, etc. [as above, no. 32].

Religionis zelus, vite ac morum honestas . . .
· *S· de Castello* / *L.* /. *L. xxx Dulcius:-*

[1] *... pridie idus Junii...;* 'idus' being inserted in the margin initialled .L.
[2] This information comes from a notwithstanding clause.

172   25 August 1499   *Reg. Lat.* 1049, fos 38^V-39^V

To William Jakson', rector of the parish church of St George the Martyr, Cranchurst [also spelt *Crauchurst*], d. Chichester. Dispensation — at his supplication — to receive and retain for life, together with the above parish church, one, or without it, any two other benefices, etc. [as above, no. 3].

Vite ac morum honestas . . .
L puccius /· V· /· V· L· De Phano:-

173   7 September 1499   *Reg. Lat.* 1049, fos 46ʳ-47ʳ

To Thomas Donyngton', scholar, d. Lincoln. Dispensation — at his supplication —
to him, who, as he asserts, is of noble birth and in his fourteenth year of age and
wishes to become a cleric, to receive and retain — after he has been duly marked
with clerical character and has reached his sixteenth year — any benefice, with cure
or otherwise incompatible or priestly,[1] even if a parish church etc. [as below, no.
240, to '... in its place receive and retain another, similar or dissimilar, benefice'],
with cure or otherwise incompatible or priestly. Notwithstanding the above defect of
age etc. With the proviso that the benefice in question shall not, on this account, be
defrauded of due services and the cure of souls therein (if any) shall not be
neglected.

Nobilitas generis, vite ac morum honestas . . .
Jo. ortega /· V· /· V· xxviij· De Phano:

[1] *presbiterale beneficium* (namely a benefice requiring the order of the priesthood)

174   18 June 1499   *Reg. Lat.* 1049, fos 59ᵛ-67ᵛ

Confirmation as below. A long while ago, letters of the tenor written below issued
from pope Alexander VIIII;[1] and a recent petition to the pope on the part of prior
John Prons and the convent of the priory of Tanntonne,[2] OSA, d. Bath and Wells,
stated that John XXIII and Boniface VIIII, as they were called in their obedience, in
which those parts then lay, made grants, respectively, [concerning][3] the celebration
of masses and other divine offices, and the ecclesiastical sacraments to be
administered to the parishioners of the parish church of B. Mary Magdalene, d. Bath
and Wells, united to the priory, in the chapels there mentioned; and concerning the
priory's not having to show its several rights and titles when it was visited; and they
otherwise granted several indults and privileges to the prior and convent, as is more
fully contained in their authentic letters drawn up in this regard, the tenors of which,
without their marks (*singnis*) and characters, the pope has caused to be inserted
verbatim in the present letters. At the supplication of prior John and the convent,
who assert that the letters are beginning to be consumed with age, to approve the
letters of pope Alexander and to confirm the letters of John and Boniface, and to
grant anew everything contained in them, the pope hereby approves and decrees to
have the force of perpetual strength the letters of pope Alexander, and he confirms

and approves the letters of John and Boniface and fortifies them with the protective power of the present writ, with all the privileges, statutes, ordinances, and concessions contained therein, and whatever flowed from them, and he renews and grants anew the contents of each letter, insofar as they are in use. Notwithstanding etc. The tenors of the letters of pope Alexander and of John and Boniface are as follows:

[At the request of prior Stephen and the brethren of the monastery of St Peter and St Paul, Taunton, Alexander III takes the monastery under his protection and that of St Peter, in the manner of Eugenius III, strengthens it by the present privilege, and establishes that all its possessions and goods, notably those named, shall endure unimpaired. Given at Montpellier, 25 May, 1162][4]

Alexander *et cetera* dilectis [fo 61[r]] filiis Stephano priori monasterii Sanctorum Petri et Pauli de Tanntonne eiusque fratribus tam presentibus quam futuris regularem vitam professis in perpetuum.

Quoniam sine vero cultu religionis nec caritatis unitas potest subsistere nec deo gratum exhibere servitium expedit apostolice auctoritati religiosos viros diligere et eorum quieti auxiliante domino salubriter providere.

Ea propter dilecti in domino filii nostri iustis postulationibus clementer communimus[5] et ad exemplar patris et predecessoris nostri sancte recordationis Eugenii pape prefatum monasterium in quo divino mancipati estis obsequio Sancti Petri et nostra protectione suscipimus et presentis scripti privilegio communimus statuentes ut quascunque possessiones quecunque bona eadem ecclesia[6] in presentiarum iuste et canonice possidet aut in futurum concessione pontificum largitione regum vel principum oblatione fidelium seu aliis justis modis deo propitio poterit adipisci firma nobis[7] /[8] vestrisque successoribus et illibata permaneat in quibus ac[9] propriis duximus exprimenda vocabulis: ecclesiam Sancte Marie Magdalene in eadem villa sitam cum omnibus pertinentiis suis quas habetis in omnibus parrochialis Tanntonne capellam Sancti Petri de Castello ecclesiam Sancti Georgii de Fonte capellam Sancti Pauli extra Castellum capellam Sancti Jacobi iuxta portam canonicorum capellam Sancti Michaelis de Orchod capellam [fo 61[v]] de Riscon capellam de Trinla ecclesiam de Lexa[10] cum pertinentiis suis ecclesiam de Ylla cum pertinentiis suis ecclesiam Sancti Laurentii de Ligiard cum omnibus pertinentiis suis ecclesiam Sancte Marie de /[11] Ringeston cum capellis et omnibus pertinentiis suis ecclesiam Sancti Andree de Pipunistre[12] cum capellis et pertinentiis suis ex dono bone memorie VVilielmi condem[13] Vniconien. episcopi terram et de Blakedonda duas hiidas terre in assia[14] cum ecclesia eiusdem ville et pertinentiis suis a Roberto Arondello vobis pietatis intuitu collatas ex dono Wuilielmi filii Oddonis terram de Vildelanda cum pertinentiis suis ad ecclesiam eiusdem ville cum pertinentiis suis ex dono Wvillelmi de Tribus Menetis terram de Tarlacon terram de Ligiardi ecclesiam de Dulnerton[15] cum omnibus capellis et pertinentiis suis terram de Gulialanda[16] ex dono Rogerii Britonis terram de Uppeccota ex dono Balduini de Cumba terram de Mora unam virgatam terre et dimidiam in /[17] Stanton' ex dono Osberti et Galfredi de Ydona terram de Midaldona ex dono Balduini de Cumba sedecim acras et ortum in

Aistercumba ex dono Hugonis de Flori viginti acras terre in Aystrcumba[18] ex dono Wuillielmi de Arco terram de Maedona terram de Aquia ex dono [fo 62ʳ] Walteri de Pral terram de Sodesaltera libertates quoque et omnium consuetudinum et servitiorum imunitates per Angliam et Normaniam in partibus marinis in civitatibus castellis burgis et extra in forestis et in omnibus aliis locis tam in aqua quam in terra sicut ab illustri rege Anglorum Henrico primo et Willeelmo et Henrico episcopis Wintonien. et aliis fidelibus devotionis intuitu vobis concessas per longa tempora rationabiliter constat esse possessas cum *soco* et *sacha* et *tol* et *theam* et *infanguensoef.*

Decernimus ergo ut nulli omnino hominum liceat prefatam ecclesiam temere perturbare aut eius possessiones auferre vel abbates[19] retinere movere[20] seu quibuslibet vexacionibus fatigare sed illibata omnia et integra conserventur eorum pro quorum gubernatione ac sustentatione concessa sunt usibus omnimodis pro futura salva sedes[21] apostolice[22] auctoritate et diocesani episcopi canonica iustitia.

Si qua igitur in futurum ecclesiastica seculari sue[23] persona hanc nostre constitutionis paginem[24] sciens contra eam temere venire temptaverit secundo tertiove commonita nisi reatum suum congrua satisfactione[25] conspexerit potestatis honorisque sui dignitate careat reamque se divino iudicio existere de perpetrata iniquitate cognoscat et a sacratissimo corpore ac sanguine dei et domini redemptoris nostri Jesu Christi aliena fiat atque in extremo examine districte ulctioni subiaceat. Cunctis autem eidem loco sua [fo 62ᵛ] iura servantibus sit pax domini nostri Jesu Christi quatinus et hic fructum bone actionis percipiunt et apud districtum judicem premia eterne pacis inveniam.[26] Amen.

Dat' apud Montem Passulanum[27] per manum[28] /[29] Hermanni[30] Sancte Romane Ecclesie subdiaconi et notarii octavo kalendas Junii indictione decima[31] incarnationis dominice anno millesimo centesimo sexagesimo secundo pontificatus vero domini[32] Alexandri pape III anno tertio.

John XXIII's letters *Ad futuram rei memoriam. Digna exauditione vota ...*, given at Constance (*Constantie*), *quinto decimo kalendas Aprilis anno quinto* [18 March 1415],[33] are as calendared in *CPL* VI, p. 486, save that the present letter has the following spellings: Tannton'; Russheton'; Corffe; and Wilcon'.

Boniface IX's letters *Ad futuram rei memoriam. Hiis que pro statu...*, given at St Peters, Rome, *decimo septimo kalendas Februarii pontificatus nostri anno duodecimo* [16 January 1401], are as calendared in *CPL* V, p. 362 (but there dated "1400. 17 Kal. Jan. "), save that the present letter has the following spellings: Tannten' (also spelt *Tannton'*); Maydenhuth; Rystecheton'; Trendell'; Hull'; Ringeston'; Pytynynstre; Hysth; Ulverton'; Thruleber'; Nyuhede; Wythoell'; Lidierd'; Dulverton'; and Maqin.

Concurrent mandate to the bishops of Worcester and Exeter and the abbot of the monastery of Glastonbury (*Glasconie*), d. Bath and Wells, or two or one of them, acting in person or by proxy, commanding them to publish the above letters when required by the prior and convent, etc.

Ad perpetuam rei memoriam. In apostolice dignitatis culmine meritis quamquam inparibus divina disponente constituti... The concurrent mandate begins: *Hodie quasdam felicis recordationis Alexandri pape III...*

· *Jo ortega; . C. de. scorciat(is) /. L. / L. L^{ta}. x. Dulcius:-*

1 *sic; recte* 'III'; probably the scribe (Bernardino Damiani) wrote *VI* (because that was the number which then usually came after 'Alexander') then, realising his mistake, *III*; but the *VI* is not deleted. The executory has *III*.

2 no 'de' before it

3 MS: *cura; recte* 'circa'?

4 unknown to Migne, *Patrologia Latina*, vol. 200: *Alexander III, Pontifex Romanus* (1855); S. Loewenfeld, *Epistolae Pontificum Romanorum ineditae* (Lipsiae,1885); Jaffé-Wattenbach, *Regesta Pontificum Romanorum*, 2nd. ed., tom. II (Lipsiae 1888); W. Holtzmann, *Papsturkunden in England*, 1 (Berlin,1930).

5 *sic*; the final 'm' converted from a 'b'; *recte* 'annuimus'?

6 *eadem ecclesia*] *sic*; even though none has been mentioned

7 *sic; recte* 'vobis'

8 *(?)vestris* deleted and initialled *L*

9 *sic*; 'h(a)ec'?

10 Lexa

11 *(?)R..* deleted but not initialled

12 Pipunistre

13 *sic; recte* 'condam' for 'quondam'

14 *in assia*] evidently a place name; but here, exceptionally, the initial is not a capital. W. Dugdale, *Monasticon Anglicanum*, ed. J. Caley, H. Ellis, and B. Bandinel, vol. VI, part I (London,1830), p. 166-7, prints a charter of Edward III enumerating the priory's holdings which has here *'apud Dissam'*

15 the 'D' over a 'V'

16 the 'G' over a 'J'

17 *T* deleted but not initialled

18 Aystrcumba

19 *sic*; 'ablatas'?

20 *sic*; 'minuere'?

21 *sic; recte* 'sedis'

22 changed (by overwriting) from *apostolica*

23 seculari sue] *sic*; 'secularisve'?

24 *sic*; for 'paginam'

25 changed (by deletion of bar) from *satisfactione(m)*

26 *sic*; 'inveniant'?

27 *sic*; 'Pessulanum'?

28 inflexion repeatedly changed

29 *sancte* deleted and initialled *L*

30 brief biographical notice in A. Ciaconius, *Vitae et Res gestae Pontificum Romanorum et SRE cardinalium*, I (Rome, 1677), col. 1087, *cf.* col. 1103; *cf.* Migne, *op. cit.*, col. 67

31 initial letter re-written

32 MS: *d(omi)ni*; 'domni' ?

33 'pontificatus nostri' does not occur

175   22 February 1499   *Reg. Lat.* 1049, fos 70ʳ-71ʳ

To Robert[1] Lathos, BTheol,[2] rector of the parish church of the Holy Trinity, Gilfordi,[3] d. Winchester. Dispensation — at his supplication — to receive and retain for life, together with the above parish church, one, and without it, any two other benefices, etc. [as above, no. 3].

Litterarum scientia, vite ac morum honestas...
. L. Puccius /· V· /· V· L· De Phano:-

[1] in the line: *Johanni* deleted, initialled *O*; in the margin: *Roberto* inserted; *Cassatum et Correctum de Mandato d(omini) Jo(hannis) Archiepiscopi Ragusini Regentis O. Marianen.*; the script of the insertion differs both from that of the enregistering scribe (Damiani) and from that of the master's note

[2] *in decretis*, deleted and initialled. *V.*, occurs between *baccalario* and *[in] theologia*

[3] the first occurrence has been changed (by deletion) from *Gilfordin'*; not initialled

176   13 November 1498   *Reg. Lat.* 1049, fos 90ʳ-91ʳ

To William, bishop of Lincoln, licence and faculty. A recent petition to the pope on bishop William's part stated that at one time he, then bishop of Coventry and Lichfield, wishing to assist those undertaking the study of letters to pursue their studies, had, by ordinary authority, instituted in a certain house, called a hospital, dedicated to St John the Baptist, founded by him outside the (?)conduits[1] of the city of Lichfield in a beautiful and lavish building, a certain college for the habitation and convenience of several scholars, chaplains and other paupers, and adequately endowed it; and had, by the same authority, published several statutes and ordinances, honest and not deviating from the sacred canons, which had to be observed in it, as is said to be more fully contained in certain authentic letters of his drawn up in that regard. At his supplication to the pope to grant faculty to him to confirm and approve the aforesaid and several other statutes and ordinances of Lincoln college (or house or like hospital) of B. Mary, vill of Oxford (*Oxonie*), and the college (etc.) of St John, vill of Northampton', d. Lincoln, of which he is the patron; curtail and transform the useless and less convenient; clarify and reform the obscure; and, for the utility and sound rule of the colleges, houses or hospitals in question and those things concerning them further, publish anew any other statutes and ordinances, the pope hereby grants licence and faculty to him to approve and confirm, by apostolic authority, the statutes and ordinances published by him and all the other statutes and ordinances of the individual colleges, houses or hospitals in question which ought to be confirmed by him; curtail, clarify, reform and transform the useless, obscure and less convenient, as it seems to him; and, for the utility and sound rule of the individual colleges, houses or hospitals in question and those things concerning them further, publish and ordain anew any other statutes and ordinances — provided that the statutes and ordinances to be confirmed as well as those to be published are honest and do not deviate from the sacred canons. Notwithstanding etc.

Tue devotionis precibus benig(n)um impartientes assensum . . .
· *Jo· ortega· /. L. /. L. Lxx. Dulcius:-*

[1] *barchas*; for 'barras'?

177   31 August 1499[1]   *Reg. Lat.* 1049, fos 135[v]-136[v]

To Robert Michell', perpetual vicar of the parish church of Bovy Tracy, d. Exeter. Dispensation — at his supplication — to receive and retain for life, together with the perpetual vicarage of the above parish church, one, and without it, any two other benefices, etc. [as above, no. 3].

Vite ac morum honestas . . .
· *L· puccius /· V· /· V·· L· De Phano:*

[1] following *nonagesimonono, Anno* deleted, initialled *V.* with *pridie Kl. Septemb. Anno octavo .V.* in the line, but in a darker ink: entered later?

178   22 August 1499   *Reg. Lat.* 1049, fo 152[r-v]

To John Kyte, BDec, rector of the parish church of Wolverton' [also spelt *Wolverton*], d. Norwich. Dispensation — at his supplication — to receive and retain for life, together with the above parish church, one, and without it, any two other benefices, etc. [as above, no. 3].

Litterarum scientia, vite ac morum honestas . . .
. *L· puccius /· V· /· V· L· De Phano:-*

179   15 May 1499   *Reg. Lat.* 1049, fos 170[r]-171[r]

Confirmation as below. A recent petition to the pope on the part of Edward, bishop of Chichester, and the dean and chapter and Nicholas Taverner, canon, of the church of Chichester, stated that at another time bishop Edward — carefully considering how harmful and dangerous ignorance of letters (especially grammar) is, particularly in churchmen, and how very useful and necessary a knowledge of it is, and desiring that the grammar-school in the city of Chichester be ruled, in perpetuity, by a suitable and learned man adept and able for teaching and instructing scholars wishing to study grammar — willed, established, and ordained, with the express consent of the dean and chapter and Nicholas, that when the canonry and prebend of Hilegh', said church, which Nicholas was (and is at present) holding was vacated through his retirement, death or other resignation, the dean of the said church for the time being (or whoever was presiding in his place) and chapter were bound, within thirty days calculated from the time of the vacancy, to nominate or present[1] to the bishop for the time being a suitable priest, learned and expert in grammar and [adept][2], able, and suitable for teaching scholars wishing to study grammar, and the bishop was bound to collate the canonry and prebend to the person so nominated or presented with the charge of reading and teaching in the city's grammar-school; and if, for any lawful impediment or other reasonable cause, the person so nominated or presented was not admitted by the bishop, the dean or president and chapter were thereupon bound[3], within the next thirty days, to present or nominate to the bishop another able and suitable person, and the bishop was bound to institute the person so nominated or presented with the above charge or to provide him with the canonry and prebend; and bishop Edward established and ordained many other reasonable and honest things with like consent, as is said to be more fully contained in his authentic letters drawn up in this regard and fortified with the [seals][4] of bishop Edward and of the chapter and the archdeacon of the said church. At this petition to add the force of apostolic confirmation to the above will, statute, and ordinance as a firmer base for them, the pope hereby approves and confirms the above will etc. and everything concerning them contained in the said letters, and supplies any defects. Notwithstanding, etc.

Ad perpetuam rei memoriam. Iniunctum nobis desuper apostolice servitutis officium. . .
P. de planca /. L. / L. xL. Dulcius:-

[1] MS *presentari*; *recte* 'presentare'
[2] MS *apud*; *recte* 'aptum'
[3] MS *debere*; *recte* 'deberent'
[4] MS *singulis*; *recte* 'sigillis'

180   16 June 1499   *Reg. Lat.* 1049, fos 179ᵛ-180ᵛ

To Edward Chambrelayn, cleric, d. Norwich. Dispensation — at his supplication — to him, who, as he asserts, is in his fifteenth year of age, to receive and retain any benefice, with cure or otherwise incompatible, etc. [as below, no. 240].[1]

Vite ac morum honestas. . .
. L. puccius /. L. /. L. xxx. Dulcius:-

[1] save that in this instance 'chantry' is not included in the list

181   15 June 1499   *Reg. Lat.* 1049, fos 191^v-193^r

To the bishops of Dunkeld and Sovana and the official of Dunkeld, mandate in favour of John, bishop of Sodor. The pope has learned that the monastery of St Columba, Hye island (*insule Hye*), OSB, d. Sodor, over which John, its late abbot, presided while he lived, is bereft of an abbot's rule by his death outside the Roman curia. Wishing to make provision of a capable and suitable person to the monastery to rule and direct it as well as to assist bishop John (who, as he asserts, cannot conveniently support himself in accordance with episcopal dignity and bear the burdens incumbent on him out of the fruits etc. of the episcopal *mensa* of Sodor the greater part of which, together with the church of Sodor over which he is understood to preside, is occupied by the English and the other part by some nobles of those parts) — the pope hereby commands that the above three, or two or one of them, in person or by proxy, shall commend the monastery, whose annual value does not exceed 20 pounds sterling, (whether vacant as above or howsoever etc.; even if its provision pertains specially or generally to the apostolic see, etc.), with all its rights and appurtenances, to bishop John to be held, ruled and governed by him for life, together with the church of Sodor and every other church, monastery, priory, provostship, dignity, *personatus*, administration, office and other ecclesiastical benefice, with and without cure, secular and regular, which he holds now or in the future; (he may — due and customary burdens of the monastery and its convent having been supported — make disposition of the rest of its fruits etc. just as abbots could and ought to do, alienation of immovable goods and precious movables being however forbidden); committing to him the care, rule and administration of the monastery in spiritualities and temporalities, and causing due obedience and reverence to be given him by the convent and customary services and rights by the vassals and other subjects of the monastery. [Curbing] gainsayers etc. Notwithstanding etc. The pope's will is, however, that divine worship and the usual number of monks and ministers in the monastery shall not, on account of this commend, be diminished, but that its aforesaid burdens and those of the convent shall be supported; and that before bishop John shall receive possession, or almost, of the rule and administration and goods of the monastery or any part of them he shall take the oath[1] of fealty in accordance with the form which the pope sends enclosed under his *bulla* before the above three (or any one of them) and that bishop John shall send the form of oath which he takes, verbatim, to the pope, at once, by his letters patent, sealed with his seal, by his own messenger.

Romani pontificis providentia circumspecta. . .
A. de Sancto Severino / F / F. Lxxxx. Sanctor(is)

[1] 'solitum' does not occur

182   27 June 1499   *Reg. Lat.* 1049, fos 223^v-224^v

Union etc. At a recent petition on the part of Richard Bryndholme, DDec, canon of the church of Ripon', d. York, the pope hereby unites etc. the parish church of Parva Wylburgh(a)m,[1] d. Ely, (whose annual value does not exceed 20 marks sterling, equivalent to 56 gold ducats of the camera or thereabouts), to the canonry and prebend of Stodely of the said church of Ripon', which he holds together with the above parish church, to the effect that Richard, in person or by proxy, may, on his own authority, take corporal possession of the parish church and its rights and appurtenances or continue in it as before and convert its fruits etc. to his own uses and those of the canonry and prebend and parish church and retain [the parish church] for as long as he holds the canonry and prebend without licence of the local diocesan or of anyone else. Notwithstanding etc. The pope's will is, however, that the parish church shall not, on account of this union etc., be defrauded of due services and the cure of souls therein shall not be neglected, but that its customary burdens shall be supported; and that on Richard's death or resignation etc. of the canonry and prebend the union etc. shall be dissolved and so deemed and the parish church shall revert to its original condition and be deemed vacant automatically.

Ad futuram rei memoriam. Decet Romanum pontificem votis illis gratum prestare assensum. . .
S. de Castello / F / F xxxv Sanctor(is)

[1] MS: *Wylburghm'*

183   27 June 1499   *Reg. Lat.* 1049, fos 225ʳ-226ʳ

To Thomas Boll, rector of the parish church of Papwortheverard, d. Ely. Dispensation — at his supplication — to receive and retain for life, together with the above parish church, one, and without it, any two other benefices, etc. [as above, no. 3].

Vite ac morum honestas. . .
F. de parma / F / F L Sanctor(is)

184   6 July 1499   *Reg. Lat.* 1049, fos 226ʳ-227ʳ

To James Boneface, rector of the parish church (or chantry) of Ruggwyke [also spelt *Ruggwike*], d. Chichester. Dispensation and indult — at his supplication — to receive and retain for life, together with the above parish church, one, and without it, any two other benefices, etc. [as above, no. 3, to '... retain them together for life, as above']; and, also for life, while residing in one of his benefices or in the Roman curia or attending a *studium generale*, not to be bound to reside in his other benefices, nor to [be liable[1]] to be compelled by anyone to do so against his will. Notwithstanding etc. and the foundation of the said church (called a chantry) etc. With the proviso that the above church and other incompatible benefices and benefices in which he shall not reside shall not, on this account, be defrauded of due services and the cure of souls in the above church and (if any) the other incompatible benefices and benefices in which he shall not reside shall not be neglected; but that customary burdens in the latter shall be supported.

Vite ac morum honestas. . .
· *L· puccius* / *F* / *F Lx. Sanctor(is)*

[1] 'possis' (or suchlike) does not occur

185   24 April 1499   *Reg. Lat.* 1049, fos 237ᵛ-238ᵛ

To Thomas Clarell', rector of the parish church of St John the Baptist, Bukton', d. Lincoln. Dispensation — at his supplication — to receive and retain for life, together with the above parish church, one, and without them, any two other benefices, etc. [as above, no. 3].[1]

Vite ac morum honestas. . .
. *P. de planca* /. *L.* /. *L. Lᵗᵃ. Dulcius:-*

[1] save that in the present instance MS wants 'cantarie libere capelle hospitalia seu annualia servitia clericis secularibus in titulum perpetui benefici ecclesiastici assignari solita aut' (or suchlike)

186   28 June 1499   *Reg. Lat.* 1050, fo 32ʳ⁻ᵛ

To John Cotell, brother of the house of the Bonshommes, Edyndon, OSA, d. Salisbury. Dispensation — at his supplication — to him, who, as he asserts, is expressly professed of the above order,[1] to receive and retain any benefice, with or without cure, usually held by secular clerics, even if a parish church or its perpetual vicarage, or a chantry, free chapel, hospital or annual service, usually assigned to secular clerics in title of a perpetual ecclesiastical benefice, if he obtains it otherwise canonically, to resign it etc. [as above, no. 32].

Religionis zelus, vite ac morum honestas. . .
S. de Castello. /. *L.* /. *L. xxx. Dulcius:-*

[1] This information comes from a notwithstanding clause.

187   1 July 1499   *Reg. Lat.* 1050, fos 69^v-70^r

To Donald Maknathtan, perpetual vicar of the parish church of Forte(r)gil,[1] d. Dunkeld. Dispensation — at his supplication — to receive and retain for life, together with the perpetual vicarage of the above parish church, one, and without it, any two other benefices, etc. [as above, no. 5].

Vite ac morum honestas. . .
A de Sancto Severino / F / F xxxx. Sanctor(is)

[1] MS: *Forte'gil* in the first instance

188   20 August 1499   *Reg. Lat.* 1050, fos 76^v-78^r

To the bishop of Dunkeld, mandate in favour of Donald Maknathan, perpetual vicar, called portionary, of the parish church of Fortergill, d. Dunkeld. A recent petition to the pope on Donald's part stated that the said church is, as is asserted, united etc. in perpetuity to the capitular *mensa* of the church of Dunkeld and the chapter receives annually <a total>[1] of more than 100 marks[2] Scots from the fruits etc. of the said parish church; and that the cure of souls of the perpetual vicarage, called a portion, of the parish church, which he, Donald, holds, is too great, heavy and onerous, particularly because the boundaries or limits of the parish of the parish church extend more than twenty miles and within the said boundaries the two churches, in which — by the same vicar — the cure of souls of parishioners of the parish church is exercised, ecclesiastical sacraments are administered to them and the bodies of their dead are buried, are more than eight miles distant <from each other>[3]; and that he, Donald, [is] alone, without a cleric, priest or chaplain to help him, and cannot exercise the cure of souls of the parishioners, serve in things divine as is fitting, and, on account of the slenderness of the fruits etc. of the vicarage, keep and support a priest or chaplain. At his supplication to the pope to erect and institute the vicarage, called a portion, into the perpetual undivided vicarage of the said parish church and to join and appropriate to it, thus erected, as its endowment, adequate fruits etc. from those of the parish church from which the holder of the undivided vicarage may keep and support a priest or chaplain, the pope hereby commands the above bishop, if and after — having summoned the chapter and others concerned — the foregoing is lawfully established before him, to erect and institute the vicarage, called a portion, into the undivided vicarage of the parish church; and to it, thus then erected, join and appropriate, as its endowment, adequate fruits etc. from those of the parish church from which the holder of the undivided vicarage may keep and support a priest or chaplain; and in the event of this erection, institution, joining and appropriation, if he finds Donald to be suitable — concerning which the pope burdens the bishop's conscience — collate and assign the newly erected undivided vicarage, being vacant, whose annual value does not exceed 7 pounds sterling, with all rights and appurtenances, to Donald, inducting him etc. having removed any unlawful detainer and causing Donald (or his proctor) to be admitted to the undivided vicarage and its fruits etc., rights and obventions to be delivered to him. [Curbing] gainsayers by ecclesiastical censure etc. Notwithstanding etc. And the pope has commanded that — if Donald be found suitable — provision of the undivided vicarage, if and when vacant, be made to him from the date of the presents.

Ex iniuncto nobis desuper. . .
A de Sancto Severino /· V· /· V· xxx De Phano:-

[1] marginal insertion by enregistering scribe, not initialled

[2] *libras* (written before *marchas*) deleted, not initialled

[3] *ab invicem* inserted in the margin by enregistering scribe, initialled . *V.*

189   26 February 1499   *Reg. Lat.* 1050, fos 189[r]-190[v]

To William Remiyan, rector of the parish church of St Peter, Hermyngh(a)m[1] Sybill', d. London. Dispensation and indult — at his supplication — to receive and retain for life, together with the above parish church, one, and without it, any two other benefices, etc. [as above, no. 3, to '... retain them together for life, as above']; and, also for life, while residing in the Roman curia or in the above church or any one of his benefices or attending a *studium generale*, not to be bound to reside in his other benefices, etc. [as above, no. 21].

Vite ac morum honestas. . .
A de Sancto Severino /· V· /· V·· Lx De Phano:

[1] MS: *Hermynghm'*

190   29 April 1499   *Reg. Lat.* 1051, fos 159[r]-160[v]

To William Douue,[1] archdeacon of the church of Aberdeen. Following the pope's reservation some time ago of all dignities and other benefices, with and without cure, vacated then and in the future at the apostolic see to his own collation and disposition, the archdeaconry of the church of Aberdeen, which Adam Elphinston', its late archdeacon, held while he lived, became vacant by his death at the said see, and is vacant at present, being reserved as above. The pope hereby collates and makes provision of the archdeaconry, which is a non-major dignity *post pontificalem* and whose annual value does not exceed 30 pounds sterling, (vacant as above or howsoever, etc.; even if it has been vacant for so long that by the Lateran statutes its collation has lawfully devolved on the apostolic see etc.), with all rights and appurtenances, to William. Notwithstanding etc.

Executory to the bishop of Moray, Thomas Regis, canon of the church of Saint-Malo, and the official of Aberdeen, or two or one of them, acting in person or by proxy.

Vite ac morum honestas. . . The executory begins: *Hodie dilecto filio Guillermo.* . .
S· de castello; · *P· de planca /. L.* . */. L. xv. x. Nonis Januarii Anno Octavo* [5 January 1500], *Dulcius:*

[1] *Dowe* in the executory

191   27 June 1499   *Reg. Lat.* 1053, fos 10ʳ-11ʳ

To John Veysye *alias* Harmon, LLD, rector of the parish church of St Mary the Virgin on the Hill, Chester (*Cestrie*), d. Coventry and Lichfield, dispensation. Some time ago, the pope dispensed him to receive and retain for life, together with the parish church of Cliston Reynys, d. Lincoln, (which[1] he was then holding), one, and without it, (any)[2] two other benefices, etc. [as above, no. 131, to '... retain them together for life'].[3] The pope — at his supplication — hereby further dispenses John, who, as he asserts, having resigned the church of Cliston, holds by the said dispensation the parish churches of St Mary the Virgin on the Hill, Chester, and St Peter, Egmon', d. Coventry and Lichfield, which at another time were canonically collated to him while vacant *certo modo*, to receive and retain for life, together with the above parish churches, or any two other incompatible benefices held together by him at the time by the said dispensation, any third benefice, etc. [as above, no. 131].

Litterarum scientia, vite ac morum honestas. . .
P. de Castello /. L. [4] */. L. Lxx. Dulcius:-*

[1] 'qui ut asserebas' (or suchlike) does not occur
[2] marginal insertion, initialled *L*
[3] below, no. 569
[4] a swung dash to the left

192   23 June 1499   *Reg. Lat.* 1053, fos 74ʳ-75ᵛ

To the dean, treasurer, and Maurice Okaraen', canon, of the church of Ferns, mandate in favour of Donald Hodii, perpetual vicar of the parish church of Rahassbuyg, d. Ferns. A recent petition to the pope on Donald's part stated that, formerly, when he was holding and in possession of the perpetual vicarage of the above parish church, (which he had acquired after it had been canonically collated to him when vacant *certo modo* and which he had held and possessed for some time), and when he had done nothing to justify his deprivation or removal, Patrick Pymd(..)gas,[1] who bore himself as a cleric or priest of Ferns, falsely related to Richard Becet,[2] archdeacon of the church of Ferns, (whom he said was a competent judge), that Donald ought to be deprived of the vicarage and removed from it on account of several excesses then expressed; that at this false report, the archdeacon, proceeding wrongly, *de facto*, and lawlessly, by his sentence, (as he called it), declared, at Patrick's instance, that Donald ought to be deprived of the vicarage and removed from it, and he deprived and removed him; that the bishop of Ferns — falsely claiming that the vicarage was <thereby>[3] vacant — then collated it, *de facto*, to Patrick, whence Donald appealed to the apostolic see; that although Donald, standing by his appeal, had recourse to Walter, archbishop of Dublin, for the protection of his right, person, and goods, and impetrated tuitorial letters from him, the bishop of Ferns — rashly disdaining his appeal, recourse, and letters (of which he was not ignorant) — bound Donald, as is said, by sentence of excommunication and certain other censures and pains then expressed and suspended him from divine service, albeit *de facto*; that Donald — not <having been informed>[4] of the <sentence>[5] of excommunication and other sentences, censures, pains, and suspension — celebrated, and Patrick, and several other clerics and laymen of the dioceses of Ferns and Dublin, unjustly deprived him of the vicarage, and inflicted certain other grave damage and injury on him, on account of which, he has, he asserts, suffered expenses and incurred serious loss. At the supplication to the pope of Donald, (who asserts that, detained by a lawful impediment, he did not prosecute his appeal within the proper time), to command that he be absolved conditionally from the excommunication, etc. by which he is deemed bound, and that he be reinstated in the vicarage, and to commit to some upright men in those parts the cases of his appeal; of everything attempted and innovated after and against it; of the nullity of the sentence, collation, excommunication, suspension, and other censures, of the bishop's and archdeacon's processes, and of everything else prejudicial to Donald done by them, Patrick, and any other judges and persons, in connection with the foregoing; and of the principal matter; also the cases which Donald intends to move against the archdeacon, Patrick, and the said clerics and laymen, jointly and severally, over the above and certain damage inflicted <on him>,[6] expenses, and other matters, the pope hereby commands that the above three (or two or one of them), having summoned Patrick and others concerned, shall, if and as it is just, for this once only, conditionally absolve Donald, if he so requests, having first received suitable security from him that if they find that the sentences of excommunication etc. were justly inflicted on him, he will obey their commands and those of the church; and, as regards the rest, if what is related about the impediment is true, having heard both sides, taking cognizance even of the principal matter, that they shall decree what is just, without appeal, causing by ecclesiastical censure what they have decreed to be strictly observed. Notwithstanding the lapse of time, etc.

Humilibus et cetera.
Puccius[7] /. *L.* [8] /. *L. xiiij. Dulcius:-*

1 'ra' obliterated by ink blot, possibly deliberately

2 or *Bocet*

3 marginal insertion by the enregistering scribe; not initialled

4 marginal insertion by the enregistering scribe; not initialled

5 marginal insertion by the enregistering scribe; not initialled

6 *et* deleted in the line; *ei* inserted above it by the enregistering scribe; not initialled

7 *sic:* no initial ('L')

8 a swung dash beneath the point to the left

193   7 April 1499   *Reg. Lat.* 1053, fos 75ᵛ-76ᵛ

To Richard Parson *alias* Wyllys, perpetual chaplain, called cantor, at the altar of the Annunciation of B. Mary the Virgin in the church of Salisbury. Dispensation and indult — at his supplication — to him (who holds one of the two perpetual chaplaincies, called chantries, at the above altar in the foundation of which it is said to be expressly laid down that the holder of either chaplaincy cannot hold it with another benefice and is bound to celebrate mass, matins, vespers and other canonical hours and several offices of the dead at certain hours then expressed) to receive and retain for life, together with the above chaplaincy, one, and without it, any two other benefices, etc. [as above, no. 3, to '... retain them together for life, as above']; and, also for life, not to be bound, while residing in either of the said benefices, to reside in his other benefices, etc. [as below, no. 238].

Vite ac morum honestas. . .
Jo ortega /. L. ¹ */. L. Lx. Dulcius:-*

1 a swung dash to the left

194   18 October 1498   *Reg. Lat.* 1053, fo 77ʳ⁻ᵛ

To William Dubler, MA, rector of the parish church of Kyrkby de Bayne [also spelt *Kirkby de Bayne*], d. Lincoln. Dispensation — at his supplication — to receive and retain for life, together with the above parish church, one, and without it, any two other benefices, etc. [as above, no. 3].

Litterarum scientia, vite ac morum honestas. . .
· L· Puccius /. L. / L. Lᵗᵃ. Dulcius:-

195   15 December 1498   *Reg. Lat.* 1053, fo 78[r-v]

To Richard Stevyns,[1] perpetual chaplain, called cantor, in the church of
Rooperchiante [also spelt *Rooperchiantre*],[2] d. Canterbury. Dispensation — at his
supplication — to him, who, as he asserts, holds a perpetual chaplaincy, called a
chantry, in the above church, which according to its foundation or custom cannot be
held with another benefice with cure or otherwise incompatible without apostolic
dispensation, to receive and retain for life, together with the above chaplaincy, one
and without it, any two other benefices, etc. [as above, no. 3].

Vite ac morum honestas. . .
. Jo. ortega /. L. /. L. L^{ta}. Dulcius:-

---

[1] or *Stenyns*
[2] *in ecclesia Rooperchiante* and, below, *in ecclesia Rooperchiantre*: the name of the chantry is evidently
confused with that of the church. A (perhaps the) Roper chantry (founded by John Roper) was in the
parish church of St Dunstan, without Westgate, Canterbury (*cf. The Register of Henry Chichele
Archbishop of Canterbury 1414-1443*, ed. E. F. Jacob, vol. I [Oxford,1943], pp. 200, 219, 260, 279, 294,
307, 311; *Valor Ecclesiasticus*, vol. VI [1834], p. 27).

196   30 April 1499   *Reg. Lat.* 1053, fos 108[v]-110[v]

To Fiocardus, abbot of the monastery of St Peter, Marcilhac (*de Marcilhaco*), OSB,
d. Cahors, dispensation. Some time ago, when the above monastery, which pertains
immediately to the Roman church, was vacant *certo modo*, the pope commanded
that it be commended etc.[1] to Fiocardus; and thereafter, by other letters, he dispensed
him to hold, together with the above monastery, two other benefices etc.[1] The pope
— at his supplication — now dispenses Fiocardus — who is a DDec and, as he
asserts, is of noble, knightly, and baronial birth, and who intends to repair the above
monastery, (which was founded by Pepin, king of the Franks, detained, formerly, for
a long time, by the English, and other, enemies of the kingdom of France, whose
fruits etc. are greatly diminished, and whose church, cloister, houses, and other
buildings are ruinous), and who offers a possible fabric fund (*operam possibilem
exhibeas*), but who, on account of the scale of the necessary expense and the
slenderness of the fruits, (which are taxed at 136 gold ducats of the camera, etc. [1]),
cannot, without great outlay and timely assistance, bring the work (*opus*) which has
been started, to the desired end — to hold, together with the above monastery, three
other benefices, etc.[1]

Personam tuam nobis et apostolice sedi devotam. . .
· N· Bregeon / ~ V /· V· C De Phano:

[1] the other information is utterly outside the scope of the Calendar

197   13 August 1499[1]   *Reg. Lat.* 1053, fos 143[V]-144[V]

To the abbots of the monasteries of Battle (*de Bello*) and Robertsbridge (*de Ponte Roberti*), d. Chichester, and the archdeacon of Lewes (*Leuuen'*) in the church of Chichester, mandate in favour of Richard Underdowne, layman, d. Chichester. A recent petition to the pope on Richard's part stated that formerly John Elphek, cleric or layman, d. Chichester — falsely asserting that Richard had, out of hatred, craftily defamed him before respectable and important people, telling them that he had committed forgery and several other crimes then expressed, or had temerariously imputed to him the crimes he (Richard) had committed — sued Richard before Hugh Peyntwyn', LLD, archdeacon of the church of Canterbury — to whom, (as he said), John, cardinal priest of St Anastasia, president of the church of Canterbury by apostolic concession, primate of all England, and legate born of the apostolic see in those parts, had, by virtue of his legation or otherwise, committed the case — praying that he be declared to have incurred the sentence of greater excommunication contained (as he said) in a certain provincial constitution of Canterbury, and to be (and have been) excommunicate; and that after false, corrupt, and perjurious witnesses who supported the case as their own, had been produced on John's part and examined, Hugh, proceeding wrongly in the case, promulgated an unjust definitive sentence by which he declared that John[2] had incurred excommunication and was excommunicate, and he condemned Richard in costs, reserving power to himself, even of taxing the costs; from which Richard appealed to the apostolic see, but having been detained (as he asserts) by lawful impediment he has not prosecuted the appeal within the proper time. At Richard's supplication to the pope to commit to some upright men in those parts the causes of the appeal, of everything perchance attempted and innovated after and against the appeal, of the nullity and invalidity of Hugh's sentence and process, and of the principal matter, the pope hereby commands that the above three (or two or one of them), having summoned John and others concerned, if what is related about the impediment is true, and having heard both sides, shall decree what is just, without appeal, causing by [ecclesiastical][3] censure what they have decreed to be strictly observed.[4] Notwithstanding the lapse of time, etc.

Humilibus et cetera.
. *L. puccius /. V.* [5] /. *V. xij De Phano:*

[1] *idibus Augusti anno septimo* apparently more heavily inked: entered later?

[2] *sic; recte* 'Richard'?

[3] MS wants 'ecclesiasticam'

[4] MS wants 'etiam de negotio principali huiusmodi cognoscentes legitime' (contemplated above); *cf.* no. 694

[5] a swung dash above the point precedes the 'V'

198   3 August 1499   *Reg. Lat.* 1053, fos 153^r-154^v

To Thomas Austell, treasurer of the church of Exeter. Some time ago, Sixtus IV by his letters dispensed him to receive and retain for life together with the parish church of Chiritoffyppayn' [also spelt *Chiritonffyppayn'*], d. Exeter, (which, as he asserted, he was then <holding>[1]), one, or having resigned it, any two other benefices, etc. [as above, no. 131, to '... as is more fully contained in those letters'].[2] The pope therefore — at his supplication — hereby further dispenses Thomas, who, as he asserts, holds by the said dispensation the treasurership of the church of [Exeter][3] and the above parish church, which at another time were canonically collated to him while vacant *certo modo*, to receive and retain for life, together with the treasurership and parish church, or without them, with any two other incompatible benefices held by him at the time by the said dispensation, any third benefice, etc. [as above, no. 131].

Vite ac morum honestas. . .
L puccius /· V· /· V· Lxx. De Phano:-

[1] marginal insertion, initialled *V*

[2] summarised in *CPL*, XIII, on p. 781

[3] Here, MS: *Oxonien*. There is a cross above the 'x' (signalling error?); *recte*: 'Exonien. '

199   8 July 1499   *Reg. Lat.* 1053, fos 167^v-168^v

Commission of cause, with absolution from excommunication etc. and relaxation of oath, in favour of Philibertus de Bone, UID, cleric, d. Lyon, following litigation over the parish church of St Peter, near Annecy (*prope Annesiacum*), d. Geneva, and his consent, through force and fear, to an agreement.

'Francis, bishop of Annaghdown, living in the city or diocese of Geneva' is one of the three judges delegate. Entry otherwise of no interest to the Calendar.

Humilibus et cetera.
S de Castello /. L· [1] */· L. xx Dulcius:-*

[1] a swung dash above the point which precedes the 'L'

200   12 June 1499   *Reg. Lat.* 1053, fos 191^r-192^v

To Richard Wilson', canon of the monastery of St Nicholas, Drax, OSA, d. York, dispensation. Some time ago, the pope by other letters of his dispensed him to receive and retain any benefice, with or without cure, usually held by secular clerics, even if a parish church or its perpetual vicarage, or a chantry, free chapel, hospital or annual service, usually assigned to secular clerics in title of a perpetual ecclesiastical benefice, if he obtained it otherwise canonically, to resign it, simply or for exchange, as often as he pleased, and in its place receive another, similar or dissimilar, benefice, with or without cure, usually assigned to secular clerics, as is more fully contained in those letters.[1] The pope therefore — at his supplication — hereby dispenses him, who, as he asserts, holds the parish church of Walkynton, d. (York),[2] by the said dispensation, and is, as he also asserts, expressly professed of the above order,[3] to receive, together with the above (church)[4] of Walkynton, or any other benefice held by him at the time by virtue of the said dispensation, any other benefice, a regular one, with or without cure, of the order of St Augustine or any other order, or one usually held by secular clerics, even if the regular benefice should be a priory, *prepositura, prepositatus,* dignity, *personatus,* administration or office, and the secular be a parish church etc. usually conferred on[5] secular clerics in title of a perpetual ecclesiastical benefice, even if the priory etc. should be customarily elective and have cure of souls, if he obtains it otherwise canonically, and retain the secular benefice, together with the above parish church, or with another secular benefice held by him (at the time)[6] by virtue of the said dispensation, or even a regular benefice, if it and the other regular benefice held at the time are dependencies of the same monastery or regular place, *in titulum* for life, to resign it, simply or for exchange, as often as he pleases, and in its place receive another, similar or dissimilar, benefice, a regular one, with or without cure, of the order aforesaid[7] or one usually held by secular clerics, and — provided that such regular benefice be not a conventual priory or other conventual dignity or a claustral office — retain it for life, as above. Notwithstanding etc. With the proviso (that the other)[8] benefice held, regular or secular, shall not, on this account, be defrauded of due services and the cure of souls therein (if any) shall not be neglected.

Religionis zelus, vite ac morum honestas . . .
S de Castello[9] / . L. / L. L^{ta}. Dulcius:-

[1] *Cf. CPL,* XVI, no. 118

[2] *Eboracen.* inserted in the margin (in different script, if not hand), initialled . *L.* ; (?)*Eboracen.,* deleted and initialled . *L.,* in the line

[3] The latter information comes from a notwithstanding clause.

[4] *ecclesia* inserted in the margin (in the same script as previous insertion); not initialled

[5] *conferri; cf. assignari* above

[6] *pro tempore* inserted in the margin (in the same script as previous insertions) initialled . *L.*

[7] *sic*

[8] *quod aliud* inserted in the margin (in the same script as previous insertions) initialled . *L*; *quod alterius,* deleted and initialled . *L* in the line

[9] the script differs somewhat from that of the letter : entered later?

201 10 December 1499   *Reg. Lat.* 1054, fos 81^V-82^r

To John Ryther, perpetual vicar of the parish church of Halstede, d. London. Dispensation — at his supplication — to receive and retain for life, together with the perpetual vicarage of the above parish church, [one],[1] and without it, any two other benefices, etc. [as above, no. 3].

Vite ac morum honestas . . .
· *L· Puccius* / · *V·* / · *V· L De Phano:*

[1] 'unum' does not occur

202 14 December 1499   *Reg. Lat.* 1054, fos 84^r-85^r

To John Wellys, rector of the parish church of Barceston' *alias* Barston',[1] d. Worcester, dispensation. Some time ago, the pope by other letters of his dispensed him to receive and retain for life, together with the parish church of Rydware Hampstall', d. Coventry and Lichfield, (which, as he asserted, he was then holding), one, and without them, any two other benefices, etc. [as above, no. 131, to '. . . as is more fully contained in those letters'].[2] The pope — at his supplication — hereby further dispenses John, who, as he asserts, having resigned the church of Rydware Hampstall', acquired, by virtue of the above dispensation, the parish church of Barceston' *alias* Barston', d. Worcester, and a perpetual benefice, called the southern moiety, in the parish church of Stoke near Granth(a)m,[3] d. Lincoln, which has cure of souls, [both of] which were canonically collated to him while vacant *certo modo*, and is holding them, to receive and retain for life, together with the parish church of Barceston' *alias* Barston' and the benefice aforesaid, and without them, with any two other incompatible benefices held by him at the time by virtue of the above dispensation, any third benefice, etc. [as above, no. 131].

Vite ac morum honestas . . .
S. de Castello / . *L.* / . *L. Lxx . Dulcius:-*

[1] MS: . . . *de Barceston' alias Barston'* (twice); subsequently . . . *de Barreston alias de Barston'* (twice)
[2] summarised in *CPL*, XV1, at no. 313
[3] MS: *Granthm'*

203 14 December 1499   *Reg. Lat.* 1054, fos 88^r-89^r

Union etc. At a recent petition on the part of Robert Spenser, canon [(?)of the church][1] of Lincoln, the pope hereby unites etc. the parish church of St John the Baptist, Nettellton', d. Lincoln, (whose annual value does not exceed 24 marks sterling, equivalent to 72 gold ducats of the camera or thereabouts) to the canonry and prebend of Myltonmante of the church of Lincoln, which he holds together with the above parish church, for as long as he holds the canonry and prebend, to the effect that Robert, in person or by proxy, may, on his own authority, take and retain corporal possession of the parish church and its rights and appurtenances, for as long as he holds the canonry and prebend, and convert its fruits etc. to his own uses and those of the parish church and the canonry and prebend without licence of the local diocesan or of anyone else. Notwithstanding etc. The pope's will is, however, that the parish church shall not, on account of this union etc., be defrauded of due services and the cure of souls therein shall not be neglected, but that its customary burdens shall be supported; and that on Robert's death or resignation etc. of the canonry and prebend the union etc. shall be dissolved and the parish church shall revert to its original condition and be deemed vacant automatically.

Ad futuram rei memoriam. Decet Romanum pontificem votis illis gratum prestare assensum . . .
P· *de Castello* / · V· / · V *xxxv De Phano:*

[1] MS: *canonici Lingolinen. diocesis*; *recte*: 'ecclesie'?

204   29 December 1499   *Reg. Lat.* 1054, fos 95[r]-96[r]

To Nicholas Channtrell, rector of the parish church of Hauukechuych [also spelt *Hanokechuych*], d. Salisbury. Dispensation and indult — at his supplication — to receive and retain for life, together with the above parish church, one, and without it, any two other benefices, etc. [as above, no. 3, to '. . . retain them together for life, as above']; and, for life, while attending a *studium generale* or residing in the Roman curia or any one of his benefices, not to be bound to reside in his other benefices, etc. [as above, no. 21].

Vite ac morum honestas . . .
· L· *Puccius* / · V· / · V· *Lx De Phano:*

205   29 December 1499   *Reg. Lat.* 1054, fos 96[r]-97[r]

To Ralph[1] Bride, perpetual vicar of the parish church of Ramsey, d. London. Dispensation — at his supplication — to receive and retain for life, together with the perpetual vicarage of the above parish church, one, and without it, any two other benefices, etc. [as above, no. 3].

Vite ac morum honestas . . .
· *L· Puccius* / *V* / *V. L· De Phano:*

[1] *Redulpho*

206   29 December 1499   *Reg. Lat.* 1054, fos 97[r]-98[r]

To William Byrde, perpetual vicar of the parish church of Bradford, d. Salisbury. Dispensation — at his supplication — to receive and retain for life, together with the perpetual vicarage of the above parish church, one, and without it, any two other benefices, etc. [as above, no. 3].

Vite ac morum honestas . . .
. *L. Puccius* / . *V.* / . *V. L. De Phano:*

207   3 January 1500   *Reg. Lat.* 1054, fo 99[r-v]

To Thomas Urmyston', MA, rector of the parish church of Lowlworth' [also spelt *Lowlworth*], d. Ely. Dispensation and indult — at his supplication — to receive and retain for life, together with the above (church),[1] one, and without it, any two other benefices, etc. [as above, no. 3, to '. . . retain them together for life, as above']; and, for life, while attending a *studium generale* or [residing][2] in the Roman curia or in any one of his benefices, not to be bound to reside [in his other benefices],[3] etc. [as below, no. 238].

Litterarum scientia, vite ac morum honestas . . .
Bregeon[4] / · *V·* / · *V· L·*[5] *De Phano:*

[1] marginal insertion, initialled . *V.*
[2] 'residendo' does not occur
[3] supplied by the editor
[4] *sic* : without initial ('F' or 'N'?)
[5] *sic* : not 'Lx' — the usual tax for a dispensation *ad duo* with indult *de non residendo*

208   3 January 1500   *Reg. Lat.* 1054, fo 100[r-v]

To Thomas Goldsmyth, perpetual vicar of the parish church of Charleton', d. Salisbury. Dispensation — at his supplication — to receive and retain for life, together with the perpetual vicarage of the above parish church, another, and having resigned them, any two other benefices, etc. [as above, no. 3].

Vite ac morum honestas . . .
L Puccius[1] */ . V· / · V· L· De Phano:-*

[1] In a different script and hand : entered later?

209   6 January 1500   *Reg. Lat.* 1054, fo 103[r-v]

To Raphael Babyngton', cleric, d. Coventry and Lichfield. Dispensation — at his supplication — to him, who, as he asserts, is [in] his nineteenth year of age or thereabouts, to receive and retain any benefice, with cure or otherwise incompatible, etc. [as below, no. 240].[1]

Vite ac morum honestas . . .
Jo Ortega / · V· / · V· xx De Phano:

[1] save that in this instance MS wants 'valeas'

210   11 January 1500   *Reg. Lat.* 1054, fos 114[r]-115[r]

To Henry Petri of Narbonne (*de Narbona*), cleric, d. London, dispensation. The pope (who, some time ago, decreed and declared that provisions, grants or mandates of provision to canonries and prebends of cathedral churches to persons who have not completed their fourteenth year of age shall be of no force except by consent of the apostolic see) hereby dispenses[1] Henry (who, as he asserts, is in his twelfth year or thereabouts, and is the son of Peter of Narbonne, barber of Henry, king of England, and intends to study letters) to receive and retain, henceforth, any canonries and prebends of any cathedral, even metropolitan, churches, and, as soon as he is in his seventeenth year, any benefice, with cure or otherwise incompatible, etc. [as below, no. 240, to '. . . if he obtains it otherwise canonically'], to resign them, at once or successively, simply or for exchange, as often as he pleases, and in their place receive and retain other canonries and prebends and another, similar or dissimilar, benefice, with cure or otherwise incompatible.[2] Notwithstanding the above defect of age etc. With the proviso that the canonries and prebends and the benefice in question shall not, on this account, be defrauded of due services and the cure of souls in the benefice (if any) shall not be neglected; but that the customary burdens of all of them shall be supported.

Laudabilia tue puerilis etatis inditia . . .
N· Bregeon / V³ / · V· xxxv De Phano:

[1] 'at his supplication' does not occur
[2] the age qualification regarding the benefice is not reiterated, but surely applies
[3] a swung dash to the right

211   18 November 1499   *Reg. Lat.* 1054, fos 128ᵛ-129ᵛ

To William[1] Ffoter, MA, rector of the parish church of Evston [also spelt *Goston*], d. Norwich. Dispensation — at his supplication — to receive and retain for life, together with the above parish church, one, and without it, any two other benefices, etc. [as above, no. 3].

Vite ac morum honestas . . . [2]
P· de Castello / · V· / . V· L· De Phano:

[1] *Guglelmo*
[2] *sic*; yet an address clause, where the recipient of the grace is designated by a degree, calls for a proem in the form 'Litterarum scientia, vite . . . '

212   19 November 1499   *Reg. Lat.* 1054, fos 129ᵛ-130ʳ

To George Symson, rector of the parish church of Warmy Worth, d. York. Dispensation — at his supplication — to receive and retain for life, together with the above parish church, one, and without it, any two other benefices, etc. [as above, no. 3].

Vite ac morum honestas . . .
. A. de. Sanctoseverino / · V· / · V· L· De Phano:-

213   16 November 1499   *Reg. Lat.* 1054, fos 131ᵛ-132ᵛ

To John Brouunesuryth,[1] LLB, perpetual vicar of the parish church of Andener, d. Winchester. Dispensation — at his supplication — to receive and retain for life, together with the perpetual vicarage of the above parish church, one, and without [it],[2] any two other benefices, etc. [as above, no. 3].

Litterarum scientia, vite ac morum honestas . . .
P· de planca / · V· / · V· L· De Phano:

[1] *rectius*: 'Brouunesmyth'?
[2] MS wants 'illa' (or suchlike)

214   16 November 1499   *Reg. Lat.* 1054, fos 132[v]-133[v]

To Richard Dampeyr, MA, perpetual vicar of the parish church of St Nicholas, Combe (*de Cumba*), d. Bath.[1] Dispensation — at his supplication — to receive and retain for life, together with the perpetual vicarage of the above parish church, one, and without it, any two other benefices, etc. [as above, no. 3].

Litterarum scientia, vite ac morum honestas . . .
L· puccius / · V· / · V· L· De Phano:

[1] *Batomen. diocesis* — 'et Wellen. ' (or suchlike) does not occur; subsequently *Batomen.* — 'diocesis' does not occur

215   5 October 1499   *Reg. Lat.* 1054, fos 135[v]-136[v]

To William Stokdale, MTheol, perpetual vicar of the parish church of Bs Peter and Paul, Westuuersey, d. London, dispensation. Some time ago, Innocent VIII by his letters dispensed him to receive and retain for life, together with the perpetual vicarage of the above parish church (which, as he asserted, he was then holding), one, or having resigned it, any two other benefices, etc. [as above, no. 131, to '. . . as is more fully contained in those letters']. The pope therefore — at his supplication — hereby dispenses him, who, as he asserts, holds the above vicarage and the parish church of St Leonard of the New Hithe, Colchester (*de Nonahyda Colestrie*), said diocese, by the above dispensation, to receive and retain for life, together with the vicarage and church held, or with two other incompatible benefices for which he is dispensed as above, any third benefice, etc. [as above, no. 131].

Litterarum scientia, vite ac morum honestas . . .
Jo ortega / . L. [1] */ L. Lxx. Dulcius:-*

[1] reworked; possibly changed from another initial ('F'?)

216   5 October 1499   *Reg. Lat.* 1054, fos 136ᵛ-137ᵛ

To Richard Moton', perpetual vicar of the parish church of Sinepe[1] in Cornwall (*in Cornubia*), d. Exeter. Dispensation — at his supplication — to receive and retain for life, together with the perpetual vicarage of the above parish church, one, and without it, any two other benefices, etc. [as above, no. 3].

Vite ac morum honestas . . .
Jo ortega / V / · V· L· De Phano:-

[1] the first occurrence has the second letter changed (by overwriting) from 'y' to 'i' or vice versa

217[1]   5 October 1499   *Reg. Lat.* 1054, fos 137ᵛ-138ᵛ

Union etc. At a recent petition on the part of William Gybins, MA, rector of the parish church of Bradley [also spelt *Bradey*], d. Coventry and Lichfield, the pope hereby unites etc. the parish church of Chyrcheytn' [also spelt *Chycheytn'*, *Chycheitn'*,[2] *Chicheytn'*], d. Coventry and Lichfield, (whose annual value does not exceed 12 marks sterling, equivalent to 37[3] gold ducats of the camera or thereabouts), to the above church of Bradley, which he holds together by apostolic dispensation, for as long as he holds that of Bradley, to the effect that William, in person or by proxy, may, on his own authority, take and retain corporal possession of the church of Chyrcheytn' and its rights and appurtenances, for as long as he holds the church of Bradley, and convert its fruits etc. to his own uses and those of the said churches without licence of the local diocesan or of anyone else. Notwithstanding etc. The pope's will is, however, that the church of Chyrcheytn' shall not, on account of this union etc., be defrauded of due services and the cure of souls therein shall not be neglected, but that its customary burdens shall be supported; and that on William's death or resignation etc. of the church of Bradley the union etc. shall be dissolved and so deemed and the church of Chyrcheytn' shall revert to its original condition automatically.

Ad futuram rei memoriam. Ex iniuncto nobis desuper apostolice servitutis officio ad ea libenter intendimus . . .
. Jo. ortega / . L. / . L. xxxv. Dulcius:-

[1] The corresponding engrossment is PRO, SC7 4/7.

[2] In one instance a deleted 'e' (not initialled) occurs before the 'y'.

[3] *triginta et septem* inserted in margin, initialled . *L.* ; *vij* deleted occurs in line

218   5 October 1499   *Reg. Lat.* 1054, fo 139^{r-v}

To Leonard Middelton, rector of the parish church of Monley'sayle [also spelt
Monley'layle[1]], d. Exeter. Dispensation — at his supplication — to receive and
retain for life, together with the above parish church, one, and without it, any two
other benefices, etc. [as above, no. 3].

Vite ac morum honestas . . .
. Jo. ortega. / . L. / L. L^{ta}. Dulcius:-

[1] the second 'l' changed (by erasure and reworking) from a long 'S'

219   5 October 1499   *Reg. Lat.* 1054, fo 140^{r-v}

To Robert Bedale, canon of the monastery of B. Mary Magdalen, Shap, OPrem, d.
Carlisle. Dispensation — at his supplication — to him, who, as he asserts, is
expressly professed of the above order,[1] to receive and retain any benefice, with or
without cure, usually held by secular clerics, etc. [as above, no. 32].

Religionis zelus, vite ac morum honestas . . .
Jo ortega / . L. / . L. xxx. Dulcius:-[2]

[1] This information comes from a notwithstanding clause.
[2] the 'D' reworked

220   26 October 1499   *Reg. Lat.* 1054, fo 162^{r-v}

To Thomas Benett, cleric, d. Salisbury. Dispensation — at his supplication — to
him, who, as he asserts, is in his fifteenth year of age, to receive and retain together
for life, henceforth, one, and as soon as he has reached his twentieth year, with it,
another, or without them, any two other benefices, with cure or otherwise mutually
incompatible, etc. [as above, no. 3, to '. . . in their place receive up to two other,
similar or dissimilar, incompatible benefices'] — viz: henceforth, one, and, in his
twentieth year, another, and without them, any two other benefices — and retain
them together for life, as above. Notwithstanding etc. With the proviso that the
incompatible benefices in question shall not, on this account, be defrauded of due
services and the cure of souls therein (if any) shall not be neglected.

Vite ac morum honestas . . .
. Jo. Ortega / . L. / . L. . Lxx. Dulcius:-

221   30 August 1499   *Reg. Lat.* 1054, fos 171^r-172^r

To the prior of the monastery, usually governed by a prior, of Chayrdownheste, d. Lismore, and the precentor and chancellor of the church of Lismore, mandate in favour of David, archbishop of Cashel. A recent petition to the pope on David's part stated that, formerly, he had obtained that the ministership of the house of St James, Achdara, OTrin, d. Limerick, (then vacant by the death outside the Roman curia of Eugene Yffaclaij, its minister), be commended to him by apostolic authority, to be held, ruled, and governed by him for life,[1] and, having acquired the house by virtue of this commend, he had held and possessed it, peacefully and quietly, for some time; that John Acclobard, who bore himself as a brother of the said order — falsely claiming that the ministership was then vacant *certo modo* and had been vacant for so long that its collation had lawfully devolved on the apostolic see, and that David was unlawfully detaining it and had done so for a certain time, with no title and no support of law, temerariously and *de facto*, and that it rightfully belonged to him and ought, by pretext of certain apostolic letters which he had surreptitiously and obreptitiously impetrated, to be collated to him — sued archbishop David by pretext of the letters before Donat Okermada, canon of the church of Limerick, whom (together with certain colleagues) he said was the judge appointed under the letters; and that canon Donat, proceeding invalidly and *de facto*, regardless of law, promulgated a definitive sentence by which he collated and made provision of the ministership to John, and declared that David was to be removed. At the supplication to the pope of David (who asserts that the sentence was null) to commit to some upright men in those parts the cases of the nullity and invalidity of the sentence, canon Donat's whole process, and everything else prejudicial to David done by Donat and John and any other judges and persons in connection with the foregoing, and of the principal matter, the pope hereby commands that the above three (or two or one of them), having summoned John and others concerned, and having heard both sides, taking cognizance even of the principal matter, shall decree what is just, without appeal, causing by ecclesiastical censure what they have decreed to be strictly observed; [and moreover compel] witnesses, etc. Notwithstanding etc.

Humilibus et cetera.
N· Bregeon / . *L.* [2] / . *L. x. Dulcius:-*

[1] *CPL* XIV, p. 254; *cf. ibid.*, p. 259
[2] *N· Bregeon* and . *L.* are written in a lighter ink : entered later? There is a swung dash above the point after the 'L'

222   3 October 1499   *Reg. Lat.* 1054, fos 180^v-181^v

To John Aspden', perpetual vicar of the parish church of Hanney [also spelt *Haney'*], d. Salisbury. Dispensation and indult — at his supplication — to receive and retain for life, together with the perpetual vicarage of the above parish church, one, and without it, any two other benefices, etc. [as above, no. 3, to '. . . retain them together for life, as above']; and, also for life, while residing in the Roman curia or in any one of his benefices or attending a *studium generale*, not to be bound to reside in his other benefices, etc. [as below, no. 238].

Vite ac morum honestas . . .
Jo. ortega | · V· | · V· Lx. De Phano:-

223   29 August 1499   *Reg. Lat.* 1054, fos 242[v]-243[r]

To Robert Lynley, MA, rector of the parish church of Esyngton' [also spelt *Esyngton*], d. Lincoln. Dispensation — at his supplication — to receive and retain for life, together with the above parish church, one, and without it, any two other benefices, etc. [as above, no. 3].

Litterarum scientia, vite ac morum honestas . . .
L puccius[1] | . L. | . L. L^{ta}. Dulcius:-

[1] written in a larger script, different hand and darker ink : entered later?

224   14 December 1499   *Reg. Lat.* 1054, fo 246[r]

To Ralph Eyre, rector of the parish church of St Bartholomew the Apostle, Sulh(a)msted, [1] d. Salisbury. Dispensation — at his supplication — to receive and retain for life, together with the above parish church, one, and without it, any two other benefices, etc. [as above, no. 3].

Vite ac morum honestas . . .
L puccius[2] | . L. | . L. L^{ta}. Dulcius:-

[1] MS: *Sulhm'sted*
[2] written in enlarged characters : entered later?

225   6 January 1500   *Reg. Lat.* 1056, fos 137[r]-140[r]

To the prior of the monastery, usually governed by a prior, of B. Mary, Galine, d. *Clonen.,*[1] and James Odurla and John Odolagan, canons of the church of *Clonen.,*[2] mandate in favour of Thady Obrog, cleric, d. Clonfert (who, as he asserts, notwithstanding a defect of birth as the son of a canon, OSA, a priest and expressly professed of this order, and an unmarried woman, has had himself dispensed first by ordinary authority to be duly marked with clerical character; and then by apostolic authority to be promoted to all even sacred orders and to hold a benefice, even if it should have cure of souls). It has been referred to the pope's audience by Thady that Donat Ohuran, canon of Clonfert, has dared to be present at the death of a single man and give help and support to it. And the pope has learned that the perpetual vicarage of the parish church of Fand, said diocese, is vacant *certo modo* at present and has been vacant for so long that by the Lateran statutes its collation has lawfully devolved on the apostolic see, although Morinanus [also spelt *Morianus*] Obrodear, who bears himself as a cleric, has detained it without any title or support of law, temerariously and *de facto*, for a certain time, as he still does. Considering that if the foregoing is true, Donat has rendered himself unworthy of the canonry and prebend of Hanacl,[3] which he holds in the church of Clonfert, the pope hereby commands that the above three (or two or one of them), if Thady will accuse Donat before them in these matters and proceed to any extraordinary pain to be imposed by their judgement, thereafter, having summoned respectively Donat and Morinanus and others concerned, shall make inquiry into all the foregoing and, if they find it to be true, deprive Donat of the canonry and prebend and remove him from them; and, in that event, collate and assign the canonry and prebend, whose annual value does not exceed 3, and the vicarage, 2, marks sterling, (whether the canonry and prebend be vacant by the said deprivation, or howsoever they and the vicarage be vacant, etc. ; [even if] the canonry and prebend have been vacant for so long that by the Lateran statutes their collation has lawfully devolved on the apostolic see etc.), with plenitude of canon law and all rights and appurtenances, to Thady, inducting him etc. having removed Donat from the canonry and prebend and Morinanus from the vicarage and any other unlawful detainers and causing Thady (or his proctor) to be received as a canon of the church of [Clonfert][4] having assigned him a stall in the choir and a place in the chapter of the said church of Clonfert, and to be admitted to the vicarage and the fruits etc., rights and obventions of the canonry and prebend and vicarage to be delivered to him. [Curbing] gainsayers by the pope's authority etc. Notwithstanding etc. Also the pope dispenses and indulges Thady to receive and retain the canonry and prebend, if conferred on him by virtue of the presents; and to have himself promoted by any catholic bishop in communion with the apostolic see to the said orders, when bound to do so by reason of any benefice; and the bishop concerned to confer them on him; notwithstanding the defect of birth etc.

Vite ac morum honestas . . .
. *S. de. Castello* / . *L.* / *L. xv. Quintodecimo kl' februarii Anno Octavo* [18 January 1500], *Dulcius:-*

[1] *recte*: 'Cluanen. ' (Clonmacnois)

[2] as above, note 1

[3] first letter — (?)'H' — blotched and reworked

[4] MS: *Clonen.* ; here, however, surely a mistake for 'Clonferten.' [!]

226   27 November 1499   *Reg. Lat.* 1056, fos 179^v-182^v

To the prior of the monastery, usually governed by a prior, of B. Mary, Saline, d. *Clonen.*,[1] and James Odurla and Cristinus Omolon, canons of the church of *Clonen.*, mandate in favour of Terence Omilaolayn, cleric, d. *Clonen.* Following the pope's reservation some time ago of all dignities major *post pontificalem* in cathedral churches vacated then and in the future to his own collation and disposition, the deanery of the church of *Clonen.*, which is a dignity major *post pontificalem* and which Eugene Mathoblayn, its late dean, held while he lived, [fell vacant] by his death, outside the Roman curia, [and it and], as the pope has learned, the perpetual vicarage of the parish church of Lodua, d. *Clonen.*, are vacant *certo modo* at present and the vicarage has been vacant for so long that by the Lateran statutes its collation has lawfully devolved on the apostolic see, the deanery being reserved as above. At a recent petition on Terence's part (which stated that the deanery's fruits etc. are so slender that the dean is unable to support himself and bear the burdens incumbent on him) to the pope to unite etc. the vicarage to the deanery, for as long as Terence holds the latter[2] — asserting that the annual value of the deanery does not exceed 12, and of the vicarage, 24, marks sterling; and that Dermot Obresel, bearing himself as a priest of the said diocese, has detained the vicarage with no title and no support of law, temerariously and *de facto*, for a certain time, as he does; and that he himself is of noble birth by both parents and in his twenty-third year of age — the pope hereby commands that the above three (or two or one of them) shall collate and assign the deanery to Terence and, having summoned Dermot and others concerned and those interested in the union, unite etc. the vicarage (whether the deanery be vacant in the above or another way and howsoever etc. it and the vicarage be vacant; even if the deanery has been vacant for so long that by the Lateran statutes its collation has lawfully devolved on the apostolic see, and it and the vicarage be specially reserved etc.), with all its rights even ancient[3] appurtenances, to the deanery, for as long as Terence holds the latter,[4] inducting him etc. having removed Dermot from [the vicarage][5] and [any] unlawful detainer from the deanery and causing Terence (or his proctor) to be admitted to the deanery and its fruits etc., rights and obventions and those of the annexed vicarage to be delivered to him. [Curbing] gainsayers by the pope's authority etc. Notwithstanding etc. Also the pope dispenses Terence to receive and retain the deanery, if conferred on him by virtue of the presents, notwithstanding the above defect of age etc. The pope's will is, however, that the deanery and the vicarage shall not, on account of this union etc., be defrauded of due services and the cure of souls in the vicarage and (if any) in the deanery shall not be neglected, but that the customary burdens of the vicarage shall be supported; and that on Terence's death or resignation etc. of the deanery the union etc. shall be dissolved and so deemed and the vicarage shall revert to its original condition and be deemed vacant automatically.

Apostolice sedis providentia circumspecta ad ea libenter intendit . . .
. *S. de. Castello* / . *L.* / *L. xxv. Quartodecimo kl' Jan' Anno Octavo* [19 December 1499] *Dulcius:-*

¹ *recte*: 'Cluanen. ' (Clonmacnois) — likewise throughout the entry

² *illam*; *recte*: 'illum' (i. e. the deanery not the vicarage)? *Cf.* below, note 4

³ *etiam antiquis* [most unexpected; usually 'et' occurs here]

⁴ *illum*; *cf.* above, note 2

⁵ *ab nexa*; for 'ab annexa' (i. e. the vicarage)

227   3 December 1499   *Reg. Lat.* 1056, fos 188^r-190^v

To the chancellor of the church of Lismore, William Obrog, canon of the church of Cloyne, and Edmund Porcel, canon of the church of Lismore, mandate in favour of Cormac Orelly, perpetual vicar of the parish church of Kykollw', d. Ossory. The pope has learned that the priorship of the monastery, usually governed by a prior, of St John the Evangelist, called the house or cell of God, outside the walls of Waterford, OSB, is vacant *certo modo* at present and has been vacant for so long that by the Lateran statutes its collation has lawfully devolved on the apostolic see, although John Derrus, who bears himself as a monk of the monastery, has detained it without any title or support of law, temerariously and *de facto*, for a certain time, as he still does. And Cormac asserts that he holds the vicarage of the said parish church and that the priory is no more than a mile distant from the church. The pope hereby commands that the above three (or two or one of them), if, having summoned John and others concerned, they find the priorship, which is conventual by custom and not by institution,¹ and whose annual value does not exceed 40 marks sterling, to be vacant (howsoever etc.) shall commend it (even if specially reserved etc.), with all rights and appurtenances, to Cormac, to be held, ruled and governed by him for life, together with the vicarage and every other benefice which he holds and shall hold; (he may — due and customary burdens of the priorship having been supported — make disposition of the rest of its fruits etc., just as those holding it *in titulum vel commendam* could and ought to do, alienation of immovable goods and precious movables being however forbidden); inducting him etc. having removed John and any other unlawful detainer and causing Cormac to be admitted to the priorship and its fruits etc., rights and obventions to be delivered to him. [Curbing] gainsayers by the pope's authority etc. Notwithstanding etc. With the proviso that the priorship shall not, on this account, be defrauded of due services and the cure of souls (if [any]) shall not be neglected; but that its aforesaid burdens shall be supported.

Vite ac morum honestas . . .
. S. de. Castello / · V· / · V· xvj: De Phano:-

¹ *hactu*; for 'actu'?

228   15 October 1499   *Reg. Lat.* 1056, fos 235^r-237^r

To the prior of the monastery, usually governed by a prior, of B. Mary, Galine,[1] d. *Clonen.*,[2] and the official of *Clonen.*, commission and mandate in favour of William[3] Offuyra, canon of the church of *Clonen.* (who, as he asserts, holds a canonry and prebend of the said church). It has been referred to the pope's audience by William that Fergal Macohegan, archdeacon of the church of *Clonen.*, has, for more than twenty years, dared to keep publicly a certain concubine, as he does, after and against canonical (?)admonitions[4] to let go of her placed on him by the local ordinary, and has dared to apply himself to secular affairs; and also that although Fergal has been very often warned by the ordinary that he must have himself promoted to the order of the diaconate (as the archdeaconry which he holds in the said church requires in accordance with the statutes and laudable customs of that church peacefully observed hitherto), nevertheless he has not troubled to do so and has continuously put the archdeaconry's fruits etc. to bad uses. Considering that if this is true, Fergal has rendered himself unworthy of the archdeaconry, the pope hereby commissions and commands that the above two (or one of them), if William will accuse Fergal over the foregoing and proceed in form of law, thereafter, having summoned Fergal and others concerned, shall make inquiry into these matters and if they find the truth of them to be substantiated, deprive Fergal of the archdeaconry and remove him from it; and in that event collate and assign the archdeaconry, which is a non-major dignity *post pontificalem*, whose annual value does not exceed 8 marks sterling, (whether vacant then by the said deprivation and removal or at another time howsoever etc., even if vacant for so long that by the Lateran statutes its collation has lawfully devolved on the apostolic see etc.), with all rights and appurtenances, to William, inducting him etc. having removed Fergal and any other unlawful detainer and causing William (or his proctor) to be admitted to the archdeaconry and its fruits etc., rights and obventions to be delivered to him. Curbing gainsayers by the pope's authority etc. Notwithstanding etc.

Vite ac morum honestas . . .
· *S· de Castello / . L. / L. xv. Septimo Id' Novembris Anno OTtavo* [7 November 1499], *Dulcius:-*

[1] the 'G' changed from 'S'; *cf.* next entry
[2] *recte*: 'Cluanen.' (Clonmacnois) — likewise throughout the entry
[3] *Guillermus*
[4] *munitiones*; *recte*: 'monitiones'?

229   19 October 1499   *Reg. Lat.* 1056, fos 237^r-239^v

To the prior of the monastery, usually governed by a prior, of Galine,[1] d. *Clonen.*,[2] and Cristinus Omilon and James Odurla, canons of the church of *Clonen.*,[3] mandate in favour of Malachy Omaytin, scholar, d. Clonfert. It has been referred to the pope's audience by Malachy that Thady Machagan, canon of Clonfert, who holds *in commendam* the monastery of B. Mary, *de Portu Puro* [Clonfert], *Clonfer(ten).*, OSA, by apostolic concession and dispensation, has dared to assemble together on a certain day a certain body of men and with it to insult and attack an adversary or several adversaries of his, in which insult deaths followed on both sides, contracting irregularity; to burn[4] or cause to be burnt several buildings of private men; to leave undone religion and the conventual way of life in the said monastery and divine offices therein; and also to appropriate the portion of several canons of his monastery and deny those portions to them, and to come and go contrary to his own oath. The pope therefore — considering that if the foregoing is true Thady has rendered himself unworthy of the rule and administration of the monastery; and wishing to make provision of a suitable governor as well as to assist Malachy (who, as he asserts, desires to become a cleric and is of noble birth by both parents) — hereby commands that the above three (or two or one of them), if Malachy will accuse Thady before them in these matters and proceed to any extraordinary pain to be imposed by their judgement, thereafter, having summoned Thady and others concerned, shall make inquiry into the above related matters and if they find the truth of them to be substantiated, make void and annul the commend and remove Thady from the said rule and administration; and, in that event, commend the monastery, whose annual value does not exceed 24 marks sterling, with all rights and appurtenances, to Malachy — after he has been duly marked with clerical character — to be held, ruled and governed by him for life; (he may — due and customary burdens of the monastery and its convent having been supported — make disposition of the rest of its fruits etc. just as abbots could and ought to do, alienation of immovable goods and precious movables being however forbidden); committing to him the care, rule and administration of the monastery in spiritualities and temporalities and causing obedience and reverence to be given him by the convent and customary services and rights by the vassals and other subjects of the monastery. [Curbing] gainsayers by ecclesiastical censure etc. Notwithstanding etc. Also the pope grants Malachy licence and faculty to be marked with clerical character by any catholic bishop of his choice in communion with the apostolic see; and the bishop concerned to confer such character on him; notwithstanding etc. With the proviso that divine worship and the usual number of ministers in the monastery shall not, on account of this commend, be diminished; but that the aforesaid burdens of the monastery and convent shall be supported.

[Romani][5] *pontificis providentia circumspecta* . . .
. *S. de castello.* / . *L.* / . *L. xxv. Septimo Id' Novembris Anno octavo* [7 November 1499], *Dulcius:-*

[1] the 'G' changed from (?)'S'; *cf.* previous entry

[2] *recte*: 'Cluanen.' (Clonmacnois)

[3] as above, note 2

[4] *comburendo*; *recte*: 'comburere' Other such oddities occur throughout the text, but are not specially

noticed here.
5 wanting in MS

230   12 November 1499   *Reg. Lat.* 1056, fos 255ᵣ-258ᵣ

To the prior of the monastery, usually governed by a prior, of B. Mary, Galine, d. *Clonen.*[1], and Cristinus Omillon and James Odurla, canons of the church of *Clonen.*,[2] mandate in favour of Donald Ochniede, cleric, d. Killaloe. The pope has learned that the rectory of the parish church of Dura, d. Killaloe, which is of lay patronage, is vacant *certo modo* at present and has been vacant for so long that by the Lateran statutes its collation has lawfully devolved on the apostolic see, although William Olaenayn', who bears himself as a priest, d. Killaloe, has detained it, with no title and no support of law, temerariously and *de facto*, for a certain time, as he does at present. At a recent petition on Donald's part to the pope to erect and institute a canonry in the church of Killaloe and the rectory, thus vacant, into a simple prebend in the same, for his lifetime, the pope hereby commands that the above three (or two or one of them), if, having summoned William and also the bishop and chapter of Killaloe and others concerned, they find the rectory to be vacant (howsoever etc.) and it to be thus, shall erect and institute a canonry in the church of Killaloe and the rectory (even if specially reserved etc.) into a simple prebend in the same, without prejudice to anyone; and, in that event, collate and assign the newly erected canonry and prebend, whose annual value does not exceed 24 marks sterling, being vacant, with plenitude of canon law and all rights and appurtenances, to Donald, inducting him etc. having removed William from the rectory and any other unlawful detainer and causing Donald (or his proctor) to be received as a canon of the church of Killaloe, with plenitude of canon law, and the fruits etc., rights and obventions of the canonry and prebend to be delivered to him. [Curbing] gainsayers by the pope's authority etc. Notwithstanding etc. The pope's will is, however, that the rectory shall not, on account of this erection and institution, be defrauded of due services and the cure of souls therein shall not be neglected, but that its customary burdens shall be supported; and that on Donald's death or resignation of the canonry and prebend, the said erection and institution shall be extinguished and so deemed and the rectory shall revert to its original condition and thus be deemed vacant automatically.

Apostolice sedis providentia circumspecta vota fidelium per que ecclesiarum presertim cathedralium decori et venustati consulitur . . .
. P. de. planca. / . L. / L. xvj. Undecimo Kl' Decembris Anno Octavo [21 November 1499], *Dulcius:-*

1 *recte*: 'Cluanen.' (Clonmacnois)
2 as above, note 1

231　28 February 1500　　　　　　　　*Reg. Lat.* 1058, fos 51^v-53^r

To the dean and John Omanna' and Renaldus Omoriele, canons, of the church of
Cork, mandate in favour of David Oeromyn, priest, d. Cork. The pope has learned
that the perpetual vicarage of the parish church of Disertsayays, d. Cork, has been
vacant *certo modo* and is vacant at present, although a certain Denis Oeromyn, who
bears himself as a priest, has detained it without any title or support of law,
temerariously and *de facto*, for a certain time, as he does. Wishing to give David —
who, as he asserts, after he had been marked with clerical character by ordinary
authority, notwithstanding a defect of birth as the son of the said Denis, then an
unmarried cleric, and an unmarried woman, had had himself dispensed by apostolic
authority to be promoted to all the higher, even sacred, orders, and to hold a
benefice, even if it should have cure of souls — a special grace, the pope hereby
commands that the above three (or two or one of them), if, having summoned Denis
and others concerned, they find the vicarage, whose annual value does not exceed 12
marks sterling, to be vacant (howsoever etc.), shall collate and assign it (even if it
has been vacant for so long that by the Lateran statutes its collation has lawfully
devolved on the apostolic see etc.), with all rights and appurtenances, to David,
inducting him etc. having removed Denis and any other unlawful detainer, and
causing David (or his proctor) to be admitted to the vicarage and its fruits etc., rights
and obventions to be delivered to him. [Curbing] gainsayers etc. Notwithstanding
etc.

Vite ac morum honestas . . .
· *S· de Castello* / F / *F· x· Quinto Id' matij' Ano' octavo* [11 March 1500], *Sanctor(is)*

232　20 June 1500　　　　　　　　*Reg. Lat.* 1058, fos 203^r-204^r

To David Arnod, provost of the church of Bochwel, Glasgow,[1] dispensation. Some
time ago, the pope by other letters of his dispensed him to receive and retain for life,
together with the perpetual vicarage of the parish church of Echt, Aberdeen, (which,
as he asserted, he was then holding),[2] one, and without it, any two other benefices,
with cure or otherwise mutually incompatible, even if parish churches or their
perpetual vicarages, or dignities, etc. [as above, no. 131, to '. . . as is more fully
contained in those letters'].[3] The pope therefore — at his supplication — hereby
dispenses David, who is a priest and, as he asserts, of noble birth by both parents
and, having resigned the said vicarage, holds the provostship of the church of
Bochwel, Glasgow, (which is a principal dignity), which was canonically collated to
him while vacant *certo modo*,[4] to receive and retain, also for life, together with the
said provostship,[5] and one other, or with any two other incompatible benefices held
by him at the time by the said dispensation, any third benefice, with cure or
otherwise incompatible, even if a parish church or its perpetual vicarage, or a

dignity, *personatus*, administration or office in a cathedral, even metropolitan, or collegiate church, even if the dignity in question should be major *post pontificalem* in a cathedral, even metropolitan, church, or principal in a collegiate church,[6] and even if the dignity etc. [as above, no. 131].

Nobilitas generis, vite ac morum honestas . . .
N bregeon / F / F . L. Sanctor(is)

[1] MS: *perpetuo vicario parochialis ecclesie de Echt' Aberdonen.* deleted and initialled *V*; with *preposito ecclesie de Bochwel Glasguen.* inserted in the margin and *Cassat(um) et Correct(um) de Mandato R(everendissimi) D(omini) Jo(hannis) Ragusini Regentis per me . V. de Phano*: after the insertion; all in *V*'s hand.

[2] MS: *etiam tunc ut asserebas perpetuam vicariam parochialis ecclesie de Echt' Aberdonen. inter alia obtinente . . . dicta vicaria* deleted and initialled *V* (and . *V*.); with *perpetua vicaria parochialis ecclesie de Echt' Alberdonen. quam tunc ut asserebas obtinebas* inserted in the margin against the second deleted passage and *Cassat(um) et Correct(um) ut supra . V.* after the insertion; all in *V*'s hand.

[3] summarised in *CPL*, XVI at no. 587

[4] MS: *dictam vicariam* changed (by deletion) to *dicta vicaria* (initialled *V*); with *per te dimissa preposituram ecclesie de Bochwel Glasguen. que inibi dignitas principalis existit primo tunc certo modo vacantem canonice tibi collatam* inserted (after *vicaria[m]*) in the margin and *Correctum ut supra V.* after the insertion; all in *V*'s hand.

[5] MS: *prepositura* inserted in the margin (*V*'s hand) initialled *V*; with *vicaria*, deleted and initialled *V*, in the line; *cf.* note 6 below

[6] MS: *vel collegiata et dignitas ipsa in cathedrali etiam metropolitana* deleted and initialled *V* ; *Cassatum et correctum Ubique ut supra V.* against it in the margin; all in *V*'s hand.

---

233   4 July 1500   *Reg. Lat.* 1058, fos 213^r-214^v

To Adam Graston, UIB, rector of the parish church of St Nicholas, Upton, d. Coventry and Lichfield, dispensation. Some time ago, Sixtus IV by his letters dispensed him to receive and retain for life, together with the perpetual vicarage of the parish church of St Alkmund (*Sancti Akk'mundi*) in the vill of Shrewsbury, (*Salapie*), d. Coventry and Lichfield, (which, as he asserted, he was then holding), one, and without it, any two other benefices, etc. [as above, no. 131, to '. . . as is more fully contained in those letters']. The pope therefore — at his supplication — hereby further dispenses Adam, who, as he asserts, having resigned the above vicarage, holds, by the above dispensation, the parish churches of St Nicholas, Upton, and St Dionis, in the city, d. London and d. Canterbury,[1] which at another time were canonically collated to him while vacant *certo modo*, to receive and retain for life, together with the churches of St Nicholas and St Dionis, or without them, with any two other incompatible benefices held by him at the time by the said dispensation, any third benefice, etc. [as above, no. 131].

Litterarum scientia, vite ac morum honestas . . .

L puccius / F / F. Lxx. Sanctor(is)

1 . . . *Sancti Dionisii civitatis Londonien. diocesis ac Cantuarien. diocesis* . . . ; this slightly odd
formulation evidently describes the position of St Dionis, Backchurch (now demolished) which was sited
locally within the diocese of London, but, as a Canterbury peculiar, came jurisdictionally within the
diocese of Canterbury

234   19 August 1500   *Reg. Lat.* 1058, fos 217[r]-219[v]

To Thomas Brunʒam and Thomas Mackyllanaha,[1] canons of the church of Tuam,
and John Odunan, canon of the church of Annaghdown, mandate in favour of
William de Burgo, canon of [the church of] Clonfert (who, as he asserts, holds a
canonry and prebend of that church). The pope has learned that the archdeaconry of
the church of Clonfert, which John Yhelay, its late archdeacon, held while he lived
(by John's death outside the Roman curia, in the kingdom of England on his way to
the curia) is vacant *certo modo* at present and the chapel of Gyllco(n)yery(n)d,[2] d.
Clonfert, is too, and the chapel has been vacant for so long that by the Lateran
statutes its collation has lawfully devolved on the apostolic see, although Eugene
Affahy,[3] who bears himself as a cleric or priest, has detained it without any title or
support of law, temerariously and *de facto*, for a certain time, as he still does. At a
recent petition on William's part to the pope to unite etc. the chapel to the
archdeaconry, for as long as William holds the archdeaconry — asserting that he is
of noble birth by both parents and that the annual value of the archdeaconry does not
exceed 16, and of the chapel, 10, marks sterling — the pope, not having certain
knowledge of the foregoing, hereby commands that the above three (or two or one of
them), if, having summoned Eugene and others concerned, they find the foregoing to
be true, shall collate and make provision of the archdeaconry, which is a non-major
dignity *post pontificalem*, to William; and unite etc. the chapel (which has cure of
souls), (howsoever the archdeaconry and chapel be vacant, etc. ; even if the
archdeaconry has been vacant for so long that by the Lateran statutes its collation
has lawfully devolved on the apostolic see, etc.), with all rights and appurtenances,
to the archdeaconry, for as long as William holds the latter, inducting him etc. having
removed Eugene from the chapel and any other unlawful detainers from it and the
archdeaconry, and causing William to be admitted to the archdeaconry and its fruits
etc., rights and obventions and those of the chapel to be annexed to be delivered to
him. [Curbing] gainsayers by the pope's authority etc. Notwithstanding etc. The
pope's will is, however, that the chapel shall not, on account of this union etc., be
defrauded of due services and the cure of souls therein shall not be neglected, but
that its customary burdens shall be supported; and that on William's death or
resignation etc. of the archdeaconry the union etc. shall be dissolved and so deemed
and the chapel shall revert to its original condition and be deemed vacant
automatically.

Decet Romanum pontificem votis illis gratum prestare assensum . . .
. S. de Castello / . V. / . V. xxv⁴ De Phano:

¹ the 'c' supralinear
² MS: *Gyllco'yery'd*
³ *Affathy*; with the 't' deleted
⁴ wants expedition date?

235   3 April 1500   *Reg. Lat.* 1059, fos 61ᵛ-62ᵛ

To the archdeacon of the church of Dromore, and Odo Ochill', canon of the church
of Connor, and William Ocua, canon of the church of Derry, mandate in favour of
Gelasius Magnassa. The pope has learned that the prebend of Claondalan in the
church of Dromore is vacant *certo modo* at present and has been vacant for so long
that by the Lateran statutes its collation has lawfully devolved on the apostolic see,
although Eugene Oruya, who bears himself as a cleric, has detained it without any
title or support of law, temerariously and *de facto*, for a certain time, as he still does.
A recent [petition]¹ to the pope on the part of Gelasius — who, by apostolic
concession and dispensation, holds *in commendam* the monastery of St Benedict,
OCist, d. Dromore, which has suffered structural collapse and is threatened with ruin
in many of its walls and whose fruits etc. are so slender that they do not suffice for
its repair and for the support of commendator Gelasius — [stated]² that if the said
prebend were to be united etc. to the Fabric of the monastery, for Gelasius's lifetime,
it would be to his benefit and the monastery's utility. The pope hereby commands
that the above three (or two or one of them), if, having summoned Eugene and other
interested parties, they find the prebend, whose annual value does not exceed 6
marks sterling, to be vacant (howsoever etc.) and the foregoing to be true, shall unite
etc. it (even if specially reserved etc.), with all rights and appurtenances, to the said
Fabric, for Gelasius's lifetime, to the effect that — having removed Eugene and any
other unlawful detainer — Gelasius may, on his own authority, take corporal
possession of the prebend and convert its fruits etc. to his own uses and those of the
Fabric and the prebend without licence of the local diocesan or of anyone else.
Notwithstanding etc. With the proviso that the prebend shall not, on account of this
union etc., be defrauded of due services and its customary burdens shall be
supported; and that on the death or resignation etc. of commendator Gelasius — to
whom as abbot or commendator of the monastery for the time being the care of the
aforesaid Fabric is understood to belong — the union etc. shall be dissolved and so
deemed and the prebend shall revert to its original condition and be deemed vacant
automatically.

Ex iniuncto nobis desuper apostolice servitutis officio ad ea libenter intendimus . . .
S de Castello³ / F / F. xx. Sanctor(is)

[1] 'petitio continebat' wanting

[2] see note 1 above

[3] in darker ink and larger letters : entered later?

236   6 April 1500   *Reg. Lat.* 1059, fo 63[r-v]

To the prior of the monastery, usually governed by a prior, of St Mary, Mochomor, d. Connor, and Maurice Ogyllamyr, canon of the church of Connor, mandate in favour of Odo Ocaeley, cleric, d. Connor (who, some time ago, as he asserts, was dispensed by apostolic authority, notwithstanding a defect of birth as the son of a priest and an unmarried woman, to be promoted to all, even sacred, orders and to hold a benefice, even if it should have cure of souls; and who afterwards was marked with clerical character, otherwise however duly). The pope has learned that the rectory of the parish church of Carrigfergussa, d. Connor, which is of lay patronage, is vacant *certo modo* at present and has been vacant for so long that by the Lateran statutes its collation has lawfully devolved on the apostolic see, although John Obeolen', who bears himself as a priest, has detained it, without any title or support of law, temerariously and *de facto*, for a certain time, as he still does. He hereby commands that the above two (or one of them), if, having summoned John and others concerned, they find the rectory, whose annual value does not exceed 8 marks sterling, to be vacant (howsoever etc.), shall collate and assign it (even if specially reserved etc., provided its collation is devolved as above, etc.), with all rights and appurtenances, to Odo, inducting him etc. having removed John and any other unlawful detainer and causing Odo (or his proctor) to be admitted to the rectory and its fruits etc., rights and obventions to be delivered to him. [Curbing] gainsayers by the pope's authority etc. Notwithstanding etc.

Vite ac morum honestas . . .
S de Castello[1] / . *F* / *F. xij.* [2] *Sanctor(is)*

[1] Marked off from rest of letter by darkness of ink and largeness of writing : entered later? *Cf.* above, no. 235

[2] wants expedition date?

237   6 December 1499   *Reg. Lat.* 1059, fos 131[r]-132[r]

To George Hopburn', treasurer of the church of Moray, dispensation. Some time ago — when the deanery of the church of Dunkeld, which is a major dignity *post pontificalem*, is customarily elective and has cure, even jurisdictional, of souls, and which Alexander Inglis, its late dean, held while he lived, was vacant by his death outside the Roman curia — the pope by other letters of his commanded provision of it, thus vacant and previously reserved to apostolic disposition, be made to George, then, as he asserted, holding the parish church of Caldar, d. St Andrews; and by the same letters dispensed George to retain the above parish church for life, together with the deanery, if conferred on him by virtue of the said letters, to resign them, at once or successively, simply or for exchange, when he pleased, and in their place receive up to two other, similar or dissimilar, incompatible benefices — provided that they be not two parish churches or their perpetual vicarages or two dignities major *post pontificalem* in cathedral, even metropolitan, churches or principal in collegiate churches — and retain them together for life, as above, as is more fully contained in those letters.[1] The pope, therefore — at his supplication — hereby dispenses him (who, as he asserts, having resigned the said parish church, holds the treasurership of the church of Moray, which is a non-major dignity *post pontificalem*, and litigating over the said deanery, which he does not possess, against a certain adversary of his in the said curia before a certain auditor of causes of the apostolic palace he left court with a definitive sentence in his favour and against the said adversary which has passed into a final judgement, letters executory in that regard having been decreed) to receive and retain for life, together with the deanery, if he acquires it, the above treasurership, and with one of them, one, and without them, any two other benefices, etc. [as above, no. 5, to '. . . at once or successively'], simply or for [exchange][2], as often as he pleases, and in their place receive up to two other, similar or dissimilar, incompatible benefices, and retain them together for life, as above. Notwithstanding etc. With the proviso that the treasurership, deanery and other incompatible benefices shall not, on this account, be defrauded of due services and the cure of souls in the treasurership and (if any) the other incompatible benefices shall not be neglected.

Vite ac morum honestas . . .
A de sancto severino[3] / · *V·* / · *V·* · *xxxx. De Phano:-*

[1] summarised in *CPL*, XVI at no. 627

[2] MS: *vel* <*dicta*> *causa [permutationis]*; oddly, *permutationis* in the line has been deleted and *dicta* inserted in the margin, both initialled . *V.*

[3] slightly shaved horizontally at the top

238   8 August 1500   *Reg. Lat.* 1059, fos 141ᵛ-142ᵛ

To William Androwe, rector of the parish church of Hanwell', d. Lincoln. Dispensation and indult — at his supplication — to receive and retain for life, together with the above parish church, one, and without it, any two other benefices, etc. [as above, no. 3, to '. . . retain them together for life, as above']; and, for life, while attending a *studium generale*, or residing in the Roman curia or in any one of his benefices, not to be bound to reside in his other benefices, nor to be liable to be compelled by anyone to do so against his will. Notwithstanding etc. With the proviso that the above church[1] and other incompatible benefices shall not, on this account, be defrauded of due services and the cure of souls in the church and (if any) the other incompatible benefices shall not be neglected; but that customary burdens of those benefices in which he shall not reside shall be supported. [2]

Vite ac morum honestas . . .
L puccius / O / O· Lx Marianen'

[1] Other such indults for non-residence are summarised in the present volume in an abridged form and refer to this entry as to the fully extended prototype. When necessary, a term appropriate to the previous content of the entry should be substituted here (e. g. in no. 345 read 'vicarage' for 'church' and in no. 193 'chaplaincy').

[2] the latter safeguard is often present (as here and in the many entries referring to this as the prototype); but some entries do not contain it (e. g. no. 21)

239   31 July 1500   *Reg. Lat.* 1059, fos 147ᵛ-148ᵛ

To William Aller, rector of the parish church of Westputtfordi, d. Exeter. Dispensation — at his supplication — to receive and retain for life, together with the above parish church, one, and without it, any two other benefices, etc. [as above, no. 3].

Vite ac morum honestas . . .
. L. puccius / · V· / V· L· De Phano:

240   8 August 1500   *Reg. Lat.* 1059, fos 161ʳ-162ʳ

To Christopher Warde, cleric, d. York. Dispensation — at his supplication — to him, who, as he asserts, is in his nineteenth year of age or thereabouts, to receive and retain any benefice, with cure or otherwise incompatible, even if a parish church or its perpetual vicarage, or a chantry, free chapel, hospital or annual service, usually assigned to secular clerics in title of a perpetual ecclesiastical benefice, or a dignity, *personatus*, administration or office in a cathedral, even metropolitan, or collegiate church, even if the dignity should be major *post pontificalem* in a cathedral, even metropolitan, church, or principal in a collegiate church, and even if the dignity etc. should be customarily elective and have cure of souls, if he obtains it otherwise canonically, to resign it, simply or for exchange, as often as he pleases, and in its place receive and retain another, similar or dissimilar, benefice, with cure or otherwise incompatible. Notwithstanding the above defect of age etc. With the proviso that the benefice in question shall not, on this account, be defrauded of due services and the cure of souls therein (if any) shall not be neglected.

Vite ac morum honestas . . .
L. puccius /· V· / V xxv De Phano:

241   8 August 1500   *Reg. Lat.* 1059, fos 167^r-168^r

To Thomas Burdale, rector of one of two portions of the parish church of Westwalton, d. Norwich, usually ruled by two rectors. Dispensation to him (who, as he asserts, holds one of two portions of the above parish church usually ruled by two rectors) — at his supplication — to receive and retain for life, together with the above church,[1] one, and without it, any two other benefices, etc. [as above, no. 3, to '. . . Notwithstanding etc']. With the proviso that the above church[2] and other incompatible benefices shall not, on this account, be defrauded of due services and the cure of souls in the church[3] and (if any) the other incompatible benefices aforesaid shall not be neglected.

Vite ac morum honestas . . .
. L. puccius /· V· / V· L· De Phano:

[1] *sic; cf.* above where he holds only a 'portion'
[2] as above, note 1
[3] as above, note 1

242   20 August 1500   *Reg. Lat.* 1059, fos 169^r-170^r

To Robert Richardson', rector of the parish church of St Laurence, Stretton super Strett [also spelt *Stretton' super Strett*], d. Coventry and Lichfield. Dispensation — at his supplication — to receive and retain for life, together with the above parish church, one, and without it, any two other benefices, etc. [as above, no. 3].

Vite ac morum honestas . . .
. L. puccius. /· V· / V. · L· De Phano:

243   30 June 1500   *Reg. Lat.* 1059, fos 194^v-195^r

To Edward Roger, cleric, d. St Andrews. Dispensation — at his supplication — to him (who, some time ago, as he asserts, was dispensed by apostolic authority notwithstanding a defect of birth as the son of an unmarried man and an unmarried woman to be promoted to all, even sacred, orders and to receive and retain a benefice, even if it should have cure of souls, if conferred on him otherwise canonically, and who afterwards was marked with clerical character otherwise however duly) to receive and retain any other benefice, without cure, even if a canonry and prebend in a cathedral or collegiate church, if he obtains it otherwise canonically, to resign it, simply or for exchange, when he pleases, and in its place receive another, similar or dissimilar, benefice, and retain it, as above. Notwithstanding etc.

Vite ac morum honestas . . .
· S· de· Castello / V / · V· xviij · De Phano:

244   2 January 1500   *Reg. Lat.* 1059, fos 237ᵛ-238ʳ

To Richard Bennet and Elisabeth Barri, his wife, lay persons,[1] d. Cloyne. [Indult] — at their supplication — to them, who, as they assert, are sixty years of age or thereabouts and infirm, and thus unable to come to the Roman curia, to choose any suitable priest, secular or regular, of any order, as their confessor [*etc.*].[2] And lest etc.[3]

Sincera fervensque devotio vestra . . .
/Jo ortega; · V· / · V· iiij · De Phano:

[1] *laicis*; 'layman' and 'woman', respectively, required by the *stilus* of the chancery

[2] 'et cetera', though required here, does not occur

[3] enregistered in abridged form

245   11 January 1500   *Reg. Lat.* 1059, fos 238ʳ-239ʳ

To John Bennet, cleric, d. Cloyne. Dispensation — at his supplication — to him, who, as he asserts, is in his nineteenth year of age or thereabouts, to receive and retain any benefice, with cure or otherwise incompatible, even if a parish church or its perpetual vicarage, or a dignity, *personatus*, administration or office in a cathedral, even metropolitan, or collegiate church, even if the dignity in question should be major *post pontificalem* in a cathedral, even metropolitan, church, or principal in a collegiate church, even if the dignity etc. should be customarily elective and have cure of souls, if he obtains it otherwise canonically;[1] and — as soon as he has reached his twenty-second year and shall be fitted (*arctatus*) — to him to have himself promoted to the order of the priesthood, and to the bishop concerned to bestow it on him. Notwithstanding the defect of age he suffers now and will do in his twenty-second year etc. With proviso that the benefice in question shall not, on this account, be defrauded of due services and the cure of souls therein (if any) shall not be neglected.

Vite ac morum honestas . . .
. S. de Castello. / · V· / · V. xx De Phano[2]

[1] i. e. no clause of exchange
[2] unlike the usual *De Phano:* or *De Phano:-*

246   8 October 1499   *Reg. Lat.* 1059, fos 294ʳ-295ᵛ

To John Matheus,[1] rector of the parish church of West Deping, d. Lincoln. Dispensation — at his supplication — to receive and retain for life, together with the above parish church, one, and having resigned it, any two other benefices, etc. [as above, no. 3].

Vite ac morum honestas . . .
F. [2] *de Castello /· V· / V· L· De Phano: —*

[1] or *Mathens*
[2] *sic*; for 'S'?

247   14 December 1499   *Reg. Lat.* 1059, fos 299ᵛ-301ʳ

To William Pye, rector of the parish church of St James the Apostle, Bardeh(a)m,[1] d. Chichester. Dispensation and indult — at his supplication — to receive and retain for life, together with the above parish church, one, and without it, any two other benefices, etc. [as above, no. 3, to '. . . retain them together for life, as above']; and, also for life, while residing in the Roman curia or in any one of his benefices or attending a *studium generale*, not to be bound to reside personally in his other benefices, etc. [as above, no. 21].

Vite ac morum honestas . . .
L. puccius[2] */ . L. / . L. Lx. Dulcius:-*

[1] MS: *Bardehm'*
[2] in a different script and hand : entered later?

248   30 January 1500   *Reg. Lat.* 1059, fos 301ʳ-302ᵛ

To William Vardelano, perpetual vicar of the parish church of Carridin [also spelt *Cariddin*], d. St Andrews. Dispensation — at his supplication — to him (who, some time ago, as he asserts, was dispensed by apostolic authority notwithstanding a defect of birth as the son of a canon, OSA, a priest, and an unmarried woman, to be promoted to all, even sacred, orders, and to receive and retain first one benefice, even if it should have cure of souls, and next another benefice, with or without cure, compatible with the said benefice, if conferred on him otherwise canonically, to resign them, at once or successively, simply or for exchange, once only when he pleased, and in their place receive and retain up to two other, similar or dissimilar, benefices, with or without cure, compatible mutually, as above; and who afterwards had himself promoted to all the orders aforesaid and acquired first the chapel of St Andrew near Ynchgall, d. Whithorn,[1] and next the perpetual vicarages of the parish churches of Carmweche[2], d. Glasgow, and, having resigned the latter, of Carridin, d. St Andrews, which were canonically collated to him while vacant *certo modo*, and holds the above chapel and the vicarage of Carridin at present and has lost the letters of dispensation) to receive and retain for life, together with the vicarage of Carridin, one, and without it, any two other benefices, with cure or otherwise mutually incompatible, even if parish churches or their perpetual vicarages, or dignities, *personatus*, administrations or offices in cathedral, even metropolitan, or collegiate churches, or a combination, even if the dignities etc. should be customarily elective and have cure of souls, if he obtains them otherwise canonically, to resign them, at once or successively, simply or for exchange, as often as he pleases, and in their place receive up to two other, similar or dissimilar, incompatible benefices — provided that such dignities be not major *post pontificalem* in cathedral, even metropolitan, churches or principal in collegiate churches — and retain them together for life, as above. Notwithstanding etc. With the proviso that the vicarage of Carridin and other incompatible benefices shall not, on this account, be defrauded of due services and the cure of souls in the vicarage and (if any) the other incompatible benefices aforesaid shall not be neglected.

Vite ac morum honestas . . .
· A· de Sancto Severino / · V· / . V. xxxxv. De Phano:

[1] *sic*; *recte*: 'St Andrews'
[2] or *Carinweche*; (?)*Carmweche*, deleted and initialled . *V*., occurs immediately before

249   18 January 1500   *Reg. Lat.* 1060, fos 114ᵛ-117ᵛ

To the prior of the monastery, usually governed by a prior, of Dumgeymin, d. Derry, John Macallan', canon of the church of Raphoe, and the official of Armagh, mandate in favour of Donat Okinaill', cleric, d. Derry. The pope has learned that the rectory

of the parish church of Leaepadrayg, d. Derry, is vacant *certo modo* at present and
has been vacant for so long that by the Lateran statutes its collation has lawfully
devolved on the apostolic see, although Nillanus Okernalan, who bears himself as a
priest, d. Derry, has detained it, without any title or support of law, temerariously and
de facto, for a certain time, as he still does. At a recent petition on Donat's part to the
pope to erect and institute a canonry in the church of Derry and the said rectory
(with the vicarage of the said parish church canonically annexed thereto) into a
simple prebend in the same, for his lifetime, the pope, not having certain knowledge
of the foregoing, hereby commands that the above three (or two or one of them), if,
having summoned Nillanus and as regards the erection the bishop and chapter of
Derry and those interested in the union,[1] they find the rectory, whose annual value
(and that of its annexed vicarage) does not exceed 6 marks sterling, to be vacant
(howsoever etc.) and the foregoing to be true, shall erect and institute a canonry in
the said church of Derry and the rectory (with the vicarage annexed thereto) into a
simple prebend in the same, for Donat's lifetime, without prejudice to anyone, even
if the rectory be specially reserved etc. ; and, in that event, collate and assign the
newly erected canonry and prebend, being vacant, with plenitude of canon law and
all rights and appurtenances, to Donat, inducting him etc. having removed Nillanus
and any other unlawful detainer from the rectory and causing Donat (or his proctor)
to be received as a canon of the church of Derry, with plenitude of canon law, and
the fruits etc., rights and obventions of the canonry and prebend to be delivered to
him. [Curbing] gainsayers by the pope's authority etc. Notwithstanding etc. With the
proviso that the rectory shall not, on this account, be defrauded of due services and
the cure of souls therein shall not be neglected, but that its customary burdens shall
be supported; and that on Donat's death or resignation etc. of the canonry and
prebend this erection and institution shall be extinguished and the rectory shall revert
to its original condition and be deemed vacant automatically.

Apostolice sedis providentia circumspecta ad ea libenter intendit . . .
· *S· de. castello / · V· / . V. xv Decimo Kl' Martii : Anno octavo* [20 February 1500],
Phano -

[1] *sic*; though no act of union is contemplated

250   23 March 1500   *Reg. Lat.* 1060, fos 137ᵛ-140ᵛ

To the abbot of the monastery of B. Mary, *Kyrieleison* [Abbeydorney], and the prior
of the monastery, usually governed by a prior, of B. Mary, Isfahalen, d. Ardfert, and
Donat Makavlly',[1] canon of the church of Cloyne,[2] mandate in favour of John
Yscolay, cleric, d. Cloyne (who, as he asserts, notwithstanding a defect of birth as
the son of a priest and an unmarried woman has been marked with clerical character
otherwise however duly). The pope has learned that the perpetual vicarage of the
parish church of Chilmyny' *alias* Chiltual, d. Ardfert, is vacant *certo modo* at

present and has been vacant for so long that by the Lateran statutes its collation has lawfully devolved on the apostolic see, although Thomas Homana', who bears himself as a cleric or priest, has detained it, without canonical title, for a certain time, but short of a three-year period, as he still does. At a recent petition on John's part to the pope to erect and institute a canonry in the church of Ardfert and the vicarage into a simple prebend in the same, for his lifetime, the pope, not having certain knowledge of the foregoing, hereby commands that the above three (or two or one of them), if, having summoned respectively Thomas and the bishop and chapter of Ardfert and others concerned, they find the vicarage, whose annual value does not exceed 12 marks sterling, to be vacant (howsoever etc.) and the foregoing to be true, shall erect and institute a canonry in the church of Ardfert and the vicarage into a simple prebend in the same, for John's lifetime, without prejudice to anyone, (even if the vicarage is specially reserved etc.); and collate and assign the newly erected canonry and prebend, being vacant, with plenitude of canon law and all rights and appurtenances, to John, inducting him etc. having removed Thomas and any other unlawful detainer from the vicarage and causing John (or his proctor) to be received as a canon of the church of Ardfert, with plenitude of canon law, and the fruits etc., rights and obventions of the canonry and prebend to be delivered to him. [Curbing] gainsayers by the pope's authority etc. Notwithstanding etc. Also the pope dispenses and indulges John to receive and retain the canonry and prebend, if conferred on him by virtue of the presents, and be promoted to all sacred orders, even the priesthood; and the local ordinary to confer them on him, notwithstanding the said defect of birth etc. With the proviso that the vicarage shall not, on account of this erection and institution, be defrauded of due services and the cure of souls therein shall not be neglected; but that its customary burdens shall be supported. The pope's will is, however, that on John's death or resignation etc. of the canonry and prebend this erection and institution and also the canonry and prebend shall be extinguished and so deemed and the vicarage shall revert to its original condition and be deemed vacant automatically.

Piis fidelium votis per que divini cultus augmentum...
· *S· de castello. /. V· /· V·* [3]. *xx. Tertio Id' Aprilis Anno octavo* [11 April 1500], *De Phano:*

[1] the 'v' written over another letter and doubtful

[2] MS here has: *Cloanen.* for 'Clonen.'

[3] *Deci⁰ I*, deleted and initialled . *V.*, occurs here

251   18 March 1500   *Reg. Lat.* 1060, fos 140ᵛ-143ᵛ

To the abbot of the monastery *de Fontevivo* [Abbeymahon], the prior of the monastery, usually governed by a prior, of B. Mary, Ross (*de̓ Rosso̓*),[1] d. Ross, and the official of Ross, mandate in favour of Thady Yhedriscoll', cleric, d. Ross. The pope has learned that a canonry of the church of Ross and the prebend of Criach in the same and also the perpetual vicarage of the parish church of Tolach, d. Ross, which are of lay patronage, and the rectory of the said church of Tolach, (in an ecclesiastical fief), are vacant *certo modo* at present and have been vacant for so long that by the Lateran statutes their collation has lawfully devolved on the apostolic see. At a recent petition on Thady's part to the pope to unite etc. the rectory and vicarage to the canonry and prebend — after provision of the canonry and prebend is made to him — for as long as Thady holds them, the pope, not having certain knowledge of the foregoing, hereby commands that the above three, or two or one of them, in person or by proxy, having summoned those interested in the union, shall inform themselves as to the foregoing and, if they find it to be thus, shall collate and assign, with plenitude of canon law, the canonry and prebend, whose annual value does not exceed 10 marks sterling, to Thady, and unite etc. the rectory and vicarage,[2] whose annual value together does not exceed 24 marks sterling, vacant howsoever etc., even if specially reserved etc., with all rights and appurtenances, to the canonry and prebend, for as long as Thady holds the canonry and prebend, inducting Thady (or his proctor) into corporal possession of the canonry and prebend and of the rectory and vicarage to be annexed thereto and of the rights and appurtenances aforesaid etc. having removed any unlawful detainers and causing Thady (or his proctor) to be received as a canon of the said church of Ross, with plenitude of canon law, and the fruits etc., rights and obventions of the canonry and prebend and of the rectory and vicarage to be annexed to be delivered to him. [Curbing] gainsayers by the pope's authority etc. Notwithstanding etc. The pope's will is, however, that the rectory and vicarage shall not, on account of this union etc., be defrauded of due services and the cure of souls therein shall not be neglected, but that their customary burdens shall be supported; and that on Thady's death or resignation etc. of the canonry and prebend the union etc. shall be dissolved and the rectory and vicarage shall revert to their original condition and be deemed vacant automatically.

Decet Romanum pontificem votis illis gratum prestare assensum...
· *S· de castello /· V· / V· xxij Sep.^{mo} Id' Aprilis Anno octavo* [7 April 1500], *De Phano:*

[1] the points occur thus in MS

[2] *rectoriam et vicarias*; *recte*: 'rectoriam et vicariam'

252   3 April 1500[1]   *Reg. Lat.* 1060, fos 143^V-147^V

To the prior of the monastery, usually governed by a prior, of B Mary,[2] Ross (*de ·Rosso·*),[3] d. Ross, and Maurice Horga and John Condon, canons of the church of Ross, mandate in favour of Cormac Makryg,[4] cleric, d. Cork. A recent petition to the pope on Cormac's part stated that some time ago he did not — while peacefully holding the perpetual vicarage of the parish church of Rygne, d. Cork, which was canonically collated to him while vacant *certo modo*, and peacefully possessing it for a year and more — on the ceasing of a lawful impediment and having obtained no dispensation in this regard, have himself promoted to the priesthood, and he detained the vicarage after the year had passed, without any title newly acquired, for months more, as he does at present, albeit *de facto*, receiving fruits etc. from it, but not more than 3 gold ducats of the camera; that the vicarage, through this lack of promotion, and, as the pope has learned, a canonry of the church of Cork and the prebend of Ryllrogan[5] in the same and the rectory of the parish church of Gauryno, said diocese, which is of lay patronage, are vacant *certo modo* at present and the canonry and prebend and rectory have been vacant for so long that by the Lateran statutes their collation has lawfully devolved on the apostolic see, although Dermot Omothuna and Thady Omorchu have detained the canonry and prebend, dividing the fruits between themselves, and Donat Mackellay, the rectory — bearing themselves as clerics — without any title or support of law, temerariously and *de facto*, for a certain time, as they still do; and, furthermore, that if the rectory and vicarage were to be united etc. to the canonry and prebend, after provision of the latter be made to Cormac, for his lifetime, it would be to his benefit. The pope — rehabilitating Cormac on account of all disability and infamy arising from the foregoing and not having certain knowledge of the foregoing — hereby commands that the above three (or two or one of them), if, having summoned respectively Dermot and Thady, Donat and other interested parties, they find the canonry and prebend, whose annual value does not exceed 12, and the vicarage and rectory, whose annual value together does not exceed 22, marks sterling, to be vacant (whether the vicarage be vacant as above, or it, the canonry and prebend and the rectory be vacant howsoever etc.) and the foregoing regarding the union etc. to be true, shall collate and assign the canonry and prebend to Cormac, and also unite etc. the vicarage and rectory (even if the vicarage has been vacant for so long that by the Lateran statutes its collation has lawfully devolved on the apostolic see, and it, the canonry and prebend and the rectory be specially reserved etc.) to the canonry and prebend, for Cormac's lifetime, with plenitude of canon law and all rights and appurtenances, inducting him etc. having removed Dermot and Thady from the canonry and prebend, Donat from the rectory and any other unlawful detainers from them and the vicarage and causing Cormac (or his proctor) to be received as a canon of Cork, with plenitude of canon law, and the fruits etc., rights and obventions of the canonry and prebend and of the rectory and vicarage to be annexed thereto to be delivered to him. [Curbing] gainsayers by the pope's authority etc. Notwithstanding etc. With the proviso that the rectory and vicarage shall not, on account of this union etc., be defrauded of due services and the cure of souls therein shall not be neglected; but that their customary burdens shall be supported. The pope's will is, however, that on Cormac's death or resignation etc. of the canonry and prebend this union etc. shall be dissolved and so deemed and the vicarage and rectory shall revert to their original condition and be deemed vacant automatically; and that before the above shall proceed to the execution of the presents in any way Cormac is bound to resign the vicarage into their hands (or those of one[6] of them) completely.

Sedes apostolica pia manter[7] recurrentibus ad eam post excessum cum humilitate...

. S. de Castello /· V· / V· xxx. [8] *De Phano:*

[1] *quadringentesimo nonagesimo nono,* deleted and initialled *V* twice, occurs directly after *millesimo* and before *quingentesimo*

[2] *Beate Marie de* inserted in the margin initialled *.V.*

[3] *sic; cf.* previous entry (esp. for the points)

[4] the 'r' overwritten and doubtful

[5] apparently changed (by deletion) from *Rylyrogan*

[6] *in manibus vestris vel alterius vestrum;* though three mandataries are named in the address clause

[7] *sic; recte:* 'mater'

[8] wants expedition date?

253   20 February 1500   *Reg. Lat.* 1060, fos 153[r]-155[v]

To Odo Ocayllt, Eugene Ohegertay and Donald Otugayll', canons of the church of Derry, mandate in favour of William Ohenahaga, priest, d. Derry. The pope has learned that the rectory of the parish church of Bengor, d. Derry, is vacant *certo modo* at present and has been vacant for so long that by the Lateran statutes its collation has lawfully devolved on the apostolic see, although Patrick Macconagaland, who bears himself as a priest, has detained it with no title, at least not a canonical one, for a certain time, but short of a year[1], as he does. At a recent petition on William's part to the pope to unite etc. the perpetual vicarage of the church of Bengor, which he holds, to the above rectory, for as long as he holds the rectory, if conferred on him by virtue of the presents — asserting that the annual value of the rectory does not exceed 3, and of the vicarage, also 3, marks sterling — the pope hereby commands that the above three (or two or one of them), if, having summoned Patrick and those interested in the union and others concerned, they find the rectory to be vacant (howsoever etc.) shall collate and assign it (even if specially reserved etc.) to William, and unite etc. the vicarage to it, with all rights and appurtenances, for as long as William holds the rectory, inducting him etc. having removed Patrick and any other unlawful detainer from the rectory and causing William (or his proctor) to be admitted to the rectory and its fruits etc., rights and obventions and those of the vicarage to be delivered to him. [Curbing] gainsayers by the pope's authority etc. Notwithstanding etc. The pope's will is, however, that the vicarage shall not, through this union etc., be defrauded of due services and the cure of souls therein shall not be neglected, but that its customary burdens shall be supported; and that on William's death or resignation etc. of the rectory the union etc. shall be dissolved and the vicarage[2] shall revert to its original condition and thereby be deemed vacant automatically.

Apostolice sedis providentia circumspecta ad ea libenter intendit...
Jo. ortega /. V· / V· xx [3] *De Phano:*

[1] *unum,* deleted and initialled *.V.,* occurs between *citra tamen* and *annum*

2 *sic*; though, above, he holds the vicarage

3 wants expedition date?

254   15 March 1500   *Reg. Lat.* 1060, fos 155ᵛ-158ʳ

To the abbot of the monastery of Tracton (*de Albetrattu*),¹ d. Cork, and Maurice Ohega and Maurice Ocullynayn, canons of the church of Ross, mandate in favour of John Omurrale, canon of the church of Cork. The pope has learned that the perpetual vicarage of the parish church of Curstrahura, d. Cork, is vacant *certo modo* at present and has been vacant for so long that by the Lateran statutes its collation has lawfully devolved on the apostolic see, although Runaldus² Orygayn, who bears himself as a priest, has detained it, without any title or support of law, temerariously and *de facto*, for a certain time, as he still does. At a recent petition on John's part to the pope to unite etc. the said vicarage to the canonry and prebend of the church of Cork which he holds, for as long as he does so — asserting that the annual value of the vicarage does not exceed 6, and of the canonry and prebend, also 6, marks sterling — the pope, not having certain knowledge of the foregoing, hereby commands that the above three (or two or one of them), if, having summoned Runaldus and others concerned, they find the vicarage to be vacant (howsoever etc.) and the foregoing to be true, shall unite etc. it (even if specially reserved etc.), with all rights and appurtenances, to the canonry and prebend, for John's lifetime, to the effect that — having removed Runaldus and any other unlawful detainer — John may, on his own authority, in person or by proxy, take and retain corporal possession of the vicarage, for as long as he holds the canonry and prebend, and convert its fruits etc. to his own uses and those of the canonry and prebend and the vicarage without licence of the local diocesan or of anyone else. Notwithstanding etc. The pope's will is, however, that the vicarage shall not, on account of this union etc., be defrauded of due services and the cure of souls therein shall not be neglected, but that its customary burdens shall be supported; and that on John's death or resignation etc. of the canonry and prebend the union etc. shall be dissolved and so deemed and the vicarage shall revert to its original condition and be deemed vacant automatically.

Decet Romanum pontificem votis illis gratum prestare assensum...
. S· de castello /· V· /· V· xij·. De Phano :

1 inserted in the margin initialled *.V.* ; (?)*Albetorattu*, deleted and initialled *.V* in the line

2 also spelt *Renaldus, Ranoldus*

255   17 March¹ 1500   *Reg. Lat.* 1060, fos 158ʳ-161ᵛ

To Maurice Ohega, Maurice Ocullenayn and John Condum, canons of the church of

Ross, mandate in favour of William Yeronyn, cleric, d. Cork (who, some time ago, as he asserts, after he had been marked — notwithstanding a defect of birth as the son of a priest and an unmarried woman — with clerical character otherwise however duly, was dispensed by apostolic authority to be promoted to all, even sacred, orders and to hold a benefice, even if it should have cure of souls). The pope has learned that the churches, called the particles, of Cornacrusi [also spelt *Cornacrusy, Cortuacsy, Gortuacsy, Cornacucy*[2] *Cortiacrusy, Comacruci*] and Balymmolann [also spelt *Balymmolayn, Balymnolayn, Ballymmolayn*[3] *Belymmolayn, Balymamolayn*[4]], and the rectory of the parish church of Treve, d. Cork, which are of lay patronage, are vacant *certo modo* at present and have been vacant for so long that by the Lateran statutes their collation has lawfully devolved on the apostolic see, although Donat Offyllyg [also spelt *Affyllyg', Offyllyg'*] — bearing himself as a priest — has detained the rectory and the church of Cornacrusi, and John Cursy [and] Donat Omongayn — bearing themselves as clerics — the church of Balymmolann, taking the fruits out of them, as whichever of them is able, without any title or support of law, temerariously and *de facto*, for a certain time, as they still do. At a recent petition on William's part to the pope to erect and institute a canonry in the church of Cork and the church of Cornacrusi into a simple prebend in the same, for his lifetime, and unite etc. to them, after they should be erected, the church of Balymmolann and the rectory, also for his lifetime, the pope, not having certain knowledge of the foregoing, hereby commands that the above three (or two or one of them), if, having summoned respectively the bishop and chapter of Cork and Donat Offyllyg, John and Donat Omongayn and other interested parties, they find the rectory, whose annual value does not exceed 12, and [the churches] of Cornacrusi [and Balymmolann], which are without cure, whose annual value does not exceed $1\frac{1}{2}$, and 1, marks sterling, to be vacant (howsoever etc.) and the foregoing to be true, shall erect and institute a canonry in the church of Cork and [the church] of Cornacrusi into a simple prebend in the same, for William's lifetime, without prejudice to anyone; collate and assign the newly erected canonry and prebend, being vacant, to William, with plenitude of canon law; and unite etc., with all rights and appurtenances, the rectory and the church of Balymmolann (even if it and the rectory and the church of Cornacrusi be specially reserved etc.) to the erected canonry and prebend, for William's lifetime, inducting him etc. having removed Donat Offyllyg from the rectory and the church of Cornacrusi and John and Donat Omongayn from the church of Balymmolann and any other unlawful detainers and causing William (or his proctor) to be received as a canon of Cork, with plenitude of canon law, and the fruits etc., rights and obventions of the canonry and prebend and of the rectory and the church of Balymmolann to be annexed to them to be delivered to him. [Curbing] gainsayers by the pope's authority etc. Notwithstanding etc. Also the pope dispenses William to receive and retain the canonry and prebend, if conferred on him by virtue of the presents, notwithstanding the said defect of birth etc. With the proviso that the churches of Cornacrusi and Balymmolann and the rectory shall not, on account of this union etc., erection and institution, be defrauded of due services and the cure of souls in the rectory shall not be neglected; but that its customary burdens and those of the said churches shall be supported. The pope's will is, however, that on William's death or resignation etc. of the canonry and prebend the union etc. shall be dissolved and the erection and institution extinguished and so deemed and the rectory and the said churches shall revert to their original condition and be deemed vacant automatically.

Piis fidelium votis per que divini cultus augumentum...
. S· de. castello /· V· | V xxv⁵ De Phano:

¹ *kalendas Aprilis* has been reworked

² uncertain reading (esp. last three letters)

³ the 'B' has been reworked

⁴ the second 'a' is uncertain and may be deleted

⁵ wants expedition date?

256   15 March 1500   *Reg. Lat.* 1060, fos 166ᵛ-169ʳ

To the abbot of the monastery *de Fontevivo* [Abbeymahon], the prior of the monastery of B. Mary the Virgin, usually governed by a prior, d. Ross, and Thady Makaryg, canon of the church of Cork, mandate in favour of Donald Ygonayn, cleric, d. Ross. The pope has learned that a canonry of the church of Ross and the prebend of Cirrogayn¹ in the same and the perpetual vicarages of the parish churches of Insula (?)Ynmdemy and of Kylle,² d. Ross, are vacant *certo modo* at present and have been vacant for so long that by the Lateran statutes their collation has lawfully devolved on the apostolic see, although Odo Ohega, who bears himself as a cleric, has detained them without any title or support of law, temerariously and *de facto,* for a certain time, as he still does. At a recent petition on Donald's part to the pope to unite etc. the vicarages to the canonry and prebend, for his lifetime, if the canonry and prebend should be conferred on him — asserting that the annual value of the canonry and prebend and of one of the vicarages and half the other together does not exceed 8 marks sterling — the pope, not having certain knowledge of the foregoing, hereby commands that the above three (or two or one of them), if, having summoned Odo and others interested, they find the canonry and prebend and the vicarages to be vacant (howsoever etc.) and the foregoing to be true, shall collate and assign the canonry and prebend to Donald, with plenitude of canon law, and unite etc. the vicarages, with all rights and appurtenances (even if they and the canonry and prebend be specially reserved etc.) to the canonry and prebend, for Donald's lifetime, inducting him etc. into corporal possession of the canonry and prebend and the vicarages to be annexed thereto and of the rights and appurtenances aforesaid, having removed Odo and any other unlawful detainers, and causing Donald (or his proctor) to be received as a canon of the church of Ross, with plenitude of canon law, and the fruits etc., rights and obventions of the canonry and prebend and of the vicarages to be annexed to be delivered to him. [Curbing] gainsayers by the pope's authority etc. Notwithstanding etc. The pope's will is, however, that the vicarages shall not, on account of this union etc., be defrauded of due services and the cure of souls therein shall not be neglected, but that their customary burdens shall be supported; and that on Donald's death or resignation etc. of the canonry and prebend the union etc. shall be dissolved and the vicarages shall revert to their original condition and be deemed vacant automatically.

Decet Romanum pontificem votis illis gratum prestare assensum...
. *S. de. Castello. |· V· |. V. xx Pridie Non' Aprilis Anno Octavo* [4 April 1500], *De Phano:*

[1] or possibly *T-*
[2] or possibly *Rylle*

257   24 March 1500   *Reg. Lat.* 1060, fos 215[r]-218[r]

To the abbots of the monastery *de Antro Sancti Fimbarri* [Gill Abbey], and of B. Mary, *de Fontevivo* [Abbeymahon] and the prior of the monastery, usually governed by a prior, of B. Mary, Ros, ds. Cork and Ross, mandate in favour of Thady Machareyg, cleric, said diocese [of Cork], (who asserts that he is of noble birth by both parents and is studying canon law (*in decretis*)). The pope has learned that the archdeaconry of the church of Ross and a canonry and the prebend of Drongaleyg of the church of Cork and the rectory in the ecclesiastical fief and the perpetual vicarage of the parish church of Scoll', d. Cork, are vacant *certis modis* at present and have been vacant for so long that by the Lateran statutes their collation has lawfully devolved on the apostolic see, although John Ohedriscoll' has detained the archdeaconry, Renaldus Omurchele the canonry and prebend, and David Oniahuna[1] the rectory — bearing themselves as clerics — and Cornelius Oskanlay', who bears himself as a priest, the vicarage, with no canonical title, for a certain time, but short of a three-year period, as they do. At a recent petition on Thady's part to the pope to unite etc. the rectory and vicarage to the archdeaconry, for as long as Thady holds the archdeaconry, if conferred on him by virtue of the presents — asserting that the annual value of the archdeaconry does not exceed 30, of the canonry and prebend, 16, and of the rectory and vicarage, 36, marks sterling — the pope hereby commands that the above three (or two or one of them), if, having summoned John, Renaldus, David and Cornelius and others concerned, they find the archdeaconry (which is a non-major dignity *post pontificalem*), canonry and prebend, rectory and vicarage to be vacant (howsoever etc.) and, [having summoned] those interested in the vicarage, the foregoing to be true, (even if they are specially reserved etc.), shall collate and assign the archdeaconry and the canonry and prebend to Thady, and unite etc., the rectory and vicarage to the archdeaconry, for as long as he holds the archdeaconry, if conferred on him as above, with all rights and appurtenances, inducting Thady (or his proctor) into corporal possession of the archdeaconry, canonry and prebend and [the rectory and vicarage] to be annexed and the rights and appurtenances aforesaid, having removed John, Renaldus, David and Cornelius from them respectively and any other unlawful detainers and causing Thady (or his proctor) to be received as a canon of the church of Cork, with plenitude of canon law, and also be admitted to the archdeaconry, rectory and vicarage and their fruits etc., rights and obventions and those of the canonry and prebend to be delivered to him. [Curbing] gainsayers by the pope's authority etc. Notwithstanding etc. The pope's will is, however, that the rectory and vicarage shall not, on account of this union etc., be defrauded of due services and the cure of souls therein shall not be neglected, but that their customary burdens shall be supported; and that on Thady's death or resignation etc. of the archdeaconry the union etc. shall be dissolved and the rectory and vicarage shall revert to their original condition automatically.

Apostolice sedis providentia circumspecta ad ea libenter intendit...
A de sancto severino[2] /. *V· /· V· xxx* [3] *De Phano:*

[1] the 'i' is dotted; for 'Omahuna'?

[2] in darker ink, perhaps not in hand of enregistering scribe (Damiani); *A de Sancto Severino* (shaved horizontally and mostly lost) written in Damiani's hand above it (in similar ink to that of the entry)

[3] wants expedition date?

258   4 April 1500[1]   *Reg. Lat.* 1060, fos 221ʳ-224ᵛ

To the treasurer of the church of Ross, mandate in favour of Thady Mackaryg, cleric, d. Cork (who, as he asserts, is of noble birth and in his seventeenth year of age or thereabouts and presently studying canon law). The pope has learned that the deanery of the church of Cork and the rectories (which are of lay patronage) of the parish churches of Ractareyn and Baryn, d. Cork, are vacant *certo modo* at present and have been vacant for so long that by the Lateran statutes their collation has lawfully devolved on the apostolic see, although Matthew Omahuna, who bears himself as a priest, [?and] John Oherlay, as a cleric, have detained the deanery, unlawfully occupied,[2] dividing its[3] fruits between themselves, without any title or support of law, temerariously and *de facto*, for a certain time, as they do at present. At a recent petition on Thady's part to the pope to unite etc. the rectories to the deanery, after provision of the deanery is made to him, for his lifetime, the pope, not having certain knowledge of the foregoing, hereby commands the above treasurer, if, having summoned respectively Matthew and John and others concerned, he finds the deanery (which is a major dignity *post pontificalem*, whose annual value does not exceed 24 marks sterling) and the rectories (whose annual value together does not exceed 17 marks sterling) to be vacant (howsoever etc.) and, having summoned those interested in the union etc., the foregoing to be true, and through diligent examination — concerning which the pope burdens the treasurer's conscience — Thady to be suitable in other respects, to collate and assign the deanery to him and unite etc. the rectories to the deanery (even if the deanery, as a major dignity, be generally reserved or it and the rectories be specially reserved, etc.), for Thady's lifetime, with all rights and appurtenances, inducting him etc. — having first received from him the oath of fealty to the pope and the Roman church in accordance with the form which the pope sends enclosed under his *bulla* — having removed Matthew and John from the deanery[4] and any other unlawful detainers from it and the [rectories][5] and causing Thady (or his proctor) to be admitted to the deanery and the fruits etc., rights and obventions [of the deanery and rectories][6] to be delivered to him. [Curbing] gainsayers by the pope's authority etc. Notwithstanding etc. Also the pope dispenses Thady to receive and retain the deanery, if conferred on him by virtue of the presents, notwithstanding the said defect of age etc. With the proviso that the deanery and rectories shall not, on this account, be defrauded of due services and the cure of souls in the deanery (if any) shall not be neglected; but that its customary burdens and those of the rectories shall be supported. The pope's will is, however, that on Thady's death or resignation etc. of the deanery the union etc. shall be dissolved and so deemed and the rectories shall revert to their original condition and be deemed vacant automatically. And the pope has commanded that provision of the deanery be made to Thady, if found suitable, from the date of the presents.

Ex iniuncto nobis desuper apostolice servitutis officio ad ea libenter intendimus...
. S· de. castello /. V· / V. xxxx Deci(m)o Octavo kl' Maii Anno octavo [14 April 1500], *de[7] Phano:*

[1] after *quingentesimo, nonagesimo* deleted, initialled *.V.* twice

[2] *occupatos*; *recte*: 'occupatum'? The plural case is inappropriate here (unless, of course, 'rectorie' omitted [but *cf.* notes 3 and 4])

[3] *sic*; *cf.* note 2

[4] no mention of John and/or Matthew needing to be removed from the rectories; *cf.* note 2

[5] *rectorie*; *recte*: 'rectoriis'

[6] *illorum*

[7] *sic*; usually 'De'

259   29 June 1500   *Reg. Lat.* 1060, fos 279[v]-282[r]

To Bernard Macbloshayd, canon of the church of Derry, mandate in favour of Donat Okahan, cleric, d. Derry (who, as he asserts, notwithstanding a defect of birth as the son of a cleric of noble birth and an unmarried woman, and that he is in his twentieth year of age, has been marked with clerical character, otherwise however duly). The pope has learned that [the monastery][1] of Machoskan *alias de Clarofonte*, OCist, d. Derry, is vacant *certo modo* at present and has been vacant for so long that in accordance with institutions of the sacred canons[2] its provision has lawfully devolved on the apostolic see, although John Machayg, who bears himself as a monk of the monastery, has detained it without any title or support of law, temerariously and *de facto*, for a certain time, as he still does. Wishing to encourage Donat — who, as he asserts, wishes to enter the monastery, under the regular habit — and to make provision of a capable and suitable person to the monastery to rule and direct it, the pope, not having certain knowledge of Donat's merits and suitability, hereby commands the above canon, if, having summoned John and others concerned, he finds the monastery, whose annual value does not exceed 8 marks sterling, to be vacant (howsoever etc., and for whatever reason its disposition pertains generally or specially to the apostolic see, etc.), to receive Donat — if he is suitable and there is no canonical obstacle — as a monk in the said monastery and bestow the regular habit on him in accordance with the custom of the monastery, and cause him to be given charitable treatment therein; and, if Donat expressly wishes to make the usual regular profession made by the monks, receive and admit it; and, thereafter, inform himself as to Donat's merits etc. and if he finds him to be capable and suitable for the rule and administration of the monastery — concerning which the pope burdens the canon's conscience — make provision of Donat to the monastery (to which this day the pope has granted that the rectory of the parish church of Drondarsi, d. Derry, vacant *certo modo* and whose annual value does not exceed 2 like marks, be united etc. for Donat's lifetime), and appoint him abbot, committing to him the care, rule and administration of the monastery in spiritualities and temporalities, and causing obedience and reverence to be given him by the convent and customary services and rights by the vassals and other subjects of the monastery. Curbing gainsayers by the pope's authority etc. Notwithstanding etc. Also the pope grants that Donat may, if provision of him to the monastery be made by virtue of the presents, receive benediction from any catholic bishop of his choice in communion with the apostolic see, and that the bishop concerned [may] impart it to him; and dispenses Donat, if he be provided and appointed as abbot, to perform and exercise the care etc. of the monastery; notwithstanding the said defects of birth and age, etc. With the proviso that divine worship and the usual number of ministers in the monastery shall not be diminished; but that its customary burdens shall be supported.

Apostolice sedis circumspecta benignitas cupientibus vitam ducere regularem...
. *S. de Castello /. L. /. L. xxxv Tertiodecimo kl' Augusti Anno Octavo* [20 July 1500], *Dulcius*

[1] 'monasterium' here wanting

[2] *iuxta sacrorum canonum institutiones*

260   19 March 1500   *Reg. Lat.* 1061, fo 1^{r-v}

To William Gilberd, prior of the priory of B. Mary, Bruton', OSA, d. Bath and Wells. Dispensation — at his supplication — to receive and retain for life *in commendam*, together with the above priory, any other secular benefice, with cure or otherwise incompatible, or a regular, with or without cure, of the aforesaid or any other order, even if the secular benefice should be a parish church or its perpetual vicarage, or a chantry, free chapel, hospital or annual service, usually assigned to secular clerics in title of a perpetual ecclesiastical benefice, or the regular benefice be a priory, *prepositura*, dignity, *personatus*, administration or office, customarily elective and with cure of souls, if he obtains it otherwise canonically, to [resign it and] cede the commend as often as he pleases, and in its place receive another, similar or dissimilar, secular benefice, with cure or otherwise incompatible, or a regular, with or without cure, of the aforesaid or any other order and — provided that such regular benefice held *in commendam* be not a conventual priory, *prepositura* or other conventual dignity or a claustral office — retain it *in commendam* for life, as above; (he may — due and customary burdens of the benefice retained *in commendam* having been supported — make disposition of the rest of its fruits etc. just as those holding it *in titulum* could and ought to do, alienation of immovable goods and precious movables being however forbidden). Notwithstanding etc. With the proviso that the secular or regular benefice retained *in commendam* shall not, on this account, be defrauded of due services and the cure of souls therein (if any) shall not be neglected; but that its aforesaid burdens shall be supported.

Religionis zelus, vite ac morum honestas...
F. de parma /· V· / V· xxxxv· De Phano:

261   20 May 1500   *Reg. Lat.* 1061, fos 39^v-40^r

To the bishops of Lincoln and Rochester, mandate in favour of Alice Chester, woman, d. London. A recent petition to the pope on Alice's part stated that, formerly, overcome by such fear and force as was capable of overcoming a steadfast woman, she contracted marriage *per verba de presenti*, albeit *de facto*, with Thomas Aderei, layman, d. London, and afterwards, as soon as she could, when the force and fear had stopped, she cried out against the marriage, and has never willingly consented to it, nor by deed, sign, or a nod, considered it valid; and that because Edward Vaughn, official of London, (before whom Alice had prayed that Thomas be summoned to trial, the marriage be declared null, and she be granted licence of contracting marriage with another man), unlawfully refused, after it had been demanded of him many times, to see Alice and administer justice in her case, she appealed to the apostolic see. At Alice's supplication to the pope to commit to some upright men in those parts the cases of her appeal, of everything perchance attempted and innovated after and against it, and of the principal matter, the pope hereby commands that the above two (or one of them), having summoned Thomas and others concerned, and having heard both sides, taking cognizance even of the principal matter, shall decree what is canonical, without appeal, causing by ecclesiastical censure what they have decreed to be strictly observed. Notwithstanding etc.

Humilibus et cetera.
L· puccius /· V· /· V· xij· De Phano

262   19 March 1500   *Reg. Lat.* 1061, fos 48ᵛ-50ʳ

To John Oxenbregge, LLB, perpetual vicar of the parish church of Columpton', d. [Exeter],[1] dispensation and indult. Some time ago, the pope by other letters of his dispensed him to receive and retain together for life any two benefices, with cure or otherwise mutually incompatible, etc. [as above, no. 131, to '... as is more fully contained in those letters'].[2] The pope — at his supplication — hereby dispenses John further and indulges him, who, as he asserts, holds the perpetual vicarages of the parish churches of Columpton', d. Exeter, and Ickyllyscham', d. Chichester, by the said dispensation, to receive and retain, also for life, together with the said vicarages, or without them, with any two other incompatible benefices held by him at the time by the said dispensation, any third benefice, etc. [as above, no. 131, to '... retain it for life, as above']; and, also for life, while attending a *studium generale*, not to be bound to reside personally in any one of the benefices held by him at the time, nor to be liable to be compelled by anyone to do so against his will. Notwithstanding etc. With the proviso that this third incompatible benefice shall not, on this account, be defrauded of due services and the cure of souls therein (if any) shall not be neglected, but that in the vicarages and the third incompatible benefice the cure shall, on account of this concession, be exercised and things divine be served by good and sufficient vicars maintained from the proceeds of these benefices.

Litterarum scientia, vite ac morum honestas...
C· de Scoractis[3] */. V· / V· Lxxx De Phano:*

[1] *Oxonien.* ; hereafter (correctly) 'Exonien.'

[2] summarised in *CPL*, XVI at no. 526

[3] *sic*; for 'Scorciatis'; the hand is not that of the enregistering scribe; entered later?

263   11 February 1500   *Reg. Lat.* 1061, fo 89ʳ⁻ᵛ

To Richard Brokysby, rector of the parish [church][1] of Bradley, d. Norwich. Dispensation

— at his supplication — to receive and retain for life, together with the above parish church, one, and without it, any <two>[2] other benefices, etc. [as above, no. 3].

Vite ac morum honestas...
Bregeon[3] */· V· / V· L· De Phano:*

[1] 'ecclesie' does not occur

[2] marginal insertion, initialled *.V.* ; *cf.* below, no. 265

[3] *sic*; *.V.* and *Bregeon* are written in a lighter ink than the entry beneath

264   5 October 1499   *Reg. Lat.* 1061, fo 106[r-v]

To Thomas Buttler *alias* Berkeley, monk of the monastery of Hyde (*de Hyda*), OSB, d. Winchester. Dispensation and indult — at his supplication — to receive and retain any benefice, with or without cure, usually held by secular clerics, even if a parish church etc. [as above, no. 32, to '... similar or dissimilar, benefice, with or without cure'], usually assigned to secular clerics; and, also for life, to bear the regular habit usually worn by monks of the above monastery, OSB, of whose number he is and is, as he asserts, expressly professed of that order, under the robe (*toga*) of a secular priest, of an honest and decent colour. Notwithstanding etc.

Religionis zelus, vite ac morum honestas...
Jo ortega / V / V· xxx De Phano:

265   11 February 1500   *Reg. Lat.* 1061, fo 122[r-v]

To Edward Haseley, rector of the parish church of Marteley, d. Worcester. Dispensation — at his supplication — to receive and retain for life, together with the above parish church, one, and without it, any [two][1] other benefices, etc. [as above, no. 3].

Vite ac morum honestas...
· P· de Castello /· V· / V· L· De Phano:

[1] MS wants 'duo'; *cf.* no. 263

266   19 March 1500   *Reg. Lat.* 1061, fos 153[v]-154[r]

To William Stokefish, perpetual vicar of the parish church of Kenton', d. Exeter.

Dispensation — at his supplication — to receive and retain for life, together with the perpetual vicarage of the above parish church, one, and without it, any two other benefices, etc. [as above, no. 3].

Vite ac morum honestas...
· *L· Puccius* |· *V·* [1] / *V· L· De Phano:*

[1] there is a point within the 'V' as well

267   20 January 1500   *Reg. Lat.* 1061, fo 162[r-v]

To Thomas Cherell, prior of the priory of St Carrok, OClun, d. Exeter. Dispensation and indult — at his supplication — to him, who, as he asserts, holds the above priory, which is a dependency of the monastery of Bs. Peter and Paul, OClun, d. Bath and Wells, of which he is a monk and, as he also asserts, expressly professed of the order, to receive and retain, (?)without[1] the said priory, any benefice, with or without cure, usually held by secular clerics, even if a parish church[2] or its perpetual vicarage, etc. [as above, no. 32, to '... usually held by secular clerics']; and also, even after he has acquired the benefice, to have a stall in the choir and a voice in the chapter of the said monastery. Notwithstanding etc.[3]

Religionis zelus, vite ac morum honestas...
ortega[4] |· *V·* |· *V· xxx*[5] *De Phano:*

[1] MS: *sine* [!]

[2] *parochiales ecclesie; recte*: 'parochialis ecclesia'

[3] *Proviso quod beneficium huiusmodi debitis propterea non fraudetur obsequiis et animarum cura,* deleted and initialled *V* twice, occurs after *indulgemus.*

[4] *sic* : 'Jo.' does not occur; *L puccius* (in a lighter ink) deleted, above it

[5] the first 'x' looks as though it may have been added later

268   20 January 1500   *Reg. Lat.* 1061, fos 162[v]-163[r]

To William Wode, canon of the monastery of the Holy Trinity, Mycchylh(a)m[1] [also spelt *Micchilh(a)m*], OSA, d. Chichester. Dispensation — at his supplication — to him, who, as he asserts, is expressly professed of the above order,[2] to receive and retain any benefice, with or without cure, usually held by secular clerics, etc. [as above, no. 32].

Religionis zelus, vite ac morum honestas...
Ortega[3] |· *V·* |· *V· xxx De Phano:*

¹ MS: *Mycchylhm'*; also: *Micchilhm'*

² This information comes from a notwithstanding clause.

³ *sic*: 'Jo.' does not occur

269   28 January 1500   *Reg. Lat.* 1061, fos 165^r-166^r

To Robert Dussyng, MA, rector of the parish church of Wykmer, d. Norwich.
Dispensation — at his supplication — to receive and retain for life, together with the
above parish church, one, and without it, any two other benefices, etc. [as above, no. 3].

Litterarum scientia, vite ac morum honestas...
C· de Scorciat' /. V· / V· L· De Phano:

270   20 January 1500   *Reg. Lat.* 1061, fos 167^v-169^r

Union etc. At a petition¹ on the part of John Nabbos, rector of the parish church of
Warton, d. *Floracen.*,² the pope hereby unites etc. the parish church of Bury, d.
Coventry and Lichfield, (whose annual value does not exceed 20 marks sterling,
equivalent to 56 gold florins of the camera or thereabouts) to the above church of
Warton, which he holds together by apostolic dispensation, for as long as he holds
that of Warton, to the effect that John, in person or by proxy, may, on his own
authority, take and retain corporal possession of the church of Bury and its rights and
appurtenances, for as long as he holds the church of Warton, and convert its fruits
etc. to his own uses and those of the said churches without licence of the local
diocesan or of anyone else. Notwithstanding etc. The pope's will is, however, that
the church of Bury shall not, on account of this union etc., be defrauded of due
services and the cure of souls therein shall not be neglected, but that its customary
burdens shall be supported; and that on John's death or resignation etc. of the church
of Warton the union etc. shall be dissolved and the church of Bury shall revert to its
original condition and be deemed vacant automatically.

Ad futuram rei memoriam. Ex iniuncto nobis desuper apostolice servitutis officio ad
ea libenter intendimus...
Jo ortega /· V· /· V· xxxv De Phano:

¹ 'nobis nuper exhibita' does not occur

² *recte*: 'Eboracen.' (York)?

271   31 January 1500   *Reg. Lat.* 1061, fos 169^r-170^v

To John <Alam>,[1] perpetual vicar of the parish church of (St)[2] Werburgh in Hoo (*Sancti Werburge in Hoo*),[3] d. Rochester, dispensation. Some time ago, Sixtus IV by his letters dispensed him to receive and retain for life, together with the perpetual vicarage of the parish church of St Nicholas, Westgoynewich' *alias* Depfford, d. Rochester, (which, as he asserted, he was then holding), one other, and without it, any two other benefices, etc. [as above, no. 131, to '... as is more fully contained in those letters']. The pope — at his supplication — hereby dispenses John who, as he also asserts, having resigned the vicarage of St Nicholas, acquired the perpetual vicarage of the above parish church of St Werburgh and the mastership of the college of Cobh(a)m,[4] said d. Rochester,[5] (in which several secular clerics are known to be associating together in a college, whose mastership is indeed, according to the college's statutes and foundation, incompatible with any other incompatible benefice), which were canonically collated to him while vacant *certo modo*, and holds them at present, to receive and [retain][6] for life, together with the above mastership and the vicarage of St Werburgh, and without them, with any two other incompatible benefices which he is dispensed to hold together as above, any third benefice, etc. [as above, no. 131].

Vite ac morum honestas...
S· de Castello /. V· /· V·· Lxx De Phano:-

[1] marginal insertion, initialled .V.

[2] *Sancti* [*sic*] inserted in the margin, initialled .V.

[3] later spelt *Sinate* [*sic*] *Werluge in Hoc*

[4] MS: *Cobhm'*

[5] MS: *Rossen.* ; for 'Roffen'.

[6] MS has a vertical line here, signalling perhaps the evident omission (of 'retinere' at the least).

272   7 January 1500   *Reg. Lat.* 1061, fos 170^v-171^v

To Eynonus Apgwaltere, LLB, rector of the parish church of Llanvailldeg, d. St David's. Dispensation — at his supplication — to receive and retain for life, together with the above parish church, one, and without it, any two other benefices, etc. [as above, no. 3].

Litterarum scientia, vite ac morum honestas...
P· de planca /· V· /· V· L· De Phano:

273   24 March 1500   *Reg. Lat.* 1061, fo 204[r-v]

To John Henyngham', professor OCarm. Dispensation — at his supplication — to receive and retain any benefice, with or without cure, usually held by secular clerics, even if a parish church or its perpetual vicarage, or a chantry, free chapel, hospital, annual service or commission of masses,[1] usually assigned to secular clerics, etc. [as above, no. 32, to '... usually held by secular clerics.'] Notwithstanding etc. and [notwithstanding] the constitutions of Otto and Ottobuono formerly legates of the apostolic see in the kingdom of England, etc.[2]

Religionis zelus, vite ac morum honestas...
A· de Sancto severino[3] / O· / O· xxxx Marianen'

[1] *commissio missarum*; unusual, but occurs also in the next entry

[2] The inclusion of these constitutions gives the recipient of the dispensation the option of holding his secular benefice in England.

[3] slightly shaved horizontally at the top

274   4 April 1500   *Reg. Lat.* 1061, fo 214[r-v]

To John Feure, professor OESA. Dispensation — at his supplication — to receive and retain any benefice, with or without cure, usually held by secular clerics, etc. [as above, no. 273].[1]

Religionis zelus, vite ac morum honestas...
F[2] parma /. V. / V xxxx De Phano:

[1] including 'commission of masses' : see note 1 of that entry; and also the constitutions of Otto and Ottobuono : see note 2 of that entry

[2] 'de' does not occur

275   16 March 1500   *Reg. Lat.* 1061, fo 229[r-v]

To Thomas Rayens, rector of the parish church of Marston Mortemayen', d. Lincoln. Dispensation — at his supplication — to receive and retain for life, together with the above parish church, one, and without it, any two other benefices, etc. [as above, no. 3].

Vite ac morum honestas...
· N· Bregeon / V / V· L· De Phano:

276   16 March 1500   *Reg. Lat.* 1061, fos 234^r-235^v

To William Wilton, DDec, rector of the parish church of Strete, d. Bath and Wells, dispensation. Some time ago, Innocent VIII by certain letters of his dispensed him to receive and retain together for life any two benefices, with cure or otherwise mutually incompatible, etc. [as above, no. 131,[1] to '... as is more fully contained in those letters']. The pope — at his supplication — hereby further dispenses William, who, as he asserts, holds the parish churches of Strete, d. Bath and Wells, and Maruchull, d. Salisbury, to receive and retain for life, together with the said two parish churches, or without them, with two other benefices, with cure or otherwise mutually incompatible, held by him at the time by virtue of the said dispensation, any third benefice, etc. [as above, no. 131].

Litterarum scientia, vite ac morum honestas...
F. de parma /. V· / V· Lxx. De Phano:

[1] as to content; though the order in which benefices are listed differs

277   28 March 1500[1]   *Reg. Lat.* 1061, fos 254^v-256^r

To Christopher Urswyke, DDec, archdeacon of NorthWillishrre' [also spelt *NorthWillishrre*] in the church of Salisbury, dispensation as below. Some time ago — after first Sixtus IV by certain letters of his[2] had dispensed him to receive and retain for life, together with the parish church of Croston, d. Norwich, (which, as he asserted, he was then holding), one, or having resigned it, any two other benefices, etc. [as above, no. 131, to '... retain them together for life']; and then Innocent VIII by letters of his had dispensed him, who, as he asserted, having resigned the church of Croston, had acquired the archdeaconry of NorthWillishrre', which is a non-major dignity *post pontificalem*), and the parish church of Cherdesey, d. Bath and Wells, which were canonically collated to him while vacant *certo modo*, and was holding them, to receive and retain — for a ten-year period — together with the archdeaconry and the church of Cherdesey aforesaid, or without them, with any two other incompatible benefices held by him at the time, any other third benefice, etc. [as above, no. 131,[3] to '... not more than two be parish churches or their perpetual vicarages — '] retain it for the said ten-year period — the [present] pope by other letters of his prorogued and extended the ten-year period for holding this third incompatible benefice to Christopher's lifetime, as is more fully contained in each of the letters aforesaid. The pope therefore — at his supplication — hereby further dispenses Christopher, who, as he asserts, holds the said archdeaconry and is a counsellor of Henry, king of England, to receive and retain for life, together with the said three incompatible benefices for which he is dispensed, as above, held by him now or at the time, any fourth benefice, with cure or otherwise incompatible, even if a parish church or its perpetual vicarage, or a chantry, free chapel, hospital or annual service, usually assigned to secular clerics in title of a perpetual ecclesiastical benefice, or a dignity, *personatus*, administration or office in a cathedral, even metropolitan, or collegiate church, even if the dignity should be major *post pontificalem* in a cathedral, even metropolitan, church, or principal in a collegiate church, and even if the dignity etc. should be customarily elective and have cure of souls, if he obtains it otherwise canonically, to resign it, simply or for exchange, as often as he pleases, and in its place receive another, similar or dissimilar, benefice, with cure or otherwise incompatible — provided that of four such incompatible benefices not more than two be parish churches or their perpetual vicarages — and retain it for life, as above. Notwithstanding etc. With the proviso that this fourth benefice, with cure or incompatible, shall not, on this account, be defrauded of due services and the cure of souls therein (if any) shall not be neglected.

Litterarum scientia, vite ac morum honestas...
. F. de. parma /. V· [4] / *V· Lxxxx. De Phano:*

[1] The script of parts of the *sanctio* and of the date clause would appear to be slightly different: entered later?

[2] lost; Index entry transcribed in *CPL* XIII, Part II, on p. 898

[3] with appropriate changes of tense

[4] a deep swung dash to the left and another odd mark to the left of that

278   16 March 1500   *Reg. Lat.* 1061, fo 263[r-v]

To Simon Yatis, BDec, perpetual vicar of the parish church of B. Mary the Virgin, within the vill of Nothinghin' [also spelt *Notinghin'*], d. York. Dispensation — at his supplication — to receive and retain for life, together with the perpetual vicarage of the above parish church, one, and without it, any two other benefices, etc. [as above, no. 3].

Litterarum scientia, vite ac morum honestas...
F de parma[1] */· V· /· V· L· De Phano:*

[1] top of 'F' and 'd' shaved horizontally

279   19 March 1500   *Reg. Lat.* 1061, fo 268[r-v]

To John Undrchill', rector, called portioner, of one of two portions of the parish church, usually ruled by two rectors, called portioners, of Honghton' Conquest, d. Lincoln. Dispensation — at his supplication — to receive and retain for life, together with the above portion, one, and without it, any two other benefices, etc. [as above, no. 3].

Vite ac morum honestas...
F de parma[1] /. V· /· V· L· De Phano:

[1] top of 'F' and 'd' shaved horizontally

280   24 March 1500   *Reg. Lat.* 1061, fos 269^v-270^r

To John Peverell', monk of the monastery of St Saviour, Bermesey, OClun, d. Winchester. Dispensation — at his supplication — to him, who, as he asserts, is expressly professed of the above order,[1] to receive and retain any benefice, with or without cure, usually held by secular clerics, etc. [as above, no. 32].

Religionis zelus, vite ac morum honestas...
F de parma /. V· /· V·[2] xxx. De Phano:

[1] This information comes from a notwithstanding clause.
[2] there is a point within the 'V' as well

281   1 May 1500   *Reg. Lat.* 1061, fos 272^r-273^r

Union etc. At a recent petition on the part of John Wyppyll, canon of London, the pope hereby unites etc. the parish church, called a rectory, of Haryngiay, d. London, to the canonry and prebend of Ialstret of the church of London, which he holds together with the above parish church, (the annual value[1] of the parish church not exceeding 8, and of the canonry and prebend, 4, marks sterling), for as long as he holds the canonry and prebend, to the effect that John, in person or by proxy, may, on his own authority, take and continue in possession[2] of the parish church and its rights and appurtenances, for as long as he holds the canonry and prebend, and convert its fruits etc. to his own uses and those of the parish church and the canonry and prebend without licence of the local diocesan or of anyone else. Notwithstanding etc. The pope's will is, however, that the parish church shall not, on account of this union etc., be defrauded of due services and the cure of souls therein shall not be neglected, but that its customary burdens shall be supported; and that on John's death or resignation etc. of the canonry and prebend the union etc. shall be dissolved and so deemed and the parish church shall revert to its original condition automatically.

Ad futuram rei memoriam. Romanum decet pontificem votis illis gratum prestare assensum...
S. de Castello[3] /· V· / V· xxxv De Phano:

[1] i. e. annual value of the fruits: MS has a mark of insertion in line; *Fructus*, (initialled *V*) *Additum De Mandato R(everendissimi) D(omini) Jo(hannis) Ragusini Regentis per me. V. De Phano*: in margin against it. However, 'redditus et proventus' does not occur.

[2] 'corporalem' does not occur

[3] shaved horizontally

282   1 May 1500   *Reg. Lat.* 1061, fos 281ᵛ-282ᵛ

Union etc. At a recent petition on the part of Robert Lowthe, rector of the parish church of Hamerton' [also spelt *Hamerton*], d. Lincoln, the pope hereby unites etc. the parish church of St Nicholas, Stretton' on Fos',[1] d. Worcester, (whose annual value does not exceed 7 marks sterling, equivalent to 21 gold ducats of the camera), to the above church of Hamerton', which he holds together by apostolic dispensation, for as long as he holds that of Hamerton', to the effect that Robert, in person or by proxy, may, on his own authority, continue in corporal possession of the church of St Nicholas and its rights and appurtenances or freely take it anew and retain it, for as long as he holds the church of Hamerton', and convert its fruits etc. to his own uses and those of the said churches, without licence of the local diocesan or of anyone else. Notwithstanding etc. The pope's will is, however, that the united church shall not, on account of this union etc., be defrauded of due services and the cure of souls therein shall not be neglected, but that its customary burdens shall be supported; and that on Robert's death or resignation etc. of the church of Hamerton' this union etc. shall be automatically dissolved and so deemed and the church of St Nicholas shall revert to its original condition.

Ad futuram rei memoriam. Ex iniuncto nobis desuper apostolice servitutis officio ad ea libenter intendimus...
C· de Scorciatis / V /· V· xxxv De Phano:

[1] or possibly *Fost'*

283   13 May 1500   *Reg. Lat.* 1061, fos 283ʳ-284ʳ

To Richard Page, prior of the priory, called the house, of B. Mary, Ederose Ivychurthe [also spelt *Edeiose Iuychurthe'*], OSA, d. Salisbury. Dispensation — at his supplication — to him, who is a canon of the above priory and, as he asserts, expressly professed of the above order,[1] to receive, together with the priory, one, and without it, any two other regular benefices, with or without cure, of the aforesaid or any other order, or with one of them, or without them, one benefice usually held by secular clerics, even if the regular benefices should be priories, *prepositure*, *prepositatus*, deaneries, dignities, *personatus*, administrations or offices, and the secular benefice be a parish church or its perpetual vicarage, or a chantry, free chapel, hospital or annual service, usually assigned to secular clerics in title of a perpetual ecclesiastical benefice, or a combination, even if the priories etc. should be customarily elective and have cure of souls, if he obtains them otherwise canonically, and to retain for life whichever one of the regular benefices he chooses, [even]² if it should be a conventual priory, *prepositura* or other conventual dignity or a claustral office, *in titulum*, and the other one of them, which may not be conventual or claustral, or the secular benefice, *in commendam*, to resign each and every one of them, at once or successively, simply or for exchange, as often as he pleases and cede the commend and in their place receive up to two other, similar or dissimilar, regular benefices, of the aforesaid or any other order, or with one of them, or without them, one benefice usually held by secular clerics — provided that the regular benefice retained *in commendam* be not a conventual priory, *prepositura*, *prepositatus* or other conventual dignity or a claustral office — and to retain for life whichever one of the regular benefices he chooses *in titulum* and the other one or a secular benefice *in commendam*, as above; (he may — due and customary burdens of the benefice retained *in commendam* having been supported — make disposition of the rest of its fruits etc. just as those holding it *in titulum* could and ought to do, alienation of immovable goods and precious movables being however forbidden). Notwithstanding etc. With the proviso that the benefice retained *in commendam* shall not, on this account, be defrauded of due services and the cure of souls therein³ shall not be neglected; but that its aforesaid burdens shall be supported.

Religionis zelus, vite ac morum honestas...
*(?)N Bregeon*⁴ */· V· / V·· L· De*⁵ *Phano:*

¹ These two items of information come from a notwithstanding clause.

² *et*; *recte*: 'etiam'

³ 'si qua illi immineat' does not occur

⁴ shaved horizontally

⁵ blotched and possibly altered (from (?)*de*)

284   1 June 1500   *Reg. Lat.* 1061, fos 301ᵛ-302ᵛ

To Thomas Adam, MA, rector of the parish church of B. Mary, Ffeltwell', d. Norwich. Dispensation — at his supplication — to receive and retain for life, together with the above parish church, one, and without it, any two other benefices, etc. [as above, no. 3].

Litterarum scientia, vite ac morum honestas...
F. de parma /. V· /· V· L· De Phano:

285   1 June 1500   *Reg. Lat.* 1061, fos 308^r-309^r

To John Ffulford, archdeacon of Tocton' in the church of Exeter, dispensation. Some time ago, Innocent VIII by his letters dispensed him to receive and retain for life, together with the perpetual vicarage of the parish church of Probus (*Sancti Probi*[1]), d. Exeter, (which, as he asserted, he was then holding), one other, and without it, any two other benefices, etc. [as above, no. 131, to '... as is more fully contained in those letters']. The pope therefore — at his supplication — hereby dispenses John, who, as he also asserts, afterwards acquired the archdeaconry of Tocton', (a non-major dignity *post pontificalem*), which was canonically collated to him while vacant *certo modo*, and holds it and the said vicarage by the said dispensation, to receive and retain for life, together with the archdeaconry and vicarage, or any two other incompatible benefices held by him at the time by virtue of the said dispensation, any third benefice, etc. [as above, no. 131].

Vite ac morum honestas...
C· de Scorciatis / V / V. Lxx De Phano:

[1] *Probi* reworked

286   10 June 1500   *Reg. Lat.* 1061, fo 311^r-v

To William Kent, perpetual vicar of the parish church of Boxe[1], d. Salisbury. Dispensation — at his supplication — to receive and retain for life, together with the perpetual vicarage of the above parish church, one, and without it, any two other benefices, etc. [as above, no. 3].

Vite ac morum honestas...
?[2] */. V· /· V· L· De Phano:*

[1] in the second occurrence the 'o' is overwritten and blotched
[2] the upper outer corner of the leaf where the name of the abbreviator should have been is shaved away entirely

287   2 May 1500   *Reg. Lat.* 1061, fos 311^v-312^r

To Geoffrey Louuyn', monk of the priory of Castellacre, OClun, d. Norwich, indult. Some time ago, the pope by other letters of his dispensed him to receive and retain any benefice, with or without cure, usually held by secular clerics, even if a parish church or its perpetual vicarage, or a chantry, free chapel, hospital or annual service, usually assigned to secular clerics in title of a perpetual ecclesiastical benefice, if he obtained it otherwise canonically, as is more fully contained in those letters.[1] The pope — at his supplication — hereby indulges him to bear the habit usually worn by monks of the above priory, OClun (of which he is a monk and, as he asserts, expressly professed of the order) or its mark[2] under garments (*vestibus*) of honest and decent colour usually worn by secular clerics. Notwithstanding etc.

Religionis zelus, vite ac morum honestas...
C· de Scorciatis / V / V xx De Phano.[3]

[1] summarised in *CPL*, XVI at no. 413

[2] *... habitum per monachos prioratus de Castellacre Cluniacensis ordinis Norwicen. diocesis cuius monachus et ut asseris ordinem ipsum expresse professus existis gestari solitum sive signum illius...* ; grammatically *illius* refers to *habitum*

[3] *sic*; usually a colon. The signature is otherwise unpunctuated.

288   22 May 1500[1]   *Reg. Lat.* 1061, fo 322[r-v]

To John Many, MA, rector of the parish church of St Tudy[2], Cornwall (*Cornubia*), d. Exeter. Dispensation — at his supplication — to receive and retain for life, together with the above parish church, one, and having resigned it, any two other benefices, etc. [as above, no. 3].

Litterarum scientia, vite ac morum honestas...
S de Castello /. V· /. V.. L· De Phano:

[1] insertion mark above *Kl.* in the line; corresponding mark in the margin with *Undecimo*, initialled *.V.*
[2] *Sancti Tudiic*

289   20 May 1500   *Reg. Lat.* 1061, fos 332[v]-333[r]

To Richard Page, rector of the parish church of Monklane [also spelt *Monkalane*], d. Hereford. Dispensation — at his supplication — to receive and retain for life, together with the above parish church, one, and without it, any two other benefices, etc. [as above, no. 3].

Vite ac morum honestas...
S· de Castello /. V· / V· L· De Phano:

290   22 April 1500   *Reg. Lat.* 1062, fos 26ʳ-27ʳ

To Henry Longforth, rector of the parish church of Longforth, d. Coventry and
Lichfield. Dispensation — at his supplication — to him (who, some time ago, as he
asserts, notwithstanding a defect of birth as the son of an unmarried man and an
unmarried woman, was dispensed by apostolic authority to be promoted to all, even
sacred, orders and to hold a benefice even if it should have cure of souls, and who,
after he was duly marked with clerical character, having acquired the above parish
church, which was canonically collated to him while vacant *certo modo*, held and
possessed it thenceforth, as he does at present) to receive and retain for life, together
with the said church, one, and without it, any two other benefices, with cure or
otherwise mutually incompatible, even if parish churches or their perpetual
vicarages, or chantries, free chapels, hospitals,[1] usually assigned to secular clerics in
title of a perpetual ecclesiastical benefice, or dignities, *personatus*, administrations
or offices in cathedral, even metropolitan, or collegiate churches, or a combination,
even if the dignities etc. should be customarily elective and have cure of souls, if he
obtains them otherwise canonically, to resign them, at once or successively, simply
or for exchange, as often as he pleases, and in their place receive up to two other,
similar or dissimilar, incompatible benefices — provided that such dignities be not
major *post pontificalem* in cathedral churches or principal in collegiate churches —
and retain them together for life. Notwithstanding etc. With the proviso that the
above church and other incompatible benefices shall not, on this account, be
defrauded of due services and the cure of souls in the church and (if any) the other
incompatible benefices aforesaid shall not be neglected.

Vite ac morum honestas...
Jo ortega[2] */· V· / V. Lx. De Phano:*

[1] 'vel annualia servitia' does not occur
[2] in lighter ink (similar to that of the magistral initial and signature) : entered later?

291   7 January 1500   *Reg. Lat.* 1062, fo 73ʳ⁻ᵛ

To Thomas, abbot of the monastery of St Mary, Waverley (*de Vauerleya* [also spelt
Vauerleia]), OCist, d. Winchester. Dispensation — at his supplication — to receive
and retain *in commendam* for life, together with the above monastery, over which he
presides, or without it, any benefice, with or without cure, usually held by secular
clerics, even if a parish church or its perpetual vicarage, or a chantry, free chapel,
hospital or annual service, usually assigned to secular clerics in title of a perpetual
ecclesiastical benefice, and of lay patronage and of whatsoever tax or annual value,
if he obtains it otherwise canonically, to resign it when he pleases and cede the
commend, and in its place receive another, similar or dissimilar, benefice, with or
without cure, usually held by secular clerics, and retain it *in commendam* for life, as

above; (he may — due and customary burdens of the benefice having been supported — make disposition of the rest of its fruits etc., just as those holding it *in titulum* could and ought to do, alienation of immovable goods and precious movables being however forbidden). Notwithstanding etc. With the proviso that this benefice shall not, on this account, be defrauded of due services and the cure of souls therein (if any) shall not be neglected; but that its aforesaid burdens shall be supported.

Personam tuam nobis et apostolice sedy[1] *devotam paterna benivolentia prosequentes illa tibi favorabiliter concedimus...*
Jo ortega[2] /. *L.* /. *L. L^{ta}. Dulcius:-*

[1] *sic*
[2] shaved horizontally

292   26 September 1499   *Reg. Lat.* 1062, fos 80^V-83^V

Confirmation and indulgence as below. A recent petition to the pope on the part of Humphrey Vuolsauve, perpetual chaplain, called cantor, at the altar of St Oswald located at the southern arch in the parish church of Asshebrun,[1] and John Reeper, perpetual chaplain, called cantor, in the newly built chapel of B. Mary the Virgin, Hoghen, d. Coventry and Lichfield, stated that formerly John Bradburn' esquire of Hoghen, co. Derby (*Derbei*), and Ann, his wife, said diocese, duly instituted and founded, in honour of the Trinity, B. Mary, St Oswald, and all other saints, a perpetual chaplaincy, called a chantry, ruled by two perpetual chaplains, who were bound to celebrate — one in the parish church at the above altar and the other in the chapel — the divine offices daily for the good estate of the late Richard, king of England, (who was then alive), and of the aforesaid couple, during their lifetimes, and for their souls after death, and also for the souls of the then late Anne, queen of England and wife of the said king while she lived, and of several others then expressed; and they nominated Humphrey, who was to celebrate in the church, and John, who was to celebrate in the chapel, as above, to rule the chaplaincy; and they appropriated and assigned, in perpetuity, certain goods, then expressed, as the endowment of the chaplaincy, to Humphrey and John respectively and their successors in the chaplaincy; and they made disposition and ordained: that the chaplaincy, [called] a chantry, and the [chaplains][2] or cantors holding it for the time being, were to be called the chaplaincy or chantry, and the [chaplains] or cantors, of John Bradburn' and Ann, his wife; that the right of patronage and of presenting suitable persons for the chaplaincy was to belong, in perpetuity, to John Bradburn' and Ann, his wife, and their heirs and successors; and that the [chaplains] holding the chaplaincy for the time being were to reside in person in certain places then expressed; and they were bound: to maintain and repair all the goods at their own expense; to recite, in the church and chapel aforesaid, in accordance with the usage and custom of those parts, the divine offices, and, once a week, the office of the dead, with certain psalms, readings, and commendatory offices, then expressed; to celebrate daily the various masses of Jesus and, sometimes, as their devotion dictated, of the Holy Cross, unless a double feast went before;[3] to say each Sunday the commemoration of the Holy Trinity and, in each mass after the offertory, before they turned aside to the (?)lavabo-dish (*lavatorium*), in a raised voice (*alta voce*), in the vernacular, certain honest words then expressed, with certain psalms, and the collect, and prayers; and every year, to solemnly celebrate, at their own expense, an anniversary for the souls of John and Ann, and their relatives and benefactors, in the said church, together with its perpetual vicar, priests, and clerics for the time being; and on the following day the vicar, or his deputy, was bound to solemnly celebrate mass there, with certain prayers and permitted musical notation (*licitis notis*), to whom, together with the other priests and clerics celebrating and serving there on the said day, a certain quantity of pennies, then expressed, was to be paid; with the proviso that the expense incurred by the chaplains in the anniversary was not to exceed a certain sum of money then expressed; and that the heirs and successors of John and Ann were bound to repair the chapel at their own expense, and to maintain the altar furnishings, missal, and other things necessary for the celebration of mass, and, in the event of their refusing to do this, the then chaplain in the chapel was, so long as they refused, bound to celebrate the divine offices, in accordance with the said ordinance, not in the chapel but in the church; and that the chaplains, on account of a life of incontinence or other demerits of theirs then expressed, must — after several warnings have first been given them by the vicar of the church and the local ordinary — be removed and severed[4] from the chaplaincy; and in the event of such a removal, as well as when any other vacancy of the chaplaincy's portions arises, the heirs must present suitable persons for them, thus vacant, to the local ordinary, within twenty days, and, if they do not, the vicar must do so within another twenty days, and, if the heirs and the vicar both refuse, the bishop of Coventry and Lichfield for the time being, or his vicar general, must, for that turn only, freely collate them to suitable persons who will carry out the above dispositions and ordinances; and the chaplains were bound, on appointment, to take an oath to inviolably observe the aforesaid ordinances, and were not able to hold another benefice under pain of deprivation of the chaplaincy or its portions; and they were to keep and conserve, at peril to themselves, the document (*instrumentum*) of the chalices, ornaments, books, and other writings of the chaplaincy and of these ordinances, in a certain place and under a certain manner and form then expressed, and were to read and publish it in a certain way each year in the church, in the presence of its priests; and, in addition, when both its portions were vacant, the fruits etc. of the chaplaincy were to be collected by the vicar and put to the repair of the books and ornaments and to other uses then expressed. And thereafter John, bishop of Coventry and Lichfield, approved and confirmed by ordinary authority the foregoing and each and every other thing arranged and ordained in the foundation, as is said to be more fully contained in, respectively, a certain public instrument drawn up in regard to the foundation and in bishop John's letters, fortified with his seal, drawn up in regard to the confirmation and approval. At Humphrey[5] and John Reeper's supplication to the pope to add the force of apostolic approval and confirmation to the foundation, appropriation, assignment, dispositions, ordinances, approval and confirmation aforesaid, as a firmer base for them, and to establish and ordain that, in perpetuity, for the inhabitants of Hoghen, mass and other divine offices may be celebrated in the chapel, infants baptized, other ecclesiastical sacraments administered, marriages solemnized, and women purified, the pope hereby approves and confirms the foundation, institution, appropriation, assignment, dispositions, ordinances, approval and confirmation, and everything concerning them contained in the above instrument and letters, fortifies them with the protective power of the present writ, and adds to them the force of perpetual and inviolable strength, supplying all defects; and he hereby establishes and ordains, without prejudice to anyone, with the express consent — lawfully proved to the pope by a public instrument — of Stephen Surteis, perpetual vicar of the said church, within the limits of whose parish the said chapel is asserted to exist, that, in perpetuity, for the said inhabitants and each one of them, mass and other divine offices may be celebrated in the said chapel, infants baptized, marriages solemnized, other ecclesiastical sacraments administered and woman purified after childbirth. Notwithstanding etc. And the pope, desiring they devoutly say one paternoster with the Angelic Salutation [for] the welfare of the souls of John and Ann, the founders, relaxes forty days of enjoined penance, every day, to those who do so. The pope's will is, however, that if, at another time, any other indulgence has been granted by him, either in perpetuity or for a limited time not yet run out, to those visiting the church or chapel in question and performing something therein for the welfare of the founders' souls, the present letters are void as regards the above relaxation. Given at Nepi.

Ad perpetuam rei memoriam. Ad singula que ad omnipotentis dei...
Jo ortega[6] */. V· /. V· Cxx De Phano:*

[1] or O-

[2] MS: *capellam*; *recte* 'capellani'?

[3] reading, tentatively, *precur[r]eret*

[4] reading, tentatively, *desecari*

[5] surname 'Vuolsauve' wanting

[6] in different ink : entered later?

293   14 December 1499   *Reg. Lat.* 1062, fos 119ʳ-120ᵛ

Union etc. At a recent petition on the part of William Boket, DDec, rector of the parish church of Mallis, d. Bath and Wells, the pope hereby unites etc. the parish church of Lymplesham [also spelt *Limplesham*], d. Bath and Wells, (whose annual value does not exceed 33 marks sterling, equivalent to 99 gold ducats of the camera), to the above church of Mallis, which he holds together by apostolic dispensation, for as long as he holds that of Mallis, to the effect that William, in person or by proxy, may, on his own authority, take and retain corporal possession of the church of

Lymplesham and its rights and appurtenances, for as long as he holds that of Mallis, and convert its fruits etc. to his own uses and those of the said churches without licence of the local diocesan or of anyone else. Notwithstanding etc. The pope's will is, however, that the church of Lymplesham shall not, on account of this union etc., be defrauded of due services and the cure of souls therein shall not be neglected, but that its customary burdens shall be supported; and that on William's death or resignation etc. of the church of Mallis the union etc. shall be dissolved and so deemed and the church of Lymplesham shall revert to its original condition automatically.

Ad futuram rei memoriam. Decet Romanum pontificem votis illis gratum prestare assensum...
S de Castello /. L. /. L. xxxv. Dulcius:-

294   14 December 1499   *Reg. Lat.* 1062, fos 120ᵛ-121ᵛ

Union etc. At a recent petition on the part of Thomas Barbur, LLB, rector of the parish church of Segebaro, d. Worcester, the pope hereby unites etc. the parish church of Braduas[1] [also spelt *Bradiuas*], d. Worcester, ([whose annual value does not exceed...][2]), to the above church of Segebaro, which he holds together by apostolic dispensation, for as long as he holds that of Segebaro, to the effect that Thomas, in person or by proxy, may, on his own authority, take and retain corporal possession of the church of Braduas and its rights and appurtenances, for as long as he holds that of Segebaro, and convert its fruits etc. to his own uses and those of the said churches without licence of the local diocesan or of anyone else. Notwithstanding etc. The pope's will is, however, that the church of Braduas shall not, on account of this union etc., be defrauded of due services and the cure of souls therein shall not be neglected, but that its customary burdens shall be supported; and that on Thomas's death or resignation etc. of the church of Segebaro the union etc. shall be dissolved and so deemed and the church of Braduas shall revert to its original condition automatically.

Ad futuram rei memoriam. Romanum decet pontificem votis illis gratum prestare assensum...
F de Parma /. L. /. L. xxxv. Dulcius:-

[1] In two instances the first minim of the 'u' is dotted; in a third *Bradeias* is a possible reading.

[2] value of the benefice and the narrative of the act of supplication omitted; the omission (which was arguably occasioned by confusion of *dicte ecclesie de Braduas* and 'dictam ecclesiam de Braduas' may be reconstructed conjecturally as follows:... *asserentis dicte ecclesie de Braduas* [fructus redditus et proventus... marcharum sterlingorum... ducatos auri de camera vel circa constituentium secundum communem extimationem valorem annuum non excedere nobis fuit humiliter supplicatum ut dictam ecclesiam de Braduas] *eidem ecclesie de Segebaro...*

295   27 December 1499   *Reg. Lat.* 1062, fos 131ᵛ-133ʳ

Union etc. At a recent petition on the part of John Luguuardyn', BDec, canon of
Wells, the pope hereby unites etc. the parish church of St John the Baptist, Axbrygg,
d. Bath and Wells, (whose annual value does not exceed 20 marks sterling,
equivalent to 60 gold ducats of the camera or thereabouts) to the canonry [of the
church of Wells][1] and the prebend of Tymberiscomb' in the same, which he holds
together with the above parish church, for as long as he holds the canonry and
prebend, to the effect that John, in person or by proxy, may, on his own authority,
take and retain corporal possession of the parish church and its rights and
appurtenances, for as long as he holds the canonry and prebend, and convert its fruits
etc. to his own uses and those of the parish church and the canonry and prebend
without licence of the local diocesan or of anyone else. Notwithstanding etc. The
pope's will is, however, that the parish church shall not, on account of this union
etc., be defrauded of due services and the cure of souls therein shall not be neglected,
but that its customary burdens shall be supported; and that on John's death or
resignation etc. of the canonry and prebend, the union etc. shall be dissolved and so
deemed and the parish church shall revert to its original condition and be deemed
vacant automatically.

*Ad futuram rei memoriam. Decet Romanum pontificem votis illis gratum prestare
assensum...*
S de Castello /· V· /· V xxxv De Phano:

[1] wanting in MS

296   6 December 1499   *Reg. Lat.* 1062, fos 135ᵛ-136ʳ

To William[1] Gimnays, LLB, rector of the parish church of Languoo [also spelt
Langnoo], d. London. Dispensation — at his supplication — to receive and retain for
life, together with the above parish church, one, and without it, any two other
benefices, etc. [as above, no. 3].

Litterarum scientia, vite ac morum honestas...
Jo ortega /· V· / V·· L· De Phano:

[1] *Guill(elm)o*

297   6 December 1499   *Reg. Lat.* 1062, fos 136ᵛ-137ᵛ

To Richard <Simon>[1], rector of the parish church of Magna Harde, d. Canterbury.
Dispensation to him (who, as he asserts, is an LLB[2]) — at his supplication — to

receive and retain for life, together with the above parish church, one, and without it, any two other benefices, etc. [as above, no. 3].

Vite ac morum honestas... [3]
Jo ortega / [-] [4] */· V·· L· De Phano:*

[1] marginal insertion initialled *.V.* ; (?)*S......*, deleted and initialled *.V.*, in the line

[2] not, strangely, designated with his degree (LLB) in the address clause

[3] accords with the address clause; but proem in the form 'Litterarum scientia, vite... ' is appropriate for a graduate

[4] no magistral initial

298   15 July 1500   *Reg. Lat.* 1062, fos 144^v-146^r

To the bishop of Lincoln and the abbots of the monasteries of Eveschin[1] and Tevukesbury, d. Worcester, mandate in favour of the abbot and convent of the monastery of Bordesley, OCist, d. Worcester. A recent petition to the pope on the abbot and convent's part stated that by special privilege of the apostolic see, (which to date has not been derogated in any way), they, their monastery, the Cistercian order, and the members and places of the order and monastery, are immediately subject to the apostolic see and totally [exempt][2] from all superiority, jurisdiction, dominion, and power of archbishops, bishops, their officials and vicars, and other judges in ordinary, to the effect that archbishops etc. cannot, by reason of a crime, contract, or disputed matter, wherever the crime is committed, the contract entered into,[3] or the matter disputed, exercise superiority, etc. over the abbot and convent, etc. ; and that the parish church of Kynfar(e) [also spelt *Kynefar(e)*], d. Coventry and Lichfield, is united, annexed, and incorporated to the monastery, and customarily governed and served by a suitable priest removable at the abbot's pleasure; that John, bishop of Coventry and Lichfield — untruthfully claiming that he had jurisdiction over the abbot and convent and that they were bound to present a suitable person to him for institution as perpetual vicar in the parish church — nevertheless suddenly [admonished][4] the abbot and convent, by certain letters of his, of a certain tenor then expressed, to present, within a certain insufficient term then expressed, a suitable person for institution as perpetual vicar, who would bear the cure of souls of the parishioners; that at the instance, as he asserted, of Richard Blokelay, William Vuolfordi of Kynfar(e), and certain other laymen, parishioners of the church, who falsely asserted that a perpetual vicar was due to be appointed, bishop John admonished the abbot and convent, (or ordered them to be cited), that if they had not presented a suitable person when the term expired they were to appear before him or his deputy, to plead their case why the bishop ought not to appoint a perpetual vicar in the church and assign a certain part of its fruits etc. to him; that the abbot and convent appealed to the apostolic see and, for the protection of their rights, affairs, and persons, they had recourse to the court of Canterbury to which, by ancient and approved custom of those parts, recourse is customarily had; that John Veysey, the bishop's official or commissary — contemptuous of their appeal and recourse (of which he was not ignorant) and while they were still well within the time for prosecuting the appeal — ordered the abbot and convent, over whom he had no jurisdiction, to be admonished and cited to appear before him, within another insufficient term, in a certain place then expressed, to plead why they ought not to be compelled over the assignment of a suitable portion of the church's fruits etc. to the vicar; and that although the abbot and convent, while not going back on their appeal, appeared before him within the prescribed term and pleaded why they were not bound in the matter of the assignment, John Veysey, proceeding illegally and *de facto* to the later stages, nevertheless declared that they were contumacious, and he decreed the sequestration, and sequestered, the church's fruits etc., taxed them in a certain way then expressed, and ordered a certain portion to be assigned annually to the perpetual vicar, whence the abbot and convent appealed to the apostolic see. At their supplication to the pope to commit to some upright men in those parts the causes of their appeals; of everything attempted and innovated after and against the appeals; of the nullity of the mandate, citation, declaration, sequestration, taxation, assignment of the portion, processes of the bishop and Veysey, and of everything else prejudicial to the abbot and convent and monastery and church done by them and by Richard and William and any other judges and persons in connection with the foregoing; and of the principal matter, the pope [hereby] commands that [the above three (or two or one of them)][5], having summoned Richard, William, the parishioners, and others concerned, and having heard both sides, taking cognizance even of the principal matter, shall decree what is just, without appeal, causing by ecclesiastical censure what they have decreed to be strictly observed; [and moreover compel] witnesses etc. Notwithstanding etc.

Humilibus et cetera.
L puccius /. V. / V. xij De Phano:

[1] or *Eveschm*

[2] MS: *exempla; recte*: 'exempta'

[3] word reworked; tentatively reading *iniatur*

[4] MS: *novit; recte*: 'monuit'?

[5] enregistration abridged : ... *supplicationibus inclinati et cetera mandamus...*

299   9 June 1500   *Reg. Lat.* 1062, fo 166[r-v]

To William Kyrkh(a)m,[1] canon of the priory of Hautrenpice [also spelt *Autremprice*], OSA, d. York. Dispensation — at his supplication — to him, who, as he asserts, is expressly professed of the above order,[2] to receive and retain any benefice, with or without cure, usually held by secular clerics, etc. [as above, no. 32].

Religionis zelus, vite ac morum honestas...

Jo ortega /. V· / V· xxx De Phano:

[1] MS: *Kirkhm'*; (*Kirk* deleted and initialled *.V.* occurs after *Guillelmo*)
[2] This information comes from a notwithstanding claus

300   10 August 1500   *Reg. Lat.* 1062, fos 258[r]-259[r]

Union etc. At a recent petition on the part of Thomas Fytzherbert, DDec, rector of the parish church of St[1] Mary, Stan Vordrynees, d. London, the pope hereby unites etc. the said church of St Mary, (whose annual value does not exceed 16 pounds in money of those parts, equivalent to 64 gold ducats of the camera <or thereabouts>[2]), to the parish church of St Helen, (?)Hallewynsm' *alias* Northuuynfeld' in Scarysdalle, d. Coventry and Lichfield, which he holds together by apostolic dispensation, for as long as he holds St Helen's, to the effect that Thomas, in person or by proxy, may, on his own authority, take [or] continue in corporal possession of St Mary's and convert its fruits etc. to his own uses and those of the said churches and retain [St Mary's], for as long as he holds St Helen's, without licence of the local diocesan or of anyone else. Notwithstanding etc. The pope's will is, however, that St Mary's shall not, on account of this union etc., be defrauded of due services and the cure of souls therein shall not be neglected, but that its customary burdens shall be supported; and that on Thomas's death or resignation etc. of St Helen's the union etc. shall be dissolved and so deemed and St Mary's shall revert to its original condition and be deemed vacant automatically.

Ad futuram rei memoriam. Ex apostolico nobis desuper iniuncto servitutis offitio ad ea libenter intendimus...
S de Castello / V /. V. xxxv. De Phano:

[1] *sancte* and *beate* variously
[2] marginal insertion initialled *.V.*

301   4 August 1500   *Reg. Lat.* 1062, fos 291[r]-293[r]

To Alexander Gifferd,[1] cleric, d. St Andrews, reservation, constitution and assignment of a pension, as below. A recent petition to the pope on Alexander's part stated that he — between whom and Roland Blacad,[2] cleric, d. Glasgow, a suit was brewing over the subdeanery of the church of Glasgow, of which formerly provision had been made to Alexander by apostolic authority when it was vacant *certo modo*, and which each was asserting rightfully belonged to him, to avoid suits, for the sake of peace, and so that Roland should remain more peacefully in the subdeanery, concerning which Roland had had provision made to him by ordinary authority at another time, by virtue of which he had acquired possession — has, spontaneously and freely, outside the Roman curia before a notary public and witnesses, ceded all right belonging to him in or to the subdeanery. Lest Alexander should suffer excessive loss from this cession, the pope hereby reserves, constitutes and assigns an annual pension of 100 marks Scots (equivalent to 20 pounds sterling) on the fruits etc. of the subdeanery (of which this pension does not, as he asserts, exceed a third part) payable in full to Alexander for life (or to his specially mandated proctor) by Roland, to which express assent has been given by David Brown', rector of the parish church of Neuay',[3] d. St Andrews (Roland's specially appointed proctor), and by his successors holding the subdeanery at the time, each year, one half on the feast of St Martin in November and the other on that of Pentecost. With decree etc. that if Roland, or any one of his successors, fails to make payment on the said feasts or within the thirty days immediately following, he shall, after this time has elapsed, incur sentence of excommunication, from which he cannot be absolved, except on the point of death, until he shall have made satisfaction in full or reached agreement in respect of it with Alexander (or his proctor) and, if he remains obdurate under that sentence for a further six months, he shall thereupon be deprived in perpetuity of the subdeanery, which shall be deemed vacant automatically. Notwithstanding etc.

Executory to the archbishop of Ragusa and the officials of St Andrews and Glasgow, or two or one of them, acting in person or by proxy.[4]

Vite ac morum honestas... The executory begins: *Hodie dilecto filio Alexandro Gifferd... C de scorciatis; N de Castello /· V· / V· xij· x De Phano:*

[1] or *Gifferdi* or *Gifferd'* : the 'd' has a tail; likewise in the executory

[2] executory: *Blacad* or *Blacadi* or *Blacad'* : the 'd' has a tail

[3] changed (by deletion) from (?) *Neuayn'*; not initialled

[4] according to the executory, the pension is payable *in certis loco et terminis*; but no place is mentioned in the principal letter

302 28 February 1500   *Reg. Lat.* 1063, fo 44[r-v]

To John Beledhey of Brigewater, BTheol, professor OFM. Dispensation — at his supplication — to him, who is a priest, to receive and retain any benefice, with cure, usually held by secular clerics, etc. [as above, no. 32, to '... similar or dissimilar, benefice'], with cure, usually assigned to secular clerics. Notwithstanding etc.

Religionis zelus, litterarum scientia, vite ac morum honestas... Jo ortega[1] / F / F· xxxx Sanctor(is)

[1] heavily inked : entered later?

303[1]   **28 February 1500**   *Reg. Lat.* 1064, fo 2[r-v]

To Robert Evedon, perpetual vicar of the parish church of Morton' [also spelt *Morton*], d. Lincoln. Dispensation — at his supplication — to receive and retain for life, together with the perpetual vicarage of the above parish church, one, and without it, any two other benefices, etc. [as above, no. 3].

Vite ac morum honestas...
· *N· Bregeon* / *F* / *F· L. Sanctor(is)*

[1] *Robertus Evedon* occurs in the index to the gathering on fo 1[r].

304[1]   **28 February 1500**   *Reg. Lat.* 1064, fo 7[r-v]

To Nicholas Fovonys, rector of the parish church of Upton' Waren' [also spelt *Upton' Wauren'*], d. Worcester. Dispensation — at his supplication — to receive and retain for life, together with the above parish church, one, and without it, any two other benefices, etc. [as above, no. 3].

Vite ac morum honestas...
· *S· de Castello* /· *V·* /. *V· L· De Phano:*

[1] *Nicolaus Fovoniis* occurs in the index to the gathering on fo 1[r].

305[1]   **28 February 1500**   *Reg. Lat.* 1064, fo 8[r-v]

To John Barney, monk of the monastery of Heye, OSB, d. Norwich. Dispensation — at his supplication — to him, who, as he asserts, is expressly professed of the above order,[2] to receive and retain any benefice, with or without cure, usually held by secular clerics, etc. [as above, no. 32, to '... similar or dissimilar, benefice'], usually assigned to secular clerics. Notwithstanding etc.

Religionis zelus, vite ac morum honestas...
· *S· de Castello* / *F* / *F· xxx Sanctor(is)*

[1] *Jo. Barney* occurs in the index to the gathering on fo 1[r].

2 This information comes from a notwithstanding clause.

306[1]   **8 February 1500**   *Reg. Lat.* 1064, fos 21^v-24^r

To the prior of the monastery, usually governed by a prior, of B Mary, Raydgaylle, d.[2] Limerick, and the prior of the secular and collegiate church of Ynyskahi, d. Killaloe, and the dean of the church of Ardfert, mandate in favour of Edmund Fismoris, cleric, d. Ardfert[3] (who, as he asserts, is of noble birth and presently a student in the university of Oxford (*Oxonie*)). Following the pope's reservation of all benefices, with and without cure, vacated then or in the future at the apostolic see to his own collation and disposition, the vicarage of the parish church of Ryndweare, d. Ardfert — by the free resignation of David Fismoris (vicar of that church, who was provided to it by apostolic authority at another time when it was vacant *certo modo* and acquired possession by virtue of the said provision) into [the pope's][4] hands and admitted by the pope at the said see — and, <as the pope has learned>[5] the rectory, called Balengary, of the said church (which is of lay patronage) have been vacant *certo modo* and are vacant at present (the vicarage being reserved as above and the rectory having been vacant for so long that by the Lateran statutes its collation has lawfully devolved on the apostolic see). A recent petition to the pope on Edmund's part stated that if a canonry were to be erected in the church of Ardfert and the rectory were to be erected into a simple prebend in that church, for his lifetime, and, after their erection, the vicarage were to be united etc. to the canonry and prebend, also for his lifetime, it would be to the increase of divine worship in the church of Ardfert and to his benefit; and supplication was made that Richard Fismoris, who has despoiled David of the vicarage, and John Bretdicach — both clerics, d. Ardfert — have detained the vicarage and rectory respectively, with no support of law, of their own temerity and *de facto*, for a certain time, as they do. At this supplication, the pope, not having certain knowledge of the foregoing, hereby commands that the above three (or two or one of them), having summoned Richard and John and others concerned, shall — howsoever the vicarage and rectory be vacant etc., even if the vicarage has been vacant for so long that its collation has lawfully devolved on the apostolic see, etc. — erect a canonry in the church of Ardfert and the rectory into a simple prebend, for Edmund's lifetime, without prejudice to anyone, and unite etc. the [?vicarage][6] to them, thus erected, also for his lifetime, and collate and assign the canonry and prebend, thus erected, the annual value of which and of its said annex does not exceed 9 marks sterling, being vacant, to Edmund, with plenitude of canon law, and the annex and all rights and appurtenances, inducting him etc. having removed any unlawful detainer and causing Edmund (or his proctor) to be received as a canon of Ardfert and the fruits etc., rights and obventions of the canonry and prebend to be delivered to him. [Curbing] gainsayers by the pope's authority etc. Notwithstanding etc.

Ex iniuncto nobis desuper apostolice servitutis officio ad ea libenter intendimus...
S. de castello. /· V· / V· xxv Sex(t)o dec(im)o kl' Aprilis Anno octavo [17 March 1500], *De Phano:*

[1] *Edemundus Fismoris* occurs in the index to the gathering on fo 1[r].

[2] *diocesis* here deleted, but comprehended in *dioc(esium)* (after *Laonen.*); similarly *ecclesie* is deleted after *collegiate*, but comprehended by *ecclesiarum* later in the address clause

[3] MS: *prefate diocesis*, with reference, presumably, to the narrative rather than the address clause.

[4] MS: *in manibus*; wanting, surely, 'nostris'

[5] marginal insertion by the enregistering scribe, initialled *.V.*

[6] *rectoriam*; *recte*: 'vicariam'?

307[1]   **24 May 1500**[2]   *Reg. Lat.* 1064, fos 40[r]-41[r]

To William Shrager,[3] perpetual vicar of the parish church of Westhan', d. London. Dispensation and indult — at his supplication — to receive and retain for life, together with the perpetual vicarage of the above parish church, one, and without it, any two other benefices, etc. [as above, no. 3, to '... retain them together for life, as above']; and for life, while attending a *studium generale* or residing in the Roman curia or any one of his benefices, not to be bound to reside in his other benefices, etc. [as above, no. 238].

Vite ac morum honestas...
F de parma /· V· / V· Lx De Phano:

[1] *Willelmus Shrager* occurs in the index to the gathering on fo. 25[r].

[2] Finally: *Millesimo quingentesimo (Nono) kalendas Junii anno octavo*; after alterations, viz: (i) *Nono* has been inserted in the margin (in the hand of the magistral signature), initialled *.V.* ; with *Nono* written over *quarto* (or perhaps *quinto*), in the line and deleted, initialled *.V.* (ii) *kalendas* changed (by overwriting) from *idus* (iii) *Junii* changed (by overwriting) from *Julii*

[3] the 'h' apparently written over a 'b'

308[1]   **15 June 1500**   *Reg. Lat.* 1064, fos 41[v]-42[v]

To Fulk Salisburi, cleric, d. St Asaph, dispensation. Some time ago, the pope by other letters of his dispensed him, who, then, as he asserted, was in his eighteenth year of age or thereabouts, to receive and retain any benefice, with cure or otherwise incompatible or requiring by foundation, statute or custom the order of the priesthood or a greater age, even if a parish church etc. [as above, no. 240, with appropriate changes of tense, to '... and in its place'] receive another, similar or dissimilar, incompatible benefice and retain it, as above, as is more fully contained in those letters. The pope — at his supplication — hereby further dispenses him, who, as he asserts, is in his twenty-fourth year, to receive and retain for life — at the lawful age — together with the above benefice, with cure or otherwise incompatible, for which he is dispensed as above, any two other benefices, with cure or otherwise mutually incompatible, even if parish churches or their perpetual vicarages, or chantries, free chapels, hospitals or annual services, usually assigned to secular clerics in title of a perpetual ecclesiastical benefice, or dignities, *personatus,* administrations or offices in cathedral, even metropolitan, or collegiate churches, even if the dignities in question should be major *post pontificalem* in cathedral, even metropolitan, churches, or principal in collegiate churches, or a combination, and even if the dignities etc. should be customarily elective and have cure of souls, if he obtains them otherwise canonically, to resign them, at once or successively, simply or for exchange, as often as he pleases, and in their place receive up to three other, similar or dissimilar, incompatible benefices — provided that of three such benefices not more than two be parish churches or their perpetual vicarages — and retain them together for life, as above. Notwithstanding etc. With the proviso that the incompatible benefices in question shall not, on this account, be defrauded of due services and the cure of souls therein ([if] any) shall not be neglected.

Vite ac morum honestas...
· *S· de Castello* /· *V·* /· *V· Lxxxx De Phano:*

1 *Fulconus Salisburi* occurs in the index to the gathering on fo. 25^r

309   15 March 1500   *Reg. Lat.* 1064, fos 80^r-81^r

Union etc. At a recent petition on the part of William Tonge, rector of the parish church of B. Mary, Langham, d. London, the pope hereby unites etc. the parish church of B. Mary, Ludgarsall' [also spelt *Ludgarsall*], d. Lincoln, to the above church of Langham, which he holds together by apostolic dispensation, (the annual value of the church of Ludgarsall' not exceeding 20, and of Langham, 24, gold ducats of the camera), for as long as he holds that of Langham, to the effect that William, in person or by proxy, may, on his own authority, take and continue in [corporal] possession of the church of Ludgarsall' and its rights and appurtenances, for as long as he holds the church of Langham, and convert its fruits etc. to his own uses and those of the said churches without licence of the local diocesan or of anyone else. With indult for life to William not to be bound, while residing in the Roman curia or one of his benefices or attending a *studium generale*, to reside personally in the said churches, nor to be liable to be compelled by anyone to do so against his will. Notwithstanding etc. The pope's will is, however, that the said churches of Langham and Ludgarsall' shall not, on account of this union etc. and indult, be defrauded of due services and the cure of souls therein shall not be neglected, but that the cure shall be exercised and things divine served by good and sufficient vicars maintained from the proceeds of those churches and that their customary burdens shall be supported; and that on William's death or resignation etc. of the church of Langham the union etc. shall be dissolved and so deemed and the church of [(?)Ludgarsall']¹ shall revert to its original condition automatically.

Ad futuram rei memoriam. Romanum decet pontificem votis illis prestare gratum assensum...
. Jo· Ortega / O· / O· xxxx Marianen'

¹ MS: *Langham*; *recte*: 'Ludgarsall''?

---

310   22 April 1500   *Reg. Lat.* 1064, fo 108ʳ⁻ᵛ

To John Chapleyn *alias* Tonker, rector of the parish church of Lutton', d. Bath and Wells. Dispensation — at his supplication — to receive and retain for life, together with the above parish church, one, and without it, any two other benefices, etc. [as above, no. 3].

Vite ac morum honestas...
· S· de Castello /· O· / O· L· Marianen'

---

311   22 April 1500   *Reg. Lat.* 1064, fo 109ʳ⁻ᵛ

To John Standerwike,¹ BDec, perpetual vicar of the parish church of Westbury, d. Bath and Wells. Dispensation — at his supplication — to receive and retain for life, together with the perpetual vicarage of the above parish church, one, and without it, any two other benefices, etc. [as above, no. 3].

Litterarum scientia, vite ac morum honestas...
· S· de· Castello / O· / O· L· Marianen'

¹ or *Standerwikt* : the final letter is blotched and perhaps redrawn

---

312   22 April 1500   *Reg. Lat.* 1064, fo 116ʳ⁻ᵛ

To Thomas Blythe, perpetual vicar of the parish church of Nasferton [also spelt *Nasferton'*], d. York. Dispensation and indult — at his supplication — to receive and retain for life, together with the perpetual vicarage of the above parish church, one, and without it, any two other benefices, etc. [as above, no. 3, to '... retain them together for life, as above']; and, also for life, while residing in the Roman curia or any one of his benefices or attending a *studium generale*, not to be bound, to reside in his other benefices, etc. [as above, no. 238].[1]

Vite ac morum honestas...
S· de Castello /· V· /· V· Lx· De Phano:

[1] save that in this instance 'incompatible' is not repeated

313   16 July 1500   *Reg. Lat.* 1064, fos 200^v-203^v

To the abbot of the monastery *de Chireleyson* [Abbeydorney], d. Ardfert, the prior of the monastery, usually governed by a prior, of Ynayscronayn, d. Killaloe, and John Thadei Machomara, canon of the church of Killaloe, mandate in favour of Thady Macconmara, cleric, d. Killaloe (who, as he asserts, is of noble birth by both parents). The pope has learned that the perpetual vicarages of the parish churches of Chovehe, Cloynlocayn and Kylnayrhe, d. Killaloe, are vacant *certo modo* at present and have been vacant for so long that by the Lateran statutes their collation has lawfully devolved on the apostolic see, although Laurence Maconmara [also spelt *Macconmara*] has detained the first vicarage, Laurence Omachayn, the second, Maurice Omulgayn[1], the third — Laurence Maconmara and Maurice bearing themselves as clerics and Laurence Omachayn, as a priest — without any title or support of law, temerariously and *de facto*, for a certain time, as they still do. At a recent petition on Thady's part to the pope to erect and institute a canonry in the church of Killaloe and out of the first vicarage a simple prebend in the same and unite etc. the second and third vicarages to them, after their erection, for his lifetime, the pope, not having certain knowledge of the foregoing, hereby commands that the above three (or two or one of them), if, having summoned respectively the bishop and chapter of Killaloe and Laurence Maconmara, Laurence Omachayn and Maurice and others concerned, they find the vicarages, whose annual value together does not exceed 20 marks sterling, to be vacant (howsoever etc.) and, having summoned those interested in the union etc., it to be thus, shall erect and institute a canonry in the church of Killaloe and the first vicarage into a simple prebend in the same, for Thady's lifetime, without prejudice to anyone; collate and assign the newly erected canonry and prebend, being vacant, to Thady; and also unite etc. the second and third vicarages (even if they and the first vicarage be specially reserved etc.) to the erected canonry and prebend, also for Thady's lifetime, with plenitude of canon law and all rights and appurtenances; inducting him etc. having removed Laurence Maconmara from the first vicarage, Laurence Omachayn[2] from the second, and Maurice from the third, and any other unlawful detainers, and causing Thady (or his proctor) to be received as a canon of the church of Killaloe, with plenitude of canon law, and the fruits etc., rights and obventions of the canonry and prebend and of the vicarages to be annexed to them to be delivered to him. [Curbing] gainsayers by the pope's authority etc. Notwithstanding etc. With the proviso that the vicarages shall not, on account of this erection, institution and union etc., be defrauded of due services and the cure of souls therein shall not be neglected; but that their customary burdens shall be supported. The pope's will is, however, that on Thady's death or resignation etc. of the canonry and prebend the canonry and prebend shall be extinguished[3] and the union etc. shall be dissolved and so deemed and the vicarages shall revert to their original condition and be deemed vacant automatically.

Piis fidelium votis per quam[4] *divini cultus augmentum...*
S· de Castello /· V· /· V· xxx· Undecimo kalendas Augusti Anno octavo [22 July 1500], *De Phano:*

[1] final letter blotched and doubtful; possibly 'o'
[2] in this instance the 'O' apparently changed (by overwriting) from a 'Y'
[3] *sic; rectius*: 'erection and institution shall be extinguished'?
[4] *sic; recte*: 'que'?

314   28 April 1500   *Reg. Lat.* 1064, fos 212[r]-213[r]

To John Mathew *alias* Norwich', monk of the monastery of Wymondh(a)m,[1] OSB, d. Norwich. Dispensation and indult — at his supplication — to receive and retain any benefice, with or without cure, usually held by secular clerics, etc. [as above, no. 32, to '... usually held by secular clerics']; and — even after he has acquired the said benefice — to bear everywhere the habit usually worn by the monks of the monastery of Wymondh(a)m [of whose number he is][2] and is, as he asserts, expressly professed of the order, under an honest vestment and habit of a secular cleric of a dark and decent colour, and not to be bound to bear the above habit [of the monks] nor to be liable to be compelled to do so against his will. Notwithstanding etc.

Religionis zelus, vite ac morum honestas...
. L. puccius /. V. / V. xxxx De Phano:

[1] MS: *Wymondh'm*
[2] 'ordinis Sancti Benedicti Norwicen. diocesis de quorum numero' (or suchlike) wanting?

315   18 April 1500   *Reg. Lat.* 1064, fos 227[v]-228[v]

To Robert Cooke, priest, d. York. Dispensation — at his supplication — to him (who, as he asserts, is a BA) to receive and retain together for life any two benefices, with cure or otherwise mutually incompatible, etc. [as above, no. 3, to '... Notwithstanding etc']. With the proviso that the incompatible benefices in question shall not, on this account, be defrauded of due services and the cure of souls therein (if any) shall not be neglected.

Vite ac morum honestas...
· *L· puccius* / *O·* / *O· L· Marianen'*

316   18 April 1500   *Reg. Lat.* 1064, fos 228ᵛ-229ᵛ

To Arthur Lacy, perpetual vicar of the parish church of Brathewell, d. York. Dispensation — at his supplication — to him (who, as he asserts, is a BA) to receive and retain for life, together with the perpetual vicarage of the above parish church, one, and without it, any two other benefices, etc. [as above, no. 3].

Vite ac morum honestas...
. *Jo· Ortega* / *O·* / *O· L· Marianen'*

317   18 April 1500   *Reg. Lat.* 1064, fos 231ʳ-232ʳ

To John Haster,[1] MA, rector of the parish church of B. Mary, Asshewell, d. Lincoln. Dispensation — at his supplication — to him (who is also a BTheol) to receive and retain for life, together with the above parish church, one, and without them, any two other benefices, etc. [as above, no. 3].

Litterarum scientia, vite ac morum honestas...
· *C· de Scorciatis* / *O·* / *O· L· Marianen'*

[1] *rectius*: 'Hafter'? *Cf.* Emden, *Oxford to 1500*, pp. 846 and 884

318   24 March 1500[1]   *Reg. Lat.* 1064, fos 257ᵛ-259ʳ

To Thomas Aphowel, LLB, archdeacon of Cardigan, in the church of St David's, dispensation. Some time ago, Innocent VIII by his letters dispensed him to receive and retain for life, together with the parish church of Llanlloycharn',[2] d. St David's, (which, as he asserted, he was then holding), one, and without them, any two other benefices, etc. [as above, no. 131, to '... as is more fully contained in those letters']. The pope therefore — at his supplication — hereby further dispenses Thomas, who, as he asserts, holds, by the said dispensation, the parish church of Llanlloycharn' still and also the archdeaconry of Cardigan, (which is a non-major dignity *post pontificalem* and was canonically collated to him while vacant *certo modo*), to receive and retain for life, together with the parish church and archdeaconry, or with any two other incompatible benefices held by him at the time by the said dispensation, any third benefice, etc. [as above, no. 131].

Litterarum scientia, vite ac morum honestas...
. L. puccius /· V· /· V· Lxx De Phano:

[1] *Nono* inserted in the margin (in the hand of the magistral signature) initialled .*V.* ; with *Non*', deleted and initialled .*V.*, in the line
[2] the first occurrence (only) written: *Llanlloy charn*'

319   28 March 1500   *Reg. Lat.* 1064, fos 259ᵛ-260ʳ

To Richard ap David, monk of the monastery of B. Mary the Virgin, Whitland (*de Albalanda*), OCist, d. St David's. Dispensation — at his supplication — to him, who, as he asserts, is a priest and expressly professed of the above order,[1] to receive and retain any benefice, with or without cure, usually held by secular clerics, etc. [as above, no. 32].

Religionis zelus, vite ac morum honestas...
. L. puccius /· V· /· V· xxx De Phano:

[1] The latter information comes from a notwithstanding clause.

320[1]   27 March 1500   *Reg. Lat.* 1064, fos 260ᵛ-262ʳ

To Maurice David, BDec, perpetual vicar of the parish church of Whitechurche, called Album Monasterium (*Albi monasterii*), d. St David's, dispensation. Some time ago, Innocent VIII by his letters dispensed him to receive and retain for life, together with the perpetual vicarage of the above parish church, (which, as he asserted, he was then holding), one, and without them, any two other benefices, etc. [as above, no. 131, to '... as is more fully contained in those letters'].[2] The pope therefore — at his supplication — hereby further dispenses Maurice, who, as he asserts, holds, by the said dispensation, the above perpetual vicarage still and a perpetual chaplaincy, called a chantry, dedicated to St Nicholas the Confessor, in the church of St David's, which is incompatible with another incompatible benefice and was canonically collated to him while vacant *certo modo*, to receive and retain for life, together with the vicarage [and][3] chaplaincy, or with any two other incompatible benefices held by him at the time by the said dispensation, any third benefice, etc. [as above, no. 131].

Litterarum scientia, vite ac morum honestas...
. L. puccius /· V· / V Lxx. De Phano:

[1] A copy (presumably made from engrossment) is published in *The Episcopal Registers of The Diocese of St David's 1397 to 1518* (Cymmrodorion Record Series, No. 6, London, 1917), Vol. II, p. 724.

[2] summarised in *CPL*, XV at no. 658

[3] though MS has *vel*

---

321   18 March 1500   *Reg. Lat.* 1064, fo 279[r-v]

To Thomas Tudenh(a)m[1] *alias* Moro, canon of the monastery of B. Mary, Langley, OPrem, d. Norwich. Dispensation — at his supplication — to him, who is a priest and, as he asserts, is expressly professed of the above order,[2] to receive and retain any benefice, with or without cure, usually held by secular clerics, etc. [as above, no. 32].[3]

Religionis zelus, vite ac morum honestas...
. L. puccius /· V· / V· xxx De Phano:

[1] MS: *Tudenhm'*

[2] The latter information comes from a notwithstanding clause.

[3] save that in this instance MS has *similiter* in error for 'simpliciter'

---

322   2 April 1500   *Reg. Lat.* 1064, fos 280[r]-281[r]

To Thomas Einster, monk of the monastery of B. Mary, Hurley, OSB, d. Salisbury, dispensation. Some time ago — after Innocent VIII by certain letters of his had dispensed him to receive and retain any benefice, with or without cure, usually ruled[1] by secular clerics, even if a parish church or its perpetual vicarage, or a chantry, free chapel, hospital or annual service, usually assigned to secular clerics in title of a perpetual ecclesiastical benefice — the pope dispensed him by other letters of his to receive together with the parish church of St John the Baptist, Dunnyquo,[2] d. Norwich, (which, as he asserted, he was then holding by the said dispensation), one, and without it, any two other benefices, with or without cure, usually held by secular clerics, even if parish churches [or] their perpetual vicarages, or chantries, free chapels, hospitals or annual services, usually assigned to secular clerics in title

of a perpetual ecclesiastical benefice, if he obtained them otherwise canonically, and
to retain for life whichever one he chooses *in titulum* and with it the other one *in
commendam*, to resign them, at once or successively, simply or for exchange, as
often as he pleased, and cede the commend, and in their place receive up to two
other, similar or dissimilar, benefices, with or without cure, usually held by secular
clerics, and retain for life whichever one he chooses *in titulum* and the other one *in
commendam*, as is more fully contained in the letters aforesaid.[3] The pope — at his
supplication — hereby dispenses[4] him,[5] who, as he asserts, still holds the said
church, to bear everywhere the habit usually worn by monks of the above monastery,
OSB, of which he is a monk and is, as he asserts, expressly professed of that order,
under an honest garment (*vestis*) and habit of a secular cleric, of a dark and decent
colour, and not to be bound to bear the above habit [of the monks] otherwise nor to
be liable to be compelled in any way to do so against his will. Notwithstanding etc.

Religionis zelus, vite ac morum honestas...
. L. puccius /· V· /· V· xx De Phano:

[1] *regi*; *cf.* below 'held' (*teneri*)

[2] *recte*: 'de Dunuyquo' for 'de Dunuico'?

[3] summarised in *CPL* XVI at no. 174

[4] *dispensamus*; *recte*: 'indulgemus' (MS has *tibi* above, *indulti* below)

[5] *de nobili genere procreatus ac* in the line deleted and initialled *.V.* thrice; *Cassat(um) de Mandato
R(everendissimi) D(omini) Jo(hannis) Ragusin' Regentis per me V. de Phano*: against it in the margin

---

323   8 April 1500   *Reg. Lat.* 1064, fos 284ᵛ-285ʳ

To William Menewynuyke, perpetual vicar of the parish church of Mylton Abbat', d.
Exeter. Indult for life — at his supplication — to him, who, as he asserts, holds the
perpetual vicarage of the above parish church, not to be bound, while residing in the
Roman curia or any one of his benefices or attending a *studium generale*, to reside
<personally>[1] in the said church,[2] nor to be liable to be compelled by anyone to do
so against his will. Notwithstanding etc. With the proviso that the vicarage shall not,
on this account, be defrauded of due services and the cure of souls therein shall not
be neglected; but that the cure shall be exercised and things divine served by a good
and sufficient vicar maintained from the proceeds of this vicarage.

Vite ac morum honestas...
. L. puccius / V / V· xx De Phano:

[1] marginal insertion, initialled *.V.*

[2] *ecclesia* ; *recte*: 'vicaria'?

324 12 April 1500 *Reg. Lat.* 1064, fo 285^{r-v}

To William Shamke, rector of the parish church of Lewtreneherd, d. Exeter. Indult for life — at his supplication — to him, who, as he asserts, holds by apostolic dispensation the parish churches of Lewtreneherd and Schyllyngford, d. Exeter, not to be bound, while residing in the Roman curia or any one of his benefices or attending a *studium generale*, to reside personally in the said churches, nor to be liable to be compelled by anyone to do so against his will. Notwithstanding etc. With the proviso that the said churches shall not, on this account, be defrauded of due services and the cure of souls therein shall not be neglected; but that the cure shall be exercised and things divine served by good and sufficient vicars maintained from the proceeds of these churches.

Vite ac morum honestas...
. L. puccius /. V· /. V· xx De Phano:-

325 12 April 1500 *Reg. Lat.* 1064, fos 293^r-294^r

To Henry Chest[1] *alias* Ris, monk of the monastery of B. Mary the Virgin, Worcester, OSB. Dispensation — at his supplication — to him, who, as he asserts, holds a place and monacal portion of the above monastery and, as he also asserts, is expressly professed of the above order,[2] to receive and retain for life, together with the above place and monacal portion, any benefice, with or without cure, usually held by [secular][3] clerics, even if a parish church or its perpetual vicarage, or a chantry, free chapel, hospital or annual service, usually assigned to secular clerics in title of a perpetual ecclesiastical benefice, and of lay patronage and of whatsoever tax or annual value, etc. [as above, no. 139, to '... retain it for life, as above']; and also — even after he has acquired the above benefice — to have, likewise for life, a stall etc. [as above, no. 139].

Religionis zelus, vite ac morum honestas...
. L. puccius /· V· / V· Lx De Phano:

[1] or possibly *Ehest* : there is a horizontal bar through the 'C' : *cf.* the 'E' of *Ecclesiasticum* (fo 293^r, line 14)

[2] The latter information comes from a notwithstanding clause.

[3] 'seculares' wanting

326 21 September 1499 *Reg. Lat.* 1064, fos 335^r-336^r

To Thomas Long, scholar, d. Canterbury. Dispensation — at his supplication — to him, who, as he asserts, wishes to become a cleric and is in his eighteenth year of age, to receive and retain for life — henceforth, after he has been duly marked with clerical character — one, and — in his twentieth year — another, and without them, any two other benefices, with cure or otherwise mutually incompatible, [as above, no. 3, to '... as often as he pleases'], and in their place receive — henceforth — one, and — in his twentieth year — up to two other, similar or dissimilar, incompatible benefices, and retain them together for life, as above. Notwithstanding the above defect of age etc. With the proviso that the incompatible benefices in question shall not, on this account, be defrauded of due services and the cure of souls therein (if any) shall not be neglected.

Vite ac morum honestas...
. L. puccius /· V· /. V· Lxx De Phano:

327   25 January 1500   *Reg. Lat.* 1064, fos 336ʳ-337ʳ

To Thomas Key, LLB, rector of the parish church of St John the Baptist, Dicheryche [also spelt *Dydrerydre*], d. Salisbury. Dispensation — at his supplication — to receive and retain for life, together with the above parish church, one, and without it, any two other benefices, etc. [as above, no. 3].

Litterarum scientia, vite ac morum honestas...
A. de Sancto Severin(o) /· V· /· V· L. De Phano:

328   4 May 1500   *Reg. Lat.* 1065, fos 29ᵛ-30ᵛ

To Thomas Dagget, rector of the parish church of Depedale, d. Norwich. Dispensation — at his supplication — to receive and retain for life, together with the above parish church, one, and without it, any two other benefices with cure, or otherwise mutually incompatible, even if parish churches or their perpetual vicarages, or chantries, free chapels, hospitals or annual services, or administrations of the sacraments,[1] usually assigned to secular clerics in title of a perpetual ecclesiastical benefice, or dignities etc. [as above, no. 3].

Vite ac morum honestas...
Jo ortega / F / F· L. Sanctor(is)

[1] *sic; cf.* no. 329

329   4 May 1500   *Reg. Lat.* 1065, fos 30[V]-31[V]

To William Taylard, Lic Dec, rector of the parish church of Abbots Ripton (*Ripton' Abbatis*), d. Lincoln. Dispensation — at his supplication — to receive and retain for life, together with the above parish church, one, and without it, any two other benefices, with cure or otherwise mutually incompatible, even if parish churches or their perpetual vicarages, or chantries, free chapels, hospitals or annual services, or administrations of the sacraments[1], usually assigned to secular clerics in title of a perpetual ecclesiastical benefice, [or] dignities etc. [as above, no. 3].

Litterarum scientia, vite ac morum honestas...
Jo ortega / F / F· L. Sanctor(is)

[1] *sic*; *cf.* no. 328

330   21 September 1499   *Reg. Lat.* 1065, fos 34[V]-37[V]

To Florence Ogervayn and Hobertus Machmiloyd, canons of the church of Clonfert, and William Ochormachan, canon of the church of Killaloe, mandate in favour of Thomas de Burgo, canon of the church of Kilmacduagh. Some time ago, the pope — having learned that the deanery of the church of Tuam was then vacant *certo modo* and had been vacant for so long that by the Lateran statutes its collation had lawfully devolved on the apostolic see, although Walter Brincheam, who was bearing himself as dean, had detained it without any title or support of law, temerariously and *de facto*, for a certain time, as he was then — charged by certain letters *ad Tuamen...*,[1] his own name not expressed, if, having summoned Walter and others concerned, they found the deanery to be vacant, to collate and make provision of it by the first of the said letters to John and by the second to Odo aforesaid.[2] Next — after representation had been made to the pope on John's part that Walter at the time of his said earlier letters had died outside the Roman curia and while he had lived was holding the deanery not without title but with canonical title; and that no mention had been made of this in the said earlier letters which had not yet then been committed for execution; and that John fears that on this account the said earlier letters [of provision][3] could be surreptitious and their effect be frustrated with the passage of time — the pope by certain other letters of his [charged] the said William and Charles and Cristianus[4] to decree by his authority that John's earlier letters, with all the clauses contained therein, be valid and have full force from the date of the later letters and to proceed to the execution of them otherwise in accordance with the tenor, form and content of John's earlier letters, in and for all things just as if it had been expressly stated in John's said earlier letters that the deanery was vacant not *certo modo* but by Walter's death, as above, and that while he lived Walter had detained[5] it not without title but with canonical title, as is more fully contained in each of the letters aforesaid in the first of which John asserted that the annual value of the deanery did not exceed 32 marks sterling and in the second Odo asserted that the deanery was not elective and its annual value did not exceed 24 marks sterling. Moreover, as a recent petition on the above Thomas's part stated, it had been customary when the deanery became vacant, in the absence of the apostolic reservations, for the appointee to be chosen by the chapter of the church of Tuam and thus the deanery was elective, and its fruits etc. at the time of the said letters were (and are) worth more, although they do not exceed a total of 40 marks sterling. The pope therefore — considering that, if it is thus, the said letters are known to be surreptitious and the collations and provisions of the deanery made to John and Odo by pretext of them and whatever ensued therefrom do not hold good, and that the deanery, which is a major dignity *post pontificalem*, is vacant *certo modo* still by Walter's death, as above; and, as the pope has learned, the monastery of Knockmoy (*Collis Victorie*), OCist,[6] aforesaid diocese, is vacant *certo modo* at present and has been vacant for so long that by canonical sanctions its provision has lawfully devolved on the apostolic see; and no-one except the pope could or can make disposition of the said [deanery][7] because he has reserved all dignities major *post pontificalem* in cathedrals vacated then and in the future to his own collation and disposition; and wishing to make provision of a suitable governor for the monastery as well as to assist Thomas (who asserts that John had detained, as he does, the monastery without any title or support of law, for a certain time; and that he, Thomas, is of exalted noble birth and holds a canonry and prebend of the church of Kilmacduagh) — hereby commands that the above three (or two or one of them), having summoned respectively John and Odo and others concerned, shall inform themselves as to all the foregoing and, if they find it to be thus, declare each of the aforesaid letters and the collations and provisions made by virtue of them to John and Odo successively as above and whatever ensued therefrom to have been and be null and void; and, in that event, commend the monastery, whose annual value does not exceed 140 marks sterling, vacant howsoever etc., to Thomas, to be held, ruled and governed by him for life; (he may — due and customary burdens of the monastery and its convent having been supported — make disposition of its fruits etc. just as those holding it *in titulum* could and ought to do, alienation of immovable goods and precious movables being however forbidden); committing to him the care, rule and administration of the monastery in spiritualities and temporalities and causing obedience and reverence to be given him by the convent and customary services and rights by the vassals and other subjects of the monastery; and collate and assign the deanery, whose annual value does not exceed 40 marks sterling, (vacant as above or howsoever etc., even if it has been vacant for so long that by the Lateran statutes its collation has lawfully devolved on the apostolic see etc.), with all rights and appurtenances, to Thomas, inducting him etc. having removed any unlawful detainer from the deanery and John and any other unlawful detainer from the monastery and causing Thomas (or his proctor) to be admitted to the deanery and its fruits etc., rights and obventions to be delivered to him. [Curbing] gainsayers etc. Notwithstanding etc. With the proviso that divine worship and the usual number of ministers in the said monastery [shall not], on account of this commend, [be diminished]⁸ and its aforesaid burdens and those of the convent shall be supported.

Romani pontificis providentia circumspecta...
S. de Castello. / L. / L. xL. Dulcius:-

¹ omission hereabouts? (*cf.* notes 2 and 4)

2 this is the first mention of John and Odo (*cf.* note 1). The letters in favour of John [OKelly] are calendared above at nos 69 and 75. Those in favour of Odo [OKelly] are lost : see no 1124 below.

³ MS *pensionis* ; *recte* : 'provisionis'

⁴ this is the first (and only) mention of William [OConcannon], Charles [OMulkerrill] and Cristianus [Spelman] (*cf.* note 1); surnames supplied from nos 69 and 75 above

⁵ *detinuerat* or possibly *detinuerit; rectius*: 'obtin... '?

⁶ 'ordinis' does not occur

⁷ *canonicatu; recte*: 'decanatu'?

⁸ supplied by editor

---

331   12 October 1499   *Reg. Lat.* 1065, fos 91ʳ-92ᵛ

To Robert Kuodi, perpetual vicar of the parish church of Lukenor, d. Lincoln. Dispensation and indult — at his supplication — to him (who is a BA) to receive and retain for life, together with the perpetual vicarage of the above parish church, one, and without it, any two other benefices, etc. [as above, no. 3, to '... retain them together for life, as above']; and, for life, while residing in the above vicarage or another of his benefices or attending a *studium generale,* not to be bound to reside personally in his other benefices, nor to be liable to be compelled by anyone to do so against his will. Notwithstanding etc. With the proviso that the above perpetual vicarage and other incompatible benefices and benefices in which he shall not reside shall not, on this account, be defrauded of due services and the cure of souls in the perpetual vicarage and (if any) in the other incompatible benefices and benefices in which he shall not reside shall not be neglected; but that customary burdens of benefices in which he shall not reside shall be supported.

Vite ac morum honestas...
F de parma /. L. / L. Lx. Dulcius:-

---

332   16 January 1500   *Reg. Lat.* 1065, fos 125ʳ-126ʳ

To John Hepburn,¹ scholar, d. St Andrews, dispensation and indult. The pope (who, some time ago, decreed and declared that provisions, grants or mandates of provision to canonries and prebends of cathedral churches to persons who have not completed their fourteenth year of age shall have no force except by consent of the apostolic see; and that any impetrations concerning canonries and prebends in collegiate churches if those impetrating be less than ten years and mention be not made of this in the impetrations shall have no force) hereby dispenses and indulges John (who, as he asserts, suffers from a defect of birth as the son of an expressly professed canon, OSA, and an unmarried woman of noble birth) — at his supplication — as soon as he has reached his eighth year — to be marked with clerical character, even by any catholic bishop of his choice in communion with the apostolic see, and, thereafter, receive any number of benefices without cure; and — as soon as he has reached his eighteenth year — one, and — his twentieth — with it, another, with cure or otherwise mutually incompatible; and — at the lawful age — be promoted to all, even sacred, orders and also receive any number of benefices, with and without cure, compatible mutually and with the incompatible benefices aforesaid, even if the compatible benefices should be canonries and prebends and they as well as the incompatible benefices should be parish churches or their perpetual vicarages, dignities, *personatus*, administrations or offices in cathedral, even metropolitan, or collegiate churches, even if the dignities in question should be major *post pontificalem* in cathedral, even metropolitan, churches, or principal in collegiate churches, or a combination, even if the dignities etc. should be customarily elective and have cure of souls, if he obtains them otherwise canonically, and retain even the incompatible benefices together for life, to resign them, at once or successively, simply or for exchange, as often as he pleases and in their place receive other, similar or dissimilar, benefices, viz. : — as soon as he has reached his eighth year — any number without cure — his eighteenth — one, and — his twentieth — with it, another, with cure or otherwise mutually incompatible and — at the lawful age — any number of other benefices, with or without cure, compatible mutually and with the incompatible benefices aforesaid, and retain even the incompatible benefices for life, as above; and not to be bound in any impetrations concerning canonries and prebends of collegiate churches to mention his defect of age and such impetrations shall not, on this account, be surreptitious, but shall be valid. Notwithstanding the defects of birth and age which he shall suffer even in his eighteenth and twentieth year etc. With the proviso that the canonries and prebends and incompatible benefices in question shall not, on this account, be defrauded of due services and the cure of souls in the said incompatible benefices (if any) shall not be neglected; but that the customary burdens of the canonries and prebends shall be supported.

Laudabilia tue infantilis etatis indicia...
F de parma /· V· /· V· Lxxx De Phano:

[1] or *Hepburr* : the 'p' and 'urn' are reworked

333   28 January 1500   *Reg. Lat.* 1065, fos 130[v]-131[v]

Restoration, as below. Some time ago, Innocent VIII, on the advice of the cardinals whose number included the present pope, erected and created the church of Glasgow into a metropolitan church with archiepiscopal dignity and other marks of metropolitan status; separated, divided and severed the church of Dunblane and several other cathedral churches and their cities and dioceses from the province of the metropolitan church of St Andrews, of which they were[1] suffragans; absolutely exempted and genuinely severed the bishops of them and the clergy and people of the said cities and dioceses from the superiority and jurisdiction of the archbishop of St Andrews at that time and for the time being; willed that these churches, thus severed, and their prelates and clergy and also the people of the said cities and dioceses thenceforth were in no way to be under the archbishop of St Andrews by metropolitical law; and granted and assigned the prelates of Dunblane and of the other churches to the archbishop of Glasgow for the time being as his suffragans, to the effect that they were subject to him by metropolitical law, as is more fully contained in the letters of the pope's predecessor drawn up in that regard.[2] Moreover, a recent [petition][3] to the pope on the part of James, administrator (deputed by apostolic authority) of the church of St Andrews, [stated] that James, bishop of Dunblane, takes the usual oath and gives due obedience and reverence to Robert, archbishop of Glasgow, as his suffragan, and if the church of Dunblane were to be restored to its original condition and be made subject to the archbishop of St Andrews as before, it would be <to the peace and quiet>[4] of the archbishop of St Andrews. At the supplication of administrator James, the pope, relaxing bishop James from the oath in question, hereby restores the church of Dunblane from the province of Glasgow — with the express consent thereto of archbishop Robert given by Thomas Halkerston', cleric, d. St Andrews, his specially appointed proctor — to its original state before the separation, to the effect that in the future the church of Dunblane and its bishop for the time being shall be subject to the archbishop of St Andrews by metropolitical law as before, and the bishop of Dunblane shall be his suffragan <in and for all things>[5] as if the separation and severance of the church of Dunblane and assignment thereof had never been done. Notwithstanding etc.

Ad perpetuam rei memoriam. Romanum decet pontificem votis illis gratum prestare assensum...
L puccius / L[6] /. L. xxx. Dulcius:-

[1] *erat*; changed (by deletion of bar) from *erant*; *recte*: 'erant'?

[2] lost; Index entry transcribed in *CPL, XV*, at no. 1448; *cf.* also no. 1446

[3] 'petitio continebat' wanting

[4] *ex hoc profecto paci et quieti* deleted from the text above, initialled *L* twice, is here inserted (in the same hand) in the margin, initialled *L* twice

[5] marginal insertion, initialled . *L*.

[6] unusually and strangely formed

334   25 January 1500   *Reg. Lat.* 1065, fos 131^v-132^v

To Richard Ranbino, rector of the parish church of Dino, d. Lincoln. Dispensation —
at his supplication — to receive and retain for life, together with the above parish
church, one, and without it, any two other benefices, etc. [as above, no. 3].[1]

Vite ac morum honestas...
L *puccius* / F / F. L^{ta}. *Sanctor(is)*

[1] save that 'or a combination' does not occur

335   27 January 1500   *Reg. Lat.* 1065, fos 133^r-134^r

To Robert Mutton', rector of the parish church of Brrowarmersche[1] [also spelt
Borrowarmersche], d. Canterbury. Dispensation — at his supplication — to receive
and retain for life, together with the above parish church, one, or without it, any two
other benefices, etc. [as above, no. 3].[2]

Vite ac morum honestas...
L *puccius* / F / F L^{ta}. *Sanctor(is)*

[1] the *B* written over a *V*

[2] save that, after the first occurrence of *metropolitanis*, MS wants 'vel collegiatis'

336   31 December 1499   *Reg. Lat.* 1065, fos 298^v-300^r

To Richard Gottis, BDec, canon of the monastery, called a priory, of Walsyngh(a)m,[1]
OSA, d. Norwich. Dispensation and indult — at his supplication — to him, who, as
he asserts, holds canonically the perpetual vicarage of the parish church of
Narsforth,[2] d. Norwich, and, as he also asserts, is expressly professed of the above
order,[3] to receive together with the above vicarage, one, and without it, any two
regular benefices, with or without cure, of any order, or with one of them, or without
them, one secular benefice, with cure, even if the [?regular][4] benefices should be
priories, *prepositure, prepositatus*, dignities, *personatus*, administrations or offices in
regular cathedral, even metropolitan, churches and the secular benefice be a parish
church or its perpetual vicarage, or a chantry, free chapel, hospital or annual service,
usually assigned to secular clerics in title of a perpetual ecclesiastical benefice, and
even if the priories, *prepositure*,[5] dignities etc. should be customarily elective and
have cure of souls, if he obtains them otherwise canonically, and to retain for life

whichever one of the regular benefices he chooses, even if it should be a priory, *prepositura* or other dignity in any of the said cathedral churches, major *post pontificalem* or conventual, or a claustral office, *in titulum*, and with it, the other regular benefice, which may not be suchlike, or a secular benefice, *in commendam*, to resign them, at once or successively, simply or for exchange, as often as he pleases, and cede the commend, and in their place receive up to two, similar or dissimilar, regular benefices as above, or with one of them, or without them, one secular benefice, with cure, and retain for life whichever one of the regular benefices he chooses, even if it should be a priory, *prepositura* or other dignity, major or conventual, or a claustral office, *in titulum*, [?and with]⁶ it, the other regular benefice, which may not be suchlike, or a secular benefice *in commendam*, as above; (he may — due and customary burdens of the benefice held *in commendam* having been supported — make disposition of the rest of its fruits etc. just as those holding it *in titulum* could and ought to do, alienation of immovable goods and precious movables being however forbidden); and, also for life, while residing in the Roman curia or one of the benefices aforesaid or attending a *studium generale*, not to be bound to reside in the other one of the benefices aforesaid, nor to be liable to be compelled by anyone to do so against his will. Notwithstanding etc. With the proviso that [the benefice] retained *in commendam* and benefices in which he shall not reside shall not, on this account, be defrauded of due services and the cure of souls in the secular benefice or (if any) in the regular benefice held *in commendam* and benefices in which he shall not reside shall not be neglected; but that the customary burdens aforesaid of the benefice held *in commendam* and of benefices in which he shall not reside shall be supported.

Religionis zelus, litterarum scientia, vite ac morum honestas...
Jo. Ortega⁷ /· V· / V· Lx. De Phano:

¹ MS: *Walsyngh'm*

² or *Norrsforth*

³ The latter information comes from a notwithstanding clause.

⁴ *secularia*; *recte*: 'regularia'?

⁵ 'prepositatus' does not occur here

⁶ *etiam*; *recte*: 'et cum'?

⁷ in enlarged characters, the form reminiscent of his signature on engrossments; perhaps written by the enregistering scribe; but later?

337   11 January 1500   *Reg. Lat.* 1065, fos 302ʳ-303ʳ

To Henry Haolt *alias* Baker, canon of the monastery of B. Mary the Virgin, Wendlyng, OPrem, d. Norwich. Dispensation — at his supplication — to him, who, as he asserts, is expressly professed of the above order,¹ to receive and retain any benefice, with or without cure, usually held by secular clerics, even if a parish church or its perpetual vicarage, or a chantry, free chapel, hospital or annual service, or an administration, called of the sacraments, with cure of souls, usually assigned to secular clerics in title of a perpetual ecclesiastical benefice, and of lay patronage and whatsoever tax or annual value, etc [as above, no. 32].

Religionis zelus, vite ac morum honestas...
Jo ortega / F / F xxxx. Sanctor(is)

[1] This information comes from a notwithstanding clause.

---

338   27 January 1500   *Reg. Lat.* 1065, fos 305^r-306^r

To Richard Halidai, perpetual vicar of the parish church of Stratton' Margarete [also spelt *Stratton' Margaete*], d. Salisbury. Dispensation — at his supplication — to him (who is a priest) to receive and retain for life, together with the perpetual vicarage of the above parish church, one, or without it, any two other benefices, etc. [as above, no. 3].

Vite ac morum honestas...
L. Puccius. [1] / F / F. L^{ta}. *Santor(is)*[2]

[1] the script (but probably not the hand) differs somewhat from that of the letter and, most unusually, there is a flourish after the point : entered later?
[2] *sic*; usually 'Sanctor(is)'

---

339   11 January 1500   *Reg. Lat.* 1065, fo 329^{r-v}

To Robert Lyttelman, brother of the pope's hospital of the Holy Spirit, in Saxia, Rome (*Sancti Spiritus in Saxia de Urbe*), OSA. Dispensation — at his supplication — to him, who is a priest and, as he asserts, originated from d. Lincoln, and who, as he also asserts, is expressly professed of the above order,[1] to receive and retain any benefice, with or without cure, usually held by secular clerics, even if a parish church or its perpetual vicarage, or a chaplaincy,[2] chantry, free chapel,[3] hospital or annual service, or an administration, called of the sacraments, with cure, usually assigned to secular clerics in title of a perpetual ecclesiastical benefice, even if of lay patronage and of whatsoever tax or annual value, etc. [as above, no. 32, to '... another, similar or dissimilar, benefice']. Notwithstanding etc. and [notwithstanding] the constitutions of Otto and Ottobuono formerly legates of the apostolic see in the kingdom of England etc.[4]

Religionis zelus, vite ac morum honestas...
N bregeon /· V· /· V· xxx De Phano:

1 This information comes from a notwithstanding clause.

2 *capellania*

3 l*acapella*; *recte*: 'capella'

4 The inclusion of these constitutions gives Lyttelman the option of holding his secular benefice in England.

340   8 August 1500   *Reg.* Lat. 1066, fos 4ʳ-5ʳ

To David Phelype, perpetual vicar of the parish church of St Nicholas, Pembroke (*de Penbrochia*), d. St David's. Dispensation — at his supplication — to receive and retain for life, together with the perpetual vicarage of the above parish church, one, and without it, any two other benefices, etc. [as above, no. 3].

Vite ac morum honestas...
. L. puccius / O. / O. L. Marianen'

341   20 April 1500   *Reg. Lat.* 1066, fos 5ᵛ-7ᵛ

To John Bury, prior, called the third, of the monastery of Chertesey, OSB, d. Winchester. Dispensation — at his supplication — to him, who, as he asserts, holds a place and monacal portion and the claustral priorship, called the third, customarily held together by one of the monks of the monastery, of whose number he is, and is expressly professed of the order, to receive, together with the above place, monacal portion and priorship, one, and without them, any two other regular benefices, with or without cure, of the said order, or with one of them, or without them, one secular benefice, with or without cure, even if the regular benefices should be priories, *prepositure, propositatus*,¹ dignities, *personatus*, administrations or offices, and the secular benefice be a parish church or its perpetual vicarage, or a chantry, free chapel, hospital or annual service, usually assigned to secular clerics in title of a perpetual ecclesiastical benefice, of lay patronage or pertaining to the presentation of the abbot and convent of the monastery, and of whatsoever tax or annual value, or a combination, and dependencies of the said monastery or of another regular place, even if the priories etc. should be customarily elective and have cure of souls, if he obtains them otherwise canonically, and to retain for life whichever one of the regular benefices he chooses, even if it be a conventual priory, *prepositura* or other conventual dignity or a claustral office, *in titulum*, and with it, the other regular, or a secular, benefice, *in commendam*, to resign them, at once or successively, simply or for exchange, as often as he pleases, and cede the commend, and in their place receive up to two other, similar or dissimilar, regular benefices of the aforesaid order, or with one of them, or without them, one secular benefice, with or without cure, and retain for life whichever one of the regular benefices he chooses *in titulum* and with it the other regular one, which may not be conventual or claustral, or a secular benefice, *in commendam*, as above; (he may — due and customary burdens of the benefice retained *in commendam* having been supported — make disposition of the rest of its fruits etc. just as those holding it [*in titulum*] could and ought to do, alienation of immovable goods and precious movables being however forbidden); and to have, also for life, even after he has acquired the secular benefice, a stall in the choir and a place [and] an active and a passive voice in the chapter of the monastery and otherwise as before, just as if he had not, or shall not have, acquired the said secular benefice. Notwithstanding etc. With the proviso that the benefice retained *in commendam* shall not, on this account, be defrauded of due services and the cure of souls therein (if any) shall not be neglected; but that its aforesaid burdens shall be supported.

Religionis zelus, vite ac morum honestas...
. L. puccius / O. /. O. Lx. Marianen'

1 *propositatus*; for 'prepositatus'

342   7 August 1500   *Reg. Lat.* 1066, fos 10ᵛ-11ᵛ

To Robert Blenkensop, rector of the parish church of Mean Stoke, d. Winchester. Dispensation — at his supplication — to receive and retain for life, together with the above parish church, one, and without it, any two other benefices, etc. [as above, no. 3].

Vite ac morum honestas...
. L. puccius /· V· /· V· L· De Phano:

343¹   1 July 1500   *Reg. Lat.* 1066, fos 20ᵛ-21ᵛ

Statute and ordinance as below. Some time ago, Boniface VIII² licensed any the then warden (*custodi*) and scholars of the college of the Annunciation of B. Mary the Virgin in the university of Cambridge (*studium Cantabrigie*), d. Ely, and all others for the time being in the college and attending it, who were priests or in sacred orders, to celebrate [in]³ the college chapel dedicated to B. Mary the Virgin mass and other divine offices, even with music and raised voice (*cum nota et alta voce*), without licence of the local diocesan or of anyone else, as is more fully contained in Boniface's letters. However, a recent petition to the pope on the part of the present warden and fellows of the college stated that the college has a house, called

Fischewyke hostel (*hospitium*), in another part of the <road>[4] opposite the college, which lawfully pertains to it and in which scholars studying letters live; and that if the scholars for the time being living in the house, and the fellows and other persons in the college for the time being, who were not in sacred orders, were able to celebrate divine office in the chapel, even with music and raised voice, it would be greatly to the advantage of scholars, house, college and those in it, facilitate the scholars' study, lessen their opportunities for wandering off, and arouse them to pious exercises, with benefit to their souls and divine worship. At the supplication of the warden and fellows, the pope hereby establishes and ordains that any the warden and fellows, the scholars of the said house, and others in the college or house for the time being, who are not in sacred [orders][5] may celebrate divine office in the chapel with music and raised voice; that the warden and fellows may keep, decently, the Eucharist in the chapel and depute a chaplain or other priest, secular or regular, of any order (even mendicant), to administer the sacraments to them and to the scholars and others in the college and house for the time being; and that they may cause the bodies of those dying in the college or house to be committed for burial in the chapel; all without the licence of the diocesan or of anyone else, but without prejudice to the parish church or any other church. Notwithstanding, etc.

Ad perpetuam rei memoriam. Piis fidelium votis...
. L. puccius / V /. V· Lxxxx De Phano:

[1] summarized briefly *ex diplomate pontificio* at p. xviii of *Academiae Historia Cantebrigiensis.* annexed to M. Parker, *De Antiquitate Britannicae Ecclesiae et Privilegiis Ecclesiae Cantuariensis*, ed S. Drake, London, 1729.

[2] MS *Bonifatius papa VIII*; *recte* 'VIIII'?

[3] MS wants 'in'

[4] *vie* inserted in the margin by the enregistering scribe, initialled .V. ; ?*aut*, deleted and initialled .V., in the line

[5] MS wants 'ordinibus'

344   8 August 1500   *Reg. Lat.* 1066, fos 22ʳ-23ʳ

To William Barton', BDec, rector of the parish church of All Saints, Monkyston' *alias* Annekeyke[1], d. Winchester. Dispensation — at his supplication — to receive and retain for life, together with the above parish church, one, and without them, any two other benefices, with cure or otherwise mutually [incompatible][2], etc. [as above, no. 3].

Litterarum scientia, vite ac morum honestas...
. L. puccius /. V· /· V·· L· De Phano:

[1] *sic*; *rectius* : 'Annebeyke' (from 'Anna de Becco' etc.)

[2] MS wants 'incompatibilia'

345   21 February 1500   *Reg. Lat.* 1066, fos 37^v-38^v

To Vincent Tothoth',[1] perpetual vicar of the parish church of Corby, d. Lincoln. Dispensation and indult — at his supplication — to receive and retain for life, together with the perpetual vicarage of the above parish church, one, and without it, any two other benefices, etc. [as above, no. 3, to '... retain them together for life, as above']; and, for life, not to be bound, while attending a *studium generale* or residing in the Roman curia or in any one of his benefices, to reside [in his other benefices],[2] etc. [as above, no. 238].

Vite ac morum honestas...
· *L· puccius / F / F· Lx Sanctor(is)*

[1] the 'T' changed (by overwriting) from a 'C' (or vice versa)
[2] supplied by editor

346   ?25 February 1500[1]   *Reg. Lat.* 1066, fos 39^r-40^r

To William Dunche, MA, perpetual vicar of the parish church of B Mary the Virgin, Overton', d. Winchester. Dispensation — at his supplication — to receive and retain for life, together with the perpetual vicarage of the above parish church, one, and without it, any two other benefices etc [as above, no. 3].

Litterarum scientia, vite ac morum honestas...
. *L. puccius / F / F· L^{ta}. Sanctor(is)*

[1] or possibly 24 February 1500; MS : *millesimo quadringentesimo nonagesimo nono primo sexto kalendas Martii anno octavo*

347   25 May 1500   *Reg. Lat.* 1066, fos 44^r-45^r

To Thomas Chirche, priest, d. Norwich. Dispensation — at his supplication — to him <who is a priest>[1] to receive and retain for life, together with one incompatible, if he holds one, one, and without it, any two other benefices, with cure or otherwise mutually incompatible, etc. [as above, no. 3, to '... Notwithstanding etc.'] With the proviso that the benefice held and other incompatible benefices in question shall not, on this account, be defrauded of due services and the cure of souls in the benefice held and (if any) the other incompatible benefices shall not be neglected.

Vite ac morum honestas...
. *L. puccius / V / V· L· De Phano:*

¹ marginal insertion (not initialled)

348   28 May 1500   *Reg. Lat.* 1066, fos 45ᵛ-46ᵛ

To Robert Dore, perpetual chaplain, called cantor, at the altar of St John the Baptist
in the parish church of Walsall, d. Coventry and Lichfield. Dispensation and indult
— at his supplication — to him (who is a priest and, [as] he asserts, holds a
perpetual chaplaincy, called a chantry, at the above altar, in the foundation of which
it is said to be laid down that the holder at the time is bound to celebrate mass each
day for the soul of the founder and for all other souls) to receive and retain for life,
together with the above chaplaincy, which is incompatible with another incompatible
benefice, one, and without it, any two other benefices, with cure or otherwise
mutually incompatible, etc. [as above, no. 3, to '... retain them together for life, as
above']; and, also for life, to serve the said chaplaincy through a capable substitute
[and], while residing in the Roman curia or one of his benefices or attending a
studium generale, not to be bound to reside personally in the said benefices, nor to
be liable to be compelled by anyone to do so against his will. Notwithstanding etc.
With derogation of the above foundation, specially and expressly, for this once only.
With the proviso that the chaplaincy and other incompatible benefices shall not, on
this account, be defrauded of due services and the cure of souls shall not be
neglected.

Vite ac morum honestas...
. L. puccius /· V· / V· Lx De Phano:

349   8 January 1500   *Reg. Lat.* 1066, fos 90ᵛ-91ᵛ

To Henry, bishop of Salisbury, whom the pope has this day translated from the
church of Bangor, over which he was then presiding, to that of Salisbury, appointing
him bishop, as is more fully contained in his letters drawn up in that regard.¹ Since,
as the pope has learned, at the time of the said translation and appointment, Henry
was holding *in commendam*, as he does, the priory of St Mary, Lantone, OSA, d.
Worcester, by apostolic concession and dispensation, the pope — wishing to assist
him to keep up his position in accordance with pontifical dignity — hereby
dispenses Henry — *motu proprio* — after he has acquired, on the strength of the said
translation and appointment, peaceful possession, or almost, of the rule and
administration and of the goods of the church of Salisbury or the greater part of
them, to retain *in commendam*, as before, the priory (whose annual value does not,
as the pope has also learned, exceed 200 marks sterling equivalent to 600 gold
ducats of the camera or thereabouts) together with the church of Salisbury, for as
long as he presides over it; notwithstanding etc. ; decreeing that the commend of the
priory docs not cease on this account. With the proviso that the priory shall not, on
this account, be defrauded of due services and the cure of souls therein (if any) shall

not be neglected; but that its customary burdens shall be supported.

Personam tuam nobis et apostolice sedi devotam tuis exigentibus meritis paterna benivolentia prosequentes illa tibi favorabiliter concedimus...
. L. puccius / Jo. / Jo. Lx. de Galves.

1 below, no. 581

350   21 May 1500   *Reg. Lat.* 1066, fos 174ᵛ-175ʳ

To the prior of the priory of B. Mary, Kellis, d. Ossory, and John Tohin and William[1] Omorissa, canons of the church of Ossory, mandate in favour of Thady Omeakir, perpetual vicar of the parish church of Kylmemanch, d. Cashel. At a recent petition on Thady's part to the pope to erect and institute a canonry in the church of Cashel and the perpetual vicarage of the above parish church, which he holds, into a simple prebend, for his lifetime, the pope, not having certain knowledge of the foregoing, hereby commands that the above three (or two or one of them), having summoned the archbishop and the dean and chapter of the church of Cashel and others concerned, shall inform themselves as to all the foregoing, and, if they find it to be thus, shall erect and institute a canonry in the church of Cashel and the said vicarage into a simple prebend in the same, for Thady's lifetime, without prejudice to anyone; and, in that event, collate and assign the newly erected canonry and prebend, whose annual value does not exceed 8 marks sterling, being vacant, with plenitude of canon law and all rights and appurtenances, to Thady, inducting him etc. having removed any unlawful detainer and causing Thady (or his proctor) to be received as a canon of the church of Cashel, with plenitude of canon law, and the fruits etc., rights and obventions of the canonry and prebend to be delivered to him. [Curbing] gainsayers etc. Notwithstanding etc. The pope's will is, however, that the vicarage shall not, on account of this erection and institution, be defrauded of due services and the cure of souls therein shall not be neglected, but that its customary burdens shall be supported; and that on Thady's death or resignation etc. of the canonry and prebend the said erection and institution shall be extinguished and so deemed and the vicarage shall revert to its original condition and be vacant automatically.

Apostolice sedis circumspecta providentia ad ea libenter intendit . . .
S de Castello / F / F. xv² Sanctor(is)

[1] *Guillermo*
[2] wants expedition date?

351   5 November 1499   *Reg. Lat.* 1068, fos 10ʳ-11ᵛ

To John Raven', DDec, rector of the parish church of All Saints, Schytlyngdor', d.

Lincoln, dispensation and indult. Some time ago, Sixtus IV by his letters dispensed him, who was then a scholar and, as he asserted, desired to become a cleric, and had completed his nineteenth year of age — after he should have been duly marked with clerical character and have completed his twentieth year — to receive and retain together for life any two benefices, with cure or otherwise mutually incompatible, etc. [as above, no. 131, to '. . . as is more fully contained in those letters'].[1] The pope therefore — at his supplication — hereby dispenses John further and indulges him, who, as he asserts, holds by the said dispensation the above parish church of All Saints and that of St Mary, Burwell, d. Norwich, to receive and retain [for life], together with the said parish churches, or with two other incompatible benefices held by him at the time, any third benefice, with cure or otherwise incompatible, even if a chantry, free chapel or hospital,[2] usually assigned to secular clerics in title of a perpetual ecclesiastical benefice, or a dignity, *personatus*, administration or office in a cathedral, even metropolitan, or collegiate church, even if the dignity in question should be major *post pontificalem* in a cathedral, even metropolitan, church, or principal in a collegiate church, and even if the dignity etc. should be customarily elective and have cure of souls, if he obtains it otherwise canonically, to resign it, simply or for exchange, when he pleases, and in its place receive another, similar or dissimilar, benefice and — provided this third incompatible benefice be not a parish church or its perpetual vicarage — retain it for life, as above; and, also for life, while residing in the Roman curia or any one of his benefices or attending a *studium generale*, not to be bound to reside personally in the above incompatible benefices and any other benefices held by him at the time, nor to be liable to be compelled by anyone to do so against his will. Notwithstanding etc. With the proviso that this third incompatible and other benefices in which he shall not reside shall not, on this account, be defrauded of due services and the cure of souls in them shall not be neglected.

Litterarum scientia, vite ac morum honestas . . .
N bregeon / F / F· Lxxx · Sanctor(is)

[1] lost; Index entry transcribed in *CPL*, XIII, Part II on p. 901
[2] 'annuale servitium' does not occur

352   27 April 1500   *Reg. Lat.* 1068, fos 17ʳ-18ʳ

To John Harrald, MA, rector of the parish church of Hasylton, d. Worcester. Dispensation — at his supplication — to receive and retain for life, together with the above parish church, one, and without it, any two other benefices, with cure or otherwise mutually incompatible, even if parish churches or their perpetual vicarages, or chantries, free chapels, hospitals or annual services, or administrations of the sacraments,[1] usually assigned to secular clerics in title of a perpetual ecclesiastical benefice, or dignities, etc. [as above, no. 3].[2]

Litterarum scientia, vite ac morum honestas . . .
Jo ortega[3] / F / F. L. Sanctor(is)

[1] *sic; cf.* nos. 328 and 329
[2] in the present instance, however, *obsequiis* ('services') is inserted in the margin, initialled F
[3] not in the enregistering scribe's hand: entered later?

353   28 April 1500   *Reg. Lat.* 1068, fo 18[r-v]

To William Picher, rector of the parish church of Bukilind [also spelt *Brikilund*], d. Bath and Wells. Indult for life — at his supplication — to him, who is a priest and, as he asserts, holds the above parish church, not to be bound, while residing in the Roman curia or in the said church or another of the benefices held by him at the time or attending a *studium generale*, to reside in his other benefices, with and without cure, nor to be liable to be compelled by anyone to do so against his will. Notwithstanding etc. With the proviso that the above church and other benefices in question shall not, on this account, be defrauded of due services and the cure of souls in the above church and (if any) the other benefices aforesaid shall not be neglected; but that their customary burdens shall be supported.

Vite ac morum honestas . . .
S de Castello / F / F . *xx. Sanctor(is)*

354   22 June 1500   *Reg. Lat.* 1068, fos 171[r]-172[r]

To William Jonys, perpetual vicar of the parish church of St John the Baptist, Pylton', d. Bath and Wells. Dispensation — at his supplication — to him, who, as he asserts, holds the perpetual vicarage of the above parish church, to receive and retain for life, together with the said church,[1] one, and without it, any two other benefices, etc. [as above, no. 3, to '. . . Notwithstanding etc. ']. With the proviso that the above church[2] and other incompatible benefices shall not, on this account, be defrauded of due services and the cure of souls in the church[3] and (if any) the other incompatible benefices aforesaid shall not be neglected.

Vite ac morum honestas . . .
L Puccius[4] / F / F. L. Sanctor(is)

¹ *ecclesia*; *recte*: 'vicaria'

² as above, note 1

³ as above, note 1

⁴ not in the enregistering scribe's hand: entered later?

---

355   14 December 1499   *Reg. Lat.* 1068, fos 175^v-176^v

To Richard Rollescon' *alias* Kollston, rector of the parish church of Stargrawerde, d. York, dispensation. Some time ago, Sixtus IV dispensed him to receive and retain together for life any two benefices, with cure or otherwise mutually incompatible, etc. [as above, no. 131, to '. . . retain them together for life'], as is more fully contained in Sixtus's letters drawn up in that regard.¹ The pope therefore — at his supplication — hereby dispenses Richard (who, as he asserts, holds by the said dispensation the above parish church and that of Weston super Trent, d. Coventry and Lichfield, which were afterwards canonically collated to him) to receive and retain for life, together with the said parish [churches],² or with two other incompatible benefices held by him at the time by virtue of the said dispensation, any third benefice, etc. [as above, no. 131].

Vite ac morum honestas . . .
L puccius / F / F· Lxx Sanctor(is)

¹ lost; Index entry transcribed in *CPL*, XIII, Part II, on p. 892

² 'ecclesiis' wanting

---

356   16 June 1500¹   *Reg. Lat.* 1069, fos 84^v-86^r

Confirmation as below. A recent petition to the pope on the part of M. Andrew Forma(n),² prior of the priory of May (*de Mayo*), OSA, d. St Andrews, papal notary, (who, as he asserts, is expressly professed of the above order)³ stated that⁴ — since formerly James, archbishop of St Andrews, primate of the whole kingdom of Scotland and legate born of the apostolic see, was bound and obliged to Andrew, during Andrew's lifetime, each year, in respect of the sum of 50 marks Scots — archbishop James, with the consent of the chapter of the church of St Andrews, OSA, gave, granted and assigned in part payment of the said 50 marks to Andrew and his assigns and [subtenants],⁵ during Andrew's lifetime, the barony and all lands of the said diocese lawfully pertaining to the archiepiscopal *mensa* of St Andrews, with their appurtenances lying in the county of the constabulary <of Hadyngton'>,⁶ with all their holdings and appurtenances, as they were and are situated, in length and breadth, with houses, buildings, vills, estates, together with their courts and other rights and appurtenances, on the agreement and condition that Andrew or his assigns or subtenants are bound to render and deliver, each year on the Nativity of B. John the Baptist, to archbishop James, but only if he requests it, a red rose upon the soil of the said lands of [. . .][7] for every other burden, exaction, request, demand, and secular service, which may be exacted and required of the said lands and their appurtenances during Andrew's lifetime, as is said to be more fully contained in certain authentic letters of archbishop James, fortified with his seal. At Andrew's supplication to the pope to add the force of apostolic confirmation to the said gift, grant and assignment as a firmer base for them, the pope hereby approves and confirms and fortifies with the protective power of the present writ the said gift etc. and everything concerning them contained in the said letters and ensuing from them, for as long as the archbishop should preside over the said church, and supplies all defects; and also dispenses Andrew to receive and retain for life the barony and lands with the rights and appurtenances. Notwithstanding etc. and the statutes and customs of the order of St Augustine, even if it was expressly laid down in them that canons of the order cannot have, or hold, lands, baronies, lordships, or any other property, and even if, for their sufficient [derogation],[8] they and their whole tenors (which the pope has as sufficiently expressed) were to be fully, expressly, specially, specifically, and individually mentioned, or expressed, word for word (and not by general clauses whose import implies full mention), the which statutes and customs the pope specially and expressly derogates for this once only.

Ad futuram rei memoriam. Apostolice servitutis <*nobis*>[9] *iniunctum desuper . . .*
A. de sancto severino[10] */ . V. / . V. L. De Phano:*

[1] a slanting stroke in the margin against the dating clause; *quingentesimo . . . octavo*] is written in the same hand, but darker ink: entered later?

[2] MS: *Forma'*

[3] This information comes from a notwithstanding clause.

[4] *ex; recte*: 'quod'?

[5] (?)*substituendis* (changed, perhaps from 'subtenendis'); thereafter, a dash struck through twice occurs — suggesting that a gap had been left and that it was only partially filled by *substituendis* (the latter part of which is written in a darker ink)

[6] *de Hadyngton* inserted in the margin by the enregistering scribe initialled . *V.* twice

[7] no name or gap occurs here

[8] *dioc(esis); recte*: 'derogatione'?

[9] *nobis* inserted in the margin by the enregistering scribe, initialled *V.*

[10] written in a darker ink (like that of marginal and other alterations): entered later?

357   19 February 1501[1]   *Reg. Lat.* 1069, fos 124[r]-125[r]

To the prior of the monastery of St Kieran (*Sancti Chirani*), Sir, usually governed by a prior, d. Ossory, and the chancellor of the church of Killaloe, and Cormac Hohea,[2] canon of the church of Emly, mandate in favour of Cornelius Ykerwayli, cleric, d. Killaloe. A recent petition to the pope on Cornelius's part stated that at one time, when the perpetual[3] rectories of the parish churches of Modrine and Berra and the perpetual vicarage of the said church of Modrine, d. Killaloe, were vacant *certo modo*, the then bishop of Killaloe by ordinary authority, for certain just reasons then expressed, united etc. the said rectories and vicarage to a certain canonry and prebend, called of Ballelochacain, of the church of Killaloe, which Cornelius holds, for his lifetime, as is said to be more fully contained in certain letters of the said bishop drawn up in that regard. Moreover since, as the said petition added, Cornelius fears that the above union etc. may, for certain reasons, not hold good; and, as the pope has learned, the rectories and vicarage are known to be still vacant as above, and that if they were to be united etc. anew to the said canonry and prebend which Cornelius holds even at present, for as long as he holds the latter, it would be to his benefit. At the supplication of Cornelius (who, as he asserts,[4] notwithstanding a defect of birth as the son of an unmarried man of noble birth and an unmarried woman had been marked with clerical character otherwise however duly and — by apostolic authority — had the said canonry and prebend (vacant *certo modo*) provided to him and himself dispensed to receive and retain them) the pope hereby grants that provision be made anew of the canonry and prebend, vacant as above, to Cornelius (who fears that they may be still vacant *sub certis modo et forma*) and commands that the above three (or two or one of them), having summoned those interested, shall unite etc. the rectories and vicarage, whose annual value together does not exceed 54 marks sterling, vacant howsoever etc., (even if they have been vacant for so long that by the Lateran statutes their collation has lawfully devolved on the apostolic see, and they be specially reserved etc.) with all rights and appurtenances, to the canonry and prebend, whose annual value does not exceed 16 marks sterling, for as long as Cornelius holds the latter; to the effect that Cornelius may, on his own authority, in person or by proxy, take corporal possession of the rectories and vicarage, or continue as before, and convert and (?)restore[5] their fruits etc. to his own uses and those of the rectories, vicarage and canonry and prebend aforesaid, for as long as he holds the canonry and prebend, without licence of the local diocesan or of anyone else. Notwithstanding etc. The pope's will is, however, that the rectories and vicarage shall not, on account of this union etc., be defrauded of due services and the cure of souls therein shall not be neglected, but that their customary burdens shall be supported; and that on Cornelius's death or resignation etc. of the canonry and prebend this union etc. shall be dissolved and so deemed and the rectories and vicarage shall revert to their original condition and be deemed vacant automatically.

Decet Romanum pontificem votis illis gratum prestare assensum . . .
S de Castello / · *V·* / . *V. xx. De Phano:*[6]

[1] a cross in each margin against the dating clause. The enregistering scribe (Boccapaduli) has written
[(?)*Anni*] *Noni* (shaved) at the base of fo 124[v], *Anni Noni* at the base of fo 125[r]
[2] preceded by *(?)Hoheg*, deleted and initialled . *V.*

^{3} *sic*

^{4} (?)*tamquam* occurs between *ut asserit* and *non obstante*

^{5} reading *restituere*

^{6} though its script differs from that of the letter the blotchiness of the signature strongly suggests that it was written by the enregistering scribe (Boccapaduli)

358   6 September 1499   *Reg. Lat.* 1070, fos 164^r-165^r

Provision, in *forma commissoria*, of Galeatius de Malvetiis, UID, cleric of Bologna, a continual commensal of the pope, to the perpetually united parish churches of St Peter and St Nicholas, Verucchio (*Castri Veruculi*), d. Rimini.

The 'bishop of Worcester' is one of the three mandataries. Entry otherwise of no interest to the Calendar.

Grata familiaritatis obsequia . . .
· *L· puccius* / . *V·* / · *V· Gratis Pro deo Nono Kl' Martij Anno octavo* [21 February 1500], *De Phano:*

359   8 April 1500   *Reg. Lat.* 1070, fos 194^v-197^r

To the prior of the monastery, usually governed by a prior, of B. Mary, Iusfaleyn, d. Ardfert, and Thady Obrusnakayn, canon of the church of Ardfert, and Donat^1 Machauli, canon of the church of Cloyne, mandate in favour of John Ymurchu, cleric, d. Ardfert. A recent petition to the pope on John's part stated that he did not — while peacefully possessing the perpetual vicarage of the parish church of Colyn, d. Ardfert, which was canonically collated to him at another time while vacant *certo modo*, for a year and more — on the ceasing of a lawful impediment and having obtained no dispensation in this regard, have himself promoted to the priesthood and he detained the vicarage after the year had passed, with no new title acquired or support of law, temerariously and *de facto*, for certain months, as he does still, receiving fruits from it; and thus the vicarage, through this lack of promotion, and, as the pope has learned, the perpetual vicarage of the parish church of Norabal,^{2} d. Ardfert, are vacant *certo modo* at present and the second vicarage has been vacant for so long that by the Lateran statutes its collation has lawfully devolved on the apostolic see, although Bernard Odal has detained it without title, for a certain time; and that if the second vicarage were to be united etc. to the first^3 for John's lifetime it would be to his benefit. The pope — rehabilitating John on account of all disability and infamy arising from the foregoing and not having certain knowledge of the foregoing — hereby commands that the above,^{4} [if], having summoned

Bernard and others concerned, they find the vicarages to be vacant (whether the first be vacant as above or otherwise, and howsoever etc. it and the second be vacant, even if the first has been vacant for so long that by the Lateran statutes its collation has lawfully devolved on the apostolic see and it and the second be specially reserved etc.) and the foregoing to be true, shall collate and assign the first vicarage, whose annual value does not exceed 10 marks sterling, to John, and unite etc. the second vicarage, whose annual value does not exceed 4 marks sterling, with all rights and appurtenances, to the first, for his lifetime, inducting John etc. having removed Bernard from the second and any unlawful detainers from it and the first and causing John (or his proctor) to be admitted to the first and its fruits etc., rights and obventions and those of the second to be annexed to it to be delivered to him. [Curbing] gainsayers by the pope's authority etc. Notwithstanding etc. With the proviso that the vicarage to be united shall not, on account of this union etc., be defrauded of due services and the cure of souls therein shall not be neglected, but that its customary burdens shall be supported; and that on John's death or resignation etc. of the said first[5] vicarage this union etc. shall be dissolved and so deemed and the vicarage to be annexed shall revert to its original condition and be deemed [vacant][6] automatically. The pope's will is, however, that before the above (or one of them)[7] shall proceed to the execution of the presents in any way, John is bound to resign the first vicarage into their hands or those of one of them genuinely and completely.

Apostolice sedis indefessa clementia recurrentibus ad eam cum humilitate . . .
. S. de Castello / V. / V. xxij Octavo Kl' Maii Anno octavo [24 April 1500], *De Phano*

[1] *Ma* deleted and initialled . *V.* immediately precedes *Donato*

[2] or possibly *Nombal*

[3] *primo [sic] dicte vicarie*

[4] *sic; see below* note 7

[5] *primo dictam vicariam*

[6] *vicare; recte*: 'vacare'

[7] The letter is addressed to three mandataries; half-way through (above, note 4) the text is simply . . . *discretioni vestre per apostolica scripta mandamus quatinus vocatis . . .;* yet here the wording is appropriate for two mandataries, namely: . . . *vos procedatis seu alter vestrum procedat . . .;* similarly, below: . . . *in manibus vestris seu alterius vestrum . . .*

360   15 March 1500   *Reg. Lat.* 1070, fos 201^r-203^r

To the priors of the monasteries, usually governed by priors, of B. Mary, *de Bello Loco* [Killagh] and of Insfalben', d. Ardfert, and Donat Machaulyn, canon of the church of Cloyne, mandate in favour of John Ysulebayn, cleric, d. Ardfert. The pope has learned that the perpetual vicarage of the parish church of Rylonayn [also spelt *Kylonaim, Kyllonaym, Kylonaym, Kylonian*[1]], d. Ardfert, is vacant at present and has been for so long that by the Lateran statutes its collation has lawfully devolved on the apostolic see, although Cornelius Osega, who bears himself as a priest of the said diocese, has detained it, with no title and no support of law, temerariously and *de facto*, for a certain time, as he still does. At a recent petition on John's part to the pope to erect and institute a canonry in the church of Ardfert and the said vicarage into a simple prebend in the same for the lifetime of John, (who, as he asserts, [holds] the perpetual vicarage of the parish church of Kylloeyn, said diocese, whose annual value does not exceed 6 marks sterling, then vacant *certo modo* which (even if generally reserved etc.) the pope has granted be united etc. to the said canonry and prebend, after their erection and institution, for his lifetime), the pope, not having certain knowledge of the foregoing — at his supplication — hereby commands that the above three (or two or one of them), if, having summoned Cornelius and others concerned, they find the aforesaid vicarage of Rylonayn to be vacant (howsoever etc.; even if specially reserved etc.) and the foregoing to be true, shall erect and institute a canonry in the church of Ardfert and the vicarage of Rylonayn into a simple prebend in the same, [having summoned] the bishop and chapter of Ardfert regarding the erection and institution, for John's lifetime and without prejudice to anyone; and collate and assign the newly erected canonry and prebend, whose annual value does not exceed 8 like marks, being vacant, to John, with plenitude of canon law and all rights and appurtenances, inducting him etc. having removed Cornelius and any other unlawful detainer and causing John (or his proctor) to be received as a canon of Ardfert, with plenitude of canon law, and the fruits etc., rights and obventions of the canonry and prebend to be delivered to him. [Curbing] gainsayers by the pope's authority etc. Notwithstanding etc. The pope's will is, however, that the said vicarage of Rylonayn shall not, on account of this erection and institution, be defrauded of due services and the cure of souls in the vicarage shall not be neglected, but that its customary burdens shall be supported; and that on John's death or resignation etc. of the canonry and prebend [the erection and institution of] the canonry and prebend shall be extinguished and so deemed and the vicarage of Rylonayn shall revert to its original condition and be deemed vacant automatically.

Piis fidelium votis per que divini cultus augmentum . . .
A. de. Sanctoseverino / . L. / . L. xv. Quarto Kl' Maii Anno Octavo [28 April 1500], *Dulcius:-*

1 the 'y' written over an 'l' (erased); the present 'l' over another letter

361   28 February 1500   *Reg. Lat.* 1070, fos 203ᵛ-205ʳ

To Laurence Ocaeylte, Donald Otuocayll' and William Ohenega, canons of the church of Derry, mandate in favour of Eugene Oduyll', cleric, d. Derry (who, as he asserts, notwithstanding a defect of birth as the son of a priest and an unmarried woman, has been marked with clerical character otherwise however duly). It has been referred to the pope's audience by Eugene that [Magonius][1] Magonuayl, perpetual vicar of the parish church of Roscercan, d. Connor,[2] has dared, while duly bound by sentence of excommunication, knowingly to celebrate mass in a certain place under public interdict by ordinary authority and otherwise take part in divine offices in contempt of the keys and to commit perjury, incurring irregularity. Considering that if the foregoing is true the said Magonius has rendered himself unworthy of the perpetual vicarage of the above parish church which he holds, the pope hereby commands that the above three (or two or one of them), if Eugene will accuse Magonius before them over the foregoing and proceed to any extraordinary pain to be determined by their judgement, thereafter shall, having summoned Magonius and others concerned, make inquiry into the above related matters and if they find the truth of them to be substantiated deprive Magonius of the vicarage and remove him from it; and in that event collate and assign the vicarage, whose annual value does not exceed 4 marks sterling, (whether vacant by the above deprivation and removal or at another time howsoever etc., even if vacant for so long that by the Lateran statutes its collation has lawfully devolved on the apostolic see, etc.), with all rights and appurtenances, to Eugene; inducting him etc. having removed any other unlawful detainer and causing Eugene (or his proctor) to be admitted to the vicarage and its fruits etc., rights and obventions to be delivered to him. [Curbing] gainsayers by the pope's authority etc. Notwithstanding etc. Also the pope dispenses Eugene to receive and retain the vicarage, if conferred on him by virtue of the presents, and to be promoted to all, even sacred, orders, otherwise however duly, notwithstanding the said defect etc.

Vite ac morum honestas . . .
S. de Castello / . L. / . L. xiiij. Tertio Id' Aprilis Anno octavo [11 April 1500], *Dulcius:-*

[1] first name wanting here; but *dictus Magonius* occurs in the text below
[2] *Convenren.*; for 'Connor'?

362   25[1] April 1500   *Reg. Lat.* 1070, fos 221[r]-222[r]

To the abbot of the monastery of B. Mary, Tracton (*de Albotrattu*), d. Cork, and the chancellor of the church of Ross, and John Vsulebayn, canon[2] of the church of Ardfert, mandate in favour of Edmund Cursy, priest, d. Cork. The pope has learned that the perpetual vicarage of the parish church of Vynsall, d. Cork, is vacant *certo modo* at present and has been vacant for so long that by the Lateran statutes its collation has lawfully devolved on the apostolic see, although Philip Copyner, who bears himself as a priest, has detained it, without [any][3] title or support of law, temerariously and *de facto*, for a certain time, as he still does. He hereby commands that the above three (or two or one of them), if, having summoned Philip and others concerned, they find the vicarage, whose annual value does not exceed 24 marks sterling, to be vacant (howsoever etc.), shall collate and assign it, (even if specially reserved etc.), with all rights and appurtenances, to Edmund, inducting him etc. having removed Philip and any other unlawful detainer and causing Edmund (or his proctor) to be admitted to the vicarage and its fruits etc., rights and obventions to be delivered to him. [Curbing] gainsayers by the pope's authority etc. Notwithstanding etc.

Vite ac morum honestas . . .
· *S· de Castello / O· / O· xv. Septimo Id' Maii Anno Octavo* [9 May 1500], *Marianen'*

[1] *Idus*, deleted but not initialled, occurs between *septimo* and *kalendas*; *cf.* date of expedition in *bullaria*
[2] *canonicis*; *recte*: 'canonico'?
[3] *alio*; *recte*: 'aliquo'?

363[1]   **12 May 1500**[2]   *Reg. Lat.* 1070, fos 266[v]-268[v]

To the bishop of Worcester, mandate in favour of Gilbert Peston *alias* Conell', monk of the monastery of B. Peter, Westminster (*Westmonasterii*), OSB, d. London. A recent petition to the pope on Gilbert's part stated that after he, then a scholar, had entered the said monastery (in whose statutes and customs it is said to be expressly laid down that those wishing to make their profession there are bound to make it after a probationary year by licence of the abbot of the monastery for the time being publicly in the chapter of the monastery before a notary public and witnesses and, thereafter, on any solemn day to bear a solemn written record of the profession to the high altar of the church of the said monastery and present it to the abbot to be subscribed by him) and had taken the tonsure and habit of the novices and the order of the subdiaconate and, for nine months or thereabouts, had conducted himself in the choir and chapter in conformity in all things with the other monks and, before the year was over, had publicly made his profession into the hands of the abbot of the monastery at that time, and — because he had made this profession without having observed the form of the statutes and customs in question and believing that on this account he was not obliged to be a religious and thinking that he could lawfully depart from the monastery — he had left and took part in secular affairs; and next, persuaded by friends and upright men, he returned to the monastery and did penance there for the things he had committed; however afterwards — since he feared that it was impossible to remain in the monastery with a clear conscience and it was asserted by several persons that the aforesaid form had not been observed when he made his profession — he returned to the world and on that account incurred apostasy and sentence of excommunication; notwithstanding which, he had himself promoted to the order of the priesthood, otherwise however duly, daily celebrating mass and other divine offices, not however in contempt of the keys; and successively when the perpetual vicarage of the parish church of Slefordie, d. Lincoln, was vacant *certo modo*, the rector, called a prebendary, of the said church (since the presentation of a suitable person for the vicarage belonged by ancient, approved and hitherto peacefully observed custom to the rector for the time being) presented Gilbert for the vicarage, vacant as above, to the bishop of Lincoln and the bishop instituted Gilbert as vicar of the church at this presentation by ordinary authority, albeit *de facto*; and Gilbert, taking possession of the vicarage by pretext of the said presentation and institution, has detained it thenceforth for five years continuously, as he does at present, receiving a few fruits from it, also *de facto*, in good faith. Moreover since, according to the foregoing, the said collation and provision do not hold good; and, as the pope has learned, the vicarage is known to be vacant still as above, supplication was made on Gilbert's part to the pope to absolve him from apostasy and the sentence of excommunication he incurred on this account and to dispense him for the irregularity contracted by him on account of the foregoing. Since Gilbert is now present in the Roman curia, the pope hereby commits and commands the bishop of Worcester above to absolve Gilbert, if he so requests, from apostasy and the sentence of excommunication and other sentences, censures and pains aforesaid, for this once only, in the customary form of the church, having enjoined a salutary penance on him, dispense him for the irregularity which he contracted on this account and to minister in the orders taken by him, and rehabilitate him on account of all disability and infamy contracted by him on account of the foregoing; and in that event collate and assign the vicarage, whose annual value does not exceed 24 gold ducats of the camera, vacant howsoever etc., even if vacant for so long that by the Lateran statutes its collation has lawfully devolved on the apostolic see etc., with all rights and appurtenances, to Gilbert, inducting him etc. having removed any unlawful detainer and causing Gilbert (or his proctor) to be admitted to the vicarage and its fruits etc., rights and obventions to be delivered to him. [Curbing] gainsayers by the pope's authority etc. Notwithstanding etc. Also the pope dispenses Gilbert to receive and retain the vicarage, if conferred on him by virtue of the presents, and, for life, to live outside the said monastery, however in honest places befitting secular clerics, and also to bear the habit usually worn by monks of the monastery under an honest cloak (*mantello*) of a decent colour usually borne by the said clerics; notwithstanding etc. The pope's will is, however, that before the bishop of Worcester shall proceed to the execution of the presents in any way, Gilbert shall resign the vicarage into his hands genuinely and completely.

Solet apostolice sedis exuberans clementia recurrentium . . .
. S. de. Castello / · *V·* [3] */ V. Lxx Quarto non' Junii Anno octavo* [2 June 1500], *De Phano:*

---

[1] Various deletions (not initialled) occur throughout the text; but are not specially noticed here.

[2] *quingententesimo; recte:* 'quingentesimo'

[3] there is a dot at either side of the left arm of the 'V'

364   22 April 1500   *Reg. Lat.* 1070, fos 310^r-312^r

Provision, in *forma gratiosa*, of Paulus Nicolai de Chivizano, continual commensal familiar of Silvester, bishop of Worcester, to the rectory of the parish church of Sts Mary and Michael, Benabbio (*de Menabio*), d. Lucca, (whose annual value, as he asserts, does not exceed 36 gold florins of the camera), which, being vacant at the apostolic see, the pope had granted to be commended to bishop Silvester, to be held, ruled, and governed by him for life, under the date *pridie nonas Aprilis, pontificatus nostri anno octavo* [4 April 1500] and who has this day, freely and spontaneously, ceded the commend into the pope's hands and the pope has admitted the cession, the relevant letters not having been drawn up. Entry otherwise of no interest to the Calendar.

Vite ac morum honestas . . . The executory begins: *Hodie dilecto filio Paulo Nicolai de Chivizano . . .*
A· de Sanctoseverino; N· de castello / O / O· xij· x· Tertio nonas Maij Anno octavo.
[5 May 1500], *Marianen'*

365   4 September 1500   *Reg. Lat.* 1071, fos 48^r-49^r

To the abbots of the monasteries of St Albans and Stratforde Langthorn', and the prior of the priory of Martond, ds Lincoln, London, and Winchester,[1] mandate in favour of John Sutton', layman, London. A recent petition to the pope on John's part stated that, formerly, Thomas Appulbii, bearing himself as rector of the parish church in Walbroke, London — untruthfully claiming that by right as also by a constitution published by the late William, bishop of London, approved by the late Thomas, archbishop of Canterbury, and confirmed by the apostolic see as well as by ancient, approved, and hitherto peacefully observed custom, any person of whatever degree, status, or condition, who inhabited any house, hospice, or shop in the city of London, and especially in the parish of the said church, whose annual payment (*pensio*) amounted to, or exceeded, the sum of 13 shillings and 4 pence sterling, or which was let or hired, or had been accustomed or able to be let or hired, for the sum of 13 shillings and 4 pence, or for a greater sum, was bound to yield (*efferre*) to the parish church in whose parish the house, hospice, or shop was situated, and pay every year to its rector,14 pence sterling for each of the nobles of the gold money of those parts making up the sum of 13 shillings and 4 pence or other greater sum for which the house, hospice, <or>[2] shop was let or had been accustomed to be let; and falsely asserting that John (who was inhabiting a certain house in the parish of the said church let to him under a certain annual payment of shillings and pence sterling then expressed) was, by pretext of the said constitution, confirmation, custom, and lease, lawfully bound to offer (*offerre*) to the said church, and give and pay to Thomas, certain quantities of pence then expressed — sued John, not through apostolic delegation, before Edward Vaghii, the then official of London, praying that he be condemned and compelled to give and pay him the said quantities of pence; that the official, proceeding wrongly and *de facto* in the case, promulgated an unjust definitive sentence, in favour of the church and Thomas and against John, by which he condemned John in the sum of 2 shillings and 4 pence sterling and costs, and from which John appealed to the apostolic see; but that John, detained, as he asserts, by lawful impediment, did not perchance prosecute his appeal within the proper time. At John's supplication to the pope to commit to some upright men in those parts the causes of the appeal; of everything attempted and innovated after and against the appeal; of the nullity of the sentence and Edward's whole process and of everything prejudicial to John done by Edward and Thomas, and any other judges and persons, in connection with the foregoing; and of the principal matter, the pope hereby commands that the above three (or two or one of them), having summoned Thomas and others concerned, if what is related about the impediment is true, and having heard both sides, taking cognizance even of the principal matter, shall decree what is just, without appeal, causing by ecclesiastical censure what they have decreed to be strictly observed. [And moreover compel] witnesses etc. Notwithstanding the lapse of time, etc.

Humilibus et cetera. [3]
L puccius / . V· / V· xij: De Phano:

[1] there is a cross (signalling error?) in the left margin opposite the line: *Lincolnien. et Londonien. ac Winctonien. diocesium salutem et cetera. Humilibus et cetera.*; refers, perhaps, to St Albans which was often (but not always) styled 'exempt' in the address clause (*cf. CPL* XVI, nos. 185, 283, and 284) and not just (as here) 'd. Lincoln'

[2] marginal insertion by the enregisterimng scribe (uninitialled)

[3] see above, note 1

366   2 September 1500   *Reg. Lat.* 1071, fos 58^V-59^V

To the dean of the church of Laronde, d. St Andrews, <and the official of St Andrews>,[1] mandate. Following the issue by Paul II of the letters, *Paulus et cetera. Ad perpetuam rei memoriam. Cum in omnibus iudiciis . . .* [2] a recent petition to the pope on the part of John Toliburnem, perpetual chaplain at the altar of B. Mary the Virgin in the parish church of Hathientonen, d. St Andrews, and Richard Toliburnen', layman, said diocese, stated that at another time he, John, wishing to provide for the utility of the perpetual chaplaincy founded at the said altar by the late Alexander Toliburnen', which is of lay patronage, and which he, John, holds, granted and let — with the consent of Adam Tuliburnen', nobleman, lord of Straling, to whom the right of patronage of the chaplaincy pertains — in fee or perpetual farm a certain little portion or piece of land called Herperseldi, lawfully belonging to the chaplaincy and of no use to it, with all its rights, liberties, exemptions and appurtenances, to Richard, for himself and his masculine heirs only, sprung or to be sprung from his body, bearing his *insignia*, for an annual payment or tax of 3 pounds 13 shillings and 4 pence Scots, each year, one half at Pentecost and the other on the feast of St Martin in the winter, to John and his successors holding the chaplaincy at the time, on the condition that if Richard and his masculine heirs become extinct the said little portion or piece of land with all its improvements, appurtenances and liberties shall revert to the chaplaincy completely, as is said to be more fully contained in the letters patent drawn up in that regard. At John and Richard's supplication to the pope to add the force of apostolic confirmation to the concession and lease aforesaid as a firmer base for them, he — not having certain knowledge of the foregoing and having the little portion or piece of land by its situation, qualities, boundaries and value[3] as expressed in the presents, hereby commands that the above two, if and after — designations and specifications of the little portion or piece of land having first been laid before them and the form of Paul's letters observed — it has been lawfully established by them, jointly, that the said concession and lease are (and have been) to the evident utility of the chaplaincy, shall approve and confirm the concession and lease and everything concerning them contained in the said instrument, and supply any defects. Notwithstanding etc.

Ex iniuncto nobis desuper apostolici servitutis offitio ad ea libenter intendimus . . .
L puccius / V / . V· xxv . De Phano:

[1] marginal insertion, initialled *V*; insertion and initial in the same hand (not enregistering scribe's)
[2] printed in *Magnum Bullarium Romanum*, I (Luxemburg, 1742), p. 381
[3] reading 'valorem'

367 16 January 1501   *Reg. Lat.* 1071, fos 136ᵛ-137ᵛ

To Hugh Grene, LLB, perpetual vicar of the parish church of St Martin, d. Hereford. Dispensation — at his supplication — to receive and retain for life, together with the perpetual vicarage of the above parish church, one, and without it, any two other benefices, etc. [as above, no. 3].

Litterarum scientia, vite ac morum honestas . . .
F de parma / Jo. / Jo. L. Electus Terracinen.

368 13 February 1501   *Reg. Lat.* 1071, fo 274ʳ⁻ᵛ

To Thomas Vynter *alias* Fynter, monk of the monastery of B. Mary the Virgin, Mellifont (*de Mellifonte*), OCist, d. Armagh. Dispensation — at his supplication — to him (who, as he asserts, notwithstanding a defect of birth as the son of a priest and an unmarried woman, has been promoted, by licence of his superior, to all, even sacred, orders and the priesthood, otherwise however duly; and is, as he also asserts, expressly professed of the said order[1]) to receive and retain any benefice, with or without cure, of the said order, even if it should be a priory, *prepositura, prepositatus,* dignity (even conventual and abbatial), administration or office, even of lay patronage and of whatsoever tax or annual value, even if it should be customarily elective and have cure of souls, if he obtains it otherwise canonically, to resign it, simply or for exchange, as often as he pleases, and in its place receive and retain another, similar or dissimilar, benefice, defined as above. Notwithstanding the above defect etc.

Religionis zelus, vite ac morum honestas . . .
. *S. de Castello / Jo / Jo xv. Electus Terracinen'*

[1] This latter information comes from a notwithstanding clause.

369   19 February 1501   *Reg. Lat.* 1071, fos 277^r-278^v

To Abraham Gechton', scholar, d. Dunkeld. Dispensation and indult — at his supplication — to him (who, as he asserts, is of noble, knightly birth and is in his fifteenth year of age and wishes to become a cleric) to receive and retain — henceforth, after he has been duly marked with clerical character — any number of chaplaincies and altars requiring sacred, even priest's, orders by foundation, statute, custom or otherwise, and — when he has reached his eighteenth year — any benefice, with cure or otherwise incompatible, even if a parish church or its perpetual vicarage, or a dignity, *personatus,* administration or office in a cathedral, even metropolitan, or collegiate church, even if the dignity in question should be major *post pontificalem* in a cathedral, even metropolitan, church or principal in a collegiate church, even if the dignity etc. should be customarily elective and have cure of souls, if he obtains them otherwise canonically, to resign them, at once or successively, simply or for exchange, as often as he pleases, and in their place receive other, similar or dissimilar, benefices, viz.: — henceforth — any number of chaplaincies and altars requiring sacred, even priest's, orders, as above, and — as soon as he has reached his eighteenth year — one benefice, with cure or otherwise incompatible, and retain them, as above. Notwithstanding the above defect of age etc. And the pope derogates the foundation, statute and custom in question, specially and expressly, for this once only. With the proviso that the chaplaincies, altars and benefice with cure in question shall not, on this account, be defrauded of due services and the cure of souls in the benefice shall not be neglected; and that customary burdens of the chaplaincies and altars shall be supported.

Nobilitas generis, vite ac morum honestas . . .
F· de parma / Jo / Jo. xxxx. Electus Terracinen'

370 13 March 1501 *Reg. Lat.* 1071, fo 296[r-v]

To Patrick Trechton',[1] scholar, d. St Andrews, indult. The pope (who, some time ago, decreed and declared that provisions or grants or mandates of provision to canonries and prebends of cathedral churches to persons who have not completed their fourteenth year of age shall have no force except by consent of the apostolic see) hereby indulges Patrick, who, as he asserts, is in his seventh year of age, of noble birth and wishes to become a cleric — at his supplication — to receive and retain — after he has been duly marked with clerical character and shall be in his tenth year — any canonries and prebends of any cathedral, even metropolitan, churches, if he obtains them otherwise canonically, to resign them, at once or successively, simply or for exchange, as often as he pleases and in their place receive and retain any other canonries and prebends of the same or other cathedral, even metropolitan, churches. Notwithstanding the defect of age which he shall suffer then in the said eighth[2] year, etc. With the proviso that the canonries and prebends in question shall not be defrauded of due services; but that their customary burdens shall be supported.

Nobilitas generis ac laudabilia tue pueris[3] etatis . . .
F· de parma / Jo / Jo· xxiiij· Electus Terracinen'

[1] the 'T' written over a 'C'; *recte*: 'C-'?
[2] *octavo*; *recte*: 'decimo'?
[3] *sic*; *recte*: 'puerilis'

371 23 March 1501 *Reg. Lat.* 1071, fos 304[v]-306[r]

To David Arnot, archdeacon of Lothian (*Landonie*) in the church of St Andrews. Indult for life — at his supplication — to him, who, as he asserts, is chaplain in the chapel of James, king of Scots, and of noble birth by both parents, [to visit][1] by suitable deputy the churches, monasteries and other ecclesiastical places within the limits of the archdeaconry of Lothian and their personnel, in which the office of visitation falls, by law or custom, to him as archdeacon, as often as the time of visitation [shall occur, even two, three or more of the places in question in the same day],[1] and to receive [the procurations due to him on visitation][1] in ready money, to a daily total not exceeding 30 silver tournois, of which 12 are worth one gold florin of Florence. Notwithstanding etc. It is, however, the pope's intention that no-one shall be compelled, by pretext of this indult, to pay a procuration beyond his means.

Executory to the abbots of the monasteries of Holyrood (*Sancte Crucis*) and Scone (*de Scona*), d. St Andrews, and the provost of the church of the Holy Trinity near Edymbruch,[2] said diocese, or two or one of them, acting in person or by proxy.

Meruit tue devotionis sinceritas . . . The executory begins: *Hodie dilecto filio David*

Arnot . . .
F· de parma; A· de Sancto severino / Jo· / Jo· xxx xx [3]

[1] The passage: 'ingruerit etiam duo tria aut plura ex locis huiusmodi eadem die visitare ac procurationes ratione visitationis huiusmodi tibi debitas ab eisdem ecclesiis monasteriis locis et personis taliter visitatis' (or suchlike) is wanting in the main body of the text; but occurs almost verbatim in the executory (wanting 'ex locis huiusmodi').

[2] or *Edyniburch*

[3] *sic*: incomplete: 'Electus Terracinen. ' (or 'Episcopus Terracinen. ') wanting

372   4 January 1501   *Reg. Lat.* 1074, fos 28^V-29^V

To John Dyllon, BDec, rector of the parish church of Newton' Fereers, d. Exeter. Dispensation — at his supplication — to receive and retain for life, together with the above parish church, one, or without it, any two other benefices, etc. [as above, no. 3].

Litterarum scientia, vite ac morum honestas . . .
L puccius / F / F· L^{ta}. Sanctor(is)

373   7 September 1500   *Reg. Lat.* 1074, fos 212^V-213^V

To Thomas Parchis, perpetual vicar of the parish church of Mikilton, d. Worcester. Dispensation — at his supplication — to receive and retain for life, together with the perpetual vicarage of the above parish church, one, and without it, any two other benefices, etc. [as above, no. 3].

Vite ac morum honestas . . .
L puccius / · V / · V· L· De Phano:

374   19 December 1500   *Reg. Lat.* 1074, fos 232^V-233^r

To William, Viscount[1] Beamow, layman, and Elizabeth, his wife, London. Indult — at their supplication — to William (who, as he asserts, although formerly he took a vow to visit Jerusalem (*Ierosolimam*) and the tombs of the Apostles Peter and Paul and of St James in Compostella, believing he could fulfil it, having been detained however by sundry impediments, has not been able to do so up to now and is not confident of being able to fulfil it further because he is prevented by decrepitude — he is a septuagenarian and valetudinarian — and has become impoverished) and

Elizabeth to choose any suitable secular priest or a regular of any order as their confessor etc.; and to the confessor of their choice to grant full remission of all their sins which they confess with a contrite heart and countenance, once only in life for obtaining the jubilee indulgence and at the point of death, while remaining in the purity of the faith, unity of the Roman church, and obedient and devoted to the pope and his canonical successors; and to their confessor to relax any oaths; and also, to them that they will — even if the current jubilee year has run out, by visiting two or three altars in a church of their choice, on three days, consecutively or at intervals, and, kneeling before them, reciting the Lord's Prayer five times and the Angelic Salutation five times — obtain every plenary indulgence, remission of sins, and jubilee, which they would have obtained, had they visited the churches and basilicas within Rome and without, appointed for it, on the appointed days, during the current year of Jubilee, and fulfilled all the other requirements for obtaining the indulgences and jubilee. And William is automatically absolved and freed from the vows taken by him in and for all things just as if he had entirely fulfilled his vows. The pope's will is, however, as regards the satisfaction which William or Elizabeth are bound to perform, as above, that the confessor shall enjoin performance by them, if they are alive, by others if they are dead.

Sincera ferven[s]que et cetera.
L puccius / · M· / · M· xxx Battiferro

1 *viscovonte*

375   12 December 1500   *Reg. Lat.* 1074, fos 233ᵛ-234ᵛ

Union etc. At a recent petition on the part of Thomas Clerlie, rector of the parish church of Westtilbury, d. London, the pope hereby unites etc. the parish church, called a rectory, of B. Mary, Abchurch' [also spelt *Abchurch*], d. London, (whose annual value does not exceed 15 marks sterling, equivalent to 45 gold ducats of the camera or thereabouts) to the parish church of Westtilbury, which he holds together with the above parish church of Abchurch' by apostolic dispensation, while he holds that of Westtilbury, to the effect that Thomas may, on his own authority, in person or by proxy, continue in or take anew and retain corporal possession of the church of Abchurch' and of its rights and appurtenances, for as long as he holds that of Westtilbury, and convert its fruits etc. to his own uses and those of the said churches without licence of the local diocesan or of anyone else. With indult for life to Thomas not to be bound, while attending a *studium generale,* to reside in the said churches (or one of them), nor to be liable to be compelled to do so against his will. Notwithstanding etc. With the proviso that the said churches shall not, on account of this union etc. and other aforesaid matters, be defrauded of due services and the cure of souls therein shall not be neglected; but that their customary burdens shall be supported. The pope's will is, however, that on Thomas's death or resignation etc. of the church of Westtilbury the above union etc. shall be dissolved and so deemed and the church of Abchurch' shall revert to its original state automatically.

Ad futuram rei memoriam. Romanum decet pontificem votis illis gratum prestare assensum . . .
F de parma / · M· / · M· xxxx. Battiferro

376   5 December 1500   *Reg. Lat.* 1074, fo 235[r-v]

To William Fayerhaer, perpetual vicar of the parish church of Sts Cyriac and Julitta, Swafpham, d. Ely. Dispensation — at his supplication — to receive and retain for life, together with the perpetual vicarage of the above parish church, one, and without it, any two other benefices, etc. [as above, no. 3].[1]

Vite ac morum honestas . . .
F de parma / · M· / · M· L. Battiferro

[1] with the addition of 'even of lay patronage' after 'or a combination'

377   24 December 1500   *Reg. Lat.* 1074, fo 236[r]

To Robert Honywodi, archdeacon of the church of Norwich. [Indult] — at his supplication — to choose any suitable priest, secular or regular, of any order, as his confessor *etc*. And lest etc.[1]

Sincera ferve[n]sque et cetera.
/ Javolateranus[2]; · M· / · M· iiij Battiferro

[1] enregistered in abridged form
[2] *sic*

378   5 December 1500   *Reg. Lat.* 1074, fos 236[r]-237[r]

To Robert Morne,[1] scholar, d. Worcester. Dispensation and indult — at his supplication — to him, who, as he asserts, is in his nineteenth year of age or thereabouts and wishes to become a cleric, to receive and retain — after he has been duly marked with clerical character — any benefice, with cure or otherwise incompatible, or requiring the order of the priesthood by foundation, statute or custom, even if a parish church, etc., [as above, no. 240, to '. . . benefice, with cure or otherwise incompatible'],[2] or otherwise requiring the order of the priesthood; and, while attending a *studium generale*, not to be bound to reside personally in the above benefice, nor to be liable to be compelled to do so by anyone against his will; notwithstanding the above defect of age etc. With the proviso that the benefice shall not, on this account, be defrauded of due services and the cure of souls therein (if any) shall not be neglected; but that its customary burdens shall be supported.

Vite ac morum honestas . . .
F de parma / · M· / · M· xxx Battiferro

[1] or *Mome*
[2] with the addition of 'and of lay patronage' after 'principal in a collegiate church'

379   20 December 1500   *Reg. Lat.* 1074, fos 237^r-238^v

Confirmation etc. as below. A recent petition on the part of Richard Tymylby, temporal lord of the place of Polum, d. Lincoln, stated that at another time — after the then abbot and the convent of the monastery of Bardeney, OSB, and Geoffrey,[1] vicar of the parish church of Edelington', d. Lincoln, and the late Robert Barkeworth, then temporal lord of Polum, had agreed together that the abbot and convent, with the vicar's consent, would grant, as they then did, to Robert and his successors in perpetuity that they could have, at their expense, a chaplain who would be in continuous residence in the chapel of Polum and fully serve them and their men in things divine, save for the right of the mother church, to which they would pay 3 shillings annually; and that all oblations, obventions and petty tithes due at the altar of the chapel remain to the rector, called chaplain, of it; and that the 3 shillings due to the mother church would be paid in two terms, viz.: half on the feast of St Martin and half on that of Pentecost, in recompense for the tithes aforesaid and for the 12 pence which they were accustomed to give and for one acre of land in the field of Polum; however the bodies of the dead of Polum and their first legacies destined to be made for the dead would remain always to the mother church; and Robert and his heirs would be bound to make provision of a suitable rector or chaplain and ornaments necessary for things divine for the chapel, and they could be compelled to do so by ecclesiastical censure; and the rector or chaplain would be bound to take an oath of fealty to the mother church on the altar of St Helen in the mother church; and that a baptismal font would be erected; and that the nomination or election of a suitable chaplain in the chapel would pertain to Robert and his heirs, and that, with the consent of the abbot of the said monastery for the time being, admission of the chaplain would pertain to the vicar for the time being of the mother church — the then bishop of Lincoln ratified and confirmed the aforesaid agreement by ordinary authority, as is more fully contained in certain letters of his, said to be drawn up in that regard, in which the tenor of the agreement was inserted verbatim as above. At the supplication on the part of Richard (who, as he asserts, is the true and legitimate heir of Robert) to the pope to add the force of apostolic confirmation to the said agreement, ratification and confirmation as a firmer base for them, the pope hereby approves and confirms the agreement etc. and everything contained in the said letters concerning them, and supplies any defects. And the pope establishes and ordains that in the future the rector or chaplain of the said chapel for the time being may administer the sacraments to Richard and his successors in the temporal lordship of Polum for the time being and to their men and subjects, familiars and domestics, of both sexes, living at the time within the limits of the chapel; without prejudice to anyone and saving always the right of the mother church. Notwithstanding etc.

Ad perpetuam rei memoriam. Hiis que pro divini cultus augumento . . .
F de parma / · M· / · M· L· Battiferro

[1] no surname

380   20 October 1500   *Reg. Lat.* 1075, fos 3ʳ-5ʳ

To the abbot of the monastery of B. Mary, *de Hunya* [Abington], d. Emly, and the dean of the church of Cashel and Andrew Cryagh, canon of the church of Limerick, mandate in favour of David Macberragoyn,[1] priest, d. Killaloe. The pope has learned that the perpetual vicarage of the parish church of Lodien'[2] [also spelt *Loden'*, *Lodon'*], d. Emly, and that of the parish church of Seradaualy *alias* Cloynacheke [also spelt *Serradaualy, Serradanaly, Sarradaualy, Sarradanaly*], d. Killaloe, are vacant *certo modo* at present and have been vacant for so long that by the Lateran statutes their collation has lawfully devolved on the apostolic see, although Richard de Burgo and Henry de Anglo *alias* Moschalaiy have detained the vicarage of Lodien' and Laurence Macchomara and Cornelius Machego that of Seradaualy, bearing themselves as clerics of the said dioceses respectively, without any title or support of law, temerariously and *de facto*, for a certain time, as they still do, dividing their fruits between themselves respectively. At a recent petition on David's part to the pope to unite etc. the vicarage of Seradaualy to that of Lodien', for as long as David holds that of Lodien', after he acquires it — asserting that the annual value of the vicarage of Lodien' does not exceed 8, and of Seradaualy, 10, marks sterling — the pope, not having certain knowledge of the foregoing, hereby commands that the above three (or two or one of them), if, having summoned respectively Richard, Henry, Laurence and Cornelius and other interested parties, they find the vicarages to be vacant (howsoever etc.) and the foregoing to be true, shall collate and assign the vicarage of Lodien' to David; and unite etc. the vicarage of Seradaualy (even if it and that of Lodien' be specially reserved etc.), with all rights and appurtenances, to that of Lodien', for as long as David holds the latter, inducting him etc. having removed respectively Richard, Henry, Laurence and Cornelius and any other unlawful detainers and causing David (or his proctor) to be admitted to the vicarage of Lodien' and its fruits etc., rights and obventions and those of Seradaualy to be delivered to him. [Curbing] gainsayers by the pope's authority etc. Notwithstanding etc. The pope's will is, however, that the said vicarage of Seradaualy shall not, on account of this union e*c., be defrauded of due services and the cure of souls therein shall not be neglected, but that its customary burdens shall be supported; and that on David's death or resignation etc. of the vicarage of Lodien' the union etc. shall be dissolved and so deemed and the vicarage of Seradaualy shall revert to its original condition and be deemed vacant automatically.

Decet Romanum pontificem votis illis gradum[3] *prestare assensum . . .*
S de Castello / Jo. / Jo. xx. de Galves

[1] the second 'r' reworked, possibly deleted

[2] final two or three letters reworked and uncertain

[3] *sic*; *recte*: 'gratum'

---

381   26 September 1500   *Reg. Lat.* 1075, fos 8ʳ-9ᵛ

To the bishop of Lismore, mandate in favour of Thomas Magra, cleric, d. Lismore (who, as he asserts, is in his fifteenth year of age). A recent petition to the pope on Thomas's part stated that at another time his relations — aspiring crookedly to a canonry of the church of Lismore and the prebend of Magdeugii, which are of lay patronage and which James Rusell then held — made a pact and agreement with James that if he resigned the canonry and prebend and provision were made of them to Thomas, they would give him a certain sum of money then expressed; [and] James, by pretext of this pact and agreement, after the money had been paid him by the relations, spontaneously resigned [the canonry and prebend] into the above bishop's hands outside the Roman curia; and the bishop, having admitted this resignation outside the said curia by ordinary authority, in ignorance of this pact and agreement, by the said authority collated the canonry and prebend, as being vacant by this resignation, to Thomas, then in his tenth year or thereabouts and ignorant of the foregoing, with the express consent thereto of the patrons who were in peaceful possession of the right of patronage, and made provision of the same, albeit *de facto*; and Thomas, by pretext of the said collation and provision, acquired the canonry and prebend, also *de facto*, without, however, receiving any fruits from them. Moreover since, according to the foregoing, the said collation and provision do not hold good; and, as the pope has learned, the canonry and prebend are known to be vacant still, as above, the pope hereby commands the above bishop, if he finds Thomas (who asserts that he has just acquired knowledge of all the foregoing) to be suitable — concerning which the pope burdens the bishop's conscience — to collate and assign the canonry and prebend, whose annual value does not exceed 14 marks sterling (vacant as above or in another way etc., even if vacant for so long that by the Lateran statutes their collation has lawfully devolved on the apostolic see etc.) with plenitude of canon law and all rights and appurtenances, to Thomas, inducting him etc. having removed any unlawful detainer and causing Thomas (or his proctor) to be received as a canon of the church of Lismore and the fruits etc., rights and obventions of the canonry and prebend to be delivered to him. [Curbing] gainsayers by the pope's authority etc. Notwithstanding etc. And the pope has commanded that — if Thomas be found suitable — provision of the canonry and prebend be made to him from the date of the presents.

Dignum arbitramur et cetera.
. L. ¹ *puccius* / . *V·* / *V· xx. Pridie kl' Novembr' Anno nono* [31 October 1500], *De Phano:*

¹ changed from 'P'

382   23 January 1501   *Reg. Lat.* 1075, fos 30ᵛ-32ʳ

Commend, in *forma commissoria*, of the Camaldolese monastery of B. Mary, d'Adelmo (*Adelmi*) d. Volterra, vacant at the apostolic see, to M. Fernandus Ponzzettus, cleric of Florence, chaplain, scriptor and familiar of the pope, cleric of the apostolic camera, secretary of the pope.

The 'bishop of Worcester' is one of the three mandataries. Entry otherwise of no interest to the Calendar.

Romani pontificis providentia circumspecta . . .
. *Jo. ortega* / *F* / *F· grat(is) p(ro) sotio Sanctor(is)*

383   31 August 1500   *Reg. Lat.* 1075, fos 147ᵛ-149ʳ

To Maurice Offlayn, canon of Limerick, mandate in favour of William d(e)ipatientia,¹ monk (formerly professor OFM, called conventuals), of the monastery of B. Mary, Monasteranenagh (*de Magio*), OCist, d. Limerick. A recent petition on William's part stated that at another time, when the said monastery was vacant *certo modo*, John Troie,² abbot of the monastery of B. Mary, Mellifont (*Millefontis*), OCist, d. Meath (to the abbot of which for the time being the provision and appointment of a suitable person to the monastery of Monasteranenagh at a time of vacancy is understood to pertain by ancient, approved and hitherto peacefully observed custom as well as in accordance with apostolic privileges granted to OCist) made provision of Wiiliam to the monastery, thus vacant, and appointed him abbot, committing to him the care, rule and administration of the monastery in spiritualities and temporalities, and William, by virtue of this provision and appointment, had benediction imparted to him, otherwise however duly, outside the Roman curia. Moreover, as the same petition added, William fears that for certain reasons the said provision and appointment do not hold good; and the pope has learned that the monastery of Monasteranenagh is vacant still, as above, and wishes to provide thereto. Not having certain knowledge of the merits and suitability of William — who, as he asserts, has been dispensed by apostolic authority to have himself transferred from OFM to OCist and, notwithstanding a defect of birth as the son of a married man and a married woman, has been dispensed to preside over a benefice OCist, with or without cure, [even] if it should be a priory, *prepositura*, dignity, even abbatial, to which he be appointed, and to perform and exercise its care etc.; and who afterwards had himself transferred from OFM to OCist; and, litigating over the said monastery of Monasteranenagh (before a certain judge *in partibus* deputed by apostolic delegation) against Gerald David de Geraldinis, who had (and is at present) intruded into it, brought back a single definitive sentence in his favour and against Gerald, which, as no appeal has been lodged, has become a *res judicata* — the pope hereby commands the above canon to inform himself as to William's merits etc. and if [he finds William to be capable and suitable][3] for the rule and administration of the monastery, whose annual value does not exceed 60 marks sterling, (vacant howsoever etc.), provide him thereto and appoint him abbot, committing to him the care etc. of the monastery in spiritualities and temporalities; and causing due obedience and reverence to be given him by the convent and customary services and rights by the vassals and other subjects of the monastery. [Curbing] gainsayers by ecclesiastical censure etc. Notwithstanding etc.

Suscepti cura regiminis . . .
S. de castello / . *V·* / *V. xxv De Phano*

[1] MS: *d'ipatientia* = (?) 'Dei patientia'
[2] changed from *Croie*, or vice versa
[3] supplied by the editor

384   7 September 1500   *Reg. Lat.* 1075, fos 151ʳ-152ʳ

To David Pindagras, David Oscara and Thomas Omurchu, canons of the church of Tuam, mandate in favour of Richard Plemen, priest and canon of the church of Tuam. A recent petition to the pope on Richard's part stated that at another time when the perpetual vicarage of the parish church of Thayn, d. Tuam or Mayo, which Miler Pindagras, canon of the monastery of B. Michael, Mayo (*de Magio*), OSA, said diocese, was recently holding *in commendam* by apostolic concession and dispensation — on the ceasing of this commend because Miler had ceded it, spontaneously and freely, into the hands of the archbishop of Tuam outside the Roman curia, and the archbishop had admitted the cession — was still then vacant in the way it had been vacant before the said commend, the archbishop by ordinary authority collated and made provision of it to Richard, albeit *de facto*, and he acquired possession of it by virtue of the said collation and provision, without receiving any fruits from it. Moreover since, according to the foregoing, the aforesaid collation and provision and whatsoever ensued therefrom do not hold good; and, as the pope has learned, the vicarage is known to be vacant still as above, the pope hereby commands that the above three, or two or one of them, in person or by proxy, shall collate and assign the vicarage, whose annual value does not exceed $2^1/_2$ marks sterling, (vacant howsoever etc., even if vacant for so long that by the Lateran statutes its collation has lawfully devolved on the apostolic see etc.), to Richard, with all rights and appurtenances, inducting him etc. having removed any [unlawful][1] detainer and causing Richard (or his proctor) to be admitted to the vicarage and its fruits etc., rights and obventions to be delivered to him. [Curbing] gainsayers by the pope's authority etc. Notwithstanding etc.

Vite ac morum honestas . . .
S. de Castello / · *V·* / *V· Gratis pro deo Tertio decimo kl' Octobr' Anno nono:* [19 September 1500], *De Phano:*

[1] 'illicito' does not occur

---

385   26 October 1500   *Reg. Lat.* 1075, fos 167^v-169^v

To the abbot of the monastery of the Holy Cross, Haerlany',[1] d. Cashel, and the precentor and the archdeacon of the church of Cashel, mandate in favour of Peter Butteller, cleric, d. Cashel. A recent petition on Peter's part stated that at one time when the deanery of the church of Cashel, which is a major dignity *post pontificalem*, was vacant *certo modo*, he was provided to it, thus vacant, by apostolic authority, and he acquired it by virtue of this provision; and then, when the rectory of the parish church of Woctherratha, d. Lismore, which is of lay patronage, was also vacant *certo modo*, he, seizing it, thus vacant, without any presentation or institution, detained it and the said deanery, without having sought title for himself, together, for a certain number of years, as he does at present, receiving fruits etc. from them (but not more than 60 ducats[2] after deduction of expenses), albeit *de facto*. Moreover, according to the foregoing, the rectory (still as above) and the deanery (by the unjust detention of the rectory) have been vacant and are vacant at present; the deanery being reserved by the pope under his reservation of all major dignities *post pontificalem* in cathedral churches vacated then and in the future to his own collation and disposition. The pope, therefore — rehabilitating Peter on account of all disability and infamy contracted by him by occasion of the foregoing — hereby commands that the above three, or two or one of them, in person or by proxy, shall collate and assign the deanery, which has cure of souls and whose annual value <and that of the canonry and prebend annexed thereto>[3] does not exceed 24, and <the said

rectory>,[4] whose annual value does not exceed 2, like marks,[5] vacant howsoever etc., even if vacant for so long that by the Lateran statutes their collation has lawfully devolved on the apostolic see etc., and provided that the express assent of the patrons is given for this, with all rights and appurtenances, to Peter, inducting him etc. having removed any unlawful detainers and causing Peter (or his proctor) to be admitted to the deanery and rectory and their fruits etc., rights and obventions to be delivered to him. [Curbing] gainsayers by the pope's authority etc. Notwithstanding etc. Also the pope dispenses Peter to receive and retain the deanery and rectory, if conferred on him by virtue of the presents, together for life, to resign them, at once or successively, simply or for exchange, as often as he pleases, and in their place receive up to two other, similar or dissimilar, benefices, with cure or otherwise incompatible, and retain them together for life, as above; and, while residing in Cashel or in the parish church in question or the other one of the benefices held by him at the time, or attending a *studium generale*, not to be bound, by reason of the deanery and rectory or any other benefices with cure or otherwise requiring sacred orders, to have himself promoted to [the orders of the diaconate and priesthood][6] for a period of seven years (calculated from the date of the presents) provided that within two years he is made a subdeacon,[7] nor to be liable to be compelled by anyone to do so against his will. Notwithstanding etc. With the proviso that the deanery, rectory and other benefices in question, incompatible or requiring sacred orders, shall not, on this account, be defrauded of due services and the cure of souls in the deanery, rectory and other aforesaid benefices (if any) shall not be neglected, but that the customary burdens of those benefices otherwise requiring sacred orders shall be supported. The pope's will is, however, that before the above three shall proceed to the execution of the presents in any way, Peter shall resign the deanery and rectory into their hands (or the hands of any of them) genuinely and completely.

Sedes apostolica, pia mater, recurrentibus ad eam post excessum cum humilitate . . .
. S. de Castello / Jo. / Jo. L. Quarto Id. ' novembr' Anno nono [10 November 1500], *de Galves*

[1] the 'ae' rewritten and uncertain

[2] *ducatorum*; changed (by deletion) from 'ducatos'

[3] 'canonicatus est annexus cuius' deleted, initialled *Jo.*; *ac illi annexorum canonicatus et prebende* inserted in the margin by the enregistering scribe, initialled *Jo.* twice

[4] *rectoriam predictos* inserted in the margin by the enregistering scribe, initialled *Jo.*

[5] *marcharum similium*; though 'ducats' occur above (see note 2)

[6] required by the context and supplied by the editor, since the passage in MS is evidently faulty: . . . *usque ad septennium . . . dummodo infra biennium fit subdiaconus et diaconus et presbyteratus ordines huiusmodi se promovere facere minime teneatur*

[7] see above, note 6

386   19 April 1501   *Reg. Lat.* 1076, fos 41^r-43^v

To the officials of Lincoln, Ely and Worcester, mandate in favour of John Cok,
BDec, priest, d. Ely. A recent petition on John's part stated that at one time when the
parish church of Wymondahm' [also spelt *Woymondahm'*, *Wymonahin'*,
Wymondhm', *Wymondahin'*, *Wimondai'*,[1] *Woymodam'*, *Woymo'dahm'*,
Wymo'dahin', *Wymondahin*, *Woymondahin*, *Wymondaym*], d. Lincoln, which is of
lay patronage, was vacant *certo modo*, its then true patron (being in peaceful
possession or almost of the right of presenting a suitable person for it at a time of
vacancy) presented John, then perpetual vicar of the parish church of Botkeshin'[2]
[also spelt *Botkeshm'*], d. Ely, for it, vacant as above, to the then bishop of Lincoln,
or his vicar general, within the lawful time, and the said bishop, or vicar, by ordinary
authority instituted John at the presentation as rector; and John, hoping that a
dispensation for holding two incompatible benefices together had been obtained on
his behalf from the apostolic see through certain friends of his, although he did not
have the support of any such dispensation, taking possession of the said church of
Wymondahm' by virtue of the said presentation and institution, has held it and the
perpetual vicarage of the said church of Botkeshin', which was canonically collated
to him at another time, for a year or thereabouts, and detained [it] contrary to pope
John XXII's constitution 'Execrabilis' (but short of the receipt of fruits — with the
exception only of those from which he has paid a certain annual pension, assigned
on the fruits of the church of Wymondahm', to Thomas Manfeld, cleric — and he
has supported the other burdens incumbent upon the church of Wymondahm').
Moreover since, according to the foregoing, the vicarage (by the acquisition of the
church of Wymondahm') and the church of Wymondahm' (by the said constitution)
have been vacant and are vacant at present, the pope — rehabilitating John on
account of all disability and infamy contracted by him by occasion of the foregoing
— hereby commands that the above three, or two or one of them, in person or by
proxy, shall collate and assign the church and vicarage, whose annual value together
does not exceed 24 gold florins of the camera, whether vacant as above or
howsoever etc., even if they have been vacant for so long that by the Lateran statutes
their collation has lawfully devolved on the apostolic see, etc., with all rights and
appurtenances, to John, inducting him etc. having removed any unlawful detainers
and causing John (or his proctor) to be admitted to the vicarage and its fruits etc.,
rights and obventions and those of the said [church][3] of Wymondahm' to be
delivered to him. [Curbing] gainsayers by the pope's authority etc. Notwithstanding
etc. Also the pope dispenses John to receive and retain the church and vicarage
aforesaid, if [conferred on][4] him by virtue of the presents, or with one of them, one,
and without them, any two other benefices, etc. [as above, no. 3, to '. . .
Notwithstanding etc.'] With the proviso that the above church and the vicarage and
other incompatible benefices shall not, on this account, be defrauded of due services
and the cure of souls in the church and vicarage and in the other incompatible
benefices (if any) shall not be neglected. The pope's will is, however, that before the
above three shall proceed to the execution of the presents in any way, John shall
resign the church and vicarage into their hands (or the hands of any of them)

genuinely and completely.

Sedes apostolica, pia mater, recurrentibus ad eam cum humilitate . . .
F. de parma / F / . F. Lxxx. Tertio Non' Aug(us)ti Ano' Nono [3 August 1501],
Sanctor(is)

[1] the first 'i' uncertain

[2] the 'k' blotched and uncertain

[3] 'ecclesie' wanting

[4] 'conferatur' wanting

387   28 May 1501   *Reg. Lat.* 1076, fos 188[r]-189[r]

To John Wytt, perpetual chaplain in the parish church of St John the Baptist,
Dambury [also spelt *Danbury*], d. London. Dispensation — at his supplication — to
him, who, as he asserts, holds a perpetual chaplaincy, called the chantry of (?)the
chalice[1] in the above parish church, to receive and retain for life, together with the
said chaplaincy, if it cannot be held with another incompatible benefice, one, and
without them, any two other benefices, etc. [as above, no. 3].

Vite ac morum honestas . . .
· L· puccius / · V· / · V· L· De Phano:

[1] . . . *perpetuam cap(ella)niam cantariam* (?)calise *nuncupatam* . . .; where (?)calise is vernacular

388   9 June 1501   *Reg. Lat.* 1076, fos 189[r]-190[r]

To Thomas Bevys, BTheol, rector of the parish church of St Clement, Norwich.
Indult — at his supplication — to him, who, as he asserts, holds the above parish
church of St Clement and the perpetual vicarage of the parish church of Worsted'
alias Wordysted', d. Norwich, by apostolic dispensation, not to be bound, for life,
while staying in the Roman curia or attending a *studium generale* or residing in the
church of St Clement or the vicarage aforesaid or one of the other benefices held by
him at the time, to reside personally in the said benefices, nor to be liable to be
compelled by anyone to do so against his will. Notwithstanding etc. With the proviso
that the church of St Clement and the vicarage shall not, on this account, be
defrauded of due services and the cure of souls therein shall not be neglected; but
that the cure shall be exercised and things divine served by good and sufficient
vicars maintained[1] from the proceeds of the church of St Clement and the vicarage.

Litterarum scientia, vite ac morum honestas . . .
· L· puccius / V / · V· xx· De Phano:

[1] supplying 'necessaria': *quibus . . . [necessaria] congrue ministrentur*

389   22 June 1501   *Reg. Lat.* 1076, fos 190ʳ-191ʳ

To Thomas Michell, MA, rector of the parish church of St Andrew, Hedyngdon, d. Salisbury. Dispensation — at his supplication — to receive and retain for life, together with the above parish church, one, and without it, any two other benefices, etc. [as above, no. 3].

Litterarum scientia, vite ac morum honestas . . .
· L· puccius / Jo. / Jo. L. Electus Terracinen'

390   26 May 1501   *Reg. Lat.* 1077, fos 35ʳ-36ʳ

To Patrick Murray, treasurer of Dunblane. Dispensation — at his supplication — to receive and retain for life, together with the treasurership of Dunblane (which is a non-major dignity *post pontificalem*), any other, and without it, any two other benefices, etc. [as above, no. 5].

Vite ac morum honestas . . .
. N. de . castello / Jo. / Jo. xxxx. Eps' Terracinen'

391   29 March 1501   *Reg. Lat.* 1077, fos 107ʳ-109ᵛ

To the abbots of the monasteries of Bangor, Mubille and Hudburryn, ds. Down and Connor, mandate in favour of William Magxan,[1] rector of the rectory of the parish church of *Sancti Chafudi* [also spelt *Chafadi*], d. Down.[2] Following the pope's reservation some time ago of all conventual priories vacated then and in the future to his own collation and disposition, the priory, called the church, of St Patrick, OSB, d. Down, which is conventual and which Robert Brechimay,[3] its late prior, held while he lived, has become vacant by his death, outside the Roman curia, and is vacant at present, being reserved as above. And, as the pope has learned, William wishes to enter the priory under the regular habit and asserts that he holds the rectorship of the rectory of the above parish church, which is without cure, and to which the rectory of the parish church of the Holy Cross, Herrethayn, said diocese, is canonically united etc. and that Gellassius[4] Magnyssa, bearing himself as a cleric, has detained the priory without any title or support of law, temerariously and *de facto*, for a certain time, and still does. Wishing to encourage William, the pope hereby commands that the above three (or two or one of them) shall receive him — if he is suitable and there is no [canonical obstacle][5] — as a monk in the said priory and bestow the regular habit on him in accordance with the custom of the priory and cause him to be received therein and given charitable treatment; and, if William spontaneously wishes to make the usual profession made by the monks, receive and admit it; and, thereafter, if, having summoned Gellassius and others concerned, they find the priory, whose annual value does not exceed 24 marks sterling, to be vacant as above or howsoever etc., shall collate and assign it, (even if it has been vacant for so long that by the Lateran statutes its collation has lawfully devolved on the apostolic see, etc.), with all rights and appurtenances, to William, inducting him etc. having removed Gellassius and any other unlawful detainer and causing William (or his proctor) to be admitted to the priory and its fruits etc., rights and obventions to be delivered to him. [Curbing] gainsayers by the pope's authority etc. Notwithstanding etc. And the pope hereby dispenses William to retain together with the priory, if conferred on him by virtue of the presents, the aforesaid rectory held by him, as before; notwithstanding etc. With the proviso that the rectory shall not be defrauded of due services; but that its customary burdens shall be supported.

Cupientibus vitam ducere regularem [. . .] consuevit adesse presidio . . .
· *S· de· Castello· / Jo. / Jo. xxx. Septimo Id' Aprilis Anno nono* [7 April 1501], *Electus Terracinen'*

[1] uncertain: the 'gx' reworked

[2] MS: *dicte diocesis* — evidently referring to Down.

[3] the 'im' uncertain: 'un'?

[4] later spelt *Gelasius*

[5] *canonicum non existat; recte*: 'canonicum non obsistat'?

392   2 April 1501   *Reg. Lat.* 1077, fos 110[r]-112[r]

To Dermot Odorna and Leonard (?)Cantim[1] and Cormac Oheaga, canons of the churches of Cloyne and Emly, mandate in favour of Richard de Geraldinis, cleric, d. Cloyne. The pope has learned that a canonry of the church of Cloyne and the prebend of (?)Chilmogonec[2] in the same are vacant at present and have been vacant for so long that by the Lateran statutes their collation has lawfully devolved on the apostolic see, although John de Geraldinis, who bears himself as a cleric or priest, has detained them without any title or support of law, temerariously and *de facto*, for a certain time, as he still does. He hereby commands that the above three (or two or one of them), if, having summoned John and others concerned, they find the canonry and prebend, whose annual value does not exceed 24 marks sterling, to be vacant (howsoever etc.), shall collate and assign them, (even if specially reserved etc.), with plenitude of canon law and all rights and appurtenances, to Richard, inducting him etc. having removed John and any other unlawful detainer and causing Richard (or his proctor) to be received as a canon of the church of Cloyne and the fruits etc., rights and obventions of the canonry and prebend to be delivered to him. [Curbing] gainsayers by the pope's authority etc. Notwithstanding etc.

Vite ac morum honestas . . .
. *S. de. castello.* / *Jo* / *Jo. xv. Septimo Idus Aprilis anno nono.* [7 April 1501], *Electus Terracinen.*

[1] or *Cantini*
[2] the 'e' is blotched and doubtful

393   3 September 1500   *Reg. Lat.* 1077, fos 219[r]-220[r]

To Hugh Ap,[1] rector of the parish church of St Machutus, (?)Nanudechell',[2] d. Bangor, dispensation. Some time ago — after, as he asserts, he was dispensed by apostolic authority notwithstanding a defect of birth as the son of a priest and an unmarried woman to be promoted to all, even sacred, orders and to receive and retain a benefice, even if it should have cure of souls, if conferred on him otherwise canonically — Sixtus IV by his letters dispensed him to receive and retain any two other benefices, even if one of the two simple benefices in question should be a canonry and prebend in a cathedral or collegiate church, if[3] conferred on him otherwise canonically; to resign them, at once or successively, simply or for exchange, as often as he pleased and in their place receive and retain likewise up to two other, similar or dissimilar, simple, mutually compatible, benefices, as is more fully contained in those letters; and afterwards he was duly promoted to all, even sacred, orders, and by virtue of the aforesaid[4] dispensation acquired the above parish church, which was canonically collated to him while vacant *certo modo*, and holds it at present. The pope hereby dispenses him — at his supplication — to receive and retain any third simple benefice, if conferred on him otherwise canonically, to resign the above parish church[5] as often as he pleases and in its place receive and retain another parish church or its perpetual vicarage, or a dignity, *personatus*, administration or office in a cathedral, even metropolitan, or collegiate church, even if the dignity, *personatus*, administration or [office] should be customarily elective and have cure of souls — provided that the dignity in question be not major *post pontificalem* in a cathedral, or principal in a collegiate church — if he obtains it otherwise canonically. Notwithstanding the above defect etc.

Vite ac morum honestas . . .
· *S· de castello* / *O·* / · *O· xx· Marianen'*

1 *sic*

2 in the first occurrence the initial letter is overwritten and unclear; in the second clearly 'N'

3 MS: *etiam si* . . . : 'etiam' surely inappropriate

4 *ex primeva; recte:* 'expresse'?

5 *sic*; somewhat disconcertingly, the passage hereafter is very reminiscent of a dispensation to hold one benefice — instead of containing the clauses to be expected in a dispensation to hold a third

394   24 August 1501   *Reg. Lat.* 1078, fos 71ʳ-80ʳ

To the bishops of Rochester and Winchester and the abbot of Glastonbury, mandate. At the petition of Richard [Kidderminster], abbot of the Benedictine monastery of Winchcombe, the pope commands the above three (or two or one of them) to establish and ordain at Winchcombe, with the licence of the local ordinary and the consent of a majority of the convent, the statutes (recited) proposed by abbot Richard.

Note. The statutes are indexed under Benedictine Order in the Index of Subjects. To facilitate reference, the editor has paragraphed and numbered them, [1] to [30]. The first page of the entry is reproduced as the frontispiece.

Alexander *et cetera* venerabilibus fratribus Roffen. et Wintonen. episcopis ac dilecto filio abbati monasterii /¹ de Glastenbery' Bathonien. et Wellen. dioc(esium) salutem *et cetera*.

Pastoralis officii debitum nobis desuper commissum nos admonet et inducit ut singularum personarum presertim sub regularis² iugo domino famulantium votis per que ecclesiarum et monasteriorum omnium statui prosperiori et regimini utiliori personarum earundem consulitur libenter annuimus et cum a nobis petitur eiusdem officii partes favorabiliter impendamus.

Exhibita siquidem nobis nuper pro parte dilecti filii Richardi abbatis monasterii Beate Marie Sanctique Kenelmi³ regis et martiris de Unichecomba ordinis Sancti Benedicti Wigornien. diocesis peticio continebat quod ipse summopere cupit in eodem monasterio ordinem monasticum eiusdem Sancti Benedicti ad honorem et gloriam omnipotentis dei semper atque feliciter cum devotione vigere et florere inibique deinceps voluntariam paupertatem summo studio ac diligentia excoli et teneri et propterea ut inibi viventes securius atque devotius vitam in futurum ducere valeant et occasiones seu pericula tribus principalibus votis dicti ordinis adversantia ab eodem monasterio maiori securitate et diligentia perpetuo excludantur ac proprietatis ambitio tollatur et premissa serventur aliqua statui et ordinari desideret.

Quare pro parte dicti Richardi abbatis nobis fuit humiliter supplicatum ut aliqua statuta et ordinationes in eodem monasterio per illius abbatem et monachos servanda statuere et ordinare ac alias impremissis oportune providere de benignitate apostolica dignaremur.

Nos igitur qui monasteriorum et religiosorum locorum [fo 71^V] omnium statum in melius dirigi nostris potissime temporibus suppremis desideramus affectibus ipsum Richardum abbatem a quibusvis excommunicationis suspensionis et interdicti aliisque ecclesiasticis sententiis censuris et penis a iure vel ab homine quavis occasione vel causa latis si quibus quomodolibet innodatus existit ad effectum presentium duntaxat consequendum harum serie absolventes et absolutum fore censentes huiusmodi supplicationibus inclinati discretioni vestre per apostolica scripta mandamus quatinus vos vel duo aut unus vestrum:

[1] quod deinceps omnes et singuli redditus decime dona oblationes legata pensiones et omnes alie spirituales et temporales eiusdem monasterii obventiones quocunque nomine vel titulo eidem monasterio aut membris eiusdem obveniant et obvenire poterunt in futurum sive ob necessitatem dicti monasterii mutuo recipiantur absque divisione aliqua in communi cista dicti monasterii quando hec in peccunia solvi debeant reponi et contegi dicteque ciste tres claves fieri quarum una apud abbatem secunda apud priorem et tertia apud precentorem eiusdem monasterii pro tempore existentes per dilectos filios ipsius monasterii conventum deputandos vel eorum vicegerentem remanere itaquod cum distributio seu solutio peccuniarum fieri contigerit id ex precepto abbatis per manus thesaurarii presentibus custodibus clavium cum annotatione et numeratione tam in receptione quam in solutione per eundem thesaurarium desuper faciendis fieri ac omnes et singule pensiones portiones redditus et[4] decime seu ecclesiarum capellarum unitates[5] officialibus dicti monasterii assignari et per eos percipi consuete deinceps cessare et pro [fo 72^r] revocatis haberi ac in communi reponi[6] debeant et quod abbas vel aliquis ex dicti monasterii monachis quicquam existis[7] in aliquos usus convertere non possit exceptis illis quem[8] itineribus compulsi necessitate et in pecuniarum collectione exponere cogerentur nisi prius in communi cista ut dictum est reponantur ac ex ista cista postmodum pro omnibus necessariis distributio fiat;

[2] quodque cellerarius per abbatem cum consilio seniorum eligendus post abbatem principalis administrator in temporalibus curis et negotiis monasterii sit itaquod omnes redditus omnesque proventus ac omnia cetera commoda quocunque nomine censceantur seu nominentur in futurum ad dictum monasterium pertinentia sive sint spiritualia sive temporalia per eundem cellerarium fideliter recipi et in usum monasterii per eum prout abbas iusserit sine diminutione sive alienatione converti necnon quecunque tam ad sacristiam quam infirmariam et vestiariam pro indumentis fratrum ac ad loca sive cellas hospitum ceteraque officia et alia loca monasterii necessaria per dictum cellerarium diligentissime provideri ab eoque vel eius vicegerente singuli officiales non in pecuniis sed in ipsis rebus omnia que ad sua sunt officia necessaria accipere ac de receptis semel in anno ad minus computum et rationem abbati presente cellerario fideliter reddere teneantur;

[3] et ut vagandi tollatur occasio quod nullus officialium dicti monasterii illius limites seu clausuram pro hiis qui[9] sunt suis officiis necessaria huiusmodi cellerario et succellerario duntaxat exceptis exire possit;

[4] et quia difficile esset [fo 72^V] quod unus singularis frater totam curam et administrationem totius monasterii tam in recipiendo quam in solvendo et necessaria providendo sufficienter gere[10] posset quod dictus cellerarius sub se coadiutorem

videlicet succellerarium unum vel si opus fuerit plures ex fratribus ut puta coquinarios seu alios ad libitum abbatis qui eum in administratione eorum que pro necessariis monasterii seu officialium providere seu etiam in necessariorum emptionibus et solutionibus diligenter adiuvare studere iuxta ipsius celerarii iussa et mandata habere de quibus omnibus eidem cellerario quotiens voluerit computum reddere debeant;

[5] quodque ipse celerarius bis in anno prima ebdomada Adventus Domini et ebdomada inmediate precedente festum Pentecostes computum ac fidelem rationem de singulis receptis et solutis ac administratis suo abbati presente tunc priore cum tribus aliis de senioribus omnino reddere teneatur et si facta fuisset aliqua diminutio in possessionibus monasterii recipiendis ex aliqua causa contingenti id totum in scriptis ostendere debeat et in hiis omnibus administrationibus cellerarius et succelerarius ac ceteri omnes sub eo administratores cavere debent ut preter abbatis voluntatem seu mandatum nichil agant sed suum preceptum et consilium in omnibus que caritati et iusticie non adversantur semper sequantur;

[6] abbas vero monasterii qui pro tempore fuerit teneatur strictissime videlicet ebdomada in Quinquagesima computum fidelem ac rationem de singulis receptionibus solutionibus ac impensis [fo 73^r] quibuscunque per eum seu cellerarium alias de bonis monasterii factis presente etiam priore cum sex de senioribus qui commode interesse possint diligenter reddere ac secunda feria prime ebdomade Quadragesime congregatis fratribus ad capitulum totius monasterii statum paucis verbis veritatem rei significantibus priore cum senioribus predictis hoc ydem testantibus suis confratribus ostendere debeat et teneatur in quo quidem computo vel alias si abbas videatur nimis liberalis vel prodigus seu vitiosus ac dissipator bonorum monasterii et quod fecerit seu fieri fecerit expensas seu solutiones superfluas tunc aliqui saltem ex fratribus qui timorem ac amorem omnipotentis dei habeant in visitationibus ordinariorum seu religionis in dicto monasterio faciendis eorum abbatis liberalitatem nimiam seu prodigalitatem aut negligentiam dictis visitatoribus quemadmodum in visitationibus fieri debet fideliter ostendere debeant; ipsique visitatores seu ordinarii vel presidentes religionis comperta veritate contra dictum abbatem secundum delicti qualitatem et ut ipsi suppremo iudici rationem super hoc erunt reddituri prout iura seu regulares constitutiones volunt procedere debeant;

[7] et licet omnia in monasterio et extra tam in spiritualibus quam in temporalibus secundum preceptum abbatis fieri debeant et in hiis omnibus abbas ipse libere agere [fo 73^v] ac ministrare dum voluerit possit magis tamen laudabile ut prefatus abbas negotia secularia ac rerum emptiones seu pecuniarum solutiones cellerario et eius coadiutoribus seu aliis committat ipsique cancellarius[11] ac ceteri omnia secundum ipsius abbatis mandata facere teneantur ac abbas ipse spiritualia magis quam temporalia curare semper ostendere ac frequenter cum fratribus in conventu divinis officiis interesse et vigilem curam ac diligentiam solicitudinem de omnibus gerere ut de officio sibi commisso dignam deo possit reddere rationem debeat;

[8] et licet ex regula quando minus sunt hospites abbas ipse possit aliquando ex monachis quos vult ad suam mensam vocare de cetero magis laudabiliter fieret si sepius cum conventu in refectorio aut misericordia seu infirmatorio refectionem sumet;

[9] ac ne de redditibus et possessionibus ac iuribus quocunque nomine seu titulo censeantur ad dictum monasterium pertinentibus alienationes diminutiones et dilapidaciones fiant diligenter curare et semel in anno vel saltem omni secundo anno in sua propria persona si non sit rationabiliter impeditus pro huius rei securitate omnia seu principalia dominia ubi possessiones monasterii iacent visitare teneatur;

[10] quodque pecunie pro victualibus vestimentis aut aliis quibuscunque rebus fratribus necessariis aut eorum recreationibus faciendis fratribus monachis infra[12] limites monasterii constitutis nisi quando sunt extra ituri nullatenus administrari possint;

[11] et si aliquis ex eis aliquas pecunias quantumcunque paucas [fo 74^r] ipsis duntaxat qui pro tempore publicas seu commissas administrationes habuerint exceptis alicubi reciperet et eas post huiusmodi receptionem si presens in monasterio seu ab ingressu si ab eo absens fuerit intra intra[13] viginti et quatuor horas suo abbati aut alteri quem super huiusmodi negotia abbas ipse constituerit totaliter non consignet atque revelet et de hoc convinctus fuerit ut proprietarius puniri debeat quodque in dicto monasterio presentes aliquid pecuniarum ad locum proprium usum seu privatam dispositionem preterquam ut supradictum est recipere aut penes se servare non possint;

[12] ipseque /[14] abbas iuxta regulam de indumentis et aliis rebus monachis necessariis diligentissime providere teneatur ac hiis[15] qui ab eodem abbate nova indumenta susceperint alia priora sibi minime retinere sed ea statim abbati vel alteri iuxta eius beneplacidum consignare ac illud quod de pane diurno et bibariis quotidianis que monachis ministrantur remanserint nullus sibi quomodolibet retinere sed ea pauperibus in elemosinis cum hiis que supererunt de vetustioribus fratrum vestimentis erogari vel saltem in utilitatem monasterii converti debeant;

[13] et ut in omnibus proprietatis ambitio evitetur quod nullus ex monachis enxenia aut quicquid sibi destinatum seu transmissum [fo 74^v] fuerit accipere sed ea abbati aut priori seu cui iusserit abbas statim assignare et in eiusdem abbatis seu prioris potestate atque discretione sit cui illud concedi aut dari mandet nec sibi invicem aut aliis personis litteras seu alia munuscula nisi id eis ratione alicuius administrationis competat sine abbatis sive eius vicegerentis licentia dari possint;

[14] et quia iuxta regulam eiusdem Beati Benedicti omnia necessaria a patre monasterii seperari debeant quod abbas ea que suis erunt fratribus necessaria oportuna tam in victualibus quam in vestimentis ac ceteris rebus omnibus cum sit minister communitatis diligentissime eis providere debeat et cum monachi eiusdem monasterii nil penitus sine ipsius abbatis licentia habere possint que sine culpa concedere potest non debet ea cum periculo denegare ea tamen discretione semper utatur ut superfluum non concedat neque ex aliqua tenaci[t]ate vel pravitate seu negligentia necessaria neget proviso semper quod propter istas reformationes nullo modo fiat diminutio divini cultus in numero fratrum seu impiis[16] operibus ut puta luminaribus ornamentis reparationibus in ecclesia seu oratorio vel capella gloriose Virginis Marie et cantoribus secularibus in eadem ac in aliis locis conventualibus [fo 75^r] aut in elemosinis seu hospitalitate servanda vel in aliis quibuscunque piis operibus sed eo melius ac devotius omnia ex hiis que in communi recipiuntur pie ac perpetuo fiant;

[15] et ut perpetue castitatis votum inviolabiliter ab omnibus servetur atque occasiones hinc inde castitati adversantes de monasterio cum diligentia expellantur quod mulieres cuiuscunque sint conditionis seu propinquitatis claustrum monachorum ubi fratres studere solent necnon et refectorium infirmitorium ac cetera loca conventualia intra limites claustri monasterii huiusmodi existentia nullatenus intrare permittantur nec licet alicui ex fratribus monachis cum eisdem mulieribus nisi fuerit reliquias ostendendo confessiones audiendo seu aliis interogationibus paucis respondendo aut abbatis presentia[17] publicas seu privatas locutiones in monasterii ecclesia seu ecclesie cimiteriis habere;

[16] quodque abbas providere debeat ut prope ianuam dicti monasterii intra illius clausuram[18] ordinetur una cella sive honesta domus et si opus fuerit plures in quibus non solum honeste vel devote seu peregrine sed etiam persone que sibi vel eius fratribus aliqua affinitate vel consanguinitate sunt coniuncte cum dicti abbatis vel eius vicegerentis expressa licentia seu mandato recipi valeant quibus in locis cum omni gravitate et religionis honestate et timore Domini benigne et humaniter tractentur nec aliquis ex fratribus monachis huiusmodi ad eas accedere aut cum eis loqui seu collationem facere possit nisi cui abbas vel eius vicegerens id iusserit;

[17] quodque abbas in loco [fo 75[v]] ad hoc congruo et apto apertum locutorium ad similitudinem inclusorum religiosorum cum fenestra et separatione ubi monachi prefati in presentia abbatis seu prioris aut alterius ad abbatis seu eius vicegerentis preceptum ex bona et honesta causa cum mulieribus sermonem habere possint ordinare ac sub pena minoris excommunicationis per contra facientes eo ipso incurrendam[19] ne alia loca intra ianuas et clausuram dicti monasterii constructa seu construenda loquendo de difficiis[20] monasterii huiusmodi nisi ad dictum publicum locutorium et ad cellas seu domos predictas ecclesia monasterii cum eius cimiteriis et capella Beate Marie seu aliis capellis in dicto monasterio seu cimiteriis in posterum edificandis exceptis mulieres intrent vel ad ea introducantur nec in ipsis cellis ad hoc deputatis valeant pernoctare strictissime percipere[21] debeat quodque abbas ipse in hoc aut aliter facere aut dispensare non possit nisi regine aut de sanguine regis fuerint vel saltem huiusmodi que vel ducibus comitibus baronibus vel militibus per matrimonium coniunctis[22] erunt cum aliis mulieribus eas pro tempore assotiantibus que sub hiis ordinationibus seu prohibitionibus non comprehendantur;

[18] quodque circa esum carnium et abstinentiam tam ex parte conventus quam abbatis serventur ea que felicis recordationis Innocentius III et Bonifatius XII Romani pontifices predecessores nostri super hoc statuerunt adiiciendo quod nemini ex illa dimidia parte conventus que ad refectorium assignatur pro illo die aut carnes seu carnea [fo 76[r]] alicubi sine expressa licentia abbatis commedere liceat declarando abbatem celerarium ac fratres infirmos seu debiles qui secundum dictam regulam carnibus vesci possint cum ceteris extra dictum monasterium ad tempus existentibus quando presumitur quod eodem die non erunt reversuri in numero conventus quorum dimidia pars diebus carnium ad refectorium assignetur non comprehendi neque computari debere secumque etiam dispensari ut antiqua consuetudo in aliquibus servetur quod solum in tribus locis videlicet in mensa seu domo abbatis in qua ipse residet in loco illo qui pro misericordia assignetur et in infirmatorio tam abbas quam singuli eius confratres monachi carnibus lice[23] vesci

possint alibi vero non intra dictum monasterium nec extra nisi in manerio quod "Cornedenia" dicitur vel infirmi aut debiles seu in studio generali vel universitate aut extra regnum constituti fuerint ubi consuetudinem loci observent ubi eos manere contingat[24] carnibus aut carneis huiusmodi vesci non possint nisi abbas ad tempus ex speciali causa aliter dispenset et cavere debet abbas ne ipse frequenter seu sine causa contrarium faciat aut cum aliis ut faciant dispenset;

[19] quodque diebus quibus carnibus non vescuntur omnes confratres nisi sint in mensa abbatis vel occupati in administrationibus vel infirmi aut debiles et si sint intra precinctum dicti monasterii ad refectorium convenire et suas ibidem refectiones sumere et tempore ieiunii regularis [fo 76ᵛ] quod stat ab idibus Septembris usque ad Pascha absque scrupulo tribus diebus in ebdomada dominico die inter eos non computato extra Quadragesimam et Adventum Domini omnes qui voluerint cenare possint hoc tamen ordine et[25] qui diebus carnium in refectorio pransi sunt ibi si sint illo die cenaturi cum cibis ad refectorium pertinentibus cenam facere debeant possint etiam lacticiniis et ovis per totum annum circulum extra Quadragesimam uti;

[20] in licentiis vero dandis monachis ut monasterium exire valeant ea serventur que Beatus Benedictus in regula et Benedictus duodecimus huiusmodi super hoc voluerunt;

[21] quodque fratres monachi qui solaciis indigent honestas recreationes et religiosa solacia intra clausuram[26] dicti monasterii secundum discretionem abbatis diebus et temporibus ad hoc congruis exclusis secularibus habere permittantur nec antiqua illa consuetudo que olim erat et[27] per quatuor vel quinque dies per vices suas a choro et austeritate regularis observantie se absentarent deinceps observari debeat ac de cetero dicto completorio a conventu in choro ab omnibus usque in crastinum secundum regulam huiusmodi silentium observetur nisi ex administratione vel speciali licentia abbatis super quo dummodo non frequenter fiat cum aliquo ex honesta causa ad tempus abbas ipse dispensare possit;

[22] quodque non frequenter aut leviter seu sine discretione cum fratribus aut[28] extra monasterii limites deambulantes suas et recreationes habeant [fo 77ʳ] dispenset sed quando id per eundem abbatem fieri contigerit ita per eum provideri debeat ut duo vel tres aut quatuor ad minus simul cum gravitate incedant et cum secularibus nisi sint ex famulis monasterii non libenter multum loquantur extra autem monasterium in huiusmodi recreationibus manducare aut bibere eis non liceat nisi fiat ex abbatis seu eius vicegerentis speciali precepto vel licentia abbas vero interdum provideat pro eis et cum eis dispenset et[29] illo loco sive manerio qui[30] "Cornedenia" dicitur possint aliquando collationes facere et honesta solatia habere;

[23] et ut premissa omnia absque per[i]culo et suspicione mali deinceps fiant ut nulla mulier cuiuscunque fuerit dignitatis aut condicionis ianuam dicti monasterii ingrediatur inhibeat nisi in vigilia Ascensionis quo die cum processione ex consuetudine intrare solent sub pena predicta exceptis pre exceptis quam incurunt intrantes claustrum dicti monasterii nec in edificiis prope sive /[31] iuxta dictum manerium erectis seu erigendis mulieres ipse nullo modo permanere permittantur;

[24] quodque in dormitorio si f[i]eri possit fratres omnes nisi fuerint propter administrationes et officia excusati dormire teneantur cellas quoque habere permittantur in eodem dummodo cellarum hostia seu fenestras aperta teneant vel in

eis habeant foramen ut possit a custodibus religionis videri si religiose se habeant in
eo autem quod vestiti dor [fo 77ᵛ] mire teneantur secum dispensetur ut eis sufficiat
si in femoralibus tunicellis longis de albo panno vel nigro laneo vel saltem in
stamineis et pro habitu regulari in scapularibus factis cum caputio vel sine caputio ad
nutum abbatis et cum cingulis sive zonis dormitant nec camiseis nec linteaminibus
lineis utantur; hec autem consuetudo ubique etiam intra monasterium et extra ad
minus ab omnibus servetur nisi abbas propter debilitatem seu infirmitatem ad tempus
aliter dispenset qui vero tunicellas laneas stamineis suis superaddent melius facient;

[25] et cum non sint³² multum laudabile ut la[i]ci seculares sive homines sive
pueri fuerint cum fratribus in locis suis conventualibus intra limites claustri maneant
quod abbas et conventus prefati si eis expedire videatur eorundem secularium et
puerorum loco laicos commissos qui se deo omnipotenti et prefato Beato Benedicto
dedicare aut commendare voluerint in congregatione fratrum suscipere possint
itaquod non teneantur ad omnes regule sive presentis reformationis austeritates sed
sufficiat eis si tria ipsa substantialia vota tamdiu firmiter servaverit³³ quamdiu in
dicta congregatione disposuerint manere; unde si eos ob aliquod delictum a dicto
monasterio expelli contingeret vel si in eodem manere diutius renuerint ad ipsa tria
vota seu ad aliquod eorum non sint amplius obligati; postquam vero tempus
probationis habuerint et deberint in congregatione recipi aperte promittant in
capitulo conventus si servaturos paupertatem voluntariam castitatem et obedientiam
donec in dicto conventu [fo 78ʳ] in servitio dei perseveraverint deturque eis signum
seu habitus ad distinctionem aliorum laicorum secundum discretionem abbatis sed
vocem in conventu seu capitulo non habeant atque deinceps in numero fratrum
computentur gaudeantque veluti ceteri fratres privilegiis indulgentiis gratiis dicto
monasterio concessis et imposterum concedendis necnon omnium bonorum
spiritualium et temporalium que in dicto monasterio fiunt et fient in futurum
comparticipes atque communes quamdiu ibidem manebunt censeantur;

[26] in coquina autem conventus ac familia abbatis et in ceteris locis et officiis
exterioribus dicti monasterii honesti homines laici atque pueri secundum antiquam
laudabilem consuetudinem dummodo sint numero competenti teneri permittantur;

[27] quodque etiam abbas qui pro tempore fuerit dum eum foras ad aliorum loca
seu civitates exire aut equitare contingeret sex aut octo famulos laicos de familia sua
secundum usum patrie secum ducere possit ultra vero dictum numerum non valeat
nisi fuerint de exteris seu pro maiori securitate dum teneret de periculo id faceret;

[28] quodque deinceps perpetuis futuris temporibus omnes et singuli monachi
dicti monasterii presentes et futuri nisi infirmitatibus detenti aut debiles aut in
confessionibus vel missarum celebrationibus seu administrationibus prepediti fuerint
aut super hoc a suo superiori licentiam obtinuerint singulis horis divinis diurnis
pariter et nocturnis diligentissime interesse;

[29] ac monachi dicti monasterii [fo 78ᵛ] tam in eo quam in universitatibus
generalibus studentes iuxta nonnulla statuta et consuetudines per prefatum
Benedictum XII super hoc edita studium continuare teneantur ipsorumque
monachorum preceptor si monachus dicti monasterii fuerit pro libris emendis aut
salario et labore suo peccunias recipere non possit sed sibi de hiis et aliis necessariis
per ipsum abbatem provideri debeat et quilibet ex dictis monachis in universitatibus

studiorum generalium residentibus decem libras monete Anglie pro portione sua annuatim iuxta eiusdem monasterii consuetudinem percipere et habere et ut sacrarum litterarum cognitio et doctrina in dicto monasterio semper incrementum suscipiant lectiones et exercitium lingue latine locis et temporibus congruis inibi frequentare ac duo ex monachis dicti monasterii nisi infirmitatis aut alia legitima seu honesta causa ad tempus prepediantur in studio generali /34 continuo residere debeant ipsique monachi sic ad studium generale pro tempore transmissi in illis locis seu collegiis nigrorum monachorum locari et perma[n]ere35 possint que ad hoc dicti monasterii abbates pro tempore duxerint eligenda /36 nec habitandi in alio loco per superiores et capitulum dicti ordinis seu presidentes illius provincie aut locorum ordinarios vel quascunque alias personas quavis auctoritate arctari valeant priores vero seu custodes aut guardiani collegiorum seu locorum huiusmodi super monachos per eorum abbatem cum eius litteris ad huiusmodi loca seu collegia missos tantam auctoritatem et potestatem in quibuscunque rebus [fo 79r] habeant quantum idem abbas super illos si in eodem monasterio constitutos habere dinoscitur;

[30] quodque abbas dicti monasterii qui pro tempore fuerit tam in dicto monasterio quam ecclesiis et capellis eidem monasterio subiectis etiam in illis que pleno iure eidem monasterio non subsint verbum dei tam in latino quam in vulgari sermone subditis suis aut populo exponere et predicare per alios et monachis37 dicti monasterii vel alias personas predicti vel cuiusvis ordinis regulares vel seculares ad id ydoneos deputare possit.

Ac omnia et singula predicta postquam in domo capitulari dicti monasterii coram dictis conventu lecta et publicata fuerint inviolabiliter observari debeant et nemini contra illa aliquid attemptare liceat ac omnes et singuli presentes et futuri in dicto monasterio professi ex tunc deinceps iuxta huiusmodi statuta <et>38 ordinationes vivere teneantur ipsique abbas et prior dicti monasterii cum sex ex primis senioribus eiusdem monasterii pro tempore existentibus sub minoris excommunicationis pena eo ipso incurrenda procurare teneantur ut per eos vel eorum aliquem presentes eidem monasterio concesse littere seu earum transumpta visitatoribus in singulis visitationibus in eodem monasterio faciendis presententur qui visitatores ea omnia publice coram prefatis conventu legi faciant examinentque diligenter singula statuta et ordinationes huiusmodi cum singulis in eis contentis clausulis faciantque ea prout eis videbitur [fo 79v] etiam in virtute sancte obedientie et sub attestatione divini iudicii atque per alia oportuna remedia et si opus fuerit per censuras ecclesiasticas omni appellatione remota ab omnibus prout ordinatum fuerit loco et tempore oportunis et congruis observare39.

Et ne ex premissis que pro dictorum monachorum salute statuenda sunt ipsis monachis periculum insurgat quod contra premissa vel eorum aliquod non ex contemptu sed humana imbecillitate venientes nisi directe contra prohibitionem in virtute sancte obedientie aut sub attestatione divini iudicii vel minoris excommunicationis pena et in ipsis ordinationibus et statutis ac presentibus litteris contentis aut tria substantialia vota huiusmodi peccatum mortale propterea non committant sed iuxta dicti abbatis vel aliorum ad quos id pro tempore spectabit arbitrium puniri debeant ac quod statuta ordinationes et cetera omnia supradicta postquam in domo capitulari huiusmodi presentate40 notario publico lecta et publicata fuerint pro confirmatis et innovatis cum suppletione defectuum habeantur et omnes presentes et futuri in dicto monasterio professi facta huiusmodi publicatione sic deinceps ad vivendum secundum ea omnino teneantur.

In ceteris vero constitutionibus atque statutis in eodem monasterio ordinatis seu in futurum ordinandis ac Benedicti XII et aliorum Romanorum pontificum pro dicte religionis conser [fo 80^r] vatione concessis presentibus non contrariis ac magistram regulam huiusmodi ubi^{41} commode loco et tempore consideratis possit observari sequi debeant de loci ordinarii licentia ac maioris partis conventus monasterii huiusmodi expresso consensu statuere et ordinare auctoritate nostra curetis.

Non obstantibus quibusvis apostolicis necnon bone memorie Ottonis et Ottoboni olim in regno Anglie apostolice sedis legatorum ac in provincialibus et sinodalibus conciliis editis generalibus vel specialibus constitutionibus et ordinationibus necnon monasterii et ordinis predictorum iuramento confirmatione apostolica vel quavis firmitate alia roboratis statutis et consuetudinibus ceterisque contrariis quibuscunque.

Datum Rome apud Sanctum Petrum anno incarnationis dominice millesimo quingentesimo primo nono kalendas Septembris anno nono.

L puccius / Jo / Jo· C· Eps' Terracinen.'

[1] *ac* or *de* deleted and initialled *Jo*

[2] *sic*; *recte*:'regulari' or 'religionis'

[3] uncertain: smudged; perhaps reworked

[4] uncertain: reworked

[5] *ecclesiarum capellarum unitates*] *sic*; *recte*: 'ecclesiarum et capellarum annuitates'?

[6] *in communi reponi*] 'cista' does not occur

[7] *sic*; *recte*: 'ex istis'

[8] *sic*; *recte*: 'que in'

[9] *sic*; *recte*: 'que'

[10] *sic*; *recte*: 'gerere'

[11] *sic*; *recte*: 'cellerarius'

[12] *sic*; *recte*: 'intra'?

[13] *sic*; not deleted

[14] *Johannes* deleted but not initialled

[15] *sic*; *recte*: 'hii' *for* 'ii'?

[16] *sic*; *for* 'in piis'

[17] *aut abbatis presentia*] 'in' does not occur

[18] changed from *claustrum*?

[19] *sic*; *recte* 'incurrenda'

[20] *sic*; *for* 'de edifficiis'

[21] *sic*; *recte*: 'precipere'

[22] *sic*; *recte*: 'coniuncte'?

[23] *sic*; *recte*: 'licite'

[24] changed (by deletion) from *contingant*

[25] *sic*; 'ut'?

[26] changed from *claustrum*?

[27] *sic*; 'ut'?

[28] *sic*; 'ut?'

[29] *sic*; 'ut?'

[30] *sic*; 'quod'?

[31] *extra* deleted but not initialled

[32] *sic*; *recte*: 'sit'

[33] *sic*; *recte*: 'servaverint'

[34] *cum* deleted but not initialled

[35] a cross (signalling error) above the position where the 'n' should be; a cross in the margin at the end of the line

[36] (?) *nec* (ill-written) deleted but not initialled

[37] *sic*; *recte*: 'monachos'?

[38] squeezed in, in the line

[39] *sic*; MS: *observar(e)*; *recte* 'observari'

[40] *sic*; *recte*: 'presentata'?

[41] over an erasure

395   12 March 1501   *Reg. Lat.* 1078, fo 157^{r-v}

To James Bethon, rector of the parish church of Glenguhon', d. Glasgow. Dispensation — at his supplication — to receive and retain for life, together with the above parish church, one, and without it, any two other benefices, etc. [as above, no. 5].

Vite ac morum honestas . . .
L putius / · B· / · B· xxxx Bolis.

396   27 April 1501   *Reg. Lat.* 1078, fos 164^{v}-165^{v}

To Richard Coluge, rector, called master, of the hospital of St John the Baptist, Radeliff *alias* Radeliffput,[1] OSA, ds. Bath and Wells. Dispensation and indult — at his supplication — to receive together with the above hospital, one, and without it, any two other regular benefices, with or without cure, of the aforesaid or any other order, or with one of them, or without them, one benefice, with or without cure, usually held by secular clerics, even if the regular benefices should be priories, *prepositure, prepositatus,* hospitals, rectories or their perpetual vicarages, dignities, *personatus,* administrations or offices in metropolitan or other cathedral churches of the said order, and the dignities in question should be major *post pontificalem* in cathedral, even metropolitan, churches, and the secular benefice should be a parish church or its perpetual vicarage, or a chantry, free chapel, hospital or annual service, usually assigned to secular clerics in title of a perpetual ecclesiastical benefice, or a canonry and prebend in a collegiate church, or a combination, even if the priories, *prepositure, prepositatus*, dignities, etc. should be customarily elective and have cure of souls, if he obtains them otherwise canonically, and to retain whichever one of the regular benefices he chooses, even if it should be a priory, *prepositura, prepositatus*, or dignity (even conventual) or a claustral office, *in titulum*, and with it the other regular benefice — which may not be suchlike — or the secular benefice, *in commendam*, for life; to resign all of them, at once or successively, simply or for exchange, as often as he pleases, and cede the commend, and in their place receive up to two other, similar or dissimilar, regular benefices, of the aforesaid or any other order, or with one of them, or without them, one secular benefice, with or without cure, and to retain whichever one of the regular benefices he chooses *in titulum*, and with it, the other — which may not be conventual or claustral — or the secular benefice, *in commendam*, for life, as above; (he may — due and customary burdens of the benefice retained *in commendam* having been supported — make disposition of the rest of its fruits etc. just as those holding it *in titulum* could and ought to do, alienation of immovable goods and precious movables being however forbidden); and henceforth, also for life, to wear under an outer robe (*toga*) or vestment (*vestis*) the particular cross of black silk thread usually worn by <preceptors>,[2] OSA, over the habit, without apostasy or sentence of excommunication, and not to be bound to bear the cross over the upper robe or vestment, nor to be liable to be compelled by anyone to do so against his will. Notwithstanding etc. With the proviso that the benefice retained *in commendam* shall not, on this account, be defrauded of due services and the cure of souls therein (if any) shall not be neglected; but that its aforesaid burdens shall be supported.

Religionis zelus, vite ac morum honestas . . .
L. putius[3] */ . V· / · V· Lxx De Phano:*

[1] MS: *alias in Radeliffput* (first occurrence); and *alias Radeliffput* (second occurrence)

[2] *canonicos* deleted; in the margin opposite, in another hand: *preceptores cass[atum] et cor(r)ect(um) de man(da)to R(everendissimi) p(at)ris d(omi)ni Jo(hannis) Archep(iscop)i Ragusini Regen(tis). F. Sanctor(is).* (slightly shaved)

[3] in enregistering scribe's hand?

397   21 August 1501[1]   *Reg. Lat.* 1078, fo 240[r-v]

To John Fyylint, prior of the monastery, usually governed by a prior, of St John the Apostle[2] and Evangelist, Pontefract (*de Pontefracto*), OClun, d. York. Indult — at his supplication — to him and his successors as priors of the said monastery —

which is immediately subject to the Roman church — to use the mitre, ring, pastoral staff, sandals and other pontifical *insignia*; and also in the said monastery and in the priories, churches and places, subject to it, albeit not by full authority, to give solemn benediction after the solemnities of mass, vespers and matins — provided that no bishop or legate of the apostolic see be present, or, if one so be, with his express consent; and to bless priestly vestments, palls, corporals, altars and other ecclesiastical ornaments necessary for divine worship in the monastery itself and in the priories, churches and chapels dependent on it. Notwithstanding the constitution [*Abbates*][3] of Alexander IV, etc.

Exposcit tue devotionis sinceritas . . .
L putius / · B· / ₁B· Lxx Bolis·

[1] *quadringentesimo* deleted, (after *millesimo*), initialled · B·

[2] changed to *apostoli* from (?)*Baptiste*, initialled · B·

[3] 'Abbates' wanting after *que incipit*

398   19 July 1501   *Reg. Lat.* 1078, fos 242ᵛ-243ᵛ

To Edward Lee, cleric, d. London. Dispensation [and indult?][1] — at his supplication — to him, who, as he asserts, is in his twentieth year of age, to receive and retain any benefice, with cure or otherwise incompatible, etc. [as above, no. 240, to '. . . another, similar or dissimilar, benefice, with cure or otherwise incompatible']; and also — as soon as he has reached his twenty-second year and be [coerced][2] by reason of a benefice with cure or requiring sacred orders held by him — to have himself promoted to all sacred orders, by any catholic bishop of his choice in communion with the apostolic [see], on three Sundays or feast days, even outside the time established by law and successively, otherwise however duly; and the pope grants licence and faculty to the bishop concerned to bestow the orders on him in the aforesaid way. Notwithstanding the defect of age regarding the priesthood which he shall suffer even in his said twenty-second year, etc. With the proviso that the benefice with cure or otherwise incompatible shall not, on this account, be defrauded of due services and the cure of souls therein (if any) shall not be neglected.

Vite ac morum honestas . . .
L putius[3] / · B· / . B. L. Bolis.

[1] MS: *dispensamus tibique pariter indu ac . . .*; indu being deleted, but not initialled

[2] MS: *aretitus*; possibly changed to *arctatus*; *recte*: 'arctatus'?

[3] or *pucius*

399   4 May 1501   *Reg. Lat.* 1078, fos 308ʳ-309ʳ

To Miles, bishop of Llandaff. Dispensation — at his supplication — to him, who, as
he asserts, holds *in commendam* the monastery of Eygemysh(a)m [also spelt
Eygenysh(a)m] alias Eynesh(a)m,[1] OSB, d. Lincoln, by apostolic concession and
dispensation, to receive and retain *in commendam* for life, together with the church
of Llandaff, over which he is understood to preside, and the above monastery, any
other benefice, with or without cure, secular or regular of the aforesaid or any other
order, even Cluniac, even if the secular benefice should be a parish church or its
perpetual vicarage, or a chantry, free chapel, hospital or annual service, usually
assigned to secular clerics in title of a perpetual ecclesiastical benefice, or a canonry
and prebend, or a dignity, *personatus*, administration or office, major *post
pontificalem*, in the aforesaid church of Llandaff or other cathedral, even
metropolitan, church, or principal in a collegiate church, and the regular benefice be
a priory, *prepositura*, dignity (even conventual), *personatus*, administration or office,
even usually held by monks of the said monastery and whose collation or
presentation pertains by reason of the above church of Llandaff to him alone as well
as by reason of the above monastery to him and to the convent of the monastery
collectively or severally, even if the priory etc. should be customarily elective and
have cure of souls, if he obtains it or it is conferred on him (even by a vicar deputed
by him in the church of Llandaff as well as in the monastery aforesaid) otherwise
canonically, to resign it as often as he pleases and cede the commend and in its place
receive another, similar or dissimilar, secular or regular benefice of any order and —
provided that such office be not claustral — retain it *in commendam* for life, as
above; he may — due and customary burdens of this benefice having been supported
— make disposition of the rest of its fruits etc. just as those holding it *in titulum*
could and ought to do, alienation of immovable goods and precious movables being
however forbidden. Notwithstanding etc. and [notwithstanding] statutes and customs
of Llandaff or another church in which the secular benefice may perchance be and of
Eygemysh(a)m or another monastery or regular place in which the regular benefice
may perchance be or from which it may depend and of the aforesaid order of St
Benedict or other order, and [notwithstanding] privileges and indults granted by the
apostolic see to the Cluniac order especially those in which it is said to be expressly
laid down that benefices of the order may be commended to none save cardinals of
the Roman church or expressly professed members of the order etc. And the pope
grants faculty to Miles to depute a vicar who shall confer the benefice in question on
him; and also derogates the privileges and indults in question, specially and
expressly, for this once only. With the proviso that this benefice shall not, on this
account, be defrauded of due services and the cure of souls therein (if any) shall not
be neglected; but that its aforesaid burdens shall be supported.

*Personam tuam nobis et apostolice sedi devotam tuis exigentibus meritis paterna
benivolentia . . .*
f de parma / Jo / Jo. C. Episcopus Terracinen.'

[1] MS: *Eygemyshm'* (also *Eygenyshm'*) *alias Eyneshm'*

400   22 June 1501[1]   *Reg. Lat.* 1078, fos 368^r-369^r

A petition[2] on the part of Richard Cheth(a)m,[3] prior, and the convent of the priory of
B. Mary and St Nicholas, Ledes, OSA, d. Canterbury, stated that if the prior of the
priory for the time being were able to confer all minor orders on its canons and bless
the altars, crosses, vestments, palls, cloths and any other ecclesiastical ornaments
necessary for divine worship in the church of the priory and in other places
dependent on it this would be to the honour of the prior and to his benefit and that of
the convent and the persons of the other places aforesaid. The pope — at this
supplication — hereby establishes that Richard and the successors or priors of the
priory for the time being, may confer all minor orders on all canons of the priory at
the time, notwithstanding any canonical obstacle; and also bless the altars, etc.; and
that the prior and individual persons of the convent and other servants and familiars
of the priory for the time being, may, in perpetuity, and also the brethren of the
confraternity, called capitular, instituted in the said church, of both sexes, who at
present are and who — within a three-year period calculated from the date of the
presents — shall be received as brethren, not exceeding a hundred in number, may,
for life, by visiting on each day of Lent and at any other time at which the Stations
are celebrated within and without Rome the seven altars of the said or another
church of the place where they (or any of them) happen to reside at the time (if there
are seven therein, otherwise as many as may be), and reciting before them seven
times the Lord's Prayer and The Angelic Salutation, obtain each and every one of the
indulgences and remissions of sins which they would have obtained if they were
visiting personally the churches appointed for this within and without Rome and
which those visiting the latter at the times <in question>[4] would have obtained.
Notwithstanding etc.

Ad perpetuam rei memoriam. Ex debito pastoralis officii meritis licet insufficientibus
nobis ex commissi . . .
. L· puccius[5] */ · M· / · M· C· xxx. Battiferro*

[1] the pontifical year has been altered (bringing it into agreement with the year of the incarnation):
decimo deleted (but not initialled); *nono* written, in a different ink, probably in the hand of the
enregistering scribe, possibly later

[2] 'nuper' does not occur

[3] MS: *Chethm'*

[4] marginal insertion by the enregistering scribe, initialled · *M·*

[5] in a lighter ink: entered later?

401   21 September 1500   *Reg. Lat.* 1079, fos 136^r-138^v

To the abbot of the monastery of St Michael, Mayo (*de Magio*), d. Tuam, and
Maurice Occullan,[1] canon of the church of Limerick, and Gilbert de Anglo, canon of

the church of [Achonry]² mandate in favour of Richard Plemen, canon of Tuam. The pope has learned that a canonry of the church of Tuam and the prebend of Chilemian³ in the same are vacant *certo modo* at present and have been vacant for so long that by the Lateran statutes their collation has lawfully devolved on the apostolic see, although Maurice Joy, ⁴ who bears himself as archdeacon of the said church of Tuam, has detained the canonry and prebend,⁵ without any title or support of law, temerariously and *de facto*, for a certain time, as he still does. He hereby commands that the above three (or two or one of them), if, having summoned Maurice and others concerned, they find the canonry and prebend, whose annual value does not exceed 1 mark sterling, to be vacant (howsoever etc.) shall collate and assign them, even if specially reserved etc., with plenitude of canon law and all rights and appurtenances, to Richard, inducting him etc. having removed Maurice and any other unlawful detainer and causing Richard (or his proctor) to be received as a canon in the said church, and the fruits etc., rights and obventions of the said canonry and prebend to be delivered to him. [Curbing] gainsayers by the pope's authority etc. Notwithstanding etc.

Vite ac morum honestas . . .
. *A. de sanctoseverino* / *Jo.* / *Jo. Grat' pro deo Tertio Id' Octobr' Anno nono.* [13 October 1500], *de Galves*

¹ preceded by (?)*op*, deleted (not initialled)
² MS: *Arkaden.*; *recte*: 'Achaden. ' or 'Akaden. '
³ the 'e' reworked and uncertain
⁴ preceded by (?)*Jly*, deleted (not initialled)
⁵ directly following *canonicatum et prebendam* there occurs (?). . . *cant*'; possibly to be read as *vacantas* (though curious here)

402   12 September 1500   *Reg. Lat.* 1079, fos 160ʳ-164ʳ

To Richard Pendeigras, David Oschara and Richard Plemen, canons of the church of Tuam, mandate in favour of David¹ Pindagras, canon of Tuam (who asserts that he is of exalted noble birth). The pope has learned that the deanery, called a rectory by some but by others a *personatus*, of the church of Mayo, and the perpetual vicarages of the parish churches of Balla and of St Gerald, Mayo (*de Maio*), d. Tuam *alias* Mayo, are vacant *certo modo* at present and have been vacant for so long that by the Lateran statutes their collation has lawfully devolved on the apostolic see, although Edmund de Sanctona has detained the first vicarage, and Walter² Cusyn, the second — bearing themselves as priests — without any title or support of law, temerariously and *de facto*, for a certain time, as they do still. At a recent petition on David's part to the pope to unite etc. the vicarages to the deanery, for as long as he holds it, after he is provided to it — asserting that the annual value of the deanery does not exceed 6, of the first vicarage, 4, and of the second, 3, marks sterling; and also that he is in his twenty-first year of age and has held the deanery united by ordinary authority at another time as a rectory *certo modo* to the canonry of the church of Tuam which he holds at present, receiving fruits from it, in good faith however — the pope, not having certain knowledge of the foregoing — at his supplication — hereby commands that the above three (or two or one of them), if, having summoned respectively Edmund and Walter and others concerned, they find the deanery, which is a dignity major *post pontificalem*, and the vicarages, to be vacant (howsoever etc.) and, having summoned those interested in the union, the foregoing to be true, shall collate and assign the deanery to David and unite etc. the vicarages (even if they and the deanery be specially reserved etc.), with all rights and appurtenances, to the deanery, for as long as David holds the deanery, inducting him etc. having removed Edmund from the first vicarage and Walter from the second and any other unlawful detainers from them and the deanery and causing David (or his proctor) to be admitted to the deanery and its fruits etc., rights and obventions and those of the vicarages to be annexed thereto to be delivered to him. [Curbing] gainsayers by the pope's authority etc. Notwithstanding etc. Also the pope dispenses David to receive and retain the deanery, if conferred on him by virtue of the presents; and not to be bound, by reason of the deanery or other benefice with cure or otherwise requiring sacred orders by right or custom held by him at the time, to have himself promoted to other sacred orders, even that of the subdiaconate, for a three-year period calculated from the date of the presents, nor to be liable to be compelled by anyone to do so against his will. Notwithstanding etc. The pope's will is, however, that the deanery and benefices — and the vicarages, on account of this union etc. — shall not, on this account, be defrauded of due services and the cure of souls in the vicarages and (if any) in the deanery and other benefice aforesaid shall not be neglected, but that their customary burdens shall be supported; and that on David's death or resignation etc. of the deanery the union etc. shall be dissolved and the vicarages shall revert to their original condition and be deemed vacant automatically.

Regiminis[3] *universalis ecclesie presidentes . . .*
· *S· de castello* / · *V·* / *V· · xxx*[4] *De Phano:*

[1] MS has *Davit* throughout, the first (and another) occurrence being changed (by overwriting) from *David*

[2] variously: *Vatherus, Valierus, Valterus*

[3] *sic*; *recte*: 'Regimini'

[4] wants expedition date?

403 13 January 1501   *Reg. Lat.* 1079, fos 170ʳ-174ʳ

To the priors of the monasteries, usually governed by priors, of St Ciaran (*Sancti Cherani*), Synr, d. Ossory, and of *Fons vivus* [Lorrha], d. Killaloe, and Cormac Oheaig, canon of the church of Emly, mandate in favour of Robert *alias* Robyn

Ycleri, cleric, d. Killaloe. The pope has learned that the perpetual vicarages of the parish churches of Bayllilocacayn and Ossquean, and also the church, (which is of lay patronage), called the rectory or particle of the lands of Medohk,[1] within the limits of the said parish church of Bayllilocacayn, d. Killaloe, are vacant at present *certo modo* and have been vacant for so long that by the Lateran statutes their collation has lawfully devolved on the apostolic see, although Philip Geydach *alias* Ocogavayn and Maurus Ohurelly have detained the vicarages and Marcus Ohuynayn the church, called a rectory — bearing themselves as clerics or priests — without any title or support of law, temerariously and *de facto*, for a certain time, as they still do. At a recent petition on Robert's part to the pope to erect and institute a canonry in the church of Killaloe and the first vicarage into a simple prebend in the same, for his lifetime, and, after their erection, unite etc. to them the second vicarage and the church called a rectory, also for his lifetime — asserting that the annual value of the vicarages and the church, called a rectory, does not exceed 20 marks sterling — the pope, not having certain knowledge of the foregoing, hereby commands that the above three (or two or one of them), if, having summoned Philip, Maurus, Marcus and others concerned, they find the vicarages and the church of Bayllilocacayn, called a rectory (which is without cure and customarily ruled by the vicar of the said parish church for the time being or by his substitute), to be vacant (howsoever etc., even if specially reserved etc.) and, having summoned those interested, the foregoing regarding the union to be true, having summoned the bishop and chapter of Killaloe, shall erect and institute a canonry in the church of Killaloe and the first vicarage into a simple prebend in the same, for Robert's lifetime and without prejudice to anyone, and, after their erection, unite etc. to them the second vicarage and the church, called a rectory, also for his lifetime; and in that event collate and assign the newly erected canonry and prebend, being vacant, to Robert, with plenitude of canon law and all rights and appurtenances, inducting him etc. into corporal possession of the canonry and prebend, annexed vicarages and church, called a rectory, rights and appurtenances aforesaid, having removed Philip and Maurus from the vicarages and Marcus from the church, called a rectory, and any other unlawful detainers, and causing Robert (or his proctor) to be received as a canon of the church of Killaloe, with plenitude of canon law, and the fruits etc., rights and obventions of the canonry and prebend, annexed vicarages and church, called a rectory, to be delivered to him. [Curbing] gainsayers by the pope's authority etc. Notwithstanding etc. The pope's will is, however, that the vicarages and the church, called a rectory, shall not, on account of this union etc. and erection and institution, be defrauded of due services and the cure of souls in the vicarages shall not be neglected; but that their customary burdens and those of the church, called a rectory, shall be supported; and that on Robert's death or resignation etc. of the canonry and prebend the union etc. shall be dissolved and erection and institution extinguished and so deemed and the vicarages and the church, called a rectory, shall revert to their original condition and be deemed vacant automatically.

Apostolice sedis providentia circumspecta ad eam libenter intendit . . .
· *S· de castello / F / F· xxx Kl' Febr' . Ano' Nono* [1 February 1501], *Sanctor(is)*

[1] the 'o' changed by overwriting; from a 'c' or 'e'?

404 9 January 1501   *Reg. Lat.* 1079, fos 176[v]-180[r]

To the prior of the monastery, usually governed by a prior, of Sire, d. Ossory, and Cormac Oheaig and Cornelius Onuchan, canons of the church of Emly, mandate in favour of Odo Ymukcan, [(?)cleric],[1] d. Cashel. The pope has learned that the perpetual vicarages of the parish churches of Killcomnayt, d. Cashel, and Kyllicuagaruan[2] *alias* Aglaysydony, d. [Killaloe][3] are vacant *certo modo* at present and have been vacant for so long that by the Lateran statutes their collation has lawfully devolved on the apostolic see, although Matheus Omukean[4] has detained the first vicarage and (?)Dermot[5] Macbiragyn, the second — bearing themselves as priests of the said dioceses — without any title or support of law, temerariously and *de facto*, for a certain time, as they still do. At a recent petition on Odo's part to the pope to erect and institute a canonry in the church of Cashel and the first vicarage into a simple prebend in the same, for his lifetime, and unite etc. the second vicarage to the canonry and prebend, after their erection, also for his lifetime — asserting that the annual value of the vicarages does not exceed 12 marks sterling — the pope, not having certain knowledge of the foregoing, hereby commands that the above three (or two or one of them), if, having summoned Matheus and (?)Dermot respectively and others concerned, they find the vicarages to be vacant (howsoever etc.) and, having summoned those interested in the union, the foregoing to be true, shall (even if the vicarages be specially reserved etc.), having summoned the archbishop and chapter of Cashel, erect and institute a canonry in the church of Cashel and the first vicarage into a simple prebend in the same, for Odo's lifetime, without prejudice to anyone, and unite etc. the second vicarage to the canonry and prebend, after their erection, also for Odo's lifetime; and in that event collate and assign the newly erected canonry and prebend, being vacant, to Odo, with plenitude of canon law and all rights and appurtenances, inducting him etc. into corporal possession of the canonry and prebend, annexed vicarage and rights and appurtenances aforesaid having removed Matheus and (?)Dermot aforesaid and any other unlawful detainers and causing Odo (or his proctor) to be received as a canon of the church of Cashel, with plenitude of canon law, and the fruits etc., rights and obventions of the canonry and prebend and annexed vicarage to be delivered to him. [Curbing] gainsayers by the pope's authority etc. Notwithstanding etc. The pope's will is, however, that the vicarages shall not, on account of this union etc., erection and institution, be defrauded of due services and the cure of souls in the vicarages shall not be neglected; but that their customary burdens shall be supported; and that on Odo's death or resignation etc. of the canonry and prebend the union etc. shall be dissolved and erection and institution shall be extinguished and so deemed and the vicarages shall revert to their original condition and be deemed vacant automatically.

Apostolice sedis providentia circumspecta ad eam libenter intendit . . .

. S· de castello / F / F xxv. Kl' Febr'. Ano' Nono [1 February 1501], *Sanctor(is)*

[1] *ecclesia* (i. e. . . . *Oddonis Ymukcan ecclesia Cassellen. diocesis* . . .); *recte*: 'clerici'?

[2] the last letter doubtful

[3] *Lagonen.* for 'Laonen.'

[4] a deleted mark above the 'n'

[5] initially spelt (?)*de Ruriaus*; but thereafter *Dermitius*; finally (?)*deBesʒintio*

405   15 July 1501   *Reg. Lat.* 1080, fos 34^r-35^r

To the bishops of Durham and Lincoln,[1] mandate in favour of John, bishop of Belley, and the convent of the provostry of B. Mary, Moncenisio (*Montis Cenisii*), OSA, d. Turin. A recent petition to the pope on the part of bishop John, who, by apostolic concession and dispensation, holds the provostship *in commendam*, and the convent stated that, formerly, the then bishop of Lincoln, by ordinary authority, united, etc., in perpetuity, the parish church of B. Mary, Vororono, called Vodesol, d. Lincoln, which was in the patronage of the then king of England, through the concession and donation of Edward, the then king, patron of the church, [to the above provostry] for the maintenance of its provost and canons and of the poor making the crossing[2] from there who are received in the provostry's hospital and have their needs attended to, and also for the maintenance of others who are unable, on account of the harshness of the place, to subsist except in the provostry and hospital; that from then on, for so long that there is no recollection to the contrary, the provosts and convent have, on the strength of this union, been in peaceful and quiet possession, or almost, of the above parish church and its rights and appurtenances; and that the then abbot and convent of the monastery of Bruern (*de Bruera*), OCist, d. Lincoln, — after they had leased the fruits etc. of the parish church for a certain time, then expressed, from the then provost and convent, or a certain proctor of theirs, for a certain annual payment, then expressed, and [had] obliged themselves to make the payment to the then provost and convent — by pretext of the dissolution of the above union, and the union of the church to the monastery, made by certain letters of Eugenius IV, which had been surreptitiously and obreptitiously impetrated, on the ground that the then provost and convent adhered to the late Amadeus, duke of Savoy, called Felix V in his obedience (in which those parts, as is asserted, lay), *de facto* despoiled the provostry of the parish church and its rights and appurtenances, intruded themselves into it, occupied it and its fruits etc., and afterwards granted it to be held and occupied by others, or allowed and caused it to be occupied — as Thomas ?K. . . .,[3] who bears himself as a cleric of Lincoln diocese, by a turn of occupation, [occupied][4] it and still does — usurping the church's fruits etc., to the danger of their souls and unbounded prejudice and damage of bishop John and the convent. At the supplication to the pope of bishop John and the convent to commit to some upright men in those parts all the cases which the bishop and convent, jointly and severally, intend to move against the abbot and convent and Thomas and certain others over the parish church and its former union, the nullity and subreption of the latter union and letters, the spoliation, intrusion, and occupation, and everything else done recklessly to the prejudice of the provost and convent, the pope hereby commands that the above two (or one of them), having summoned the abbot and convent, Thomas, and others concerned, and having heard both sides, taking cognizance even of the principal matter, shall decree what is just, without appeal, causing by ecclesiastical censure what they have decreed to be strictly observed; [and moreover compel] witnesses, etc. Notwithstanding etc.

Humilibus et cetera.
F de parma[5] / *F* / *F· xii· Sanctor(is)*

[1] the address clause (which occupies two lines) has evidently been entered later (though by the scribe of the rest of the letter): the words are 'stretched' and it has been extended to *benedictionem* to fill the space left for it. (Ordinarily, enregistration was abridged — with an 'et cetera' — at 'salutem'). Enough space had been left for the names of three mandataries — the usual number. *Cf.* note 5

[2] i. e. of the Alps

[3] surname altered and now uncertain; possibly originally *Hnrey*, with the 'H' now changed to *K* and the '-nrey' overwritten

[4] word illegible

[5] the writing 'stretched': entered later? *Cf.* note 1 above

406   25 June 1501   *Reg. Lat.* 1080, fo 37[r-v]

To Richard Smyth, rector of the parish church of Waltham, d. Lincoln. Dispensation — at his supplication — to receive and retain for life, together with the above parish church, one, and without it, any two other benefices, etc. [as above, no. 3].

Vite ac morum honestas . . .
L puccius[1] / *[-]*[2] / *F . L. Sanctor(is)*

[1] in a lighter ink: entered later?
[2] no magistral initial

407   10 March 1501   *Reg. Lat.* 1080, fos 57[v]-59[r]

To William Turnbull, cleric, d. Glasgow, reservation, constitution and assignment of a pension, as below. William — between whom (as a recent petition to the pope on his part stated) and Robert Schanwel, perpetual vicar of the parish [church][1] of

Kyrkcayde, d. St Andrews, a suit was brewing over the [vicarage of the said church][2] concerning which at another time when it was vacant *certo modo* provision had been granted to be made to William by apostolic authority and provision had been made to Robert by ordinary authority, to avoid the tortuosity of litigation, spare labour and expense and for the implementation of a certain honest agreement brought about between William and Robert through the intervention of several upright men at the pleasure of the apostolic see — has left Robert peacefully in the vicarage and does not intend to pursue further the right belonging to him from the said grant. Lest William should suffer excessive loss on this account, the pope hereby reserves, constitutes and assigns an annual pension of 20 pounds Scots (not exceeding 6 pounds sterling) on the fruits etc. of the vicarage (of which this pension does not, as he asserts, exceed a third part) payable in full to William for life (or to William's specially mandated proctor) by Robert, to which express assent has been given by M. Paul Tuba, papal scriptor and familiar (Robert's specially appointed proctor), and his successors holding the vicarage at the time, each year, one half on the Nativity of St John the Baptist and the other on that of Jesus Christ. With decree etc. that if Robert, or any one of his successors, fails to make payment on the said feasts or within the thirty days immediately following, he shall, after this time has elapsed, incur sentence of excommunication, from which he cannot be absolved, except on the point of death, until he shall have made satisfaction in full or reached agreement in respect of it with William (or his proctor) and, if he remains obdurate under that sentence for a further six months, he shall thereupon be deprived in perpetuity of the said vicarage, which shall be deemed vacant automatically. Notwithstanding etc.

Executory to the archbishop of Ragusa, the abbot of the monastery of Holyrood (*Sancte Crucis*), d. St Andrews, and the archdeacon of Lothian (*Landonie*) in the church of St Andrews, or two or one of them, acting in person or by proxy.

Vite ac morum honestas . . . The executory begins: *Hodie dilecto filio Willelmo Turnbull* . . .
N de Castello; C de S[c]ortiatis / Jo. / Jo. xij. x. Electus Terracinen'

[1] 'ecclesie' wanting?

[2] MS: *super dicta ecclesia; recte*: '. . . vicaria' (as in the text below and the executory)

---

408   23 March 1501   *Reg. Lat.* 1080, fos 63ʳ-64ʳ

To Alexander Stewart, scholar, d. Glasgow, dispensation and indult. The pope (who, some time ago, decreed and declared that provisions, grants or mandates of provision to canonries and prebends of cathedral churches to persons who have not completed their fourteenth year of age shall have no force except by consent of the apostolic see; and that any impetrations concerning canonries and prebends in collegiate churches if those impetrating be less than ten years and express mention be not made of this in the impetrations shall have no force) hereby dispenses and indulges Alexander (who, as he asserts, is in his eighth year, suffers from a defect of birth as the son of the unmarried king of Scots and an unmarried woman, and desires to become a cleric) — at his supplication — to be promoted at the lawful age — after he has been duly marked with clerical character — to all, even sacred, orders; and to receive and retain — after he has reached his twelfth year — any dignity, *personatus*, administration with cure or office, and — henceforth — any number of benefices without cure, and — when he has reached the lawful age — any number, with and without cure, compatible mutually, even if canonries and prebends, dignities, *personatus*, administrations or offices in cathedral, even metropolitan, or collegiate churches, even if the dignities in question should be major *post pontificalem* in cathedral, even metropolitan, churches, or principal in collegiate churches, even if the dignities etc. should be customarily elective and have cure of souls, if he obtains them otherwise canonically, to resign them, at once or successively, simply or for exchange, as often as he pleases, and in their place receive and retain — henceforth — any number of similar or dissimilar benefices without cure — and — when he has reached the lawful age — any number of benefices, with and without cure, compatible mutually, and — as soon as he has reached his twelfth year — a dignity, *personatus*, administration with cure or an office; and not to be bound in any impetrations concerning canonries and prebends of [collegiate][1] churches to mention his defect of age, and such impetrations shall not, on this account, be surreptitious, but shall be valid and efficacious. Notwithstanding the defects of birth and age which he shall suffer even in his twelfth year etc. With the proviso that the canonries and prebends and the dignity etc. shall not, on this account, be defrauded of due services and the cure of souls in the dignity or *personatus* (if any) shall not be neglected; and that customary burdens of the canonries and prebends shall be supported.

Laudabilia tue puerilis etatis indicia . . .
F de parma / · V· / V· Lxxxx De Phano

[1] *cathedralium*; *recte*: 'collegiatarum'

409   13 March 1501   *Reg. Lat.* 1080, fo 64[r-v]

To Michael Lornisen, monk of the monastery of Dunfermlen', OSB, d. St Andrews. Dispensation — at his supplication — to him, who, as he asserts, is expressly professed of the above order,[1] to receive and retain any benefice, with or without cure, usually held by secular clerics, even if a parish church or its perpetual vicarage, even of lay patronage, if he obtains it otherwise canonically, etc. [as above, no. 32].

Religionis zelus, vite ac morum honestas . . .
F de parma / . V / V xxx De Phano:

[1] This information comes from a notwithstanding clause.

410   23 March 1501   *Reg. Lat.* 1080, fos 64^v-65^r

To Elizabeth Hoin, nun of the monastery of Eccles (*de Ecclesiis*), OCist, d. St Andrews. Dispensation — at her supplication — to her, who, as she asserts, is in her twentieth year of age or thereabouts and is of noble, baronial birth, to receive and retain the priory of the above monastery, usually governed by a prioress, (of which she is a nun and, as she also asserts, expressly professed of the said order), or any other conventual dignity of the order, even if it should be customarily elective, if she obtains it otherwise canonically. Notwithstanding the above defect of age etc.

Digna reddimur attentione soliciti vota earum ad exauditionis gratiam admittere . . .
Lpuccius / V / V . xx . De Phano:

411   23 March 1501   *Reg. Lat.* 1080, fos 65^v-66^r

To William, bishop of Aberdeen, indult. A recent petition to the pope on William's part stated that it often happens that churches, cemeteries and other sacred places of his diocese of Aberdeen are polluted by bloodshed or otherwise and as often as such pollutions occur he is unable, on account of the poverty of the places as well as even the inconvenience to himself, to conveniently go there in person to reconcile them. The pope therefore — at his supplication — hereby indulges William, for as long as he shall preside over the church of Aberdeen, to cause any churches, cemeteries and other ecclesiastical places of his diocese polluted by bloodshed or adultery at the time to be reconciled by any suitable secular priest, whom he shall depute for this at the time, the water having been blessed by him beforehand in accordance with the constitution of Gregory IX. Notwithstanding etc. The pope's will is, however, that this shall not be to the prejudice of the aforesaid constitution which lays down[1] that this may only be done by bishops.

Tue devotionis sinceritas benignum prebentes assensum . . .
L puccius / Jo / Jo. L. Electus Terracinen'

[1] *percipit; recte*: 'precipit'?

412   16 March 1501   *Reg. Lat.* 1080, fo 66^{r-v}

To Robert Elphinston, cleric, Glasgow. Dispensation — at his supplication — to him, who, as he asserts, is in his twentieth year of age or thereabouts, to receive and retain a sacerdotal canonry and prebend of any cathedral or metropolitan church, if he obtains them otherwise canonically. Notwithstanding the above defect of age etc. With the proviso that the above canonry and prebend shall not, on this account, be defrauded of due services; but that their customary burdens shall be supported.

Vite ac morum honestas . . .
L puccius / . V· / V· xx· De Phano:

413   29 March 1501   *Reg. Lat.* 1080, fo 225^{r-v}

Relaxation as below. The pope — desiring that the chapel of Aston, otherwise called the chapel of grace, within the parish boundary of the parish church [of] Alfyngton, d. Exeter, which William Russel, perpetual vicar of the chapel, holds and to which he is singularly devoted, is visited with fitting respect and that Christ's faithful of both sexes flock to it more willingly because they see themselves abundantly refreshed there from the gift of celestial grace, assured of the mercy of Almighty God and the authority of BB. Peter and Paul his apostles — relaxes, in perpetuity, for all Christ's faithful who, truly penitent and confessed, devotedly visit the chapel on the feasts of the Annunciation, Assumption, Nativity, and Purification of B. Mary the Virgin, from first to second vespers on each of the feastdays, seven years and as many quarantines of enjoined penance for every feastday they do it, annually. The pope's will is, however, that if any other indulgence has been granted by him for those visiting the chapel or extending a helping hand to it, whether perpetual or for a certain time not yet elapsed, the present letters are void.

Universis Christifidelibus presentes litteras inspecturis . . . Licet is de cuius munere . . .
Ja Volateranus; F / F. L^{ta}. Sanctor(is)

414^1 28 March 1501   *Reg. Lat.* 1080, fos 240^r-241^r

To Edmund Cook, rector of one of two portions of the parish church, usually governed by two rectors, of Bradfelde, d. Norwich. Dispensation — at his supplication — to receive and retain for life, together with the above portion, one, and without it, any two other benefices, etc. [as above, no. 3].

Vite ac morum honestas . . .
[-]^2 / F / F L^{ta}. Sanctor(is)

[1] The engrossment survives: Sayers, pp. 40-41 (no. 114).

[2] no abbreviator's name

415   30 March 1501   *Reg. Lat.* 1080, fos 241[r]-242[r]

To William Burdelewer, perpetual chaplain, called *persona* or cantor, at the altar of Sts Andrew and Cuthbert, in the church of York. Dispensation — at his supplication — to him (who, as he asserts, holds a perpetual chaplaincy, called a chantry, in the above church) to receive and retain together for life any two benefices, with cure or otherwise mutually incompatible, etc. [as above, no. 3, to '. . . Notwithstanding etc. ']. With the proviso that the incompatible benefices in question shall not, on this account, be defrauded of due services and the cure of souls therein (if any) shall not be neglected.

Vite ac morum honestas . . .
S de Castello / F / F. L^{ta}. Sanctor(is)

416   6 March 1501   *Reg. Lat.* 1080, fos 266[r]-267[v]

To the bishop of Worcester, commission and mandate in favour of John Cosyn, brother of the hospital of the *Cruciferi Sancti Johannis cum stella*, of the new vill near Trixin,[1] OSA, d. Meath (who, as he asserts, is expressly professed of the above order)[2]. A petition[3] to the pope on John's part stated that at another time he, eager to visit the tombs of B. Peter and of B. Paul, had betaken himself, with his superior's licence, to Rome to visit them and, thence, to the kingdom of England where for a certain time, having laid aside the habit of his order and put on the usual dress worn by secular clerics, he had, in this secular dress, served several persons for a certain time; nevertheless afterwards, having had a change of heart and laid aside secular dress, he returned to the said hospital and afterwards had lived therein for a certain time in his regular habit; [but] — on account of seeing the dishonest life which the prior of the hospital was leading; and also because of several grave infirmities which he had sustained after his return to the hospital; and also because of the austerity of the rule of the said order which he was unable to endure; and also because the hospital, on account of the wars and other sinister events by which, alas, those parts had been grieviously afflicted and its utter devastation, [4] had been so reduced in its income that food and other necessities could not be supplied to him and the other brothers — he left the hospital with his said superior's licence, and again laid aside his habit and appeared in secular dress, serving in parish churches and performing the cure of souls of their parishioners, incurring apostasy and also sentence of excommunication in accordance with the regular institutes of the said order, and contracting irregularity because, bound by censures, he celebrated mass and other divine offices, for all of which he is deeply sorry. At the supplication on the part of John (who, as he asserts, notwithstanding a defect of birth as the son of a priest and an unmarried woman has been promoted to all, even sacred, orders and the priesthood, likewise with his said superior's licence), the pope hereby commissions and commands the above bishop to absolve John, if he so requests, from apostasy and the censures arising therefrom, in the customary form of the church, having enjoined a salutary penance on him; dispense him on account of irregularity contracted by him by occasion of the foregoing and to receive and retain any benefice, with or without cure, usually held by secular clerics, if with cure a parish church or its perpetual vicarage and if without cure a chantry, free chapel or annual service, usually assigned to secular clerics in title of a perpetual ecclesiastical benefice, even if of lay patronage and of whatsoever tax or annual value, if he obtains it otherwise canonically, to resign it, simply or for exchange, as often as he pleases, and in its place receive and retain another, similar or dissimilar, benefice, as above, notwithstanding the defect of birth, etc.; and rehabilitate him on account of all disability and infamy arising from the foregoing.

Sedes apostolica pia mater recurentibus ad eam cum humilitate . . .
S de castello | F | F. xxv. Sanctor(is)

¹ or *Tuxin*; for 'Trym' (or suchlike)?
² This information comes from a notwithstanding clause.
³ 'nuper' does not occur
⁴ the syntax is clumsy hereabouts

417   27 April 1501   *Reg. Lat.* 1082, fos 117ʳ-120ʳ

Provision anew, in *forma commissoria*, following litigation at the Roman curia, of Andreas Naso, cleric of Palermo, to one of two perpetual portions, called chaplaincies, of the parish church, usually ruled by two rectors, called chaplains, of St Laurence, Trapani (*Drepanij*), d. Maz(z)ara del Vallo (*Mazarien.*).

The 'bishop of Worcester' is one of the three mandataries. Entry otherwise of no interest to the Calendar

Vite ac morum honestas . . .
· *F· de parma | . B· | ¡ B· gratis pro deo. Quarto Id(us) octobr(is) anno decimo·* [12 October 1501], *Bolis·*

418   21 August 1501   *Reg. Lat.* 1082, fo 211ʳ⁻ᵛ

To Richard Panter, BTheol, rector of the parish church of Semley, d. Salisbury.

Dispensation — at his supplication — to receive and retain for life, together with the above parish church, one, and without it, any two othcr benefices, etc. [as above, no. 3].

Litterarum scientia, vite ac morum honestas . . .
F. de parma[1] */ Jo / Jo. L. Eps' Terracinen'*

[1] in a lighter ink: entered later?

419   21 August 1501   *Reg. Lat.* 1082, fo 212[r-v]

To Roger Godenow, rector of the parish church of Wissyngsette, d. Norwich. Dispensation — at his supplication — to receive and retain for life, together with the above parish church, one, and without it, any two other benefices, etc. [as above, no. 3].[1]

Vite ac morum honestas . . .
Jo ortega[2] */ Jo / Jo. L. Eps' Terracinen'*

[1] save that 'chantries' are not mentioned
[2] in a lighter ink: entered later?

420   21 August 1501   *Reg. Lat.* 1082, fos 215[v]-216[r]

To William Huntrodys, rector of the parish church of Tuduuorth', d. Salisbury. Dispensation — at his supplication — to receive and retain for life, together with the above parish church, one, and without it, any two other benefices, etc. [as above, no. 3].[1]

Vite ac morum honestas . . .
· L· puccius / · B· / . B. L. Bolis.

[1] save that in the present instance MS wants 'cura' and also 'ecclesia' in the last clause summarised

421   21 August 1501   *Reg. Lat.* 1082, fos 217[v]-218[v]

To William Chubbe, MA, rector of the parish church of the Holy Trinity, Exeter. Dispensation — at his supplication — to receive and retain for life, together with the above parish church, one, and without it, any two other benefices, etc. [as above, no. 3].

Litterarum scientia, vite ac morum honestas . . .
F. de parma / *. B·* / *. B. L. Bolis.*

422   21 August 1501   *Reg. Lat.* 1082, fos 221^r-222^v

Union etc. At a recent petition on the part of Roger Cherche, DDec, rector of the free chapel, Lashebarow, d. Worcester, the pope hereby unites etc. the parish church of Bisshopestor, d. Canterbury, (whose annual value and that of the chapel of Barh(a)m[1] [also spelt *Bachin*] annexed to it does not exceed 30 marks sterling, equivalent to 90 gold ducats of the camera or thereabouts) to the free chapel, which he holds together with the above parish church, for as long as he holds the free chapel, to the effect that Roger, in person or by proxy, may, on his own authority, continue in or take anew and retain corporal possession of the church and its annex and rights and appurtenances, for as long as he holds the free chapel, and convert its fruits etc. to his own uses and those of the church, chapel or free chapel without licence of the local diocesan or of anyone else. With indult to Roger not to be bound, while residing in the Roman curia or other benefices held by him at the time or attending a *studium generale*, to reside in the remaining benefices, nor to be liable to be compelled by anyone to do so against his will. Notwithstanding etc. With the proviso that the above church and other benefices in which he shall not reside shall not, on this account, be defrauded of due services and the cure of souls in the church and (if any) the other benefices shall not be neglected, but that their customary burdens shall be supported. The pope's will is, however, that on Roger's death or resignation etc. of the free chapel the union etc. shall be dissolved and so deemed and the church shall revert to its original state automatically.

Ad futuram rei memoriam. Romanum decet pontificem votis (?)illius[2] *prestare assensum* . . .
F. de parma / *. B·* / *· B· xxxxv Bolis·*

[1] MS: *Barhm'*
[2] *recte*: 'illis'

423   15 May 1501   *Reg. Lat.* 1082, fo 223^{r-v}

To the bishop of Lincoln and the dean and James Withston', canon, of the church of Lincoln, commission and mandate in favour of the noblewoman Margaret, countess of Richmond (*Richemondie*),[1] mother of Henry, king of England. A recent petition to the pope on her part stated that several statutes and ordinances formerly ordained and published for the benefit of the church of the Holy Trinity, Tateshall, d. Lincoln, of which she is patroness, are, on account of the changes of the times and the conditions, reforms or changes of the church itself and its personnel, inadequate and it is expedient for the tranquillity and benefit of the church and its personnel and also for the increase of divine worship therein to make and ordain new statutes. The pope therefore — at this supplication — hereby commissions and commands that the above three (or two or one of them), having summoned the chapter of the church and others concerned, shall themselves (or two or one of them) diligently examine and discuss the church's statutes and ordinances hitherto made, published or even approved, by ordinary as well as by apostolic authority, and correct, change, make new and (?)enlarge[2] them; and make, establish and ordain other similar, or even dissimilar, statutes and ordinances (not deviating from the sacred canons) which they regard as expedient for the church's tranquillity and benefit and the benefit of its personnel and for the increase and conservation of divine worship in it; concerning which the pope grants the above three faculty and authority by the presents. Notwithstanding etc.

Eximie devotionis affectus . . .
F de parma[3] / F / · F· xxx Sanctor(is)

[1] *comitissa Richemondie*; Derby not mentioned

[2] apparently *enormetis*

[3] in a lighter ink: entered later?

424   6 March 1501   *Reg. Lat.* 1082, fos 224^r-225^r

To Thomas Wodyngton, UID, rector of the parish church of St Helen, Worcester, dispensation. Some time ago, Innocent VIII by his letters dispensed him to receive and retain together for life any two benefices, with cure or otherwise mutually incompatible, etc. [as above, no. 131, to '. . . as is more fully contained in those letters'].[1] The pope — at his supplication — hereby dispenses Thomas, who is a priest and, as he asserts, holds by the said dispensation the above parish church of St Helen and that of St James the Apostle, Horwood Magna', [d.][2] Lincoln, which were canonically collated to him while successively vacant *certis modis*, to receive and retain together with the said parish churches now, or with any two other incompatible benefices held by him at the time by virtue of the said dispensation, any third benefice, etc. [as above, no. 131]. [3]

Litterarum scientia, vite ac morum honestas . . .
F de parma / F / F. Lxx Sanctor(is)

[1] lost; Index entry transcribed in *CPL*, XV at no. 996

[2] 'diocesis' wanting

[3] with the addition of: 'even of lay patronage' after 'principal in a collegiate church'

425   15 July 1501   *Reg. Lat.* 1082, fos 251^v-254^r

Confirmation etc. as below. A recent petition to the pope on the part of the abbot and convent of the monastery of Peterborough (*de Burgo Sancti Petri*),[1] OSB, d. Lincoln, stated that at another time Boniface, called the Ninth, in his obedience, from which those parts then were, indulged the abbot of the monastery then and for the time being and the convent, first by certain apostolic letters of his,[2] to farm out all the fruits etc., tithes and obventions of churches, chapels, portions, pensions and other possessions belonging to them and the monastery itself at the time to clerics or laymen, even before the fruits were separated or taken from the soil or the nine parts, and to give at farm or as an annual pension or lease and sell, without licence of the local ordinaries and of any others; and then, by other apostolic letters of his,[2] to use the mitre, ring, pastoral staff and other pontifical *insignia* anywhere; and in the said monastery, priories subject to that monastery and parish and other churches belonging to them, collectively or severally, albeit not subject to them by full authority, to give solemn benediction after the solemnities of mass, vespers and matins and in the *mensa* of the abbot himself — provided that no bishop or legate of the apostolic see be present; to consecrate the aforesaid [churches] and the churches and oratories of the monastery and priories and the chapels and altars in the same and also the vestments and other ornaments and apparel of the said monastery, priories, churches, oratories, chapels and altars and any not yet consecrated at the time; and to reconcile them and the cemeteries of the said churches any number of times that happen to be polluted or violated by bloodshed or adultery, without licence of the local diocesan or of anyone else, even in this regard; and Eugenius III approved and confirmed those things which had been granted concerning the right of the abbot and convent and of the sacristy of the monastery and which Eugenius himself had granted; and Thomas of good memory, archbishop of Canterbury, primate of all England and legate of the apostolic see, and several other archbishops, legates and nuncios of the said see, and also kings, queens, princes, dukes and other temporal lords granted and confirmed the many privileges, liberties, immunities, concessions, *gabelle*, pensions, revenues, tithes and other goods to the monastery and its abbot for the time being and the convent. And, latterly, also the late Thomas, archbishop of York, and John, bishop of Lincoln, united etc., in perpetuity, the parish churches of Northeolynghin, Brynghurste *alias* Eston' and Undyll' *alias* Oundyll', ds. York and Lincoln, with all their chapels, lands, tithes, oblations, produce, emoluments, rights and appurtenances — save portions fit for three perpetual vicars of the said parish churches — and several other pensions or annual revenues and rights payable annually to the archbishop of York and the bishop and their successors respectively, with the consent of those interested; and also former kings and princes of the kingdom of England, the first founders of the monastery, gave by their letters patent, to God and to the monastery in pure and perpetual alms all the dwellings located in that part of the vill or town of Stamford (*Stamfordie*) which is towards the said burgh and in that part the abbots of the monastery for the time being and the convent founded, built and erected one monastery dedicated to St John the Baptist with a chapel dedicated to St Thomas the Martyr and another monastery with a house of lepers to St Giles, called hospitals, and also a monastery of nuns dedicated to St Michael. And afterwards the late Richard I, then king of England, confirmed the concessions in question made by the said kings and princes by his royal letters patent for the honour of God and the Apostles Peter and Paul by his royal authority, specially and perpetually, as is said to be more fully contained in the letters patent and instruments of the said popes Boniface and Eugenius and the archbishops, bishops and kings respectively drawn up in this regard. At the abbot and convent's suppplication to the pope to add the force of apostolic confirmation to the privileges, concessions, donations, faculties, immunities, unions, annexations and incorporations as a firmer base for them, the pope hereby, with certain knowledge, approves and confirms the privileges etc. and everything concerning them contained in each of the instruments and letters aforesaid, save as regards those things which concern consecration; and decrees that they ought to be observed in perpetuity and inviolably, and supplies any defects. And, as a greater precaution, the pope hereby grants licence and faculty to and indulges the said abbot of the monastery of Peterborough, now and for the time being, to give benediction, as above, in the said monastery, and in the priories subject to it and also in those in which the monastery receives any portion or pension and which are known to pertain to the presentation of the abbot and convent, collectively or severally, and in the other churches pertaining to the said monastery and mediately or immediately subject to it, albeit not by full authority; and also to reconcile the churches of the monastery of Peterborough and priories aforesaid and the churches subject to portions and pensions pertaining to their presentation, and also the oratories, chapels and altars of the same polluted by bloodshed or adultery, the water having been blessed beforehand however by any catholic bishop, as the custom is; and also to bless the vestments and other ornaments and ecclesiastical apparel in them as often and as many times as opportune. Notwithstanding the constitution "Abbates" of Alexander IV, etc. The pope's will is, however, that this shall not be to the prejudice of this constitution which lays down that such reconciliations may only be done by bishops.

Ad perpetuam rei memoriam. Divina propitiatione disponente regimini universalis ecclesie meritis licet insufficientibus presidentes . . .
F. de parma | Jo | . Jo. CCC. Eps' Terracinen'

[1] later simply referred to as *Burgo*
[2] summarized in *CPL*, V, on pp. 511 and 548 respectively

426   24 April 1501   *Reg. Lat.* 1082, fos 283ʳ-284ʳ

To Thomas Brady, perpetual chaplain in the church of London, validation as below. Some time ago, the pope by other letters of his dispensed him to receive and retain for life, together with the perpetual chaplaincy in the church of London, which, as he asserted, he was then holding — if it could not be held with another incompatible benefice — one, and without it, any two other benefices, etc. [as above, no. 131, to '. . . as is more fully contained in those letters'].[1] However — since, as the pope has learned, in the foundation of the said chaplaincy, called the chantry of Roger Walden', it is expressly laid down that the chaplaincy cannot be held with another benefice, even a compatible one; and, as a recent petition to the pope on Thomas's part stated, because in the said letters no mention was made of this foundation, he fears that the letters could be branded surreptitious and he could be molested over this with the passage of time — the pope — at his supplication — hereby wills and grants to him that the letters and dispensation aforesaid with the clauses of exchange and other clauses therein shall be valid and have full force in and for all things from the date of the presents, just as if express mention had been made in them of the aforesaid foundation and it had been specially and expressly derogated. Notwithstanding etc.

Vite ac morum honestas ...
. *L. Puccius / Jo / Jo. xvj. Electus Terracinen'*

[1] *Cf.* below, no. 1167

427   26 June 1501   *Reg. Lat.* 1082, fos 296^V-297^V

To Thurstan Smyth, perpetual vicar of the parish church of Haburgh, d. Lincoln. Dispensation — at his supplication — to receive and retain for life, together with the perpetual vicarage of the above parish church, one, and without it, any two other benefices, etc. [as above, no. 3].

Vite ac morum honestas ...
. *L. puccius / Jo / Jo. L. Electus Terracinen'*

428   26 June 1501   *Reg. Lat.* 1082, fos 315^V-317^r

Union etc. At a recent petition on the part of Edmund Wylfordi, MTheol, canon of Lichfield, the pope hereby unites etc. the parish church of Byfeldi', d. Lincoln, (whose annual value does not exceed 84 gold ducats of the camera), to the canonry and prebend of (?)Voolni[1] in the church of Lichfield, which he holds together with the above parish church, for as long as he holds the canonry and prebend, to the effect that Edmund, in person or by proxy, may, on his own authority, take and retain corporal possession of the parish church and its rights and appurtenances, for as long as he holds the canonry and prebend, and convert its fruits etc. to his own uses and those of the canonry and prebend and the parish church without licence of the local diocesan or of anyone else. Notwithstanding etc. The pope's will is, however, that the parish church shall not, on account of this union etc., be defrauded of due services and the cure of souls therein shall not be neglected, but that its customary burdens shall be supported; and that on Edmund's death or resignation etc. of the canonry and prebend the union etc. shall be dissolved and so deemed and the parish church shall revert to its original condition automatically.

Ad futuram rei memoriam. Romanum decet pontificem votis illis gratum prestare assensum . . .
L puccius[2] */ . B. / . B. xxxv. Bolis.*

[1] penultimate letter (changed by overwriting?) doubtful
[2] in lighter ink: entered later?

429   8 July 1501   *Reg. Lat.* 1083, fos 8ᵛ-9ᵛ

To Richard, bishop of Durham, licence and faculty. A recent petition to the pope on bishop Richard's part stated that among certain places formerly founded and instituted for pious uses in his diocese of Durham, the late <Ranulph>[1], bishop of Durham, founded a hospital, called the hospital of Kepyer; that next, Ranulph's successor, the late Hugh, bishop of Durham, approved the said foundation or, by ordinary authority, founded the said hospital anew, for the support of one rector, called a master, and thirteen brothers professed of a certain religion or regular observance (not otherwise approved by law [having] only three essentials of religion), and made and published certain statutes and ordinances for the direction and conservation of the hospital; and that after this bishop Hugh founded and instituted a certain other hospital, called the hospital of Scherbone [also spelt *Sherbone*], for eight chaplains, who were to devote themselves to the divine offices therein and receive up to fifty-five lepers and attend to their needs; and also that the late Thomas, bishop of Durham, for certain reasons, reformed the statutes and ordinances in question by ordinary authority as well as by apostolic authority perchance granted to him in that regard and made and published new statutes and ordinances. Moreover, as the same petition added, they are not brothers or religious of the said religion in the hospital of Kepyer because those willing to be professed of the whole regular profession are not easily found; and on account of the slenderness, scarcity or dimunition of the goods, fruits and other emoluments of the hospital of Scherbone or for other reasons its statutes and ordinances are not observed and it is unlikely that they will be so in the future; and — for the conservation of the said hospitals and the works of piety to be performed in them — it is expedient to reform their statutes and ordinances or make and ordain others anew. At bishop Richard's supplication to the pope to grant him licence and faculty to reform, by apostolic authority, each and every one of the statutes and ordinances of the said hospitals made and published both by ordinary and by apostolic authority, or quash and revoke them in full or in part, the pope — who seeks to conserve hospitals and whatsoever pious places for the assistance of the Christian poor — hereby grants licence and faculty to him, acting in person or by proxy, to reform each and every one of the statutes and ordinances of the said hospitals made and published both by ordinary and by apostolic authority, or quash and revoke them in whole or in part; to make, ordain and publish, by apostolic authority, other new statutes and ordinances, honest and not deviating from the sacred canons, as seems to him expedient for the conservation of the said hospitals and the works of piety to be performed in them; to cause those which he makes and ordains to be observed; to otherwise moderate and limit these statutes; and to do and execute the other things which in the foregoing seem necessary to him. Notwithstanding etc.

Exigentibus meritis tue devotionis . . .
F de parma[2] / · *V·* / · *V· L· De Phano:*

[1] *Ranulphus* inserted in the margin by the enregistering scribe, initialled . *V.*
[2] in lighter ink: entered later?

430   9 July 1501   *Reg. Lat.* 1083, fos 31[r]-32[r]

To Robert Ayshecum, perpetual vicar of the parish church of Bannewelle, d. Bath and Wells. Dispensation and indult — at his supplication — to receive and retain for life, together with the perpetual vicarage of the above parish church, one, and without it, any two other benefices, etc. [as above, no. 3, to '. . . retain them together for life, as above']¹; and for life, while attending a *studium generale* or residing in the Roman curia or any one of his benefices, not to be bound to reside in his other benefices, (even defined as above and requiring personal residence, continuously or at certain times of the year, by privilege, foundation, statute, custom or otherwise), nor to be liable to be compelled by anyone to do so against his will. Notwithstanding etc. With the proviso that the above vicarage and other incompatible benefices in question shall not, on this account, be defrauded of due services and the cure of souls in the church² and (if any) the other incompatible benefices aforesaid shall not be neglected; but that the customary burdens of those benefices in which he shall not reside shall be supported.

Vite ac morum honestas . . .
N. de Castello / *Jo* / *Jo. Lx. Electus Terracinen'*

[1] with the addition of 'and of lay patronage and of whatsoever tax or annual value' after 'or a combination'
[2] *ecclesia; recte:* 'vicaria'

431   7 July 1501   *Reg. Lat.* 1083, fos 32[v]-33[r]

To James Bottiler, rector of the parish church of Kynwarton [also spelt *Kynwarton'*],

d. Worcester. Dispensation — at his supplication — to receive and retain for life, together with the above parish church, two, and without it, any three other benefices, etc. [as above. no. 17]. [1]

Vite ac morum[2] *honestas . . .*
N. de Castello[3] */ Jo / Jo. C. Electus Terracinen.* '

[1] with the addition of: 'even of lay patronage' after 'two of them be parish churches or their perpetual vicarages'
[2] *morum* written twice (erroneously) in MS
[3] in lighter ink: entered later?

432   7 July 1501   *Reg. Lat.* 1083, fos 38[v]-39[v]

To William Hancok,[1] rector of the parish church of St Clement, Worcester. Dispensation — at his supplication — to receive and retain for life, together with the above parish church, one, and without it, any two other benefices, etc. [as above, no. 3].

Vite ac morum honestas . . .
F. de parma / Jo / Jo. L. Electus Terracinen'

[1] blotched and partially corroded

433   18 May 1501   *Reg. Lat.* 1083, fos 52[v]-53[r]

To Hugh Walbrond, rector of the parish church of St Andrew the Apostle, Cromehale, d. Worcester. Dispensation — at his supplication — to receive and retain for life, together with the above parish church, one, and without it, any two other benefices, etc. [as above, no. 3].

Vite ac morum honestas . . .
F de parma / · V· / · V· · L· De Phano:

434   15 May 1501   *Reg. Lat.* 1083, fos 53[v]-55[r]

To Edward Willu'ghby, MA, dean of the church of Exeter, dispensation. Some time ago, first Sixtus IV by certain letters[1] dispensed him to receive and retain for life, together with the perpetual vicarage of the parish church of Milton Abbot, d. Exeter (which, as he asserted, he was <then>[2] holding), one other, and having resigned it, any two other benefices, etc. [as above, no. 131, to '. . . retain them together for life']; and then Innocent VIII by other letters[3] dispensed him to receive and retain for life, together with the above perpetual vicarage and another benefice, with cure or otherwise incompatible, which perchance he was holding by the said dispensation, or having resigned them, any two other benefices, with cure or otherwise incompatible, for which he had been dispensed, as above, any third benefice, etc. [as above, no. 131,[4] to '. . . in its place receive another, similar or dissimilar, incompatible benefice'] and retain it for life, as is more fully contained in each of the above letters respectively. The [present] pope, therefore — at his supplication — hereby further dispenses Edward (who, as he asserts, is of noble birth and holds by the aforesaid dispensations the deanery of the church of [Exeter],[5] which is a major dignity *post pontificalem* and is customarily elective, and the archdeaconry of Stafford (*Staffordie*) in the church of Lichfield, which is a non-major dignity *post pontificalem*, and the parish church of Jagford *alias* Jugforth', said diocese) to receive and retain for life, together with the deanery, [archdeaconry][6] and church held, or without them, any three other benefices, with cure or otherwise incompatible, for which he is dispensed, as above, any fourth benefice, etc. [as above, no. 277].[7]

Nobilitas generis, litterarum scientia, vite ac morum honestas . . .
Jo ortega / Jo. / Jo. C. Electus Terracinen'

[1] summarised in *CPL*, XIII, Part II on p. 779

[2] marginal insertion, initialled *Jo.*

[3] summarised in *CPL*, XV, at no. 218

[4] with appropriate changes of tense

[5] *Oxonien.*; *recte*: 'Exonien.'

[6] *archipresbyteratus*; *recte*: 'archidiaconatus'

[7] in the present instance, additionally, it is specified that the archdeaconry — as well as the dignity etc. — may be customarily elective and that it and the deanery also may have cure of souls

435   10 June 1501   *Reg. Lat.* 1083, fos 74ʳ-75ʳ

To the bishop of Aberdeen and *Decanum*[1] Guthre, canon of the church of Aberdeen, mandate in favour of William, lord of Graha(m)me,[2] nobleman, d. Dunblane. A recent petition to the pope on William's part stated that although he was under no legal obligation to Elizabeth Dru(m)mond,[3] woman, d. Dunblane, she — falsely asserting that he was lawfully bound, for reasons then expressed, to give and pay her a certain sum of money, then expressed — nevertheless sued William, not through apostolic delegation, before Henry Quhite, official of Dunblane, whom she said was a competent judge, praying that he be condemned and compelled to give and pay her the money; that the official, proceeding wrongly in the case, promulgated an unjust definitive sentence in Elizabeth's favour and against William, from which he appealed to the apostolic see; and that the official unlawfully refused to defer to his appeal (to which, by right, deference was due). At William's supplication to the pope to commit to some upright men in those parts the causes of the appeal; of everything perchance attempted and innovated after and against it; of the nullity of the sentence, of the official's whole process, and of everything else prejudicial to William done by him and Elizabeth and any others; and of the principal matter, the pope hereby commands that the above two (or one of them), having summoned Elizabeth and others concerned, and having heard both sides, taking cognizance even of the principal matter, shall decree what is just, without appeal, causing by ecclesiastical censure what they have decreed to be strictly observed; [and moreover compel] witnesses etc. Notwithstanding etc.

Humilibus et cetera.
F de parma / · V· / · V· / · xij· De Phano:

[1] *sic*; possibly for 'Duncano' (Duncan); or *recte* 'David'? (*cf. Registrum Episcopatus Aberdonensis,* I [Spalding Club, Edinburgh, 1845], pp. 337-8)

[2] MS: *Graha'me*

[3] MS: *Drum'ond*

436   12 June 1501   *Reg. Lat.* 1083, fos 77ᵛ-78ᵛ

To James Adam, LLB,[1] perpetual vicar of the parish church of Dunsford, d. Exeter. Dispensation and indult — at his supplication — to receive and retain for life, together with the perpetual vicarage of the above parish church, one, and without it, any two other benefices, etc. [as above, no. 3, to '. . . retain them together for life, as above']; and, for life, not to be bound, while attending a *studium generale* or residing in the Roman curia or any one of his benefices, with or without cure, [to reside][2] in his other benefices, etc. [as above, no. 238].

Litterarum scientia, vite ac morum honestas . . .
F. de parma / · V· / V· Lx De Phano:

[1] *bacallario in legibus*; *decretis* has been deleted, initialled . *V.* after *in*

[2] 'residere' wanting

437   12 June 1501   *Reg. Lat.* 1083, fos 78ᵛ-79ᵛ

To William Fareyway, rector of the parish church of Mydley, d. Canterbury.

Dispensation and indult — at his supplication — to receive and retain for life, together with the above parish church, one, and without it, any two other benefices, etc. [as above, no. 3, to '. . . retain them together for life, as above']; and, for life, not to be bound, while attending a *studium generale* or residing in the Roman curia or any one of his benefices, to reside in his other benefices etc. [as above, no. 238].

Vite ac morum honestas . . .
f. de parma / . V. / V. Lx De Phano:

438   12 June 1501   *Reg. Lat.* 1083, fo 92[r-v]

To John Trappe, canon of the monastery of the Holy Cross, Heryngg. m,[1] OSA, d. Chichester. Dispensation — at his supplication — to him, who, as he asserts, is expressly professed of the above order,[2] to receive and retain any benefice, with or without cure, usually held by secular clerics, etc. [as above, no. 32].

Religionis zelus, vite ac morum honestas . . .
N. de Castello / . V· / · V. xxx. De Phano:

[1] penultimate letter blotched; 'a'?
[2] This information comes from a notwithstanding clause.

439   4 March 1501[1]   *Reg. Lat.* 1083, fo 123[r-v]

To Richard Gaunte, MA, rector of the parish church of Esthenreth', d. Salisbury, indult. Some time ago, the pope by other letters of his dispensed him to receive and retain for life, together with the above parish church (which, as he asserted, he was then holding), one, and without it, any two other benefices, etc. [as above, no. 131, to '. . . if he obtained them otherwise canonically'], as is more fully contained in those letters.[2] The pope — at his supplication — hereby indulges him not to be bound, while residing in the Roman curia or any one of his benefices or attending a *studium generale*, to reside in the said church or in the other benefices held by him now and at the time, nor to be liable to be compelled by anyone to do so against his will. Notwithstanding etc. and [notwithstanding] the oath perchance taken by him to reside in the above church or benefices held by him. And the pope relaxes the said oath in this regard. With the proviso that the parish church and other benefices in which he shall not reside shall not, on this account, be defrauded of due services and the cure of souls in the church and (if any) the other benefices aforesaid shall not be neglected; but that their customary burdens shall be supported.

Litterarum scientia, vite ac morum honestas . . .

f de parma[3] / *Jo.* / *Jo. xx. Electus Terracinen'*

[1] dating clause in the hand of enregistering scribe; but writing differs slightly from that of rest of letter; entered later? (*cf.* note 2 below)

[2] *cf.* no. 1132 below

[3] *L. puccius*, deleted, above; *cf.* writing of dating clause (note 1 above)

440[1]   **20 April 1501**   *Reg. Lat.* 1083, fos 158[v]-159[r]

To John Johnson[2], rector of the parish church of Uffyngton' [also spelt *Uffyngton*], d. Lincoln. Dispensation — at his supplication — to receive and retain for life, together with the above parish church, one, and without it, any two other benefices, etc. [as above, no. 3].

Vite ac morum honestas . . .
F. de parma / *Jo.* / *Jo. L. Electus Terracinen'*

[1] The engrossment survives: Sayers, p.41 (no. 115).

[2] *Johannes Johnson* occurs in the index to the gathering on fo. 153[r].

441   **9 February 1501**   *Reg. Lat.* 1083, fos 177[r]-178[v]

Licence, in *forma commissoria*, to Silvester, bishop of Worcester, facilitating the rebuilding, partly at his own expense, of the priory of S. Michele in Foro (*in foro civitatis*), Lucca, OSA, which he holds *in commendam* by apostolic concession and dispensation. Entry otherwise of no interest to the Calendar.

Ex iniuncto nobis desuper apostolice servitutis officio . . .
. L· pucius / *V·* / *V· L· De Phano*

442   **16 February 1501**   *Reg. Lat.* 1083, fos 205[v]-207[r]

To the bishops of Hereford and St David's, and the abbot of the monastery of St Peter, Gloucester (*Gloucestrie*), d. Worcester, mandate in favour of Henry, bishop of Salisbury, and the convent of the monastery, usually governed by a prior, of B. Mary near Gloucester (*iuxta Gloucestriam*), OSA, d. Worcester, the priorship of which Henry holds *in commendam* by apostolic concession and dispensation. A recent petition to the pope on the part of bishop Henry and the convent stated that the parish churches of Volcke [also spelt *Wolcke*] and Colpe, together with the places or granges of Volcke and Colpe, d. Meath, and all their other rights and appurtenances, are united etc., in perpetuity, to the monastery of B. Mary, and the priors (or commendatory priors) and vicars of the parish churches for the time being and convent are not bound (and cannot be compelled) to pay any annual payment, portion, pension, or spiritual exaction to the bishop of Meath for the time being by reason of the said churches, etc., and to date have never been accustomed to pay anything; that because John, bishop of Meath — falsely asserting that the monastery, or Henry and the convent, were lawfully bound to give and pay to the bishop of Meath a certain annual payment, etc. and other rights then expressed by reason of the churches, etc. — was nevertheless unlawfully disturbing Henry and the convent and the vicars and others appointed by them in the churches, etc., causing them serious trouble and damage, Henry and the convent sued him over this and other matters before Octavian, archbishop of Armagh, the local metropolitan, and primate of Ireland; that the archbishop and primate, proceeding duly in the case, promulgated a definitive sentence (which as no lawful appeal was made became a final judgement), in favour of Henry and the convent and against bishop John, by which he declared that the churches were free and exempt from the exaction etc., and nothing was due to the bishop of Meath by reason of the churches etc., imposing perpetual silence on bishop John; and that, notwithstanding the sentence (which has become a final judgement), bishop John is endeavouring, unlawfully and unjustly, to extort the annual payment, portion, and other rights from Henry etc., to molest and disturb them and the churches etc. in various ways, and to cause them serious trouble, whence Henry and the convent have appealed, respectively, to the apostolic see. At their supplication to the pope to commit to some upright men in those parts the cases of the appeals; of everything attempted and innovated after and against the appeals; of the molestation, disturbances, and harassment, and of the nullity of everything else prejudicial to Henry and the convent done by bishop John in connection with the foregoing; and of the principal matter; also, <the cases>[1] which Henry and the convent intend to move, jointly or severally, against bishop John and clerics and laymen of the city and diocese of Meath adhering to him in this, over the molestation, disturbances, hindrance, damage, injuries, rights, jurisdiction, property, places, granges, and other matters; and to cause the sentence to be properly executed, the pope hereby commands that the above three (or two or one of them), having summoned bishop John, the clerics and laymen, and others concerned, and having heard both sides, taking cognizance even of the principal matter, shall decree what is just, without appeal, causing by ecclesiastical censure what they have decreed to be strictly observed; and, if it is established that the sentence has become a final judgement they shall cause it to be strictly observed as if it was duly published. Notwithstanding etc.

Humilibus et cetera.
F de parma / Jo: / Jo. xij. Electus Terracinen'

[1] *ac quas* inserted in the margin by the enregistering scribe initialled *Jo.*

**443	27 February 1501**						*Reg. Lat.* 1083, fo 319^{r-v}

To William Craufurde, canon of the monastery of Holyrood (*Sancte Crucis*) near Edemburgh [also spelt *Edeynburgh*[1]], OSA, d. St Andrews, who has expressly professed the said order and, as he asserts, holds the perpetual vicarage of the parish church of Faukerk, d. St Andrews, which is customarily governed by canons of the said monastery of which he is one, faculty — at his supplication — to bequeath and make disposition of any movable and immovable goods acquired by him, otherwise lawfully, from the fruits etc. of the said vicarage and other benefices which he holds now or in the future — movable goods assigned to the ministry of the altar or altars of the said benefices or to divine worship or use for a special altar of the same excepted — and also of the fruits etc. of the benefices held by him now and at the time which are collected in the year of his death, as the secular clerics of the kingdom of Scotland are accustomed to make disposition, up to the sum of 300 gold ducats of the camera, for the decent and honest expenses of his funeral and for the remuneration of those who have served him during his lifetime, whether blood relations or others, in accordance with the deserts of their service; and — after deductions have been made from the said goods for debts and (as appropriate) for the houses and buildings in the places of the said benefices which stand in need of repair as a result of the fault or negligence aforesaid[2] — otherwise to convert them to pious and other[3] lawful uses. Notwithstanding etc. The pope's will is, however, that in the disposition of the said goods he is liberal towards the said benefices in accordance with the amount of the residue, as his conscience dictates and he sees fit for the health of his soul.

Quia presentis vite conditio . . .
A de sancto Severino / F / F xvj· Sanctor(is)

[1] the 'e' deleted?

[2] as a result . . . aforesaid] *sic*; as originally enregistered the condition read: prius tamen de omnibus predictis bonis ere alieno et hiis [for (?)'iis'] que pro reparandis domibus et edifficiis consistentibus in locis dictorum beneficiorum *culpa vel negligentia tua seu tuorum procuratorum destructis vel deterioratis nec non restaurandis iuribus eorundem beneficiorum depredictis* [for 'depredatis'] ex culpa vel negligentia supradictis fuerint oportuna deductis; but the passage here *italicised* was then deleted. (The deletion is initialled *F* in seven places.) The mistake — whatever its nature — was apparently triggered by the repetition of the phrase 'culpa vel negligentia'

[3] marginal insertion by the enregistering scribe; not initialled

**444	15 March 1501**						*Reg. Lat.* 1084, fos 39^r-40^v

To Andrew Bessat, priest, d. Aberdeen, reservation, constitution and assignment of a pension, as below. A recent petition to the pope on Andrew's part stated that he at another time, spontaneously and freely, resigned the perpetual vicarage of the parish church of Eurowry,[1] d. Aberdeen, which he was then holding, into the hands of the then bishop of Aberdeen, or his vicar general, outside the Roman curia, and the bishop, or his vicar having, as he said, special power from the bishop by his letters, by virtue of it, having admitted the resignation outside the said curia by ordinary authority, by that authority collated and made provision of the vicarage, vacant by the resignation, to Gilbert Cranston,[2] perpetual vicar of this church; and he, by virtue of this collation and provision, acquired possession of the vicarage. Lest Andrew should suffer excessive loss from this resignation, the pope hereby reserves, constitutes and assigns an annual pension of 10 marks Scots (which, as he asserts, do not exceed 2 pounds sterling) on the fruits etc. of the vicarage (of which, as he also asserts, this pension does not exceed a third part) payable in full to Andrew for life (or to Andrew's specially mandated proctor), by Gilbert, to which express assent has been given by William Turnbul, cleric, d. Glasgow, (Gilbert's specially appointed proctor), and his successors holding the said vicarage at the time, each year, one half on the Nativity of B. John the Baptist and the other on that of Jesus Christ. With decree etc. that if Gilbert, or any one of his successors, fails to make payment on the said feasts, or within the thirty days immediately following, he shall, after this time has elapsed, incur sentence of excommunication from which he shall be denied absolution, except on the point of death, until he shall have made satisfaction in full or reached agreement in respect of it with Andrew (or his proctor) and, if he remains obdurate under that sentence for a further six months, he shall thereupon be deprived in perpetuity of the said perpetual vicarage, which shall be deemed vacant automatically. Notwithstanding etc.

Executory to the archdeacon of the church of Ross and Duncan Scherat, canon of the church of Aberdeen, and the offical of Aberdeen, or two or one of them, acting in person or by proxy.

Vite ac morum honestas . . . The executory begins: *Hodie dilecto filio Andree Bessat* . . . *f de parma; A de sanctoseverino | · B· | . B· xij. · x· Bolis.*

[1] the 'E' written over .*V*.; spelt *Curowry* in the executory

[2] or *Crenston*

445   5 May 1501   *Reg. Lat.* 1084, fo 41[r-v]

To Ralph Heylysdon', professor OFM and of theology. Dispensation and indult — at his supplication — to receive and retain any benefice, with or without cure, usually held by secular clerics, etc. [as above, no. 32, to '. . . similar or dissimilar, benefice'], usually assigned to secular clerics; and also — after he has acquired the said benefice — to have an active and a passive voice in the general and provincial chapters as well as in those of the houses OFM and in the congregations and acts; to be elected etc. to any prelacies and offices of the said order; to perform and exercise them for life or for the time for which they should be consigned to him; and to use and enjoy all the privileges, indults, immunities and exemptions of the order and granted by any authority to professors thereof, as if he had not acquired the benefice. Notwithstanding etc. and [notwithstanding] the constitutions of Otto and Ottobuono formerly legates of the apostolic see in the kingdom of England etc.[1]

Religionis zelus, litterarum scientia, vite ac morum honestas . . .
L. puccius / . B· / · B· xxxx Bolis·

[1] The inclusion of these constitutions gives Heylysdon' the option of holding his secular benefice in England.

446   6 August 1502   *Reg. Lat.* 1084, fos 112^v-113^r

To Christopher Hylle, professor OFM. Dispensation — at his supplication — to receive and retain any benefice, with or without cure, usually held by secular clerics, even if a parish [church] or its perpetual vicarage, etc. [as above, no. 32, to '. . . similar or dissimilar, benefice'], usually assigned to secular clerics. Notwithstanding etc. and [notwithstanding] the constitutions of Otto and Ottobuono formerly legates of the apostolic see in the kingdom of England etc.[1]

Religionis zelus, vite ac morum honestas . . .
L puccius / · B· / · B· xxxx Bolis·

[1] The inclusion of these constitutions gives Hille the option of holding his secular benefice in England.

447   5 December 1500   *Reg. Lat.* 1084, fo 240^{r-v}

To Thomas Garforth, monk of the monastery of B. Mary, Kirkested[1] [also spelt *Kyrkested*], OCist, d. Lincoln, (who, as he asserts, is expressly professed of the said order),[2] indult. Some time ago, Sixtus IV by his letters dispensed him to receive and retain any benefice usually held by secular clerics, if conferred on him otherwise canonically, as is more fully contained in those letters.[3] Wishing to enable Thomas to live among secular clerics more honestly and without scandal to the people, the pope — at his supplication — hereby indulges him for life to wear his religious habit under an honest priestly vestment and to (?)proceed[4] in other respects in the manner of secular priests; notwithstanding etc.

Religionis zelus, vite ac morum honestas . . .
. F. de parma / Jo / Jo. xx. Electus Terracinen'.

[1] or *Ro-*
[2] This information comes from a notwithstanding clause.
[3] summarised in *CPL*, XIII, Part II, on p. 814
[4] reading 'incedere'

448   20 July 1501   *Reg. Lat.* 1085, fo 298^{r-v}

To William Omurgissa, Nellanus Oquervalan and Maurice Oquervalan, canons of the church of Derry, mandate in favour of Henry Ogarmilegayd, cleric, d. Derry. The pope has learned that the perpetual vicarage of the parish church of Cyllcayrayld, d. Derry, is vacant *certo modo* at present and has been vacant for so long that by the Lateran statutes its collation has lawfully devolved on the apostolic see, although John Omogan, who bears himself as a priest of the said diocese, has detained it, without any title or support of law, temerariously and *de facto*, for a certain time, as he still does. He hereby commands that the above three (or two or one of them), if, having summoned John and others concerned, they find the vicarage, whose annual value does not exceed 4 marks sterling, to be vacant (howsoever etc.), shall collate and assign it, (even if specially reserved etc.), with all rights and appurtenances, to Henry, inducting him etc. having removed John and any other unlawful detainer and causing Henry (or his proctor) to be admitted to the vicarage and its fruits etc., rights and obventions to be delivered to him. [Curbing] gainsayers etc. Notwithstanding etc.

Vite ac morum honestas . . .
S de Castello / · B· / · B· x Quinto Id' aug^{ti} anno nono [9 August 1501], · *Bolis*

449   23 August 1501   *Reg. Lat.* 1085, fos 311^r-312^r

To the bishop of Kilmacduagh, the chancellor of the church of Kilmacduagh and Maurice Ohoney,[1] canon of the church of Ardfert, mandate in favour of Matthew Ubryen, canon of Kilfenora, (who, some time ago, as he asserts, notwithstanding a defect of birth as the son of an unmarried man of noble birth and an unmarried woman, was dispensed first by ordinary authority to be marked with clerical character and then by apostolic authority to be promoted to all, even sacred, orders and the priesthood, and to receive and retain a benefice, even if it should have cure of souls, if conferred on him otherwise canonically; and afterwards was duly marked with clerical character and acquired the said canonry and prebend , which were canonically collated to him while vacant *certo modo*). The pope has learned that the perpetual vicarages of the parish churches of Killnafearbay [also spelt *Killnafernbay*] and Killarda[2] and a certain perpetual <simple>[3] benefice, called a rectory of an ecclesiastical fief, in the said church of Killnafearbay, and also a certain portion called Moynneor of the church of Ynyskay [also spelt *Inyschay*] in which several clerics are known to be forming a college and holding certain portions therein, d. Killaloe, have been vacant *certo modo* and are vacant at present, although the layman Dermot Obrien is taking and usurping the fruits of the vicarage of Killnafearbay and Gillasius[4] Oknyllay, who bears himself as a priest, and Donat Ogriffa [also spelt *Ogryffa*], as a cleric, have detained the vicarage of Killarda, each taking its fruits as he can, and Donat Offlamyagayn [also spelt *Offlannagayn*], as a cleric, has detained the benefice and Thady Macahayn [also spelt *Mackahayn*], who bears himself as a priest, d. Killaloe, the aforesaid portion, without any title or support of law, temerariously and *de facto*, as they still detain them. At a recent petition on Matthew's part to the pope to unite etc. the vicarages, benefice and portion to the canonry and prebend of the church of Kilfenora, which he holds, for as long as he does so, the pope, not having certain knowledge of the foregoing, hereby commands that the above three (or two or one of them), if, having summoned Dermot, Gillasius, Donat Ogriffa, Donat Offlamyagayn, Thady and others concerned, they find the vicarages and <the benefice> and the portion <which is with cure>, [5] the annual value of all of which together does not exceed 18 marks sterling, to be vacant (howsoever etc.) and, having summoned those interested in the union etc., it to be thus, unite etc. the vicarages, benefice and portion (even if vacant for so long that by the Lateran statutes their collation has lawfully devolved on the apostolic see, etc.), with all rights and appurtenances, to the canonry and prebend, for as long as Matthew holds the canonry and prebend; to the effect that Matthew may, on his own authority, in person or by proxy, take and retain corporal possession of the vicarages, benefice and portion and rights and appurtenances aforesaid, for as long as he holds the canonry and prebend, and convert their fruits etc. to his own uses and those of the vicarages, benefice and portion and the canonry and prebend without licence of the local diocesan or of anyone else. Notwithstanding etc. The pope's will is, however, that the vicarages, benefice and portion shall not, on account of this union etc., be defrauded of due services and the cure of souls in the vicarages[6] shall not be neglected; but that their customary burdens and those of the benefice and portion shall be supported; and that on Matthew's death or resignation etc. of the canonry and prebend the union etc. shall be dissolved and so deemed and the vicarages, portion and benefice shall revert to their original condition and be deemed vacant automatically.

*Ex iniuncto nobis desuper apostolice servitutis officio ad ea libenter intendimus . . .
A de Sanctoseverino / · B· / . B. xxv. Octavo Kl' octobr' anno decimo* [24 September 1501], *Bolis.*

[1] or (?)*Ohoneyo* or (?)*Ohoneyy*: ends in a blotched or deleted letter

[2] the final 'a' written over a 'y'

[3] *simplex* inserted in the margin in the hand of the enregistering scribe; *Correctum de Mandato R(everendissimi) p(atris) D(omini) Jo(hannis) ragusini regentis . B. Bolis.*

[4] also spelt *Gelasius, Gellasius*

[5] It looks as if the description 'with cure' was initially applied to the benefice and then corrected to apply to the portion. A deletion in the line: (?)*quod* (?)*curatum* (?)*existit* (?)*beneficium*, initialled . *B.* twice (the number of deleted words also being conjectural) immediately before *et portionem*, is accompanied by the marginal correction: *beneficium et que curata existit* in a different hand, initialled *.B.; Cassatum et correctum de mandato ut supra . B. Bolis* However, cf. note 6.

[6] i. e. the cure of only the vicarages is explicitly safeguarded here.

450   26 June 1501   *Reg. Lat.* 1086, fos 3ᵛ-4ᵛ

To John Denh(a)m,[1] BTheol, rector of the parish church of Kylworth Rabbas *alias*
North Kilworth [also spelt *Kilworth Rabbas alias North Kilworth*], d. Lincoln.
Dispensation —at his supplication— to receive and retain for life, together with the
above parish church, one, and without it, any two other benefices, etc. [as above, no. 3].

Litterarum scientia, vite ac morum honestas . . .
. L. Puccius / Jo / Jo. L. Electus Terracinen'

[1] MS: *Denhm'*

451   26 June 1501   *Reg. Lat.* 1086, fo 5ʳ⁻ᵛ

To John Morwyn, canon of the monastery of the Holy Trinity, Kirkh(a)m [also spelt
Kirkl(a)m],[1] OSA, d. York. Dispensation —at his supplication— to him, who, as he
asserts, is expressly professed of the above order,[2] to receive and retain any benefice,
with or without cure, usually held by secular clerics, etc. [as above, no. 32].[3]

Religionis zelus, vite ac morum honestas . . .
. L. puccius / Jo. / Jo. xxx. Electus Terracinen'

[1] MS: *Kirkhm'* also *Kirklm'*

[2] This information comes from a notwithstanding clause.

[3] save that in the present instance 'and of lay patronage and of whatsoever tax or annual value' does not
occur

452   14 July 1501   *Reg. Lat.* 1086, fos 11ᵛ-13ʳ

Union etc. At a recent petition on the part of Alexander Inell *alias* Gylis, BDec,
rector of the parish church of Culmyngtowe [also spelt *Culmyntowe, Culmyngtwe*]
alias Culmyngton', d. Bath and Wells, the pope hereby unites etc. the parish church
of St Tydfil the Virgin (*Sancte Tudeville Virginis*)[1], Merther Tudefeld, d. Llandaff,
(whose annual value does not exceed 14 1/4 gold ducats of the camera) to the above
parish church of Culmyngtowe, which he holds together by apostolic dispensation,
for as long as he holds that of Culmyngtowe, to the effect that Alexander, in person
or by proxy, may, on his own authority, (?)retain[2] or take anew corporal possession
of the church of St Tydfil and its rights and appurtenances, for as long as he holds
the church of Culmyngtowe, and convert its fruits etc. to his own uses and those of
the said churches without licence of the local diocesan or of anyone else.
Notwithstanding etc. The pope's will is, however, that the church of St Tydfil shall
not, on account of this union etc., be defrauded of due services and the cure of souls
therein shall not be neglected, but that its customary burdens shall be supported; and

that on Alexander's death or resignation etc. of the church of Culmyngtowe the union etc. shall be dissolved and so deemed and the church of St Tydfil shall revert to its original condition automatically.

Ad futuram rei memoriam. Romanum decet pontificem votis illis gratum prestare assensum . . .
N. de Castello[3] / *Jo* / *Jo. xxxv. Electus Terracinen'*

[1] Yet St Tydfil is described as a Martyr and a wife in *The Book of Saints*, (compiled by the Benedictines of Ramsgate, London, 1921).

[2] MS: *libere /(?)tinere*; for 'libere re / tinere'

[3] in lighter ink: written later?

453   14 July 1501   *Reg. Lat.* 1086, fos 13[v]-14[r]

To Elias Bartrame, brother of the hospital of St John the Baptist, Briggewatir, OSA, d. Bath and Wells. Dispensation —at his supplication— to him, who, as he asserts, is expressly professed of the above order,[1] to receive and retain any benefice, with or without cure, usually held by secular clerics, etc. [as above, no. 32,[2] to '. . . similar or dissimilar, benefice'], usually assigned to secular clerics. Notwithstanding etc.

Religionis zelus, vite ac morum honestas . . .
· *L· puccius* / *Jo* / *Jo. xxx. Electus Terracinen'*

[1] This information comes from a notwithstanding clause.

[2] save that in the present instance MS wants 'taxe'

454   10 November 1500[1]   *Reg. Lat.* 1086, fo 37[r-v]

To Severus Maris, professor OP. Dispensation —at his supplication— to receive and retain any benefice, with or without cure, usually held by secular clerics, etc. [as above, no. 32, to '. . . similar or dissimilar, benefice'], usually assigned to secular clerics. Notwithstanding etc. and [notwithstanding] the constitutions of Otto and Ottobuono, formerly legates of the apostolic see in the kingdom of England etc.[2]

Religionis zelus, vite ac morum honestas . . .
L. puccius[3]/ *Jo.* / *Jo. xxxx. de Galves*

[1] *quingentesimo . . . nono*] written in darker ink: entered later?

[2] The inclusion of these constitutions gives Maris the option of holding his secular benefice in England.

[3] heavily inked; *cf.* note 1

455   11 September 1500   *Reg. Lat.* 1086, fos 45ᵛ-46ᵛ

To Laurence Potter, rector of the parish church of Manesyn Rydware [also spelt *Menesyn Ridware*], d. Coventry and Lichfield. Dispensation —at his supplication— to receive and retain for life, together with the above parish church, one, and without it, any two other benefices, etc. [as above, no. 3].

Vite ac morum honestas . . .
. L· puccius / · V· / · V· L· De Phano:

456   12 September 1500   *Reg. Lat.* 1086, fos 47ʳ-48ʳ

To the bishop of Coventry and Lichfield, the abbot of the monastery of Bukkelonde, d. Exeter, and the dean of the church of Exeter, mandate in favour of John Hikkys [also spelt *Hykkys, Hirkkys*], MA, cleric, d. Exeter. A recent petition to the pope on John's part stated that, formerly — since the presentation of a suitable person for the parish church of Exmstre,[1] d. Exeter, at a time of vacancy, pertains, by ancient, approved, and hitherto peacefully observed custom, to the prior for the time being and convent of the priory of Bs. Peter and Paul the Apostles, Phympton', OSA, d. Exeter — he was repeatedly presented for the church, then vacant *certo modo*, by the present prior and convent, within the proper time, firstly to John Nance, the then vicar of the bishop of Exeter (who was then absent from his city and diocese) and thereafter, when he had returned, to the bishop, and he duly requested that he be instituted rector; that after the bishop and vicar had, without reasonable cause, refused to institute him, or unduly delayed, and John had had recourse to the local metropolitical court of Canterbury, and Humphrey Hauuardyn, the court official, had, by certain letters of his, of a certain tenor, duly ordered the bishop or vicar to administer [justice][2] to him in the case of his institution, the official temerariously assigned an excessively long term to the bishop or vicar for inquiring into the prior and convent's right of presentation, whence John appealed to the apostolic see. At John's supplication to the pope to commit to some upright men in those parts the cases of his appeal; of everything attempted and innovated after and against the appeal; of the nullity of the assignment of the term, processes of the bishop and vicar, process of the official after the assignment, and of everything else prejudicial to John done by the bishop, vicar, and official, and any other judges and persons, in connection with the foregoing; and of the principal matter, the pope hereby commands that the above three (or two or one of them), having summoned the bishop, vicar, and others concerned, and having heard both sides, taking cognizance even of the principal matter, shall decree what is just, without appeal, causing [by ecclesiastical censure][3] what they have decreed [to be strictly observed; and moreover compel] witnesses etc. . Notwithstanding etc.

Humilibus et cetera.

· *L· puccius* / . *V·* / . *V. xij. De Phano:*

[1] *sic*

[2] MS: *instantiam; recte* 'justitiam'?

[3] or ['by the pope's authority in the bishop's case, by ecclesiastical censure in the case of others']: enregistration abridged by *et cetera*

457   24 October 1500   *Reg. Lat.* 1086, fos 61[r]-62[v]

To Robert Wylloghby, cleric, d. Norwich. Dispensation and indult —at his supplication— to him, who, as he asserts, is a BA, to receive and retain together for life any three benefices, etc. [as above, no. 17, to '. . . retain them together for life, as above']¹; and also for life, while residing in the Roman curia or any one of his benefices or attending a *studium generale,* not to be bound to reside personally in his other benefices, nor to be liable to be compelled by anyone to do so against his will. Notwithstanding etc. With the proviso that the incompatible benefices in question shall not, on this account, be defrauded of due services and the cure of souls therein shall not be neglected.

Vite ac morum honestas . . .
· *L. puccius* / *Jo.* / *Jo. Cx. de Galves*

[1] as to content; though the order of words is not identical

458   24 October 1500   *Reg. Lat.* 1086, fos 63[r]-64[r]

To William Dalton, scholar, d. York. Dispensation —at his supplication— to him, who, as he asserts, is below his eighteenth year of age and wishes to become a cleric, to receive and retain, after he has been duly marked with clerical character and reached his eighteenth year, any benefice, with cure or otherwise incompatible, or requiring sacred, even priest's, orders, by statute or foundation, even if a parish church etc. [as above, no. 240, to '. . . receive and retain another benefice'], incompatible or requiring sacred, even priest's, orders, by statute or foundation; notwithstanding the above defect of age etc. With the proviso that the benefice in question shall not, on this account, be defrauded of due services and the cure of souls therein (if any) shall not be neglected.

Vite ac morum honestas . . .
. *L. puccius* / *Jo.* / *Jo. xx. de Galves*

459 6 March 1501   *Reg. Lat.* 1086, fos 71^r-72^r

To William Smyth', rector of the parish church of St Peter, North Walton', d. Winchester. Dispensation —at his supplication— to receive and retain for life, together with the above parish church, one, and without it, any two other benefices, etc. [as above, no. 3].

Vite ac morum honestas . . .
. *L. Puccius* / · *V·* / *V.* · *L· De Phano:*

460 6 March 1501   *Reg. Lat.* 1086, fos 72^r-73^r

To William Bowen, MA, rector of the parish church of Ranuernach' super Cave [also spelt *Rannernch' super Cave,*], d. St David's. Dispensation — at his supplication— to receive and retain for life, together with the above parish church, one, and without it, any two other benefices, etc. [as above, no. 3].

Litterarum scientia, vite ac morum honestas . . .
. *F. de Parma* / · *V·* / *V· L· De Phano*

461 21 March 1501   *Reg. Lat.* 1086, fos 73^r-74^v

To Richard Mader, perpetual vicar of the parish church of Pitimuster, d. Bath and Wells. Dispensation and indult —at his supplication— to receive and retain for life, together with the perpetual vicarage of the above parish church, one, and without it, any two other benefices, etc. [as above, no. 3, to '. . . retain them together for life, as above']; and for life, while attending a *studium generale* or residing in the Roman curia or any one of his benefices, not to be bound to reside in his other benefices, etc. [as above, no. 238].

Vite ac morum honestas . . .
· *L· puccius* / *Jo.* / . *Jo. Lx. Electus Terracinen'*

462 27 March 1501   *Reg. Lat.* 1086, fos 74^v-75^v

To John Hunte, rector of the parish church of All Saints, Batlesden', d. Lincoln. Dispensation —at his supplication— to receive and retain for life, together with the above parish church, one, and without it, any two other benefices, etc. [as above, no. 3].

Vite ac morum honestas . . .
. *L. puccius* / . *V·* / . *V· L· De Phano:*

463   28 March 1501   *Reg. Lat.* 1086, fo 76^{r-v}

To Thomas Whynby, rector of the parish church of Karsyngton', d. Coventry and Lichfield. Dispensation —at his supplication— to receive and retain for life, together with the above parish church, one, and without it, any two other benefices, etc. [as above, no. 3].

Vite ac morum honestas . . .
. *L. Puccius* / . *V·* / · *V· L· De Phano:*

464   28 March 1501   *Reg. Lat.* 1086, fo 78^{r-v}

To Nicholas Ursewik, rector of the parish church of St Nicholas Acon, near Lombard strete,[1] London' [also spelt *Londonen'*], d. London. Dispensation —at his supplication— to receive and retain for life, together with the above parish church, one, and without it, any two other benefices, etc. [as above, no. 3].

Vite ac morum honestas . . .
. *L. puccius* / · *V·* / . *V· L· De Phano*

[1] thus in MS

465   28 March 1501   *Reg. Lat.* 1086, fo 79^{r-v}

To Nicholas Mullet, canon of the priory of St Peter, Ipswich (*de Gipwico*), OSA, d. Norwich. Dispensation — at his supplication — to him, who, as he asserts, is expressly professed of the above order,[1] to receive and retain any benefice, with or without cure, usually held by secular clerics, etc. [as above, no. 32, to '. . . similar or dissimilar, benefice'], usually assigned to secular clerics. Notwithstanding etc.

Religionis zelus, vite ac morum honestas . . .
. *L. puccius* / · *V·* / . *V. xxx De Phano:*

[1] This information comes from a notwithstanding clause.

466   29 August 1500[1]   *Reg. Lat.* 1086, fos 87^r-88^r

To John Lere, rector of the parish church of St James, Claufeldi[2] [also spelt *Claudefeldi*], d. Winchester. Dispensation —at his supplication— to receive and retain for life, together with the above parish church, one, and without them, any two other benefices, etc. [as above, no. 3].

Vite ac morum honestas . . .
. L. puccius[3] */ · V· / · V· L· De Phano:*

[1] *quarto . . . nono*] written in a different ink, not in the hand of the enregistering scribe: entered later?
[2] changed (by deletion of the 'de') from *Claudefeldi*; initialled . *V.*
[3] not in the hand of the enregistering scribe: entered later? *Cf.* note 1.

467   29 August 1500[1]   *Reg. Lat.* 1086, fos 88^v-89^v

To Henry Hunt, rector of the parish church of All Saints, Nettyswell, d. London. Dispensation —at his supplication— to receive and retain for life, together with the above parish church, one, and without it, any two other benefices, etc. [as above, no. 3].

Vite ac morum honestas . . .
. L. puccius.[2] */ . V· / · V· · L· De Phano:*

[1] *quarto . . . nono*] written in a different ink, not in the hand of the enregistering scribe: entered later?
[2] not in the hand of the enregistering scribe: entered later? *Cf.* note 1.

468   29 August 1500   *Reg. Lat.* 1086, fos 92^v-93^r

To John Clyderowe, monk of the monastery of B. Mary, Crokysden', OCist, d. Coventry and Lichfield. Dispensation —at his supplication— to him, who, as he asserts, is expressly professed of the above order[1] to receive and retain any benefice, with or without cure, usually held by secular clerics, etc. [as above, no. 32, to '. . . similar or dissimilar, benefice'], usually assigned to secular clerics. Notwithstanding etc.

Religionis zelus, vite ac morum honestas . . .
· S·[2] *de Scorciatis / O· / O· xxx Marianen'*

[1] This information comes from a notwithstanding clause.
[2] *sic; recte:* 'C'

469   14 July 1501   *Reg. Lat.* 1086, fos 119ᵛ-120ᵛ

To Richard Robertson', perpetual vicar of the parish church of B. Mary the Virgin, Gedney[1] [also spelt *Geduey*], d. Lincoln. Dispensation and indult —at his supplication— to receive and retain for life, together with the perpetual vicarage of the above parish church, one, and without it, any two other benefices, etc. [as above, no. 3, to '. . . retain them together for life, as above']; and, while residing in the Roman curia or any one of his benefices or attending a *studium generale*, not to be bound to reside personally in his other benefices, nor to be liable to be compelled by anyone to do so[2] against his will etc. [as above, no. 238].

Vite ac morum honestas . . .
. L. puccius / . V· / V· Lx De Phano:

[1] *Gendey* deleted; initialled . *V*
[2] *ad residendum in illis*; (in place of the usual 'ad id')

470   14 July 1501   *Reg. Lat.* 1086, fos 121ʳ-122ʳ

To John Wildon', perpetual vicar of the parish church of Tyrfeldi,[1] d. Lincoln. Dispensation and indult —at his supplication— to receive and retain for life, together with the perpetual vicarage of the above parish church, one, and without it, any two other benefices, etc. [as above, no. 3, to '. . . retain them together for life, as above']; and, for life, while attending a *studium generale* or residing in the Roman curia or any one of his benefices, not to be bound to reside in his other benefices, nor to be liable to be compelled by anyone to do so[2] against his will etc. [as above, no. 238].

Vite ac morum honestas . . .
. L. Puccius / . V· / · V· Lx De Phano:

[1] in the second occurrence, the 'T' written over an (?)'L'
[2] *ad munus* (in place of the usual 'ad id')

471   12 February 1501   *Reg. Lat.* 1086, fo 141ʳ⁻ᵛ

To Walter[1] Woliner, rector of the parish church of St Andrew, Blyclyng, d. Norwich. Dispensation —at his supplication— to receive and retain for life, together with the above parish church, one, and without it, any two other benefices, etc. [as above, no. 3].

Vite ac morum honestas . . .
N· de castello / · V· / V· L· De Phano:

[1] *Gualtero*

472   14 February 1501   *Reg. Lat.* 1086, fo 142[r-v]

To John Bulkeley, rector of the parish church of Sutton Maundevyle, d. Salisbury. Dispensation —at his supplication— to receive and retain for life, together with the above parish church, one, and without it, any two other benefices, etc. [as above, no. 3].

Vite ac morum honestas . . .
. L. puccius /. V· / V· L· De Phano:

473   3 March 1501   *Reg.Lat.* 1086, fos 160[r]-161[r]

Union etc. At a recent petition on the part of Walter Knygheley, MMed, canon of Wells, the pope hereby unites etc. the parish church of Kelston, d. Bath and Wells, (whose annual value does not exceed 23 marks in money of those parts, equivalent to 69 gold ducats of the camera), to the canonry and prebend of Haselbery in the church of Wells, which he holds together with the above parish church, for as long as he holds the canonry and prebend, to the effect that Walter, in person[1] or by proxy, may, on his own authority, take and retain corporal possession of the parish [church][2] and its rights and appurtenances, for as long as he holds[3] the canonry and prebend[4], and convert its fruits etc. to his own uses and those of the parish church and the canonry and prebend without licence of the local diocesan or of anyone else. Notwithstanding etc. The pope's will is, however, that the parish church shall not, on account of this union etc., be defrauded of due services and the cure of souls therein shall not be neglected, but that its customary burdens shall be supported; and that on Walter's death or resignation etc. of the canonry and prebend the union etc. shall be dissolved and so deemed and the parish church shall revert to its original condition automatically.

Ad futuram rei memoriam. Romanum decet pontificem votis illius[5] gratum prestare assensum . . .
. L. puccius / V /. V. xxxv De Phano:

[1] *per seu; recte*: 'per se'
[2] 'ecclesie' does not occur
[3] *obtinere*; for 'obtineret' or 'obtinuerit'?
[4] 'prebendam' wanting
[5] *sic; recte*: 'illis'

474   6 March 1501   *Reg. Lat.* 1086, fos 161ᵛ-162ᵛ

To Robert Crafford, perpetual vicar of the parish church of Moreton', d. London.
Dispensation —at his supplication— to receive and retain for life, together with the
perpetual vicarage of the above parish church, one, and without it, any two [other]
benefices, etc. [as above, no. 3].

Vite ac morum honestas . . .
. L. Puccius / · V· / . V· · L· De Phano:

475   6 March 1501   *Reg. Lat.* 1086, fos 162ᵛ-164ʳ

Union etc. At a recent petition on the part of James Stanley, rector of the parish
church of Wineswyk [also spelt *Wyneswyk*], d. Coventry and Lichfield, the pope
hereby unites etc. the parish church of Rotherston' [also spelt *Rotherston*][1], d.
Coventry and Lichfield, (whose annual value does not exceed 57 gold ducats of the
camera), to the above parish church of Wineswyk, which he holds together by
apostolic dispensation, for as long as he holds that of Wineswyk, to the effect that
James (who asserts that he is of noble birth by both parents), in person or by proxy,
may, on his own authority, take and retain corporal possession of the church of
Rotherston' and its rights and appurtenances, for as long as he holds the church of
Wineswyk, and convert its fruits etc. to his own uses and those of the said churches
without licence of the local diocesan or of anyone else. Notwithstanding etc. The
pope's will is, however, that the church of Rotherston' shall not, on account of this
union etc., be defrauded of due services and the cure of souls therein shall not be
neglected, but that its customary burdens shall be supported; and that on James's
death or resignation etc. of the church of Wineswyk the union etc. shall be dissolved
and so deemed and the church of Rotherston' shall revert to its original condition
automatically.

*Ad futuram rei memoriam. Romanum decet pontificem votis illis gratum prestare
assensum . . .*
N² de castello / · V· / · V xxxv · De Phano:

[1] in one instance changed (by overwriting) from *Rosherston*; not initialled

[2] changed (by overwriting) from (?)*P*; the whole of the abbreviator's name is written by a different hand
(in a different ink) from the entry : entered later?

476   21 March 1501   *Reg. Lat.* 1086, fos 167ᵛ-168ᵛ

To John Tayler, rector of the parish church of Sthorisbroke [also spelt *Storisbroke*],

d. Salisbury. Dispensation —at his supplication— to receive and retain for life, together with the above parish church, one, and without it, any two other benefices, etc. [as above, no. 3].

Vite ac morum honestas . . .
· *L· puccius / F / F. L. Sanctor(is)*

477   23 April 1501   *Reg. Lat.* 1086, fos 178^v-179^v

To Walter Cotton', LLB, rector of the parish church of St Nicholas, Glatton', d. Lincoln. Dispensation —at his supplication— to receive and retain for life, together with the above parish church, one, and without it, any two other benefices, etc. [as above, no. 3].

Litterarum scientia, vite ac morum honestas . . .
A. de s^{to} sev^{no} / Jo. / Jo. L. Electus Terracinen.'

478   12 January 1501   *Reg. Lat.* 1086, fos 185^r-186^r

To William Toft, of the chapel royal, succentor of the church of Salisbury. Dispensation —at his supplication— to him (who, as he asserts, holds the succentorship of the above church of Salisbury, which is an office and is incompatible and to which the parish church of Ebbesburne, d. Salisbury, is annexed in perpetuity) to receive and retain for life, together with the above succentorship, one, and without it, any two other benefices, etc. [as above, no. 3, to '. . . Notwithstanding etc.']. With the proviso that the succentorship <and other>[1] incompatible benefices in question shall not, on this account, be defrauded of due [services][2] and the cure of souls therein shall not be neglected.

Vite ac morum honestas . . .
. *F. de parma*[3] / *Jo.* / *Jo. L. Electus Terracinen'*

[1] marginal insertion (different hand?); initialled *Jo.*
[2] 'obsequiis' wanting
[3] in a darker ink: entered later?

479   9 January 1501   *Reg. Lat.* 1086, fos 186^r-187^r

To William Ffrankleyn, cleric, d. Lincoln. Dispensation —at his supplication— to him, who, as he asserts, is in his twentieth year of age, to receive and retain any benefice, with cure or otherwise incompatible, or requiring sacred,[1] even priest's, orders by statute or otherwise,[2] even if this benefice with cure should be a parish church or its perpetual vicarage, or a <chantry>,[3] free chapel, etc. [as above, no. 240, to '. . . receive and retain another, similar or dissimilar, benefice'], incompatible or requiring sacred, even priest's, orders by statute or otherwise; and —as soon as he has reached his twenty-second year and acquired a benefice by reason of which he is otherwise bound to celebrate— to have himself promoted to the priesthood. Notwithstanding etc. and [notwithstanding] general or special constitutions etc. especially those in which it is said to be laid down that no-one may receive and retain a parish church or its perpetual vicarage unless he is in the order of the diaconate —and William is not— the which constitutions etc. the pope hereby derogates, specially and expressly, for this once only. With the proviso that the benefice in question shall not, on this account, be defrauded of due services and the cure of souls therein (if any) shall not be neglected.

Vite ac morum honestas . . .
. *L. puccius*[4] / *Jo.* / *Jo. xxxv. Electus Terracinen'*

[1] *ordines* here deleted, initialled *Jo.*
[2] *fundatione* here deleted, but not initialled
[3] marginal insertion by enregistering scribe, initialled *Jo.*
[4] in darker ink (like marginal insertion): entered later?

480   12 January 1501   *Reg. Lat.* 1086, fos 187^v-188^v

To Thomas Edwardes, BDec, rector of the parish church of Grasham [also spelt *Graham*],[1] d. Chichester. Dispensation —at his supplication— to receive and retain for life, together with the above parish church, two, and without it, any three other <secular>[2] benefices, etc. [as above, no. 17, to '. . . retain them together for life, as above'].[3] Notwithstanding etc. With the proviso that the above <church>[4] and other incompatible benefices in question shall not, on this account, be defrauded of due services and the cure of souls in the church and (if any) the other incompatible benefices aforesaid shall not be neglected.

Litterarum scientia, vite ac morum honestas . . .
. *L. puccius*[5] / *Jo* / *Jo. C. Electus Terracinen.*

[1] *Grasham Cicestren.* and, below, *dGraham* [= 'de Graham'] are written in darker ink: entered later?
[2] marginal insertion (in darker ink: *cf.* note 1), initialled *Jo.*; however the inclusion of 'secularia' is surely unnecessary in a straightforward dispensation *ad tria* and is not often found
[3] as usual, parish churches and their perpetual vicarages are specifically limited to two, early on in the entry; though in the present instance the usual clause: 'provided that of three such benefices not more than two be parish churches or their perpetual vicarages' does not occur below

[4] marginal insertion (in darker ink: *cf.* note 1), initialled *Jo.*
[5] in darker ink: *cf.* note 1

481   23 January 1501   *Reg. Lat.* 1086, fos 192[r]-193[r]

To Reginald West, rector of the parish church of St Ebba the Virgin, d. Lincoln. Dispensation —at his supplication— to him, who, as he asserts, is of noble birth by both parents, to receive and retain for life, together with the above parish church, one, and without it, any two other benefices, etc. [as above, no. 3].

Nobilitas generis, vite ac morum honestas . . .
A.[1] *de sanctoseverino*[2] / *Jo.* / *Jo. L Electus Terracinen'*

[1] converted from an 'L'; *cf.* next note
[2] written above *puccius* (which is deleted but not initialled); *cf.* previous note; both names are written in the same ink and hand — which differ from those of the entry: entered later?

482   24 January 1501   *Reg. Lat.* 1086, fos 197[r]-198[r]

To William Spencer, perpetual vicar, called of the northern part,[1] of the parish church of St Wulfram, Graham *alias* Grantham, d. Lincoln. Dispensation —at his supplication— to him, who, [as] he asserts, holds the perpetual vicarage, called of the northern part, of the above parish church, to receive and retain for life, together with the above perpetual vicarage, one, and without it, any two other benefices, etc. [as above, no 3].

Vite ac morum honestas . . .
. *L. puccius* / *F* / *F. L. Sanctor(is)*

[1] MS: . . . *perpetuo vicario ex parte boriali nuncupato parrochialis ecclesie* . . .

483   26 January 1501   *Reg. Lat.* 1086, fos 200[r]-201[v]

Union etc. At a recent petition on the part of Geoffrey Helis[1], canon of St Asaph, the pope hereby unites etc. the parish churches of Llanvarchell' and (?)Botuatria, d. St Asaph, (whose annual value does not exceed 13 marks in money of those parts, equivalent to 39 gold ducats of the camera), to the canonry [and] prebend of Minot, otherwise cursal, of the church of St Asaph, which he holds with the above parish churches by apostolic dispensation, for as long as he holds the canonry and prebend, to the effect that Geoffrey, in person or by proxy, may, on his own authority, continue in or take anew corporal possession of the parish churches and their rights and appurtenances and convert their fruits etc. to his own uses and those of the parish churches and the canonry and prebend without licence of the local diocesan or of anyone else. Notwithstanding etc. With the proviso that the parish churches shall not, on account of this union etc., be defrauded of due services and the cure of souls therein shall not be neglected, but that their customary burdens shall be supported. The pope's will is, however, that on Geoffrey's death or resignation etc. of the canonry and prebend this union etc. shall be dissolved and so deemed and the parish churches shall revert to their original condition automatically.

Ad futuram rei memoriam. Votis fidelium omnium [. . .] libenter annuimus . . . . L puccius. [2] */ Jo. / Jo. xxxx. Electus Terracinen.*

[1] written *He lis*

[2] in a hand (Damiani's?) other than that of the enregistering scribe (and different ink)

484   19 January 1[501][1]   *Reg. Lat.* 1086, fos 201[v]-203[r]

To John Robson', prior of the priory of the Holy Cross, Reygate, OSA, d. Winchester. Dispensation —at his supplication— to receive together with the above priory, one, and without it, any two other regular benefices, with or without cure, of the said order, or with one of them, or without them, one benefice, with or without cure, usually held by secular clerics, even if the regular benefices should be priories, *prepositure, prepositatus,*[2] administrations or offices and depending from one and the same monastery or regular place, and the secular benefice be a parish church or its perpetual vicarage, or a chantry, free chapel, hospital or annual service, usually assigned to secular clerics in title of a perpetual ecclesiastical benefice, even if the priories, *prepositure, prepositatus,*[3] administrations or offices should be customarily elective and have cure of souls, if he obtains them otherwise canonically, and retain for life whichever one of the regular benefices he chooses, even if it be a priory or other conventual dignity or a claustral office, *in titulum,* and the other regular or a secular benefice, with or without cure, *in commendam,* to resign them, at once or successively, simply or for exchange, as often as he pleases, and to cede the commend, and in their place receive up to two other, similar or dissimilar, regular benefices of the said order, or with one of them, or without them, one secular benefice, with or without cure, and retain for life whichever one of the said regular benefices he chooses *in titulum,* and the other, even regular —provided that it be not a priory or other conventual dignity or a claustral office— or secular, *in commendam,* as above; he may —due and customary burdens of the benefice retained *in commendam* having been supported— make disposition of the rest of its fruits etc., just as those holding it *in titulum* could and ought to do, alienation of immovable goods and precious movables being however forbidden. Notwithstanding etc. With the proviso that the benefice retained *in commendam* shall not, on this account, be defrauded of due services and the cure of souls in it[4] (if any) shall not be neglected; but that its aforesaid burdens shall be supported.

Religionis zelus, vite ac morum honestas . . .
. *F. de parma | F | F. L. Sanctor(is)*

[1] *millesimo* ['quingentesimo'] *quarto* [changed (by overwriting) from *quin(to)?*] *decimo kalendas Februarii anno nono*

[2] *dignitates personatus* here deleted and initialled *F; cf.* , note 3

[3] following *prepositatus*, MS again has *dignitates personatus* deleted and initialled *F; cf.*, note 2

[4] *in eo* inserted in the margin by the enregistering scribe, initialled *F*.

485   5 September 1500   *Reg. Lat.* 1086, fos 264[r]-265[r]

To Maurice Flellain, canon of the church of Limerick, mandate in favour of Maurice Ymulcorcny, chancellor of the church of Limerick. The pope has learned that the perpetual vicarage of the parish church of Killsca'nyll', d. Limerick, has been vacant *certo modo* and is vacant at present, although Thady Offlahud, who bears himself as prior[1] of Rageell, OSA, d. Limerick, has detained it without any title or support of law, temerariously and *de facto*, for a certain time, as he still does. A recent petition on Maurice's part to the pope to unite etc. the vicarage to the chancellorship, which Maurice was holding, for as long as he should hold it, asserted that, engaged in sundry places for the defence of his country and of the rights of the chancellorship and of his temporal lord, he was present, defending himself and his own, where there were killings, robberies, thefts, fires, acts of pillage and sacrilege and other evils customarily done in time of war against the enemy; that he did not, however, kill or wound anyone, or cut off anyone's limbs, or commit any robbery, theft or act of sacrilege; and also that he took part, with certain cleric and lay associates, in certain conspiracies against the then bishop of Limerick (who was then in the Roman curia), and, on this account, was excommunicated by the bishop's then vicar general and bound by other ecclesiastical sentences, censures and pains and was afterwards canonically absolved from them; that, when he was bound by them, he was present, actively and passively, at mass and other divine offices, not however in contempt of the keys; that at another time he had himself dispensed by apostolic authority to be promoted within a seven-year period to any of the sacred orders, provided that within the first two years he was promoted to the subdiaconate; that he was provided to the chancellorship by the said authority; and that he did not have himself promoted to the above orders as he was not advised by the ordinary to do so. At his supplication, the pope, not having certain knowledge of the foregoing, hereby commands the above canon,[2] to absolve Maurice, if he so requests, from the above excesses, for this once only, in the customary form of the church, having enjoined a salutary penance on him etc.; to dispense him on account of the irregularity contracted and not to be bound to have himself promoted, by reason of the chancellorship, for a seven-year period calculated from the date of the presents, to any of the sacred orders, even the priesthood, provided that within a year he has himself promoted to the subdiaconate, nor to be liable to be compelled by anyone to do so against his will; and to rehabilitate him on account of all disability and infamy contracted by occasion of the foregoing; and if, in the event of this absolution etc., having summoned Thady and others interested, the above canon finds the vicarage, whose annual value does not exceed 6 marks sterling, to be vacant (howsoever etc.) and the foregoing to be true, to unite etc. it (even if it has been vacant for so long that by the Lateran statutes its collation has lawfully devolved on the apostolic see, etc.) to the chancellorship, whose annual value does not exceed 60 marks sterling, with all rights and appurtenances; to the effect that —having removed Thady and any other unlawful detainer— Maurice may, on his own authority, take corporal possession of the vicarage and convert its fruits etc. to his own uses and those of the vicarage and chancellorship, without licence of the local diocesan or of anyone else. Notwithstanding etc. The pope's will is, however, that the chancellorship and the vicarage shall not, on this account, be defrauded of due services and the cure of souls therein shall not be neglected; but that the customary burdens of the vicarage shall be supported; and that on Maurice's death or resignation etc. of the chancellorship this union etc. shall be dissolved and so deemed and the vicarage shall revert to its original condition and be deemed vacant automatically.

Sedes apostolica, pia mater, recurrentibus ad eam cum humilitate . . .
S de Castello[3] / · *V·* / · *V· Lx De Phano:*

[1] *pro priore de Rageell*; 'monasterii' (or suchlike) does not occur

[2] *vestre; recte:* 'tue'

[3] written with deliberation: entered later?

---

486   28 September 1500   *Reg. Lat.* 1086, fos 268[r]-269[r]

To Maurice Flellayn, canon of Limerick, mandate in favour of Maurice de Geraldinis the younger (son of Maurice the elder), cleric, d. Ardfert. The pope has learned that the precentorship and a canonry of the church of Limerick and the prebend of Tollebrache in the same are vacant *certo modo* at present and have been vacant for so long that by the Lateran statutes their collation has lawfully devolved on the apostolic see, although William de Mivrey *alias* Hohounyn, who bears himself as a cleric, has detained them with no title and no support of law, of his own temerity and *de facto*, for a certain time, as he still does. At a recent petition on the part of Maurice the younger to the pope to unite etc. the precentorship to the canonry and prebend, if conferred on him by virtue of the presents, for as long as he holds them —asserting that the annual value of the canonry and prebend does not exceed 12, and of the precentorship, 60, marks sterling; that certain laymen are taking the fruits of the precentorship; that he, notwithstanding a defect of birth as the son of an unmarried nobleman and an unmarried woman has been dispensed by ordinary authority to be marked with clerical character and has been duly so marked; and that he, who is powerful in those parts, can truly recover the fruits of the precentorship from the hands of the said laymen and restore them to its ownership— the pope, not having certain knowledge of the foregoing, hereby commands the above canon, if, having summoned William and others concerned and those interested in the union etc., he finds the canonry and prebend and precentorship to be vacant (howsoever etc.) and the foregoing to be true and Maurice the younger to be suitable — concerning which the pope burdens the canon's conscience— to collate and assign the canonry and prebend, with plenitude of canon law, to Maurice the younger, and unite etc. the precentorship, which is a non-major dignity *post pontificalem* (even if it and the canonry and prebend be specially reserved etc.), with all rights and appurtenances, to the canonry and prebend, for as long as Maurice holds the canonry and prebend, inducting him etc. having removed William from the canonry and prebend and any other unlawful detainers from them and the precentorship, and causing Maurice (or his proctor) to be received as a canon of the church of Limerick, with plenitude of canon law, and the fruits etc., rights and obventions of the canonry and prebend and annexed precentorship to be delivered to him. [Curbing] gainsayers by the pope's authority etc. Notwithstanding etc. Also the pope dispenses Maurice the younger to receive and retain the canonry and prebend, if conferred on him by virtue of the presents, notwithstanding the said defect etc. His will is, however, that the precentorship shall not, on account of this union etc., be defrauded of due services and the cure of souls therein (if any) shall not be neglected, but that its burdens shall be supported; and that on Maurice's death or resignation etc. of the canonry and prebend this union etc. shall be dissolved and the precentorship shall revert to its original condition and be deemed vacant automatically. And the pope has commanded that — if Maurice be found suitable — provision of the canonry and prebend be made to him from the date of the presents.

Apostolice sedis providentia circumspecta ad ea libenter intendit...
A de Sanctoseverino / Jo. / Jo. xxx. [1] *de Galves.*

[1] wants expedition date?

487[1]   **29 October 1500**   *Reg. Lat.* 1086, fos 270[v]-271[r]

To William Watson, perpetual vicar of the parish church of Birling, [d.][2] Canterbury.[3] Dispensation —at his supplication— to receive and retain for life, together with the perpetual vicarage of the above parish church, one, and without it, any two other benefices, etc. [as above, no. 3, to '. . . or principal in collegiate churches'], even if of the patronage of princes or other laymen,[4] or a combination etc. [as above, no. 3].[5]

Vite ac morum honestas . . .
S de Castello / Jo. / Jo. L. de Galves

[1] Textual oddities common to the present entry and to nos. 489 and 490 suggest that the drafting and enregistration of the three letters —all enregistered by the same scribe— was closely linked.

[2] 'diocesis' does not occur here, but does below

[3] *sic*

[4] *etiam si de iure patronatus principum vel aliorum laicorum*; 'principum vel aliorum' is a rare elaboration (which recurs below, at nos. 489 and 490)

[5] save that 'together for life' is not repeated

488   3 November 1500   *Reg. Lat.* 1086, fo 271[r-v]

To Thomas Hegge, BDec, rector of the parish church of Whelmeth(a)m[1] Parva, d. Norwich. Dispensation and indult —at his supplication— to receive and retain for life, together with the above parish church, one, and without it, any two other benefices, etc. [as above, no. 3, to '. . . retain them together for life, as above'][2]; and, for life, while attending a *studium generale* or residing in the Roman curia or any one of his benefices, not to be bound to reside [in his other benefices],[3] nor to be liable to be compelled by anyone to do so etc. [as above, no. 238].

Litterarum scientia, vite ac morum honestas . . .
L puccius / · V· / V· Lx De Phano:

[1] MS: *Whelmethm'*

[2] save that in this instance MS wants 'vel collegiatis et dignitates ipse in cathedralibus etiam metropolitanis'

[3] supplied by the editor

489[1]   23 January 1501   *Reg. Lat.* 1086, fos 279[v]-280[r]

To John Holt, MA,[2] rector of the parish church of St Michael, Smardeyn, d. Canterbury. Dispensation —at his supplication— to receive and retain for life, together with the above parish church, <one>,[3] and without it, any two other benefices, etc. [as above, no. 3, to '. . . or principal in collegiate churches'], even if of the patronage of princes or other laymen,[4] or a combination, etc. [as above, no. 3].[5]

Litterarum scientia, vite ac morum honestas . . .
S de Castello / Jo. / Jo. L. Electus Terracinen.

[1] See above, no. 487, note 1.

[2] positioned thus in MS (though ordinarily in the address clause the designation by degree (if any) comes at the end — i. e. after that by benefice (or clerical status))

[3] marginal insertion by the enregistering scribe; initialled *Jo.*

[4] See above, no. 487, note 4; also no. 490 below.

[5] save that 'together for life' is not repeated

490[1]   24 January 1501   *Reg. Lat.* 1086, fo 280[r-v]

To Leonard Eglifeld, MA,[2] perpetual vicar of the parish church of St Mary, Reculu',[3] d. Canterbury. Dispensation —at his supplication— to receive and retain for life, together with the above <vicarage>,[4] one, and without it, any two other benefices, etc. [as above, no. 3, to '. . . or principal in collegiate churches'], even of the patronage of princes or other laymen,[5] or a combination, etc. [as above, no. 3, to '. . . Notwithstanding etc. ']. With the proviso that the <vicarage>[6] held and other incompatible benefices in question shall not, on this account, be defrauded of due services and the cure of souls <in the vicarage held>[7] and (if any) in the other incompatible benefices shall not be neglected.

Litterarum scientia, vite ac morum honestas . . .
S de Castello / Jo. / . Jo. L Electus Terracinen.

[1] See above, no. 487, note 1.

[2] positioned thus in MS; *cf.* above, no. 489, note 1

[3] in the first instance, a mark (which is on the line after the second 'u') resembles an 's' and at first glance suggests the reading *Reculus*; in the second instance, a mark which again resembles an 's' is suspended after the final 'u': *Reculv(er)*?

[4] inserted in the margin by the enregistering scribe, initialled *Jo*; like insertions of 'vicarage' occur throughout the entry, as do related deletions of or adjustments to 'parish church(es)'

[5] See above, no. 487, note 4; also no. 489.

[6] *parochialis ecclesia*, deleted and initialled *Jo.* occurs in the line; with *vicaria* inserted by the enregistering scribe in the margin initialled *Jo*; *cf.* above, note 4

[7] *in parochiali*, deleted and initialled *Jo.* occurs in the line; with *in vicaria obtenta* inserted in the margin by the enregistering scribe, initialled *Jo* and *Jo.*; *cf.* above, note 4

491   3 November 1500   *Reg. Lat.* 1086, fo 301[r-v]

To John Thwaytis, perpetual vicar of the parish church of Feversam, [d.][1] Canterbury. Dispensation and indult —at his supplication— to receive and retain for life, together with the perpetual vicarage of the above parish church, one, and without it, any two other benefices, etc. [as above, no. 3, to '. . . retain them together for life, as above']², and, also for life, while residing in the Roman curia or any one of his benefices or attending a *studium generale,* not to be bound to reside personally in the above vicarage or other benefices, defined as above, also held by him at the time, nor to be liable to be compelled by anyone to do so against his will. Notwithstanding etc. and statutes and customs of churches in which the incompatible and other benefices may perchance be —especially those in which it is said to be expressly laid down that those holding a dignity etc. or benefice with cure in the churches or dioceses in question are bound to reside in it continuously, or at least for a certain time each year— which John (or his proctor) has perchance sworn to observe. The pope hereby derogates the statutes and customs aforesaid, specially and expressly, for this once only; and also relaxes any such oath perchance taken by John or which he may take in the future. With the proviso that the above vicarage and other incompatible [benefices] shall not, on this account, be defrauded of due services and the cure of souls in the vicarage and (if any) the other incompatible benefices aforesaid shall not be neglected; but that the customary burdens of the aforesaid benefices (without cure)³ shall be supported.

Vite ac morum honestas . . .
L puccius / . V / V. Lx. De Phano:-

1 'diocesis' does not occur here, but does below

2 save that MS wants 'et dignitates ipse in cathedralibus etiam metropolitanis post pontificales maiores aut collegiatis' (or suchlike); the omission only partially supplied in the margin: *post pontificales maiores* (in the hand of the enregistering scribe), initialled . *V.* and *V.*

3 MS (inappropriately?): *sed sine cura beneficiorum predictorum . . .*

492   15 March 1501   *Reg. Lat.* 1086, fos 323ʳ-324ʳ

To Thady Machrgan, <Maurice>¹ Machnayn² and David Ologan', canons of the church of Clonfert, mandate in favour of Malachy Ocell', cleric, d. Clonfert (who asserts that he is of noble birth by both parents and in his fourteenth year of age). Following the pope's reservation some time ago of all conventual priories vacated then and in the future to his own disposition, the priory, as the pope has learned, of the monastery, usually governed by a prior, of Atrohomane, OSA, d. Clonfert, which John Yolei, its late prior, held while he lived, became vacant by his death, outside the Roman curia, and is vacant at present, being reserved as above. Wishing to assist Malachy —who asserts that Carbericus [also spelt *Cornelius*]³ Machkyth, who bears himself as a canon of the said order, has detained the priory without any title or support of law, temerariously and *de facto,* for a certain time, as he still does— to support himself more decently, the pope hereby commands that the above three (or two or one of them), if, having summoned Carbericus and others concerned, they find the priory, which is conventual by custom and not by institution and whose annual value does not exceed 40 marks sterling, to be vacant (whether as above or howsoever etc.; even if vacant for so long that by the Lateran statutes its collation has lawfully devolved on the apostolic see, etc.), shall commend it, with all rights and appurtenances, to Malachy to be held, ruled and governed by him for life; (<he may>[4] —due and customary burdens of the priory having been supported— make disposition of the rest of its fruits etc. just as those holding it *in titulum* could and ought to do, alienation of immovable goods and precious movables being however forbidden); inducting him etc. having removed Carbericus and any other unlawful detainer and causing Malachy (or his proctor) to be admitted to the priory and its fruits etc., rights and obventions to be delivered to him. [Curbing] gainsayers etc. Notwithstanding etc. With the proviso that the priory shall not, on account of this commend, be defrauded of due services and the cure of souls therein (if any) shall not be neglected; but that its aforesaid burdens shall be supported.

Nobilitas generis, vite ac morum honestas . . .
S de Castello[5] */ Jo / Jo. xx.* [6] *Electus Terracinen'*

[1] *Mauricio* inserted in the margin, perhaps in the hand of the master; initialled *Jo.*

[2] the first 'n' reworked and uncertain

[3] *Carberic[us]* thrice; finally, once: *prefato Cornelio*

[4] *liceat sibi* inserted in the margin by the enregistering scribe; initialled *Jo.*

[5] written with deliberation: entered later?

[6] wants expedition date?

493   2 March 1501   *Reg. Lat.* 1086, fos 333[v]-334[r]

Statute and ordinance as below. A recent petition to the pope on the part of James Skeymgeour, rector, and John Skeymgeour, lay patron, of the parish church of Kylleneur, d. Lismore, stated that the church is in a quite wooded place and near the sea-shore and on the edges of land open to the sea and near it and even within the limits of its parish live wild men who cannot be coerced or punished by secular judge or power and within the said limits and surrounding vicinity, especially at the side of the mountain of Latyrewern', at the castle of Fynchaers and the lake of Lochquho, at the ford of the rivulet of Anygray and also the places of Strovesk,[1] Terroner, and at Lochclea, Soctocha, Brenowc and Glusner, d. Lismore— habitually carry out many homicides, thefts, robberies, burnings, oppressions, vulgarly called *lesornyng,*[2] and other similar evils which it is impossible to prevent by judge or power; and that the said men, albeit wild and up to a point ungovernable, are, however, exceedingly afraid of censures promulgated by apostolic authority; and that if it were to be established and ordained that everyone there of both sexes committing such homicides, thefts, burnings, oppressions and other evils would incur sentence of excommunication, many homicides would be avoided and it would also be to the good of souls because from dread of the censures they would abstain from homicides etc. The pope —at this supplication— hereby establishes and ordains, in perpetuity, that each and every one, of both sexes and wherever they may be from, and of whatsoever condition, religion and quality, who, within the limits of the parish, church and surrounding vicinity shall —after the present letters have been published in the church and surrounding vicinity— commit, or command and cause to be committed, such robberies etc.,[3] or anyone of them, shall automatically incur sentence of excommunication from which they shall be denied absolution save by the local ordinary after satisfaction has been made. Notwithstanding etc.

Ad perpetuam rei memoriam. Commissum nobis desuper . . .
F de parma / Jo / Jo˙ xxxx. Electus Terracinen'

[1] preceded by (?)*Strovesk et de* deleted and initialled *Jo.*

[2] later written: *le sornyng*; (two words?); *cf.* Jamieson's *Scottish Dictionary* (1867): sorning - the act of exacting free lodging

[3] the same items are listed here as are first listed above though the word order differs

494   21 March 1501[1]   *Reg. Lat.* 1086, fos 358ʳ-359ʳ

To Peter Bradsha, BDec, perpetual vicar of the parish church of St Nicholas, Plumsted, d. Rochester. Dispensation —at his supplication— to him, who, as he asserts, is of noble birth, to receive and retain for life, together with the perpetual vicarage of the above parish church, one, and without it, any two other benefices, etc. [as above, no. 3].

Nobilitas generis, vite ac morum honestas . . . [2]
. L. puccius / . V· / V· · L· De Phano:

[1] *duodecimo . . . nono*] written in much smaller letters, possibly entered later, squeezed into a space between *quingentesimo* and the start of the magistral signature

[2] *sic*; yet an address clause, where the recipient of the grace is designated by a degree, calls for a proem in the form 'Litterarum scientia . . . ' (i. e. in the present instance: 'Nobilitas generis, litterarum scientia, vite . . . ')

495   23 December 1500   *Reg. Lat.* 1087, fos 23ʳ-24ᵛ

To William Walter, [UID],[1] perpetual vicar of the parish church of Odyham, d. Winchester. Some time ago, Innocent VIII dispensed him —who, formerly, as he asserted, had been dispensed by apostolic authority notwithstanding a defect of birth as the son of an unmarried man and an unmarried woman to be promoted to all, even sacred, orders, and to hold a benefice, even if it should have cure of souls, and afterwards had been duly marked with clerical character and was holding the perpetual vicarage of the above parish church, having acquired it when it was canonically collated to him while vacant *certo modo* — to receive and retain together with the said vicarage, one other, and having resigned it, any two other benefices, etc. [as above, no. 131, to '. . . as is more fully contained in those letters'].[2] The pope therefore —at his supplication— hereby further dispenses William, who, as he asserts, holds the archdeaconry of Brecon (*Brechonie*), d. St David's, and the above vicarage, to receive and retain for life, together with the archdeaconry and vicarage, or without them, with any two other incompatible benefices held at the time by virtue of the said dispensation, any third benefice, etc. [as above, no. 131].[3]

Litterarum scientia, vite ac morum honestas . . .
. L. puccius / F / F· Lxx. Sanctor(is)

[1] *utriusque doctor*; 'iuris' wanting
[2] summarised in *CPL*, XV at no. 498
[3] with the addition of 'even of lay patronage' after 'in title of a perpetual ecclesiastical benefice'

496[1]   29 August 1501   *Reg. Lat.* 1087, fos 46[v]-47[v]

To Thomas Ortons, BDec, perpetual chaplain, called cantor, in the parish church of St Michael, Co(n)ventre[2] [also spelt *Conventrie*], d. Coventry and Lichfield. Dispensation[3] —at his supplication— to him, who, as he asserts, holds the perpetual chaplaincy, called the chantry of Hugh Merinton, in the above parish church, to receive and retain for life, together with the above chaplaincy, if it cannot be held with another incompatible benefice, one, and without it, any two other benefices etc. [as above, no. 3, to '. . . retain them together for life, as above']; and, also for life, not to be bound, while staying in the Roman curia or attending a *studium generale* or residing in any one of his benefices, to reside personally in his other benefices, etc. [as above, no. 21].

Litterarum scientia, vite ac morum honestas . . .
L puccius / · B / . B. L. [4] *Bolis.*

[1] See below, no. 715.
[2] MS: *Co'ventre*
[3] 'tibique pariter indulgemus' (or suchlike) does not occur; neither does 'indulti' (or 'concessionis') in the *sanctio*; *cf.* note 4 below
[4] *sic*; 'Lx' for such a dispensation and indult; but *cf.* note 3 above

497   29 August 1501   *Reg. Lat.* 1087, fo 48[r-v]

To Andrew Saun'der, rector of the parish church of Cottysbech, [d.][1] Lincoln.

Dispensation —at his supplication— to receive and retain for life, together with the above parish church, one, and without it, any two other benefices, with cure or otherwise mutually incompatible, even if parish churches or their perpetual vicarages, or chantries, free chapels, hospitals or annual services, usually assigned to secular clerics in title of a perpetual ecclesiastical benefice, or . . . [2] the dignities, *personatus*, administrations or offices should be customarily elective etc. [as above, no. 3].

Vite ac morum honestas . . .
L puccius / · B· / · B. L. Bolis.

[1] 'diocesis' does not occur here, but does below

[2] 'dignitates personatus administrationes vel officia in cathedralibus etiam metropolitanis vel collegiatis et dignitates ipse in cathedralibus etiam metropolitanis post pontificales maiores seu in collegiatis ecclesiis huiusmodi principales aut talia mixtim fuerint et ad' (or suchlike) wanting; *cf.* above, no. 3

498   15 June 1501   *Reg. Lat.* 1087, fos 67^v-68^r

To Robert Holdirnessa, rector of the parish church of All Saints, Braybrote, d. Lincoln. Dispensation —at his supplication— to receive and retain for life, together with the above parish church, one, and without them, any two other benefices, etc. [as above, no. 3].

Vite ac morum honestas . . .
L. puccius / · V· / · V· L· De Phano:

499   7 April 1501   *Reg. Lat.* 1087, fos 81^r-82^r

To Thomas Tame, rector of the parish church of Castelleton', d. Salisbury. Dispensation —at his supplication— to receive and retain for life, together with the above parish church, one, and without it, any two other benefices, etc. [as above, no. 3].[1]

Vite ac morum honestas . . .
L putius[2] / Jo / Jo. L. Electus Terracinen'

[1] save that MS has *dignitas* for 'dignitates' in the first occurrence; *cf.* next entry
[2] *sic; cf.* next entry

500   7 April 1501   *Reg. Lat.* 1087, fos 82^r -83^r

To Robert Stokesley, cleric, d. York. Dispensation — at his supplication — to receive and retain together for life any two benefices, with cure or otherwise mutually incompatible, etc. [as above, no. 3,[1] to '. . . Notwithstanding etc.'] With the proviso that the incompatible benefices in question shall not, on this account, be defrauded of due services and the cure of souls therein (if any) shall not be neglected.

Vite ac morum honestas . . .
. L. putius[2] */ Jo. / Jo. L. Electus Terracinen'*

[1] save that MS has *dignitas* for 'dignitates' in the first occurrence; *cf.* the previous entry
[2] *sic; cf.* previous entry

501   7 April 1501   *Reg. Lat.* 1087, fos 83^r-84^r

To William Mason, Lic UI, rector of the parish church of Tynwell', d. Lincoln. Dispensation — at his supplication — to receive and retain for life, together with the above parish church, one, and without it, any two other benefices, etc. [as above, no. 3].

Litterarum scientia, vite ac morum honestas . . .
. L. putius[1] */ Jo / Jo. L. Electus Terracinen'*

[1] *sic*

502   14 July 1501   *Reg. Lat.* 1087, fos 98^v-99^v

To John Perot, B<A>,[1] rector of the parish church of Woldham [also spelt *Voldam*], d. Rochester. Some time ago Pius II dispensed him to receive and [retain][2] together for life any two benefices, with cure or otherwise mutually incompatible, even if parish churches or their perpetual vicarages, or dignities, etc. [as above, no. 131, to '. . . retain them together for life'][3] — by certain [letters][4] in which it was expressed that he was of noble birth. Next, Paul II — after representation had been made to him on John's part that he was not of noble birth — wishing to provide lest the effect of the said letters be frustrated on this account, willed and granted John, by other letters of his, that the letters of Pius and the dispensation in question and their content should be valid and have full force in and for all things, just as if no mention had been made in them that he was of noble birth by both parents, as is more fully contained in the separate letters. The pope therefore — at his supplication — hereby further dispenses John, who, as he asserts, holds the above parish church and the archdeaconry of Colchester (*Colchestrie*) in the church of London by the said dispensation, to receive and retain for life, together with the church of Woldham and the archdeaconry, or any two other incompatible benefices, held by him at the time by the said dispensation, any third benefice, etc. [as above, no. 131].

Litterarum scientia,[5] *vite ac morum honestas . . .*
L. puccius / Jo / Jo. Lxx. Electus Terracinen'

[1] *artibus* in the line deleted by the master and initialled *Jo.*; as *artibus* was inserted in the margin by the master, initialled *Jo*, the sense of the deletion is obscure. Perhaps the intention was to insert 'decretis' (see below, note 5).

[2] 'retinere' wanting

[3] though in the present instance MS several times has the present tense where the past is required

[4] summarised in *CPL*, XII on pp. 224-5

[5] There is a want of accord between the proem (which is in the form — 'Litterarum scientia' — reserved for graduates) and the address clause where the petitioner is designated BA (not recognized as a degree by the chancery). Perot was in fact a BDec (Emden, *Oxford to 1500*, p. 1465).

503   8 July 1496   *Reg. Lat.* 1087, fos 99[v]-100[v]

To Richard Seynt John', perpetual chaplain, called Gilbert Keymer's cantor, in the church of Salisbury, dispensation and indult. The pope has learned that in the statutes and customs of the church of Salisbury and in the foundation of the perpetual chaplaincy, called the chantry of Gilbert Keymer, in the said church, published canonically, it is expressly laid down that holders of the chaplaincy cannot hold another benefice or office and are bound to reside in the said church and may not absent themselves without the express licence of the dean of the church for the time being. He hereby dispenses and indulges Richard (who, as he asserts, is a BA, and holds the chaplaincy and, on admission to it, took the oath to observe the statutes and foundation) — at his supplication — <relaxing the oath>[1] to receive and retain for life, together with the chaplaincy, two, and without it, any three other benefices, etc. [as above, no. 17, to '. . . retain them together for life, as above'][2]; and also for life, while residing in the Roman curia or any one of his benefices or attending a *studium generale*, not to be bound to reside personally in his other benefices, nor to be liable to be compelled by anyone to do so against his will. Notwithstanding etc. The pope derogates the said statutes and foundation specially and expressly, for this once only. With the proviso that the above chaplaincy and other benefices shall not, on this account, be defrauded of due services and the cure of souls therein shall not be neglected; but that the cure shall be exercised and things divine served by good and sufficient vicars maintained from the proceeds of these benefices.

Vite ac morum honestas . . .

L. puccius / . Jo / Jo. Cx. Electus Terracinen'

¹ marginal insertion, initialled *Jo*

² as to content; though the order of words is not identical

504 — ¹   *Reg. Lat.* 1087, fo 104ᵛ

Beginning of letter addressed to John Bryme, rector of the parish church of St Nicholas at the bridge, Gilforde, d. Winchester. Extends no farther than first part of recital: *Hinc est . . . inter alia obtines* [ends]. Proem: *Vite ac morum honestas . . .*; no abbreviator's name; no magistral initial.

Occupies 9½ lines at top of otherwise blank page; deleted; no explanatory note. Spelling of names apart, identical, so far as it goes, with the dispensation and indult, dated 9 July 1496, in favour of John Brime enregistered (by same scribe) at fo 311ʳ⁻ᵛ of *Reg. Lat.* 1008 (= *CPL* XVI, no. 795). In all probability, an abortive enregistration of it.

The registral context of the letter in *Reg. Lat.* 1008 indicates that its expedition was delayed. (Until 1500, 18. xii at the earliest: *cf. CPL* XVI, p. cv, note 33). The fragment's presence in *Reg. Lat.* 1087 — a *liber* of the ninth year [1500, 26. viii-1501, 25. viii] — tends to corroborate it.

¹ no dating clause

505¹   **5 May 1501**²   *Reg. Lat.* 1087, fo 154ʳ⁻ᵛ

To Ambrose Weston, monk of the monastery of St Peter, Gloucester (*Glocestrie*),³ OSB, d. Worcester. Dispensation — at his supplication — to him (who, as he asserts, holds a place and monacal portion of the above monastery and, as he also asserts, is expressly professed of the above order)⁴ to receive and retain for life, together with his place and monacal portion, any benefice, with or without cure, usually held by secular clerics, etc. [as above, no. 32, to '. . . Notwithstanding etc.'] With the proviso that the benefice and monacal portion in question shall not, on this account, be defrauded of due services and the cure of souls in the benefice (if any) shall not be neglected; but that its customary burdens and those of the place and monacal portion shall be supported.

Religionis zelus, vite ac morum honestas . . .
L. puccius / Jo. / Jo. L. Electus Terracinen'

¹ In seven places in the course of the entry various small-scale additions or alterations have been made in, apparently, the hand of the enregistering scribe; but in a quite different ink, sometimes in pre-existant

spaces.

2 *primo . . . anno nono*] in a different ink: entered later? *Cf.* note 1.

3 thus the second occurrence; previously: *Glocestee* or possibly *Glocestre*

4 The latter information comes from a notwithstanding clause.

506   19 May 1501   *Reg. Lat.* 1087, fos 158^V-159^V

To John Smyth' *alias* Gogh, MA, perpetual chaplain in the church of the Holy Trinity, d. Coventry and Lichfield. Dispensation and indult — at his supplication — to him, who, as he asserts, holds a chaplaincy, called the half chantry of Nicholas Percy in the church [aforesaid],[1] d. Coventry and Lichfield, to receive and retain for life, together with the chaplaincy, if it cannot be held with another incompatible benefice, one, and without it, any two other benefices, etc. [as above, no. 3, to '. . . retain them together for life, as above']; and, also for life, while residing in the Roman curia or any one of his benefices or attending a *studium generale*, not to be bound to reside personally in his other benefices, etc. [as above, no. 238].

Litterarum scientia, vite ac morum honestas laudabilia etc.[2]
[-][3] */ Jo / Jo. Lx. Electus Terracinen.'*

1 . . . *cappellaniam dimidiam cantariam Nicolay Percy nuncupatam in ecclesia Conventren. et Lichfelden. dioc(esium)*

2 abridgement of this proem is unusual; but *cf.* no. 507 below

3 no abbreviator's name; *cf.* no. 507 below

507   19 May 1501   *Reg. Lat.* 1087, fos 159^V-160^V

To Thomas Ba(m)buri,[1] rector of the parish church of Convvnde' [also spelt *Co'vvnde'*], d. Rochester. Dispensation — at his supplication — to receive and retain for life, together with the above parish church, one, and without it, any two other benefices, etc. [as above, no. 3].

Vite ac morum honestas etc.[2]
[-][3]*/ Jo / Jo. L. Electus Terracinen'*

1 MS: *Ba'buri*

2 abridgement of this proem is unusual; but *cf.* previous entry

3 no abbreviator's name; *cf.* previous entry

508[1]   **8 November 1500**   *Reg. Lat.* 1087, fos 311^r-312^v

To Richard Bryte, rector of the parish church of St Michael the Archangel, . . . [2] d. *Oxonien.,*[3] dispensation. Some time ago, the pope by other letters of his dispensed him to receive and retain together for life any two benefices, with cure or otherwise mutually incompatible, even if parish churches or their perpetual vicarages,[4] or dignities, etc. [as above, no. 131, to '. . . two other, similar or dissimilar, benefices,'] and retain them for life, as above, as is more fully contained in those letters.[5] The pope — at his supplication — hereby further dispenses Richard, who, as he asserts, is of noble birth, and holds by the said dispensation the parish churches of St Michael the Archangel, . . . [6] and of B. Mary, . . . [7] d. *Oxonien.,* [8] to receive and retain for life, together with the two parish churches aforesaid or any two other incompatible benefices, held by him at the time by virtue of this dispensation, any third benefice, etc. [as above, no. 131].

Nobilitas generis, vite ac morum honestas . . .
[-][9] */ [-]*[10] */ [-]*[11]

[1] the entry struck through; no explanation; *cf.* below, notes 8, 9 and 10 below

[2] blank space in MS

[3] *recte*: 'Exonien.' (Exeter)

[4] *vicarie aut*] 'cantarie libere capelle hospitalia vel annualia servitia clericis secularibus in titulum perpetui beneficii ecclesiastici assignari solita' (or suchlike) does not occur

[5] lost; Index entry transcribed below at no. 1218

[6] blank space in MS

[7] blank space in MS

[8] see above, note 3

[9] no magistral initial; *cf.* note 1 above and notes 9 and 10 below

[10] no abbreviator's name; *cf.* notes 1 and 8 above and 10 below

[11] no magistral signature; *cf.* notes 1, 8 and 9 above

509   **6 July 1501**   *Reg. Lat.* 1088, fos 14^v-16^v

To the abbot of the monastery of Tongland, d. Whithorn, mandate in favour of William Cranfurd, canon of the monastery of Holyrood (*Sancte Crucis*), near Edinburg, OSA, d. St Andrews. It has been referred to the pope's audience by William that John Cranfurd, prior of the priory of St Mary's Isle (*Insule Beate Marie*), OSA, d. Whithorn, has dared to dilapidate and alienate immovable goods and precious movables of the said priory which he holds. Considering that if this is true, John has rendered himself unworthy of the priory, the pope hereby commands the above abbot, if William will accuse John before him over the foregoing and proceed in form of law, thereafter, having summoned John and others concerned, to make inquiry into these matters and, if he finds the truth of them to be substantiated, deprive John of the priory and remove him from it; and, in that event, if through diligent examination he finds William to be suitable — concerning which the pope burdens the abbot's conscience — collate and assign the priory, which is conventual and is a dependency of the above monastery and whose annual value does not exceed 90 pounds sterling (whether vacant by the above deprivation and removal or at another time howsoever etc.; even if vacant for so long that by the Lateran statutes its collation has lawfully devolved on the apostolic see, etc.), with all rights and appurtenances, to William, inducting him etc. having removed any unlawful detainer — having first received from William the usual oath of fealty in the name of the pope and the Roman church in accordance with the form which the pope sends enclosed under his *bulla* — and causing William (or his proctor) to be admitted to the priory and its fruits etc., rights and obventions to be delivered to him. [Curbing] gainsayers by the pope's authority etc. Notwithstanding etc. The pope has commanded that — if John resigns the priory after the above accusation etc. and the first definitive sentence of deprivation has been laid against him — such resignation be deemed made in evasion of future deprivation and the judge (or judges) before whom the case is brought may proceed to the execution of the present letters in all things just as if John had [not][1] made such resignation and the priory had been made vacant not by resignation but by deprivation; and if William be found suitable, as above, provision of the priory (if and when vacant) be made to him from the date of the presents.

Dignum et cetera.
. *F. de parma* / *Jo* / *Jo. L. pridie kl' Augusti anno nono* [31 July 1501], *Electus Terracinen'*

[1] *nunc*; *recte*: 'non'?

510   14 March 1501   *Reg. Lat.* 1088, fos 55^r-56^r

To the prior of the monastery, usually governed by a prior, of B. Mary, Achamacharte, d. Ossory, and John Magillapadrie and William Ossian, canons of the church of Ossory, mandate in favour of Malachy Obergyn, cleric, d. Ossory (who, as he asserts, notwithstanding a defect of birth as the son of an unmarried cleric and an unmarried woman, has been duly marked with clerical character). The pope has learned that the parish church of Rosconyll, d. Ossory, which Thady Obergyn, its late rector, held while he lived, has become vacant by his death outside the Roman curia and is vacant at present, although Cornelius Obergyn, who bears himself as a cleric, has detained it with no title, at least no canonical title, for more than five months, but short of a year, as he still does. Therefore he hereby commands that the above three (or two or one of them), if, having summoned Cornelius and others concerned, they find the said church, annual value not exceeding 10 marks sterling, to be vacant (as above or howsoever etc.), shall collate and assign it (even if it has been vacant for so long that by the Lateran statutes its collation has lawfully devolved on the apostolic see etc.), with all rights and appurtenances, to Malachy, inducting him etc. having removed Cornelius and any other unlawful detainer and causing the church's fruits etc., rights and obventions to be delivered to him. [Curbing] gainsayers by the pope's authority etc. Notwithstanding etc. Also the pope dispenses Malachy to be promoted to all, even sacred, orders and the priesthood and to receive and retain the said church, if conferred on him by virtue of the presents. Notwithstanding etc.

Vite ac morum honestas . . .
Jo ortega / · V· / V xij Quintodecimo kl' Aprilis Anno nono [18 March 1501], *de Phano:*

511 19 March 1501 *Reg. Lat.* 1088, fos 69ʳ-71ʳ

To the prior of the monastery, usually governed by a prior, of *Fons vivus*, Lora, d. Killaloe, and Cormac Oheyga, canon of the church of Emly, and the official of Killaloe, mandate in favour of Edmund Okynayth, cleric, d. Killaloe (who, as he asserts, notwithstanding a defect of birth as the son of a priest and an unmarried woman, has been marked with clerical character, otherwise however duly). The pope has learned that the perpetual vicarage of the parish church of Cyllbarrayn, d. Killaloe, is vacant at present and has been vacant for so long that by the Lateran statutes its collation has lawfully devolved on the apostolic see, although Aulanus Okennedy, who bears himself as a cleric, has detained it without canonical title, for more than a year, but short of a three-year period, as he still does. He hereby commands that the above three (or two or one of them), if, having summoned Aulanus and others concerned, they find the vicarage, whose annual value does not exceed 14 marks sterling, to be vacant (howsoever etc.), shall collate and assign it, with all rights and appurtenances, to Edmund, inducting him etc., having removed Aulanus and any other unlawful detainer and causing Edmund (or his proctor) to be admitted to the vicarage and its fruits etc., rights and obventions to be delivered to him. [Curbing] gainsayers by the pope's authority etc. Notwithstanding etc. Also the pope dispenses Edmund to receive and retain the vicarage, if conferred on him by virtue of the presents, and to have himself promoted to all, even sacred, orders and the priesthood; and also not to be bound, by reason of the vicarage, while attending a *studium generale vel particulare* (there being, as he likewise asserts, no *studia generalia*[1] in Ireland), and studying letters, to have himself promoted to any of the sacred orders, even the subdiaconate, for a period of up to seven years (calculated from the date of the presents), provided that within the first two years he shall be promoted to the subdiaconate, nor to be liable to be compelled by anyone to do so against his will; notwithstanding the said defect of birth etc. With the proviso that meanwhile the vicarage shall not, on this account, be defrauded of due services and the cure of souls therein shall not be neglected.

Vite ac morum honestas . . .
· *S· de castello* / *[-]*[2] / *Jo. xx. Tertio kl' Aprilis Anno nono* [30 March 1501], *Electus Terracinen'*

[1] MS: *generalia studia*
[2] no magistral initial

512   8 March 1501   *Reg. Lat.* 1088, fos 167[r]-172[r]

To Lucanus Oconray, precentor of the church of Killaloe, Florence Ogerranayn, canon of the church of Clonfert, and Cormac Oheaga, canon of the church of Emly, mandate in favour of Dermot Yfahy, canon of Clonfert. Some time ago, the pope — having learned that the archdeaconry of the church of Clonfert, which John Okellayd, its late archdeacon, held while he lived, has become vacant by his death, outside the Roman curia, in the kingdom of England on his way to the curia, and was vacant then — by other letters of his charged certain judges that they (or either of them) were to collate and make provision of the archdeaconry, thus vacant, to William[1] de Burgo, canon of Clonfert, as is more fully contained in those letters. Moreover, a recent petition to the pope on Dermot's part stated that William, who at the date of the said letters was holding a certain canonry and prebend of the said church, did not mention that another canonry and prebend of the church had been canonically annexed to the archdeaconry, and, on this account, the said letters are known to be surreptitious, and therefore they and the mandate of provision in them are void. And the pope has learned that the archdeaconry is vacant still, as above; and also that the priorship of the monastery, usually governed by a prior, of St Catherine, Accumomane, OSA, [and] the perpetual vicarage of the parish church of Loctriach [also spelt *Lochriach, Locryach*], d. Clonfert, have been vacant *certo modo* and are vacant at present, and the vicarage has been vacant for so long that by the Lateran statutes its collation has lawfully devolved on the apostolic see, although William Obroghy [also spelt *Obroghyd, Obroghid, Obrogyd*] has detained the archdeaconry, Carbric(us)[2] Mackehic, the priorship, and William Odarnussihy [also spelt *Odannussihy, Odamussihy, Odimussihy*], the vicarage — bearing themselves as priests — for a certain time, short however of a three-year period, [(?)without][3] canonical title, as they do. Supplication was made on Dermot's part to the pope to unite etc. the said vicarage to a certain canonry and prebend which he holds in the church of Clonfert, for as long as he holds the canonry and prebend — asserting that he, notwithstanding a defect of birth as the son of a priest and an unmarried woman, has been marked with clerical character, otherwise however duly; that, by apostolic authority, in the church of Clonfert a canonry has been erected and instituted and the perpetual vicarage of the parish church of Ballenakille *alias* Kilccumpim,[4] d. Clonfert, vacant *certo modo*, has been erected and instituted into a prebend in the church of Clonfert, for his lifetime, both of which he holds as above, and the perpetual vicarage of the parish church of Dumdayre, d. Clonfert, has been united etc. to them, also for his lifetime, and the newly erected canonry and prebend, being vacant, collated and provided to him; and that he has been dispensed to receive and retain them by the said authority. Wishing to honour Dermot further in the said church, the pope hereby commands that the above three (or two or one of them), if, having summoned respectively William Obroghy, Carbric(us) and William Odarnussihy and, as regards the subreption of the letters, William de Burgo, and those interested in the union, they find the priorship, which is conventual and has cure of souls, whose annual value does not exceed 70 marks sterling, and the archdeaconry, which is a non-major dignity *post pontificalem*, the annual value of which and of the canonry and prebend annexed thereto does not exceed 20, and of the vicarage of Loctriach, 9, marks sterling, to be vacant (whether as above or otherwise etc.) and the foregoing to be true, shall declare the aforesaid letters to be surreptitious and those letters and the mandate of provision in them to be (and have been) void; and, in that event, commend the priorship to Dermot, to be held, ruled and governed by him for life; (he may — due and customary burdens of the priorship having been supported — make disposition of the rest of its fruits etc. just as those holding it *in titulum vel commendam* could and ought to do, alienation of immovable goods and precious movables being however forbidden); and collate and assign the archdeaconry (even if it and the priorship have been vacant for so long that by the Lateran statutes their collation has lawfully devolved on the apostolic see) to Dermot; and unite etc. the vicarage, (even if it and the archdeaconry and priorship be specially reserved etc.), with all rights and appurtenances, to the canonry and prebend held, (the annual values of which and of the annexes thereto do not exceed 16 marks sterling), for as long as Dermot holds the canonry and prebend, inducting him etc. having removed William Obroghy from the archdeaconry, Carbric(us) from the priorship and William Odarnussihy from the vicarage and any other unlawful detainers and causing Dermot (or his proctor) to be admitted to the archdeaconry and priorship and their fruits etc., rights and obventions and those of the vicarage to be annexed to be delivered to him. [Curbing] gainsayers etc. Notwithstanding etc. Also the pope dispenses Dermot to receive and retain the priorship and archdeaconry, if the priorship is commended to and the archdeaconry conferred on him by virtue of the presents, and, together with them and the canonry and prebend annexed to the archdeaconry, the canonry and prebend held by him; and not to be bound, by reason of the archdeaconry or any other benefices having cure of souls [or] otherwise requiring sacred orders held at the time, to have himself promoted for a seven-year period calculated from the date of the presents to any of the sacred orders, even the subdiaconate, nor to be liable to be compelled by anyone to do so against his will, provided that he is a subdeacon within the first two years; notwithstanding the above defect of birth etc. The pope's will is, however, that the vicarage to be annexed and also the archdeaconry, priorship, canonry and prebend held and benefices to be held at the time shall not be defrauded of due services, and the cure of souls in the vicarage, priorship and (if any) archdeaconry and other benefices shall not be neglected, but that the customary burdens of the priorship, archdeaconry, vicarage, canonry and prebend and other benefices aforesaid shall be supported; and that on Dermot's retirement or his resignation of the canonry and prebend the union etc. shall be dissolved and so deemed and the vicarage shall revert to its original condition automatically.

Decet Romanum pontificem votis illis gradum[5] *prestare assensum . . .*
. S. de. Castello. / Jo / Jo. xxxx. Sexto kl' Aprilis anno nono [27 March 1501], *Electus Terracinen'*

[1] MS: *Wllialm(us), Wlhalm(us) Wlhan(us), Whalm(us),* or *Willealm(us)*
[2] also spelt *Carbirite(us)*
[3] MS: ?*super; recte*: 'absque'?
[4] the second 'c' is uncertain
[5] *sic; recte*: 'gratum'

513   2 March 1501   *Reg. Lat.* 1088, fos 174[v]-177[r]

To Dermot Osuyllybayn', Cormac Hohe and David Olongan, canons of, respectively, the churches of Ardfert, Emly and Clonfert, mandate in favour of Henry Jeurmachan, canon of the monastery of B. Mary, *de Portu Puro* [Clonfert], OSA, d. Clonfert (who, as he asserts, holds a place and canonical portion of the said monastery, suffers from a defect of birth as the son of an unmarried man and an unmarried woman, and, as he also asserts, is expressly professed of the said order)[1]. The pope has learned that the perpetual vicarages of the parish churches of Dunocta and Chilmolonog, (?)which [are] of lay patronage,[2] and the rectory, of the parish church of Kymiayd *alias* Kylmolonog, d. Clonfert, are vacant *certo modo* at present and have been vacant for so long that by the Lateran statutes their collation has lawfully devolved on the apostolic see, although John Ocorra'chan,[3] who bears himself as a cleric, has detained the rectory, without any title or support of law, temerariously and *de facto*, for a certain time, as he still does. At a recent petition on Henry's part to the pope to unite etc. to the first vicarage, for as long as he holds it, the second vicarage and the (?)rectories,[4] after he acquires the first vicarage — asserting that the annual value of the vicarage[s][5] and (?)rectories[6] together does not exceed 8 marks sterling — the pope, not having certain knowledge of the foregoing, hereby commands that the above three (or two or one of them), if, having summoned John and those interested in the union, they find the vicarage[s][7] and rectory to be vacant (howsoever etc.; [even if] specially reserved etc.) shall unite etc. the second vicarage and the rectory to the first vicarage, while he holds the latter; and in that event collate and assign to Henry the first vicarage with the second vicarage and the rectory to be annexed thereto, inducting him etc. having removed John from the rectory and any other unlawful detainers from it and the vicarages, and causing Henry to be admitted to the first vicarage and its fruits etc., rights and obventions and those of the second vicarage and the rectory to be delivered to him. [Curbing] gainsayers etc. Notwithstanding etc. Also the pope dispenses Henry to receive the [first] vicarage, if conferred on him by virtue of the presents, and retain with it the place and canonical portion aforesaid, notwithstanding the defect of birth etc. The pope's will is, however, that the second vicarage and rectory shall not, on account of this union etc., be defrauded of due services and the cure of souls therein shall not be neglected, but that their customary burdens shall be supported; and that on Henry's death or resignation etc. of the first vicarage the union etc. shall be dissolved and so deemed and the second vicarage and rectory shall revert to their original condition and be deemed vacant automatically.

Decet Romanum pontificem votis illis gratum prestare assensum . . .
· S· *de Castello* / . V· / V· xxxx *De Phano:*[8]

[1] The latter information comes from a notwithstanding clause.

[2] *perpetue vicarie que de iure patronatus laicorum existit; recte*: 'existunt'? But the text is so confused hereabouts that the phrase could be taken to refer to the rectory (or even rectories)! See note 4.

[3] the central part of the name is overwritten and uncertain

[4] *rectorie* The occurrence of 'rectory' in the plural here may be suggestive of an omission earlier in the narrative. But the entry is so riddled throughout with alterations, confusion of cases and other errors of omission and commission that any such suggestion can only be tentative.

[5] *vicaria; recte*: 'vicarie'? (Two vicarages being clearly named above)

[6] see note 4

[7] see note 5

[8] wants expedition date?

---

514   2 April 1501   *Reg. Lat.* 1088, fos 209[r]-211[r]

To the abbot of the monastery of B. Mary, *de Castro dei* [Fermoy], d. Cloyne, and William Okwym and Dermot Odorana, canons of the church of Cloyne, mandate in favour of Peter Roche, perpetual vicar of the parish church of Bellacaha', d. Cloyne. The pope has learned that a canonry of the church of Cloyne and the prebend of Culheay in the same are vacant at present and have been for so long that by the Lateran statutes [their][1] collation has lawfully devolved on the apostolic see, although John Oduny, who bears himself as a cleric or priest, has detained them without any title or support of law, temerariously and *de facto*, for a certain time, as he still does. At a recent petition on Peter's part to the pope to unite etc. the perpetual vicarage of the said parish church, which he holds, to the canonry and prebend, after he acquires them, for his lifetime — asserting that the annual value of the canonry and prebend does not exceed 8 marks sterling — the pope hereby commands that the above three (or two or one of them), if, having summoned John and others concerned and those interested in the union, they find the canonry and prebend to be vacant (howsoever etc.) and the foregoing to be true, shall collate and assign the canonry and prebend (even if specially reserved etc.), with plenitude of canon law, to Peter; and, in that event, [unite etc.]² the vicarage, with all rights and appurtenances, to the canonry and prebend, [inducting him etc. into corporal possession of the canonry and prebend],³ vicarage to be annexed and rights and appurtenances aforesaid, having removed John and any other unlawful detainer from the canonry and prebend and causing Peter (or his proctor) to be received as a canon of the church of Cloyne, with plenitude of canon law, and the fruits etc., rights and obventions of the canonry and prebend and vicarage to be annexed to be delivered to him. [Curbing] gainsayers etc. Notwithstanding etc. The pope's will is, however, that the vicarage shall not, on account of this union etc., be defrauded of due services and the cure of souls therein shall not be neglected, but that its customary burdens shall be supported; and that on Peter's death or resignation etc. of the canonry and prebend the union etc. shall be dissolved and so deemed and the vicarage shall revert to its original condition and be deemed vacant automatically.

Decet Romanum pontificem votis illis gratum prestare assensum . . .
· *S· de castello / Jo / Jo. xxv. Septimo Id' Aprilis Anno nono* [7 April 1501], *Electus Terracinen'*

¹ *eius; recte*: 'eorum'?

² evidently a sizable passage is wanting in the text, here supplied, conjecturally, by the editor in brackets

³ see above, note 2

---

515   17 November 1500   *Reg. Lat.* 1089, fos 1ʳ-3ʳ

To the bishop of Worcester, John Leba',¹ canon of the church of Rennes, and the official of Winchester, mandate in favour of John Brebanh² [also spelt *Brehanh*], monk of the monastery of B. Mary, Bosquen (*de Boquiano*), OCist, d. Saint-Brieuc. A recent petition to the pope on John's part stated that at another time when the priory of St Helier (*Sancti Elerii*) in the isle of Jersey (*de Jaeseyo*), OSA, once d. Coutances and now d. Winchester, was vacant *certo modo*, Henry, king of England — since the collation and provision of the said priory at a time of vacancy pertain by apostolic privilege to him and the kings of England for the time being — collated and made provision of the priory, vacant as above, to John (who previously, as he asserts, had been dispensed by apostolic authority to receive and retain any benefice, with or without cure, usually held by secular clerics, if conferred on him otherwise canonically), albeit *de facto*. And John, believing that he could do this by pretext of the collation and [provision]³ and dispensation aforesaid, detained it thenceforth for two years or thereabouts, as he does, receiving fruits from it, also *de facto*, contracting disability. Moreover since, according to the foregoing, the said collation and provision do not hold good and, as the pope has learned, the priory is known to be vacant still as above, the pope, rehabilitating John on account of all disability and infamy contracted by him by occasion of the foregoing, hereby commands that the above three, or two or one of them, in person or by proxy, shall commend the priory, which is not conventual and is a dependency of the monastery of Chereboure, OSA, d. Coutances, whose annual value does not exceed 40[4] gold ducats of the camera, (vacant howsoever etc., even if it has been vacant for so long that by the Lateran statutes its collation has lawfully devolved on the apostolic see etc.), with all rights and appurtenances, to John, to be held, ruled and governed by him for life; (he may — due and customary burdens of the priory having been supported — make disposition of the rest of its fruits etc. just as those holding it *in titulum* could and ought to do, alienation of immovable goods and precious movables being however forbidden); inducting him etc. having removed any unlawful detainer and causing John (or his proctor) to be admitted to the priory and its fruits etc., rights and obventions to be delivered to him. [Curbing] gainsayers etc. Notwithstanding etc. With the proviso that the priory shall not, on account of this commend, be defrauded of due services and the cure of souls therein (if any) shall not be neglected; but that its aforesaid burdens shall be supported. The pope's will is, however, that before the above three shall proceed to the execution of the presents in any way John Brebanh shall resign the priory into their hands genuinely and completely.

Sedes apostolica, pia mater, recurrentibus ad eam cum humilitate . . .
F de parma / · V· / V xxxx de phano[5]

[1] possibly *Lebam*

[2] or *Brebauh*

[3] *collationis et collationis; recte*: 'collationis et provisionis'

[4] *proventus quadraginta*; the first word (at end of line) unnaturally elongated; the second (at start of line) partly in margin: entered later?

[5] *sic* (usually 'De Phano'); and otherwise unlike 'his' hand

516   11 April 1501   *Reg. Lat.* 1090, fos 6[V]-7[V]

To John Kuyvet, rector of the parish church of Boxworth, d. Ely. Dispensation — at his supplication — to him, who, as he asserts, is in his twentieth year of age and holds the above parish church by apostolic dispensation, to receive and retain for life, together with the above parish church, one, and without it, any two other benefices, etc. [as above, no. 3, to '. . . retain them together for life, as above'].[1] Notwithstanding the above defect of age etc. With the proviso that the incompatible benefices in question shall not, on this account, be defrauded of due services and the cure of souls therein shall not be neglected.

Vite ac morum honestas . . .
N de castello / V / V· Lxx De Phano:

[1] with the addition of 'even of lay patronage' after 'or principal in collegiate churches'

517   30 December 1500   *Reg. Lat.* 1090, fos 10[V]-11[V]

To James Bromuoych, BDec, rector of the parish church of Hampton', d. Hereford, dispensation. Some time ago, the pope by other letters of his dispensed him to receive and retain for life, together with the parish church of Stokelacy, d. Hereford, (which he was then holding), one, and having resigned it, any two other benefices, etc. [as above, no. 131, to '. . . as is more fully contained in those letters'].[1] The pope therefore — at his supplication — hereby further dispenses James (who, as he asserts, having afterwards resigned the said church [of Stokelacy], holds by the said dispensation, the parish church of Hampton' and also the perpetual vicarage of the parish church of Volchoppe,[2] d. Hereford, which were canonically collated to him) to receive and retain for life, together with the church of Hampton' and the vicarage aforesaid, or two other incompatible benefices, for which he is dispensed as above, held by him at the time, any third benefice, etc. [as above, no. 131].

Litterarum scientia, vite ac morum honestas . . .
N de Castello[3] */ Jo. / Jo. Lxx. Electus Terracinen'*[4]

[1] summarised in *CPL*, XVI at no. 386
[2] or *Volchope*
[3] much fainter ink and touching the first line: entered later?
[4] *Electus Terracinen'* in much darker ink than the rest of the magistral signature: entered later?

518   21 April 1501   *Reg. Lat.* 1090, fos 26[V]-27[V]

To Nicholas Curleus, perpetual chaplain, called cantor, at the altar of B. Mary the Virgin, in the church of London. Dispensation and indult — at his supplication — to him (who, as he asserts, holds the perpetual chaplaincy, called a chantry, at the above altar near the tomb of the late John Beauchinp',[1] knight, in whose foundation it is said to be expressly laid down that the holder cannot hold another benefice with it) to receive and retain for life, together with the above chaplaincy, one, and without it, any two other benefices, etc. [as above, no. 3, to '. . . Notwithstanding etc.'][2] The pope derogates the above foundation, specially and expressly, for this once only. With the proviso that the above chaplaincy and other incompatible benefices shall not, on this account, be defrauded of due services and the cure of souls in the said incompatibles shall not be neglected; but that the customary burdens of the chaplaincy shall be supported.

Vite ac morum honestas . . .
F de parma / · V / V· · Lx De Phano:

[1] the 'p' is written over a (?)'y'
[2] with the addition of 'and of lay patronage and of whatsoever tax or annual value' after 'or a

combination'. The additional passage is more typical of a dispensation *ad unum seculare* than an *ad duo*

519   6 May 1501   *Reg. Lat.* 1090, fos 49^r-50^r

To Richard Clerke, cleric invested with a perpetual benefice (*clerico perpetuo beneficiato*), called cantor, in the parish church of All Saints, Maldon', d. London. Dispensation — at his supplication — to him (who, as he asserts, holds a certain perpetual benefice, called the chantry of Dareyes in the above parish church) to receive and retain for life, together with the above benefice, called a chantry, if it is incompatible with another benefice,[1] one, or without it, any two other benefices, etc. [as above, no. 3].

Vite ac morum honestas . . .
S. de Castello / · V· / V· L· De Phano:

[1] *si cum alio incompatibile existit* [possibly corrected to 'existat']; an unusual formulation found also in no. 528

520   18 May 1501   *Reg. Lat.* 1090, fo 55^{r-v}

To James Horton', rector, called master, of the hospital of St John the Baptist, city of Bath (*Bathonie*), d. Bath and Wells. Dispensation — at his supplication — to him, who, as he asserts, holds the above hospital, usually assigned to secular clerics in title of a perpetual ecclesiastical benefice, to receive and retain for life, together with the hospital, if it is incompatible, one, and without it, any two other benefices, etc. [as above, no. 3].

Vite ac morum honestas . . .
F de parma / . V· / V· L· De Phano

521   6 May 1501   *Reg. Lat.* 1090, fo 56^{r-v}

To Cuthbert Turistall,[1] rector of the parish church of Claghton [also spelt *Claghton*'], d. York. Dispensation — at his supplication — to receive and retain for life, together with the above parish church, one, and without it, any two other benefices, etc. [as above, no. 3].[2]

Vite ac morum honestas . . .
· *S·*[3] *de Castello* / . *V·* / *V. L. de Phano:*

[1] *sic*

[2] save that in the present instance 'retain' only occurs where no. 3 repeats 'receive and retain'

[3] in the form of an 'F' without crossbar

522   7 April 1501   *Reg. Lat.* 1090, fo 86[r-v]

To Henry Rydyng,[1] rector of the parish church of B. Mary the Virgin, Gravisende, d. *Rossen.*[2] Dispensation — at his supplication — to receive and retain for life, together with the above parish church, one, and without it, any two other benefices, etc. [as above, no. 3].

Vite ac morum honestas . . .
F. de parma / *Jo* / *Jo. L Electus Terracinen'*

[1] second letter blotched; probably a 'y' written over another letter

[2] *recte*: 'Roffen' (Rochester)

523   7 April 1501   *Reg. Lat.* 1090, fo 87[r-v]

To Walter Reddman',[1] BTheol, rector of the parish church of Plumlonde, d. Carlisle. Dispensation — at his supplication — to receive and retain for life, together with the above parish church, one, and without it, any two other benefices, etc. [as above, no. 3].

Litterarum scientia, vite ac morum honestas . . .
. *F. de parma* / *Jo* / . *Jo. L. Electus Terracinen'*

[1] or possibly *Redolman'*

524   9 January 1501   *Reg. Lat.* 1090, fos 102[r]-103[r]

To John Chaundeler, prior of the priory of St Michael the Archangel, Bromor, OSA, d. Winchester. Dispensation — at his supplication — to receive together with the above priory, one, and without it, any two other regular benefices, with or without cure, of the said order, or, with one of them or without them, one secular benefice, with or without cure, even if the regular benefices should be priories, *prepositure, prepositatus*, dignities, *personatus*, administrations or offices, and the secular benefice be a parish church or its perpetual vicarage, or a chantry, free chapel, hospital or annual service, usually assigned to secular clerics in title of a perpetual ecclesiastical benefice, and of lay patronage and of whatsoever tax or annual value, even if the priories etc. should be customarily elective and have cure of souls, if he obtains them otherwise canonically, and retain for life whichever one of the regular benefices he chooses, even if it be a priory, *prepositura* or other conventual dignity or a claustral office, in *titulum*, and with it the other regular benefice, which may not be a conventual dignity or a claustral office, or a secular benefice, in *commendam,* to resign them, at once or successively, simply or for exchange, as often as he pleases, and cede the commend, and in their place receive up to two other, similar or dissimilar, regular benefices, with or without cure, of the said order, or, with one of them or without them, one secular benefice, with or without cure, and retain for life whichever one of the regular benefices he chooses, even if it should be a priory, *prepositura* or other conventual dignity or a claustral office, in *titulum*, and with it the other regular benefice, which may not be conventual or claustral, or a secular benefice, in *commendam,* as above; he may — due and customary burdens of the benefice held in *commendam* having been supported — make disposition of the rest of its fruits etc. just as those holding it in *titulum* could and ought to do, alienation of immovable goods and precious movables being however forbidden. Notwithstanding etc. With the proviso that the benefice retained in *commendam* shall not, on this account, be defrauded of due services and the cure of souls therein (if any) shall not be neglected; but that its aforesaid burdens shall be supported.

Religionis zelus, vite ac morum honestas . . .
. Jo. ortega / . V· / V· L· De Phano:

525   24[1] March 1501   *Reg. Lat.* 1090, fos 119[v]-120[r]

To Thomas Yermoth *alias* Ludhnn', canon of the monastery of B. Mary, Langley, OPrem, d. Norwich. Dispensation — at his supplication — to him, who, as he asserts, is expressly professed of the above order,[2] to receive and retain any benefice, with or without cure, usually held by secular clerics, etc. [as above, no. 32].

Religionis zelus, vite ac morum honestas . . .
N. de Castello / . V· / V. xxx De Phano:

---

[1] . . . *Nono* [altered (by deletion and overwriting) from ?*Decimo*; not initialled] *kalendas Aprilis* . . .

[2] This information comes from a notwithstanding clause.

526   1 April 1501   *Reg. Lat.* 1090, fos 121^r-122^r

To Thomas Haroppe, MA, rector of the parish church of Stooke[1] Talmache, d. Lincoln. Dispensation — at his supplication — to receive and retain for life, together with the above parish church, one, and without it, any two other benefices, etc. [as above, no. 3].

Litterarum scientia, vite ac morum honestas . . .
F de parma / V / · V· · L· De Phano:

[1] the second occurrence altered (by deletion of 't') from *Stootke*; not initialled

527   27 March 1501   *Reg. Lat.* 1090, fo 122^{r-v}

To John Goodwyne', abbot of the monastery of B. Mary, Robertsbridge (*de Ponteroberti*), OCist, d. Chichester. Dispensation — at his supplication — to receive and retain *in commendam* for life, together with the above monastery, or without it, any benefice, with or without cure, usually held by secular clerics, even if a parish church or its perpetual vicarage, or a chantry, free chapel, hospital or annual service, usually held[1] by secular clerics in title of a perpetual ecclesiastical benefice, even if of lay or clerical patronage and of whatsoever tax or annual value, if he obtains it otherwise canonically, to resign it when[2] he pleases and cede the commend, and in its place receive another, similar or dissimilar, benefice, usually held by secular clerics, and retain it *in commendam* for life, as above; he may — due and customary burdens of this benefice having been supported — make disposition of the rest of its fruits etc. just as those holding it *in titulum* could and ought to do, alienation of immovable goods and precious movables being however forbidden. Notwithstanding etc. With the proviso that the benefice shall not, on this account, be defrauded of due services and the cure of souls therein (if any) shall not be neglected; but that its aforesaid burdens shall be supported.

Personam tuam nobis et apostolice sedi devotam tuis exigentibus meritis paterna benivolentia prosequentes illa tibi favorabiliter concedimus . . .
S· de Castello / F / F. L. Sanctor(is)

[1] *obtineri;* (though 'assignari' usually deployed here)
[2] *illudque quando;* 'simpliciter vel ex causa permutationis' does not occur

528   6 May 1501   *Reg. Lat.* 1090, fos 141^v-142^v

To Thomas Gunby, cleric invested with a perpetual benefice (*clerico perpetuo beneficiato*), called cantor, in the parish church of Dambury, d. London. Dispensation — at his supplication — to him (who, as he asserts, holds a certain perpetual benefice, called the chantry of Wyses, in the above parish church) to receive and retain for life, together with the above benefice, called a chantry, if it is incompatible with another benefice,[1] one, and without them, any two other benefices, etc. [as above, no. 3].

Vite ac morum honestas . . .
F. de parma / Jo / Jo. L. Electus Terracinen.'

[1] *si . . . existit]; as above, no. 519*

---

529   22 August 1501   *Reg. Lat.* 1090, fos 169^V-171^V

To the abbot of the monastery [of] Deveshm',[1] d. Worcester, the precentor of the church of Lichfield, and the prior of the church of Worcester, mandate in favour of the present provost and chapter of the church of Briggenorth' [also spelt *Briggenerth', Briggenorth*], d. Coventry and Lichfield, and Richard Knotte, cleric, their official and commissary. A recent petition to the pope on the part of the provost and chapter and Richard stated that by special privilege of the apostolic see, (which to date has not been derogated in any way), the church of Briggenorth', its provost for the time being and chapter, canons, subordinate ecclesiastics (*ministri*), chaplains (*servitores*), resident clerics (*habituati*), and persons, as well as all the parishioners and inhabitants living within the boundary of the parish of the church (which is parochial) and in the neighbourhood of the prebends, are immediately subject to the apostolic see and totally exempt from all jurisdiction, correction, dominion, and power, of the archbishop of Canterbury (the local metropolitan), the bishop of Coventry [and]^2 Lichfield, and, when the see is vacant, of the prior and chapter of the church of Canterbury and their stewards, generals, and other officials and commissaries, and of any judges in ordinary, to the effect that the archbishop, etc. cannot, by reason of a crime, contract, or disputed matter, wherever the crime is committed, the contract entered into, or the matter disputed, exercise any ordinary jurisdiction or power over the provost etc.; that by ancient, approved, and hitherto peacefully observed custom, the correction and punishment of the canons, etc., persons, and inhabitants, as well as the probate, refusal of probate, registration, and execution, of the last wills and testaments of the persons and inhabitants, and the committing to another, in legal form, of the administration of all the goods of those dying intestate there, the receiving of the computation or account of the administration, and the granting of the quittance to the administrators, and all other exercisable jurisdiction, lawfully pertains to the provost and chapter and their specially appointed commissaries and officials; and that the provost and chapter have been in peaceful possession (or almost) of the above exemption and jurisdiction from the time when the privilege was granted and for so long that there is no recollection to the contrary; that Hugh Peyntwyn', who bears himself as steward or official of the prior and chapter of the church of Canterbury, nevertheless endeavoured, when the see was vacant, to disturb and upset Richard and the provost and chapter in their possession of the exemption and jurisdiction, impede them, so that they were unable to peacefully enjoy the exemption and franchise (*libertate*) and freely exercise the jurisdiction, and inflict damage on them; that Richard, aggrieved and fearful, for good reason, that he could be further damaged in the future, appealed to the apostolic see and, for the protection of his right, person, and affairs, had recourse to the court of Canterbury in accordance with the custom of those parts; that Hugh, contemptuous of the appeal (of which he was not ignorant) and while Richard was still well within the time for prosecuting it, proceeding to the later stages, *ex officio*, as he said, and at the instance of Thomas Malpas, layman of Hereford, suspended Richard from divine service, excommunicated him, and ordered him to be publicly denounced as excommunicate, whence Richard appealed anew to the apostolic see. At the provost and chapter and Richard's supplication to the pope to command that Richard be absolved, simply or conditionally, from the sentences of suspension and excommunication, and any other ecclesiastical censures inflicted on him by Hugh and otherwise, and to commit to some upright men in those parts the causes (and everything connected with them) of the appeals; of everything attempted and innovated after and against the appeals; of the nullity of the suspension, excommunication, and other censures, and of the impediments and everything else prejudicial to the provost and chapter and Richard done by Hugh and any others in connection with the foregoing; and of the principal matter; also the causes which the provost and chapter and Richard intend to move, jointly and severally, against Hugh, Thomas, and any others, over the unlawful impediments and molestation, and the damages, expenses, and just interest payments, which they have suffered, and other matters, the pope hereby commands that the above three (or two or one of them), having summoned Hugh and Thomas and others concerned, shall [if and][3] as it is just, for this once only, conditionally absolve Richard, if he so requests, having first received suitable security from him, that if it appears to them that the sentences etc. were justly inflicted on him, he will obey their commands and those of the church; and, as regards the rest, that they shall hear and duly determine all the cases, without appeal, causing by ecclesiastical censure what they have decreed to be strictly observed, but without prejudice to lawful execution; [and moreover compel] witnesses. Notwithstanding etc.

Humilibus et cetera.
Jo ortega / Jo / Jo· xiiij. Eps' Terracinen'

[1] the capital letter overwritten in lighter ink; 'de' + 'Evesh(a)m' evidently conflated

[2] MS wants 'et' (or suchlike)

[3] MS wants 'si et'

530   7 August 1501   *Reg. Lat.* 1090, fos 179^V-180^V

To Bernard Andree,[1] cleric of Toulouse — who, as he asserts, is preceptor and poet laureate of the noble Arthur, prince of Wales (*Wallie*), first born of Henry, king of England — dispensation and indult. Some time ago, the pope, by other letters of his, dispensed him, (who, as was asserted, was sightless), to receive and retain any number of mutually compatible benefices, with and without cure, even if [?chantries],[2] free chapels, hospitals or annual services, usually assigned to secular clerics in title of a perpetual ecclesiastical benefice and called preceptorships (*preceptorie*), or canonries and prebends, dignities, *personatus*, administrations or offices in cathedral, even metropolitan, or collegiate churches, even if the dignities in question should be major *post pontificalem* in cathedral, even metropolitan, churches or principal in collegiate churches, even if the dignities etc. should be customarily elective and have cure of souls, if he obtained them otherwise canonically, to resign them, at once or successively, simply or for exchange, as often as he pleased, and in their place receive and retain any number of other, similar or dissimilar, mutually compatible benefices, with and without cure, as is more fully contained in those letters. The pope — at his supplication — hereby dispenses him further and indulges him to receive and retain for life, together with an incompatible benefice,[3] if he holds it by the said dispensation, one, and without them, any two other benefices, with cure or otherwise mutually incompatible, even if parish churches or their perpetual vicarages, or chantries, free chapels, hospitals or annual services, usually assigned to secular clerics in title of a perpetual ecclesiastical benefice, even of lay patronage, or dignities, *personatus*, administrations or offices in cathedral, even metropolitan, or collegiate churches, even if the dignities in question should be major *post pontificalem* in cathedral, even metropolitan, churches or principal in collegiate churches, or a combination, and of whatsoever tax or annual value, if he obtains them otherwise canonically, to resign them, at once or successively, simply or for exchange, as often as he pleases, and in their place receive up to two other, similar or dissimilar, mutually incompatible benefices, and retain them together for life, as above; and, for life, not to be bound by reason of those or any other benefices, with cure or otherwise requiring sacred orders, held by him at the time, to have himself promoted to any of the sacred orders or to reside personally in them or any one of them, nor to be liable to be compelled by anyone to do so against his will; and to be able — provided that the local ordinary has expressly consented thereto — to preach and publicly expound the word of God to the people, without any other licence required. Notwithstanding etc. and [notwithstanding] the constitutions of Otto and Ottobuono, formerly legates of the apostolic see in the kingdom of England etc.[4] With the proviso that the incompatible and other benefices in question shall not, on this account, be defrauded of due services and the cure of souls therein (if any) shall not be neglected; but that the customary burdens of benefices in which he shall not reside shall be supported.

Vite ac morum honestas . . .
F. de parma / · B· / . B. Lxxxx Bolis

[1] No mention in letter of his being OESA; *cf.* Emden, *Oxford to 1500*, p. 33

[2] *cantorie; recte:* 'cantarie'

[3] MS: *una cum duo curata seu alias incompatibili si quod ex premissa dispensatione obtineas; duo curata seu alias* an intrusion of unknown origin? (The 'pro habentes expressis' clause mentions: *unum cum cura seu alias incompatibile.*)

[4] The inclusion of these constitutions gives André the option of holding his benefices in England.

531   5 June 1501   *Reg. Lat.* 1090, fo 225[r-v]

To Robert Barbour, MTheol,[1] perpetual vicar of the parish church of St Petroc, Bodmyn', d. Exeter. Dispensation and indult — at his supplication — to receive and retain for life, together with the perpetual vicarage of the above parish church, one, and without it, any two other benefices, etc. [as above, no. 3, to '. . . retain them together for life, as above']; and, for life, while attending a *studium generale* or residing in the Roman curia or any one of his benefices, not to be bound to reside in his other benefices, etc. [as above, no. 238].

Litterarum scientia, vite ac morum honestas . . .
F. de parma / F / F. Lx. Sanctor(is)

[1] altered to *in theologia magistro; (sacre* having been deleted and *theologie* changed to *in theologia)*

532   7 July 1501   *Reg. Lat.* 1090, fo 226[r-v]

To Richard Wyatt, rector of the parish church of Hardyngham, d. Norwich. Dispensation and indult — at his supplication — to receive and retain for life, together with the above parish church, one, and without it, any two other benefices, etc. [as above, no. 3, to '. . . retain them together for life, as above']; and, for life, while attending a *studium generale* or residing in the Roman [curia][1] or any one of his benefices, not to be bound to reside in his other benefices, etc. [as above, no. 238].

Vite ac morum honestas . . .
f. de parma / F / F. Lx Sanctor(is)

[1] wanting in MS

533   12 June 1501   *Reg. Lat.* 1090, fo 229[r-v]

To Roger Squyer, rector of the parish church of All Saints, Canterbury. Dispensation

— at his supplication — to receive and retain for life, together with the above parish church, one, and without it, any two other benefices, etc. [as above, no. 3].

Vite ac morum honestas . . .
F. de parma | Jo | Jo. L. Electus Terracinen.'

534   12 June 1501   *Reg. Lat.* 1090, fo 230^{r-v}

To Humphrey Stanley, cleric, d. Coventry and Lichfield. Dispensation — at his supplication — to him, who, as he asserts, is in his nineteenth year of age, to receive and retain any benefice, with cure or otherwise incompatible, etc. [as above, no. 240].

Vite ac morum honestas . . .
N· de Castello | Jo | Jo. xxij. Electus Terracinen.'

535   24 July 1501   *Reg. Lat.* 1090, fos 282^{v}-284^{r}

To John Howme, monk, recently prior of the priory of Coldingham,[1] OSB, d. St Andrews, reservation etc. and indult, as below. This day John has, through a certain specially appointed proctor of his, <spontaneously and>[2] freely, resigned the above priory, which is conventual and which he was holding at the time, into the pope's hands, and the pope, admitting the resignation, has commanded that provision of the priory, vacant by the said resignation and previously reserved to apostolic disposition, be made to Ninian Howme, cleric, d. St Andrews, with display (*exhibitione*) of the habit and admission of the regular profession and otherwise *sub certis modo et forma* then expressed, as is more fully contained in the pope's letters drawn up in that regard.[3] Lest John should suffer excessive loss from this resignation, the pope hereby reserves, grants and assigns to him, with Ninian's express assent, half of all fruits etc. of the priory's lands and tithes to be received, collected and levied by him (or others in his name) for life, on his own authority, for his own use, in place of an annual pension; and indulges John that — on Ninian's death or resignation etc., or the priory falling vacant in any way, even at the apostolic see — he may have free re-entry and freely take corporal possession of the priory, in person or by proxy, on his own authority, and retain it as before, as much by virtue of his earlier title as of the present letters, without having to be provided anew, in and for all things, just as if he had not resigned the priory. Notwithstanding etc.

    Executory to the archbishop of Glasgow and the officials of St Andrews and Brechin, or two or one of them, acting in person or by proxy.

Religionis zelus, vite ac morum honestas . . . The executory begins: *Hodie cum dilectus filius Johannes Howme* . . .

F de parma; A de sanctoseverino / F / F· xxx xx Sanctor(is)

[1] end of second occurrence overwritten and unclear

[2] marginal insertion by the enregistering scribe, initialled *F*.

[3] *Cf.* below, no. 1217.

536   23 April 1501   *Reg. Lat.* 1091, fos 81^r-82^v

To the bishop of Ross, mandate in favour of James Barri, monk of the monastery of B. Mary, Tracton (*de Albotractu*), OCist, d. Cork. The pope has learned that the above monastery, over which John Barri, its late abbot, presided while he lived, by his death outside the Roman curia, is vacant *certo modo* at present, as are the rectories of the parish churches of <Inisscoganayn>[1] and of <Lyeamhune>,[2] d. Cork, (which are of lay patronage), and the rectories have been vacant for so long that by the Lateran statutes their collation has lawfully devolved on the apostolic see, although Edmund Barri, who bears himself as a monk of the said order, has detained the monastery without any title or support of law, temerariously and *de facto*, for a certain time, as he still does. At a recent petition on James's part to the pope to unite etc. the rectories to the abbatial *mensa*, for as long as James presides over the monastery, if he acquires it — asserting that the annual value of the monastery does not exceed 100, and of the rectories, 20, marks sterling — the pope, wishing to make provision of a capable and suitable person to the monastery to rule and direct it and not having certain knowledge of the merits and suitability of James (who, as he asserts, is expressly professed of the above order), hereby commands <the above bishop>,[3] if, having summoned Edmund and others concerned and those interested in the union, he finds the monastery to be vacant (howsoever etc.) and the foregoing to be true, shall unite etc. the rectories (even if specially reserved etc.), with all their rights and appurtenances, to the *mensa*, for as long as James presides over the monastery; and, in that event, inform himself as to James's merits etc. and if he finds him to be capable and suitable for the rule and administration of the monastery — concerning which the pope burdens the bishop's conscience — make provision of James to the monastery and appoint him abbot, committing to him the care, rule and administration of the monastery in spiritualities and temporalities, inducting him etc. having removed Edmund from the monastery and any other unlawful detainers from it and the rectories and causing the fruits etc., rights and obventions of the rectories to be delivered to him and obedience and reverence to be given him by the convent and customary services and rights by the vassals and other subjects of the monastery. [Curbing] gainsayers etc. Notwithstanding etc. Also the pope dispenses James not to be bound, by reason of any benefices having cure of souls or otherwise requiring sacred orders held by him at the time or of attending a *studium generale vel particulare*, to have himself promoted to the orders of the diaconate and priesthood[4] — <provided that he is a subdeacon within a two-year period>[5]; and grants and indulges that James may — if provision of him be made and he be appointed abbot — receive benediction from any catholic bishop of his choice in communion with the apostolic see, and that the bishop concerned may impart it to him; and that this may not be to the prejudice of the bishop of Cork, to whom the monastery is understood to be subject by ordinary law. The pope's will is, however, that the rectories shall not, on account of this union etc., be defrauded of due services and the cure of souls therein shall not be neglected, but that their customary burdens shall be supported; and that on James's death or resignation etc. of the monastery the union etc. shall be dissolved and so deemed and the rectories shall revert to their original condition and be deemed vacant automatically.[6]

Romani pontificis providentia circumspecta . . .
S de Castello / F / F· L.[7] *Sanctor(is)*

[1] inserted in the margin by the enregistering scribe, initialled *F.*; (?)*Miscogarri* in the line has been deleted, initialled *F.*

[2] inserted in the margin by the enregistering scribe (the 'a' supralinear); (?)*Ly* . . . in the line has been deleted, initialled *F*

[3] *fraternitati tue* inserted in the margin by the enregistering scribe, initialled *F.*; *discretioni vestre* in the line has been deleted, initialled *F.*

[4] Deletion of: *nec non ad* (?)*triennium cogi et compelli possit* (initialled *F.*) has left this without a time-scale.

[5] *dummodo infra biennium sit subdiaconus* inserted in the margin by the enregistering scribe, initialled *F.*

[6] Alterations, deletions and marginal insertions occur throughout the text (but are not necessarily noticed in this summary).

[7] wants expedition date?

537   11 May 1501   *Reg. Lat.* 1091, fos 89[v]-90[v]

To the abbot of the monastery of B. Mary, Kenlys, d. Meath, and Thady Orodochan, canon of the church of Ardagh, and the official of Meath, mandate in favour of John Ogoband, cleric, d. Kilmore (who asserts that notwithstanding a defect of birth as the son of a simple, <unmarried>[1] cleric and an unmarried woman he has been marked with clerical character otherwise however duly). The pope has learned that the vicarage[2] of the parish church of St Patrick, Kylldrumaferthayn, d. Kilmore, has been vacant *certo modo* and is vacant at present, although Cormac Ogoband, who bears himself as a cleric or priest, has detained it without any title or support of law, temerariously and *de facto*, for a certain time, as he still does. At a recent petition on John's part to the pope to erect and institute a canonry in the church of Kilmore and the said vicarage into a simple prebend in the same for his lifetime, the pope hereby

commands that the above three (or two or one of them), if, having summoned
Cormac and others concerned and the bishop and chapter of Kilmore regarding the
erection, they find the vicarage, whose annual value does not exceed 7 marks
sterling, to be vacant (howsoever etc.), and the foregoing to be true, shall erect and
institute a canonry in the church of Kilmore and the said vicarage into a simple
prebend in the same, for John's lifetime, without prejudice to anyone (even if the
vicarage has been vacant for so long that by the Lateran statutes its collation has
lawfully devolved on the apostolic see etc.); and in that event collate and assign the
newly erected canonry and prebend, being vacant, to John, with plenitude of canon
law and all rights and appurtenances, inducting him etc. having removed Cormac
and any other unlawful detainer and causing John (or his proctor) to be received as a
canon of the church of Kilmore, with plenitude of canon law, and causing the fruits
etc., rights and obventions of the canonry and prebend to be delivered to him.
[Curbing] gainsayers etc. Notwithstanding etc. Also the pope dispenses John to
receive and retain the canonry and prebend, if conferred on him by virtue of the
presents, notwithstanding the said defect etc. The pope's will is, however, that the
vicarage shall not, on account of this erection and institution, be defrauded of due
services and the cure of souls therein shall not be neglected, but that its customary
burdens shall be supported; and that on John's death or resignation etc. of the
canonry and prebend, the said erection and institution shall be extinguished and so
deemed and the vicarage shall revert to its original condition and be deemed vacant
automatically.

Apostolice sedis providentia circumspecta ad ea libenter intendit . . .
S *de Castello*[3] / *Jo* / *Jo. xxv. Octavo Id' Junii anno nono* [6 June 1501], *Electus
Terracinen'*

[1] marginal insertion by enregistering scribe, initialled *Jo.*

[2] *perpetua* does not occur

[3] written with deliberation: entered later?

538   5 May 1501   *Reg. Lat.* 1091, fos 127ᵛ-128ᵛ

To the prior of the monastery, usually governed by a prior, of B. Mary, Druymleham,
d. Kilmore, Corbanus Magmahuna,[1] canon of the church of Clogher, and Gellassius
Oscyiridan, canon of the church of Kilmore, mandate in favour of Fergal Yscrydan',
cleric, d. Kilmore. The pope has learned that the rectory of the parish church of
Narnayd *alias* Ched, d. Kilmore, has been vacant *certo modo* and is vacant at
present. At a recent petition on Fergal's part to the pope to erect and institute the said
rectory into a simple prebend in the church of Kilmore, for his lifetime — asserting
that the annual value of the rectory does not exceed 8 marks sterling — the pope, not

having certain knowledge of the foregoing, hereby commands that the above three (or two or one of them), if, having summoned the bishop and chapter of Kilmore and others concerned, they find it to be thus, shall erect and institute the said rectory (vacant howsoever etc.), into a simple prebend of the church of Kilmore, for Fergal's lifetime, without prejudice to anyone (even if the rectory has been vacant for so long that by the Lateran statutes its collation has lawfully devolved on the apostolic see etc.); and, in that event, collate and assign a canonry of the church of Kilmore and the newly erected prebend, being vacant, with plenitude of canon law and all rights and appurtenances, to Fergal, inducting him etc. having removed any unlawful detainer from the canonry and prebend and causing Fergal (or his proctor) to be received as a canon of the church of Kilmore, with plenitude of canon law, and the fruits etc., rights and obventions of the canonry and prebend to be delivered to him. [Curbing] gainsayers etc. Notwithstanding etc.[2]

Apostolice sedis providentia circumspecta ad ea libenter intendit . . .
S de Castello[3] / Jo / Jo. xvj. *Tertio Id' maii anno nono* [13 May 1501],   *Electus Terracinen'*

[1] or *Maginahuna*
[2] no mention of safeguarding the rectory's services and cure of souls after its erection into a prebend
[3] written with deliberation: entered later?

539   23 March 1501   *Reg. Lat.* 1091, fo 167[r-v]

To the abbot of the monastery of B. Mary, *de Castro Dei* [Fermoy], d. Cloyne, and Cormac Oheaga and Dermot Odorna, canons of the churches of Emly and Cloyne, mandate in favour of George Roche, cleric, d. Cork (who, as he asserts, is in his eighteenth year of age). The pope has learned that the archdeaconry of the church of Cork has been vacant *certo modo* and is vacant at present, although John de Geraldinis, who bears himself as a cleric, has detained it for a certain time, but short of a three-year period, without canonical title, as he still does. He hereby commands that the above three (or two or one of them), if, having summoned John and others concerned, they find the archdeaconry, which is a major dignity *post pontificalem* and whose annual value does not exceed 50 marks sterling, to be vacant (howsoever etc.), shall collate and assign it, (even if it has been vacant for so long that by the Lateran statutes its collation has lawfully devolved on the apostolice see etc.), with all rights and appurtenances, to George, inducting him etc. having removed John and any other unlawful detainer, and causing George (or his proctor) to be admitted to the archdeaconry and its fruits etc., rights and obventions to be delivered to him. [Curbing] gainsayers etc. Notwithstanding etc. Also the pope dispenses George (in his eighteenth year, as above) to receive and retain the archdeaconry, if conferred on him by virtue of the presents, notwithstanding the defect of age, etc. With the proviso that the archdeaconry shall not, meanwhile, be defrauded of due services and the cure of souls therein (if any) shall not be neglected; but that its customary burdens shall be supported.

Vite ac morum honestas . . .
S de Castello / Jo. / Jo. xxx. Octavo Id' Aprilis Anno nono [6 April 1501], *Electus Terracinen'*

540   21 March 1501   *Reg. Lat.* 1091, fos 170^V-171^V

To the abbot of the monastery of B. Mary, *de Castro Dei* [Fermoy], d. Cloyne, and the prior of the monastery, usually governed by a prior, of Inistalhuhlin, d. Ardfert, and Dermot Odornay, canon of the church of Cloyne, mandate in favour of Eugene Mecharri, cleric, d. Ardfert. The pope has learned that the vicarage of the parish church of Drisoun *alias* Chilmide, d. Ardfert, is vacant at present and has been vacant for so long that by the Lateran statutes its collation has lawfully devolved on the apostolic see, although Cornelius Ormrdayn, who bears himself as a priest, has detained it, without any title or support of law, temerariously, for a certain time, as he does. At a recent petition on Eugene's part to the pope to erect and institute a canonry in the church of Ardfert and the said vicarage into a simple prebend in the same, for his lifetime — asserting that the annual value of the vicarage does not exceed 14 marks sterling — the pope, not having certain knowledge of the foregoing, hereby commands that the above three (or two or one of them), if, having summoned respectively Cornelius and as regards the erection and institution the bishop and chapter of Ardfert and others concerned, they find the vicarage to be vacant (howsoever etc.) and the foregoing to be thus, shall erect and institute a canonry in the church of Ardfert and the vicarage (even if specially reserved etc.) into a simple prebend in the same, for Eugene's lifetime, without prejudice to anyone; and, in that event, collate and assign the newly erected canonry and prebend, being vacant, with plenitude of canon law and all rights, to Eugene, inducting him etc. having removed Cornelius and any other unlawful detainer from the vicarage and causing Eugene (or his proctor) to be received as a canon of the church of Ardfert, with plenitude of canon law, and the fruits etc., rights and obventions of the canonry and prebend to be delivered to him. [Curbing] gainsayers etc. Notwithstanding etc. The pope's will is, however, that the vicarage shall not, on account of this erection and institution, be defrauded of due services and the cure of souls therein shall not be neglected, but that its customary burdens shall be supported; and that on Eugene's death or resignation etc. of the canonry and prebend, this erection and institution shall be extinguished and so deemed and the vicarage shall revert to its original condition and be deemed vacant automatically.

Apostolice sedis providentia circumspecta ad ea libenter intendere consuevit . . .
S de Castello[1] / *Jo. / Jo. xx. Tertio Kl' Aprilis Anno nono* [30 March 1501], *Electus Terracinen'*

541   23 March 1501   *Reg. Lat.* 1091, fos 175ᵛ-176ᵛ

To the abbots of the monasteries of B. Mary, *de Castro Dei* [Fermoy], and *de Antro Sancti Fanbarri* [Gill Abbey], ds. Cloyne and Cork, and the chancellor of the church of Cork, mandate in favour of John Yherlahe, cleric, d. Cloyne. The pope has learned that the perpetual vicarage of the parish church of Burrneach, d. Cloyne, is vacant *certo modo* at present and has been vacant for so long that by the Lateran statutes its collation has lawfully devolved on the apostolic see, although Donat Oherlahe, who bears himself as a priest, has detained it, without any title or support of law, temerariously and *de facto*, for a certain time, as he still does. At a recent petition on John's part to the pope to erect and institute a canonry in the church of Cloyne and the said vicarage into a simple prebend in the same, for his lifetime — asserting that the annual value of the vicarage does not exceed 7 marks sterling — the pope, not having certain knowledge of the foregoing, hereby commands that the above three (or two or one of them), if, having summoned Donat and as regards the erection the bishop and chapter of Cloyne and others concerned, they find the vicarage to be vacant (howsoever etc.) and the foregoing regarding the erection to be true, (even if the vicarage be specially reserved etc.) shall erect and institute a canonry in the church of Cloyne and the vicarage into a simple prebend in the same, for John's lifetime, without prejudice to anyone; and, in that event, collate and assign the newly erected canonry and prebend, being vacant, with plenitude of canon law and all rights and appurtenances, to John, inducting him etc. having removed Donat and any other unlawful detainer and causing John (or his proctor) to be received as a canon of the church of Cloyne, with plenitude of canon law, and the fruits etc., rights and obventions of the canonry and prebend to be delivered to him. [Curbing] gainsayers etc. Notwithstanding etc. The pope's will is, however, that the vicarage shall not, on account of this erection and institution, be defrauded of due services and the cure of souls therein shall not be neglected, but that its customary burdens shall be supported; and that on John's death or resignation etc. of the canonry and prebend the said erection and institution shall be extinguished and so deemed and the vicarage shall revert to its original condition and be deemed vacant automatically.

Apostolice sedis circumspecta benignitas ad ea libenter intendit . . .
S de Castello / Jo. / Jo. xx. Tertio non' Aprilis Anno nono [3 April 1501], *Electus Terracinen'*

542   1 September 1500   *Reg. Lat.* 1091, fos 183ʳ-184ʳ

To the abbot of the monastery of Monasteranenagh (*de Maio*), d. Limerick, and

Maurice Ffelayn, canon of the church of Limerick, and John Condon, canon of the church of Cloyne, mandate in favour of Denis Ochacheri, canon of the monastery of B. Mary the Virgin, Ragell', OSA, d. Limerick. It has been referred to the pope's audience by Denis that Thady Oflayterah,[1] prior of the said monastery, usually governed by a prior, has refused to be obedient to his father abbot or, while he is away on business, to the abbot's vicar general and *locum tenens*, and to pay him the procuration and refection or expenses which he is obliged to by reason of the monastery and of the vicarage of Kill'sgantayll',[2] which he possesses, and had, on this account, been excommunicated by the said abbot or vicar and publicly denounced as such, and Thady — while not unaware of this and bound by the censures and wallowing in them for a year and more — dared to hear masses and cause them to be celebrated and otherwise take part in divine offices in contempt of the keys, contracting irregularity. Therefore the pope — considering that if the above related matters are true, Thady has rendered himself unworthy of the priory, and wishing to give a special grace to Denis, who, as he asserts, is expressly professed of the said order — hereby commands that the above three (or two or one of them), if Denis will accuse Thady over the foregoing before them and proceed in form of law to any pain, shall, thereafter, having summoned Thady and others concerned, make inquiry into the truth of the foregoing and if they find it to be substantiated, deprive Thady of the priory and remove him from it; and, in that event, collate and assign the priory, which is a conventual dignity, whose annual value does not exceed 12 marks sterling (whether vacant by the above deprivation and removal or in any other way, etc., even if vacant for so long that by the Lateran statutes its collation has lawfully devolved on the apostolic see, etc.) with all rights and appurtenances, to Denis, inducting him etc. having removed Thady and any other unlawful detainer, causing Denis (or his proctor) to be admitted to the priory and its fruits etc., rights and obventions to be delivered to him. [Curbing] gainsayers etc. Notwithstanding etc.

Religionis zelus, vite ac morum honestas . . .
S de Castello / · V· / · V· xxv Quarto kl' Octobr' Anno nono [28 September 1500], *De Phano:*

[1] or *Oflaytemh*
[2] diocese not mentioned

543   17 October 1500   *Reg. Lat.* 1091, fos 193ᵛ-194ᵛ

To Maurice Okmayn,[1] cleric, d. Ossory (who, as he asserts, notwithstanding a defect of birth as the son of an abbot, OSA, and an unmarried woman, has been duly marked with clerical character). Some time ago, the pope by other letters of his made provision to Nicholas Fwin [also spelt *Fwyn*], canon of Waterford — while he was also then holding the canonry and prebend of Corvaly [also spelt *Corvali*][2], church of Waterford — of the deanery of the said church, which is a major dignity *post pontificalem*, vacant by the death, outside the Roman curia, of (?)Rupert[3] Bruyn, its late dean, as is more fully contained in those letters. The pope has learned that this canonry and prebend, which Nicholas still holds, are expected to be vacant by the acquisition of the deanery to which another canonry and prebend of the said church are united in perpetuity. He hereby reserves, by apostolic donation, the above canonry and prebend of Corvaly, whose annual value does not exceed 3 marks sterling, as soon as they fall vacant, as above or in any other way except by Nicholas's death, to be conferred on Maurice, with plenitude of canon law and all rights and appurtenances, strictly inhibiting the bishop and chapter of Waterford and those to whom the collation, provision, presentation or other disposition of the said canonry and prebend pertains, collectively or severally, from presuming to make disposition of them contrary to this reservation. Notwithstanding etc. Also the pope dispenses Maurice to receive and retain the reserved canonry and prebend, if conferred on him by virtue of the presents, notwithstanding the said defect etc.

Executory to the bishop of Limerick, the dean of the church of Cashel and Maurice Felayn, canon of the church of Limerick, or two or one of them, acting in person or by proxy.

Vite ac morum honestas . . . The executory begins: *Hodie cum nos nuper dilecto filio Nicolao Fwyn . . .*
Jo Ortega; Jo Ortega[4] / *Jo.* / *Jo. xviij. decimo octavo kl' decembr' Anno nono* [14 November 1500], *de Galves*

[1] (?)*clerico* heavily deleted, initialled *Jo*

[2] (?)*Cornali* deleted, initialled *Jo.*

[3] MS here has *Ruperti*; executory has *Ruberti* (for Robert?)

[4] there is a cross adjacent (signalling error?)

544 22 November 1500[1] *Reg. Lat.* 1091, fo 197[r-v]

To John Smyth, BDec, rector of the parish church of Knapton, d. Norwich. Dispensation — at his supplication — to receive and retain for life, together with the above [parish church],[2] one, and without it, any two other benefices, etc. [as above, no. 3].

Litterarum scientia, vite ac morum honestas . . .
L puccius / J. [3] *o.* / *Jo. L. de Galves*

[1] *Datum Rome anno . . .*; 'apud Sanctum Petrum' (or suchlike) does not occur

[2] *dicta unum . . .*; ('ecclesia' does not occur)

[3] *sic*

545   2 March 1500   *Reg. Lat.* 1091, fos 207[v]-209[r]

To the priors of the monasteries, usually governed by priors, of B. Mary, Kenll' and of Instyog, d. Ossory, and the official of Ossory, mandate in favour of John Mohl'an, canon of Ossory. Some time ago, the pope — having learned that the chancellorship of the church of Ossory, the perpetual vicarage of the parish church of Downkyt and the rectory of the parish church of Kyllokech'an (which is of lay patronage), d. Ossory, were then vacant *certo modo* and had been vacant for so long that by the Lateran statutes their collation had lawfully devolved on the apostolic see, although the late William Clyntown' had detained the chancellorship and John Grawnt the vicarage and rectory — bearing themselves as priests — with no title and no support of law, of their own temerity and *de facto*, for a certain time, as they were then; and after representation made on the part of Hoellus Brenagh', priest, d. Ossory, to the pope to unite etc. the <vicarage and>[1] rectory to the chancellorship, for as long as he holds the chancellorship, if conferred on him — at Hoellus's supplication, charged by other letters of his the priors of the monasteries, usually governed by priors, of B. Mary, *de Insula Viventium* [Monaincha], d. Killaloe, and the said B. Mary, Kenll', d. Ossory, and of St Catherine, d. Waterford, their own names not expressed, with a clause that they (or two or one of them), if, having summoned William and John and others interested, they found the chancellorship, vicarage and rectory to be vacant, were to unite etc. the vicarage and rectory to the chancellorship, for Hoellus's lifetime; and, in that event, collate and make provision of the chancellorship with the annexes to Hoellus, as is more fully contained in the said letters.[2] And, as a recent petition to the pope on John's part stated, since it is quite untrue that at the time of the said letters William was holding the chancellorship without any title or support of law, as above; on the contrary, he had a strong title, though not a canonical one in that he was holding it from someone who did not then have faculty of collating, and, on this account, the said letters are known to be surreptitious and whatever ensued by pretext of them does not hold good and the chancellorship is vacant still, as above; and, as the pope has learned, the perpetual vicarage of the parish church of Ieriponte, said diocese, which James Hedyan', its late perpetual vicar, held while he lived, has become vacant, by his death outside the Roman curia, and is vacant at present, although Thomas O Corregan' has, by pretext of a certain collation made of it *de facto* to him by someone who did not have faculty to do so, detained it for a certain time, as he still does. The pope hereby commands that the above three (or two or one of them), having summoned William, Thomas and Hoellus and others concerned, shall inform themselves as to all the foregoing and if they find the truth of it to be substantiated, declare the said letters to be and have been surreptitious and they and whatsoever ensued by pretext of them null and void; and, in that event, collate and assign the chancellorship which is a non-major dignity *post pontificalem*, has cure of souls, is not customarily elective, and is of annual value not exceeding 10 marks sterling, and the last vicarage, of annual value not exceeding 8 marks sterling, (vacant howsoever etc.; even if the last vicarage has been vacant for so long that by the Lateran statutes its collation has lawfully devolved on the apostolic see, and it and the chancellorship be specially reserved to apostolic disposition or the last vicarage be generally reserved because, [as] is asserted by several persons, James, its holder, was the collector, or one of the subcollectors, of the fruits and proceeds due in those parts to the apostolic camera, etc.), with all rights and appurtenances, to John, inducting him etc. having removed William from the chancellorship, Thomas from the last vicarage and any other unlawful detainers, and causing John (or his proctor) to be admitted to the chancellorship and last vicarage and their fruits etc., rights and obventions to be delivered to him. [Curbing] gainsayers by the pope's authority etc. Notwithstanding etc. Also the pope dispenses John to receive and retain together for life the chancellorship and last vicarage, if conferred on him by virtue of the presents, to resign them, at once or successively, simply or for exchange, as often as he pleases, and in their place receive up to two other, similar or dissimilar, incompatible benefices and retain them together for life, as above. Notwithstanding etc. With the proviso that the chancellorship and last vicarage and other benefices shall not, on this account, be defrauded of due services and the cure of souls in the chancellorship and vicarage and (if any) the other incompatible benefices aforesaid shall not be neglected.

Vite ac morum honestas . . .
S de Castello[3] / *F.* / *F· xxx. Pridie Id' matii' Ano' Octavo* [14 March 1500], *Sanctor(is)*

[1] marginal insertion by enregistering scribe, initialled *F.*

[2] above, no. 157

[3] written with deliberation: entered later?

546   18 January 1501   *Reg. Lat.* 1092, fos 254^r-256^r

To Thomas, formerly bishop of London, [archbishop] elect of York. Consistorial translation, [though absent from the Roman curia][1] from the church of London to that of York, vacant by the death, outside the Roman curia, of the late archbishop Thomas, during whose rule the said church of York was specially reserved by the pope to his own disposition. The pope hereby appoints Thomas archbishop, committing to him the care and administration of the church of York in spiritualities and temporalities and granting him licence to transfer thereto. His will is, however, that — before Thomas receives possession or almost of the rule, administration and goods of the said church — he shall take the usual oath of fealty before the bishops of Durham and Salisbury, in accordance with the form the pope sends enclosed under his *bulla*; and the pope, by other letters, commands the said bishops that they (or one of them) shall receive the oath from Thomas in his name and that of the Roman church.

Conclusions to: (i) the chapter of the church of York, (ii) the clergy of the city and diocese, (iii) the people of the city and diocese (iv) the vassals of the said church, (v) the suffragans of the said church, (vi) Henry, king of England.

Romani pontificis quem pastor ille celestis . . . The conclusions begin: *(i), (iv) Hodie venerabilem fratrem nostrum Thomam* . . . *(ii), (iii), (v) Hodie et cetera. (vi) Gratie divine premium* . . .
. *F. de parma | Jo | Jo. xxv. xij÷xij÷xij÷xij÷xij÷xij÷ Electus Terracinen'*

[1] *Cf.* below, no. 547

547   18 January 1501   *Reg. Lat.* 1092, fo 256[r-v]

To the bishops of Durham and Salisbury, mandate. Since the pope has this day translated Thomas, lately bishop of London, from the church of London to that of York, appointing him archbishop, as is more fully contained in his letters drawn up in that regard,[1] he — wishing to spare archbishop Thomas, who lives in those parts, the labour and expense of being compelled on that account to come in person to the apostolic see — hereby commissions and commands that the above two (or one of them) shall receive from him in the name of the pope and the Roman church the usual oath of fealty in accordance with the form the pope sends enclosed under his *bulla* and shall cause the form of oath which archbishop Thomas takes to be sent, verbatim, to the pope, at once, by his own messenger, by his letters patent, marked with his seal.

Cum nos hodie . . .
. *L[2]. puccius | Jo. | Jo. xvj Electus Terracinen'*

[1] above, no. 546
[2] changed from a (?)'C'

548   18 January 1501   *Reg. Lat.* 1092, fos 256[v]-257[r]

To Thomas, bishop of London. Since the pope, on the advice of the cardinals, intends this day to translate Thomas from the church of London, over which he is understood to preside, to that of York, vacant *certo modo*, and to appoint him archbishop, he hereby absolves him from any [sentences] of excommunication etc. under which he may perchance lie, so far only as regards the taking effect of the said translation and appointment and each of the relevant letters. Notwithstanding etc.

Apostolice sedis consueta clementia ne dispositiones . . .
L· puccius | Jo· | Jo. xxv. Electus Terracinen'

549   10 July 1500   *Reg. Lat.* 1092, fos 336ʳ-338ʳ

To Edward Stowart, BDec, canon of Orkney, consistorial appointment as coadjutor and provision on the bishop's death etc. The pope — wishing to safeguard the church of Orkney, over which Andrew, bishop of Orkney, (who is in his eightieth year of age or thereabouts and is unable on account of his age and other infirmities to support by himself the burdens incumbent on him by reason of the church), presides — with bishop Andrew and the chapter's express consent, hereby appoints, establishes and deputes Edward (who also[1] is a MA and bishop Andrew's vicar general) coadjutor of the rule and administration of the church and its goods, for as long as bishop Andrew presides over it, in spiritualities and temporalities; and grants Edward faculty to do and execute everything which pertains to the office of coadjutor by right or custom (though he shall abstain from <alienating>[2] the church's immovable goods and precious movables). His will is, however, that Edward shall be bound to render account of what he has done by reason of the office, in accordance with Boniface VIII's constitution *Pastoralis*; and that he shall apply himself to the rule and administration of the church during his coadjutorship. And on bishop Andrew's death or resignation etc. or the church being vacant in any way, even at the apostolic see, the pope now as of then and then as of now makes provision of Edward to the church and appoints him bishop, committing to him the care and administration of the church in spiritualities and temporalities.

Conclusions to: (i) the chapter of the church of Orkney, (ii) the clergy of the city and diocese, (iii) the vassals of the said church, (iv) the people of the said city and diocese, (v) James, king of Scots, (vi) the archbishop of St Andrews

Romanus pontifex in potestatat(is)[3] plenitudine . . . The conclusions begin: (i), (ii), (iii), (iv) Hodie dilectum filium . . . (v) Gratie divine premium . . . (vi) Ad cumulum et cetera.
F de parma / F / F . Lᵗᵃ. x. x. x. x. x. x. Sanctor(is)

[1] *in decretis bacallarius et* deleted; initialled *F*
[2] marginal insertion by the enregistering scribe; initialled *F*.
[3] *sic; recte*: 'potestatis'?

550   10 July 1500   *Reg. Lat.* 1092, fo 338v

To Edward Stowart, BDec, canon of Orkney. Since the pope intends this day to appoint Edward (who also is a MA and, as he asserts, bishop Andrew's vicar general) coadjutor while bishop Andrew presides over the church of Orkney and on his death or resignation etc. thenceforth to make provision of Edward to the said church and appoint him bishop, he hereby absolves Edward from any sentences of excommunication, suspension and interdict and other ecclesiastical sentences, censures and pains under which he may perchance lie, so far only as the taking effect of the said appointments and provision and <each>[1] of the relevant letters. Notwithstanding etc.

Apostolice sedis consueta clementia ne dispositiones . . .
F de parma | F | F· xx. Sanctor(is)

[1] *singule* inserted by the enregistering scribe at end of line, not initialled

551   11 July 1500   *Reg. Lat.* 1092, fo 339[r-v]

To Edward Stowart, canon of Orkney. Since the pope has recently appointed Edward coadjutor for as long as bishop Andrew presides over the church of Orkney and on his death or resignation etc. made provision of Edward to the said church, as is more fully contained in his letters drawn up in that regard, [1] he hereby grants faculty to Edward — at his supplication — to receive (by reason of the said provision) consecration from any catholic bishop etc. [as above, no. 57, with appropriate changes, to '. . . marked with his seal'] and that the above shall not be to the prejudice of the archbishop of St Andrews, to whom the aforesaid church is understood to be subject by metropolitical law. With the form of oath appended.

Cum nos pridem . . .
F de parma | F | F. xxviij. Sanctor(is)

[1] above, no. 549

552   10 July 1500   *Reg. Lat.* 1092, fos 340[r]-341[v]

To Edward Stowart, BDec, canon of Orkney, whom the pope has this day appointed coadjutor for as long as bishop Andrew presides over the church of Orkney and on his death or resignation etc. provided to the said church, as is more fully contained in his letters drawn up in that regard.[1] The pope — *motu proprio* — with bishop Andrew's express consent, hereby reserves, grants and assigns to Edward (who is also a MA) all fruits etc. and any emoluments arising from goods within the limits of the archdeaconry of Shetland (*Zetlandie*), d. Orkney, and customarily received and levied by bishop Andrew and the bishop of Orkney for the time being, by reason of the said church, whose annual values do not exceed 40[2] pounds sterling, and also the collation, provision, presentation and all manner of disposition of every benefice, with and without cure, secular and regular of any order, located within the limits of the archdeaconry, pertaining to the collation, provision, presentation, election or any other disposition of bishop Andrew and the bishop of Orkney for the time being by reason of the said church, to the effect that Edward has nothing further to receive by reason of the coadjutorship; and the pope dispenses Edward to retain as before — even after he has, on the strength of the said provision and appointment, acquired corporal possession, or almost, of the rule and administration and goods of the said church or the greater part of them — the parish church of St Mary, Sande, d. Orkney, which he holds, whose annual value and that of the basilica or chapel of St Laurence, d. Orkney, canonically united etc. thereto, do not exceed 3 like pounds; decreeing that Edward cannot be molested over [?the receipt][3] of fruits and emoluments <and the collation of benefices aforesaid>[4] and that the church of St Mary is not made vacant on this account. Notwithstanding etc. With the proviso that St Mary's shall not, on this account, be defrauded of due services and the cure of souls therein shall not be neglected; but that its customary burdens shall be supported.

Executory — likewise *motu proprio* — to the bishops of Moray, Aberdeen and Brechin, or two or one of them, acting in person or by proxy.

Personam tuam nobis et apostolice sedi devotam tuis exigentibus meritis paterna benivolentia prosequentes illa tibi favorabiliter concedamus[5] . . . The executory begins: *Hodie dilecto filio . . .*
F de parma; A de sanctoseverino / F / F. Lxxxx . xxx. Sanctor(is)

[1] above, no. 549
[2] *quadraginta* has been changed (by erasure and overwriting) from a number which did not (apparently) begin 'qua-'; not initialled
[3] *super per promotionem* (reading uncertain); *recte:* 'super perceptione'?
[4] marginal insertion by the enregistering scribe
[5] *sic*

553   14 June 1499   *Reg. Lat.* 1092, fos 389ᵛ-391ᵛ

To Thomas, elect of Norwich. Consistorial provision of him — archdeacon of Essex (*Execie*) and canon of the church of London, DDec, counsellor and Master of Requests of Henry, king of England — to the church of Norwich, vacant by the death, outside the Roman curia, of the late bishop James, during whose rule the said church was specially reserved by the pope to his own disposition; and appointment of Thomas as bishop, committing to him the care and administration of the church of Norwich in spiritualities and temporalities.

Conclusions to: (i) the chapter of the church of Norwich, (ii) the clergy of the city and diocese, (iii) the people of the city and diocese, (iv) the vassals of the said church, (v) the archbishop of Canterbury, (vi) Henry, king of England.

Apostolatus officium quamquam insufficientibus meritis nobis ex alto commissum . . .
The conclusions begin: *(i) Hodie ecclesie vestre. . . (ii) Hodie ecclesie Norwicen. . . .*
(iii), (iv) Hodie et cetera. (v) Ad cumulum et cetera. (vi) Gratie divine et cetera.

S· de Castello / . L. / L. xx. x. x. x. x. x. x. Dulcius:-

554   15 June 1499   *Reg. Lat.* 1092, fo 392^{r-v}

To Thomas, elect of Norwich. Since the pope, on the advice of the cardinals, has recently made provision of Thomas to the church of Norwich, as is more fully contained in his letters drawn up in that regard,[1] he hereby grants faculty to Thomas — at his supplication — to receive consecration from any catholic bishop etc. [as above, no. 57, with appropriate changes, to '. . . marked with his seal;'] and that the above shall not be to the prejudice of the archbishop of Canterbury, to whom the aforesaid church is understood to be subject by metropolitical law. With the form of oath appended.

Cum nos pridem . . .
· *S· de Castello / L. / . L. xxviij Dulcius:-*

[1] above, no. 553

555   14 June 1499   *Reg. Lat.* 1092, fos 392^{v}-393^{r}

To Thomas Ian', DDec, archdeacon of Essex (*Execie*) in the church of London. Since the pope, on the advice of the cardinals, intends this day to make provision of Thomas to the church of Norwich, vacant *certo modo,* and to appoint him bishop, he hereby absolves him from any [sentences] of excommunication, etc. [as above, no. 53].

Apostolice sedis indefessa clementia ad ea libenter intendit . . .
S. de Castello / . L. / . L. xx. Dulcius:-

556   20 June 1497   *Reg. Lat.* 1093, fos 93^{r}-94^{v}

To John Lanton', layman, d. Coventry and Lichfield, dispensation and indult. A recent petition to the pope on John's part stated that, at another time, when he was intent upon secular affairs, he occasionally, in criminal causes, received accusations [and] reports (*insinuationes*), whether true or false, extending (*tenentes*) to punishments of bloodshed, and he was secretary (*dictator*) and scribe in those in which several persons of both sexes were dragged before secular judges, questioned, and tortured, and, as their faults and demerits demanded, condemned to death, and some, perchance, to mutilation of limbs, in accordance with the statutes, constitutions, and laws of the kingdom of England, and perchance with several of them the sentences have been executed;[1] that he thereby contracted irregularity; and that he wishes to become a cleric. At his supplication, the pope hereby dispenses John, (who, as he asserts, at another time, was presented for the parish church of Asburi,[2] which is of lay patronage, when it was vacant *certo modo*, by its patrons, to the local ordinary, albeit *de facto*, but institution and possession, by pretext of the presentation, never followed), to be promoted to all, even sacred, orders, and to minister therein, even in the ministry of the altar, and, if the above or another [parish church] is not held by him, to receive and retain any other benefice, with or without cure, even if a parish church, or its perpetual vicarage, or a chaplaincy, chantry, free chapel, hospital or annual service[3], usually assigned to secular clerics in title of a perpetual ecclesiastical benefice, or a canonry and prebend, dignity, *personatus*, administration or office in a cathedral, even metropolitan, or collegiate church, even if the dignity in question should be major *post pontificalem* in a cathedral, even metropolitan, church, or principal in a collegiate church, and even if the dignity etc. should be customarily elective and have cure of souls, if he obtains it otherwise canonically, to resign it, simply or for exchange, as often as he pleases, and in its place receive and retain another, similar or dissimilar, benefice, defined as above; and he indulges John, while attending a *studium generale*, not to be bound, by reason of any benefice canonically held by him, with cure or otherwise requiring sacred orders by foundation or custom, to have himself promoted to any of the higher (*ulterioribus*) sacred orders for a period of seven years (calculated from the time he acquired peaceful possession of the benefice), provided that within the first two years he be duly promoted to the subdiaconate, and not to be bound to reside in the benefice, nor to be liable to be compelled by anyone to do so against his will. With the proviso that the benefice shall not, meanwhile, be defrauded of due services and the cure of souls therein (if any) shall not be neglected, but that its customary burdens shall be supported.

Vite ac morum honestas . . .
. S. de. Castello / . L. / . L. Lx. Dulcius:-

[1] this, and other, passages have been altered

[2] diocese not stated

[3] *hospitalia vel annualia servitia; recte:* 'hospitale vel annuale servitium'

557   23 December 1496   *Reg. Lat.* 1093, fos 110^v-111^r

To John Andrew, BTheol, perpetual vicar of the parish church of St John the Baptist, Bradwynsour, d. Salisbury. Dispensation — at his supplication — to receive and retain for life, together with the perpetual vicarage of the above parish church, one, and having resigned it, any two other benefices, etc. [as above, no. 3].

Litterarum scientia, vite ac morum honestas . . .
N· Bregeon / B. / B. L. Bagarothus Proton'

558[1]   **30 May 1497**   *Reg. Lat.* 1093, fos 153^v-154^v

To the abbot of the monastery of Scone (*de Scona*), d. St Andrews, and the dean of the church of Aberdeen, mandate. Following the issue by Paul II of the letters, *Paulus et cetera. Ad perpetuam rei memoriam. Cum in omnibus judiciis . . . ,*[2] a recent petition to the pope on the part of George, bishop of Dunkeld, and Thomas Tourys,[3] layman, and Elisabeth, his wife, d. Dunkeld, stated that the bishop, with the consent of the chapter of Dunkeld, granted a lease of certain lands, called the lands of Nentoun [and] Crrigtone, (with all rights and appurtenances), in the barony of Oche'tuyle, county of Fife, said diocese, lawfully pertaining to his episcopal *mensa,* to Thomas and Elisabeth for themselves, their heirs and successors, and those to whom they (or one of them) may wish to grant a lease of the lands or put in their place, for nineteen years, for an annual payment or tribute of 10 pounds 13 shillings and 4 pence of the money current in Scotland, and three sheep customarily given and thirty-six capons, payable each year to the bishop, as is said to be more fully contained in certain public instruments drawn up in that regard. At the supplication of the bishop, Thomas and Elisabeth — asserting that the said grant of a lease is (and has been) to the evident utility of the *mensa* — to the pope to add the force of apostolic confirmation to the grant, as a firmer base for it, the pope — who does not have certain knowledge of the foregoing — hereby commands that the above two, proceeding jointly, having observed the form of Paul's letters and summoned the chapter and others concerned and after specifications of the lands, with their rights and appurtenances, have first been laid before them, if and when it has been lawfully established that the grant is (and has been) to the evident utility of the *mensa*, shall approve and confirm the grant and supply any defects. Notwithstanding etc.

Ex debito ministerii pastoralis . . .
A de Sancto severino / . L. / L. xxx Dulcius:-

[1] 'Georgius Episcopus Deukalden cum aliis' occurs in the index to the gathering on fo 142^r.
[2] printed in *Magnum Bullarium Romanum,* I (Luxemburg, 1742), p. 381
[3] or *Tonrys*

559   **29 May 1497**   *Reg. Lat.* 1093, fos 156^r-157^r

To Roger Lubbenh(a)m,[1] perpetual cantor of the chantry, called "Louergues channtre",[2] at the altar of B. Mary the Virgin in the parish church of All Hallows at the Hay (*Omnium Sanctorum ad fenum*), city of London, d. London. Dispensation and indult — at his supplication — to him (who, as he asserts, holds the above chantry, in whose foundation it is said to be expressly laid down that its holder is bound to reside in it continuously and take an oath to reside, as Roger has done) to receive and retain for life, together with the above chantry, one, and without it, any two other benefices, etc. [as above, no. 3, to '. . . retain them together for life, as above']; and, while attending a *studium generale* or residing in the Roman curia or any one of his benefices, not to be bound to reside in his other benefices, nor to be compelled by anyone to do so against his will. Notwithstanding etc. The pope derogates the aforesaid foundation, specially and expressly, for this once only; and relaxes the oath. With the proviso that the above chantry and other benefices shall not be defrauded of due services and the cure of souls (if any) in the incompatible benefices aforesaid shall not be neglected; but that the cure of the other benefices in which he shall not reside [shall be exercised] by suitable vicars to whom a fitting portion from the proceeds of the said benefices shall be given and that the customary burdens shall be supported.

Vite ac morum honestas . . .
· *S· de Castello* / *. L.* / *. L. Lxx. Dulcius:-*

1 MS: *Lubbenhm'*
2 also spelt 'chantre'

560   15 August 1497   *Reg. Lat.* 1093, fo 165[r-v]

To Thomas Hunden', MA, rector of the parish church of Holwele, d. Lincoln. Dispensation and indult — at his supplication — to receive and retain for life, together with the above parish church, any other, and having resigned them, any two other benefices, etc. [as above, no. 3, to '. . . retain them together for life, as above']; and for life, while attending a *studium generale* or residing in the Roman curia or any one of his benefices, not to be bound to reside in his other benefices, etc. [as above, no. 238].

Litterarum scientia, vite ac morum honestas . . .
f de parma / *. L.* / *. L. Lx. Dulcius:-*

561   5 August 1497   *Reg. Lat.* 1093, fo 166[r-v]

To Robert Dedworth, BDec, perpetual vicar of the parish church of St Michael the Archangel, Mylverton', d. Bath and Wells. Dispensation and indult — at his supplication — to receive and retain for life, together with the above church,[1] any other, and having resigned them, any two other benefices, etc. [as above, no. 3, to '. . . retain them together for life, as above']; and for life, while attending a *studium generale* or residing in the Roman curia or any one of his benefices, not to be bound to reside in his other benefices, nor to be liable to be compelled by anyone to do so against his will. Notwithstanding etc. With the proviso that the above church[1] and incompatible and other benefices in which he shall not reside shall not, on this account, be defrauded of due services and the cure of souls in the above church and (if any) the incompatible and other benefices aforesaid shall not be neglected; but that customary burdens of those benefices in which he shall not reside shall be supported.

Litterarum scientia, vite ac morum honestas . . .
. f de parma / . L. / . L. Lx. Dulcius:-

[1] *ecclesia; recte:* 'vicaria'

562   15 August 1497   *Reg. Lat.* 1093, fo 167[r-v]

To Christopher Plominer, rector of the parish church of Shyrbek, d. Lincoln. Dispensation — at his supplication — to receive and retain for life, together with the above parish church, another, and having resigned them, any two other benefices, etc. [as above, no. 3].

Vite ac morum honestas . . .
f. de parma / . L. / . L. L^{ta}. Dulcius:-

563   18 February 1497   *Reg. Lat.* 1093, fos 167[v]-168[r]

To Edmund Sterne, canon of the monastery of St Peter, Annscapus, OSA, d. Lincoln. Dispensation — at his supplication—to him, who, as he asserts, is expressly professed of the above order,[1] to receive and retain any benefice, with or without cure, usually held by secular clerics, etc. [as above, no. 32].

Religionis zelus, vite ac morum honestas . . .
S. de Castello / . L. / L. xxx. Dulcius:-

[1] This information comes from a notwithstanding clause.

564   11 August 1497   *Reg. Lat.* 1093, fos 168^v-169^r

To John Hayne, brother of New Hospital of B. Mary the Virgin without Bisshopsgate, OSA, d. London. Dispensation — at his supplication — to him, who, as he asserts, is expressly professed of the above order,[1] to receive and retain any benefice, with or without cure, usually held by secular clerics, etc. [as above, no. 32].

Religionis zelus, vite ac morum honestas . . .
f. de. parma / . L. / . L. xxx. Dulcius:-

[1] This information comes from a notwithstanding clause.

565   5 August 1497   *Reg. Lat.* 1093, fo 169^{r-v}

To Roger Sondyfordy, UIB, rector of one of two portions of the parish church of Fareby [also spelt *Farebi*], d. Lincoln, usually governed by two rectors. Dispensation — at his supplication — to receive [and retain for life],[1] together with the said rectory,[2] another, and having resigned them, any two other benefices, etc. [as above, no. 3, to '. . . Notwithstanding etc.']. With the proviso that the above portion and other incompatible benefices in question shall not, on this account, be defrauded of due services and the cure of souls in the portion and (if any) the other incompatible benefices shall not be neglected.

Litterarum scientia, vite ac morum honestas . . .
. F. de parma / . L. / . L. L^{ta}. Dulcius:-

[1] 'et etiam quoadvixeris retinere' occurs below, but is wanting here
[2] *dicta rectoria; recte:* 'dicta portio'

566   13 February 1497   *Reg. Lat.* 1093, fos 211^v-212^r

To Henry Grymston, rector of the parish church of All Saints, Goodmadanie, d. York. Dispensation — at his supplication — to receive and retain for life, together with the above parish church, another, and having resigned them, any two other benefices, etc. [as above, no. 3].

Vite ac morum honestas . . .
. S. de. Castello / . L. / . L. L^{ta}. Dulcius:-

567   7 March 1497   *Reg. Lat.* 1093, fo 212^{r-v}

To John Gerard, rector of the parish church of All Saints, Sestarffordi, d. Coventry
and Lichfield. Dispensation (and indult)[1] — at his supplication — to him, who is in
the order of the subdiaconate, to receive and retain for life, together with the above
parish church, any other, or without them, any two other benefices, etc. [as above,
no. 3, to '. . . retain them together for life, as above']; and, not to be bound, while
residing in the Roman curia or any one of his benefices or attending a *studium
generale*, by reason of the above church or any other benefices, with or without cure,
held by him at the time, requiring sacred orders, to be promoted to the orders of the
diaconate or priesthood for a period of up to seven years (calculated from the date of
the presents) and to reside in the other benefices, with and without cure, held by him
at the time, nor to be liable to be compelled by anyone to do so against his will.
Notwithstanding etc. With the proviso that the church of All Saints and other
benefices, even incompatible, shall not, on this account, be defrauded of due services
and the cure of souls in the above church and (if any) the other incompatible
benefices shall not be neglected; but that the customary burdens of those benefices in
which he shall not reside shall be supported.

Vite ac morum honestas . . .
. f de. parma / . L. / . L. Lxx. Dulcius:-

[1] *tibique pariter indulgemus* inserted in the margin by the enregistering scribe; initialled *. L.*

568   14 February 1497   *Reg. Lat.* 1093, fos 230^{v}-231^{v}

To Thomas Borgh, MA, rector of the parish church of Okfford, d. Exeter.
Dispensation — at his supplication — to receive and retain for life, together with the
above parish church, another, and having resigned them, any two other benefices,
etc. [as above, no. 3].

Litterarum scientia, vite ac morum honestas . . .
. P. de Castello. / . L. / L. L^{ta}. Dulcius:-

569   16 December 1497[1]   *Reg. Lat.* 1093, fo 296^{r-v}

To John Weysi *alias* Harmon, LLD, rector of the parish church of Cliston' Reynys,
d. Lincoln. Dispensation — at his supplication — to receive and retain for life,
together with the above parish church, one, and without it, any two other benefices,
etc. [as above, no. 3].[2]

Litterarum scientia, vite ac morum honestas . . .
A de Sanctoseverino[3] */ . L. / . L. L^{ta} . Dulcius:-*

[1] *decimo septimo kalendas Januarii anno sexto* is written in somewhat heavier ink and larger letters than the rest of the dating clause: entered later? *cf.* note 3, below, and next entry

[2] save that 'or a combination' does not occur; *cf.* next entry

[3] *S de Castello*, deleted, above it; the two names and the end of the dating clause were written in different inks: entered at various times?

570   16 December 1497[1]   *Reg. Lat.* 1093, fos 296^v-297^v

To Andrew Roode, rector of the parish church of Wischaston, d. Coventry and Lichfield. Dispensation — at his supplication — to receive and retain for life, together with the above parish church, one, and without it, any two other benefices, etc. [as above, no. 3].[2]

Vite ac morum honestas . . .
A de Sanctoseverino[3] */ . L. / . L. L^{ta} . Dulcius:-*

[1] *decimo septimo kalendas Januarii anno sexto* is written in somewhat heavier ink and larger letters than rest of dating clause: entered later? *cf.* note 3 below and previous entry

[2] save that 'or a combination' does not occur; *cf.* previous entry

[3] *S de Castello* changed (by overwriting) to *A de Sanctoseverino* and deleted above it; the ink of the abbreviators' names is much heavier than that of the letter: entered later? *Cf.* note 1, above, and previous entry

571   20 October 1497   *Reg. Lat.* 1093, fos 297^v-298^r

To Nicholas Done, canon of the monastery of St Peter, Donstaple, OSA, d. Lincoln. Dispensation — at his supplication — to him, who, as he asserts, is expressly professed of the above order,[1] to receive and retain any benefice, with or without cure, usually held by secular clerics, etc. [as above, no. 32, to '. . . Notwithstanding etc.']. Given at Ostia.

Religionis zelus, vite ac morum honestas . . .
S. de Castello / . L. / L. xxx. Dulcius:-

[1] This information comes from a notwithstanding clause.

572   22 April 1497   *Reg. Lat.* 1093, fos 316[r]-317[r]

To Patrick Blacader, cleric of Glasgow, dispensation and indult. The pope (who, some time ago, decreed and declared that <provisions>,[1] grants or mandates of provision to canonries and prebends of cathedral churches to persons who have [not][2] completed their fourteenth year of age shall have no force except by consent of the apostolic see) hereby dispenses and indulges Patrick, who, as he asserts, is of noble birth by both parents [and] in his eighth year — at his supplication — to receive and retain any benefice, even if a canonry and prebend, dignity, *personatus*, administration or office in a cathedral, even metropolitan, or collegiate, church — provided that such dignity be not major *post pontificalem* in a cathedral, even metropolitan, church, or principal in a collegiate church — if he obtains it otherwise canonically, to resign it, simply or for exchange, when he pleases, and in its place receive and retain another, similar or dissimilar, benefice; and — until he has reached his fourteenth year — to have the said benefice served <in things divine>[3] by a suitable cleric. Notwithstanding the above defect of age etc. With the proviso that the said benefice shall not, on this account, be defrauded of due services; but that its customary burdens shall be supported.

Nobilitas generis ac laudabilia tue puerilis etatis . . .
Jo ortega. / . L. / . L. xxx. Dulcius:-

[1] marginal insertion by the enregistering scribe, not initialled
[2] 'non' wanting
[3] marginal insertion by the enregistering scribe, not initialled

573   26 February 1498   *Reg. Lat.* 1093, fos 372[r]-374[r]

To the abbot of the monastery *de Choro Benedicti* [Midleton], d. Cloyne, mandate in favour of John Yhacgeryn, canon of the monastery of Molana (*de Insula Sancti Melansyd*), OSA, d. Lismore. A petition[1] to the pope on John's part stated that although he had had himself provided by apostolic authority to the said monastery, vacant *certo modo*, had been appointed abbot and had had the care, rule and administration of the monastery commended to him, nevertheless Donat Mnacarnara[2] and Edmund Fisgybon, who bear themselves as clerics, ds. Lismore and Cloyne, falsely asserting that the monastery rightfully belonged to them, sued John over this before divers judges in those parts by apostolic delegation, praying that the monastery be declared to belong rightfully to one of them, perpetual silence be imposed on John over the rule and administration and he be removed from them; and these judges proceeding wrongly in the cases promulgated unjust sentences successively in favour of Donat and Edmund and against John, from which sentences John appealed to the pope and the apostolic see. Moreover, as the same petition added, John, detained by just impediment, did not prosecute these appeals or receive benediction within the lawful times and also because — in a certain conflict undertaken by him in defence of the monastery and in which he assisted, several murders and mutilations were perpetrated — although he did not kill or mutilate anyone with his own hands, nevertheless he fears that he has incurred irregularity. At John's supplication, the pope — not having certain knowledge [of the foregoing] — hereby commands the above abbot to dispense John for irregularity, if he contracted it by occasion of the foregoing, rehabilitate him on account of all disability and infamy arising therefrom, and, having summoned Donat, Edmund and others concerned and after lawful impediment has been demonstrated to him, hear, decide and duly determine the causes of the appeals, causing what he decrees [to be observed] by ecclesiastical censure etc.; and, moreover, [compel] witnesses etc.; and, if, after the case has been brought before the abbot, through the outcome of the suit it is established by him that neither John, Donat nor Edmund has the right of it in or to the rule and administration of the monastery and he finds John to be suitable — concerning which the pope burdens the abbot's conscience — to make provision of John to the monastery, whose annual value does not exceed 40 marks sterling, (vacant howsoever etc.), and appoint him abbot, committing to him the care, rule and administration of the monastery in spiritualities and temporalities and causing obedience and reverence to be given him by the convent and customary services and rights by the vassals and other subjects of the monastery and grant that he may use the benediction imparted to him. [Curbing] gainsayers by ecclesiastical censure etc. Notwithstanding etc. The pope's will is, however, that before the abbot proceeds to the execution of the aforesaid in any way John is bound to cede the rule and administration of the monastery into his hands genuinely and completely.

Apostolice sedis indefessa clementia recurrentibus ad eam cum humilitate . . .
. S. de. Castello / . B. / . B. xxx. Bagarothus Proton'

[1] 'nuper' wanting?

[2] the second 'a' doubtful

574   7 March 1498   *Reg. Lat.* 1093, fos 387[r]-391[v]

To the dean of the church of Ossory, mandate in favour of John Omulvardayn *alias* Abrohe, cleric, d. Cashel (who, as he asserts, is in his twenty-third year of age or thereabouts and notwithstanding a defect of birth as the son of an unmarried man and an unmarried woman has been marked with clerical character, otherwise however duly). The pope has learned that the monastery of the Holy Cross, An'ficampo *alias* Cilleule, OCist, d. [Cashel][1] and the perpetual vicarage of the parish church of St Nicholas, Casleandriohc',[2] d. Ossory, are vacant at present and have been for so long that by canonical sanctions the provision of the monastery and by the Lateran statutes the collation of the vicarage have lawfully devolved on the apostolic see, although Donat Omulvardayn *alias* Obrohe, who bears himself as a monk of the monastery, by pretext of a certain election of himself by the convent of this monastery and confirmation by the abbot of the monastery of Jerpoint (*de Geroponte*), said order, d. Ossory (to which by special apostolic privilege, which has not yet been derogated, the monastery of the Holy Cross is understood to be immediately subject) made in that regard *de facto*, has detained the monastery, for a certain time, but short of a two-year period, and William Clynton,[3] who bears himself as a priest of d. Ossory, the vicarage, [each] without any title or support of law, temerariously and *de facto*, for a certain time, as they still do; and that the above John wishes to enter the monastery of the Holy Cross, under the regular habit. Supplication has been made on the part of John — who, as he asserts, at another time when he was studying letters in a certain *studium*, had stolen a certain amount of money not exceeding three or four *carlini* in total from an associate of his, although he swore — even on a certain image — that he had not taken it at all, nevertheless he afterwards restored it to his associate, incurring perjury — to the pope to absolve him from perjury and excess and rehabilitate him on account of all disability and infamy arising therefrom; and to unite etc. the vicarage to the monastery of the Holy Cross (to which this day the pope has granted that the rectory of the parish church of St Kieran (*Sancti Cherani*), Glascro,[4] d. Ossory, whose annual value does not exceed 8 marks sterling, vacant *certo modo*, be united etc.) while John presides over its rule and administration. Wishing to encourage John and to make provision of a suitable person to the monastery to rule and direct it, the pope not having certain knowledge of John's merits and suitability — at this supplication — hereby commands the above dean to absolve John, if he so requests, from the perjury and excess aforesaid, for this once only, in the customary form of the church, having enjoined a salutary penance on him etc.; and also to rehabilitate him on account of all disability and infamy arising therefrom; and, in that event, receive John — if he is suitable and there is no canonical obstacle — as a monk in the monastery and bestow the regular habit on him in accordance with the custom of the monastery and cause him to be given charitable treatment therein; and also, if John spontaneously wishes to make the usual regular profession made by the monks, receive and admit it; and, thereafter, inform himself as to John's merits etc. and if he finds John to be capable and suitable for the rule and administration of the monastery — concerning which the pope burdens the dean's conscience — and if, having summoned respectively Donat and William and other interested parties as regards the union, the monastery, whose annual value does not exceed 20, and the vicarage, 8, like marks, to be vacant (howsoever etc.), and the foregoing to be true, (for whatever reason the provision of the monastery pertains specially or generally to the apostolic see and the vicarage be specially reserved, etc.), make provision of John to the said monastery and appoint him abbot, committing to him the care, rule and administration of the monastery in spiritualities and temporalities and causing obedience and reverence to be given him by the convent and customary services and rights by the vassals and other subjects of the monastery; and unite etc. the vicarage, with all rights and appurtenances, to the monastery, for as long as John presides over it, to the effect that he may, on his own authority, in person or by proxy, having first removed Donat from the monastery and William from the vicarage and any other unlawful detainers, take corporal possession of the vicarage, and convert its fruits etc. to his own uses and those of the vicarage and the monastery without licence of the local diocesan or of anyone else. [Curbing] gainsayers by ecclesiastical censure etc. Notwithstanding etc. Also the pope grants that John may, if provided to the said monastery by virtue of the presents, receive benediction from any catholic bishop of his choice in communion with the apostolic see and that the bishop concerned may [impart][5] it to him. Also the pope dispenses John, if provided to the monastery and appointed abbot, to preside over it and perform [and] exercise its care etc., notwithstanding the said defects [of age and birth] etc. With the proviso that the monastery and the vicarage, on account of this union etc., shall not, on this account, be defrauded of due services and the cure of souls in the vicarage shall not be neglected; but that its customary burdens and those of the convent shall be supported. The pope's will is, however, that on John's death or resignation etc. of the monastery the union etc. shall be dissolved and the vicarage shall revert to its original condition and be deemed vacant automatically.

Apostolice sedis indefessa clementia recurrentibus ad eam cum humilitate . . .
. S. de Castello / . L. / . L. xxxv. Dulcius:-

[1] supplied by the editor; MS has — directly after the name of the parish church — . . . *et Oxorien. dioc(esium) vacent*

[2] uncertain reading; the '-hc'' blotched

[3] *Cf. CPL,* XV, no. 673, mandate in favour of William Elinton (or Elmton).

[4] *Cf.* (as in previous note) *CPL,* XV. no. 673: rectory of St Kieran, Glayferon (tentatively identified in the index as ?Glashare); *cf.* also *Annates, Ossory* no. 27, p. 7: Glascro (identified in the notes beneath as Clashacrow).

[5] *impedire; recte:* 'impendere'; other such slips occur throughout the entry, but are not specially noticed here

---

575   3 March 1498   *Reg. Lat.* 1093, fos 391[V]-394[V]

To the abbot of the monastery of Jerpoint (*de Geroponte*), d. Ossory, and Robert Edegayn, canon of the church of Cashel, and Nicholas White, canon of the church of Waterford, mandate in favour of Edmund Conmerforth, dean of the church of Ossory. The pope has learned that the priorship of the monastery, called a house or hospital, usually governed by a prior, of St John the Evangelist, near Kilkenny (*iuxta Kylherna(m)*[1]), OSA, and the perpetual vicarage of the parish church of B. Mary, Calayn *alias* Kylbride, d. Ossory, are vacant *certo modo* at present and have been vacant for so long that by the Lateran statutes their collation has lawfully devolved on the apostolic see, although John Cantuel has detained the priorship, and Dermot Oclere, the vicarage — bearing themselves as priests — with no title and no support of law, but of their own temerity and *de facto*, for a certain time, as they do. Wishing to assist Edmund, who, as he asserts, holds the deanery of the church of Ossory, which is a principal dignity, to support himself more conveniently, the pope hereby commands that the above three (or two or one of them), if, having summoned John and Dermot and others concerned, they find the vicarage, whose annual value does not exceed 20, and the priorship, which is conventual and whose annual value does not exceed 100, marks sterling, to be vacant (howsoever etc.), shall collate the vicarage and commend the priorship, (even if specially reserved etc.), to Edmund, with all rights and appurtenances, to be held, ruled and governed by him for life, even together with the deanery and every other benefice — secular, without cure, which he holds as above, and secular, with and without cure, and regular of the aforesaid and any other order which he shall hold (even by any apostolic concessions and dispensations) in the future — and with annual pensions on any ecclesiastical fruits etc. which he receives and shall receive; (he may — due and customary burdens of the priorship having been supported — make disposition of the rest of its fruits etc. just as those holding it *in titulum* could and ought to do, alienation of immovable goods and precious movables being however forbidden); inducting him etc. having removed John from the priorship and Dermot from the vicarage and any other unlawful detainers and causing Edmund (or his proctor) to be admitted to the priorship and vicarage and their fruits etc., rights and obventions to be delivered to him. [Curbing] gainsayers by the pope's authority etc. Notwithstanding etc. Also the pope dispenses Edmund to receive and retain for life, together with the said vicarage, if [conferred on him] by virtue of the presents, the deanery, [or] with either of them, one, and without them, any two other benefices, with cure or otherwise mutually incompatible, even if parish churches or their perpetual vicarages, or dignities, etc. [as above, no. 3, to '. . . retain them together for life as above']; notwithstanding etc. With the proviso that the deanery, vicarage and other incompatible benefices and also the priorship shall not, on this account, be defrauded of due services and the cure of souls in the vicarage and (if any) the deanery and other incompatible benefices and also the priorship shall not be neglected; but that the aforesaid burdens of the priorship shall be supported.

Vite ac morum honestas . . .
. Jo. ortega. | L. | . L. xxxv. [2] *Dulcius:-*

[1] MS: *Kylherna'*
[2] wants expedition date?

576   19 February 1498   *Reg. Lat.* 1093, fos 403[v]-406[v]

To the dean of the church of Ossory and the treasurer and Gerald Macduyll, canon, of the church of Leighlin, mandate in favour of William . . . [1] (who, as he asserts, notwithstanding a defect of birth as the son of a priest and an unmarried woman, has been marked with clerical character, otherwise however duly). The pope has learned that the perpetual vicarages of the parish churches of Balleaculleaym, Thamohoc *alias* Baleuatibenda and Rayasbuyc,[2] d. Leighlin, are vacant at present and have been for so long that by the Lateran statutes their collation has lawfully devolved on the apostolic see, although John Ochellay [has detained] the first vicarage, Donat Olamyr, the second, and Rory[3] Odulayud,[4] the third — [bearing themselves] as priests of the said diocese — [without any title or support of law, temerariously and *de facto*, for a certain time, as they still do. At a recent petition on William's part] [to the pope to collate and assign the first and second vicarages to William and][5] to unite etc. the third vicarage to the first, for William's lifetime, the pope — not having certain knowledge of the foregoing — hereby commands that the above three (or two or one of them), if, having summoned respectively John, Donat and Rory and others concerned, they find the first vicarage, whose annual value does not exceed 6, and the second, 9, and the third, 4, marks sterling, to be vacant (howsoever etc.) and having summoned those interested regarding the union, the foregoing to be true, shall, (even if the vicarages be specially reserved etc.), collate and assign the first and second vicarages, with all [their rights and appurtenances][6], to William, and unite etc. the third vicarage to the first, for William's lifetime, inducting him etc. having removed John from the first, Donat from the second and Rory from the third and any other unlawful detainers, and causing William (or his proctor) to be admitted to the first and second vicarages, and their fruits etc., rights and obventions and those of the vicarage to be annexed to the first to be delivered to him. [Curbing] gainsayers by the pope's authority etc. Notwithstanding etc. And the pope dispenses William to receive and retain together for life the first and second vicarages, if conferred on him by virtue of the presents; and not to be bound, while attending a *studium generale*, to have himself promoted by reason of the first and second vicarages and of any other benefices acquired at the time having cure of souls or requiring sacred orders by law, statute [or] foundation, to have himself promoted to any of the higher sacred orders for a seven-year period, calculated from the date of the presents, provided that within the first three years he has himself promoted to the subdiaconate, nor to be liable to be compelled by anyone to do so against his will; notwithstanding the defect of birth etc. With the proviso that the third vicarage shall not, on account of this union etc., and also the first and second vicarages and other benefices aforesaid, on this account, be defrauded of due services and the cure of souls therein shall not be neglected, but that the aforesaid burdens[7] of the third vicarage shall be supported; and that on William's death or resignation etc. of the first vicarage the union etc. shall be dissolved and the third vicarage shall revert to its original condition and be deemed vacant automatically.

Decet Romanum pontificis[8] votis illis gratum prestare assensum . . .
. S. de castello / . B. / B. xxxv. Bagarothus Proton'

[1] lacuna which may be supplied conjecturally as follows: 'se gerunt absque aliquo titulo sive iuris adminiculo sibi desuper suffragante immo temere et de facto per certum tempus detinuerint prout adhuc detinent indebite occupatas. Et sicut exhibita nobis nuper pro parte dilecti filii Willelmi N' (or suchlike) at least; the tenor of which is supplied below by the editor within brackets

[2] *(?)Rayasb* deleted; not initialled

[3] *Roricus;* *(?)Rodericus* deleted before second occurrence, not initialled

4 after the 'd', a letter (?'a') now blotched appears to be deleted

5 'nobis fuit humiliter supplicatum' wanting at least; the text below indicates that reference to the collation of the first and second vicarages would be appropriate too

6 supplied by the editor

7 *onera antedicta;* however MS contains no previous mention of this vicarage having burdens

8 *sic; recte:* 'pontificem'

577   4 May 1500   *Reg. Lat.* 1094, fos 19ᵛ-21ᵛ

Commend, to Ludovicus, bishop of Maurienne, of the monastery of B. Mary, Ambronay (*Ambrumaci*), OSB, d. Lyon, vacant at the apostolic see.

He is to take the usual oath of fealty, to the pope and the Roman church, before the bishops of Geneva and Annaghdown, and by other letters the pope is commanding them (or one of them) to receive it. Entry otherwise of no interest to the Calendar.

Conclusions to: (i) the convent; (ii) vassals; (iii) Ludovicus, king of the Franks; (iv) archbishop of Lyon.

Romani pontificis providentia circumspecta . . . The conclusions begin: *(i) Hodie monasterium vestrum . . .; (ii) (iii) (iv) Hodie et cetera.*
· *N· Bregeon /. V· / · V· L· viij. viij. viij. viij De Phano:-*

578   4 May 1500   *Reg. Lat.* 1094, fos 21ᵛ-22ʳ

Mandate to the bishops of Geneva and Annaghdown informing them that the pope has this day commended the monastery of B. Mary, Ambronay (*Ambrumaci*), OSB, d. Lyon, to Ludovicus, bishop of Maurienne, and commanding them (or one of them) to receive his oath of fealty. Entry otherwise of no interest to the Calendar.

Cum nos hodie . . .
· *N· Bregeon / · V· / V· xij· De Phano:*

579   21 August 1500   *Reg. Lat.* 1094, fos 65ʳ-66ᵛ

To Francis of Cordova (*de Corduba*), elect of Glendalough. Consistorial provision of him — professor OP, DTheol, in priest's orders — to the church of Glendalough, vacant by the death, outside the Roman curia, of the late bishop Ivo, during whose rule the said church was specially reserved by the pope to his own disposition; and appointment of Francis as bishop, committing to him the care and administration of the church in spiritualities and temporalities.

Conclusions to: (i) the chapter of the church of Glendalough, (ii) the clergy of the city and diocese,[1] (iii) the vassals of the said church, (iv) the people of the city and diocese, (v) the archbishop of Dublin.[2]

Apostolatus officium meritis quamquam insufficientibus nobis ex alto commissum . . .
The conclusions begin: *(i) Hodie ecclesie vestre . . . (ii), (iii), (iv) Hodie et cetera. (v) Ad cumulum . . .*
F. de parma / O· / O · xx x x x x x Marianen.

[1] The conclusions to the clergy, vassals and people are each enregistered much abridged.

[2] Most unusually, a conclusion to the king of England was enregistered elsewhere (below, no. 776).

580   21 August 1500   *Reg. Lat.* 1094, fos 66^v-67^r

To Francis of Cordova (*de Corduba*), DTheol, professor OP. Since the pope, on the advice of the cardinals, intends this day to make provision of Francis to the church of Glendalough, vacant *certo modo*, and appoint him bishop, he hereby absolves him from any sentences of excommunication, etc. [as above, no. 53].

Apostolice sedis indefessa clementia ad ea libenter intendit . . .
[-]¹ / O· / O· xx Marianen.

[1] no abbreviator's name

581   8 January 1500   *Reg. Lat.* 1094, fos 117^v-119^v

To Henry, bishop of Salisbury. Consistorial translation, though absent [from the Roman curia], from the church of Bangor to that of Salisbury, vacant by the death, outside the Roman curia, of the late bishop John, during whose rule the church of Salisbury was specially reserved by the pope to his own disposition. The pope hereby appoints Henry bishop, committing to him the care and administration of the church of Salisbury in spiritualities and temporalities and granting him licence to transfer thereto. His will is, however, that — before Henry involves himself in the rule and administration of the said church — he shall take the usual oath of fealty before the bishops of Lincoln and Worcester in accordance with the form the pope sends enclosed under his *bulla*; and the pope by other letters of his commands the

said bishops that they (or one of them) shall receive the oath from Henry in his name
and that of the Roman church.

Conclusions to: (i) the chapter of the church of Salisbury, (ii) the clergy of the
city and diocese, (iii) the people of the city and diocese, (iv) the vassals of the said
church, (v) the archbishop of Canterbury, (vi) Henry, king of England.[1]

Quam sit onusta dispendiis . . . The conclusions begin: *(i) Hodie venerabilem fratrem
nostrum . . . (ii), (iii), (iv) Hodie et cetera. (v) Ad cumulum . . . (vi) Gratie et cetera.
· L· Puccius / . V.* [2] */ · V· · xxiiij· xij· xij· xij· xij· xij· xij· De Phano:-*

[1] The conclusion to Henry VII is PRO Papal Bulls SC. 7/37(6).

[2] a swung dash below the point to the left

582   8 January 1500   *Reg. Lat.* 1094, fo 120[r]

To the bishops of Lincoln and Worcester, mandate. Since the pope has this day
translated bishop Henry from the church of Bangor to that of Salisbury, as is more
fully contained in his letters drawn up in that regard,[1] he — wishing to spare Henry,
who lives in those parts, the labour and expense of being compelled on that account
to come in person to the apostolic see — hereby commissions and commands that
the above two (or one of them) shall receive from him in the name of the pope and
the Roman church the usual oath of fealty etc. [as above, no. 547, with appropriate
changes].

Cum nos hodie . . .
· L· Puccius / · V· / · V· xvj· De Phano:

[1] above, no. 581

583   8 January 1500   *Reg. Lat.* 1094, fo 120[v]

To Henry, bishop of Bangor. Since the pope, on the advice of the cardinals, intends
this day to translate Henry from the church of Bangor, over which he is understood
to preside, to that of Salisbury, vacant *certo modo,* and to appoint him bishop, he
hereby absolves him from any sentences of excommunication, suspension and
interdict and other ecclesiastical censures, sentences and pains under which he may
perchance lie, so far only as regards the taking effect of the said translation and
appointment and each of the relevant letters. Notwithstanding etc.

Romani pontificis circumspecta benignitas ad ea libenter intendit . . .
· L· Puccius / · V· [1] */ V· xxiiij De Phano:*

[1] a mark above

584   3 June 1500   *Reg. Lat.* 1094, fos 127ᵛ-130ʳ

To George, abbot of the monastery of Holyrood (*Sancte Crucis*), OSA, d. St
Andrews. Consistorial provision of him — at the time abbot of the monastery of
Donfermilin, OSB, said diocese — to Holyrood. Following the pope's reservation of
provisions of all churches and monasteries vacated then and in the future at the
apostolic see to his own disposition, the monastery of Holyrood was bereft of the
rule of an abbot at the apostolic see, because Robert, recently abbot, spontaneously
and freely ceded its rule and administration, over which he was then presiding, into
the pope's hands, and the pope admitted the cession; and this day James, archbishop
of St Andrews — to whom at another time the pope (on the advice of the cardinals)
by other letters of his, *sub certis modo et forma*, commended the monastery when
vacant by Robert's death or resignation etc. — spontaneously and freely ceded the
commend into the pope's hands, and the pope admitted the cession. The pope (on the
advice of the cardinals) hereby makes provision of George to the monastery of
Holyrood, reserved as above, and appoints him abbot, committing to him the care,
rule and administration of the monastery in spiritualities and temporalities. His will
is, however, that before George involves himself in any way in the rule and
administration of the monastery of Holyrood he shall take the <usual>¹ oath of
fealty before the bishops of Aberdeen and Dunblane in accordance with the form
which the pope sends enclosed under his *bulla* and by other letters of his commands
them (or one of them) to receive the oath in the name of the pope and the Roman
church; and that — as soon as he has peacefully acquired possession of the rule and
administration and the goods of the monastery of Holyrood, or the greater part of
them, or almost, by virtue of the presents — he shall receive and wear the habit worn
in the monastery of Holyrood and conform to its regular institutes.
    Conclusions to: (i) the convent of the monastery of Holyrood, (ii) the vassals of
the said monastery, (iii) the archbishop of St Andrews, (iv) James, king of Scots.

Summi dispositione rectoris ad regimen universalis . . . The conclusions begin: *(i)*
Hodie monasterio vestro . . . *(ii), (iii), (iv) Hodie et cetera.*
N . Bregeon / V² / · V· xvj viij · viij · viij · viij · De Phano

¹ *solitum* inserted in margin by enregistering scribe, initialled · V·
² a swung dash to the left

585   3 June 1500   *Reg. Lat.* 1094, fo 130ʳ⁻ᵛ

Motu proprio decree that the monastery of Donfermilyn, OSB,¹ d. St Andrews —
over which George, abbot of the monastery of Holyrood (*Sancte Crucis*), OSA, said
diocese, was presiding at the time of the pope's provision and appointment of him to
Holyrood — be vacant at the apostolic see by [this] single appointment [to
Holyrood] of George only. Notwithstanding the constitutions etc. of the monastery

of Donfermilyn and the Benedictine order etc.

Ad futuram rei memoriam. Romanus pontifex ad quem ecclesiarum et monasteriorum omnium plenaria dispositio pertinere dinoscitur . . .
Bregeon[2] / *V* / *V · xvj*[3] · *De Phano:*

[1] *Augustini*, deleted but not initialled, occurs directly before *Benedicti*

[2] *sic;* no initial; *cf.* nos. 586, 587 and 589

[3] the 'j' reworked

---

586   3 June 1500   *Reg. Lat.* 1094, fos 130[v]-131[r]

To George, abbot of the monastery of Donfermilyn, OSB, d. St Andrews. Since the pope, on the advice of the cardinals, intends this day to make provision of George to the monastery of Holyrood (*Sancte Crucis*), OSA, d. St Andrews, bereft of the rule of an abbot *certo modo*, and appoint him abbot, he hereby absolves him from any [sentences] of excommunication etc. [as above, no. 53].

Romani pontificis gratiosa benignitas . . .
Bregeon[1] / *V*[2] / *V xvj · De Phano ·*

[1] *sic;* no initial; *cf.* nos. 585, 587 and 589
[2] a swung dash to the left

---

587   3 June 1500   *Reg. Lat.* 1094, fo 131[r-v]

To the bishops of Aberdeen and Dunblane,[1] mandate. Since the pope has this day made provision of George to the monastery of Holyrood (*Sancte Crucis*), d. St Andrews, bereft of the rule of an abbot *certo modo*, as is more fully contained in his letters drawn up in that regard,[2] he — wishing to spare George, who lives in those parts, the labour and expense of being compelled on that account to come in person to the apostolic see — hereby commands that the above two (or one of them) shall receive from him in the name of the pope and the Roman church the usual oath of fealty etc. [as above, no. 547, with appropriate changes].

Cum nos hodie . . .
Bregeon[3] / · *V*· / *V xij De Phano:*

[1] MS: *Sumblanen.*
[2] above, no. 584
[3] *sic;* no initial; *cf.* nos. 585, 586 and 589

588   3 June 1500   *Reg. Lat.* 1094, fos 131^V-133^V

To James, archbishop of St Andrews. Following the pope's reservation of provisions of all churches and monasteries vacated then or in the future at the apostolic see to his own disposition, the pope decreed by other letters of his the monastery of Donfermilyn, OSB, d. St Andrews, to be vacant by the provision and appointment made by him this day of George, abbot of the monastery of Holyrood (*Sancte Crucis*), OSA, said diocese, (who was presiding over Donfermilyn at the time of his provision and appointment to Holyrood), only, as is more fully contained in those letters. [1] Wishing to provide the monastery of Donfermilyn — left vacant at the apostolic see and reserved as above — with a capable and suitable governor to rule and direct it as well as to assist James to keep up his position in accordance with pontifical dignity, the pope, on the advice of the cardinals, hereby commends the monastery of Donfermilyn, thus vacant, with all rights and appurtenances, to James, to be held, ruled and governed by him for life, even together with the church of St Andrews, over which he presides, for as long as he does so, and any other monasteries, priories, *prepositure*, dignities and offices and other ecclesiastical benefices, with and without cure, secular and regular of any order, which he holds and shall hold in the future *in titulum, commendam vel administrationem*, and with annual pensions on any ecclesiastical fruits etc. which he receives and shall receive in the future, committing the care, rule and administration of the monastery to him in spiritualities and temporalities. The pope's will is, however, that divine worship and the usual number of monks and ministers in the monastery of Donfermilyn shall not, on account of this commend, be diminished, but that the customary burdens of the monastery and its convent shall be supported; and that James may — the burdens having been supported — make disposition of the rest of the fruits etc. of the monastery, just as its abbots could and ought to do, alienation of immovable goods and precious movables being however forbidden; and that before James involves himself in any way in the rule and administration of the monastery of Donfermilyn he shall take the usual oath of fealty before the bishops of Aberdeen and Ross (or one of them) in accordance with the form which the pope sends enclosed under his *bulla*. And the pope has commanded by other letters of his[2] that they (or one of them) shall receive the oath in [the name] of the pope and the Roman church; and hereby commands archbishop James to rule and exercise (personally or by proxy) this care etc. solicitously.

Conclusions to: (i) the convent of the monastery of Donfermilyn, (ii) the vassals of the said monastery, (iii) James, king of Scots.

Romani pontificis providentia circumspecta . . . The conclusions begin: *(i) Hodie monasterium vestrum . . . (ii), (iii) Hodie et cetera.*
N· Bregeon / . V· / V· L· viij· viij· viij De Phano:

[1] above, no. 585
[2] below, no. 590

589   3 June 1500   *Reg. Lat.* 1094, fo 133[v]

To James, archbishop of St Andrews. Since the pope intends this day to commend the monastery of Donfermilyn,[1] OSB, d. St Andrews, at present bereft of the rule of an abbot *certo modo*, to James to be held, ruled and governed by him for life, he hereby absolves him from any [sentences] of excommunication etc. under which he may perchance lie, so far only as regards the taking effect of the said commend and each of the relevant letters. Notwithstanding etc.

Apostolice sedis consueta clementia ad ea libenter intendit . . .
Bregeon[2] / - V· / V xvj · De Phano·

[1] *Fon* occurs, deleted but not initialled, directly prior to *Donfermilyn*
[2] *sic;* no initial; *cf.* above, nos. 585-587

590   3 June 1500   *Reg. Lat.* 1094, fo 134[r]

To the bishops of Aberdeen and Ross, mandate. Since the pope has this day commended the monastery of Donfermilyn, OSB, d. St Andrews, then vacant *certo modo*, to James, archbishop of St Andrews, to be held, ruled and governed by him for life, as is more fully contained in his letters drawn up in that regard,[1] he — wishing to spare the archbishop, who lives in those parts, the labour and expense of being compelled on that account to come in person to the apostolic see — hereby commands that the above two (or one of them) shall receive from him in the name of the pope and the Roman church the usual oath of fealty etc. [as above, no. 547, with appropriate changes].

Cum nos hodie . . .
· N· Bregeon / . V· / V. xij· De Phano:

[1] above, no. 588

591   17 April 1499   *Reg. Lat.* 1094, fos 142[r]-143[r]

To George, bishop of Elphin. Consistorial translation, though absent [from the Roman curia], from the church of Dromore to that of Elphin, vacant by the cession by the recent bishop Nicholas of the rule and administration of the church of Elphin into the pope's hands, and the pope's admission of this cession at the [apostolic][1] see, provision being reserved to the pope's disposition under his reservation of provisions of all churches vacated then and in the future at the apostolic see. The pope hereby appoints George bishop, committing to him the care and administration of the church of Elphin in spiritualities and temporalities, and granting him licence to transfer thereto. His will is, however, that — before George involves himself in the rule and administration of the said church — he shall take the usual oath of fealty before the bishops of Killala and Clonfert in accordance with the form which the pope sends enclosed under his *bulla*; and the pope by other letters of his commands that the said bishops (or one of them) shall receive the oath in his name and that of the Roman church.

Conclusions to: (i) the chapter of the church of Elphin, (ii) the people of the city and diocese, (iii) the clergy of the city and diocese, (iv) the vassals of the said church, (v) the archbishop of Tuam, (vi) Henry, king of England.[2]

Quam sit onusta dispendiis . . . The conclusions begin: *(i), (iv) Hodie venerabilem fratrem nostrum* . . . *(ii), (iii) Hodie et cetera. (v) Ad cumulum et cetera. (vi) Gratie divine et cetera.*
L puccius; D Scarsius[3] */ F / F xxiiij .*[4]*. xij . xij . xij . xij . xij . xij . Sanctor(is)*

[1] MS wants 'predictam' (or suchlike)

[2] *Anglie regi;* i. e. not notified as king or lord of Ireland

[3] the second name — that of the abbreviator *de parco minori* who expedited the conclusions — rarely enregistered

[4] *viij . viij* deleted

592   17 April 1499[1]   *Reg. Lat.* 1094, fo 143[v]

To the bishops of Killala and Clonfert, mandate. Since the pope has this day translated bishop George from the church of Dromore to that of Elphin, as is more fully contained in his letters drawn up in that regard,[2] he — wishing to spare George, who lives in those parts, the labour and expense of being compelled on that account to come in person to the Roman curia — hereby commissions and commands that the above two (or one of them) shall receive from him in the name of the pope and the Roman church the usual oath of fealty etc. [as above, no. 547, with appropriate changes].

Cum nos hodie . . .
L puccius / F. / F xvj · Sanctor(is)

[1] The dating clause is written by the enregistering scribe (Boccapaduli) with deliberation, in larger letters and much less cursively than the text above: entered later?

[2] above, no. 591

593   17 April 1499[1]   *Reg. Lat.* 1094, fo 144[r]

To George, bishop of Dromore. Since the pope, on the advice of the cardinals, intends this day to translate George from the church of Dromore, over which he is understood to preside, to that of Elphin, vacant *certo modo*, and to appoint him bishop, he hereby absolves him from any sentences of excommunication, etc. [as above, no. 583].

Romani pontificis circumspecta benignitas ad ea libenter intendit. . .
L puccius:- / F / F xxiiij . Sanctor(is)

[1] written as described above, no. 592, note 1

594   8 January 1500   *Reg. Lat.* 1094, fos 151[r]-153[r]

To David, elect of St Asaph. Consistorial provision of him — abbot of the monastery of Valle Crucis *alias* Ryneguvesteyll', OCist, d. St Asaph, in priest's orders — to the church of St Asaph, vacant by the death, outside the Roman curia, of the late bishop Michael, during whose rule provision of the said church was specially reserved by the pope to his own disposition; and appointment of David as bishop, committing to him the care and administration of the church in spiritualities and temporalities.

    Conclusions to: (i) the chapter of the church of St Asaph, (ii) the clergy of the city and diocese, (iii) the people of the city and diocese, (iv) the vassals of the said church, (v) the archbishop of Canterbury, (vi) Henry, king of England.

Apostolatus officium quamquam insufficientibus meritis nobis ex alto commissum . . .
The conclusions begin: *(i) Hodie ecclesie vestre . . . (ii) Hodie ecclesie Assanen. (iii),*
(iv) Hodie et cetera. (v) Ad cumulum . . . (vi) Gratie divine et cetera.
L puccius / · V· / · V· xx · x · x · · x · x · x · x · De Phano:

595   9 January 1500   *Reg. Lat.* 1094, fos 153[v]-154[r]

To David, elect of St Asaph. Since the pope has recently made provision of David to the church of St Asaph, as is more fully contained in his letters drawn up in that regard,[1] he hereby grants faculty to David — at his supplication — to receive consecration from any catholic bishop etc. [as above, no. 57, to '. . . marked with his seal;'] and that the above shall not be to the prejudice of the archbishop of Canterbury, to whom the aforesaid church is understood to be subject by metropolitical law. With the form of oath appended.

Cum nos pridem . . .
L puccius / · V· / · V· xxviij De Phano:

[1] above, no. 594

596   8 January 1500   *Reg. Lat.* 1094, fos 154^r-155^r

To David, elect of St Asaph, whom the pope has this day provided to the church of St Asaph and appointed bishop, as is more fully contained in his letters drawn up in that regard. [1] Since, as the pope has learned, at the time of the said provision and appointment, David was presiding, as he does, over the monastery of Valle Crucis *alias* Rynegwesteyll', OCist, d. St Asaph, whose annual value does not exceed 40 marks of the money current in England, and was holding, as he does, *in commendam*, by apostolic concession and dispensation, the church, called a custodianship or guardianship, of St Peter, Ruthyn', d. Bangor, whose annual value does not exceed 10 pounds of the money current in England, the pope — *motu proprio* — hereby dispenses David to retain — after he has, on the strength of the said provision and appointment, acquired peaceful possession, or almost, of the rule and goods of the church of St Asaph or the greater part of them, and received consecration — the church of St Peter *in commendam* as before and also the above monastery likewise *in commendam*, together with the church of St Asaph, for as long as he presides over the latter; (he may — due and customary burdens of the monastery having been supported — make disposition of the rest of its fruits etc. just as he could until now and as others who were abbots at the time could and ought to do, alienation of immovable goods and precious movables being however forbidden); notwithstanding etc.; decreeing that the monastery is not made vacant and the commend of the church of St Peter does not cease on this account. With the proviso that divine worship in the monastery and the usual number of monks and ministers shall not be diminished; and that the church of St Peter shall not, on this account, be defrauded of due services; but that the aforesaid burdens of the church and of the monastery and its convent shall be supported.

Personam tuam nobis et apostolice sedi devotam tuis exigentibus meritis paterna benivolentia prosequentes illa tibi favorabiliter concedimus . . .
L puccius / · V· / · V· Lxx De Phano:-

[1] above, no. 594

597   8 January 1500   *Reg. Lat.* 1094, fo 155^v

To David, abbot of the monastery of Valle Crucis *alias* Rynegwesteyll', OCist, d. St Asaph. Since the pope intends this day to make provision of David to the church of St Asaph, vacant *certo modo*, and to appoint him bishop, he hereby absolves him from any [sentences] of excommunication etc. [as above, no. 53].

Apostolice sedis circumspecta benignitas de statu personarum ecclesiasticarum quarumlibet . . .
L puccius / · V· / · V· · xx De Phano:

598   8 January 1500   *Reg. Lat.* 1094, fos 156^r-158^v

To Miles, elect of Llandaff. Consistorial provision of him — abbot of the monastery of Eygomyshyn' *alias* Eyneshin', OSB, d. Lincoln, in priest's orders — to the church of Llandaff, vacant by the death, outside the Roman curia, of the late bishop John, during whose rule the said church was specially reserved by the pope to his own disposition; and appointment of Miles as bishop, committing to him the care and administration of the church in spiritualities and temporalities.

Conclusions to: (i) the chapter of the church of Llandaff, (ii) the clergy of the city and diocese, (iii) the people of the city and diocese, (iv) the vassals of the said church, (v) the archbishop of Canterbury, (vi) Henry, king of England.

Apostolatus offitium quamquam insufficientibus meritis nobis ex alto commissum . . .
The conclusions begin: *(i) Hodie ecclesie vestre . . . (ii), (iii), (iv) Hodie et cetera. (v) Ad cumulum . . . (vi) Gratie divine et cetera.*
L puccius / · V· / V. xx. x[1]*. x. x. x. x. x. De Phano:*

[1] apparently changed (by insertion of point and oblique stroke as separator) from *xxx*

599   9 January 1500   *Reg. Lat.* 1094, fos 158^v-159^r

To Miles, elect of Llandaff. Since the pope has recently made provision of Miles to the church of Llandaff, as is more fully contained in his letters drawn up in that regard,[1] he hereby grants faculty to Miles — at his supplication — to receive consecration from any catholic bishop etc. [as above, no. 57, with appropriate changes, to '. . . marked with his seal;'] and that the above shall not be to the prejudice of the archbishop of Canterbury to whom the aforesaid church is understood to be subject by metropolitical law. With the form of oath appended.

Cum nos pridem . . .
L puccius / . V· / . V· xxviij De Phano:

[1] above, no. 598

600   8 January 1500   *Reg. Lat.* 1094, fos 159^v-160^r

To Miles, elect of Llandaff, whom the pope has this day provided to the church of Llandaff and appointed bishop, as is more fully contained in his letters drawn up in that regard.[1] Since, as the pope has learned, at the time of the said provision and appointment, Miles was presiding, as he does, over the monastery of Eygenysh(a)m *alias* Eynesh(a)m,[2] OSB, d. Lincoln, whose annual value does not exceed 100 marks of the money current in England, the pope — *motu proprio* — hereby dispenses Miles to retain — after he has, on the strength of the said provision and appointment, acquired peaceful possession, or almost, of the rule and goods of the church of Llandaff or the greater part of them, and received consecration — the above monastery *in commendam*, together with the church of Llandaff, for as long as he presides over the latter; (he may — due and customary burdens of the monastery having been supported — make disposition of the rest of its fruits etc. just as he could until now and as others who were abbots at the time could and ought to do, alienation of immovable goods and precious movables being however forbidden); notwithstanding etc.; decreeing that the monastery is not, on this account, made vacant. With the proviso that divine worship in the monastery and the usual number of monks and [ministers][3] shall not, on this account, be diminished; but that its aforesaid burdens and those of the convent of the monastery shall be supported.

Personam tuam nobis et apostolice sedi devotam tuis exigentibus meritis paterna benivolentia prosequentes illa tibi favorabiliter concedimus . . .
L puccius / V / · V· Lx De Phano:

[1] above, no. 598
[2] MS: *Eygenyshm' alias Eyneshm'*
[3] *mon(asteri)orum; recte:* 'ministrorum'

601   8 January 1500   *Reg. Lat.* 1094, fo 160[v]

To Miles, abbot of the monastery of Eygenysh(a)m *alias* Eynesh(a)m,[1] OSB, d. Lincoln. Since the pope intends this day to make provision of Miles to the church of Llandaff, vacant *certo modo*, and to appoint him bishop, he hereby absolves him from any [sentences] of excommunication etc. [as above, no. 53].

Apostolice sedis circumspecta benignitas de statu personarum ecclesiasticarum quarumlibet . . .
L puccius / · V· / · V· xx De Phano:-

[1] MS: *Eygenyshm' alias Eyneshm'*

602   4 May 1500   *Reg. Lat.* 1094, fos 164[r]-165[v]

To Thomas, elect of Bangor. Consistorial provision of him — abbot of the monastery of St Peter, Chertesey, OSB, d. Winchester, in priest's orders — to the church of Bangor, vacant by the translation of bishop Henry to the church of Salisbury from that of Bangor, over which he was then presiding and which formerly had been reserved by the pope to his own disposition under his reservation of provisions of all churches vacated by his translations then and in the future; and appointment of Thomas as bishop, committing to him the care, rule and administration of the church of Bangor in spiritualities and temporalities.

   Conclusions to: (i) the chapter of the church of Bangor, (ii) the clergy of the city and diocese, (iii) the people of the city and diocese, (iv) the vassals of the said church, (v) the archbishop of Canterbury, (vi) Henry, king of England.

Apostolatus officium quamquam insufficientibus meritis nobis ex alto commissum . . .
The conclusions begin: *(i) Hodie ecclesie vestre . . . (ii), (iii), (iv) Hodie et cetera. (v) Ad cumulum et cetera. (vi) Gratie divine et cetera.*
f de parma / F / F. xx. x. xxxxx . Sanctor(is)

603   5 May 1500   *Reg. Lat.* 1094, fo 166[r-v]

To Thomas, elect of Bangor. Since the pope has recently made provision of Thomas to the church of Bangor, as is more fully contained in his letters drawn up in that regard,[1] he hereby grants faculty to Thomas — at his supplication — to receive consecration from any catholic bishop etc. [as above, no. 57, with appropriate changes, to '. . . marked with his seal;'] and that the above shall not be to the prejudice of the archbishop of Canterbury, to whom the aforesaid church is understood to be subject by metropolitical law. With the form of oath appended.

Cum nos pridem . . .
F de parma / F / F· xxviij· Sanctor(is)

[1] see above, no. 602

604   4 May 1500   *Reg. Lat.* 1094, fos 166[v]-167[r]

To Thomas, abbot of the monastery of St Peter, Chertesi, OSB, d. Winchester. Since the pope, on the advice of the cardinals, intends this day to make provision of Thomas to the church of Bangor, vacant *certo modo*, and appoint him bishop, he hereby absolves him from any [sentences] of excommunication etc. [as above, no. 53[1]].

Apostolice sedis consueta clementia ne dispositiones . . .
f de parma / F / F . xx . Sanctor(is)

[1] but here enregistered in a slightly abridged form

605   4 May 1500   *Reg. Lat.* 1094, fos 167^r-168^r

To Thomas, elect of Bangor, whom the pope has this day provided to the church of Bangor and appointed bishop, as is more fully contained in his letters drawn up in that regard.[1] Since, as the pope has learned, at the time of the said provision and appointment, Thomas was presiding over, as he does, the monastery of St Peter, Chertesey, OSB, d. Winchester, whose annual value does not exceed 90 gold florins of the camera, the pope — *motu proprio* — hereby dispenses Thomas to retain the monastery *in commendam* — even after he has, on the strength of the said provision and appointment, acquired possession, or almost, of the rule and administration and of the goods of the church of Bangor or the greater part of them, and received consecration — together with the church of Bangor, for as long as he presides over the latter; (he may — due and customary burdens of the monastery and its convent having been supported — make disposition of the rest of its fruits etc. as abbots could and ought to do, alienation of immovable goods and precious movables being however forbidden); notwithstanding etc.; decreeing that the monastery is not, on this account, made vacant. With the proviso that divine worship and the usual number of monks and ministers in the monastery shall not, on this account, be diminished; but that its aforesaid burdens and those of the convent shall be supported.

Personam tuam nobis et apostolice sedi devotam tuis exigentibus meritis paterna benivolentia prosequentes illa tibi libenter concedimus . . .
F de parma / F / F . Lx . Sanctor(is)

[1] above, no. 602

606[1]   3 June 1500   *Reg. Lat.* 1094, fos 177^r-179^r

To Thomas Clerk, elect of Killala. Consistorial provision of him — archdeacon of the church of Sodor — to the church of Killala, vacant by the death, outside the Roman curia, of the late bishop Thomas, during whose rule it was specially reserved by the pope to his own disposition; and appointment of Thomas as bishop, committing to him the care and administration of the church of Killala in spiritualities and temporalities.

   Conclusions to: (i) the chapter of the church of Killala, (ii) the clergy of the city and diocese, (iii) the people of the city and diocese, (iv) the vassals of the said church, (v) the archbishop of Tuam, (vi) Henry, king of England.

Apostolatus offitium meritis licet insufficientibus nobis ex alto commissum . . . The conclusions begin: *(i) Hodie ecclesie vestre . . . (ii), (iv) Hodie ecclesie Aladen . . . (iii) Hodie et cetera. (v) Ad cumulum . . . (vi) Gratie divine et cetera.*
S de Castello / V· [2] */ V· xx· x· x· x· x· . x .* [3] *De Phano:*

[1] *Thomas Electus Aladen'* occurs in the index to the gathering on fo. 169[r]

[2] a swung dash to the left

[3] 'x' occurs only five times; in error for six?

607   4 June 1500   *Reg. Lat.* 1094, fos 179[v]-180[r]

To Thomas, elect of Killala. Since the pope has recently made provision of Thomas to the church of Killala, as is more fully contained in his letters drawn up in that regard,[1] he hereby grants faculty to Thomas — at his supplication — to receive consecration from any catholic bishop etc. [as above, no. 57, with appropriate changes, to '. . . marked with his seal;'] and that the above shall not be to the prejudice of the archbishop of Tuam to whom the aforesaid church is understood to be subject by metropolitical law. With the form of oath appended.

Cum nos pridem . . .
S de Castello / . V· / V. xxviij. De Phano:-

[1] above, no. 606

608   3 June 1500   *Reg. Lat.* 1094, fos 180[r]-181[r]

To Thomas Clerk, elect of Killala, whom the pope has this day provided to the church of Killala and appointed bishop, as is more fully contained in his letters drawn up in that regard.[1] The pope — *motu proprio* — hereby dispenses Thomas to receive and retain *in commendam* for life, together with the church of Killala, any number of secular benefices, with and without cure, compatible mutually, and regular benefices of any order, even if the secular benefices should be canonries and prebends, dignities, *personatus*, administrations or offices in cathedral, even metropolitan, or collegiate churches, or parish churches or their perpetual vicarages, and the regular be priories, *prepositure, prepositatus,* dignities, *personatus,* administrations or offices, and the priories etc. be customarily elective and have cure of souls, of annual value not exceeding 300 gold florins of the camera, if he obtains them otherwise canonically — provided that the secular benefices be not major *post pontificalem* in cathedral, even metropolitan, churches, or principal in collegiate churches, and the regular be not conventual dignities or claustral offices; (he may —

due and customary burdens of the benefices having been supported — make disposition of the rest of their fruits etc. just as those holding these benefices *in titulum* could and ought to do, alienation of immovable goods and precious movables being however forbidden); notwithstanding etc. With the proviso that the benefices held *in commendam* shall not, on this account, be defrauded of due services and the cure of souls therein [if any][2] shall not be neglected; but that their aforesaid burdens shall be supported.

Personam tuam nobis et apostolice sedi[3] devotam tuis exigentibus meritis paterna benivolentia prosequentes illam tibi gratiam libenter concedimus . . .
S[4] de Castello / . V· / . V· · C· De Phano:

[1] above, no. 606

[2] *. . . in eis quibus . . .*; wanting 'si' before *quibus*?

[3] changed (by deletion of 's') from *sedis*; not initialled

[4] changed (by overwriting) from *C*

609   3 June 1500   *Reg. Lat.* 1094, fo 181[r-v]

To Thomas Clerk, archdeacon of the church of Sodor. Since the pope, on the advice of the cardinals, intends this day to make provision of Thomas to the church of Killala and to appoint him bishop, he hereby absolves him from any [sentences] of excommunication etc. [as above, no. 53].

Romani pontificis copiosa benignitas ad ea libenter intendit . . .
S de Castello / . V· / . V· xx De Phano:

610   15 February 1499   *Reg. Lat.* 1094, fos 250[v]-253[r]

To Patrick, elect of Cork and Cloyne. Consistorial provision of him — abbot of the monastery of B. Mary, *de Castrodei* [Fermoy], OCist, d. Cloyne, of noble birth by both parents — to the canonically mutually united churches of Cork and Cloyne, vacant by the death, outside the Roman curia, of the late bishop Jordan, during whose rule the said united churches were specially reserved by the pope to his own disposition; and appointment of Patrick as bishop, committing to him the care and administration of the said churches in spiritualities and temporalities.

Conclusions to: (i) the chapters of the united churches of Cork and Cloyne, (ii) the clergy of the city and diocese,[1] (iii) the vassals of the said churches,[2] (iv) the peoples of the cities and dioceses, (v) the archbishop of Cashel.

Apostolatus officium quamquam insufficientibus meritis nobis ex alto commissum . . .
The conclusions begin: *(i) Hodie ecclesiis . . . (ii), (iii), (iv) Hodie et cetera. (v) Ad cumulum et cetera.*
S· de Castello / V / V· xx x x x x x x De Phano:-

[1] *sic:* singular

[2] The conclusions to the clergy and vassals are each enregistered much abridged. Unusually, the conclusion to the vassals does not follow that to the people.

611   15 February 1499   *Reg. Lat.* 1094, fo 253[r-v]

To Patrick Cantun, abbot of the monastery of B. Mary, *de Castro Dei* [Fermoy], OCist, d. Cloyne. Since the pope, on the advice of the cardinals, intends this day to make provision of Patrick to the canonically mutually united churches of Cork and Cloyne, vacant at present, and to appoint him bishop, he hereby absolves him from any [sentences] of excommunication etc. [as above, no. 53[1]].

Apostolice sedis consueta clementia ne dispositiones . . .
S· de Castello / · V· / · V· xx De Phano:-

[1] but here enregistered in a slightly abridged form

612[1]   26 June 1499   *Reg. Lat.* 1094, fos 312[r]-313[v]

To John Edemundi de Geraldinis, elect of Cork and Cloyne.[2] Consistorial provision (under the pope's reservation of provisions of all churches vacated then and in the future at the apostolic see to his own disposition) of him — [(?)cleric],[3] d. Cloyne, in minor orders — to the mutually united churches of Cork and Cloyne, vacant because Gerard, recently bishop, spontaneously and freely ceded the rule and administration of the said churches, over which he was then presiding, into the pope's hands and the pope admitted the cession at the said see; and appointment of John Edemundi as bishop, committing to him the care and administration of these churches in spiritualities and temporalities.

Conclusions to: (i) the chapters of the united churches of Cork and Cloyne, (ii) the clergy of the cities and dioceses, (iii) the archbishop of Cashel.

Apostolatus officium quamquam insuficientibus[4] meritis nobis ex alto commissum . . .
The conclusions begin: *(i) Hodie ecclesiis vestris . . . (ii) Hodie Corkagen. et Cloanen. ecclesiis . . . (iii) Ad cumulum et cetera.*
L puccius / Jo. / Jo. xx . x . x . x . de Galves

[1] *Johannes Edemundi electus Corkagen' et Cloanen' idem idem idem* occurs in the index to the gathering on fo. 311[r]

[2] *Cluanen.* or *Cloanen.* throughout

[3] MS: *ecclesiam* (i. e. . . . *ad te ecclesiam Cluanen. diocesis* . . .); *recte:* 'clericum'? *Cf.* below, no. 614 where he is designated cleric.

[4] *sic*

613[1]   **27 June 1499**   *Reg. Lat.* 1094, fos 313[v]-314[v]

To John, elect of Cork and Cloyne.[2] Since the pope, on the advice of the cardinals, has recently made provision of John to the mutually united churches of Cork and Cloyne, as is more fully contained in his letters drawn up in that regard,[3] he hereby grants faculty to John, who is in minor orders only — at his supplication — to have himself promoted by any catholic bishop of his choice in communion with the apostolic see on any Sunday or other feast day to the orders, successively, of the subdiaconate, diaconate and priesthood; and also to receive consecration from the same, or other, catholic bishop similarly in communion assisted by two or three catholic bishops etc. [as above, no. 57, with appropriate changes, to '. . . marked with his seal;'] and that the above shall not be to the prejudice of the archbishop of Cashel, to whom the aforesaid united churches are understood to be subject by metropolitical law. With the form of oath appended.

Cum nos pridem . . .
L puccius / Jo. / Jo. xxviij. de Galves

[1] See above, no. 612, note 1.
[2] *Cloanen.* or *Cluanen.* throughout
[3] above, no. 612

614[1]   **26 June 1499**   *Reg. Lat.* 1094, fos 314[v]-315[r]

To John Edemundi de Geraldinis, cleric, d. Cloyne.[2] Since the pope intends this day to make provision of John Edemundi to the united churches of Cork and Cloyne, vacant *certo modo*, and appoint him bishop, and, as the pope has learned, John Edemundi is in his twenty-eighth year of age, he — *motu proprio* — hereby dispenses him henceforth to be appointed to the said churches, preside over them as bishop, perform and exercise the care and administration of them in spiritualities and temporalities and also receive and use consecration. Notwithstanding the defect of age etc.

Supereminens[3] *divina largitas . . .*
L puccius / Jo. / Jo . xxx . de Galves

[1] See above, no. 612, note 1
[2] *Cluanen.*
[3] *sic; cf.* 'Superveniens'

615[1]   **26 June 1499**   *Reg. Lat.* 1094, fo 315[r]

To John Edemundi de Geraldinis, cleric, d. Cloyne.[2] Since the pope intends this day
to make provision of John Edemundi to the mutually united churches of Cork and
Cloyne, vacant *certo modo*, and to appoint him bishop, he hereby absolves him from
any sentences of excommunication, etc. [as above, no. 53].

Apostolice sedis circumspecta benignitas de statu personarum ecclesiasticarum
quarumlibet . . .
L puccius / Jo. / Jo. xx. de Galves

[1] See above, no. 612, note 1.
[2] *Cloanen.* or *Cluanen.* throughout

616   18 June 1500   *Reg. Lat.* 1095, fos 100[r]-101[v]

Provision, in *forma commissoria*, of Johannes Fabri, cleric, d. Trier, (who, as he
asserts, is a continual commensal familiar of M. Fernandus Poncetus, scriptor and
abbreviator of apostolic letters), to the parish church of Vinningen (*in Vinningen'*), d.
Metz.
    The 'bishop of Worcester' is one of the three mandataries. Entry otherwise of no
interest to the Calendar.

Vite ac morum honestas . . .
. *Jo· ortega / . B· / ¡ B· gratis pro deo· Tertio Id(us) decembr(is) anno decimo·* [11
December 1501]*, Bolis·*

617   20 October 1501   *Reg. Lat.* 1096, fos 5[r]-7[r]

To William, elect of London. Consistorial provision (under the pope's reservation of provisions of all churches vacated then and in the future at the apostolic see to his own disposition) of him — archdeacon of Hunttingdon' in the church of Lincoln, LLD, Keeper of the Rolls of the Chancery of Henry, king of England, in priest's orders — to the church of London — (vacant because Thomas <arch>bishop[1] of York, then [bishop] of London, was translated, from the church of London, over which he was then presiding, to that of York, and appointed <arch>bishop,[2] as is more fully contained in the pope's letters drawn up in that regard[3] — and appointment of William as bishop,[4] committing to him the care and administration of the church of London in spiritualities and temporalities.

Conclusions to (i) the chapter of the church of London, (ii) the clergy of the city and diocese, (iii) the people of the city and diocese, (iv) the vassals of the said church, (v) the archbishop of Canterbury, (vi) Henry, king [of England].[5]

Divina disponente clementia . . . The conclusions begin: *(i) Hodie ecclesie vestre . . . (ii) Hodie et cetera. (iii) Quocirca . . .*[6] *(iv) Hodie ecclesie Londonien. (v) Ad cumulum et cetera. (vi) Gratie divine et cetera.*
L puccius / F / F. xx. x. x. x. x. x. x. Sanctor(is)

[1] *Thomam* is smudged (but not deleted); *Archi* is inserted in the margin (by enregistering scribe); initialled *F*; *cf.* below, note 4

[2] *Archi* inserted in the margin (by enregistering scribe) at start of line; not initialled

[3] above, no. 546

[4] The narrative has: *Thomam <Archi>episcopum Eboracen. tunc Londonien.* and also (presumably in error) *Willelmum eidem ecclesie Londonien. in <Archi>episcopum* (in both instances *Archi* is inserted in the margin by enregistering scribe, initialled *F*.)

[5] 'Anglie' does not occur

[6] i. e. 'Hodie et cetera' (or suchlike) does not occur here

618   20 October 1501   *Reg. Lat.* 1096, fo 7ʳ⁻ᵛ

To William Warh(a)m,[1] LLD, archdeacon of Huntingdon' in the church of Lincoln. Since the pope intends this day to make provision of William to the church of London, vacant *certo modo*, and to appoint him bishop, he hereby absolves him from any sentences of excommunication, etc. [as above, no. 53].

Apostolice sedis circumspecta benignitas de statu personarum ecclesiasticarum quarumlibet . . .
L puccius / F / F . xx . Sanctor(is)

[1] MS: *Warhm'*

619　21 October 1501　　　　　　　　　　　*Reg Lat.* 1096, fos 7^v-8^r

To William, elect of London. Since the pope has recently made provision of William to the church of London, as is more fully contained in his letters drawn up in that regard,[1] he hereby grants faculty to William — at his supplication — to receive consecration from any catholic bishop etc. [as above, no. 57, with appropriate changes, to '. . . marked with his seal;'] and that the above shall not be to the prejudice of the archbishop of Canterbury, to whom the aforesaid church is understood to be subject by metropolitical law. With the form of oath appended.

Cum nos pridem . . .
L puccius / F / F · xxviij· Sanctor(is)

[1] above, no. 617

620　26 November 1501　　　　　　　　　　*Reg. Lat.* 1096, fos 16^v-18^v

To Andrew Stewart, elect of Caithness. Consistorial provision of him — canon of Glasgow, in the order of the diaconate only, in his twenty-fifth year of age and a kinsman of James, king of Scots — to the church of Caithness, vacant by the death, outside the Roman curia, of the late elect John, during whose rule the said church was specially reserved by the pope to his own disposition; and appointment of Andrew as bishop, committing to him the care and administration of the church in spiritualities and temporalities.

Conclusions to: (i) the chapter of the church of Caithness, (ii) the clergy of the city and diocese, (iii) the people of the city and diocese, (iv) the vassals of the said church, (v) the archbishop of St Andrews, (vi) James, king of Scots.

Apostolatus officium quamquam insuficentibus[1] *meritis nobis ex alto commissum . . .*
The conclusions begin: *(i) Hodie ecclesie vestre . . . (ii), (iii), (iv) Hodie ecclesie Cathenen. et cetera. (v) Ad cumulum et cetera. (vi) Gratie divine et cetera.*
F de parma / . B· / ١ B · xx x · x x x x x Bolis.

[1] *sic*

621　27 November 1501　　　　　　　　　　*Reg. Lat.* 1096, fos 18^v-19^r

To Andrew, elect of Caithness. Since the pope has recently made provision of Andrew to the church of Caithness, as is more fully contained in his letters drawn up in that regard,[1] he hereby grants faculty to Andrew, who is in the order of the diaconate — at his supplication — to be promoted to the priesthood, even outside the times established by law, by any catholic bishop of his choice in communion with the apostolic see, and to receive consecration from the bishop, assisted by two or three catholic bishops etc. [as above, no. 57, with appropriate changes, to '. . . marked with his seal;'] and that the above shall not be to the prejudice of the archbishop of St Andrews, to whom the aforesaid church is understood to be subject by metropolitical law. With the form of oath appended.

Cum nos pridem . . .
F de parma / · B· / · B· xxviij· Bolis

[1] above, no. 620

622   26 November 1501   *Reg. Lat.* 1096, fo 19[v]

To Andrew Stewart, canon of Glasgow (who is, as he asserts, a kinsman of James, king of Scots). Since the pope, on the advice of the cardinals, intends this day to make provision of Andrew to the church of Caithness, at present vacant *certo modo,* and to appoint him bishop, he hereby absolves him from any sentences of excommunication, etc. [as above, no. 53].

Apostolice sedis consueta clementia ne dispositiones . . .
F de parma / · B· /ı B· xx Bolis

623   26 November 1501   *Reg. Lat.* 1096, fo 20[r-v]

To Andrew Steward, canon of Glasgow. Since the pope, on the advice of the cardinals, intends this day to make provision of Andrew to the church of Caithness, at present vacant *certo modo,* and to appoint him bishop, he — *motu proprio* — hereby dispenses Andrew — who, as the pope has learned, is in his twenty-fifth year of age, is a kinsman of James, king of Scots, and some time ago, was dispensed by apostolic authority notwithstanding a defect of birth as the son of a priest of illustrious birth and an unmarried woman to be promoted to all, even sacred, orders and to receive and retain any number of mutually compatible benefices, even if canonries and prebends, dignities, *personatus*, administrations or offices in cathedral, even metropolitan, or collegiate churches, even if the dignities in question should be major *post pontificalem* in cathedral, even metropolitan, churches, or principal in collegiate churches, even if the dignities etc. should be customarily elective and have cure of souls, if he obtained them otherwise canonically; and afterwards was duly promoted to the order of the diaconate and acquired a canonry and prebend of the church of Glasgow, which was canonically collated to him while vacant *certo modo* — to be appointed to and preside over the church of Caithness and rule and govern it in spiritualities and temporalities and receive and use consecration. Notwithstanding the said defects of age and birth etc.

Divina supereminens[1] *largitas . . .*
F de parma / · *B·* / . *B. Lx Bolis.*

[1] *sic; cf.* 'superveniens'

624   20 August 1501   *Reg. Lat.* 1096, fo 32^r

To Richard, bishop of Durham. Since the pope, on the advice of the cardinals, intends this day to translate Richard from the church of Durham, over which he is understood to preside, to that of Winchester, OSB, vacant *certo modo,* and to appoint him bishop, he hereby absolves him from any sentences of excommunication, etc. [as above, no. 583].

Apostolice sedis circumspecta clementia ne dispositiones . . .
L[1] *puccius* / · *B·* / · *B · xxiiij · Bolis*

[1] written over *p*

625   20 August 1501   *Reg. Lat.* 1096, fo 32^v

To the bishops of Norwich and of Coventry [and] Lichfield. Since the pope has this day translated bishop Richard, from the church of Durham to that of Winchester, OSB, as is more fully contained in his letters drawn up in that regard,[1] he — wishing to spare Richard, who lives in those parts, the labour and expense of being compelled on that account to come in person to the apostolic see — hereby commissions and commands that the above two (or one of them) shall receive from him in the name of the pope and the Roman church the usual oath of fealty etc. [as above, no. 547, with appropriate changes].

Cum nos hodie . . .
L puccius / *[-]*[2] / . *B· xvj· Bolis*

[1] below, no. 626
[2] no magistral initial

626 20 August 1501[1] *Reg. Lat.* 1096, fos 33^r-35^r

To Richard, bishop of Winchester. Consistorial translation, though absent [from the Roman curia], from the church of Durham to that of Winchester, vacant by the death, outside the Roman curia, of the late bishop Thomas, during whose rule the said church of Winchester, OSB, was specially reserved by the pope to his own disposition. The pope hereby appoints Richard bishop, committing to him the care and administration of the church of Winchester in spiritualities and temporalities and granting him licence to transfer thereto. His will is, however, that — before Richard involves himself in the rule and administration of the church of Winchester — he shall take the usual oath of fealty before the bishops <of Norwich and of Coventry and Lichfield>[2] in accordance with the form which the pope sends enclosed under his *bulla*; and the pope has, by other letters of his, commanded the said bishops (and each of them) that they (or one of them) shall receive the oath from Richard in his name and that of the Roman church.

  Conclusions to: (i) the chapter of the church of Winchester, (ii) the clergy of the city and diocese, (iii) the people of the city and diocese, (iv) the vassals of the said church, (v) the archbishop of Canterbury, (vi) Henry, king of England.

Quam sit onusta[3] *dispendiis* . . . The conclusions begin: *(i), (ii) Hodie venerabilem fratrem nostrum* . . . *(iii), (iv) Hodie et cetera. (v) Hodie et cetera. Ad cumulum et cetera.* [4] *(vi) Gratie divine premium* . . .
L puccius / . *B·* / · *B· xxiiij · xij xij · xij · xij · xij · xij · Bolis·*

[1] *Datum Rome* . . . *anno nono*] the italicised passage evidently squeezed into a limited space: entered later?

[2] *Cicestren. et Exonien.* deleted and initialled . *B.* twice; in the margin opposite: . *B. Noruuicen. et conuentren. Lich'efelden. casatum et corectum de Ma(n)d(a)to d(omi)ni rege(n)tis . B. Bolis.; Jo. ra* [the start of 'Jo. ragusin. '?] deleted after *regentis*

[3] changed (by deletion of 'h') from *honusta*

[4] the narrative should follow the proem and not (as here) precede it

627 26 May 1501 *Reg. Lat.* 1096, fos 53^r-55^v

To Richard, bishop of Ely. Consistorial translation, though absent [from the Roman curia], from the church of Exeter to that of Ely, vacant by the death, outside the Roman curia, of the late bishop John, during whose rule the said church of Ely was specially reserved by the pope to his own disposition. The pope hereby appoints Richard bishop, committing to him the care and administration of the church of Ely in spiritualities and temporalities and granting him licence to transfer thereto. His will is, however, that — before Richard involves himself in the rule and administration of the church of Ely — he shall take the usual oath of fealty before the bishops of Coventry and Lichfield[1] in accordance with the form which the pope sends enclosed under his *bulla*; and the pope has, by other letters of his, commanded the said bishops (and each of them) that they (or one of them) shall receive the oath from Richard in his name and that of the Roman church.

Conclusions[2] to: (i) the chapter of the church of Ely, (ii) the clergy of the city and diocese, (iii) the people of the city and diocese, (iv) the vassals of the said church, (v) the archbishop of Canterbury, (vi) Henry, king of England.

Quam sit onusta dispendiis . . . The conclusions begin: *(i), (ii), (iii) Hodie venerabilem fratrem nostrum* . . . *(iv) Hodie venerabilem et cetera. (v) Ad cumulum et cetera. (vi) Gratie divine et cetera.*
L puccius / . *V·* / *V. xxiiij · xij · xij · xij · xij· xij· xij* —*De Phano:*

[1] *sic*

[2] The first four conclusions, oddly, refer to Richard as 'elect'; *recte:* 'bishop'?

628   26 May 1501   *Reg. Lat.* 1096, fos 55[v]-56[r]

To the bishops of Coventry and Lichfield.[1] Since the pope has this day translated bishop Richard, from the church of Exeter to that of Ely, as is more fully contained in his letters drawn up in that regard,[2] he — wishing to spare Richard, who lives in those parts, the labour and expense of being compelled on that account to come in person to the apostolic see — hereby commissions and commands that the above two (or one of them) shall receive from him in the name of the pope and the Roman church the usual oath of fealty etc. [as above, no. 547, with appropriate changes].

Cum nos hodie . . .
L puccius / . *V·* / *V· xv· De Phano:*

[1] *Conventren. et Lichfelden.*: treated throughout as two separate sees each with its own bishop
[2] above, no. 627

629   26 May 1501   *Reg. Lat.* 1096, fo 56[r-v]

To Richard, bishop of Exeter. Since the pope, on the advice of the cardinals, intends this day to translate Richard from the church of Exeter, over which he is understood to preside, to that of Ely, vacant *certo modo*, and to appoint him bishop, he hereby absolves him from any sentences of excommunication, etc. [as above, no. 583].

Apostolice sedis circumspecta clementia ne dispositiones . . .
L puccius / · *V·* / *V· xxiiij De Phano:*

630   26 November 1501   *Reg. Lat.* 1096, fos 105^r-107^v

To Andrew,[1] elect of Moray. Consistorial provision of him — prior of the priory of Mayo *alias* Petynveyn, OSA, d. St Andrews, Lic A, in priest's orders and of noble birth — to the church of Moray, vacant by the death, outside the Roman curia, of the late bishop Andrew, during whose rule it was specially reserved by the pope to his own disposition; and appointment of Andrew as bishop, committing to him the care and administration of the church in spiritualities and temporalities.

Conclusions to: (i) the chapter of the church of Moray, (ii) the people of the city and diocese, (iii) the clergy of the city and diocese,[2] (iv) the vassals of the said church, (v) the archbishop of St Andrews, (vi) James, king of Scots.

Apostolatus officium quamquam insufficientibus meritis nobis ex alto commissum . . .
The conclusions begin: *(i) Hodie ecclesie vestre* . . . *(ii) Hodie et cetera. (iii), (iv) Hodie ecclesie Moravien.* . . . *(v) Ad cumulum* . . . *(vi) Gratie*[3] *divine premium* . . .
F de parma / · B· / . B· xx x x x x x x Bolis.

[1] Unusually, the conclusion to the chapter gives his surname: Forman (MS: *Forma'*)

[2] usually enregistered before conclusion to people

[3] *Hodie et cetera* deleted, initialled *B*

631   27 November 1501   *Reg. Lat.* 1096, fos 107^v-108^r

To Andrew, elect of Moray. Since the pope has [recently][1] made provision of Andrew to the church of Moray, as is more fully contained in his letters drawn up in that regard,[2] he hereby grants faculty to Andrew — at his supplication — to receive consecration from any catholic bishop etc. [as above, no. 57, with appropriate changes, to '. . . marked with his seal;'] and that the above shall not be to the prejudice of the archbishop of St Andrews, to whom the aforesaid church is understood to be subject by metropolitical law. With the form of oath appended.

Cum nos idem[3] . . .
F de parma / · B· / B· xxviij· Bolis·

[1] *idem; recte:* 'pridem'

[2] above, no. 630

[3] *sic; cf.* note 1

632   26 November 1501   *Reg. Lat.* 1096, fos 108ᵛ-109ʳ

To Andrew, elect of Moray, whom the pope has this day provided to the church of
Moray and appointed bishop, as is more fully contained in his letters drawn up in
that regard.[1] Since, as the pope has learned, at the time of the said provision and
appointment Andrew was holding, as he does, the priory of Mayo *alias*
Petynveymen, OSA, d. St Andrews, *in titulum*, and the rectory of the parish church
of Totinczhanen, d. York, *in commendam*, by apostolic concession and dispensation,
the pope — *motu proprio* — hereby dispenses Andrew to retain as before — even
after he has, on the strength of the said provision and appointment, received
consecration and peacefully acquired possession, or almost, of the rule and
administration and of the goods of the church of Moray or the greater part of them
— the priory, which is conventual and is a dependency of the church of St Andrews,
said order, and the rectory, whose annual values do not exceed 130 and 30 pounds
sterling [respectively], (even if the priory is customarily elective and has cure of
souls) together with the church of Moray, for as long as he presides over it;
notwithstanding etc. and [notwithstanding] the constitutions of Otto and Ottobuono
formerly legates of the apostolic see in the kingdom of England.[2] With decree that
the priory and vicarage[3] are not made vacant and the commend does not cease on
this account. With the proviso that the priory and rectory shall not, on this account,
be defrauded of due services and the cure of souls in the rectory and (if any) the
priory shall not be neglected; but that their customary burdens shall be supported.[4]

Personam tuam nobis et apostolice sedi devotam tuis exigentibus meritis paterna
benivolentia prosequentes illa tibi libenter concedimus . . .
F. de parma / · B· / · B· Lxx· Bolis·

[1] above, no. 630

[2] These constitutions are included here — in this essentially 'Scottish' entry — because the rectory
Forman is holding is in England.

[3] *sic:* vicarage; in error for 'rectory'?

[4] Relatively unusually for a letter of this type there is an executory; most unusually it was enregistered
elsewhere (below, no. 698).

633   26 November 1501   *Reg. Lat.* 1096, fo 109ᵛ

To Andrew Forman, prior of the priory of Mayo *alias* Petynveymen,[1] OSA, d. St
Andrews. Since the pope, on the advice of the cardinals, intends this day to make
provision of Andrew to the church of Moray, at present vacant *certo modo*, and to
appoint him bishop, he hereby absolves him from any sentences of
excommunication etc. [as above, no. 53[2]].

Apostolice sedis consueta clementia ne dispositiones . . .

F de parma /. B· / B· xx· Bolis·

[1] changed (by deletion) from *Peyt-*; not initialled
[2] but here enregistered in a slightly abridged form

634   26 February 1501   *Reg. Lat.* 1096, fos 244^r-246^r

To Richard, elect of Norwich. Consistorial provision of him — archdeacon of the church of Wells and in priest's orders — to the church of Norwich, vacant by the death, outside the Roman curia, of the late bishop Thomas, during whose rule the said church was specially reserved by the pope to his own disposition; and appointment of Richard as bishop, committing to him the care and administration of the church in spiritualities and temporalities.

   Conclusions to: (i) the chapter of the church of Norwich, (ii) the clergy of the city and diocese, (iii) the people of the city and diocese, (iv) the vassals of the said church, (v) Henry, king of England, (vi) the archbishop of Canterbury.

Apostolatus officium quamquam insuficientibus[1] *meritis nobis ex alto commissum . . .*
The conclusions begin: *(i) Hodie ecclesie vestre . . . (ii), (iv) Hodie ecclesie Norwicen. . . . (iii) Hodie et cetera. (v) Gratie divine premium . . .* [2] *(vi) Ad cumulum et cetera.*
. A. de Sanctoseverino /. V. / V· · · xx· x x x x x x De Phano:

[1] *sic*
[2] The engrossment is PRO Papal Bulls, SC. 7/37(30).

635   26 February 1501   *Reg. Lat.* 1096, fo 246^v

To Richard Nikke, archdeacon of the church of Wells. Since the pope, on the advice of the cardinals, intends this day to make provision of Richard to the church of Norwich, vacant *certo modo*, and <to appoint>[1] him bishop, he hereby absolves him from any sentences of excommunication, etc. [as above, no. 53].

Apostolice sedis circumspecta benignitas de statu personarum ecclesiasticarum quarumlibet . . .
A de sancto severino /. V· / V· xx· De Phano:

[1] marginal insertion by the enregistering scribe; initialled . *V.*

636   27 February 1501   *Reg. Lat.* 1096, fo 247[r-v]

To Richard, [elect][1] of Norwich. Since the pope has recently made provision of Richard to the church of Norwich, as is more fully contained in his letters drawn up in that regard,[2] he hereby grants faculty to Richard — at his supplication — to receive consecration from any catholic bishop etc. [as above, no. 57,[3] with appropriate changes, to '. . . marked with his seal;'] and that the above shall not be to the prejudice of the archbishop of Canterbury, to whom the aforesaid church is understood to be subject by metropolitical law. With the form of oath appended.

Cum nos pridem . . .
A de sancto severino / . *V· / V· xxviij · De Phano:*

[1] 'electo' wanting

[2] above, no. 634

[3] though here MS wants 'apostolice'; and *quamtocius* is inserted in the margin by the enregistering scribe; initialled . *V.*

637   14 March 1498   *Reg. Lat.* 1096, fos 272[r]-273[r]

To John Frisel, elect of Ross. Consistorial provision of him — canon of Glasgow and in priest's orders — to the church of Ross, vacant by the death, outside the Roman curia, of the late bishop John (Gulture),[1] during whose rule the said church was specially reserved by the pope to his own disposition; and appointment of the above John as bishop, committing to him the care and administration of the church in spiritualities and temporalities.

Conclusions to: (i) the chapter of the church of Ross, (ii) the clergy of the city and diocese, (iii) the people of the city and diocese, (iv) the vassals of the said church, (v) the archbishop of St Andrews, (vi) James, king of Scotland.[2]

Apostolatus officium quamquam insufficientibus meritis nobis ex alto commissum . . .
The conclusions begin: *(i) Hodie ecclesie vestre . . . (ii), (iii), (iv) Hodie et cetera. (v) Ad cumulum et cetera. (vi) Gratie divine et cetera.*
F de parma[3]; *Jo de Turchis*[4] */ . B. / . B. xx x x x x x x Bagarothus Proton'.*

[1] this name is supplied in the conclusion to the chapter — unusually, but presumably to distinguish the late bishop John from John the elect

[2] *Scotie* (not 'Scotorum')

[3] upper part shaved away

[4] an abbreviator *de parco minori* (the one, presumably, who expedited the conclusions); not usually noted in the register

638   15 March 1498   *Reg. Lat.* 1096, fo 273[r]

To John Frisel, elect of Ross. Since the pope has recently made provision of John to the church of Ross, as is more fully contained in his letters drawn up in that regard,[1] he hereby grants faculty to John — at his supplication — to receive consecration from any catholic bishop etc. [as above, no. 57, with appropriate changes, to '. . . marked with his seal;'] and that the above shall not be to the prejudice of the archbishop of St Andrews, to whom the aforesaid church is understood to be subject by metropolitical law. With the form of oath appended.

Cum nos pridem . . .
F. de parma /. B. /. B. xxvijj Bagarothus Proton.'

[1] above, no. 637

639   14 March 1498   *Reg. Lat.* 1096, fo 273[v]

To John Frisel, canon of Glasgow. Since the pope, on the advice of the cardinals, intends this day to make provision of John to the church of Ross, vacant *certo modo*, and to appoint him bishop, he hereby absolves him from any sentences of excommunication, etc. [as above, no. 53].

Apostolice sedis consueta clementia ne dispositiones . . .
F de parma[1] /. B. /. B. xx . Bagarothus Proton. '

[1] upper part shaved away

640   14 March 1498   *Reg. Lat.* 1096, fo 273[v]

To John Frisel, canon of Glasgow. Since the pope, on the advice of the cardinals, intends this day to make provision of John to the church of Ross, vacant *certo modo*, and to appoint him bishop, he — *motu proprio* — hereby dispenses him (who, some time ago, as the pope has learned, was dispensed by apostolic authority notwithstanding a defect of birth as the son of a priest, then an unmarried man, and a married woman, to be promoted to all, even sacred, orders, and afterwards was duly promoted to the said orders) to be appointed to and preside over the said church, perform and exercise its care and administration in spiritualities and temporalities and receive and use consecration. Notwithstanding the said defect etc.

Divina supereminens[1] *largitas . . .*
F de parma / . B. / . B. xxx . Bagarothus Proton.'

[1] *sic; cf.* 'superveniens'

641   23 March 1501   *Reg. Lat.* 1097, fos 73ʳ-74ᵛ

To Edward Scot, LLD, rector of the parish church of Sutton in Colfeld, d. Coventry
and Lichfield, papal familiar. Dispensation and indult — at his supplication — to
him, who is also a continual commensal and a *cubicularius* of the pope, to receive
and retain for life, together with the above parish church, two, or without it, any
three other benefices, etc. [as above, no. 17, to '. . . retain them together for life, as
above'][1]; and also for life, not to be bound, while residing in the Roman curia or any
one of his benefices, or attending a *studium generale*, to reside personally in the
church of Sutton or other benefices held by him at the time, even if defined as above,
nor to be liable to be compelled by anyone to do so against his will; and not to be
bound, by reason of the church of Sutton and any other benefices held by him at the
time having cure of souls or requiring sacred orders by foundation or otherwise, to
have himself promoted henceforth for a seven-year period to any of the sacred orders
in question, provided that he shall be a subdeacon within two years. Notwithstanding
constitutions etc., even if he (or his proctor) perchance has taken or shall take an
oath to observe them and not to impetrate apostolic letters contrary to them and not
to make use of such letters even if impetrated by another (or others) or granted in
any other way, etc. With the proviso that the above church and the incompatible and
other benefices in question shall not, on this account, be defrauded of due services
and the cure of souls in the above church and (if any) the incompatible and other
benefices aforesaid shall not be neglected; but that customary burdens of benefices
requiring sacred orders and those in which he shall not reside shall be supported.

Grata familiaritatis obsequia que nobis hactenus inpe[n]disti . . .
N. de Castello / · B· / · B· Grat(is) de man(da)to. Bolis̄

[1] as to content; though the order of words is not identical

642   21 August 1501   *Reg. Lat.* 1097, fos 133ᵛ-135ʳ

To the bishop of Agia (*Agien.*), the abbot of the monastery of Kelso (*de Calco*), d. St
Andrews, and the dean of the church of Glasgow, mandate in favour of John
Duncani, priest, d. Glasgow. The pope has learned that a certain perpetual simple
ecclesiastical benefice, called a clerkship (*officium clericatus*), in the parish church,

called a chapel, of Melros, said diocese, is vacant *certo modo* at present and has been vacant for so long that by the Lateran statutes its collation has lawfully devolved on the apostolic see. He hereby commands that the above three, or two or one of them, in person or by proxy, shall collate and assign the benefice, whose annual value does not exceed 2²/3 pounds sterling, vacant howsoever etc., even if specially reserved etc., with all rights and appurtenances, to John, inducting him etc. having removed any unlawful detainer and causing John (or his proctor) to be admitted to the benefice and its fruits etc., rights and obventions to be delivered to him. [Curbing] gainsayers by the pope's authority etc. Notwithstanding etc.

Vite ac morum honestas . . .
· *L· puccius / B / · B· xx Id' Septembr' anno Vndecimo.* [13 September 1502], *Bolis.*

643[1]   **4 May 1502**   *Reg. Lat.* 1097, fos 401ʳ-403ᵛ

To James Murray, MA, canon of Ross, *motu proprio* collation and provision, and reservation. The pope, wishing the present letters to operate as if granted *sub data kalendis Martii pontificatus nostri anno quarto* [1 March 1496], hereby collates to James (who, as he has learned, is of noble birth and does not hold another expectative grace from him) a canonry of the church of Ross,[2] with plenitude of canon law, and makes provision of it; and he reserves to apostolic donation, for collation to James after his acceptance, with all their rights and appurtenances, a prebend and a dignity, *personatus*, administration, or office of the same church, and also another benefice, with or without cure, even a rural deanery or archpresbytry, or vicarage, or perpetual chaplaincy,[3] which are reputed dignities, even with cure, though outside a cathedral church, or a dignity, or *personatus*, or any one of them, canonry and prebend, administration, or office, in a cathedral or collegiate church, even if the dignities, etc. should be customarily elective and have cure of souls — provided that any dignity aforesaid be not major *post pontificalem* in the church of Ross or other cathedral church, or principal in a collegiate church — and the annual value of this benefice (according to the taxation of the tenth) shall not exceed 35 marks sterling, if it be with cure or a dignity or *personatus*, and 25 marks, if not, and pertaining to the collation, provision, presentation, election, or other disposition of the bishop of Brechin and the dean, provost, chapter, and individual canons and persons of the church of Brechin, even by reason of the dignities, *personatus*, administrations, and offices which they hold in that church, collectively or severally, if they are vacant at present or when they fall vacant, at once or successively, which James, in person or by his lawfully appointed proctor, accepts within the space of one month after their vacancy shall have become known to him or his proctor, strictly inhibiting the bishop and chapter of Ross and those to whom, collectively or severally, the collation, etc. pertains, from making disposition of the prebends, dignity, etc. in the church of Ross, and also the bishop, dean, etc. of Brechin, from making disposition of the other benefice, in the interim, even before James's acceptance, unless they are certain that he or his proctor has refused them. Notwithstanding etc. It is the pope's will that as soon as James has peacefully acquired possession, on the strength of the presents, of any one of the dignities, *personatus*, administrations, and offices, or of a benefice with cure, the present letters are void as regards a benefice incompatible with it, etc.

Executory to the archbishop of Ragusa, the dean of the church of Moray, and the official of Moray, or two or one of them, acting in person or by proxy.

Nobilitas generis, litterarum scientia, vite ac morum honestas . . . The executory begins: *Hodie dilecto filio Jacobo Murray . . .*
N de Castello; P de Planca / · B· / ¡ B· xij· x Quarto Id(us) Junij anno decimo [10 June 1502], · *Bolis*

[1] *Ex(pectati)va* in left margin at beginning of letter, in a contemporary hand (but not enregistering scribe's?)

[2] in its recital the executory has here, erroneously, canonry *and prebend* [my italics] of the church of Ross

[3] MS: *vicaria vel capellania perpetua: recte* 'perpetua vicaria vel capellania'?

644   22 January 1502   *Reg. Lat.* 1098, fos 60^v-62^v

To the bishop of Sagone, the archdeacon of the church of Worcester and the vicar general of the bishop of Worcester, mandate in favour of Hugh Moris, priest of Worcester. A recent petition to the pope on Hugh's part stated that at another time — after he had been dispensed by ordinary authority notwithstanding a defect of birth as the son of an unmarried man and an unmarried woman to be promoted to minor orders and had had himself duly promoted to the said orders; and a certain count palatine, asserting that he had power to dispense over this, had dispensed Hugh to inherit paternal and maternal goods in a certain way then expressed and to have himself promoted to sacred orders — Hugh, believing that this was permissible for him, simple and ignorant of law and without having obtained any dispensation in this regard, had himself promoted to all sacred orders, otherwise however duly, and ministered therein.[1] Then — without having obtained any dispensation in regard to the irregularity in question[2] — M. Hadrian Castellesi (*Castellen.*), cleric of Corneto, papal notary, then nuncio of the apostolic see in the kingdom of England, having, as he asserted, special faculty for this from the said see through its letters, by pretext of them dispensed Hugh, who asserted that he had been promoted to the said orders by a canonical dispensation, to hold any two benefices otherwise mutually compatible. Next, the then prior of the church of Worcester, OSB, by ordinary authority, collated and made provision of the parish church of St Martin, d. Worcester, then vacant *certo modo* — since its collation and provision at a time of vacancy pertains by ancient, approved and hitherto peacefully observed custom to the prior of the church of Worcester for the time being — to Hugh, albeit *de facto*; and he, taking possession of the parish church by pretext of this collation and provision, thenceforth detained it, receiving fruits therefrom, likewise *de facto*, contracting disability. Moreover since, according to the foregoing, Hadrian's dispensation and also the collation and provision aforesaid do not hold good; and, as the pope has learned, the said parish church is known to be vacant still, as above, the pope — rehabilitating Hugh on account of all disability and infamy contracted by him by occasion of the foregoing — hereby commands[3] that the above three, or two or one of them, in person or by proxy, shall collate and assign the parish church, whose annual value does not exceed 15 marks sterling, equivalent to 45 gold ducats of the camera or thereabouts, (vacant howsoever etc., even if it has been vacant for so long that by the Lateran statutes its collation has lawfully devolved on the apostolic see etc.), with all rights and appurtenances, to Hugh, inducting him etc. having removed any unlawful detainer and causing its fruits etc., rights and obventions to be delivered to Hugh.[4] [Curbing] gainsayers by the pope's authority etc. Notwithstanding etc. The pope dispenses Hugh — if the said collation and provision be carried out by the above three by virtue of the presents — to minister in the orders he has taken and receive and retain the church, if conferred on him by virtue of the presents, notwithstanding the above defect of birth etc. The pope's will is, however, that before the above three shall proceed to the execution of the presents in any way, Hugh shall resign the parish church into their hands (or the hands of any one of them) genuinely and completely.

Sedes apostolica pia mater recurrentibus ad eam cum humilitate . . .
F. de. parma / · *B·* / · *B· xxx decimo KL' Maij anno Vndecimo·* [22 April 1502], *Bolis·*

[1] *irregularitatem contrahendo* deleted and initialled *B.* and . *B*
[2] *Cf.* note 1
[3] 'discretioni vestre per apostolica scripta' wanting
[4] no mention of his being admitted

645   14 May 1502   *Reg. Lat.* 1098, fos 109[r]-110[r]

To the prior of the monastery, usually governed by a prior, of Imistyok, d. Ossory, the dean of the church of Waterford and Robert Hedyan, canon of the church of Cashel, mandate in favour of William Comerford, cleric, d. Ossory (who, as he asserts, notwithstanding a defect of birth as the son of the dean, then a chaplain, of the church of Ossory, and an unmarried woman, has been duly marked with clerical character). The pope has learned that the rectory of the parish church of Culcrahyn, d. Ossory, which is of lay patronage, is vacant *certo modo* at present and has been vacant for so long that by the Lateran statutes its collation has lawfully devolved on the apostolic see, although Maurus Olealonyr, who bears himself as a priest, has detained it, with no title and no support of law, temerariously and *de facto*, for a certain time, as he does. At a recent petition on William's part to the pope to erect and institute a canonry in the church of Ossory and the said rectory into a simple prebend of the same, for his lifetime, the pope hereby commands that the above three (or two or one of them), if, having summoned Maurus and the bishop and chapter of Ossory as regards the erection and institution and others concerned, they find the rectory, whose annual value does not exceed 8 marks sterling, to be vacant (howsoever etc.), shall (even if the rectory be specially reserved etc.) erect and institute a canonry in the said church of Ossory and the rectory into a simple prebend of the same, for his lifetime; and, in that event, collate and assign the newly erected canonry and prebend, being then vacant, to William, with plenitude of canon law and all rights and appurtenances, inducting him etc. having removed Maurus and any other unlawful detainer from the rectory and causing William (or his proctor) to be received as a canon of the church of Ossory, with plenitude of canon law, and the fruits etc., rights and obventions of the canonry and prebend to be delivered to him. [Curbing] gainsayers etc. Notwithstanding etc. Also the pope dispenses William to be promoted to all, even sacred, orders, and to receive and retain the canonry and prebend, if conferred on him by virtue of the presents. Notwithstanding the said defect of birth etc. and that William's father is the dean of the church of Ossory, etc. The pope's will is, however, that the rectory shall not, on account of this erection and institution, be defrauded of due services and the cure of souls therein shall not be neglected, but that its customary burdens shall be supported; and that on William's death or resignation etc. of the canonry and prebend [the erection and institution of] the canonry and prebend shall be extinguished and the rectory shall revert to its original condition automatically.

Ex debito pastoralis officii nobis licet inmeritis superna dispositione commissi ad ea libenter intendimus . . .

A de S^{to} Severino | · B· | · B· xxx non' Kl' Junij anno decimo [24 May 1502], · *Bolis*

---

646   12 May 1502   *Reg. Lat.* 1098, fos 110^V-111^V

To the prior of the monastery, usually governed by a prior, of Inisconayn, d. Killaloe, mandate in favour of Magonius Yfflaytbertay, cleric, d. [Annaghdown],[1] (who, as he asserts, is in his eleventh year of age, is of noble birth by both parents and is studying both laws at a *studium generale* in a certain place). The pope has learned that the perpetual vicarages of the parish churches of Kylleomyn and Kyllardun, d. Annaghdown, are vacant *certo modo* at present and have been vacant for so long that by the Lateran statutes their collation has lawfully devolved on the apostolic see. At a recent petition on Magonius's part to the pope to erect and institute a canonry in the church of Annaghdown and the vicarages into a simple prebend of that church, for his lifetime, the pope (who, some time ago, decreed and declared that provisions or grants or mandates of provision to canonries and prebends of cathedral churches to persons who have not completed their fourteenth year shall have no force except by consent of the apostolic see) hereby commands the above prior,[2] if he finds

Magonius to be suitable (having taken his age into account) — concerning which the pope burdens the prior's conscience — having summoned the bishop and chapter of Annaghdown and others concerned, to erect and institute a canonry in the church of Annaghdown and the vicarages, whose annual value together does not exceed 3 marks sterling, (vacant howsoever etc., even if by the death of the late Roger Yco'mimayn,[3] outside the Roman curia, etc.; even if specially reserved etc.), into a simple prebend of the church of Annaghdown, without prejudice to anyone; and, in that event, collate and assign the newly erected canonry and prebend, being vacant, to Magonius, with plenitude of canon law and all rights and appurtenances, inducting him etc. having removed any unlawful detainer and causing Magonius (or his proctor) to be received as a canon of the church of Annaghdown, with plenitude of canon law, and the fruits etc., rights and obventions of the canonry and prebend to be delivered to him. [Curbing] gainsayers etc. Notwithstanding etc. Also the pope indulges Magonius to receive and retain the canonry and prebend, if conferred on him by virtue of the presents, notwithstanding the above defect of age etc. The pope's will is, however, that the vicarages and canonry and prebend shall not, on this account, be defrauded of due services and the cure of souls in the vicarages shall not be neglected, but that the customary burdens of the canonry and prebend shall be supported; and that on Magonius's death or resignation etc. of the canonry and prebend this erection and institution shall be extinguished and the vicarages shall revert to their original condition automatically. And the pope has commanded that — if Magonius be found suitable — provision of the canonry and prebend be made to him from the date of the presents.

Ex debito pastoralis officii nobis licet inmeritis superna dispositione commissi ad ea libenter intendimus . . .
A de S^{to} Severino / · B· / · B· xxxx Quinto Kl' Junij anno decimo· [28 May 1502], Bolis·

1 *dicte diocesis* evidently referring to Annaghdown (the word-order of the text not being strictly adhered to in this summary)

2 *discretioni vestre; recte:* 'discretioni tue'

3 i. e. *Yco(m)mimayn;* the 'im' doubtful

647   18 May 1502   *Reg. Lat.* 1098, fo 113^{r-v}

To William Fuye, James Scyortal and William Ohallmarayl, canons of the churches of Limerick, Ossory and Annaghdown, mandate in favour of James Macnamara[1] *alias* Scyda, canon of the church of [Killaloe].[2] The pope has learned that the treasurership of the church of Killaloe is vacant *certo modo* at present and has been vacant for so long that by the Lateran statutes its collation has lawfully devolved on the apostolic see, although Rory Mathanamara, who bears himself as a cleric, has detained it, without any title or support of law, temerariously and *de facto*, for a certain time, as he still does. At a recent petition on James's part to the pope to unite etc. the treasurership to the canonry and prebend which he holds in the said church, for as long as he holds the canonry and prebend — asserting that the annual value of the treasurership does not exceed 12, and of the canonry and prebend and annexes thereto, 26, marks sterling — the pope — not having certain knowledge of the foregoing — hereby commands that the above three (or two or one of them), having summoned Rory and others concerned and those interested in the union, shall inform themselves as to the foregoing and if they find it to be thus [and] find the treasurership (which is a non-major dignity *post pontificalem*) to be vacant (howsoever etc.), shall unite etc. it[3] (even if specially reserved etc.), with all rights and appurtenances, to the canonry and prebend, for as long as James holds the canonry and prebend; to the effect that James may, on his own authority, in person or by proxy, take corporal possession of the treasurership and convert its fruits etc. to his own uses and those of the treasurership and the canonry and prebend, and retain [it] for as long as he holds the canonry and prebend, without licence of the local diocesan or of anyone else. Notwithstanding etc. The pope's will is, however, that the treasurership shall not, on account of this union etc., be defrauded of due services and the cure of souls therein (if any) shall not be neglected, but that its customary burdens shall be supported; and that on James's death or resignation etc. of the canonry and prebend this union etc. shall be dissolved and so deemed and the treasurership shall revert to its original condition and be deemed vacant automatically.

Decet Romanum pontificem illis gratum prestare assensum . . .
A de S^to Severino / · B· / · B· xx octavo Kl' Junij anno· decimo· [25 May 1502],
Bolis·

[1] (?)*Macnamara* deleted and initialled *B*

[2] *dicte ecclesie* evidently referring to Killaloe (the word-order of the text not being strictly adhered to in this summary)

[3] no mention of Rory (the alleged detainer) or any other detainer being removed

648   31 May 1502   *Reg. Lat.* 1098, fos 127^r-129^r

To the abbot of the monastery of B. Mary, Kylthanna, d. Kilfenora, Maurice Obrien, canon of Killaloe, and the official of Kilfenora, mandate in favour of Cormac Ykyhyr, cleric, d. Kilfenora. The pope has learned that the canonry and prebend of the church of Kilfenora and the perpetual vicarage of the parish church of Kylthalbach, d. Kilfenora, which the late canon Dermot Obrien and the late perpetual vicar Denis Odea held while they lived, became vacant by their deaths outside the Roman curia, and are vacant at present, although Donald Oday has detained the vicarage without any title or support of law, of his own temerity and *de facto*, for a certain time, as he does. At a recent petition on Cormac's part to the pope to unite etc. the vicarage to the canonry and prebend, for as long as he holds the canonry and prebend, after he acquires them — asserting that some time ago he was dispensed by apostolic authority notwithstanding a defect of birth as the son of a <cleric>[1] and an unmarried woman to be promoted to all, even sacred, orders, and to hold a benefice, even if it should have cure of souls; that he afterwards had himself duly marked with clerical character; and that the annual value of the canonry and prebend does not exceed 2, and of the vicarage, also 2, marks sterling — the pope hereby commands that the above three (or two or one of them), if, having summoned Donald and others concerned and those interested in the union, they find the canonry and prebend and the vicarage to be vacant, (as above or howsoever etc.), shall (even if the canonry and prebend have been vacant for so long that by the Lateran statutes their collation has lawfully devolved on the apostolic see, and they and the vicarage be specially reserved etc.) unite etc. the vicarage to the canonry and prebend, for as long as Cormac holds the canonry and prebend; and collate and assign the canonry and prebend, with the annex and plenitude of canon law and all rights and appurtenances, to Cormac, inducting him etc. having removed Donald and any other unlawful detainers and causing Cormac (or his proctor) to be received as a canon of the church of Kilfenora, with plenitude of canon law, and the fruits etc., rights and obventions of the canonry and prebend and annexed vicarage to be delivered to him. [Curbing] gainsayers etc. Notwithstanding etc. Also the pope dispenses Cormac to receive and retain the canonry and prebend, if conferred on him by virtue of the presents, notwithstanding the above defect etc. The pope's will is, however, that the vicarage shall not, on account of this union etc., be defrauded of due services and the cure of souls therein shall not be neglected, but that its customary burdens shall be supported; and that on Cormac's death or resignation etc. of the canonry and prebend the union etc. shall be dissolved and so deemed and the vicarage shall revert to its original condition automatically.

Apostolice sedis providentia circumspecta votis illis . . .
F de parma / · B· / · B· xxx Septimo Kl' Junij anno decimo [26 June 1502], ｜*Bolis.*

[1] *soluto* in the line deleted; *clerico* inserted in the margin by the enregistering scribe initialled *B*

---

649   31 May 1502   *Reg. Lat.* 1098, fos 129ʳ-130ʳ

To the dean and archdeacon and Eugene Odalle, canon, of the church of Kilfenora, mandate in favour of <Maurice Obrien>,[1] canon of the church of Killaloe (who, as he asserts, holds the canonry and prebend of Rablanich <in the same>[2] and is of noble birth by both parents). The pope has learned that the monastery of B. Mary, Kyltanna, OSA, d. Kilfenora, over which Dermot Obriel, its late abbot, presided while he lived, has become vacant by his death outside the Roman curia and is vacant at present. Wishing to make provision of a capable and suitable person to the monastery to rule and direct it as well as to assist Maurice to support himself, the pope hereby commands that the above three, or two or one of them, in person or by proxy, shall commend the monastery, whose annual value does not exceed 16 marks sterling, whether vacant as above or howsoever etc., with all rights and appurtenances, to Maurice, to be held, ruled and governed by him for life; (he may — due and customary burdens of the monastery and its convent having been supported — make disposition of the rest of its fruits etc. just as those holding it *in titulum* could and ought to do, alienation of immovable goods and precious movables being however forbidden); committing to him the care, rule and administration of the monastery in spiritualities and temporalities, and causing due obedience and reverence to be given him by the convent and customary services and rights by the vassals and other subjects of the monastery. [Curbing] gainsayers etc. Notwithstanding etc. The pope's will is, however, that divine worship and the usual number of ministers in the monastery shall not, on account of this commend, be diminished, but that its aforesaid burdens and those of the convent shall be supported.

Romani pontificis providentia circumspecta . . .
S de Castello /· B. /· B· xxv· Bolis·

[1] *filio Mauritio Obrien* inserted in the margin by the enregistering scribe initialled *B* twice; *Dermitio* in the line deleted and initialled *B*; below, in the second instance: *Mauritium* inserted in the margin, with *Dermitium* in the line deleted and initialled *B*; in the three remaining instances: *Mauriti* — has simply been written over *Dermiti* — in the line, without initial
[2] marginal insertion by the enregistering scribe initialled *B*

650   2 July 1502   *Reg. Lat.* 1098, fos 133^v-135^r

To the prior of the monastery, usually governed by a prior, of Inniscronan', d. Killaloe, and the dean of [the church of] Cloyne and Maurus Obrien, canon of [the church of][1] Kilfenora, mandate in favour of Cornelius *alias* Curnea Macnamara, cleric, d. Killaloe (who, some time ago, as he asserts, was dispensed by apostolic authority notwithstanding a certain accidental homicide committed by him to be promoted to all sacred orders, and to receive and retain any benefices, even if they should be canonries and prebends in cathedral churches, if conferred on him otherwise canonically). The pope has learned that a canonry of the church of Killaloe and the prebend of Tullachannasbach[2] in the same and the perpetual vicarages of the parish churches of Clonroy[s][3] and Inyschalcra [also spelt *Inischaltra*] and also Nova Sancte Trinitatis, d. Killaloe, are vacant *certo modo* at present and have been vacant for so long that by the Lateran statutes their collation has lawfully devolved on the apostolic see, although John Macnamara has detained the canonry and prebend, Rory Oflannira, the vicarage of Clonroys, Odo Machsyda, that of Inyschalcra, and James *alias* Syda Macnamara, that of B. Mary *alias* of the Holy Trinity — bearing themselves as clerics — with no title and no support of law, of their own temerity and *de facto*, for a certain time, as they still do. At a recent petition on Cornelius's part to the pope to unite etc. the vicarages to the canonry and prebend, if conferred on him by virtue of the presents and he acquires them, for as long as he holds the canonry and prebend — asserting that the annual value of the canonry and prebend does not exceed 12, and of the vicarages together, 18, marks sterling — the pope hereby commands that the above three (or two or one of them), if, having summoned the aforesaid detainers and others concerned and those interested in the union, they find the canonry and prebend and vicarages to be vacant (howsoever etc.), shall collate and assign the canonry and prebend (even if they and the vicarages be specially reserved etc.), with plenitude of canon law and all rights and appurtenances, to Cornelius, and unite etc. the vicarages to the canonry and prebend, for as long as Cornelius holds the canonry and prebend, inducting him etc. having removed the aforesaid and any other unlawful detainers and causing Cornelius (or his proctor) to be received as a canon of the church of Killaloe, with plenitude of canon law, and the fruits etc., rights and obventions of the canonry and prebend and vicarages to be delivered to him. [Curbing] gainsayers etc. Notwithstanding etc. The pope's will is, however, that the vicarages shall not, on account of this union etc., be defrauded of due services and the cure of souls therein shall not be neglected, but that their customary burdens shall be supported; and that on Cornelius's death or resignation etc. of the canonry and prebend the union etc. shall be dissolved and so deemed and the vicarages shall revert to their original condition and be deemed vacant automatically.

Apostolice sedis providentia circumspecta ad ea libenter intendit . . .
N de Castello / Jo / Jo. xxx. Eps' Terracinen'

[1] 'ecclesiarum' does not occur

[2] the *-anna-* uncertain

[3] (?)*Cloro* deleted but not initialled just before the first occurrence of *Clonroy[s]* (the final [s] of which is blotched and detached)

651 28 June 1502   *Reg. Lat.* 1098, fos 137ᵛ-138ᵛ

To the precentor and the treasurer and John Macco'mara, canon, of the church of Killaloe, mandate in favour of Thady Ybryen, canon of Kilfenora. The pope has learned that the perpetual vicarage of the parish church of St (?)Findchu (*Sancte Ffynchie*), [1] d. Killaloe, is vacant *certo modo* at present and has been vacant for so long that by the Lateran statutes its collation has lawfully devolved on the apostolic see, although Roderick Ocwynd, priest, d. Killaloe, has detained it, without any title or support of law, temerariously and *de facto*, for a certain time, as he still does. At a recent petition on Thady's part to the pope to unite etc. the vicarage to the canonry and prebend of the church of Kilfenora which he holds, for as long as he holds the canonry and prebend — asserting that the annual value of <the vicarage>[2] does not exceed 8, and of the canonry and prebend, 1, marks sterling — the pope hereby commands that the above three (or two or one of them), if, having summoned Roderick and others concerned and those interested in the union, they find the vicarage to be vacant (howsoever etc.), shall unite etc. it (even if specially reserved etc.), with all rights and appurtenances, to the canonry and prebend, for as long as Thady holds the latter, to the effect that he may, on his own authority, in person or by proxy, take corporal possession of the vicarage and rights and appurtenances aforesaid, having removed Roderick and any other unlawful detainer and retain [it] for as long as he holds the canonry and prebend and convert its fruits etc. to his own uses and those of the canonry and prebend and vicarage, without licence of the local diocesan or of anyone else. Notwithstanding etc. The pope's will is, however, that the vicarage shall not, on this account, be defrauded of due services and the cure of souls therein shall not be neglected, but that its customary burdens shall be supported; and that on Thady's death or resignation etc. of the canonry and prebend this union etc. shall be dissolved and the vicarage shall revert to its original condition automatically.

Romanum decet pontificem votis illis gratum prestare assensum . . .
A de Sancto Severino / · B· / · B· xv· Bolis·

[1] or *Ffynclue*
[2] marginal insertion initialled . *B*.

652   27 July 1502[1]   *Reg. Lat.* 1098, fos 141[r]-142[v]

To the precentor, treasurer and John Tatei Macco(n)mara,[2] canon, of the church of Killaloe, mandate in favour of Cornelius *alias* Cunca Macco(n)marra,[3] cleric, d. Killaloe. The pope has learned that a canonry and the prebend of Donaomar[4] [of the church][5] of Limerick and the perpetual vicarages of the parish churches of Kyllyelly [also spelt *Kyllelly*], Kilfhyntanayn [also spelt *Kylfhyntanayn*], Cunthy, Cloynlokayn and Bym[r]athy[6] [also spelt *Bunrathyn*], ds. Limerick and Killaloe, are vacant *certis modis* at present and have been vacant for so long that by the Lateran statutes their collation has lawfully devolved on the apostolic see, although John Macomara [also spelt *Machomara*] has detained the canonry and prebend and the vicarages of Kyllyelly and Kilfhyntanayn, Thady Macomara, the vicarage of Cunthy, Laurence Omachayn, that of Cloynlokayn, and John Okyngrigayn [also spelt *Okyngrygayn*] that of Bym[r]athy, respectively — bearing themselves as clerics and priests — without any title or support of law, temerariously and *de facto*, for a certain time, as they still do. At a recent petition on Cornelius's part to the pope to unite etc. the vicarages to the canonry and prebend, for as long as Cornelius holds [the latter], if conferred on him by virtue of the presents — asserting that he, notwithstanding a defect of birth as the son of a cleric and an unmarried woman of noble birth related in the third and fifth degrees of consanguinity and affinity, has been duly marked with clerical character; and that the annual value of the canonry and prebend and vicarages does not exceed 40 marks sterling — the pope hereby commands that the above three (or two or one of them), if, having summoned John Macomara, Thady, Laurence and John Okyngrigayn respectively and others concerned and those interested in the union, they find the canonry and prebend and the vicarages to be vacant (howsoever etc.) and it to be true regarding the union, shall collate and assign the canonry and prebend (even if specially reserved etc.), with plenitude of canon law and all their rights and appurtenances, to Cornelius; and unite etc. the vicarages to the canonry and prebend, for as long as Cornelius holds the canonry and prebend, if conferred on him as above, inducting him etc. having removed John Macomara, Thady, Laurence and John Okyngrigayn respectively and any other unlawful detainers and causing Cornelius (or his proctor) to be received as a canon of the church of Limerick, with plenitude of canon law, and be admitted to the vicarages and their fruits etc., rights and obventions and those of the canonry and prebend to be delivered to him. [Curbing] gainsayers etc. Notwithstanding etc. Also the pope dispenses Cornelius to be promoted to all, even sacred, orders and receive and retain the canonry and prebend, if conferred on him by virtue of the presents, notwithstanding the above defect etc. The pope's will is, however, that the vicarages shall not, on this account, be defrauded of due services and the cure of souls therein shall not be neglected, but that their customary burdens shall be supported; and that on Cornelius's death or resignation etc. of the canonry and prebend the union etc. shall be dissolved and the vicarages shall revert to their original condition automatically.

Vite ac morum honestas . . .
A de S^{to} Severino / · B· / · B· xxx. Vndecimo Kl' Septembr' anno decimo· [22 August 1502], *Bolis·*

1 The date clause is markedly less cursive than the rest of the entry and may have been entered later (after the magistral signature?) in a pre-existant space; and there is a line between *kalendas* and *Augusti* which again is suggestive of filling in space

2 MS: *Macco'mara*

3 MS: *Macco'marra*

4 or *Donnomar*

5 'ecclesie' does not occur

6 the fourth letter blotched, perhaps 'o'

653   5 April 1502   *Reg. Lat.* 1099, fos 24^v-25^v

To Thomas Dalison, LLB, rector of the parish church of Brandon, d. Exeter. Dispensation — at his supplication — to receive and retain for life, together with the above parish church, one, and without it, any two other benefices, etc. [as above, no. 3].

Litterarum scientia, vite ac morum honestas . . .
L pucceus^1 / F / F · L . Sanctor(is)

1 *sic*

654[1]   **<21 September 1501>**[2]   *Reg. Lat.* 1099, fos 185^r-186^r

To Robert Wekis, <MA>,[3] perpetual vicar of the parish church of St Cyriac, Lacok, d. Salisbury. Dispensation and indult — at his supplication — to receive and retain for life, together with the perpetual vicarage of the above parish church, one, and without it, any two other benefices, etc. [as above, no. 3, to '. . . retain them together for life, as above']⁴; and for life, while attending a *studium generale* or residing in the Roman curia or any one of his benefices, not to be bound to reside in his other benefices, etc. [as above, no. 238]. Given at <St Peters, Rome>.⁵

<Litterarum scientia>,⁶ *vite ac morum honestas . . .*
*L pucceus*⁷ / · *B·* / . *B. Lx Bolis*

¹ This letter has been enregistered twice (by mistake?). The two entries were made in separate registers by different scribes (the one here by Marasca, the one below (summarised at no. 772) by Boccapaduli). Neither has been cancelled. The present entry has been much corrected by order of the regent of the chancery, the corrections being made by Marasca himself. As corrected, this entry is essentially the same as the other entry which did not have to be corrected. The corrections to this entry were added in the margin and have been incorporated into the summary above, with the original version noted below (notes 2-4, 6).

² Originally dated: *Civitatis Castellane* [i. e. Civita Castellana] *Anno Incarnationis dominice Millesimo quingentesimo primo Quarto kalendas Octobris Anno Decimo* [28 September 1501] (the deletion being initialled . *B.* in six places); corrected (in the margin) to . *B. Rome apud Sanctum Petrum Anno Incarnationis dominice Millesimo quingentesimo primo undecimo kalendas Octobris Anno Decimo. Adictum de mandato ut supra . B. Bolis.* .

³ Marginal addition: *B. Magister in artibus Aditum de mandato R(everendissimi) p(atris) D(omini) Jo(hannis) ragusini regent(is) . B. Bolis.*

⁴ part of the text being, in the present instance, added in the margin, namely: *B. in cathedralibus etiam metropolitanis vel collegiatis et dignitates ipse in cathedralibus etiam metropolitanis post pontificales maiores seu collegiatis ecclesiis huiusmodi principales seu talia mixtim fuerint et ad dignitates personatus administrationes vel officia Aditum ut supra . B. Bolis.*

⁵ see above, note 2

⁶ Marginal addition: *. B. Litterarum scientia Aditum de mandato ut supra . B. Bolis*

⁷ *sic*

655   1 February 1502   *Reg. Lat.* 1099, fos 344^v-345^r

To the bishop of Norwich, mandate. A recent petition presented to the pope on the part of Henry Rabett, layman, and Olive Chappeleyʒ, woman, of Norwich, stated that they desire to be joined together in marriage, but that — because formerly the late Helen, then Henry's wife, now deceased, had been godmother to a certain child of Olive by her first husband, a spiritual relationship arose — they cannot fulfil their desire in this matter without an apostolic dispensation. The pope therefore, not having certain knowledge of the foregoing, on the aforesaid and several other reasonable grounds demonstrated to him on the part of Henry and Olive (who, as they assert, are not rich) — at their supplication — hereby commands the above bishop — if it is so and Olive has not been ravished on this account — to dispense Henry and Olive to contract marriage together and remain therein, notwithstanding the impediment of the above spiritual relationship, etc., declaring the offspring of the marriage legitimate.

Oblate nobis nuper pro parte [. . .] petitionis series continebat . . .
A de sancto severino / · B· ¹ / . B. Lx Bolis

¹ a swung dash to the left

656   10 March 1502   *Reg. Lat.* 1099, fo 367^{r-v}

To Robert Wadyluff, perpetual vicar of the parish church of Ravensthorppe, d. Lincoln. Dispensation — at his supplication — to receive and retain for life, together with the said [church],¹ one, and without it, any two other benefices, etc. [as above, no. 3]. Given at Civitavecchia, d. Viterbo.

Vite ac morum honestas . . .
L puccius / F / F. L^{ta}. Sanctor(is)

¹ *ecclesia; recte:* 'vicaria' (as, consistently, above and below)

657   25 September 1501   *Reg. Lat.* 1100, fo 8^{r-v}

To William Theccher, BDec, rector of the parish church of Westden' [also spelt *Vestden'*], d. Chichester. Dispensation — at his supplication — to receive and retain for life, together with the above parish church, one, and without it, any two other benefices, etc. [as above, no. 3].

Litterarum scientia, vite ac morum honestas . . .
F de parma / · B· /₁B. L. Bolis.

658   25 September 1501   *Reg. Lat.* 1100, fo 9^{r-v}

To William Benett, monk of the monastery of St Andrew, Bromholme', OClun, d. Norwich. Dispensation — at his supplication — to him, who, as he asserts, is expressly professed of the above order,[1] to receive and retain any benefice, with or without cure, usually held by secular clerics, etc. [as above, no. 32].

Religionis zelus, vite ac morum honestas . . .
F de parma / . B· / . B. xxx. Bolis.

[1] This information comes from a notwithstanding clause.

659   31 December 1501   *Reg. Lat.* 1100, fo 23^{r-v}

To Nicholas Sueede,[1] perpetual vicar of the parish church of Salforde, d. Worcester. Dispensation and indult — at his supplication — to receive and retain for life, together with the perpetual vicarage of the above parish church, one, and without it, any two other benefices, etc. [as above, no. 3, to '. . . retain them together for life, as above']; and, for life, while attending a *studium generale* or residing in the Roman curia or any one of his benefices, not to be bound to reside in his other benefices, etc. [as above, no. 238].

Vite ac morum honestas . . .
F. de parma / . B· / · B. Lx . Bolis

[1] or *Sneede*

660   31 December 1501   *Reg. Lat.* 1100, fos 26^{r}-27^{r}

To John Alenson', rector of the parish church of St Margaret, Shattyshm [also spelt *Shattyhm*], d. Norwich. Dispensation — at his supplication — to receive and retain for life, together with the above parish church, one, and without it, any two other benefices, etc. [as above, no. 3].

Vite ac morum honestas . . .
F. de parma / · B· /\B L. Bolis.

661   13 January 1502   *Reg. Lat.* 1100, fos 35^{r}-36^{v}

To the bishops of Winchester and London and the abbot of the monastery of St Peter, Wostm', d. London, mandate in favour of the dean and chapter of the church of Chichester and John Body of Weseden', cleric or layman, d. Chichester. A recent

petition to the pope on the part of the dean and chapter and John stated that
<although>[1] all the tithes which come from fruits of the fields of Weseden', and
from Wesefelde, Chestfelden', Southgasten', Estgaston', Nodylfeld', Malecomys,
and Northfelde, within the boundary of the parish church of Estden', d. Chichester,
and the right of receiving them, lawfully pertain to the capitular *mensa* of the church
of Chichester through sundry pious gifts and grants made to the dean and chapter
and confirmed by apostolic authority, and otherwise, by ancient, approved, and
hitherto peacefully observed custom; and although the deans for the time being and
chapter have been in peaceful possession, or almost, of the right of receiving the
tithes, and of the aforesaid grants, for so long that there is no recollection to the
contrary; nevertheless Thomas Campion' *alias* Campio', who bears himself as rector
of the parish church — falsely claiming that the tithes by right belong to him and
that John, who had been duly deputed collector or farmer of the tithes by the dean
and chapter, had unlawfully gathered and removed them — sued John before
Humphrey Halbarden', official of the episcopal[2] court of Canterbury, whom he said
was a competent judge, praying that the tithes be declared to belong to him by right
and that John be condemned and compelled to restore them; and although the official
had admitted the dean and chapter with John to the defence of the case, he —
unlawfully refusing to allow the dean and chapter to prove their title and possession,
as had been lawfully prayed on their part, and wrongly proceeding to the later stages
in the cause — nevertheless promulgated an unjust definitive sentence by which he
pronounced that the tithes belong to Thomas, that John had collected and removed
them illegally, and that he was bound to restore them or their true value to Thomas,
condemning John in expenses; from which appeal was made on John's part to the
apostolic see, but the official — contemptuous of the appeal (of which he was not
ignorant) and when John was still well within the time for prosecuting it —
endeavoured (and is endeavouring), albeit *de facto* and temerariously, to have the
sentence executed and to compel John to obey it by ecclesiastical censures. At the
supplication to the pope on the part of the dean and chapter and John to command
that John be absolved conditionally from the sentence of excommunication and any
other ecclesiastical sentences, censures, and pains perchance inflicted on him by the
official, and to commit to some upright men in those parts the causes of the appeal;
of everything attempted and innovated after and against the appeal; of the nullity of
the refusal, definitive sentence, sentence of excommunication, and other sentences,
etc. ; of the official's whole process and of everything prejudicial to the dean and
chapter and John done by him and Thomas and any others in connection with the
above; and of the principal matter, the pope hereby commands that the above three
(or two or one of them), having summoned Thomas and others concerned, shall, if
and as it is just, for this once only, conditionally absolve John, if he so requests,
having first received suitable security from him that if it appears to them that the
sentences, etc. were justly inflicted on him, he will obey their commands and those
of the church; and, as regards the rest, having heard both sides, taking cognizance
even of the principal matter, that they shall decree what is just, without appeal,
causing by ecclesiastical censure what they have decreed to be strictly observed;
[and moreover compel] witnesses etc. Notwithstanding, etc.

Humilibus et cetera.
Jo ortega[3] / - *B·* / . *B· xiiij· Bolis*

[1] marginal insertion by the enregistering scribe; not initialled
[2] MS *episcopalis; recte* 'archiepiscopalis'
[3] in different ink : entered later?

662   14 September 1501   *Reg. Lat.* 1100, fo 43[r-v]

To John Clerck,[1] cleric, d. Norwich. Dispensation — at his supplication — to him, who, as he asserts, is in his nineteenth year of age, to receive and retain any benefice, with cure or otherwise incompatible, etc. [as above, no. 240]. [2]

Vite ac morum honestas . . .
F de parma[3] / . *B·* / . *B· xxiiij. Bolis*

[1] or *Clerk* : the second 'c' possibly deleted (though not initialled)
[2] save that in this instance MS wants 'valeas'
[3] in a lighter ink : entered later?

663   10 September 1501   *Reg. Lat.* 1100, fos 65[v]-66[v]

Union etc. At a recent petition on the part of Christopher Wyngho, canon of Exeter[1], the pope hereby unites etc. the parish church of Kyngesdon', d. Bath and Wells, (whose annual value does not exceed 27[2] marks sterling, equivalent to 81[3] gold ducats of the camera or thereabouts), to the canonry and prebend of the church of Exeter, which he holds together with the above parish church, for as long as he holds the canonry and prebend, to the effect that Christopher, in person or by proxy, may, on his own authority, continue in or take anew and retain corporal possession of the parish church and its rights and appurtenances, for as long as he holds the canonry and prebend, and convert[4] its fruits etc. to his own uses and those of the canonry and prebend and the parish church without licence of the local diocesan or of anyone else. Notwithstanding etc. The pope's will is, however, that the parish church shall not, on account of this union etc., be defrauded of due services and the cure of souls therein shall not be neglected, but that its customary burdens shall be supported; and that on Christopher's death or resignation etc. of the canonry and prebend the union etc. shall be dissolved and so deemed and the parish church shall revert to its original condition automatically.

Ad futuram rei memoriam. Romanum decet pontificem votis[5] *gratum prestare*

assensum . . .
F. de parma[6] */ · B· / ⎮ B· xxxv Bolis·*

[1] *dioc(esis)* deleted, but not initialled

[2] *quindecim* in line deleted and initialled *B*; . *Vigintiseptem* inserted in margin, initialled *B*; *Cassatum et corectum de Mandato R(everendissimi) p(atris) d(omini) Jo(hannis) ragusin regent(is) per me . B Bolis* against the insertion

[3] *quadraginta quinque* in line deleted and initialled *B*. ; *Octuaginta unum* inserted in margin; the insertion sandwiched between *B* and *Bolis*

[4] *convertendo*

[5] *illis* does not occur

[6] in lighter ink : entered later?

664   10 September 1501   *Reg. Lat.* 1100, fos 67ʳ-68ʳ

Union etc. At a recent petition on the part of Philip Josselyne, BDec, perpetual cantor, called warden (*custos*) or master, in the parish church of Halstede, d. London, the pope hereby unites etc. the parish church of Drynskton', d. Norwich, (whose annual value does not exceed 15 marks sterling, equivalent to 45 gold ducats of the camera or thereabouts), to the perpetual chantry, called (?)Beurschieres[1] Chantre[2], in the above church of Halstede, which he holds with the above church of Drynskton', for as long as he holds the chantry, to the effect that Philip, in person or by proxy, may, on his own authority, continue in or take anew and retain corporal possession of· the church of Drynskton' and its rights and appurtenances, for as long as he holds the chantry, and convert its fruits etc. to his own uses and those of the church of Drynskton' and the chantry without licence of the local diocesan or of anyone else. Notwithstanding etc. With the proviso that the church of Drynskton' shall not, on account of this union etc., be defrauded of due services and the cure of souls therein shall not be neglected, but that its customary burdens shall be supported. The pope's will is, however, that on Philip's death or resignation etc. of the chantry, the union etc. shall be dissolved and so deemed automatically and the church of Drynskton' shall revert to its original condition.

Ad futuram rei memoriam. Romanum decet pontificem votis illis gratum prestare assensum . . .
F. de parma. [3] */ . B· / ⎮ B· xxxv Bolis·*

[1] the first 'e' doubtful

[2] *sic*

[3] in lighter ink : entered later?

665   11 September 1501   *Reg. Lat.* 1100, fos 72ᵛ-73ᵛ

To William Bewe, rector of the parish church of St Mildred in Bread Street (*Bredstrete* [also spelt *Bedstrete*]), London. Dispensation — at his supplication — to receive and retain for life, together with the above parish church, one, and without it, any two other benefices, etc. [as above, no. 3].

Vite ac morum honestas . . .
F de parma / . B· / . B. L. Bolis

666   24 September 1501   *Reg. Lat.* 1100, fos 73ᵛ-74ᵛ

To Thomas Fyshewyke, BDec, rector of the parish church of Bueuuardescote [also spelt *Buewardescote*], d. Salisbury. Dispensation — at his supplication — to receive and retain for life, together with the above parish church, one, and without it, any two other benefices, etc. [as above, no. 3].

Litterarum scientia, vite ac morum honestas . . .
F de parma / · B· /₁ B. L. Bolis

667   25 September 1501   *Reg. Lat.* 1100, fos 74ᵛ-75ʳ

To John Cocke, BDec, rector of the parish church of St Mary, Norton', d. Canterbury. Dispensation — at his supplication — to receive and retain for life, together with the above parish church, one, and without it, any two other benefices, etc. [as above, no. 3].

Litterarum scientia, vite ac morum honestas . . .
F. de parma¹ / . B· / B. L. Bolis.

¹ in a lighter ink : entered later?

668   11 September 1501   *Reg. Lat.* 1100, fos 75ᵛ-76ʳ

To William Loddon' *alias* Galys, canon of the monastery of B. Mary, Langley, OPrem, d. Norwich. Dispensation — at his supplication — to him, who, as he asserts, is expressly professed of the above order,¹ to receive and retain any benefice, with or without cure, usually held by secular clerics, etc. [as above, no. 32].

Religionis zelus, vite ac morum honestas . . .
F. de parma / B / . B. xxx. Bolis⸗

[1] This information comes from a notwithstanding clause.

669   4 December 1501   *Reg. Lat.* 1100, fos 91ᵛ-92ᵛ

To Richard Quynby, MA, rector of the parish church of Pittuam,[1] d. Winchester. Dispensation and indult — at his supplication — to receive and retain for life, together with the above parish church, one, and without it, any two other benefices, etc. [as above, no. 3, to '. . . retain them together for life, as above']; and for life, while attending a *studium generale* or residing in the Roman curia or any one of his benefices, not to be bound to reside in his other benefices etc. [as above, no. 238].

Litterarum scientia, vite ac morum honestas . . .
. Jo. Ortega / . B· / ₁ B. Lx. Bolis⸗

[1] or *Pittnam*

670   4 December 1501   *Reg. Lat.* 1100, fos 92ᵛ-93ᵛ

To Thomas Nicolson, rector of the parish church of Pakelhesham, d. London. Dispensation and indult — at his supplication — to receive and retain for life, together with the above parish church, one, and without it, any two other benefices, etc. [as above, no. 3, to '. . . retain them together for life, as above']; and for life, while attending a *studium generale* or residing in the Roman curia or any one of his benefices, not to be bound to reside in his other benefices, etc. [as above, no. 238].

Vite ac morum honestas . . .
N. de Castello / · B· / ₁ B. Lx⸗ Bolis⸗

671   4 December 1501   *Reg. Lat.* 1100, fo 94ʳ⁻ᵛ

To Thomas Jackeson, rector of the parish church of Thormerton', d. Worcester. Dispensation — at his supplication — to receive and retain for life, together with the above parish church, one, and without it, any two other benefices, etc. [as above, no. 3].

Vite ac morum honestas . . .
N. de Castello / . B· / . B. L. Bolis

672　15 January 1502　　　　　　　　*Reg. Lat.* 1100, fos 120^v-121^r

To William, elect of London, whom some time ago the pope provided to the church of London and appointed bishop, as is more fully contained in his letters drawn up in that regard.[1] Since, as the pope has learned, at the time of the said provision and appointment, William was holding, as he does at present, the rectory of the parish church of Shirborn', d. Winchester, whose annual value does not exceed 45 gold ducats of the camera, the pope — *motu proprio* — hereby dispenses William to retain the rectory as before — even after he has, on the strength of the said provision and appointment, received consecration and peacefully acquired possession,[2] or almost, of the rule and administration and of the goods of the church of London, or the greater part of them — together with the church of London, for as long as he presides over the latter; notwithstanding etc. ; decreeing that the rectory is not made vacant through the provision, appointment, consecration or acquisition aforesaid. With the proviso that the rectory shall not, on this account, be defrauded of due services and the cure of souls therein be neglected.

Personam tuam nobis et apostolice sedi devotam tuis exigentibus meritis paterna benivolentia prosequentes illa tibi favorabiliter concedimus . . .
A^3 de Castello^4 / . B / ╷ B. Lx. Bolis.

[1] above, no. 617
[2] *professionem; recte:* 'possessionem'
[3] *sic*
[4] written in a different ink by a different hand : entered later?

673　14 June 1502　　　　　　　　*Reg. Lat.* 1100, fo 135^{r-v}

To John Cole, rector of the parish church of Pertenay, d. Lincoln. Dispensation — at his supplication — to receive and retain for life, together with the above parish church, one, and without it, any two other benefices, etc. [as above, no. 3].

Vite ac morum honestas . . .
F. de parma / · M· / · M· L. Battiferro

674   14 June 1502   *Reg. Lat.* 1100, fo 136[r-v]

To John Hadynh(a)m,[1] rector of the parish church of St Thomas, Wynchelsee, d. Chichester. Dispensation — at his supplication — to receive and retain for life, together with the above parish church, one, and without it, any two other benefices, etc. [as above, no. 3].

Vite ac morum honestas . . .
F. de parma | · M· | · M· L· Battife(r)ro

[1] MS: *Hadynhm'*

675   14 June 1502   *Reg. Lat.* 1100, fo 137[r-v]

To Thomas Norbery, rector of the parish church of Albury, d. Winchester. Dispensation — at his supplication — to receive and retain for life, together with the above parish church, one, and without it, any two other benefices, etc. [as above, no. 3].

Vite ac morum honestas . . .
F. de parma | · M· | · M· L. [1] *Battiferro*

[1] *M* deleted, not initialled

676   14 June 1502   *Reg. Lat.* 1100, fo 142[r-v]

To John Hancok, rector of the parish church of St (?)Senan (*Sancti Simani*),[1] Hellond' [also spelt *Hellond*], d. Exeter. Dispensation — at his supplication — to receive and retain for life, together with the above parish church, one, and without it, any two other benefices, etc. [as above, no. 3].

Vite ac morum honestas . . .
F. de parma | · B· | · B. L. Bolis·

[1] or *Sunani*

677   14 June 1502   *Reg. Lat.* 1100, fo 143[r-v]

To Laurence Corttis,[1] perpetual vicar of the parish church of Fynthin' [also spelt *Fynchin'*], d. Norwich. Dispensation — at his supplication — to receive and retain for life, together with the perpetual vicarage of the above parish church, one, and without it, any two other benefices, etc. [as above, no. 3].

Vite ac morum honestas . . .
F. de parma /. B. /. B. L. Bolis

¹ or *Coittis*

678   15 March 1502   *Reg. Lat.* 1100, fos 172ʳ-173ʳ

To John Johannis, rector of the parish church of Okley, d. Winchester. Dispensation — at his supplication — to receive and retain for life, together with the above parish church, one, and without it, any two other benefices, etc. [as above, no. 3].

Vite ac morum honestas . . .
N. de Castello /· M· /· M· L. Battiferro

679   15 March 1502   *Reg. Lat.* 1100, fos 173ʳ-174ʳ

To John Geffrey, rector of the parish church of Henton' Bluet, d. Bath and Wells. Dispensation — at his supplication — to receive and retain for life, together with the above parish church, one, and without it, any two other benefices, etc. [as above, no. 3].

Vite ac morum honestas . . .
F. de parma /· M· /· M· L. Battiferro

680   15 March 1502   *Reg. Lat.* 1100, fos 174ʳ-175ʳ

To William Hedygton', rector of the parish church of St Michael, Wey, d. Winchester. Dispensation — at his supplication — to receive and retain for life, together with the above parish church, one, and without it, any two other benefices, etc. [as above, no. 3].

Vite ac morum honestas . . .
F. de parma /· M· /· M· L. Battiferro

681   3 November 1501   *Reg. Lat.* 1100, fos 189[r]-190[r]

To John Hobyll, MTheol, perpetual vicar of the parish church of Ensyld, d. London. Dispensation and indult — at his supplication — to receive and retain for life, together with the perpetual vicarage of the above parish church, one, and without it, any two other benefices, etc. [as above, no. 3, to '. . . retain them together for life, as above']; and for life, while attending a *studium generale* or residing in the Roman curia or any one of his benefices, not to be bound to reside in his other benefices, etc. [as above, no. 238].

Litterarum scientia, vite ac morum honestas . . .
Jo orteg[a][1] /· *M·* / *M Lx. Battiferro*

[1] written beneath *N. de Castello* which is deleted; the final 'a' of 'Ortega' shaved away

682[1]   **3 November l50l**   *Reg. Lat.* 1100, fos 190[v]-191[v]

To Thomas Wuley, MA, rector of the parish church of Lymyngton', d. Bath and Wells. Dispensation and indult — at his supplication — to receive and retain for life, together with the above parish church, one, and without it, any two other benefices, etc. [as above, no. 3, to '. . . retain them together for life, as above']; and, also for life, while attending a *studium generale* or residing in the Roman curia or any one of his benefices, not to be bound to reside in his other benefices etc. [as above, no. 238].

Litterarum scientia, vite ac morum honestas . . .
N· de Castello /· *M·* /· *M· Lx. Battiferro*

[1] The corresponding engrossment is PRO Papal Bulls, SC. 7/4(5).

683   4 November 1501   *Reg. Lat.* 1100, fos 196[v]-198[r]

Union etc. At a petition[1] on the part of Edward Willughby, MA, dean of the church of Exeter, the pope hereby unites etc. the parish church of Jagford *alias* Jagfourth, d. Exeter, (whose annual value does not exceed 36 English pounds, equivalent to 162 gold ducats[2] of the camera or thereabouts) to the canonry and prebend of Wyvelestom' of the church of Wells, which he holds together with the deanship of the church of Exeter (which is a major dignity *post pontificalem*) and the above parish church by apostolic dispensation, for as long as he holds the canonry and prebend, to the effect that Edward (who asserted that he was of noble birth by both

parents), in person or by proxy, may, on his own authority, continue in or take anew
and retain corporal possession of the parish church and its rights and appurtenances,
for as long as he holds the canonry and prebend, and convert its fruits etc. to his own
uses and those of the canonry and prebend and the parish church without licence of
the local diocesan or of anyone else. Notwithstanding etc. The pope's will is,
however, that the parish church shall not, on account of this union etc., be defrauded
of due services and the cure of souls therein shall not be neglected, but that its
customary burdens shall be supported; and that on Edward's death or resignation etc.
of the canonry and prebend the union etc. shall be dissolved and so deemed and the
parish church shall revert to its original condition automatically.

Ad futuram rei memoriam. Romanum decet pontificem votis illis gratum prestare
assensum . . .
F. de. parma / . B· / ₁ B· xxxv Bolis

[1] 'nuper' does not occur

[2] *centum sexaginta duos ducatos*, the latter two words being changed (by overwriting) from *duorum*
ducatorum; not initialled

684   12 February 1502   *Reg. Lat.* 1100, fos 214ʳ-215ʳ

Union etc. At a recent petition on the part of John Nans, UID, perpetual beneficed
cleric (*clerici perpetui beneficiati*), called prebendary, in the church of Exeter, the
pope hereby unites etc. the parish church of St Illogan (*Sancti Illogani*), d. Exeter,
(whose annual value does not exceed 30 English marks, equivalent to 90 gold ducats
of the camera or thereabouts), to a certain perpetual simple benefice, called a
prebend, in the said church of Exeter, (whose annual value does not exceed 6 like
marks), both of which he holds, for as long as he holds the benefice, to the effect that
John (who asserts that he also holds the perpetual vicarage of the parish church of St
Gluvias (*Sancti Cluviati*), d. Exeter, by apostolic dispensation), in person or by
proxy, may, on his own authority, continue in, or take anew, corporal possession of
the church of St Illogan and its rights and appurtenances and convert its fruits etc. to
his own uses and those of the benefice and the church of St Illogan, without licence
of the local diocesan or of anyone else. Notwithstanding etc. The pope's will is,
however, that the church of St Illogan shall not, on account of this union etc., be
defrauded of due services and the cure of souls therein shall not be neglected, but
that its customary burdens shall be supported; and that on John's death or resignation
etc. of the benefice this union etc. shall be dissolved and so deemed and the church
of St Illogan shall revert to its original condition automatically.

Ad futuram rei memoriam. Romanum decet pontificem votis illis gratum prestare
assensum . . .
N. de Castell[o][1] */ · B· / ₁ B· xxxv Bolis*

[1] shaved

685   17 February 1502   *Reg. Lat.* 1100, fos 217^V-218^V

Union etc. At a recent petition on the part of Thomas Urmeston', MA, rector of the parish church of Bryngton', d. Lincoln, the pope hereby unites etc. the parish church of Lolleworth', d. Ely, (whose annual value does not exceed 24 gold ducats of the camera), to the above church of Bryngton', which he holds together by apostolic dispensation, for as long as he holds that of Bryngton', to the effect that Thomas,[1] may, on his own authority, continue in or take anew corporal possession of the church of Lolleworth' and its rights and appurtenances and convert its fruits etc. to his own uses and those of the said churches without licence of the local diocesan or of anyone else. Notwithstanding etc. The pope's will is, however, that the church of Lolleworth' shall not, on account of this union etc., be defrauded of due services and the cure of souls therein shall not be neglected, but that its customary burdens shall be supported; and that on Thomas's death or resignation etc. of the church of Bryngton' the union etc. shall be dissolved and so deemed and the church of Lolleworth' shall revert to its original condition automatically.

Ad futuram rei memoriam. Romanum decet pontificem votis illis prestare gratum assensum . . .
N· de Castello / . B· / ₁ B· xxxv Bolis.

[1] 'per se vel alium seu alios' does not occur

686   19 October 1501   *Reg. Lat.* 1100, fos 234^V-235^V

To abbot Richard and the convent of the monastery of St John the Apostle and Evangelist, Haghmo(n)de,[1] OSA, ds. Coventry and Lichfield. Indult and grant of faculty — at their supplication — to the abbot and his successors as abbots for the time being to use the mitre, ring, pastoral staff and other pontifical *insignia*; and also — in the said monastery as well as in any other priories and churches subject to the monastery and dependencies of it, albeit not beneath the abbot and his successors by full authority, even called portions, and also pertaining at a time of vacancy to their presentation, and also in which they may have some superiority, and in any other ecclesiastical places in which the abbot and his successors shall celebrate in pontificals at the time — to give solemn benediction after the solemnities of mass, vespers, matins and other divine offices over the people then present there and in the *mensa* of the abbot and his successors — provided that no bishop or legate of the apostolic see be present, or, if one so be, with his express consent; to promote each and every one of the canons, servants and novices of the monastery and, with the consent and licence of the local ordinaries, any others, to the four minor orders, at once and a single time or separately, as expedient, at times established by law; to confer the said orders on them; to bless images, crosses, and all ecclesiastical ornaments, even priestly robes, and bells and any vestments and vases and tabernacles, even in which the sacrament of the Eucharist is served and relics are held, of altars and churches and all other ecclesiastical places dedicated to divine worship, and of the aforesaid monastery; and to reconcile churches of the monastery and any other individual secular and regular churches subject to the monastery and dependencies of it and over which the abbot and his successors shall have superiority, and which shall pertain to their presentation, as well as those which the abbot and his successors shall require, even if they are not beneath them in any way and then with the consent of their superior, and cemeteries and other ecclesiastical places polluted by bloodshed or adultery and in any other way, the water having been blessed beforehand by any catholic bishop, as the custom is. Notwithstanding the constitution "Abbates" of Alexander IV, etc. This shall not be to the prejudice of this constitution which lays down that such reconciliations may only be done by bishops. Moreover the pope's will and decree is that — because it may perchance be difficult to deliver the present letters to each of the places where they may be necessary — exactly the same trustworthiness both in trials and not in trials shall adhere to a transumpt of the present letters fortified with the seal of any ecclesiastical prelate and subscribed by the hand of a notary public as would have adhered to the originals had they been exhibited or shown.

Exposcit vestre devotionis sinceritas . . .
F. de parma / . *B·* / . *B. CC. Bolis.*

[1] MS: *Haghmo'de*

687   11 December 1501   *Reg. Lat.* 1100, fos 262[v]-263[r]

To John Brady, priest of St Andrews. Dispensation — at his supplication — to him — who, as he asserts, is litigating over the parish church of Tanadas,[1] d. St Andrews, provision of which was made to him by ordinary authority at another time while vacant *certo modo* and which he possesses, in the Roman curia against a certain adversary of his before a certain auditor of causes of the apostolic palace — to receive and retain for life, together with the above parish church, if he wins it, one, and without it, any two other benefices, etc. [as above, no. 5].

Vite ac morum honestas . . .
A. de Sanctoseverino / · *B·* / *B· xxxx* ı *Bolis·*

[1] or *Tavadas*

688   31 December 1501   *Reg. Lat.* 1100, fo 282[r-v]

To John Bray, scholar, d. London, indult. The pope (who, some time ago, decreed and declared that provisions, grants or mandates of provision to canonries and prebends of cathedral churches to persons who have not completed their fourteenth year of age shall have no force except by consent of the apostolic see) hereby indulges John, who, as he asserts, has not yet completed his seventh year and wishes to become a cleric — at his supplication — to receive and retain — as soon as he has completed his seventh year and been duly marked with clerical character — any canonries and prebends of any cathedral, even metropolitan, churches, if conferred on him otherwise canonically. Notwithstanding the above defect of age etc. [With the proviso] that the canonries and prebends in question shall not, on this account, be defrauded of due services; but that their customary burdens shall be supported.

Spes future probitatis . . .
· *F· de. parma* / · *B·* / . *B· xx · Bolis·*

689   31 December 1501   *Reg. Lat.* 1100, fo 282ᵛ-283ʳ

To Reginald Bray, scholar, d. London, indult, etc. [as above, no. 688, with appropriate change of name].[1]

Spes future probitatis . . .
F. de parma /. *B·* / . *B· xx Bolis·*

[1] Both letters are identically formulated and were enregistered by the same scribe.

690   31 December 1501   *Reg. Lat.* 1100, fos 283ʳ-284ʳ

To Robert Peryns, cleric, d. Coventry and Lichfield. Dispensation — at his supplication — to him, who, as he asserts, is in his eighteenth year of age, to receive and retain any benefice, with cure or otherwise incompatible, etc. [as above, no. 240].

Vite ac morum honestas . . .
F. de parma /. *B·* /ᵢ *B· xxiiij· Bolis·*

691   1 June 1502   *Reg. Lat.* 1100, fos 286ᵛ-288ʳ

To the bishops of Dunkeld and Brechin, mandate in favour of John Myll, priest, d. St Andrews. A recent petition to the pope on John's part stated that formerly, when a certain perpetual chaplaincy, which is of lay patronage, at a certain altar in the church of St Salvator, St Andrews, was vacant by the death, outside the Roman curia, of Thomas Esplane, the perpetual chaplain, John had been presented for it, within the proper time, by John, earl of Crawford (*Craufurdie*), nobleman (the chaplaincy's true and only patron, who was in peaceful possession, or almost, of the right of presenting a suitable person for it, at a time of vacancy) to the present provost of St Salvator's, since, by ancient, approved, and hitherto peacefully observed custom the institution of persons presented for the chaplaincy lawfully pertains to the provost for the time being; that Walter Lamey, who bears himself as a cleric, had been presented for the chaplaincy to the provost by the present abbot and convent of the monastery of Lindores (*Lundorum*), OSB, d. St Andrews, (who falsely claimed that the right of patronage belonged to them and that they were in peaceful possession, or almost, of the right of presentation), and had been *de facto* instituted by him as perpetual chaplain at the altar; that the provost, with a view to the retraction, quashing, and cancellation of the institution, had ordered Walter to appear before him, and had put up a certain edict about it; that a suit (not through apostolic delegation) had arisen between them before the provost; that the provost, proceeding lawlessly, wrongly, and *de facto*, declared by his unjust, interlocutory [sentence], as he called it, that the institution was not to be retracted, and John appealed to the apostolic see, but detained, as he asserts, by a lawful impediment, he did not prosecute his appeal within the proper time.[1] At the supplication of John and the earl of Crawford to the pope to command that John be absolved conditionally from the sentence of excommunication and any other ecclesiastical censures perchance inflicted on him by the provost, and to commit to some upright men in those parts the cases of the appeal; of everything attempted and innovated after and against the appeal; of the nullity of the institution, declaration, provost's whole process, and of everything else prejudicial to the earl of Crawford and John done by the provost, abbot and convent, Walter, and any others, in connection with the foregoing; and of the whole principal matter; also the cases which the earl and John intend to move against the abbot and convent and Walter, and any other clerics of the dioceses of St Andrews and Brechin, over the right of patronage and damage which they have jointly suffered, the pope hereby commands that the above two (or one of them), if what is related about the impediment is true, and having summoned Walter and the abbot and convent and others concerned, shall, if and as it is just, for this once only, conditionally absolve John, if he so requests, having first received suitable security from him that if it appears to them that the sentence of excommunication and other censures were justly inflicted on him, he will obey their commands and those of the church; and, as regards the rest, having heard both sides, taking cognizance even of the principal matter, that they shall decree what is just, without appeal, causing by ecclesiastical censure what they have decreed to be strictly observed; [and moreover compel] witnesses, etc. Notwithstanding the lapse of time, etc.

Humilibus et cetera.
. *Jo. ortega /. B· / · B· xiiij· Bolis*

1 *but detained . . . time*] this information comes, curiously, from the second part of the narrative (where the operative part of the supplication is recited); ordinarily it is found at the end of the first part (where the events leading up to the supplication are narrated).

692   21 May 1502   *Reg. Lat.* 1100, fo 292^{r-v}

To John Wardroper, UIB, archdeacon of Stafford (*Staffordii*) in the church of Coventry and Lichfield. Dispensation — at his supplication — to receive and retain for life, together with the archdeaconry in the above church, one, and without it, any two other benefices, etc. [as above, no. 3].

Litterarum scientia, vite ac morum honestas . . .
F. de parma[1] /. *B·* / · *B· L. Bolis*

1 in a lighter ink : entered later?

693   21 May 1502   *Reg. Lat.* 1100, fo 293^{r-v}

To John Alyson', perpetual vicar of the parish church of Multon', by Northampton', d. Lincoln. Dispensation — at his supplication — to receive and retain for life, together with the perpetual vicarage of the above parish church, one, and without it, any two other benefices, etc. [as above, no. 3].

Vite ac morum honestas . . .
F. de parma[1] /· *B·* / . *B. L. Bolis*

1 in a lighter ink : entered later?

694   6 June 1502   *Reg. Lat.* 1100, fos 299^{r}-300^{r}

To the prior of the priory of St John, Kilinovan, d. Dublin, and the dean and the archdeacon of the church of Dublin, mandate in favour of John Warde, DDec, rector of the parish church of St Patrick, Tryme [also spelt *Triyme*], d. Meath. A recent petition to the pope on John's part stated that at the denunciation of the late Edward Welsley, cleric, d. Meath — who falsely asserted that the late Richard Walshe, formerly rector of St Patrick's, Tryme, had perpetrated several excesses and crimes then expressed and ought therefore to be deprived — the archdeacon of the church of Meath (then vacant), asserting that he had sufficient power, had descended *ex officio* to inquiry against Richard *de facto*, and the then prior of the priory of St John near Tryme, d. Meath, to whom, as he said, the archdeacon had committed the inquiry, proceeding *de facto* and lawlessly, promulgated an unjust definitive sentence by which he deprived Richard and, as is said, collated St Patrick's to Edward; that Richard appealed to the apostolic see, impetrated apostolic letters to certain judges in those parts, sued Edward before them, and the judges, proceeding duly, promulgated a definitive sentence in Richard's favour and against Edward; that Walter Welsley, who bore himself as a cleric — falsely asserting that St Patrick's was then vacant by the death, outside the Roman curia, of Edward, and had been vacant for so long that its collation had lawfully devolved on the apostolic see and that by pretext of certain apostolic letters (which he had impetrated by *suggestio falsi* and *suppressio veri*) provision should be made of it to him — thereupon sued Richard before certain other judges in those parts whom he said were the judges appointed under the letters; and that these judges cited Richard to appear before them in a place known to be unsafe for him and he appealed to the apostolic see, but detained, as John asserts, by a lawful impediment, he did not prosecute this latter appeal within the proper time. At the supplication to the pope of John (who asserts that the church of St Patrick was canonically collated to him when it was vacant by Richard's death and that he should like, in his own interest, to prosecute the latter appeal) to commit to some upright men in those parts the cases of the appeal; of everything attempted and innovated after and against the appeal; of the nullity of the last judges' process and of everything else prejudicial to Richard and John done by them, Walter, and any other judges and persons, in connection with the foregoing; and of the principal matter; also the cases which John intends to move against Walter and certain other clerics and laymen over the subreption and obreption of the letters, and the annoyance and hindrance caused him over the church, the pope hereby commands that the above three (or two or one of them), having summoned Walter and others concerned, if what is related about the impediment is true, and having heard both sides, [taking cognizance even of the principal matter],[1] shall decree what is just, without appeal, causing by ecclesiastical censure what they have decreed to be strictly observed. Notwithstanding the lapse of time, etc.

Humilibus et cetera.
· *L· puccius* / · *B·* / . *B· xij· Bolis.*

[1] MS wants 'etiam de negotio principali huiusmodi cognoscentes legitime' (contemplated above); *cf.* no. 197

695   23 October 1501   *Reg. Lat.* 1100, fos 337r-338r

To Nicholas Farley, perpetual vicar of the parish church of Harpery,[1] d. Worcester. Dispensation — at his supplication — to receive and retain for life, together with the perpetual vicarage of the above parish church, one, and without it, any two other benefices, etc. [as above, no. 3].

Vite ac morum honestas . . .
. F. de. parma / F / . F. L. Sanctor(is)

[1] the first occurrence has a vertical stroke above the 'p'

696   18 September 1501   *Reg. Lat.* 1100, fo 338[r-v]

To Roger Layburn', BTheol, cleric, d. Durham. Indult for life — at his supplication — not to be bound, while residing in the Roman curia or one of the benefices, with and without cure, held by him now and at the time or attending a *studium generale*, to reside in his other benefices, nor to be liable to be compelled by anyone to do so against his will. Notwithstanding etc. With the proviso that the benefices in which he shall not reside shall not, on this account, be defrauded of due services and the cure of souls therein (if any) shall not be neglected.

Litterarum scientia, vite ac morum honestas . . .
Jo Ortega / F / F. xx. Sanctor(is)

697   30 April 1502   *Reg. Lat.* 1101, fos 200[r]-202[v]

Provision, in *forma gratiosa*, of Orsinius de Orsiniis, notary of the pope, to the rectory of the parish church of St Mary, Stazzema (*de Stazema*), d. Lucca, vacant at the apostolic see.
    The 'bishop of Worcester' is one of the three mandataries of the executory. Entry otherwise of no interest to the Calendar.

Grata devotionis obsequia . . . The executory begins : *Hodie dilecto filio Orsinio de Orsiniis . . .*
S de Castello; A de Sanctoseverino / · B· / · B· xx x pridie Id(us) Maij anno decimo [14 May 1502], | *Bolis*

698   26 November 1501   *Reg. Lat.* 1103, fos 15[v]-16[v]

Executory — in respect of the *retentio* in favour of Andrew, elect of Moray, above[1] — to the abbot of the monastery of Holyrood (*Sancte Crucis*), d. St Andrews, the archdeacon of the church of Ross and the official of Glasgow, or two or one of them, acting in person or by proxy.

The executory begins: *Hodie cum ecclesia*[2] *Moravien. . . .*

*L pucius*³ / · *B·* / · *B· xv Bolis̄*

¹ enregistered, most unusually, elsewhere (above, no. 632) The spellings of proper names in the executory — *Maio alias Petinveyn* and *Cotigham* — may be compared with those of the principal letter.

² *sic; recte*: 'ecclesie'?

³ *sic*; written in lighter ink : entered later?

699¹   **2 October 1501**   *Reg. Lat.* 1103, fos 21ᵛ-22ʳ

To George Chadworth, BDec, rector of the parish church of Campe [also spelt *Champe*], near Guysnes in county Guysnes,² d. Thérouanne.³ Dispensation — at his supplication — to receive and retain for life, together with the above parish church, one, and without it, any two other benefices, etc. [as above, no. 3].⁴

Litterarum scientia, vite ac morum honestas . . .
*[-]*⁵ / · *B·* / ₁ *B· L. Bolis.*

¹ *Georgius Cadworth* occurs in the index to the gathering on fo. 19ʳ.

² *in comitatu Guysnes* (changed by overwriting from *Guysnien.*) in the first instance; *in comitatu Guysnien.* in the second

³ in the first instance, initially written *Morenen.*, then changed (by overwriting) to *Moranen.* and *seu Moranien.* added in the margin (the addition initialled . *B.* and *B*); in the second *Moranien.*

⁴ The constitutions of Otto and Ottobuono are mentioned in a notwithstanding clause, giving Chadworth the option of holding benefices in England.

⁵ no abbreviator's name

700¹   **2 October 1501**   *Reg. Lat.* 1103, fos 22ᵛ-23ʳ

To John Leycetyr,² BDec, rector of the parish church of Stoneham Aspal [also spelt *Aspall*] *alias* Lambard, d. Norwich. Dispensation and indult — at his supplication — to receive and retain for life, together with the above parish church, one, and without it, any two other benefices, etc. [as above, no. 3, to '. . . retain them together for life, as above']; and, for life, while residing in the Roman curia or any one of his benefices or attending a *studium generale*, to reside in his other benefices, etc. [as above, no. 238].

Litterarum scientia, vite ac morum honestas . . .
N. de castello / · *B·* / · *B· Lx. Bolis̄*

¹ *Johannes Leycetir* occurs in the index to the gathering on fo. 19ʳ.

² the 'c' written over another letter ('r'?); *tyr* is deleted directly after *Leycetyr;* neither alteration is initialled

701   2 October 1501   *Reg. Lat.* 1103, fo 31^{r-v}

To William Spicer, BDec, rector of the parish church of Clopton' [also spelt *Clopton*], d. Ely. Dispensation — at his supplication — to receive and retain for life, together with the above parish church, one, and without it, any two other benefices, etc. [as above, no. 3].

Litterarum scientia, vite ac morum honestas . . .
L. puccius / · B· / ₁ B. L. Bolis

702   15 January 1502   *Reg. Lat.* 1103, fos 61^{r}-62^{r}

Union etc. At a recent petition on the part of Thomas Martyn', DDec, rector of the parish church of St Peter, Fauleston, d. Salisbury, the pope hereby unites etc. the perpetual vicarage of the parish church of St Michael, Wyluesfordi, d. Salisbury, (whose annual value does not exceed 9 gold ducats of the camera), to the above parish church of St Peter, which he holds together by apostolic dispensation, for as long as he holds St Peter's, to the effect that Thomas, in person or by proxy, may, on his own authority, take or continue in and retain corporal possession of the vicarage and its rights and appurtenances, for as long as he holds St Peter's, and convert its fruits etc. to his own uses and those of St Peter's and the vicarage without licence of the local diocesan or of anyone else. Notwithstanding etc. The pope's will is, however, that the vicarage shall not, on account of this union etc., be defrauded of due services and the cure of souls therein shall not be neglected, but that its customary burdens shall be supported; and that on Thomas's death or resignation etc. of St Peter's the union etc. shall be dissolved and so deemed and the vicarage shall revert to its original condition automatically.

Ad futuram rey memoriam. Romanum decet pontificem votis illis gratum prestare assensum . . .
A. de Sancto Seve[rino][1] / *Jo* / *Jo· xxxv Eps' Terracinen'*

[1] shaved

703   15 January 1502   *Reg. Lat.* 1103, fos 62^{v}-63^{v}

Union etc. At a recent petition on the part of Richard Lathes, BDec, perpetual vicar of the parish church of St Mary Magdalen, Eschin'[1], d. London, the pope hereby unites etc. the parish church of St Andrew, Thorisby, d. Lincoln, (whose annual value does not exceed 20 gold ducats of the camera), to the perpetual vicarage of the above church of St Mary Magdalen, which he holds together by apostolic dispensation, for as long as he holds the vicarage, to the effect that Richard, in person or by proxy, may, on his own authority, take or continue in and retain corporal possession of St Andrew's and its rights and appurtenances, for as long as he holds the vicarage, and convert its fruits etc. to his own uses and those of St Andrew's and the vicarage without licence of the local diocesan or of anyone else. Notwithstanding etc. The pope's will is, however, that St Andrew's shall not, on account of this union etc., be defrauded of due services and the cure of souls therein shall not be neglected, but that its customary burdens shall be supported; and that on Richard's death or resignation etc. of the vicarage the union etc. shall be dissolved and so deemed and St Andrew's shall revert to its original condition automatically.

Ad futuram rey memoriam. Romanum decet pontificem votis illis gratum prestare assensum . . .
A de Sancto Severino / Jo / Jo. xxxv. Eps' Terracinen'

[1] or, possibly, *Eschin^a* or, despite the dot, *Eschm'*

704   11 September 1501   *Reg. Lat.* 1103, fos 64^r-65^r

To Thomas Hare, LLD, rector of the parish church of St Peter, Heydon, d. Norwich. Dispensation — at his supplication — to receive and retain for life, together with the above parish church, two, and without them, any three other secular benefices, with cure or otherwise mutually incompatible, etc. [as above. no. 17].[1]

Litterarum scientia, vite ac morum honestas . . .
S de Castello / · B· / · B· C. Bolis·

[1] as usual, parish churches and their perpetual vicarages are specifically limited to two early on in the entry, though in the present instance the usual clause: 'provided that of three such benefices not more than two be parish churches or their perpetual vicarages' is not to be found below

705   15 January 1502   *Reg. Lat.* 1103, fos 65^r-66^r

To Robert Duxbery, rector of the parish church of St George, Heth, d. Lincoln. Dispensation — at his supplication — to receive and retain for life, together with the above parish church, one, and without it, any two other benefices, etc. [as above, no. 3].

Vite ac morum honestas . . .
A de S^to Severi[no][1] / · B· / \B. L. Bolis.

[1] shaved

706   15 January 1502   *Reg. Lat.* 1103, fos 66ʳ-67ʳ

To Richard Dighton', perpetual vicar of the parish church of Ingham, d. Lincoln. Dispensation — at his supplication — to receive and retain for life, together with the perpetual vicarage of the above parish church, one, and without it, any two other benefices, etc. [as above, no. 3].

Vite ac morum honestas . . .
A. de Sᵗᵒ Severino / · B· / ₁ B. L. Bolis

707   11 January 1502   *Reg. Lat.* 1103, fos 71ʳ-72ʳ

To Thomas, abbot of the monastery of B. Mary and St John the Evangelist, Tychefeld, OPrem, d. Winchester. Dispensation — at his supplication — to receive together with the above monastery, one, and without it, any two other regular benefices, with or without cure, of the said order, or with one of them, or without them, one secular benefice, with or without cure, even if the regular benefices should be priories, *prepositure, prepositatus,* dignities, *personatus,* administrations or offices, and the secular benefice should be a parish church or its perpetual vicarage, or a chantry, free chapel, hospital or annual service, usually assigned to secular clerics in title of a perpetual ecclesiastical benefice, and of lay patronage and of whatsoever tax or annual value, even if the priories etc. should be customarily elective and have cure of souls, if he obtains them otherwise canonically, and to retain for life whichever one of the regular benefices he chooses, even if it be a priory, *prepositura* or other conventual dignity or a claustral office, *in titulum,* and the other regular benefice, which may not be a conventual dignity or claustral office, or the secular benefice, *in commendam,* to resign them, at once or successively, simply or for exchange, as often as he pleases, and to cede the commend, and in their place receive up to two other, similar or dissimilar, regular benefices, with or without cure, of the said order, or with one of them, or without them, one secular benefice, with or without cure, and retain for life, whichever one of the regular benefices he chooses *in titulum,* and the other regular benefice, which may not be conventual or claustral, or the secular benefice, *in commendam,* as above; (he may — due and customary burdens of the benefice held *in commendam* having been supported — make disposition of the rest of its fruits etc. just as those holding it *in titulum* could and ought to do, alienation of immovable goods and precious movables being however forbidden). Notwithstanding etc. With the proviso that the benefice retained *in commendam* shall not, on this account, be defrauded of due services and the cure of souls therein (if any) shall not be neglected; but that its aforesaid burdens shall be supported.

Personam tuam nobis et apostolice sedi devotam . . .
L puccius / · B· / · B· L. Bolis

708   15 January 1502   *Reg. Lat.* 1103, fos 72^v-73^v

To George Staxeley, perpetual vicar of the parish church of Bs. Peter and Paul, Westleton, d. Norwich. Dispensation — at his supplication — to receive and retain for life, together with the perpetual vicarage of the above parish church, one, and without it, any two other benefices, etc. [as above, no. 3].

Vite ac morum honestas . . .
A de S^{to} Severino / · B· / ı B· L. Bolis

709   15 January 1502   *Reg. Lat.* 1103, fos 73^v-74^v

To Henry Andeleyn, perpetual vicar of the parish church of Meltone Moubrey [also spelt *Meltone Mo'brey*], d. Lincoln. Dispensation — at his supplication — to receive and retain for life, together with the perpetual vicarage of the above parish church, one, and without it, any two other benefices, etc. [as above, no. 3].

Vite ac morum honestas . . .
A. de S^{to} Severino / · B· / ı B· L. Bolis

710   15 January 1502   *Reg. Lat.* 1103, fos 75^r-76^r

To John Looder, perpetual vicar of the parish church of B. Mary, Wurthswanewych', d. Salisbury. Dispensation — at his supplication — to receive and retain for life, together with the perpetual vicarage of the above parish church, one, and without it, any two other benefices, etc. [as above, no. 3].

Vite ac morum honestas . . .
A. de S^{to} Severino / . B· / ı B· L. Bolis

711   15 January 1502   *Reg. Lat.* 1103, fos 76^r-77^r

To Thomas Brereton, cleric, d. Coventry and Lichfield. Dispensation — at his supplication — to him, who, as he asserts, is of noble birth and in his fifteenth year of age, to receive and retain any benefice, with cure or otherwise incompatible, etc. [as above, no. 240].

Nobilitas generis, vite ac morum honestas . . .
L puccius / · B· / B· xxx Bolis·

712   27 November 1501   *Reg. Lat.* 1103, fo 91^{r-v}

To Henry Baron, canon of the priory of Bemwell [also spelt *Bemwel*], OSA, d. Ely.
Dispensation — at his supplication — to him, who, as he asserts, is expressly
professed of the above order,[1] to receive and retain any benefice, with or without
cure, usually held by secular clerics, etc. [as above, no. 32].

Religionis zelus, vite ac morum honestas . . .
L puccius / · M· / · M· xxx Battiferro

[1] This information comes from a notwithstanding clause.

713   1 December 1501   *Reg. Lat.* 1103, fos 96^{v}-97^{r}

To Robert Bernardi, MA, rector of the parish church of Overwalop, d. Winchester.
Dispensation — at his supplication — to receive and retain for life, together with the
above parish church, one, and without it, any two other benefices, etc. [as above, no. 3].

Litterarum scientia, vite ac morum honestas . . .
L puccius / · B· / ₁ B· L. Bolis·

714   27 November 1501   *Reg. Lat.* 1103, fos 97^{v}-98^{r}

To John Aplien, perpetual vicar of the parish church of Peterborough (*de Burgo
Sancti Petri*), d. Lincoln. Dispensation — at his supplication — to receive and retain
for life, together with the above church,[1] one, and without it, any two other
benefices, etc. [as above, no. 3].

Vite ac morum honestas . . .
G.[2] de Castello / · B· / . B· L. Bolis·

[1] strangely, *vicaria* has been deleted, initialled . B. and is followed by *ecclesia; recte :* 'vicaria'?
[2] error for 'S'

715[1]   29 August 1501   *Reg. Lat.* 1103, fos 99[v]-100[v]

To Thomas Orton, BDec, perpetual chaplain, called cantor, in the parish church of St
Michael, Coventry *(Co(n)ve(n)trie)*,[2] d. Coventry and Lichfield. Dispensation — at
his supplication — to him (who, as he asserts, holds a perpetual chaplaincy, called the
chantry of Hugh Meruiton,[3] in the above parish church), to receive and retain for life,
together with the above chaplaincy, if it cannot be held with another incompatible
benefice, one, and without it, any two other benefices, etc. [as above, no. 3].

Litterarum scientia, vite ac morum honestas . . .
L. puccius / B / · B· L· Bolis·

[1] See above, no. 496. The existence, here, of another dispensation *ad duo* for Orton drawn under the
same date argues a mix-up. Deficiencies of formulary in 496 (a dispensation *ad duo* with indult for non-
residence) suggest that it was modelled on a simple dispensation *ad duo* (this one?) That its tax mark
should also be for a simple *ad duo* (L not Lx) is decidedly curious. Both letters were enregistered by the
same scribe.

[2] MS: *Co've'trie*

[3] or *Merniton*

716   28 March 1502[1]   *Reg. Lat.* 1103, fos 113[v]-114[v]

To John Tailar, rector of the parish church of More,[2] d. Lincoln. Dispensation and
indult — at his supplication — to receive and retain for life, together with the above
parish church, one, and without it, any two other benefices, etc. [as above, no. 3, to '.
. . retain them together for life, as above']; and for life, while residing in the Roman
curia or any one of his benefices or attending a *studium generale*, not to be bound to
reside personally in his other benefices, etc. [as above, no. 21].

Litterarum scientia,[3] vite ac morum honestas . . .
L: puccius / · B· / · B · Lx· Bolis·

[1] *p(rim)o* deleted, but not initialled; *secundo quinto . . . decimo*] written by the enregistering scribe, but
in a different ink : entered later?

[2] both occurrences inserted in the margin by the enregistering scribe, initialled . *B.* ; (?)*monte*, in the
line, deleted and initialled . *B.*

[3] the form appropriate for a graduate, but no degree mentioned; he had one (*cf.* Emden, *Oxford to 1500*,
p. 1851)

717   29 August 1501   *Reg. Lat.* 1103, fos 131[r]-132[r]

Union etc. At a recent petition on the part of Thomas Gilbert, DDec, canon of

Exeter, the pope hereby unites etc. the parish church of Lympysham, d. Bath and Wells, (whose annual value does not exceed 18 English marks, equivalent to 52[1] gold ducats of the camera), to the canonry and prebend of the church of Exeter, which he holds together with the above parish church, for as long as he holds the canonry and prebend, to the effect that Thomas, in person or by proxy, may, on his own authority, take and retain corporal possession of the parish church and its rights and appurtenances, for as long as he holds the canonry and prebend, and convert its fruits etc. to his own uses and those of the canonry and prebend and the parish church without licence of the local diocesan or of anyone else. Notwithstanding etc.[2] The pope's will is, however, that the parish church shall not, on account of this union etc., be defrauded of due services and the cure of souls therein shall not be neglected, but that its customary burdens shall be supported; and that on Thomas's death or resignation etc. of the canonry and prebend the union etc. shall be dissolved and so deemed and the parish church shall revert to its original condition and be deemed vacant automatically.

Ad futuram rey memoriam. Romanum decet pontificem votis[3] *gratum prestare assensum* . . .
A. de Sancto Severino / . *B·* / · *B· xxxv . Bolis*

[1] *quadraginta* in the line deleted and initialled . *B.* twice; *Quinquaginta* inserted in the margin; *Cassatum et corectum de mandato R(everendissimi) p(atris) d(omini) J(ohannis) Ragusini regentis B. Bolis.* against it (*duos*, next to *quadraginta* in the line, being untouched)

[2] The constitutions of Otto and Ottobuono are not mentioned.

[3] 'illis' does not occur

718   28 August 1501   *Reg. Lat.* 1103, fo 132[r-v]

To James Haryngton, rector of the parish church of Baddysworth', d. York. Dispensation — at his supplication — to receive and retain for life, together with the above parish church, one, and without it, any two other benefices, etc. [as above, no. 3].

Vite ac morum honestas . . .
[-][1] / *Jo* / *Jo. L. Eps' Terracinen'*

[1] no abbreviator's name

719   28 August 1501   *Reg. Lat.* 1103, fos 133[r]-134[r]

To Thomas Martini, DDec, rector of the parish church of St Peter, Ffouleston', d.

Salisbury, dispensation. Some time ago, the pope by other letters of his dispensed him to receive and retain for life, together with the perpetual vicarage of the parish church of Northmoreton, d. Salisbury, (which, as he asserted, he was then holding), one, and without it, any two other benefices, etc. [as above, no. 131, to '. . . as is more fully contained in those letters'].[1] The pope therefore — at his supplication — hereby dispenses Thomas (who, as he asserts, having resigned the said vicarage, holds by the said dispensation the above parish church of St Peter and the perpetual vicarage of the parish church of St Michael, Wyluesfordi, d. Salisbury, having acquired them at another time when they were canonically collated to him while successively vacant *certo modo*), to receive and retain for life, together with the second vicarage and the church of St Peter, or without them, with any two other incompatible benefices held by him at the time by virtue of the said dispensation, any third benefice, etc. [as above, no. 131].

Litterarum scientia, vite ac morum honestas . . .
[-][2] / Jo. / Jo. Lxx. Eps' Terracinen'

[1] lost; Index entry transcribed in *CPL*, XVI at no. 1213.
[2] no abbreviator's name

720   28 August 1501   *Reg. Lat.* 1103, fos 134[v]-135[r]

To Christopher Crosley, BDec, perpetual vicar of the parish church of Sutturton', d. Lincoln. Dispensation — at his supplication — to receive and retain for life, together with the perpetual vicarage of the above parish church, one, and without it, any two other benefices, etc. [as above, no. 3].

Litterarum scientia, vite ac morum honestas . . .
[-][1] / Jo / Jo. L. Eps' Terracinen. '

[1] no abbreviator's name

721   2[1] September 1501   *Reg. Lat.* 1103, fo 135[r-v]

To the bishop of Lincoln, commission and mandate in favour of Richard Baker, scholar, of his diocese. A recent petition to the pope on Richard's part stated that he, who has been deprived of sight in his left eye, through no fault of his own, but through various infirmities and, perchance, assiduous study — leaving the eye with some white film[2] or blemish and a not particularly notable deformity — is eager to be promoted to all, even sacred and priest's, orders and to minister in them, even in the ministry of the altar. At his supplication, (asserting that he is a BA), to the pope to dispense him to be duly promoted and to minister, as above, and to receive and retain any benefice, with or without cure, even if a parish church etc. [as above, no. 240, to '. . . or principal in a collegiate church'], if he obtains it otherwise canonically, to resign it, simply or for exchange, as often as he pleases, and in its place receive and retain another, similar or dissimilar, benefice, as above, the pope, not having certain knowledge of the foregoing, hereby commissions and commands the above bishop to inspect the eye diligently and, if he finds it to be thus, act and make disposition in the aforesaid matters as shall seem to him expedient. Notwithstanding etc.

Vite ac morum honestas . . .
[-]³/ Jo / Jo . xxv . Eps' Terracinen.

[1] date altered : *quinto* in the line deleted and initialled *Jo.* ; *quarto* inserted in the margin by the enregistering scribe initialled *Jo.*

[2] *albudine*; *cf.* 'albugo'

[3] no abbreviator's name

722   28 August 1501   *Reg. Lat.* 1103, fo 136^r-v

To William Ayleuoard, perpetual vicar of the parish church of B. Mary, Piddiltouon,[1] d. Salisbury. Dispensation — at his supplication — to receive and retain for life, together with the perpetual vicarage of the above parish church, one, and without it, any two other benefices, etc. [as above, no. 3].

Vite ac morum honestas . . .
[-]² / Jo / Jo. L. Eps' Terracinen. '

[1] the second occurrence of the name is in a marginal insertion (*Beate Marie de Piddiltouon Saresbirien. diocesis*) by the enregistering scribe initialled *Jo.* and *Jo*

[2] no abbreviator's name

723   28 September 1501[1]   *Reg. Lat.* 1103, fos 139^v-140^r

To John Wich', UIB, rector of the parish church of St Margaret, Teyntyhull [also spelt *Teyntyhulle*], d. Bath and Wells. Dispensation — at his supplication — to receive and retain for life, together with the above parish church, one, and without it, any two other benefices, etc. [as above, no. 3]. Given at Civita Castellana.[2]

Litterarum scientia, vite ac morum honestas . . .
L pucius[3] */· B· / ₁ B· L. Bolis·*

[1] after *Datum*, entire dating clause in lighter ink (as is the abbreviator's name, see below, note 3) : entered later?

[2] see above, note 1

[3] *sic*; in lighter ink : entered later? See above, note 1; and *cf.* below, no. 724, note 2.

724   28 September 1501   *Reg. Lat.* 1103, fos 140[v]-141[v]

To Cornelius Arpur, rector of the parish church of Waltun,[1] d. Coventry and Lichfield. Dispensation — at his supplication — to receive and retain for life, together with the above parish church, one, and without it, any two other benefices, etc. [as above, no. 3]. Given at Civita Castellana.

Vite ac morum honestas . . .
L pucius[2] */ · B· / ₁ B · L. Bolis.*

[1] in both occurrences the 'u' has been written over another letter (now blotched) possibly 'o'

[2] *sic*; entered later? (*cf.* no. 723, note 2)

725   28 September[1] 1501   *Reg. Lat.* 1103, fo 143[r-v]

To John Cradoc, rector of the parish church of Henellan Amgoed, d. St David's. Dispensation — at his supplication — to receive and retain for life, together with the above parish church, one, and without it, any two other benefices, etc. [as above, no. 3].[2] Given at Civita Castellana.

Vite ac morum honestas . . .
L puccius[3] */ · B· / ₁ B· L. Bolis·*

[1] *quarto kalendas Octobris* ; *quinto* in the line has been deleted, initialled . *B.* and *quarto* inserted (in lighter ink : later?) in the margin by the enregistering scribe, initialled *B*

[2] save that the first occurrence of 'or offices' is wanting

[3] in lighter ink : entered later?

726 14 September 1501 *Reg. Lat.* 1103, fo 152^r-v

To Thomas Re'pe, BDec, rector of the parish church of Northbarsham, d. Norwich. Dispensation — at his supplication — to receive and retain for life, together with the above parish church, one, and without it, any two other benefices, etc. [as above, no. 3].

Litterarum scientia, vite ac morum honestas ...
L. puccius / · B· / . B· L. Bolis

727 28 August 1501 *Reg. Lat.* 1103, fo 153^r-v

To John Parker, LLB, perpetual vicar of the parish church of B. Mary, Beneflete Magna [also spelt *Benefilet Magna*], d. London. Dispensation and indult — at his supplication — to receive and retain for life, together with the perpetual vicarage of the above parish church, one, and without it, any two other benefices, etc. [as above, no. 3, to '. . . retain them together for life, as above']; and for life, while residing in the Roman curia or any one of his benefices, or attending a *studium generale*, not to be bound to reside personally in his other benefices, etc. [as above, no. 238].

Litterarum scientia, vite ac morum honestas ...
. *L. pucius*[1] /· *B· / · B· Lx · Bolis*

[1] *sic*

728 28 August 1501 *Reg. Lat.* 1103, fo 160^r-v

To John Edmond, canon of the priory, order of St Gilbert, Sempryagham [also spelt *Semprymgara*], d. Lincoln. Dispensation — at his supplication — to him, who, as he asserts, is expressly professed of the above order,[1] to receive and retain any benefice, with or without cure, usually held by secular clerics, etc. [as above, no. 32, to '. . . another, similar or dissimilar, benefice'], usually assigned to secular clerics. Notwithstanding etc.

Religionis zelus, vite ac morum honestas ...
[-][2] /· *B· / · B xxx Bolis*

[1] This information comes from a notwithstanding clause.
[2] no abbreviator's name

729   6 August 1502   *Reg. Lat.* 1103, fos 223[r]-224[r]

To John Jackeson,[1] perpetual vicar of the parish church of Empynghm [also spelt *Empynghm'*] in Ruttlande, d. Lincoln. Dispensation — at his supplication — to receive and retain for life, together with the [perpetual vicarage of the above parish church],[2] one, and without it, any two other benefices, etc. [as above, no. 3].

Vite ac morum honestas . . .
L puccius / · B· / · B· L. Bolis

1 or *Jackoson*; the 'e' or 'o' apparently squeezed in
2 MS: *unacum dicta unum*; i. e. wanting 'vicaria'

730   30 July 1502   *Reg. Lat.* 1103, fos 231[v]-232[v]

To John Twyforth[1] *alias* Colyns, canon of the monastery of B. Mary the Virgin, *in Prat(is)*,[2] near the vill [of] Laycestet [also spelt *Laycestre*], OSA, d. Lincoln, dispensation. Some time ago, as he asserts, the pope by other letters of his dispensed him to receive and retain any benefice, with or without cure, usually held by secular clerics, even if a parish church or its perpetual vicarage, or a chantry, free chapel, hospital or annual service, usually assigned to secular clerics in title of a perpetual ecclesiastical benefice, and of lay patronage and of whatsoever tax or annual value, if he obtained it otherwise canonically, to resign it, simply or for exchange, as often as he pleased, and in its place receive and retain another, similar or dissimilar, benefice, usually assigned to secular clerics, as above, and to receive the canonical portion usually received by canons of the above monastery, just as if he had not acquired the benefice, as is more fully contained in those letters.[3] The pope therefore — at his supplication — hereby dispenses him, who, as he asserts, holds the parish church of Ryther, d. York, to receive and retain for life, in place of the said canonical portion, together with the church of Ryther, or with another secular benefice held by him at the time by virtue of the said dispensation, one other secular benefice, even if a parish church etc. [as above, this entry, but with appropriate changes of tense, to '. . . receive and retain'] for life, together [with the secular benefice held], another, similar or dissimilar, benefice, usually held by secular clerics, as above. Notwithstanding etc. With the proviso that the above church and other benefices in question shall not, on this account, be defrauded of due services and the cure of souls in the church and (if any) the other benefices aforesaid shall not be neglected.

Religionis zelus, vite ac morum honestas . . .
L puccius / · B· / . B· xxxx Bolis.

¹ *Cf. Tunyforth* (*CPL*, XVI, no. 583)

² MS: *in Prat'*

³ summarised in *CPL*, XVI at no. 583

731   25 June 1502   *Reg. Lat.* 1103, fos 235ᵛ-236ᵛ

To Thomas Everard, BDec, perpetual vicar of the parish church of Vaplod, d. Lincoln. Dispensation — at his supplication — to receive and retain for life, together with the perpetual vicarage of the above parish church, one, and without it, any two other benefices, etc. [as above, no. 3].

Litterarum sciencia, vite ac morum honestas . . .
S de Castello / · B· / ₁ B· L. Bolisˑ

732   2 July 1502   *Reg. Lat.* 1103, fos 249ᵛ-250ᵛ

To Edward Wetton, perpetual vicar of the parish church of St Laurence, Lechelade, d. Worcester. Dispensation — at his supplication — to receive and retain for life, together with the perpetual vicarage of the above parish church, one, and without it, any two other benefices, etc. [as above, no. 3].

Vite ac morum honestas . . .
L. puccius / Jo / Jo. L. Eps' Terracinen.'

733   29 June 1502   *Reg. Lat.* 1103, fos 251ʳ-252ᵛ

Union etc. At a recent petition on the part of John Hyslington, rector of the parish church of St Romuald (*sancti Rumvoldi*),¹ d. Salisbury, the pope hereby unites etc. the perpetual vicarage of the parish church of St John, Tysbury, d. Salisbury, (whose annual value does not exceed 5 English marks, equivalent to 15 gold ducats of the camera or thereabouts), to the above church of St Romuald, which he holds together by apostolic dispensation, for as long as he holds St Romuald's, to the effect that John, in person or by proxy, may, on his own authority, take and retain possession² of the vicarage and its rights and appurtenances, for as long as he holds St Romuald's, and convert its fruits etc. to his own uses and those of the said vicarage and church without licence of the local diocesan or of anyone else. Notwithstanding etc. The pope's will is, however, that the vicarage shall not, on account of this union etc., be defrauded of due services and the cure of souls therein shall not be neglected, but that its customary burdens shall be supported; and that on John's death or resignation etc. of St Romuald's the union etc. shall be dissolved and so deemed and the vicarage shall revert to its original condition and be deemed vacant automatically.

Ad futuram rey memoriam. Romanum decet pontificem votis illis gratum prestare assensum . . .
L puccius / Jo / Jo. xxxv. Eps' Terracinen'

[1] also spelt: *Ruyoldy, Runyvoldy, Rumuoldi, (?)Rumuoldy, Rumoldi*
[2] 'corporalem' does not occur

734   26 May 1502   *Reg. Lat.* 1103, fos 256ʳ-257ʳ

To John Dowman', LLD, rector of the parish church of Upuoay, d. Salisbury. Dispensation — at his supplication — to receive and retain for life, together with the above parish church, one, and without it, any two other benefices, etc. [as above, no. 3].

Litterarum scientia, vite ac morum honestas . . .
Jo ortega / · B· / · B· L. Bolis

735   2 June 1502   *Reg. Lat.* 1103, fo 257ʳ⁻ᵛ

To Thomas Bradschauu, canon of the monastery of Heryngham or Herdham, OSA,[1] d. Chichester. Dispensation — at his supplication — to him, who, as he asserts, is expressly professed of the above order,[2] to receive and retain any benefice, with or without cure, usually held by secular clerics, etc. [as above, no. 32, to '. . . another, similar or dissimilar, benefice'], usually assigned to secular clerics. Notwithstanding etc.

Religionis zelus, vite ac morum honestas . . .
L puccius / · B· / · B· xxx Bolis

[1] *Cistercien.* deleted and initialled *B* and . *B.* occurs between *Augustini* and *Cicestren.*
[2] This information comes from a notwithstanding clause.

736   26 May 1502   *Reg. Lat.* 1103, fos 261^r-262^v

Union etc. At a recent petition on the part of William Ketilton,[1] MA, rector of the parish church of St Peter in Shaftesbury (*in Shaftonia*), d. Salisbury, the pope hereby unites etc. the parish church of St Mary, Vilton in Bredstret, d. Salisbury, (whose annual value does not exceed <16>[2] English marks, equivalent to 46 gold ducats of the camera or thereabouts), to St Peter's, which he holds together with St Mary's, for as long as he holds St Peter's; to the effect that he may, on his own authority, in person or by proxy, take and retain corporal [possession] of St Mary's and its rights and appurtenances, for as long as he holds St Peter's, and convert its fruits etc. to his own uses and those of St Mary's and St Peter's, without licence of the local diocesan or of anyone else. Notwithstanding etc. The pope's will is, however, that St Mary's shall not, on account of this union etc., be defrauded of due services and the cure of souls therein shall not be neglected, but that its customary burdens shall be supported; and that on William's death or resignation etc. of St Peter's this union etc. shall be dissolved and so deemed and St Mary's shall revert to its original condition and be deemed vacant automatically.

Ad futuram rey memoriam. Romanum decet pontificem votis illis gratum prestare assensum . . .
L puccius / · B· / · B· xxxv Bolis·

[1] or *R-*
[2] *quindecim* in the line deleted, initialled *B*; *sedecim* inserted in the margin by the enregistering scribe, initialled *. B*

737   3 June 1502   *Reg. Lat.* 1103, fos 263^r-264^r

To David Barker, MA, rector of the parish church of Westwrethin' [also spelt *Westwrethm'*], d. Norwich. Dispensation — at his supplication — to receive and retain for life, together with the above parish church, one, and without it, any two other benefices, etc. [as above, no. 3].

Litterarum scientia, vite ac morum honestas . . .
L puccius / · B· / · B· L. Bolis·

738   3 June 1502   *Reg. Lat.* 1103, fos 264^v-265^v

To John Heyly, rector of one of two portions of the parish church, usually ruled by two rectors, of B. Mary the Virgin, Burford, d. Hereford. Dispensation — at his supplication — to receive and retain for life, together with the above portion, one, and without it, any two other benefices, etc. [as above, no. 3].

Vite ac morum honestas . . .
L puccius / · *B·* / · *B·*   *L. Bolis*

739   2 November 1501   *Reg. Lat.* 1103, fos 265ᵛ-267ᵛ

To Thomas Aphowell, LLB, rector of the parish church of Llanllaychayarin' [also spelt *Llanlloychayarn'*, *Llanlloychayran'*, *Llanlloychayarn*], d. St David's, validation. Some time ago, Innocent VIII by certain letters[1] dispensed Thomas to receive and retain for life, together with the parish church of Curcheoner [also spelt *Churᵉcheover*][2], d. Coventry and Lichfield, (which, as he asserted, he was then holding), one, and without it, any two other benefices, etc. [as above, no. 131, to '. . . retain them together for life']; and then the pope by his letters[3] dispensed him to receive and retain for life, together with the above parish church of Llanllaychayarin' and the archdeaconry of Cardigan in the church of St David's (which, as he asserted, he was then holding), or with any two other incompatible benefices held by him at the time by the said dispensation, any third benefice, etc. [as above, no. 131, to '. . . simply or for exchange'], as often as he pleased, and in its place receive and retain for life another, similar or dissimilar, benefice, as is more fully contained in each of the aforesaid letters. Moreover, as a recent petition to the pope on Thomas's part stated, at the time of Innocent's letters Thomas had resigned and parted with the church of Curcheoner and was holding the parish church of Llanllaychayarin' and no mention had been made of this resignation etc. of Curcheoner and holding of Llanllaychayarin' in the said letters of Innocent, and, on this account, Thomas fears that these letters as well as those of the pope could be branded surreptitious and he be molested over them with the passage of time. The pope — at his supplication — hereby wills and grants Thomas, (who, as he asserts, holds the church of Llanllaychayarin' and the archdeaconry aforesaid), that the earlier and later dispensations and the letters of Innocent and of the pope, with all clauses contained therein, be valid and have full force, in and for all things, just as if it had been expressed in Innocent's letters that he was holding not the church of Curcheoner, but that of Llanllaychayarin', and the same narrated in the pope's letters as in those of Innocent. Notwithstanding etc.

Litterarum sciencia[4], vite ac morum honestas . . .
L puccius /· *B·* / · *B· xx Bolis*

[1] summarised in *CPL*, XV, at no. 135
[2] thus written (once only)

3 above, no. 318
4 *sic*

740   4 June 1502   *Reg. Lat.* 1103, fos 267ᵛ-268ᵛ

To John Trotter, scholar, d. London. Dispensation and indult — at his supplication — to him, who, as he asserts, is in his eighteenth year of age and wishes to become a cleric, to receive and retain for life — after he has been duly marked with clerical character — one, and — as soon as he has reached his twenty-first year — together with it, another, and without them, any two other benefices, etc. [as above, no. 3, to '. . . as often as he pleases'], and in their place receive up to two other, similar or dissimilar, incompatible benefices, viz. : — after he has been duly marked with clerical character — one, and — when he has reached his twenty-first year — another, and retain them together for life, as above; and, also for life, while residing in the Roman curia or any one of his benefices or attending a *studium generale*, not to be bound to reside personally in his other benefices, and not to be liable to be compelled to do so by anyone against his will. Notwithstanding the said defect of age etc. With the proviso that the incompatible benefices in question shall not, on this account, be defrauded of due services and the cure of souls therein ([if] any) shall not be neglected.

Vite ac morum honestas . . .
L puccius / · B· / · B· Lxxx Bolis·

741   30 May 1502   *Reg. Lat.* 1103, fos 269ʳ-270ʳ

To John Burgis, professor OESA, dispensation. Some time ago, Sixtus IV by letters of his dispensed him to receive and retain any benefice, with or without cure, usually held by secular clerics, even if a parish church or its perpetual vicarage, or a chantry, free chapel, hospital or annual service, usually assigned to secular clerics in title of a perpetual ecclesiastical benefice, and of lay patronage and of whatsoever tax or annual value, if he obtained it otherwise canonically, to resign it, simply or for exchange, as often as he pleased, and in its place receive and retain another, similar or dissimilar, benefice, usually ruled by secular clerics, as is more fully contained in those letters.[1] The pope — at his supplication — hereby further dispenses him, (who, as he asserts, holds the parish church of Asby, d. Carlisle, by the said dispensation), to receive and retain *in commendam* for life, together with the above church, or other benefice held by him at the time by virtue of the said dispensation, any other benefice, with or without cure, usually held by secular clerics, even if a parish church or its perpetual vicarage, or a chantry, free chapel, hospital or annual service, usually assigned to secular clerics in title of a perpetual ecclesiastical benefice, and of lay patronage and of whatsoever tax or annual value, if he obtains it otherwise canonically, to resign it when he pleases, <and to cede the commend>,[2] and in its place receive and retain *in commendam* for life another, similar or dissimilar, benefice; (he may — due and customary burdens of the benefice retained *in commendam* having been supported — make disposition of the rest of its fruits etc. just as those holding it [*in titulum*] could and ought to do, alienation of immovable goods and precious movables being however forbidden). Notwithstanding etc. and [notwithstanding] the constitutions of Otto and Ottobuono formerly legates of the apostolic see in the kingdom of England etc.[3] With the proviso that the benefice retained *in commendam* shall not, on this account, be defrauded of due services and the cure of souls therein (if any) shall not be neglected; but that its aforesaid burdens shall be supported.

Religionis zelus, vite ac morum honestas . . .
L puccius / · *B·* / · *B·* · *L. Bolis·*

[1] summarised in *CPL*, XIII, Part II, on p. 853

[2] marginal insertion by the enregistering scribe, initialled *B.* and *B*

[3] Inclusion of these constitutions gives Burgis the option of holding (as he does) benefice(s) in England.

742   5 September 1495[1]   *Reg. Lat.* 1103, fos 287[r]-288[r]

To Simon Senouse, canon of the monastery or priory of St John the Evangelist, Hellaghe or Helley, OSA, d. York, (who, as he asserts, is expressly professed of the above order),[2] dispensation. Some time ago, Sixtus IV by letters of his dispensed him to receive and retain any benefice, with or without cure, usually held by secular clerics, etc. [as above, no. 741, to '. . . as is more fully contained in those letters']. The pope — at his supplication — hereby further dispenses him, (who, as he asserts, holds by the said dispensation the perpetual vicarage of the parish church of Eversham, d. York, having acquired it when it was vacant *certo modo* and canonically collated to him), to receive, together with the above vicarage, one, and without it, any two other benefices, with or without cure, regular of the said order or secular, even if the regular benefices should be priories, *prepositura*,[3] dignities, *personatus*, administrations or offices, and the secular benefices be parish churches or their perpetual vicarages, or chantries, free chapels, hospitals or annual services, usually assigned to secular clerics in title of a perpetual ecclesiastical benefice, even if the priories etc. should be customarily elective and have cure of souls, if he obtains them otherwise canonically, and to retain for life whichever one of the regular or secular benefices he chooses, even if the regular benefice should be a priory, *prepositura* or other conventual dignity or a claustral office, *in titulum*, and with it, the other regular benefice, which may not be suchlike, or the secular benefice, *in commendam*, to resign them, at once or successively, simply or for exchange, as often as he pleases, and to cede the commend, and in their place receive up to two, other, similar or dissimilar, benefices, with or without cure, regular of the said order or secular, and retain for life whichever one of the regular or secular benefices he chooses *in titulum* and with it the other regular benefice, which may not be a priory, *prepositura* or other conventual dignity or a claustral office, or the secular benefice, *in commendam*, as above; (he may — due and customary burdens of the benefice held *in commendam* having been supported — make disposition of the rest of its fruits etc. just as those holding it *in titulum* could and ought to do, alienation of immovable goods and precious movables being however forbidden). Notwithstanding etc. With the proviso that the benefice retained *in commendam* shall not, on this account, be defrauded of due services, and the cure of souls therein (if any) shall not be neglected; but that its aforesaid burdens shall be supported.

Religionis zelus, vite ac morum honestas . . .
S de Castello[4] */ · B· / . B. L. Bolis·*

[1] *quingentesimo p(rim)o* deleted, initialled . *B.* ; the rest of the dating clause being in darker ink : entered later?

[2] This information comes from a notwithstanding clause.

[3] *sic; recte:* 'prepositure'

[4] in darker ink (*cf.* dating clause): entered later?

743   18 January 1502[1]   *Reg. Lat.* 1103, fos 288ᵛ-289ʳ

To Thomas Chaundeler, MTheol, monk of the monastery called Christchurch, OSB, Canterbury. Dispensation — at his supplication — to him, who, as he asserts, holds a place and monacal portion of the above monastery and is expressly professed of the above order,[2] to receive and retain for life, together with the above place and monacal portion, any benefice, with or without cure, usually held by secular clerics, etc. [as above, no. 32, to '. . . usually held by secular clerics']; and, also for life, to have as before — even after he has acquired the benefice — a stall in the choir and a place and an active and a passive voice in the said monastery and any chapters in other congregations of the order, in and for all things, just as if he had not acquired the benefice. Notwithstanding etc. With the proviso that this benefice shall not, on this account, be defrauded of due services and the cure of souls therein (if any) shall not be neglected; but that its customary burdens shall be supported.

Religionis zelus, litterarum scientia, vite ac morum honestas . . .
S de Castello[3] */ · B· / | B· L. Bolis·*

[1] after *Datum*, entire dating clause in darker ink : entered later?

[2] The latter information comes from a notwithstanding clause.

[3] in darker ink (*cf.* dating clause) : entered later?

744   5 February[1] 1502   *Reg. Lat.* 1103, fos 289[v]-290[v]

To Richard Willeys, UIB, rector of the parish church of B. Mary the Virgin, Ramesduncrays, d. London. Dispensation — at his supplication — to receive and retain for life, together with the above parish church, one, and without it, any two other benefices, etc. [as above, no. 3].

Litterarum scientia, vite ac morum honestas . . .
L puccius[2] /· B· / . B. L. Bolis.

[1] *nonis Februarii anno decimo* in darker ink : entered later?

[2] in darker ink (*cf.* dating clause) : entered later?

745   5 February 1502[1]   *Reg. Lat.* 1103, fos 290[v]-291[r]

To Henry Bukarawl, monk of the monastery of St Saviour, Bermyssey [also spelt *Benmyssey*], OSB,[2] d. Winchester. Dispensation — at his supplication — to him, who, as he asserts, is expressly professed of the above order,[3] to receive and retain any benefice, with or without cure, usually held by secular clerics, etc. [as above, no. 32, to '. . . another, similar or dissimilar, benefice'], usually assigned to secular clerics. Notwithstanding etc.

Religionis zelus, vite ac morum honestas . . .
L puccius[4] / · B· / . B· xxx Bolis

[1] *non' . . . decimo*] in darker ink : entered later?

[2] *sic;* yet Bermondsey is usually styled Cluniac (*cf. CPL,* XVI, no. 614)

[3] This information comes from a notwithstanding clause.

[4] in darker ink (*cf.* dating clause): entered later?

746   5 February 1502[1]   *Reg. Lat.* 1103, fos 291[v]-292[r]

To Edward Redmayn, cleric, d. Carlisle. Dispensation — at his supplication — to him, who, as he asserts, is of noble birth and in his nineteenth year of age, to receive and retain any benefice, with cure or otherwise incompatible, etc. [as above, no. 240].

Nobilitas generis, vite ac morum honestas . . .
L puccius[2] / · B· / . B. xx. Bolis.

[1] *non' februarii* in darker ink : entered later?

[2] in darker ink : entered later?

747   3 June 1502   *Reg. Lat.* 1103, fos 303^r-304^r

To Thomas, abbot of the monastery of St Saviour,[1] Tor, OPrem, d. Exeter. Dispensation — at his supplication — to receive, together with the above monastery of St Saviour,[2] one, and without it, any two other regular benefices, with or without cure, of the said order, or with one of them, or without them, one secular benefice, with or without cure, etc. [as above, no. 707]. [3]

Personam tuam nobis et apostolice sedi devotam . . .
L puccius / · B· / . B· L. Bolis

[1] *Beate Marie* deleted and initialled . *B.* ; *Sancti Salvatoris* inserted in the margin, initialled . *B.* ; *Cassatum et corectum de Mandato R(everendissimi) p(atris) d(omini) Jo(hannis) ragusin' regentis per me . B. Bolis.* ; insertion and note in Bolis's hand

[2] *Beate Marie* deleted and initialled . *B.* ; *Sancti Salvatoris* (between . *B* and *Bolis.*) inserted in the margin; insertion in Bolis's hand

[3] substituting here: 'which may not be a monastery or be conventual or claustral' where no. 707 has: 'which may not be conventual or claustral'

748   2 June 1502   *Reg. Lat.* 1103, fos 304^v-305^v

To Peter Willyam, perpetual chaplain, called cantor, of the perpetual chaplaincy, called the chantry of Philip and Fulk Bassett [also spelt *Basset*] and Peter Newport at the altar of St George in the church of London. Dispensation and indult — at his supplication — to receive and retain for life, together with the said chaplaincy or chantry, if it cannot be held with another incompatible benefice, one, and without it, any two other benefices, etc. [as above, no. 3, to '. . . retain them together for life, as above']; and for life, while residing in the Roman curia or any one of his benefices, or attending a *studium generale*, not to be bound to reside personally in his other benefices, etc. [as above, no. 238].

Vite ac morum honestas . . .
S de Castello / · B· / · B· Lx Bolis

749   13 June 1502   *Reg. Lat.* 1103, fos 317^v-319^r

Union etc. At a recent petition on the part of John Cutler, canon of the church of St

Margaret near Leicester (*Leycestriam*), d. Lincoln, the pope hereby unites etc. [the perpetual vicarage of][1] the parish church of Craste, d. Lincoln, (whose annual value does not exceed 20 English marks, equivalent to 58 gold ducats of the camera or thereabouts), to the canonry and prebend of the above church of St Margaret, which he holds together with the above vicarage, for as long as he holds the canonry and prebend, to the effect that John, in person or by proxy, may, on his own authority,take corporal possession of the vicarage and its rights and appurtenances, and convert its fruits etc. to his own uses and those of the vicarage and the canonry and prebend without licence of the local diocesan or of anyone else. Notwithstanding etc. The pope's will is, however, that the vicarage shall not, on account of this union etc., be defrauded of due services and the cure of souls therein shall not be neglected, but that its customary burdens shall be supported; and that on John's death or resignation of the canonry and prebend the union etc. shall be dissolved and so deemed and the vicarage shall revert to its original condition and be deemed [vacant][2] automatically.

Ad futuram rey memoriam. Romanum decet pontificem votis illis gratum prestare assensum . . .
N. de castello | · B· | · B· xxxv· Bolis·

[1] MS : *ecclesiam predictam; recte* : 'vicariam predictam' (consistently a vicarage elsewhere in MS)
[2] MS : *vicaria; recte* : 'vacare'

750   16 June 1502   *Reg. Lat.* 1103, fos 319ᵛ-320ᵛ

To Gabriel Silvestro, rector of the parish church of Wedyngton,d. London. Dispensation and indult —at his supplication— to receive and retain for life, together with the above parish church, one, and without it, any two other benefices, etc. [as above, no. 3, to '. . . retain them together for life, as above']; and for life, while residing in the Roman curia or any one of his benefices, or attending a *studium generale*, not to be bound to reside personally in his other benefices, etc. [as above, no. 238].

Vite ac morum honestas . . .
L puccius | · B | . B· Lx· Bolis·

751   16 June 1502   *Reg. Lat.* 1103, fos 321ʳ-322ʳ

To Thomas Thyndyn', rector of the parish church of St Andrew, Acryng, d. York. Dispensation —at his supplication— to receive and retain for life, together with the above parish church, one, and without it, any two other benefices, etc. [as above, no. 3].

Vite ac morum honestas . . .
L puccius | B | · B· L. Bolis·

752   16 June 1502   *Reg. Lat.* 1103, fos 323^r-324^v

Union etc. At a recent petition on the part of George Sitzhugh, canon of Lincoln, the pope hereby unites etc. the parish church of Aldyngh(a)m,[1] d. York, (whose annual value does not exceed 193 gold ducats of the camera), to the canonry and prebend of Cropperedy in the church of Lincoln, which he holds with the above parish church, for as long as he holds the canonry and prebend, to the effect that George, (who asserted that he was of noble birth), in person or by proxy, may, on his own authority, take and retain corporal possession of the parish church and its rights and appurtenances, for as long as he holds the canonry and prebend, and convert its fruits etc. to his own uses and those of the canonry and prebend and the parish church without licence of the local diocesan or of anyone else. Notwithstanding etc. The pope's will is, however, that the parish [church] shall not, on account of this union etc., be defrauded of due services and the cure of souls therein shall not be neglected, but that its customary burdens shall be supported; and that on George's death or resignation etc. of the canonry and prebend the union etc. shall be dissolved and so deemed and the parish church shall revert to its original condition and be deemed vacant automatically.

Ad futuram rey memoriam. Romanum decet pontificem votis illis gratum prestare assensum . . .
L puccius / · B· / . B. xxxv · Bolis

[1] MS: *Aldynghm'*

753   16 June 1502   *Reg. Lat.* 1103, fos 325^r-326^v

Union etc. At a recent petition on the part of John Mane, rector of the parish church of St Tudy (*Sancti Tudii*), county Cornwall (*Cornubie*), d. Exeter, the pope hereby unites etc. the perpetual vicarage of the parish church of St Cuby (*Sancti Cuvy*), said county and diocese, (whose annual value does not exceed 44 gold ducats of the camera), to the above parish church of St Tudy, which he holds together by apostolic dispensation, for as long as he holds that of St Tudy, to the effect that John, in person or by proxy, may, on his own authority, take and retain corporal possession of the vicarage and its rights and appurtenances, for as long as he holds the church of St Tudy, and convert its fruits etc. to his own uses and those of the said vicarage and church without licence of the local diocesan or of anyone else. Notwithstanding etc. The pope's will is, however, that the vicarage shall not, on account of this union etc., be defrauded of due services and the cure of souls therein shall not be neglected, but that its customary burdens shall be supported; and that on John's death or resignation etc. of the church of St Tudy the union etc. shall be dissolved and so deemed and the vicarage shall revert to its original condition and be deemed vacant automatically.

Ad futuram rey memoriam. Romanum decet pontificem votis illis gratum prestare

assensum . . .
L puccius / · B· / · B· xxxv Bolis

754   16 June 1502   *Reg. Lat.* 1103, fos 326^v-327^v

To John, abbot of the monastery of B. Mary, Miravall, OCist, d. Coventry and Lichfield. Dispensation —at his supplication— to receive together with the above monastery, one, and without it, any two other regular benefices, with or without cure, of the said order, or with one of them, or without them, one secular benefice, with or without cure, etc. [as above, no. 707]. [1]

Personam tuam nobis et apostolice sedis[2] devotam . . .
L. puccius / · B· / · B· L. Bolis

[1] substituting here: 'which may not be a monastery or be conventual or claustral' where no. 707 has : 'which may not be conventual or claustral'

[2] *sic; recte:* 'sedi'

755   16 June 1502   *Reg. Lat.* 1103, fos 328^r-329^r

To Edward Bradeley, rector of the parish church of St Laurence, Lokeford [also spelt *Lockeford*], d. Norwich. Dispensation and indult —at his supplication— to receive and retain for life, together with the above parish church, one, and without it, any two other benefices, etc. [as above, no. 3, to '. . . retain them together for life, as above']; and also[1] not to be bound, while residing in the Roman curia or any one of his benefices, or attending a *studium generale*, to reside personally in his other benefices, etc. [as above, no. 21].

Vite ac morum honestas . . .
L puccius / · B· / . B· Lx Bolis

[1] 'quoadvixeris' does not occur here

756   7 June 1502   *Reg. Lat.* 1103, fos 332^v-333^v

To Ewart[1] Redmayn, scholar, d. Carlisle. Dispensation —at his supplication— to him, (who, as he asserts, is in his nineteenth year of age and regarding whom it was recently commanded that he be dispensed by apostolic authority, notwithstanding a defect of birth as the son of an unmarried man and an unmarried woman, to be promoted to all orders, even of the subdiaconate and diaconate and — as soon as he has reached his twenty-third year — of the priesthood, and — at the lawful age — to hold a benefice, even if it should have cure of souls), to receive and retain — after he has been duly marked with clerical character by virtue of this dispensation — any benefice, with cure or otherwise incompatible or requiring sacred and priest's orders by statute, foundation or otherwise, even if a parish church etc. [as above, no. 240, to '. . . benefice, with cure or otherwise incompatible']² or requiring sacred orders. Notwithstanding the above defects of age and birth etc. With the proviso that the benefice in question shall not, on this account, be defrauded of due services and the cure of souls therein (if any) shall not be neglected.

Vite ac morum honestas . . .
L puccius / · B· / . B· xx Bolis·

¹ *Ewardo*; (a slip for 'Edwardo'?) *Cf.* Emden, *Oxford 1501 to 1540*, p. 483 : 'Redmayne, Edward'

² save that in this instance 'to secular clerics' does not occur

---

757   25 June 1502   *Reg. Lat.* 1103, fos 333ᵛ-334ᵛ

To John Emley, priest, d. Lincoln. Dispensation —at his supplication— to receive and retain together for life any two benefices, with cure or otherwise mutually incompatible, etc. [as above, no. 3, to '. . . Notwithstanding etc. ']. With the proviso that the incompatible benefices in question shall not, on this account, be defrauded of due services and the cure of souls therein shall not be neglected.

Vite ac morum honestas . . .
L : puccius / · B· / . B· L. Bolis·

---

758   21 June 1502   *Reg. Lat.* 1103, fos 334ᵛ-335ᵛ

To William Burra, canon of the priory or monastery of B. Mary Magdalen, Tortington [also spelt *Tortyngton*], OSA, ¹ d. Chichester. Dispensation —at his supplication— to him, who, as he asserts, is expressly professed of the above order, ² to receive and retain any benefice, with or without cure, usually held by secular clerics etc. [as above, no. 32, to '. . . another, similar or dissimilar, benefice'], usually assigned to secular clerics. Notwithstanding etc.

Religionis zelus, vite ac morum honestas . . .
L. puccius / · B· / · B· xxx Bolis·

¹ *Cistercien.* , deleted and initialled . *B.* , occurs between *Augustini* and *Cicestren.*

² This information comes from a notwithstanding clause.

759   19 May 1502   *Reg. Lat.* 1103, fos 335ᵛ-336ᵛ

To William Cowper, rector of the parish church of Wyke [also spelt *Wilke*], d. Worcester. Dispensation —at his supplication— to receive and retain for life, together with the above parish church, one, and without it, any two other benefices, etc. [as above, no. 3].

Vite ac morum honestas . . .
L. puccius /· B· / . B. L. Bolis·

760   6 August 1502   *Reg. Lat.* 1103, fos 378ᵛ-379ᵛ

To Robert Dokett, BTheol, rector of the parish church of B. Mary, Chevenyng, d. Canterbury. Dispensation and indult —at his supplication— to receive and retain for life, together with the above parish church, one, and without it, any two other benefices, etc. [as above, no. 3, to '. . . retain them together for life, as above']; and for life, while residing in the Roman curia or any one of his benefices, or attending a *studium generale*, not to be bound to reside personally in his other benefices, etc. [as above, no. 238].

Litterarum scientia, vite ac morum honestas . . .
L puccius / . B. / . B. Lx. Bolis.

761   6 August 1502   *Reg. Lat.* 1103, fo 380ʳ⁻ᵛ

To Brian Stapylton, cleric, d. York. Dispensation —at his supplication— to him, who, as he asserts, is in his seventeenth year of age, to receive and retain any benefice, with cure or otherwise incompatible, etc. [as above, no. 240].

Vite ac morum honestas . . .
[-]¹ /· B· /· B· xxv Bolis·

¹ no abbreviator's name

762   26 July 1502   *Reg. Lat.* 1103, fo 381ʳ⁻ᵛ

To John Laure(n)ce, ¹ rector of the parish church of St Erme (*Sancti Ermetis*), in the county of Cornwall, ² d. Exeter. Dispensation — at his supplication — to receive and retain for life, together with the above parish church, one, and without it, any two other benefices, etc. [as above, no. 3].

Vite ac morum honestas . . .
L puccius / · B· / · B· L. Bolis

[1] MS: *Laure'ce*

[2] *in com(itatu) Cornub(ie)* twice inserted in the margin by the enregistering scribe, initialled in the first instance *B* and in the second . *B*.

763   26 December 1501   *Reg.Lat.* 1104, fos 183[v]-184[v]

To the abbot of the monastery *de Flumine Dei* [Abbeyshrule], d. Meath, the prior of the priory of Dearg, d. Ardagh, and Odo Oberyn, canon of the church of Elphin, mandate in favour of <John Hofergil, cleric, d. Ardagh>[1]. The pope has learned that the perpetual vicarage of the parish church of Kyllechassy, said diocese [of Ardagh], which Donald Ofirgil, its late perpetual vicar, held while he lived, has become vacant by his death, outside the Roman curia, and is vacant at present. He hereby commands that the above three, or two or one of them, in person or by proxy, shall collate and assign the vicarage, whose annual value does not exceed 6 marks sterling, (whether vacant as above etc., or by the said Donald's free resignation or that of Donald Ymorrij, formerly its perpetual vicar, or of anyone else, etc. ; even if it has been vacant for so long that by the Lateran statutes its collation has lawfully devolved on the apostolic see etc.), with all rights and appurtenances, to John, inducting him etc. having removed any unlawful detainer and causing John (or his proctor) to be admitted to the vicarage and its fruits etc., rights and obventions to be delivered to him. [Curbing] gainsayers etc. Notwithstanding etc.

Vite ac morum honestas . . .
A de S[to] Severino / · B· / ǀ B· x pridie Id' Februar' anno decimo [12 February 1502],
ǀ *Bolis*

[1] marginal insertion by the enregistering scribe initialled . *B*. twice

764   22 February 1502   *Reg. Lat.* 1105, fos 66[v]-68[r]

To Henry Bounde, rector of the parish church of Torleston, [1] d. York. Dispensation — at his supplication— to receive and retain for life, together with the above parish church, one, and without it, any two other benefices, etc. [as above, no. 3]. Given at Piombino, d. Massa Marittima.

Vite ac morum honestas . . .
· Jo ortega / B / . B. L. Bolis

or *Torlestone'*; in the first occurrence the end of the name is reworked and uncertain

765   19 March 1502   *Reg. Lat.* 1105, fos 72^r-74^v

Mandate to the abbot of Holyrood, d. St Andrews, and the archdeacon of Lothian in the church of St Andrews, concerning the endowment by James [IV] of the chapel royal, Stirling, recently erected into a collegiate church.

Ex iniuncto nobis desuper apostolice servitutis officio . . .
F. de parma / Jo / Jo. L. Eps' Terracinen'

Printed in full, from the copy in the *Registrum Capellae Regiae Strivelinensis*, by C. Rogers, *History of the Chapel Royal of Scotland* [= Grampian Club, no. 20], Edinburgh, 1882, pp. 66-71 (item 11. Bulla si in Evidentem).

Trifling discrepancies apart, the copy in the papal register follows that in print, save that the recital of Paul II's letters is (as usual) abridged, and Lothian is spelt *Laudonien'*, Kintyre *Kyntyr*, and Lochaber *Lochabyr*.

766   18 March 1502   *Reg. Lat.* 1105, fos 74^v-75^v

To Walter Stewart, MA, cleric, d. Glasgow. Dispensation —at his supplication— to him (who, some time ago, was dispensed by apostolic authority notwithstanding a defect of birth as the son of a priest and an unmarried woman to be promoted to all, even sacred, orders and to retain a benefice, even if it should have cure of souls, and who afterwards was marked with clerical character) to receive and retain together for life any two benefices, with cure or otherwise mutually incompatible, and also any number of other benefices, with and without cure, compatible mutually and with the said incompatibles, even if the [(?)compatibles][1] should be canonries and prebends and they as well as the incompatibles should be dignities, *personatus*, administrations or offices in cathedral, even metropolitan, or collegiate churches, even if the dignities in question should be major *post pontificalem* in cathedral, even metropolitan, churches, or principal in collegiate churches, or parish churches or their perpetual vicarages, or a combination, if he obtains them otherwise canonically, to resign each and every one of them, at once or successively, simply or for exchange, as often as he pleases, and in their place receive up to two other, similar or dissimilar, mutually incompatible benefices and also any number of other benefices compatible mutually and with the said incompatibles, as above, and retain them together for life, as above. Notwithstanding the above defect of birth etc. With the proviso that the incompatible benefices in question shall not, on this account, be defrauded of due services and the cure of souls therein ([if] any) shall not be neglected. [2]

Litterarum scientia, vite ac morum honestas . . .
L. puccius / Jo / Jo. · Lxxx Eps' Terracinen'.

[1] *incompatibilia; recte:* 'compatientia' (or suchlike)?

[2] The text of the entry has been corrected in various places by order of the regent: firstly (fos 74^v-75^r): *omnia et singula beneficia ecclesiastica* in the line deleted and initialled *Jo* and in the margin opposite: *Jo* then *quodcunque beneficii [sic] ecclesiasticum* then *casatu(m) et correctu(m) de m[andato] R(everendissimi) p(atris) d(omini) Jo(hannis) Ragusin' Regen(tis) p(er) me Jo(hannem) E(pisco)p(u)m Terracinen' r(e)g(ist)ri mag(istrum)*; half a dozen words later a reference mark is inserted above the line, and in the margin opposite : *Jo* then *forsan ex premissa dispen(sation)e* then *casatu(m) et correctu(m) ut supra* then *Jo.* ; and below there are more corrections in the same hand (but not explicitly noted as being by the regent's order).

767   16 April 1502   *Reg. Lat.* 1105, fo 76^r-v

Letters conservatory, addressed to the abbots of Holyrood, Cambuskenneth, and Paisley, ds. St Andrews and Glasgow, in favour of the chapel royal, Stirling.

Millitanti[1] ecclesie . . .
F· de parma / Jo / Jo· C· Eps' Terracinen'

Printed in full, from the copy in the *Reg. Cap. Reg. Striv.* , by C. Rogers, *op. cit.* (above, no. 765), pp. 29-33 (item 3. Conservatoria Ecclesie Collegiate de Striueling)

The copy in the papal register is (as usual in the case of such letters) much abridged. So far as it goes, it agrees (trifling discrepancies apart) with the printed copy, save that Cambuskenneth is spelt *Cambuschinet*, Stirling *Stirling*.

[1] *sic*

768   16 April 1502   *Reg. Lat.* 1105, fos 76^v-83^r

Separation, after reservation of specified sums, of residues of fruits of named canonries and prebends of Glasgow, Aberdeen, Dunkeld, and Moray, and their appropriation to the chapel royal, Stirling.
    Executory to the abbots of Cambuskenneth and Paisley and the archdeacon of the church of St Andrews.

Ad perpetuam rei memoriam. Ad ea ex iniuncto nobis desuper apostolice servitutis officio intendimus . . . The executory begins: *Hodie ex certis causis . . .*

F. de parma; . A. de sanctoseverino / Jo / Jo· xxxx xx Eps' Terracinen'

Printed in full, from the copy in the *Reg. Cap. Reg. Striv.* , by C. Rogers, *op. cit.* (above, no. 765). The principal letter is at pp. 60-66 (item 10. Applicacio prima fructuum de Aire Kincardin Creif et Petty Brachlee); the executory at pp. 71-72 (item 12. Conservatoria penes applicacionem fructuum de Air Kincardin Creif et Pettybrachlie).

About forty words are omitted in error from the copy of the principal letter in the papal register. Otherwise, it agrees (minor discrepancies apart) with the printed copy, as does the executory, save that in the papal register Stirling is spelt *Stirling*, Dunbar *Dumbar* and *Du'bar*, Lothian *Lodonie*, Crieff *Creyff*, Kincardine *Kyncarden'*, Petty-Brackley *Petty Brauchele*, Duthel *Duthel*, and Cambuskenneth (?) *Cambuschinent*.

769   15 March 1502   *Reg. Lat.* 1105, fos 108^V-110^V

To Alexander Stewart, cleric, d. Glasgow, dispensation. Some time ago, the pope by other letters of his dispensed and indulged him (who was then [not yet][1] marked with clerical character and, as he asserted, in his eighth year of age, suffered a defect of birth as the son of the unmarried king of Scots and an unmarried woman, and who desired to become a cleric) to be promoted, after he had been duly marked with clerical character — at the lawful age — to all, even sacred, orders, and to receive and retain — as soon as he had reached his twelfth year — any dignity, *personatus*, administration with cure, or office, etc. [as above, no. 408, with appropriate changes of tense, to '. . . administration with cure, or an office'], as is more fully contained in those letters. The pope therefore — at his supplication — hereby further dispenses[2] him (who, as he asserts, afterwards was duly marked with clerical character and is in his ninth year or thereabouts) to receive and retain — henceforth — any dignity, *personatus*, administration with cure, or office in a cathedral, even metropolitan, or collegiate church, even if the dignity etc. should be customarily elective and have cure of souls, if he obtains it otherwise canonically — provided that the dignity be not major *post pontificalem* in a metropolitan or other cathedral church, or principal in a collegiate church. Notwithstanding the above defects of birth and age etc. With the proviso that the dignity etc. in question shall not, on this account, be defrauded of due services and the cure of souls therein (if any) shall not be neglected.

Laudabilia tue puerilis etatis indicia . . .
F. de parma / Jo / Jo. xx. Eps' Terracinen'

[1] *modum*; *recte*: 'nondum'?
[2] mention of absolution is wanting in the text here (and in the final clauses)

770   2 June 1502   *Reg. Lat.* 1105, fo 209^{r-v}

To Henry Curll, rector of the parish church of Yelverton, d. Norwich. Dispensation

— at his supplication — to receive and retain for life, together with the above parish church, one, and without it, any two other benefices, etc. [as above, no. 3].[1]

Vite ac morum honestas . . .
L. puccius / · B· / ₁ B· L. Bolis

[1] with the addition of: 'and of lay patronage and of whatsoever tax or annual value' after 'perpetual ecclesiastical benefice'

---

771   7 September 1501   *Reg. Lat.* 1105, fos 245ᵛ-246ʳ

To Thomas Rede, MA, rector of the parish church of Carletonrode, d. Norwich. Dispensation —at his supplication— to receive and retain for life, together with the above parish church, one, and without it, any two other benefices, etc. [as above, no. 3].

Litterarum scientia, vite ac morum honestas . . .
L puccius / · B· / · B· L. Bolis

772[1]   21 September 1501   *Reg. Lat.* 1105, fos 252ᵛ-253ʳ

To Robert Wykes, MA, perpetual vicar of the parish church of St Cyriac, Lacok, d. Salisbury. Dispensation and indult —at his supplication— to receive and retain for life, together with the perpetual vicarage of the above parish church, one, and without it, any two other benefices, etc. [as above, no. 3, to '. . . retain them together for life, as above']; and for life, while attending a *studium generale* or residing in the Roman curia or any one of his benefices, not to be bound to reside in his other benefices, etc. [as above, no. 238].

Litterarum scientia, vite ac morum honestas . . .
L puccius / · B· / ₁ B· Lx Bolis

[1] This letter has been enregistered twice, the other enregistration being summarised above at no. 654 (see, especially, note 1).

---

773   18 June 1502   *Reg. Lat.* 1106, fos 128ʳ-129ʳ

To John Fabell, priest, d. London. Dispensation and indult —at his supplication— to receive and retain for life, together with one incompatible benefice perchance held by him, one, and without them, any two other benefices, etc. [as above, no. 3, to '. . . retain them together for life, as above']; and for life, while attending a *studium generale* or residing in the Roman curia or any one of his benefices, not to be bound to reside in his other benefices, etc. [as above, no. 238].

Vite ac morum honestas . . .
L puccius / F / F· Lx Sanctor(is)

774   11 June 1502   *Reg. Lat.* 1106, fos 129^r-130^r

To Robert Bryght, LLD, perpetual vicar of the parish church of Est Alta, d. London. Dispensation and indult —at his supplication— to receive and retain for life, together with the perpetual vicarage of the above parish church, one, and without it, any two other benefices, etc. [as above, no. 3, to '. . . retain them together for life, as above']; and for life, while attending a *studium generale* or residing in the Roman curia or any one of his benefices, not to be bound to reside in his other benefices, etc. [as above, no. 238].

Litterarum scientia, vite ac morum honestas . . .
L puccius / F / F· Lx Sanctor(is)

775   18 June 1502   *Reg. Lat.* 1106, fos 130^v-131^v

To Thomas Abbot, priest, d. London. Dispensation and indult —at his supplication— to receive and retain for life, together with one incompatible benefice perchance held by him, one, and without them, any two other benefices, etc. [as above, no. 3, to '. . . retain them together for life, as above']^1; and for life, while attending a *studium generale* or residing in the Roman curia or any one of his benefices, not to be bound to reside in his other benefices, etc. [as above, no. 238].

Vite ac morum honestas . . .
L puccius / F / F· Lx Sanctor(is)

^{1} save that 'chantries' does not occur

776^1 21 August 1500   *Reg. Lat.* 1106, fo 232^r

Conclusion to Henry, king of England, in respect of the consistorial provision of Francis of Cordova (*de Corduba*) to the church of Glendalough. ^{2}

Gratie divine premium . . .
Menendez /· M· / · M xx. Battiferro

[1] *Henricus anglie regi* occurs in the index to the gathering; (?)*Rex*, in different ink, after *regi* (fo. 209[r])

[2] Most unusually, the principal letter and other conclusions were enregistered elsewhere (above, no. 579).

777   8 January 1502   *Reg. Lat.* 1107, fos 80[r]-81[r]

Statute and ordinance, as below. The pope has learned that it is expressly laid down in the foundation of the chapel, called a chantry, of Sts John the Baptist and John the Evangelist in the cemetery of the church of Norwich that those holding this chapel or any of the five perpetual chaplaincies, called portions, in the same cannot hold another benefice with them. And a recent petition to the pope on the part of Thomas Grone, rector, [called][1] master, of the said chapel, and all the chaplains, called portionaries, in the same, stated that although at one time adequate revenues from which one rector and five perpetual chaplains, priests, could be comfortably supported had been assigned to the chapel — to which all the bones of the dead from all the parish churches of the city of Norwich were carried and for the conservation of which it was founded — nevertheless the said revenues had become so meagre[2] that scarcely two chaplains are able to be comfortably supported. At the supplication on the part of Thomas and the chaplains, the pope hereby establishes and ordains that hereafter in perpetuity the chapel and chaplaincies are compatible with all other benefices, with and without cure, to the effect that those holding them at the time may receive and retain any number of benefices, with cure and otherwise compatible mutually and with the chapel and chaplaincies, even if parish churches or their perpetual vicarages, or chantries, free chapels, hospitals or annual services, usually assigned to secular clerics in title of a perpetual ecclesiastical benefice, if conferred on them otherwise canonically. Notwithstanding the above foundation etc.

Ad perpetuam rei memoriam. Ex debito pastoralis officii meritis licet insufficientibus nobis ex alto commissi ad ea libenter intendimus . . .
. L. puccius. / · M· / · M· L. Battiferro

[1] 'nuncupati' wanting
[2] *ex illos; recte*: 'exiles'

778   14 December 1501   *Reg. Lat.* 1107, fos 127[r]-129[v]

To John Anderson, priest, d. St Andrews, reservation, constitution and assignment of a pension, as below. A recent petition to the pope on John's part stated that he — between whom and Thomas Maywel, perpetual vicar of the parish church of

Rothtmariel[1] and Kiawthtimonth, d. Aberdeen, a suit was brewing over the vicarage of the said church which each of them asserted rightfully belonged to him, and for which (at another time when it was vacant *certo modo*) John had been presented by the abbot and convent of the monastery of Lundo[r]is, [2] OSB, d. St Andrews, to whom the presentation of a suitable person for the vicarage at a time of vacancy pertains by ancient, approved and hitherto peacefully observed custom, to the local ordinary, within the lawful time — to avoid future suits has spontaneously and freely ceded into the hands of the ordinary, outside the Roman curia, all right belonging to him in or to the vicarage, and left Thomas in peaceful possession. Lest John should suffer excessive loss on this account, the pope hereby reserves, constitutes and assigns to him an annual pension of 10 marks Scots, equivalent to 3 pounds sterling or thereabouts, on the fruits etc. of the vicarage (of which this pension does not, as he asserts, exceed a third part) payable (in the town of Ediniburg, [3] d. St Andrews) in full to John, for life (or to John's specially mandated proctor) by Thomas, to which express assent has been given by Thomas Halkerston', cleric, d. St Andrews, (Thomas's specially appointed proctor) and by his successors as vicars for the time being, each year, one half on the Nativity of Jesus Christ and the other on that of St John the Baptist. With decree etc. that if Thomas, or any one of his successors, fails to make payment on the said feasts, or within the thirty days immediately following, he shall, after this time has elapsed, incur sentence of excommunication, from which he shall be denied absolution, except on the point of death, until he shall have made satisfaction in full or reached agreement in respect of it with John (or his proctor) and, if he remains obdurate under that sentence for a further six months, he shall thereupon be deprived in perpetuity of the vicarage, which shall be deemed vacant automatically. Notwithstanding etc.

Executory to the archbishop of Ragusa, the dean of the church of Dunkeld and the official of St Andrews, or two or one of them, acting in person or by proxy.

Vite ac morum honestas . . . The executory begins: *Hodie dilecto filio Johanni Anderson* . . .
. *p. de planca.* ; *N· de Castello / · B· / ₁ B· xij· x· Bolis·*

[1] spelt *Rothtinuriel* (the '-nu' being doubtful) in the executory
[2] blotched
[3] or possibly -*gi*; also the 'ini' doubtful

779   24 February 1502   *Reg. Lat.* 1107, fos 136ᵛ-137ᵛ

Licence etc., in *forma commissoria*, to the sisters Anna and Leonora, and their grand-daughter Francisc(i)a, women, Cordova, to build, in that city or outside it, a monastery, OCist, dedicated to St Mary *de populo*, with church, etc., for themselves and others who make the regular profession usually made by Cistercian nuns. Given at Piombino (*Plombini*), d. Massa.

The 'bishop of Glendalough' is the sole mandatary. Entry otherwise of no interest to the Calendar.

Inter curas multiplices ...
L. puccius. / · B· / ↓B· xxxx Bolis

780   20 February 1502   *Reg. Lat.* 1107, fos 162^r-164^r

To John Spens, succentor of the church of Moray. Indult —[1] at his supplication — to him (who, as he asserts, holds by apostolic dispensation the succentorship of the church of Moray and the parish church of Iboston', d. Glasgow) while residing in the Roman curia or one of his benefices or attending a *studium generale*, to receive for life all the fruits etc. of the above parish church and succentorship and of any other benefices, with and without cure, which he holds and shall hold in any churches or places, even if they should be canonries and prebends, or dignities, *personatus*, administrations or offices in cathedral, even metropolitan, or collegiate churches, even if the dignities in question should be major *post pontificalem* in cathedral, even metropolitan, churches, or principal in collegiate churches, and even if the dignities etc. should be customarily elective and have cure of souls, the daily distributions alone excepted, as if he were resident personally in the said churches or places and not to be bound meanwhile to reside in them, nor to be liable to be compelled by anyone to do so against his will. Notwithstanding that he may not have made the customary first residence in the said churches or places personally and the constitution of Boniface VIII prohibiting grants of this type without a limit set on their duration and also [notwithstanding] the foundation of the said succentorship by which it is said to be laid down that the succentor for the time being is bound to serve the succentorship personally, otherwise he shall receive no fruits, and [notwithstanding] constitutions etc., [even][1] if he (or his proctor) has perchance taken or shall take an oath to observe them and to not impetrate apostolic letters contrary to them or make use of such letters even if impetrated by another or others or granted in any other way, etc. With the proviso that the parish church, succentorship and other benefices in question shall not, on this account, be defrauded of due services and the cure of souls in the parish church and (if any) the succentorship and other benefices shall not be neglected; but that the cure shall be exercised and things divine served by good and sufficient vicars maintained from the proceeds of the parish church, succentorship and other benefices in question. Given at Corneto. [2]

Executory to the archbishop of Ragusa and the bishops of Brechin[3] and Ross, [4] or two or one of them, acting in person or by proxy.

Vite ac morum honestas ... The executory begins: *Hodie dilecto filio Johanni Spens ...*
. A· de. sanctoseverino; · p de planca / · M· / · M· xxx xx Battiferro

[1] MS has no 'pro expressis habentes' clause; numerous other oddities are to be found in the text, but have not been specially noted here

[2] *Rome apud sanctum Petrum*, deleted and initialled . *V*. in the line; *Corneti* . . . follows directly thereafter

[3] *Brichinen.*

[4] *Rosten.*

781   16 April 1502   *Reg. Lat.* 1107, fos 265ᵛ-275ʳ

Confirmation of erection of chapel royal, Stirling, into a collegiate church; erection of cantorship therein.

Ad perpetuam rei memoriam. Apostolice nobis desuper meritis licet sufficientibus[1]
iniuncte servitutis officium . . .
F de parma / Jo / Jo. CL. Eps' Terracinen'

Printed in full, from the copy in the *Reg. Cap. Reg. Striv.*, by C. Rogers, *op. cit.* (above, no. 765), pp. 18-29 (item 2. Confirmacio erectionis ecclesie collegiate de Striueling cum ereccione cantorie).

Trifling discrepancies apart, the copy in the papal register follows that in print, save that Stirling is spelt *Sterlyng*, Restennet *Rensenot*, Lothian *Landome*, Kirk-Andrews *Kyckandris*, Balmaclellan *Ballmaclellen'* and *Balmaclellen'*, Glenholm *Glenquhom'* and *Glenquhom'*, Southwick *Swyphtyk*, Bute *Bwyt*, Cranshaws *Crauschawis*, Pinkerton *Pyncarton'*, and Dunse *Dwns'*

[1] *sic; recte* 'insufficientibus'

782   10 June 1502   *Reg. Lat.* 1107, fos 354ʳ-356ʳ

To Martin Wans, priest of Aberdeen, reservation etc., as below. This day Martin has, through a certain specially appointed proctor of his, spontaneously and freely resigned the deanery of the church of Ross, which he was holding at the time, into the pope's hands, and the pope, admitting the resignation, has, by other letters of his, made provision of the deanery, vacant by this resignation and previously reserved to apostolic disposition, to Hugh Grenlau, [1] dean of this church, as is more fully contained in those letters. [2] Lest Martin (who, as he asserts, is worn out with old age) should suffer excessive loss on account of this resignation, the pope hereby reserves, constitutes and assigns a fourth part of the tithes of corn of the churches of Rosmarky[3] and Cromache, belonging to the deanery, and also all fruits etc. of the church of Kilmore, d. Ross, annexed to the deanery, (which do not, as he asserts, exceed a third part of all the deanery's fruits etc.) to be paid and assigned —in place of an annual pension— to Martin, in full, for life (or to his specially mandated proctor) by Hugh (who has given his express assent thereto) and by his successors holding the deanery at the time, each year, on the feast of St Martin in the winter and that of Pentecost. With decree etc. that if Hugh, or any one of his successors, fails to make payment on the said feasts, or within the thirty days immediately following, he shall, after this time has elapsed, incur sentence of excommunication, from which he cannot be absolved, except on the point of death, until he shall have made satisfaction in full or reached agreement in respect of it with Martin (or his proctor) and, if he remains obdurate under that sentence for a further six months, he shall thereupon be deprived in perpetuity of the deanery, which shall be deemed vacant automatically. Notwithstanding etc.

Executory to the bishop of Cesena, the prior of the church of St Andrews and the dean of the church of Moray, or two or one of them, acting in person or by proxy.

Vite ac morum honestas . . . The executory begins: *Hodie dilectus filius Martinus Wans* . . .
Jo ortega; . N. de castello. / . B. / · B· xij· x Bolis

1 spelt *Greulan* in the executory
2 below, no. 839; *cf.* , however, no. 840
3 spelt *Rosenarky* in the executory

783   6 May 1502   *Reg. Lat.* 1108, fos 141^V-142^V

To the dean and James Macnamara and Thomas Ograda, canons, of the church of Killaloe, mandate in favour of Maurice Omulleampuyll, cleric, d. Cashel (who, some time ago, as he asserts, was dispensed by apostolic authority, notwithstanding a defect of birth as the son of a priest and an unmarried woman, and having been duly marked with clerical character, to be promoted to all, even sacred, orders and the priesthood, and to hold a benefice, even if it should have cure of souls). The pope has learned that the perpetual vicarage of the parish church of Tempullacallay *alias* Caladama'rain, d. Cashel, is vacant *certo modo* at present and has been vacant for so long that by the Lateran statutes its collation has lawfully devolved on the apostolic see, although Donat Ohogayn, who bears himself as a priest, has detained it with no title and no support of law, temerariously and *de facto*, for a certain time, as he does. He hereby commands that the above three (or two or one of them), if, having summoned Donat and others concerned, they find the vicarage, whose annual value does not exceed 12 marks sterling, to be vacant (howsoever etc.), shall collate and assign it (even if specially reserved etc.), with all rights and appurtenances, to Maurice, inducting him etc. having removed Donat and any other unlawful detainer and causing Maurice (or his proctor) to be admitted to the vicarage and its fruits etc., rights and obventions to be delivered to him. [Curbing] gainsayers etc.

Notwithstanding etc.

Vite ac morum honestas . . .
A de S^{to} Severino / · B· / | B· xij· Quinto decimo Kl' <Junij>[1] *anno decimo* [18 May 1502], *Bolis*

[1] *Maii* deleted and initialled . *B.* ; *Junij* inserted (at end of line) by same hand as rest of magistral signature; initialled . *B.*

784   19 April 1502   *Reg. Lat.* 1108, fo 151^{r-v}

To Malachy, William and John Otontenynd, canons of the church of Tuam, mandate in favour of Cornelius Oceally, canon of Elphin (who, as [he asserts], [1] holds a canonry and prebend of the church of Elphin). The pope has learned that the perpetual vicarage of the parish church of Teacboych, d. Elphin, which the late Cornelius Oddowelyan [also spelt *Oddwelyan, Odonelyan*[2]], perpetual vicar of it, held while he lived, by his death outside the Roman curia, is vacant at present and has been vacant for so long that by the Lateran statutes its collation has lawfully devolved on the apostolic see. He hereby commands that the above three, or two or one of them, in person or by proxy, shall collate and assign the vicarage, whose annual value does not exceed 3 marks sterling, (vacant as above or by the death, outside the Roman curia, of the late Charles Ialbim, perpetual vicar of it while he lived, or in any other way, etc., or by the free resignation of Cornelius Oddowelyan or of Charles; even if specially reserved etc.), with all rights and appurtenances, to Cornelius Oceally, inducting him etc. having removed any unlawful detainer and causing Cornelius Oceally (or his proctor) to be admitted to the vicarage and its fruits etc., rights and obventions to be delivered to him. [Curbing] gainsayers etc. Notwithstanding etc.

Vite ac morum honestas . . .
A de S^{to} Severino / · B· / | B · x nonis Maii anno decimo [7 May 1502], | *Bolis*

[1] 'asserit' wanting
[2] or — in view of previous spelling — *Odouelyan*

785   20 April 1502   *Reg. Lat.* 1108, fos 153^{v}-154^{v}

To the abbot of the monastery of Motallea, d. Lismore, and James Styortal and John Thobym, [1] canons of the church of Ossory, mandate in favour of Walter Buttyler, cleric, d. Lismore. The pope has learned that the perpetual vicarages of the parish churches of Hylsylhayn and Lonayn *alias* Balenoe, d. Lismore, are vacant *certo modo* at present and have been vacant for so long that by the Lateran statutes their collation has lawfully devolved on the apostolic see, although Thomas Ochayll, monk, [2] OCist, has detained the first vicarage and Maurice Ochayll, priest, [3] the second, with no title and no support of law, temerariously and *de facto,* for a certain time, as they do. At a recent petition on the part of Walter (to whom this day the pope has commanded by other letters of his that the monastery of B. Mary, Suir (*de Surio*), said order and diocese, whose annual value does not exceed 80 marks sterling, vacant *certo modo* at the time, be commended to be held, ruled and governed by him for life, as is more fully contained in those letters;[4] and who, as he asserts, is of noble, even comital and baronial, birth), to the pope to erect and institute a canonry in the church of Lismore and the said vicarages into a prebend of that church, for his lifetime, the pope hereby commands that the above three (or two or one of them), if, having summoned Thomas and Maurice, the bishop and chapter of Lismore as regards the erection, and others concerned, they find the vicarages, whose annual value together does not exceed 14 like marks, to be vacant (howsoever etc. ; even if specially reserved etc.) to erect and institute a canonry in the church of Lismore and the vicarages into a prebend of the said church without prejudice to anyone; and, in that event, collate and assign the newly erected canonry and prebend, being vacant, to Walter, with plenitude of canon law and all rights and appurtenances, inducting him etc. having removed Thomas and Maurice and any other unlawful detainers and causing Walter (or his proctor) to be received as a canon of Lismore, with plenitude of canon law, and the fruits etc., rights and obventions of the canonry and prebend to be delivered to him. [Curbing] gainsayers etc. Notwithstanding etc. The pope's will is, however, that the said vicarages shall not, on this account, be defrauded of due services and the cure of souls therein shall not be neglected, but that their customary burdens shall be supported; and that on Walter's death or resignation etc. of the canonry and prebend [the erection and institution of] the canonry and prebend shall be extinguished and the vicarages shall revert to their original condition automatically.

Ex debito pastoralis officii nobis licet inmeritis superna dispositione commissi ad ea libenter intendimus . . .
A de S^{to} Severino | · B· | ¡ B · xx · Quarto · Id Maii anno decimo [12 May 1502], · *Bolis ·*

[1] last letter doubtful : apparently changed from -*n* by addition of minim

[2] *Thomas Ochayll monachus* . . . ; unusual to express a detainer's designation straightforwardly thus, instead of by means of 'se gerere pro'; likewise below (note 3)

[3] *sic*; see above, note 2

[4] below, no. 789

786   19 April 1502   *Reg. Lat.* 1108, fos 155^r-156^r

To the abbot of the monastery of the Holy Cross, Huochtarlawan, [1] d. Cashel, and the archdeacon and James Saprtall, canon, of the church of Ossory, mandate in favour of Henry Mocleyr, rector of the parish church of Kazdaglas [also spelt

Kacdaglas] *alias* Maclerystown', d. Cashel. The pope has learned that the perpetual vicarages of the parish churches of Ballimunora[2] *alias* Murtown,[3] Downachinor' and Coloram[4] *alias* Kystye, ds. Cashel and Lismore, are vacant *certo modo* at present and have been vacant for so long that by the Lateran statutes their collation has lawfully devolved on the apostolic see, although Philip Brydach has detained the first vicarage, William Obuoe,[5] the second, and John Loweys, the third —bearing themselves as priests — with no title and no support of law, temerariously and *de facto*, for a certain time, as they do. At a recent petition on Henry's part to the pope to erect and institute a canonry in the church of Cashel and the rectory of the said church of Kazdaglas, which Henry holds, into a prebend of the church of Cashel, for his lifetime; and to unite etc. the vicarages to the erected canonry and prebend, for as long as Henry holds the canonry and prebend, if conferred on him by virtue of the presents — asserting that the annual value of the vicarages together does not exceed 15, and of the rectory, 5, marks sterling — the pope hereby commands that the above three (or two or one of them), if, having summoned Philip, William and John and the archbishop and chapter of Cashel (regarding the erection) and others concerned, they find the vicarages to be vacant (howsoever etc.) and the foregoing regarding the union to be true, shall (even if the vicarages be specially reserved etc.) erect and institute a canonry in the church of Cashel and the rectory into a prebend of the same, without prejudice to anyone; and, in that event, collate and assign the newly erected canonry and prebend, being vacant, to Henry; and unite etc. the vicarages to the canonry and prebend, for as long as he holds the latter, if conferred on him as above, with plenitude of canon law and all rights and appurtenances, inducting him etc. having removed Philip, William, John and any other unlawful detainers from the vicarages, and causing Henry (or his proctor) to be received as a canon of the church of Cashel, with plenitude of canon law, and the fruits etc., rights and obventions of the canonry and prebend and annexes to be delivered to him. [Curbing] gainsayers etc. Notwithstanding etc. The pope's will is, however, that the rectory and vicarages shall not, on account of this <erection, institution>[6] and union etc., be defrauded of due services and the cure of souls therein shall not be neglected, but that their customary burdens shall be supported; and that on Henry's death or resignation etc. of the canonry and prebend, the union etc. shall be dissolved, [the erection and institution of] the canonry and prebend[7] be extinguished and the vicarages and rectory shall revert to their original condition automatically.

Ex debito pastoralis officii nobis meritis licet insufficientibus ex alto commissi ad ea libenter intendimus . . .
A de *S^{to}* Severino / · B· / · B· *xxxv pridie Id' Maij anno decimo* [14 May 1502], *Bolis*

[1] the 'r' uncertain

[2] only *Ball-* certain

[3] the 'r' uncertain

[4] only *Colo-* certain

[5] blotched and doubtful

[6] marginal insertion by the enregistering scribe initialled . B.

[7] *sic; rectius* : 'erection and institution' ?

787   4 May 1502   *Reg. Lat.* 1108, fos 156^V-157^V

To Robert and Henry Hedyan and Thady Omuchyre, canons of the church of Cashel, mandate in favour of James Scyortall, canon of Ossory. The pope has learned that the rectories of the parish churches of Bellemartin and Belyta(r)sny, [1] which are of lay patronage and which John Grant, their late rector, held while he lived, are vacant by his death, outside the Roman curia, and the perpetual vicarages of the parish churches of Killcolun [also spelt *Kilcollum, Kylcolum*] *alias* Kylcolbyn, Thomastown' [also spelt *Tomastown'*], Deynyarluan [also spelt *Dungaruwan, Dunygervan'*], and also Kylmanach [also spelt *Kilmanach*], d. Ossory, are vacant *certo modo* at present and have been vacant for so long that by the Lateran statutes their collation has lawfully devolved on the apostolic see, although William Omorisa, who bears himself as a cleric, has detained the vicarage of Killcolun, and Robert Omiday[2] and Philip Ochayll — bearing themselves as priests — the vicarages of Deynyarluan and Kylmanach [respectively], with no title and no support of law, temerariously and *de facto*, for a certain time, as they do. At a recent petition on James's part to the pope to unite etc. the said rectories and vicarages to the canonry and prebend of St Maul's (*de Sancta Mala*) of the church of Ossory, which he holds, for as long as he does so — asserting that the annual value of the rectories and vicarages does not exceed 35 marks sterling — the pope hereby commands that the above three (or two or one of them) shall unite etc. the rectories and the vicarage of Thomastown' and, having summoned William, Robert and Philip and others concerned, the vicarages of Killcolun, Deynyarluan and Kylmanach, whether the rectories be vacant as above or otherwise, and they and the vicarages be vacant howsoever etc., even if specially reserved etc., <with all their rights and appurtenances to the said canonry and prebend, for as long as James holds them>, [3] to the effect that James may, on his own authority, in person or by proxy, take and retain corporal possession of the rectories and vicarages and rights and appurtenances aforesaid, for as long as he holds the canonry and prebend, and convert their fruits etc. to his own uses and those of the canonry and prebend, rectories and vicarages without licence of the local diocesan or of anyone else. Notwithstanding etc. The pope's will is, however, that the rectories and vicarages shall not, on this account, be defrauded of due services and the cure of souls therein shall not be neglected, but that their customary burdens shall be supported; and that on James's death or resignation etc. of the canonry and prebend the union etc. shall be dissolved and the rectories and vicarages shall revert to their original condition automatically.

Romanum decet pontificem votis illis gratum prestare assensum . . .
A de S^{to} Severino / . B. /· B· xx Sexto Id' Maij anno decimo [10 May 1502], *Bolis·*

[1] MS: *Belyta'sny*

[2] the 'mi' uncertain

[3] marginal insertion by the enregistering scribe; initialled . *B*. twice

788   19 April 1502   *Reg. Lat.* 1108, fos 160^V^-161^r^

To Malachy, William and John Oconcenynd, canons of the church of Tuam, mandate in favour of Donat Ocealli, canon of Elphin (who, as he asserts, holds a canonry and prebend of the church of Elphin). The pope has learned that the perpetual vicarage of the parish church of Foynach, d. Clonfert, [1] is vacant *certo modo* at present and has been vacant for so long that by the Lateran statutes its collation has lawfully devolved on the apostolic see, although Cornelius Ocealli, who bears himself as a cleric, has detained it, with no title and no support of law, temerariously and *de facto*, for a certain time, as he does. He hereby commands that the above three (or two or one of them), if, having summoned Cornelius and others concerned, they find the vicarage, whose annual value does not exceed 3 marks sterling, to be vacant (howsoever etc.), shall collate and assign it, (even if specially reserved etc.), with all rights and appurtenances, to Donat, inducting him [. . .][2] to be admitted to the vicarage and its fruits etc., rights and obventions to be delivered to him. [Curbing] gainsayers etc. Notwithstanding etc.

Vite ac morum honestas . . .

A de S^to Severino / Jo / Jo. xiij . Sexto Id' maij anno decimo [10 May 1502], *Eps' Terracinen'*

[1] *Clonnerten.*

[2] There is evidently an omission here: *suum eius* is deleted; and thereafter 'suum eius nomine in corporalem possessionem vicarie iuriumque et pertinentiarum predictorum et defendentes inductum amoto a dicta vicaria Cornelio et quolibet alio illicito detentore ac facientes Donatum vel pro eo procuratorem' (or suchlike) is wanting. The deletion of *suum eius* suggests that the omission may not be an error of the enregistering scribe and that the passage may have been wanting in MS which formed the basis of the enregistration.

789   20 April 1502   *Reg. Lat.* 1108, fos 161^V^-162^V^

To the abbot of the monastery of Motalea, d. Lismore, and James Scyortal and John Tobin, canons of the church of Ossory, mandate in favour of Walter Buttiller, cleric, d. Lismor,[1] (to whom this day the pope by other letters of his commanded provision be made of a certain canonry and prebend of the church of Lismore, of annual value not exceeding 14 marks sterling, and which [he commanded] be erected and instituted therein, as is more fully contained in those letters;[2] and who, as he asserts, is of noble, even comital and baronial, birth). The pope has learned that the monastery of B. Mary, Suir (*de Surio*), OCist, d. Lismore, is vacant[3] *certo modo* at present and has been vacant for so long that by canonical sanctions its provision has lawfully devolved on the apostolic see, although William Odonchw, who bears himself as a priest and monk of the said order, has detained it with no title and no support of law, temerariously and *de facto*, for a certain time, as he does. He hereby commands that the above three (or two or one of them), if, having summoned William and others concerned, they find the monastery, whose annual value does not exceed 80 like marks, to be vacant (howsoever and by whatsoever person), shall commend it, (even if its provision pertains specially or generally to the apostolic see, etc.), with all rights and appurtenances, to Walter to be held, ruled and governed by him for life, even together with the canonry and prebend; (he may — due and customary burdens of the monastery and its convent having been supported — make disposition of the rest of its fruits etc. just as abbots of the monastery at the time could and ought to do, alienation of immovable goods and precious movables being however forbidden); committing the care, rule and administration of the monastery to him in spiritualities and temporalities and causing obedience and reverence to be given him by the convent and customary services and rights by the vassals and other subjects of the monastery. [Curbing] gainsayers etc. Notwithstanding etc. and the apostolic privileges and indults granted to the Cistercian order, in particular those in which it is said to be expressly laid down that when the order's monasteries are vacant provision of suitable persons who have expressly professed the order can and ought to be made by the father abbots and diffinitors in accordance with the regular institutes of the order and the apostolic privileges granted to it; that those monasteries may be commended to no-one save cardinals of the Holy Roman Church or those expressly professed of the order and [only then] with the express consent of the abbot for the time being and convent of the monastery of Cîteaux, d. Chalons-sur-Saône, and commends of them made otherwise, even by the apostolic see, are void, the commendators being bound to cede the commends within a certain time then expressed; that the order's privileges and indults cannot — even with the cardinals' advice and assent — be derogated except under certain ways, forms and words expressed therein and only with insertion of their whole tenors; and that if they are derogated it is deemed to be done in a certain way and the derogation must first be intimated by divers letters to the order's superiors at certain intervals; the which privileges etc. the pope specially and expressly derogates for this once only. With the proviso that divine worship and the usual number of monks and ministers in the monastery shall not, on account of this commend, be diminished; but that its aforesaid burdens and those of the convent shall be supported.

Romani pontificis providentia circumspecta . . .
A de S^to Severino / Jo / Jo · xxxv · Eps' Terracinen'

[1] MS: *dicte diocesis* — evidently referring to Lismore, the word order of the Latin not being strictly followed in this summary

[2] above, no. 785

³ *vacent; recte:* 'vacet'?

790   20 April 1502[1]   *Reg. Lat.* 1108, fos 162ᵛ-164ʳ

To the abbot of the monastery of Motallea, d. Lismore, and James Styortall and John Thobyn, canons of the church of Ossory, mandate in favour of Philip Stack [also spelt *Stak*], cleric, d. Ardfert (who, some time ago, as he asserts, was dispensed by apostolic authority notwithstanding a defect of birth as the son of a cleric and an unmarried woman — having at the time been duly marked with clerical character — to be promoted to all, even sacred, orders, and to hold a benefice, even if it should have cure of souls). The pope has learned that the perpetual vicarages of the parish churches of Kykonayn and Kylkassy, d. Lismore, are vacant *certo modo* at present and have been vacant for so long that by the Lateran statutes their collation has lawfully devolved on the apostolic see, although John Philippi de Geraldinis, who bears himself as a cleric, has detained the first vicarage, and Maurice Machaestyn, as a priest, the second, with no title and no support of law, temerariously and *de facto*, for a certain time, as they do. At a recent petition on Philip Stack's part to the pope to erect and institute a canonry in the church of Lismore and the said vicarages into a prebend of that church, for as long as he holds the canonry and prebend, if conferred on him by virtue of the presents, the pope hereby commands that the above three (or two or one of them), if, having summoned John and Maurice and the bishop and chapter of Lismore (regarding the erection) and others concerned, they find the first vicarage, whose annual value does not exceed 8, and the second, 6, marks sterling, to be vacant (howsoever etc.), shall erect and institute a canonry in the church of Lismore and the said vicarages (even if specially reserved etc.) into a prebend of that church, without prejudice to anyone; and, in that event, collate and assign the newly erected canonry and prebend, being vacant, to Philip Stack, with plenitude of canon law and all rights and appurtenances, inducting him etc. having removed John and Maurice and any other unlawful detainers and causing Philip Stack (or his proctor) to be received as a canon of the church of Lismore, with plenitude of canon law, and the fruits etc., rights and obventions of the canonry and prebend to be delivered to him. [Curbing] gainsayers etc. Notwithstanding etc. Also the pope dispenses Philip Stack to receive and retain the said canonry and prebend, if conferred on him by virtue of the presents, to resign them, simply or for exchange, as often as he pleases, and in their place receive and retain [an]other, similar or dissimilar, canonry and prebend,[2] even if they should have cure of souls, notwithstanding the said defect etc. The pope's will is, however, that the vicarages shall not, on this account, be defrauded of due services and the cure of souls therein shall not be neglected, but that their customary burdens shall be supported; and that on Philip Stack's death or resignation etc. of the canonry and prebend [the erection and institution of] the canonry and prebend shall be extinguished and the vicarages shall revert to their original condition automatically.

Ex debito pastoralis officii nobis licet inmeritis superna dispositione commissi ad ea libenter intendimus . . .
A de Sanctoseverino / · *B·* / . *B· xxv Quintodecimo Kl' Junij anno decimo.* [18 May 1502], *Bolis*

[1] Dating clause in same hand as rest of letter; but script much less cursive : added later?
[2] the Latin hereabouts treats 'canonry and prebend' both as a singular and a plural

791   27 December 1501   *Reg. Lat.* 1108, fos 247^r-248^v

To the bishop of Agia (*Agien.*), the archdeacon of Valdemeriel in the church of Leon and the official of Dunkeld, mandate in favour of John Duncani, cleric, d. Glasgow. The pope has learned that the parish church, called a rectory, of Weyme', d. Dunkeld, which is of lay patronage, is vacant *certo modo* at present and has been vacant for so long that by the Lateran statutes its collation has lawfully devolved on the apostolic see. He hereby commands that the above three, or two or one of them, in person or by proxy, shall collate and assign the said church, whose annual value does not exceed 20 pounds sterling, (vacant howsoever etc., even if specially reserved etc.), with all rights and appurtenances, to John, inducting him etc. having removed any unlawful detainer and causing the fruits etc., rights and obventions of the said church to be delivered to John. [1] [Curbing] gainsayers by the pope's authority etc. Notwithstanding etc.

Vite ac morum honestas . . .
Jo ortega / *Jo* / *Jo xx Sexto decimo kl' maij anno decimo* [16 April 1502], *Eps' Terracinen'*

[1] no mention of his being admitted

792   6 July 1502   *Reg. Lat.* 1109, fos 1^r-2^v

To the prior of the church of St Andrews, and the deans of the churches of Glasgow and Brechin, mandate in favour of David Spens, rector of the parish church of Convecth, d. St Andrews. A recent petition to the pope on David's part stated that, formerly, the late John Naper of Merchinston, layman, d. St Andrews —falsely asserting that David was unlawfully refusing to pay and restore to him, as he was lawfully bound, 200 pounds of the money of those parts paid by him (unless he was lying) on the occasion of a certain guarantee entered into for David with the commonalty of Edinbrugh, d. St Andrews— sued David, (not through apostolic delegation), for the payment and restoration of the money, before the then external official in the district of Lothian (*Laudonie*), d. St Andrews, appointed by the then archbishop of St Andrews; that the official, proceeding wrongly and *de facto* in the case, declared, by his unjust, definitive (as he called it), sentence, that David was obliged to relieve John and indemnify him, from which David appealed to the archiepiscopal court of St Andrews; that after the suit had been lawfully quieted and John had desisted utterly from his molestations, and otherwise, for fourteen years and more, Archibald Naper, layman, d. St Andrews, who bears himself as John's son and the executor of his will — falsely claiming that he was entitled to prosecute the sentence and suit and that they were transferrable to him— had, on John's death, sued David before the same official; that the official, having temerariously rejected certain lawful allegations and relevant exceptions put before him on David's part, by his unjust, interlocutory [sentence] (as he called it), declared that the sentence and suit were transferrable to Archibald, from which David appealed anew to the archiepiscopal court of St Andrews and sued Archibald before the court's present official; that the official, by his unjust, interlocutory [sentence] (as he called it), declared that certain relevant, lawful, and legally admissible petitions and allegations formally put before him on David's part at a suitable time and place, were inadmissible and that it was time to proceed to the later stages, from which David appealed to the apostolic see; and that the official, contemptuous of the appeal lodged by David (of which he was not ignorant) and while David was still well within the time for prosecuting it, proceeding to the later stages, promulgated an unjust definitive sentence in favour of Archibald and against David, from which David again appealed to the apostolic see. At David's supplication to the pope to command that he be conditionally absolved from the sentence of excommunication and any other ecclesiastical censures and pains perchance inflicted on him by the officials, and to commit to some upright men in those parts the cases of each of the later appeals; of everything attempted and innovated after and against them; of the nullity of the sentences, censures, and pains, and of the officials' processes, and of everything else prejudicial to David done by them and Archibald and any others in connection with the foregoing; and of the principal matter, the pope hereby commands that the above three (or two or one of them), having summoned Archibald and others concerned, shall, if and as it is just, for this once only, conditionally absolve David, if he so requests, having first received * *1 from him that if it appears to them that the sentence etc. were justly inflicted on him, he will obey their commands and those of the church; and, as regards the rest, having heard both sides, taking cognizance even of the principal matter, shall decree what is just, causing by ecclesiastical censure what they have decreed to be strictly observed; [and moreover compel] witnesses, etc. Notwithstanding etc.

Humilibus et cetera.
L· puccius / · B· / · B· xiiij· Bolis·

1 *cautione ydonea* (which is needed here) deleted and initialled . *B*. ; odd

793   6 July 1502   *Reg. Lat.* 1109, fos 2ᵛ-4ʳ

To the bishops of Aberdeen and Moray, and David Guthre, canon of the church of
Aberdeen, mandate in favour of Hugh Martini, canon of Brechin. A recent petition
to the pope on Hugh's part stated that although an annual pension of 100 marks of
the money of those parts on the fruits etc. of the parish church of Ellone, d.
Aberdeen, which is united, annexed, and incorporated in perpetuity to the monastery
of Kinlos, OCist, d. Moray, payable to him for life, had been reserved, established,
and assigned by apostolic authority, and the tithes of corn, pertaining to the parish
church, of Alathone, Petmedane, Craghed, Vodland, Tulymod, Torry, Eselmud', and
Dumbreh, and of Argram, Uthtirelone, and Vatirtone, with their appurtenances and
annexes, had been especially reserved, etc. for the 100 marks; nevertheless, because
abbot Thomas and the convent of the monastery have unlawfully refused to pay him
the pension, (which has been lawfully demanded), for many years, and were also, by
pretext of certain apostolic letters surreptitiously and obreptitiously impetrated by
them, unlawfully presuming to molest and disturb <him>[1] over it and to cause him
serious damage, injury, and loss, Hugh appealed to the apostolic see. At Hugh's
supplication to the pope to commit to some upright men in those parts the causes of
the appeal; of everything perchance attempted and innovated after and against the
appeal; of the surreptitious and obreptitious fraudulence of the letters impetrated by
the abbot and convent; of the nullity and invalidity of the letters and of everything
prejudicial to Hugh done by the abbot and convent and any other judges and persons
in connection with the foregoing; of the principal matter; and the causes which Hugh
intends to move, both jointly and severally, against the abbot and convent over their
unlawful molestation and the damage, injuries, and losses, and other aforesaid
matters; and to command that the abbot and convent be compelled by the censures
and pains in the letters granted to Hugh to pay him the pension, even for the time
which has run out, the pope hereby commands that the above three (or two or one of
them), having summoned the abbot and convent and others concerned, and having
heard both sides, taking cognizance even of the principal matter, shall decree what is
just, without appeal, causing by ecclesiastical censure what they have decreed to be
strictly observed; [and moreover compel] witnesses etc. Notwithstanding etc.

Humilibus et cetera.
Jo ortega / . *B·* / · *B· xij· Bolis·*

[1] marginal insertion by the enregistering scribe initialled . *B.*

794   10 May 1502   *Reg. Lat.* 1109, fo 44ʳ⁻ᵛ

To Gilbert[1] Andrenoson, [2] BTheol, perpetual vicar of the parish church of Hendon',
d. London. Dispensation and indult — at his supplication — to receive and retain for
life, together with the perpetual vicarage of the above parish church, one, and

without it, any two other benefices, etc. [as above, no. 3, to '. . . retain them together for life, as above']; and for life, while attending a *studium generale* or residing in the Roman curia or any one of his benefices, not to be bound to reside in his other benefices, etc. [as above, no. 238].

Litterarum scientia, vite ac morum honestas . . .
F. de parma / Jo. / Jo. Lx. Eps' Terracinen

[1] *Gisberto*
[2] the *-no-* uncertain : possibly *-uo-*

795   7 May[1] 1502   *Reg. Lat.* 1109, fos 71[v]-72[r]

To John Russell, cleric, d. Bath and Wells. Dispensation — at his supplication — to him, who, as he asserts, is in his twentieth year of age, to receive and retain any benefice, with cure or otherwise incompatible, etc. [as above, no. 240].

Vite ac morum honestas . . .
N. de Castello / · B· / · B· xx Bolis

[1] *Aprilis*, in the line, has been deleted, initialled . *B*. ; with *Maii* inserted in the margin, initialled . *B*.

796   7 May 1502   *Reg. Lat.* 1109, fos 72[r]-73[r]

To William Danyell', rector of the parish church of Clovelly, d. Exeter. Dispensation —at his supplication— to receive and retain for life, together with the above parish church, one, and without it, any two other benefices, etc. [as above, no. 3].

Vite ac morum honestas . . .
f de parma / . B· /. B· L. Bolis

797   6 May 1502   *Reg. Lat.* 1109, fos 73[r]-74[r]

Union etc. At a recent petition on the part of William Rokeby, DDec, rector of the parish church of St Peter, Fakenhamdin', d. Norwich, the pope hereby unites etc. the parish church of St Swithin, Sprotley, d. York, (whose annual value does not exceed 24 marks sterling, equivalent to 72 gold ducats of the camera or thereabouts), to the above church of St Peter, which he holds together by apostolic dispensation, for as long as he holds St Peter's, to the effect that William, in person or by proxy, may, on his own authority, continue in or take anew corporal possession of St Swithin's and its rights and appurtenances, and convert its fruits etc. to his own uses and those of the said churches without licence of the local diocesan or of anyone else. Notwithstanding etc. The pope's will is, however, that St Swithin's shall not, on account of this union etc., be defrauded of due services and the cure of souls therein shall not be neglected, but that its customary burdens shall be supported; and that on William's death or resignation etc. of St Peter's the union etc. shall be dissolved and so deemed and St Swithin's shall revert to its original condition automatically.

Ad futuram rei memoriam. Romanum decet pontificem votis illis gratum prestare assensum . . .
N. de Castello / · *B·* / · *B· xxxv Bolis*

---

798   7 May 1502   *Reg. Lat.* 1109, fo 76^{r-v}

To John Morlandi, canon of the monastery of Tupholme, OPrem, d. Lincoln. Dispensation —at his supplication— to him, who, as he asserts, is expressly professed of the above order,[1] to receive and retain any benefice, with or without cure, usually held by secular clerics, etc. [as above, no. 32].

Religionis zelus, vite ac morum honestas . . .
F. de parma / · *B·* / · *B· xxx Bolis*

[1] This information comes from a notwithstanding clause.

---

799   10 May 1502   *Reg. Lat.* 1109, fos 78^r-79^r

To John Atkyngson, perpetual vicar of the parish church of Adelyngflete, d. York. Dispensation —at his supplication— to receive and retain for life, together with the perpetual vicarage of the above parish church, one, and without it, any two other benefices, etc. [as above, no. 3].

Vite ac morum honestas . . .
F. de parma / · *B·* / . *B· L. Bolis*

---

800   1 July 1502   *Reg. Lat.* 1109, fos 85^r-86^r

To William Richardson,[1] perpetual chaplain, called cantor, at the altar of the Holy

Spirit, in the church of London. Dispensation and indult — at his supplication — to him, (who is a priest and, as he asserts, holds one of three portions of the perpetual chaplaincy, called a chantry, at the above altar, usually ruled by three perpetual chaplains, called cantors, and founded for the souls of the late Roger Holme and Adam[2] Bury, in the foundation of which it is said to be expressly laid down that the holder of any of the portions cannot hold another benefice with it and is bound to reside continuously in the said church), to receive and retain together for life any two benefices, etc. [as above, no. 3, to '. . . retain them together for life']^3; and[4] not to be bound, while residing in the Roman curia, or the said church or another benefice of his, or attending a *studium generale*, to reside in the said church or other benefices held by him, nor to be liable to be compelled by anyone to do so against his will. Notwithstanding etc. and the aforesaid foundation etc. With the proviso that the incompatible and other benefices in question shall not, on this account, be defrauded of due services and the cure of souls therein shall not be neglected; but that customary burdens of those benefices in which he shall not reside shall be supported.

Vite ac morum honestas . . .
N· de Castello / · B· / ₁ B· Lx Bolis

[1] the 'd' changed (by erasure and overwriting) from a long 's'

[2] changed to *Ade* (by deletion) from (?)*Adest*; not initialled

[3] with the addition of: 'and of lay patronage and of whatsoever tax or annual value' after 'or a combination'; (however, 'usually' does not occur before 'assigned' in this instance)

[4] 'quo ad vixeris' does not occur here

801   16 July 1502   *Reg. Lat.* 1109, fos 93^v-94^v

To Henry Molyneux, rector of the parish church of Asshemere, d. Salisbury. Dispensation and indult — at his supplication — to him, who, as he asserts, is a BA, to receive and retain for life, together with the above parish church, one, and without it, any two other benefices, etc. [as above, no. 3, to '. . . retain them together for life, as above']; and for life, while attending a *studium generale* or residing in the Roman curia or any one of his benefices, not to be bound to reside in his other benefices, etc. [as above, no. 238].

Vite ac morum honestas . . .
F de. parma / · B· / B · Lx · Bolis

802   1 April 1502   *Reg. Lat.* 1109, fo 120^r

To Robert Chambyr, canon of the monastery of B. Mary, Hyckelyng, OSA, d.

Norwich. Dispensation — at his supplication — to him, who, as he asserts, is expressly professed of the above order,[1] to receive and retain any benefice, with or without cure, usually held by secular clerics, etc. [as above, no. 32].

Religionis zelus, vite ac morum honestas . . .
N de Castello / · B· / ₁ B· xxx Bolis

[1] This information comes from a notwithstanding clause.

803   1 April 1502   *Reg. Lat.* 1109, fos 124ᵛ-125ᵛ

To Thomas Cobaldi, BTheol, perpetual vicar of the parish church of Staverton' [also spelt *Stauerton'*], d. Exeter. Dispensation — at his supplication — to receive and retain for life, together with the perpetual vicarage of the above parish church, one, and without it, any two other benefices, etc. [as above, no. 3].

Litterarum scientia, vite ac morum honestas . . .
F. de parma / · B· / · B . L . Bolis ·

804   1 April 1502   *Reg. Lat.* 1109, fos 125ᵛ-126ʳ

To Nicholas Calverley, perpetual vicar of the parish church of All Saints,[1] Batley, d. York. Dispensation — at his supplication — to receive and retain for life, together with the perpetual vicarage of the above parish church, one, and without it, any two other benefices, etc. [as above no. 3].

Vite ac morum honestas . . .
F. de parma / B· / ₁ B· L. Bolis

[1] de Batley Omnium Sanctorum

805   1 April 1502   *Reg. Lat.* 1109, fos 126ᵛ-127ʳ

To Richard Frecce, rector of the parish church of Monyton' *alias* Monyngton', d. Hereford. Dispensation — at his supplication — to receive and retain for life, together with the above [parish church],[1] one, and without it, any two other benefices, etc. [as above, no. 3].

Vite ac morum honestas . . .
N. de Castello[2] */ . B· / ¡ B· L. Bolis*

[1] 'ecclesia' (at the least) wanted here
[2] in a lighter ink: entered later?

806   1 April 1502   *Reg. Lat.* 1109, fos 127^v-128^r

To Edward Derby, MA, rector of the parish church of Resynden Parva, d. Worcester. Dispensation and indult — at his supplication — to receive and retain for life, together with the above parish church, one, and without it, any two other benefices, etc. [as above, no. 3, to '. . . retain them together for life, as above']¹; and for life, while attending a *studium generale*, or residing in the Roman curia or any one of his benefices, not to be bound to reside in his other benefices, etc. [as above, no. 238].

Litterarum scientia, vite ac morum honestas . . .
f. de parma[2] */ · B· / ¡ B· Lx Bolis*

[1] save that 'ecclesiastical' does not occur
[2] in a different ink: entered later?

807   15 May 1501   *Reg. Lat.* 1109, fos 131^r-132^v

Translation of indulgences, as below. Some time ago, the pope — having learned that the noblewoman, Margaret, countess of Richmond (*Richimundie*) and Derby (*Derbie*), mother of Henry, king of England, was proposing to found, build and sufficiently endow a chapel in the town of Windesore, d. Salisbury, lavishly, from her own goods, and also to endow it properly with books, chalices and other ecclesiastical ornaments necessary for divine worship — by other letters of his bestowed on the priests who celebrated therein at the time and prayed for Margaret's well-being in this life and for her soul after death that indulgence which the celebrants for the dead in the chapel of *Scala Celi* in the church of the monastery of Tre Fontane (*Trium Fontium*), outside the walls of Rome (*Urbis*), OCist, have; and for all the faithful, of both sexes, who shall, being truly penitent and having confessed, devotedly visit the chapel on the feasts of the Purification, Annunciation, Assumption and Conception of B. Mary the Virgin, from first to second vespers, annually, and, as above, pray on each day of the said feasts, relaxed ten years and as many quarantines of enjoined penance, as is more fully contained in the said letters drawn up in that regard. Moreover, as the pope has learned, countess Margaret, swayed by certain reasonable causes, does not intend to cause the aforesaid chapel in the said town further to be built; but proposes to adorn and endow another chapel, to be chosen by her, with chalices, books and other ecclesiastical ornaments — in the way in which she had proposed to adorn and endow the aforesaid chapel which was to be built — and to choose her tomb in it. Wishing that fitting honours may be visited upon the chapel in which countess Margaret happens to choose or have her tomb, as above, and that priests may be induced to celebrate therein and the faithful to visit the chapel for the purpose of devotion more gladly, the pope, by the presents, translates the indulgences aforesaid granted by him to the priests who [(?)were to celebrate] in the chapel which countess Margaret intended to have built in the said town, and who were to pray for her, as above, and likewise to visitors to that chapel on the said feasts, as above, to the other chapel, of her choice, in which she happens to have her tomb. And the pope, as a stronger precaution, establishes and ordains that the priests in the chapel in which countess Margaret shall choose the tomb ([who] shall celebrate in perpetuity and [pray] for her well-being in this life and for her soul after death) and the souls of the faithful (who die in the charity of God and for whom the said priests shall celebrate and pray) have precisely the same indulgences and remissions of sins which the celebrants in the said chapel of Scala Celi and the souls for whom celebrations and prayers are undertaken there have; and all the faithful, of both sexes, who shall, being penitent and having confessed, devotedly visit the chapel of countess Margaret's choice on each day of the said feasts and of those of the Nativity and the Visitation of B. Mary the Virgin, from first to second vespers inclusively, and pray, as above, on each day of the said feasts attain [a relaxation of] ten years and as many quarantines of enjoined penance. The pope's will is, however, that if at another time any other indulgence in perpetuity, or for a certain time, shall be granted by the pope to those visiting the chapel to be chosen or to the priests celebrating therein or to all for whom prayers shall be said therein, the present letters shall be void.

Ad perpetuam rei memoriam. Ascensurus in celum Christus dominus noster . . .
F. de parma | B | . B· Cxx Bolis·

808   12 February 1502   *Reg. Lat.* 1109, fos 160^v-161^v

To Gonzalo[1] Ferdinandi, rector of the parish church of Bradwell', d. London, dispensation. Some time ago, the pope by other letters of his dispensed him, who then, as he asserted, was in his twentieth year of age, to receive and retain for life, any two benefices, with cure or otherwise mutually incompatible, etc. [as above, no. 131, to '. . . as is more fully contained in those letters']. [2] The pope therefore — at his supplication — hereby further dispenses Gonzalo, (who, as he asserts, is in his twenty-first year and is the son of the ambassador of Ferdinand, king of Castile and Leon, to Henry, king of England, and holds the above parish church of Bradwell', by the said dispensation), to receive and retain for life, together with the said parish church and another benefice, with cure or otherwise incompatible, perchance held by him now, or with any two other incompatible benefices held by him at the time by virtue of the said dispensation, any third benefice, etc. [as above, no. 131, to '. . . retain it for life, as above']. Notwithstanding the defect of age which he — in his twenty-first year — suffers etc. and [notwithstanding] the constitutions of Otto and Ottobuono formerly legates of the apostolic see in the kingdom of England etc.[3] With the proviso that this third incompatible benefice shall not, on this account, be defrauded of due services and the cure of souls therein (if any) shall not be neglected.

Vite ac morum honestas . . .
F· de parma / . B· / B. Lxxxx ┆ Bolis.

[1] *Gundisalvo*

[2] with the addition of 'and of lay patronage' after 'or principal in collegiate churches'

[3] The inclusion of these constitutions gives Gonzalo the option of holding (as he does) benefice(s) in England.

809   21 November 1501   *Reg. Lat.* 1109, fo 176[r-v]

To Hugh Saunders, MTheol, perpetual vicar of the parish church of Mepham, d. Rochester.[1] Dispensation — at his supplication — to receive and retain for life, together with the perpetual vicarage of the above parish church, one, and without it, any two other benefices, etc. [as above, no. 3].

Litterarum scientia, vite ac morum honestas . . .
F. de parma / B / B. L. Bolis·

[1] in the first instance *Rossen.* altered (by a stroke over the long 'SS' in darker ink — added later?) to *Roffen.*; but the second instance unaltered

810   20 November 1501   *Reg. Lat.* 1109, fo 177[r-v]

To Edmund Cowp(er),[1] rector of the parish church of Pebemerche, d. London. Dispensation — at his supplication — to receive and retain for life, together with the above parish church, one, and without it, any two other benefices, etc. [as above, no. 3].

Vite ac morum honestas . . .
· N· de Castello / Jo / Jo. L. Eps' Terracinen'

[1] MS: *Cowp'*

811   23 January 1502   *Reg. Lat.* 1109, fos 209^v-210^v

To the bishop of Ross, and James, bishop of Clogher, residing in the diocese of Ross, mandate in favour of John Bouett, cleric, warden of the new college of clerics of B. Mary, Johoill', d. Cloyne. A recent petition to the pope on John's part stated that, formerly, after Joan Vhytt, woman, and several blood relations of hers, d. Lismore, had defamed him in front of respectable and important people, falsely asserting that he had lawfully contracted marriage with her *per verba de presenti*, connection having followed, and that he was her lawful husband, <Thomas>[1] bishop of Lismore, by ordinary authority, had, at John's instance, firstly committed the case over the defamation and marriage bond (*federe*) to Maurice Offlavin, and had then committed it, *ex officio,* to Jordan Porcell, canon of the church of Lismore, together with Maurice, to be heard, examined, and duly determined; that while John was absent, (not through contumacy but because he was no longer summoned or cited), Jordan proceeded without Maurice, invalidly and *de facto*, to the later stages, and, as soon as this came to his notice, John appealed to the apostolic see; and that Jordan is said to have proceeded to later stages in contempt of this appeal, of which he was not ignorant, and while John was still well within the time for prosecuting it. At John's supplication to the pope to commit to some prelates in those parts the cases of the appeal; of everything attempted and innovated after and against it; of the nullity of [Jordan's] process [and of everything else] prejudicial to John done [by him], the bishop, Joan, her blood relations, and any other judges and persons in connection with the foregoing;[2] and of the principal matter; also the cases which John intends to move against Joan, (who, as is asserted, is joined to John in the third or fourth degree of consanguinity), and certain other clerics and laymen, jointly and severally, over the above and the nullity and invalidity of the marriage, the pope hereby commands that the above two (or one of them), having summoned Joan, her blood relations, and others concerned, and having heard both sides, taking cognizance even of the principal matter, shall decree what is canonical, without appeal, causing by ecclesiastical censure what they have decreed to be strictly observed. Notwithstanding etc.

Humilibus et cetera.
Jo ortega / · B· / · B· xij | *Bolis*

[1] marginal insertion by the enregistering scribe; not initialled

[2] omission supplied conjecturally: . . . *nullitatisque* [fo 210^r] *processus per dictum Jordanum* [(desuper) *habiti omniumque aliorum et singulorum per eum*] *et episcopum ac Johannam et consanguineos prefatos et quoscunque alios judices et personas in ipsius Johannis prejudicium circa premissa gestorum*

812   23 January 1502   *Reg. Lat.* 1109, fos 210^v-212^r

To Thomas Erskyn, canon of the church of Glasgow, Thomas Farsyltht,[1] canon of the church of Ross living in the city of Glasgow, and the official of Glasgow, mandate in favour of Walter Abirnethy, provost of the church of Dumberthem,[2] d. Glasgow. A recent petition to the pope on Walter's part stated that, formerly, the abbot and convent of the monastery of Landoris, OSB or other order, d. St Andrews — falsely asserting that Walter, then coadjutor appointed by ordinary and apostolic authority to the late John Abirnethy, the then rector of the parish church of Tanadas, d. St Andrews, was, for certain reasons then expressed, lawfully bound to give and pay them a certain sum of money, then expressed — sued Walter, then John's coadjutor, before Robert de Fontibus, archdeacon of the church of St Andrews, to whom, as they said, the archbishop of St Andrews had, by ordinary authority, committed the case to be heard and duly determined, praying that he be condemned and compelled to give and pay the money to them; that archdeacon Robert, proceeding wrongly in the case, promulgated an unjust definitive sentence in favour of the abbot and convent and against Walter, from which Walter appealed to the apostolic see; that archdeacon Robert — contemptuous of this appeal (of which he was not ignorant) and while Walter was still well within the time for prosecuting it — proceeding to the later stages, bound Walter by sentence of excommunication and commanded him to be published as excommunicate, and is said to have proceeded otherwise against him; and that Walter, having been detained, as he asserts, by lawful impediment, did not prosecute his appeal within the proper time. At Walter's supplication to the pope to command that he be conditionally absolved from the sentence of excommunication and the other censures and pains inflicted on him, and to commit to some upright men in those parts the cases of the appeal; of everything attempted and innovated after and against the appeal; of the nullity of the sentence, censures, declaration, and publication; of the nullity of the archdeacon's whole process, and of everything prejudicial to Walter done by him, and by the abbot and convent, and any other judges and persons, in connection with the foregoing; and of the principal matter, the pope hereby commands that the above three (or two or one of them), having summoned the abbot and convent and others concerned, shall, if and as it is just, for this once only, conditionally absolve Walter, if he so requests, having first received suitable security from him that if they find that the sentence etc. was justly inflicted on him, he will obey their commands and those of the church; and, as regards the rest, if what is related about the impediment is true, and having heard both sides, taking cognizance even of the principal matter, shall decree what is just, without appeal, causing by ecclesiastical censure what they have decreed to be strictly observed; [and moreover compel] witnesses etc. Notwithstanding the lapse of time etc.

Humilibus et cetera.
L. puccius / B / ⸗ B· xiiij· Bolis

[1] the 'a' reworked
[2] the 'm's reworked and uncertain

813   27 January 1502   *Reg. Lat.* 1109, fo 212[r-v]

To Richard Tresh(a)m,[1] rector of the parish church of Rendecombe, d. Worcester.

Dispensation — at his supplication — to receive and retain for life, together with the above parish church, one, and without it, any two other benefices, [with cure][2] or otherwise mutually incompatible, etc. [as above, no. 3]. Given at <Frascati, d. Tusculum>.[3]

Vite ac morum honestas . . .
F de parma / · B· / ₁ B· L. Bolis

[1] MS: *Treshm'*

[2] 'curata' wanting

[3] inserted in the margin by the enregistering scribe initialled . *B.*; *Rome apud Sanctum Petrum* in the line deleted and initialled . *B.*

---

814   21 June 1502   *Reg. Lat.* 1109, fos 260[v]-262[r]

To William Foster, perpetual vicar of the parish church of St Withburga, Hokh(a)m,[1] d. Norwich. Dispensation and indult — at his supplication — to receive and retain for life, together with the perpetual vicarage of the above parish church, one, and without it, any two other benefices, etc. [as above, no. 3, to '. . . retain them together for life, as above']; and for life, while attending a *studium generale,* or residing in the Roman curia or any one of his benefices, not to be bound to reside in his other benefices, etc. [as above, no. 238].

Vite ac morum honestas . . .
. L· puccius / · B· / · B· Lx Bolis

[1] MS: *Hokhm'*

---

815   31 August 1501   *Reg. Lat.* 1109, fos 337[v]-339[r]

To Matthew Obryen and Thomas Oneyllayn, canons of the church of Kilfenora, and Maurice Ohonayn, canon of the church of Ardfert, mandate in favour of Andrew Craenach, canon of Limerick. The pope has learned that the perpetual vicarage of the parish church of St Michael, just outside the walls of Limerick, has been vacant *certo modo* and is vacant at present, although John Macraych, who bears himself as a priest, d. Limerick, has detained it with no title and no support of law, temerariously and *de facto*, for a certain time, as he still does. A recent petition to the pope on Andrew's part stated that at one time — after the rectory of the parish church and of the hospital of lepers[1] of St Laurence, outside the walls of Limerick, which is of the patronage of laymen (viz.: of the mayors, bailiffs and commonalty of the city of Limerick) and which the late Richard (?)Warnygtiu(m),[2] rector of this church,[3] held while he lived, had become vacant by his death, outside the Roman curia, and was then vacant, and the said patrons, being in peaceful possession, or almost, of the right of patronage and of presenting a suitable person for the said church[4] at a time of vacancy, [had] presented Andrew for it, thus vacant, to the then bishop of Limerick, and at this presentation the bishop had instituted Andrew as rector of the said church — the bishop created Andrew a canon of the church of Limerick; erected and instituted the said parish church into a prebend of the church of Limerick, for his lifetime; and granted and assigned [it] to him as the prebend for a canonry, as is said to be more fully contained in a certain public instrument. At this same petition to the pope to unite etc. the vicarage to the canonry and prebend of the church of Limerick, which Andrew holds, for as long as he does so, the pope, not having certain knowledge of the foregoing, hereby commands that the above three (or two or one of them), if, having summoned John and others concerned, they find the vicarage, whose annual value does not exceed 4 [marks sterling], to be vacant (howsoever etc.), and, having summoned those interested in the union etc., it to be thus, shall unite etc. [the vicarage] (even if it has been vacant for so long that by the Lateran statutes its collation has lawfully devolved on the apostolic see, etc.), with all rights and appurtenances, to the canonry and prebend, whose annual value does not exceed 3 marks sterling, for as long as Andrew holds the canonry and prebend; to the effect that Andrew may, on his own authority, in person or by proxy, take and retain corporal possession of the vicarage and its rights and appurtenances, for as long as he holds the canonry and prebend, and convert its fruits etc. to his own uses and those of the vicarage and the canonry and prebend without licence of the local diocesan or of anyone else. Notwithstanding etc. The pope's will is, however, that the vicarage shall not, on account of this union etc., be defrauded of due services and the cure of souls therein shall not be neglected, but that its customary burdens shall be supported; and that on Andrew's death or resignation etc. of the canonry and prebend the union etc. shall be dissolved and so deemed and the vicarage shall revert to its original condition and be deemed vacant automatically.

Ex iniuncto nobis desuper apostolice servitutis officio ad ea libenter intendimus . . .
p de planca / - B· / ₁ B· xviij· Bolis·

[1] *rectoria parochialis ecclesie et hospitalis leprosorum*; the words 'et hospitalis leprosorum' are nowhere else deployed to describe the rectory

[2] MS: *Warnygtiu'* (the letters after the 't' are uncertain)

[3] *sic; cf.* above, note 1

[4] *sic; cf.* above, note 1

816   31 January 1502   *Reg. Lat.* 1109, fos 355[v]-356[r]

To the abbot of the monastery of B. Mary, *de Andro* [Gill Abbey], d. Cork, and John Oherlahe, canon of the church of Cork, commission and mandate in favour of Donat

Macaryg, canon of the church of Cork. It has been referred to the pope's audience by Donat that Gerald, recently bishop of the mutually united churches of Cork and Cloyne and this day administrator of St Finbar's church fabric just outside the walls of Cork has not been ashamed to convert and dissipate goods, even immovable ones, lawfully pertaining to the fabric of the church (which is understood to be in need of no little repair to its structures) to his own uses, not the fabric's. Considering that if the foregoing is true bishop Gerald has rendered himself unworthy of the administration, the pope hereby commissions and commands that the above two (or one of them), if Donat will accuse bishop Gerald over the foregoing before them and proceed in form of law, thereafter shall, having summoned bishop Gerald and others concerned, inquire into the foregoing and, if they find it to be thus, deprive bishop Gerald of the administration and remove him from it; and, in that event, create, establish and depute Donat adminstrator of the fabric for life, with power of doing, performing and exercising everything that pertains, by law as well as by custom, to the office of administrator of the fabric. Notwithstanding etc.

Inter cetera nostri desideria cordis . . .
S de Castello / · B· / ∣ B· xij· Quinto decimo Kl' Marcij anno decimo· [15 February 1502], *Bolis*

817   7 May 1502   *Reg. Lat.* 1110, fos 88^r-89^v

To the bishops of Bath, Worcester and *Rossen.* ,[1] mandate in favour of Ralph Leonardi, professor OP and of theology. A recent petition to the pope on Ralph's part stated that at another time — after he had been dispensed by apostolic authority to receive any secular benefice with cure, or a regular one, with or without cure, of any order, even Cluniac, even if the secular benefice should be a parish church or its perpetual vicarage, and the regular should be a priory, *prepositura*, dignity, *personatus*, administration or office, even if the priory etc. should be customarily elective and have cure of souls, if he obtains the benefice otherwise canonically, and, if a secular, retain it *in titulum*, and if a regular, *in commendam*, for life — when the priory of B. Mary, Lyhou, OSB, island of Gernesey, once d. Coutances, now d. Winchester, was vacant *certo modo*, the then abbot of the monastery of Mont St Michel (*Montis Sancti Michaelis*), OSB, d. Avranches — since the collation, provision and every disposition of the priory at a time of vacancy pertains by ancient, approved and hitherto peacefully observed custom to the abbot for the time being of the said monastery, of which the priory is a dependency — by ordinary authority collated and made provision of the priory, vacant as above, to Ralph, and he received it, conferred on him as above, *in commendam*, by virtue of this dispensation, and holds it at present. Moreover, as the same petition added, Ralph fears that the said collation, provision and receipt *in commendam* for certain reasons do not hold good; and, as the pope has learned, the priory is known to be vacant still as above. The pope hereby commands that the above three, or two or one of them, in person or by proxy, shall commend the priory, which is not conventual and whose annual value does not exceed 20 gold ducats of the camera, vacant howsoever etc., even if it has been vacant for so long that by the Lateran statutes its collation has lawfully devolved on the apostolic see etc., with all rights and appurtenances, to Ralph, to be held, ruled and governed by him for life; (he may — due and customary burdens of the priory having been supported — make disposition of the rest of its fruits etc. just as those holding it *in titulum* could and ought to do, alienation of immovable goods and precious movables being however forbidden); inducting him etc. having removed any unlawful detainer and causing Ralph (or his proctor) to be admitted to the priory and its fruits etc., rights and obventions to be delivered to him. [Curbing] gainsayers etc. Notwithstanding etc. and [notwithstanding] the constitutions of Otto and Ottobuono formerly legates of the apostolic see in the kingdom of England etc. With the proviso that the priory shall not, on this account, be defrauded of due services and the cure of souls therein (if any) shall not be neglected; but that its aforesaid burdens shall be supported.

Religionis zelus, litterarum scientia, vite ac morum honestas . . .
N. de Castello / · B· / B· xxx Bolis.

[1] *recte:* 'Roffen.' (Rochester)?

---

818   5 September 1501   *Reg. Lat.* 1111, fos 5[r]-6[r]

To the abbot of the monastery of B. Mary, *de Kirieleison* [Abbeydorney], d. Ardfert, and the archdeacon and Maurice Ochavaym, canon, of the church of Ardfert, mandate in favour of Cornelius Machayn, priest, d. Killaloe. The pope has learned that the perpetual vicarage of the parish church of Killsfebrach and the sacerdotal portion of the secular and collegiate church of Inyskachy [also spelt *Iniskachy*, *Iniskachi*, *Iniskathy*] which is (?)called[1] Gleandbannam,[2] vulgarly (?)Ileraunr',[3] d. Killaloe, are vacant *certo modo* at present and have been vacant for so long that by the Lateran statutes their collation has lawfully devolved on the apostolic see, although Maurice Oberyn, bishop of Kilfenora, has detained the vicarage, and John Obechayn and Cornelius Macmabona [also spelt *Macmahona*], who bear themselves as priests of the said diocese, have detained the portion, with no title and no support of law, of their own temerity and *de facto*, for a certain time, as they do, receiving fruits etc. from them respectively. He hereby commands that the above three (or two or one of them), if, having summoned bishop Maurice and John and Cornelius Macmabona and others concerned, they find the vicarage and the portion, (which is sacerdotal, as above), whose annual values together do not exceed 14 marks sterling, to be vacant (howsoever etc.), shall collate and assign them, (even if specially reserved etc.), with all rights and appurtenances, to Cornelius Machayn, inducting him etc. having removed bishop Maurice from the vicarage and John and Cornelius

Macmabona from the portion and any other unlawful detainers and causing Cornelius Machayn to be admitted to the vicarage and portion and their fruits etc., rights and obventions to be delivered to him. [Curbing] gainsayers etc. Notwithstanding etc.

Vite ac morum honestas . . .
· *p de planca* / . *B* / . *B. xvij. duodecimo Kl' octobr' anno decimo.* [20 September 1501], . *Bolis.*

[1] blotched and uncertain; reading: 'nominatur'

[2] the 'nd' blotched and doubtful; perhaps 'nn'

[3] uncertain reading

819   6 September 1501   *Reg. Lat.* 1111, fos 10[v]-11[r]

To the prior of the monastery, usually governed by a prior, of Contoscyardomane [also spelt *Clontosoeyedomane*], d. Clonfert, and William Obrogy and John Omallay, canons of the church of Clonfert, mandate in favour of Donald Omaynyn, cleric, d. Clonfert. The pope has learned that the perpetual vicarage of the parish church of Oryac *alias* Suchyhyn, Clonfert,[1] is vacant *certo modo* at present and has been vacant for so long that by the Lateran statutes its collation has lawfully devolved on the apostolic see, although Kynetus[2] Odulcayn,[3] who bears himself as a canon of the above monastery, OSA, has detained the vicarage without any title or support of law, for a certain time, as he still does. He hereby commands that the above three (or two or one of them), if, having summoned Kynetus and others concerned, they find the vicarage, whose annual value does not exceed 2 marks sterling, to be vacant (howsoever etc.), shall collate and assign it, (even if specially reserved etc.), with all rights and appurtenances, to Donald, inducting him etc. having removed Kynetus and any other unlawful detainer and causing Donald (or his proctor) to be admitted to the vicarage and its fruits etc., rights and obventions to be delivered to him. [Curbing] gainsayers etc. Notwithstanding etc.

Vite ac morum honestas . . .
p de planca / · *B·* / . *B. xv Quarto Kl' octobr' anno decimo.* [28 September 1501], *Bolis*

[1] 'diocesis' wanting?

[2] immediately prior to the first occurrence *Kynetus* blotched and deleted, initialled . *B.*

[3] possibly *Odulrayn* in one instance

820   24 September 1501   *Reg. Lat.* 1111, fos 16[v]-17[v]

To Matthew Obryey and Thomas Oneyllayn, canons of the church of Kilfenora, and

Maurice Hohenayn, canon of the church of Ardfert,[1] mandate in favour of Philip Makehycayn, perpetual vicar of the parish church of Killaressy [also spelt *Killaryssy, Kyllaryssy*], d. Limerick. The pope has learned that the perpetual vicarages of the parish churches of Killmalayne[2] [also spelt *Killmalayn*] and Killbradarayn, d. Limerick, are vacant *certo modo* at present and have been vacant for so long that by the Lateran statutes their collation has lawfully devolved on the apostolic see, although Donald Maclanchi has detained the vicarage of Killmalayne, and William Odunagayn, that of Killbradarayn — bearing themselves as priests, d. Limerick — without any title or support of law, temerariously and *de facto*, for a certain time, as they still do. At a recent petition on Philip's part to the pope to unite etc. the said vicarages to the perpetual vicarage of the said church of Killaressy, which Philip holds, for as long as he does so — asserting that the annual value of the vicarages of Killmalayne and Killbradarayn does not exceed 12, and of Killaressy, 6, marks sterling — the pope, not having certain knowledge of the foregoing, hereby commands that the above three (or two or one of them), if, having summoned Donald and William and others concerned, they find the vicarages of Killmalayne and Killbradarayn to be vacant (howsoever etc.) and as regards the union etc., having summoned those interested, it to be thus, shall unite etc. the said vicarages, (even if specially reserved etc.), with all rights and appurtenances, to that of Killaressy, for as long as Philip holds it; to the effect that Philip may, on his own authority, in person or by proxy, take and retain corporal possession of the vicarages of Killmalayne and Killbradarayn and their rights and appurtenances, for as long as he holds that of Killaressy, and convert their fruits etc. to his own uses and those of the said vicarages without licence of the local diocesan or of anyone else. Notwithstanding etc. The pope's will is, however, that the vicarages of Killmalayne and Killbradarayn shall not, on account of this union etc., be defrauded of due services and the cure of souls therein shall not be neglected; but that their customary burdens shall be supported; and that on Philip's death or resignation etc. of the vicarage of Killaressy, the union etc. shall be dissolved and so deemed and the vicarages of Killmalayne and Killbradarayn shall revert to their original condition and be deemed vacant automatically.

Apostolice sedis providentia circumspecta ad ea libenter intendit . . .
P de planca[3] / · *B* / . *B· xx non' octobr' anno decimo* [7 October 1501], *Bolis*

[1] *Harteferten.*

[2] immediately prior to the first occurrence (?)*Killmarayne* has been deleted, initialled . *B.*

[3] in lighter ink and larger letters: entered later?

821   29 November 1501   *Reg. Lat.* 1111, fos 22ʳ-23ᵛ

To Patrick Macbrady and Odo Omulmochere, canons of the church of Kilmore, and the official of Kilmore, mandate in favour of Adam Offegail, cleric, d. Kilmore (who asserts that formerly he was dispensed by apostolic authority notwithstanding a defect of birth as the son of an unmarried man and an unmarried woman to be promoted to all orders and hold a benefice, even if it should have cure of souls, and afterwards was duly marked with clerical character). The pope has learned that the perpetual vicarage of the parish church of Sts Molanus (*Sanctorum Marlani* . . .) and Queranus, Eaga, called the *plebs* of Ytharture, and the church, called a chapel, of Sts Patrick, Columba and Canicus, Tolach, d. Kilmore, which the late Odo Offegail, their last rector, held while he lived, have become vacant by his death, outside the Roman curia, and are vacant at present. At a recent petition on Adam's part to the pope to erect and institute a canonry in the church of Kilmore and the church, called a chapel, into a simple prebend in the same, for his lifetime; and, thereafter, unite etc. the vicarage to the canonry and prebend, for as long as he holds the canonry and prebend — asserting that the annual value of the vicarage does not exceed 6 marks sterling, and of the church, called a chapel, 1 mark sterling — the pope — not having certain knowledge of the foregoing — hereby commands that the above three, or two or one of them, in person or by proxy, if, having summoned the bishop and chapter of Kilmore regarding the erection and also others concerned regarding the union, they find it to be thus, shall erect etc. a canonry in the church of Kilmore and the said vicarage into a simple prebend in the same, for Adam's lifetime; and thereafter, unite etc. the church, called a chapel, to the erected canonry and prebend, (whether vacant as above or howsoever etc.; even if they have been vacant for so long that by the Lateran statutes their collation has lawfully devolved on the apostolic see, etc.); and, in the event of this erection etc. and union etc., collate and assign the newly erected canonry and prebend, being vacant, with plenitude of canon law, the annexed vicarage and all rights and appurtenances, to Adam, inducting him etc. having removed any unlawful detainers from them and causing Adam (or his proctor) to be received as a canon of the church of Kilmore, with plenitude of canon law, and the fruits etc., rights and obventions of the canonry and prebend and annexed vicarage to be delivered to him. [Curbing] gainsayers etc. Notwithstanding etc. Also the pope dispenses Adam to receive and retain the canonry and prebend, if conferred on him by virtue of the presents, notwithstanding the said defect etc. His will is, however, that the vicarage and the church, called a chapel, shall not, on account of this union etc. and erection etc., be defrauded of due services and the cure of souls in the vicarage shall not be neglected, but that its customary burdens and those of [the church], called a chapel, shall be supported; and that on Adam's death or resignation etc. of the canonry and prebend this union etc. shall be dissolved and erection etc. shall be extinguished and so deemed and the vicarage and the church, called a chapel, shall revert to their original condition and be deemed vacant automatically.

Apostolice sedis providentia circumspecta ad ea libenter intendit . . .
S de Castello / B / · B· xxxv Tertio Id' Januar' anno decimo. [11 January 1502], *Bolis*

822   15 January 1502   *Reg. Lat.* 1111, fos 27^V-28^V

To the abbot of the monastery of B. Mary, *de Andro* [Gill Abbey], d. Cork, and John
Oherlahe and Donald Omurhu, canons of the church of Cork, mandate in favour of
Donat Macharyg, canon of the church of Cork. The pope has learned that the
archdeaconry of the church of Cork and the rectory of the parish church of
Ynseonnyn,[1] d. Cork, which is of lay patronage, are vacant *certo modo* at present
and have been vacant for so long that by the Lateran statutes their collation has
lawfully devolved on the apostolic see, although James Barri, who bears himself as a
monk or as the abbot of the monastery of B. Mary, Tracton (*de Albotractu*),[2] d. Cork,
has detained the archdeaconry and rectory, for a certain time, without any title or
support of law, temerariously and *de facto*, as he does. At a recent petition on
Donat's part to the pope to unite etc. the archdeaconry and rectory to the canonry
and prebend of Ynserem, which Donat holds in the said church of Cork, for as long
as he does so — asserting that the annual value of the archdeaconry and rectory does
not exceed 37, and of the canonry and prebend, 3, marks sterling — the pope, not
having certain knowledge of the foregoing, hereby commands that the above three
(or two or one of them), if, having summoned James and others concerned and those
interested in the union, they find the archdeaconry, which is a non-major dignity *post
pontificalem*, and the rectory, to be vacant (howsoever etc.) and the foregoing to be
true, shall unite etc. the archdeaconry and rectory (even if specially reserved etc.),
with all rights and appurtenances, to the canonry and prebend, for as long as Donat
holds the canonry and prebend; to the effect that — having removed James and any
other unlawful detainers — Donat may, on his own authority, in person or by proxy,
take possession[3] of the archdeaconry and rectory, and convert their fruits etc. to his
own uses and those of the canonry and prebend, archdeaconry and rectory and retain
them, for as long as he holds the canonry and prebend, without licence of the local
diocesan or of anyone else. Notwithstanding etc. The pope's will is, however, that
the archdeaconry and rectory shall not, on account of this union etc., be defrauded of
due services and the cure of souls in the rectory and (if any) the archdeaconry shall
not be neglected, but that their customary burdens shall be supported; and that on
Donat's death or resignation etc. of the archdeaconry and rectory the union etc. shall
be dissolved and so deemed and the archdeaconry and rectory shall revert to their
original condition and be deemed vacant automatically.

Decet Romanum pontificem votis illis gratum prestare assensum . . .
S de Castello / · B· / | · B· xx Quarto Kl' februar' anno decimo. [29 January 1502],
Bolis

[1] or *Ynseonayn*
[2] order not mentioned
[3] 'corporalem' does not occur

823   8 January 1502[1]   *Reg. Lat.* 1111, fos 30^V-31^V

To the abbot of the monastery of B. Mary, *de Andro* [Gill Abbey], d. Cork, and John

Ocherlahe and John Dermitii, canons of the church of Cork, mandate in favour of Cornelius Ymurhu, cleric, d. Cork. The pope has learned that the perpetual vicarage of the parish church of Mocromuhu, d. Cloyne, which is of lay patronage, is vacant *certo modo* at present and has been vacant for so long that by the Lateran statutes its collation has lawfully devolved on the apostolic see, although a certain Donald Oconuhur, who bears himself as a priest, has detained it, without any title or support of law, temerariously and *de facto*, for a certain time, as he does. At a recent petition on Cornelius's part to the pope to erect and institute a canonry in the church of Cloyne and the said vicarage into a simple prebend in the same, for his lifetime — asserting that the annual value of the vicarage does not exceed 6 marks sterling — the pope, not having certain knowledge of the foregoing, hereby commands that the above three (or two or one of them), if, having summoned Donald and as regards the erection the bishop and chapter of Cloyne and others concerned, they find the vicarage to be vacant (howsoever etc.) and the foregoing to be true, shall erect and institute a canonry in the church of Cloyne and the vicarage (even if specially reserved etc.) into a simple prebend in the same, for the lifetime of Cornelius, without prejudice to anyone; and, in that event, collate and assign the newly erected canonry and prebend, being vacant, with plenitude of canon law and all rights and appurtenances, to Cornelius, inducting him etc. having removed Donald and any other unlawful detainer from the vicarage and causing Cornelius (or his proctor) to be received as a canon of the church of Cloyne, with plenitude of canon law, and the fruits etc., rights and obventions of the said canonry and prebend to be delivered to him. [Curbing] gainsayers etc. Notwithstanding etc. The pope's will is, however, that the vicarage shall not, on account of this erection and institution, be defrauded of due services and the cure of souls therein (if any) shall not be neglected, but that its customary burdens shall be supported; and that on Cornelius's death or resignation etc. of the canonry and prebend the said erection and institution shall be dissolved and so deemed and the vicarage shall revert to its original condition and be deemed vacant automatically.

Apostolice sedis providentia circumspecta ad ea libenter intendit . . .
S de Castello /· M· /· M· xviii pridie nonas februarii anno decimo [4 February 1502], *Battiferro*

[1] the script of the dating clause is noticeably less cursive than that of the rest of the letter; but the hand is almost certainly the same: entered later?

824 15 January 1502   *Reg. Lat.* 1111, fos 34^v-36^r

To the bishop of Cloyne and Donat Omwrhow and Thomas Ogiellyry, canons of the church of Cloyne, mandate in favour of Richard Yhunwnan, cleric, d. Limerick. The pope has learned that the perpetual vicarages of the parish churches of Kyllide and Kyllochelean, d. Limerick, are vacant *certo modo* at present and have been vacant for so long that by the Lateran statutes their collation has lawfully devolved on the apostolic see, although Maurice Offyellan has detained the first vicarage and Donald Ohunwnan the second — bearing themselves as priests — with no title and no support of law, temerariously and *de facto*, for a certain time, as they do. At a recent petition on Richard's part to the pope to erect and institute a canonry in the church of Limerick and the first vicarage into a simple prebend of that church, for as long as he holds the canonry and prebend, if conferred on him by virtue of the presents; and to unite etc. the second vicarage to the erected canonry and prebend, also for as long as he holds them, as above — asserting that the annual value of the first vicarage does not exceed 8, and of the second, 4, marks sterling — he hereby commands that the above three (or two or one of them), if, having summoned Maurice and Donald and the bishop and chapter of Limerick and others concerned, they find the vicarages to be vacant (howsoever etc.), and regarding the union, having summoned those interested, the foregoing to be true, shall, (even if the vicarages be specially reserved etc.), erect and institute a canonry in the church of Limerick and the first vicarage into a simple prebend of that church, for as long as Richard holds the canonry and prebend, without prejudice to anyone; and unite etc. the second vicarage to the canonry and prebend thus erected; and collate and assign the newly erected canonry and prebend, being vacant, to Richard, with plenitude of canon law and all rights and appurtenances, inducting him etc. having removed Maurice from the first vicarage and Donald from the second and any other unlawful detainers, and causing Richard (or his proctor) to be received as a canon of the church of Limerick, with plenitude of canon law, and the fruits etc., rights and obventions of the canonry and prebend and annex aforesaid to be delivered to him. [Curbing] gainsayers etc. Notwithstanding etc. The pope's will is, however, that the vicarages shall not, on account of this erection, institution and union etc., be defrauded of due services and the cure of souls therein shall not be neglected, but that their customary burdens shall be supported; and that on Richard's death or resignation etc. of the canonry and prebend, the union etc. shall be dissolved and erection and institution extinguished and the vicarages shall revert to their original condition automatically.

Ex iniuncto nobis desuper apostolice servitutis officio ad ea libenter intendimus. . .
A de Sancto Severino / · B· / ǀ · B· xxx Quinto decimo Kl' marcij anno decimo· [15 February 1502], *Bolis·*

825   31 January 1502   *Reg. Lat.* 1111, fos 36ʳ-37ᵛ

To the abbot of the monastery of B. Mary, *de Andro* [Gill Abbey], d. Cork, and Donat Macharyg and John Dermitii, canons of the church of Cork, mandate in favour of John Oherlahe, the elder, priest, d. Cork. A recent petition to the pope on John's part stated that at one time when the perpetual vicarage of the parish church of Culmoneayn, d. Cork, was vacant *certo modo* outside the Roman curia, Gerald, bishop of Cork and Cloyne, by ordinary authority collated and made provision of it, thus vacant, to John, outside the said curia, and he acquired possession of it by virtue of this collation and provision. Moreover since, as the same petition added, John fears that for certain reasons the said collation and provision do not hold good; and, as the pope has learned, the said vicarage is vacant still, as above, and the perpetual vicarage of the parish church of Achynach', d. Cloyne, which is of lay patronage, is vacant at present, and this second vicarage has been vacant for so long that by the Lateran statutes its collation has lawfully devolved on the apostolic see, although Donat Ocronyn, who bears himself as a priest, has detained it, without any title or support of law, temerariously and *de facto*, for a certain time, as he still does. The pope hereby commands that the above three (or two or one of them), having summoned Donat and others concerned regarding the second vicarage, shall collate and assign the vicarages, whose annual value together does not exceed 12 marks sterling, (howsoever they should be vacant etc.; even if the first one has been vacant for so long that its collation has lawfully devolved on the apostolic see, and even if they be specially reserved etc.), with all rights and appurtenances, to John, inducting him etc. having removed Donat from the second vicarage and any other unlawful detainers from it and the first vicarage and causing John (or his proctor) to be admitted to the vicarages and their fruits etc., rights and obventions to be delivered to him. [Curbing] gainsayers etc. Notwithstanding etc. Also the pope dispenses John to receive and retain the vicarages together for life, if conferred on him by virtue of the presents, and to resign them, at once or successively, simply or for exchange, as often as he pleases, and in their place receive and retain another (or other), similar or dissimilar, perpetual vicarage (or vicarages) or parish church (or churches), notwithstanding etc. With the proviso that the said vicarages (and other vicarages or parish churches in place of them) shall not, on this account, be defrauded of due services and [the cure][1] of souls in the aforesaid vicarages (and other vicarages or parish churches in place of them) shall not be neglected.

Vite ac morum honestas . . .
· *S· de Castello* /· *B·* / ǀ *B· xxxv· Tertio·* · *decimo Kl' marcij anno decimo·* [17 February 1502], *Bolis·*

[1] *cura* wanting

826   3 February 1502   *Reg. Lat.* 1111, fos 38^V-39^V

To the abbots of the monasteries of St Michael, Mayo (*de Magyo*), of the Holy Trinity, *de Fonte Sancti Patritii* [Ballintober], and of B. Mary, Cong (*de Conga*), d. Tuam, mandate in favour of Theobald de Burgo, cleric, d. Tuam. The pope has learned that the rectories of the parish churches of Locmask[1] and of Portmen' *alias* Ennosmeon, d. Tuam, which are of lay patronage, are vacant *certo modo* at present and have been vacant for so long that by the Lateran statutes their collation has

lawfully devolved on the apostolic see, although Edmund Joy has detained the first
rectory, and Maurice Joy the second, bearing themselves as priests, with no title and
no support of law, temerariously and *de facto*, for a certain time, as they do. At a
recent petition on Theobald's part to the pope to erect and institute a canonry in the
church of Tuam and the rectories into a simple prebend of the said church, for as
long as he holds the erected canonry and prebend, if conferred on him by virtue of
the presents — asserting that the annual value of the first rectory does not exceed 8,
and of the second, 6, marks sterling — the pope hereby commands that the above
three (or two or one of them), if, having summoned the bishop[2] and chapter of
Tuam, Edmund, Maurice and others concerned, they find the rectories to be vacant
(howsoever etc.), shall erect and institute a canonry in the church of Tuam and the
rectories (even if specially reserved etc.) into a simple prebend of the said church,
without prejudice to anyone; and, in that event, collate and assign the newly erected
canonry and prebend, being vacant, to Theobald, with plenitude of canon law and all
rights and appurtenances, inducting him etc. having removed Edmund and Maurice
and any other unlawful detainers and causing Theobald (or his proctor) to be
received as a canon of Tuam, with plenitude of canon law, and the fruits etc., rights
and obventions of the canonry and prebend to be delivered to him. [Curbing]
gainsayers etc. Notwithstanding etc. The pope's will is, however, that the rectories
shall not, on this account, be defrauded of due services, but that their customary
burdens shall be supported; and that on Theobald's death or resignation etc. of the
canonry and prebend this erection and institution shall be extinguished and so
deemed and the rectories shall revert to their original condition automatically.

Ex debito pastoralis officii quamquam insufficientibus meritis nobis ex alto commissi . . .
A de Sancto Severino / · B· / · B· xxv nono Kl' marcij anno decimo [21 February
1502], *Bolis*

[1] (?)*Locmas* deleted (but not initialled)
[2] *sic; recte:* 'archbishop'

827   5 February 1502   *Reg. Lat.* 1111, fos 40[r]-41[v]

To the abbots of the monasteries of St Michael, Mayo (*de Magio*), of the Holy
Trinity, *de Fonte Sancti Patritii* [Ballintober], and of B. Mary, Cong (*de Conga*), d.
Tuam, mandate in favour of Ilialmus[1] de Stantona, cleric, d. Tuam. The pope has
learned that the perpetual vicarage of the parish church of Oue,[2] d. Tuam, is vacant
certo modo at present and has been vacant for so long that by the Lateran statutes its
collation has lawfully devolved on the apostolic see, although Hebertus[3] de
Stantona, who bears himself as a priest, has detained it, with no title and no support
of law, temerariously and *de facto*, for a certain time, as he does. At a recent petition
on the part of Ilialmus to the pope to apply and appropriate a certain particle, also
called Oue,[4] located within the limits of the parish of the said church and pertaining

at present to the rectory of the parish church of Portmen', d. Tuam, to the said vicarage, for the lifetime of Ilialmus; and to erect and institute a canonry in the said church of Tuam and the vicarage (after this appropriation) into a simple prebend of that church, for as long as Ilialmus holds the erected canonry and prebend, if conferred on him by virtue of the presents — asserting that the annual value of the vicarage and particle aforesaid does not exceed 5 marks sterling — the pope hereby commands that the above three (or two or one of them), if, having summoned the archbishop and chapter of Tuam and Hebertus and others concerned, they find the vicarage to be vacant (howsoever etc.) and the foregoing to be true, shall apply and appropriate the particle to the vicarage, (even if the vicarage be specially reserved etc.), for the lifetime of Ilialmus, provided that the express assent of the present rector of the church of Portmen' is given thereto; and erect and institute a canonry in the church of Tuam and the vicarage into a simple prebend of that church, for as long as Ilialmus holds the said canonry and prebend, if conferred on him as above, without prejudice to anyone; and in that event collate and assign the newly erected canonry and prebend, with plenitude of canon law and all rights and appurtenances, to Ilialmus, inducting him etc. having removed Hebertus and any other unlawful detainer and causing Ilialmus (or his proctor) to be received as a canon of the church of Tuam, with plenitude of canon law, and the fruits etc., rights and obventions of the canonry and prebend to be delivered to him. [Curbing] gainsayers etc. Notwithstanding etc. The pope's will is, however, that the vicarage shall not, on account of this erection and institution, be defrauded of due services and the cure of souls shall not be neglected, but that its customary burdens shall be supported; and that on Ilialmus's death or resignation etc. of the canonry and prebend, the above application, appropriation, erection and institution shall be extinguished and the vicarage and particle shall revert to their original condition automatically.

Ex debito pastoralis officii nobis licet insufficientibus meritis ex alto commissi . . .
A de S^{to} Severino / . B· / ₁ B· xxx nono Kl' marcii anno decimo [21 February 1502],
Bolis

[1] *Ilialm-* or *Illialm-* occurs throughout; (*cf.* , of course, 'Willialmus')

[2] or *One* (*cf.* note 4)

[3] also spelt *Hubert*

[4] or *One* (*cf.* note 2)

---

828   16 February 1502   *Reg. Lat.* 1111, fos 43^v-44^r

To the abbot of the monastery of the Holy Trinity, *de Fonte Sancti Patritii* [Ballintober], d. Tuam, and Walter Cusin and David Onilleayn, canons of the church of Tuam, mandate in favour of Restardus[1] [Richard] de Burgo, canon of Tuam, (who, as he asserts, holds a canonry of the church of Tuam, to which the perpetual vicarage of the parish church of Kylfynaym, d. Tuam, is united etc. by ordinary authority). The pope has learned that the rectory of the parish church of Boychoholan, d. Achonry, which is of lay patronage and which John Ymurchw, its late rector, held while he lived and which by his death, outside the Roman curia, is vacant at present and has been vacant for so long that by the Lateran statutes its collation has lawfully devolved on the apostolic see. He hereby commands that the above three, or two or one of them, in person or by proxy, shall collate and assign the rectory, whose annual value does not exceed 8 marks sterling, (vacant as above, or howsoever etc., even if specially reserved etc.), with all rights and appurtenances, to Restardus, inducting him etc. having removed any unlawful detainer and causing Restardus to be admitted to the rectory and its fruits etc., rights and obventions to be delivered to him. Curbing [gainsayers] etc. Notwithstanding etc.

Vite ac morum honestas . . .
A de S^{to} Severino / · B· / . B. x Kl' Marcij anno decimo. [1 March 1502], *Bolis.*

1 also spelt *Ristardus*

---

829   24 February 1502   *Reg. Lat.* 1111, fo 45^{r-v}

To the dean and Thomas de Burgo and John Odowna, canons, of the church of Annaghdown, mandate in favour of William Oclmuran,[1] cleric, d. Annaghdown. The pope has learned that the chapel of B. Mary, Bougalia, d. Annaghdown, is vacant *certo modo* at present and has been vacant for so long that by the Lateran statutes its collation has lawfully devolved on the apostolic see. He hereby commands that the above three, or two or one of them, in person or by proxy, shall collate and assign the chapel, which is with cure and whose annual value does not exceed 6 marks sterling, (vacant howsoever etc., even if specially reserved etc.), with all rights and appurtenances, to William, inducting him etc. having removed any unlawful detainer and causing the chapel's fruits etc., rights and obventions to be delivered to him.[2] [Curbing] gainsayers etc. Notwithstanding etc. Given at Piombino, d. Massa Marittima.

Vite ac morum honestas . . .
A de S^{to} Severino / . B· / . B· x Quinto non' marcij anno decimo. [3 March 1502], *Bolis·*

1 the 'mu' doubtful
2 no mention of William being admitted

---

830   27 November 1501   *Reg. Lat.* 1111, fos 53^{v}-54^{r}

To Cormac Magragalli, John Macgillarni and William Odonallan, canons of the church of Elphin, mandate in favour of Cornelius Mac. ard,[1] priest, d. Elphin. The pope has learned that the parish church of Chillerulan, d. Elphin, is vacant *certo modo* at present and has been vacant for so long that by the Lateran statutes its collation has lawfully devolved on the apostolic see, although Donald Okellay, who bears himself as a cleric, has detained it without any title or support of law, temerariously and *de facto*, for a certain time, as he still does. He hereby commands that the above three (or two or one of them), if, having summoned Donald and others concerned, they find the church, whose annual value does not exceed 4 marks sterling, to be vacant (howsoever etc.; even if specially reserved etc.), shall collate and assign it, with all rights and appurtenances, to Cornelius, inducting him etc. having removed Donald and any other unlawful detainer and causing the church's fruits etc., rights and obventions to be delivered to him.[2][Curbing] gainsayers etc. Notwithstanding etc.

Vite ac morum honestas . . .
S de Castello / . B· / ₁ B. x Quarto non' decembr' anno decimo · [2 December 1501], *Bolis·*

[1] the fourth letter entirely obscured by ink blot; *Macdard*?
[2] no mention of Cornelius being admitted

831   18 November 1501   *Reg. Lat.* 1111, fos 64^v-65^r

To Patrick Macbradi and Odo Omulmothore, canons of the church of Kilmore, and the official of Kilmore, mandate in favour of Nicholas Magbraday, priest, d. Kilmore. A recent petition to the pope on Nicholas's part stated that at one time when the perpetual vicarage of the parish church of St Bridget, Vornay *alias* Kede, and the rectory of the church, called the *plebs*, of Cuacaynde *alias* Clacerogarde, d. Kilmore, were vacant *certo modo*, the bishop of Kilmore, or his vicar general by virtue of special power for this from the bishop by his letters, by ordinary authority, collated and made provision of the vicarage and rectory, vacant as above, to Nicholas and he acquired possession of them by virtue of the said collation and provision. Moreover since Nicholas fears that for certain reasons the said collation and provision do not hold good; and, as the pope has learned, the vicarage and rectory are known to be vacant still as above, the pope hereby commands that the above three, or two or one of them, in person or by proxy, shall collate and assign the vicarage and the rectory (which is without cure), whose annual value together does not exceed 7 marks sterling, (vacant howsoever etc.; even if they have been vacant for so long that by the Lateran statutes their collation has lawfully devolved on the apostolic see, etc.), with all rights and appurtenances, to Nicholas, inducting him etc. having removed any unlawful detainers from them and causing Nicholas (or his proctor) to be admitted to the vicarage and rectory and their fruits etc., rights and obventions to be delivered to them. Curbing [gainsayers] etc. Notwithstanding etc.

Vite ac morum honestas . . .
S de Castello / . B· / . B· xij· Tertio Id' decembr' anno decimo · [11 December 1501],
Bolis ·

832   18 November 1501   *Reg. Lat.* 1111, fos 65ᵛ-66ʳ

To Patrick Magbraday and Adam Offegayd, canons of the church of Kilmore, and
the official of Kilmore, mandate in favour of Eugene Magbraday, priest, d. Kilmore.
A recent petition to the pope on Eugene's part stated that at one time when the
vicarage[1] of the parish church of St Patrick, Druymduyn, otherwise called the *plebs*
of Macharembahyr, d. Kilmore, was vacant *certo modo*, the then bishop of Kilmore,
or his vicar general, by virtue of special power from the bishop by his letters, by
ordinary authority collated and made provision of the church,[2] thus vacant as above,
to Eugene, and he acquired possession of the said church[3] by virtue of the said
collation and provision. Moreover since, as the same petition added, Eugene fears
that for certain reasons the said collation and provision do not hold good; and, as the
pope has learned, the said church[4] is known to be vacant still as above, the pope
hereby commands that the above three, or two or one of them, in person or by proxy,
shall collate and assign the vicarage, whose annual value does not exceed 5 marks
sterling, (vacant howsoever etc., even if it has been vacant for so long that by the
Lateran statutes its collation has lawfully devolved on the apostolic see etc.), with all
rights and appurtenances, to Eugene, inducting him (or his proctor) into corporal
possession of the vicarage etc. having removed any unlawful detainer and causing
Eugene to be admitted thereto and the fruits etc., rights and obventions of this
church[5] to be delivered to him. [Curbing] gainsayers etc. Notwithstanding etc.

Vite ac morum honestas . . .
S de Castello / · B· / ₁ B· x decimo nono Kl' Januar' anno decimo [14 December
1501], ₁ *Bolis ·*

[1] *olim vicaria;* 'perpetua' does not occur; variously: 'vicarage' or 'church' (see notes 2-5); rightly:
vicarage?
[2] *sic: ecclesiam*; *cf.* notes 3-5 below; *recte*: 'vicariam'?
[3] *sic*
[4] *sic*
[5] *sic*; there is a cross in the margin (signalling error?)

833   28 November 1501   *Reg. Lat.* 1111, fos 66ᵛ-67ᵛ

To the abbot of the monastery of Knockmoy (*Collii*[1] *Victorie*), d. Tuam, and Thomas

Omolain and John Orauri, canons of the church of Tuam, mandate in favour of Wolmus Otonconnan, canon of [the church of][2] Tuam. A recent petition to the pope on Wolmus's part stated that formerly — after he had been dispensed by apostolic authority notwithstanding a defect of birth as the son of a priest and an unmarried woman, first to be promoted to all, even sacred, orders and the priesthood and to hold a benefice, even if it should have cure of souls; and then to receive and retain any number of benefices, with and without cure, compatible mutually and with the said benefice, even if they should be canonries and prebends in cathedral or metropolitan churches, if conferred on him otherwise canonically; and had been duly marked with clerical character — when the parish church of Kyltaryn, d. Tuam, which is of lay patronage, became vacant by the free resignation of Tyichironus, brother of the third order of B. Francis, called *de Penitentia*, which he then [held][3] canonically, made spontaneously into the hands of the then archbishop of Tuam, or his vicar general, outside the Roman curia, and admitted by ordinary authority by the said archbishop or vicar (having, as he asserted, special power from the archbishop by his letters [and] by virtue of it), outside the said curia, the archbishop or vicar, by the said ordinary authority, collated and made provision of the said church, thus vacant, to Wolmus, and he acquired possession by virtue of the said collation and provision, and held and possessed it thereafter, as he does at present. Moreover since, as the same petition added, Wolmus fears that for certain reasons the said collation and provision do not hold good; and, as the pope has learned, the church is known to be vacant still as above, and its fruits etc. and also those of the canonry and prebend of the church of Tuam, which Wolmus holds by the said later dispensation, and of the perpetual vicarages of the parish churches of Calioco *alias* Tempul Antoter[4] and of Cluanbectii, d. Tuam, [?annexed][5] to the said canonry and prebend are so slender and meagre — in that the annual values do not exceed 14 marks sterling — that Wolmus can scarcely support himself from them and on this account divine worship in the church of Tuam has been neglected and shall be so in the future unless the parish church named above be united to the canonry and prebend, and if it were to be united etc. to the canonry and prebend, for as long as Wolmus holds the canonry and prebend, he would be able to support himself more comfortably and divine worship in the church of Tuam would be increased. The pope — who does not have certain knowledge of the foregoing — therefore hereby commands that the above three (or two or one of them), having summoned those concerned, shall inform themselves as to each and every one of the aforesaid matters, and if they find them to be true, shall unite etc. the parish church named first, (whether vacant as above or howsoever etc., even if it has been vacant for so long that by the Lateran statutes its collation has lawfully devolved on the apostolic see, etc.,) — provided that the express assent of the patrons be given thereto — with all its rights and appurtenances to the said canonry and prebend, for as long as Wolmus holds the canonry and prebend, to the effect that Wolmus may, on his own authority, in person or by proxy, take or continue in and retain corporal possession of the parish church and rights and appurtenances aforesaid, for as long as he holds the canonry and prebend, and convert its fruits etc. to his own uses and those of the parish church and the canonry and prebend without licence of the local diocesan or of anyone else. Notwithstanding etc. The pope's will is, however, that the parish church named first shall not, on account of this union etc., be defrauded of due services and the cure of souls therein shall not be neglected, but that its customary burdens shall be supported; and that on Wolmus's death or resignation etc. of the canonry and prebend the union etc. shall be dissolved and the parish church shall revert to its original condition and be deemed vacant automatically.

Romanum decet pontificem votis illis gratum prestare assensum . . .
A de S^{to} Severino / · B· / ₁ B· xiij· Bolis·

[1] *sic*

[2] MS here has: *canonici Tuamen. diocesis; recte*: 'canonici ecclesie Tuamen.'? (*Cf.* the text below where he holds a canonry and prebend of the church of Tuam)

[3] *obtinet; recte*: 'obtinebat'

[4] MS *Tempul | Antoter*; last letter doubtful

[5] *cum earum; recte*: 'annexarum'?

834   27 November 1501   *Reg. Lat.* 1111, fos 68^r-69^r

To Odo Mactalie and Patrick Macbradi, canons of the church of Kilmore, and the official of Kilmore, mandate in favour of Gilbert Macbraday, cleric, d. Kilmore. Some time ago, the pope — after he had learned that the rectory of the parish church of St Bridget, Nornay *alias* Kede, d. Kilmore, had been vacant *certo modo*, and was then vacant; and after representation made on the part of Fergal Ysiridan, cleric, d. Kilmore, to him to erect and institute the said rectory into a simple prebend in the church of Kilmore, for Fergal's lifetime — at Fergal's supplication, by other letters of his charged the prior of the monastery, usually governed by a prior, of B. Mary, Idruymlehan, d. Kilmore, and Corbanus Magniahuna, canon of the church of Clogher, and Gelasius Oseyndan, canon of the church of Kilmore, that they (or one of them),[1] if, having summoned the bishop and chapter of Kilmore and others concerned, they found it to be thus, were to erect and institute the rectory (vacant howsoever etc.) into a simple prebend in the church of Kilmore, for Fergal's lifetime; and, thereafter, collate and assign a canonry of the said church and the newly erected prebend, being vacant, to Fergal, as is more fully contained in the said letters. Moreover since, as a recent petition to the pope on Gilbert's part stated, Fergal made no mention in the said letters that his father had been the immediate predecessor in the rectory, the pope — considering that, if the foregoing is true, the said letters are known to be surreptitious and the erection, collation and provision perchance made by pretext of them do not hold good; and, as the pope has learned, the said simple rectory is known to be vacant still as above — hereby commands that the above three (or two or one of them), if, having summoned Fergal and others concerned, they find the foregoing to be true, shall declare the letters to be surreptitious and the erection, collation and provision null and void; and in that event collate and assign the rectory, whose annual value does not exceed 8 marks sterling, (vacant howsoever etc., even if it has been vacant for so long that by the Lateran statutes its collation has lawfully devolved on the apostolic see etc.), with all rights and appurtenances, to Gilbert, inducting him etc. having removed Fergal and any other unlawful detainer and causing Gilbert (or his proctor) to be admitted to the rectory and its fruits etc., rights and obventions to be delivered to him. [Curbing] gainsayers etc. Notwithstanding etc.

Vite ac morum honestas . . .
S de Castello / · B· / . B. x. *Quinto decimo Kl' Januar' anno decimo* [18 December 1501], · *Bolis·*

[1] *ipsi vel eorum alter*

835   15 December 1501   *Reg. Lat.* 1111, fos 74[v]-75[r]

To Malachy Ocontennan, Thomas Omolan and Nemeas Malignyl, canons of the church of Tuam,[1] mandate in favour of William, archbishop of Tuam. It has been referred to the pope's audience by archbishop William that Miler, abbot of the monastery of B. John the Evangelist, OSA, d. Tuam, has dared to impose several pacts and agreements on the reception of canons and thereby seek and receive divers goods, movable and immovable, from the canons themselves or their relations, incurring simony, and to alienate certain of the monastery's immovable goods or precious movables in cases not permitted by law and convert the proceeds to his own uses; and has failed to repair the church, refectory, dormitory and other structures and buildings of the monastery which are suffering (or are threatened with) ruin, and to be in continuous residence therein. A recent petition to the pope on archbishop William's part stated that the demesne tax and possessions lawfully pertaining to the archiepiscopal *mensa* of Tuam are detained *de facto* by several powerful laymen and the fruits etc. of the *mensa* are so slender and meagre that out of them he cannot conveniently prosecute and defend his rights and those of the *mensa*, keep up his position in accordance with archiepiscopal dignity and bear the burdens incumbent on him; and that if the monastery were to be united etc. to the *mensa*, for as long as he presides over the church of Tuam, he would repair the monastery and its structures and buildings and reform it, and could the better support himself, keep up his position and bear the aforesaid burdens; and it is asserted that the annual value of the monastery does not exceed 24 marks sterling. The pope — considering that if the above related matters are true, abbot Miler has rendered himself unworthy of the rule and administration of the monastery over which he is understood to preside; and not having certain knowledge of the other aforesaid matters — hereby commands that the above three (or two or one of them), if archbishop William will accuse abbot Miler over the above related matters before them and proceed in form of law, thereafter shall, having summoned abbot Miler and others concerned, inquire into these matters and if they find the truth of them to be substantiated, deprive abbot Miler of the said rule and administration and remove him from them; and, in that event, inform themselves as to each and every one of the other aforesaid matters and all the circumstances thereof, and if they find them to be true, unite etc. the monastery, (whether vacant by the said deprivation and removal or at another time in any other way etc.), with all rights and appurtenances, to the *mensa*, for as long as archbishop William presides over the said church; to the effect that the archbishop may, on his own authority, in person or by proxy, take and retain corporal possession of the monastery (and rights and appurtenances aforesaid), for as long as he presides over the said church; and convert its fruits etc. to his own uses and those of the *mensa* and monastery without licence of the local diocesan[2] or of anyone else. Notwithstanding etc. The pope's will is, however, that the monastery shall not, on account of this union etc., be defrauded of due services and the usual number of monks and ministers therein shall not be diminished, but that the customary burdens shall be supported; and that on archbishop William's death or resignation etc. of the said church this union etc. shall be dissolved and the monastery shall revert to its original condition and be deemed vacant automatically.

Pastoralis officii debitum nos excitat et inducit . . .
A de S^{to} Severino / · *B* / ₁ *B* · *L. Bolis.*

[1] the address clause is inserted in the margin by the enregistering scribe initialled . *B.* twice; there are several other marginal insertions in the course of the entry

[2] *diocesani loci* — standard formula, but odd here as grantee is the diocesan

836   11 December 1501   *Reg. Lat.* 1111, fos 75^v-76^v

To the prior of the priory of Dearg, d. Ardagh, and Peter Oscingyn, canon of the church of Elphin, and Thomas Omolan, canon of the church of Tuam, mandate in favour of Fantutius Ofergyl, canon of the monastery of B. Mary, Saints Island (*de Insula Omnium Sanctorum*), OSA, d. Ardagh. The pope has learned that the priorship of the said monastery, usually governed by a prior, is vacant *certo modo* at present, although Thomas Ofergyl, who bears himself as a canon of the said order, has detained it with no title and no support of law, temerariously and *de facto*, for a certain time, as he does. He hereby commands that the above three (or two or one of them), if, having summoned Thomas and others concerned, they find the priorship, which is conventual and whose annual value does not exceed 60 marks sterling, to be vacant (howsoever etc.), shall collate and assign it ([even] if it has been vacant for so long that by the Lateran statutes its collation has lawfully devolved on the apostolic see, etc.), with all rights and appurtenances, to Fantutius, inducting him etc. having removed Thomas and any other unlawful detainer, and causing Fantutius (or his proctor) to be admitted to the priorship and its fruits etc., rights and obventions to be delivered to him. [Curbing] gainsayers etc. Notwithstanding etc.

Religionis zelus, vite ac morum honestas . . .
A de Sancto Severino / · B / ₁ B· xx· Vndecimo Kl' Januar' anno decimo· [22 December 1501], *Bolis·*

837   18 December 1501   *Reg. Lat.* 1111, fos 76ᵛ-77ᵛ

To Peter Oscingyn and Charles Ofallwy, canons of the church of Elphin, and Thomas Omolan, canon of the church of Tuam, mandate in favour of Roceus Offergil, canon of the monastery of B. Mary, Saints Island (*de Insula Omnium Sanctorum*), OSA, d. Ardagh. The pope has learned that the priorship of the monastery, usually governed by a prior, of B. Mary, Inchcleraun (*de Insula Clo'xii*),[1] said order and diocese, is vacant *certo modo* at present, although Maurus Offergil, who bears himself as a canon of the order, has detained it with no title and no support of law, temerariously and *de facto*, for a certain time, as he does. He hereby commands that the above three (or two or one of them), if, having summoned Maurus and others concerned, they find the priorship, which is conventual and whose annual value does not exceed 8 marks sterling, to be vacant (howsoever etc.), shall collate and assign it, (even if it has been vacant for so long that by the Lateran statutes its collation has lawfully devolved on the apostolic see, etc.), with all rights and appurtenances, to Roceus, inducting him etc. having removed Maurus and any other unlawful detainer, and causing Roceus (or his proctor) to be admitted thereto; and transfer Roceus — as soon as he has peacefully acquired possession of the priorship by virtue of the presents — from the monastery of Saints Island (of which he is a canon, as above, and, as he asserts, expressly professed of this order) to that of Inchcleraun, and cause him to be received there as a canon and given charitable treatment, and the fruits etc., rights and obventions of the priorship to be delivered to him. [Curbing] gainsayers etc. Notwithstanding etc.

Religionis zelus, vite ac morum honestas . . .
A de Sᵗᵒ Severino[2] / · B· / ₁ B· xx· Tertio Kl' januar' anno. decimo. [30 December 1501], *Bolis·*

[1] thus in the first instance; later: *Beate Marie Clorxii*
[2] enlarged letters written in lighter ink: entered later?

838   15 December 1501   *Reg. Lat.* 1111, fos 80ʳ-81ʳ

To the abbot of the monastery *de Castro Dei* [Fermoy], d. Cloyne, Edmund de Burgo, canon of the church of Cashel, and John Benet, canon of the church of Cork, mandate in favour of Raymond de Burgo, canon of the church of Emly (who, as he asserts, is in his eighteenth year of age, is of noble birth and holds a canonry and prebend of the said church [of Emly]). The pope has learned that the deanery of the said church is vacant *certo modo* at present and has been vacant for so long that by the Lateran statutes its collation has lawfully devolved on the apostolic see, although William Machibren, who bears himself as a cleric, has detained it, without any title or support of law, for a certain time, as he still does. He hereby commands that the above three (or two or one of them), if, having summoned William and others concerned, they find the deanery, which is a non-major dignity *post pontificalem* and whose annual value does not exceed 16 marks sterling, to be vacant (howsoever etc.), shall collate and assign it, ([even] if specially reserved etc.), with all rights and appurtenances, to Raymond, inducting him etc. having removed William and any other unlawful detainer and causing Raymond (or his proctor) to be admitted to the deanery and its fruits etc., rights and obventions to be delivered to him. [Curbing] gainsayers etc. Notwithstanding etc. Also the pope dispenses Raymond to receive and retain the deanery, if conferred on him by virtue of the presents, notwithstanding the said defect of age etc. With the proviso that the deanery shall not, on this account, be defrauded of due services and the cure of souls therein (if any) shall not be neglected.

Nobilitas generis, vite ac morum honestas . . .
S de Castello*1* / · B· / . B· xxv· Tertio Id' Januar' anno decimo· [11 January 1502], Bolis·

1 enlarged letters written in a lighter ink: entered later?

839   10 June 1502   *Reg. Lat.* 1111, fos 133*r*-135*r*

To Hugh Grenlau, dean of the church of Ross, (who is a priest), collation and provision. Following the pope's reservation some time ago to his own collation and disposition of all dignities and other benefices, with and without cure, vacated then or in the future at the apostolic see, the deanery of the church of Ross has become vacant by the free resignation of Martin Wans, its late dean, which he held at the time, made through M. Leonard de Bertinis, scriptor and papal familiar, his specially appointed proctor, spontaneously into the pope's hands, and admitted by the pope at the said see, and is vacant at present, being reserved as above. The pope therefore hereby collates and makes provision of the deanery, which is a major dignity *post pontificalem*, the annual value of which and of the church*1* of Kilmere*2* and other annexes thereto does not exceed 36 pounds sterling, (whether vacant as above or howsoever etc., even if it has been vacant for so long that by the Lateran statutes its collation has lawfully devolved on the apostolic see etc.), with all rights and appurtenances, to Hugh. Notwithstanding etc.

Executory to the bishop of Cesena, the prior of the church of St Andrews and the dean of the church of Moray, or two or one of them, acting in person or by proxy.

Vite ac morum honestas . . . The executory begins: *Hodie dilecto filio Hugoni Grenlau* . . .

Jo ortega; . N de castello / · B· / · B· xx x Septimo Kl. Julii anno decimo [25 June 1502], *Bolis*

[1] *sic*: 'parochialis' does not occur

[2] diocese not stated; *cf.* no. 782 'd. Ross'

---

840   16 June 1502   *Reg. Lat.* 1114, fos 25ʳ-26ʳ

To Martin Wans, cleric, d. Ross, reservation of fruits etc., as below. This day Martin has, through a certain specially appointed proctor of his, spontaneously and freely, resigned the deanery of the church of Ross, which he was holding at the time, into the pope's hands, and the pope, admitting the resignation, has, by other letters of his, commanded that the deanery, vacant by the said resignation and previously reserved to apostolic disposition, be provided to Robert Fresel, priest, d. Glasgow, as is more fully contained in those letters.[1] Lest Martin should suffer excessive loss from this resignation, the pope hereby reserves, grants and assigns all fruits etc. of the church of Kylmore and a fourth part of the tithes of corn of the churches of Rosmarky and Cromathy,[2] pertaining [to][3] the deanery, not exceeding 9 pounds sterling annually, to Martin, for life — in place of an annual pension — to be received, collected and levied, by him, in person or by proxy, on his own authority, and be converted to his own uses, with Robert's express consent. Notwithstanding etc.

Executory to the bishop of Ross and the provost of the church of St Martin, Embrica, d. Utrecht, and the official of Moray, or two or one of them, acting in person or by proxy.

Vite ac morum honestas . . . The executory begins: *Hodie dilecto filio Martinus Wans* . . . *A de sancto severino; A. de Colotius*[4] */ Jo / Jo. xij. x. Eps' Terracinen'*

[1] below, no. 841; *cf.*, however, above, nos. 782 and 839

[2] diocese not stated; *cf.* no. 782: 'd. Ross'

[3] *de dictum* . . .; *recte*: 'ad dictum . . .'

[4] both names in a different ink from that of the text: entered later?

---

841   16 June 1502   *Reg. Lat.* 1114, fos 27ʳ-29ʳ

To the official of Ross, mandate in favour of Robert Fresel, priest, d. Glasgow. Following the pope's reservation some time ago to his own collation and disposition of all dignities and other benefices, with and without cure, vacated then or in the future at the apostolic see, the deanery of the church of Ross became vacant by the free resignation of Martin Wans, its late dean, which he held at the time, made through Leonard de Bertinis, scriptor of apostolic letters, his specially appointed proctor, spontaneously into the pope's hands, and admitted by the pope at the said see, and is vacant at present, being reserved as above. The pope therefore hereby commands the above official, if by diligent examination he finds Robert to be suitable — concerning which the pope burdens the official's conscience — to collate and assign the deanery, which is a major dignity *post pontificalem* and whose annual value does not exceed 24 pounds sterling, (whether vacant as above or howsoever etc., even if it has been vacant for so long that by the Lateran statutes its collation has lawfully devolved on the apostolic see etc.), with all rights and appurtenances, to Robert, inducting him etc. — having first received from him the usual oath of fealty in the name of the pope and the Roman church, in accordance with the form which the pope sends enclosed under his *bulla* — having removed any unlawful detainer and causing Robert (or his proctor) to be admitted to the deanery and its fruits etc., rights and obventions to be delivered to him. [Curbing] gainsayers etc. Notwithstanding etc.

Dignum et cetera.
. A. de sanctoseverino / Jo / Jo. xxx. Non' novembr' anno Vndecimo [5 November 1502], *Eps' Terracinen'*

842   11 December 1501   *Reg. Lat.* 1114, fos 105ᵛ-106ʳ

To William Preston, MA, perpetual vicar of the parish church of Newbirn, d. St Andrews. Dispensation — at his supplication — to him, who, as he asserts, holds the perpetual vicarage of the above parish church, to receive and retain for life, together with the said church,[1] one, and without it, any two other benefices, etc. [as above, no. 5, to '. . . Notwithstanding etc. ']. With the proviso that the church held and other incompatible benefices shall not be defrauded of due services and the cure of souls in the church held and (if any) the other incompatible benefices shall not be neglected.

Litterarum scientia, vite ac morum honestas . . .
F de parma / · B· / · B· xxxx. Bolis

[1] *ecclesia; recte*: 'vicaria'; *ecclesia (-e)* in fact occurs four times in the course of the entry where 'vicaria' ('-e') might be expected; *ecclesia (-e)* is, however, appropriate in the next entry (also for a graduate, d. St Andrews, and of the same date) which was enregistered by the same scribe (Boccapaduli) — i. e. the present entry is possibly linked with the next (no. 843). For a discussion of linkage between entries see my Introduction to *CPL*, XVI, particularly Appendix II *The Intricacies of Enregistration: Batches and Drafts*, pp. xli-xlviii

843[1]   **11 December 1501**   *Reg. Lat.* 1114, fo 106[r-v]

To Thomas Dikson, MA, rector of the parish church of Idwy, d. St Andrews. Dispensation — at his supplication — to receive and retain for life, together with the above parish church, one, and without it, any two other benefices, etc. [as above, no. 5].

Litterarum scientia, vite ac morum honestas . . .
L *puccius* / · *B·* / . *B· xxxx Bolis·*

[1] possibly linked with the previous entry; see especially note 1

844   **5**[1] **August 1502**   *Reg. Lat.* 1114, fos 113[v]-114[v]

To Thomas Halkerston, provost of the church of Creithton [also spelt *Creython*][2], d. St Andrews, reservation, constitution and assignment of a pension. This day Thomas — to whom, as he asserts, by apostolic authority, provision had been made (or mandated or granted to be made) of the succentorship of the church of Moray, then vacant *certo modo*, and who had appealed extrajudicially to the apostolic see from the occupation or possession of the succentorship which John Spens, succentor of that church, had acquired, and against whose appeal (which perchance had not yet been committed to anyone) John caused the case which he intended to move against Thomas over the succentorship to be committed to a certain auditor of causes of the apostolic palace, (the citation not yet having been executed) — has (to avoid the later twists and turns of suits, spare labour and expense, and for the sake of peace and for the implementation of a certain honest agreement entered into by himself and John) spontaneously and freely ceded the suit and case and all right belonging to him in or to the succentorship into the pope's hands, leaving John in peaceful possession, and the pope has caused the cession to be admitted. Lest Thomas (who, as he also asserts, holds the *prepositura* of the above church of Creithton) should suffer excessive loss on this account, the pope hereby reserves, constitutes and assigns an annual pension of 45 marks Scots, equivalent to 9 pounds sterling or thereabouts, on the fruits etc. of the succentorship (of which this pension does not allegedly exceed one third) payable (in the town of Edinburgh (*Edinburgi*), d. St Andrews) in full to Thomas for life (or to his specially mandated proctor) by John (who has expressly consented and has specially appointed Alexander of Bologna (*de Bononia*), cleric of Bologna, as his proctor) and by his successors holding the succentorship at the time, each year, one half on the feast of St Martin in November and the other on that of Pentecost. With decree etc. that if John (or one of his successors) fails to make payment on the said feasts, or within the thirty days immediately following, he shall, after this time has elapsed, incur sentence of excommunication, from which he shall be denied absolution, except on the point of death, until he shall have made satisfaction in full or reached agreement in respect of it with Thomas (or his proctor) and if he remains obdurate under that sentence for a further six months, he shall thereupon be deprived in perpetuity of the succentorship, which shall be deemed vacant automatically. Notwithstanding etc.

Executory to the dean of the church of Moray and the archpriest of the church of St Prosper, Collécchio (*de Colliculo*), d. Parma, and the official of St Andrews, or one or two of them, acting in person or by proxy.

Vite ac morum honestas . . . The executory begins: *Hodie dilecto filio Thome Halkerston* . . .
F de parma; L puccius[3] / *F* / *F· xii· x· Sanctor(is)*

[1] date altered from *primo* (in the line, deleted but not initialled) to *secundo* (inserted above the line by the enregistering scribe but not initialled) *nonis Augusti*; *secundo* is written in a different ink: entered later?

[2] spelt thus also in the executory

[3] both names in a different ink (*cf.* above note 1): entered later?

---

845   14 June 1503   *Reg. Lat.* 1114, fos 120ᵛ-121ʳ

Union as below. The pope has learned that the perpetual vicarages of the parish churches of Kyllromayn and Kyllardun, d. Annaghdown, which Magonius Oflachyrdayd, their late perpetual vicar, held while he lived, have become vacant by his death outside the Roman curia and are vacant at present. At a recent petition on the part of Odo Oflacharthyd, canon of Annaghdown, to the pope to unite etc. the vicarages to the canonry and prebend of the church of Annaghdown, which he holds, for as long as he does so — asserting that the annual value of the vicarages together does not exceed 3 marks sterling — the pope hereby unites etc. the vicarages, (vacant as above or howsoever etc.; even if they have been vacant for so long that by the Lateran statutes their collation has lawfully devolved on the apostolic see, etc.), with all rights and appurtenances, to the canonry and prebend, for as long as Odo holds the canonry and prebend; to the effect that he may, on his own authority, in person or by proxy, take possession[1] of the vicarages and the rights and appurtenances aforesaid, and convert their[2] fruits etc. to his own uses and those of the vicarages and retain them for as long as he holds the canonry and prebend, without licence of the local diocesan or of anyone else. Notwithstanding etc. The pope's will is, however, that the vicarages shall not, on account of this union etc., be defrauded of due services and the cure of souls therein shall not be neglected, but that their customary burdens shall be supported; and that on Odo's death or resignation etc. of the canonry and prebend the union etc. shall be dissolved and so deemed and the vicarages shall revert to their original condition and be deemed vacant automatically.

Ad futuram rei memoriam. Decet Romanum pontificem votis illis gratum prestare assensum . . .

S de Castello | · B· | · B· xx Bolis

1 'corporalem' does not occur

2 *illius; recte*: 'illarum'?

846   19 March 1503   *Reg. Lat.* 1114, fos 127ᵛ-128ᵛ

To the dean of the church of Elphin, commission and mandate in favour of Malachy
Macgillakyeran, canon of the monastery *Insule Sancte Trinitatis* [Trinity Island],
Lochlie, OPrem, d. Elphin (who, some time ago, as he asserts, was dispensed by
apostolic authority notwithstanding a defect of birth as the son of a priest, a canon,
<said order>,1 and an unmarried woman, to receive and retain the priorship of the
said monastery, if conferred on him otherwise canonically). It has been referred to
the pope's audience by Malachy that Magonius, abbot of the monastery, has dared to
alienate, dilapidate and dissipate several of its immovable goods and precious
movables in cases not permitted by law. And, as a recent petition on Malachy's part
stated, at one time — following the renewal by Paul II of all papal sentences of
excommunication, suspension and interdict and other ecclesiastical sentences,
censures and pains against simoniacs (his will being that every simoniac, manifest or
occult, should incur them) and his reservation of their absolution and relaxation —
except on the point of death — to himself and his successors — Malachy, wrongly
aspiring to the perpetual vicarage of the parish church of Culdea, d. Elphin, vacant
certo modo, reached a pact and agreement with the then local ordinary that if he
would unite the vicarage to the monastery Malachy would give and pay him a
certain amount of money by reason of the first year's fruits of the vicarage, as he
afterwards did, incurring simony and excommunication and the other sentences,
censures and pains aforesaid. At Malachy's supplication to the pope to absolve him
from simony etc. incurred on this account, and to dispense him on account of
irregularity, if he contracted it by occasion of the foregoing, the pope — considering
that if the above related matters are true, Magonius has rendered himself unworthy
of the rule and administration of the monastery, over which he presides; and wishing
to make provision of a suitable person to the monastery to rule and direct it; and not
having certain knowledge of Malachy's merits and suitability — hereby
commissions and commands the above dean to absolve Malachy, if he so requests,
from simony and excommunication and the other sentences, censures and pains
aforesaid, incurred on this account, for this once only, in the customary form of the
church, having enjoined a salutary penance on him etc., dispense him on account of
irregularity, if he contracted it by occasion of the foregoing, and rehabilitate him on
account of all disability and infamy contracted by him by the said occasion; and, in
the event of this absolution, dispensation and rehabilitation, if Malachy will accuse
Magonius before him and proceed in form of law and, thereafter, to any
extraordinary pain to be regulated by his judgement, having summoned Magonius

and others concerned, make inquiry into the above related matters, and if he finds them to be true, deprive Magonius of the rule and administration of the monastery and remove him from them; and, if this deprivation and removal be carried out by virtue of the presents, inform himself as to Malachy's merits etc., and if he finds him to be capable and suitable for the rule and administration of the monastery — concerning which the pope burdens the dean's conscience — make provision of Malachy to the monastery (whose annual value does not exceed 30 marks sterling and to which this day the pope has commanded by other letters of his that the above perpetual vicarage of Culdea and the perpetual vicarage of the parish church of Kyllamemery,[2] d. Ardagh, whose annual values do not exceed 5 and 6 marks sterling, then vacant *certo modo,* be united etc. to the monastery, over which — if provided thereto by virtue of the presents — he presided), whether vacant then by the said deprivation and removal or at another time howsoever etc., and appoint him abbot, committing to him the care, rule and administration of the monastery in spiritualities and temporalities and causing obedience and reverence to be given him by the convent and customary services and rights by the vassals and other subjects of the monastery. [Curbing] gainsayers etc. Notwithstanding etc. Also the pope dispenses Malachy to be appointed to and preside over the monastery by virtue of the presents, perform and exercise its care etc., and receive and use benediction; notwithstanding the above defect etc. And he grants that Malachy may receive benediction from any catholic bishop of his choice in communion with the apostolic see; and that the bishop concerned may impart it to him. The pope's will is, however, that this shall not be to the prejudice of the bishop of Elphin to whom the monastery is understood to be subject by ordinary law.

Sedes apostolica, pia mater, recurrentibus[3] ad eam post excessum cum humilitate . . .
A de S^{to} Severino / · B· /. B· xxxx Bolis

[1] marginal insertion by the enregistering scribe initialled *B*

[2] seemingly; but only *Kyll-* and *-ry* certain

[3] *sic; recte*: 'recurrentium'?

847   19 April 1503   *Reg. Lat.* 1114, fos 146^v-147^r

To William Jeffrey, rector of the parish church of Withyam,[1] d. Chichester. Dispensation and indult — at his supplication — to receive and retain for life, together with the above parish church, one, and without it, any two other benefices, etc. [as above, no. 3, to '. . . retain them together for life, as above']; and for life, while attending a *studium generale* or residing in the Roman curia or any one of his benefices, not to be bound to reside in his other benefices, etc. [as above, no. 238].

Vite ac morum honestas . . .
L puccius / · B· / . B· Lx Bolis

[1] *Wyth* deleted and initialled *B*

848   5 April 1502   *Reg. Lat.* 1114, fo 184ᵛ

To James, elect of St Andrews, faculty. Some time ago, when the church of St Andrews was vacant by the death of the late archbishop William, outside the Roman curia, the pope, on the advice of the cardinals — lest the said church (by reason of which the archbishop of St Andrews for the time being is understood to be primate of the whole kingdom of Scotland and legate born therein by apostolic privilege) be exposed to the inconvenience of a long vacancy — constituted and appointed James, then in his nineteenth year of age or thereabouts and marked with clerical character only, administrator in spiritualities and temporalities of the said church until he reached the lawful age; and then, on like advice, as soon as he has reached it, made provision of him to the said church thenceforth as from that day, and appointed him archbishop, as is more fully contained in those letters thereupon drawn up.[1] Since, as has been represented to the pope on his part, James is still below the lawful age and only marked with the said character and it often happens that churches and cemeteries of his city and diocese are violated by bloodshed or adultery, which he cannot reconcile for the said reason as well as because the diocese of St Andrews is so large and wide-spread, the pope — at his supplication — by the presents grants faculty to James to reconcile the churches and cemeteries aforesaid by any suitable priest, secular or regular of any order, deputed or nominated by him at the time, as often as opportune, the water having been blessed by him or another bishop beforehand, as the custom is. The pope's will is, however, that this shall not be to the prejudice of the constitution which lays down that this may only be done by bishops;[2] the presents shall only be valid for as long as he shall preside over the said church, even after he has been consecrated archbishop.

Tue devotionis precibus benignum inpartientes assensum . . .
A de Sᵗᵒ Severino / · B· / · B· xxx Bolis·

[1] summarised in *CPL*, XVI, at no. 837
[2] *Cf.* above, no. 411.

849   16 July 1502   *Reg. Lat.* 1114, fos 299ʳ-300ʳ

To John Brady, rector of the parish church of Tana'das [also spelt *Tana'des*],[1] d. St Andrews, dispensation. Some time ago, the pope by other letters of his dispensed him (who then, as he asserted, was litigating over the above parish church — provision of which had been made to him by ordinary authority at another time when vacant *certo modo*, and which he then possessed — in the Roman curia against a certain adversary of his [before][2] a certain auditor of causes of the apostolic palace) to receive and retain for life, together with the above parish church, if he won it, one, and without it, any two other benefices, with cure or otherwise mutually incompatible, even if parish churches or their perpetual vicarages, or dignities, etc. [as above, no. 131, to '. . . as is more fully contained in those letters'].[3] The pope therefore — at his supplication — hereby dispenses him to receive and retain for life, together with the above parish church (which, as he asserts, he holds still), and perchance another incompatible, or even any two other incompatible benefices held by him at the time by the said dispensation, any third benefice, with cure or otherwise incompatible, even if a parish church or its perpetual vicarage, or a dignity, etc. [as above, no. 131].

Vite ac morum honestas . . .
· *A· de S(an)cto Severino* / · *B·* / · *B· Lx Bolis·*

[1] i. e. *Tan(n)adas, Tan(n)ades?*
[2] *contra*; *recte:* 'coram'
[3] above, no. 687

---

850   27 May 1502   *Reg. Lat.* 1114, fos 301ᵛ-303ʳ

To Robert Forman, precentor of the church of Glasgow, papal familiar. Licence and faculty — at his supplication — to him (who is in the service of Johannes Baptista, cardinal priest of S. Crisogono, is also a continual commensal of the pope, and, as he asserts, holds the precentorship of the church of Glasgow) to resign the precentorship, simply or for exchange for another or other, similar or dissimilar, benefice or benefices with any person willing to exchange with him — in which exchange, however, there may not be any illicit pact or simony — into the hands of the local ordinary, or a canon of a metropolitan or other cathedral church, or a person established in an ecclesiastical dignity, to be chosen by himself (or his proctor), outside the Roman curia, without the licence of the apostolic see or of anyone else; and to the ordinary, or canon or person established in a dignity, licence and faculty to receive and admit such resignation and to collate and make provision of the precentorship to a suitable person to be nominated by Robert (or his proctor), even a person holding or expecting benefices, if Robert shall have resigned it simply, and to the person exchanging with him, if Robert shall have resigned it for exchange; also to collate and make provision to Robert of those benefices which the person exchanging with him shall have resigned for exchange, even if canonries and prebends, dignities, *personatus*, administrations, or offices in cathedral even metropolitan, or collegiate churches, even if the dignities, etc. should be customarily elective and have cure of souls, provided that these dignities be not major *post pontificalem* in metropolitan or cathedral churches or principal in collegiate churches, and provided that the benefices of the person exchanging with him and not having a like faculty be not generally reserved to apostolic disposition; and to do and execute whatever is necessary and convenient in connection with the foregoing. Notwithstanding etc. The pope's will is, however, that if the fruits etc. of the precentorship exceed 24 gold florins of the camera in annual value, those collating it and he to whom it is collated, and — if resignations are made for exchange and the fruits etc. of the benefices then collated to Robert be unequal and of greater value, even if the inequality does not exceed 24 such florins — the above collators and Robert, are to inform (*certificare*) the personnel (*gentes*) of the apostolic camera, or the collectors or sub-collectors of the fruits etc. due to the camera appointed in those parts for the time being, within the time expressed in the letters of Sixtus IV and Innocent VIII published in this regard, of the names and surnames of the persons, names of the benefices collated to Robert in exchange, and of the days such collations were made; otherwise the precentorship and benefices thus collated shall be deemed vacant automatically.

Grata familiaritatis obsequia . . .
F de parma / · B· / . B. xxx Bolis·

851   11 December 1501   *Reg. Lat.* 1115, fo 37[r-v]

To James Kyneragy,[1] rector of the parish church of Kyrbforthyr [also spelt *Kyrkforthyr*], d. St Andrews. Dispensation — at his supplication — to receive and retain for life, together with the above parish church, one, and without them, any two other benefices, etc. [as above, no. 5].

Vite ac morum honestas . . .
S de Castello / · B· / . B· xxxx Bolis·

[1] or *Kyncragy*

852   1 January 1503   *Reg. Lat.* 1116, fos 85[r]-86[r]

To the abbot of the monastery of Molana (*de Insula Sancti Mellanfyd*), d. Lismore, and the dean and Philip Oketk, canon, of the church of Lismore, mandate in favour of Philip Whyte, cleric, d. Cloyne. The pope has learned that a canonry of the church of Cloyne and the prebend of Chylmodonoc,[1] in the same are vacant *certo modo* at present and have been vacant for so long that by the Lateran statutes their collation has lawfully devolved on the apostolic see, although Richard Giraldi Willelmi de Geraldinis, who bears himself as a cleric, has detained the canonry and prebend without any title or support of law, temerariously and *de facto*, for a certain time, as he still does. He hereby commands that the above three (or two or one of them), if, having summoned Richard and others concerned, they find the canonry and prebend, whose annual value does not exceed 24 marks sterling, to be vacant (howsoever etc.), shall collate and assign them, (even if specially reserved etc.), with plenitude of canon law and all rights and appurtenances, to Philip, inducting him etc. having removed Richard and any other unlawful detainer and causing Philip (or his proctor) to be received as a canon of the church of Cloyne, with plenitude of canon law, and the fruits etc., rights and obventions of the canonry and prebend to be delivered to him. [Curbing] gainsayers etc. Notwithstanding etc.

Vite ac morum honestas . . .
S de Castello /· B· / · B· xv· Septimo Id(us) Januar(ii) anno Vndecimo. [7 January 1503], *Bolis·*

853   7 September 1502   *Reg. Lat.* 1116, fo 88^r-v

To Florence Ogervan and Maurice Macvaney, canons of the church of Clonfert, and the official of Clonfert, mandate in favour of John Magnay,[1] cleric, d. Clonfert (who, as he asserts, suffers a defect of birth as the son of a priest and a married woman). The pope has learned that the perpetual vicarage of the parish church of Donderey, d. Clonfert, is vacant *certo modo* at present and has been vacant for so long that by the Lateran statutes its collation has lawfully devolved on the apostolic see, although Maurus Macvaney, who bears himself as a priest, has detained it with no title and no support of law, temerariously and *de facto*, for several years, as he still does. He hereby commands that the above three (or two or one of them), shall collate and assign the vicarage, whose annual value does not exceed 4 marks sterling, if, having summoned[2] Maurus and others concerned, it is vacant (howsoever etc.); even if specially reserved etc., with all rights and appurtenances, to John, inducting him etc. having removed Maurus and any other unlawful detainer and causing John to be admitted to the vicarage and its fruits etc., rights and obventions to be delivered to him. [Curbing] gainsayers etc. Notwithstanding etc. Also the pope dispenses John to receive and retain the vicarage, if conferred on him by virtue of the presents, notwithstanding the said defect etc.

Vite ac morum honestas . . .
S de Castello / Jo / Jo. . x. Tertio decimo Kl' Januar' anno Vndecimo [20 December 1502], *Eps' Terracinen.*

[1] or *Maguay*

[2] *vocato; recte*: 'vocatis'? The Latin hereabouts is unusually constructed.

854 16 May 1503 *Reg. Lat.* 1116, fos 161^r-163^r

Provision, in *forma gratiosa*, of Augustinus Grimaldus, Genoese, canon of the monastery of St Th(e)odorus, OSA, Lateran Congregation, and, as he asserts, continual commensal of Federicus, cardinal deacon of St Theodorus, to the parish church, called archpresbytery, of St Mary, Treglio (*del Treglo*), d. Chieti, vacant at the apostolic see.

The 'bishop of Worcester' is one of the three mandataries of the executory. Entry otherwise of no interest to the Calendar.

Religionis zelus, vite ac morum honestas . . . The executory begins: *Hodie dilecto filio Augustino Grimaldo* . . .
F de parma; L. puccius / · B / . B· xxx xx decimo Kl' Junij anno Vndecimo [23 May 1503], . *Bolis*

855 25 March 1503 *Reg. Lat.* 1116, fos 276^r-277^v

Provision, in *forma gratiosa*, of Antonius Mangneri, (who, as he asserts, is a continual commensal familiar of M. Fernandus Poncetus, scriptor and familiar of the pope), to the rectory of the chapel of Sts Clarus and Blasius, ?Monfavrey (*Montisfabritii*), d. Lyon, vacant at the apostolic see.

The 'bishop of Worcester' is one of the three mandataries of the executory. Entry otherwise of no interest to the Calendar.

Vite ac morum honestas . . . The executory begins: *Hodie dilecto filio Antonio (?)Mangeri* . . .
. *F de parma; . L. puccius / Jo / Jo. Grat(is) pro deo Sexto Id(us) Aprilis anno undecimo* [8 April 1503], *Eps' Terracinen'*

856 19 April 1503 *Reg. Lat.* 1117, fos 13^v-14^v

To William Tactorm', perpetual chaplain at the altar of B. Mary in the crypt (*criptis*) of the church of London. Dispensation and indult — at his supplication — to him, who, as he asserts, holds the perpetual chaplaincy founded at the above altar by the late William Say (then dean of the church), to receive and retain for life, together with the above chaplaincy, which is incompatible with another incompatible benefice, one, and without them, any two other benefices, with cure or otherwise mutually incompatible, etc. [as above, no. 3, to '. . . retain them together for life, as above']; and for life, while residing in the Roman curia or any one of his benefices or attending a *studium generale*, not to be bound to reside personally in his other benefices, etc. [as above, no. 238].

Vite ac morum honestas . . .
L. puccius / · B· / · B· Lx Bolis

857   19 April 1503   *Reg. Lat.* 1117, fos 14ᵛ-15ʳ

To William Baker, canon of the monastery of B. Mary, Gyseburn'[1] [also spelt *Giseburn'*], OSA, d. York. Dispensation — at his supplication — to him, who, as he asserts, is expressly professed of the above order,[2] to receive and retain any benefice, with or without cure, usually held by secular clerics, etc. [as above, no. 32, to '. . . another, similar or dissimilar, benefice'], usually assigned to secular clerics. Notwithstanding etc.

Religionis zelus, vite ac morum honestas . . .
L. puccius / · B· / · B· xxx Bolis·

[1] the 'y' reworked
[2] This information comes from a notwithstanding clause.

858   7 February 1503   *Reg. Lat.* 1117, fos 35ᵛ-36ᵛ

To William Irelond, rector of the parish church of the Holy Cross, Cuxham, d. Lincoln. Dispensation — at his supplication — to receive and retain for life, together with the above parish church, one, and without it, any two other benefices, etc. [as above, no. 3].

Vite ac morum honestas . . .
L· puccius / · B· / . B· L. Bolis·

859   10 April 1503   *Reg. Lat.* 1117, fo 44ʳ⁻ᵛ

To Thomas Tanfeld, prior of the monastery, usually governed by a prior, of B. Mary, Thornholme *alias* Thornh(a)m,[1] OSA, d. Lincoln. Dispensation — at his supplication — to receive together with the priorship of the above monastery, one, and without it, any two other regular benefices, with or without cure, of the said order, or with one of them, or without them, one secular benefice, with or without cure, etc. [as above, no. 707].

Religionis zelus, vite ac morum honestas . . .
L. puccius / P / . P. L. Thomarotius:

1 MS: *Thornhm'*

860 —[1] *Reg. Lat.* 1117, fo 67[r-v]

Unfinished dispensation *ad duo* (at the least: there might, for instance, have been an indult for non-residence as well) addressed to and in favour of Edmund Mandvell, MTheol, perpetual vicar of the parish church of Burnham, d. Lincoln. Stops abruptly in mid-clause, in middle of *dispositiva*: . . . *aut talia mixtim* [ends]. Proem: *Litterarum sientia,*[2] *vite ac morum honestas* . . . Abbreviator: L. puccius No magistral initial.

Stops with first word of third line of second page (the rest of which is blank). Unclear why abandoned: not deleted; no explanatory note.

Belongs, probably, to the eleventh year (26, viii. 1502-18. viii. 1503): thus the *liber* and the adjacent letters. Cannot be matched with any other letter in an extant chancery register; or with an entry in the *rubricellae* of registers now lost. (This fragment is rubricated at *Ind.* 343, fo 112[r]). Probably the fully enregistered copy was in a lost register which was only incompletely rubricated (*cf. CPL* XVI, p. lii, note 21). Possibly the letter was never expedited, at least by the chancery.

1 dating clause wanting
2 *sic; recte*: 'scientia'

861 11 June 1503 *Reg. Lat.* 1117, fo 68[r-v]

To John Kynton, professor OFM and of theology. Dispensation — at his supplication — to receive and retain any benefice, with or without cure, usually held by secular clerics, etc. [as above, no. 32, to '. . . another, similar or dissimilar, benefice'], usually assigned to secular clerics. Notwithstanding etc. and [notwithstanding] the constitutions of Otto and Ottobuono formerly legates of the apostolic see in the kingdom of England etc.[1]

Religionis zelus, vite[2] *ac morum honestas . . .*
L. puccius / P / P. xxxx. Thomarotius:

1 The inclusion of these constitutions gives Kington the option of holding his secular benefice in

England.

² *sic*; '. . . litterarum scientia, vite . . . ' would be appropriate for a graduate

862   2 June 1503   *Reg. Lat.* 1117, fos 68ᵛ-70ʳ

To Richard Bulkeley, LLB, archdeacon <of Bangor>¹ in the church of Bangor, dispensation. Some time ago, Innocent VIII by his letters dispensed him to receive and retain for life, together with the archdeaconry of Meryonyth' in the church of Bangor (which, as he asserted, he was then holding), one, and without it, any two other benefices, etc. [as above, no. 131, to '. . . as is more fully contained in those letters'].² The pope therefore — at his supplication — hereby further dispenses him (who, as he asserts, <having resigned the archdeaconry [of Meryonyth'] acquired the archdeaconry of Bangor which was canonically collated to him while vacant *certo modo*>³ and holds it and the parish church of Chedill, d. Coventry and Lichfield, by the said dispensation) to receive and retain for life, together with the archdeaconry <held>⁴ and the parish church, or with any two other incompatible benefices held by him at the time by the said dispensation, any third benefice, etc. [as above, no. 131].

Litterarum sientia, ⁵ *vite ac morum honestas . . .*
L. puccius / P / · P· Lxx Thomarotius:

¹ in the line: *Meryonyth'* deleted and initialled . *B.*; in the margin: . *B.* then (in a different hand) *Bangorie* then *Cassatu(m) et corectu(m) de Man(da)to R(everendissimi) p(atris) d(omini) A(ndree) e(pisco)pi cotronen' reg(en)t(is) Bolis*

² summarized in *CPL*, XIV on p. 321

³ in the line: *dictum archidiaconatum* [i. e. Meryonyth'] *adhuc* deleted and initialled . *B.* twice; in the margin opposite: . *B* then (in the different hand) *dicto archidiaconatu* [i. e. Meryonyth'] *dimmisso archidiaconatum Bangorie in dicta ecclesia tunc certo [modo] vacantem canonice tibi collatum assecutus* then *Bolis*. This correction is of a piece with the first (note 1); but, unusually, the authority is not repeated.

⁴ *obtento* (in the different hand) inserted in the margin, sandwiched between . *B.* and *Bolis*; again, authority not repeated

⁵ *sic*; *recte*: 'scientia'

863   27 May 1503   *Reg. Lat.* 1117, fos 70ʳ-71ᵛ

To Richard Spryngo, prior of the monastery, usually governed by a prior, of Woyspiynge [also spelt *Woispiynge*], OSA, d. Bath and Wells, dispensation. Some time ago, Innocent VIII by his letters dispensed him to receive and retain *in commendam* for life, together with the priorship of the above monastery (which, as he asserted, he was then holding), or with any other priory or monastery over which he perchance presided, of the aforesaid order, held by him at the time, or without it, any benefice, with or without cure, usually held by secular clerics, even if a parish church or its perpetual vicarage, or a chantry, free chapel, hospital or annual service, usually assigned to secular clerics in title of a perpetual ecclesiastical benefice, and of [(?)lay][1] patronage and of whatsoever tax or annual value, if he obtained it otherwise canonically, to resign it, simply or for exchange, as often as he pleased,[2] and in its place receive, another, similar or dissimilar, benefice, with or without cure, usually held by secular clerics, and retain it *in commendam* for life, as above, as is more fully contained in those letters. The pope therefore — at his supplication — hereby dispenses him (who,<as he asserts>,[3] holds by the said dispensation the above priorship, which is an office, and also the perpetual vicarage of the parish church of Vurlle, said diocese) to receive together with the priorship and vicarage, one, and without them, any three other regular benefices, with or without cure, of the aforesaid or any other order, or with one or two of them, or without them, one secular benefice, with or without cure, usually held by secular clerics, even if the regular benefices should be priories, *prepositure, prepositatus*, dignities, *personatus*, administrations or offices in cathedral, even metropolitan, churches, of his order, and the dignities be major *post pontificalem* in cathedral, even metropolitan, churches, or conventual, and the secular benefice be a parish church or its perpetual vicarage, or a chantry, free chapel, hospital or annual service, usually assigned to secular clerics in title of a perpetual ecclesiastical benefice, and even if the dignities etc. should be customarily elective and have cure of souls, if he obtains them otherwise canonically, and to retain whichever one of the regular benefices he chooses, even if it be a dignity major *post pontificalem* or conventual, or a claustral office, *in titulum*, and the other two regular benefices, which may not be suchlike, or the secular benefice, *in commendam*, for life; to resign them, at once or successively, simply or for exchange, as often as he pleases, and cede the commend, and in their place receive [up to three] other, similar or dissimilar, regular benefices, of the aforesaid or any other order, or with one or two of them, or without them, one secular benefice, with or without cure, and retain whichever one of the regular benefices he chooses *in titulum*, and with it the other two, which may not be conventual dignities or claustral offices, or the secular benefice, *in commendam*, also for life, as above; he may — due and customary burdens of the benefices retained *in commendam* having been supported — make disposition of the rest of their fruits etc. just as those holding them *in titulum* could and ought to do, alienation of immovable goods and precious movables being however forbidden. Notwithstanding etc. With the proviso that the benefices retained *in commendam* shall not, on this account, be defrauded of due services and the cure of souls therein ([if] any) shall not be neglected; but that their aforesaid burdens shall be supported.

Religionis zelus, vite ac morum honestas . . .
L puccius / P / P· Lxx Thomarotius:

[1] *laicorum* (required here?) deleted (strangely) but not initialled
[2] *et commende huiusmodi cedere* deleted and initialled *P*.
[3] marginal insertion by the enregistering scribe initialled *P*

864   22 July 1503   *Reg. Lat.* 1117, fos 91ᵛ-92ᵛ

To John Podynger, LLB, rector of the parish church of Aldaham, d. London.
Dispensation and indult — at his supplication — to receive and retain for life,
together with the above parish church, one, and without it, any two other benefices,
etc. [as above, no. 3, to '. . . retain them together for life, as above']; and also for life,
while residing in the Roman curia or any one of his benefices or attending a *studium
generale*, not to be bound to reside personally in his other benefices, etc. [as above,
no. 238].

Litterarum scientia, vite ac morum honestas . . .
p. de planca / · B· / · B· Lx· Bolis·

865   26 November 1502   *Reg. Lat.* 1117, fos 111ʳ-112ʳ

To William Eduard, MA, canon of London. ¹ Dispensation and indult — at his
supplication — to him, who, as he asserts, holds a canonry and prebend of the
church of London, to receive and retain for life any two benefices, with cure or
otherwise mutually incompatible, etc. [as above, no. 3, to '. . . retain them together
for life, as above']; and also for life, while residing in the Roman curia or any one of
his benefices or attending a *studium generale*, not to be bound to reside personally in
his other benefices, nor to be liable to be compelled by anyone to do so against his
will. Notwithstanding etc. With the proviso that the incompatible benefices in
question shall not, on this account, be defrauded of due services and the cure of souls
therein shall not be neglected; but that the customary burdens of those benefices in
which he shall not reside shall be supported.

Litterarum scientia, vite ac morum honestas . . .
[-]² / · B· / · B· Lx· Bolis·

¹ *Bondonien.; recte*: 'Londonien'.
² no abbreviator's name

866   9 September 1502   *Reg. Lat.* 1117, fos 120ᵛ-121ᵛ

To John Beyto, MA, rector of the parish church of Stokchertte, d. Winchester.
Dispensation and indult — at his supplication — to receive and retain for life,
together with the above parish church, one, and without it, any two other benefices,
etc. [as above, no. 3, to '. . . retain them together for life, as above']; and for life,
while attending a *studium generale* or residing in the Roman curia or any one of his

benefices, not to be bound to reside in his other benefices, etc. [as above, no. 238, to '. . . shall be supported']. Given at Nepi.

Litterarum scientia, vite ac morum honestas . . .
L puccius / F / F· Lx Sanctor(is)

867   30 December 1502   *Reg. Lat.* 1117, fo 145^{r-v}

To John Warde, monk of the monastery of St Mary, Coventry (*de Conventa*), OSB, d. Coventry and Lichfield. Dispensation — at his supplication — to him, who, as he asserts, is expressly professed of the above order,[1] to receive and retain any benefice, with or without cure, usually held by secular clerics, etc. [as above, no. 32].

Religionis zelus, vite ac morum honestas . . .
F· de parma / · B· / · B· xxx Bolis·

[1] This information comes from a notwithstanding clause.

868[1]   **21 May 1503**   *Reg. Lat.* 1117, fos 169^r-170^r

To John (?)Brereton,[2] cleric, d. Coventry and Lichfield, dispensation. Some time ago, the pope by other letters of his dispensed him — then a scholar, as he asserted, in his fifteenth year of age — to receive and retain — as soon as he is in his sixteenth year and has been duly marked with clerical character — any benefice, with cure or otherwise incompatible or priestly, even if it should be a parish church or its perpetual vicarage, or a chantry, free chapel, hospital or annual service, usually assigned to secular clerics in title of a perpetual benefice, or a dignity, *personatus*, administration or office in a cathedral, even metropolitan, or collegiate church, even if the dignity should be major *post pontificalem* in a cathedral, even metropolitan, church, or principal in a collegiate church, and the dignity etc. should be customarily elective and have cure of souls, if he obtained it otherwise canonically, to resign it, simply or for exchange, as often as he pleased, and in its place receive and retain another, similar or dissimilar, benefice, with cure or otherwise incompatible or priestly, as is more fully contained in those letters.[3] The pope therefore — at his supplication — hereby further dispenses him (who, as he asserts, was afterwards duly marked with clerical character and is of noble birth and in his nineteenth year) to receive and retain for life, together with the one benefice, with cure or otherwise incompatible, which perchance he holds by the said dispensation, as above, one, and without them, any two other benefices, etc. [as above, no. 3, to '. . . retain them together for life, as above']. Notwithstanding the above defect of age etc. With the proviso that the benefice perchance held and other incompatible benefices in question shall not, on this account, be defrauded of due services, and the cure of souls in the benefice perchance held and (if any) the other incompatible benefices aforesaid shall not be neglected.

Nobilitas generis, vite ac morum honestas . . .
L. puccius / · B· / . B. Lxx Bolis

[1] The engrossment is British Library, Stowe Charter 582. (I am indebted to the Keeper, Dr D. P. Waley, for this reference.)

[2] the 'e's overwritten and indistinct

[3] Not traced. A dispensation to *Joannes Brereton*, described as *ad incompatibilia* is entered in the Index, transcribed in *CPL*, XVI, at no. 1424 .

869   21 May 1503   *Reg. Lat.* 1117, fos 170^v-171^v

To William Coventry, rector of the parish church of Manyngsford, d. Salisbury. Dispensation — at his supplication — to receive and retain for life, together with the above parish church, one, and without it, any two other benefices, etc. [as above, no. 3].

Vite ac morum honestas . . .
L. puccius / · B· / . B· L. Bolis

870   25 May 1503   *Reg. Lat.* 1117, fos 171^v-172^v

To John Levokenore, rector of the parish church of B. Mary, Brodewater, d. Chichester. Dispensation and indult — at his supplication — to receive and retain for life, together with the above parish church, one, and without it, any two other benefices, etc. [as above, no. 3, to '. . . retain them together for life, as above']; and also for life, while residing in the Roman curia or any one of his benefices or attending a *studium generale,* not to be bound to reside personally in his other benefices, etc. [as above, no. 238].

Vite ac morum honestas . . .
L. puccius / · B· / ₁ B· Lx Bolis

871   15 April 1503   *Reg. Lat.* 1117, fo 193^r-v

To Thomas Starkey, canon of the monastery of Tunbrigge, OSA, d. Rochester.

Dispensation — at his supplication — to him, who, as he asserts, is expressly professed of the above order,[1] to receive and retain any benefice, with or without cure, usually held by secular clerics, etc. [as above, no. 32, to '. . . another, similar or dissimilar, benefice'], usually assigned to secular clerics. Notwithstanding etc.

Religionis zelus, vite ac morum honestas . . .
F· Bregion[2] */ P· / · P· xxx· Thomarotius:*

[1] This information comes from a notwithstanding clause.

[2] *sic*: usually 'Bregeon'

872   26 November 1502   *Reg. Lat.* 1117, fos 206ʳ-207ᵛ

Union etc. At a recent petition on the part of Thomas Hare, LLD, canon of the church of B. Mary in the Fields (*de Campis*), d. Norwich, the pope hereby unites etc. the perpetual vicarage of the parish church of B. Mary, Twykenh(a)m,[1] d. London, (whose annual value does not exceed 24 gold ducats of the camera), to the canonry and prebend <of the said church in the Fields>[2], which he holds together with the above vicarage, for as long as he holds the canonry and prebend, to the effect that Thomas, in person or by proxy, may, on his own authority, take and retain corporal possession of the vicarage and its rights and appurtenances, for as long as he holds the canonry and prebend, and convert its fruits etc. to his own uses and those of the vicarage and the canonry and prebend without licence of the local diocesan or of anyone else. Notwithstanding etc. The pope's will is, however, that the vicarage shall not, on account of this union etc., be defrauded of due services and the cure of souls therein shall not be neglected, but that its customary burdens shall be supported; and that on Thomas's death or resignation etc. of the canonry and prebend the union etc. shall be dissolved and so deemed and the vicarage shall revert to its original condition and be deemed vacant automatically.

Ad futuram rey memoriam. Ex iniu[n]cto nobis desuper apostolice servitutis officio ad ea libenter intendimus . . .
p. de planca / Jo / Jo. xxxv. Eps' Terracinen'

[1] MS: *Twykenhm'*

[2] *ac ipsius ecclesie de Campis* inserted in the margin, initialled *Jo* twice; *et dictos*, deleted and initialled *Jo* in the line

873   24 January 1499[1]   *Reg. Lat.* 1117, fos 207ᵛ-209ʳ

Union etc. At a recent petition on the part of William Haryngton, LLD, canon of

London, the pope hereby unites etc. the parish church of Great Langton (*Magna Langtona*),[2] d. York, (whose annual value does not exceed 36 gold florins of the camera), to the canonry and prebend of Iseldon *alias* Islington[3] in the church of London, which he holds together with the above parish church, for as long as he holds the canonry and prebend, to the effect that William, in person or by proxy, may, on his own authority, take and retain corporal possession of the parish church and its rights and appurtenances, for as long as he holds the canonry and prebend, and convert its fruits etc. to his own uses and those of the canonry and prebend and the parish church without licence of the local diocesan or of anyone else. Notwithstanding etc. The pope's will is, however, that the parish church shall not, on account of this union etc., be defrauded of due services and the cure of souls therein shall not be neglected, but that its customary burdens shall be supported; and that on William's death or resignation etc. of the canonry and prebend the union etc. shall be dissolved and so deemed and the parish church shall revert to its original condition and be deemed vacant automatically.

Ad futuram rey memoriam. Romanum decet pontificem votis illis gratum prestare assensum . . .
L. pucius[4] / *Jo* / *Jo. xxxv. Eps' Terracinen'*

[1] *quingentesimo*, deleted and initialled *Jo.* , occurs after *millesimo*

[2] also occurs variously abridged: *M(agna) La'tona, M(agna) Langtona, M(agna) La(ngtona)*

[3] *Iseldon alias Islington* is written (by the enregistering scribe) in darker ink apparently over existing writing now obscured: entered later?

[4] *sic*; the abbreviator's name and the magistral initial are in darker ink (*cf.* note 3): entered later?

874   1 April 1503   *Reg. Lat.* 1117, fos 213[r]-214[r]

To Thomas Sawndurs, prior of the priory of Sts Peter and Paul, Chacombe (*de Chaconba*), OSA, d. Lincoln. Dispensation — at his supplication — to receive together with the said priory, one, and without it, any two other regular benefices, with or without cure, of the aforesaid or any other order, or with one of them, or without them, one benefice, with or without cure, usually held by secular clerics, even if the regular benefices should be priories, *prepositure, prepositatus*, dignities, *personatus*, administrations or offices, even in metropolitan, or other cathedral, churches, of the said order, and the dignities should be major *post pontificalem* in metropolitan, or other cathedral, churches, and the secular benefice should be a parish church or its perpetual vicarage, or a chantry, free chapel, hospital or annual service, usually assigned to secular clerics in title of a perpetual ecclesiastical benefice, or a canonry and prebend in a collegiate church, or a combination, even if the priories etc. should be customarily elective and have cure of souls, if he obtains them otherwise canonically, and, for life, to retain whichever one of the regular benefices he chooses, even if it should be a priory or other conventual dignity or a claustral office, *in titulum*, and the other regular benefice, which may not be conventual or claustral, or the secular benefice, *in commendam*, to resign them, at once or successively, simply or for exchange, as often as he pleases, and cede the commend, and in their place receive up to two other, similar or dissimilar, regular benefices, of the aforesaid or any other order, or with one of them, or without them, one benefice, with or without cure, usually held by secular clerics, and to retain whichever one of the regular benefices he chooses *in titulum*, and the other regular benefice — provided it be not a priory or other conventual dignity or a claustral office — or the secular benefice, *in commendam*, for life as above; he may — due and customary burdens of the benefice retained *in commendam* having been supported — make disposition of the rest of its fruits etc. just as those holding it *in titulum* could and ought to do, alienation of immovable goods and precious movables being however forbidden. Notwithstanding etc. With the proviso that the benefice retained *in commendam* shall not, on this account, be defrauded of due services and the cure of souls therein (if any) shall not be neglected, but that its aforesaid burdens shall be supported.

Religionis zelus, vite ac morum honestas . . .
F de parma / · B· / · B· L. Bolis

875   26 November 1502   *Reg. Lat.* 1117, fos 224^V-225^V

To John Lunbard, perpetual chaplain, called cantor, at the altar of B. Mary the Virgin in the parish church of Ledbury, d. Hereford. Dispensation — at his supplication — to receive and retain for life, together with the chaplaincy at the above altar, which is incompatible with another incompatible benefice, one, and without it, any two other benefices, with cure or otherwise mutually incompatible, etc. [as above, no. 3].

Vite ac morum honestas . . .
L puccius / · B· / . B· L. Bolis

876   26 November 1502   *Reg. Lat.* 1117, fos 225^V-226^V

To William Brenex, perpetual vicar of the parish church of St Peter, Hereford. Dispensation — at his supplication — to receive and retain for life, together with the perpetual vicarage of the above parish church, one, and without it, any two other benefices, etc. [as above, no. 3].

Vite ac morum honestas . . .
L puccius / · B· / · B· L. Bolis

877   26 November 1502   *Reg. Lat.* 1117, fos 230^r-231^r

Union etc. At a recent petition on the part of Peter, abbot of the monastery of B.
Mary and St John the Baptist, Netteley, OSA, d. Lincoln, the pope hereby unites etc.
the parish church of Lamport, d. Lincoln, (which he was holding[1] *in titulum vel
commendam* by apostolic concession and dispensation and whose annual value does
not exceed 40 marks in money of those parts, equivalent to 120 gold ducats of the
camera or thereabouts) to the above monastery, for as long as he presides over it, to
the effect that abbot Peter, in person or by proxy, may, on his own authority, take and
retain corporal possession of the church and its rights and appurtenances, for as long
as he presides over the monastery, and convert its fruits etc. to his own uses and
those of the church and monastery without licence of the local diocesan or of anyone
else. Notwithstanding etc. The pope's will is, however, that the church shall not, on
account of this union etc., be defrauded of due services and the cure of souls therein
shall not be neglected, but that its customary burdens shall be supported; and that on
abbot Peter's death or resignation etc. of the monastery the union etc. shall be
dissolved and so deemed and the church shall revert to its original condition
automatically.

*Ad futuram rey memoriam. Ex iniuncto nobis desuper apostolice servitutis officio ad
ea libenter intendimus . . .*
N· de castello / · B· / · B· xxxv Bolis·

[1] *obtinebat* (not 'obtinet' as usual)

878   29 November 1502   *Reg. Lat.* 1117, fos 234^v-235^r

To William Cumberton, rector of the parish church of St Andrew, Russal, d.
Salisbury. Dispensation — at his supplication — to receive and retain for life,
together with the above parish church, one, and without it, any two other benefices,
etc. [as above, no. 3].

Vite ac morum honestas . . .
F de parma / Jo / Jo. L. Eps' Terracinen'

879   18 October 1502   *Reg. Lat.* 1117, fos 247^v-249^r

To John Milde, perpetual chaplain at the altar of All Saints in the church of York,
dispensation and indult. Some time ago, the pope by other letters of his dispensed
him to receive and retain for life, together with the parish church of Skerpenbek

[also spelt *Skerp'ebek*], d. York, (which, as he asserted, he was then holding), one, and without them, any two other benefices, etc. [as above, no. 131, to '. . . as is more fully contained in those letters']. The pope — at his supplication — hereby further dispenses John and indulges him (who, as he asserts, holds by the said dispensation the church of Skerpenbek still and also the perpetual chaplaincy at the above altar in the church of York — in whose statutes and customs it is said to be expressly laid down that the holder of the chaplaincy cannot hold another benefice, with or without cure, and is bound to reside personally in it — which was canonically collated to him at another time while vacant *certo modo*) to receive and retain, together with the church of Skerpenbek and chaplaincy aforesaid, or without them, with any two other incompatible benefices, for which he is dispensed as above, any third incompatible benefice, even if a parish church, etc. [as above, no. 131, to '. . . retain it for life, as above ']; and for life, while residing in the Roman curia or any one of his benefices or attending a *studium generale*, not to be bound to reside personally in his other benefices, nor to be liable to be compelled by anyone to do so against his will. Notwithstanding etc. and [notwithstanding] statutes and customs etc. of the church of York etc. With the proviso that this third incompatible benefice shall not, on this account, be defrauded of due services and the cure of souls shall not be neglected; but that customary burdens of those benefices in which he shall not reside shall be supported.

Vite ac morum honestas . . .
p. de planca / Jo / Jo. Lxxx. Eps' Terracinen'

880   18 October 1502   *Reg. Lat.* 1117, fos 249^V-250^V

To Thomas Bunt, LLB, rector of the parish church of Cholocomb [also spelt *Cholocob'*], d. Exeter. Dispensation and indult — at his supplication — to receive and retain for life, together with the above parish church, one, and without it, any two other benefices, etc. [as above, no. 3, to '. . . retain them together for life, as above']; and for life, while residing in the Roman curia or any one of his benefices or attending a *studium generale*, not to be bound [to reside]^1 personally in his other benefices, etc. [as above, no. 238].

Litterarum scientia, vite ac morum honestas . . .
L puccius / Jo / Jo. Lx. Eps' Terracinen'

^{1} 'residere' wanting

881   12 November 1502   *Reg. Lat.* 1117, fos 252^r-253^r

To Stephen Whytraw, MA, rector of the parish church of B. Mary, Estvokyngton, d.

Exeter. Dispensation and indult — at his supplication — to receive and retain for life, together with the above parish church, one, and without it, any two other benefices, etc. [as above, no. 3, to '. . . retain them together for life, as above']; and for life, while residing in the Roman curia or any one of his benefices or attending a *studium generale*, not to be bound to reside personally in his other benefices, etc. [as above, no. 238].

Litterarum scientia, vite ac morum honestas . . .
L pucius[1] */ · B· / . B· Lx Bolis*

[1] *sic*

882   5 November 1502   *Reg. Lat.* 1117, fos 253ʳ-254ʳ

To William Bisshop' *alias* Leynham, prior of the church of Rochester, OSB. Dispensation — at his supplication — to receive together with the priorship of the above church, or with a monastery or any other regular benefice or ecclesiastical office of the said order held by him at the time, or without it, any other benefice, with or without cure, usually held by secular clerics, even if a parish church or its perpetual vicarage, or a chantry, free chapel, hospital or annual service, usually assigned to secular clerics in title of a perpetual ecclesiastical benefice, and of lay patronage and of whatsoever tax or annual value, if he obtains it otherwise canonically, and to retain it *in commendam* for life, to resign it, simply or for exchange, when he pleases, and cede the commend and in its place receive another, similar or dissimilar, benefice, with or without cure, usually assigned to secular clerics, and retain it *in commendam* for life, as above; he may — due and customary burdens of the benefice retained *in commendam* having been supported — make disposition of the rest of its fruits etc. just as those holding it *in titulum* could and ought to do, alienation of immovable goods and precious movables being however forbidden. Notwithstanding etc. With the proviso that the benefice retained *in commendam* shall not, on this account, be defrauded of due services and the cure of souls therein (if any) shall not be neglected; but that its aforesaid burdens shall be supported.

Religionis zelus, vite ac morum honestas . . .
. N. de Castello / · B· / · B· L. Bolis

883   17 January 1503   *Reg. Lat.* 1117, fo 283ʳ⁻ᵛ

To Laurence Dobyll, rector of the parish church of Southbradon, d. Bath and Wells.

Dispensation — at his supplication — to receive and retain for life, together with the above parish church, one, and without it, any two other benefices, etc. [as above, no. 3].

Vite ac morum honestas . . .
L. puccius / · B· / . B. L. Bolis

884   17 January 1503   *Reg. Lat.* 1117, fos 284ʳ-285ʳ

To William Chechester, rector of the parish church of Arlyngton, d. Exeter. Dispensation and indult — at his supplication — to receive and retain for life, together with the above parish church, one, and without it, any two other benefices, etc. [as above, no. 3, to '. . . retain them together for life, as above']; and for life, while residing in the Roman curia or any one of his benefices or attending a *studium generale*, not to be bound to reside personally in his other benefices, etc. [as above, no. 238, to '. . . Notwithstanding etc. ']. With the proviso that the above church and other incompatible and other benefices shall not be neglected[1]; but that customary burdens of those benefices in which he shall not reside shall be supported.

Vite ac morum honestas . . .
L. puccius / · B· / · B· Lx Bolis

[1] cure of souls is not mentioned explicitly

885   17 January 1503   *Reg. Lat.* 1117, fos 285ʳ-286ʳ

To James Rogers, LLB, rector of the parish church of Ffalley, d. Lincoln. Dispensation and indult — at his supplication — to receive and retain for life, together with the above parish church, one, and without it, any two other benefices, etc. [as above, no. 3, to '. . . retain them together for life, as above']; and for life, while residing in the Roman curia or any one of his benefices or attending a *studium generale*, not to be bound to reside personally in his other benefices, etc. [as above, no. 238].

Litterarum sientia,[1] vite ac morum honestas . . .
L. puccius / · B· / · B· Lx Bolis

[1] sic

886   17 January 1503   *Reg. Lat.* 1117, fos 286ʳ-287ʳ

To John Jennyn,[1] LLD, perpetual vicar of the parish church of Quenecauunell,[2] d.

Bath and Wells. Dispensation — at his supplication — to receive and retain for life, together with the perpetual vicarage of the above parish church, one, and without it, any two other benefices, etc. [as above, no. 3].

Litterarum scientia, vite ac morum honestas . . .
L. puccius / · B· / . B· L· Bolis·

[1] preceded by (?)*Jenneyn*, deleted and initialled . *B*.
[2] or *Quenecanuuell*

887   17 January 1503   *Reg. Lat.* 1117, fos 287[v]-288[r]

To John Scotton, perpetual chaplain, called cantor, at the altar of St Catherine in the church of St John, Beverley (*Beverlacy*), d. York. Dispensation — at his supplication — to receive and retain for life, together with the perpetual chaplaincy at the above altar, which[1] is incompatible with another incompatible benefice, one, and without it, any two other benefices, with cure or otherwise mutually incompatible, etc. [as above, no. 3].[2]

Vite ac morum honestas . . .
L puccius / · B· / · B· L. Bolis·

[1] *quecumque*; *recte*: 'que cum'
[2] save that in the present instance MS has 'vel officia' once only

888   17 January 1503   *Reg. Lat.* 1117, fos 288[v]-289[r]

To William Wilkes,[1] canon of the monastery of Peter and Paul the Apostles, Dorchester, OSA, d. Lincoln. Dispensation — at his supplication — to him, who, as he asserts, is expressly professed of the above order,[2] to receive and retain any benefice, with or without cure, usually held by secular clerics, etc. [as above, no. 32, to '. . . another, similar or dissimilar, benefice'], usually assigned to secular clerics. Notwithstanding etc.

Religionis zelus, vite ac morum honestas . . .
L. puccius / · B· / · B· xxx Bolis·

[1] the 'k' somewhat doubtful
[2] This information comes from a notwithstanding clause.

889   16 January 1503   *Reg. Lat.* 1117, fos 289^r-290^r

To John Magryche,[1] rector of the parish church of St Mary, Wylbond, d. Exeter.
Dispensation — at his supplication — to receive and retain for life, together with the
above parish church, one, and without it, any two other benefices, etc. [as above, no. 3].

Vite ac morum honestas . . .
L. puccius / · B· / · B· L. Bolis·

[1] or possibly *Mo-*

890   1 February 1503[1]   *Reg. Lat.* 1117, fos 294^r-295^r

To John Prud, BTheol, rector of the parish church of Parkeham, d. Exeter.
Dispensation and indult — at his supplication — to receive and retain for life,
together with the above parish church, one, and without it, any two other benefices,
etc. [as above, no. 3, to '. . . retain them together for life, as above']; and for life,
while residing in the Roman curia or any one of his benefices or attending a *studium
generale*, not to be bound to reside personally in his other benefices, etc. [as above,
no. 238].

Litterarum scientia, vite ac morum honestas . . .
L. puccius / . B· / · B· Lx Bolis·

[1] *Kl . . . undecimo*] written in a different ink: entered later?

891   18 January 1503   *Reg. Lat.* 1117, fos 295^r-296^r

To Thomas Long, scholar, d. Salisbury. Dispensation — at his supplication — to him
(who, as he asserts, is below his sixteenth year of age and wishes to become a cleric)
to receive and retain together for life — after he has been duly marked with clerical
character and shall be in his sixteenth year — one and — as soon as he has reached
his twentieth year — with it, another, and without them, any two other benefices, etc.
[as above, no. 3, to '. . . as often as he pleases'], and in their place receive and retain
together for life up to two other, similar or dissimilar, incompatible benefices, viz.:
— after he has been duly marked with clerical character and shall be in his sixteenth
year — one and — when he has reached his twentieth year — another, as above.
Notwithstanding the above defect of age, etc. With the proviso that the incompatible
benefices in question shall not, on this account, be defrauded of due services and the
cure of souls therein ([if] any) shall not be neglected.

Vite ac morum honestas . . .
L puccius | · B· | · B· Lxxx Bolis·

892   20 January 1503   *Reg. Lat.* 1117, fos 298ᵛ-300ʳ

To Maurice Adam, BDec, perpetual vicar of the parish church of Llandylovaure, d. St David's, dispensation. Some time ago, as he asserts, he had been dispensed by apostolic authority first, notwithstanding a defect of birth as the son of a married man and an unmarried woman, to be promoted to all, even sacred, orders, and to the priesthood, and [to hold]¹ a benefice, even if it should have cure of souls; and next — [since] he, simple and ignorant of law, had, by virtue of this dispensation, had himself promoted to the said orders before the lawful age, otherwise however duly at the times established by law, and had ministered therein, even in the ministry of the altar, and taken part in divine offices and, after he had reached the lawful age, had, without having otherwise obtained rehabilitation in respect of the foregoing, acquired the vicarage of the above parish church, vacant *certo modo* and collated to him otherwise canonically — to be absolved from the excesses in question and on account of the irregularity contracted; and to hold the vicarage, and, with it, another incompatible benefice; and he holds the vicarage at present. The pope — at his supplication — hereby dispenses and indulges him to receive and retain for life, together with the vicarage, one, and without it, any two other benefices, etc. [as above, no. 3, to '. . . retain them together for life, as above']; and for life, while residing in the Roman curia or any one of his benefices or attending a *studium generale*, not to be bound to reside personally in his other benefices, etc. [as above, no. 21].

Litterarum scientia, vite ac morum honestas . . .
² *S. Castello*³ *| · B· | . B· Lxx Bolis·*

¹ verb wanting
² above, *L pucius (sic)* deleted; not initialled
³ *sic*: no 'de'

893   20 January 1503   *Reg. Lat.* 1117, fos 300ʳ-301ᵛ

To Maurice Gwyn, MA, perpetual vicar of the parish church of LLanbadarne Vawr, d. St David's. Dispensation and indult — at his supplication — to him — who, some time ago, as he asserts, was dispensed by apostolic authority, first, notwithstanding a defect of birth as the son of a priest and an unmarried woman to be promoted to all, even sacred, orders and the priesthood and to receive and retain a benefice, even if it should have cure of souls, and then (after he was dispensed in respect of the foregoing and was unable to support himself comfortably from the fruits to be had from this benefice) to receive and retain another benefice compatible with the aforesaid, even if it should have cure of souls, and be in a cathedral, even metropolitan, church, (but short of a canonry and prebend), or a canonry and prebend of a collegiate church, an administration or office, to resign them, for exchange or otherwise, at once or successively, once only, and in their place receive and retain up to two other, similar or dissimilar, mutually compatible benefices; and who afterwards, by virtue of the said dispensation, was duly promoted to all, even sacred, orders, and holds the vicarage of the above parish church and a canonry and prebend of the church of Abergwyli, d. St David's — to receive and retain for life, together with the above vicarage, one, and without them, any two other benefices, with cure or otherwise mutually incompatible, etc. [as above, no. 3, to '. . . retain them together for life']; and, also for life, while residing in the Roman curia or any one of his benefices, or attending a *studium generale*, not to be bound to reside personally in his other benefices, etc. [as above, no. 21].[1]

Litterarum sientia,[2] *vite ac morum honestas . . .*
L. pucius[3] */ · B· / · B· Lxx Bolis*

[1] in the present instance, the Notwithstanding clauses include mention of Maurice's defect of birth
[2] *sic; recte*: 'scientia'
[3] *sic*

---

894   31 December 1502   *Reg. Lat.* 1117, fos 301ᵛ-302ᵛ

To Robert Coren, perpetual vicar of the parish church of Billesdon, d. Lincoln. Dispensation — at his supplication — to receive and retain for life, together with the perpetual vicarage of the above parish church, one, and without it, any two other benefices, etc. [as above, no. 3].

Vite ac morum honestas . . .
L. puccius / · B· / · B· L. Bolis

---

895   20 January 1503   *Reg. Lat.* 1117, fos 302ᵛ-303ᵛ

To John Lokton,[1] scholar, d. Canterbury, dispensation. A recent petition to the pope on John's part stated that — at another time, while he was a scribe of trial or temporal justice — he was present at the examination of several persons who were being detained, in prison or otherwise, for certain crimes perpetrated by them while they were examined about those crimes; that he drafted and reduced to public form the process and confession and deposition of witnesses made in that regard and the sentences which were passed; that he publicly read the said processes and sentences and did other things[2] usually done in like offices; and that those who were examined were condemned on account of the above, getting their deserts, and were handed over for capital punishment or otherwise were mutilated,[3] contracting irregularity; and that he is eager to become a cleric. Wherefore supplication was made on his part to the pope to dispense him for the said irregularity.[4] The pope therefore — at his supplication — hereby dispenses him to be promoted to all, even sacred, orders, otherwise however duly and minister in them, even in the ministry of the altar; and to receive and retain any number of mutually compatible benefices, with and without cure, even if canonries and prebends, dignities, *personatus*, administrations or offices in cathedral, even metropolitan, or collegiate churches, even if the dignities in question should be major *post pontificalem* in cathedral, even metropolitan, churches, or principal in collegiate churches, and even if the dignities etc. should be customarily elective and have cure of souls, if he obtains them otherwise canonically, to resign them, at once or successively, simply or for exchange, as often as he pleases, and in their place receive and retain any number of mutually compatible benefices, with or without cure, as above. Notwithstanding etc.

Vite ac morum honestas . . .
L. puccius / Jo / Jo. xxxv. Eps' Terracinen'

[1] the 'k' seemingly written over an 'o' or possibly 'b'

[2] *alias; recte*: 'alia' ('alia' had, in fact, been written before the recasting, *cf.* note 3)

[3] The whole narrative has been recast, with deletions and insertions throughout.

[4] There is, however, no mention in the operative part of the letter of the pope dispensing him for irregularity.

896   15 September 1502   *Reg. Lat.* 1118, fos 13[v]-14[r]

To William Thorpe', MA, perpetual chaplain, called cantor, in the church of Lincoln. Dispensation — at his supplication — to receive and retain for life, together with a perpetual chaplaincy in the above church, which is incompatible with another incompatible benefice, one, and without it, any two other benefices, with cure or otherwise mutually incompatible, etc. [as above, no. 3]. Given at Civita Castellana.

Litterarum scientia, vite ac morum honestas . . .
L puccius / · B· / · B· L. Bolis·

897   3 September 1502   *Reg. Lat.* 1118, fo 33[r-v]

To John Docura, BDec, rector of the parish church of Upmynster [also spelt

Upmyster], d. London. Dispensation — at his supplication — to receive and retain for life, together with the above parish church, one, and without it, any two other benefices, etc. [as above, no. 3].

Litterarum scientia, vite ac morum honestas . . .
L puccius | · B· / | B· L. Bolis.

898   8 September 1502   *Reg. Lat.* 1118, fo 38^{r-v}

To John Wardall, BTheol, rector of the parish church of B. Mary, Sperham, d. Norwich. Dispensation — at his supplication — to receive and retain for life, together with the above parish church, one, and without it, any two other benefices, etc. [as above, no. 3].

Litterarum scientia, vite ac morum honestas . . .
L puccius | · B· / | B· L. Bolis·

899   10 September 1502   *Reg. Lat.* 1118, fo 42^{r-v}

To William Goodicwyn, canon of the priory of B. Mary, Combuell, OSA, d. Canterbury. Dispensation — at his supplication — to him, who, as he asserts, is expressly professed of the above order,[1] to receive and retain any benefice, with or without cure, usually held by secular clerics, etc. [as above, no. 32, to '. . . another, similar or dissimilar, benefice'], usually assigned to secular clerics. Notwithstanding etc. Given at Nepi.

Religionis zelus, vite ac morum honestas . . .
L puccius | · B· / · B· xxx Bolis·

[1] This information comes from a notwithstanding clause.

900   1 July 1503   *Reg. Lat.* 1118, fos 43^r-44^r

To Richard Carlyon, perpetual vicar of the parish church of Straton, d. Exeter. Dispensation and indult — at his supplication — to receive and retain for life, together with the perpetual vicarage of the above parish church, one, and without it, any two other benefices, etc. [as above, no. 3, to '. . . retain them together for life, as above']; and for life, while residing in the Roman curia or any one of his benefices or attending a *studium generale*, not to be bound to reside personally in his other benefices, etc. [as above, no. 238].

Vite ac morum honestas . . .
L. puccius / *B·* / · *B· Lx Bolis·*

901 —[1]   *Reg. Lat.* 1118, fo 47[V]

Beginning of letter addressed to Thomas Darcy, rector of the parish church of the Most Blessed Virgin Mary, Mamudebylyston, d. Armagh. The fragment does not extend beyond start of proem: *Vite ac morum honestas* [ends]. Consistent with a grace in Thomas's favour. Perhaps a dispensation to hold two incompatible benefices. Adjacent letters suggest a date in the eleventh year (1502, 26. viii-1503, 18. viii). No abbreviator's name. And no magistral initial.

Unclear why unfinished. Space apparently left to finish it: occupies four lines at top of otherwise blank page; next page also blank. Not deleted. No explanatory note. Enregistration never completed rather than abandoned. Reminiscent of next entry (same scribe).

[1] dating clause wanting

902 —[1]   *Reg. Lat.* 1118, fo 48[V]

Beginning of letter addressed to Christopher Rosynalde (*or* Rosyualde), rector of the parish church of Calkton, d. Winchester. The fragment does not extend beyond start of proem: *Vite ac morum* [ends]. Consistent with a grace in Christopher's favour. Probably a dispensation to hold two incompatible benefices. Adjacent letters suggest a date in the eleventh year (1502, 26. viii- 1503, 18. viii). No abbreviator's name. And no magistral initial.

Unclear why unfinished. Space apparently left to finish it: occupies three lines and start of fourth at top of otherwise blank page; next page also blank. Not deleted. No explanatory note. Reminiscent of previous entry (same scribe).

[1] dating clause wanting

903   8 July 1503   *Reg. Lat.* 1118, fos 52[V]-53[r]

To the bishops of Winchester and London and the dean of the church of Salisbury, mandate. A recent petition to the pope on the part of the present abbot and the convent of the monastery of B. Mary the Virgin and St Egwin (*Sancti Enwini*), [Evesham, OSB, d. Worcester][1] and of (?). . . burg'[2] and also Peter Tarkii, guardians, and the other brothers of the confraternity or society, called a guild (*gilde*), of the Drapers' Company (*artis pannariorum*), established in the parish church of St Michael the Archangel in Cornehill', London, stated that the right of presentation of a suitable person for the said church at a time of vacancy pertains to the abbot for the time being and the convent of the said monastery by ancient, approved and hitherto peacefully observed custom; and that if licence were granted to the abbot and convent to exchange the right of presentation with the said guardians and brothers for certain other immovable goods, from which an annual pension or annual income of 106 shillings and 8 pence of English money would be received, or to grant that right to them for the said goods, it would be to the abbot and convent's benefit. At the supplication of the abbot and convent and guardians and brothers, the pope, not having certain knowledge of the foregoing, hereby commands that the above three (or two or one of them), if and after the said representations to the pope have been lawfully established before them, shall grant licence to the abbot and convent [to exchange] the right of presentation with the guardians and brothers for other immovable goods, from which the above annual pension or income would be received, or to grant this right — with the consent of interested parties — to the guardians and brothers for the said goods. Notwithstanding etc.[3]

Ex iniuncto nobis desuper . . .
L. puccius / · B· / · B· xxxxv Bolis.

[1] Evident hiatus between *Enwini* and *burg'*; the text runs: *Sancti Enwini burg' necnon Petri Tarkii guardianorum* . . . The order of the monastery is wanting; and is not specified elsewhere although the Notwithstanding clauses refer (as might be expected) to 'the statutes and customs of the monastery and order aforesaid'. The editor has supplied both the order and whereabouts of the monastery — namely the Benedictine house at Evesham — from other sources, notably Dugdale — which mentions the monastery's seal: ". . . Sancte Marie et Sancti Ecgwini . . . " and a pension "Ecclesie Sancti Michaelis de Cornehill" (Dugdale, *Monasticon*, ed. Caley, Ellis, and Bandinel, II [1819], pp. 13, 48) — and the *Valor* — which likewise mentions a pension "ex Rectoria Sancti Michaelis Cornhill" (*Valor Ecclesiasticus*, Record Commission, VI [1834], p. 189). *burg'* would appear to be the end of a proper name of one of the guardians.

[2] see above, note 1

[3] see above, note 1

904   24 December 1502   *Reg. Lat.* 1118, fos 71^V-72^V

To John, abbot of the monastery of B. Mary, *in Pratis*, Leicester (*Leicestre*), OSA, d. Lincoln. Dispensation — at his supplication — to receive together with the above monastery, one, and without it, any two other regular benefices, with or without cure, of the said order, or with one of them, or without them, one secular benefice, with or without cure, etc. [as above, no. 707].[1]

Personam tuam nobis et apostolice sedi devotam . . .
N. de Castello / · B· / . B· L. Bolis

[1] substituting here: 'which may not be a monastery or be conventual or claustral' where no. 707 has: 'which may not be conventual or claustral'

905[1]   **28 December 1502**   *Reg. Lat.* 1118, fos 74ʳ-75ʳ

To the bishops of London and Winchester, mandate in favour of Margaret Keble, woman, d. London. A recent petition to the pope on Margaret's part stated that, formerly, she sued (not through apostolic delegation) Roger Vernon of Westminster (*de West Monasterii*), layman, d. London, who was falsely claiming that he had lawfully contracted marriage with her *per verba de presenti*, before Thomas Ely, archdeacon of the archdeaconry within the limits of the jurisdiction of the monastery of St Peter, Westminster, d. London, (since by ancient, approved, and hitherto peacefully observed custom, cognizance of such cases arising from time to time between such persons pertains to the archdeacon for the time being), praying that it be declared that no marriage had been contracted between them; that Roger, falsely asserting that Margaret was lawfully his wife, counter-sued (*reconvenit*) her before the same archdeacon, praying that she be adjudged his lawful wife; that the archdeacon — who assigned a certain term to Margaret for the examination or hearing of her replies to certain accusations (*possicionibus*) and articles, or matter drawn up in articles, exhibited before him, as he said, on Roger's part, after she had already made her replies, and who ordained that she was to appear personally before him in the parish church of St Margaret, Westminster, d. London, for the examination or hearing of the replies she had made, after she had already appeared (having been lawfully cited) — wrongly, *de facto*, lawlessly, and without lawful cause, at Roger's instance, as he said, when the term had expired, bound Margaret by sentence of excommunication, and frequently threatened that he was minded to order that she be denounced and published as excommunicate by certain letters of his fortified with his seal; and that Margaret appealed to the apostolic see. At Margaret's supplication to the pope to command that she be absolved conditionally from the sentence of excommunication and other censures and pains by which she is deemed bound, and to commit to some upright men in those parts the cases of the appeal; of everything attempted and innovated after and against the appeal; of the nullity of the excommunication, threats, publication, denunciation, archdeacon's whole process, and everything else prejudicial to Margaret done by him, Roger, and any other judges and persons, in connection with the foregoing; and of the principal matter, the pope hereby commands that the above two (or one of them), having summoned Roger and others concerned, shall, if and as it is just, for this once only, conditionally absolve Margaret, if she so requests, having first received suitable security from her that if they find that the excommunication and other sentences etc. were justly inflicted on her, she will obey their commands and those of the church; and, as regards the rest, having heard both sides, taking cognizance even of the principal matter, that they shall decree what is canonical, without appeal, causing by ecclesiastical censure what they have decreed to be strictly observed. Notwithstanding etc.

Humilibus supplicum [*et cetera.*]
L puccius / · B· / · B· xiiij· Bolis·

[1] *Cf.* below, no. 988.

906   24 December 1502   *Reg. Lat.* 1118, fos 75ʳ-76ʳ

To the bishop of Exeter, the archdeacon of Shropshmc,[1] and Peter Grenes, canon of the church[2] of London, mandate in favour of Peter Vasor, LLB, rector of the parish church of Henley on Thames (*supra Themisiam*), d. Lincoln. A recent petition to the pope on Peter Vasor's part stated that formerly he sued, not through apostolic delegation, Thomas Hales, layman, parishioner of his church, for unlawfully refusing certain tithes and oblations then expressed which he was lawfully bound to pay and give to him by reason of his church, before Hugh Peyntwyn, LLD, cleric, then auditor of causes and matters of the late John, archbishop of Canterbury, primate of all England and legate born of the apostolic see, (to whom belongs, by ancient, approved, and hitherto peacefully observed custom, cognizance of causes and suchlike moved by rectors of the parish churches of Lincoln diocese against their parishioners), praying that he be condemned and compelled to give and pay the tithes and oblations. After the death of archbishop John, Hugh — bearing himself as auditor of the chapter of the church of Canterbury to whom, as he said, jurisdiction and cognizance of such causes pertains when the see was vacant — reassuming the case, as he asserted, and proceeding wrongfully in it to the later stages, promulgated an unjust definitive sentence by which he absolved Thomas from Peter's accusation, and from which, on Peter's part, appeal was made to the apostolic see; but Peter, detained, as he asserts, by a lawful impediment, did not prosecute the appeal within the proper time. At the supplication on Peter's part to the pope to commit to some upright men in those parts the causes of the appeal; of anything attempted and innovated after and against the appeal; of the nullity of the sentence and whole process of Hugh; of everything prejudicial to Peter done in connection with the above by Hugh, Thomas, and any other judges and persons; and of the principal matter; also the causes which Peter intends to move against Thomas and certain other clerics of the said diocese, jointly and severally, the pope hereby commands that the above three (or two or one of them), having summoned Thomas and others concerned, if what is related about the impediment is true, and having heard both sides, taking cogizance even of the principal matter, shall decree what is just without appeal, causing by ecclesiastical censure what they have decreed to be strictly observed. Notwithstanding the lapse of time, etc.

Humilibus et cetera.
L puccius / · B· / · B· xiiij· Bolis

[1] penultimate letter doubtful
[2] MS *ecclesiarum; recte* 'ecclesie' (unless there is an omission)

**907	31 December 1502**					*Reg. Lat.* 1118, fos 76^v-77^r

To Edward Banys, rector of the parish church of St James, Stove,[1] d. Exeter. Dispensation — at his supplication — to receive and retain for life, together with the above parish church, one, and without it, any two other benefices, etc. [as above, no. 3].

Vite ac morum honestas . . .
L. puccius / . B· / · B· L. Bolis

[1] in the first instance the 'v' blotched and perhaps reworked

**908	24 December 1502**					*Reg. Lat.* 1118, fos 81^r-82^v

Union etc. At a recent petition on the part of Richard Neuporte,[1] LLB, canon of Salisbury, the pope hereby unites etc. the parish church of Mildenhal, d. Salisbury, (whose annual value does not exceed 20 English marks, equivalent to 57 gold ducats of the camera or thereabouts), to the canonry and prebend of Ffaryngdon *alias* Ffarendon of the church of Salisbury, which he holds together with the above parish church, for as long as he holds the canonry and prebend, to the effect that Richard, in person or by proxy, may, on his own authority, take and retain corporal possession of the parish church and its rights and appurtenances, for as long as he holds the canonry and prebend, and convert its fruits etc. to his own uses and those of the parish church and the canonry and prebend without licence of the local diocesan or of anyone else. Notwithstanding etc. The pope's will is, however, that the parish church shall not, on account of this union etc., be defrauded of due services and the cure of souls therein shall not be neglected, but that its customary burdens shall be supported; and that on Richard's death or resignation etc. of the canonry and prebend the union etc. shall be dissolved and the parish church shall revert to its original condition and be deemed vacant automatically.

Ad futuram rey memoriam. Ex iniuncto nobis desuper apostolice servitutis officio ad ea libenter intendimus . . .

A. de Sancto Severino / Jo / Jo. xxxv. Eps' Terracinen'

[1] or *Nenporte*

909   24 December 1502   *Reg. Lat.* 1118, fos 82ᵛ-85ʳ[1]

Union etc. At a recent petition on the part of John Burton, canon of the church of Exeter, the pope hereby unites etc. the parish church of Wymple, d. Exeter, (whose annual value does not exceed 22 marks sterling, equivalent to 60 gold ducats of the camera or thereabouts), to the canonry and prebend of the church of Exeter, which he holds together with the above parish church, for as long as he holds the canonry and prebend, to the effect that John, in person or by proxy, may, on his own authority, take and retain corporal possession of the parish church and its rights and appurtenances, for as long as he holds the canonry and prebend, and convert its fruits etc. to his own uses and those of the canonry and prebend and the parish church without licence of the local diocesan or of anyone else. Notwithstanding etc. The pope's will is, however, that the parish church shall not, on account of this union etc., be defrauded of due services and the cure of souls therein shall not be neglected, but that its customary burdens shall be supported; and that on John's death or resignation etc. of the canonry and prebend the union etc. shall be dissolved and so deemed and the parish church shall revert to its original condition and be deemed vacant automatically.

Ad futuram rey memoriam. Romanum decet pontificem votis illis gratum prestare assensum . . .
S. de Castello / Jo / Jo. xxxv. Eps' Terracinen'

[1] fos 83ᵛ and 84ʳ are blank and struck through: in turning over fo 83ʳ the scribe evidently turned over fo 84ʳ as well

910   18 February 1503   *Reg. Lat.* 1118, fos 94ʳ-95ʳ

To John Judson, perpetual vicar of the parish church of B. Mary, Kensyngton, d. London. Dispensation and indult — at his supplication — to receive and retain for life, together with the perpetual vicarage of the above parish church, one, and without it, any two other benefices, etc. [as above, no. 3, to '. . . retain them together for life, as above']; and for life, while residing in the Roman curia or any one of his benefices or attending a *studium generale*, not to be bound to reside personally in his other benefices, etc. [as above, no. 238].

Vite ac morum honestas . . .
L. pucius[1] / · *B·* / · *B· Lx Bolis*

[1] *sic*

911   18 February 1503   *Reg. Lat.* 1118, fos 95^r-96^v

To Richard Gawnt, MA, rector of the parish church of Eschenreth' [also spelt *Eschemeth, Eschenreth*], d. Salisbury, dispensation. Some time ago, the pope by other letters of his dispensed him to receive and retain for life, together with the above parish church (which, as he asserted, he was then holding), one, and without it, any two other benefices, etc. [as above, no. 131, to '. . . as is more fully contained in those letters'].[1] The pope therefore — at his supplication — hereby further dispenses Richard (who, as he asserts, holds by virtue of the said dispensation, the said church still and also the perpetual vicarage of the parish church of Sutton, d. Salisbury, canonically collated to him at another time when vacant *certo modo*) to receive and retain for life, together with the church of Eschenreth' and the vicarage aforesaid, or without them, with any two other incompatible benefices held by him at the time by the said dispensation, any third benefice, etc. [as above, no. 131].

Litterarum sientia,[2] *vite ac morum honestas . . .*
L pucius[3] / · *B·* / . *B. Lxx Bolis*

[1] *Cf.* no. 1132 below.
[2] *sic; recte:* 'scientia'
[3] *sic*

912   7 February 1503   *Reg. Lat.* 1118, fos 100^v-101^v

To John Pinchibek, rector of the parish church of Aldeburgh, d. Norwich. Dispensation — at his supplication — to receive and retain for life, together with the above parish church, one, and without it, any two other benefices, etc. [as above, no. 3].

Vite ac morum honestas . . .
N. de Castello / · *B·*[1] / · *B· L. Bolis*

[1] blotched

913   21 May 1503   *Reg. Lat.* 1118, fos 117^v-118^r

To John Ungram, perpetual vicar of the parish church of the Apostles Peter and Paul,

Hornedon' on the Hill (*super Montem*), d. London. Dispensation — at his supplication — to receive and retain for life, together with the perpetual vicarage of the above parish church, one, and without it, any two other benefices, etc. [as above, no. 3].

Vite ac morum honestas . . .
A. *collocius* / · *B·* / · *B· L. Bolis*

914   21 May 1503   *Reg. Lat.* 1118, fos 118ᵛ-119ʳ

To Thomas Marshal, monk of the monastery of St Erkenwald, Cherchesey, OSB,[1] d. Winchester. Dispensation — at his supplication — to him, who, as he asserts, is expressly professed of the above order,[2] to receive and retain any benefice, with or without cure, usually held by secular clerics, etc. [as above, no. 32, to '. . . another, similar or dissimilar, benefice'], usually assigned to secular clerics. Notwithstanding etc.

Religionis zelus, vite ac morum honestas . . .
p planca[3] / · *B.* / · *B· xxx Bolis*

[1] *Augustini* deleted (but not initialled) precedes *Benedicti*.
[2] This information comes from a notwithstanding clause.
[3] *sic*; no 'de'

915   13 May 1503   *Reg. Lat.* 1118, fos 121ʳ-122ʳ

To Richard Syndmor,[1] MA, perpetual vicar of the parish church of Ermyngton', d. Exeter. Dispensation — at his supplication — to receive and retain for life, together with the perpetual vicarage of the above parish church, one, and without it, any two other benefices, etc. [as above, no. 3].

Litterarum scientia, vite ac morum honestas . . .
N. *de castello* / · *B·* / · *B· L· Bolis.*

[1] the 'm' overwritten and doubtful; possibly 'n'

916   13 May 1503   *Reg. Lat.* 1118, fos 122ʳ-123ʳ

To John Hyde, perpetual vicar of the parish church of B. Mary, Wynsh(a)m,[1] d. Bath

and Wells. Dispensation and indult — at his supplication — to receive and retain for
life, together with the perpetual vicarage of the above parish church, one, and
without it, any two other benefices, etc. [as above, no. 3, to '. . . retain them together
for life, as above']² ; and also for life, while residing in the Roman curia or any one
of his benefices, or attending a *studium generale*, not to be bound to reside
personally in his other benefices, etc. [as above, no. 238].

Vite ac morum honestas . . .
L. puccius / B / · B· Lx Bolis

¹ MS: *Wynshm'*
² save that in this instance MS wants 'permutationis' ('exchange')

917   9 September 1502   *Reg. Lat.* 1118, fo 135ʳ⁻ᵛ

To Thomas Grene, LLB, rector of the parish church of Sundrich, Canterbury.¹
Dispensation and indult — at his supplication — to receive and retain for life,
together with the above parish church, one, and without it, any two other benefices,
etc. [as above, no. 3, to '. . . retain them together for life, as above']² ; and also for
life, while residing in the Roman curia or any one of his benefices, or attending a
studium generale, not to be bound to reside personally in his other benefices, etc. [as
above, no. 238, to '. . . shall be supported']. Given at Nepi.

Litterarum scientia, vite ac morum honestas . . .
L puccius / Jo / Jo· Lx Eps' Terracinen. '

¹ 'diocesis' does not occur
² save that here 'even metropolitan' is wanting in the first instance

918   15 September 1502   *Reg. Lat.* 1118, fos 138ʳ-139ʳ

To Edward Jenney, rector of the parish church of Kyrkeley, d. Norwich, validation.
Some time ago, Innocent VIII by his letters dispensed him to receive and retain for
life, together with one of two portions of the parish church of Pakefelde, usually
ruled by two rectors, d. Norwich, (which he was then holding), one, and without it,
any two other benefices, etc. [as above, no. 131, to '. . . as is more fully contained in
those letters'].¹ Moreover, as a recent petition to the pope on Edward's part stated, at
the time of Innocent's letters he had resigned and parted with the portion, and was
holding the above parish church of Kyrkeley, and because in the said letters no
mention was made of the resignation etc. of the portion and holding of the church of

Kyrkeley Edward fears that the letters could be branded surreptitious and he be molested over them with the passage of time. The pope therefore — at his supplication — hereby wills and grants to him (who, as he asserts, holds the church of Kyrkeley and portion[2] aforesaid by the said dispensation) that Innocent's dispensation and letters, with all the clauses contained therein — from the date of the presents — be valid and have full force in and for all things, just as if it had been expressed in them that he was holding not the portion but the church of Kyrkeley. Notwithstanding etc. Given at Civita Castellana.

Vite ac morum honestas . . .
L. puccius / · B· / · B· xvj· Bolis·

[1] summarised in *CPL*, XV at no. 570

[2] *sic*; but not necessarily at odds with the purport of the letter. He could have reacquired it.

919   1 October 1502   *Reg. Lat.* 1118, fos 143ᵛ-144ʳ

To William Beverley, layman, d. Chichester, indult. The pope has learned that in provincial and synodal constitutions or constitutions of the episcopal curia of [Chichester][1] it is expressly laid down that no married man may exercise the office of notary in the said curia. He hereby — at his supplication — indulges William (who, as he asserts, after bishop Edward and the chapter of Chichester had appointed him for life to exercise the office of notary of the curia, which was then vacant *certo modo*, or which perchance he was then exercising, lawfully contracted marriage with a certain woman *per verba de presenti* and consummated it, and afterwards has exercised the office, as he does at present) to exercise the office of notary in accordance with the said appointment made by the bishop and chapter, as above. The pope specially and expressly derogates the aforesaid constitutions for this once only. Notwithstanding that William is a married man, etc.

Laudabilia probitatis et virtutum merita . . .
L puccius / · B· / · B· xx Bolis·

[1] *Cistren.; recte*: 'Cicestren.'

920   13 May 1503   *Reg. Lat.* 1118, fos 175ᵛ-176ᵛ

To William Synkclare,[1] perpetual vicar of the parish church of St Andrew, Milburne and Dewlych',[2] d. Salisbury. Dispensation and indult — at his supplication — to receive and retain for life, together with the perpetual vicarage of the above parish

church, one, and without it, any two other benefices, etc. [as above, no. 3, to '. . .
retain them together for life, as above']; and for life, while residing in the Roman
curia or any one of his benefices or attending a *studium generale*, not to be bound to
reside personally in his other benefices, etc. [as above, no. 238].

Vite ac morum honestas . . .
L. *puccius* / . *B·* / · *B· L.* [3] *Bolis*

[1] *syn* has been deleted (but not initialled)

[2] MS: *de Wlych'*

[3] *sic;* (such a letter could be expected to carry a tax of *Lx*)

921   1 December 1502   *Reg. Lat.* 1118, fos 183[V]-184[V]

To the precentor <and>[1] archdeacon of the church of Dunkeld, and the provost of the
church of B. <Mary>[2], Edemborg, d. St Andrews, mandate in favour of Henry
Wardlaw, knight, of St Andrews or another diocese. A recent petition to the pope on
Henry's part stated that, formerly, a dispute had arisen, not through apostolic
delegation, between himself and the present prior and chapter of the church of St
Andrews, OSB[3], over certain tithes and other things then expressed, which the prior
and chapter were unlawfully endeavouring to extort from him, before David
Medrum, official of St Andrews; and the official, proceeding wrongly in the case,
promulgated an unjust definitive sentence in favour of the prior and chapter and
against Henry, from which Henry appealed to the apostolic see; but the official
unlawfully refused to defer to the appeal (to which, by right, deference was due). At
the supplication on Henry's part to commit to some upright men in those parts the
causes of the appeal; of everything attempted and innovated after and against the
appeal; of the nullity of the sentence and any censures perchance promulgated
against Henry and of the official's whole process; of everything prejudicial to Henry
done by the official and the prior and chapter and any others in connection with the
foregoing; and of the principal matter, the pope hereby commands that the above
three (or two or one of them), having summoned the prior and chapter and others
concerned and having heard both sides, taking cognizance even of the principal
matter, shall decree what is just, without appeal, causing by ecclesiastical censure
what they have decreed to be strictly observed; [and moreover compel] witnesses
etc. Notwithstanding, etc.

Humilibus et cetera.
L. *puccius* / · *B·* / ₁ *B· xij· Bolis*

[1] supralinear insertion by the enregistering scribe initialled . *B.*

[2] marginal insertion by the enregistering scribe initialled . *B*

[3] *sic; recte* OSA

922   3 December 1502   *Reg. Lat.* 1118, fo 186^{r-v}

To Stephen Quogno, rector of the parish church of Saxlyngh(a)m[1] next the Sea (*iuxta Mare*), d. Norwich. Dispensation — at his supplication — to receive and retain for life, together with the above parish church, one, and without it, any two other benefices, etc. [as above, no. 3][2].

Vite ac morum honestas . . .
F de parma / Jo / . Jo. L. Eps' Terracinen'

[1] MS: *Saxlynghm'*
[2] with the addition of: 'and of lay patronage' after 'or principal in collegiate churches'

923   3 December 1502   *Reg. Lat.* 1118, fos 193^{r}-194^{r}

To Thomas Branmount, MA, rector of the parish church of St Clement Danes without the Bars of New Temple, London, d. London, dispensation. Some time ago, the pope by other letters of his dispensed him to receive and retain for life, together with the above parish church (which, as he asserted, he was then holding), one, and without it, any two other benefices, etc. [as above, no. 131, to '. . . as is more fully contained in those letters']. The pope therefore — at his supplication — hereby further dispenses him (who, as he asserts, afterwards acquired the perpetual vicarage of the parish church of Olstoon, d. Worcester, canonically collated to him when vacant *certo modo*, and holds it and the above church of St Clement) to receive and retain for life, together with the church of St Clement and the vicarage aforesaid, or with any two other incompatible benefices held by him at the time by virtue of the said dispensation, any third benefice, etc. [as above, no. 131].

Litterarum scientia, vite ac morum honestas . . .
F de parma / · B· / . B. Lxx. Bolis.

924   12 November 1502   *Reg. Lat.* 1118, fos 227^{v}-228^{v}

To the bishops of Winchester and Exeter, and the abbot of the monastery of Westminster (*Vestmonasterii*), d. London, mandate in favour of Joan Marowte, woman, London. A recent petition to the pope on Joan's part stated that although the late John Crosby, layman, d. London, appointed her sole executrix in his last will, and although William Barocis,[1] then commissary or auditor of Henry, archbishop of Canterbury, primate of all England, and legate born of the apostolic see, — after he had, at Joan's instance and in the presence of William Arowsmithe [also spelt

Arowsmith], layman, city or diocese of London, examined several witnesses as to the will's validity, in accordance with the custom of the archbishop's court of audience of causes and matters, and had approved and confirmed it — proceeding duly, committed its execution solely to her, or declared that it belonged to her, nevertheless, subsequently, either William Wylton' or Hugh Peyntwyn', (who bore themselves as the archbishop's commissaries or auditors), proceeding wrongly and *de facto*, at the instance of William Arowsmithe, who falsely asserted that he was appointed executor, admitted several unsuitable witnesses for examination, or ordered and caused them to be admitted and their depositions to be received, and then, temerariously and *de facto*, regardless of law, in Joan's absence, when she had been neither summoned nor cited, at least lawfully, and was not absent through contumacy, appointed William Arowsmithe executor, whence appeal was made on Joan's part to the apostolic see. At her supplication to the pope to commit to some upright men in those parts the cases of her appeal; of everything attempted and innovated after and against it; of the nullity of William Wylton''s, or Hugh's, process, examination of witnesses, and appointment of executor, and of everything else prejudicial to Joan done by them and by William Arowsmithe and any other judges and persons in connection with the foregoing; and of the principal matter, the pope hereby commands that the above three (or two or one of them), having summoned William Arowsmithe and others concerned, and having heard both sides, taking cognizance even of the principal matter, shall decree what is just, without appeal, causing by ecclesiastical censure what they have decreed to be strictly observed; [and moreover compel] witnesses etc. Notwithstanding etc.

Humilibus et cetera.
L· puccius / Jo / Jo. xij. Eps' Terracinen'

[1] the *-ci-* changed (by overwriting) from (?)*n* and uncertain

925   13 November 1502   *Reg. Lat.* 1118, fo 231[r-v]

To the noblewoman, Margaret, countess of Richmond (*Richemundie*) and Derby (*Derbie*). Indult — at her supplication — for the five priests whom she — the mother of Henry, king of England — has appointed as her chaplains not to be bound, for life and while they remain in her service, to reside personally in any benefices held by [them][1] at the time, of whatsoever quality, even requiring [personal][2] residence by statute or foundation or otherwise, nor to be liable to be compelled by anyone to do so against their will. Notwithstanding etc. With the proviso that the benefices held by the said [(?)chaplains][3] shall not, on this account, be defrauded of due services and the cure of souls therein (if any) shall not be neglected; but that their customary burdens shall be supported.

Eximie devotionis affectus . . .

F de parma / Jo / . Jo. xxxx. Eps' Terracinen.

1 *nos* or *vos; recte:* 'eos'?

2 *personatum; recte:* 'personalem'?

3 *cano(nica)tus; recte:* 'capellanos'?

926   22 November 1502[1]   *Reg. Lat.* 1118, fos 243^v-244^r

To Robert Bekeryng *alias* Sandherst, monk of the monastery of B. Mary, Robardis Bridge, OCist, d. Chichester. Dispensation — at his supplication — to him, who, as he asserts, is expressly professed of the said [order],[2] to receive and retain any benefice, with or without cure, usually held by secular clerics, etc. [as above, no. 32].

Religionis zelus, vite ac morum honestas . . .
N de Castello / · B· / . B· xxx Bolis

1 supralinear reference mark between *secundo* and *kalendas;* with *decimo* inserted (with corresponding reference mark) in the margin by the enregistering scribe, initialled . *B.*

2 This information comes from a notwithstanding clause. 'Ordinis' wanting.

927   27 August 1502   *Reg. Lat.* 1118, fos 272^v-274^r

To the archbishop of Dublin, the abbot of the monastery of B. Mary, near Dublin (*iuxta Dublinam*), and the prior of the priory of the Holy Trinity, Dublin, mandate in favour of Catherine Puscon, woman, d. Meath. A recent petition to the pope on Catherine's part stated that, formerly, by virtue of a dispensation granted to them by apostolic authority, she had lawfully contracted marriage *per verba de presenti*, publicly, *in facie ecclesie*, with Christopher Plunket, layman, d. Meath, (who was related to her in the third and fourth degree of consanguinity), connection followed, and they cohabited, as a married couple, for fourteen years; that, afterwards, when Catherine had been sent away on account of her rash conduct,[1] and Christopher was unlawfully refusing to have her back, (when she wanted to return), and to show her conjugal affection, robbing her of the latter, she sued him (not through apostolic delegation) over this and the marriage bond (*federe*) before, firstly, John, bishop of Meath, and then Octavian, archbishop of Armagh, the local metropolitan, (then in provincial council), to whom the case had been remitted by bishop John and had otherwise been lawfully devolved, praying that she be restored to conjugal affection and to enjoyment of the marriage; that the archbishop, proceeding duly, promulgated a definitive sentence in Catherine's favour and against Christopher, by which he declared that Catherine was to be restored to enjoyment of the marriage, ordered Christopher to show Catherine conjugal affection, and condemned him in costs, which he lawfully taxed at a certain sum then expressed, and ordered him, under pain of excommunication, to pay them to Catherine; that Christopher — belittling the sentence of excommunication by which he had been bound and falsely asserting that the letters which he and Catherine had obtained over the dispensation were surreptitious or obreptitious, and that for several reasons (none legitimate) their dispensation, made by virtue of the letters, was invalid — sued Catherine over this and other matters then expressed, by pretext of certain apostolic letters which he had surreptitiously or obreptitiously impetrated, before the present bishop of Ardagh, whom he said was the judge appointed by the letters; that the bishop of Ardagh, having rejected, at least tacitly, certain exceptions and relevant defences exhibited before him on Catherine's part at a suitable time and place, which ought, by right, to have been admitted, proceeding wrongly and *de facto*, promulgated an unjust definitive sentence, as he called it, in Christopher's favour and against Catherine, by which he declared that they ought to be separated, and from which Catherine appealed to the apostolic see. At Catherine's supplication to the pope to commit to some upright men in those parts the cases (and everything connected with them) of her appeal; of everything attempted and innovated after and against the appeal; of the nullity of the later sentence, bishop of Ardagh's whole process, and everything else prejudicial to her done by him, Christopher, and any other judges and persons, in connection with the foregoing; and of the principal matter, the pope hereby commands that the above three (or two or one of them), having summoned Christopher and others concerned, and having heard both sides, taking cognizance even of the principal matter, shall decree what is canonical, without appeal, causing by ecclesiastical censure what they have decreed to be strictly observed. Notwithstanding that the above abbot and prior are not persons to whom such cases are usually committed,[2] etc.

Humilibus et cetera.
L· Puccius / · B· / . B· xij· Bolis·

[1] MS *temeritas; recte*: 'temeritate'
[2] matrimonial cases were usually only committed to bishops

928   28 June 1503   *Reg. Lat.* 1119, fos 17ʳ-20ʳ

To Hugh Martini, canon of Brechin, reservation, constitution and assignment of a pension, as below. Some time ago, Innocent VIII by his letters, for certain reasons then expressed, reserved, constituted and assigned to Hugh, an annual pension of 100 marks Scots on the fruits etc. of the parish church of Flone [also spelt *Ellon*], d. Aberdeen, united in perpetuity to the monastery of Kinlos,[1] OCist, d. Moray, especially for the 100 marks the tithes of corn, pertaining to the parish church, of the places of Alathan,[2] Pertinendam,[3] Craghed, Voudland, Inlymad, Torry, Esilmud', with the annex Dunbrek and annexes Argrom, Wthertllon and Wattirtonn', for life or until canonical provision be made of benefices whose fruits etc. are annually worth 100 pounds Scots (after deduction of expenses), payable in full to him (or his specially mandated proctor) by the late William (whom Innocent had provided to the monastery, then vacant *certo modo*) and his successors as abbots, each year, in certain terms then expressed, under sentence of excommunication and then pain of deprivation, with William's express consent, as is more fully contained in those letters.[4] Subsequently, as a recent petition to the pope on the part of Hugh and of Thomas, the present abbot, and the convent of the monastery stated, a dispute arose between Hugh and the said Thomas and convent over the pension: abbot Thomas and the convent asserted that, on account of the collation of some ecclesiastical [benefices][5] whose fruits (as they asserted) are annually worth 100 pounds Scots, the pension has ceased and become extinct and they are not bound to pay it; whereas Hugh asserted that the pension is lawful and that abbot Thomas and his successors are obliged to pay it; and the pope, at abbot Thomas's instance, committed the case — notwithstanding that it had not lawfully devolved to the Roman curia and was not, by legal necessity, due to be dealt with and finished at it — to the late William de Pereriis, papal chaplain and auditor [of causes][6] of the apostolic palace, to be duly determined; and the auditor (or his substitute) is said to have proceeded in the case to several acts, but short of a conclusion. The pope — treating the state of the cause as expressed, and hereby calling it to himself, (abbot Thomas and the convent and Hugh having, for the implementation of a certain honest agreement, expressly consented to this through John Duncarii, priest, d. Glasgow, their specially constituted proctor), and extinguishing, quashing and annulling the case and the pension and decreeing that abbot Thomas and his successors are not bound to pay it and do not incur excommunication or deprivation on account of non-payment — lest Hugh, (who, as is asserted, holds a canonry and prebend of the church of Brechin), should suffer excessive loss on account of the quashing of the pension, hereby reserves, etc. to him — in place of the previous pension — an annual pension of 50[7] like marks, not exceeding 11 pounds sterling, and for it the tithes of corn of Alathane[8] with the appurtenances of Ardmore, Ly Houss [Syd and, with its mill, Wetno', Utherellon also][9] with their appurtenances of Ly Mains, ʒotidest[10] Utherellon, Caterstonn',[11] Modele with their mill, and also Vattytonn',[12] pertaining to Alexander Banat Nan,[13] with the appurtenances of Vattytonn' and Trehed[14] [and of Tulyma' and Traig likewise with appurtenances][15] and tithes of corn pertaining to the monastery by reason of the said parish church of Flone and not exceeding 50 marks, annually, with their appurtenances, to be collected, levied and received by Hugh for life, in person or by proxy — even notwithstanding any benefices Hugh acquires before or after the agreement — and be converted to his own uses, with abbot Thomas and the convent's express consent through the said John their specially appointed proctor; decreeing that Hugh cannot and must not be molested by abbot Thomas and his successors and the convent over the tithes of corn assigned to him latterly for the pension of 50 marks. Notwithstanding etc. and privileges and indults granted to the monastery and order and to the abbot and convent, even if they have been granted *motu proprio*, of certain knowledge, and under [disqualifying][16] decrees, even stronger, more efficacious, and unusual decrees, even if granted on the advice of the cardinals in consistory, and even if it is expressly laid down in them that annual pensions on the fruits of the order's monasteries cannot be reserved, the which privileges etc. the pope (having their true tenors as expressed), specially and expressly, derogates for this once only.

Executory to the bishops of Agia[17] and Aberdeen and the official of Moray, or two or one of them, acting in person or by proxy.

Vite ac morum honestas . . . The executory begins: *Hodie dilecto filio Hugoni Martini* . . . *F de parma; · P· de planca / · B· / · B· xxx xx Bolis·*

[1] spelt *Kynlos* in the executory

[2] (?)*Alla* deleted and initialled *B.* before *Alathan*

[3] *sic*; for 'Petmedan'? *Cf*. no. 793

[4] Innocent's letters are exemplified above, at no. 144; *cf*. also, above, no. 793

[5] 'beneficiorum' wanting

[6] *ecc(lesi)ar(um); recte*: 'causarum'

[7] *quinquaginta* written at start of line; *quin-* in the margin: entered later?

[8] spelt *Allathari* in the executory

[9] at this point the executory has: *Syd et cum molendino eiusdem Wetno' Vtherellon etiam'*

[10] spelt *Ʒondir* in the executory

[11] spelt *Culustonn'* in the executory

[12] spelt *Vattirtonn'* in the executory

[13] spelt *Bananna'* in the executory

[14] spelt *Crethed* in the executory

[15] at this point the executory has: *ac de Tulyma' et Traig similter cum pertinentiis*

[16] *inhabitationibus; recte*: 'inhabilitationibus'?

[17] *Agnien.*; for 'Agien. '

929   19 January 1503   *Reg. Lat.* 1119, fos 21ʳ-23ᵛ

To John Duncani, rector of the parish church, called a rectory, of Annand, d. Glasgow. Following the pope's reservation of all benefices, with and without cure, vacated then and in the future at the apostolic see to his own collation and disposition, the above parish church has become vacant by the free resignation of William Turnbul, its late rector, who then held it, made spontaneously into the hands of the pope, (who has suspended, and decreed to have no place or effect in the above vacancy, any special or general reservations, expectative graces, unions, etc., in perpetuity or for a time, suppressions, extinctions, appointments of coadjutors without William's consent, nominations, faculties of nominating and collating to nominees and others, and other faculties, mandates, and indults, even ones with provisions or other [dispositions][1] as from the day when it shall have become vacant by William's cession, death, resignation, or otherwise, hitherto granted by the pope, apostolic see, or its legates, to any persons, even cardinals of the Holy Roman Church, and to continual commensal familiars, even of a (?) scriptor ((?) *descriptoris*), even to officials of the Roman curia, even to those actually exercising their offices, even ones granted in contemplation or consideration of kings, queens, dukes, or other princes, or on account of remuneration of labour and services, even labour and services performed for the pope and the apostolic see, or ones in recompense for ceded or lost rights,[2] even to no one's favour or advantage, even ones granted *motu proprio, ex certa scientia*, and *de apostolice potestatis plenitudine*, with clauses derogatory of derogatory clauses, and other stronger, more efficacious, and unusual clauses, and with nullifying decrees,[3] in general or in particular, or even ones extending expressly to the above parish church), and admitted by him, and is vacant at present, being reserved as above. The pope hereby collates the above parish church, whose annual value does not exceed 14 pounds sterling, whether vacant as above or howsoever etc., even if it has been vacant for so long that by the Lateran statutes its collation has lawfully devolved on the apostolic see, etc., with all its rights and appurtenances, to John, and makes provision of the same. Notwithstanding etc.

Executory to the bishop of Agia (*Agien.*) and the archdeacon of the church of Ross and the official of Glasgow, or two or one of them, acting in person or by proxy.

Vite ac morum honestas . . .
F de parma; L. puccius / · B· / · B· xx. x. Quinto KL' aprilis anno Vndecimo [28 March 1503], · *Bolis*

[1] MS: *dispen(sationi)bus* (apparently); *recte* 'dispositionibus'?

[2] *in recompense . . . rights*] repeated verbatim below, seemingly in error; the repetition ignored by this summary

[3] *unusual clauses . . . decrees*] repeated almost verbatim below, seemingly in error; the repetition ignored by this summary

930   7 February 1503   *Reg. Lat.* 1119, fos 61ᵛ-64ᵛ

To the bishop of Ossory, the prior of the monastery, usually governed by a prior, of B. Mary, *de Insula Viventium* [Monaincha], d. Killaloe, and Matthew Obrien, canon of the church of Killaloe, mandate in favour of Rory Omaynnachan,[1] cleric, d. Ossory,[2] (who, as he asserts, notwithstanding a defect of birth as the son of an unmarried cleric and an unmarried woman, has been marked with clerical character, otherwise however duly). The pope has learned that the priorship of the monastery, usually governed by a prior, of St Kieran, Sayr,[3] OSA, d. Ossory, is vacant *certo modo* at present and has been vacant for so long that by the Lateran statutes its collation has lawfully devolved on the apostolic see, although Odo Okeacboyll, who bears himself as prior, has detained it without any title or support of law, temerariously and *de facto*, for a certain time, as he still does; and that Rory wishes to enter the monastery, under the regular habit. Wishing to encourage Rory, the pope hereby commands that the above three (or two or one of them), if, having summoned Odo and others concerned, [they find] the priorship, which is conventual and whose annual value does not exceed 28 marks sterling, to be vacant (howsoever etc.), and Rory to be suitable and there to be no canonical obstacle, shall cause him to be received as a canon, the regular habit to be bestowed on him in accordance with the custom of the monastery, and Rory to be given charitable treatment therein; and, if Rory wishes to make the usual regular profession made by the said canons, receive and admit it; and collate and assign the priorship, (even if it has been vacant for so long that by the Lateran statutes its collation has lawfully devolved on the apostolic see, etc.), with all rights and appurtenances, to Rory, inducting him etc. having removed Odo and any other unlawful detainer, and causing Rory (or his proctor) to be admitted to the priorship and its fruits etc., rights and obventions to be delivered to him. [Curbing] gainsayers etc. Notwithstanding etc. Also the pope dispenses Rory — a secular cleric — to receive the priorship, if conferred on him by virtue of the presents, and retain it without having taken the habit and made his profession for six months (calculated from the day of his taking peaceful possession); notwithstanding the defect of birth etc. The pope's will is, however, that, after the said six-month period has elapsed, Rory shall — unless he has previously been received as a canon of the said monastery by virtue of the presents, the habit has been bestowed on him, and he has made his profession — be bound to resign the priorship — which the pope decrees vacant thenceforth — completely.

Apostolice sedis circumspecta benignitas regularem vitam ducere cupientibus . . .
. S. de Castello / · B· / . B. xxx. Quinto Id' Martij anno Vndecimo. [11 March 1503], *Bolis*

[1] another letter ((?) 'n') at the end may be deleted

[2] MS: *dicte diocesis*, evidently referring to Ossory, the word order of the text not being strictly adhered to in this summary

[3] the 'r' doubtful

---

931   22 September 1502   *Reg. Lat.* 1119, fos 119[r]-121[r]

To Adam Gordone, cleric, d. Moray, reservation, constitution and assignment of a pension, as below. This day Adam has, through a certain specially appointed proctor of his, spontaneously and freely, resigned the precentorship of the church of Moray, which he was holding at the time, into the pope's hands, and the pope, admitting the resignation, has, by other letters of his, collated and made provision of the precentorship, vacant by the said resignation and previously reserved to apostolic disposition, to Alexander Gordone, precentor of this church, as is more fully contained in those letters. Lest Adam should suffer excessive loss on this account, the pope hereby reserves, constitutes and assigns to him an annual pension of a third part of the gross fruits etc. of the precentorship, equivalent to 20 pounds sterling or thereabouts, payable in full to Adam for life (or to his specially appointed proctor) by Alexander (who has given his express assent thereto) and by his successors holding the precentorship at the time, each year, one half on the Nativity of Jesus Christ and the other on that of B. John the Baptist. With decree etc. that if Alexander, or any one of his successors, fails to make payment on the said feasts, or within the thirty days immediately following, he shall, after this time has elapsed, incur sentence of excommunication, from which he cannot be absolved, except on the point of death, until he shall have made absolution in full or reached agreement in respect of it with Adam (or his proctor) and, if he remains obdurate under that sentence for a further six months, he shall thereupon be deprived in perpetuity of the precentorship, which shall be deemed vacant automatically. Notwithstanding etc.

Executory to the archbishop of Ragusa, the dean of the church of Ross and the official of Moray, or two or one of them, acting in person or by proxy.

Vite ac morum honestas . . . The executory begins: *Hodie dilecto filio Adam Gordone* . . . . *A. de sancto severino; A. Colotius* / · *B·* / · *B· xij· x Bolis·*

---

932   2 November 1502   *Reg. Lat.* 1119, fos 152ᵛ-153ʳ

To the abbot of the monastery *de Legedei* [Abbeyleix], d. Leighlin, and the archdeacon of the church of Leighlin and Florence Ogerrwayn, canon of the church of Clonfert, mandate in favour of William Oeluana,[1] priest, d. Leighlin (who, some time ago, as he asserts, was dispensed by apostolic authority notwithstanding a defect of birth as the son of a priest and an unmarried woman to be promoted to all, even sacred, orders and to hold a benefice, even if it should have cure of souls; and, by virtue of the dispensation, was afterwards promoted to all sacred orders and acquired a certain benefice vacant *certo modo* which was canonically collated to him, and later resigned it). The pope has learned that the perpetual vicarages of the parish churches of Kylsnalay and Muanay, d. Leighlin, have been vacant *certo modo* and are vacant at present. He hereby commands that the above three, or two or one of them, in person or by proxy, shall collate and assign the vicarages, whose annual value does not exceed 6 marks sterling, (vacant howsoever etc., even if they have been vacant for so long that by the Lateran statutes their collation has lawfully devolved on the apostolic see, etc.), with all rights and appurtenances, to William, inducting him etc. having removed any unlawful detainers and causing William (or his proctor) to be admitted to the vicarages and their fruits etc., rights and obventions to be delivered to him. [Curbing] gainsayers etc. Notwithstanding etc. Also the pope dispenses William to receive the vicarages, if conferred on him by virtue of the presents, and retain them together for life, notwithstanding etc. With the proviso that the said vicarages shall not be defrauded of due services and the cure of souls therein shall not be neglected.

Vite ac morum honestas . . .
S de Castello / . B. / · B· xx Quinto decimo KL.' decembr' anno Vndecimo · [17 November 1502], *Bolis·*

[1] *sic*; 'Ocluana'?

933   15 October 1502   *Reg. Lat.* 1119, fos 154ᵛ-156ʳ

To Thomas Bremeche(n)ni[1] and William Ocaassay, canons of the church of Tuam, and Florence Ogerwayn, canon of the church of Kilmacduagh, mandate in favour of Walter de Burgo, cleric, d. Clonfert (who, as he asserts, is of noble, even comital, birth by both parents and suffers a defect of birth as the son of an unmarried man and an unmarried woman). The pope has learned that a canonry and the prebend of Kuymara of the church of Kilmacduagh and a chantry of the said church and also the perpetual vicarages of the parish churches of Beach [also spelt *Beache*] *alias* Chumalay[2] and Clonre[u]s[3] [also spelt *Clonrus, Clorus*] and also the chapel of St Mary, <Bougalve> [4] ds. Kilmacduagh, Killaloe and Annaghdown respectively, are vacant *certo modo* at present and have been vacant for so long that by the Lateran statutes their collation has lawfully devolved on the apostolic see, although Nemeas Occhanassoy,[5] who bears himself as a cleric, has detained the canonry and prebend, the chantry and the vicarage of Beach, and Rory Oflanura, as a priest, the vicarage of Clonre[u]s, and the guardian and friars of the house of Galway (*de Gallvia*), Order of Minors, the chapel, with no title and no support of law, for a certain time, as they do. At a recent petition on Walter's part to the pope to unite etc. the chantry, vicarages and chapel to the canonry and prebend, if conferred on him by virtue of the presents, for as long as he holds the canonry and prebend, the pope, not having certain knowledge of the foregoing, hereby commands that the above three (or two or one of them), if, having summoned Nemeas and Rory and also the guardian and friars and others concerned, they find the canonry and prebend, annual value not exceeding 6, the chantry, 5, the vicarage of Beach, 12, the vicarage of Clonre[u]s, 4, and the chapel, 6, marks sterling, to be vacant (howsoever etc.; even if specially reserved etc.) shall collate[6] the canonry and prebend, with plenitude of canon law, to Walter; and unite etc. the chantry, vicarages and chapel (which is without cure)[7] to the canonry and prebend, if conferred on him by virtue of the presents, for as long as Walter holds the canonry and prebend, with all rights and appurtenances, inducting him etc. having removed Nemeas from the canonry and prebend, the chantry and the vicarage of Beach, Rory from the vicarage of Clonre[u]s, the guardian and friars from the chapel and any other unlawful detainers from them and causing Walter (or his proctor) to be admitted to the prebend[8] in the church of Kilmacduagh and the fruits etc., rights and obventions of the canonry and prebend and annexes to be delivered to him. [Curbing] gainsayers etc. Notwithstanding etc. Also the pope dispenses Walter to receive and retain the canonry and prebend for life, if conferred on him by virtue of the presents, notwithstanding the above defect etc. The pope's will is, however, that the chantry, vicarages and chapel shall not, on account of this union etc., be defrauded of due services and the cure of souls in the vicarages and (if any) the chantry and chapel[9] shall not be neglected, but that their customary burdens shall be supported; and that on Walter's death or resignation etc. of the canonry and prebend the union etc. shall be dissolved and so deemed and the chantry, vicarages and chapel shall revert to their original condition and be deemed vacant automatically.

Vite ac morum honestas . . .
p de planca / · *B·* / · *B· xxx. pridie KL' nove'br' anno Vndecimo·* [31 October 1502], *Bolis.*

[1] MS: *Bremeche'ni*

[2] only 'Ch-', '-l-' and '-y-' certain; otherwise a row of minims capable of various readings

[3] the penultimate letter obscured by the magistral initial

[4] inserted in the margin by the enregistering scribe initialled . *B.*; (?)*Bokgallvie* in the line has been deleted, initialled *B*

[5] the '-ana-' uncertain

[6] 'et assignare' does not occur

[7] *sic; cf.* below, note 9

[8] 'in canonicum recipi et in fratrem' wanting

[9] *sic; cf.* above, note 7

934   10 December 1502   *Reg. Lat.* 1119, fos 160ᵛ-162ʳ

To the abbot of the monastery of B. Mary, *de Lege dei* [Abbeyleix], d. Leighlin, Florence Ogerwayn, [(?)canon][1] of the church of Clonfert, and Gerald Macduyl, [(?)canon][2] of the church of (?)d. [3] Leighlin, mandate in favour of Peter Maclanthlaym, priest, d. [(?)Kildare][4] (who, some time ago, as he asserts, was dispensed by apostolic authority notwithstanding a defect of birth as the son of a priest and an unmarried woman to be promoted to all, even sacred, orders, and to hold a benefice; and who afterwards by virtue of this dispensation was duly promoted to all orders, and acquired a certain perpetual vicarage of a certain parish church, canonically collated to him while vacant *certo modo*, which he afterwards resigned). The pope has learned that the rectory of the parish church of St James, Ballisonan, (which is of lay patronage), and the perpetual vicarages of the parish churches of St Patrick, Norchac and St Fintan, Tapinan, ds. [(?)Kildare] and Dublin

(*Andubleren.*), are vacant *certo modo* at present and have been vacant for so long that by the Lateran statutes their collation has lawfully devolved on the apostolic see, although Thomas Newel, who bears himself as a priest, has detained the rectory with no title and no support of law, of his own temerity and *de facto*, for a certain time, as he still does. At a recent petition on Peter's part to the pope to erect and institute a canonry in the church of [(?)Kildare] and the rectory into a simple prebend in the same and to unite etc. the vicarages to them, after their erection, for as long as he holds them, if erected and conferred on him by virtue of the presents — asserting that the annual value of the rectory and vicarages together does not exceed 24 marks sterling — the pope, not having certain knowledge of the foregoing, hereby commands that the above three (or two or one of them), if, having summoned Thomas,[5] [they][6] find the rectory and vicarages to be vacant (howsoever etc.) and the foregoing to be true, and [if, having summoned] the bishop and chapter of [(?)Kildare] regarding the erection and institution and those interested in the union, [they][7] find the foregoing to be true, shall erect and institute a canonry in the church of [(?)Kildare] and the rectory into a simple prebend in the same, for Peter's lifetime; and unite etc. the vicarages to them, after their erection, for as long as he [holds][8] them, if conferred on him as above, even if they and the rectory be specially reserved, etc.; and, in that event, collate and assign the newly erected canonry and prebend, being vacant, to Peter, with plenitude of canon law[9] and all rights and appurtenances, inducting him etc. having removed Thomas from the [rectory][10] and any other unlawful detainers and causing Peter (or his proctor) to be received as a canon of the church of [(?)Kildare], with plenitude of canon law, and the fruits etc., rights and obventions of the canonry and prebend and the vicarages to be annexed to be delivered to him. [Curbing] gainsayers etc. Notwithstanding etc. Also the pope dispenses Peter to receive and retain the canonry and prebend, if conferred on him by virtue of the presents, notwithstanding the above defect of birth etc. His will is, however, that [the rectory and vicarages][11] shall not, on account of this erection and institution and union etc., be defrauded of due services and the cure of souls therein shall not be neglected, but that their customary burdens shall be supported; and that on Peter's death or resignation etc. of the canonry and prebend the erection and institution shall be extinguished, the union etc. shall be dissolved and so deemed, and [the rectory and vicarages][12] shall revert to their original condition and be deemed vacant automatically.

Apostolice sedis providentia circumspecta ad ea libenter intendit . . .
S de Castello / . *B·* / · *B· xxx Quinto decimo KL' Januar' a'no Vndecimo.* [18 December 1502], *Bolis*

[1] see below, note 3

[2] see below, note 3

[3] the latter part of the address clause is evidently muddled: *Florentio Ogerwayn Clonferten. et Geraldo Macduyl Leglinen. dioc(esis) ecclesiarum salutem . . .*; i. e. 'canonicis' (or suchlike) does not occur, whereas *dioc(esis)* does!

[4] MS: *Deren.* repeatedly throughout the entry; but almost certainly *recte*: 'Daren.' (Kildare)

[5] 'et aliis qui fuerint evocandi' wanting

[6] *repereris; recte*: 'repereritis'; likewise next note

[7] as above, previous note

[8] verb wanting

[9] hereafter the text is confused by the (seemingly irrelevant and nonsensical) inclusion of the words: *necnon ab ea et vicariis huiusmodi et annexis vicariis*

[10] *vicaria; recte*: 'rectoria'

[11] *rectorie et vicaria; recte*: 'rectoria et vicarie'; likewise next note

[12] as above, previous note

935   23 November 1502   *Reg. Lat.* 1119, fos 164^r-165^r

To Florence Ogenwayn, Thady Machyachayn and Hobertus Macmyloyd, canons of the church of Clonfert, mandate in favour of Ristardus [Richard] de Burgo, canon of Annaghdown (who, as he asserts, holds a canonry and the prebend of Surmiricor[1] of the church of Annaghdown). The pope has learned that a canonry and the prebend called of the small churches (*ecclesiarum parvarum prebenda nuncupata*) of the church of Kilmacduagh and the rectory of the parish church of Tiraglas and the perpetual vicarages of the parish churches of Kynmara and Bellenelare [also spelt *Balanelara*,[2] *Balamura*, *Bellamo'clare*[3]], ds. Annaghdown, Killaloe and Kilmacduagh, are vacant *certo modo* at present and have been vacant for so long that by the Lateran statutes their collation has lawfully devolved on the apostolic see, although Philip Ohanle, who bears himself as a priest, has detained the rectory, and Theoderic Oberen, as a cleric, the canonry and prebend and the vicarage of Kynmara, and the warden and chapter of the church of St Nicholas, Galway (*Gallvie*), d. Annaghdown, have detained the vicarage of Bellenelare, with no title and no support of law, temerariously and *de facto*, for a certain time, as they still do. At a petition[4] on the part of Ristardus to the pope to unite etc. the rectory and vicarages to the canonry and prebend, if conferred on him by virtue of the presents, for as long as he holds the canonry and prebend, the pope, not having certain knowledge of the foregoing, hereby commands that the above three (or two or one of them), if, having summoned Theoderic, Philip, the warden and chapter and others concerned, they find the canonry and prebend and the rectory and vicarages, whose annual value together does not exceed 32 marks sterling, to be vacant howsoever etc. [and] it to be thus, shall, (even if they be specially reserved etc.)[5] collate[6] the canonry and prebend to Ristardus, with plenitude of canon law, and unite etc. the rectory and vicarages to the canonry and prebend, if conferred on him by virtue of the presents, for as long as he holds the canonry and prebend, with all rights and appurtenances, inducting him etc. having removed Theoderic from the canonry and prebend and the vicarage of Kynmara, Philip from the rectory, the warden and chapter from the vicarage of Bellenelare and any other unlawful detainers and causing Ristardus (or his proctor) to be received as a canon for the prebend of the small churches in the church of Kilmacduagh and the fruits etc., rights and obventions of the canonry and [the prebend] of the small churches and the vicarages and rectory[7] to be delivered to him. [Curbing] gainsayers etc. Notwithstanding etc. The pope's will is, however, that the rectory and vicarages shall not, on this account, be defrauded of due services, and the cure of souls therein shall not be neglected, but that their customary burdens shall be supported; and that on Ristardus's death or resignation etc. of the canonry and prebend the union etc. shall be dissolved and so deemed and the rectory and vicarages shall revert to their original condition and be deemed vacant automatically.

Vite ac morum honestas . . .
S de Castello | · B· | · B· xxx Quinto decimo KL' Januar' anno Vndecimo. [18 December 1502], *Bolis·*

[1] only *Sur-* and *-ricor* certain

[2] the 'e' uncertain

[3] *-mo'c-*

[4] 'nuper' does not occur

[5] applying to the canonry and prebend, rectory and vicarages

[6] 'et assignare' does not occur

[7] *vicarie et rectoriarum; recte*: 'vicariarum et rectorie'

936   17 December 1502   *Reg. Lat.* 1119, fos 165[v]-167[v]

To the abbot of the monastery of B. Mary, Boyle (*de Buleo*) and the prior of the monastery, usually governed by a prior, of Kylmor, d. Elphin, and Florence Ogerwayn, canon of the church of Clonfert, mandate in favour of Theoderic Otontuyr, cleric, d. Elphin. It has been referred to the pope's audience by Theoderic that Thomas Ohadean *alias* Ofyne, dean of the church of Elphin, has dared to commit perjury; that he and Dermot Oflandegayn, provost of the church of Elphin, have dared — after being excommunicated and publicly denounced as such, of which they were not ignorant — to celebrate [mass] in contempt of the keys and otherwise take part in divine offices, contracting irregularity; that Thomas — to whom, by reason of the deanery which he holds, the collation, provision and every disposition of vacant [canonries and prebends][1] of the church of Elphin pertain by ancient, approved and hitherto peacefully observed custom — has dared, for a certain sum of money given him, to collate and make provision of a certain vacant canonry and prebend of that church to one Dermot Oflandegayn, incurring simony and the sentences, censures and pains promulgated by the pope's predecessors against perpetrators of such things; that provost Dermot and Thomas Obenathayn, prior of the priory of Insimyceryneyn[2] *alias* Mitnere, OSA, d. Elphin, have dared to keep a concubine publicly; and that prior Thomas has dared to alienate and dissipate the priory's immovable goods.[3] And the pope has learned that the rectory and vicarage of the parish churches of Clontonpuyr[4] and Godellw, d. Elphin, are vacant *certo modo* at present and have been vacant for so long that by the Lateran statutes their collation has lawfully devolved on the apostolic see, although Lewis Oflandegayn has detained the rectory and Nemeas Ofinchua, the vicarage — bearing themselves as clerics — without any title or support of law, temerariously and *de facto*, for a certain time, as they still do; and a recent petition on Theoderic's part stated that if the *prepositura*, rectory and vicarage were to be united etc. to the deanery, for as long as he holds the deanery, if conferred on him by virtue of the presents, he would be able to support himself comfortably and bear more easily the burdens incumbent on him by reason of the deanery, which is a major dignity *post pontificalem*. At Theoderic's supplication — asserting that he is in his twenty-fourth year of age; that he is of noble birth by both parents; that at another time he was taken and imprisoned by certain friends of dean Thomas, even at the dean's instance, and was unable to secure his release until he had taken an oath not to impetrate the deanery; and that the annual value of the deanery does not exceed 16, of the *prepositura*,12, of the priory, 30, and of the rectory and vicarage together also 16, marks sterling — to him to relax the oath and unite etc. the *prepositura*, rectory and vicarage to the deanery, as above, the pope — considering that if the above related matters are true, dean Thomas, provost Dermot and prior Thomas have rendered themselves unworthy of the deanery, *prepositura* and priory — not having certain knowledge of the foregoing, hereby commands that the above three (or two or one of them), if Theoderic will accuse dean Thomas, provost Dermot and prior Thomas before him over the foregoing, and proceed in form of law, thereafter, having summoned respectively dean Thomas, provost Dermot, prior Thomas, Lewis and Nemeas and those interested in the union, shall make inquiry into the aforesaid matters and, if they find the truth of them to be substantiated, deprive dean Thomas of the deanery, provost Dermot of the *prepositura* and prior Thomas of the priory and remove from them; relax the oath taken by Theoderic; and then unite etc. the *prepositura*, vicarage and rectory to the deanery, for as long as Theoderic holds the deanery, as above; and, in the event of this deprivation and removal, relaxation, and union etc., commend (?)the deanery[5] and the priory, which is conventual, (even if they and the *prepositura* (which is a non-major dignity *post pontificalem*) be vacant by the above deprivation and removal or otherwise etc., even if they have been vacant for so long that by the Lateran statutes the collation of the deanery, *prepositura* and priory has lawfully devolved on the apostolic see, etc.), to Theoderic to be held, ruled and governed by him for life; (he may — due and customary burdens of the priory having been supported — make disposition of its fruits etc. just as those holding it *in titulum* could and ought to do, alienation of immovable goods and precious movables being however forbidden); and collate and assign the deanery, with the *prepositura*, rectory and vicarage annexed thereto and all rights and appurtenances, to Theoderic, inducting him etc. having removed Lewis from the rectory, Nemeas from the vicarage and any unlawful detainers from the deanery, *prepositura* and priory and causing Theoderic to be admitted to the deanery and priory and the fruits etc., rights and obventions of the deanery and its annexes and those of the priory to be delivered to him. [Curbing] gainsayers etc. Notwithstanding etc. Also the pope dispenses Theoderic to receive and retain the deanery, if conferred on him by virtue of the presents, notwithstanding the above defect [of age] etc. His will is, however, that the deanery and, on account of this union etc., the *prepositura,* rectory and vicarage and, on account of this commend, the priory shall not be defrauded of due services and the cure of souls in the rectory and vicarage and (if any) in the deanery, *prepositura* and priory shall not be neglected, but that the customary burdens of the *prepositura,* rectory and vicarage and the aforesaid burdens of the priory shall be supported; and that on Theoderic's death or resignation etc. of the deanery the union etc. shall be dissolved and so deemed and the *prepositura,* rectory and vicarage shall revert to their original condition and be deemed vacant automatically.

Decet ex benignitate sedis apostolice ...
S de Castello / · B· /: B· xxxx Tertio non' Januar' anno decimo. [3 January 1502], *Bolis·*

¹ *canonicatum et prebendam ... vacantium; recte:* 'canonicatuum et prebendarum ... vacantium'

² uncertain reading

³ Remarkably dean Thomas, provost Dermot and prior Thomas are termed *iniquitatis filii* (instead of 'dilecti filii').

⁴ uncertain reading

⁵ Text apparently confused: here: *decanatum et qu(i) conventualis est ———prioratum predictos ...;* yet below, seemingly, only the priory is to be commended, and the deanery is to be collated. Perhaps significantly, there is a short space before *prioratum* (enough for one or two words), now filled by three roughly horizontal lines.

937   11 February 1503   *Reg. Lat.* 1119, fos 171ᵛ-172ʳ

To Patrick Panter, perpetual vicar of the parish church of Kylmany, d. St Andrews, collation and provision. Following the pope's reservation to his own collation and disposition of all benefices, with and without cure, vacated then and in the future at the apostolic see, the perpetual vicarage of the above parish church of Kylmany, has become vacant by the free resignation of Alexander Dobi, its late perpetual vicar, which he held at the time, through M. Leonard de Bertinis, priest of Siena, scriptor and papal familiar, his specially appointed proctor, spontaneously into the pope's hands, and admitted by him at the said see, and is vacant at present, being reserved as above. The pope therefore hereby collates and makes provision of the vicarage, whose annual value does not exceed 9 pounds sterling, (vacant as above, or howsoever etc., even if it has been vacant for so long that by the Lateran statutes its collation has lawfully devolved on the apostolic see, etc.), with all rights and appurtenances, to Patrick. Notwithstanding etc.

Executory to the archbishop of Ragusa, the prior of the church of St Andrews and the dean of the church of Dunkeld, or two or one of them, acting in person or by proxy.

Vite ac morum honestas . . . The executory begins: *Hodie dilecto filio Patritio Panter . . .*
A de S^{to} Severino; A colotius[1] */ · B· / · B· xij· x· nono Kl' Martij anno Vndecimo* [21
February 1503], · *Bolis·*

[1] both names written in a different ink from that of the text: entered later?

938   14 February 1503   *Reg. Lat.* 1119, fos 176^{r}-177^{v}

To the prior of the monastery, usually governed by a prior, of B. Mary, Kathgrell, d.
Limerick, and Maurice Offellayn, canon of the church[1] of Limerick, and Matthew
Obrien, canon of the church of Killaloe, mandate in favour of Thomas Oduir, cleric,
d. Cashel,[2] (who, as he asserts, notwithstanding a defect of birth as the son of an
unmarried, noble cleric and an unmarried noblewoman, has been marked with
clerical character by ordinary authority). The pope has learned that the preceptorship
of the house of Cloynhawlii, d. Cashel, of the Hospital of St John of Jerusalem, is
vacant *certo modo* at present and has been vacant for so long that by the Lateran
statutes its collation has lawfully devolved on the apostolic see, although
Redmundus Odwir, who bears himself as a brother of the Hospital, has detained the
preceptorship with no title and no support of law, of his own temerity and *de facto*,
for many years, as he still does; and also that Thomas wishes to enter the Hospital
and join the Master and Convent of Rhodes therein, under the regular habit. He
hereby commands that the above three (or two or one of them), if, having summoned
Redmundus and others concerned, they find the preceptorship, which is not
conventual and whose annual value does not exceed 40 marks sterling, to be vacant
(howsoever, etc.) shall commend it (even if specially reserved etc.), with all rights
and appurtenances, to Thomas, to be held, ruled and governed by him for up to six
months calculated from the day of taking peaceful possession; (meanwhile, he may
— due and customary burdens of the preceptorship having been supported — make
disposition of the rest of its fruits etc., just as those holding it *in titulum* could and
ought to do, alienation of immovable goods and precious movables being however
forbidden); and next, or even before, if Thomas so chooses, create him a knight of
the Hospital, bestow military *insignia* on him, and then — if he is suitable and there
is no canonical obstacle — receive him as a brother, bestow the regular habit on him
in accordance with the custom of the Hospital, and give him charitable treatment
therein and, if he wishes to make the usual regular profession made by the brothers,
receive and admit it; and, thereafter, collate and assign the preceptorship to him,
inducting him etc. having removed Redmundus and any other unlawful detainer and
causing Thomas (or his proctor) to be admitted to the preceptorship and its fruits
etc., rights and obventions to be delivered to him. [Curbing] gainsayers etc.
Notwithstanding etc. and [notwithstanding] statutes, customs, legislation, uses and

natures of the Hospital fortified by oath, apostolic confirmation, or by any other strengthening, or privileges, indults and apostolic letters granted to the Hospital and its master for the time being and convent, and confirmed and renewed — even ones granted, etc. by way of statute, ordinance and contract, even *motu proprio,* of certain knowledge, of the plenitude of apostolic power and on the advice of the cardinals — by which it is said to be expressly laid down that henceforth, in perpetuity, provision of the preceptories and other benefices of the Hospital at a time of vacancy is only (and not otherwise) to be made by the master and convent, in accordance with the Hospital's legislation, to brothers of the Hospital, preferably veterans, who had first worn the habit shown them by the master and convent for a certain time and made their profession into the master's hands; that no one could assume the military *insignia* and habit save at the hands of the master or other superiors of the Hospital; that collations, provisions, and any other dispositions, of the preceptories and other benefices of the Hospital, as well as exhibitions of the *insignia* and habit, performed by anyone other than the master and convent — even if done by the Roman pontiff, even *motu proprio* and of certain knowledge and with an express derogation of the statute, ordinance and privileges — are void (and so deemed) and confer no right or colour of title to possession on anyone; that the privileges and legislation of the Hospital cannot be derogated by any clauses, even by clauses derogatory of derogatory clauses, or by stronger, more efficacious, and unusual clauses, unless the tenor of the privileges etc., is fully inserted, word for word (and not by general clauses whose import implies full insertion), and the derogation is made on the advice of the cardinals, and not even then unless the master and convent have expressly assented and the letters of derogation have been subscribed by the master, and the same has been intimated by sundry apostolic letters in *forma brevis* presented at various times at certain intervals; and that derogations, even ones done on the advice of cardinals, are deemed to contain a clause that they take effect from the consent of the master and convent, and not otherwise or in any other way; the which privileges etc. the pope specially and expressly hereby derogates and wills to be derogated for this once only. Also the pope dispenses Thomas to receive and retain the preceptorship, if commended to him by virtue of the presents and then conferred as above, notwithstanding the said defect etc. With the proviso that the preceptorship shall not, during the commend, be defrauded on this account of due services; but that its aforesaid burdens shall be supported. The pope's will is, however, that Thomas shall be bound, within the said six months, to take the habit and make his profession; otherwise, the months having elapsed, the preceptorship shall be vacant and the commend shall cease.

Apostolice sedis providentia circumspecta . . .
N de Castello / · B· / · B· xxxv pridie non' Martij anno Vndecimo [6 March 1503], *· Bolis*

[1] *ecclesie* (not repeated); *recte*: 'ecclesiarum' (Limerick and Killaloe)

[2] MS: *dicte diocesis* — evidently referring to Cashel, the word order of the Latin not being strictly followed in this summary.

939   23 May 1503   *Reg. Lat.* 1119, fos 187^r-189^r

To the abbot of the monastery of B. Mary, *de Kirieleison* [Abbeydorney], and the priors of the monasteries, usually governed by priors, *de Bello Loco* [Killagh] and Ynnschfallyn, d. Ardfert, mandate in favour of Edmund de Gerardinis [also spelt *Geraldinis*], cleric, d. Ardfert. A recent petition to the pope on Edmund's part stated that he, at one time rector of the parish church of Ardwalebeg, d. Ardfert, having canonically acquired the rectory of the said church, which is of lay patronage, and peacefully possessing it for a year and more, did not, on lawful impediment ceasing and without having obtained any dispensation in this regard, have himself promoted to the priesthood; and subsequently, after the year had passed, detained it, for another two years, as he does at present, without having sought anew any other title in it, receiving fruits from it (but not exceeding 16 marks sterling), albeit *de facto*. Moreover, according to the foregoing, the rectory of Ardwalebeg through the non-promotion in question, and, as the pope has learned, the rectories of the parish churches of Eglasnalame *alias* Balyytayg and of Kyllury, which are also of lay patronage, and the particle of land of Killcolin,[1] usually assigned to secular clerics in title of a perpetual ecclesiastical benefice, d. Ardfert, are vacant *certis modis* at present and have been vacant for so long that by the Lateran statutes their collation has lawfully devolved on the apostolic see, although David Ffysmoris, priest, has detained the third[2] rectory, and Maurice Ffismoris, cleric, the second,[3] and Edmund Ffismoris, cleric, the particle, with no title and no support of law, temerariously and *de facto*, for a certain time, as they still do. At this petition on the part of Edmund de Gerardinis to the pope to erect and institute a canonry in the church of Ardfert, and the first rectory into a simple prebend of that church for his lifetime; and to unite etc. the second and third rectories and the particle to the erected canonry and prebend, for as long as he holds [the latter],[4] if conferred on him by virtue of the presents — asserting that he is of noble birth by both parents and that the annual value of the first rectory does not exceed 14, and of the second and third rectories and the particle 46, like marks — the pope — rehabilitating Edmund de Gerardinis on account of all disability and infamy contracted by occasion of the foregoing — hereby commands that the above three (or two or one of them), having summoned David, Maurice and Edmund Ffismoris and the bishop and chapter of Ardfert and those interested, respectively, and others concerned, if it is thus, shall erect and institute a canonry in the church of Ardfert and the first rectory into a simple prebend of that church, for the lifetime of Edmund de Gerardinis, without prejudice to anyone; and, in that event, collate and assign the newly erected canonry and prebend, thus then vacant to Edmund de Gerardinis; and unite etc. the second and third rectories and also the particle, which is without cure, (whether the first rectory is vacant as above or it and the other rectories and the particle are vacant howsoever etc.; even if specially reserved etc.), with plenitude of canon law and all rights and appurtenances, to the erected canonry and prebend, for as long as Edmund de Gerardinis holds the latter, if conferred on him as above, inducting him etc. having removed David from the second[5] and Maurice from the third[6] rectory and Edmund Ffismoris from the particle and any other unlawful detainers and causing Edmund de Gerardinis (or his proctor) to be received as a canon of the church of Ardfert, with plenitude of canon law, and causing the fruits etc., rights and obventions of the canonry and prebend and annexed rectories and particle to be delivered to him. [Curbing] gainsayers etc. Notwithstanding etc. The pope's will is, however, that the rectories and particle shall not, on this account, be defrauded of due services and the cure of souls in the rectories shall not be neglected; but that their customary burdens and those of the particle shall be supported; and that on the death of Edmund de Gerardinis or his resignation etc. of the canonry and prebend this erection and institution shall be extinguished and union etc. dissolved and the rectories and particle shall revert to their original condition automatically; and that before the above three shall proceed[7] to the execution of the presents, Edmund de Gerardinis shall resign the first rectory into their hands (or those of one of them) genuinely and completely.

Sedes apostolica, pia mater, ad ea libenter intendit . . .
A de S^{to} Severino / . B. / . B. xxxv. Kl' Junij anno Vndecimo. [1 June 1503], *Bolis.*

[1] second letter blotched and indistinct

[2] MS: *David Ffysmoris presbyter tertiam ac Mauritius etiam Ffismoris secundam rectorias . . .; cf.* below, note 5

[3] *sic*; see above, note 2

[4] 'illos' wanting

[5] MS: *amotis a secunda David et Mauritio a tertia . . .* Likewise David is associated with the second and Maurice with the third rectory in the 'pro expressis habentes' clause; however, *cf.* above, note 2.

[6] *sic*; see above note 5

[7] *procedas; recte*: 'procedatis'

940   22 February 1503   *Reg. Lat.* 1119, fo 189^{r-v}

To Odo and Gillatius Omulinochory, canons of the church of Kilmore, mandate in favour of Fergal Megauran, priest, d. Kilmore (who, some time ago, as he asserts, was dispensed by apostolic authority notwithstanding a defect of birth as the son of a bishop and an unmarried woman to be promoted to all, even sacred, orders and to hold a benefice, [even] if it should have cure of souls; and afterwards was duly promoted to the said orders). The pope has learned that the perpetual vicarage of the parish church of Tempulpuirt *alias* Ynesbrachyn, d. Kilmore, is vacant *certo modo* at present and has been vacant for so long that by the Lateran statutes its collation has lawfully devolved on the apostolic see. He hereby commands that the above two, or one of them, in person or by proxy, shall collate and assign the vicarage, whose annual value does not exceed 8 marks sterling, (vacant howsoever etc.; even if specially reserved etc.), with all rights and appurtenances, to Fergal, inducting him etc. having removed any unlawful detainer and causing Fergal (or his proctor) to be admitted to the vicarage and its fruits etc., rights and obventions to be delivered to him. [Curbing] gainsayers etc. Notwithstanding etc.

Vite ac morum honestas . . .
A de *S*^*to* *Severino* / *[-]*^1 / · *B*· *x· Kl' Junij anno Vndecimo* [1 June 1503], *Bolis*

1 no magistral initial

941   4 March 1503   *Reg. Lat.* 1119, fos 200^r-201^r

To the prior of the monastery, usually governed by a prior, of B. Mary, Rattgell,1 d. Limerick, the dean of the church of Lismore and William Hanlayn, canon of the church of Cloyne, mandate in favour of Philip Hanlayn, cleric, d. Cloyne (who, as he asserts, notwithstanding a defect of birth as the son of an unmarried cleric and an unmarried woman, has been duly marked with clerical character by ordinary authority). The pope has learned that the perpetual vicarages of the parish churches of Dirwylleayn [also spelt *Dirwilleayn*] and Kylidariri [also spelt *Kyllydariri*], d. Cloyne, are vacant *certo modo* at present and have been vacant for so long that by the Lateran statutes their collation has lawfully devolved on the apostolic see, although Richard Flemyng *alias* Plemyn has detained the vicarage of Dirwylleayn and Thady Myninayn2 and Donat Ohenassa that of Kylidariri, dividing the fruits between themselves — bearing themselves as priests — with no title and no support of law, of their own temerity and *de facto*, for many years, as they still do. He hereby commands that the above three (or two or one of them), if, having summoned Richard, Thady and Donat and others concerned, they find the vicarages, whose annual value together does not exceed 12 marks sterling, to be vacant (howsoever etc.), shall collate and assign them, (even if specially reserved etc.), with all rights and appurtenances, to Philip, inducting him etc. having removed Richard, Thady and Donat and any other unlawful detainers and causing Philip (or his proctor) to be admitted to the vicarages and their fruits etc., rights and obventions to be delivered to him. [Curbing] gainsayers etc. Notwithstanding etc. Also the pope dispenses Philip to receive and retain the vicarages together for life, if conferred on him by virtue of the presents, to resign them, at once or successively, simply or for exchange, as often as he pleases, and in their place receive up to two other, similar or dissimilar, benefices, with or without cure, and retain them together for life, as above; notwithstanding the said defect etc. With the proviso that the said vicarages and other benefices shall not, on this account, be defrauded of due services and the cure of souls in the vicarages and (if any) the other benefices aforesaid shall not be neglected.

Vite ac morum honestas . . .
N de *Castello* / · *B* / · *B*· *xxxx· Septimo Id' Martij anno Vndecimo·* [9 March 1503], *Bolis·*

1 or *Rathgell*
2 only *My-* and *-ayn* certain; the five intervening minims of uncertain value

942[1] **1 March 1503**[2] *Reg. Lat.* 1119, fos 202[r]-203[v]

To the prior of the monastery, usually governed by a prior, of St Mary, Rachel, d. Limerick, and Philip Odwir, canon of the church of Cashel, and William Hanlan, canon of the church of Cloyne, mandate in favour of James Radmundi[3] Mauritii de Geraldinis, cleric, d. Limerick. The pope has learned that the perpetual vicarages of the parish churches of <Cloymcoma(r)tha>[4] [also spelt <Cloyncoma(r)tha>,[5] <Cloyncomartha>,[6] <Cloycoma(r)tha>,[7] <Cloyncomard>],[8] ds. Limerick and Cloyne,[9] (which Davit[10] Os. . ayn,[11] the late perpetual vicar held while he lived, [and which] by his death outside the Roman curia) and of Balincheyn [also spelt *Balinchtyn, Balinchthy,*[12] *Balynchtyn, Balynchty,* <(?)Balinchechyn>[13]] *alias* Cormootin[14] [also spelt *Cormootyn*], d. Limerick, are vacant *certo modo* at present, and the vicarage of Balincheyn *alias* Cormootin has been vacant for so long that by the Lateran statutes its collation has lawfully devolved on the apostolic see, although Thomas Offaeyn, who bears himself as a priest, d. Limerick, has detained the vicarage of Cloymcoma(r)tha for many months, but short of a year, without canonical title, and James Oronayn, as a cleric, d. Limerick, that of Balincheyn *alias* Cormootin, for many months, with no title and no support of law, of their own temerity and *de facto*, as they still do. At a recent petition on the part of James Radmundi to the pope to erect and institute the vicarage of Cloymcoma(r)tha into a canonry and prebend of the church of Limerick, and unite etc. the vicarage of Balincheyn *alias* Cormootin to the erected canonry and prebend, for as long as he holds [the latter], if conferred on him by virtue of the presents — asserting that the annual value of the vicarage of Cloymcoma(r)tha does not exceed 3, and that of Balincheyn *alias* Cormootin, 12, marks sterling — the pope hereby commands that the above three (or two or one of them), if, having summoned Thomas and James Oronayn and others concerned, they find the vicarages to be vacant (howsoever etc.; even if the vicarage of Cloymcoma(r)tha has been vacant for so long that by the Lateran statutes its collation has lawfully devolved on the apostolic see, and the vicarages be specially reserved etc.), shall, having summoned the bishop and chapter of Limerick, erect and institute the vicarage of Cloymcoma(r)tha into a canonry and prebend of the church of Limerick, without prejudice to anyone; collate and assign the erected canonry and prebend, with plenitude of canon law, to James Radmundi; and, having summoned those interested, unite etc. the vicarage of Balincheyn, with all rights and appurtenances, to the erected canonry and prebend, for as long as he holds the canonry and prebend; inducting him etc. having removed Thomas and James Oronayn and any other unlawful detainers, and causing James Radmundi (or his proctor) to be received as a canon of the said church, with plenitude of canon law, and the fruits etc., rights and obventions of the canonry and prebend and vicarage to be delivered to him. [Curbing] gainsayers etc. Notwithstanding etc. The pope's will is, however, that the vicarages shall not, on account of this erection and union etc., be defrauded of due services, <and the cure of souls therein shall not be neglected>,[15] but that their customary burdens shall be supported; and that on James Radmundi's death or resignation etc. of the canonry and prebend this erection and institution shall be extinguished and union etc. shall be dissolved and the vicarages shall revert to their original condition and be deemed vacant automatically.

Ex iniuncto nobis desuper apostolice servitutis officio ad ea libenter intendimus . . .
N de Castello / · B· / · B· xxxv Bolis

[1] Throughout the entry place names in the line are deleted (sometimes in the dark ink used in the entry, sometimes in a lighter ink); with altered forms written in the margin by the enregistering scribe (Boccapaduli). Marginal insertions are initialled *B* - in the same ink as the magistral initial and signature; this ink is lighter than the text, but not clearly the same as the insertions.

[2] the latter part of the dating clause (*secundo kalendas Martii anno decimo*) in lighter ink than the text above: entered later?

[3] also spelt *Redmundi*

[4] MS: *Cloymcoma'tha* — inserted in the margin by the enregistering scribe initialled . *B.*; (?)*Cl.* . *syloynsyonew* in the line deleted and initialled *B*; the second occurrence of *Cloymcoma'tha* similarly inserted in the margin by the enregistering scribe initialled . *B.*; (?)*Cl.* . *sil. ynsyonew* in the line deleted and initialled *B*

[5] MS: *Cloyncoma'tha* — inserted in the margin by the enregistering scribe initialled *B*; (?)*Clunsyloynsyonew* in the line deleted and initialled *B*; the second occurrence of *Cloyncoma'tha* similarly inserted in the margin by the enregistering scribe initialled *B*; , (?)*Cl. ysyloynsyo.* . *yw* in the line deleted and initialled *B*

[6] inserted in the margin by the enregistering scribe initialled . *B.*; (?)*Cl.* . *syloynsyonew* in the line deleted and initialled *B*; second occurrence of *Cloyncomartha* inserted in the margin by the enregistering scribe initialled *B*; (?)*Cl.* . *syloynsyonnyw* in the line deleted and initialled *B*

[7] MS: *Cloycoma'tha* — inserted in the margin by the enregistering scribe initialled . *B*; (?)*Cl.* . *syloynsy.* . *ew* in the line deleted and initialled *B*

[8] inserted in the margin by the enregistering scribe initialled *B*; (?)*Cl.* . *syloynsyo.* . *w* in the line deleted and initialled *B*

[9] *Limiricen. et Clonen. dioc(esium)*

[10] or *David*: changed from *-t* to *-d* or vice versa

[11] uncertain reading

[12] (?)*Balynthyy* deleted and initialled *B*

[13] inserted in the margin by the enregistering scribe initialled *B*

[14] in one instance, (?)*Cor. . . otin* deleted and initialled . *B.*

[15] marginal insertion by the enregistering scribe initialled . *B.*

943   22 April 1503   *Reg. Lat.* 1119, fos 209ʳ-210ᵛ

To the abbot of the monastery of B. Mary, Boyle (*de Buellio*), d. Elphin, mandate in favour of Donald Obiugil, monk of the monastery of B. Mary, Assaroe (*de Sameria*), OCist, d. Raphoe. A recent petition to the pope on Donald's part stated that, formerly — after he, then rector of the parish churches of Cyllomardi and Inwer, d. Raphoe, had been dispensed by apostolic authority not to be bound, by reason of these churches, (which he held by apostolic <dispensation>[1]), to have himself promoted to either the diaconate or the priesthood for a period of up to five years (calculated from the end of the year prefixed by law), provided that within two years he was promoted to the subdiaconate, nor to be liable to be compelled by anyone to do so against his will — he did not, while holding the churches, have himself promoted subdeacon within the two year period, there being no lawful impediment and not having obtained another dispensation, and he received, *de facto*, the fruits, (not exceeding 7 marks sterling), after the churches had become vacant by his non-promotion, thereby incurring disability; and that — when the aforesaid monastery of Assaroe, which the late John Olaste, canon of Raphoe, held *in commendam* by apostolic concession, was vacant *certo modo*, by his death outside the Roman curia, still in the way in which it was vacant when it had been commended to him — the convent, after everyone who wanted, was able, and ought, properly to be present at the election had been summoned, assembling, as is the custom, to elect the future abbot on the day prefixed for the election, *de facto* unanimously elected Donald, who had expressly professed the order and was of lawful age, as abbot, and Donald, consenting to the election when the election decree had been presented to him, had himself confirmed as father abbot by the then abbot of the monastery of B. Mary, Boyle, OCist, d. Elphin, in accordance with the order's regular institutes, (which had been approved by apostolic authority), and the apostolic privileges and indults granted to it, everything being done at the legal times. However, according to the foregoing, the aforesaid election and confirmation do not hold good, and, as the pope has learned, the monastery of Assaroe is still, as above, known to be vacant, although Nigel Ogaltabayr, priest, d. Elphin, is detaining it without canonical title and has done so for a certain time, but short of a year. The pope — wishing to make provision of a capable and suitable person to the monastery to rule and direct it and not having certain knowledge of Donald's merits and suitability, and rehabilitating Donald on account of all disability and infamy contracted by him in the aforesaid matters — hereby commands that the above abbot shall diligently inform himself as to Donald's merits and suitability, and if he finds him to be capable and suitable for the rule and administration of the above monastery — concerning which the pope burdens the abbot's conscience — he is to make provision of Donald to the monastery, whose annual value does not exceed 24 marks sterling, howsoever vacant and by whatever person, even if vacant by the death outside the Roman curia of Arthur Ogalrabayr, its abbot, and even if its provision pertains, specially or generally, to the apostolic see, etc., and appoint him abbot, committing the care, rule, and administration of the monastery to him, in spiritualities and temporalities, and causing obedience and reverence to be given him by the convent and customary services and rights by the vassals and other subjects of the monastery. [Curbing] gainsayers, etc. Notwithstanding etc. and [notwithstanding] the privileges, indults, and apostolic letters, granted to the Cistercian order, especially those in which it is said to be expressly laid down that when the order's monasteries are vacant suitable persons who have expressly professed the order can and ought to be provided to them by the father abbots or diffinitors of the order in accordance with the regular institutes and privileges granted to the order, and provisions made otherwise, even by the apostolic see, are void; and that the order's privileges and indults cannot — even with the advice and assent of cardinals of the Holy Roman Church — be derogated, (and if they are derogated they are deemed not to be derogated in any way), except under certain ways, forms, and expressions of words, expressed therein, and with the insertion of their whole tenor, and the derogation must first be communicated, by sundry letters, to the order's superiors, at certain intervals; the which privileges etc. (which otherwise are to remain in force), even if they and their whole tenors should be fully, expressly, specially, specifically, and individually, mentioned, word for word, or otherwise expressed, and not incorporated by general clauses implying full insertion, the pope, having their tenors as sufficiently expressed, for this once only, specially and expressly derogates, etc. Also, the pope grants that if Donald is provided to the above monastery and appointed abbot on the strength of the presents he may receive benediction from any catholic bishop in communion with the apostolic see and the bishop concerned may impart it to him.

Sedes apostolica, pia mater, recurrentibus . . .
A de Sancto Severino /· B· / · B· xxx Bolis·

[1] marginal insertion by the enregistering scribe, initialled *B*

---

944   23 May 1503   *Reg. Lat.* 1119, fos 218^r-219^r

To the chancellor and the treasurer of the church of Limerick and William Offlawan', canon of the church of Lismore, mandate in favour of David <Offahym>,[1] canon of the monastery, usually governed by a prior, of B. Mary, Rachȝell', OSA, d. Limerick (who, some time ago, as he asserts, was dispensed by apostolic authority notwithstanding a defect of birth as the son of a cleric and an unmarried woman to be promoted to all, even sacred, orders and to hold a benefice, even if it should have cure of souls). The pope has learned that the priorship of the said monastery is vacant *certo modo* at present and has been vacant for so long that by the Lateran statutes its collation has lawfully devolved on the apostolic see, although Maurice Offelathayn, priest,[2] d. Limerick, has detained it without canonical title, for a certain time, but short of a year, as he does. He hereby commands that the above three (or two or one of them), if, having summoned Maurice and others concerned, they find the priorship, which is conventual and whose annual value does not exceed 12 marks sterling, to be vacant (howsoever etc., even if by the deaths, outside the Roman curia, of Thady Ylathym or Gerard Ymolierayn,[3] successively priors of it while they lived), shall collate and assign it, (even if specially reserved etc.), with all rights and appurtenances, to David, inducting him etc. having removed Maurice and any other unlawful detainer and causing David (or his proctor) to be admitted to the priorship and its fruits etc., rights and obventions to be delivered to him. [Curbing] gainsayers etc. Notwithstanding etc. Also the pope dispenses David to receive and retain the priorship, if conferred on him by virtue of the presents, notwithstanding the said defect etc.

Religionis zelus, vite ac morum honestas . . .
A de S^{to} Severino[4] / *B* / · *B· xx Tertio non'. Junii anno Vndecimo* [3 June 1503],
Bolis

[1] marginal insertion, initialled . *B.*; *Ylathym* in the line, deleted and initialled *B*

[2] unusual for a detainer to be described thus (i. e. without the 'pro se gerere' formula)

[3] the 'li' and 'a' doubtful

[4] the 'A' blotched, perhaps changed from another letter; the 'S' preceded by a blot — another letter deleted? The whole name written in a lighter ink: entered later?

---

945   3 May 1503   *Reg. Lat.* 1119, fos 221^V-222^V

To the priors of the monasteries, usually governed by priors, of B. Mary, *de Belloloco* [Killagh], of Inyschfallyn and of St Michael, *de Rupe* [Ballinskelligs], d. Ardfert, mandate in favour of Gerald de Geraldinis, cleric, d. Ardfert (who, as he asserts, is of noble birth by both parents). The pope has learned that the archdeaconry of the church of Ardfert is vacant *certo modo* at present and has been vacant for so long that by the Lateran statutes its collation has lawfully devolved on the apostolic see, although Gerald Stak, cleric, d. Ardfert, has detained it with no title and no support of law, temerariously and *de facto*, for a certain time, as he does. He hereby commands that the above three (or two or one of them), if, having summoned Gerald Stak and others concerned, they find the archdeaconry, which is a non-major dignity *post pontificalem*, has cure of souls and whose annual value does not exceed 24 marks sterling, to be vacant (howsoever etc.), shall collate and assign it, (even if specially reserved etc.), with all rights and appurtenances, to Gerald de Geraldinis, inducting him etc. having removed Gerald Stak and any other unlawful detainer, and causing Gerald de Geraldinis (or his proctor) to be admitted to the archdeaconry and its fruits etc., rights and obventions to be delivered to him. [Curbing] gainsayers etc. Notwithstanding etc.

Nobilitas generis, vite ac morum honestas . . .
A de S^{to} Severino / . *B.* / . *B. xv. nono Kl' Junij anno Vndecimo.* [24 May 1503],
Bolis.

---

946   21 May 1503   *Reg. Lat.* 1119, fos 224^r-225^r

To the abbot of the monastery of Sts Coan and Brogan, Mothel (*de Motalia*), d. Lismore, <commission and>[1] mandate in favour of William Oflawan, cleric, d. Lismore. A recent petition to the pope on William's part stated that at one time — following the renewal by Paul II of all papal sentences of excommunication, suspension and interdict and other sentences, censures and pains against simoniacs (his will being that every simoniac — manifest or occult — should incur them automatically) and his reservation of their absolution and relaxation — except on the point of death — to himself and his successors alone — he, improperly aspiring to the perpetual vicarages of the parish churches of Modelyg [also spelt *Modelag*][2] and

Luoran [also spelt *Lictoran, Lyctoran*], d. Lismore, then vacant *certo modo*, reached a pact and agreement with the then local ordinary that if the ordinary would confer the vicarages on him he would give and pay him a certain amount of money, as he afterwards did, incurring simony and sentence of excommunication and the other sentences, censures and pains aforesaid. And then the ordinary — to implement this prior pact and agreement — by ordinary authority collated and made provision of the vicarages, thus vacant, to William, (who was bound by the sentences and censures), albeit *de facto*; and William, taking possession of them on pretext of the said collation and provision, detained them thenceforth, as he does at present, receiving fruits, not however exceeding $1^1/2$ marks sterling (equivalent to 4 gold florins of the camera), from them, also *de facto*. Moreover, according to the foregoing, the said collation and provision do not hold good; and the vicarages are known to be vacant still as above. At William's supplication — asserting that he deeply regrets the foregoing and that the annual value of the vicarage of Luoran does not exceed 2, and of Modelyg, 5, marks sterling — to the pope to absolve him from simony and sentence of excommunication and the other sentences, censures and pains aforesaid; to erect and institute a canonry in the church of Lismore and the vicarage of Luoran into a simple prebend of that church, for his lifetime; and to unite etc. the vicarage of Modelyg to the canonry and prebend thus then erected, for as long as William holds them, if conferred on him as above — the pope — rehabilitating William on account of all disability and infamy contracted by him by occasion of the foregoing[3] — hereby <commissions and>[4] commands the above abbot to absolve William, if he so requests, from simony and sentence of excommunication and the other sentences, censures and pains, for this once only, in the customary form of the church, having enjoined a salutary penance on him, and rehabilitate him on account of all disability and infamy contracted by him by the said occasion;[5] and, in the event of this absolution and rehabilitation, having summoned the bishop and chapter of Lismore and those interested in the union and others concerned, if it is thus, erect and institute a canonry in the said church of Lismore and the vicarage of Luoran into a simple prebend of that church, for William's lifetime, without prejudice to anyone; and, in the event of this erection and institution, collate and assign the newly erected canonry and prebend, being vacant, to William, and unite etc. the vicarage of Modelyg, (howsoever the vicarages be vacant etc.; even if they have been vacant for so long that by the Lateran statutes their collation has lawfully devolved on the apostolic see, etc.) to the canonry and prebend thus then erected, for as long as William holds the canonry and prebend, if conferred on him as above, with plenitude of canon law and all rights and appurtenances, inducting him etc. having removed any unlawful detainers and causing William (or his proctor) to be received as a canon of the church of Lismore, with plenitude of canon law, and the fruits etc., rights and obventions of the canonry and prebend and annexed vicarage to be delivered to him. [Curbing] gainsayers etc. Notwithstanding etc. The pope's will is, however, that before the above abbot shall proceed to the execution of the presents William shall resign the said vicarages into his hands genuinely and completely; and that the vicarages shall not, on account of this erection and institution and union etc., be defrauded of due services and the cure of souls therein shall not be neglected, but that their customary burdens shall be supported; and that on William's death or resignation etc. of the canonry and prebend this erection and institution shall be extinguished and union etc. dissolved and the vicarages shall revert to their original condition automatically.

Sedes apostolica, pia mater, ad ea libenter intendit . . .
A de Sancto Severino / · *B·* / *B· xxx Sexto KL' Junij anno Vndecimo* [27 May 1503], *Bolis·*

[1] see below, note 4

[2] penultimate letter doubtful

[3] *sic*; yet, below, the pope commissions and commands this be done (see note 5)

[4] *committimus et* inserted in the margin by the enregistering scribe initialled . *B*

[5] *sic*; yet, above, the pope has already done so (see note 3). Note also that there is no mention of his being dispensed for irregularity.

947   21 February 1503   *Reg. Lat.* 1119, fos 257[v]-258[r]

To the dean and John Ohergedayn and Bernard Omori, canons, of the church of Elphin, mandate in favour of Maurice Omilkerayn, priest, d. Elphin. The pope has learned that the perpetual vicarage of the parish church of Thuinnia *alias* Thomuay, d. Elphin, is vacant *certo modo* at present and has been vacant for so long that by the Lateran statutes its collation has lawfully devolved on the apostolic see, although Thomas Ocolla, who bears himself as a priest, d. Elphin, has detained it, for twenty years and more,[1] but short of twenty-one, without any title or support of law, as he still does. He hereby commands that the above three, or two or one of them, in person or by proxy, having summoned Thomas and others concerned, shall collate and assign the vicarage, whose annual value does not exceed 5 marks sterling, (vacant howsoever etc., even if specially reserved etc.), with all rights and appurtenances, to Maurice, inducting him etc. having removed Thomas and any other unlawful detainer and causing Maurice to be admitted to the vicarage and its fruits etc., rights and obventions to be delivered to him. [Curbing] gainsayers etc. Notwithstanding etc.

Vite ac morum honestas . . .
. *S. de Castello* / *P* / *P. Grat(is) p(ro) Deo. Octavo Id(us) Aprilis Anno Vndecimo* [6 April 1503], *Thomarot(ius)* .

[1] reading 'ultra'

948   3 March 1503   *Reg. Lat.* 1119, fos 321[v]-322[r]

To the prior of the monastery, usually governed by a prior, of Inyscronayn, d.

Killaloe, and the precentor and Matthew Obrien, canon, of the church of Killaloe, mandate in favour of Matthew Ohehyr, cleric, d. Killaloe. The pope has learned that the perpetual vicarages of the parish churches of Kyllemuyr and Kyllesind,[1] d. Killaloe, are vacant *certo modo* at present and have been vacant for so long that by the Lateran statutes their collation has lawfully devolved on the apostolic see, although Rory Okaelly has detained the first vicarage and Dermot Mackynracta, the second — bearing themselves as priests of the said diocese — without any title or support of law, temerariously and *de facto*, for a certain time, as they still do. He hereby commands that the above three (or two or one of them), if, having summoned respectively Rory and Dermot and others concerned, they find the vicarages, whose annual value together does not exceed 10 marks sterling, to be vacant (howsoever etc.), shall collate and assign them, (even if specially reserved etc.), with all rights and appurtenances, to Matthew, inducting him etc. having removed Rory and Dermot respectively and any other unlawful detainers and causing Matthew (or his proctor) to be admitted to the vicarages and their fruits etc., rights and obventions to be delivered to him. [Curbing] gainsayers etc. Notwithstanding etc. Also the pope dispenses Matthew to receive and retain[2] the vicarages, if conferred on him by virtue of the presents, to resign them, at once or successively, simply or for exchange, as often as he pleases, and in their place receive another (or other) similar perpetual vicarage (or vicarages) or parish church (or churches) and retain them together for life as above,[3] notwithstanding etc. With the proviso that the aforesaid and other vicarages or parish churches held in place of them at the time shall not be defrauded of due services and the cure of souls in any of them shall not be neglected.

Vite ac morum honestas . . .
S de Castello[4] / · *B·* / . *B. xxxv. Quarto Id' Julij anno Vndecimo.* [12 July 1503], *Bolis*

[1] *et Kyllesind*: 'de' does not occur
[2] *sic; cf.* note 3
[3] *quoadvixerit* here, but not above (*cf.* note 2)
[4] not in the hand of the enregistering scribe; and in lighter ink: entered later?

949   24 April 1503   *Reg. Lat.* 1120, fos 100[r]-101[v]

To the abbot of the monastery of Suir (*de Surio*), d. Lismore, and the chancellor and Walter Buttiller, canon, of the church of Lismore, mandate in favour of Thady Oflyijd[1] [also spelt *Ofryijd*], cleric, d. Lismore. The pope has learned that the perpetual vicarages of the parish churches of Kylbarrymedyn and Rosmyr, d. Lismore, are vacant *certo modo* at present and have been vacant for so long that by the Lateran statutes their collation has lawfully devolved on the apostolic see, although Thady Okyneala *alias* Mackyneala, priest, d. Lismore, has detained them with no title and no support of law, of his own temerity and *de facto*, for a certain time, as he does. He hereby commands that the above three (or two or one of them), if, having summoned Thady Okyneala *alias* Mackyneala and others concerned, they find the vicarages, whose annual values do not exceed 15 marks sterling, to be vacant (howsoever etc. or by the free resignation of Thady Okyneala *alias* Mackyneala), shall collate and assign them, (even if specially reserved etc.), with all rights and appurtenances, to Thady Oflyijd, inducting him etc. having removed Thady Okyneala *alias* Mackyneala and other unlawful detainers and causing Thady Oflyijd to be admitted to the vicarages and their fruits etc., rights and obventions to be delivered to him. [Curbing] gainsayers by the pope's authority etc. Notwithstanding etc. Also the pope dispenses Thady Oflyijd to receive the vicarages, if conferred on him by virtue of the presents, to resign them, at once or successively, simply or for exchange, as often as he pleases, and receive others in their place and retain[2] them together for life, as above. Notwithstanding etc. With the proviso that the vicarages shall not, on this account, be defrauded of due services.[3]

Vite ac morum honestas . . .
A. de Sancto severino / · B· / . B· xxx non' Kl' Junij anno Vndecimo [24 May 1503], *. Bolis*

[1] last letter uncertain: changed by overwriting
[2] first mention of 'retain'
[3] no mention of safeguarding the cure of souls

950   23 May 1503   *Reg. Lat.* 1120, fos 106^v-108^r

To Tancred Obingill, Toroletus Macaedh and Bernard Obingill, canons of the church of Derry, mandate in favour of Donald, abbot of the monastery of B. Mary, Assaroe (*de Samena, recte*: 'Sameria'), OCist, d. Raphoe. The pope has learned that the parish church of Cyllomaird, called a union, d. Raphoe, which is of lay patronage, is vacant *certo modo* at present and has been vacant for so long that by the Lateran statutes its collation has lawfully devolved on the apostolic see, although Patrick Macgyllage *alias* Ogallcubayr, who bears himself as a priest, has detained it, with no title and no support of law, temerariously and *de facto*, for a certain time, but short of a year, as he does. At a recent petition on abbot Donald's part to the pope to unite etc. the said church to the above monastery, for as long as he presides over its rule and administration, the pope, not having certain knowledge of the foregoing, hereby commands that the above three (or two or one of them), if, having summoned Patrick and others concerned, they find the church, whose annual value does not exceed 4 marks sterling, to be vacant (howsoever etc.), and, having summoned those interested in the union etc., it to be thus, shall unite etc. the church (even if specially reserved etc.), with all rights and appurtenances, to the monastery, for as long as abbot Donald presides over its rule and administration, to the effect that abbot Donald may, on his own authority, in person or by proxy, take and retain corporal possession of the church and rights and appurtenances aforesaid, for as long as he presides over the said rule and administration, and convert its fruits etc. to his own uses and those of the church and the monastery without licence of the local diocesan or of anyone else. Notwithstanding etc. The pope's will is, however, that the church shall not, on account of this union etc., be defrauded of due services and the cure of souls therein shall not be neglected, but that its customary burdens shall be supported; and that on abbot Donald's death or resignation etc. of the rule and administration of the monastery the union etc. shall be dissolved and so deemed and the church shall revert to its original condition and be deemed vacant automatically.

Ex iniuncto nobis desuper apostolice servitutis officio meritis licet insufficientibus ad ea libenter intendimus . . .
F Bregeon / Jo / . Jo. xij. nono kl' Junii anno undecimo [24 May 1503], *Eps' Terracinen'*

951   8 April 1503   *Reg. Lat.* 1120, fos 145ᵛ-146ᵛ

Provision, in *forma commissoria*, of Hercules de Ciampantibus, cleric of Lucca, to the hospital, usually assigned to secular clerics in title of a perpetual ecclesiastical benefice, of St Michael, Cortesora (*de Co'tesora*), d. Lucca, (which is without cure and whose annual value does not, as he asserts, exceed 24 gold ducats of the camera), vacant at the apostolic see by the free resignation, made spontaneously into the pope's hands and admitted by him, of Silvester, bishop of Worcester, who was holding it by apostolic dispensation. Entry otherwise of no interest to the Calendar.

Laudabilia dilecti filii . . . puerilis etatis indicia . . .
A. de Sanctoseverino / · B· / · B. xx. Sexto non(as) Maij anno Vndecimo [2 May 1503], ₁*Bolis*

952   1 November 1502   *Reg. Lat.* 1121, fos 33ᵛ-34ʳ

To Edmund Aleyns, rector of the parish church of Swanton' Abbat', [1] d. Norwich. Dispensation and indult — at his supplication — to receive and retain for life, together with the above parish church, one, and without it, any two other benefices, etc. [as above, no. 3, to '. . . retain them together for life, as above']; and for life, while attending a *studium generale* or residing in the Roman curia or any one of his benefices, not to be bound to reside in his other benefices, etc. [as above, no. 238]. [2]

Vite ac morum honestas . . .
F de parma / Jo / Jo. Lx. Eps' Terracinen.'

[1] i. e. *Abbat(is)*?

[2] the present letter is given *apud Sanctum Petrum*, but 'Rome' is wanting in MS

953   1 November 1502   *Reg. Lat.* 1121, fos 34^v-35^r

To Thomas Tybenh(a)m,[1] MA, rector of the parish church of Preston' [also spelt *Preston*], d. Norwich. Dispensation — at his supplication — to receive and retain for life, together with the above parish church, one, and without it, any two other benefices, etc. [as above, no. 3].

Litterarum scientia, vite ac morum honestas . . .
F. de parma / Jo / . Jo. L. Eps' Terracinen. '

[1] MS: *Tybenhm'*

954   13 June 1503   *Reg. Lat.* 1121, fo 60^{r-v}

To Leonard Yeo, rector of the parish church of Hwysch, d. Exeter. Dispensation — at his supplication — to receive and retain for life, together with the above parish church, one, and without it, any two other benefices, etc. [as above, no. 3][1].

Vite ac morum honestas . . .
F de parma[2] / P· / · P· L· Thomarotius:

[1] with the addition of: 'even of lay patronage' after 'or a combination'
[2] ascender tops shaved away

955   24 December 1502   *Reg. Lat.* 1121, fos 69^v-70^r

To Thomas Wellis, MA, rector of the parish church of Heyford' Magna, d. Lincoln. Dispensation and indult — at his supplication — to receive and retain for life, together with the above parish church, one, and without it, any two other benefices, etc. [as above, no. 3, to '. . . retain them together for life, as above'][1]; and for life, while attending a *studium generale* or residing in the Roman curia or any one of his benefices, not to be bound to reside in his other benefices, etc. [as above, no. 238]. [2]

Litterarum scientia, vite ac morum honestas . . .

– N· de Castello[3] */ · B· / . B· Lx· Bolis·*

[1] with the addition of 'and of lay patronage and whatsoever tax or annual value' after 'or a combination'

[2] The notwithstanding clauses include, unusually: *necnon fundationibus eorundem beneficiorum in quibus non resideris*

[3] written in a different hand (and ink): entered later? *Cf.* nos. 956 and 957.

956   20 December 1502   *Reg. Lat.* 1121, fos 74ᵛ-75ʳ

To John Lacy, rector of the parish church of Dessheforde, d. Lincoln. Dispensation and indult — at his supplication — to receive and retain for life, together with the above parish church, one, and without it, any two other benefices, etc. [as above, no. 3, to '. . . retain them together for life, as above']¹; and for life, while attending a *studium generale* or residing in the Roman curia or any one of his benefices, not to be bound to reside in his other benefices, etc. [as above, no. 238].

Vite ac morum honestas . . .
F. de parma[2] */ Jo / . Jo. Lx. Eps' Terracinen'*

[1] with the addition of 'even of lay patronage' after 'or a combination'

[2] *N de Castello* deleted occurs above *F. de parma*; both names are written in the same hand and ink which differ from those of the entry; the *N de Castello* here is similar in appearance to that of nos. 955 and 957: entered later?

957   9 September 1502   *Reg. Lat.* 1121, fos 76ᵛ-77ᵛ

To John Yong, LLD, rector of the parish church of St Martin, d. Lincoln. Dispensation and indult — at his supplication — to receive and retain for life, together with the above parish church, two, and without them, any three other benefices, etc. [as above, no. 17, to '. . . retain them together for life, as above']¹; and, also for life, not to be bound, while residing in the Roman curia or any one of his benefices, or attending a *studium generale*, to reside personally in the church of St Martin or other benefices held by him at the time, defined as above, and requiring continuous residence by foundation, statute, custom or otherwise, nor to be liable to be compelled by anyone to do so against his will. Notwithstanding constitutions etc. and foundations of benefices in which he shall not reside, etc., even if he (or his proctor) perchance has taken or shall take an oath to observe them and not to impetrate apostolic letters contrary to them and not to make use of such letters even if impetrated by another (or others) or granted in any other way, etc. With the proviso that the church of St Martin and other incompatible benefices in which he shall not reside shall not, on this account, be defrauded of due services and the cure of souls in the said church and (if any) the other incompatible benefices shall not be neglected; but that customary burdens of those benefices in which he shall not reside shall be supported. Given at Nepi.

Litterarum scientia, vite ac morum honestas . . .
N· de Castello[2] */ · B· / . B· Cx· Bolis·*

[1] with the addition of: 'and of lay patronage' after 'in title of a perpetual ecclesiastical benefice'
[2] in a different hand and ink from the entry: entered later? *Cf.* nos. 955 and 956.

958   8 February 1503   *Reg. Lat.* 1121, fos 104ʳ-105ʳ

Union etc. At a recent petition on the part of John Tyak, BDec, rector of the parish church of St Andrew, Kenne, d. Exeter, the pope hereby unites etc. the parish church of St George, Maneton', d. Exeter, (whose annual value does not exceed 18 marks sterling, equivalent to 54 gold ducats of the camera or thereabouts), to the above parish church of St Andrew, which he holds together by apostolic dispensation, for as long as he holds St Andrew's, to the effect that John, in person or by proxy, may, on his own authority, continue in or take anew and retain corporal possession of St George's and its rights and appurtenances, for as long as he holds St Andrew's, and convert its fruits etc. to his own uses and those of the said churches without licence of the local diocesan or of anyone else. Notwithstanding etc.[1] The pope's will is, however, that St George's shall not, on account of this union etc., be defrauded of due services and the cure of souls therein shall not be neglected, but that its customary burdens shall be supported; and that on John's death or resignation etc. of St Andrew's the union etc. shall be dissolved and so deemed and St George's shall revert to its original condition automatically.

Ad futuram rei memoriam. Romanum decet pontificem votis illis gratum prestare assensum . . .
N· de Castello / · B· / · B· xxxv· Bolis·

[1] the usual clause relating to the constitutions of Otto and Ottobuono is inserted in the margin (in the enregistering scribe's hand) initialled . *B* and . *B*.

959   24 February 1503   *Reg. Lat.* 1121, fo 120ʳ⁻ᵛ

To Thomas Tompson, BTheol, rector of the parish church of Nyton, d. Winchester. Dispensation — at his supplication — to receive and retain for life, together with the above parish church, one, and without it, any two other benefices, etc. [as above, no. 3][1].

Litterarum scientia, vite ac morum honestas . . .
· F· de· Parma / · B· / B· L. Bolis·

[1] with the addition of: 'even of lay patronage' after 'or a combination'

960   11 March 1503   *Reg. Lat.* 1121, fos 122[r]-123[r]

To Edward Crakyntroppe, rector of the parish church of Musgrave, d. Carlisle. Dispensation — at his supplication — to receive and retain for life, together with the above parish church, one, and without it, any two other benefices, etc. [as above, no. 3].[1]

Vite ac morum honestas . . .
F. de parma / · B· / . B. L. Bolis·

[1] with the addition of: 'even of lay patronage' after 'or a combination'

961[1]   11 March 1503   *Reg. Lat.* 1121, fo 123[r-v]

To John Smales, monk of the monastery of B. Mary, Roche (*de Rupe*), OCist, d. York. Dispensation — at his supplication — to him, who, as he asserts, is expressly professed of the above order,[2] to receive and retain any benefice, with or without cure, usually held by secular clerics, etc. [as above, no. 32].

Religionis zelus, vite ac morum honestas . . .
F de parma / · B· / · B· xxx Bolis·

[1] *Cf.* next entry, especially note 1.
[2] This information comes from a notwithstanding clause.

962   11 March 1503   *Reg. Lat.* 1121, fos 123[v]-124[r]

To William Anstyn', monk of the monastery of B. Mary, Robertsbridge (*Pontis Roberti*), OCist, d. Chichester. Dispensation etc. [as previous entry]. [1]

Religionis zelus, vite ac morum honestas . . .
F. de parma / · B· / · B· xxx Bolis·

[1] Both entries appear to derive from the same draft: this entry has *de Rupe C* deleted (initialled . *B*.) before *Pontis Roberti* (second occurrence only); and both entries have the same abbreviator and date.

963   8 March 1503   *Reg. Lat.* 1121, fos 124[V]-126[V]

To Ralph, elect of Ascalon (who, as the pope has learned, is expressly professed OFM),[1] reservation etc. of a pension. Since the pope has, on the advice of the cardinals, this day provided Ralph to the church of Ascalon (at the time vacant *certo modo*) and appointed him bishop, as is more fully contained in his letters drawn up in that regard, and Ralph cannot receive anything from the fruits etc. of the said church, which is *in partibus infidelium*, the pope — *motu proprio* — hereby reserves, constitutes and assigns to Ralph — whom some time ago he dispensed by other letters[2] of his [to receive and retain][3] any benefice, with or without cure, usually held by secular clerics, even if a parish church etc., and of lay patronage and of whatsoever tax or annual value, as is more fully contained in those letters — an annual pension of 150 gold ducats of the camera on the fruits etc. of the episcopal *mensa* of Worcester, for life (or until he has acquired regular or secular benefices, with or without cure, of an annual value of 200 like gold ducats) or to his specially mandated proctor, to be paid in full each year by Silvester, bishop of Worcester, whose express assent has been given thereto, and by his successors as bishops of Worcester for the time being, one half on the Nativity of B. John the Baptist and the other on that of Jesus Christ, and to be received, exacted and levied by Ralph for life, even together with the said church [of Ascalon], for as long as he holds it. With decree etc. that if bishop Silvester, or any one of his successors, fails to make payment on the said feasts or within the thirty days immediately following, he shall, after this time has elapsed, be utterly interdicted from church,[4] and be denied relaxation, except on the point of death, until he shall have made satisfaction in full or reached agreement in respect of it with Ralph (or his proctor) and, if he remains obdurate under this interdict for a further six months, he shall thereupon be automatically suspended from the rule and administration of his church of Worcester. Notwithstanding the constitutions of Otto and Ottobuono etc. Also the pope dispenses Ralph to receive the said pension for life, together with the church of Ascalon, even after he has received consecration on the strength of the said provision and appointment; and to receive any two benefices, with and without cure, usually held by secular clerics, or regular benefices of any order, even if the secular benefices be parish churches or their perpetual vicarages, or chantries, free chapels, hospitals or annual services, usually assigned to secular clerics in title of a perpetual ecclesiastical benefice, or even of lay patronage, and the regular benefices be priories, *prepositure*, *prepositatus*, dignities, even conventual, *personatus*, administrations or offices, or a combination, of whatsoever tax or annual value, and [even if] the priories etc. be customarily elective and have cure of souls, if he obtains them otherwise canonically, and — provided that the offices be not claustral — retain them *in commendam* for life, even together with the church of Ascalon; (he may — due and customary burdens of those benefices having been supported — make disposition of the rest of their fruits etc. just as those holding them *in titulum* could and ought to do, alienation of immovable goods and precious movables being however forbidden). Notwithstanding etc. The pope's will is, however, that as soon as he has acquired secular or regular benefices of this [annual] value of 200 ducats (whether he acquires them together at the same time up to the said value of 200 ducats or separately to amount to this) the said pension shall be extinguished; and that the benefices retained *in commendam* shall not, on this account, be defrauded of due services and the cure of souls in them (if any) shall not be neglected; but that their aforesaid burdens shall be supported.

Executory — *motu proprio* — to the dean and archdeacon of the church of London and the vicar general of the bishop of St David's, or two or one of them, acting in person or by proxy.

Personam tuam nobis et apostolice sedi devotam tuis exigentibus meritis paterna benivolentia prosequentes illa tibi libenter concedimus . . . The executory begins: *Hodie dilecto filio* . . .
F. de parma; . L. puccius / · B· / · B· Cxx Bolis·

1 This information comes from a notwithstanding clause.

2 above, no. 445

3 wanting; *cf.* no. 445

4 The syntax is defective hereabouts, but the meaning is clear.

964   8 October 1502   *Reg. Lat.* 1121, fos 150^r-151^v

To the prior of the priory of St John of Jerusalem, near Dublin (*iuxta Dublinam*), d. Dublin, and the deans of the churches of Dublin and Derry, mandate in favour of the noble man the mayor, aldermen, sheriffs of the county, and commonalty, of the vill, town, or borough of Drogheda, ds. Armagh and Meath, joint parties to a suit. A recent petition to the pope on the joint parties' part stated that although it is laid down in the canonically enacted foundation of the hospitals of the poor, called pious places, of St Mary, Dise[1], and St Laurence the Martyr, outside the walls of the vill, etc. of Drogheda, that the appointment, removal, and deposition of the warden and infirm of the hospitals pertains to the mayor for the time being of the aldermen, sheriffs of the county, and commonalty, of the vill, etc., of Drogheda,[2] and both the joint parties and their predecessors have been in peaceful possession, or almost, of the appointment, etc., from the time when the hospitals were founded, the present archbishop of Armagh, primate of Ireland (*Ibernie*), nevertheless came with a large cavalcade to visit the hospitals and their chapels, and to extort undue, unusual, and not[3] excessive procurations from their wardens, extorted them by pretext of certain letters of his, by which he ordered them to be paid under certain censures and pains then expressed, and exacted them from the wardens, otherwise seriously molesting and injuring the joint parties and their common rights, whence they appealed to the apostolic see. At the joint parties' supplication to the pope to commit to some upright men in those parts the cases of their appeal; of everything attempted and innovated after and against the appeal; of the nullity of the extortion, letters, censures, archbishop's whole process, and everything else prejudicial to the joint parties and the places and hospitals done by him and any other judges and persons in connection with the foregoing; and of the principal matter; also the cases which the joint parties intend to move against the archbishop and other clerics over certain impediments, molestation, disturbances, common rights, damage, expenses, goods, and other matters, the pope hereby commands that the above three (or two or one of them), having summoned the archbishop and others concerned, and having heard both sides, taking cognizance even of the principal matter, shall decree what is just, without appeal, causing — by the pope's authority in the archbishop's case, by ecclesiastical censure in the case of others — what they have decreed to be strictly observed; [and moreover compel] witnesses, etc. Notwithstanding etc.

Humilibus et cetera.
L· puccius / · B· / . B· xij· Bolis̄

[1] or *Drse*
[2] *pertains . . . Drogheda*] *sic*
[3] MS: *minus*; *recte*: 'nimis' ('too')?

965   13 June 1503   *Reg. Lat.* 1121, fos 164ᵛ-165ᵛ

Union etc. At a recent petition on the part of David Knollys, BDec, rector, called warden (*custos*), of the hospital of St John the Baptist in Shaftesbury (*Shafftonia*), d. Salisbury, usually held in title of a perpetual ecclesiastical benefice, the pope hereby unites etc. the perpetual vicarage of the parish church of St Michael, Mylkeshme', d. Salisbury, (whose annual value does not exceed 12 marks sterling, equivalent to 36 gold ducats of the camera or thereabouts) to the above hospital, which he holds together, for as long as he holds the hospital, to the effect that David, in person or by proxy, may, on his own authority, continue in or take anew and retain corporal possession of the vicarage and its rights and appurtenances, for as long as he holds the hospital, and convert its fruits etc. to his own uses and those of the hospital and vicarage without licence of the local diocesan or of anyone else. Notwithstanding etc. The pope's will is, however, that the vicarage shall not, on account of this union etc., be defrauded of due services and the cure of souls therein shall not be neglected, but that its customary burdens shall be supported; and that on David's death or resignation etc. of the hospital the union etc. shall be dissolved and so deemed and the vicarage shall revert to its original condition automatically.

Ad futuram rei memoriam. Ex iniuncto nobis desuper apostolice servitutis officio ad ea libenter intendimus . . .
N. de Castello / · B· / · B· xxxv Bolis̄

966   4 July 1503   *Reg. Lat.* 1121, fos 178ʳ-179ʳ

To Henry Sleford,[1] rector of the parish church of Cherinton' [also spelt *Cherynton'*],
d. Winchester. Dispensation and indult — at his supplication — to receive and retain
for life, together with the above parish church, one, and without it, any two other
benefices, etc. [as above, no. 3, to '. . . retain them together for life, as above']²; and
for life, while attending a *studium generale* or residing in the Roman curia or any
one of his benefices, not to be bound to reside in his other benefices, etc. [as above,
no. 238].

Vite ac morum honestas . . .
N· de Castello / · B· / . B. Lx Bolis

[1] with an 'i' squeezed in (later?) after the 'd' in a lighter ink
[2] with the addition of 'even of lay patronage' after 'or a combination'

967   4 July 1503   *Reg. Lat.* 1121, fos 179ʳ-180ʳ

To Robert Ffreuill'[1] or Norbourne, prior of the monastery, usually governed by a
prior, of St Martin, New Work (*Novi Operis*), Dover (*Dovorie*) [also spelt *Dovorre*],
OSB, d. Canterbury. Dispensation — at his supplication — to receive together with
the priorship of the above monastery (which is conventual), any other benefice, with
or without cure, usually held by secular clerics, even if a parish church or its
perpetual vicarage, or a chantry, free chapel, hospital or annual service, usually
assigned to secular clerics in title of a perpetual ecclesiastical benefice, even of lay
patronage and of whatsoever tax or annual value, if he obtains it otherwise
canonically, and retain it even together with the priorship *in commendam* for life, or,
having resigned the priorship, *in titulum*, to resign it as often as he pleases and cede
the commend, and in its place receive another, similar or dissimilar, benefice, with or
without cure, usually held by secular clerics, and retain it *in commendam* or, having
resigned the priorship, *in titulum*, for life, as above; he may — due and customary
burdens of the benefice retained *in commendam* having been supported — make
disposition of the rest of its fruits etc. just as those holding it *in titulum* could and
ought to do, alienation of immovable goods and precious movables being however
forbidden. Notwithstanding etc. With the proviso that the benefice retained *in
commendam* shall not, on this account, be defrauded of due services and the cure of
souls therein (if any) shall not be neglected; but that the aforesaid burdens shall be
supported.

Religionis zelus, vite ac morum honestas . . .
F de parma / · B· / · B· L. Bolis

[1] a thin horizontal stroke through the 'll': added later?

968   30 May 1503   *Reg. Lat.* 1121, fos 218^v-219^r

To John Sowthwode, BTheol, rector of the parish church of the Holy Trinity, Gillford' [also spelt *Willford'*], d. Winchester. Dispensation — at his supplication — to receive and retain for life, together with the above parish church, one, and without it, any two other benefices, etc. [as above, no. 3].[1]

Litterarum scientia, vite ac morum honestas . . .
N. de Castello / P / P. L. Thomarotius.

[1] with the addition of: 'even of lay patronage' after 'or a combination'

969   16 May 1503   *Reg. Lat.* 1121, fo 223^r-v

To Edward Pontesbury, rector of the parish church of St Andrew Hubert at Eschepe, within the city of London, d. London. Dispensation [and indult][1] — at his supplication — to receive and retain for life, together with the above parish church, one, and without it, any two other benefices, etc. [as above, no. 3, to '. . . retain them together for life, as above'][2]; and for life, while attending a *studium generale* or residing in the Roman curia or any one of his benefices, not to be bound to reside in his other benefices, etc. [as above, no. 238].

Vite ac morum honestas . . .
. F. de. parma / · B· / · B· Lx· Bolis·

[1] supplied by the editor
[2] with the addition of 'and of lay patronage' after 'or a combination'

970   16 May 1503   *Reg. Lat.* 1121, fo 224^r-v

To Humphrey Combe, perpetual vicar of the parish church of St Nicholas within the castle of Castrisbrok [also spelt *Carisbrok*], Isle of Wight (*Insule Vecte*), d. Winchester. Dispensation and indult — at his supplication — to receive and retain for life, together with the perpetual vicarage of the above parish church, one, and without it, any two other benefices, etc. [as above, no. 3, to '. . . retain them together for life, as above'];[1] and for life, while attending a *studium generale* or residing in the Roman curia or any one of his benefices, not to be bound to reside in his other benefices, etc. [as above, no. 238].

Vite ac morum honestas . . .

F de Parma / · B· / · B· Lx Bolis

[1] with the addition of 'and of lay patronage' after 'or a combination'

971   5 September 1502   *Reg. Lat.* 1121, fos 264[r]-265[r]

To the bishop of Ross, the sub-dean of the church of Dunkeld, and the official of
Dunblane, mandate in favour of Andrew Lundy [also spelt *Lundi*] of Carnbo,[1] Alan
Cowits,[2] Thomas Dindson, William Sibbald,[3] Alexander Stot, John Aytonn',
William Stephani, Henry Philpi,[4] Thomas Mylne', William Robertson, John
Radnaldson',[5] and Andrew Colȝony,[6] also of Elizabeth Sibbaldi[7] of Balgony,[8]
Elizabeth Stot, Agnes Sibbald, and Margaret Kynloch', women, joint parties to a
suit, d. St Andrews. A recent petition to the pope on the part of the joint parties
stated that formerly, when David Lormonth't, chamberlain of the monastery of St
Andrew, OSA, city of St Andrews, falsely reported to David Meldrum, official of St
Andrews, that they were injuring him over certain tithes of corn or tithe fruits (which
he said belonged to him or to the monastery) arising in the places or vills of Balgony,
le Mylicton' of Balgony, and Spittale, or had unjustly meddled with them, the
official had, at the chamberlain's instance, illegally and *de facto* commanded the
joint parties to be cited to appear before him, in a certain term then expressed, on a
certain day at harvest or vintage festival time, to see themselves excommunicated
and be declared excommunicates or be published and denounced as
excommunicates; and then, by his unjust, interlocutory [sentence] (as he called it),
he had pronounced that the citation which had been made for the festival day, as
above, was valid, (?) as was their appearing and answering.[9] Appeal was made to the
apostolic see on the part of the joint parties, and again on the part of Andrew Lundy
of Balgorny and Elizabeth Sibbaldi[10] aforesaid,[11] because after the prior and
convent had sued them over production of certain rights, instruments, or letters of
lease, then expressed, (which they falsely asserted Andrew and Elizabeth were
bound to produce), praying that they be condemned and compelled to produce the
rights etc. at the trial, the official — proceeding wrongly and *de facto* in the case —
by his interlocutory [sentence] (as he called it) pronounced that certain lawful
exceptions on Andrew and Elizabeth's part, which had been produced before him at
a suitable time and place and which by right were admissible, ought not to be
admitted; but the joint parties have not prosecuted their appeals (or perchance one of
them) within the proper time. At the supplication to the pope on the joint parties'
part, to commit to some upright men in those parts the causes of the appeals; of
everything attempted and innovated after and against the appeals; of the nullity of
the interlocutory [sentences] and of the official's whole process; of everything done
to the joint parties' prejudice by the official, the chamberlain, prior and convent, and
any other judges and persons in connection with the foregoing; and of the principal
matter, the lapse of time notwithstanding, the pope hereby commands that the above
three (or two or one of them), having summoned the prior and convent, and

chamberlain, and others concerned, if what is related about the said impediment[12] is true and having heard both sides, taking cognizance even of the principal matter, shall decree what is just, causing by ecclesiastical censure what they have decreed to be strictly observed. [And moreover compel] witnesses, etc. Notwithstanding, etc.

Humilibus et cetera.
. L. puccius[13] */ . B. / B. xij. Bolis.*

[1] thus the first mention; but mentioned later as 'Andrew Lundy of Balgorny': *cf.* note 11 below

[2] the '-its' uncertain; possibly '-tts'

[3] a final 'o' deleted

[4] the final 'i' reworked

[5] the first 'd' reworked

[6] the 'y' reworked

[7] the final 'i' perhaps deleted

[8] thus the first mention; but mentioned later as plain 'Elizabeth Sibbaldi'; *cf.* note 11 below

[9] MS: *(. . . citationem . . . factam . . . valere) et eorum comparere et responder [!] . . . pronuntiasset. . .*

[10] the final 'i' perhaps deleted

[11] *Andrew Lundy . . . Sibbaldi aforesaid] sic*; *de Balgorny* here transposed? *cf.* notes 1 and 8 above

[12] this is the first mention of an impediment — presumably one which prevented the appellants from prosecuting their appeals within the proper time

[13] written in lighter ink: entered later?

972   13 September 1502   *Reg. Lat.* 1121, fos 266[r]-267[r]

To the provost of the church of Cesena, commission and mandate in favour of Damianus de Cesena, canon of the monastery of St Mary in Portico (*in Portichu*), Ravenna, OSA. A recent petition[1] to the pope on the part of Damianus stated that at one time, after he (then called John) had entered the monastery, taken the habit usually worn by its canons, and made the regular profession usually made by them, he went, while still a young man, with a certain canon of the monastery, in whose care he was, to the university of Paris to study; that, exhausted by the journey and enfeebled of foot, he was unable to follow the other canon and had been deserted by him on the way and deprived of his advice and help; that he was for some time uncertain what to do and had at length resumed his journey and reached Paris; that the canons of the order's monasteries and places there had refused to receive him; that deprived of all hope, he put aside the regular habit, assumed lay dress, and studied letters in the university; that he made such progress that on account of his learning and skill in healing he was summoned by James, king of Scotland, and honourably received by him in his court for many months, and is still in the king's service and in secular dress, involving himself in secular affairs, incurring apostasy and excommunication. The pope — at his supplication — hereby commissions and commands <the above provost>² to absolve Damianus, if he so requests, from apostasy and excommunication and other censures and pains, for this once only, in the customary form of the church, having enjoined a salutary penance on him etc.; and dispense and indulge him for irregularity contracted as above, and to receive and retain any benefice with cure, usually held by secular clerics, even if a parish church or its perpetual vicarage, if he obtains it otherwise canonically, to resign it, simply or for exchange, when he pleases, and in its place receive and retain another similar benefice with cure, usually held by secular clerics, as above; and meanwhile to serve the king's chapel, and to wear over the regular habit, when he has reassumed it, an honest robe (*toga*) or other priestly vestment, of a dark colour, without apostasy and incurring any ecclesiastical censures; and not to be bound to wear the habit usually worn by the canons nor to be liable to be compelled by anyone to do so against his will. Notwithstanding etc. Given at Gallese, d. Civita Castellana.

Sedes apostolica, pia mater, recurrentibus ad eam cum humilitate . . .
L· pucius³ / . B· / · B· Lxxx Bolis.

¹ *petitio continebat* inserted in margin; before it: . *B.*; after it: *Aditum de Man(da)to R(everendissimi) p(atris) d(omini) d(ominici) dela porta regent(is) Bolis.*; the insertion is in a hand other than the enregistering scribe's; the surrounding note in a third hand
² *discretioni tue* inserted in the margin by the enregistering scribe initialled . *B.*
³ in a different ink: entered later?

973   9 September 1502   *Reg. Lat.* 1121, fos 276ᵛ-277ʳ

To John Ffranck, monk of the monastery of B. Mary, Medmeham [also spelt *Medmehan*], OCist, d. Lincoln. Dispensation — at his supplication — to him (who, as he asserts, made his regular profession in the monastery of B. Mary the Virgin, Fürstenfeld (*Campi Principum*), OCist, d. Freising, and afterwards was canonically translated from that monastery to Medmeham) to receive and retain any benefice, with or without cure, usually held by secular clerics, etc. [as above, no. 32, to '. . . Notwithstanding etc. ']. Given at Nepi.

Religionis zelus, vite ac morum honestas . . .
– L· puccius / Jo / Jo· xxx Eps' Terracinen.'

974   9 September 1502¹   *Reg. Lat.* 1121, fos 277ᵛ-278ʳ

To Richard Bexyll', abbot of the monastery of B. Mary, Beghin' [also spelt *Beghin*], OPrem, d. Chichester. Dispensation — at his supplication — to receive together with the said monastery, or without it, any benefice, with or without cure, usually held by secular clerics, even if a parish church or its perpetual vicarage, or a chantry, free chapel, hospital or annual service usually held by secular clerics in title of a perpetual ecclesiastical benefice, even if of lay or clerical patronage, and of whatsoever tax or half-value,[2] if he obtains it otherwise canonically, and to retain it *in commendam* for life, to resign it when he pleases, and cede the commend, and in its place receive another, similar or dissimilar, benefice, usually held by secular clerics, and retain it *in commendam* for life, as above; he may — due and customary burdens of the benefice having been supported — make disposition of the rest of its fruits etc. just as those holding it *in titulum* at the time could and ought to do, alienation of immovable goods and precious movables being however forbidden. Notwithstanding etc. With the proviso that the benefice in question shall not, on this account, be defrauded of due services and the cure of souls therein (if any) shall not be neglected; but that its aforesaid burdens shall be supported. Given at Nepi.

Personam tuam nobis et apostolice sedi devotam . . .
N. *de Castello*[3] / F / F. L. *Sanctor(is)*

[1] *anno incarnationis dominice millesimo quingentesimo secundo* inserted in the margin by the enregistering scribe, initialled *F*.

[2] *seu dimidii valoris* — unusual; usually 'seu annui valoris'

[3] in lighter ink: entered later?

975   22 September 1502   *Reg. Lat.* 1121, fos 284[v]-285[r]

To John Dussyng, cleric, d. Chichester. Dispensation — at his supplication — to him, who, as he asserts, is in his twenty-first year of age, to receive and retain any benefice, with cure or otherwise incompatible, etc. [as above, no. 240].

Vite ac morum honestas . . .
F. *de parma*[1] / · B· / · B· *xviii· Bolis.*

[1] in lighter ink: entered later?

976   10 April 1503   *Reg. Lat.* 1121, fos 288[v]-289[r]

To Thomas Legh', BTheol, perpetual vicar of the parish church of Forset, d. York. Dispensation — at his supplication — to receive and retain for life, together with the perpetual vicarage of the above parish church, one, and without it, any two other benefices, etc. [as above, no. 3].[1]

Litterarum scientia, vite ac morum honestas . . .
F de parma / . B. / . B. L. Bolis.

1 with the addition of: 'and of lay patronage' after 'or a combination'

---

977   8 April 1503   *Reg. Lat.* 1121, fo 291^{r-v}

To Thomas Ffox, rector of the parish church of Ffarthyngston [also spelt *Ffartyngston*], d. Lincoln. Dispensation — at his supplication — to receive and retain for life, together with the above parish church, one, and without it, any two other benefices, etc. [as above, no. 3].

Vite ac morum honestas . . .
L· puccius / · B· / · B· L. Bolis

---

978   19 April 1503   *Reg. Lat.* 1121, fo 306^{r-v}

To Richard Gay, perpetual vicar of the parish church of St Andrew, Pershoure, d. Worcester. Dispensation — at his supplication — to receive and retain for life, together with the perpetual vicarage of the above parish church, one, and without it, any two other benefices, etc. [as above, no. 3].[1]

Vite ac morum honestas . . .
N. de Castello / P / . P. L. Thomarotius:

1 with the addition of: 'and of lay patronage' after 'or a combination'

---

979   28 August 1502   *Reg. Lat.* 1122, fo 2^{r}

To John Wallas', perpetual vicar of the parish church of Linlithquew, d. St Andrews. Dispensation — at his supplication — to receive and retain for life, together with the perpetual vicarage of the above parish church, one, and without it, any two other benefices, etc. [as above, no. 5].

Vite ac morum honestas . . .
A de S^{to} Severino / · B· / · B· xxxx Bolis.

980   5 November 1502   *Reg. Lat.* 1122, fo 10^{r-v}

To Cornelius Oconenar and Matthew and Donald Macgyllysacdy, canons of
Kilfenora, mandate in favour of Maurus Obryen, canon of Kilfenora (who, as he
asserts, is of noble birth by both parents and holds a canonry of the church of
Kilfenora). The pope has learned that the monastery of B. Mary, Kyllsenayd, OSA,
d. Kilfenora, which the late Dermot Bryen, cleric, held *in commendam* by apostolic
concession while he lived, the commend ceasing on his death outside the Roman
curia, is known to be vacant at present still in the way in which it was when
commended to him. Wishing to make provision of a capable and suitable person to
the monastery to rule and direct it and [wishing] to assist Maurus to support himself,
the pope hereby commands that the above three, or two or one of them, in person or
by proxy, shall commend the monastery, whose annual value does not exceed 20
marks sterling, vacant howsoever, even if by the deaths, outside the said curia, of the
late Bernard or Cormac, successively abbots while they lived, etc. and [even if]
specially or generally reserved etc., with all rights and appurtenances, to Maurus, to
be held, ruled and governed by him for life; (he may — due and customary burdens
of the monastery and its convent having been supported — make disposition of its
fruits etc. just as abbots for the time being could and ought to do, alienation of
immovable goods and precious movables being however forbidden); committing the
care, rule and administration of the monastery to him in spiritualities and
temporalities, and causing obedience and reverence to be given him by the convent
and customary services and rights by the vassals and other subjects of the monastery.
[Curbing] gainsayers etc. Notwithstanding etc. The pope's will is, however, that
divine worship and the usual number of ministers and canons in the monastery shall
not, on account of this commend, be diminished; but that its aforesaid burdens and
those of the convent shall be supported.

Romani pontificis providentia circumspecta . . .
A de S^{to} Severino / Jo / Jo. xx. Eps' Terracinen'

981   2 November 1502   *Reg. Lat.* 1122, fo 12^{r-v}

To the treasurer and Gerald Machdil, canon, of the church of Leighlin, mandate in
favour of Donat Ymillam, cleric, d. Leighlin. Following the issue by Paul II of the
letters, *Paulus episcopus [. . .] ad perpetuam rei memoriam. Cum in omnibus
judiciis . . . ,*[1] a recent petition to the pope on Donat's part stated that if several
possessions of the grange of Ballam,[2] lawfully belonging to the priory of B. Mary,
Glassarge, OSB, d. Ferns, customarily given by its prior in farm or rent under a
certain annual pension payable to him were to be granted to Donat in like farm or
rent under the usual annual pension, he, Donat, would take care that the said
possessions would — to the priory's evident utility — be not merely conserved but

improved; and supplication was made to the pope to cede the possessions to Donat for life in farm or rent etc. The pope — not having certain knowledge of the foregoing and not having the sites, situations, values, quality, boundaries and names of the possessions sufficiently expressed in the presents — hereby commands the above two, jointly, after the possessions have been first specified and expressed before them and the form of Paul's letters observed, to inform themselves as to each and every one of the aforesaid matters and all the circumstances thereof; and, if they find them to be thus and that to cede the foregoing would be to the priory's evident utility, grant and assign, with the prior and convent's express consent, the possessions to Donat for life in farm or rent under the usual annual payment payable by Donat to the prior for the time being. Notwithstanding etc.

Ex iniuncto nobis desuper apostolice servitutis officio ad ea [. . .] libenter intendimus . . .
S de Castello / · B· / ⎸B· x Bolis⁻

¹ See above, no. 558.

² MS: *possessiones Grange Da ballam; recte*: 'possessiones grangie de Ballam'?

982   8 November 1502   *Reg. Lat.* 1122, fos 16ʳ-17ᵛ

To Maurice Offaellayn, canon of Limerick,¹ mandate² in favour of Edmund Omillayn, cleric, d. Leighlin.³ The pope has learned that the perpetual vicarages of the parish churches of Kalyn, Kerrach and Kellasna, d. Leighlin, are vacant *certo modo* at present and have been vacant for so long that by the Lateran statutes their collation has lawfully devolved on the apostolic see, although Thady Occurrin has detained the first two vicarages, and Henry Omyllayn, the third — bearing themselves as clerics — with no title and no support of law, of their own temerity and *de facto*, for a certain time, as they do. And, as a recent petition to the pope on Edmund's part stated, at one time he — after he, notwithstanding a defect of birth as the son of a priest and an unmarried woman, had been marked with clerical character otherwise duly — was present at a certain conflict in which several men were killed and others had limbs mutilated, nevertheless he did not kill or mutilate anyone with his own hands. At Edmund's supplication — asserting that the annual value of the vicarages does not exceed 12 marks sterling — to the pope to absolve him from the excess; dispense him on account of the irregularity contracted by him by occasion of the foregoing; erect and institute a canonry in the church of Leighlin and the first vicarage into a simple prebend of the said church, like its other prebends; and unite etc. the other two vicarages to the erected canonry and prebend, for as long as Edmund holds the canonry and prebend — the pope — who does not have certain knowledge of the foregoing — hereby commands⁴ the above [canon] to absolve Edmund, if he so requests, from the excess, for this once only, in the customary form of the church, having enjoined a salutary penance on him etc.; dispense him on account of the irregularity which he contracted on this account and to receive and retain the canonry and prebend (if erected by virtue of the presents and conferred on him); rehabilitate him on account of all disability and infamy contracted by him by the said occasion; and, if and after — having summoned the bishop and chapter of Leighlin, Thady, Henry and also those interested in the union and others concerned — he lawfully establishes the foregoing, erect a canonry in the said church of Leighlin and the first vicarage into a simple prebend of the same, like its other prebends, without prejudice to anyone; and unite etc. the other vicarages (howsoever they be vacant etc.; even if specially reserved etc.) to the erected canonry and prebend, for as long as Edmund holds the latter; and, in the event of this absolution, dispensation, erection and union etc., collate and assign the newly erected canonry and prebend, being vacant, with plenitude of canon law and the annexes and all their rights and appurtenances, to Edmund, inducting him etc. having removed Thady and Henry and any other unlawful detainers from them; and cause Edmund (or his proctor) to be received as a canon of the church of Leighlin, with plenitude of canon law, and the fruits etc., rights and obventions of the collated canonry and prebend and annexes to be delivered to him. [Curbing] gainsayers etc. Notwithstanding etc. The pope's will is, however, that the vicarages shall not, on account of this erection and union etc., be defrauded of due services and the cure of souls therein shall not be neglected, but that their customary burdens shall be supported; and that on Edmund's death or resignation etc. of the canonry and prebend the union etc. shall be dissolved and erection cease and the vicarages shall revert to their original condition and the canonry and prebend shall be extinguished automatically.

Sedes apostolica, pia mater, recurrentibus ad eam cum humilitate . . .
L puccius / · *B·* / · *B· xxxx Bolis.*

[1] *Florentio Ugerrimayn* [or *Ugerrunayn*] *canonico Clonferten.* in the line has been deleted and initialled . *B.* , . *B* and *B*; and, inserted in the margin, is: *Mauricio Offaellayn canonico Limericen.* (in a hand other than the enregistering scribe's) with, below: *Cassatum et corectum de Mandato R(everendissimi) p(atris) d(omini) Jo(hannis) Ragusin. regentis per me . B. Bolis*

[2] see below, note 4

[3] MS: *dicte diocesis* — evidently referring to Leighlin, the word order of the text not being strictly followed in this summary

[4] *mandamus* only; 'committimus et' does not occur

983   17 September 1502   *Reg. Lat.* 1122, fos 23ᵛ-24ʳ

To Geoffrey de Burgo, canon of the church of Kilmacduagh, union etc. Following the pope's reservation some time ago of all benefices, with and without cure, vacated then and in the future at the apostolic see to his own collation and disposition, the perpetual vicarage of the parish church of Disterkellay, d. Kilmacduagh, became vacant by the free resignation of Florence Ygervayn, its late perpetual vicar, who was holding it at the time, made spontaneously into the pope's hands and admitted by him at the said see, and is vacant at present, being reserved as above. At a recent petition on Geoffrey's part to the pope to unite etc. the said vicarage to the canonry and prebend of Disterkellay, church of Kilmacduagh, which he holds, for as long as he holds them — asserting that the annual value of the canonry and prebend does not exceed 3, and of the vicarage, 2, marks sterling, the pope hereby unites etc. the vicarage, (vacant as above or howsoever etc., even if it has been vacant for so long that by the Lateran statutes its collation has lawfully devolved on the apostolic see etc.), with all rights and appurtenances, to the canonry and prebend, for as long as he holds the canonry and prebend; to the effect that he may, on his own authority, in person or by proxy, take and have corporal possession of the vicarage and rights and appurtenances aforesaid, for as long as he holds the canonry and prebend, and convert its fruits etc. to his own uses and those of the vicarage and of the canonry and prebend, without licence of the local diocesan and of anyone else. Notwithstanding etc. The pope's will is, however, that the vicarage shall not, on account of this union etc., be defrauded of due services and the cure of souls therein shall not be neglected, but that its customary burdens shall be supported; and that on [Geoffrey's][1] death or resignation etc. of the canonry and prebend this union etc. shall be dissolved and so deemed and the vicarage shall revert to its original condition and be deemed vacant automatically. Given at[2] Civita Castellana.

Vite ac morum honestas . . .
S de Castello / · B· / · B· xv Bolis·

[1] MS wants his name; a cross in the margin signals the omission.
[2] Following *Datum*: *R* [the start of 'Rome'] deleted, initialled *B*

984   24 October 1502   *Reg. Lat.* 1122, fos 24^V-25^V

To Florence Ogerwayn, canon of Clonfert, mandate in favour of Matthew Ybrien, canon of Killaloe (who, as he asserts, notwithstanding a defect of birth as the son of an unmarried cleric of noble birth and an unmarried woman, has been marked with clerical character otherwise however duly; and who by apostolic authority obtained provision of a canonry and prebend of the church of Killaloe, vacant *certo modo*, and commend of the archdeaconry of the said church, vacant likewise, to be held and governed by him for life; and by the same authority has had himself dispensed to receive and retain the canonry and prebend and archdeaconry; and holds and possesses them at present). The pope has learned that the priorship of the monastery, usually governed by a prior, of St John the Baptist, at Lenanach, OSA, d. Killaloe, is vacant *certo modo* at present and has been vacant for so long that by the Lateran statutes its collation has lawfully devolved on the apostolic see, although William Okynmede, who bears himself as a cleric, has detained it without any title or support of law, temerariously and *de facto*, for a certain time, as he still does. And a recent petition to the pope on Matthew's part stated that although at another time he —

having taken up arms at the command of his lord (whom he could not refuse) — was
present at several conflicts in which several persons had been killed and mutilated,
nevertheless he did not himself kill or mutilate anyone. At Matthew's supplication,
the pope hereby commands the above canon to absolve him from the excess, if he so
requests, in the customary form of the church, having enjoined a salutary penance on
him etc.; dispense him on account of the irregularity contracted by occasion of the
foregoing and to receive the priorship, if commended to him by virtue of the
presents, and retain it together with the canonry and prebend and archdeaconry
aforesaid, notwithstanding the above defect etc.; and rehabilitate him on account of
all disability and infamy arising from the foregoing; and, in that event, and if, having
summoned William and others concerned, he finds the priorship, which is
conventual and whose annual value does not exceed 120 marks sterling, to be vacant
(howsoever etc.), to commend it (even if it has been vacant for so long that by the
Lateran statutes its collation has lawfully devolved on the apostolic see etc.), with all
rights and appurtenances, to Matthew, to be held, ruled and governed by him for life;
(he may — due and customary burdens of the priorship having been supported —
make disposition of the rest of its fruits etc. just as those holding it *in titulum vel
commendam* could and ought to do, alienation of immovable goods and precious
movables being however forbidden); inducting him etc. having removed William
and any other unlawful detainer and causing Matthew (or his proctor) to be admitted
to the priorship and its fruits etc., rights and obventions to be delivered to him.
[Curbing] gainsayers etc. Notwithstanding etc. With the proviso that the priorship
and its convent shall not, on this account, be defrauded of due services and the cure
of souls therein (if any) shall not be neglected; but that its aforesaid burdens and
those of the convent shall be supported.

Sedes apostolica, pia mater, recurrentibus ad eam cum humilitate . . .
S de Castello / · B· / . B. L. Bolis·

---

985   14 February 1503   *Reg. Lat.* 1122, fo 38ʳ

To John Dyneley, rector of the parish church of Borough Clere, d. Winchester.
Dispensation — at his supplication — to receive and retain for life, together with the
above parish church, one, and without them, any two other benefices, etc. [as above, no. 3].

Vite ac morum honestas . . .
L puccius / · B· / · B· L. Bolis·

---

986   20 May 1503   *Reg. Lat.* 1122, fo 63ʳ⁻ᵛ

To Robert Martini, perpetual vicar of the parish church of Garvok, d. St Andrews.

Dispensation — at his supplication — to receive and retain for life, together with the perpetual vicarage of the above parish church, one, and without it, any two other benefices, etc. [as above, no. 5].

Vite ac morum honestas ...
p de planca / · B· / . B· xxxx Bolis·

987[1]   **11 July 1503**   *Reg. Lat.* 1122, fos 81ᵛ-83ʳ

To the bishops of Bath and Wells and *Turen.*[2] and Thomas Gilberti, canon of the church of Wells, mandate in favour of John Vaghan, MA, perpetual vicar of the parish church of Bedmynster, d. Bath and Wells. A recent petition to the pope on John's part stated that, formerly, William Russell, DDec, canon of Salisbury, who, as he asserts, holds the rectory of the above parish church, which has been erected into a prebend of a canonry of the church of Salisbury, and the canonry — falsely asserting that John had deprived, and was depriving, him unjustly of a certain annual portion, pension, or payment, then expressed, which was customarily paid, and payable annually, by vicar John to William, and the holder for the time being of the canonry and prebend, and had deprived, and was depriving, them of their rights, and that John had thereby automatically incurred sentence of excommunication under the provincial constitutions of Canterbury promulgated against such deprivers — sued John *de facto* over this and other matters then expressed before doctor Hugh Peyntwhyn, then auditor of causes and matters of the audience of the archbishop of Canterbury, primate of all England and legate born of the apostolic see; that Hugh, [proceeding][3] wrongly and *de facto*, without following the legal procedure usually followed in such cases, promulgated an unjust definitive sentence, in William's favour and against John, by which he declared that John had deprived William of the pension, diminished (*fregisse*) the rights (*libertatem*) of the church, thereby incurred excommunication, and ought to be published as excommunicate, condemning him in costs; that John appealed to the apostolic see; and that after Hugh, having assigned a legal term and certain place to John, (which he had duly requested), for receiving the *apostolos*, had unlawfully refused to give them and appear in the said place, John again appealed to the apostolic see, from a certain injury, then expressed, inflicted on him *de facto* by Hugh. At John's supplication to the pope to command that he be absolved conditionally from the sentence of excommunication, and other censures and pains by which he is perchance deemed bound, and to commit to some upright men in those parts the cases of his appeals; of everything attempted and innovated after and against the appeals; of the nullity of Hugh's process[4], and everything else prejudicial to John done by him and William, and any other judges and persons, in connection with the foregoing; and of the principle matter, the pope hereby commands that the above three (or two or one of them), having summoned William and others concerned, shall, if and as it is just, for this once only, conditionally

absolve John, if he so requests, having first received suitable security from him that
if they find that the sentence of excommunication, etc. were justly inflicted on him,
he will obey their commands and those of the church; and, as regards the rest, having
heard both sides, taking cognizance even of the principal matter, that [they shall
decree] what is just, [without appeal, causing by ecclesiastical censure what they
have decreed to be strictly][5] observed; [and moreover compel] witnesses, etc.
Notwithstanding etc.

Humilibus et cetera.
L· Puccius / · B / . B· xiiij· Bolis

[1] there is a cross (signalling error?) at the top of fo 81[v], in the middle, before the start of the entry

[2] *sic; recte* 'Tinen.' (Tinos)?

[3] MS wants 'procedens'

[4] usually 'whole process'; *cf.* no. 989

[5] enregistration abridged by *et cetera*

988[1]   **15 July 1503**   *Reg. Lat.* 1122, fos 85[r]-86[v]

To the bishop of [Exeter],[2] mandate in favour of Roger Vernen', layman, d. Coventry
and Lichfield. A recent petition to the pope on Roger's part stated that, formerly,
Margaret Kebull' *alias* Vernon', woman, with whom he had lawfully contracted
marriage *per verba de presenti*, consummated it with connection, and cohabited for
some time — falsely asserting that she had contracted marriage with him through
such force and fear as was capable of overcoming a steadfast woman — sued Roger
(not through apostolic delegation) before Thomas Ely, archdeacon of the monastery
of B. Peter, Westminster (*Westmonasterii*), d. London, (to whom, as she said,
cognizance of such a case pertained, by ancient, approved, and hitherto peacefully
observed custom), praying that they be separated for ever and that the marriage be
decreed null; that after Margaret had appealed to the apostolic see from a certain
insufficient injury, then expressed, inflicted on her, as she said, by the archdeacon, it
had been duly requested on Roger's part that Margaret — who, according to her
plea, had been induced to contract marriage with Roger by certain of his blood
relations, through force and fear — be removed from the fellowship of his relations
and kept safely in some decent place so that she might freely say what she wanted;
and that the archdeacon unlawfully refused to do this, and Roger appealed to the
apostolic see. At Roger's supplication to the pope to commit to some prelates in
those parts the cases of his appeal; of everything attempted and innovated after and
against it; of the nullity of the archdeacon's process and everything else prejudicial
to Roger done by him, Margaret, and any other judges and persons in connection
with the foregoing; and of the principal matter, the pope hereby commands that the
above bishop, having summoned Margaret and others concerned, and having heard
both sides, [taking cognizance even of the principal matter],[3] shall [decree what is]

canonical [without appeal, causing by ecclesiastical censure what he has decreed to be strictly] observed.[4] Notwithstanding etc.

Humilibus et cetera.
L. Puccius / . B. / . B. xij. Bolis.

[1] *Cf.* above, no. 905.

[2] MS: *Oxonen.; recte* 'Exonien.'? It is unusual for a rescript of justice to have only one mandatary

[3] contemplated above, but wanting in MS

[4] enregistration abridged by *et cetera*

989   8 June 1503   *Reg. Lat.* 1122, fos 96[r]-97[v]

To the prior of the monastery, usually governed by a prior, of the Holy Trinity, Dublin, and Henry Lenat *alias* Lenet, canon of the church of Dublin, and William Ffyhan', canon of the church of Ossory, mandate in favour of prior Patrick Baldewyn' and the convent of the monastery, called a house, usually governed by a prior, of Sts Peter and Paul, Seleskyr, near Weysford, OSA, Arroasian Congregation (*de Arowacen.*),[1] d. Ferns. A recent petition to the pope on prior Patrick and the convent's part stated that, formerly, when the priory of Seleskyr was vacant by the death, outside the Roman curia, of Thomas Aleyn', its prior, the convent, (to which the election of a prior at a time of vacancy belongs by privileges — which to date have not been derogated in any way — granted to the monastery by the apostolic see), after everyone who wanted, was able, and ought, properly to be present at the election, had been summoned, assembling, as is the custom, on the day prefixed for it, unanimously, or by a majority, elected Patrick, a canon of the monastery, as prior; that Patrick, consenting to the election when the election decree had been presented to him, had it confirmed, by ordinary authority, by the bishop of Ferns to whom, under the above privileges, confirmation of the election of the prior pertains; and that everything was done at the legal times; that, previously, Richard Browne, treasurer of the church of Ferns — falsely asserting that the priory was vacant and had been vacant for so long that its collation had lawfully devolved on the apostolic see, that Thomas Aleyn' was unlawfully detaining it, and that under certain apostolic letters, which he had surreptitiously or obreptitiously impetrated, the priory ought to be commended to him, to be held, ruled, and governed, for life — by pretext of the letters had sued Thomas over this and other matters, then expressed, before William Omurrysse, canon of Ossory, whom, he said, was (with certain colleagues), the judge appointed by the letters; that canon William, proceeding wrongly, *de facto*, and lawlessly, had promulgated an unjust definitive sentence in favour of Richard and against Thomas, by which he declared that the priory was vacant and due to be commended to Richard, (which he had done), from which Thomas had appealed, by due right, to the apostolic see; that Richard then acquired *de facto* possession of the priory by lay power, intruded himself into it, and is unlawfully detaining it and its goods, receiving certain of its fruits and converting them to his own damnable uses, to the danger, unbounded prejudice, and damage of his soul;[2] and that Patrick and the convent appealed, jointly and severally, to the apostolic see. At their supplication to the pope to commit to some upright men in those parts the cases of their appeals; of everything attempted and innovated after and against the appeals; of the nullity of the sentence, canon William's process,[3] and everything else prejudicial to Patrick and the convent done by him, Richard, and all other judges and persons, in connection with the foregoing; of the subreption and obreption of the apostolic letters; and of the principal matter; and also the cases which Patrick and the convent intend to move against Richard and other clerics and laymen of the city and diocese of Ferns, jointly and severally, over the occupation and detention of the priory and its goods, fruits, etc., and over the damage, injuries, acts of violence, expenses, and other matters pertaining to the monastery, the pope hereby commands that the above three (or two or one of them), having summoned Richard and others concerned, and having heard both sides, taking cognizance even of the principal matter, <shall decree> what is just, <without appeal, causing by ecclesiastical censure what they have decreed to be strictly observed>;[4] [and moreover compel] witnesses, etc. Notwithstanding, etc.

Humilibus et cetera.
L· *Puccius* / · B / · B· xij· Bolis·

[1] designation by congregation is rare

[2] originally 'to the danger of his soul, and the monastery's unbounded prejudice and damage'; *et dicti monasterii* then deleted and initialled . *B*

[3] usually 'whole process'

[4] marginal insertion by the enregistering scribe, initialled . *B* and . *B*.

990[1]   10 June 1503   *Reg. Lat.* 1122, fos 100[r]-101[r]

To the abbot of the monastery of Walley and the priors of the monasteries, usually governed by priors, of Cartinell and Helay, ds. Coventry and Lichfield, and York, mandate as below. A recent [petition][2] to the pope on the part of Thomas Banes, cleric or layman, executor of the will of the late Thomas Nelson [also spelt *Nelso(n)*], perpetual vicar [of the parish church of N, N diocese, stated that, formerly, after] a dispute [between Thomas Banes, on the one] part, [and Thomas Ormeston (also spelt *Ormestu(n)*), the church's present perpetual vicar], on the other, over the dilapidation or bad administration of Thomas Nelson's personal property which he had ordered to be put to sundry uses by his executor, and over other matters then expressed, [had arisen] before a certain competent ecclesiastical judge in those parts, the judge, proceeding wrongly in the dispute, promulgated an unjust definitive sentence in favour of Thomas Ormeston and against Thomas Banes, from which the latter appealed to the apostolic see. At Thomas's supplication to the pope to commit to some upright men in those parts the cases of the appeal; of everything attempted and innovated after and against it; of the nullity of the sentence and the judge's process and of everything else prejudicial to Thomas done by him and Thomas Ormeston and any other judges and persons in connection with the foregoing; and of the principal matter, the pope hereby commands that the above three (or two, or one of them), having summoned Thomas Ormeston and others concerned, and having heard both sides, taking cognizance even of the principal matter, shall decree what is just, without appeal, causing by ecclesiastical censure what they have decreed to be strictly observed; and moreover compel witnesses etc.[3] Notwithstanding etc.

Humilibus et cetera.
L· Puccius· / B / . B· xij· Bolis·

[1] enregistered, so far as it goes, by the same scribe in another register and then deleted: see no. 999

[2] there is an omission in the opening part of the narrative which is supplied, conjecturally, as follows: . . . *perpetui vicarii* ['(dum viveret) parochialis ecclesie de N, N diocesis, petitio continebat quod olim orta inter eum ex una et dilectum filium Thomam Ormeston modernum (perpetuum vicarium)'] *dicte ecclesie* . . . . The omission occurs, strangely, at the point where the abortive enregistration (at no. 999) breaks off.

[3] this clause, which is usually abridged (with an *et cetera*) in the register, is, most unusually, enregistered here in full

991   4 August 1503   *Reg. Lat.* 1122, fos 138^V-139^V

To the bishop of Sodor, the prior of the priory of Birkenhede, ds. Coventry and Lichfield, and Edward Underwode, canon of the church of London, mandate in favour of John Fowler, rector of the parish church of Cristilton, ds. Coventry and Lichfield. A recent petition to the pope on John's part stated that, formerly, after he had acquired the above parish church, which had been canonically collated to him, and while he was holding and possessing it, peacefully and quietly, as he had for some time, Richard Salter and Philip Agarde — at the instance, as they said, of Thomas, bishop of Killala (who falsely asserted that John had intruded into the parish church and was unlawfully detaining it) — bearing themselves as clerics, and sometimes as keepers in spirituals of the dioceses of Coventry and Lichfield, sometimes as vicars or officials of the chapter of the church of Coventry and Lichfield (which was then vacant) — *de facto* ordered John to be cited to appear before them, to answer certain articles, or matter drawn up in articles, which had been exhibited, as they asserted, in the case they were trying; that Richard and Philip, proceeding wrongly and *de facto*, unlawfully refused to assign John a competent term, (which he had duly requested), for considering and answering the articles and accusations (*posicionibus*), and then, by their sentence, as they called it, declared that he had intruded into the parish church and, thereafter, albeit invalidly and *de facto,* they ordered the fruits etc. of the church to be sequestered, whence John appealed to the apostolic see. At John's supplication to the pope to commit to some upright men in those parts the cases of the appeal; of everything attempted and innovated after and against the appeal; of the nullity of the sentence, sequestration, Richard and Philip's whole process, and of everything else prejudicial to John done by them and bishop Thomas, in connection with the foregoing; and of the principal matter, the pope hereby commands that the above three (or two or one of them), having summoned Thomas and others concerned, and having heard both sides, taking cognizance even of the principal matter, [shall decree] what is just, [without appeal, causing — by the pope's authority in bishop Thomas's case, by ecclesiastical censure, in the case of others — what they have decreed] to be [strictly][1] observed; [and moreover compel] witnesses. Notwithstanding etc.

Humilibus et cetera.
L· Puccius· / · B· / · B· xij· Bolis·

[1] or '[without appeal, causing by ecclesiastical censure what they have decreed] to be [strictly]': enregistration abridged by *et cetera*

**992	5 October 1502[1]**					*Reg. Lat.* 1123, fos 117[v]-119[r]

To the dean of the church of Moray, mandate in favour of William Liell, priest, d. Aberdeen. Following the pope's reservation some time ago of all benefices, with and without cure, vacated then and in the future at the apostolic see to his own collation and disposition, the perpetual vicarage of the parish church of Logidurno, d. Aberdeen, became vacant by the free resignation of Andrew Liell, its late perpetual vicar, made of the vicarage, which he then held, through John Fabri, solicitor of apostolic letters, his specially appointed proctor, spontaneously, into the pope's hands, and admitted by him at the said see, and is vacant at present, being reserved as above. The pope hereby commands the above dean if through diligent examination he finds William to be suitable — concerning which the pope burdens the dean's conscience — to collate and assign the vicarage, whose annual value does not exceed 9 pounds sterling, (whether vacant as above or howsoever etc., even if it has been vacant for so long that by the Lateran statutes its collation has lawfully devolved on the apostolic see, and the vicarage is specially reserved to apostolic disposition or generally reserved at another time even because, as is asserted, the said Andrew was, while holding it, acolyte [and][2] chaplain of the pope and the said see, etc.), with all rights and appurtenances, to William, inducting him etc. having removed any [unlawful][3] detainer and causing William (or his proctor) to be admitted to the vicarage and its fruits etc., rights and obventions to be delivered to him. [Curbing] gainsayers by the pope's authority etc. Notwithstanding etc.

Dignum et cetera.
A de sanctoseverino / Jo / Jo. xx. //[4] Tertio decimo Kl' Octobrn'[5] anno Vndecimo [19 September 1502], *Eps' Terracinen'*

1 Should predate the date of expedition in the *bullaria*; in fact post-dates it!

2 *accolitus capellanus*; 'et' (or suchlike) does not occur

3 'illicito' wanting?

4 *Eps' T* deleted and initialled *Jo*

5 *sic; cf.* note 1

993   27 April 1503   *Reg. Lat.* 1123, fos 143ᵛ-144ᵛ

To the priors of the monasteries, usually governed by priors, of B. Mary, *de Belloloco* [Killagh], Inischfallyn and St Michael, *de Rupe* [Ballinskelligs], <d. >¹ Ardfert, mandate in favour of Philip de Geraldinis, cleric, d. Ardfert. The pope has learned that the chancellorship of the church of Ardfert and the perpetual vicarages of the parish churches of Offanach, Kilmaelte adye² and Garyfynach, d. Ardfert, are vacant *certis modis* at present and have been vacant for so long that by the Lateran statutes their collation has lawfully devolved on the apostolic see, although David Fysmoris and Gerald Stack have detained the chancellorship, dividing or occupying its fruits between themselves, and Thomas Omurchw, the second vicarage, and John de Geraldinis the third, priests and clerics,³ d. Ardfert, with no title and no support of law, temerariously and *de facto*, for a certain time, as they do. At a recent petition on Philip's part to the pope to unite etc. the vicarages to the chancellorship, for as long as he holds it, if conferred on him by virtue of the presents — asserting that the annual value of the chancellorship and vicarages together does not exceed 32 marks sterling — the pope hereby commands that the above three (or two or one of them), having summoned David, Gerald, Thomas, John and those interested in the union and others concerned, shall collate and assign the chancellorship, (which is a non-major dignity *post pontificalem* and has cure of souls), to Philip; and unite etc. the said vicarages (vacant howsoever etc.) to the chancellorship, for as long as Philip holds it, if conferred on him as above, with all rights and appurtenances; inducting him etc. having removed David and Gerald from the chancellorship, Thomas from the second vicarage, John from the third and any other unlawful detainers and causing Philip (or his proctor) to be admitted to the chancellorship and its fruits etc., rights and obventions and those of the vicarages to be delivered to him. [Curbing] gainsayers etc. Notwithstanding etc. The pope's will is, however, that the vicarages shall not, on this account, be defrauded of due services and the cure of souls therein shall not be neglected, but that their customary burdens shall be supported; and that on Philip's death or resignation etc. of the chancellorship the union etc. shall be dissolved and the vicarages shall revert to their original condition and be deemed vacant automatically.

Vite ac morum honestas . . .

A de Sᵗᵒ Severino / · B· / · B· xxx Tertio non' maij anno Vndecimo [5 May 1503], *Bolis·*

1 marginal insertion by the enregistering scribe initialled . *B*.

2 thus in MS

3 no 'qui se gerere' formula; *cf.* no. 994

994   30 May 1503   *Reg. Lat.* 1123, fos 145ʳ-146ʳ

To Thady Obrosoacan, John Davit de Geraldinis and Davit Trawt, canons of the
church of Ardfert, mandate in favour of Brendan Macconcour, perpetual vicar of the
parish church of Balli moth hilligoyd¹ [also spelt *Ballimeth killygod*], d. Ardfert
(who some time ago, as he asserts, was dispensed by apostolic authority
notwithstanding a defect of birth as the son of an unmarried man and an unmarried
woman to be promoted to all, even sacred, orders and to hold a benefice, even if it
should have cure of souls; and afterwards was duly promoted to the said orders and
holds by the said dispensation the perpetual vicarage of the above parish church
which was canonically collated to him while vacant *certo modo*). The pope has
learned that the rectory of the parish church of Ballyduyff *alias* Glenquhaw, d.
Ardfert, which is of lay patronage, is vacant *certo modo* at present and has been
vacant for so long that by the Lateran statutes its collation has lawfully devolved on
the apostolic see, although Donald² Offyn, priest,³ has detained it with no title and
no support of law, temerariously and *de facto*, for a certain time, as he does. He
hereby commands that the above three (or two or one of them), if, having summoned
the said [(?)Donald]⁴ and others concerned, they find the rectory, whose annual
value does not exceed 6 marks sterling, to be vacant (howsoever etc.) shall collate
and assign it (even if specially reserved etc.), with all rights and appurtenances, to
Brendan, inducting him etc. having removed the said [(?)Donald]⁵ and any other
unlawful detainer and causing Brendan (or his proctor) to be admitted to the rectory
and its fruits etc., rights and obventions to be delivered to him. [Curbing] gainsayers
etc. Notwithstanding etc. Also the pope dispenses Brendan to retain the vicarage
together with the rectory, if conferred on him by virtue of the presents, for life, to
resign them, simply or for exchange, when he pleases and in the place of a resigned
one receive another parish church or its perpetual vicarage, and retain [them]
together for life as above; notwithstanding the said defect etc. With a protective
proviso.⁶

Vite ac morum honestas . . .
A de Sᵗᵒ Severino / · *B·* / · *B· xv· decimo octavo Kl' Julij anno Vndecimo.* [14 June
1503], *Bolis·*

1 thus in MS

2 *Donaldus*

3 *presbyter*; unusual: no diocese; and usually 'qui se gerere' formula. *Cf.* no. 993

4 here *Davit*; but named above: 'Donaldus'; *cf.* note 2

[5] here *Donato* (immediately following *Brandano* deleted and initialled *B*); but named above: 'Donaldus'; *cf.* note 2

[6] Unintelligible: *Proviso quod vacans et alia rectorie obtenta et alia vacans et parochialis ecclesia huiusmodi debitis propterea non fraudentur . . .; vacans* in error for 'vicari(a)'?

995   19 March 1503   *Reg. Lat.* 1123, fo 161^r-v

To the dean and Bernard Omori,[1] canon, of the church of Elphin, and Maurice Offergill, canon of the church of Ardagh, mandate in favour of Malachy Macgyllakieran, canon of the monastery *Insule Sancte Trinitatis* [Trinity Island], Loch Ke, OPrem, d. Elphin. The pope has learned that the perpetual vicarages of the parish churches of Culdea and Kyllumomeri, ds. Elphin and Ardagh, are vacant *certo modo* at present and have been vacant for so long that by the Lateran statutes their collation has lawfully devolved on the apostolic see, although Eugene Maglocyn, priest,[2] d. Kilmore, has detained the second vicarage with no title and no support of law, temerariously and *de facto*, for more than a two-year, but short of a three-year, period, as he does. At a recent petition on Malachy's part to the pope to unite etc. the vicarages to the monastery, for as long as Malachy (to whom this day the pope has commanded by other letters of his *sub certis modo et forma* provision of the monastery be made) presides over it — asserting that the annual value of the monastery does not exceed 30, of the first vicarage, 5, and of the second, 6, marks sterling — the pope (who also this day by the same letters has commanded Malachy be absolved from a certain stain of simony and sentence of excommunication and other sentences, censures and pains which he incurred by occasion of the foregoing,[3] and be dispensed on account of irregularity if contracted on this account and be rehabilitated on account of all disability and infamy contracted by the said occasion) hereby commands that the above three (or two or one of them) having summoned Eugene and those interested in the union and others concerned, shall unite etc. the vicarages (vacant howsoever etc.; even if specially reserved etc.), with all rights and appurtenances, to the monastery, for as long as Malachy presides over it; to the effect that Malachy may, on his own authority, in person or by proxy, take and retain corporal possession of the vicarages and rights and appurtenances aforesaid, for as long as he presides over the monastery, and convert their fruits etc. to his own uses and those of the monastery and the vicarages without licence of the local diocesan or of anyone else. Notwithstanding etc. The pope's will is, however, that the vicarages shall not, on this account, be defrauded of due services and the cure of souls therein shall not be neglected, but that their customary burdens shall be supported; and that on Malachy's death or resignation etc. of the monastery the union etc. shall be dissolved and the vicarages shall revert to their original condition automatically.

Romanum decet pontificem votis illis gratum prestare assensum . . .
A de S^to Severino / · B· / . B· xv Tertio Id' Maij anno Vndecimo. [13 May 1503], *Bolis*

1 the second 'o' blotched and uncertain

2 no 'qui se gerere' formula

3 *Cf.* the letters referred to, summarised above at no. 846.

996   4 October 1502 [!]   *Reg. Lat.* 1123, fos 166ʳ-167ʳ

Provision, in *forma commissoria*, of M. Ferdinandus Ponzetus, cleric of Florence, chaplain of the pope, cleric of the apostolic camera, MTheol, (who is also a scriptor of apostolic letters), to the parish church, called archpresbytery, of St Bartholomew, *de Cassano*, d. Nocera (*Nuserin.*).

The 'bishop of Worcester' is one of the three mandataries. Entry otherwise of no interest to the Calendar.

Grata devotionis et familiaritatis obsequia . . .
F de parma / · *B·* / | *B· Grat(is) pro Scriptor(e) octavo Kl' octobr(is) anno Vndecimo.*
[24 September 1502 (!)] *Bolis.*

997   9 June 1503   *Reg. Lat.* 1124, fos 121ᵛ-122ʳ

To John Legate, canon of the monastery of Thoruton, OSA, d. Lincoln. Dispensation — at his supplication — to him, who, as he asserts, is expressly professed of the above order,[1] to receive and retain any benefice, with or without cure, customarily ruled[2] by secular clerics, even if a parish church or its portion[3] or perpetual vicarage, etc. [as above, no. 32].

Religionis zelus, vite ac morum honestas . . .
. *F. Bregeon.* / *Jo* / *Jo. xxx. Eps' Terracinen'*

1 This information comes from a notwithstanding clause.

2 *regi consuetum* — slightly unusual

3 *vel eius portio* — unusual

998   11 February 1503   *Reg. Lat.* 1124, fos 235ʳ-236ᵛ

Union etc. as below. The pope has learned that the perpetual vicarages of the churches[1] of Bachischyean and Horrey, ville Kaylke' and Trompostan', d. Cashel, are vacant *certo modo* at present and have been vacant for so long that by the

Lateran statutes their collation has lawfully devolved on the apostolic see. At a recent petition on the part of David, archbishop of Cashel, to the pope to unite etc. the vicarages to the archiepiscopal *mensa* of Cashel, for as long as he presides over the church of Cashel — asserting that the annual value of the vicarages together does not exceed 12 marks sterling — the pope hereby unites etc. the vicarages (vacant howsoever etc. or still by the deaths, outside the Roman curia, of, respectively, the late Richard Elibarde[2] or Thomas Itahylle',[3] once perpetual vicars of those churches while they lived, or by their free resignations etc.; even if the vicarages be specially reserved, etc.), to the archiepiscopal *mensa* of Cashel, for as long as archbishop David presides over the church of Cashel; to the effect that he, in person or by proxy, may, on his own authority, take and retain corporal possession of the vicarages and their rights and appurtenances, for as long as he presides over the church of Cashel, and convert their fruits etc. to his own uses and those of the *mensa* and the vicarages without licence of the local diocesan or of anyone else. Notwithstanding etc. The pope's will is, however, that the vicarages shall not, on account of this union etc., be defrauded of due services and the cure of souls therein shall not be neglected, but that their customary burdens shall be supported; and that on archbishop David's death or resignation etc. of the church of Cashel the union etc. shall be dissolved and the vicarages shall revert to their original condition and be deemed vacant automatically.

Ad futuram rei memoriam. Romanum decet pontificem et cetera.[4]
· *N· de castello* / · *B·* / ı *B· xxxx Bolis*

[1] 'parochialium' does not occur hereabouts or in the relevant annates entry

[2] uncertain reading

[3] the 'I' reworked and uncertain

[4] proem abridged thus: most unusual

999   —[1]   *Reg. Lat.* 1125, fo 19[v]

Start of a mandate addressed 'to the abbot of the monastery of Walley, and the priors of the monasteries, usually governed by priors, of Cartinell and Helay, ds. Coventry and Lichfield, and York.' The text of the letter, which is a rescript of justice in the form *Humilibus*, does not extend beyond the opening part of the narrative. It is drawn in favour of 'Thomas Banes, cleric or layman, executor of the will of the late Thomas Nelso(n), perpetual vicar [ends].' No abbreviator's name; no magistral initial.

Occupies last seven lines of page, ending (with *vicarii*) at end of last line; but the next leaf (the last of the *quinternus*) is blank.

Crossed through; no explanatory note; but clearly misplaced: letters of justice were ordinarily enregistered in *libri de diversis*. The present register is a *liber de vacantibus*; hence abortive?

Identical, so far as it goes, with no. 990 (*q.v.*) which was enregistered by the same scribe. That letter, curiously, has an omission at the point where this one ends.

[1] dating clause wanting

1000   22 December 1502   *Reg. Lat.* 1125, fos 174^V-177^V

To the abbots of the monasteries *de Castrodei*[1] [Fermoy] and *de Choro Benedicti* [Midleton] and the prior of the monastery, usually governed by a prior, of Bridgetown (*Villepontis*), d. Cloyne, mandate in favour of John Power, cleric, d. Cloyne (who, as he asserts, is of noble birth by both parents). A recent petition to the pope on John's part stated that at one time — when the church, called a particle, of Ferrebiythi, and the rectory of the parish church of Hinche, d. Cloyne, which are of lay patronage, were vacant outside the Roman curia *certo modo* — the bishop of Cloyne by ordinary authority erected and instituted the said church, called a particle, into a simple prebend of the church of Cloyne, for John's lifetime, with the consent of the chapter of Cloyne and of its patrons, and united etc. the rectory to the prebend thus erected, with like consent, also for John's lifetime, by the said authority, outside the said curia, and collated and made provision of a canonry of the church of Cloyne [and] the newly erected prebend, being vacant, with the rectory annexed thereto, to John. Moreover, as the same petition added, John fears that the erection and institution and also the collation and provision aforesaid for certain reasons do not hold good; and, as the pope has learned, the canonry and prebend are known to be vacant still as above. At his supplication to the pope to erect and institute anew the said church, called a particle, [into a simple prebend] in the church of Cloyne, for his lifetime; and to unite etc. anew the rectory to it after erection, likewise for his lifetime, the pope hereby commands that the above three (or two or one of them), having summoned the bishop and chapter regarding the erection and others concerned and those interested in the union, shall erect and institute the church, called a particle, into a simple prebend in the church of Cloyne, without prejudice to anyone; and unite etc. the rectory to it after erection, (howsoever the rectory and the church, called a particle, be vacant etc.; even if they have been vacant for so long that by the Lateran statutes their collation has lawfully devolved on the apostolic see, etc.); and, in the event of this erection and institution and union etc., collate and assign a canonry of the church of Cloyne and the newly erected prebend, being vacant, the annual value of which and of the rectory to be annexed does not exceed 16 marks sterling, with plenitude of canon law and all rights and appurtenances, to John, inducting him etc. having removed any unlawful detainer and causing John (or his proctor) to be received as a canon of the church of Cloyne, with plenitude of canon law, and their[2] fruits etc., rights and obventions to be delivered to him. [Curbing] gainsayers etc. Notwithstanding etc. The pope's will is, however, that the church, called a particle, and the rectory shall not, on account of this union etc., be defrauded of due services and the cure of souls in the rectory shall not be neglected, but that its customary burdens and those of the church, called a particle, shall be supported; and that on John's death or resignation etc. of the canonry and prebend this union etc. shall be dissolved and [erection][3] shall be extinguished and the church, called a particle, and the rectory shall revert to their original condition and be deemed vacant automatically.

Apostolice sedis providentia circumspecta ad ea libenter intendit . . .
S de Castello / · B / · B· xxv non' Januar' anno Vndecimo [5 January 1503], *Bolis·*

[1] preceded by (?)*Castrodei* deleted and initialled . *B.*

[2] *illorum* (referring to the canonry and the prebend and annexed rectory)

[3] *unio; recte:* 'erectio'?

1001   28 March 1503

Reg. Lat. 1125, fos 283[r]-288[v]

Provision, in *forma gratiosa*, of Wlffgangus Goler, continual commensal familiar of M. Fer(di)nandus Ponzectus, notary, scriptor, and familiar of the pope, to a canonry and prebend of the church of the Holy Trinity, Speyer, vacant at the apostolic see by Ponzectus's resignation.

The 'bishop of Worcester' is one of the three mandataries of the executory. Entry otherwise of no interest to the Calendar.

Vite ac morum honestas . . . The executory begins: *Hodie dilecto filio Wolgfango Goleri . . .*
F de parma; L. Puccius. / P / P. Grat(is) p(ro) deo p(ro) fam(ilia)ri Script(oris).
Thomarotius [deleted] *Decimo Kl' Maij Anno Vndecimo* [22 April 1503], *Thomaroti(us)*

1002   15 October 1502

Reg. Lat. 1126, fos 122[v]-124[r]

Provision, in *forma gratiosa*, of Sebastianus Bartholomei de Massaroza, to a canonry and prebend of the church of Lucca, (whose annual values do not exceed 40 gold ducats of the camera), vacant at the apostolic see by the free resignation, made spontaneously into the pope's hands and admitted by him, of Silvester, bishop of Worcester, who was holding them by apostolic concession and dispensation. Entry otherwise of no interest to the Calendar.

Vite ac morum honestas . . . The executory begins: *Hodie dilecto filio Sebastiano Bartholomei de Massaroza . . .*
N. de Castello; F Bregeon / · B· / · B· xij· x. Tertio decimo KL' novembr(is) anno Vndecimo. [20 October 1502], *Bolis·*

1003   21 May 1503   *Reg. Lat.* 1126, fos 277^r-278^v

Union etc. At a petition[1] on the part of Thomas, bishop of Tinos (*Tinen.*), the pope
hereby unites etc. the perpetual vicarage of the parish church of St Andrew, Ipylpen',
d. Exeter, (whose annual value does not exceed 27 marks sterling, equivalent to 70
gold ducats of the camera or thereabouts), to the canonry and prebend of Compton
(?)Ducudien'[2] of the church of Wells, which he holds together with the above
perpetual vicarage *in titulum vel commendam* by apostolic concession and
dispensation, for as long as he holds the canonry and prebend, to the effect that
bishop Thomas, in person or by proxy, may, on his own authority, take and retain
corporal possession of the vicarage and its rights and appurtenances, for as long as
he holds the canonry and prebend, and convert its fruits etc. to his own uses and
those of the vicarage and the canonry and prebend without licence of the local
diocesan or of anyone else. Notwithstanding etc. The pope's will is, however, that
the vicarage shall not, on account of this union etc., be defrauded of due services and
the cure of souls therein shall not be neglected, but that its customary burdens shall
be supported; and that on bishop Thomas's death or resignation etc. of the canonry
and prebend the union etc. shall be dissolved and so deemed and the vicarage shall
revert to its original condition and be deemed vacant automatically.

*Ad futuram rey[3] memoriam. Romanum decet pontificem votis illis gratum prestare
assensum* . . .
A Collocius[4] / P / · P· xxxv· Thomarotius:

[1] 'nuper' does not occur
[2] the 'cu' is doubtful
[3] apparently changed by overwriting from *rei*
[4] in different ink: entered later?

1004   21 March 1503[1]   *Reg. Lat.* 1126, fos 307^v-308^v

To Nicholas Mytford', cleric, d. Durham. Dispensation — at his supplication — to
him, who, as he asserts, is in his nineteenth year of age, to receive and retain any
benefice, with cure or otherwise incompatible, etc. [as above, no. 240].

Vite ac morum honestas . . .
p. de planca / · B. / · B· xx· Bolis·

[1] the middle of the dating clause — *duo decimo kalendas aprilis* — is in a slightly different script and
ink: entered later?

1005   28 March 1503[1]   *Reg. Lat.* 1126, fos 308ᵛ-310ᵛ

To the bishop of Ossory, the prior of the priory of St John, Kilmanni, near Dublin (*prope Dublinam*), d. Dublin, and the precentor of the church of Dublin, mandate in favour of John, bishop of Meath. A recent petition to the pope on John's part stated that the archbishop of Armagh and his officials for the time being can in no wise take cognizance of cases pending between subjects of his suffragans, except by way of appeals lodged at the court of Armagh — the local metropolitical court; that when there is an appeal from the suffragan bishops and their officials to the court of Armagh, the archbishop and his official ought in no wise to summon the parties, in the cause of the appeal, before definitive sentence, nor commit the appeal case to others when a plausible or lawful ground of appeal has not been expressed;[2] that if, when the parties have been summoned, it is submitted that there was no appeal, or not one within ten days after the interlocutory or definitive sentence, and the matter was not therefore devolved to the archbishop or his officials by appeal, they ought not to presume to inhibit unless it has first been established by them that the case has indeed devolved to them by appeal; and that if it is brought up that the appeal was lodged before definitive sentence for an unjust or illegal reason and was not on that account admissible, they cannot inhibit and may not proceed, unless they have first taken cognizance, on receipt of the appeal, of whether it is truly grounded on a plausible case;[3] that Octavian, archbishop of Armagh, and his officials, have nevertheless unjustly presumed, and are presuming, to take cognizance of cases pending between bishop John's subjects, and —- when there is an appeal from bishop John and his officials to the court of Armagh by bishop John's subjects before definitive sentence — to summon the parties and to commit the cases to others, when a plausible or lawful ground of appeal has not been expressed,[4] and also to inhibit when — after the parties have been summoned — it is submitted that there was no appeal or not one within the ten days, and they have not established that the matter has devolved to them, and to take cognizance of the principal matter where it is brought up that the appeal was lodged for an unjust or illegal reason, and it was not received as one grounded on a plausible case, and to proceed recklessly and *de facto*, and, regardless of law, to absolve subjects of the bishop of Meath who have been duly excommunicated by him and his officials, and to unlawfully extort large sums of money from the bishop's subjects by pretext of visitation (which, contrary to the form of law, he does not carry out personally, but by certain of his officials), and to occasion serious annoyance, confusion, disturbance, and injury over the above and other rights and jurisdiction belonging to the bishop of Meath [and] the episcopal *mensa*; and that archbishop Octavian, his officials, and several other clerics and laymen of the dioceses of Armagh and Meath, have damaged him over certain annual revenues, income, sums of money, goods, and other things, lawfully belonging to the episcopal *mensa* of Meath and otherwise to the bishop. At the bishop's supplication to the pope to commit to some upright men in those parts the cases which he intends to bring against archbishop Octavian, his officials, and other clerics and laymen, jointly and severally, over the above and other matters, the pope hereby commands that the above three (or two or one of them), having summoned archbishop Octavian, his officials, clerics, laymen, and others concerned, and having heard both sides, [shall] decree[5] what is just, without appeal, causing — in the archbishop's case by the pope's authority, by ecclesiastical censure in the case of others — what they have decreed to be strictly observed; [and moreover compel] witnesses, etc. Notwithstanding etc.

Humilibus et cetera.
L. puccius / · B· / · B· x Bolis·

[1] originally *millesimo quingentesimo secundo; secundo* deleted and *tertio* inserted in the margin by the enregistering scribe; the change initialled B twice (variously punctuated); the rest of the dating clause in a different ink: entered later?

[2] *nec etiam aliis illam committere appellationis eiusdem cause probabili seu legitima non expresse committere* !

[3] *nisi prius appellatione recepta veluti ex causa probabili emissa* [changed from *emisse*] *cognoscere inceperint <de causa* [inserted in the margin; (?)*de causa* deleted in the line]*> huiusmodi <an* [supralinear insertion]*> sit vera.*

[4] *aliis committere cause probabili sive legitime* [changed from *legitima*] *non expressa*

[5] MS: *decernentes*; 'decernatis'?

1006   27 June[1] 1502   *Reg. Lat.* 1128, fos 53[v]-56[r]

To William, bishop of Durham. Consistorial translation, though absent [from the Roman curia], from the church of Carlisle to that of Durham, left — following the pope's reservation some time ago of provisions to all churches vacated then and in the future at the apostolic see to his own disposition — vacant at the said see by the consistorial translation of bishop Richard from the church of Durham to that of Winchester. The pope hereby appoints William bishop, committing to him the care and administration of the church of Durham in spiritualities and temporalities and granting him licence to transfer thereto. His will is, however, that — before William involves himself in the rule and administration of the church of Durham in any way — he shall take the oath[2] of fealty before the bishops of Bangor and Whithorn (or one of them) in accordance with the form which the pope sends enclosed under his *bulla*; and the pope has, by other letters of his, commissioned the said bishops (and each of them) that they (or one of them) shall receive the oath from William in his name and that of the Roman church.

Conclusions to: (i) the chapter of the church of Durham, (ii) the clergy of the city and diocese of Durham, (iii) the people of the said city and diocese, (iv) the vassals of the said church, (v) the archbishop of York, (vi) Henry, king of England.

Quam sit onusta dispendiis . . . The conclusions begin: *(i), (ii), (iii), (iv) Hodie venerabilem fratrem nostrum . . . (v) Ad cumulum et cetera. (vi) Gratie divine et cetera.*
L puccius[3] / · B· / · B· xxiiij· xij· xij· xij· · xij· xij· xij· Bolis·

[1] The script of *Julii* is different and there is ample space on either side: entered later in a pre-existant space? *cf.* abbreviator's name (below, note 3) *cf.* also below, nos. 1007 and 1008

[2] 'solitum' does not occur

[3] different script; entered later? *cf.* note 1

1007   27 June[1] 1502   *Reg. Lat.* 1128, fo 56[v]

To the bishops of Bangor and Whithorn, mandate. Since the pope has this day translated bishop William, though absent [from the Roman curia], from the church of Carlisle to that of Durham, as is more fully contained in his letters drawn up in that regard,[2] he — wishing to spare William, who lives in those parts, the labour and expense of being compelled on that account to come in person to the Roman curia — hereby commissions and commands that the above two (or one of them) shall receive from him in the name of the pope and the Roman church the usual oath of fealty etc. [as above, no. 547, with appropriate changes].

Cum hodie[3] . . .
L puccius[4] / · *B·* / · *B· xvj· Bolis̄*

[1] the script of *quinto kalendas Julii anno decimo* is different: entered later? *cf.* abbreviator's name (below, note 4) *cf.* also principal letter of provision (above, no. 1006)

[2] above, no. 1006

[3] 'nos' does not occur

[4] different script: entered later? *cf.* dating clause (above, note 1)

1008   27 June[1] 1502   *Reg. Lat.* 1128, fo 57[r-v]

To William, bishop of Carlisle. Since the pope, on the advice of the cardinals, intends this day to translate William from the church of Carlisle, over which he is understood to preside, to that of Durham, vacant *certo modo* at present, and appoint him bishop, he hereby absolves him from any sentences of excommunication, etc. [as above, no. 548].

Apostolice sedis consueta clementia ne dispositiones . . .
L puccius[2] / · *B·* / · *B· xxiiij· Bolis̄*

[1] the script of *quinto kalendas Julii anno decimo* is different: entered later? *cf.* abbreviator's name (below, note 2) *cf.* also principal letter of provision (above, no. 1006)

[2] different script: entered later? *cf.* dating clause (above, note 1)

1009   27 April 1502   *Reg. Lat.* 1128, fos 72ʳ-74ᵛ

To Robert, archbishop of Glasgow, commend. Some time ago, during the rule of the late abbot Thomas, the pope specially reserved provision to the monastery of B. Mary, Jedword,[1] OSA, d. Glasgow, to his own disposition; and afterwards the monastery was left vacant by the death of abbot Thomas outside the Roman curia, being reserved as above. Wishing to make provision of a capable and suitable governor to the monastery to rule and direct it, as well as to assist Robert to keep up his position in accordance with pontifical dignity, the pope, on the advice of the cardinals, hereby commends the monastery, thus vacant, to Robert, to be held, ruled and governed by him for life, even together with the church of Glasgow, over which he is understood to preside, committing to him the care, rule and administration of the monastery in spiritualities and temporalities. The pope's will is, however, that divine worship and the usual number of canons and ministers in the monastery shall not, on account of this commend, be diminished; that Robert may — due and customary burdens of the monastery and its convent having been supported — make disposition of the rest of its fruits etc. just as abbots could and ought to do, alienation of immovable goods and precious movables being however forbidden; and that, before he involves himself in the rule and administration of the monastery in any way, Robert shall take the usual oath of fealty before the bishops of Aberdeen and Moray (or one of them) in accordance with the form which the pope sends enclosed under his *bulla*; and the pope, by other letters of his, commands the said bishops that they (or one of them) shall receive the oath from him in the name of the pope and the Roman church.

Conclusions to (i) the convent of the monastery of Jedword, (ii) the vassals of the monastery, (iii) James, king of Scots.

Romani pontificis providentia circumspecta . . . The conclusions begin: *(i) Hodie monasterium vestrum . . . (ii) Hodie et cetera. (iii) Cum nos hodie et cetera.*
. F. de parma; Al. de Acre[2] / · *B·* / · *B· xxxxvj.* [3] · *viij· viij· viij· Bolis*

[1] (?)*Gea Jedd* (deleted and initialled *B*) precedes the first occurrence of *Jedword*

[2] it is unusual for the name of the abbreviator *de parco minori* who expedited the conclusions to be noted in the register

[3] *xvj. xvj. xvj. Bolis.* deleted and initialled . *B.*

1010   27 April 1502   *Reg. Lat.* 1128, fos 74ᵛ-75ʳ

To Robert, archbishop of Glasgow. Since the pope intends this day to commend the monastery of B. Mary, Jedword, OSA, d. Glasgow, bereft of the rule of an abbot *certo modo* at present, to be held, ruled and governed by him for life, he hereby absolves him from any [sentences] of excommunication etc. under which he may perchance lie, only so far as the taking effect of the commend and each of the relevant letters. Notwithstanding etc.

Apostolice sedis consueta clementia ad ea libenter intendit . . .
f. de parma / . B. / · B· xvj· Bolis·

1011   27 April 1502   *Reg. Lat.* 1128, fos 75ᵛ-76ʳ

To the bishops of Aberdeen and Moray, mandate. Since the pope has this day commended the monastery of B. Mary, Jedword, OSA, d. Glasgow, to Robert, archbishop of Glasgow, to be held, ruled and governed by him for life, as is more fully contained in his letters drawn up in that regard,[1] he — wishing to spare Robert, archbishop and commendatory, who lives in those parts, the labour and expense of being compelled on that account to come in person to the apostolic see — hereby commands that the above two (or one of them) shall receive from him in the name of the pope and the Roman church the usual oath of fealty etc. [as above, no. 547, with appropriate changes].

Cum nos hodie . . .
. F. de parma / . B. / . B. xij. Bolis·

[1] above, no. 1009

1012   21 June[1] 1503   *Reg. Lat.* 1128, fos 150ʳ-152ᵛ

To Roger Layburii, elect of Carlisle. Consistorial provision of him — cleric of Carlisle, BTheol, in the priesthood, chaplain of Henry, king of England — to the church of Carlisle, left — following the pope's reservation some time ago of provisions to all churches vacated then and in the future at the apostolic see to his own disposition — vacant at the said see by the consistorial translation of bishop William from the church of Carlisle to that of Durham.[2] The pope hereby appoints Roger bishop, committing to him the care and administration of the church of Carlisle in spiritualities and temporalities.

Conclusions to: (i) the chapter of the church of Carlisle, (ii) the clergy of the city and diocese of Carlisle, (iii) the vassals of the said church, (iv) the archbishop of York, (v) Henry, king of England.

Divina disponente clementia . . . The conclusions begin: (i) Hodie ecclesie vestre . . .
(ii) Hodie ecclesie Carleolen. et cetera. (iii) Hodie et cetera. (iv) Ad cumulum . . . (v)
Gratie divine premium . . .
L puccius³ / . B. / . B· xx x x x x x x ⁴ Bolis.

1 *undecimo kalendas Julii pontificatus nostri* written in lighter ink: entered later? *cf.* abbreviator's name (below, note 3) *cf.* also below , no. 1013, note 1

2 above, no. 1006

3 written in lighter ink: entered later? *cf.* above, note 1

4 *sic*: tax marks for six conclusions: only five enregistered: that to people wanting

1013   22 May![1] **1503**   *Reg. Lat.* 1128, fos 152^v-153^r

To Roger <Lanburi>[2], cleric of Carlisle. Since the pope intends this day to make provision of Roger to the church of Carlisle and to appoint him bishop, he hereby absolves him from any [sentences] of excommunication etc. [as above, no. 53].

Apostolice sedis circumspecta benignitas de statu personarum ecclesiasticarum quarumlibet . . .
[-][3] */ · B· / · B· xx* [4] *Bolis*

1 *Cf.* above, no. 1012. MS here now reads: *undecimo kalendas Junii* — following alterations, namely: *undecimo* in the line deleted, initialled *B.*; but inserted in the margin, initialled . *B.* with *nono* deleted and initialled *B*, in the margin beside it (regarding 'nono': *cf.* below, no. 1014, note 1); both *undecimo* and *nono* in the margin are in the hand of the enregistering scribe.

2 inserted in the margin by the enregistering scribe; next to magistral initial at start of letter; not separately initialled

3 no abbreviator's name

4 changed (by deletion of the 'viij') from *xxviij* (*cf.* below, no. 1014); the deletion initialled . *B.*

1014   23 June[1] **1503**   *Reg. Lat.* 1128, fo 153^r

To Roger, elect of Carlisle. Since the pope has recently made provision of Roger to the church of Carlisle, as is more fully contained in his letters drawn up in that regard,[2] he [hereby grants faculty] to Roger — at his supplication — [to receive consecration] from any catholic bishop of his choice *et cetera*.[3]

Cum nos pridem . . .
L puccius / . B. / . B. xxviij. Bolis

1 *nono kalendas Julii*; *cf.* above, no. 1013

2 above, no. 1012

3 thus abridged (quite unusually)

1015   1 February 1503   *Reg. Lat.* 1128, fos 168^V-172^r

To William, abbot of the monastery of B. Mary, Melros, OCist, d. Glasgow, surrogation etc. and provision etc., as below. Some time ago, when the above monastery was vacant *certo modo*, Innocent VIII, on the advice of the cardinals whose number included the present pope, made provision of Bernard Bel, then a monk of the monastery, (whom the convent had elected abbot of the monastery, then vacant *certo modo*, as the convent could in accordance with the regular institutes of the said order and the privileges granted to it by the apostolic see); and appointed him abbot, committing to him the care, rule and administration of the monastery in spiritualities and temporalities.[1] Next, after Bernard had, by virtue of the said provision and appointment, acquired peaceful possession or almost of the rule and administration of the monastery, and had presided over it for some time, a dispute arose between himself and David Brown, who bears himself as a cleric, over the rule and administration of the monastery, to which Bernard asserted he had been provided and that he had been appointed its abbot and had acquired possession or almost of its rule and administration, as above; yet David asserted that the monastery rightfully belonged to him. After Innocent's death, the pope called the case to the late Battista, bishop of Tusculum; and subsequently, because of his absence from the Roman curia, to Oliviero, bishop of Sabina; and then from bishop Oliviero to Giovanni Antonio, cardinal priest of SS Nereo e Achilleo, to be resumed by him in due state and be heard further and duly determined. And, since Cardinal Giovanni Antonio, for certain reasons, had remitted the case to the apostolic chancery, the pope committed it to Antoniotto, cardinal priest of S Prassede, likewise to be resumed by him in due state and be heard further and duly determined. And Cardinal Antoniotto, proceeding in the case — the rights of Bernard, then absent, not having been produced or discussed — promulgated a certain sentence by which he adjudged the monastery to David and imposed perpetual silence over it upon Bernard; and since it was claimed that the sentence had, in the absence of an appeal, become a final judgement he decreed letters executory and declared Bernard caught by the censures contained in them on account of his non-appearance. However afterwards, the pope, at Bernard's instance, committed the case of the nullity of the said sentence, etc. to Giovanni Battista, cardinal priest of SS Giovanni e Paolo, to be heard and duly determined, and Cardinal Giovanni Battista proceeding in the case lawfully promulgated a definitive sentence by which he declared Cardinal Antoniotto's sentence etc. to be (and have been) null; from which sentence David appealed to the said see. And the pope committed the case of this appeal to Juan, cardinal priest of S Balbina, to be heard and duly determined; and Cardinal Juan is said to have proceeded to several acts, but short of a conclusion. Moreover since, while this suit before Cardinal Juan was thus pending undecided, Bernard, spontaneously and freely, ceded the suit and case and all right belonging to him in or to the rule and administration into the pope's hands, and the pope admitted the cession, the pope — lest, with the case undefended, the rule and administration be handed over to an intruder; and lest the monastery be exposed to the inconveniences of a long vacation — on the advice of the cardinals, hereby surrogates William (perpetual vicar of the parish church of Enerlchtan, d. Glasgow, at the lawful age and in the priesthood; whom, also this day, the pope has dispensed, by other letters of his, to be surrogated — even without having taken the habit and made the profession — in the right belonging to Bernard in or to the rule and administration, and to be appointed to and preside over the monastery as abbot, as is more fully contained in those letters)[2] in and to all right that belonged (or could belong) to Bernard in or to the rule and administration; and grants the right to William, and admits him: to the right; to the prosecution and defence of the right, suit and case in that state, whatever it was, in which Bernard was able and due to be admitted at the time of his cession, as if he had not ceded; and to Bernard's possession, or almost, of the rule and administration; and wills and commands that he be so admitted. And the pope, on like advice, makes provision of William to the monastery and appoints him abbot, committing to him its care, rule and administration in spiritualities and temporalities. His will is, however, that — before William involves himself in the said rule and administration in any way — he shall be bound to take the habit and make the profession; otherwise the pope decrees the monastery to be vacant automatically.

　　　Conclusions to: (i) the convent of the said monastery of Melros, (ii) the vassals of the said monastery, (iii) the abbot of the monastery of Cîteaux, d. Chalon-sur-Saône, (iv) James, king of Scots.

Summi dispositioni rectoris . . . The conclusions begin: *(i), (ii), (iii), (iv) Hodie cum dilectus filius* . . .
F de parma / F / F· xvj· viij· viij· viij· viij Sanctor(is)

[1] *Cf. CPL*, XV, no. 1220 (an *Indice* entry).
[2] below, no. 1020

1016　　1 February 1503　　　　　　　　　*Reg. Lat.* 1128, fos 172[v]-173[r]

To William, abbot of the monastery of B. Mary, Melros, OCist, d. Glasgow, faculty as below. This day Bernard Bel, monk, recently abbot, of the above monastery — between whom and David Brown, who bears himself as a cleric, a suit over the rule and administration of the monastery was pending undecided in the Roman curia before a certain judge deputed by apostolic delegation — had, spontaneously and freely, ceded the suit and case and all right in or to the said rule and administration belonging to him into the pope's hands; and the pope, then admitting the cession, has, on the advice of the cardinals, surrogated William in and to all right that belonged (or could belong) to Bernard in or to the rule and administration, and, on like advice, made provision of William to the monastery, and appointed him abbot, as is more fully contained in his letters drawn up in that regard.[1] The pope hereby grants faculty to William — at his supplication — to receive benediction from any catholic bishop of his choice in communion with the apostolic see; and to the bishop concerned to impart it to him.

Cum hodie dilectus filius Bernardus Bel...
F de parma / F / F. xij. Sanctor(is)

[1] above, no. 1015

1017   1 February 1503   *Reg. Lat.* 1128, fo 173^{r-v}

To the bishop of Agia (*Agien.*), the abbots of the monasteries of Newbotyl, d. St Andrews, and Sweetheart (*Dulcis Cordis*), d. Glasgow, mandate in favour of William Turnbul, perpetual vicar of the parish church of Enerlethan, d. Glasgow. The pope has learned that William wishes to enter the monastery of B. Mary, Melros, OCist, d. Glasgow, under the regular habit. Wishing to encourage him, the pope hereby commands that the above three, or two or one of them, in person or by proxy, shall receive William — if he is suitable and there is no canonical obstacle — as a monk in the monastery and bestow the regular habit on him in accordance with the custom of the monastery and cause him to be given charitable treatment therein; and, if William spontaneously wishes to make the usual regular profession made by the monks, receive and admit it. [Curbing] gainsayers by ecclesiastical censure etc. Notwithstanding etc.

Cupientibus vitam ducere regularem apostolicum decet adesse presidium...
F de parma / F / F. xij. Sanctor(is)

1018   1 February 1503   *Reg. Lat.* 1128, fos 173^{v}-174^{v}

To William Turnbal, perpetual vicar of the parish church of Enerlerthan, d. Glasgow, absolution as below. This day Bernard Bel, monk, recently abbot, of the monastery of B. Mary, Melros, OCist, d. Glasgow — between whom and David Brown, who bears himself as a cleric, a suit over the rule and administration of the monastery was pending undecided in the Roman curia before a certain judge deputed by apostolic delegation — has, spontaneously and freely, ceded the suit and case and all right in or to the said rule and administration belonging to him into the pope's hands; and the pope has admitted the cession and intends, also this day, on the advice of the cardinals, to surrogate William in and to all right that belonged (or could belong) to Bernard in the rule and administration, and to make provision of William to the monastery even by a grace "Si Neutri" and appoint him abbot. The pope hereby absolves William from any [sentences] of excommunication, suspension and interdict *et cetera* under which he may perchance lie so far only as regards the taking effect of the said surrogation, provision and appointment and each of the relevant letters. Notwithstanding etc.

Apostolice sedis consueta clementia ne dispositiones. . .
F de parma / F / F. xvj. Sanctor(is)

1019   1 February 1503   *Reg. Lat.* 1128, fos 174^v-175^v

To William, abbot of the monastery of B. Mary, Melros, OCist, d. Glasgow, *motu proprio* dispensation. This day Bernard Bel, monk, recently abbot, of the above monastery — between whom and David Brown, who bears himself as a cleric, a suit over the rule and administration of the monastery was pending undecided in the Roman curia before a certain judge deputed by apostolic delegation — has, spontaneously and freely, ceded the suit and case and all right in or to the said rule and administration belonging to him into the pope's hands; and the pope, admitting the cession, has, on the advice of the cardinals, surrogated William in and to all right which belonged (or could belong) to Bernard in or to the rule and administration, and made provision of William to the monastery and appointed him abbot. And the pope has learned that at the time of the said provision and appointment, William was receiving (and does receive) annual pensions reserved, established and assigned to him by apostolic authority, one of 20 pounds Scots on the fruits etc. of the perpetual vicarage of the parish church of Kyrkcande, d. St Andrews, and the other of 10 marks Scots on those of the canonry [and] prebend of Aberlady, church of Dunkeld. Wishing to assist William to keep up his position in accordance with abbatial dignity, the pope — *motu proprio* — hereby dispenses William — whom also this day he has dispensed, *sub certis modo et forma*, to be appointed abbot without his having taken the habit usually worn by monks of the said monastery and made the regular profession, as is more fully contained in each of the letters thereupon drawn up[1] — to receive — even after he has taken the habit and made the profession and acquired peaceful possession, or almost, of the rule and administration of the monastery and of its goods or the major part of them — together with the monastery, for as long as he presides over it, the aforesaid pensions, not exceeding 9 pounds sterling annually, for life, as before. Notwithstanding etc. With decree that these pensions shall not expire on this account.

Personam tuam nobis et apostolice sedi devotam tuis exigentibus meritis paterna benivolentia prosequentes illa tibi favorabiliter concedimus . . .
F de parma / F / F. xx. Sanctor(is)

[1] below, no. 1020

1020   1 February 1503   *Reg. Lat.* 1128, fos 175^v-177^r

To William Turnbul, perpetual vicar of the parish church of Enerleithan, d. Glasgow, dispensation and indult. Bernard Bel, monk, recently abbot, of the monastery of B. Mary, Melros, OCist, d. Glasgow — between whom and David Brown, who bears himself as a cleric, a suit over the rule and administration of the monastery was pending undecided in the Roman curia before a certain judge deputed by apostolic delegation — has this day, spontaneously and freely, ceded into the pope's hands the suit and case and all right in or to the said rule and administration belonging to him and the pope has admitted the cession; and the pope intends this day, on the advice of the cardinals, to surrogate William — even without his having taken the regular habit or made his profession — to Bernard's right to the rule and administration and to provide William to the monastery and appoint him abbot, even if it appears after the surrogation that neither has [the right]; and, as the pope has learned, it is expressly laid down in the privileges, indults, and letters granted to the Cistercian order by several Roman pontiffs or otherwise by the apostolic see and approved, renewed and confirmed by Innocent VIII or other pontiffs that no one may be appointed to or preside over any Cistercian monastery unless he has been on probation in the order for at least a year, made the regular profession and worn the habit of the professed, and that provisions made otherwise by the apostolic see are void; that the convents and persons of Cistercian monasteries are not bound to obey those who have been provided otherwise than as above, even by the apostolic see, whatever their dignity, state, grade, order or condition, and are not liable to be compelled to do so against their will or be interdicted, suspended or excommunicated on this account, and sentences passed on the strength of such letters of provision against persons refusing obedience are void; that convents may proceed to the election or postulation of other abbots as if the letters of provision had never issued; that it is not possible for the order's privileges, indults and letters — even if they and their whole tenors are mentioned in the letters of provision, whether specially, specifically, individually, and expressly, or by clauses whose import implies it and they are derogated with the clauses *motu proprio, ex certa scientia, de plenitudine potestatis*, and others and it is done on the advice of the cardinals of the Holy Roman Church — to be derogated without the express consent of the abbot for the time being and convent of the monastery of Cîteaux, d. Chalon-sur-Saône; and that if they are derogated the derogations are of no help to anyone unless they have been intimated by sundry letters (expedited even in *forma brevis* and under sundry dates), at certain intervals of days, to the abbot and convent of Cîteaux and to the diffinitors of the order's general chapter. The pope — *motu proprio* — hereby dispenses and indulges William to be surrogated to Bernard's right and appointed abbot and to preside over the monastery without his having taken the habit and made the regular profession and that the surrogation, provision, and appointment due to be made are valid and efficacious; and, in order that the surrogation, etc. and the relevant letters take full effect, the pope — also *motu proprio* — for this once only, hereby specially and expressly derogates the order's privileges and indults (which otherwise remain in force and whose tenors he deems to be sufficiently inserted and expressed [in the presents][1]) howsoever granted, even ones with the clauses *motu proprio, ex certa scientia*, and *de plenitudine potestatis* and ones with stronger, more efficacious, and unusual clauses derogatory of derogatory clauses and with the decree *irritans*, and even if, for their sufficient derogation, special, specific, express and individual mention (or other expression) should be made of them, word for word, their tenor being inserted in full and not by general clauses whose import implies full insertion, or other recherché form should be observed. Notwithstanding, etc.

Exigit tue devotionis sinceritas . . .
F de parma | F | F. xxxx. Sanctor(is)

[1] MS wants 'presentibus'

1021   10 January 1502   *Reg. Lat.* 1128, fos 188[r]-190[r]

To Edmund, bishop of Salisbury. Consistorial translation, though absent [from the Roman curia], from the church of Hereford[1] to that of Salisbury, left — following the pope's reservation some time ago of provisions to all churches vacated then and in the future at the apostolic see to his own disposition — vacant at the said see by the consistorial translation of Henry, archbishop of Canterbury (then bishop of Salisbury) from the church of Salisbury to that of Canterbury. The pope hereby appoints Edmund bishop, committing to him the care and administration of the church of Salisbury in spiritualities and temporalities and granting him licence to transfer thereto. His will is, however, that — before Edmund involves himself in the rule and administration of the church of Salisbury[2] — he shall take the usual oath of fealty before the bishops of Winchester and of Coventry and Lichfield[3] in accordance with the form which the pope sends enclosed under his *bulla*; and the pope has, by other letters of his, commanded the said bishops (and each of them) that they (or one of them) shall receive the oath from Edmund in his name and that of the Roman church.

    Conclusions to: (i) the chapter of the church of Salisbury, (ii) the clergy of the city and diocese of Salisbury, (iii) the people of the said city and diocese, (iv) the vassals of the said church, (v) Henry,[4] archbishop of Canterbury, (vi) Henry, king of England.

Romani pontificis quem pastor ille celestis . . . The conclusions begin: *(i) Hodie venerabilem fratrem nostrum . . . (ii), (iii), (iv) Hodie et cetera. (v) Hodie et cetera.*[5] *(vi) Gratie divine et cetera.*
F de parma | · B· | ₁B· xxiiij· xij· xij· xij· xij· xij· xij· Bolis·

[1] *Erfoden.*

[2] 'in aliquo' does not occur

[3] 'seu alterius eorumdem' (or suchlike) does not occur

[4] unusual for the archbishop to be named in the conclusion to him; seemingly the scribe found it unexpected for he wrote and deleted *archie* before writing *Henrico archiepiscopo*

5 'Ad cumulum et cetera' wanting (or comprehended in the 'et cetera' after *salutem*)

1022   10 January 1502[1]   *Reg. Lat.* 1128, fo 190[r-v]

To Edmund, bishop of Hereford.[2] Since the pope, on the advice of the cardinals, intends this day to translate Edmund from the church of Hereford, over which he is understood to preside, to that of Salisbury, vacant *certo modo* at present, and to appoint him bishop, he hereby absolves him from any [sentences] of excommunication *et cetera*[3] under which he may perchance lie. Notwithstanding etc.

Apostolice sedis consueta clementia ne dispositiones . . .
F de parma / · B· / ͺ B· xxiiij· Bolis

[1] *quadrin* deleted before *quingentesimo*, initialled *B*
[2] *Erfoden.*
[3] the entry much abridged hereafter

1023   10 January 1502   *Reg. Lat.* 1128, fos 190[v]-191[r]

To the bishops of Winchester and of Coventry and Lichfield. Since the pope has this day translated bishop Edmund, though absent [from the Roman curia], from the church of Hereford[1] to that of Salisbury, as is more fully contained in his letters drawn up in that regard,[2] he — wishing to spare Edmund, who lives in those parts, the labour and expense of being compelled on that account to come in person to the Roman curia — hereby commands that the above two (or one of them) shall receive from him in the name of the pope and the Roman church the usual oath of fealty etc. [as above, no. 547, with appropriate changes].

Cum nos hodie . . .
F de parma / · B· / ͺ B· xvj· Bolis

[1] *Erfoden.*
[2] above, no. 1021

1024   29 March 1503   *Reg. Lat.* 1128, fos 275[v]-277[v]

To David, abbot of the monastery of B. Mary, Cambuskynneth [also spelt

Canbuskynneth], OSA, d. St Andrews. Consistorial provision of him (archdeacon of
the archdeaconry of Lothian (*Loudonie*), said diocese, of noble, even baronial, birth
by both parents, the issue of a lawful marriage, in the priesthood and of lawful age;
whom this day the pope has dispensed — *motu proprio* — by other letters of his, to
be appointed to the monastery as abbot — even without having taken the usual habit
worn by the canons and made the usual profession made by them — and to preside
over it — without having taken the habit and made the profession — for eight
months calculated from the date of having peaceful possession of the rule and
administration and goods of the monastery or the greater part of them, as is more
fully contained in those letters[1]) to the above monastery, vacant by the death, outside
the Roman curia, of the late abbot Henry, during whose rule the monastery was
specially reserved by the pope to his own disposition. The pope hereby appoints
David abbot, committing to him the care, rule and administration of the monastery in
spiritualities and temporalities. His will is, however, that David shall be bound —
within the said eight months — to take the habit and make the profession; otherwise,
he decrees — the said months having elapsed — the monastery vacant automatically.

Conclusions to: (i) the convent of the monastery of B. Mary, Cambuskynneth, (ii)
the vassals of the said monastery, (iii) James, king of Scots, (iv) the archbishop of St
Andrews.

Summi disposicione rectoris . . . The conclusions begin: *(i) Hodie monasterio vestro . . .*
(ii), (iii) Hodie et cetera. (iv) Cum igitur . . .
F. de parma / P. / . P. xvi. viij. viij. viij. viij. Thomarotius:

[1] below, no. 1025

1025   29 March 1503   *Reg. Lat.* 1128, fo 278[r-v]

To David Arnot, archdeacon of the archdeaconry of Lothian (*Laudone*), d. St
Andrews, dispensation. Since the pope, on the advice of the cardinals, intends this
day to make provision of David to the monastery of B. Mary, Cannbuskynneth,
OSA, d. St Andrews, at present vacant *certo modo*, and appoint him abbot, he —
motu proprio — hereby dispenses David to be appointed to the monastery as abbot
— even without having taken the usual habit worn by the canons and without having
made the usual profession made by them — and to preside over it — even without
having taken the habit and made the profession — for eight months calculated from
the date of having peaceful possession of the rule and administration and goods of
the monastery or the greater part of them, and to rule and exercise it in spiritualities
and temporalities. Notwithstanding etc. The pope's will is, however, that David shall
be bound — within the said eight months — to take the habit and make the
profession; otherwise — the said eight months having elapsed — the monastery
shall be deemed vacant automatically.

Exigit tue devocionis sinceritas . . .
F de parma / P / . P. xx. Thomarotius:

1026   29 March 1503   *Reg. Lat.* 1128, fos 278ᵛ-279ʳ

To David Arnot, archdeacon of the archdeaconry of Lothian (*Laudonie*), d. St Andrews. Since the pope, on the advice of the cardinals, intends this day to make provision of David to the monastery of B. Mary, Cambuskynneth, OSA, d. St Andrews, vacant *certo modo* at present, and to appoint him abbot, he hereby absolves him from any [sentences] of excommunication etc. [as above, no. 53].

Apostolice sedis consueta clementia ne [dispositiones][1] *. . .*
[-][2] */ [-]*[3] */ P. xvj. Thomarotius:*

[1] MS: (?)*dispensaciones; recte*: 'dispositiones'
[2] no abbreviator's name
[3] no magistral initial

1027   29 March 1503   *Reg. Lat.* 1128, fos 279ᵛ-280ʳ

To David, abbot of the monastery of B. Mary, Cambuskynneth, OSA, d. St Andrews. Since the pope has this day made provision of David to the above monastery, as is more fully contained in his letters drawn up in that regard,[1] he hereby grants faculty to David — at his supplication — to receive benediction from any catholic bishop of his choice in communion with the apostolic see; and to the bishop concerned to impart it to him. The pope's will is, however, that the bishop who imparts benediction to David shall, after he has imparted it, [receive][2] from David the usual oath of fealty in the name of the pope and the Roman church in accordance with the form which the pope sends enclosed under [his][3] *bulla*, and shall cause the form of oath which David takes to be sent, verbatim, to the pope, at once, by his letters patent, marked with his seal; and that the above shall not be to the prejudice of the <arch>bishop[4] of St Andrews, to whom the monastery is understood to be subject by ordinary law.

Cum nos hodie . . .
F. de parma / P / P. xij. Thomarotius:

[1] above, no. 1024
[2] 'recipiat' wanting
[3] 'nostra' wanting

[4] *archi* inserted above the line by the enregistering scribe, not initialled

1028   29 March 1503   *Reg. Lat.* 1128, fo 280[r-v]

To the bishop of Aberdeen and the abbots of the monasteries of Holyrood (*Sancte Crucis*) and Scone (*de Scona*), d. St Andrews. Since, as the pope has learned, David Arnot, archdeacon of the archdeaconry of Lothian (*Laudone*), d. St Andrews, wishes to enter the monastery of B. Mary, Cambuskynneth, OSA, said diocese, under the regular habit, the pope, wishing to encourage him, hereby commands that the above three, or two or one of them, in person or by proxy, shall receive David — if he is suitable and there is no canonical obstacle — as a canon in the monastery and bestow the regular habit on him in accordance with the custom of the monastery and cause him to be given charitable treatment therein; and if David spontaneously wishes to make the usual regular profession made by the canons, receive and admit it. [Curbing] gainsayers by [ecclesiastical] censure etc. Notwithstanding etc.

Cupientibus vitam ducere regularem apostolicum decet adesse presidium . . .
F. de parma / *P* / . *P. xij. Thomaroti(us):*

1029   5 May 1503   *Reg. Lat.* 1129A, fos 1[r]-4[r]

To Geoffrey, elect of Coventry and Lichfield. Consistorial provision of him — dean of the church of York, MTheol, in the priesthood, chaplain and counsellor of Henry, king of England — to the mutually united churches of Coventry and Lichfield, left — following the pope's reservation some time ago of provisions to all churches vacated then and in the future at the apostolic see to his own disposition — vacant at the said see by the consistorial translation of bishop John from the united churches of Coventry and Lichfield to the church of Exeter. The pope hereby appoints Geoffrey bishop, committing to him the care and administration of the said united churches in spiritualities and temporalities.

Conclusions to: (i) the chapters of the mutually united churches of Coventry and Lichfield, (ii) the clergy of the cities and dioceses of Coventry and Lichfield, (iii) the people of the said cities and dioceses, (iv) the vassals of the said churches, (v) the archbishop of Canterbury, (vi) Henry, king of England.

Divina disponente clementia . . . The conclusions begin: (i) *Hodie ecclesiis vestris . . .*
(ii), (iii), (iv) Hodie et cetera. (v) Ad cumulum . . . (vi) Gratie divine premium . . .
. *L. puccius;* . *Jo de peleg'*[1] / · *B* / · *B· xx· xx*[2] · *x x x x x Bolis*

[1] it is unusual for the name of the abbreviator *de parco minori* who expedited the conclusions to be

noted in the register
[2] *sic*; an error for 'x'?

1030 5 May 1503   *Reg. Lat.* 1129A, fo 4^{r-v}

To Geoffrey Blythe, dean of the church of York. Since the pope intends this day to make provision of Geoffrey to the mutually united churches of Coventry and Lichfield and to appoint him bishop, he hereby absolves him from any [sentences] of excommunication etc. [as above, no. 53].

Apostolice sedis circumspecta benignitas de statu personarum ecclesiasticarum quarumlibet . . .
L . puccius / · B· / · B· xx Bolis

1031 14 May 1503   *Reg. Lat.* 1129A, fos 4^v-6^r

To Geoffrey, elect of Coventry and Lichfield. Since the pope has recently made provision of Geoffrey to the mutually united churches of Coventry and Lichfield, as is more fully contained in his letters drawn up in that regard,[1] he hereby grants faculty to Geoffrey — at his supplication — to receive consecration from any catholic bishop etc. [as above, no. 57, with appropriate changes, to '. . . marked with his seal;'] and that the above shall not be to the prejudice of the archbishop of Canterbury, to whom the aforesaid church is understood to be subject by metropolitical law. With the form of oath appended in full.

Cum nos pridem . . .
. L. puccius / · B· / · B· xxviij· Bolis

[1] above, no. 1029

1032 5 May 1503   *Reg. Lat.* 1129A, fos 278^r-280^r

To John Turnbul,[1] cellarer of the monastery of Newbotil,[2] OCist, d. St Andrews, designation as coadjutor and provision as abbot. The pope — having regard for the position and indemnity of the above monastery, which is presided over by abbot Andrew, who, on account of his feebleness and increasing age, cannot comfortably by himself rule and exercise its care, rule and administration and pay attention thereto; and hoping that John, who is a monk of the monastery and its cellarer, expressly professed of this order, in the priesthood and of lawful age, has the knowledge and capacity to rule and govern the monastery — on the advice of the cardinals and with abbot Andrew's express consent, hereby gives, designates and deputes John as coadjutor for life for abbot Andrew in the said rule and administration in spiritualities and temporalities with full and free power and faculty in every way to perform, exercise, make disposition of and execute everything pertaining to the office of coadjutor by law or custom or otherwise in any way; to the effect that he may — by reason of the coadjutorship — receive moderate expenses from the fruits of the monastery. The pope's will is, however, that John shall wholly abstain from alienation of the monastery's immovable goods and precious movables; and that he shall be bound to render account of things done and administered by him by reason of the office of coadjutor in accordance with Boniface VIII's constitution "Pastoralis". And, on abbot Andrew's death or resignation etc. or on the monastery being vacant in any way, [even][3] at the apostolic see, even if it is actually vacant at present, the pope, on like [advice],[4] hereby makes provision of John to the monastery now as of then and then as of now and appoints him abbot; and decrees that provision of John is made and he is appointed abbot, committing to him the care, rule and administration of the monastery in spiritualities and temporalities.

Conclusions to: (i) the convent of the monastery of Newbotil, (ii) the vassals of the said monastery, (iii) the abbot of the monastery of Melros, OCist, d. Glasgow, (iv) James, king of Scots.

Ex debito pastoralis officii circa ecclesiarum et monasteriorum quorumlibet ac illis presidentium personarum statum solicite vigilantes . . . The conclusions begin: *(i) <Hodie dilecto filio Andree abbati . . . >*[5] *(ii) Hodie dilecto filio Andree abbati et cetera. (iii), (iv) Hodie et cetera.*
F. de parma / · B· / · B· xxxxvj· · viij· viij· viij· viij· Bolis

[1] spelt *Turribul* in a conclusion

[2] also spelt *Neubotil, Neuubotil* in conclusions

[3] 'etiam' wanting

[4] *consensu; recte:* 'consilio'? (as in the conclusion to the convent)

[5] *Hodie dilecto filio Andree abbati vestri monasterii de Neubotil Cistercien. ordinis Sancti andree diocesis* inserted in the margin by the enregistering scribe, initialled *B* and . *B*.

1033   5 May 1503   *Reg. Lat.* 1129A, fo 280[v]

To John Turnbul, cellarer of the monastery of Newbotil, OCist, d. St Andrews. Since the pope has this day designated John as coadjutor for life of the above monastery and, on abbot Andrew's death or resignation etc. or on the monastery being vacant in any way, even at the apostolic see, thenceforth provided and appointed John thereto and decreed him appointed, as is more fully contained in the pope's letters drawn up in that regard,[1] he hereby grants faculty to John — at his supplication — in the event of the vacation and appointment in question, to receive benediction from any catholic bishop etc. [as above, no. 1027, with appropriate changes, to '. . . enclosed under his *bulla*;'] and John shall send the form of oath taken by him, verbatim, to the pope, at once, by his letters patent, by his own messenger, marked with his seal.

Cum nos hodie . . .
F. de parma / · B· / · B· xij· Bolis·

[1] above, no. 1032

1034   5 May 1503   *Reg. Lat.* 1129A, fo 281[r]

To John Turnbul, cellarer of the monastery of Neuubotil, OCist, d. St Andrews. Since the pope, on the advice of the cardinals, intends for certain reasons this day to give, designate and depute John as coadjutor for abbot Andrew in the rule and administration of the above monastery and, on abbot Andrew's death or resignation etc. or on the monastery being vacant in any way, even at the apostolic see, on like advice, make provision of John thenceforth and appoint him abbot, the pope hereby absolves John from any [sentences] of excommunication etc. under which he may perchance lie, so far only as regards the taking effect of the said designation etc. and provision etc. and each of the relevant letters. Notwithstanding etc.

Apostolice sedis consueta clementia ad ea libenter intendit . . .
F. de parma / · B· / ﹐B· xvj· Bolis·

1035   1 August 1504   *Reg. Lat.* 1150, fos 169[v]-171[r]

Union etc. At the recent petition of James Whitston', DDec, canon of the church of Lincoln, the pope hereby unites etc. the parish church of Sts Peter and Paul, Keteryng, d. Lincoln, whose annual value does not exceed 28 pounds sterling, to the canonry of the church of Lincoln and the prebend of St Mary, Banbury, in the same . . . [as calendared in *CPL* XVIII, no. 397 where, by virtue of the date under which it is drawn and its presence in a *liber* of Julius II, it is treated as a letter of Julius II].

Ad futuram rei memoriam. Romanum decet pontificem votis illis gratum prestare assensum . . .
. S. de Castello / Jo / Jo. xxxv. Episcopus Terracinen'

The dating clause puts the letter in 1 Julius II: *Rome apud Sanctum Petrum anno incarnationis dominice millesimo quingentesimo quarto kalendis Augusti anno primo*; but it is drawn in the name of Alexander [VI], not Julius. As the registry scribe had been writing *Julius et cetera* for at least a year he is unlikely to have written *Alexander et cetera* through sheer inadvertence. The contradiction is real and not easily resolved. Internal evidence is unhelpful: Whitstones held these benefices in both pontificates. (J. Le Neve, *Fasti Ecclesiae Anglicanae 1300-1541*, I, *Lincoln Diocese*, compiled by H. P. King (London, 1962), p. 32; Emden, *Oxford to 1500*, III, p. 2039). Likewise, the evidence of the bureaucracy: abbreviator, master of the registry, and registry scribe (Resta) concerned all held office under Alexander as well as Julius (*cf. CPL*, XVI, pp. cii, civ and cvii). Until more data turns up we must guess. The letter is the first in a run of four English letters (nos. 397-400) all expedited by the same abbreviator (S. de Castello), signed by the same master (Jo. Episcopus Terracinen.) and enregistered by the same scribe (Resta). The second and third letters also bear the same date. It is therefore possible that our's is a letter of Alexander which was expedited late and attracted the date of the others in the batch. Alternatively, and perhaps more probably, the letter was enregistered from a draft which had been drawn up in Alexander's pontificate; and the error was missed when the register entry was collated with the engrossment.

1036   16 April 1502   *Reg. Lat.* 2463, fos 242^v-244^r

To Roger Payntoure, BA, rector of the parish church of All Saints,[1] Chyngelford, d. London. Dispensation — at his supplication — to receive and retain for life, together with the above parish church, one, and without it, any two other benefices, etc. [as above, no. 3].

Litterarum scientia,[2] *vite ac morum honestas . . .*
· *A· de Sanctoseverino* / · *B·* / · *B· L. Bolis·*

[1] *Omnium Sanctorum*; *cf.* next entry which has 'Omnium Sanctorum' deleted!

[2] 'Litterarum scientia' (kept for graduates) inappropriate for a BA (not regarded as a degree by the chancery); *cf.* next entry where it is used, appropriately, for an MA

1037   16 April 1502   *Reg. Lat.* 2463, fos 244^r-245^r

To John Bacheler, MA, perpetual vicar of the parish church of the Holy Trinity, Magna Wenlok [also spelt *Magna We'lok*], d. Hereford. Dispensation — at his supplication — to him, who, as he asserts, holds the perpetual vicarage of the parish church[1] of the Holy Trinity, Magna Wenlok, to receive and retain for life, together with the above vicarage, one, and without it, any two other benefices, etc. [as above, no. 3].

Litterarum scientia,[2] *vite ac morum honestas . . .*
. A. de Sanctoseverino / . B. /. B. L. Bolis.

[1] directly hereafter, *Omnium Sanctorum* is deleted, initialled *B*; *cf.* 'Omnium Sanctorum' in previous entry

[2] appropriate here; *cf.* previous entry where the proem 'Litterarum scientia' is, inappropriately, associated with a BA

1038 —[1]   *Reg. Lat.* 2463, fo 245[v2]

Union as below. At a recent petition on the part of John Veysy, DDec, canon of the church of Dericton [also spelt *Dericton'*] *alias* Derlyngton [also spelt *Derlyngton'*], d. Durham, to the pope to unite etc. the parish church of Egmond, d. Coventry and Lichfield, to the canonry and prebend of the above church, both of which he holds, for as long as he holds the latter — asserting that the annual value of the parish church does not exceed 103 gold ducats of the camera . . . [3]

Ad futuram rei memoriam. Romanum decet pontificem votis . . .
A. de Sancto Severino / . B. / [-][4]

[1] Probably tenth year (26. viii. 1501-25. viii. 1502): the fragment comes from a register rubricated in the eighteenth century as *liber XI Anni X* (*cf. Ind.* 343, fos 37[v],106[r]; on the descriptive value of the *signatura* see *CPL* XVI, pp. lii-liii). Certainly, the letter was not enregistered before 31 July 1501: Bolis, whose initial occurs at the start of the letter, was not appointed master until then (*cf. CPL* XVI, p. civ). The date under which a letter is drawn can considerably pre-date enregistration (*ibid.*, pp. xxxv-xxxviii). Veysey did not acquire the benefices until 1497-98 (Emden, *Oxford to 1500*, III, pp. 1947-8)

[2] previously *cclxiiij*[v]; originally *ccxxiij*[v]

[3] mutilated: ceases (with *dignaremur*) at end of last line of first page; rest (on another leaf) lost

[4] magistral signature (of Bolis) and tax mark, which would have been at end of the letter, lost

Note. Where a letter can be identified from other sources (not searched exhaustively) the reference is given in a footnote. (The date, usually in parentheses, is that under which the letter is drawn.)

On the losses and the extent to which they can be supplied from the *Index* see *CPL* XVI, pp. xlix-liv.

	Ind.	DIOCESE	PERSON	MATTER	LIBER	FOLIO
				SEVENTH YEAR [1] **1498, 26. viii - 1499, 25. viii**		
1039	341, fo 10^v	*Aberdeen*	Willelmus [Elphinstone] episcopus Aberdonen.	Concessio nonnullarum decimarum cuiusdam loci ad mensam Aberdonen. spectantium	I Anni VII	23
1040	341, fo 120^v	*Lincoln*	Edmundus Wylford	Dispensatio ad incompatibilia	I Anni VII	26
1041	341, fo 200^v	*St Andrews*	Vivianus Hovine	*The like*	I Anni VII	31
1042	34l, fo 120^v	*Lincoln*	Joannes Ynyago	*The like*	I Anni VII	39
1043	341, fo 150^r	*Norwich*	Willelmus Bewirley	*The like*	I Anni VII	50
1044	341, fo 73^v	*York*	Joannes Aleshe	*The like*	I Anni VI [2]	51
1045	341, fo 150^r	*Norwich*	Laurentius Gretyngham	*The like*	I Anni VII	52
1046 [3]	341, fo 67^r	*Durham*	Rogerus Layburn	*The like*	I Anni VII	68
1047	341, fo 234^v	*Worcester*	Joannes More	*The like*	I Anni VII	69
1048	341, fo 73^v	*Exeter*	Thomas Hareys	Unio parochialis canonicatui per dictum Thomam obtento ad eius vitam tantum	I Anni VI [4]	70
1049	34l, fo 234^v	*Worcester*	Richardus More	Dispensatio ad incompatibilia	I Anni VII	72
1050	341, fo 10^v	*Armagh*	Thomas Waren	Commissio vigore appellationis	I Anni VII	75
1051	34l, fo 51^r	*Canterbury*	Richardus Draper	*The like*	I Anni VII	78
1052	341, fo 150^r	*Nullius*	Joannes Undyrwod	Dispensatio ad incompatibilia	I Anni VII	80
1053 [5]	341, fo 150^r	*Nullius perpetua*	Minister provincialis custodes et fratres Provincie Anglie Conventuales nec non commissarius Ultramuntanorum de Observantia nuncupatorum	Conferentie inter eos inite super nonnullis iurisdictionibus	I Anni VII	141
1054	341, fo 200^v	*St Andrews*	Willelmus Donglas	Dispensatio ad incompatibilia	I Anni VII	254
1055	341, fo 200^v	*Same*	Joannes Donglas	*The like*	I Anni VII	275
1056	341, fo 120^v	*Lincoln*	Joannes Dey	*The like*	I Anni VII	320
1057	341, fo 73^v	*Exeter*	Joannes Pikeman	Unio parochialis canonicatui per dictum Joannem obtento ad sui vitam	II Anni VII	28
1058	341, fo 73^v	*York*	Robertus Boude	Dispensatio ad incompatibilia	II Anni VII	29

	Ind.	DIOCESE	PERSON	MATTER	LIBER	FOLIO
1059	341, fo 234^v	Worcester	Gargridus Joannis	The like	II Anni VII	53
1060	341, fo 29^r 234^v	Bath and Wells	Joannes Marowod	The like	II Anni VII	68
1061	341, fo 201^r	Salisbury	Philippus David	The like	II Anni VII	69
1062	341, fo 150^r	Norwich	Simon Fineham	The like	II Anni VII	190
1063	341, fo 235^r	Winchester	Robertus Elesmere	The like	II Anni VII	191
1064	341, fo 121^r	Lincoln	Willelmus Elys	The like	II Anni VII	224
1065	341, fo 137^v	St David's	Owenus Apdd	The like	II Anni VII	228
1066	341, fo 235^r	Winchester	Richardus Suthyke	The like	II Anni VII	230
1067	341, fo 235^r	Worcester	Joannes Gryffith	The like	II Anni VII	249
1068 [6]	341, fo 29^v 235^r	Bath and Wells	Joannes Vanghan	The like	II Anni VII	250
1069	341, fo 29^v 235^r	Same	Willelmus Horsey	The like	II Anni VII	316 306
1070 [7]	341, fo 12^r	Ardfert Unio	Donatus Oconnyll	Unio vicarie canonicatui ad vitam dicti Donati tantum	V Anni VII	169
1071 [8]	341, fo 12^r	Ardfert	Connachus Magearyg	Erectio vicarie in simplicem prebendam ad vitam dicti Connachii tantum	V Anni VII	171
1072	341, fo 12^r	Killala	Willelmus Oheuacham	Erectio vicarie in simplicem prebendam ad vitam dicti Willelmi	V Anni VII	177
1073 [9]	341, fo 68^r	Dublin	Prior et capitulum ecclesie Dublinen. ordinis S. Augustini	Commissio vigore appellationis	XIV Anni VII	113
1074	341, fo 190^v	Rathluren.	Thomas [?Ingleby] episcopus Rathluren.	Ampliatio dispensationis ad incompatibilia	XIV Anni VII	118
1075 [10]	341, fo 75^r	Exeter Unio	Joannes Fulford	Unio parochialis canonicatui per dictum Joannem obtento ad eius vitam tantum	XIV Anni VII	127
1076	341, fo 124^r	Lincoln	Robertus Spenser	Dispensatio ad incompatibilia	XIV Anni VII	129
1077	341, fo 238^v	Winchester	Nicolaus Bradbriga	The like	XIV Anni VII	157
1078	341, fo 68^r	Dublin	Joannes Upinam	The like	XIV Anni VII	159
1079	341, fo 152^v	Norwich perpetua	Prior et fratres domus de Inghem ordinis Sancte Trinitatis Redemptionis Captivorum Norwicen. diocesis	Confirmatio erectionis dicte domus et unionis parochialis eidem domui	XIV Anni VII	175
1080	341, fo 152^v	Norwich	Joannes Ruynet	Dispensatio ad incompatibilia	XIV Anni VII	183

	Ind.	DIOCESE	PERSON	MATTER	LIBER	FOLIO
1081	341, fo 68[r]	*Durham*	Eduardus Stranguais	Unio parochialis alteri per dictum Eduardum obtente ad eius vitam	XIV Anni VII	192
1082	341, fo 124[r]	*London*	Richardus Picherd	Dispensatio ad incompatibilia	XIV Anni VII	204
1083	341, fo 124[r]	*Lincoln*	Joannes Thomson	*The like*	XIV Anni VII	205
1084[11]	341, fo 58[r]	*Cashel*	Patritius Stapulton	Monasterium et prioratus regularis certo modo	XIV Anni VII	206
1085[12]	341, fo 58[r] 124[r]	*Coventry and Lichfield*	Joannes Greislei	Dispensatio ad incompatibilia	XIV Anni VII	209
1086	341, fo 152[v]	*Norwich*	Thomas Cryppyng	*The like*	XIV Anni VII	216
1087	341, fo 75[r]	*York*	Joannes Hastyng	*The like*	XIV Anni VII	217
1088	341, fo 203[v]	*Salisbury*	Guillelmus Dunster	*The like*	XIV Anni VII	218
1089	341, fo 124[r]	*Lismore*	Thomas Portell	*The like*	XIV Anni VII	229
1090	341, fo 124[r]	*Same*	Jordanus Portell	*The like*	XIV Anni VII	230
1091	341, fo 124[r]	*Lincoln*	Joannes Longe	Unio parochialis alteri per dictum Joannem o[bten]te[13]ad eius vitam tantum	XIV Anni VII	237
1092	341, fo 204[r]	*Salisbury Unio*	Joannes Gryse	Unio parochialis alteri per dictum Joannem obtente ad eius vitam ad futuram	XV Anni VII	9
1093	341, fo 75[r]	*York*	Thomas Barker	Dispensatio ad incompatibilia	XV Anni VII	19
1094	341, fo 152[v]	*Norwich*	Henricus Norton	*The like*	XV Anni VII	21
1095	341, fo 91v	*Glasgow*	Wynninus Morwel	*The like*	XV Anni VII	22
1096	341, fo 124[v]	*Lincoln*	Willelmus Freston	*The like*	XV Anni VII	22
1097	341, fo 58[v]	*Canterbury*	Joannes Wilcok	Littere apostolice in forma Provisionis nostre - ad futuram	XV Anni VII	23
1098	341, fo 152[v]	*Norwich*	Robertus Honywood	Indultum deputandi personam seu personas ad officium visitandi loca sui archidiaconatus	XV Anni VII	25
1099	341, fo 75[r]	*York*	Radulphus Bulmer	Dispensatio ad incompatibilia	XV Anni VII	111
1100	341, fo 75[r]	*Exeter perpetua*	Joannes Serlo prior prioratus S. Germano in Carumbia ordinis S. Augustini Exonien. diocesis	Indultum utendi mitra baculo aliisque insigniis pontificalibus	XV Anni VII	112
1101	341, fo 124[v]	*Lincoln*	Elias abbas monasterii S. Joannis Apostoli de Croyston Premonstraten. ordinis Lincomen. diocesis	Dispensatio ad incompatibilia	XV Anni VII	113
1102	341, fo 238[v]	*Winchester*	Joannes Toppyng	*The like*	XV Anni VII	114
1103	341, fo 91[v]	*Glasgow*	Joannes Carlile	Commissio vigore appellationis	XV Anni VII	138

	Ind.	DIOCESE	PERSON	MATTER	LIBER	FOLIO
1104	341, fo 124ᵛ	*London*	Joannes Kelouz	Dispensatio ad incompatibilia	XV Anni VII	164
1105	341, fo 32ᵛ 239ʳ	*Bath and Wells*	Willelmus Norbury	*The like*	XV Anni VII	179
1106	341, fo 153ʳ	*Norwich*	Joannes Harrys	*The like*	XV Anni VII	179
1107	341, fo 32ᵛ 239ʳ *perpetua*	*Bath and Wells*	Thomas Spenfer magister et confratres hospitalis Domus Dei nuncupati S. Joannis siti apud Brigewater Bathonien. et Vellen. diocesis	Confirmatio donationis nonnullarum ecclesiarum eidem hospitali	XV Anni VII	243
1108	341, fo 32ᵛ 239ʳ *perpetua*	*Bath and Wells*	Joannes Prons prior monasterii Tauutonne ordinis S. Augustini. Bathonien. et Wellen diocesis	Indultum retinendi altare portatile pro se et successoribus	XV Anni VII	252
1109[14]	341, fo 32ᵛ 239ʳ *perpetua*	*Bath and Wells*	Joannes Prons et conventus monasterii et cetera ut supra [15]	Indultum utendi mitra baculo aliisque insigniis pontificalibus	XV Anni VII	253
1110	341, fo 75ᵛ	*York*	Christophorus Radclif	Dispensatio ad incompatibilia	XIX Anni VII	48
1111	341, fo 125ᵛ	*Lincoln*	Joannes Baptista de Basodonys	Indultum non residendi in locis in quibus beneficiatus extiterit	XIX Anni VII	53
1112	341, fo 125ᵛ	*Lichfield*	Willelmus Middelton	Dispensatio ad incompatibilia	XIX Anni VII	55
1113	341, fo 60ᵛ	*Carlisle*	Willelmus Draylow	*The like*	XIX Anni VII	66
1114	341, fo 204ᵛ	*Sodor*	Malcolinus Margillespy	Nova provisio rectorie parochialis	XIX Anni VII	213
1115	341, fo 204ᵛ	*Same*	Donaldus Matefaill	Prioratus regularis per obitum	XIX Anni VII	214
1116	341, fo 16ᵛ	*Ardfert*	Donaldus Ohyngardayll	Vicaria parochialis certo modo	XIX Anni VII	240
1117	341, fo 191ᵛ	*Raphoe*	Edmundus Oddomayll	Parochialis per privationem	XXI Anni VII	3
1118 [16]	341, fo 61ʳ	*Clonfert*	Thomas de Burgo	Monasterium et parochiales certo modo	XXI Anni VII	5
1119 [17]	341, fo 126ʳ	*Killaloe Unio*	Richardus de Burgo	Unio vicarie monasterio ad vitam dicti Richardi	XXI Anni VII	77
1120 [18]	341, fo 126ʳ	*Lismore Unio*	Thomas Pwer	Unio vicarie alteri ad vitam tantum dicti Thome	XXI Anni VII	108
1121	341, fo 68ᵛ 126ʳ	*Dublin Leighlin*	Patritius Olerahur	Erectio vicarie in canonicatum et simplicis in simplicem prebendam ad vitam tantum dicti Patritii	XXI Anni VII	135
1122 [19]	341, fo 76ʳ	*Annaghdown*	Thomas de Burgo	Unio vicariarum canonicatui ad vitam tantum dicti Thome	XXI Anni VII	145
1123	341, fo 68ᵛ	*Kildare*	Joannes Macgyllabryde	Monasterium per obitum	XXI Anni VII	176
1124 [20]	341, fo 222ᵛ	*Tuam*	Odo Ykallayd	Decanatus per obitum	XXI Anni VII	188

	Ind.	DIOCESE	PERSON	MATTER	LIBER	FOLIO
1125	341, fo 126^r	*Leighlin*	Reruallus Omona	Vicaria et rectoria certo modo	XXI Anni VII	190
1126	341, fo 126^r	*Same*	Edmundus Okella	Erectio vicarie in canonicatum et alterius in simplicem prebendam ad eius vitam	XXI Anni VII	193
1127 [21]	341, fo 191^v	*Raphoe*	Joannes Magyllabryde	Erectio rectorie in simplicem prebendam ecclesie Rapoten. ad vitam dicti Joannis	XXI Anni VII	253
1128	341, fo 142^r	*Moray*	Georgius Cicheton	Nova provisio vicarie	XXI Anni VII	317
1129	341, fo 126^v	*Lincoln*	Joannes Ffaukener	Dispensatio ad incompatibilia	XXV Anni VII	35
1130	341, fo 76^r	*Exeter*	Rogerus Horde	*The like*	XXV Anni VII	37
1131	341, fo 154^r	*Norwich*	Robertus Pokyswell	*The like*	XXV Anni VII	45
1132	341, fo 205^r	*Salisbury*	Riccardus Sanunt	*The like*	XXV Anni VII	69
1133 [22]	341, fo 34^v 241^v	*Bath and Wells*	Joannes Benet	*The like*	XXV Anni VII	71
1134	341, fo 241^v	*Worcester*	Thomas Neuuman	*The like*	XXV Anni VII	101
1135	341, fo 126^v	*London*	Joannes Lavage	*The like*	XXV Anni VII	153
1136	341, fo 62^v	*Chichester*	Joannes Austen	*The like*	XXV Anni VII	154
1137	341, fo 18^v	*Killala*	Restardus Baret	Expectativa ad quecumque	XXVIII Anni VII [23]	312
1138	341, fo 242^v	*Worcester*	Joannes Witthens	Dispensatio ad incompatibilia	XXVIII Anni VII [23]	317

EIGHTH YEAR [24]
1499, 26. viii - 1500, 25. viii

	Ind.	DIOCESE	PERSON	MATTER	LIBER	FOLIO
1139	342, fo 100^r	*London* Unio	Joannes Martyr	Unio parochialis canonicatui per dictum Joannem obtento ad eius vitam [-] ad futuram	I Anni VIII	20
1140	342, fo 100^r	*Lincoln*	Joannes Marchyell	Dispensatio ad incompatibilia	I Anni VIII	21
1141	342, fo 100^r	*London*	Joannes Forster	*The like*	I Anni VIII	41
1142	342, fo 60^r	*Exeter*	Thomas Laurrey	*The like*	I Anni VIII	55
1143 [25]	342, fo 1^r	*Aberdeen* perpetua	Scotorum rex illustris	Facultas et licentia quibuscumque ecclesiis [26] legendi audiendi ac studendi iuri civili in universitate dicte civitatis	I Anni VIII	98
1144 [27]	342, fo 1^r	*Aberdeen*	Magistri et alii universitatis studii generalis civitatis Aberdonen.	Commissio vigore recursus	I Anni VIII	99
1145	342, fo 100^r	*London*	Henricus Mayheu	Dispensatio ad incompatibilia	I Anni VIII	100
1146	342, fo 76^r	*Glasgow*	Andreas Madorack	Pensio super archidiaconatu	I Anni VIII	103

	Ind.	DIOCESE	PERSON	MATTER	LIBER	FOLIO
1147	342, fo 176^r	*St Andrews*	Stephanus de Wglas	Dispensatio ad incompatibilia	I Anni VIII	106
1148	342, fo 100^r	*London*	Willelmus Thorneburgh	*The like*	I Anni VIII	168
1149	342, fo 100^r	*Lincoln*	Robertus Wayfleot	*The like*	I Anni VIII	210
1150 [28]	342, fo 101^r	*Lismore Unio*	Wilhelmus Omorissa	Unio nonnullarum vicariarum canonicatui ad eius vitam	VI Anni VIII	26
1151 [29]	342, fo 140^r	*Ossory*	Riccardus Porol	Unio vicariarum canonicatui ad eius vitam	VI Anni VIII	32
1152 [30]	342, fo 140^r	*Same*	Joannes Grunt	Erectio canonicatus ad eius vitam	VI Anni VIII	39
1153	342, fo 205^v	*Waterford*	Willerius Omorissa	Vicaria certo modo	VI Anni VIII	193
1154	342, fo 101^r	*Lismore*	Thomas Aplialo	*The like*	VI Anni VIII	194
1155 [31]	342, fo 205^v	*Waterford*	Joannes Dugin	Cancellariatus per resignationem	VI Anni VIII	200
1156 [32]	342, fo 140^v	*Ossory*	Joannes Yhily	Erectio canonicatus ad eius vitam	IX Anni VIII	158
1157	342, fo 55^v	*Dunkeld*	Henricus Wod	Precentoria per permutationem	IX Anni VIII	193
1158	342, fo 55^v	*Same*	Robertus Boissunel	Decanatus per permutationem	IX Anni VIII	195
1159	342, fo 131^v	*Norwich*	Joannes Penton	Dispensatio ad incompatibilia	XII Anni VIII	17
1160	342, fo 102^v	*Lincoln*	Thomas ?Ulreby	*The like*	XII Anni VIII	20
1161	342, fo 131^v	*Norwich*	Thomas Thaverner	*The like*	XII Anni VIII	165
1162	342, fo 56^r	*Dublin*	Robertus Barnel	Commissio vigore appellationis	XII Anni VIII	170
1163	342, fo 102^v	*London*	Thomas Johuson	Dispensatio ad incompatibilia	XII Anni VIII	194
1164	342, fo 3^v 118^v	*Armagh Meath*	Octavianus [de Palatio] archiepiscopus Armachan. cum alio	Commissio vigore appellationis	XII Anni VIII	198
1165	342, fo 38^r	*Whithorn*	Archibaldus Stenvart	Parochialis certo modo	XVII Anni VIII	305
1166	342, fo 56^v	*Durham*	Joannes Cuttelar	Dispensatio ad incompatibilia	XVIII Anni VIII	51
1167	342, fo 104^v	*London*	Thomas Brady	*The like*	XVIII Anni VIII	88
1168	342, fo 21^r 209^r	*Bath and Wells*	Riccardus [33] Marschall	*The like*	XVIII Anni VIII	89
1169	342, fo 62^r	*York Unio*	Robertus Picherdi	Unio parochialis canonicatui per eum obtento ad eius vitam	XVIII Anni VIII	90
1170	342, fo 62^r	*Exeter*	Robertus Awyten	Dispensatio ad incompatibilia	XVIII Anni VIII	92
1171	342, fo 21^r 209^r	*Bath and Wells*	Joannes Kymer	*The like*	XVIII Anni VIII	93
1172	342, fo 62^r	*Exeter*	Willelmus Couuanni	Indultum non residendi in locis in quibus beneficiatus extitit	XVIII Anni VIII	94
1173	342, fo 104^v	*Lincoln perpetua*	Joannes abbas monasterii de Ramesey ordinis S. Benedicti	Facultas promovendi sex monachos in dicto monasterio nec non deputandi unum clericum ad	XVIII Anni VIII	96

Ind.		DIOCESE	PERSON	MATTER	LIBER	FOLIO
			Lincolinen. diocesis	officium tabellionatus		
1174	342, fo 104ᵛ	*Lincoln*	*Same*	Indultum exercendi pontificalia in dicto monasterio	XVIII Anni VIII	98
1175	342, fo 132ᵛ	*Norwich perpetua*	Willelmus abbas et conventus monasterii S. Edmundi de Bury ordinis S. Benedicti Norwicen. diocesis	Indultum applicandi certas missas pro aliis benefactoribus	XVIII Anni VIII	107
1176	342, fo 132ᵛ	*Norwich perpetua*	*Same*	?Conf(eren)tie super iurisdictione cuiusdam ville ad dictum monasterium pertinente	XVIII Anni VIII	108
1177	342, fo 104ᵛ	*Lincoln*	Thomas Dey	Dispensatio ad incompatibilia	XVIII Anni VIII	117
1178	342, fo 209ʳ	*Winchester*	Willelmus Parkins	*The like*	XVIII Anni VIII	118
1179	342, fo 132ᵛ	*Norwich*	Willelmus Dershin	*The like*	XVIII Anni VIII	127
1180	342, fo 179ᵛ	*Salisbury*	?Oddowinus [34] Woarson	*The like*	XVIII Anni VIII	128
1181 [35]	342, fo 209ʳ	*Worcester*	Robertus Ychyngton	*The like*	XVIII Anni VIII	156
1182	342, fo 21ʳ 209ʳ	*Bath and Wells*	Thomas Whyte [36]	*The like*	XVIII Anni VIII	157
1183	342, fo 62ʳ	*Ely*	Willermus Gearges	*The like*	XVIII Anni VIII	167
1184	342, fo 38ʳ	*Chichester Unio*	Willelmus N. [37]	Unio parochialis decanatui per eum obtento ad eius vitam Ad futuram	XVIII Anni VIII	189
1185	342, fo 119ᵛ	*St David's*	Joannes Stoltdale [38]	Dispensatio ad incompatibilia	XVIII Anni VIII	189
1186	342, fo 104ᵛ	*Lincoln*	Thomas Nicolson	*The like*	XVIII Anni VIII	197
1187	342, fo 179ᵛ	*Salisbury*	Joannes Louer	*The like*	XVIII Anni VIII	205
1188	342, fo 56ᵛ	*Dunblane*	Joannes ?Delly	Simplex per privationem	XVIII Anni VIII	210
1189	342, fo 209ʳ	*Winchester*	Joannes Grigge	Dispensatio ad incompatibilia	XVIII Anni VIII	213
1190	342, fo 104ᵛ	*Lincoln*	Robertus Kyngesley	*The like*	XVIII Anni VIII	216
1191	342, fo 38ʳ 105ʳ	*Coventry and Lichfield*	Joannes Wright	*The like*	XVIII Anni VIII	250
1192	342, fo 105ʳ	*Lichfield*	Georgius Vronon	*The like*	XVIII Anni VIII	251
1193 [39]	342, fo 38ᵛ	*Clonfert Unio*	Edmundus de Burgo	Unio prioratus canonicatui ad eius vitam tantum	XIX Anni VIII	19
1194	342, fo 38ᵛ	*Cashel*	Edmundus Morlier	Erectio ecclesie in prebendam	XIX Anni VIII	38
1195 [40]	342, fo 38ᵛ	*Clonfert*	Willelmus de Burgo	Vicaria devoluta	XIX Anni VIII	54
1196	342, fo 169ᵛ	*Raphoe*	Oddo Margilabryde	Vicaria parochialis certo modo	XXV Anni VIII	31
1197 [41]	342, fo 106ᵛ	*Limerick*	Beraldus Thome	Canonicatus certo modo	XXV Anni VIII	80
1198	342, fo 133ᵛ	*Norwich*	Joannes Pluttinger	Dispensatio ad incompatibilia	XXV Anni VIII	262
1199	342, fo 195ʳ	*Tuam*	Thomas Olarnyn [42]	Nova provisio vicarie parochialis	XXVII Anni VIII [43]	15

	Ind.	DIOCESE	PERSON	MATTER	LIBER	FOLIO
1200	342, fo 181ᵛ	St Andrews	Willelmus Monorgono'	Canonicatus per assequutionemXXVII Anni VIII [43]		88

NINTH YEAR [44]
1500, 26. viii - 1501, 25. viii

	Ind.	DIOCESE	PERSON	MATTER	LIBER	FOLIO
1201	342, fo 98ʳ	Kilmore	Gelasius Osidereau	Prioratus regularis certo modo	V Anni IX	25
1202	342, fo 98ʳ	Same	Joannes Margoryne	Vicaria certo modo	V Anni IX	37
1203	342, fo 170ᵛ	Raphoe	Laurentius Ogaleur	Parochialis certo modo	V Anni IX	119
1204	342, fo 57ᵛ	Kilmacduagh	Odo Ochayllyn	Vicaria certo modo	V Anni IX	129
1205	342, fo 43ᵛ	Clogher	Donatus Ocullen	Parochialis certo modo	V Anni IX	146
1206	342, fo 43ᵛ	Same Unio	Donatus Oslannagail	Unio vicarie alteri ad eius vitam tantum	V Anni IX	153
1207	342, fo 196ᵛ	Tuam	Milerius Prindragas	Vicaria et sine cura ecclesia certo modo	V Anni IX	199
1208	342, fo 9ᵛ	Aberdeen	Alexander Symson	Pensio	VI Anni IX	332
1209 [45]	342, fo 45ʳ	Canterbury Ecclesia	Henricus [Dean] electus Cantuarien.	Ecclesia per obitum	IX Anni IX	233
1210	342, fo 45ʳ	Same	Same	Absolutio	IX Anni IX	233
1211	342, fo 45ʳ	Same	Same	Munus	IX Anni IX	233
1212	342, fo 45ʳ	Same	Same	Commissio	IX Anni IX	233
1213	342, fo 58ʳ	Kildare	Mauritius Oqueronaten'	Decanatus per privationem	XIV Anni IX	87
1214 [46]	342, fo 184ʳ	St Andrews perpetua	Jacobus Scotorum rex illustris	Erectio cappelle regie in collegiatam cum unione pre(positu)re	XIV Anni IX	95
1215 [47]	342, fo 47ʳ	Clogher	Bernardus Mangynsenan	Monasterium per privationem	XIV Anni IX	225
1216 [48]	342, fo 110ʳ	Limerick	Joannes Militis	Archidiaconatus certo modo	XIV Anni IX	243
1217	342, fo 184ʳ	St Andrews	Ninianus Hovvme	Prioratus regularis per resignationem	XIV Anni IX	316
1218	342, fo 65ʳ	Exeter	Riccardus Brite	Dispensatio ad incompatibilia	XV Anni IX	21
1219	342, fo 65ʳ	York	Thomas Cunstable	The like	XV Anni IX	22
1220	342, fo 87ʳ	Hereford	Robertus Whitleg	The like	XV Anni IX	24
1221	342, fo 135ᵛ	Norwich	Alanus ?Thelau [49]	The like	XV Anni IX	25
1222	342, fo 215ʳ	Worcester	Riccardus Bilmer	The like	XV Anni IX	26
1223	342, fo 125ʳ	St David's	Matthias Hugan	The like	XV Anni IX	111
1224	342, fo 184ʳ	St Andrews	Niuianus Hobbine	Commissio	XV Anni IX	268
1225	342, fo 184ʳ	Same	Georgius Leomonth	Dispensatio ad incompatibilia	XV Anni IX	316
1226	342, fo 12ʳ	Aberdeen	Duncanus Thome de Anthinhamper	Concessio si in evidentem	XV Anni IX	317

	Ind.	DIOCESE	PERSON	MATTER	LIBER	FOLIO
1227	342, fo 26^v	Brechin	Guillelmus [Meldrum] episcopus Brechinen.	Concessio in evidentem	XV Anni IX	330
1228	342, fo 110^v	*London*	Willelmus Arosmith	Dispensatio ad incompatibilia	XVII Anni IX	16
1229	342, fo 48^r 110^v	*Coventry and Lichfield* (Unio)[51]	Jacobus Stanley	Unio parochialis alteri per eum obtente ad eius vitam (Ad futuram)[50]	XVII Anni IX	17
1230	342, fo 216^r	*Worcester*	Guillelmus Yonis	Unio parochialis canonicatui per eum obtento ad eius vitam Ad futuram	XVII Anni IX	19
1231	342, fo 65^r	*York*	Radulphus Butternuorth	Dispensatio ad incompatibilia	XVII Anni IX	22
1232	342, fo 110^v	*London*	Joannes Ruttur	*The like*	XVII Anni IX	35
1233	342, fo 136^r	*Norwich*	Thomas Bingrey	*The like*	XVII Anni IX	37
1234	342, fo 48^r	*Chichester*	Guillelmus Bounter	*The like*	XVII Anni IX	70
1235	342, fo 216^r	*Worcester*	Wilelmus Hebran	*The like*	XVII Anni IX	70
1236	342, fo 65^r	*York*	Thomas [Savage] episcopus olim Londonien. in archiepiscopum Eboracen. electus	Traditio pallii	XVII Anni IX	79
1237	342, fo 65^r	*Same*	*Same*	Commissio traditionis pallii	XVII Anni IX	79
1238	342, fo 65^v	*Exeter*	Willelmus Stoliefish	Indultum non residendi in locis in quibus beneficiatus extituit	XVII Anni IX	99
1239	342, fo 65^r	*Same*	Joannes Redmayne	Dispensatio ad incompatibilia	XVII Anni IX	101
1240	342, fo 27^r 216^r	*Bath and Wells*	Willelmus Combe	*The like*	XVII Anni IX	125
1241	342, fo 48^v	*Canterbury*	Joannes Picton	*The like*	XVII Anni IX	145
1242	342, fo 136^r	*Norwich*	Joannes Untum	*The like*	XVII Anni IX	202
1243	342, fo 58^v	*Durham*	Joannes Claimondi	*The like*	XVII Anni IX	206
1244	342, fo 136^r	*Norwich*	Thomas Walsohayn	*The like*	XVII Anni IX	212
1245	342, fo 111^r	*Lincoln*	Edmundus Stainbauke	*The like*	XVII Anni IX	213
1246	342, fo 65^v	*Ely*	Riccardus Wyart	*The like*	XVII Anni IX	217
1247	342, fo 13^r	*Achonry*	Thomas [Ford] episcopus Arhaden.	*The like*	XVII Anni IX	252
1248	342, fo 186^v	*Salisbury*	Joannes Leshugton	*The like*	XXVI Anni IX	12
1249	342, fo 29^v 219^r	*Bath and Wells*	Willelmus Ruffel	Unio parochialis alteri per eum obtente ad eius vitam Ad futuram	XXVI Anni IX	61
1250	342, fo 52^v	*Canterbury*	Henricus [Dean] episcopus nuper Saresbirien. in archiepiscopum	Traditio pallii	XXVI Anni IX	89

	Ind.	DIOCESE	PERSON	MATTER	LIBER	FOLIO
			Cantuarien. electus			
1251	342, fo 66^v	*York*	Riccardus Cook	Dispensatio ad incompatibilia	XXVI Anni IX	143
1252	342, fo 66^v	*Exeter*	Thomas Callow	*The like*	XXVI Anni IX	152
1253	342, fo 82^v	*Glasgow*	Robertus Elphinston	*The like*	XXVI Anni IX	329
1254	342, fo 59^r	*Dunblane*	Andreas Mahbrak	*The like*	XXVI Anni IX	332

TENTH YEAR [52]
1501, 26. viii - 1502, 25. viii

1255	343, fo 176^v	*St Andrews*	Guillelmus Craufurd	Res(ervati)o decimarum monasterii	VI Anni X	79
1256	343, fo 77^v	*Glasgow*	Jacobus Marchaston	Pensio	VI Anni X	116
1257	343, fo 77^v	*Same*	Joannes Scherar	Canonicatus per promotionem	VI Anni X	144
1258	343, fo 77^v	*Same*	Georgius Ker	Dispensatio ad incompatibilia	VI Anni X	188
1259	343, fo 77^v	*Same*	Thomas Ker	*The like*	VI Anni X	188
1260	343, fo 176^v	*St Andrews*	Andreas monacus nuper abbas monasterii B. Marie de Lundotis ordinis S. Benedicti	Reserv(ati)o fructuum monasterii	VI Anni X	302
1261	343, fo 4^r	Archaden.	Eugenius Maccamilii	Vicaria certo modo	XI Anni X	18
1262	343, fo 206^r	*Winchester*	Antonius abbas monasterii de Luirreae in Insula Vecte Cistercien. ordinis	Dispensatio ad incompatibilia	XI Anni X	240
1263	343, fo 121^r	*St David's*	Owinus Apris	Unio parochialis alteri per eum obtente ad eius vitam Ad futuram	XI Anni X	242
1264	343, fo 106^r	*Lincoln*	Thomas Davy	Dispensatio ad incompatibilia	XI Anni X	245
1265	343, fo 37^v	*Canterbury*	Riccardus Chethin	*The like*	XI Anni X	247
1266	343, fo 62^r	*Exeter*	Joannes Tregulan	*The like*	XI Anni X	266
1267	343, fo 62^r	*Ely*	Thomas Hyne	*The like*	XI Anni X	270
1268	343, fo 37^v	*Carlisle*	Riccardus Redinayd	*The like*	XI Anni X	271
1269	343, fo 106^r	*Lincoln*	Thomas abbas monasterii B. M. de Woburma ordinis Cistercien. Lincolinen. diocesis	*The like*	XI Anni X	272
1270	343, fo 37^v	*Carlisle*	Robertus Lonthree	*The like*	XI Anni X	274
1271	343, fo 134^v	*Norwich*	Thomas Exsalle	*The like*	XI Anni X	276
1272	343, fo 134^v	Nullius	Joannes Goryng	*The like*	XI Anni X	277
1273	343, fo 62^r	*York*	Willelmus Haryngton	*The like*	XI Anni X	282

Ind.		DIOCESE	PERSON	MATTER	LIBER	FOLIO
1274	343, fo 106^r	*Lincoln*	Patritius Hodgeson	*The like*	XI Anni X	289
1275	343, fo 37^v	*Chichester*	Villelmus Atkynson	*The like*	XI Anni X	295
1276	343, fo 37^v 106^r	*Coventry and Lichfield*	Joannes Stubis	*The like*	XI Anni X	316
1277	343, fo 106^r	*Lincoln*	Joannes Hamond	*The like*	XI Anni X	317
1278	343, fo 62^r	*York*	Thomas Strykland	*The like*	XI Anni X	318
1279	343, fo 62^v	*Exeter*	Joannes Soriano	Archipresbiteratus per obitum	XVIII Anni X	75

ELEVENTH YEAR [53]
1502, 26. viii - 1503, 18. viii

1280	343, fo 101^r	*Kilmore*	Patritius Iuacbradayd	Erectio vicarie in canonicatum ad vitam tantum dicti Patritii	I Anni XI	116
1281	343, fo 101^r	*Same*	Guardianus et fr[atr]es domus S. Francisci de Canayn ordinis Minorum Kilmoren. diocesis	Commissio	IV Anni XI	47
1282 [54]	343, fo 110^v	*Lismore*	Willelmus [55]	Erectio canonicatus ad eius vitam tantum	IV Anni XI	137
1283 [56]	343, fo 195^v	*Tuam*	Thomas de Burgo	Monasterium per dissolutionem unionis	IV Anni XI	143
1284 [57]	343, fo 110^v	*Limerick*	Mauritius Fellaim	Prioratus regularis per resignationem	IV Anni XI	179
1285 [58]	343, fo 110^v	*Killaloe*	Donatus Iharadgreyn	Erectio vicarie in canonicatum ad eius vitam	IV Anni XI	185
1286	343, fo 64^v	*Annaghdown*	Edmundus de Burgo	Unio vicarie portioni canonicali monasterii ad eius vitam tantum	IV Anni XI	322
1287	343, fo 145^v	*Ossory*	Cornelius Ykayl	Unio vicarie monasterio ad eius vitam tantum	IV Anni XI	327
1288	343, fo 80^v	*Glasgow*	Willelmus Valastz	Pensio	VII Anni XI	127
1289	343, fo 171^v	Rossen.	Thomas Kilsensz	Canonicatus per resignationem	VII Anni XI	161
1290	343, fo 182^r	*St Andrews*	Nouianus Hovvint	Perinde	VII Anni XI	285
1291	343, fo 112^v	*Lincoln*	Riccardus Carpentier	Dispensatio ad incompatibilia	XII Anni XI	12
1292	343, fo 112^v	*Lichfield*	Joannes Wardroper	*The like*	XII Anni XI	13
1293	343, fo 112^v	*Lincoln*	Robertus Lawnd	*The like*	XII Anni XI	15
1294	343, fo 47^v	*Canterbury*	Martinus Raynar	*The like*	XII Anni XI	22
1295	343, fo 81^v	*Glasgow*	Abbas et conventus monasterii B. M. de Melros Cistercien. ordinis	Licentia locandi nonnulla bona ad dictum monasterium spectantia	XII Anni XI	77
1296	343, fo 128^r	*Moray*	Alexander Gordone	Precentoria per resignationem	XII Anni XI	163

	Ind.	DIOCESE	PERSON	MATTER	LIBER	FOLIO
1297	343, fo 11ʳ	Aberdeen	Willelmus Rollandi	Dispensatio ad incompatibilia	XII Anni XI	179
1298	343, fo 172ʳ	Ross	Joannes Wans	The like	XIII Anni XI	12
1299	343, fo 74ʳ	Ferns	Riccardus Kawall	Dispensatio pro illegitimo	XIII Anni XI	159
1300	343, fo 183ᵛ	St Andrews	Joannes Bradi	Unio vicarie prep(ositu)re	XVI Anni XI	3
1301	343, fo 183ᵛ	Same	Jacobus Achison	Pensio	XVI Anni XI	5
1302	343, fo 139ʳ	Norwich	Willelmus Cobbe	Dispensatio ad incompatibilia	XVI Anni XI	151
1303	343, fo 139ʳ	Same	Walterus Braye	The like	XVI Anni XI	152
1304	343, fo 214ᵛ	Winchester	Joannes Pimburton	The like	XVI Anni XI	158
1305	343, fo 183ᵛ	Salisbury	Joannes Hallo	Unio parochialis alteri ad eius vitam	XVI Anni XI	159
1306	343, fo 49ᵛ	Cloyne	Joannes Odoni	Commissio	XVI Anni XI	177
1307	343, fo 58ʳ	Dunkeld	Jacobus Crethoun	The like	XVI Anni XI	181
1308	343, fo 139ʳ	Norwich	Joannes Wayen	Dispensatio ad incompatibilia	XVI Anni XI	218
1309	343, fo 113ᵛ	Lincoln	Thomas Hutton	Indultum deputandi personam seu personas ad officium visitandi loca sui archidiaconatus	XVI Anni XI	250
1310	343, fo 114ʳ	London	Hugo Trufodi	Dispensatio ad incompatibilia	XIX Anni XI [59]	228
1311	343, fo 216ʳ	Winchester Worcester	Eduardus electus Caliporen.	Retentio parochialis et pensionis super mensa	XXV Anni XI [59]	12
1312	343, fo 185ʳ	St Andrews	Georgius Knowis	Dispensatio ad incompatibilia	XXV Anni XI [59]	201
1313 [60]	343, fo 52ʳ	Cork	Donaldus Omurckw	Unio vicarie canonicatui ad eius vitam tantum	XXV Anni XI [59]	398
1314	343, fo 14ʳ	Ardfert	Joannes Mare'lligoid	Erectio vicarie in canonicatum ad eius vitam	XXV Anni XI [59]	400

TWELFTH YEAR [61]

1315 [62]	343, fo 67ʳ	Ecclesia Exouien.	Joannes [Arundel] episcopus Exouien.	Ecclesia per translationem	I Anni XII	28
1316	343, fo 67ʳ	Same	Same	Commissio	I Anni XII	30
1317	343, fo 67ʳ	Same	Same	Absolutio	I Anni XII	30
1318 [63]	343, fo 185ᵛ	Monasterium Sancti Andree	Henricus Orme	Monasterium per cessionem	I Anni XII	51
1319	343, fo 185ᵛ	Same	Same	Munus	I Anni XII	53
1320	343, fo 185ᵛ	Same	Same	Absolutio	I Anni XII	53
1321 [64]	343, fo 185ᵛ	Monasterium Sancti Andree	Jacobus [Stewart] archiepiscopus Sancti Andree	Monasterium per obitum	I Anni XII	154

	Ind.	DIOCESE	PERSON	MATTER	LIBER	FOLIO
1322	343, fo 185ᵛ	*Same*	*Same*	Absolutio	I Anni XII	155
1323	343, fo 140ᵛ	*Norwich*	Edmundus [Connesburgh] electus Calcedonien.	Retentio prioratus regularis	I Anni XI⁶⁶	104
1324	343, fo 141ʳ	Ecclesia Nigropontin.	Joannes Hatton electus Nigropontem.	Ecclesia certo modo	I Anni XII	209
1325	343, fo 141ʳ	*Same*	*Same*	Munus	I Anni XII	210
1326	343, fo 116ʳ 174ʳ	*London* *Rochester*	Joannes [Hatton] electus Nigroponten.	Retentio parochialis et simplicium	I Anni XII	210
1327	343, fo 141ʳ	Ecclesia Nigropontin.	Joannes Hatton electus Nigropontem.	Absolutio	I Anni XII	213
1328	343, fo 141ʳ	*Same*	*Same*	Indultum non residendi	I Anni XII	213
1329 ⁶⁶	343, fo 83ᵛ	Monasterium Glasgnien.	Robertus Schw	Monasterium per cessionem	II Anni XII	62
1330	343, fo 83ᵛ	*Same*	*Same*	Munus	II Anni XII	67
1331	343, fo 83ᵛ	*Same*	*Same*	Absolutio	II Anni XII	67
1332	343, fo 83ᵛ	*Same*	*Same*	Derogatio statutorum	II Anni XII	67
1333	343, fo 83ᵛ	*Same*	*Same*	Commissio receptionis in religionem	II Anni XII	67
1334	343, fo 83ᵛ	*Same*	*Same*	Retentio vicarie	II Anni XII	67
1335 ⁶⁷	343, fo 217ʳ	Ecclesia Vigornien.	Joannes [de' Gigli] electus Vigornien.	Ecclesia per obitum	II Anni XII	84
1336	343, fo 217ʳ	*Same*	*Same*	Absolutio	II Anni XII	85
1337	343, fo 54ʳ 116ᵛ	*Coventry and Lichfield*	Joannes [de' Gigli] electus Vigorinen.	Retentio parochialis ⁶⁸	II Anni XII	86
1338	343, fo 54ʳ	Ecclesia Clocen.	Vincentius electus Clocen.	Ecclesia per translationem	II Anni XII	166
1339	343, fo 54ʳ	*Same*	*Same*	[--] ⁶⁹	II Anni XII	168
1340 ⁷⁰	343, fo 131ᵛ	Moranien. Monasterium	Thomas Vawan	Monasterium per cessionem	II Anni XII	314
1341	343, fo 131ᵛ	*Same*	*Same*	Munus	II Anni XII	317
1342	343, fo 131ᵛ	*Same*	*Same*	Absolutio	II Anni XII	317

[1] probably the original year of the *liber* unless otherwise indicated

[2] *Sic; recte* 'VII'

[3] *Cf. The Register of Richard Fox Lord Bishop of Durham 1494-1501*, ed. M. P. Howden [= Surtees Society, vol. CXLVII], 1932, pp. 121-123 (26 December 1498).

[4] *Sic; recte* 'VII'

[5] i. e. *Super gregem* of 12 January 1499 (*cf.* Wadding, *Annales Minorum*, XV [Quaracchi, 1933], pp. 215-220 [from liber 174 (= I Anni VII), fo. 141])

[6] *Cf. Regs. King & Castello*, no. 321 (4 April 1499)

[7] *Cf. Annates, Ardfert*, no. 122 (28 December 1498)

[8] *Cf. Annates, Ardfert*, no. 123 (30 December 1498)

[9] *Cf. The Twentieth Report of the Deputy Keeper of the Public Records in Ireland*, HMSO, Dublin, 1888. Appendix VII: Calendar to Christ Church Deeds, p. 105, no. 370 (30 July 1499)

[10] *Cf.* M. R. James, *A Descriptive Catalogue of the Manuscripts in the Library of Corpus Christi College Cambridge*, I (Cambridge, 1912), no. 170: Letter-Book of N. Collys, Notary, item 39 (n. d.)

[11] *Cf.* Brady, *Episcopal Succession*, II, pp. 245-6 (8 June 1499)

[12] *Cf.* dispensation of 6 July 1499 to John Gresley, cleric, d. Coventry and Lichfield, in his seventeenth year, or thereabouts, enabling him to hold a benefice with cure (Lichfield Joint Record Office, B/A/1/13. Register of John Arundel, fos 242^v-243^r)

[13] MS corroded

[14] J. Sayers, *Original Papal Documents in Lambeth Palace Library. A Catalogue* (= Bulletin of the Institute of Historical Research, Special Supplement, 6), London, 1967, p. 40, no. 112 and *Victoria County History of Somerset*, II (1911), p. 143 both refer to a bull of 1498-99 granting use of the ring and staff (but not mitre). This letter, despite discrepancy?

[15] thus fo 32^v (*Bathonien.*), with reference to previous entry (no. 1108); fo 239^r (*Wellen.*) has only *ydem*

[16] *Cf.* Brady, *Episcopal Succession*, II, p. 247 (9 August 1499)

[17] *Cf. Annates, Killaloe*, no. 230 (24 July 1499)

[18] *Cf. Annates, Lismore*, no. 76 (13 July 1499)

[19] *Cf. Annates, Tuam Province*, no. 321 (17 August 1499)

[20] *Cf. Annates, Tuam Province*, no. 318 (10 June 1499)

[21] *Cf. Annates, Ulster*, pp. 269-70, no. 1 (9 August 1499)

[22] *Cf. Regs. King & Castello*, no. 251 (7 July 1499)

[23] probably a *liber* of the eighth year

[24] probably the original year of the *liber* unless otherwise indicated

[25] i. e. *Eximie devotionis* of 4 July 1500; printed from engrossment in *Fasti Aberdonenses*, ed. C. Innes [Spalding Club, 26], Aberdeen, 1854, pp. 36-38

[26] *sic; recte* 'ecclesiasticis'

[27] i. e. *Militanti ecclesie* of 4 July 1500; printed from engrossment in *Fasti* . . . (above, note 25), pp. 33-36

[28] *Cf. Annates, Ossory*, no. 103 (15 June 1500)

[29] *Cf. Annates, Ossory*, no. 104 (30 June 1500)

[30] *Cf. Annates, Ossory*, no. 105 (6 July 1500)

[31] *Cf. Annates, Waterford*, no. 22 (1 June 1500)

[32] *Cf. Annates, Ossory*, no. 101 (26 January 1500)

[33] thus fo 21^r (*Bathonien.*); fo 209r (Wellen.) has *Richardus*

[34] blotched: *Oddowinus*

[35] *Cf.* dispensation of 17 March 1500 to Robert Ychyngton', prior of the priory of St Sepulchre, Warwick, OSA, d. Worcester, enabling him to hold two regular benefices or one regular and one secular; one regular to be held *in titulum* the other, regular or secular, *in commendam* (HWRO, BA. 2648/8(i): register of Silvestro de' Gigli, fos 104^v-105^r, pp. 206-207)

[36] thus fo 21^r (*Bathonien.*); fo. 209^r (*Wellen.*) has *White*

[37] *sic*

[38] blotched: *Stoltdale*

[39] *Cf. Annates, Clonfert*, no. 71 (3 September 1499)

[40] *Cf. Annates, Clonfert*, no. 70 (1 September 1499)

[41] *Cf. Annates, Limerick*, no. 116 (17 July 1499)

[42] or *Olamyn*

[43] possibly a *liber* of the ninth, tenth, or eleventh year

[44] probably the original year of the *liber*

[45] *Cf.* Brady, *Episcopal Succession*, I, p. 3 (26 May 1501)

[46] i. e. *Inter cetera* of 2 May 1501; printed from copy in *Reg. Cap. Reg. Striv.* by C. Rogers, *op. cit.* (above, no. 765), pp. 2-11 (from item 1. Processus super ereccione ecclesie Collegiate de Striueling)

[47] *Cf. Annates, Ulster*, Clogher, 1501, no. 4 (12 July 1501)

[48] *Cf. Annates, Limerick*, no. 119 (10 August 1501)

49 blotched: Thelau

[50] fo 110^v (*Lichefelden.*) only

[51] fo 48^r (*Conventren.*) only

[52] probably the original year of the *liber*

[53] probably the original year of the *liber* unless otherwise indicated

[54] *Cf. Annates, Lismore*, no. 80 (21 May 1503)

[55] *sic*; no surname or title; 'Offlaban'? (see reference in previous note)

[56] *Cf. Annates, Tuam Province*, no. 328 (23 May 1503)

[57] *Cf. Annates, Limerick*, no. 122 (7 February 1503)

[58] *Cf. Annates, Killaloe*, no. 236 (16 February 1503)

[59] probably a *liber* of various years

[60] *Cf. Annates, Cork*, no. 95 (15 April 1503)

[61] fictitious: in no case the original year of the *liber*

[62] *Cf.* Brady, *Episcopal Succession*, I, p. 41 (8 April 1502)

[63] *Cf.* Brady, *Episcopal Succession*, I, p. 197 (12 June 1502)

[64] *Cf.* Brady, *Episcopal Succession*, I, p. 164 (7 July 1503)

[65] *sic*; *recte* 'XII'

[66] *Cf.* Brady, *Episcopal Succession*, I, p. 205-6 (20 July 1498)

[67] the principal bull (dated 30 August 1497) and the concurrent conclusions to the chapter, clergy, people, and vassals, are enregistered in Gigli's register: HWRO, BA. 2648/7 (iii), pp. 4-6; the conclusion to the king is extant: PRO SC7 37(40)

[68] i. e. Rostherne, Cheshire (ASV, *Annatae*, 42, fo. 75^v [Rowstorne]); *cf.* Emden, *Oxford to 1500*, II. p. 764

[69] MS blank as to matter (e. g. 'Munus', 'Absolutio') of other letter(s)

[70] *Cf.* Brady, *Episcopal Succession*, I, pp. 193-4 (13 January 1500)

INDEX OF PERSONS AND PLACES

Note. The present index has been compiled largely in accordance with the convention for record publications followed by earlier volumes in the *CPL* series. All references are to serial numbers of calendar entries. Irish surnames are under their Mac and O prefixes. However, the index differs from its predecessors in two major respects.

Firstly, the index collects the names of places under counties (given only rarely in the letters) as well as under dioceses. Secondly, the names of *all* (and not just selected) persons are collected under dioceses. The sub-entries (emboldened) of the relevant main entries are, typically: "cathedral church"; "bishop"; "diocese". Under "diocese, persons of" the reader will find listed, as before : (i) persons who are locally designated by diocese alone; and (ii) persons entered under that diocese in the *rubricellae* of lost letters. He will also now find (iii) persons beneficed in that diocese, either currently or prospectively (e.g. by virtue of a mandate of provision), or otherwise connected with it. (The inclusion of the prospectively beneficed brings the indexing of letters into conformity with the established indexing of the *rubricellae*). To avoid wasteful repetition, persons encountered elsewhere in the main entry (e.g. as canons under "cathedral church") are excluded from the listing under diocese. Archdeacons are entered below "bishop", not under "cathedral church".

It is hoped that these innovations will enable readers whose interests are limited by county and diocesan boundaries to exploit the material more efficiently.

A

Abbeyderg (Dearg) [*in* Taghsheenod, co. Longford], [Augustinian] priory of, prior of, papal mandatary, 763, 836

Abbeydorney [*in* ODorney, co. Kerry], [Cistercian] monastery of, abbot of, papal mandatary, 250, 313, 818, 939

Abbeygormacan (Ogorlakane)[co. Galway], [Augustinian] monastery of, abbot of, papal mandatary, 16

Abbeyknockmoy [co. Galway], Cistercian monastery of, 330
......, ..., abbot of, papal mandatary, 833
......, ..., commendatory abbot of *see* de Burgo, Thomas; OKelly, John
......, ..., parish church of the Great Gate at, 122

Abbeyleix [co. Laois], [Cistercian] monastery of, abbot of, papal mandatary, 932, 934

Abbeymahon [co. Cork], [Cistercian] monastery of, abbot of, papal mandatary, 251, 256, 257

Abbeyshrule [co. Longford], [Cistercian] monastery of, abbot of, papal mandatary, 763

Abbot, Thomas, priest of London diocese, 775

Abbots Bromley *see* Bromley, Abbots

Abbots Ripton *see* Ripton, Abbots

[Abdie, co. Fife], place in *see* Lindores

Aberdeen, **city** of [*now* Old Aberdeen, co. Aberdeen], university in, faculty for churchmen to study civil law in, 1143
......, ..., ..., masters and others of, letters conservatory for, 1144
......, **new vill** of [*now* Aberdeen, co. Aberdeen], 64
......, ..., parish church to be erected in, 64
......, ..., proposal of James [IV] to establish

Aberdeen, **new vill** (*contd*)
market at, 64

......, **[cathedral] church** of [*at* Old Aberdeen], dean of, papal mandatary, 558

......, ..., treasurer of, papal mandatary, 155

......, ..., canons of *see* Bog, Patrick; Forbes, Alexander and John; Guthrie, David; Guthrie, *Decanum* [*recte* David?]; Shearer, Duncan; Wauvri, William; Wawane, William; Young, Alexander

......, ..., prebends in *see* Kearn and Forbes; Kincardine O'Neil

......, **bishop** (or his vicar general) of, refusal of, to institute patron's presentee, 50, 68

......, ..., resignation admitted by, 444

......, ..., collation by, 444

......, bishop of, as local ordinary, presentation to, *cf.* 778

......, ..., ..., cession into hands of, *cf.* 778

......, ..., papal mandatary, 64, 552, 793, 928

......, ..., papal judge delegate, 435

......, ..., to receive oath of fealty in pope's name, 584, 587, 588, 590, 1009, 1011

......, ..., to receive intending religious as canon, bestow habit, and receive profession, 1028

......, ..., *mensa* of, 1039

......, ..., *see* Elphinstone, William

......, official of, papal mandatary, 190, 444

......, church of, archdeaconry of, 190

......, ..., archdeacons of *see* Dowe, William; Elphinstone, Adam

......, **diocese** of, churches, cemeteries, etc. of, pollution of, 411

......, ..., persons of *see* Anderson, John; Arnot, David; Bannerman, Alexander; Bisset, Andrew; Cranston, Gilbert; Lyell, Andrew and William; Maywel, Thomas; Otterburn, Gilbert; Rolland, William; Simson, Alexander; Stewart, James; Strachan, William; Thomson,

Aberdeen, **diocese** (*contd*)
Duncan; Vaus, Martin

......, ..., places in *see* Allathan [*in* Udny]; Ardgrain [*in* Ellon]; Ardmore [*in* Udny]; Auchterellon [*in* Ellon]; Chapel of Garioch; ?Collieston [*in* Slains]; Craig [*in* Udny]; ?Craigheid [*in* Ellon]; Dumbreck [*in* Udny]; Echt; Ellon; Esslemont [*in* Ellon]; Forvie; Housieside [*in* Udny]; Inverurie; Logie Durno; Mains (of Aucterellon) [*in* Ellon]; ?Meikle [*in* Slains]; Pitmedden [*in* Udny]; Rathmuriel and Kinnethmont; Slains; Tilliemaud [*in* Udny]; Torry [*in* Udny]; ?Udny; Waterton [*in* Ellon]; Woodland [*in* Udny]; Yonder Aucterellon [*now* Yonderton *in* Ellon]

[Aberdeen, co. of], places in *see* Aberdeen; Auchindoir; Forbes; Kearn; Kincardine O'Neil; Tullynessle; *and* places *listed above under* Aberdeen, diocese of

[Aberdour], place in *see* Inchcolm

Abergwili (Abergwyli) [co. Carmarthen], [collegiate] church of, canon and prebendary of *see* Gwynn, Maurice

Aberlady [co. Haddington], canonry and prebend of in Dunkeld cathedral, 1019

......, ..., pensioner of *see* [Turnbull], William

Abington [co. Limerick], [Cistercian] monastery of, abbot of, papal mandatary, 380

[ab Iorwerth], David *see* David [ab Iorwerth]

Abirnethy, John, the late, rector of Tannadice, 812

......, ..., ..., ..., coadjutor to *see* Abirnethy, Walter

Abirnethy (*contd*)
......, Walter, provost of Dumbarton, 812
......, ..., coadjutor to John Abirnethy, *q.v.*
......, ..., ..., appeal of, 812

Abrohe *see* OBrophy

Acclobard *see* Appleyard

Accumomane *see* Aughrim

Achamacharte *see* Aghmacart

Achdara *see* Adare

Achison *see* Aitchison

Achonry [co. Sligo], [cathedral] church of,
canon of *see* de Anglo, Gilbert
......, bishop of *see* [Ford], Thomas
......, diocese of, persons of *see* de Burgo,
Richard / Restardus; OMurphy, John;
and see MacCawell, Eugenius
......, ..., place in *see* Bohola

?Achonry (*Archaden.*) [co. Sligo], diocese
of, person of *see* MacCawell, Eugenius

Achyarta *see* Aghiart

Achynach' *see* Aghinagh

de Acre, Alfonsus, *abbreviator de parco
minori* , conclusions expedited by, 1009

Acryng *see* Eakring

Adam, James, vicar of Dunsford, 436
......, Thomas, rector of St Mary's, Feltwell,
284

Adams (Adam), Maurice, vicar of
Llandeilo Vawr, 892

Adare (Achdara) [co. Limerick], Trinitarian
house of, ministership of, 221

Adare (*contd*)
......, ..., ministers of *see* Appleyard, John;
[Creagh], David; OPhelan, Maurice

d'Adelmo [*or* Badia Elmi, *modern* Villa
Landi, *near* Certaldo, province of
Florence, Italy], Camaldolese
monastery of B. Mary, 382

Adelyngflete *see* Adlingfleet

Aderei, Thomas, layman of London
diocese, 261
......, ..., marriage of, to Alice Chester, 261

Adlingfleet (Adelyngflete) [Yorks], parish
church of, 799

Affahy *see* OFahy

Agard (Agarde), Philip, ostensible keeper
in spirituals of the dioceses of Coventry
and Lichfield, litigation before, 991
......, ..., ostensible vicar or official of the
chapter of the church of Coventry and
Lichfield, *sede vacante*, litigation
before, 991

[Aghadoe, co. Kerry], place in *see*
Innisfallen

Aghiart (Achyarta) [*in* Ballynakill, co.
Galway], appurtenances of, of the
parish church of Killererin *alias
Muinter Murchada*, 69, 75

Aghinagh (Achynach', Athinach) [co.
Cork], parish church of, to be erected
into prebend in Cloyne cathedral, 15
....., ..., vicarage of, 825

Aghmacart (Achamacharte) [co. Laois],
[Augustinian] monastery of, prior of,
papal mandatary, 510

Agia (*Agien.*) [*or Cydonien. or Caneen.* ,

Agia (*contd*)
    near Khania (on site of ancient
    Kydonia) in the island of Crete], bishop
    of, papal mandatary, 642, 791, 928, 929
    ......, ..., to receive intending religious as
    monk, bestow habit, and admit his
    profession, 1017

Aglaysdony, alias of Killeenagarriff, *q.v.*

Aglish *or* Aglishmartin (Bellemartin) [co.
    Kilkenny], parish church of, rectory of,
    787
    ......, ..., ..., to be united to canonry and
    prebend of St Maul's in Ossory
    cathedral, 787

Ahascragh (Hathasecuth) [co. Galway],
    parish church of, rectory of, 164
    ......, ..., ..., to be united to proposed
    prebend of Killosolan in Elphin
    cathedral, 164

Aherne (Ochacheri), Denis, canon of the
    Augustinian monastery of Rathkeale, to
    be prior, 542

Air(e) *see* Ayr

Aistercumba *see* Hestercombe

Aitchison (Achison), James, reservation of
    pension for, St Andrews diocese, 1301

Alan (Alam), John, master of Cobham
    college, vicar of Hoo St Werburgh,
    sometime vicar of Deptford St
    Nicholas, 271

Alathan, Alathan', Alathane, Alathone *see*
    Allathan

Album Monasterium see Whitchurch

Albury [Surrey], parish church of, 675

[Alcock], John, bishop of Ely, death of, 627

Aldaham *see* Aldham

Aldborough (Aldeburgh) [Norf], parish
    church of, 912

[Alderbury, Wilts], place in *see* Ivychurch

Aldham (Aldaham) [Essex], parish church
    of, 864

Aldingham (Aldyngh(a)m) [Lancs], parish
    church of, union of, to the canonry and
    prebend of Cropredy in Lincoln
    cathedral, 752

Alenson', John, rector of Shottisham, 660

Aleshe, John, of York diocese, dispensed
    for plurality, 1044

Alexander III, letters of, 174

Alexander IV, constitution "Abbates" of,
    397, 425, 686

[Alexander VI], household etc. of :
    chaplain : Ponzettus, Fer(di)nandus;
    and see de Pereriis, William
    continual commensals *see* Forman,
    Robert; Malvezzi, Galeatius; Scott,
    Edward
    cubicularius see Scott, Edward
    familiars *see* de Bertinis, Leonard;
    Forman, Robert; Ponzettus,
    Fer(di)nandus; Scott, Edward; Tuba,
    master Paul

Aleyn' *see* Allen

Aleyns, Edmund, rector of Swanton Abbot,
    952

Alfyngton *see* West Alvington

Alison (Alyson'), John, vicar of Moulton, 693

Allathan (Alathan, Alathan', Alathane, Alathone) [*in* Udny, co. Aberdeen], tithes of pertaining to Ellon parish church, 144, 793, 928

Allen (Aleyn'), Thomas, prior / detainer of the Augustinian priory of Selsker near Wexford, death of, 989
......, ..., appeal of, 989

Aller, William, rector of West Putford, 239

Alnwick (Alnewik) [Northumb], [Premonstratensian] monastery of, abbot of, papal judge delegate, 94

[Alps], crossing of, 405
......, pass of *cf.* Mont - Cenis

Althinelek *see* Auchinleck

Alveston (Olstoon) [Warw], parish church of, 923

Alvington, West (Alfyngton) [Devon], parish church of, 413
......, ..., chapel within the parish of *see* ?Easton

Alyson' *see* Alison

Amadeus, duke of Savoy *see* Felix V

Amalle *see* OMalley

Ambronay [*in dép.* of Ain, France], Benedictine monastery of, commend of, 577, 578
......, ..., convent and vassals of, conclusions to, 577

Anachdrilin *see* Annagh

Andeleyn, Henry, vicar of Melton Mowbray, 709

Andener *see* Andover

Anderson, John, priest of St Andrews diocese, presentation of, for vicarage of Rathmuriel and Kinnethmont, 778
......, ..., cession by and assignment to, of pension on vicarage's fruits, 778
......, *cf.* Andrenoson

Andover (Andener) [Hants], parish church of, 213

André (Andree), Bernard, cleric of Toulouse, preceptor and poet laureate of Arthur, prince of Wales, 530

Andrenoson, Gilbert, vicar of Hendon, 794
......, *cf.* Anderson, Andrewson

Andrew (Androw, Androwe), John, vicar of Broadwindsor, 557
......, Peter, rector of Roborough, 89
......, William, rector of Hanwell, 238
......, ..., rector of West Coker, 77
......, *cf.* Andrewes

Andrew, abbot of Newbattle *see* [Longant], Andrew
......, [bishop-] elect of Caithness *see* [Stewart], Andrew
......, late bishop of Moray *see* [Stewart], Andrew
......, [bishop-] elect of Moray *see* [Forman], Andrew
......, bishop of Orkney *see* [Painter], Andrew

Andrewes *cf.* Andrew

Andrewson *cf.* Andrenoson

Androw(e) *see* Andrew

An'ficampo *alias* Cilleule *see* Kilcooly

Angersleigh (Lexa) [Som], church of, 174

[Anglesey, co. of] place in *see* ?Llanfechell

Angliam see England

de Anglo, Gilbert, canon of Achonry, papal mandatary, 401
......, *cf.* Nangle

de Anglo *alias* Moschalaiy, Henry, ostensible cleric of Emly diocese, detainer, with Richard de Burgo, of the vicarage of Ludden, 380

Anian, bishop of Bangor, synodal constitution concerning *gologoith* published by, 118

Annacalla   (Hanacl)   [*modern* ?Annaghcallow *in* Clonfert, co. Galway], prebend of in Clonfert cathedral, 225

Annagh (Eaga) [co. Cavan], parish church of Sts Molanus and Queranus, called the plebs of Ytharture, vicarage of, 821
......, ..., ..., ..., to be united to canonry of Kilmore and prebend of 'Tolach', 821

Annagh (Anachdrilin) [church in Annies townland, parish of Robeen, co. Mayo], parish church of, vicarage of, 127

?Annaghcallow *see* Annacalla

Annaghdown [co. Galway], Augustinian monastery of B. Mary *de Portu Patrum*, 163
......, ..., abbots of *see* [de Burgo], Thomas; de Burgo, William

......, [cathedral] church of, dean of, papal mandatary, 829

Annaghdown, [cathedral] church (*contd*)
......, ..., chapter of, to be summoned over erection of canonry and prebend, 163, 646
......, ..., canons of *see* de Burgo, Richard [Ristardus], Thomas, and William; Mors, William; Oberen, Theoderic; Odunan, John; OFlaherty, Magonius and Odo; Ohallmarayl, William
......, ..., prebends in *see* ?Kilcummin and Killeroon; Lackagh; Oranmore
......, ..., canonry and prebend (unnamed) of, union to, of vicarages of ?Kilcummin and Killeroon, 845
......, ..., vicarage of, to be united to proposed prebend of Lackagh, 163

......, bishop of, to be summoned over erection of canonry and prebend, 163, 646
......, ..., to receive oath of fealty, 577, 578
......, ..., *see* [Brunand], Francis

......, diocese of, persons of, *see* de Burgo, Edmund and Walter; Maicha, Aulanus; Oclmuran, William; Yco'mimayn, Roger
......, ..., places in *see* Claregalway; Galway; Kilcoona; ?Kilcummin; Killeroon; Lackagh

Annan (Annand) [co. Dumfries], parish church of, rector of, 929
......, ..., collation of, 929

Anne, queen of England, the late, wife of Richard [III], divine offices to be celebrated for the soul of, 292

Annecy [*in dép.* of Haute Savoie, France], parish church of St Peter near, 199

Annekeyke [*rectius* Annebeyke], alias of Monxton, *q.v.*

[Annies townland *in* Robeen, co. Mayo],

Annies (*contd*)
  place in *see* Annagh

Annscapus *see* Dunstable

Anstyn', William, monk of the Cistercian monastery of Robertsbridge, 962

Anthinhamper *see* Auchinhamper

Antoniotto, cardinal priest of S. Prassede *see* [Pallavicini], Antoniotto

Antony, abbot of the Cistercian monastery of Quarr, dispensed for plurality, 1262

[Antrim, co. of], places in *see* Carrickfergus; Connor; Muckamore; Rasharkin; Woodburn

Anygray *see* Ford

Ap, Hugh *see* Hugh ap [patronymic wanting]

Ap D[avi]d, Owen *see* Owen ap D[avi]d

Ap David, Richard *see* Richard ap David

Apgwaltere, Eynonus *see* Eynon ap Gwalter

Aphowel, Aphowell *see* Howell

Aplialo, Thomas, to have vicarage in Lismore diocese, 1154

Aplien, John, vicar of Peterborough, 714

[Appin, co. Argyll] *see* Lismore

[Appleby, Lincs], place in *see* Thornholme

Appleyard (Acclobard), John, ostensible brother of the Trinitarian order, provision to, of the ministership of

Appleyard (*contd*)
  Adare, 221

Appulby (Appulbii), Thomas, ostensible rector of the parish church of [St John the Baptist], Walbrook, London, litigant, 365

Apris, Owen *see* Owen ap Rhys

'Aquia' [*unidentified*], land of, gifted to Taunton priory, 174

Archaden. *see* ?Achonry

de Arco, William, property gifted to Taunton priory by, 174

Ardagh [co. Longford], [cathedral] church of, canons of *see* OFarrell, Maurice; Orodochan, Thady
......, bishop of, litigation before, 927
......, diocese of, persons of *see* Maglocyn, Eugene; OFarrell, Donald, Fantutius, John, Maurus, Roceus, and Thomas; Ymorrij, Donald
......, ..., places in *see* Abbeyderg; Inchcleraun; ?Kilglass; Killanummery; Saints Island

Ardchattan (Ardkathan') [co. Argyll], [Valliscaulian] priory of, prior of, papal mandatary, 116

Arden, Ardern *cf.* Ardion'

Ardern', Robert, layman of Coventry and Lichfield diocese, litigant, 28
......, ..., wife of *see* Rose, Joan

Ardfert [co. Kerry], **[cathedral] church** of, dean of, papal mandatary, 306
......, ..., chancellorship of, 993
......, ..., chancellors of *see* FitzMaurice, David; de Geraldinis, Philip; Stack, Gerald

Ardfert, **[cathedral] church** (*contd*)

......, ..., chapter of, to be summoned over erection of canonry and prebend, 72, 250, 540, 939

......, ..., canons of *see* FitzMaurice, Edmund; de Geraldinis, Edmund and John Davit; MacCarthy, Cormac and Eugene; MacElligott, John; OBrosnan, Thady; OConnell, Donat and Galfrigidus; OHonan, Maurice; OScully, John; OSullivan, Dermot and John; Trant, Davit

......, ..., prebend to be erected in, 1071

......, ..., prebends in *see* ?Ballingarry; Drishane *alias* Kilmeedy; ?Killinane; Kilmeen; 'Kylldacu(m) *alias* Turere'; Stradbally

......, **bishop** of, to be summoned over erection of canonry and prebend, 72, 250, 540, 939

......, church of, archdeaconry of, 945

......, ..., archdeacon of, papal mandatary, 818

......, ..., archdeacons of *see* de Geraldinis, Gerald; Stack, Gerald

......, **diocese** of, persons of *see* Bretdicach, John; FitzMaurice, Maurice and Richard; de Geraldinis, John and Maurice the younger; Homana', Thomas; MacConnor, Brendan; ODaly, Bernard; OFinn, Donald; OHingerdell, Donald; OHoulihan, Edmund; OMurphy, John and Thomas;ORiordan, Cornelius; OScolayn, Dermot; OShea, Cornelius; OSullivan, Florence; Stack, Philip

......, ..., places in *see* Abbeydorney; Ballinskelligs; Ballyduff *alias* Glennahoo; Ballymacelligott; Barrow; *Beara*; Cullen; Drishane *alias* Kilmeedy; Dromtariff; *Eaglais-na-lainne alias* Ballyheige; ?Feohanagh [*in* Kilquane]; Garfinny; Innisfallen; Killagh; 'Killcolin'; ?Killinane;

Ardfert, **diocese** (*contd*)

Killury; ; Kilmalkedar; Kilmeen; 'Kylldacu(m) *alias* Turere'; 'Kylloeyn'; Nohaval-Daly; *Rinn-bheara* ; Stradbally

Ardgrain (Argram, Argrane, Argrom) [*in* Ellon, co. Aberdeen], annex of, 928

......, tithes of pertaining to Ellon parish church, 144, 793, 928

Ardion', Ann, intended marriage of, to John Stanley, 76

......, *cf.* Arden, Ardern

Ardkathan' *see* Ardchattan

?Ardkeen (Herrethayn) [co. Down], parish church of the Holy Cross, rectory of, united to parish church of [?Ardquin], 391

Ardmore [*in* Udny, co. Aberdeen], tithes of, 928

[?Ardquin, co. Down], parish church of *Sancti Chafudi*, rector of, 391

......, ..., ?Ardkeen parish church united to, 391

Ardwalebeg *see* Stradbally

Argram, Argrane, Argrom *see* Ardgrain

[Argyll, bishopric of] *see* Lismore

[Argyll, co. of], places in *see* Iona; Kilmartin;Kilmichael Glassary;Kintyre;Lismore; Loch a' Choire; Loch Awe; Torran; *and* places *listed below under* Lismore, diocese of

[de Arianis] de Parma, Franciscus, *abbreviator de parco maiori*, letters expedited by:
F. *de Parma* , 8, 29, 30, 41, 48, 52-54,

[de Arianis] (contd)
61-66, 68, 87, 144,145, 183, 260, 274
(F Parma), 276-280, 284, 294, 307,
331, 332, 367, 369-371, 375, 376, 378,
379, 386, 399, 405, 408, 409, 417, 418,
421, 422, 424, 425, 429, 432, 433, 435-
437, 439, 440, 442, 444, 447, 460, 478,
484, 493, 509, 515, 518, 520, 522, 523,
526, 528, 530-533, 535, 549-552, 560-
562, 564, 565, 567, 579, 602-605, 620-
623, 630-633, 637-640, 644, 648, 657-
660, 662-668, 673-677, 679, 680, 683,
686, 688-690, 692, 693, 695, 765, 767-
769, 781, 794, 796, 798, 799, 801, 803,
804, 806-809, 813, 842, 844, 850, 854,
855, 867, 874, 878, 922, 923, 925, 928,
929, 952-954, 956, 959-963, 967, 969,
970, 975, 976, 996, 1001, 1009-1011,
1015- 1025, 1027, 1028, 1032-1034

Arlington (Arlyngton) [Devon], parish
church of, 884

Armagh [co. Armagh], archbishop of,
visitation of [Cruciferi] hospitals
(named) outside the walls of Drogheda
by, 964
......, ..., metropolitical jurisdiction of, 1005
......, ..., metropolitical court of, 1005
......, ..., appeals to from sentences of
suffragans, 1005
......, ..., primate of Ireland, 964
......, ..., see [Spinelli (de Palatio)],
Octavian
......, official of, papal mandatary, 249
......, ..., cf. 1005

......, diocese of, persons of see Darcy,
Thomas; Vynter alias Fynter, Thomas;
Waren, Thomas
......, ..., places in see Drogheda;
Mansfieldstown; Mellifont
......, province of, council of, 927

[Armagh, co. of], place in see Armagh

Arnot (Arnod), David, archdeacon of
Lothian, 371, 1024-1026, 1028
......, ..., indulged to visit archdeaconry by
deputy, 371
......, ..., provost of Bothwell, 232
......, ..., sometime vicar of Echt, 232
......, ..., chaplain in chapel of James [IV],
371
......, ..., provision of, to the Augustinian
monastery of Cambuskenneth, 1024
......, ..., dispensed to be abbot for eight
months without taking habit and
making profession, 1025
......, ..., reception as canon of, bestowal of
habit on, and reception of profession of,
mandate over, 1028
......, ..., absolution of, preliminary to
provision, 1026
......, ..., faculty for benediction of, 1027
......, ..., to take oath of fealty to pope, 1027

[Arnot], Henry, abbot of the Augustinian
monastery of Cambuskenneth, death of,
1024

'Arodmuneach' [unidentified ; perhaps
obsolete ; probably in the barony of
Moycarn, co. Roscommon or barony of
Longford, co. Galway, near the
confluence of the Suck and Shannon],
ecclesiastical lands abutting belonging
to the episcopal mensa of Clonfert,
grant of, 146

Arondello see Arundel

Arosmith, Arowsmithe see Arrowsmith

Arpur see Harper

Arrowsmith (Arosmith, Arowsmithe),
William, of London diocese, dispensed
for plurality, 1228
......, ..., layman of the city or diocese of
London, executor of the will of John
Crosby, 924

Arthur, prince of Wales, first born of Henry [VII], 530

......, ..., preceptor and poet laureate of *see* André, Bernard

[Arundel], John, bishop of Coventry and Lichfield, 298

......, ..., ..., Bordesley abbey admonished by, to present person for institution as vicar of Kinver, 298

......, ..., ..., official or commissary of *see* Veysey *alias* Harman, John

......, ..., ..., translation of, to Exeter, 1029, 1315

......, ..., ..., absolution of preliminary to translation, 1317

......, ..., ..., oath of fealty of, commission for receipt of, 1316

......, ..., ..., *and see* [Hales *or* Arundel], John

Arundel (Arondello), Robert, property gifted to Taunton priory by, 174

[?Arundel], Thomas, the late, archbishop of Canterbury, constitution approved by, 365

......, ..., ..., ..., primate of all England, legate of the apostolic see, grant and confirmation of privileges by, 425

Asburi *see* Astbury

Asby [Westm], parish church of, 741

Ascalon [*now* 'Askalān, in Palestine], church of, *in partibus infidelium*, 963

......, [bishop-] elect of *see* [Heylesdon], Ralph

Ascanius Maria, cardinal deacon of S. Vitus in Macello Martirum *see* [Sforza], Ascanius Maria

Ascham *cf.* Ayshecum

Ashbourne (Ashburne, Asshebrun) [Derb], parish church of, 35

......, ..., vicar of, 292

......, ..., southern arch in, altar of St Oswald at, chaplain at, 292

......, ..., chantry of John Bradburn and his wife Ann in, 292

......, ..., parish of, chapel of ?Hognaston in, 292

Ashe (Assh') [Hants], parish church of, rector of, 34

Ashmore (Asshemere) [Dors], parish church of, 801

Ash Priors (Assia, Hysth) [Som], land in, 174

......, vill of, church of, 174

Ashwell (Asshewell) [Rut], parish church of, 317

Aspden', John, vicar of Hanney, 222

Assaroe [*in* Kilbarron, co. Donegal], Cistercian monastery of, 943

......, ..., convent of, election of abbot by, 943

......, ..., ..., ..., confirmation of by abbot of Boyle, 943

......, ..., abbots of *see* OBoyle, Donald; [?OBoyle], Donald; OGallagher, Arthur and Nigel; OLasty, John

......, ..., monk of *see* OBoyle, Donald

......, ..., vassals of, 943

......, ..., proposed union to, of the parish church of Killymard, 950

Assh' *see* Ashe

Asshebrun *see* Ashbourne

Asshemere *see* Ashmore

Asshewell *see* Ashwell

Assia *see* Ash Priors

Astbury (Asburi) [Ches], parish church of, person presented by patrons for, 556

Astingg' *see* Hastings

Aston *see* ?Easton

Athinach *see* Aghinagh

Athlone (Hathluam) [*in* St Peter's, co. Roscommon], Benedictine monastery of Bs. Peter and Paul the Apostles, prior and convent of, detainer of rectories of Ahascragh and Killosolan, 164

Atkinson (Atkynson), William, of Chichester diocese, dispensed for plurality, 1275

Atkyngson, John, vicar of Adlingfleet, 799

Atkynson *see* Atkinson

Atrohomane *see* Aughrim

[Attercliff], Elias, abbot of the Premonstratensian monastery of Croxton, dispensed for plurality, 1101

Aubrey (Auubrey), Joan, woman, London, litigant, 8

Auchindoir *see* Kearn

Auchinhamper (Anthinhamper) [*in* Inverkeithny, co. Banff], person of *see* Thomson, Duncan

Auchinleck (Althinelek) [co. Ayr], church of, fruits etc. of pertaining to Cluniac monastery of Paisley, grant of, 63

[Auchterderran, co. Fife], place in *see* Spittal

Auchterellon (Utherellon, Uthtirelone, Wthertllon) [*in* Ellon, co. Aberdeen], annex of, 928
......, tithes of pertaining to Ellon parish church, 144, 793, 928
......, *and see* Mains (of Auchterellon); Yonder Auchterellon

Auchtertool (Oche'tuyle) [co. Fife], barony of, lands (named) in, 558

[Auchtertool, co. Fife], places in *see* Craigton; Newtown

[Audley], Edmund, bishop of Hereford, translation of, to Salisbury, 1021, 1023
......, ..., ..., ..., ..., to take oath of fealty, 1021
......, ..., ..., ..., ..., reception of oath of fealty of, mandate over, 1023
......, ..., ..., ..., ..., absolution of preliminary to translation, 1022

Aughrim (Accumomane, Atrohomane) [co. Galway], Augustinian priory of, 492, 512
......, ..., priors of *see* MacKeogh, Carb(e)ricus / Cornelius; OFahy, Dermot; OKelly, Malachy; Yolei, John

Aurifabri *see* Goldsmith

Austell, Thomas, treasurer of Exeter and incumbent of Cheriton Fitzpaine, 198

Austen, John, of Chichester diocese, dispensed for plurality, 1136

Autun *see Eduen.*

Auubrey *see* Aubrey

Avranches [*dép.* of La Manche, France], diocese of, place in *see* Mont St Michel

Awe *see* Loch Awe

Awyten, Robert, of Exeter diocese, dispensed for plurality, 1170

Axbridge (Axbrygg) [Som], parish church of, union of, to the canonry and prebend of Timberscombe in Wells cathedral, 295

[Axminster, Devon], place in *see* Newenham

Ayleuoard, William, vicar of Puddletown, 722

Aylward *cf.* Ayleuoard

Ayr (Air(e)) [co. Ayr], prebend in Glasgow cathedral, appropriation of residue of fruits of to chapel royal, Stirling, 768

Ayr (Air), county of, places (named) stated to be in, 63

[Ayr, co. of], places in *see* Auchinleck; Ayr; Braidstane [*in* ?Beith]; Craigie; Dalmilling; Dundonald; Largs; Monkton (and Prestwick); Riccarton; (?)St Quivox

Ayshecum, Robert, vicar of Banwell, 430
......, *cf.* Ascham

Aystrcumba *see* Hestercombe

Ayton (Aytonn'), John, of St Andrews diocese, appeal of, 971

B

Babyngton', Raphael, cleric of Coventry and Lichfield diocese, 209

Bacheler, John, vicar of Much Wenlock, 1037

Bachischyean *see* Ballysheehan

Backer, John, layman of the city and diocese of Hereford, proceedings against, 9

Badsworth (Baddysworth') [Yorks], parish church of, 718

Bagarothus, Baptista, *magister registri*, letters signed by:
    B. Bagarothus Proton(otarius), 5, 557, 573, 576, 637-640

Bailey (Baylli), William, layman of Winchester diocese, litigant, 28
......, ..., wife of *see* Rose, Joan

Bains *cf.* Banes, Banys

Baker, Richard, scholar of Lincoln diocese, 721
......, William, canon of the Augustinian monastery of Guisborough, 857
......, alias of Haolt, Henry, *q.v.*

Baldwin (Baldewyn'), Patrick, prior, formerly canon, of the Augustinian monastery of Sts Peter and Paul, Selsker near Wexford, appeal of, 989
......, ..., election of, as prior, 989

Balengary *see* ?Ballingarry

Balenoe *see* Newtown Lennan

Baleuatibenda *see* Timahoe

Balgonie (Balgony, Balgorny) [*in* Markinch, co. Fife], place or vill of, tithes of belonging to the Augustinian monastery of St Andrews, 971
......, *and see* Milton of Balgonie
......, Andrew Lundy of, *q.v.*
......, Elizabeth Sibbald of, *q.v.*

Balincheyn *see* ?Ballycahane

Balla [co. Mayo], parish church of, vicarage of, to be united to deanery of Mayo, 402

Ballam *see* Ballon

Balleaculleaym *see* Ballycoolan

Ballelochacain *see* Ballyloughnane

Ballenakille *alias* Kilccumpim *see* Ballynakill

Balli moth hilligoyd *see* Ballymacelligott

Ballimunora *alias* Murtown *see* Moorstown

[Ballinchalla, co. Mayo], place in *see* Inishmaine

?Ballingarry (Balengary) [*in* Ballyheige, co. Kerry], rectory of, to be erected into prebend in Ardfert cathedral, 306
......, rectory of parish church of *Rinn-bheara* so called, 306

[Ballingry, co. Fife], place in *see* Inchegall

Ballinrobe (Ropba in Concnecule Obeara, *i.e. Rodhba in Conmaicne Cuile* 'Obeara') [the parish in part of Ballinrobe south of the river Robe; subsequently the barony of Kilmaine, co. Mayo], parish church of, vicarage of, 127

Ballinskelligs [*in* Prior, co. Kerry], [Augustinian] monastery of St Michael, prior of, papal mandatary, 72, 945, 993

Ballintober [co. Mayo], [Augustinian] monastery of, abbot of, papal mandatary, 826-828

Ballisonan *see* Ballyshannon

Ballon (Ballam) [co. Carlow], grange of, possessions of belonging to Glascarrig priory, 981

Ballybeg [*in* Buttevant, co. Cork], Augustinian monastery of St Thomas the Martyr, priorship of, 128
......, ..., prior of, papal mandatary, 74, 156
......, ..., ..., *see* Barry, Thomas; Magner, David

Ballybritt, barony of *see* Cenél arga

?Ballycahane (Balincheyn *alias* Cormootin) [co. Limerick], parish church of, vicarage of, to be united to the proposed canonry and prebend of *Cluain Comarda* in Limerick cathedral, 942

Ballycoolan (Balleaculleaym) [*in* Timogue, co. Laois], parish church of, vicarage of, Rathaspick vicarage to be united to, 576

Ballyduff (Ballyduyff) [co. Kerry] *alias* Glennahoo (Glenquhaw) [*in* Ballyduff, co. Kerry], parish church of, rectory of, 994

Ballyhay (Bellacaha') [co. Cork], parish church of, vicarage of, to be united to canonry of Cloyne and prebend of Cooliney, 514
......, ..., vicar of, 514

Ballyheige (Balyytayg), alias of *Eaglais-na- lainne* , *q.v.*

[Ballyheige, co. Kerry], place in *see* ?Ballingarry

Ballyloughloe (Lodua) [co. Westmeath], parish church of, vicarage of, to be united to deanery of Cloyne (*recte* Clonmacnois), 226

Ballyloughnane (Ballelochacain) [*in* Lockeen, co. Tipperary], prebend of in Killaloe cathedral, rectories of Birr and Modreeny and vicarage of Modreeny to be united anew to, 357

Ballymacelligott (Balli moth hilligoyd) [co. Kerry], parish church of, vicarage of, 994
......, ..., vicar of, 994

Ballymoney, *once* Corrsruhara, *q.v.*

?Ballymountain (Balymmolann) [*in* Inishannon, co. Cork], church, called particle of, to be united to the proposed canonry and prebend of Gortnacrusha in Cork cathedral, 255

Ballynakill (Ballenakille *alias* Kilccumpim) [*in* Leitrim barony, co. Galway], parish church of, vicarage of, erected into prebend in Clonfert cathedral, 512
......, ..., ..., ..., vicarage of Duniry united to, 512

[Ballynakill, co. Galway], place in *see* Aghiart

[Ballynakill, co. Sligo], place in *see* Coola

Ballyquillane *cf.* Ballycoolan

Ballyshannon (Ballisonan) [co. Kildare],

Ballyshannon (*contd*)
parish church of, rectory of, to be erected into prebend of Derry (*recte* Kildare), 934
......, ..., ..., ..., vicarages of Norragh and Tippeenan to be united to, 934

Ballysheehan (Bachischyean) [co. Tipperary], church of, vicarage of, union of, to the archiepiscopal *mensa* of Cashel, 998

Ballytarsney (Belyta(r)sny) [co. Kilkenny], parish church of, rectory of, to be united to canonry and prebend of St Maul's in Ossory cathedral, 787
......, place in *see* Kilcraggan

Ballyvourney (Burrneach) [co. Cork], parish church of, vicarage of, to be erected into prebend in Cloyne cathedral, 541

[Ballyvourney, co. Cork], place in *see* Fuhiry

Balmaclellan [co. Kirkcudbright], [parish church of], 781

Balymmolann *see* ?Ballymountain

Balyytayg *see* Ballyheige

Ba(m)buri, Thomas, rector of Cowden, 507

Banagher (Bengor) [co. Londonderry], parish church of, rectory of, 253
......, ..., vicarage of, to be united to rectory, 253

Banat Nan *see* Bannerman

Banbury [Oxon], prebend of in Lincoln cathedral, union to, of Kettering parish church, 1035

Banes, Thomas, cleric or layman, executor of the will of Thomas Nelson, appeal of, 990, 999
......, cf. Banys

[Banff, co. of], place in see Auchinhamper [in Inverkeithny]

Bangchier', Clement, rector of Ashe, 34
......, cf. Bourchier

Bangor [co. Carnarvon], [cathedral] church of, dean and chapter of, consent of to episcopal statute abolishing gologoith, 118
......, ..., ..., to be summoned over confirmation of episcopal statute abolishing gologoith, 118
......, ..., chapter of, conclusion to, 602
......, ..., statutes and customs of, cf. 118
......, ..., tithes due to, 118
......, ..., synod celebrated in, 118

......, bishops of, absolution reserved to, 118
......, ..., vicars or commissaries general of, absolution reserved to, 118
......, bishop of, to receive oath of fealty in pope's name, 1006, 1007
......, bishops of, see Anian; [Deane], Henry; [Pigot], Thomas
......, church of, statutes and customs of, 118
......, ..., subjection of, to archbishop of Canterbury, 603
......, ..., vassals of, conclusion to, 602
......, ..., archdeacon of Bangor in see Bulkeley, Richard
......, ..., archdeacon of Merioneth in see Bulkeley, Richard

......, city and diocese of, parish churches of, rectors and vicars of, tithes due to, 118
......, ..., ..., tithes of, 118
......, ..., clergy of, consent of, to episcopal statute abolishing gologoith, 118

Bangor, city and diocese (contd)
......, ..., ..., conclusion to, 602
......, ..., people of, conclusion to, 602
......, diocese of, persons of see David [ab Iorwerth]; Hugh ap [patronymic wanting]
......, ..., places in see ?Llanfechell; Ruthin

Bangor [co. Down], [Augustinian] monastery of, abbot of, papal mandatary, 391

Bannerman (Banat Nan), Alexander, of Waterton, 928

Banwell (Bannewelle) [Som], parish church of, 430

Banys, Edward, rector of ?Jacobstowe, 907
......, cf. Bains; Banes

'baptized islands' [unidentified ; near Inchcolm in the Firth of Forth], 108

Barbour (Barbur, Borbol), John, commissary of the late Robert [Morton], bishop of Worcester, litigation before, 29
......, ..., cleric of Glasgow diocese, familiar of cardinal Ascanius Maria [Sforza], SRE vicechancellor, to have hospital of Duns and its annexed parish church of Ellem, 130
......, Robert, vicar of Bodmin, 531
......, Thomas, rector of Sedgeberrow and incumbent of Broadwas, 294

Barcheston (Barceston' alias Barston') [Warw], parish church of, 202

Bardeh(a)m see Birdham

Bardney (Bardeney) [Lincs], Benedictine monastery of, abbot and convent of, grant of, to Robert Barkeworth, lord of Poolham, and his successors, enabling

Bardney (*contd*)
   them to have a resident chaplain in the
   chapel of Poolham, save for the right of
   the mother church of Edlington, 379
......, ..., ..., consent of, to admission of
   chaplain pertaining to vicar of
   Edlington, 379

Baret *see* Barrett

Barham (Barh(a)m) [Kent], chapel of,
   annexed to parish church of
   Bishopsbourne, 422

Barker, David, rector of West Wretham,
   737
......, Thomas, of York diocese, dispensed
   for plurality, 1093

Barkeworth, Robert, the late, lord of
   Poolham, and his successors, grant to
   by Bardney abbey enabling them to
   have a resident chaplain in the chapel of
   Poolham, save for the right of the
   mother church of Edlington, 379
......, ..., nomination of chaplain to pertain
   to, 379
......, ..., heir of *see* Thimbleby, Richard

Barmondesey *see* Bermondsey

Barnel, Robert, of Dublin diocese,
   commission by virtue of an appeal,
   1162

Barney, John, monk of the Benedictine
   monastery of Eye, 305

Barnwell (Bemwell) [*in* St Andrew the
   Less, Cambridge, Cambs], Augustinian
   priory of, 712
......, ..., canon of *see* Baron, Henry

Barocis, William, commissary or auditor of
   Henry [Deane], archbishop of
   Canterbury, etc., probate of will by, 924

Barocis (*contd*)
......, *cf.* Barons

Baron, Henry, canon of the Augustinian
   priory of Barnwell, 712

Barons *cf.* Barocis

Barrett (Baret), Restardus, expectative
   grace for, Killala diocese, 1137

[Barrett], Thomas, bishop of Killala, death
   of, 606

Barri *see* Barry

Barrow *see Rinn bheara*

Barry (Barri, Barrus), Edmund, ostensible
   Cistercian monk, detainer of the
   Cistercian monastery of Tracton, 536
......, Elisabeth, lay person of Cloyne
   diocese, 244
......, ..., husband of *see* Bennett, Richard
......, James, monk of the Cistercian
   monastery of Tracton, 536
......, ..., ..., to be abbot of Tracton and
   have rectories of Inishannon and
   Leighmoney united to abbatial *mensa*,
   536
......, ..., ostensible monk or abbot of
   Tracton, detainer of archdeaconry of
   Cork and Inishannon parish church, 822
......, John, detainer of rectory of
   Ringcurran, 71
......, ..., cleric of Cork diocese, to be abbot
   of Tracton and have vicarage of Brinny
   united thereto, 67
......, ..., abbot of Tracton, death of, 536
......, Thomas, ostensible prior and detainer
   of the Augustinian monastery of St
   Thomas the Martyr, Ballybeg, 128

Barsham, North (Northbarsham) [Norf],
   parish church of, 726

Barston', alias of Barceston', *q.v.*

Barton (Barton'), William, rector of Monxton, 344

Bartram (Bartrame), Elias, brother of the Augustinian hospital of Bridgwater, 453

Baryn *see* Burren

[Baslick, co. Roscommon], place in *see Clann conchobair*

de Basodonys, John Baptist, of Lincoln diocese, indulged for non-residence, 1111

Bassett, Fulk, chantry of in London cathedral, 748
......, Philip, chantry of in London cathedral, 748

Bassingbourn (Bassingbron') [Cambs], parish church of, vicar of, 81

Bath [Som], city of, hospital of St John the Baptist in, 520

[Bath and] Wells, **[cathedral] church** of [*at* Wells, Som], dean of, *cf.* Cosyn, William
......, ..., canons of *see* [Cornish], Thomas; Gilbert, Thomas; Knyghtley, Walter; Lugwardyn, John; Pykeman, John; Willoughby, Edward
......, ..., prebends in *see* Compton Dundon; Haselbere; Timberscombe; Wiveliscombe

Bath (and Wells), **bishop** of, papal mandatary, 817
......, ..., papal judge delegate, 987
[Bath and] Wells, church of, archdeacon of *see* [Nykke], Richard

Bath (and Wells), (canonically united) **diocese(s)** of, persons of *see* Andrew, William; Ayshecum, Robert; Bartram, Elias; Benet, John; Board, John; Boket, William; Chaplain *alias* Tonker, John; Cherell, Thomas; Coluge, Richard; Combe, William; Dampeyr, Richard; Dedworth, Robert; Dobyll, Laurence; Fox, John; Geffrey, John; Gilbert, Thomas and William; Harww, John; Horsey, William; Horton, James; Hyde, John; Inell *alias* Giles, Alexander; Jenynges, John; Jones, William; Kymer, John; Lynton', William; Mader, Richard; Marshall, Richard; Marwood, John; Morris, William; Norbury, William; Picher, William; Prowse, John; Russell, John and William; Spenser, Thomas; Spring, Richard; Standerwike, John; Urswick, Christopher; Vaughan, John; White, Thomas; Wilton, William; Wolsey, Thomas; Wyche, John; Wyngho, Christopher
......, ..., places in *see* Axbridge; Banwell; Bath; Bedminster; Bradon, South; Bridgwater; Bristol (Redcliff); Bruton; Buckland St Mary; Camel, Queen; Chedzoy; Coker, West; Combe St Nicholas; Corston; Glastonbury; Hinton Blewett; Kelston; Kilmington; Kingsdon; Limington; Litton; Lympsham; Mells; Milverton; [Montacute]; Pilton; Pitminster; Porlock; Spaxton; Street; Taunton; Tintinhull; Wells; Westbury (sub Mendip); Winsham; Woodspring; Worle; *and see* Angersleigh; Ash Priors; Blagdon; Corfe; Dulverton; Gulland [*in* Dulverton]; Hestercombe [*in* Kingston]; Hull, Bishop's; Kingston; Lydeard (St Lawrence); Milton; Nynehead; Orchard Portman; Ruishton; Thurlbear; Thurloxton; Trull; ?Upcott; ?Westmoor; Wilton;

Bath (and Wells), **diocese(s)** (*contd*)
Withiel Florey; and *cf.* 'Aquia';
'Maedona';'Sodesaltera'

Batlesden' *see* Battlesden

Batley [Yorks], parish church of, 804

de Battiferro, Matheus, *magister registri* ,
letters signed by:
M. Battiferro, 374-379, 673-675, 678-
682, 712, 776, 777, 780, 823

Battista, bishop of Tusculum *see* [Zeno],
Battista

Battle [Sussex], [Benedictine] monastery
of, abbot of, papal judge delegate, 197

Battlesden (Batlesden') [Beds], parish
church of, 462

Bayham (Beghin') [*in* Frant, Sussex],
Premonstratensian monastery of, abbot
of *see* Bexyll', Richard

Baylli *see* Bailey

Bayllilocacayn *see* Loughkeen

Beagh (Beach) *alias Cliath-Ceallayd*
(Chumalay) [co, Galway], parish
church of, vicarage of, to be united to
canonry of Kilmacduagh and prebend
of Kinvarra, 933

Beamow *see* Beaumont

Beara see Rinn-bheara

'Bearnduamlegynd' [*unidentified* ; *perhaps
obsolete* ; *probably* in the barony of
Moycarn, co. Roscommon or the
barony of Longford, co.Galway, near
the confluence of the Suck and
Shannon], ecclesiastical lands abutting

'Bearnduamlegynd' (*contd*)
belonging to the episcopal *mensa* of
Clonfert, grant of, 146

Beaton *cf.* Betonen'; Betoun

Beauchamp (Beauchinp'), John, knight,
tomb of, altar of B. Mary the Virgin
near, chantry at, in London cathedral,
foundation of, 518

[Beaufort], Margaret, countess of
Richmond (and Derby), 423, 807, 925
......, ..., mother of Henry [VII], 423, 807,
925
......, ..., proposed chapel of, at Windsor
and elsewhere, 807
......, ..., patroness of Tattershall church,
petition of, concerning reform of its
statutes, 423
......, ..., chaplains of, 925

Beaumont (Beamow), viscount, William,
layman of London, and Elizabeth, his
wife, indulged to choose confessor, 374
......, ..., ..., vow of, to visit Jerusalem,
Rome, and Santiago de Compostela,
374

Beaumont (Branmount), Thomas, rector of
St Clement Danes, London and vicar of
Alveston, 923

Beckett (Becet), Richard, archdeacon of
Ferns, litigation before, 192

Bedale, Robert, canon of the
Premonstratensian monastery of Shap,
219

[Bedford, co. of], places in *see* Battlesden;
Dunstable; ?Holcot; Holwell; Houghton
Conquest; Marston Moretaine; Potton;
Shillington; Sutton; Woburn; *and see*
Dean

Bedminster (Bedmynster) [Som], parish church of, rectory of, erected into prebend of Salisbury cathedral, 987
......, ..., vicar of, 987
......, prebendary of, annual portion payable by vicar to, 987

Beghin' see Bayham

[?Beith, cos. Ayr and Renfrew], place in see Braidstane

Bekeryng alias Sandherst, Robert, monk of the Cistercian monastery of Robertsbridge, 926

Bel see Bell

Belach see Templevalley

Beledhey, John, of Bridgwater, OFM, 302

Bell (Bel), Bernard, monk of the Cistercian monastery of Melrose, 1015, 1018
......, ..., ..., election and provision of, as abbot, 1015
......, ..., ..., cession of, 1015, 1016, 1018-1020
......, Thomas, rector of Papworth Everard, 183
......, cf. Boll

Bellacaha' see Ballyhay

Bellemartin see Aglish or Aglishmartin

[Bellenden], Robert, abbot of Holyrood, resignation of, 584

Bellenelare see Claregalway

Belley [in dép. of Ain, France], bishop of see [de Varax], John

Belyta(r)sny see Ballytarsney

Bemwell see Barnwell

Benabbio [in Bagni di Lucca, province of Lucca, Italy], parish church of, rectory of, 364
Benedict XII, will of concerning exeats for monks, 394 [20]
......, statutes of concerning monk-students, 394 [29]

Beneflete Magna see South Benfleet

Benet, John, of Bath and Wells diocese, dispensed for plurality, 1133
......, see Bennett

Benett, Thomas, cleric of Salisbury diocese, 220
......, William, monk of the Cluniac monastery of Broomholm, 658

Benfleet, South (Beneflete Magna) [Essex], parish church of, 727

Bengor see Banagher

Bennett (Benet, Bennet, Bouett), John, canon of Cork, papal mandatary, 838
......, ..., cleric of Cloyne diocese, 245
......, ..., cleric, warden of the new college of clerics of B. Mary, Youghal, litigant, 811
......, ..., ..., ..., alleged wife and blood relation of see White, Joan
......, ..., ..., ..., appeal of, 811
......, Richard, lay person of Cloyne diocese, 244
......, ..., wife of see Barry, Elisabeth

Berkeley, alias of Buttler, Thomas, q.v.

[Berkshire], places in see Blewbury; Buscot; Faringdon; Hanney, West; Hendred, East; Hurley; Moreton, North; Shottesbrooke; Sulhampstead Abbots;

[Berkshire] (*contd*)
    Sutton Courtenay; Tilehurst; Wallingford; Windsor

Bermesey *see* Bermondsey

Bermingham (Bremeche(n)ni, Bremichiam, Bremichian, Brincheam, Brunʒam, Premichiam), Thomas, canon of Tuam, papal mandatary, 234, 933
......, Walter, dean of Tuam, 69, 75, 330
......, ..., ..., vicar of 'Kilelonne', 69, 75
......, ..., ..., ..., death of, 69, 330
......, William, ostensible archdeacon of Tuam, 166
......, ..., ..., detainer of Premonstratensian monastery outside the walls of Tuam and of ?chaplaincy in Tuam cathedral, 166

Bermondsey (Barmondesey, Bermesey, Bermyssey) [Surrey], Cluniac monastery of St Saviour, 745
......, ..., called Benedictine [!], 745
......, ..., monks of *see* Bukarawl, Henry; Peverell, John
......, parish church of St Mary Magdalene near, 105

Bernardi, Robert, rector of Over Wallop, 713

Bernard, the late, abbot of Kilshanny *see* [OConnor], Bernard

Berra *see* Birr

de Bertinis, Leonard, priest of Siena, 937
......, ..., scriptor of apostolic letters, 839, 841, 937
......, ..., papal familiar, 839, 937
......, ..., proctor of Martin Vaus, 839, 841
......, ..., proctor of Alexander Doby, 937

[Berwick, co. of], places in *see* Coldingham; Cranshaws; Duns; Eccles;

[Berwick, co.] (*contd*)
    Ellem; Longformacus

Bessat *see* Bisset

Bethon *see* Betoun

Betonen', Robert, rector of Lundie, 65

Betoun (Bethon), James, rector of ?Quothquan, 395
......, *cf.* Betonen'

?Beurschieres Chantre *see* Bourchier chantry

Beverley [Yorks], [collegiate] church of St John at, altar of St Catherine in, 887

Beverley (Bewirley), William, of Norwich diocese, dispensed for plurality, 1043
......, ..., layman of Chichester diocese, appointment of as notary in the episcopal curia, 919
......, ..., ..., ..., marriage of, 919

Bevys, Thomas, rector of St Clement's [at the bridge], Norwich and vicar of Worsted, 388

Bew (Bewe), William, rector of St Mildred, Bread Street, London, 665

Bewirley *see* Beverley

Bexley *cf.* Bexyll'

Bexwike, Thomas, vicar of Harrowden, 95

Bexyll', Richard, abbot of the Premonstratensian monastery of Bayham, 974
......, *cf.* Bexley

Beyto, John, rector of Stoke Charity, 866

Billesdon [Leics], parish church of, 894

Bilmer, Richard, of Worcester diocese, dispensed for plurality, 1222

Bingrey, Thomas, of Norwich diocese, dispensed for plurality, 1233

Birdham (Bardeh(a)m) [Sussex], parish church of, 247

Birkenhead (Birkenhede) [Ches], [Benedictine] priory of, prior of, papal judge delegate, 991

Birling [Kent], parish church of, 487

Birr (Berra) [co. Offaly], parish church of, rectory of, to be united anew to canonry of Killaloe and prebend of Ballyloughnane, 357

Birton' see Burton Bradstock

Bishopsbourne (Bisshopestor) [Kent], parish church of, union of, to the free chapel of Lasborough, 422
......, ..., Barham chapel annexed to, 422

Bishop's Hull see Hull, Bishop's

Bishop's Lydeard see Lydeard

Bisset (Bessat), Andrew, priest of Aberdeen diocese, 444
......, ..., ..., resignation of as vicar of Inverurie, and assignment to of pension on fruits of vicarage, 444

Bisshop' see Bysshope

Bisshopestor see Bishopsbourne

Blackadder (Blacad, Blacader), Patrick, cleric of Glasgow diocese, 572

Blackadder (contd)
......, Robert, archbishop of Glasgow, 80, 333, 1009-1011
......, ..., ..., commend to of Augustinian monastery of Jedburgh, 1009
......, ..., ..., ..., to take oath of fealty to pope, 1009
......, ..., ..., ..., ..., mandate over, 1011
......, ..., ..., absolution of preliminary to appointment as commendatory abbot, 1010
......, ..., ..., oath to, of bishop of Dunblane as suffragan, 333
......, ..., ..., consent of, to restoration of Dunblane to province of St Andrews, 333
......, ..., ..., proctor (named) of, 333
......, ..., ..., collation by, of precentorship of Glasgow, 80
......, ..., ..., appeal of, 80
......, Roland, cleric of Glasgow diocese, 301
......, ..., subdean of Glasgow, 301
......, ..., ..., assent of to payment of pension on fruits of subdeanery, 301
......, ..., ..., proctor (named) of, 301

Blacktoft (?Blalitoff) [Yorks], chapel of, united to parish church of Brantingham, 94
......, ..., tithes of, 94

Blagdon (Blakedonda) [in Pitminster, Som], land of, 174

Blakedonda see Blagdon

?Blalitoff see Blacktoft

Blebery see Blewbury

Bledlow [Bucks], parish church of, 135

Blenkinsop (Blenkensop), Robert, rector of Meonstoke, 342

B. John the Evangelist, Augustinian monastery of *see* Tuam

B. Mary Magdalene, parish church of *see* [Taunton]

B. Mary the Virgin, monastery of *see* Ross Carbery

B. Mary *alias* of the Holy Trinity, parish church of *see* Ogonnelloe

B. Paul, tomb of *see under* Rome, [S Paolo fuori le Mura, Basilica of]

B. Peter, tomb of *see under* Rome, [S Pietro in Vaticano, Basilica of]

Bs. Peter and Paul, the apostles, 413
......, Cluniac monastery of *see* [Montacute]

Blewbury (Blebery) [Berks], prebend of in Salisbury cathedral, union to, of parish church of Sutton, 91

Blickling (Blyclyng) [Norf], parish church of, 471

[de Blois], Henry, bishop of Winchester, 174

Blokelay, Richard, layman, parishioner of Kinver, 298

Blount (Blownt), Walter, rector of All Saints', Worcester, 39

Blyclyng *see* Blickling

Blythe, Geoffrey, dean of York, 1029, 1030
......, ..., ..., chaplain and counsellor of Henry [VII], 1029
......, ..., ..., ..., provision of, to bishopric of Coventry and Lichfield, 1029
......, ..., ..., ..., absolution of preliminary

Blythe (*contd*)
to provision, 1030
......, ..., ..., ..., faculty for consecration of, 1031
......, ..., ..., ..., to take oath of fealty to pope, 1031
......, John, bishop of Salisbury, 28, 581
......, ..., ..., papal judge delegate, litigation before, 28
......, ..., ..., ..., sub-delegate of *see* Draper, Richard
......, ..., ..., death of, 581
......, Thomas, vicar of Nafferton, 312

Board (Borde), John, rector of Limington, 23

Boccapaduli, [Evangelista], registry scribe, 129 *note* , 357 *note* , 592 *note*

Bochwel *see* Bothwell

Boderoffe, alias of Hungersord', *q.v.*

?Bodfari (?Botuatria) [cos. Denbigh and Flint], parish church of, incumbent of, 483
......, ..., union of, to canonry of St Asaph and prebend of ?Meifod, otherwise cursal, 483

Bodley, Thomas, vicar of St Neot, 147

Bodmin (Bodmyn') [Corn], parish church of, 531

Body, John, of West Dean, cleric or layman of Chichester diocese, 661
......, ..., ..., ..., collector or farmer deputed by dean and chapter of tithes of fields of West Dean and of fields (named) in East Dean, appeal of, 661

Bog, Patrick, priest of Aberdeen diocese, to have canonry of Aberdeen and prebend of Kearn and Forbes, 68

Bohola (Boychoholan) [co. Mayo], parish church of, rectory of, 828

Boissunel *see* Boswell

Boket, William, rector of Mells and incumbent of Lympsham, 293

de Bolis, Bartholomeus, *magister registri*, letters signed by:
B.*Bolis*, 395, 397, 398, 417, 420-422, 428, 444-446, 448, 449, 496, 497, 530, 616, 620-624, 625 (initial wanting at beginning), 626, 630-633, 641-649, 651, 652, 654, 655, 657-672, 676, 677, 683-694, 697-701, 704-711, 713-717, 723-731, 734-764, 770-772, 778, 779, 782-787, 790, 792, 793, 795-809, 811-822, 824-839, 842, 843, 845-852, 854, 856-858, 864, 865, 867-870, 874-877, 881-891, 893, 894, 896-900, 903-907, 910-916, 918-921, 923, 926-946, 948, 949, 951, 955, 957-967, 969-972, 975-977, 979, 981-983, 985-991, 993-996, 998, 1000, 1002, 1004-1014, 1021-1023, 1030-1034, 1036-1038
......, ..., ..., correction of register ordered by regent of chancery done by, 144, 449, 626, 654, 663, 717, 747, 862, 972, 982

Boll *cf.* Bell

Bologna [*in* province of Bologna, Italy], Alexander of, cleric of Bologna, proctor of John Spens, 844
......, [city] of, person of *see* Bologna, Alexander of; Malvezzi, Galeazzo

Bondleigh (Bonleghe) [Devon], parish church of, 111

de Bone, Philibertus, litigant over parish church of St Peter near Annecy, 199

Boneface *see* Boniface

Boniface VIII, constitution *Pastoralis* of, 549, 1032
......, constitution of, prohibiting mendicants from receiving new places, 1
......, ..., prohibiting indults *de fructibus percipiendis in absentia*, 147, 780
......, [*recte* IX?], letters of, 343

Boniface IX, obedience of, 174, 425
......, letters of, 174, 425; *and see* 343 note

Boniface XII, statute concerning abstinence of, 394 [18]

Boniface (Boneface), James, rector of Rudgwick, 184

Bonleghe *see* Bondleigh

Borbol *see* Barbour

Borde *see* Board

Bordesley [*in* Tardebigg, Worcs], Cistercian monastery of, parish church of Kinver united to, 298
......, ..., abbot and convent of, admonished by bishop of Coventry and Lichfield to present person for institution as vicar of Kinver, 298
......, ..., ..., appeal of, 298
......, ..., ..., recourse of, to court of Canterbury, for protection, 298

Borgh, Thomas, rector of Oakford, 568

[Borgue, co. Kirkcudbright], place in *see* Kirk-Andrews

Borough Clere *see* Burghclere

Bosquen [*in dép.* of Côtes du Nord, France], Cistercian monastery of, monk

Bosquen (*contd*)
  of *see* Brehault, John

Boswell (Boissunel), Robert, to have
  deanery in Dunkeld diocese, 1158

Boteller *see* Butler

Bothwell (Bochwel) [co. Lanark], church
  of, 232

Botkeshin' *see* Bottisham

Bottiler *see* Butler

Bottisham (Botkeshin') [Cambs], parish
  church of, vicarage of, 386
......, ..., vicar of, 386

Botuatria *see* ?Bodfari

Boude, Robert, of York diocese, dispensed
  for plurality, 1058

Bouett *see* Bennett

Bougalia, Bougalve *see* Galway

Boughton (Bukton') [Northants], parish
  church of, 185

Bound (Bounde), Henry, rector of
  Tollerton, 764

Bounter, William, of Chichester diocese,
  dispensed for plurality, 1234

Bourchier chantry (?Beurschieres Chantre),
  in Halstead parish church, 664

Bourchier *cf.* Bangchier'

Bourney (Buorm) [co. Tipperary] *alias*
  Ogarryn [*now represented by* Ikerrin
  barony, co. Tipperary], parish church
  of, vicarage of, 14

Bourney *alias* Ogarryn (*contd*)
......, ..., ..., to be united to canonry of
  Cashel and prebend of Killea, 14

Bovey Tracy (Bovy Tracy) [Devon], parish
  church of, 177

Bowen, William, rector of Llanfyrnach on
  Taff, 460

Box (Boxe) [Wilts], parish church of, 286

Boxwell [with] Leighterton (Boxuuel
  Leyghtterten') [Glos], parish church
  [and chapel] of, 153

Boxworth [Cambs], parish church of, rector
  of, 516

Boychoholan *see* Bohola

Boyle [co. Roscommon], Cistercian
  monastery of, abbot of, confirmation of
  abbot- elect of Assaroe by, 943
......, ..., ..., papal mandatary, 936, 943
......, place in *see* Inchmacnerin

Brackley *see* Petty-Brackley

Bradbridge (Bradbriga), Nicholas, of
  Winchester diocese, dispensed for
  plurality, 1077

Bradburn (Bradburn'), John, esquire, of
  ?Hognaston, 292
......, ..., ..., ..., Ann his wife, 292
......, ..., ..., ..., ..., foundation by, of
  chantry in Ashbourne parish church and
  ?Hognaston chapel, 292
......, ..., ..., ..., ..., ..., ..., episcopal and
  papal confirmation of, 292
...., ..., ..., ..., ..., indulgence for those
  saying one paternoster with the Angelic
  salutation for the welfare of the souls
  of, 292

Bradeley *see* Bradley

Bradfield (Bradfelde) [Norf], parish church of, 414

Bradford-on-Avon (Bradford) [Wilts], parish church of, vicar of, 206

Bradi *see* Brady

Bradley [Staffs], parish church of, union to, of the parish church of Church Eaton, 217

Bradley [*probably* Great ~, Suff], parish church of, rector of, 263

Bradley (Bradeley), Edward, rector of Lackford, 755

Bradon, South (Southbradon) [Som], parish church of, 883

Bradshaw (Bradschauu, Bradsha, Bradshawe), James, rector of Kettleburgh, 102
......, Peter, vicar of Plumstead, 494
......, Thomas, canon of the Augustinian monastery of Heryngham, 735

Braduas *see* Broadwas

Bradwell on Sea (Bradwell') [Essex], parish church of, 808

Bradwynsour *see* Broadwindsor

Brady (Bradi), John, priest of St Andrews, litigant over parish church of Tannadice, 687
......, ..., rector of Tannadice, 849
......, ..., union for, of vicarage to provostship, St Andrews diocese, 1300
......, Thomas, of London diocese, dispensed for plurality, 1167

Brady (*contd*)
......, ..., chaplain of the chantry of Roger Walden in London cathedral, 426

Braidstane (Bravidestare) [*modern* Broadstone Hall *in* ?Beith, cos. Ayr and Renfrew], person of *see* Montgomery, Alexander

Braithwell (Brathenvell) [Yorks], parish church of, 316

[de Brana] *see* [Braua]

Brandon *see* Brendon

Branmount *see* Beaumont

Brant' *see* Grant

Brantingham (Brantynghn') [Yorks], parish church of, 94
......, ..., chapels of Blacktoft and Ellerker united to, 94
......, ..., united, with its annexed chapels, to Durham capitular *mensa*, 94
......, ..., tithes of, prior and chapter robbed of by William Stewardi of Howden, 94
......, place in *see* Ellerker

Brathenvell *see* Braithwell

[Braua *or* de Brana], George, bishop of Dromore, 591-593
......, ..., ..., translation of to Elphin, 591-593
......, ..., ..., ..., to take oath of fealty, 591
......, ..., ..., ..., ..., commission over, 592
......, ..., ..., absolution of preliminary to translation, 593

Bravidestare *see* Braidstane

Bray, John, scholar of London diocese, 688
......, Reginald, scholar of London diocese, 689

Bray (*contd*)
......, *cf.* Braye

Braybrooke (Braybrote) [Northants], parish
church of, 498

Braye, Walter, of Norwich diocese,
dispensed for plurality, 1303
......, *cf.* Bray

Breaghwy Island (Ynesbrachyn), alias of
Templeport, *q.v.*

Breamore (Bromor) [Hants], Augustinian
priory of, prior of *see* Chaundeler, John

Breathnach *cf.* Brennagh; Brydach

Brebanh *see* Brehault

Brechimay, Robert, prior of the Benedictine
priory of Downpatrick, death of, 391
......, *cf.* MacBritany

Brechin [co. Forfar], **[cathedral] church**
of, dean of, papal judge delegate, 792
......, ..., dean, provost, chapter, and canons
of, reservation of benefice in gift of,
643
......, ..., canon of *see* Martin, Hugh

......, **bishop** of, papal mandatary, 552, 780
......, ..., papal judge delegate, 691
......, ..., *see* [Meldrum], William
......, official of, papal mandatary, 535

......, **diocese** of, persons of *see*
Scrimgeour, James; *and see* Murray,
James
......, ..., clerics (unnamed) of, 691

Brecon [co. Brecon], archdeacon of in
church of St David's, *q.v.*

[Brecon, co. of], place in *see* Brecon

Bregeon, Franciscus, *abbreviator de parco
maiori*, letters expedited by:
F. Bregeon, 871 (*F. Bregion*), 950, 997,
1002

......, Nicolaus, *abbreviator de parco maiori*,
letters expedited by:
N. Bregeon, 9, 55-58, 86, 147, 196, 210,
221, 232, 275, 283, 303, 339, 351 (*N
bregeon*), 557, 577, 578, 584, 588, 590

......, Franciscus *or* Nicolaus, *abbreviator de
parco maiori*, letters expedited by:
Bregeon, 207, 263, 585-587, 589

Brehault (Brebanh), John, monk of the
Cistercian monastery of Bosquen, 515
......, ..., ..., collation to of the Augustinian
priory of St Helier, Jersey, 515
......, ..., ..., to have same *in commendam*,
515

Bremeche(n)ni, Bremichiam, Bremichian
see Bermingham

Brenache, Brenagh' *see* Brennagh

Brendon (Brandon) [Devon], parish church
of, 653

Brenex, William, vicar of St Peter's,
Hereford, 876

Brennagh (Brenache, Brenagh'), Hoellus,
priest of Ossory diocese, 157, 545
......, ..., ..., collation to, of Pollrone
vicarage, invalidity of, 157
......, ..., ..., to have chancellorship of
Ossory with Pollrone and Dunkitt
vicarages and Kilcraggan rectory united
thereto, 157
......, ..., ..., grant to, of chancellorship of
Ossory with vicarage of Dunkitt and
rectory of Kilcraggan united thereto,
impetration of, alleged subreption of, 545

Brennock *cf.* Brennagh

'Brenowc', Lismore diocese [*unidentified*; *in vicinity of* head of Loch Awe, co. Argyll], place of, 493

Brent, John, monk of the Benedictine priory of Monmouth, 20

?Brereton, John, cleric of Coventry and Lichfield diocese, 868

Brereton, Thomas, cleric of Coventry and Lichfield diocese, 711

Bretdicach, John, detainer of rectory of ?Ballingarry, 306

le Breton (Britonis), Roger, property gifted to Taunton priory by, 174

Breyny *see* Brinny

Bride, Ralph, vicar of Ramsey, 205

Bridgetown [co. Cork], [Augustinian] monastery of, prior of, papal mandatary, 1000

Bridgnorth (Briggenorth') [Salop], [collegiate] church of, provost and chapter of, 529
......, ..., ..., probate and criminal jurisdiction of, 529
......, ..., ..., official and commissary of *see* Knott, Richard
......, ..., canons, subordinate ecclesiastics, chaplains, resident clerics, and persons of, 529
......, ..., prebends of, 529
......, ..., immediately subject to the apostolic see , 529
......, ..., exemption of, from jurisdiction of metropolitan and diocesan bishop, 529
......, ..., parish of, 529

Bridgwater (Brigewater, Briggewatir) [Som], Augustinian hospital of St John the Baptist, 453
......, ..., gift of churches to, confirmation of, 1107
......, ..., master of *see* Spenser, Thomas
......, ..., brother of *see* Bartram, Elias
......, person of *see* Beledhey, John

Briggenorth' *see* Bridgnorth

Briggewatir *see* Bridgwater

Bright (Brite, Bryght, Bryte), Richard, of Exeter diocese, dispensed for plurality, 1218
......, ..., of noble birth, rector of the parish church of St Michael the Archangel, [*place wanting*] and incumbent of the parish church of B. Mary, [*place wanting*], Exeter diocese, 508
......, Robert, vicar of High Easter, 774

Brime (Bryme), John, rector of St Nicholas's, Deptford, 504

Brincheam *see* Bermingham

Bringhurst (Brynghurste) [Leics] *alias* Easton Magna (Eston') [*or* Great Easton, *in* Bringhurst, Leics], parish church of, union of, to the Benedictine monastery of Peterborough, 425
......, ..., vicar of, portion for, 425

Brington (Bryngton') [Hunts], parish church of, union of Lolworth to, 685
......, ..., rector of, 685

de Brinis, Antonius, *abbreviator de parco minori*, conclusions expedited by: *A de brinis*, 52

Brinny (Breyny) [co. Cork], parish church of, vicarage of, 67

Brinny (*contd*)
......, ..., to be united to Cistercian monastery of Tracton, 67

Bristol (Bristott) [cos. Gloucester and Somerset], Augustinian hospital of St John the Baptist, Redcliff, master of *see* Coluge, Richard
......, parish church of All Saints, vicar of, 106

Brite *see* Bright

Britonis *see* le Breton

Broadstone Hall *see* Braidstane

Broadwas (Braduas) [Worcs], parish church of, union of, to the parish church of Sedgeberrow, 294

Broadwater (Brodewater) [Sussex], parish church of, 870

Broadwindsor (Bradwynsour) [Dors], parish church of, 557

Brocklesby (Brokelsby) [Lincs], parish church of, incumbent of, 131

Broder, Broderick *cf.* Obrodear

Brodewater *see* Broadwater

Brokelsby *see* Brocklesby

Brokesby (Brokysby), Richard, rector of Bradley [*probably* Great], 263

Bromholm, Bromholme' *see* Broomholm

Bromley, Abbots (Abbatis Bromley) [Staffs], vill of, parish church of, 150

Bromor *see* Breamore

Bromuoych, James, rector of Hampton Bishop, vicar of Woolhope, and sometime incumbent of Stoke Lacy, 517

Bromwich *cf.* Bromuoych

Broomholm (Bromholme') [*in* Bacton, Norf], Cluniac monastery of, 658
......, ..., monk of *see* Benett, William

Brouunesuryth *see* Brownesmyth

Browder *cf.* Obrodear

Brown (Brown', Bruyn), David, cleric, abbacy of Melrose disputed by, 1015, 1016, 1018-1020
......, ..., rector of Nevay, 301
......, ..., ..., proctor of Roland Blackadder, 301
......, George, bishop of Dunkeld, lease of lands by, 558
......, John, chaplain in Lechlade parish church, 119
......, Rupert, dean of Waterford, death of, 543

Browne, Richard, treasurer of the cathedral church of Ferns, 989
......, ..., commendatory prior of the Augustinian priory of Selsker near Wexford, 989

Brownesmyth (Brouunesuryth), John, vicar of Andover, 213

Broxholme (Broxhome) [Lincs], parish church of, 110

Brrowarmersche *see* Burmarsh

'Bruachtalach' [*unidentified*; *perhaps obsolete*; *probably in* the barony of Moycarn, co. Roscommon *or the*

'Bruachtalach' (*contd*)
     barony of Longford, co. Galway, *near
     the confluence of the Suck and
     Shannon*], gorge *apud Syliam* called,
     146

Bruern [Oxon], Cistercian monastery of,
     abbot and convent of, lease to, from the
     provost and convent of Moncenisio, of
     the fruits of the parish church of
     Wootton, 405
......, ..., union to, of the parish church of
     Wootton, 405
......, ..., abbot and convent of, grant of
     Wootton church by, 405

[Brunand], Francis, bishop of
     Annaghdown, papal judge delegate, 199
......, ..., ..., living in the city or diocese of
     Geneva, 199

Brundholm (Bryndholme), Richard, canon
     of Ripon, prebendary of Studley, and
     incumbent of Little Wilbraham, 182

Brunʒam *see* Bermingham

Bruton (Bruton') [Som], Augustinian priory
     of, prior of *see* Gilbert, William

Bruyn *see* Brown

Brydach, Philip, detainer of vicarage of
     Moorstown, 786,
......, *cf.* Breathnach

Bryen *see* OBrien

Bryght *see* Bright

Bryme *see* Brime

Bryndholme *see* Brundholm

Brynghurste *see* Bringhurst

Bryngton' *see* Brington

Bryte *see* Bright

[Buckingham, co. of], places in *see*
     Bledlow; Burnham; Clifton Reynes;
     Fawley; Horwood, Great; Ludgershall;
     Medmenham; Missenden; Notley;
     Oakley; Penn; Turville

Buckland (Bukkelonde) [*in* Buckland
     Monachorum, Devon], [Cistercian]
     monastery of, abbot of, papal judge
     delegate, 456

Buckland St Mary (Bukilind) [Som], parish
     church of, rector of, 353

Bueuuardescote *see* Buscot

Bukarawl, Henry, monk of the [Cluniac]
     monastery of St Saviour, Bermondsey,
     745

Bukilind *see* Buckland St Mary

Bukkelonde *see* Buckland [Devon]

Bukton' *see* Boughton

Bulin' *see* Bulmer

Bulkeley, John, rector of Sutton
     Mandeville, 472
......, Richard, archdeacon of Bangor,
     incumbent of Cheadle, and sometime
     archdeacon of Merioneth, 862

Bulmer (Bulin') [Yorks], parish church of,
     incumbent of, 143

Bulmer, Ralph, of York diocese, dispensed
     for plurality, 1099

Bunratty (Bym[r]athy) [co. Clare], parish

Bunratty (*contd*)
　church of, vicarage of, to be united to
　canonry of Limerick and prebend of
　Donaghmore, 652

Bunt, Thomas, rector of Challacombe, 880

[Bunting], alias of [Codenham], William,
　q.v.

Buorm *alias* Ogarryn *see* Bourney

Burdale, Thomas, portioner of West
　Walton, 241

Burdelewer, William, chaplain in York
　cathedral, 415

Burford [Salop], parish church of, 738

?...burg', [*Christian name wanting*],
　guardian of the guild of the Drapers'
　Company in St Michael, Cornhill,
　London, 903

Burghclere (Borough Clere) [Hants], parish
　church of, 985

Burgis, John, OESA, incumbent of Asby,
　741

de Burgo, Edmund, to have vicarage united
　to canonical portion of monastery,
　Annaghdown diocese, 1286
......, ..., canon of Cashel, papal mandatary,
　838
......, ..., cleric of Clonfert diocese, to be
　canon of Clonfert and have vicarage of
　Loughrea erected into a prebend, with
　archdeaconry of Clonfert and rectories
　of Finnoe and Terryglass united thereto,
　16
......, ..., to have priory united to canonry,
　Clonfert diocese, 1193
......, Geoffrey, canon of Kilmacduagh and
　prebendary of Isertkelly, 983

de Burgo (*contd*)
......, John, canon of Tuam, papal
　mandatary, 165
......, ..., detainer of church, called prebend,
　of place of 'Tilmadim', Upper and
　Lower Umall, 165
......, Miler, abbot of the Augustinian
　monastery of B. John the Evangelist,
　[Tuam], to be deprived for alleged
　misdeeds, 835
......, Raymond, canon and prebendary of
　Emly, to be dean, 838
......, Richard / Ristardus / Restardus, holder
　of canonry of Tuam with Kilvine
　vicarage united thereto, 828
......, ..., ..., to have rectory of Bohola, 828
......, ..., canon of Annaghdown and
　prebendary of Oranmore, 935
......, ..., ..., to have canonry of
　Kilmacduagh and prebend of the small
　churches with the rectory of Terryglass
　and the vicarages of Kinvarra and
　Claregalway united thereto, 935
......, ..., ostensible cleric of Emly diocese,
　detainer, with Henry de Anglo *alias*
　Moschalaiy, of the vicarage of Ludden,
　380
......, ..., canon of Killala, papal mandatary,
　124
......, ..., to have vicarage united to
　monastery, Killaloe diocese, 1119
......, ..., abbot of the Augustinian
　monastery of Cong, to be deprived for
　alleged misdeeds, 127
......, Theobald, cleric of Tuam diocese, to
　be canon of Tuam and have rectories of
　Lough Mask and Inishmaine erected
　into prebend, 826
......, Thomas, to be canon of Annaghdown
　and have church, called prebend, of
　Lackagh erected into simple prebend,
　with vicarages of *Tempull na Scrine*,
　Kilcoona, and Annaghdown united
　thereto, 163
......, ..., [another] detainer of vicarage of
　Tempull na Scrine and vicarage of

de Burgo (*contd*)

Annaghdown cathedral, 163

......, ..., to be commendatory abbot of the Augustinian monastery of B. Mary *de Portu Patrum*, Annaghdown, 163

......, ..., canon of Annaghdown, papal mandatary, 829

......, ..., to have vicarage of Annaghdown diocese united to canonry [of Kilmacduagh?], 1122

......, ..., to have monastery and parish churches, Clonfert diocese, 1118

......, ..., canon and prebendary of Kilmacduagh, to be commendatory abbot of the Cistercian monastery of Knockmoy and dean of Tuam, 330

......, ..., canon of the Augustinian monastery of Cong and commendatory vicar of Ballinrobe and Annagh, to be abbot of Cong, 127

......, ..., to have monastery, Tuam diocese, 1283

......, Walter, cleric of Clonfert diocese, to be canon of Kilmacduagh and prebendary of Kinvarra with chantry in Kilmacduagh cathedral, chapel of St Mary, Galway, and vicarages of Beagh *alias* Cliath-Ceallayd and Clonrush united thereto, 933

......, William, canon of Annaghdown, papal commissary and mandatary, 127

......, ..., detainer and ostensible abbot of the Augustinian monastery of Annaghdown, and detainer of the church, called prebend, of Lackagh, 163

......, ..., canon and prebendary of Clonfert, to have archdeaconry of Clonfert and Kilconierin chapel united thereto, 234

......, ..., ..., grant to, of the archdeaconry of Clonfert, impetration of, alleged subreption of, 512

......, ..., to have vicarage, Clonfert diocese, 1195

......, ..., canon of Tuam, papal mandatary, 126

Burmarsh (Brrowarmersche) [Kent], parish church of, 335

Burnham [Bucks], parish church of, vicar of, 860

Burnham Deepdale (Depedale) [Norf], parish church of, 328

Burra, William, canon of the Augustinian priory of Tortington, 758

Burren (Baryn) [*in* Rathclarin, co. Cork], parish church of, rectory of, to be united to deanery of Cork, 258

Burrneach *see* Ballyvourney

Burton, John, canon and prebendary of Exeter and incumbent of Whimple, 909

Burton Bradstock (Birton') [Dors], parish church of, union of, to the canonry and prebend of Nassington in Lincoln cathedral, 154

......, ..., incumbent of, 154

Burwell St Mary [*now* part of Burwell, Cambs], parish church of, 351

Bury [Lancs], parish church of, union of, to the parish church of Warton, 270

Bury, Adam, chantry of in London cathedral, 800

......, John, third prior of the Benedictine monastery of Chertsey, 341

Bury St Edmunds (Bury) [Suff], Benedictine monastery of St Edmund, abbot William and convent of, indulged to apply certain masses for other benefactors, 1175

......, ..., ..., ?conferences [*recte* confirmation?] concerning the

Bury St Edmunds (*contd*)
monastery's jurisdiction of a vill, 1176
......, ..., abbot of *see* [Codenham *alias* Bunting], William

Buscot (Bueuuardescote) [Berks], parish church of, 666

Bute [an island, co. Bute], [parish church of], 781

[Bute, co. of], places in *see* Bute; ?Cumbray

Butler (Bottiler, Butteller, Buttiller, Buttyler), James, rector of Kinwarton, 431
......, Peter, cleric of Cashel diocese, to have deanery of Cashel and rectory of Outeragh, 385
......, Walter, cleric of Lismore diocese, 785, 789
......, ..., ..., to be commendatory abbot of the Cistercian monastery of Inishlounaght, 785, 789
......, ..., ..., to be canon and prebendary of Lismore, 789
......, ..., ..., to be canon of Lismore and have vicarages of Kilsheelan and Newtown Lennan erected into prebend, 785
......, ..., canon of Lismore, papal mandatary, 949
......, *and see* Butler *alias* Okynale; Buttler *alias* Berkeley

Butler (Boteller) *alias* Okynale, William, ostensible cleric or priest of Lismore, detainer of deanery of Lismore, 159

Butteller *see* Butler

Butterworth (Butternuorth), Ralph, of York diocese, dispensed for plurality, 1231

Buttevant [co. Cork], [Augustinian]

Buttevant (*contd*)
monastery of St Thomas the Martyr near *see* Ballybeg
......, place in *see* Ballybeg

Buttiller *see* Butler

Buttler *alias* Berkeley, Thomas, monk of the Benedictine monastery of Hyde, Winchester, 264

Buttyler *see* Butler

Byfield (Byfeldi') [Northants], parish church of, union of, to the canonry and prebend of Wolvey in Lichfield cathedral, 428

Byford, David, vicar of Monkton, 88

Bym[r]athy *see* Bunratty

Byrde, William, vicar of Bradford-on-Avon, 206

Bysshope (Bisshop') *alias* Leynham, William, prior of the Benedictine cathedral priory of Rochester, 882

C

[de Caccialupis] de Sancto Severino, Antonius, *abbreviator de parco maiori*, letters expedited by:
A *de Sancto Severino*, 17, 18, 22, 43, 61, 63, 83, 90, 112, 115, 116, 155, 168, 181, 187-189, 212, 237, 248, 257, 273, 327, 356, 360, 364, 371, 401, 443, 444, 449, 477, 481, 486, 535, 552, 558, 569, 570, 634-636, 645-647, 651, 652, 655, 687, 697, 702, 703, 705, 706, 708-710, 717, 763, 768, 780, 783-790, 824, 826-829, 833, 835-837, 840, 841, 846, 848, 849, 908, 931, 937, 939, 940, 943-946, 949, 951, 979, 980, 992-995, 1036-1038

Caher (Chayrdownheste) [co. Tipperary], [Augustinian] monastery of, prior of, papal judge delegate, 221

[Cahir, co. Kerry], place near see 'Kylldacu(m) alias Turere'

Cahors [dép. of Lot, France], place in see Marcilhac

Cairns (Carnis) [in Mid Calder, co. Midlothian], James Crichton of, q.v.

Caithness, [cathedral] church of [at Dornoch, co. Sutherland], chapter of, conclusion to, 620

......, bishop of see Stewart, Andrew
......, [bishop-] elect of see [Sinclair], John
......, church of, subjection of, to the archbishop of St Andrews, 621
......, ..., vassals of, conclusion to, 620

......, city and diocese of, clergy of, conclusion to, 620
......, ..., people of, conclusion to, 620

Caladama'rain see Callathamery

Calayn see Callan

Calcedonien. see Chalcedon

Calder (Caldar) [now East Calder (and Kirknewton), Mid Calder, and West Calder, co. Midlothian], parish church of, incumbent of, 237

[Calder, Mid, co. Midlothian], place in see Cairns

Calioco alias Templetogher, q.v.

Caliporen. see Gallipoli

Calkton see Chalton

Callan (Calayn) [co. Kilkenny] alias Kilbride (Kylbride) [in Callan, co. Kilkenny], parish church of, vicarage of, 575

Callathamery (Caladama'rain), alias of Templeachally, q.v.

Callow, Thomas, of Exeter diocese, dispensed for plurality, 1252

Calverley, Nicholas, vicar of Batley, 804

Cambridge [Cambs], university of, college of the Annunciation of B. Mary the Virgin in [i.e. Gonville (now Gonville and Caius)], warden and scholars of, 343
......, ..., ..., warden and fellows of, 343
......, ..., ..., chapel of, 343
......, ..., ..., Physwick (Fischewyke) hostel of, 343
......, and see Barnwell

[Cambridge, co. of], places in see Barnwell; Bassingbourn; Bottisham; Boxworth; Burwell; Cambridge; Clopton; Lolworth; Papworth Everard; Swaffham; Wilbraham, Little

Cambuskenneth (Cambuskynneth, Cannbuskynneth) [or Abbey, in Stirling, co. Stirling], Augustinian monastery of, 1024, 1025
......, ..., subjection of, to the archbishop of St Andrews, 1027
......, ..., abbot of, papal mandatary, 767, 768
......, ..., ..., see [Arnot], David and Henry
......, ..., convent of, conclusion to, 1024
......, ..., canon of see Arnot, David

Cambuskenneth (*contd*)
......, ..., vassals of, conclusion to, 1024

[Campbell], John, bishop of Sodor, to be commendatory abbot of the Benedictine monastery of Iona, 181

Campe *see* Guemps

Campion (Campion' *alias* Campio'), Thomas, ostensible rector of East Dean, litigant, 661

Canayn *see* Cavan

[Candidus], Otto *see* Otto [Candidus]

Caneen. see Khania

Cannbuskynneth *see* Cambuskenneth

Cant (Cantun), Patrick, abbot of the Cistercian monastery of Fermoy, 610, 611
......, ..., ..., provision of, to the bishopric of Cork and Cloyne, 121, 610
......, ..., ..., absolution of, preliminary to promotion to episcopate, 611
......, ..., ..., to retain Fermoy *in commendam*, 121

Canterbury [co. Kent], **city** of, parish church of All Saints in, 533
......, ..., hospital of poor priests in, 101
......, ..., [parish church of St Dunstan without Westgate of], Roper chantry (Rooperchiante) in, 195

......, [Benedictine **cathedral**] **church** of, (prior and) chapter of, *sede vacante* jurisdiction of, 906
......, ..., ..., ..., exemption from, 529
......, ..., ..., steward or official of *sede vacante see* Peynthwyn, Hugh
......, ..., ..., auditor of *see* Peynthwyn, Hugh

Canterbury (*contd*)
......, Benedictine monastery of Christ Church [i.e. the cathedral priory], 743
......, ..., monk of *see* Chaundler, Thomas
......, **archbishop** of, primate of all England and legate born of the apostolic see, 987
......, ..., subjection to, of the church of Bangor, 603
......, ..., ..., of the united churches of Coventry and Lichfield, 1031
......, ..., ..., of the church of Llandaff, 599
......, ..., ..., of the church of London, 619
......, ..., ..., of the church of Norwich, 554, 636
......, ..., ..., of the church of St Asaph, 595
......, ..., conclusion to, 59, 553, 581, 594, 598, 602, 617, 626, 627, 634, 1029
......, ..., jurisdiction of, exemption from, 529
......, ..., court of audience of causes and matters of, custom of, 924
......, ..., audience of, auditor of causes and matters of *see* Peynthwyn, Hugh
......, [archi]episcopal court of, official of *see* Hawardyn, Humphrey
......, metropolitical court of, recourse to, 456; *and cf.* 298, 529
......, ..., official of *see* Hawardyn, Humphrey
......, court of, recourse to, for protection, 298, 529
......, ..., *see* [?Arundel], Thomas; [Dean(e)], Henry; [Morton], John
......, archbishops of [named], commissaries and auditors of *see* Barocis, William; Peynthwyn, Hugh; Wilton, William
......, church of, president of *see* [Morton], John
......, ..., archdeacon of *see* Peynthwyn, Hugh
......, **diocese** of, persons of *see* Byford, David; Chetham, Richard; Churche, Roger; Clerk, John; Cocke, John; Dokett, Robert; Draper, Richard; Eglifield, Leonard; Fareyway, William; Ffreuill' or Norbourne, Robert;

Canterbury **diocese** (*contd*)
 Gardener, Richard; Goodwyn, William;
 Grafton, Adam; Grene, Thomas; Holt,
 John; Lokton, John; Long, Thomas;
 Mutton, Robert; Pickton, John; Rayner,
 Martin; Simon, Richard; Squyer, Roger;
 Stevyns, Richard; Thwaytes, John;
 Watrer, Thomas; Watson, William;
 Wilcock, John
......, ..., places in *see* Barham; Birling;
 Bishopsbourne; Burmarsh; Chevening;
 Chiddingstone; Combwell; Dover;
 Faversham; Hardres, Great *now* Upper;
 London (St Dionis Backchurch);
 Midley; Monkton; Norton; Reculver;
 Smarden; Sundridge; Thanet, Isle of
......, province of, constitutions of, 197, 987;
 and see 919

Canton (?Cantim), Leonard, canon of
 Cloyne, papal mandatary, 392
......, *cf.* Condon

Cantuel *see* Cantwell

Cantun *see* Cant

Cantwell (Cantuel), John, detainer of
 priorship of the Augustinian monastery
 of St John the Evangelist near
 Kilkenny, 575

Capaccio [*in* province of Salerno, Italy],
 bishop of, papal mandatary, 147

[Capra], A[loysius bishop of] Pesaro,
 regent of the chancery, correction of
 register ordered by, 13, 35, 61, 91

[Caraffa], Oliviero, [cardinal] bishop of
 Sabina, suit before, 1015

Cardigan [co. Cardigan], archdeaconry of
 in the church of St David's, 739
......, archdeacon of *see* Howell, Thomas

[Cardigan, co. of], places in *see* Cardigan;
 Llanbadarn Fawr; Llanllwchaiarn

Carisbrooke (Castrisbrok) [Isle of Wight,
 Hants], castle of, parish church of St
 Nicholas within, 970

Carleton Rode (Carletonrode) [Norf],
 parish church of, 771

Carlile, John, of Glasgow diocese,
 commission by virtue of an appeal,
 1103

Carlisle [Cumb], **[cathedral] church** of,
 chapter of, conclusion to, 1012

......, **bishops** of *see* Layburne, Roger;
 [Sever *or* Senhouse], William
......, church of, vassals of, conclusion to,
 1012

......, **city and diocese** of, clergy of,
 conclusion to, 1012
......, diocese of, persons of *see* Bedale,
 Robert; Burgis, John; Crakyntroppe,
 Edward; Draylow, William; Lowther,
 Robert; Redinayd, Richard; Redman,
 Walter; Redmayn, Edward; Redmayne,
 Ewart
......, places in *see* Asby; Musgrave, Great;
 Plumbland; Shap

[Carlow, co. of], place in *see* Ballon

Carlyon, Richard, vicar of Stratton, 900

[Carmarthen, co. of], places in *see*
 Abergwili; Henllan-Amgoed; Llandeilo
 Vawr; Llanfallteg; Whitland

Carmichael (Carmechet [*recte* Carmechel])
 [co. Lanark], James, nobleman, of, 80

Carmweche *see* Carnwath

[Carnarvon,co. of], place in *see* Bangor

Carnbo [*in* Fossoway,co. Kinross],Andrew Lundy of, *q.v.*

Carnis *see* Cairns

Carnwath (Carmweche) [co. Lanark], parish church of, vicarage of, 248

Carpenter (Carpentier), Richard, of Lincoln diocese, dispensed for plurality, 1291

Carrickfergus (Carrigfergussa) [co. Antrim], parish church of, rectory of, 236
......,place in *see* Woodburn

Carriden (Carridin) [co. Linlithgow], parish church of, vicarage of, 248
......, ..., vicar of, 248

Carrigfergussa *see* Carrickfergus

Carsington (Karsyngton') [Derb], parish church of, 463

Cartmel (Cartinell) [Lancs], [Augustinian] monastery of, prior of, papal judge delegate, 990, 999

[Cashel, co. Longford], places in *see* Inchcleraun; Saints Island

Cashel [co. Tipperary], **[cathedral] church** of, deanery of, 385
......, ..., ..., canonry and prebend annexed to, 385
......, ..., dean of, to be summoned over erection of canonry and prebend, 350
......, ..., ..., papal mandatary, 380, 543
......, ..., ..., *see* Butler, Peter
......, ..., precentor of, papal mandatary, 385
......, ..., chapter of, to be summoned over erection of canonry and prebend, 350,

Cashel, **[cathedral] church** (*contd*) 404, 786
......, ..., canonry of, annexed to deanery, 385
......, ..., canons of *see* de Burgo, Edmund; Mockler, Henry; ODwyer, Philip; OHedian, Henry and Robert; OMeagher, John, Thady and William; Omuchyre, Thady; Ymukcan, Odo
......, ..., prebend in, annexed to deanery, 385
......, ..., prebends in *see* ?Kilcomenty; Killea; 'Kylmemanch'; ?Mocklerstown

......, **archbishopric** of, *mensa* of, union to, of the vicarages of Ballysheehan, ?Erry, Railstown, and Crumpstown, 998
......, archbishop of, to be summoned over erection of canonry and prebend, 350, 404, 786
......, ..., subjection to, of the churches of Cork and Cloyne, 613
......, ..., conclusions to, 52, 610, 612
......, ..., *see* [Creagh], David
......, church of, archdeacon of, papal mandatary, 385

......, **diocese** of, persons of *see* Brydach, Philip; Butler, Peter; Everard, Richard; Morlier, Edmund; OCahill, Thomas; ODwyer, Redmundus and Thomas; OHogan, Donat; OMullanphy, Maurice; OMulwarden *alias* OBrophy, Donat and John; Omukean, Matheus; Stapleton, Patrick; Ymukcan, Odo; *and see* Loweys, John; OBogue, William
......, ..., places in *see* Ballysheehan; Clonoulty; Crumpstown; ?Erry; Holycross; ?Kilcomenty; Kilcooly; Killea; 'Kylmemanch'; ?Mocklerstown; Moorstown; Railstown; Templeachally *alias* Callathamery; *and see* ?Colman; Donaghmore

Casleandriohc' *see* Odagh

'Cassano', diocese of Nocera

'Cassano' (*contd*)
[*unidentified*], parish church of, 996

Castellacre *see* Castle Acre

Castellesi, master Hadrian, cleric of Corneto, papal notary, sometime nuncio of the apostolic see in the kingdom of England, dispensation by, 644

Castelleton' *see* Castle Eaton

de Castello, A [*recte* 'N', 'P', *or* 'S'; probably 'N'], *abbreviator de parco maiori*, letter expedited by, 672

de Castello, F [*recte* 'N', 'P', *or* 'S'; probably 'S'], *abbreviator de parco maiori*, letter expedited by, 246

de Castello, G [*recte* 'N', 'P', *or* 'S'; probably 'S'], *abbreviator de parco maiori*, letters expedited by, 155, 714

de Castello, Nicolaus Olivius, *abbreviator de parco maiori,* letters expedited by:
N. *de Castello,* 301, 364, 390, 430, 431, 438, 452, 471, 475, 516, 517, 525, 534, 641, 643, 650, 670, 671, 678, 682, 684, 685, 700, 749, 778, 782, 795, 797, 800, 802, 805, 810, 817, 839, 877, 882, 904, 912, 915, 926, 938, 941, 942, 955, 957, 958, 965, 966, 968, 974, 978, 998, 1002; *and see* 681 *note*, 956 *note* ; *see also under* de Castello, A

de Castello, Paulus Amadei de Iustinis, *abbreviator de parco maiori*, letters expedited by:
P. *de Castello,* 10, 19, 59, 60, 82, 128, 136, 137, 147, 161, 191, 203, 211, 265, 568; *and see* 475 *note*

de Castello, Saldonus de Saldis, *abbreviator de parco maiori*, letters expedited by:

de Castello, Saldonus de Saldis (*contd*)
S. *de Castello,* 6, 7, 11-16, 28, 47, 67, 69-75, 80, 88, 89, 108, 115, 117, 121-127, 129, 146, 156, 158-160, 162-167, 169-171, 182, 186, 190, 199, 200, 202, 225-229, 231, 234-236, 243, 245, 249-252, 254-256, 258, 259, 271, 281, 288, 289, 293, 295, 300, 304-306, 308, 310-313, 330, 350, 353, 357, 359, 361-363, 368, 380, 383-385, 391-393, 402-404, 407, 415, 416, 448, 485, 487, 489, 490, 492, 511-514, 519, 521, 527, 536-542, 545, 553-556, 559, 563, 566, 571, 573, 574, 576, 606-611, 649, 697, 704, 731, 742, 743, 748, 816, 821-823, 825, 830-832, 834, 838, 845, 851-853, 892 (*S. Castello*), 909, 930, 932, 934-936, 947, 948, 981, 983, 1000, 1035; *and see* 569 *note* , 570 *note* ; *see also under* de Castello, F and G

de Castello, Sancti Petri see under [Taunton]

extra Castellum, Sancti Pauli see under [Taunton]

Castile and Leon, king of *see* Ferdinand [V]

Castle Acre (Castellacre) [Norf], Cluniac priory of, monk of *see* Louuyn', Geoffrey

Castleconor [co. Sligo], parish church of, vicarage of, 124

Castle Eaton (Castelleton') [Wilts], parish church of, 499

Castrisbrok *see* Carisbrooke

Caterstonn' *see* ?Collieston

[Caueris], Andrew, monk, recently abbot, of the Benedictine monastery of Lindores, reservation of fruits for, 1260

Cavan (Canayn) [*in* Urney, co. Cavan], Franciscan house of, guardian and friars of, commission [in virtue of an appeal?] for, 1281

[Cavan, co. of], places in *see* Annagh; Cavan; Drumgoon; Drumlane; Kildrumferton *or* Crosserlough; Kilmore; Magheranure; Templeport *alias* Breaghwy Island; Urney; Urney *alias* Keadew *or* Keadue

[Caversham], Peter, abbot of the Augustinian monastery of Notley and holder of Lamport parish church, 877

? *Cell cairill* (Cyllcayrayld) [*modern* Termonamongan, co. Tyrone], parish church of, vicarage of, 448

Cenél arga (Chinallarga) [*modern* Ballybritt barony, co. Offaly; *also* an alias of Kinnitty, co. Offaly], rectory of, in a lay fief, 162
......, ..., to be erected into prebend in Killaloe cathedral, with rectory of Lynally and vicarages of Kilcomin and Loughkeen united thereto, 162

Cerne (Serne) [*in* Cerne Abbas, Dors], Benedictine monastery of, 139
......, ..., monk of *see* Trebel, John

[Cerne Abbas, Dors], place in *see* Cerne

Cesena [*in* province of Forlì, Italy], [cathedral] church of, provost of, papal commissary and mandatary, 972
......, bishop of, papal mandatary, 782, 839

de Cesena, Damianus *see* [de Falcutiis *or* Falcariis], Damianus

Chacombe [Northants], Augustinian priory of, prior of *see* Saunders, Thomas

Chadworth, George, rector of Guemps, 699

Chagford (Jagford *alias* Jugforth', Jagford *alias* Jagfourth) [Devon], parish church of, 434
......, ..., union of, to the canonry and prebend of Wiveliscombe in Wells cathedral, 683

Chalcedon (*Calcedonien.*) [titular see in ancient Bithynia; *modern* Kadiköy, a suburb of Constantinople], [bishop-] elect of *see* [Connesburgh], Edmund

Challacombe (Cholocomb) [Devon], parish church of, 880

Chalon-sur-Saône [*in dép.* of Saône et Loire, France], diocese of, place in *see* Cîteaux

Chalton (Calkton) [Hants], parish church of, rector of, 902

Chamber(s) *cf.* Chambyr

Chamberlain (Chambrelayn), Edward, cleric of Norwich diocese, 180

Chambyr, Robert, canon of the Augustinian monastery of Hickling, 802
......, *cf.* Chamber(s)

[Channel Islands] *see* Guernsey; Jersey; Lihou

Chantrell (Channtrell), Nicholas, rector of Hawkchurch, 204

Chapel of Garioch *see* Logie Durno

Chaplain (Chapleyn) *alias* Tonker, John, rector of Litton, 310

Chapman (Chapman'), Thomas, rector of

Chapman (contd)
Conington and canon and prebendary of
Newark College, Leicester, 17

Chappeley3, Olive, woman of Norwich, 655
......, ..., ..., first husband of, 655
......, ..., ..., child by, 655
......, ..., ..., ..., ..., godmother to see
Rabett, Henry, Helen, deceased wife of
......, ..., ..., future husband of see Rabett,
Henry

Charlton (Charleton') [Wilts], parish
church of, 208

Chaundler (Chaundeler), John, prior of the
Augustinian priory of Breamore, 524
......, Thomas, monk of the Benedictine
monastery of Christ Church,
Canterbury, 743

Chayrdownheste see Caher

Cheadle (Chedill) [Ches], parish church of,
862

Chechester, William, rector of Arlington,
884
......, cf. Chichester

Checkendon (C3akenden) [Oxon], parish
church of, rector of, 46

Ched see Keadew

Chedill see Cheadle

Chedyngstone see Chiddingstone

Chedzoy (Cherdesey) [Som], parish church
of, 277

Cherbourg (Chereboure) [in dép. of La
Manche, France], Augustinian
monastery of, dependency of see St
Helier

Cherche see Churche

Cherchesey see Chertsey

Cherdesey see Chedzoy

Chereboure see Cherbourg

Cherell, Thomas, monk of the Cluniac
monastery of Bs Peter and Paul,
[Montacute], 267
......, ..., prior of the Cluniac priory of St
Carrok, 267

Cheriton (Cherinton') [Hants], parish
church of, 966

Cheriton Fitzpaine (Chiritoffyppayn')
[Devon], parish church of, 198

Chertsey (Cherchesey, Chertesey, Chertesi)
[Surrey], Benedictine monastery of, 914
......, ..., to be held in commendam, 605
......, ..., (commendatory) abbot of see
[Pigot], Thomas
......, ..., third prior of see Bury, John
......, ..., monk of see Marshall, Thomas

Chest alias Ris, Henry, monk of the
Benedictine monastery of B. Mary the
Virgin, Worcester [i.e. the cathedral
priory], 325

Chester [Ches], parish church of St Mary
the Virgin on the Hill, 191

[Chester, co. of], places in see Astbury;
Birkenhead; Cheadle; Chester;
Christleton; Rostherne; Sandbach;
Warmingham; Wistaston

Chester, Alice, woman of London diocese,
appeal of, 261
......, ..., marriage of, to Thomas Aderei,
261

?Chesterfield (Sestarffordi) [Derb], parish church of All Saints, rector of, 567

'Chestfelden'' [*unidentified; in* East Dean, West Sussex], fields of, tithes from, 661

Cheswyk *see* Chiswick

Chetham (Chethin), Richard, of Canterbury diocese, dispensed for plurality, 1265

Chevening (Chevenyng) [Kent], parish church of, 760

Chichester [Sussex], **city** of, grammar school in, 179
......, ..., ..., canonry of Chichester and prebend of Highleigh destined for teacher in, by statute of bishop Edward [Story], 179

......, **[cathedral] church** of, dean and chapter of, 179, 661
......, ..., ..., consent of, to statute of bishop Edward [Story] whereby canonry and prebend of Highleigh destined for teacher at the grammar school, 179
......, ..., ..., to nominate priest learned in grammar as teacher, 179
......, ..., chapter of, letters of bishop Edward [Story] fortified with seal of, 179
......, ..., ..., notary in episcopal curia appointed by (with bishop), 919
......, ..., ..., *mensa* of, tithes from fields of West Dean and from fields (named) in East Dean pertain to, 661
......, ..., ..., collector or farmer of tithes deputed by *see* Body, John
......, ..., ..., appeal of, 661
......, ..., canon of *see* Taverner, Nicholas
......, ..., prebend in *see* Highleigh
......, **bishop** of, to collate canonry and prebend of Highleigh with charge of teaching at city's grammar school to

Chichester, **bishop** (*contd*)
priest nominated by dean and chapter, 179
......, ..., to institute priest nominated by dean and chapter as teacher at city's grammar school or provide him with canonry and prebend of Highleigh, 179
......, ..., curia of, constitutions of, 919
......, ..., ..., office of notary in, barred to married men, 919
......, ..., 626 *note*
......, ..., *see* [Story], Edward
......, church of, archdeacon of, letters of bishop Edward [Story] fortified with seal of, 179
......, ...archdeacon of Lewes in *q.v.*

......, **diocese** of, persons of *see* Anstyn', William; Atkinson, William; Austen, John; Bekeryng *alias* Sandherst, Robert; Beverley, William; Bexyll', Richard; Body, John; Boniface, James; Bounter, William; Bradshaw, Thomas; Burra, William; Campion, Thomas; Dussyng, John; Edimundi, John; Edwardes, Thomas; Elphick, John; Goodwyn, John; Hadynh(a)m, John; Jackson, William; Jeffrey, William; Levokenore, John; Morris, John; N [= *nomen*? (Cosyn?)], William; Oxenbregge, John; Pye, William; Thatcher, William; Trappe, John; Underdown, Richard; Wode, William

......, ..., places in *see* Battle; Bayham; Birdham; Broadwater; 'Chestfelden'' [*in* East Dean]; Crowhurst; Dean, East and West [West Sussex]; Dean, West [East Sussex]; 'Estgaston'' [*in* East Dean]; Graffham; Hastings; Heryngham; Icklesham; Malecomb [*in* East Dean]; Michelham; 'Nodylfeld'' [*in* East Dean]; 'Northfelde' [*in* East Dean]; Petworth; Robertsbridge; Rudgwick; 'Southgasten'' [*in* East Dean]; Telscombe; Tortington;

Chichester, **diocese** (*contd*)
'Wesefelde' [*in* East Dean];
Winchelsea;Withyham

Chichester *cf.* Chechester

Chiddingstone (Chedyngstone) [co. Kent],
parish church of, 168

Chieti [Italy], diocese of, persons of *see*
Grimaldi, Agostino
......, ..., place in *see* Treglio

Chilemian *see* Kilcurnan

Chilenanna *see* Kilcoona

Chiller *see* Killea

Chillerulan *see* Killeroran

Chilmide *see* Kilmeedy

?Chilmogonec *see* Kilmacdonogh

Chilmolonog *see* Kilmalinoge

Chilmyny' *alias* Chiltual *see* Kilmeen

Chilsane *see* Kilshannig

Chiltual, alias of Kilmeen, *q.v.*

Chinallarga *see* Cénel arga

Chingford (Chyngelford) [Essex], parish
church of, 1036

Chirche *see* Church

Chiritoffyppayn' *see* Cheriton Fitzpaine

[Chisholm], James, bishop of Dunblane,
oath of, as suffragan of archbishop of
Glasgow, relaxation of, 333

Chiswick (Cheswyk) [Midd], parish church
of, 99

de Chivizano *see* da ?Civezzano

Cholocomb *see* Challacombe

Chovehe *see* Quin

Christleton (Cristilton) [Ches], parish
church of, litigation over, 991
......, ..., rector of, 991

[Chrystal], alias of [Wawain], Thomas, *q.v.*

Chubbe, William, rector of Holy Trinity,
Exeter, 421

Chumalay *see* Cliath-ceallayd

Church (Chirche), Thomas, priest of
Norwich diocese, 347

Churche (Cherche), Roger, rector of the
free chapel of Lasborough and
incumbent of Bishopsbourne with
Barham, 422

Church Eaton *see* Eaton, Church

Church Island *see* Inchmacnerin

Churchover (Curcheoner) [Warw], parish
church of, incumbent of, 739

Churchstanton (Stanton') [Devon], land in,
174

Church Stretton *see* Stretton, Church

Chylmodonoc *see* Kilmacdonogh

Chyltoloch *see* Kiltullagh

Chyngelford *see* Chingford

Chyrcheytn' *see* Church Eaton

de Ciampantibus, Hercules, cleric of Lucca, provision of to the hospital of St Michael, Cortesora, 951

Cicheton, George, provided anew to vicarage in Moray diocese, 1128
......, *cf.* Crichton

Cilleule *see* Kilcooly

Cirrogayn *see* Curragranemore

Cîteaux [*in dép.* of Côte d'Or, France], monastery of, abbot and convent of, Cistercian privileges cannot be derogated without consent of, 1020
......, ..., ..., Cistercian monasteries may not be commended without consent of, 121
......, ..., ..., commends of Cistercian monasteries to cardinals need consent of, 789
......, ..., abbot of, conclusion to, 1015

da ?Civezzano (de Chivizano) [*in* province of Trent, Italy], Paolo di Niccolò, continual commensal familiar of Silvester [de' Gigli], bishop of Worcester, 364
......, ..., ..., ..., provision of, to the rectory of Benabbio, 364

Civita Castellana [*in* province of Viterbo, Italy], letters dated at, 654 *note*, 723-725, 896, 918
......, diocese of, place in *see* Gallese

Civitavecchia [*in* province of Rome, Italy], letter dated at, 656

'Clacerogarde', alias of 'Cuacaynde', *q.v.*

[?Clachan, on Lismore island, co. Argyll] *see* Lismore

Claghton *see* Claughton

Claimondi *see* Claymond

Clanfield (Claufeldi) [Hants], parish church of, 466

Clann conchobair (Clontonpuyr) [*in* Baslick, co. Roscommon], parish church of, rectory of, to be united to deanery of Elphin, 936

Claondalan *see* Clonallan

Clapton *see* Clopton

[Clare, co. of], places in *see* Bunratty; Clonloghan; Clonrush; Inchicronan; Inishcaltra; Kilcarragh; Kilfarboy; Kilfearagh; Kilfenora; Kilfintinan; Killaloe; Killard; Killimer; [Killinaboy]; Killeely; Killofin; ?Kilmaleery; Kilshanny; Kiltoraght; Moanmore [*in* Kilrush]; Ogonnelloe; Quin; Rath; Scattery Island [*in* Kilrush]; Tulla

Claregalway (Bellenelare) [co. Galway], parish church of, vicarage of, to be united to canonry of Kilmacduagh and prebend of the small churches, 935

Clarell', Thomas, rector of Boughton, 185

Clashacrow (Glascro) [co. Kilkenny], parish church of, rectory of, union of, to the Cistercian monastery of Kilcooly, 574

Clashmore (Clasmor) [co. Waterford], prebend of in Lismore cathedral, 159
......, ..., vicarage of Kilronan annexed to, 159
........, ..., to be united to the deanery of Lismore, 159

Claufeldi *see* Clanfield

Claughton (Claghton) [Lancs], parish church of, 521

Claymond (Claimondi), John, of Durham diocese, dispensed for plurality, 1243

Clayton (Clayton'),Nicholas, vicar of Bassingbourn, 81

Clear Island (Clery) [co. Cork], parish church of, rectory of, to be united to canonry of Ross and prebend of Clear Island, 129
......, ..., vicarage of, to be erected into prebend in Ross cathedral, with rectories of Clear Island, Creagh, and Gortnaclohy united thereto, 129

?Clee (Klay) [Lincs], parish church of, vicarage of, 41

Clement V, constitution of concerning hospitals published at council of Vienne, 130

Clerk (Clerck), John, cleric of Norwich diocese, 662
......, ..., master of the Augustinian hospital of Maison Dieu, Dover, 7

Clerke (Clerk, Clerlie), Richard, cleric in All Saint's, Maldon, 519
......, Thomas, archdeacon of the church of Sodor, 606, 609
......, ..., ..., provision of, to the bishopric of Killala, 606
......, ..., ..., absolution of, preliminary to provision, 609
......, ..., ..., [bishop-] elect of Killala, faculty for consecration of, 607
......, ..., ..., ..., dispensed to receive and retain benefices *in commendam*, 608
......, ..., bishop of Killala, litigant over

Clerke (*contd*)
parish church of Christleton, 991
......, ..., rector of West Tilbury and incumbent of St Mary Abchurch, London, 375

Clery *see* Clear Island

Cliath-Ceallayd (Chumalay), alias of Beagh, *q.v.*

Cliff (Clyff), John, rector of St Mary's, East Raynham, 3

Clifton Reynes (Cliston Reynys, Cliston' Reynys) [Bucks], parish church of, 191, 569

Clinton (Clinchon, Clynton, Clyntown'), William, detainer of chancellorship of Ossory, 157
......, ..., ..., the late, 545
......, ..., ostensible priest of Ossory diocese, detainer of vicarage of Odagh, 574

Cliston Reynys, Cliston' Reynys *see* Clifton Reynes

Clitherow (Clyderowe), John, monk of the Cistercian monastery of Croxden, 468

Clocen. see ?Clogher

Clogher [co. Tyrone], [cathedral] church of, canon of *see* MacMahon, Corbanus
......, bishop of *see* [MacMahon], James
......, diocese of, persons of *see* MacGilsenan, Bernard; OCullen, Donat; Oslannagail, Donat

?Clogher (*Clocen.*) [co. Tyrone], bishop of *see* Vincent

Clonallan (Claondalan) [co. Down], prebend of in Dromore cathedral, to be united to the Fabric of the Cistercian

Clonallan (*contd*)
monastery of [Newry], 235

Clonbern (Cluanbectii) [co. Galway],
parish church of, vicarage of, 833
......, ..., ..., [?annexed] to a canonry and
prebend of Tuam, 833

Clonfert [co. Galway], walls of, lands by,
146
......, square of, 146
......, Augustinian monastery of B. Mary *de
Portu Puro*, commendatory abbots of
see MacEgan, Thady; Omaytin,
Malachy
......, ..., convent of, 229
......, ..., canons' portions of, 229
......, ..., canon of *see* Jeurmachan, Henry
......, ..., vassals of, 229
......, place in *see* Annacalla

......, **[cathedral] church** of, dean and
chapter of, consent of, to grant of
mensal lands anew by bishop, 146
......, ..., ..., to be summoned over erection
anew of canonry and prebend, 167
......, ..., chapter of, to be summoned over
erection of canonry and prebend, 16,
167
......, ..., ..., to be summoned over
confirmation of grant of mensal lands,
146
......, ..., ..., *mensa* of, tithes of 'Ycluelin'
belonging to, 167
......, ..., canons of *see* de Burgo, Edmund
and William; MacEgan, Thady;
MacEvilly, Hobertus; Machnayn,
Maurice; Macvaney, Maurice; OBrogy,
Thady and William; OFahy, Dermot
and Thady; OGarvan, Florence;
OHoran, Donat; OLongan, David;
OMalley, John; OMannin, Malachy;
OMullally, John and Magonius
......, ..., canonry and prebend annexed to
archdeaconry, 512
......, ..., prebends in *see* Annacalla;

Clonfert, **[cathedral] church** (*contd*)
Ballynakill; Loughrea; 'Ycluelin'; *see
also* 512

......, **bishop** of, to be summoned over
erection of canonry and prebend, 16,
167
......, ..., to be summoned over erection
anew of canonry and prebend, 167
......, ..., to be summoned over confirmation
of grant of mensal lands, 146
......, ..., to receive oath of fealty in pope's
name, 591, 592
......, ..., *see* [OBrogy], Gregory; [OKelly],
Thomas
......, ..., *mensa* of, lands belonging to, grant
of, 146
......, ..., ..., ..., *see* 'Glochmor';
'Gortuaglothbg''; '?Goven'
......, official of, papal mandatary, 853
......, church of, archdeaconry of, to be
united to proposed canonry and prebend
of Loughrea, 16
......, ..., ..., grant of, impetration of,
alleged subreption of, 512
......, ..., ..., Kilconierin chapel to be united
to, 234
......, ..., ..., canonry and prebend annexed
to, 512
......, ..., ..., Kiltullagh vicarage ?to be
severed from, 16
......, ..., archdeacons of *see* de Burgo,
William; OBrogy, William; OFahy,
Dermot; OKelly, John

......, **diocese** of, persons of *see* de Burgo,
Thomas and Walter; Jeurmachan,
Henry; MacEgan, Thady; MacKeogh,
Carb(e)ricus / Cornelius; Macvaney,
Maurus; Magnay, John; Obrodear,
Morinanus; OBrogy, James of the clan
of; OBrogy, Odo; OBrogy, William
Jacobi viventis; Ocorra'chan, John;
ODempsey, William; Odulcayn,
Kynetus; OFahy, Eugene; OKelly,
Cornelius, Donat, and Malachy;

Clonfert, **diocese** (*contd*)
OMannin, Donald; Omaytin, Malachy;
OMulkerrill, Charles; Yolei, John
......, ..., places in *see* [Abbeygormacan];
Aughrim; Ballynakill; Clontuskert;
Creagh; Donanaghta; Duniry; Fahy;
Fohanagh; Kilconierin; Kilmalinoge;
Kiltullagh; Loughrea; 'Ycluelin'; *and
see* 'Arodmuneach'; 'Bearnduamlegynd';
'Bruachtalach'; 'Glochmor';
'Gortnuybg''; 'Gortuaglothbg'';
'?Goven';*Muinter Chineith;* 'Syliam'

Clonloghan (Cloynlocayn, Cloynlokayn)
[co. Clare], parish church of, vicarage
of, to be united to proposed canonry
and prebend of Quin in Killaloe
cathedral, 313
......, ..., ..., to be united to canonry of
Limerick and prebend of Donaghmore,
652

Clonmacnois (*Cluanen.*; often, erroneously,
Clonen. [Cloyne]) [co. Offaly],
[cathedral] church of, deanery of,
proposed union to, of Ballyloughloe
vicarage, 226
......, ..., deans of *see* Mathoblayn, Eugene;
Omilaolayn, Terence
......, ..., canons of *see* ODollaghan, John;
ODoorley, James; Offuyra, William;
OMullan, Cristinus
......, ..., prebends (unnamed) in, 228

......, **diocese** of, persons of *see* Obresel,
Dermot; Omilaolayn, Terence;
......, ..., places in *see* Ballyloughloe;
Gallen
......, *and see* ?Clonmacnois

?Clonmacnois (*Clonen.* [Cloyne] *recte
Cluanen.*?) [co. Offaly], **[cathedral]
church** of, dean of, papal mandatary,
146
......, ..., statutes and customs of, *cf.* 228
......, official of, papal mandatary, 228

?Clonmacnois (*contd*)
......, church of, statutes and customs of, 228
......, ..., archdeaconry of, 228
......, ..., archdeacons of *see* MacEgan,
Fergal; Offuyra, William

Clonoulty (Cloynhawlii) [co. Tipperary],
Hospitaller house of, preceptorship of,
938
......, ..., preceptors of *see* ODwyer,
Redmundus and Thomas

Clonrush (Clonre[u]s, Clonroy[s]) [co.
Galway], parish church of, vicarage of,
650, 933
......, ..., ..., to be united to canonry of
Killaloe and prebend of Tulla, 650
......, ..., ..., to be united to canonry of
Kilmacduagh and prebend of Kinvarra,
933

Clontonpuyr *see Clann conchobair*

Clontuskert (Contoscyardomane) [co.
Galway], [Augustinian] monastery of,
prior of, papal mandatary, 819
......, ..., canon of *see* Odulcayn, Kynetus

[Cloon Island *in* Stradbally, *q.v.*]

Clopton (Clopton') [*or* Clapton *now part* of
Croydon cum Clapton, Cambs], parish
church of, 701

[Clounclieffe *in* Stradbally, *q.v.*]

Clovelly [Devon], parish church of, 796

Cloymcoma(r)tha *see Cluain Comarda*

'Cloynacheke', alias of Stradbally, *q.v.*

Cloyne (*Clonen.*) [co. Cork], **[cathedral]
church** of, dean of, papal mandatary,
650
......, ..., treasurer of, papal mandatary, 156

Cloyne, **[cathedral] church** (*contd*)

......, ..., chapter of, to be summoned over erection of canonry and prebend, 15, 160, 541, 823

......, ..., ..., ..., anew, 1000

......, ..., ..., consent of, to bishop's erection of prebend and union thereto, 1000

......, ..., canons of *see* Canton, Leonard; Condon, John; de Geraldinis, John, Richard, Richard Giraldi Willelmi; Hanlon, William; MacAuliffe, Donat; MacCarthy, Felmicus; Magner, Edmund; OBrogy, William; Odorna, Dermot; ODowney, John; Ogiellyry, Thomas; OHerlihy, John; Okwym, William; OLongan, Maurice; OMurphy, Cornelius, Donat, Edmund, and Philip; Power, John; Roche, Peter; White, Philip

......, ..., prebends in *see* Aghinagh; Ballyvourney; Cooliney; 'Ferrebiythi'; Kilmacdonogh; Macroom; Templevalley

......, **bishop** of, erection of prebend by, with union thereto, 1000

......, ..., collation by, of canonry and prebend with annex, 1000

......, ..., to be summoned over erection of canonry and prebend, 15, 160, 541, 823

......, ..., ..., anew, 1000

......, ..., papal mandatary, 824

......, **diocese** of, persons of *see* Barry, Elisabeth and Thomas; Bennett, John and Richard; [Cant], Patrick; Fitzgibbon, Edmund; Fleming, Philip; de Geraldinis, James Radmundi Mauritii; de Geraldinis, John Edemundi; [de Geraldinis?], John Odoni[s]; Hanlon, Philip; Magner, David; Myninayn, Thady; OConnor, Donald; OCronin, Donat; Offaeyn, Thomas; OFlynn, Donat; OHennessy, Donat; OHerlihy, Donat and John the elder; OMurphy, Thady; ONoonan,

Cloyne, **diocese** (*contd*)

John and Thady; OScully, John; OSheehan, Dermot; Os..ayn, Davit;

......, ..., places in *see* Aghinagh; Ballybeg; Ballyhay; Ballyvourney; Bridgetown; *Cluain Comarda* [*now* ?Colmanswell]; Derryvillane; Fermoy; 'Ferrebiythi'; Inch; Kildorrery; Kilshannig; Macroom; Midleton; Templevalley [*in* Mogeely]; Tullylease; Youghal

......, *and see* Cork (and Cloyne); *and see under* Clonmacnois *and* ?Clonmacnois

Cloynhawlii *see* Clonoulty

Cloynlocayn, Cloynlokayn *see* Clonloghan

Cluain Comarda (Cloymcoma(r)tha) [*now* ?Colmanswell, co. Limerick], parish church of, vicarage of, to be erected into canonry and prebend of Limerick, with vicarage of ?Ballycahane united thereto, 942

Cluanbectii *see* Clonbern

Cluny [Saône-et-Loire], monastery of, abbot and convent of, commends of Cluniac benefices void without consent of, 138

Clyderowe *see* Clitherow

Clyff *see* Cliff

Clynton, Clyntown' *see* Clinton

Cobaldi, Thomas, vicar of Staverton, 803

Cobbald *cf.* Cobaldi

Cobbe, William, of Norwich diocese, dispensed for plurality, 1302

Cobham (Cobh(a)m) [Kent], college of, 271

Cockburn (Cokburn', Toliburnem, Toliburnen', Tuliburnen'), Adam, nobleman, lord of Skirling, 366
......, ..., ..., ..., patron of the chaplaincy at the altar of B. Mary the Virgin in Haddington parish church, consent of, 366
......, Alexander, chaplaincy at the altar of B. Mary the Virgin in Haddington parish church founded by, 366
......, Edward, rector of the hospital of Duns, death of in the Roman curia, 130
......, John, chaplain at the altar of B. Mary the Virgin in Haddington parish church, 366
......, ..., ..., grant of land belonging to chaplaincy by, 366
......, Richard, layman of St Andrews diocese, grant to, of land called 'Herperseldi', 366

Cocke, John, rector of Norton, 667

[Codenham alias Bunting], William, abbot of the Benedictine monastery of Bury St Edmunds, 1175, 1176

Cok see Cook

Cokburn' see Cockburn

Coke (Cooki), Thomas, commissary of John [Morton], cardinal legate, litigation before, 29
......, ..., death of, 29
......, and see Cook(e)

Cokefford see Coxford

Coker, West (Westcoker) [Som], parish church of, rector of, 77

Colchester [Essex], [Augustinian] priory of St Botolph, prior of, papal judge delegate, 8

Colchester (contd)
......, ..., prior of see Stampe, John
......, parish church of St Leonard of the New Hithe, 215
......, archdeacon of in the church of London, q.v.

Coldingham [co. Berwick], Benedictine priory of, 535
......, ..., fruits of, assignment of half of in place of pension, 535
......, ..., prior of, papal judge delegate, 80
......, ..., ..., see Home, John and Ninian
......, ..., monk of see Home, John

Cole, John, rector of Partney, 673

Coll (Ocolla), Thomas, priest of Elphin diocese, detainer of vicarage of Tumna, 947

Collécchio (Colliculo) [in province of Parma, Italy], church of St Prosper of, archpriest of, papal mandatary, 68, 844

?Collieston (Caterstonn') [in Slains, co. Aberdeen], tithes of, 928

Collingham, North (Northeolynghin) [Notts], parish church of, union of, to the Benedictine monastery of Peterborough, 425
......, ..., vicar of, portion for, 425

Collins cf. Colyns, OCullane

Collocius see Colotius

[Colman, co. Tipperary], place in see ?Mocklerstown
......, and see ?Colman

?Colman (Coloram alias Kystye) [co. Tipperary], parish church of, vicarage of, to be united to canonry of Cashel and prebend of ?Mocklerstown, 786

?Colman (*contd*)
......, *and see* Colman

Colman, Robert, monk of the Benedictine monastery of St Mary, Coventry, 133

?Colmanswell, co. Limerick *see Cluain Comarda*

Coloram *alias* Kystye *see* ?Colman

Colotius, Angelus, *abbreviator de parco maiori*, letters expedited by:
A. *Colotius* , 840 (*A. de Colotius*), 913 (*A. Collocius*), 931, 937, 1003 (*A Collocius*)
......, ..., *magister registri,*correction of register ordered by regent of chancery done by, 111 *note*

Colp (Colpe) [co. Meath], parish church of, united to Augustinian monastery of Lanthony II by Gloucester, 442
......, ..., vicar of, exempt from payment to bishop of Meath, 442
......, grange of, likewise united, 442

[Colquhoun], Robert, bishop of Lismore, death of, 55

Coluge, Richard, master of the Augustinian hospital of St John the Baptist, Redcliff, [Bristol], 396

Columpton' *see* Cullompton

Colvend [co. Kirkcudbright] *see* Southwick

Colvil, Alexander, cleric of St Andrews diocese, 66

Colyn *see* Cullen

Colyns, Martin, cleric of York diocese, counsellor of Henry [VII], 117
......, ..., official and commissary general of

Colyns (*contd*)
Thomas [Rotherham], archbishop of York and legate, litigation before, 94
......, ..., ..., ..., commissary of *see* Metcalfe, Thomas
......, alias of Twyforth, John, *q.v.*
......, *cf.* Collins

Colȝony, Andrew, of St Andrews diocese, appeal of, 971

Combe, Humphrey, vicar of St Nicholas, Carisbrooke Castle, 970
......, William, of Bath and Wells diocese, dispensed for plurality, 1240

Combe St Nicholas (Cumba) [Som], parish church of, 214

Combwell (Combuell) [*in* Goudhurst, Kent], Augustinian priory of, 899
......, ..., canon of *see* Goodwyn, William

Comerford (Conmerforth), Edmund, dean of Ossory, 575, 645
......, ..., ..., to be vicar of Callan *alias* Kilbride and have priorship of the Augustinian monastery of St John the Evangelist near Kilkenny *in commendam*, 575
......, ..., chaplain, 645
......, ..., son of *see* Comerford, William
......, William, cleric of Ossory diocese, 645
......, ..., ..., to be canon of Ossory and have rectory of Coolcraheen erected into prebend, 645
......, ..., ..., father of *see* [Comerford, Edmund]

Compostella *see* Santiago de Compostela

Compton Dundon (Compton ?Ducudien') [Som], prebend of in Wells cathedral, union to, of the vicarage of Ipplepen, 1003

Condon (Condum), John, canon of Ross,

Condon (*contd*)
  papal mandatary, 252, 255
......, ..., canon of Cloyne, papal mandatary,
  542
....., *cf.* Canton

Conell', alias of Peston, Gilbert, *q.v.*

Conesgrave *see* Cosgrove

Cong [co. Mayo], Augustinian monastery
  of, subjection of, to the archbishop of
  Tuam, 127
......, ..., abbot of, papal mandatary, 826,
  827
......, ..., ..., *see* de Burgo, Richard and
  Thomas
......, ..., convent of, 127
......, ..., canon of *see* de Burgo, Thomas
......, ..., vassals of, 127

Conington (Conyngton') [Hunts], parish
  church of, 17

Conmerforth *see* Comerford

Connayl *see* Greatconnell

[Connesburgh], Edmund, [bishop-] elect of
  Chalcedon, to retain regular priory in
  Norwich diocese, 1323

Connor [co. Antrim], **[cathedral] church**
  of, canons of *see* Ochill', Odo;
  Ogyllamyr, Maurice
......, **diocese** of, persons of *see* Magonuayl,
  [Magonius]; Obeolen', John; Ocaeley,
  Odo; Oduyll', Eugene
......, ..., places in *see* Carrickfergus;
  Muckamore; Rasharkin; Woodburn

Constable (Cunstable), Thomas, of York
  diocese, dispensed for plurality, 1219

Constance [Germany], letters dated at, 174

Contoscyardomane *see* Clontuskert

Convecth *see* Conveth

Co(n)ventre, ?Conventre *see* Coventry *and*
  under (Coventry and) Lichfield

Conveth (Convecth) [*now* Laurencekirk,
  co. Kincardine], parish church of, rector
  of, 792

Convvnde' *see* Cowden

Conyngton' *see* Conington

Cook (Cok), Edmund, portioner of
  Bradfield, 414
......, John, priest of Ely diocese, to have
  vicarage of Bottisham and rectory of
  Wymondham anew, 386
......, Richard, of York diocese, dispensed
  for plurality, 1251
......, *and see* Coke

Cooke, Robert, of York diocese, 315
......, *and see* Coke

Cooki *see* Coke

Coola (Culdea) [*in* Ballynakill, co. Sligo],
  parish church of, vicarage of, 846, 995
......, ..., ..., to be united to
  Premonstratensian monastery of Lough
  Key, 846, 995
......, ..., ..., simoniacal union of, to Lough
  Key, 846

Coolcraheen (Culcrahyn) [co. Kilkenny],
  parish church of, rectory of, to be
  erected into prebend in Ossory
  cathedral, 645

[Coolderry *in* Creagh, co. Roscommon] *see*
  Muinter Chineith

Cooliney (Culheay) [co. Cork], prebend of in Cloyne cathedral, 514

......, ..., vicarage of Ballyhay to be united to, 514

Copping, John, vicar of Tannington, 25

Coppinger (Copyner), Philip, detainer of vicarage of Kinsale, 362

[Corbally, co. Tipperary], place in *see* Monaincha

Corbally (Corvaly) [co. Waterford], prebend of in Waterford cathedral, 543

Corby [Lincs], parish church of, 345

Cordova [*in* Cordova province, Spain], city of, licence to build Cistercian nunnery of St Mary *de populo* in or outside, 779

......, person of *see* [?FitzJohn], Francis

Coren, Robert, vicar of Billesdon, 894

Corfe (Corffe) [Som], [chapel of], 174

Cork [co. Cork], [Augustinian] monastery of B. Mary [i.e. Gill Abbey], abbot of, papal commissary and mandatary, 816

......, ..., ..., papal mandatary, 15, 71, 257, 541, 822, 823, 825

......, St Finbar's church outside the walls of, disrepair of, 816

......, ..., fabric of, administrators of *see* [FitzGerald], Gerald; MacCarthy, Donat

Cork (and Cloyne), [cathedral] church of, deanery of, 258

......, ..., dean of, papal mandatary, 231

......, ..., ..., *see* MacCarthy, Thady; OHerlihy, John; OMahoney, Matthew

......, ..., chancellor of, papal mandatary, 541

......, ..., chapter of, to be summoned over erection of canonry and prebend, 71, 255

Cork (and Cloyne), [cathedral] church (*contd*)

......, united [cathedral] churches of, chapters of, conclusions to, 610, 612

......, [cathedral] church of, canons of *see* Bennett, John; Dermitii, John; ?Giulus, Philip; MacCarthy, Cormac, Donat and Thady; Makterrelaigh, John; OCronin, William; OHerlihy, John; OMahony, Dermot; Omanna', John; OMurilly, John and Renaldus; OMurphy, Donald, Edmund, and Thady; OSullivan, Eugene; Ykayllis, Nicholas

......, ..., prebends in, 254

......, ..., ..., *see* Dromdaleague *or* Drimoleague; Gortnacrusha; Inishkenny; Kilbrogan; Ringcurran

......, **bishop** of, subjection to, of Cistercian monastery of Tracton, 536

......, ..., to be summoned over erection of canonry and prebend, 71, 255

......, ..., *see* [Cant], Patrick; [FitzGerald], Gerald or Gerard; de Geraldinis, John Edemundi; [Purcell], Jordan

......, united churches of, subjection of, to the archbishop of Cashel, 613

......, ..., vassals of, conclusion to, 610

......, church of, archdeaconry of, 539

......, ..., ..., to be united to canonry and prebend of Inishkenny, 822

......, ..., archdeacons of *see* Barry, James; de Geraldinis, John; Roche, George

......, **city(ies) and diocese(s)** of, clergy of, conclusion to, 610, 612

......, ..., peoples of, conclusion to, 610

......, diocese of, persons of *see* Barry, Edmund and John;Coppinger, Philip; de Courcy, Edmund and John; Mackellay, Donat; Oeromyn, David and Denis; Offyllyg, Donat; OHerlihy, John the elder; OLeary, Dermot and Matthew; OMahony, David; OMongan, Donat; OMurphy, Cornelius; ORegan, Runaldus; OScanlan, Cornelius; Roche, William

Cork (and Cloyne), **city(ies) and diocese(s)** (*contd*)
......, ..., places in *see* Ballymoney; ?Ballymountain [*in* Inishannon]; Brinny; Burren; Cork; Corrsruhara; Desertserges; Fermoy; Garrynoe; Gortnacrusha [*in* Templetrine]; Inishannon; Kilmoney; Kinsale; Leighmoney; Rathclarin; Ringcurran; ?Ringrone; Schull *or* Skull; Templetrine; Tracton
......, *and see* Cloyne

[Cork, co. of], places in *see* Abbeymahon; Aghinagh; Ballybeg; Ballyhay; Ballyvourney; Bridgetown; Clear Island; Cloyne; Cooliney; Creach; Creagh; Cullen; Curragranemore; Derryvillane; Drishane; Dromdaleague *or* Drimoleague; Dromtariff; Fuhiry; Gortnaclohy; Inch; Inchydoney Island; Inishkenny; Kilbrogan; Kildorrery; ?Kilgarriff; Kilmacdonogh; Kilmeedy; Kilmeen; Kilnamanagh; Kilshannig; Macroom; Midleton; Nohaval-Daly; Ross Carbery; Templevalley [*in* Mogeely]; Tullagh; Tullylease; Youghal; *and* places *listed above under* Cork (and Cloyne), diocese of

Cormac, the late, abbot of Kilshanny *see* [OCahir], Cormac

Cormootin *see* ?Ballycahane

Cornacrusi *see* Gortnacrusha

Corndean (Cornedenia) [*in* Winchcombe, Glos], manor of, 394:[18], [22]

Corneto [*now* Tarquinia, province of Viterbo, Italy], letters dated at, 780
......, cleric of *see* Castellesi, Hadrian

[Cornish], Thomas, bishop of Tinos, holder of the vicarage of Ipplepen and the

[Cornish] (*contd*)
canonry and prebend of Compton Dundon in Wells cathedral, 1003

Cornwall (*Carumbia*), places stated to be in, 147, 216, 288, 1100
......, county of, places stated to be in, 753, 762

[Cornwall, co. of], places in *see* Bodmin; Cuby; Glasney; Gwennap; Helland; Illogan; Minster; Penryn; Probus; St Carrok; St Erme; St Germans; St Gluvias; St Neot; St Tudy; St Veep; Stratton; Talcarne; Tregony

Corrsruhara [*now* Ballymoney, co. Cork], parish church of, vicarage of, to be united to canonry and prebend of Cork, 254

Corston (Coston') [Som], parish church of, 21

Cortesora [*in* commune and province of Lucca, Italy], hospital of St Michael of, 951

Corttis, Laurence, vicar of Fincham [*probably* St Martin's], 677

Corvaly *see* Corbally

Cosgrove (Conesgrave) [Northants], parish church of, 112

Coston' *see* Corston

[Cosyn, William] *cf.* N. [= *nomen* ? (Cosyn?)], William
Cosyn *see* Cussen; *cf.* Cousin

Cotell, John, brother of the house of the Bonshommes, Edington, 186

Cotesbach (Cottysbech) [Leics], parish

Cotesbach (*contd*)
church of, 497

Cotigham *see* Cottingham

Cotrone (*Cotronen'*) [*now* Crotone,
province of Catanzaro, Italy], bishop of
see [de Valle], A[ndreas]

Cottingham (Cotigham, Totincȝhanen)
[Yorks], parish church of, rectory of,
632, 698
......, ..., commendator of *see* [Forman],
Andrew

Cotton (Cotton'), Walter, rector of Glatton,
477

Cottysbech *see* Cotesbach

de Courcy (Cursy), Edmund, priest of Cork
diocese, to have vicarage of Kinsale,
362
......, John, detainer, with Donat OMongan,
of the church of ?Ballymountain, 255

[?Courtenay], William, the late, bishop of
London, constitution published by, 365

Cousin *cf.* Cosyn

Coutances [*in dép.* of La Manche, France],
diocese of, places in *see* Cherbourg;
Lihou, Guernesey; St Helier, Jersey

Coutts (Cowits), Alan, of St Andrews
diocese, appeal of, 971

Couuanni, William, of Exeter diocese,
indulged for non-residence, 1172

Coventry (Co(n)ventre) [Warw],
Benedictine monastery of St Mary, 867
......, ..., monks of *see* Colman, Robert;
Warde, John
......, church of the Holy Trinity, 506

Coventry (*contd*)
......, ..., Percy chantry in, 506
......, parish church of St Michael, 496, 715
......, ..., chaplain in, 496
......, ..., chantry of Hugh Merinton in, 496,
715
......, archdeaconry of *see below under*
Coventry and Lichfield

(Coventry and) Lichfield, **[cathedral]**
church of [*at* Lichfield, Staffs],
precentor of, papal judge delegate, 529
......, ..., treasurer of, papal judge delegate, 94
......, ..., chapter of, *sede vacante* vicars or
officials of *see* Agard, Philip; Salter,
Richard
......, united [cathedral] churches of,
chapters of, conclusion to, 1029
......, [cathedral] church of, canon of *see*
Wyllesford, Edmund; *and see* Jonys,
William
......, ..., prebend in *see* Wolvey

......, **bishop** of, jurisdiction of, exemption
from, 529
......, bishop (or his vicar general) of,
devolution upon, of collation of
chaplains to Bradburn chantry in
Ashbourne parish church and
?Hognaston chapel, 292
......, bishop of, as local ordinary,
presentation to by patron of person for
parish church, *cf.* 556
......, bishop (named) of, official or
commissary of *see* Veysey *alias*
Harman, John
......, bishop(s) of, to receive oath of fealty
in pope's name, 625-628, 1021, 1023
......, ..., papal judge delegate, 456
......, ..., *see* [Arundel], John; [Blythe],
Geoffrey; [Hales], John; [Smith],
William
......, united churches of, subjection of, to
the archbishop of Canterbury, 1031
......, ..., vassals of, conclusion to, 1029
......, church of, archdeaconry of Coventry

(Coventry and) Lichfield, **bishop** (*contd*) (?Conventre) in, holder of, 143

......, ..., archdeacon of Coventry in *see* Strangways, George

......, ..., archdeacon of Salop in *see under* Shropshire

......, ..., archdeaconry of Stafford in, 434

......, ..., archdeacons of Stafford in *see* Wardroper, John; Willoughby, Edward

......, **cities and dioceses** of, clergy of, conclusion to, 1029

......, ..., people of, conclusion to, 1029

......, dioceses of, keepers in spirituals of *see* Agard, Philip; Salter.Richard

......, diocese of, persons of *see* Ardern', Robert; Babyngton', Raphael; Blokelay, Richard; Bradburn, John, and wife Ann; Brereton, Thomas; ?Brereton, John; Bulkeley, Richard; [Clerke], Thomas; Clitherow, John; Colman, Robert; Dore, Robert; Eliston', Robert; Fitz Herbert, Thomas; Fowler, John; Fydkoc, Henry; Gerard, John; de' Gigli, John; Grafton, Adam; Gresley, John; Gybbons, William; Harper, Cornelius; Howell, Thomas; Lauton, John; Longforth, Henry; Meynoryng, John; Middleton, William; Nabbos, John; Orton, Thomas; Perrins, Robert; [?Pontisbury], Richard; Potter, Laurence; Reeper, John; Rolleston, Richard; Roode, Andrew; Scott, Edward; Smyth *alias* Gogh, John; Stanley, Humphrey and James; Stubbs, John; de Surteys, Stephen; Vernon, Roger; Vronon, George; Vuolsauve, Humphrey; Warde, John; Wellys, John; Whynby, Thomas; Wolford, William; Wright, John; [*unknown*], John, abbot of Merevale; *and see* Knott, Richard; Richardson, Robert

......, ..., places in *see* Ashbourne; Astbury; Birkenhead; Bradley; Bridgnorth; Bromley, Abbots; Bury; Carsington; Cheadle; Chester; ?Chesterfield;

(Coventry and) Lichfield, **cities and dioceses** (*contd*) Christleton; Churchover; Coventry; Croxden; Eaton, Church; Edgmond; ?Hallewynsm'; Haughmond; ?Hognaston; Kinver; Longford; Merevale; Ridware, Hamstall; Ridware, Mavesyn; Rostherne; Sandbach; Scarsdale; Shrewsbury; Sutton Coldfield; Upton Magna; Walsall; Walton; Warmingham; Weston-on-Trent; Whalley; Wingfield, North; Winwick; Wistaston; *and see* Church Stretton

Coventry, William, rector of Manningford, 869

Cowden (Convvnde') [Kent], parish church of, 507

Cowits *see* Coutts

Cowley, Thomas, rector of Poulshot, 98

Cowper (Cowp(er)), Edmund, rector of Pebmarsh, 810

......, William, rector of Droitwich, 759

Coxford (Cokefford) [*in* East Rudham, Norf], Augustinian priory of, 48

......, ..., prior of *see* Mileham, Henry

Cradoc, John, rector of Henllan-Amgoed, 725

Craenach, Andrew, rector of the parish church [of St Michael?] and of the leper hospital of St Laurence outside the walls of Limerick, 815

......, ..., canon of Limerick and prebendary of the parish church [of St Michael?], 815

......, ..., to have vicarage of the parish church of St Michael outside the walls of Limerick united to his canonry and prebend, 815

......, *cf.* Creagh

Crafford, Robert, vicar of Moreton, 474

Craghed *see* ?Craigheid

Cragyn' *see* Craigie

Craig (Traig) [*now represented by* Old Craig and West Craig *in* Udny, co. Aberdeen], tithes of, 928

?Craigheid (Craghed, Eraghed, Trehed) [*probably now obsolete*; *in* the old barony of Esslemont, *in* Ellon parish, co. Aberdeen], tithes of pertaining to Ellon parish church, 144, 793, 928

Craigie (Cragyn') [co. Ayr], church of, fruits of pertaining to Cluniac monastery of Paisley, 63
......, ..., ..., grant of, 63

Craigton (Crrigtone) [*in* Auchtertool, co. Fife], lands of pertaining to episcopal *mensa* of Dunkeld, lease of, 558

Crakyntroppe, Edward, rector of Musgrave, 960

Crampscastle, *once* Crumpstown, *q.v.*

Cranchurst *see* Crowhurst

Cranfurd *see* Crawford

Cranshaws [co. Berwick], [parish church of], 781

Cranston, Gilbert, collation to, of the vicarage of Inverurie, 444
......, ..., assent of to payment of pension on fruits of vicarage, 444
......, ..., proctor of *see* Turnbull, William
......, Thomas, abbot of the Augustinian monastery of Jedburgh, death of, 1009

Craste *see* Croft

Crawford (Cranfurd, Craufurd(e)), John, earl of *see* [Lindsay], John
......, ..., prior of the Augustinian priory of St Mary's Isle, to be deprived for alleged misdeeds, 509
......, William, canon of the Augustinian monastery of Holyrood and vicar of Falkirk, faculty to bequeath and make disposition of goods and fruits for, 443
......, ..., canon of the Augustinian monastery of Holyrood, to be prior of the Augustinian priory of St Mary's Isle, 509
......, ..., tithes of monastery in St Andrews diocese reserved for, 1255

Creagh (Criach, Cribach) [co. Cork], prebend of in Ross cathedral, 251
......, ..., vicarage and rectory of Tullagh to be united to, 251
......, parish church of, vicarage of, to be united to prebend of Kilnamanagh in Ross cathedral, 70
......, *and see* Creagh and Gortnaclohy

Creagh (Crybach) [co. Cork] and Gortnaclohy (Gornaclohy) [*in* Creagh, co. Cork], parish church of, rectory of, to be united to canonry of Ross and prebend of Clear Island, 129

Creagh (Oryac *alias* Suchyhyn) [co. Roscommon], parish church of, vicarage of, 819
......, places in *see* Coolderry; Culliaghbeg; Gortnasharvoge

Creagh (Cryagh), Andrew, canon of Limerick, papal mandatary, 380
......, David, archbishop of Cashel, 221, 998
......, ..., ..., vicarages of Ballysheehan, ?Erry, Railstown, and Crumpstown united to archiepiscopal *mensa* for as

Creagh (*contd*)

long as he is archbishop, 998

......, ..., ..., commendatory minister of the Trinitarian house of Adare, to be removed, 221

......, ..., ..., ..., appeal of, 221

......, *cf.* Craenach

Creithone', Creithonen *see* Crichton

Creithton *see* Crichton, co. Midlothian

[Crendon, Long, Bucks], place in *see* Notley

[Crete, island of], place in *see* Agia

Crethoun *see* Crichton

Criach, Cribach *see* Creagh

Crichton (Creithton) [co. Midlothian], [collegiate] church of, provost of *see* Halkerston, Thomas

Crichton (Creithone', Creithonen, Crethoun), George, abbot of the Benedictine monastery of Dunfermline, 584-586, 588

......, ..., ..., provision of, to the Augustinian monastery of Holyrood, 584, 587

......, ..., ..., absolution of preliminary to provision, 586

......, ..., ..., to take oath of fealty, 584

......, ..., ..., ..., commission over, 587

......, ..., abbot of Holyrood, 585, 588

......, James, knight, the late, 86

......, ..., ..., ..., wife of *see* Semple, Margaret

......, ..., ..., ..., son of *see* Crichton, James, of Cairns

......, ..., of Cairns, nobleman, knight, litigant, 86

......, ..., father of *see* Crichton, James

......, ..., of Dunkeld diocese, commission

Crichton (*contd*)

[by virtue of an appeal?], 1307

......, *cf.* Cicheton, Gechton', Trechton'

Crieff [co. Perth], prebend of in Dunkeld, fruits of, appropriation of residue of to chapel royal, Stirling, 768

Cristilton *see* Christleton

Croft (Craste) [*probably* Lincs, *possibly* Leics], parish church of, vicarage of, union of, to the canonry and prebend of Leicester St Margaret in Lincoln cathedral, 749

Crokysden' *see* Croxden

Cromarty (Cromache, Cromathy) [co. Ross and Cromarty], church of, tithes of belonging to deanery of Ross, 782, 840

[Cromarty, co. of] *see* [Ross and Cromarty]

Cromhall (Cromehale) [Glos], parish church of, 433

Cropredy (Cropperedy) [Oxon], prebend of in Lincoln cathedral, union to, of the parish church of Aldingham, 752

Crosby, John, the late, layman of London diocese, 924

......, ..., ..., will of, executrix of *see* Marowte, Joan

......, ..., ..., ..., executor of *see* Arrowsmith, William

Crosley, Christopher, vicar of Sutterton, 720

[Crossboyne, co. Mayo], place in *see* Kilcurnan

Crosserlough *see* Kildrumferton

Croston *see* Croxton

Crouulandi, alias of Garford, Thomas, *q.v.*

Crowhurst (Cranchurst) [Sussex], parish church of, 172

Croxden (Crokysden') [Staffs], Cistercian monastery of, 468
......, ..., monk of *see* Clitherow, John

Croxton (Croxton', Croyston) [*in* Croxton Keyrial, Leics], Premonstratensian monastery of, abbot of, papal judge delegate, 46
......, ..., ..., *see* [Attercliff], Elias

Croxton (Croston) [Norf], parish church of, 277

Croydon cum Clapton *see* Clopton

Croyston *see* Croxton

Crrigtone *see* Craigton

Crumpstown (Trompostan') [*now* Crampscastle *in* Peppardstown, co. Tipperary], church of, vicarage of, union of, to the archiepiscopal *mensa* of Cashel, 998

Cryagh *see* Creagh

Crybach *see* Creagh, co. Cork

Cryppyng, Thomas, of Norwich diocese, dispensed for plurality, 1086

'Cuacaynde' *alias* 'Clacerogarde', diocese of Kilmore [*unidentified*], church, called plebs, of, rectory of, 831

Cuby (St Cuby) [*now* Tregony with St Cuby, Corn], vicarage of, union of, to the parish church of St Tudy, 753

Culcrahyn *see* Coolcraheen

Culdea *see* Coola

Culheay *see* Cooliney

Cullen (Colyn) [*in* Duhallow barony, co. Cork], parish church of, vicarage of, 359
......, ..., ..., vicarage of Nohaval-Daly to be united to, 359

[Culliaghbeg *in* Creagh, co. Roscommon] *see Muinter Chineith*

Cullompton (Columpton') [Devon], parish church of, 262

Cully *see* Coll

Culmoneayn *see* Kilmoney

Culmyngtowe *alias* Culmyngton' *see* Kilmington

Culross, William, election and appointment of, as abbot of the Cistercian monastery of Kinloss, 144
......, ..., monk, recently abbot, of Kinloss, 155
......, ..., ..., ..., ..., cession of, 155
......, ..., ..., ..., ..., assignment to, of pension on fruits of abbatial *mensa* of Kinloss and vill of Hatton, 155
......, ..., the late, abbot of Kinloss, 928
......, ..., ..., ..., consent of to payment of pension on fruits of Ellon parish church, 928

Cumba *see* Combe St Nicholas

Cumba, Baldwin de, property gifted to Taunton priory by, 174

[Cumberland, co. of], places in *see* Carlisle; Plumbland

Cumberton, William, rector of Rushall, 878

?Cumbray (Cumray) [islands of Great and Little Cumbray, co. Bute], church of, fruits of pertaining to Cluniac monastery of Paisley, grant of, 63

Cunningham (Cuunyglan'), David, official of Glasgow, 86
......, ..., ..., commissary of *see* Knox, James

Cunthy *see* Quin

Curcheoner *see* Churchover

Curleus, Nicholas, chaplain in London cathedral, 518

Curll, Henry, rector of Yelverton, 770

?Curragh [*in* Killeshin, co. Laois], parish church of, vicarage of, to be united to proposed canonry of Leighlin and prebend of ?Killeen, 982

Curragranemore (Cirrogayn) [*in* Desert, co. Cork], prebend of in Ross cathedral, vicarages of Inchydoney Island and ?Kilgarriff to be united to, 256

[Curry Rivel, Som], place in *see* ?Westmoor

Curstrahura *see* Corrsruhara

Cursy *see* de Courcy

Cussen (Cosyn, Cusin, Cusyn), John, brother of the Augustinian hospital of the *Cruciferi Sancti Johannis cum stella* at Newtown Trim, 416
......, ..., ..., visits Rome and England, 416
......, ..., ..., repeated apostasy of, 416
......, Walter, canon of Tuam, papal

Cussen (*contd*)
mandatary, 828
......, ..., detainer of vicarage of St Gerald, Mayo, 402

Cutfolde (Gutfold'), Thomas, rector of Georgeham, 40

Cutler, John, canon [of Lincoln] and prebendary of Leicester St Margaret, incumbent of Croft, 749

Cuttler (Cuttelar), John, of Durham diocese, dispensed for plurality, 1166

Cuunyglan' *see* Cunningham

Cuxham [Oxon], parish church of, 858

[*Cydonien. see* Kydonia]

Cyllbarrayn *see* Kilbarron

Cyllcayrayld *see* ? *Cell cairill*

Cyllomaird, Cyllomardi *see* Killymard

C3akenden *see* Checkendon

D

Dagget, Thomas, rector of Burnham Deepdale, 328

Dalison, Thomas, rector of Brendon, 653
......, *cf.* Dalyson

Dalmilling [*in* ?St Quivox, co. Ayr], place of, lordship or territory of, lands etc. pertaining to Cluniac monastery of Paisley in, grant of, 63

Dalton, William, scholar of York diocese, 458

Dalyson *cf.* Dalison

Dambury *see* Danbury

Damian, John *see* [de Falcutiis *or* Falcariis], Damianus

Damiani, Bernardino, registry scribe, 174 *note*, 483 *note*

Damianus de Cesena *see* [de Falcutiis *or* Falcariis], Damianus

Dampeyr, Richard, vicar of Combe St Nicholas, 214

Danbury (Dambury) [Essex], parish church of, 387, 528
......, ..., chaplain in *see* Witt, John
......, ..., cleric in *see* Gunby, Thomas
......, ..., Wyses chantry in, 528
......, ..., chantry of ?the chalice in, 387

Daniell (Danyell'), William, rector of Clovelly, 796

Darby (Derby), Edward, rector of Little Rissington, 806

Darcy, Thomas, rector of Mansfieldstown, 901

Darcy (Dareyes), chantry of, in All Saints', Maldon, 519

Darlington (Dericton) [Durh], [collegiate] church of, canonry and prebend of, union to, of the parish church of Edgmond, 1038
......, ..., canon and prebendary of *see* Veysey *alias* Harman, John

David, Maurice, vicar of Whitchurch and chaplain in St David's cathedral, 320
......, Philip, of Salisbury diocese, dispensed for plurality, 1061

David [ab Iorwerth], abbot of the Cistercian monastery of Valle Crucis, 594, 596, 597
......, ..., provision of, to the bishopric of St Asaph, 594

David [ab Iorwerth] (*contd*)
......, ..., absolution of preliminary to provision, 597
......, [bishop-] elect of St Asaph, faculty for consecration of, 595
......, ..., to retain Valle Crucis and St Peter's, Ruthin *in commendam* , 596

David, abbot of Cambuskenneth *see* [Arnot], David
......, archbishop of Cashel *see* [Creagh], David
......, [bishop-] elect of Lismore *see* [Hamilton], David
......, [bishop-] elect of St Asaph *see* David [ab Iorwerth]

Davy, Thomas, of Lincoln diocese, dispensed for plurality, 1264
......, ..., prebendary of Blewbury in Salisbury cathedral and incumbent of Sutton, 91

[Deacon], Michael, bishop of St Asaph, death of, 594

Dean, East (Estden') [West Sussex], parish church of, rector of, 661
......, ..., ..., boundary of, fields within *see* 'Chestfelden''; 'Estgaston''; Malecomb; 'Nodylfeld''; 'Northfelde'; 'Southgasten''; 'Wesefelde'

Dean, West (Westden') [East Sussex], parish church of, 657

Dean, West (Weseden') [West Sussex], fields of, tithes from, 661
......, ..., person of *see* John Body

[Deane], Henry, bishop of Bangor, 118, 581-583, 602
......, ..., ..., statute abolishing *gologoith* published in synod by, 118
......, ..., ..., translation of, to Salisbury, 349, 581, 582, 602
......, ..., ..., absolution of preliminary to translation, 583
......, ..., ..., to take oath of fealty, 581, 582
......, ..., ..., ..., commission over, 582
......, ..., ..., to retain Augustinian priory of

[Deane] (*contd*)
Lanthony II by Gloucester *in commendam*, 349
......, ..., bishop of Salisbury, 349, 442, 1250
......, ..., ..., commendatory prior of Lanthony II, appeal of, 442
......, ..., ..., translation of, to Canterbury, 1021, 1209
......, ..., ..., absolution of preliminary to translation, 1210
......, ..., ..., faculty for consecration of, 1211
......, ..., ..., oath of fealty of, commission over, 1212
......, ..., archbishop of Canterbury, formerly bishop of Salisbury, delivery of pallium to, 1250
......, ..., ..., primate of all England, legate born of the apostolic see, 924
......, ..., ..., ..., ..., commissary or auditor of *see* Barocis, William
......, ..., ..., conclusion to, 1021

Dearg *see* Abbeyderg

Dedworth, Robert, vicar of Milverton, 561

Deeping, West (West Deping) [Lincs], parish church of, 246

Deipatientia [!], William, monk of the Cistercian monastery of Monasteranenagh, to be provided anew as abbot, 383
......, ..., ..., formerly OFM, 383
......, ..., litigant over Monasteranenagh, 383

?Delly, John, to have simple benefice in Dunblane diocese, 1188

[Denbigh, co. of], places in *see* ?Bodfari; Llandysilio; ?Llanfarchell; Ruthin; Valle Crucis

Denh(a)m, John, rector of North Kilworth, 450

Depedale *see* Burnham Deepdale

Deptford (Depfford), alias of West Greenwich, *q.v.*

Derby, county of, place stated to be in, 292

[Derby, co. of], places in *see* Ashbourne; Carsington; ?Chesterfield; ?Hognaston; Longford; Scarsdale; Walton upon Trent; Weston-on-Trent; Wingfield, North

Derby *see* Darby

Derby, Margaret, countess of *see* [Beaufort], Margaret

Dericton *see* Darlington

Dermitii, John, canon of Cork, papal mandatary, 823, 825

Derrus, John, detainer and ostensible monk of the Benedictine monastery of St John the Evangelist outside the walls of Waterford, 227

Derry, **[cathedral] church** of [*at* Derry *or* Londonderry, co. Londonderry], dean of, papal judge delegate, 964
......, ..., chapter of, to be summoned over erection of canonry and prebend, 249; *and see* 934
......, ..., canons of *see* MacCloskey, Bernard; MacKee, Toroletus; OBoyle, Bernard and Tancred; OCarolan, Maurice and N(e)(i)llanus; Ocua, William; OHegarty, Eugene; Ohenega, William; Okinaill', Donat; OMorrissey, William; OQuilty, Laurence and Odo; Otuocayll', Donald; *and see* Maclanthlaym, Peter
......, ..., prebend in *see* Leckpatrick; *and see* Ballyshannon
......, **bishop** of, to be summoned over erection of canonry and prebend, 249; *and see* 934

......, **diocese** of, persons of *see* Macconagaland, Patrick; Machayg, John; OCahan, Donat; Oduyll', Eugene;

Derry, **diocese** (*contd*)
Ogarmilegayd, Henry; Omogan, John
......, ..., places in *see* Banagher; ?*Cell cairill* [*now* Termonamongan]; *Druim tairsigh*; Dungiven; Leckpatrick; Macosquin

[Derry *or* Londonderry, co. of], places in *see* Banagher; Derry; Dungiven; Killowen; Macosquin; Maghera

Derryvillane (Dirwylleayn) [co. Cork], parish church of, vicarage of, 941

Dersham (Dershin), William, of Norwich diocese, dispensed for plurality, 1179

[Desert, co. Cork], place in *see* Curragranemore

Desertserges (Disertsayays) [co. Cork], parish church of, vicarage of, 231
......, part of *see* Garrynoe

Desford (Dessheforde) [Leics], parish church of, 956

Deuuleyse *see* Dewlish

Deveshm' *see* Evesham

[Devon, co. of], places in *see* Alvington, West; Arlington; Bondleigh; Bovey Tracy; Brendon; Buckland; Chagford; Challacombe; Cheriton Fitzpaine; Churchstanton; Clovelly; Cullompton; Dodbrooke; Dunkeswell; Dunsford; ?Easton; Ermington; Exeter; Exminster; Georgeham; Hawkchurch; Huish; Ipplepen; ?Jacobstowe; Kenn; Kenton; Lewtrenchard; Manaton; Milton Abbot; Moreton Hampstead; Newenham; Newton Ferrers; Oakford; Parkham; Plympton; Putford, West; Roborough; Shillingford St George; Shobrooke; Staverton; Torre; Whimple; Willand; Worlington, East; Zeal Monachorum; *and see* Forde [*now* Dorset]

Dewlish (Deuuleyse) [Dors], parish church of, 82

Dewlish (*contd*)
......, *and see* Milborne St Andrew and Dewlish

Dewlych' *see* Milborne St Andrew and Dewlish

Dey, John, of Lincoln diocese, dispensed for plurality, 1056
......, ..., chantry chaplain, 51
......, Thomas, of Lincoln diocese, dispensed for plurality, 1177

Deynyarluan *see* Dungarvan

Dicheryche *see* Ditteridge

Dickson (Dikson), Thomas, rector of Idvie(s), 843

Dighton (Dighton'), Richard, vicar of Ingham, 706

Dikson *see* Dickson

Dindson, Thomas, of St Andrews diocese, appeal of, 971

'Dino', diocese of Lincoln [*unidentified* ; *probably either* Dean, Beds *or* Deene, Northants], parish church of, rector of, 334

Dirwylleayn *see* Derryvillane

Disertsayays *see* Desertserges

Disterkellay *see* Isertkelly

Ditteridge (Dicheryche) [Wilts], parish church of, 327

Doby (Dobi), Alexander, vicar of Kilmany, resignation of, 937
......, ..., ..., proctor of *see* de Bertinis, Leonard

Dobyll, Laurence, rector of South Bradon, 883

Docura, John, rector of Upminster, 897

Dodbrooke (Dodbroke) [Devon], parish church of St Thomas the Martyr, rector of, 41

Doderoffe, alias of Hungersord', Thomas, *q.v.*

Dodson *cf.* Dotson'

Dodyne (Dodyn'), Benedict, canon of Hereford, papal sub-delegate, litigation before, 8

Doget, Thomas, abbot of the Premonstratensian monastery of Leiston, 42

Dokett, Robert, rector of Chevening, 760

Donaghmore (Donaomar) [co. Limerick], prebend of in Limerick cathedral, 652
......, ..., vicarages of Killeely, Kilfintinan, Quin, Clonloghan, and Bunratty, to be united to, 652

Donaghmore (Downachinor') [co. Tipperary], parish church of, vicarage of, to be united to canonry of Cashel and prebend of ?Mocklerstown, 786

[Donaghmore, co. Wexford], place in *see* Glascarrig

Donald, abbot of Assaroe *see* [?OBoyle], Donald

Donanaghta (Dunocta) [co. Galway], parish church of, vicarage of, 513
......, ..., ..., rectory and vicarage of Kilmalinoge to be united to, 513

Donaomar *see* Donaghmore [co. Limerick]

Donderey *see* Duniry

Done, Nicholas, canon of the Augustinian monastery of St Peter, Dunstable, 571

[Donegal, co. of], places in *see* Assaroe; Inver; Killymard

Donfermilin, Donfermilyn *see* Dunfermline

Donglas *see* Douglas

Donstaple *see* Dunstable

Donyngton', Thomas, scholar of Lincoln diocese, 173

Dorchester [Oxon], Augustinian monastery of Peter and Paul the Apostles, 888
......, ..., canon of *see* Wilkes, William

Dore, Robert, chaplain in Walsall parish church, 348

[Dornoch, co. Sutherland] *see* Caithness

Dorrha (Dura) [co. Tipperary], parish church of, rectory of, to be erected into prebend in Killaloe, 230

[Dorset, co. of], places in *see* Ashmore; Broadwindsor; Burton Bradstock; Cerne; Dewlish; Hawkchurch; Marnhull; Milborne St Andrew; Puddletown; Shaftesbury; Silton; Swanage; Totnes; Upway; Worth; *and see* Forde [*formerly in* Devon]

Dotson', Laurence, vicar of Penn, 62
......, *cf.* Dodson

Douglas (de Wglas, Donglas), John, of St Andrews diocese, dispensed for plurality, 1055
......, Stephen, of St Andrews diocese, dispensed for plurality, 1147
......, William, of St Andrews diocese, dispensed for plurality, 1054

Douue *see* Dowe

Dover (Dovor') [Kent], Benedictine monastery of St Martin, *Novi Operis*, prior of *see* Ffreuill' or Norbourne, Robert
......, hospital of Maison Dieu, OSA, called of those marked with a Cross, 7
......, ..., ..., ..., master of *see* Clerk, John

Dowe (Douue), William, collation to, of archdeaconry of Aberdeen, 190

Dowman (Dowman'), John, rector of Upway, 734

Down, **[cathedral] church** of [*at* Downpatrick, *in* Down, co. Down], Benedictine priory of, 391
......, ..., priors of *see* Brechimay, Robert; Magennis, Gellassius; Magxan, William

......, **diocese** of, places in *see* ?Ardkeen; [?Ardquin]; Bangor; Downpatrick; Moville

[Down, co. of], places in *see* Clonallan; Dromore; [Newry]; *and* places *listed above under* Down, diocese of

Downachinor' *see* Donaghmore

Downkyt *see* Dunkitt

Downpatrick *see under* Down

Doyle (Macduyl, Macduyll, Machdil), Gerald, canon of Leighlin, papal mandatary, 576, 934, 981
......, *cf.* MacDowell

Draper, Richard, of Canterbury diocese, commission by virtue of an appeal, 1051
......, ..., papal sub-delegate, litigation before, 28

Drax [Yorks], Augustinian monastery of, canon of *see* Wilson, Richard

Draylow, William, of Carlisle diocese, dispensed for plurality, 1113

Drimoleague *see* Dromdaleague

Drinkstone (Drynskton') [Suff], parish church of, union of, to the Bourchier chantry in Halstead parish church, 664

Drishane (Drisoun) [co. Cork] *alias*

Drishane (*contd*)
Kilmeedy (Chilmide) [*in* Drishane, co. Cork], parish church of, vicarage of, to be erected into prebend in Ardfert cathedral, 540

Drogheda [co. Louth], vill, town, or borough of, mayor, aldermen, and sheriffs of the county, and commonalty, of, appeal of, 964
......, ..., ..., ..., ..., ..., ..., ..., appointment etc. of warden and infirm of [Cruciferi] hospitals of St Mary de Urso and St Laurence the Martyr outside the walls of Drogheda pertain to, 964
......, ..., ..., ..., [Cruciferi] hospital of St Mary de Urso (*de Dise*) outside the walls of, warden and infirm of, appointment etc. of, 964
......, ..., ..., ..., ..., chapel of, 964
......, ..., ..., ..., ..., visitation of, 964
......, ..., ..., ..., [Cruciferi] hospital of St Laurence the Martyr outside the walls of, warden and infirm of, appointment etc. of, 964
......, ..., ..., ..., ..., chapel of, 964
......, ..., ..., ..., ..., visitation of, 964

Droitwich (Wyke) [Worcs], parish church of, rector of, 759

Dromdaleague *or* Drimoleague (Drongaleyg) [co. Cork], prebend of in Cork cathedral, 257

Dromore [co. Down], [cathedral] church of, canon and prebendary of, *cf.* Oruya, Eugene
......, ..., prebends in *see* Clonallan

......, bishop of *see* [Braua *or* de Brana], George
......, church of, archdeacon of, papal mandatary, 235
......, diocese of, person of, *cf.* Magennis, Gelasius
......, ..., place in *see* [Newry]

Dromtariff (Drumtaryf) [co. Cork], parish church of, vicarage of, 125

Drondarsi *see Druim tairsigh*

Drongaleyg *see* Dromdaleague

Drons *see* Duns

Druim tairsigh (Drondarsi) [*now part of* Killowen, co. Derry], parish church of, rectory of, to be united to Cistercian monastery of Macosquin, 259

Drumgoon (Druymduyn) [co. Cavan] otherwise called the *plebs* of Magheranure (Macharembahyr) [*in* Drumgoon, co. Cavan], parish church of St Patrick, vicarage of, 832

Drumlane (Druymleham, Idruymlehan) [co. Cavan], [Augustinian] monastery of, prior of, papal mandatary, 538, 834

Drummond (Dru(m)mond), Elizabeth, woman of Dunblane diocese, litigant, 435

Drumtaryf *see* Dromtariff

Druymduyn *see* Drumgoon

Druymleham *see* Drumlane

Drynskton' *see* Drinkstone

Dubler, William, rector of Kirkby on Bain, 194

Dublin [co. Dublin], [Cistercian] monastery of B. Mary near, abbot of, papal judge delegate, 927
......, priory of St John of Jerusalem near *see* Kilmainham

......, [cathedral] church and priory of Holy Trinity [i.e. Christ Church] of, OSA, prior of, papal judge delegate, 927, 989
......, ..., ..., prior and chapter of, commission by virtue of an appeal, 1073

......, [cathedral] church [i.e. St Patrick's]

Dublin [cathedral] church (*contd*)
of, dean of, papal judge delegate, 694, 964
......, ..., precentor of, papal judge delegate, 1005
......, ..., canon of *see* Lenat *alias* Lenet, Henry; *cf.* Olerahur, Patrick

......, **archbishop** of, papal judge delegate, 927
......, ..., conclusion to, 579
......, ..., *see* [FitzSimons], Walter
......, church of, archdeacon of, papal judge delegate, 694

......, **diocese** of, clerics and laymen (unnamed) of, 192
......, ..., persons of *see* Barnel, Robert; Maclanthlaym, Peter; Upinam, John
......, ..., places in *see* Fontstown; Kilmainham; Narraghmore; Norragh; Tippeenan

[Dublin, co. of] places in *see* Dublin; Kilmainham

Dubrovnik *see* Ragusa

Dugin *see* ODuggan

Dulcius, Lucas, *magister registri*, letters signed by:
L.Dulcius, 2-4, 6-13, 35-40, 49, 55-58, 84, 97-100, 131, 138, 144, 145, 154, 160, 171, 174, 176, 179, 180, 185, 186, 190-195, 199, 200, 202, 215, 217-221, 223-226, 228-230, 247, 259, 291, 293, 294, 330, 331, 333, 360, 361, 553-556, 558- 572, 574, 575
......, ..., ..., correction of register ordered by regent of chancery done by, 97
......, ..., ..., register entry annotated by, 96 *note*

Duleek (Volcke) [co. Meath], parish church of, united to Augustinian monastery of Lanthony II by Gloucester, 442
......, ..., vicar of, exempt from payment to bishop of Meath, 442
......, grange of, likewise united, 442

Dulverton (Dulnerton, Dulverton', Ulverton) [Som], church of, 174
......, place in *see* Gulland

Dumbarton (Dumbertane', Dumberthem) [co. Dumbarton], [collegiate] church of, provost of, papal judge delegate, 86
......, ..., ..., *see* Abirnethy, Walter

[Dumbarton, co. of], place in *see* Dumbarton

Dumbreck (Dumbred, Dumbreh, Dunbrek) [*in* Udny, co. Aberdeen], annex of, tithes of pertaining to Ellon parish church, 144, 793, 928

Dumdayre *see* Duniry

[Dumfries, co. of], places in *see* Annan; Johnstone

Dumgeymin *see* Dungiven

Dunbar [co. Haddington], [collegiate church of], 768
......, ..., [canonries and prebends in] *see* Duns(e); Pinkerton
......, place in *see* Pinkerton

Dunblane [co. Perth], **cathedral church of**], treasurer of *see* Murray, Patrick

......, **bishop** of, to receive oath of fealty in pope's name, 584, 587
......, ..., *see* [Chisholm], James
......, official of, papal judge delegate, 971
......, ..., *see* White, Henry
......, church of, separation of, from province of St Andrews, 333
......, ..., assignment of, as suffragan, to archbishop of Glasgow, 333
......, ..., restoration of, from province of Glasgow to that of St Andrews, 333
......, ..., re-assignment of, to archbishop of St Andrews, as his suffragan, 333

......, **diocese** of, persons of *see* ?Delly, John; Drummond, Elizabeth; Makbrek, Andrew; William, lord of Graham

Dunbrek *see* Dumbreck

Duncanson (Duncani, Duncarii), John, cleric of Glasgow diocese, to have rectory of Weem, 791
......, ..., collation to, of parish church of Annan, 929
......, ..., priest of Glasgow diocese, 642, 928
......, ..., ..., to have clerkship in parish church of Melrose, 642
......, ..., ..., proctor of abbot and convent of Kinloss and Hugh Martin, 928

Dunche, William, vicar of Overton, 346

Dundonald [co. Ayr], church of, fruits of pertaining to Cluniac monastery of Paisley, grant of, 63

Dunfermline (Dunfermiling, Donfermilin, Donfermilyn, Dunfermlen', Du(n)fermlyn') [co. Fife], Benedictine monastery of, 409
......, ..., vacancy of at the apostolic see, 588
......, ..., ..., decree over, 585
......, ..., constitutions of, reference to, 585
......, ..., commendation of, 588-590
......, ..., ..., abbot of, papal mandatary, 61, 63
......, ..., ..., *see* [Crichton], George
......, ..., commendation of *see* [Stewart], James
......, ..., convent of, conclusion to, 588
......, ..., monks of *see* Lornisen, Michael; Swynton, Robert
......, ..., vassals of, conclusion to, 588

Dungarvan (Deynyarluan) [co. Kilkenny], parish church of, vicarage of, to be united to canonry and prebend of St Maul's in Ossory cathedral, 787

Dungiven (Dumgeymin) [co. Derry], [Augustinian] monastery of, prior of, papal mandatary, 249

Duniry (Donderey, Dumdayre) [co. Galway], parish church of, vicarage of, 853
......, ..., ..., united to canonry of Clonfert and prebend of Ballynakill, 512

Dunkeld [co. Perth], **[cathedral] church** of, deanery of, litigation over, 237

......, ..., dean of, papal mandatary, 778, 937

......, ..., ..., *see* Boswell, Robert; Inglis, Alexander; *and see* Hepburn, George

......, ..., sub-dean of, papal judge delegate, 86, 971

......, ..., precentor of, papal judge delegate, 86, 921

......, ..., ..., *see* Wood, Henry

......, ..., chapter of, consent of to lease by bishop of lands pertaining to episcopal *mensa*, 558

......, ..., ..., to be summoned over erection of vicarage into undivided vicarage, 188

......, ..., ..., *mensa* of, Fortingall parish church united to, 188

......, ..., canonry and prebend of Aberlady in, pensioner of *see* [Turnbull], William

......, ..., prebends in *see* Aberlady; Crieff

......, **bishop** of, papal judge delegate, 691

......, ..., papal mandatary, 181, 188

......, ..., *see* [Brown], George

......, ..., *mensa* of, lands of Newtown and Craigton pertaining to, 558

......, official of, papal mandatary, 181, 791

......, church of, archdeacon of, papal judge delegate, 86, 921

......, **diocese** of, persons of *see* Betonen', Robert; Crichton, James, (of Cairns); Duncanson, John; Gechton', Abraham; Macnaughton, Donald; Touris, Thomas and wife Elisabeth

......, ..., places in *see* Auchtertool; Craigton; Fortingall; Inchcolm; Lundie; Newtown; Weem

Dunkeswell (Dunkeswell', Dunxwy) [Devon], Cistercian monastery of, monk, recently abbot, of *see* Hooper *alias* Pittemyster, Richard

......, ..., monk of *see* Fowler, John

Dunkitt (Downkyt, Dunket) [co. Kilkenny], parish church of, vicarage of, 157, 545

......, ..., ..., proposed union of to chancellorship of Ossory, 157

......, ..., ..., ..., grant of, impetration of,

Dunkitt (*contd*) alleged subreption of, 545

Du(n)mow, John, layman of the city and diocese of Hereford, proceedings against, 9

Dunne *see* ODunn

Dunnyquo *see* Dunwich

Dunocta *see* Donanaghta

Duns(e) (Drons) [co. Berwick], hospital of the poor of, 130

......, ..., parish church of Ellem annexed to, 130

......, [canonry and prebend of in the collegiate church of Dunbar], 781

Dunsford [Devon], parish church of, 436

Dunstable (Annscapus, Donstaple) [Beds], Augustinian monastery of St Peter, 571

......, ..., canon of *see* Done, Nicholas; Sterne, Edmund

Dunster, William, of Salisbury diocese, dispensed for plurality, 1088

Dunwich (Dunnyquo) [Suff], parish church of St John the Baptist, 322

Dunxwy *see* Dunkeswell

Dura *see* Dorrha

Durham [Durh], [parish of St Giles], place in *see* Kepier

......, **[cathedral] church** of, prior and chapter of, litigants, 94

......, ..., ..., holders of parish church of Brantingham and its chapels of Blacktoft and Ellerker, and receivers of their tithes, 94

......, ..., chapter of, *mensa* of, parish church of Brantingham, with its annexed chapels of Blacktoft and Ellerker, united to, 94

Durham [cathedral] church (*contd*)
......, ..., ..., conclusion to, 1006

......, **bishop** of, to receive oath of fealty in pope's name, 546, 547
......, ..., papal judge delegate, 405
......, ..., commissary of cardinal John [Morton], legate, litigation before, 28
......, ..., *see* [Flambard], Ranulph; [Fox], Richard; [Langley], Thomas; [du Puiset *or* Pudsey], Hugh; [Sever *or* Senhouse], William
......, church of, vassals of, conclusion to, 1006

......, **city and diocese** of, clergy of, conclusion to, 1006
......, ..., people of, conclusion to, 1006
......, diocese of, persons of *see* Claymond, John; Cuttler, John; Layburne, Roger; Mitford, Nicholas; Strangways, Edward; Veysey *alias* Harman, John
......, ..., places in *see* Alnwick; Darlington; Kepier; Newminster; Sherburn

[Durham, co. of], places in *see* Darlington; Durham; Kepier; Sherburn

Durham, Martin, canon of the Augustinian priory of [Newtown] Trim, 22

Dussyng, John, cleric of Chichester diocese, 975
......, Robert, rector of Wickmere, 269

Duthel [cos. Elgin and Inverness], prebend of in Moray, fruits of, appropriation of residue of to chapel royal, Stirling, 768

Duxbery, Robert, rector of Hethe, 705

[Dyer], Thomas, abbot of the Premonstratensian monastery of Torre, 747

Dyllon, John, rector of Newton Ferrers, 372

Dyneley, John, rector of Burghclere, 985

[Dysart, co. Fife], place in *see* Redford

E

Eaga *see* Annagh

Eaglais-na-lainne (Eglasnalame) *alias* Ballyheige (Balyytayg) [co.Kerry], parish church of, rectory of, to be united to canonry of Ardfert and prebend of Stradbally, 939
......, *cf. Rinn-bheara*

Eakring (Acryng) [Notts], parish church of, 751

Ealdstreet (Ialstret), prebend of in London cathedral, 281

Ealing (Elyng) [Midd], parish church of, 107

Easington (Esyngton') [Oxon], parish church of, 223

[Eassie] *see* Nevay

[East Calder] *see* Calder

East Dean [West Sussex] *see* Dean, East

Easter, High (Est Alta) [Essex], parish church of, 774

East Ham *see* Ham, East

East Hendred *see* Hendred, East

[East Lothian, co. of] *see* [Haddington, co. of]

East Raynham *see* Reynham

East Rudham *see* Rudham, East

East Worlington *see* Worlington, East

?Easton (Aston) [*in* West Alvington, Devon], chapel of, otherwise called the chapel of grace, indulgence for, 413
......, ..., vicar of, 413

Easton Magna *or* Great Easton (Eston'), alias of Bringhurst, *q.v.*

Eaton, Church (Chyrcheytn') [Staffs], parish church of, union of, to the parish church of Bradley, 217

Ebbesborne (Ebbesburne) [now Ebbesborne Wake, Wilts], parish church of, 478

[Ebrard], Fiocardus, abbot of the Benedictine monastery of Marcilhac, 196
......, ..., ..., his projected repair of the monastery, 196

Eccles [co. Berwick], Cistercian monastery of, nun of see Hoin, Elizabeth

Echt [co. Aberdeen], parish church of, 232

Edegayn see OHedian

Edelington' see Edlington

Edemborg, Edemburgh see Edinburgh

Ederose Ivychurthe see Ivychurch

Edgmond (Egmon', Egmond) [Salop], parish church of, 191, 1038
......, ..., union of, to a canonry and prebend of Darlington, 1038
......, ..., incumbent of, 1038

Edimundi, John, rector of Petworth, 33
......, cf. Edmonds, Edmondson

Edinburgh (Edemborg, Edemburgh, Edinbrugh, Edinburg, Ediniburg, Edymbruch) [co. Midlothian], town of, pension payable in, 778, 844
......, commonalty of, guarantee entered into with, 792
......, [collegiate] church of B. Mary of, provost of, papal judge delegate, 921
......, [collegiate] church of Holy Trinity near, provost of, papal mandatary, 371
......, Augustinian monastery of Holyrood, commend of, to James [Stewart], archbishop of St Andrews, 584
......, ..., abbot of, to receive intending religious as canon (elsewhere), bestow

Edinburgh (contd)
habit on him and receive his profession, 1028
......, ..., ..., papal mandatary, 371, 407, 698, 765, 767
......, ..., ..., see [Bellenden], Robert; [Crichton], George;
......, ..., convent of, conclusion to, 584
......, ..., canon of see Crawford, William
......, ..., vassals of, conclusion to, 584
......, ..., vicarage of Falkirk customarily governed by canons of, 443
......, ..., dependency of see St Mary's Isle
......, and see Merchiston

[Edinburgh, co. of] see [Midlothian, co. of]

Edington (Edyndon) [Wilts], house of the Bonshommes, brother of see Cotell, John

Ediniburg see Edinburgh

Edlington (Edelington') [Lincs], parish church of, altar of St Helen in, 379
......, ..., mother church of chapel of Poolham, 379
......, ..., vicar of, 379
......, ..., ..., admission of chaplain in Poolham chapel to pertain to, 379

Edmond, John, canon of the Gilbertine priory of Sempringham, 728

Edmonds, Edmondson cf. Edimundi

Edmund, bishop of Hereford, afterwards bishop of Salisbury see [Audley], Edmund

Eduard, William, canon and prebendary of London cathedral, 865
......, cf. Edwards

Eduen. (Autun) recte 'Exonien.' ('Exeter'), 148, note

Edward [I], king of England, patron of the parish church of Wootton, called Woodstock, donation of, 405

Edward, bishop of Chichester *see* [Story], Edward

......, [bishop-] elect of Gallipoli, to retain parish church and pension over [episcopal?] *mensa*, dioceses of Winchester and Worcester, 1311

Edwardes, Thomas, rector of Graffham, 480

Edwards *cf.* Eduard

Edymbruch *see* Edinburgh

Edyndon *see* Edington

Eglasnalame *see* Eaglais-na-lainne

Eglifeld, Leonard, vicar of Reculver, 490

Egmon', Egmond *see* Edgmond

Einster, Thomas, monk of the Benedictine monastery of Hurley and incumbent of St John the Baptist's, Dunwich, 322

Elberkat *see* Ellerker

Elesmere, Robert, of Winchester diocese, dispensed for plurality, 1063

[Elgin and Nairn, co. of] *see* [Moray *or* Elgin and Nairn, co. of]

Elias, abbot of Croxton *see* [Attercliff], Elias

Elibarde *see* Everard

Eliston', Robert, vicar of Sandbach, 38

Ellam *see* Ellem

Ellbardi, Thomas, OESA, 138

Ellem (Ellam) [*now part of* Longformacus, co. Berwick], parish church of, annexed to hospital of Duns(e), 130

Ellerker (Elberkat) [*in* Brantingham,

Ellerker (*contd*)
Yorks], chapel of, united to parish church of Brantingham, 94

......, ..., tithes of, 94

Ellis *cf.* Helis

Ellon (Ellone, Elone, Flone) [co. Aberdeen], parish church of, united to Cistercian monastery of Kinloss, 144, 793

......, ..., fruits of, pension over, 144, 793, 928

......, ..., tithes pertaining to *see* Allathan, Ardgrain, Auchterellon, ?Craigheid, Dumbreck, Esslemont, Pitmedden, Tilliemaud, Torry, Waterton, and Woodland; *and see* Ardmore, ?Collieston, Craig, Housieside, Mains (of Auchterellon), ?Meikle, ?Udny, Yonder Auchterellon [*now* Yonderton]

......, places *in see* Ardgrain; Auchterellon; ?Craigheid; Esslemont; Mains (of Auchterellon); Waterton; Yonder Auchterellon [*now* Yonderton]

Elphick (Elphek), John, cleric or layman of Chichester diocese, litigant, 197

Elphin [co. Roscommon], **[cathedral] church** of, deanery of, 936

......, ..., ..., provostry of Elphin, rectory of *Clann conchobair* and vicarage of Ogulla to be united to, 936

......, ..., ..., holder of, collation of canonries and prebends pertains to, 936

......, ..., dean of, papal commissary and mandatary, 846

......, ..., ..., papal mandatary, 947, 995

......, ..., ..., *see* OConnor, Theoderic; OHedian *alias* Ofyne, Thomas

......, ..., provostry of, 936

......, ..., ..., to be united to deanery, 936

......, ..., provost of *see* OFlanagan, Dermot

......, ..., chapter of, to be summoned over erection of prebend, 164

......, ..., ..., conclusion to, 591

......, ..., canons of *see* Macgillarni, John; Magragalli, Cormac; Oberyn, Odo; ODonnellan, William; OFallon, Charles; OFlanagan, Dermot;

Elphin, **[cathedral] church** (*contd*)
Ohergedayn, John; OKelly, Cornelius and Donat; Omori, Bernard; OScingin, Peter
......, ..., canonries and prebends of, collation of pertains to dean, 936
......, ..., prebend in *see* Killosolan

......, **bishop** of, Premonstratensian monastery of Lough Key subject to, 846
......, ..., to be summoned over erection of prebend, 164
......, ..., as local ordinary, simoniacal pact of, *cf.* 846
......, ..., *see* [Braua *or* de Brana], George; [OFlanagan], Nicholas
......, church of, vassals of, conclusion to, 591

......, **city and diocese** of, clergy of, conclusion to, 591
......, ..., people of, conclusion to, 591
......, diocese of, persons of *see* Coll, Thomas; Ialbim, Charles; [MacDonagh], Magonius; MacElheron, Malachy; Mac.ard, Cornelius; Oddowelyan, Cornelius; Ofinchua, Nemeas; OFlanagan, Lewis; OGallagher, Nigel; OKelly, Donald; Omilkerayn, Maurice
......, ..., places in *see* Ahascragh; Athlone; Boyle; *Clann conchobair* [*in* Baslick]; Coola [*in* Ballynakill]; Inchmacnerin; Killeroran; Killosolan; Kilmore; Lough Key; Ogulla; Taghboy; Tumna

Elphinstone (Elphinston, Elphinston', Elphinstonen'), Adam, archdeacon of Aberdeen, death of at the apostolic see, 190
......, John, 134 *note*
......, Robert, scholar and prospective cleric of Glasgow diocese, 134
......, ..., cleric of Glasgow, 412
......, ..., of Glasgow diocese, dispensed for plurality, 1253
......, William, bishop of Aberdeen, indult for, to reconcile churches by deputy, 411
......, ..., ..., concession of tithes belonging to *mensa*, 1039

Ely [Cambs], **[cathedral] church** of, chapter of, conclusion to, 627

......, **bishop** of *see* [Alcock], John; [Redman], Richard
......, official of, papal mandatary, 386
......, church of, vassals of, conclusion to, 627

......, **city and diocese** of, clergy of, conclusion to, 627
......, ..., people of, conclusion to, 627
......, diocese of, persons of *see* Baron, Henry; Bell, Thomas; Brundholm, Richard; Clayton, Nicholas; Cook, John; Fayerhaer, William; Gearges, William; Hyne, Thomas; Kuyvet, John; Ormeston, Thomas; Spicer, William; Wyatt, Richard
......, ..., places in *see* Barnwell; Bassingbourn; Bottisham; Boxworth; Cambridge; Clopton; Lolworth; Papworth Everard; Swaffham; Wilbraham, Little

Ely, Thomas, archdeacon of the [Benedictine] monastery of St Peter, Westminster, litigation before, 905, 988
......, ..., ..., ..., seal of, 905
......, ..., ..., ..., litigant to appear before him in St Margaret's, Westminster, 905

Elyng *see* Ealing

Elys, John, rector of Silton, 109
......, William, of Lincoln diocese, dispensed for plurality, 1064

Embrica *see* Emmerich

Emley, John, priest of Lincoln diocese, 757

Emly [co. Tipperary], **[cathedral] church** of, deanery of, 838
......, ..., deans of *see* de Burgo, Raymond; MacBrien, William
......, ..., chapter of, conclusion to, 52
......, ..., canons of *see* de Burgo, Raymond; MacBrien, Charles; OHea, Cormac; OMeehan, Cornelius

Emly (*contd*)
......, **bishop** of *see* MacBrien, Charles;
[OCahill], Philip

......, **city and diocese** of, clergy of,
conclusion to, 52
......, ..., people of, conclusion to, 52
......, diocese of, persons of *see* de Anglo
alias Moschalaiy, Henry; de Burgo,
Richard; Macberragoyn, David
......, ..., places in *see* Abington; Ludden

Emmerich (Embrica) [*in* Rhine province,
Germany], church of St Martin, provost
of, papal mandatary, 840

Empingham (Empynghm) [Rut], parish
church of, 729

Enerlchtan, Enerleithan, Enerlerthan,
Enerlethan *see* Innerleithen

Enfield (Ensyld) [Midd], parish church of,
681

England (*Angliam*), kingdom of, statutes,
constitutions, and laws of, 556
......, ..., kings and princes of, founders of
the Benedictine monastery of
Peterborough, 425
......, ..., ..., ..., gift to Peterborough of
dwellings in Stamford-Baron, 425
......, kings of, collation of religious house
pertaining to, 515
......, ..., parish church of Wootton, called
Woodstock, in the patronage of, 405
......, ..., *see* Edward [II]; Henry [VII];
Richard [I]; Richard [III]; *and see under*
English, king of the
......, queens of *see* Anne
......, kingdom of, legate of the apostolic see
in *see* [Morton], John
......, ..., quondam legates of the apostolic
see in *see* [Fieschi], Ottobuono; Otto
[Candidus]
......, ..., nuncio of the apostolic see in *see*
Castellesi, Hadrian
......, kingdom of, primate of the whole *see*
[Morton], John
......, primate of all *see* [?Arundel], Thomas;
[Deane], Henry; [Morton], John

England (*contd*)
......, primate of *see* [Rotherham], Thomas
......, Augustinian Eremite province of,
minister (and general?) of, 138
......, Franciscan province of, minister
provincial, guardians, and friars
Conventual of, and the commissary of
the ultramontane Observants,
conferences over jurisdiction between,
1053
......, kingdom of, Irish apostate in, 416
......, ..., Irishman *en route* to Roman curia
dying in, 512
......, ..., death in, of person *en route* to
Roman curia, 234
......, ..., cleric living in *see* Wiltan, William
......, 174

English, the, king of *see* Henry I
......, ..., enemies of the kingdom of France,
196
......, ..., detention of Benedictine
monastery of Marcilhac by, 196

Ennosmeon *see* Inishmaine

Ensyld *see* Enfield

Eraghed *see* ?Craigheid

Ermington (Ermyngton') [Devon], parish
church of, 915

?Erry (Horrey) [co. Tipperary], church of,
vicarage of, union of, to the
archiepiscopal *mensa* of Cashel, 998

Erskine (Erskyn), Thomas, canon of
Glasgow, papal judge delegate, 812

Ervyc *see* Hervey

Eschenreth' *see* East Hendred

Eschin' *see* East Ham

Eselmud', Esilmud', Esil<mund> *see*
Esslemont

Esplane, Thomas, chaplain in St Salvator's,
St Andrews, death of, 691

Essex, archdeacon of in the church of London, *q.v.*

[Essex, co. of], places in *see* Aldham; Benfleet, South; Bradwell on Sea; Chingford; Colchester; Danbury; Easter, High; Halstead; Ham, East and West; Horndon on the Hill; Langenhoe; Langham; Leighs, Little; Maldon; Mersea, West; Moreton; Netteswell; Paglesham; Pebmarsh; Ramsden Crays; Ramsey; Sible Hedingham; Stanford Rivers; Stratford Langthorne; Tilbury, West; Upminster; Widdington

Esslemont (Eselmud', Esilmud', Esil<mund>) [*in* Ellon, co. Aberdeen], tithes of pertaining to Ellon parish church, 144, 793, 928
......, old barony of, place in *see* ?Craigheid

Est Alta *see* High Easter

Estden' *see* Dean, East [West Sussex]

'Estgaston'' [*unidentified*; *in* East Dean, West Sussex], fields of, tithes from, 661

Esthenreth' *see* Hendred, East

Eston' *see* Easton Magna

Estvokyngton *see* Worlington, East

Esyngton' *see* Easington

[Euboea] *see* Negropont

Eugenius III, confirmation of, 425
......, letter of protection after the manner of, 174

Eugenius IV, letters of, 146, 405

Eurowry *see* Inverurie

Euston (Evston) [Suff], parish church of, 211

Evedon (Evedon') [Lincs], parish church of, 103

Evedon, Robert, vicar of Morton (by Bourne), 303

Everard (Elibarde), Richard, the late, once vicar of one or more of the following : Ballysheehan; Crumpstown; ?Erry; Railstown, 998
......, Thomas, vicar of Whaplode, 731

Eversham *see* Heversham

Evesham (Deveshm', Eveschin, Evyshin') [Worcs], Benedictine monastery of, abbot of, papal judge delegate, 29, 298, 529
......, ..., abbot and convent of, to exchange with guild of Drapers' Company patronage of St Michael, Cornhill, London for goods yielding annual pension, 903

Evston *see* Euston

Evyshin' *see* Evesham

Excester, alias of Wherre, William, *q.v.*

Exeter [Devon], parish church of Holy Trinity in, 421

......, [cathedral] church of, deanery of, 434
......, ..., dean of, papal judge delegate, 456
......, ..., ..., *see* Willoughby, Edward
......, ..., treasurer of *see* Austell, Thomas
......, ..., canonry and prebend of, union to, of the parish church of Illogan, 684
......, ..., ..., ..., of the parish church of Kingsdon, 663
......, ..., ..., ..., of the parish church of Lympsham, 717
,......, ..., ..., ..., of the parish church of Whimple, 909
......, ..., canons and prebendaries of *see* Burton, John; Fulford, John; Gilbert, Thomas; Harrys, Thomas; Nans, John; Wyngho, Christopher
......, **bishop** of, absence of, 456
......, ..., refusal of, to institute person presented for parish church, 456

Exeter **bishop** (*contd*)

......, ..., assignment to by official of metropolitical court of Canterbury of term to inquire into right of presentation, 456

......, ..., papal judge delegate, 906, 924, 988

......, ..., papal mandatary, 174

......, ..., vicar of *see* Nans, John

......, ..., *see* [Arundel], John; [Redman], Richard

......, ..., 626 *note*

......, official of, papal mandatary, 147

......, church of, archdeacon of Totnes in *see* Fulford, John

......, **diocese** of, persons of *see* Adam, James; Aller, William; Andrew, Peter; Awyten, Robert; Banys, Edward; Barbour, Robert; Bodley, Thomas; Borgh, Thomas; Bright, Richard; Bunt, Thomas; Callow, Thomas; Carlyon, Richard; Chechester, William; Cherell, Thomas; Chubbe, William; Cobaldi, Thomas; [Cornish], Thomas; Couuanni, William; Cutfolde, Thomas; Dalison, Thomas; Daniell, William; [Dyer], Thomas; Dyllon, John; Freste, Robert; Garlond, Richard; Hancock, John; Hicks, John; Hooper *alias* Pittemyster, Richard; Horde, Roger; Laure(n)ce, John; Laury, Thomas; Magryche, John; Many, John; Menewynuyke, William; Michell, Robert; Middleton, Leonard; More, Richard; Morton, Nicholas; Moton', Richard; Oxenbregge, John; Prud, John; Pykeman, John; Redmayne, John; Ruer, Thomas; Russell, William; Serlo, John; Shamke, William; Soriano, John; Speke, Christopher; Stockfish, William; Stoliefish, William; Sydnor, Richard; Tregulan, John; Tyake, John; Wherre *alias* Excester, William; Whitrow, Stephen; Yeo, Leonard

......, ..., places in *see* Alvington, West; Arlington; Bodmin; Bondleigh; Bovey Tracy; Brendon; Buckland; Chagford; Challacombe; Cheriton Fitzpaine; Clovelly; Cornwall; Cuby; Cullompton; Dodbrooke; Dunkeswell; Dunsford;

Exeter **diocese** (*contd*)

?Easton; Ermington; Exminster; Forde; Georgeham; Glasney; Gwennap; Helland; Huish; Illogan; Ipplepen; ?Jacobstowe; Kenn; Kenton; Lewtrenchard; Manaton; Milton Abbot; Minster; Moreton Hampstead; Newenham; Newton Ferrers; Oakford; Parkham; Plympton; Probus; Putford, West; Roborough; St Carrok;St Erme; St Germans; St Gluvias; St Neot; St Tudy; St Veep; Shillingford St George; Shobrooke; Staverton; Stratton; Talcarne; Torre; Totnes; Whimple; Willand; Worlington, East; Zeal Monachorum; *and see* Churchstanton

Exminster (Exmstre) [Devon], parish church of, rectory of, 456

......, ..., presentation of person for pertains to the prior and convent of the Augustinian priory of Plympton, 456

......, ..., right of presentation for, inquiry into, 456

Exsalle, Thomas, of Norwich diocese, dispensed for plurality, 1271

Eye (Heye) [Suff], Benedictine monastery of, 305

......, ..., monk of *see* Barney, John

Eye [*now part of* Stornoway] *see* 'Li'

Eygemysh(a)m, Eygenysh(a)m *alias* Eynesh(a)m, Eygomyshyn' *alias* Eyneshin' *see* Eynsham

Eynon ap Gwalter (Eynonus Apgwaltere), rector of Llanfallteg, 272

Eynsham (Eygemysh(a)m, Eygenysh(a)m *alias* Eynesh(a)m, Eygomyshyn' *alias* Eyneshin') [Oxon], Benedictine monastery of, (commendatory) abbot of *see* [Salley], Miles

Eyre, Ralph, rector of Sulhampstead Abbots, 224

F

Fabell, John, priest of London diocese, 773

Fabri, John, solicitor of apostolic letters, proctor of Andrew Lyell, 992
......, ...[another?], cleric of Trier diocese, familiar of Fer(di)nandus Ponzettus, 616
......, ..., ..., ..., provision of to the parish church of Vinningen, 616

Fahy (Fand) [co. Galway], parish church of, vicarage of, 225

Fakenham (Fakenhamdin') [Norf], parish church of, union to, of the parish church of Sproatley, 797

[de Falcariis] see [de Falcutiis or Falcariis]

Falconer cf. Faulkener

[de Falcutiis or Falcariis] de Cesena, Damianus (once John), canon of the Augustinian monastery of St Mary in Portico, Ravenna, 972
......, ..., ..., ..., sometime student at Paris university, 972
......, ..., ..., ..., ..., in service of James [IV], 972

Falkirk (Faukerk) [co. Stirling], parish church of, vicarage of, customarily governed by canons of the Augustinian monastery of Holyrood, 443
......, ..., vicar of, 443

Fand see Fahy

Fano [in province of Pesaro e Urbino, Italy] see [de Lanciarinis] de Fano, Ulixes

Fareby see Ferriby

Fareyway, William, rector of Midley, 437

Faringdon (Ffaryngdon alias Ffarendon) [Berks], prebend of in Salisbury cathedral, union to, of the parish church of Mildenhall, 908

Farley, Nicholas, vicar of Hartpury, 695

?Farmington (Thormerton') [Glos], parish church of, rector of, 671

Farsyltht see Forsyth

Farthingstone (Ffarthyngston) [Northants], parish church of, 977

Faukerk see Falkirk

Fauleston see Fugglestone

Faulkener (Ffaukener), John, of Lincoln diocese, dispensed for plurality, 1129
......, cf. Falconer

Faversham (Feversam) [Kent], parish church of, 491

Fawley (Ffalley) [Bucks], parish church of, 885

Fayerhaer, William, vicar of St Cyriac and Julitta's, Swaffham, 376

Federicus, cardinal deacon of St Theodorus see [Sanseverinas], Federicus

Felayn see OPhelan

Felix V (Amadeus, duke of Savoy), obedience of, 405
......, adherents of, 405

Fellaim see OPhelan

Feltwell (Ffeltwell') [Norf], parish church of B. Mary, 284

?Feohanagh (Offanach) [in Kilquane, co. Kerry], parish church of, vicarage of, to be united to chancellorship of Ardfert, 993

Ferdinand [V], king of Castile and Leon, ambassador of, to Henry [VII], 808

Ferdinandi, Gonzalo, incumbent of Bradwell on Sea, 808

Ferdinandi (*contd*)
......, ..., ..., son of the ambassador of Ferdinand [V], king of Castile and Leon, to Henry [VII], 808

Fermoy [co. Cork], Cistercian monastery of, abbot of, papal mandatary, 74, 128, 514, 539-541, 838, 1000
......, ..., ..., see [Cant], Patrick

Ferns [co. Wexford], **[cathedral] church** of, dean of, papal judge delegate, 192
......, ..., treasurer of, papal judge delegate, 192
......, ..., ..., see Browne, Richard
......, ..., canon of see OCarran, Maurice

......, **bishop** of, *de facto* collation by, 192
......, ..., *de facto* excommunication and suspension by, 192
......, ..., confirmation of election of prior of the Augustinian monastery of Selsker near Wexford by, 989
......, church of, archdeacon of see Beckett, Richard

......, **diocese** of, clerics and laymen (unnamed) of, 192
......, ..., persons of see Allen, Thomas; Baldwin, Patrick; Browne, Richard; Hodii, Donald; Kawall, Richard; Prendergast, Patrick
......, ..., places in see Glascarrig; Rathaspick; Selsker near Wexford; Wexford

[de Ferrariis], Johannes (Baptista), cardinal priest of S. Crisogono, 850
......, ..., ..., servant of see Forman, Robert
......, ..., bishop of Modena, 97
......, ..., ..., regent [of the chancery], 97
......, ..., ..., ..., correction of register ordered by, 97

'Ferrebiythi', diocese of Cloyne [*un-identified; possibly* Fuhiry *in* Ballyvourney, co. Cork], church, called particle, of, 1000
......, ..., ..., ..., erection of into prebend of Cloyne cathedral with union of rectory of Inch thereto, 1000

'Ferrebiythi' (*contd*)
......, ..., ..., ..., patrons of, consent of, 1000
......, ..., ..., ..., to be erected etc. anew, 1000

Ferriby (Fareby) [*now* South Ferriby, Lincs], parish church of, 565

Feure, John, OESA, 274

Feversam see Faversham

Ffalley see Fawley

Ffarendon, alias of Ffaryngdon, *q.v.*

Ffarthyngston see Farthingstone

Ffaryngdon *alias* Ffarendon see Faringdon

Ffaukener see Faulkener

Ffelayn see OPhelan

Ffeltwell' see Feltwell

Ffismoris see Fitzmaurice

Ffolsham see Foulsham

Fforde see Forde

Ffoter, William, rector of Euston, 211

Ffouleston' see Fugglestone

Ffouuler see Fowler

Ffox see Fox

Ffranck see Franck

Ffrankleyn see Franklin

Ffreuill' or Norbourne, Robert, prior of the Benedictine monastery of St Martin, Dover, 967

Ffulford see Fulford

Ffyhan', William, canon of Ossory, papal

Ffyhan' (*contd*)
  judge delegate, 989
......, *cf.* OFeehan

Ffysmoris *see* Fitzmaurice

Fhynunc *see* Finnoe

[Fieschi], Ottobuono *see* Otto [Candidus] and Ottobuono [Fieschi]

Fife, county of, places (named) stated to be in, 558

[Fife, co. of], places in *see* Auchtertool; Balgonie [*in* Markinch]; Craigton; Dunfermline; Inchcolm; Inchegall [*in* Ballingry]; Kilmany; Kirkcaldy; Kirkforthar; Lindores [*in* Abdie]; Markinch; May *alias* Pittenweem; Milton of Balgonie; Newburn; Newtown; Redford [*in* Dysart]; St Andrews; Spittal [*in* Auchterderran]; 'Spittale'

Fincham (Fynthin') [Norf], parish church [*probably* St Martin's] of, 677

Fincharn (Fynchaers) [*in* Kilmichael Glassary, co. Argyll], castle of, 493

Fineham, Simon, of Norwich diocese, dispensed for plurality, 1062

Finnoe (Fhynunc) [co. Tipperary], parish church of, rectory of, to have been erected into prebend in Killaloe cathedral with rectory of Terryglass united thereto, 16
......, ..., ..., to be united to proposed canonry and prebend of Loughrea in Clonfert cathedral, 16

Fiocardus, abbot of Marcilhac *see* [Ebrard], Fiocardus

[Firth of Forth], islands in *see* St Columba; 'baptized islands'

Fisgybon *see* Fitzgibbon

Fishwick (Fyshewyke), Thomas, rector of Buscot, 666

Fismoris *see* Fitzmaurice

Fisshwike *cf.* Fishwick

[FitzGerald], Gerald or Gerard, bishop of Cork and Cloyne, collation and provision by, 825
......, ..., ..., cession of, 612,
......, ..., recently bishop of Cork and Cloyne, 816
......, ..., ..., administrator of the fabric of St Finbar's, Cork, 816
......, ..., ..., ..., to be deprived for alleged misdeeds, 816
......, *and see* de Geraldinis

Fitzgibbon (Fisgybon), Edmund, ostensible cleric of Cloyne diocese, litigant over abbacy of the Augustinian monastery of Molana, 573

Fitz Herbert (Fytzherbert), Thomas, rector of Stanford Rivers and incumbent of North Wingfield, 300

Fitz Hugh (Sitzhugh), George, canon of Lincoln, prebendary of Cropredy, and incumbent of Aldingham, 752

[?FitzJohn], Francis, OP, of Cordova, provision of, to bishopric of Glendalough, 579, 776
......, ..., ..., ..., absolution of preliminary to provision, 580

Fitzmaurice (Ffismoris, Ffysmoris, Fismoris, Fysmoris), David, detainer, with Gerald Stack, of the chancellorship of Ardfert, 993
......, ..., detainer of rectory of Killury, 939
......, ..., vicar of *Rinn-bheara*, resignation of, 306
......, Edmund, cleric of Ardfert-diocese, student at Oxford university, 306
......, ..., ..., ..., to be canon of Ardfert, have rectory of ?Ballingarry erected into prebend and vicarage of *Rinn-bheara*

Fitzmaurice (*contd*)
united thereto, 306
......, ..., detainer of particle of 'Killcolin',
939
......, Maurice, detainer of rectory of
Eaglais-na-lainne alias Ballyheige, 939
......, Richard, detainer of vicarage of *Rinn-bheara*, 306

[FitzSimons], Walter, archbishop of
Dublin, tuitorial letters of, 192

[Flambard], Ranulph, the late, bishop of
Durham, foundation of Kepier hospital
by, 429

Flellain, Flellayn *see* OPhelan

Fleming (Flemyng *alias* Plemyn), Richard,
detainer of vicarage of Derryvillane,
941
......, *cf.* Plemen

[Flint, co. of], places in *see* ?Bodfari; St
Asaph

Flint (Fyylint), John, prior of the Cluniac
priory of Pontefract, 92
......, ..., ..., indulged to use mitre etc., 397

Flone *see* Ellon

Florence [*in* province of Florence, Italy],
city of, person of *see* Ponzettus,
Fer(di)nandus

Flury (Flori) [*cf.* Fleury, France], Hugh de,
property gifted to Taunton priory by,
174

Fohanagh (Foynach) [co. Galway], parish
church of, vicarage of, 788

de Fonte see Wilton

de Fontibus *see* Fountains

[Fontstown, co. Kildare], place in *see*
Tippeenan

Forbes [co. Aberdeen] *see* Kearn

Forbes [*now in* Tullynessle and Forbes, co.
Aberdeen], lord of, canonry and
prebend of Kearn and Forbes in
Aberdeen cathedral in patronage of, 68

Forbes, Alexander, the late, once canon of
Aberdeen and prebendary of Kearn and
Forbes, 68
......, John, canon of Aberdeen and
prebendary of Kearn and Forbes, death
of, 68

?Forcett (Forset) [Yorks], parish church of,
vicar of, 976

Ford (Anygray) [*at head of* Loch Awe, *in
parishes of* Kilmichael Glassary and
Kilmartin, co. Argyll], rivulet of, ford
of, 493

[Ford], Thomas, bishop of Achonry,
dispensed for plurality, 1247

Forde (Fforde) [*in* Thorncombe, Dors
formerly Devon], Cistercian monastery
of, monk of *see* Wherre *alias* Excester,
William

[Forfar, co. of], places in *see* Brechin;
Idvie(s); Kirkden; Lundie; Nevay;
Restennet; Tannadice

Forman (Forma(n), Forman'), Andrew,
master, papal notary, 356
......, ..., ..., ..., prior of the Augustinian
priory of May or Pittenweem, 356, 630,
632, 633
......, ..., ..., ..., ..., grant to, of barony and
lands in St Andrews diocese pertaining
to archiepiscopal *mensa*, confirmation
of, 356
......, ..., ..., ..., ..., provision of to the
bishopric of Moray, 630
......, ..., ..., ..., ..., absolution of
preliminary to provision, 633
......, ..., commendatory rector of
Cottingham, 632
......, ..., [bishop-] elect of Moray, 631, 632
......, ..., ..., faculty for consecration of, 631
......, ..., ..., to retain May *alias* Pittenweem

Forman (*contd*)
and Cottingham, 632, 698
......, Robert, collation to, of precentorship of Glasgow, 80
......, ..., precentor of Glasgow, 850
......, ..., ..., familiar and continual commensal of the pope, 850
......, ..., ..., ..., servant of Johannes Baptista [de Ferrariis], cardinal of S. Crisogono, 850
......, ..., ..., ..., ..., licensed to resign and exchange precentorship, 850

de Fornariis *or* Furnariis, Octavianus, bishop of Mariana, *magister registri* , letters signed by:
O Marianen., 238, 273, 309-311, 315-317, 340, 341, 362, 364, 393, 468, 579, 580
......, ..., ..., ..., correction of register ordered by regent of chancery done by, 175 *note*

Forset *see* ?Forcett

Forster, John, of London diocese, dispensed for plurality, 1141

Forsyth (Farsyltht), Thomas, canon of Ross living in Glasgow, papal judge delegate, 812

Fortingall (Forte(r)gil, Fortergill) [co. Perth], parish church of, 187
......, ..., united to capitular *mensa* of Dunkeld, 188
......, ..., vicarage, called portion, of, cure of souls of, 188
......, ..., ..., ..., ..., to be erected into perpetual undivided vicarage and adequately endowed, 188

Fortrose *see* Ross [Scotland]

Forvie *see* Slains

Fosse (Fos'), Stretton on the, *q.v.*

[Fossoway, co. Kinross], place in *see* Carnbo

Foster, William, vicar of Holkham, 814

Foulsham (Ffolsham) [Norf], parish church of, rector of, 31

Fountains (de Fontibus), Robert, archdeacon of the church of St Andrews, commissary of the archbishop, litigation before, 812

Fovonys, Nicholas, rector of Upton Warren, 304

Fowler (Ffouuler), John, rector of Christleton, appeal of, 991
......, ..., monk of the Cistercian monastery of Dunkeswell, 13

Fox (Ffox), John, vicar of Corston, 21
......, Richard, bishop of Durham, 429, 625, 626
......, ..., ..., licensed to reform statutes of the hospitals of Kepier and Sherburn, 429
......, ..., ..., translation of to Winchester, 625, 626
......, ..., ..., absolution of preliminary to translation, 624
......, ..., ..., to take oath of fealty, 626
......, ..., ..., ..., commission over, 625
......, ..., ..., afterwards bishop of Winchester, 1006
......, Thomas, rector of Farthingstone, 977

Foynach *see* Fohanagh

France, kingdom of, English and other enemies of, 196
......, ..., *and see below under* Franks

Francis, bishop of Annaghdown *see* [Brunand], Francis

Francis of Cordova, [bishop-] elect of Glendalough *see* [?FitzJohn], Francis

Francis of Sassello, OFM, dispensation and indult for, 97

Franck (Ffranck), John, monk of the Cistercian monastery of Medmenham,

Franck (*contd*)
973
......, ..., ..., translated there from the Cistercian monastery of Fürstenfeld, 973

Franklin (Ffrankleyn), William, cleric of Lincoln diocese, 479

Franks, kings of *see* Louis [XII]; Pepin

[Frant, Sussex], place in *see* Bayham

Frascati [*in* province of Rome, Italy], letters dated at, 813
......, *see* Tusculum

Fraser (Fresel, Frisel), John, canon of Glasgow, 637, 639, 640
......, ..., ..., provision of to the bishopric of Ross, 637
......, ..., ..., absolution of preliminary to provision, 639
......, ..., ..., dispensation of over illegitimacy preliminary to provision, 640
......, ..., [bishop-] elect of Ross, faculty for consecration of, 638
......, Robert, priest of Glasgow diocese, 840, 841
......, ..., ..., provision of to deanery of Ross, 840, 841
......, ..., ..., consent of, to assignment of fruits and tithes pertaining to deanery in place of pension, 840

Frecce, Richard, rector of Monnington on Wye, 805

Fresel *see* Fraser

Freste, Robert, rector of Shobrooke, 149

Freston, William, of Lincoln diocese, dispensed for plurality, 1096

Frisel *see* Fraser

Fugglestone (Fauleston, Ffouleston') [*now* Fugglestone St Peter, Wilts], parish church of, 719

Fugglestone (*contd*)
......, ..., union to, of the vicarage of Wilsford, 702

[Fuhiry *in* Ballyvourney] *see* 'Ferrebiythi'

Fulford (Ffulford), John, archdeacon of Totnes and vicar of Probus, 285
......, ..., union for, of parish church in Exeter diocese to his canonry [of Exeter], 1075

de Furnariis *see* de Fornariis

Furneux Pelham *see* Pelham, Furneux

Fürstenfeld [*in* Upper Bavaria (near Munich), Germany], Cistercian monastery of, 973
......, ..., monk of *see* Franck, John

Fuye, Fwin *see* White

Fydkoc, Henry, vicar of Abbots Bromley, 150

Fynchaers *see* Fincharn

Fynter, alias of Vynter, Thomas, *q.v.*

Fynthin' *see* Fincham

Fyshewyke *see* Fishwick

Fysmoris *see* Fitzmaurice

Fytzherbert *see* Fitz Herbert

Fyylint *see* Flint

G

Gallen (Gabine, Galine) [co. Offaly], [Augustinian] monastery of B. Mary, prior of, papal mandatary, 146, 225, 226, 228-230

Gallese [*in* province of Viterbo, Italy], letters dated at, 972

Gallipoli (*Caliporen.*) [a titular see; on the

Gallipoli (*contd*)
Dardanelles in European Turkey],
[bishop-] elect of *see* Edward

de Galves, Johannes, bishop of Terracina,
magister registri, letters signed by:
Jo. de Galves, 118, 349, 380, 385, 401,
454, 457, 458, 486, 487, 543, 544, 612-
615
Jo. Electus Terracinen., 121, 367-370,
389, 391, 392, 407, 411, 426, 427, 430-
432, 434, 439, 440, 442, 447, 450-453,
461, 477-481, 483, 489, 490, 492, 493,
499-503, 505-507, 509, 511, 512, 514,
517, 522, 523, 528, 533, 534, 537-541,
547, 548
Jo. Episcopus Terracinen., 390, 394,
399, 418, 419, 425, 529, 650, 702, 703,
718-722, 732, 733, 765-769, 781, 788,
789, 791, 794, 810, 840, 841, 853, 855,
872, 873, 878-880, 895, 908, 909, 917,
922, 924, 925, 950, 952, 953, 956, 973,
980, 992, 997, 1035
Jo. [incomplete], 371
......, ..., ..., ..., corrections of register
ordered by regent of chancery done by:
Jo. Episcopus Terracinen., 766
Jo., 154 *note*

Galway (Bougalia, Bougalve) [co.
Galway], [collegiate] church of St
Nicholas, warden and chapter of,
vicarage of Glaregalway detained by,
935
......, Franciscan house of, guardian and
friars of, chapel of St Mary, Galway,
detained by, 933
......, chapel of B. *or* St Mary, 829, 933
......, ..., to be united to canonry of
Kilmacduagh and prebend of Kinvarra,
933
......, chapel of B. Mary *Templi Collis* at,
166
......, ..., annexed to Premonstratensian
monastery of the Holy Trinity outside
the walls of Tuam, 166

[Galway, co. of], places in *see*
Abbeygormacan; Abbeyknockmoy;
Aghiart; Ahascragh; Annaghcallow;
Annaghdown; Aughrim; Ballynakill;

Galway, co. of (*contd*)
Beagh *alias Cliath-Ceallayd* ;
Claregalway; Clonbern; Clonfert;
Clonrush; Clontuskert; Donanaghta;
Duniry; Fahy; Fohanagh; Galway;
Inishcaltra; Inishmaine [*in* Ballinchalla];
Isertkelly; Kilconierin; Kilcoona;
?Kilcummin; Kilkerrin; Killannin;
Killeelaun; Killererin *alias Muinter
Murchada* ; Killeroon; Killeroran;
Killoscobe; Killosolan; Kilmacduagh;
Kilmalinoge; Kiltullagh; Kinvarra;
Lackagh; Laghtgannon; Lough Mask;
Loughrea; Omey; Oranmore; Taghboy;
Templetogher; *Tempull-na-Scrine*;
Tisaxon *alias* Templegaile [*in
Monivea*]; Tuam; *and see* Longford,
barony of, places in

Galys, alias of Loddon, William, *q.v.*

Garard (Gerard), Thomas, rector of
Stokesby, 47

Gardener, Richard, rector of Chiddingstone,
168

Garfinny (Garyfynach) [co. Kerry], parish
church of, vicarage of, to be united to
chancellorship of Ardfert, 993

Garford *alias* Crouulandi, Thomas, canon
of the Augustinian priory of Stonely, 12

Garforth, Thomas, monk of the Cistercian
monastery of Kirkstead, 447

Garlond, Richard, monk of the Cistercian
monastery of Newenham, 37

Garrynoe (Gauryno) [*part of modern*
Desertserges, co. Cork], parish church
of, rectory of, to be united to canonry
and prebend of Kilbrogan in Cork
cathedral, 252

Garvock (Garvok) [co. Kincardine], parish
church of, 986

Garyfynach *see* Garfinny

Gascoigne (Gaysconye), Humphrey, rector
of Newton Kyme, 100

Gaunt (Gaunte, Gawnt, Sanunt), Richard,
rector of East Hendred, 439, 911
......, ..., ..., vicar of Sutton Courtenay, 911
......, ..., of Salisbury diocese, dispensed for
plurality, 1132

Gauryno see Garrynoe

Gawnt see Gaunt

Gay, Richard, vicar of Pershore, 978

Gaysconye see Gascoigne

Gearges, William, of Ely diocese,
dispensed for plurality, 1183

Gechton', Abraham, scholar of Dunkeld
diocese, 369
......, cf. Crichton

Geddac alias Ocoggobayn (Geydach alias
Ocogavayn), Pilapus / Philip, detainer
of vicarage of Loughkeen, 162, 403
......, cf. OHaugh

Gedney [Lincs], parish church of, 469

Geffrey, John, rector of Hinton Blewett,
679

Geneva [Switzerland], bishop of, to receive
oath of fealty, 577, 578
......, city or diocese of, Francis [Brunand],
bishop of Annaghdown, living in, 199
......, diocese of, place in see Annecy

Genoa [Italy], person of see Grimaldi,
Agostino

Geoffrey [no surname], vicar of Edlington,
379
......, ..., consent of, to grant by abbot and
convent of Bardney to Robert
Barkeworth, lord of Poolham, and his
successors, enabling them to have a
resident chaplain in Poolham chapel,

Geoffrey (contd)
save for the right of the mother church
of Edlington, 379

George, bishop of Dunkeld see [Brown],
George
......, bishop of Elphin, previously bishop of
Dromore see [Braua or de Brana],
George
......, abbot of Holyrood, formerly abbot of
Dunfermline see [Crichton], George

Georgeham (Ham') [Devon], parish church
of St George, rector of, 40

Gerald, (recently) bishop of Cork and
Cloyne see [FitzGerald], Gerald or
Gerard

de Geraldinis ([de Geraldinis?], de
Gerardinis, de Gerarldinis), Beraldus
[recte Geraldus] Thome, to have
canonry of Limerick, 1197
......, Edmund, cleric of Ardfert diocese and
detainer of rectory of Stradbally, 939
......, ..., ..., to be canon of Ardfert and
have the rectory of Stradbally erected
into a prebend, with the rectories of
Eaglais-na-lainne alias Ballyheige and
Killury and the particle of 'Killcolin'
united thereto, 939
......, Gerald, cleric of Ardfert diocese, to be
archdeacon of Ardfert, 945
......, ..., sometime dean of Lismore, 159
......, ..., and see [FitzGerald], Gerald or
Gerard
......, Gerald David, intruder into Cistercian
monastery of Monasteranenagh and
litigant over it, 383
......, Gerald Johannis, cleric of Lismore
diocese, to have precentorship of
Lismore, 158
......, [Geraldus] Thome see de Geraldinis,
Beraldus Thome
......, James, sometime dean of Lismore, 159
......, James Radmundi Mauritii, cleric of
Limerick diocese, to have vicarage of
Cluain Comarda erected into a canonry
and prebend of Limerick with the
vicarage of ?Ballycahane united thereto,
942

de Geraldinis (*contd*)

......, John, detainer of archdeaconry of Cork, 539

......, ..., detainer of canonry of Cloyne and prebend of Kilmacdonogh, 392

......, ..., detainer of vicarage of Garfinny, 993

......, John Davit, canon of Ardfert, papal mandatary, 994

......, John Edemundi, cleric of Cloyne diocese, 612, 614, 615

......, ..., provision of to the bishopric of Cork and Cloyne, 612

......, ..., absolution of preliminary to provision, 615

......, ..., dispensation for minority of preliminary to provision, 614

......, ..., [bishop-] elect of Cork and Cloyne, faculty for promotion to sacred orders and for consecration of, 613

......, John Odoni[s], of Cloyne diocese, commission [by virtue of an appeal?], 1306

......, John Philippi, canon of Lismore, papal mandatary, 159, 160

......, ..., ..., prebendary of Clashmore, 159

......, ..., ..., ..., to be dean of Lismore and have his canonry and prebend, with vicarage of Kilronan annexed thereto, united to the deanery, 159

......, ..., detainer of vicarage of Kilronan, 790

......, Maurice, the younger (son of Maurice the elder), cleric of Ardfert diocese, to be canon of Limerick and prebendary of Tullabracky and have precentorship of Limerick united thereto, 486

......, Maurice the elder, son of *see* de Geraldinis, Maurice the younger

......, Philip, cleric of Ardfert diocese, to have chancellorship of Ardfert with vicarages of ?Feohanagh, Kilmalkedar, and Garfinny united thereto, 993

......, Richard, cleric of Cloyne diocese, to be canon of Cloyne and have prebend of Kilmacdonogh, 392

......, Richard Giraldi Willelmi, detainer of canonry of Cloyne and prebend of Kilmacdonogh, 852

......, *and see* [FitzGerald]; *see also Militis* [i.e. of the Knight (of Glin de

de Geraldinis (*contd*) Geraldinis)], John

Gerard, John, rector of All Saints', ?Chesterfield, 567

......, *and see* Garard

Gerard, (recently) bishop of Cork and Cloyne *see* FitzGerald, Gerald *or* Gerard

de Gerardinis, de Gerarldinis *see* de Geraldinis

Gernesey *see* Guernesey

Geydach *alias* Ocogavayn *see* Geddac *alias* Ocoggobayn

[de Gherardis de Vulterris], Jacobus, apostolic secretary, letters expedited by: *Ja Volateranus*, 377, 413

Gibson (Gibson'), John, canon of Glasgow, papal judge delegate, 86

[Giffard], William, bishop of Winchester, the late, 174

Gifferd, Alexander, cleric of St Andrews diocese, provision of to subdeanery of Glasgow, 301

......, ..., ..., cession of, 301

......, ..., ..., assignment to of pension on fruits of subdeanery, 301

de' Gigli (de Giglis), John, provision of to the bishopric of Worcester, 1335

......, ..., absolution of preliminary to provision, 1336

......, ..., to retain [Rostherne] parish church in Coventry and Lichfield diocese, 1337

......, ..., bishop of Worcester, death of, 59

......, Silvester, archpriest of Lucca cathedral, 59, 60

......, ..., canon (and prebendary) of Lucca cathedral, 59

......, ..., ..., resignation of, 1002

......, ..., provision of to the bishopric of Worcester, 59

......, ..., absolution of preliminary to

de' Gigli (*contd*)
provision, 60

......, ..., bishop of Worcester, 364, 441, 951, 963, 1002

......, ..., ..., assent of, to payment of pension on fruits of episcopal *mensa*, 963

......, ..., ..., commend to of rectory of Benabbio, cession of, 364

......, ..., ..., commendatory prior of the Augustinian priory of S. Michele in Foro, Lucca, 441

......, ..., ..., ..., licence to, facilitating the rebuilding of the priory, 441

......, ..., ..., resignation of, of hospital of St Michael, Cortesora, 951

......, ..., ..., continual commensal familiar of *see* da ?Civezzano, Paolo di Niccolò

Gilbert (Gilberd, Gilberti), Robert, rector of Saltfleetby (All Saints), 140

......, Thomas, canon and prebendary of Exeter and incumbent of Lympsham, 717

......, ..., canon of Wells, papal judge delegate, 987

......, William, prior of the Augustinian priory of Bruton, 260

Giles (Gylis), alias of Inell, *q.v.*

Gilforde, Gilfordi *see* Guildford

[Gill Abbey] *see* Cork

Gillford' *see* Guildford

Gimnays, William, rector of Langenhoe, 296

Giovanni Antonio, cardinal priest of SS Nereo e Achilleo *see* [de Sangiorgio], Giovanni Antonio

Giovanni Battista, cardinal priest of SS Giovanni e Paolo *see* [Orsini], Giovanni Battista

?Giulus, Philip, canon of Cork cathedral, papal mandatary, 15

[Glamorgan, co. of], place in *see* Merthyr Tydfil

Glascarrig (Glassarge) [*in* Donaghmore, co. Wexford], Benedictine priory of, possessions of the grange of Ballon belonging to, 981

......, ..., prior and convent of, possessions of Ballon to be granted in farm with consent of, 981

Glascro *see* Clashacrow

Glasgow [co. Lanark], **[cathedral] church** of, dean of, papal mandatary, 642, 792

......, ..., subdeanery of, 301

......, ..., ..., fruits of, pension on, 301

......, ..., subdeans of *see* Blackadder, Roland; Gifferd, Alexander

......, ..., precentorship of, 80

......, ..., precentors of *see* Forman, Robert; Goldsmith, John

......, ..., chancellor of, papal judge delegate, 86

......, ..., canons of *see* Erskine, Thomas; Fraser, John; Gibson, John; Shearer, John; Stewart, Andrew

......, ..., prebends in *see* Ayr

......, ..., invasion and sacrilege of, 80

......, **archbishop** of, subjection to, of the church of Lismore, 57

......, ..., assignment to, of Dunblane as suffragan, 333

......, ..., papal mandatary, 535

......, ..., conclusion to, 55

......, ..., *see* [Blackadder], Robert

......, official of, papal judge delegate, 812

......, ..., papal mandatary, 301, 698, 929

......, ..., *see* Cunningham, David

......, church of, erection of, into metropolitan church with archiepiscopal dignity, 333

......, archdeaconry of, *cf.* 1146

......, archdeacons of *cf.* Madorack, Andrew

......, **city** of, person living in *see* Forsyth, Thomas

......, **diocese** of, persons of *see* Abirnethy, Walter; Arnot, David; Barbour, John;

Glasgow, **diocese** (*contd*)
Bell, Bernard; Betoun, James; Blackadder, Patrick and Robert; Brown, David; Carlile, John; Carmichael, James of; [Cranston], Thomas; Duncanson, John; Elphinstone, Robert; Fraser, Robert; Goldsmith, John; Hamilton, David; Ker, George and Thomas; Madorack, Andrew; Merchinston, James; Montgomery, Alexander, of Braidstane; Montgomery, Hugh, lord of; Montgomery, John, knight; Montgomery, Robert; Morwel, Wynninus; Pannetter, Thomas; Scott, John; Semple, Margaret; Shaw, George and Robert; Spens, John; Stewart, Alexander and Walter; Turnbull, William; Valastz, William; Wardlaw, William

......, ..., places in *see* Annan; Auchinleck; Bothwell; Braidstane; Carmichael; Carnwath; Craigie; ?Cumbray; Dalmilling; Dumbarton; Dundonald; Glen; Glenholm; Innerleithen; Jedburgh; Johnstone; Largs; Lochwinnoch; Melrose; Monkton; Paisley; Prestwick; ?Quothquan; Riccarton; St Quivox; Southwick; Sweetheart

......, province of, restoration from, of church of Dunblane, to province of St Andrews, 333

Glasney [*in* St Gluvias, at Penryn, Corn], [collegiate] church of St Thomas the Martyr of, 85

Glassarge *see* Glascarrig

Glastonbury (Glastenbery') [Som], [Benedictine] monastery of, abbot of, papal mandatary, 174, 394

Glasvaar (Glusner) [*in* Kilmichael Glassary, co. Argyll], place of, 493

Glatton (Glatton') [Hunts], parish church of, 477

'Gleandbannam', vulgarly '?Ileraunr', diocese of Killaloe [*unidentified*; but *cf.*

'Gleandbannam' (*contd*)
Glenbane *in* Shanagolden, co. Limerick], portion of in the collegiate church of Scattery Island, 818

Glen (Glen') [*now represented by* Glenhead *in* Lochwinnoch, co. Renfrew], lands of pertaining to Cluniac monastery of Paisley, fruits of, grant of, 63

Glenbane *see* 'Gleandbannam'

Glendalough [co Wicklow], [cathedral] church of, chapter of, conclusion to, 579

......, bishop of, papal mandatary, 779

......, ..., *see* [?FitzJohn], Francis; [Ruffi], Ivo

......, church of, vassals of, conclusion to, 579

......, city and diocese of, clergy of, conclusion to, 579

......, ..., people of, conclusion to, 579

Glenguhon' *see* ?Quothquan

Glenhead *see* Glen

Glenholm [co. Peebles], [parish church of], 781

Glennahoo (Glenquhaw), alias of Ballyduff, *q.v.*

Glentham (Glenth(a)m) [Lincs], parish church of, vicar of, 2

[Glin, *in* Kilfergus, co. Limerick], knight of *see* Militis

'Glochmor' [*unidentified; perhaps obsolete; probably in* the barony of Moycarn, co. Roscommon *or* barony of Longford, co. Galway, *near* the confluence of the Suck and Shannon], ecclesiastical lands of belonging to the episcopal *mensa* of Clonfert, grant of, 146

Gloucester [Glos], Benedictine monastery of St Peter, 505

......, ..., abbot of, papal judge delegate, 442

Gloucester (*contd*)
......, ..., monk of *see* Weston, Ambrose
......, Augustinian monastery of B. Mary near *see* Lanthony II by Gloucester

[Gloucester, co. of], places in *see* Boxwell; Bristol; Cromhall; ?Farmington; Gloucester; Hartpury; Haselton; Lanthony II by Gloucester; Lasborough; Lechlade; Leighterton; Mickleton; Rendcombe; Rissington, Little; Sodbury; Tewkesbury; Tirley; Winchcombe

Glusner *see* Glasvaar

Godellw *see* Ogulla

Godenow *see* Goodnow

Goff *cf.* Gogh

Gogh, alias of Smyth, John, *q.v.*
......, *cf.* Gough

Goldsmith (Aurifabri, Goldsmyth), John, ostensible priest of Glasgow diocese, claimant to precentorship of Glasgow, 80
......, ..., supporters (named) of, 80
......, Thomas, vicar of Charlton, 208

[Goldwell], James, bishop of Norwich, death of, 553

Goler, Wolffgangus, familiar of Fer(di)nandus Ponzettus, 1001
......, ..., ..., provision of to a canonry and prebend of the church of Holy Trinity, Speyer, 1001

Goodicwyn *see* Goodwyn

Goodmanham (Goodmadanie) [Yorks], parish church of, 566

Goodnow (Godenow), Roger, rector of Whissonsett, 419

Goodwyn (Goodicwyn, Goodwyn', Goodwyne'), John, abbot of the

Goodwyn (*contd*)
Cistercian monastery of Robertsbridge, 527
......, ..., chaplain in the parish church of St Clement, Hastings, 79
......, William, canon of the Augustinian priory of Combwell, 899

Gordon (Gordone), Adam, cleric of Moray diocese, 931
......, ..., resignation of, of precentorship of Moray, 931
......, ..., assignment to, of pension on fruits of precentorship, 931
......, ..., proctor (unnamed) of, 931
......, Alexander, collation to, of precentorship of Moray, 931, 1296
......, ..., assent of, to assignment of pension on fruits of precentorship, 931

Gornaclohy *see* Gortnaclohy

[de Gorrevodo], Ludovicus, bishop of Maurienne, commend to, of the Benedictine monastery of Ambronay, 577, 578
......, ..., to take oath of fealty, 577, 578

Gortnaclohy (Gornaclohy) *see* Creagh [co. Cork]

Gortnacrusha (Cornacrusi) [*in* Templetrine, co. Cork], church, called particle of, to be erected into prebend in Cork cathedral, with church of ?Ballymountain and rectory of Templetrine united thereto, 255

[Gortnasharvoge *in* Creagh, co. Roscommon] *see* Muinter Chineith

'Gortnuybg'' [*unidentified*; *perhaps obsolete*; *probably in* the barony of Moycarn, co. Roscommon *or* the barony of Longford, co. Galway, *near* the confluence of the Suck and Shannon], ecclesiastical lands abutting belonging to the episcopal *mensa* of Clonfert, grant of, 146

'Gortuaglothbg'' [*unidentified*; *perhaps*

'Gortuaglothbg" (contd)
obsolete; probably in the barony of Moycarn, co. Roscommon or the barony of Longford, co. Galway, near the confluence of the Suck and Shannon], ecclesiastical lands of belonging to the episcopal mensa of Clonfert, grant of, 146

Goryng, John [the Franciscan?], dispensed for plurality, 1272

Gottis, Richard, canon of the Augustinian priory of Walsingham, 336
......, ..., ..., vicar of Narford, 336

[Goudhurst, Kent], place in see Combwell

Gough cf. Gogh

?Goven' [unidentified; perhaps obsolete; probably in the barony of Moycarn, co. Roscommon or the barony of Longford, co. Galway, near the confluence of the Suck and Shannon], ecclesiastical lands of belonging to the episcopal mensa of Clonfert, grant of, 146

Graffham (Grasham) [Sussex], parish church of, 480

Grafton (Graston), Adam, rector of Upton Magna, incumbent of St Dionis [Backchurch], London, and sometime vicar of St Alkmund's, Shrewsbury, 233

Graham (Graha(m)me), William, lord of, nobleman, appeal of, 435

Graham alias Grantham see Grantham

Graha(m)me see Graham

Grant (Brant', Grawnt, Grunt), John, to be canon of Ossory, 1152
......, ..., detainer of vicarage of Dunkitt and rectory of Kilcraggan, 157, 545
......, ..., late rector of Aglishmartin and Ballytarsney, 787

Grantham (Graham alias Grantham, Granth(a)m) [Lincs], parish church of, 482
......, place near, 202

Grasham see Graffham

Graston see Grafton

Gravesend (Gravisende) [Kent], parish church of, 522

Grawnt see Grant

Great Bradley see Bradley

Greatconnell (Connayl) [co. Kildare], Augustinian monastery of, prior and convent of, rectory of Lynally detained by, 162

Great Easton see Easton Magna

Great Hardres see Hardres, Great

Great Horwood see Horwood, Great

Great Langton see Langton, Great

Great Milton see Milton, Great

Great Missenden see Missenden

Great Musgrave see Musgrave

Greenlaw (Grenlau), Hugh, provision of, to the deanery of Ross, 782, 839
......, ..., assent of, to assignment of tithes and fruits belonging to deanery, 782

Greenwich, West (Westgoynewich') alias Deptford (Depfford) [now Deptford, Kent], parish church of St Nicholas, 271

Gregory IX, constitution of concerning reconciliation of polluted churches, 411; cf. 848

Gregory, bishop of Clonfert see [OBrogy], Gregory

Greislei *see* Gresley

Grene, Hugh, vicar of St Martin's, Hereford, 367
......, ..., cleric living in the city or diocese of Hereford, 9
......, ..., ..., commissary of the dean of Hereford, proceedings by, 9
......, ..., ..., appeal of, 9
......, Thomas, rector of Sundridge, 917

Grenes *see* Greves

Grenlau *see* Greenlaw

Gresley (Greislei), John, of Coventry and Lichfield diocese, dispensed for plurality [i.e. dispensed for a benefice with cure], 1085

Gretyngham, Laurence, of Norwich diocese, dispensed for plurality, 1045

Greves (Grenes), Peter, canon of London, papal judge delegate, 906

Grice (Gryse), John, union for, of one of his parish churches to the other, Salisbury diocese, 1092

Griffith (Gryffith), John, of Worcester diocese, dispensed for plurality, 1067

Grigg (Grigge), John, of Winchester diocese, dispensed for plurality, 1189

Grimaldi, Agostino, Genoese, canon of the Augustinian monastery (Lateran Congregation) of St Th(e)odorus [*diocese unstated*] and continual commensal of Federicus [Sanseverinas], cardinal deacon of St Theodorus, 854
......, ..., ..., ..., ..., provision of to the parish church of Treglio, 854

Grimoldby (Grymolbe) [Lincs], parish church of, 141

Grove (Grone), Thomas, master of the chapel of Sts John the Baptist and John

Grove (*contd*)
the Evangelist in the cemetery of Norwich cathedral, 777

Grunt *see* Grant

Gryffith *see* Griffith

Grymolbe *see* Grimoldby

Grymston, Henry, rector of Goodmanham, 566

Gryse *see* Grice

Guemps (Campe) [*in dép.* of Pas-de-Calais, France], parish church of, 699

Guernesey (Gernesey) [Channel Islands], island of, 817

Guildford (Gilforde, Gilfordi, Gillford') [Surrey], parish church of St Nicholas at the bridge, rector of, 504
......, parish church of the Holy Trinity of, 175, 968

Guînes (Guysnes) [*in dép.* of Pas-de-Calais, France], place near, 699
......, county of, 699

Guisborough (Gyseburn') [Yorks], Augustinian monastery of, canon of *see* Baker, William

Gulland (Gulialanda) [*in* Dulverton, Som], land of, 174

Gulture *see* Guthrie

Gunby, Thomas, cleric in Danbury parish church, 528

Gutfold' *see* Cutfolde

Guthrie (Gulture, Guthre), David, canon of Aberdeen, papal mandatary, 793
......, *Decanum* [*recte* David?], canon of Aberdeen, papal judge delegate, 435
......, John, bishop of Ross, death of, 637

Gwennap [Corn], parish church of, 85

Gwynn (Gwyn), Maurice, vicar of Llanbadarn Fawr and canon and prebendary of Abergwili, 893

Gybbons (Gybins), William, rector of Bradley and incumbent of Church Eaton, 217

Gylis *see* Giles

Gyllco(n)yery(n)d *see* Kilconierin

Gyseburn' *see* Guisborough

H

Habrough (Haburgh) [Lincs], parish church of, 427

Haddington (Hadyngton', Hathientonen) [co. Haddington], parish church of, altar of B. Mary the Virgin in, chaplaincy at founded by Alexander Cockburn, 366
......, ..., ..., ..., land called 'Herperseldi' belonging to, 366
......, ..., ..., ..., patron (named) of, 366
......, ..., ..., chaplain at, 366
......, place in *see* Harperdean
......, constabulary of, county of, 356

[Haddington *or* East Lothian, co. of], places in *see* Aberlady; Dunbar; Haddington; Pinkerton

Hadynh(a)m, John, rector of St Thomas's, Winchelsea, 674

Haerlany *see* Holycross

Hafter (Haster), John, rector of Ashwell, 317

Haghmo(n)de *see* Haughmond

[Hailsham, Sussex], place in *see* Michelham

Halbarden' *see* Hawardyn

Hales, John, bishop of Coventry and Lichfield *see* [Hales *or* Arundel], John
......, Thomas, layman, parishioner of Henley on Thames, litigant, 906

[Hales *or* Arundel], John, bishop of Coventry and Lichfield, approval and confirmation by, of chantry founded by John Bradburn and his wife Ann in Ashbourne parish church and ?Hognaston chapel, 292

Haliday (Halidai), Richard, vicar of Stratton St Margaret, 338

Halkerston (Halkerston'), Thomas, cleric of St Andrews diocese, 333, 778
......, ..., ..., proctor of Robert [Blackadder], archbishop of Glasgow, 333
......, ..., ..., proctor of Thomas Maywel, 778
......, ..., provost of Crichton, 844
......, ..., ..., provision of to succentorship of Moray, 844
......, ..., ..., cession of, 844
......, ..., ..., assignment to, of pension on fruits of succentorship, 844

?Hallewynsm', North Wingfield *alias, q.v.*

Hallo, John, union for, of one of his parish churches to the other, Salisbury diocese, 1305

Halstead (Halstede) [Essex], parish church of, 201, 664
......, ..., Bourchier chantry in, 664
......, ..., ..., union to, of the parish church of Drinkstone, 664

Haltemprice (Hautrenpice) [Yorks], Augustinian priory of, 299
......, ..., canon of *see* Kirkham, William

Haltowm' *see* Hatton

Ham' *see* Georgeham

Ham, East (Eschin') [Essex], vicarage of,

Ham, East (*contd*)
union to, of the parish church of South
Thoresby, 703

Ham, West (Westhan')[Essex], parish
church of, 307
......, ..., place in *see* Stratford Langthorne

Hamerton (Hamerton') [Hunts], parish
church of, union to, of the parish church
of Stretton on the Fosse, 282

Hamilton (Hamilton', Hamulton), David,
cleric of Glasgow diocese, 55, 56, 58
......, ..., ..., provision of, to the bishopric
of Lismore, 55
......, ..., ..., absolution of preliminary to
provision, 56
......, ..., ..., dispensation of over
illegitimacy and minority preliminary to
provision, 58
......, ..., [bishop-] elect of Lismore, faculty
for consecration of, 57

Hammond (Hamond), John, of Lincoln
diocese, dispensed for plurality, 1277

[Hampshire], places in *see* Andover; Ashe;
Breamore; Burghclere; Carisbrooke;
Chalton; Cheriton; Clanfield; Heckfield;
Meonstoke; Monxton; Niton; Odiham;
Overton; Sherborne St John; Stoke
Charity; Titchfield; Wallop, Over;
Waltham, ?North; Weyhill; Winchester

Hampton Bishop (Hampton') [Heref],
parish church of, 517

Hamstall Ridware *see* Ridware, Hamstall

Hamulton *see* Hamilton

Hanacl *see* Annacalla

Hancock (Hancok), John, rector of Helland,
676
......, William, rector of St Clement's,
Worcester, 432

Hanlon (Hanlan, Hanlan', Hanlayn), Philip,
cleric of Cloyne diocese, to have

Hanlon (*contd*)
vicarages of Derryvillane and
Kildorrery, 941
......, William, canon of Cloyne, papal
mandatary, 159, 160, 941, 942

Hanney [*now* West Hanney, Berks], parish
church of, 222

Hanwell (Hanwell') [Oxon], parish church
of, 238

Haolt *alias* Baker, Henry, canon of the
Premonstratensian monastery of
Wendling, 337

Hardham (Herdham), alternative name of
Heryngham, *q.v.*

Hardham [Sussex], place in *see* Heryngham

Hardingham (Hardyngham) [Norf], parish
church of, 532

Hardres, Great (Magna Harde) [*now* Upper
Hardres, Kent], parish church of, 297

Hardyngham *see* Hardingham

Hare, Thomas, rector of Heydon, 704
......, ..., canon and prebendary of B. Mary
in the Fields, Norwich, and vicar of
Twickenham, 872

Hareodon' *see* Harrowden

Hareys *see* Harrys

Harington (Haryngton), James, rector of
Badsworth, 718
......, William, canon of London and
prebendary of Islington and incumbent
of Great Langton, 873
......, ..., of York diocese, dispensed for
plurality, 1273
......, *cf.* Haryndon

Harman (Harmon), alias of Veysey, John,
q.v.

Haroppe *see* Harrop

Harper (Arpur), Cornelius, rector of Walton, 724

Harperdean [*in* Haddington, co. Haddington] *see* 'Herperseldi'

Harpery *see* Hartpury

Harrald, John, rector of Haselton, 352

Harringay (Haryngiay) [*now* Hornsey, Midd], parish church of, union of, to the canonry and prebend of Ealdstreet in London cathedral, 281

Harrison (Harrison'), Hugh, rector of Evedon, 103

Harrop (Haroppe), Thomas, rector of Stoke Talmage, 526

Harrowden (Hareodon') [*now* Great Harrowden, Northants], parish church of, 95

Harrys (Hareys), John, of Norwich diocese, dispensed for plurality, 1106
......, Thomas, union for, of his parish church [in Exeter diocese?] to his canonry of Exeter, 1048

Hartpury (Harpery) [Glos], parish church of, 695

Harww, John, canon of the Augustinian priory of Taunton, 6

Haryndon *cf.* Harington

Haryngiay *see* Harringay

Haryngton *see* Harington

Haselbere (Haselbery), prebend of in Wells cathedral, union to, of the parish church of Kelston, 473

Haselbury Plucknett [Som] *cf.* Haselbere

Haseley, Edward, rector of Martley, 265

Haselton (Hasylton) [Glos], parish church of, 352

Haster *see* Hafter

Hasting (Hastyng), John, of York diocese, dispensed for plurality, 1087

Hastings (Astingg') [Sussex], parish church of St Clement of, chaplain in, 79

Hastyng *see* Hasting

Hasylton *see* Haselton

Hathasecuth *see* Ahascragh

Hathientonen *see* Haddington

Hathluam *see* Athlone

Hatton (Haltowm') [*in* Kinloss, co. Elgin], vill of, pertaining to Cistercian monastery of Kinloss, 155
......, ..., assignment of, 155

Hatton, John, provision of, to bishopric of Negropont, 1324
......, ..., absolution of preliminary to provision, 1327
......, ..., faculty for consecration of, 1325
......, ..., to retain parish church and simple benefices in London and Rochester dioceses, 1326
......, ..., indulged for non-residence, 1328

Haughmond (Haghmo(n)de) [*in* Haughmond Demesne, Salop], Augustinian monastery of, abbots of, faculty to, to use mitre, etc., 686
......, ..., abbot of, *mensa* of, 686
......, ..., ..., *see* [?Pontisbury], Richard
......, ..., convent of, 686
......, ..., canons, servants, and novices of, 686

Hautrenpice *see* Haltemprice

Hawardyn (Halbarden', Hauuardyn), Humphrey, official of the [archi]

Hawardyn (*contd*)
episcopal court of Canterbury, litigation
before, 661
......, ..., official of the metropolitical court
of Canterbury, proceedings by, 456
......, ..., ..., assignment by, of term to
bishop of Exeter or his vicar to inquire
into right of presentation, 456

Hawkchurch (Hawkechuych) [Dors *now*
Devon], parish church of, 204

Hawlay, Robert, rector of Cosgrove, 112

Hayne, John, brother of the new hospital of
B. Mary the Virgin without
Bishopsgate, London, OSA, 564

Healaugh (Helay, Hellaghe or Helley)
[Yorks], Augustinian priory of, prior of,
papal judge delegate, 990, 999
......, ..., canon of *see* Senhouse, Simon

Hebran, William, of Worcester diocese,
dispensed for plurality, 1235

Hebrides, Outer *see* Lewis

Heckfield (Hekfelde, Helifelde) [Hants],
parish church of, 84, 96

Heddington (Hedyngdon') [Wilts], parish
church of, 389

Hedge (Hegge), Thomas, rector of Little
Whelnetham, 488

Hedingham, Sible (Hermyngh(a)m Sybill')
[Essex], parish church of, 189

Hedyan, Hedyan' *see* OHedian

Hedygton', William, rector of Weyhill, 680

Hedyngdon' *see* Heddington

Hegge *see* Hedge

Hekfelde *see* Heckfield

Helay *see* Healaugh

Helifelde *see* Heckfield

Helis, Geoffrey, canon of St Asaph and
prebendary of ?Meifod, otherwise
cursal, and incumbent of ?Llanfarchell
and ?Bodfari, 483
......, *cf.* Ellis

Hellaghe or Helley *see* Healaugh

Helland (Hellond') [Corn], parish church
of, 676

Helley, alias of Hellaghe, *q.v.*

Hellond' *see* Helland

Helmsley (Helmesley), Henry, monk of the
Cistercian monastery of Revesby, 171

Helwys, Richard, portioner of Grimoldby,
141

Helysdon *cf.* Heylesdon

Hendon (Hendon') [Midd], parish church
of, 794

Hendred, East (Eschenreth', Esthenreth')
[Berks], parish church of, rector of, 439,
911

Henellan Amgoed *see* Henllan-Amgoed

Henley on Thames [Oxon], parish church
of, rector of, 906
......, ..., parishioner of, 906
......, ..., tithes payable by reason of,
litigation over, 906

Henllan-Amgoed (Henellan Amgoed) [co.
Carmarthen], parish church of, 725

Henry I, king of the English, 174

Henry [VII], king of England, first born of
see Arthur, prince of Wales
......, ..., mother of *see* [Beaufort], Margaret
......, ..., collation of religious house by,
515
......, ..., conclusion to, 59, 546, 553, 579

Henry [VII] (*contd*)
  note, 581, 591, 594, 598, 602, 606, 617, 626, 627, 634, 776, 1006, 1012, 1021, 1029
  ......, ..., ambassador to, of Ferdinand [V], king of Castile and Leon, 808
  ......, ..., barber of *see* Narbonne, Peter of
  ......, ..., chapel of, [member] of *see* Toft, William
  ......, ..., chaplains of *see* [Blythe], Geoffrey; Layburne, Roger
  ......, ..., counsellors of *see* [Blythe], Geoffrey; Colyns, Martin; [Jane], Thomas; Urswick, Christopher
  ......, ..., Master of Requests of *see* [Jane], Thomas
  ......, ..., keeper of the rolls of the chancery of *see* [Warham], William

Henry, bishop of Bangor *see* [Dean(e)], Henry
  ......, archbishop of Canterbury *see* [Dean(e)], Henry
  ......, bishop of Salisbury *see* [Dean(e)], Henry
  ......, bishop of Winchester *see* [de Blois], Henry
  ......, late abbot of Cambuskenneth *see* [Arnot], Henry

Henton' Bluet *see* Hinton Blewett

Henyngham', John, OCarm, 273

Hepburn (Hopburn'), George, treasurer of Moray, incumbent of Calder, and litigant over deanery of Dunkeld, 237
  ......, John, scholar of St Andrews diocese, 332

Herbert *alias* Newlond, James, canon of the Augustinian priory of Merton, 87

Herdham *see* Hardham

Hereford [Heref], [Benedictine] priory of St Guthlac of, prior of, papal judge delegate, 9
  ......, parish churches in:
    St Martin's, 367

Hereford (*contd*)
  St Peter's, 876
  ......, [**cathedral**] **church** of, deanery of, district of, 9
  ......, ..., dean of, inquisition of crimes committed within the deanery pertains to, 9
  ......, ..., ..., papal judge delegate, 8
  ......, ..., ..., *see* Hervey, John
  ......, ..., canon of *see* Dodyne, Benedict

  ......, **bishop** of, papal judge delegate, 29, 442
  ......, ..., *see* [Audley], Edmund
  ......, [church of], archdeacon of Shropshire in, *q.v.*

  ......, **diocese** of, persons of *see* Bacheler, John; Backer, John; Brenex, William; Brent, John; Bromuoych, James; Du(n)mow, John; Frecce, Richard; Grene, Hugh; Heyly, John; Lunbard, John; Malpas, Thomas; Page, Richard; Spicer, Robert; Whitelegg, Robert; *cf.* Richardson, Robert
  ......, ..., places in *see* Burford; Hampton Bishop; Ledbury; Monkland; Monmouth; Monnington on Wye; Stoke Lacy; Wenlock, Much; Woolhope; *cf.* Church Stretton

[Hereford, co. of], places in *see* Hampton Bishop; Hereford; Ledbury; Monkland; Monnington on Wye; Stoke Lacy; Woolhope

Hermannus, S.R.E. subdiaconus et notarius, 174

Hermyngh(a)m Sybill' *see* Sible Hedingham

'Herperseldi', St Andrews diocese? [*unidentified; possibly now represented by* Harperdean (*in* Haddington, co. Haddington)], lands called belonging to chaplaincy in Haddington parish church, grant of, 366

Herrethayn *see* ?Ardkeen

[Hertford, co. of], places in *see* Holwell;
Pelham, Furneux; St Albans

Hervey (Ervyc, Hervye), John, dean of
Hereford, 8, 9
......, ..., ..., commissary of *see* Grene,
Hugh
......, ..., ..., papal judge delegate, litigation
before, 8
......, ..., ..., ..., sub-delegate of *see*
Dodyne, Benedict

Heryngham or Hardham (Herdham,
Heryngg.m) [*in* Hardham, Sussex],
Augustinian monastery of, 438, 735
......, ..., canons of *see* Bradshaw, Thomas;
Trappe, John

Hestercombe (Aistercumba, Aystrcumba)
[*in* Kingston, Som], land and garden in,
174

Hethe (Heth) [Oxon], parish church of, 705

Heversham (Eversham) [Westm], parish
church of, vicarage of, 742

Heydon [Norf], parish church of, rector of,
704

Heye *see* Eye

Heyford Warren (Heyford' Magna) [Oxon],
parish church of, 955

Heylesdon (Heylysdon'), Ralph, OFM,
445, 963
......, ..., ..., provision of, to the [titular]
bishopric of Ascalon, 963
......, ..., ..., [bishop-] elect of Ascalon, 963
......, ..., ..., ..., assignment to, of pension
on fruits of episcopal *mensa* of
Worcester, 963
......, *cf.* Helysdon

Heyly, John, portioner of Burford, 738

Heylysdon' *see* Heylesdon

Hickling (Hyckelyng) [Norf], Augustinian
monastery of, 802

Hickling (*contd*)
......, ..., canon of *see* Chambyr, Robert

Hicks (Hikkys), John, cleric of Exeter
diocese, 456
......, ..., ..., presentation of, for parish
church of Exminster, 456
......, ..., ..., institution of refused, 456
......, ..., ..., appeal of, 456

de Hidona (de Ydona), Geoffrey and
Osbert, property gifted to Taunton
priory by, 174

High Easter *see* Easter, High

Highleigh (Hilegh') [*in* Sidlesham, Sussex],
prebend of in Chichester cathedral, 179
......, ..., destined for teacher at Chichester
grammar school, 179

Hikkys *see* Hicks

Hilegh' *see* Highleigh

Hill (Hill'), John, canon of London, 8
......, ..., ..., papal sub-delegate, litigation
before, 8

Hille (Hylle), Christopher, OFM, 446

Hinche *see* Inch

Hinton Blewett (Henton' Bluet) [Som],
parish church of, 679

Hobbine *see* Home

Hobyll, John, vicar of Enfield, 681

Hodgson (Hodgeson), Patrick, of Lincoln
diocese, dispensed for plurality, 1274
......, *cf.* [Hogeson]

Hodii, Donald, vicar of Rathaspick, 192
......, ..., ..., deprivation, excommunication,
and suspension of, 192
......, ..., ..., appeal of, 192
......, ..., ..., recourse of, to archbishop of
Dublin, 192

Hofergil *see* OFarrell

[Hogeson], Thomas, abbot of the Cistercian monastery of Woburn, dispensed for plurality, 1269
......, *cf.* Hodgson

?Hognaston (Hoghen) [Derb], chapel of B. Mary the Virgin, chaplain in, 292
......, ..., chantry of John Bradburn and his wife Ann in, 292
......, inhabitants of, divine offices to be celebrated and sacraments administered in the chapel for, 292
......, ..., in the parish of Ashbourne, 292
......, person of *see* Bradburn, John

Hohe, Hohea *see* OHea

Hohenayn *see* OHonan

Hohounyn, de Mivrey *alias, see* OHonan

Hoin, Elizabeth, nun of the Cistercian monastery of Eccles, 410
......, ..., ..., dispensed with a view to her becoming prioress, 410
......, *cf.* Home

Hokh(a)m *see* Holkham

?Holcot (Holcote) [Beds], parish church of, rector of, 114

Holdirnessa, Robert, rector of Braybrooke, 498

Holkham (Hokh(a)m) [Norf], parish church of, 814

Holme, Roger, chantry of, in London cathedral, 800

Holt, John, rector of Smarden, 489

Holwell (Holwele) [Beds *now* Herts], parish church of, 560

Holycross (Haerlany, Huochtarlawan) [co. Tipperary], [Cistercian] monastery of,

Holycross (*contd*)
abbot of, papal mandatary, 385, 786

Holyrood *see* Edinburgh

Holy Trinity, parish church of *see* Ogonnelloe

Homana', Thomas, detainer of the vicarage of Kilmeen, 250
......, *cf.* OManahan

Home (Hobbine, Hovine, Hovvint, Hovvme, Howme), John, monk, recently prior, of the Benedictine priory of Coldingham, 535
......, ..., cession of, 535
......, ..., assignment to of half fruits of priory's lands and tithes in place of pension, 535
......, ..., to have re-entry, 535
......, Ninian, provision of to regular priory in St Andrews diocese, 1217
......, ..., cleric of St Andrews diocese, 535
......, ..., ..., provision of to the Benedictine priory of Coldingham, 535
......, ..., ..., assent of, to assignment of half fruits of priory's lands and tithes in place of pension, 535
......, ..., of St Andrews diocese, commission [by virtue of an appeal?], 1224
......, Nouianus [*recte* Ninian], of St Andrews diocese, validation for, 1290
......, Vivian [*recte* Ninian], of St Andrews diocese, dispensed for plurality, 1041
......, *cf.* Hoin

Honghton' Conquest *see* Houghton Conquest

Honghton' super Hill *see* Houghton on the Hill

Honywood (Honywodi, Honywoode), Robert, archdeacon of Norwich, 36, 377
......, ..., indulged to visit his archdeaconry of Norwich by deputy, 1098

Hoo [Kent], parish church of St Werburgh in, 271

Hooper (Hoper) *alias* Pittemyster, Richard, monk, recently abbot, of the Cistercian monastery of Dunkeswell, 148

Hopburn' *see* Hepburn

Hoper *see* Hooper

Horde, Roger, of Exeter diocese, dispensed for plurality, 1130

Horga *see* OHea

Hornby, Henry, canon of Lincoln and prebendary of Nassington, incumbent of Burton Bradstock, 154

Horndon on the Hill (Hornedon' on the Hill) [Essex], parish church of, 913

Hornsey *see* Harringay

Horrey *see* ?Erry

Horsey, William, of Bath and Wells diocese, dispensed for plurality, 1069

Horton (Horton'), James, rector of the hospital of St John the Baptist, Bath, 520

Horwood, Great (Horwood Magna) [Bucks], parish church of, 424

Houghton Conquest (Honghton' Conquest) [Beds], parish church of, 279

Houghton on the Hill (Honghton' super Hill) [Leics], parish church of, 152

Housieside (Ly Houss Syd) [*in* Udny, co. Aberdeen], tithes of, 928

Hovine, Hovvint, Hovvme *see* Home

Howden (Howeden') [Yorks], William Stewardi of, *q.v.*

Howell (Aphowel, Aphowell), Thomas, archdeacon of Cardigan, 318, 739

Howell (*contd*)
......, ..., ..., rector of Llanllwchaiarn, 318, 739
......, ..., ..., ..., sometime incumbent of Churchover, 739
......, *cf.* ap Hywel

Howme *see* Home

Hudburryn *see* Woodburn

Hugan *see* Wogan

Hugh Ap [*patronymic wanting*], rector of ?Llanfechell, 393

Hugh, bishop of Durham *see* [du Puiset], Hugh

Huish (Hwysch) [Devon], parish church of, 954

Hull, Bishop's (Hull', Ylla) [Som], church of, 174

Hunden', Thomas, rector of Holwell, 560

Hungerford *cf.* Hungersord'

Hungersord' *alias* Doderoffe (*or* Boderoffe), Thomas, rector of St Mary Magdalen's near Bermondsey, 105

Hunt (Hunte), Henry, rector of Netteswell, 467
......, John, rector of Battlesden, 462

Huntingdon (Huntingdon', Hunttingdon'), archdeacon of in the church of Lincoln, *q.v.*

[Huntingdon, co. of], places in *see* Conington; Glatton; Hamerton; Orton Longueville; Ramsey; Ripton, Abbots; Stonely; *cf.* Brington

[Huntingdon], John, abbot of the Benedictine monastery of Ramsey, faculty for, 1173
......, ..., ..., indult for, 1174

Huntrodys, William, rector of Tidworth, 420

Hunttingdon' *see* Huntingdon

Huochtarlawan *see* Holycross

Hurley [Berks], Benedictine monastery of, monk of *see* Einster, Thomas

Hussey (Husse), Thomas, vicar of Oakley (Bucks), 170

Hutton (Hutten'), Thomas, indulged to visit his archdeaconry of Lincoln by deputy, 1309
......, ..., cleric living in the city or diocese of Lincoln, 46
......, ..., ..., commissary of the bishop of Lincoln, litigation before, 46

Hwysch *see* Huish

Hyckelyng *see* Hickling

Hyde *see* Winchester

Hyde, John, vicar of Tilehurst, 26
......, ..., vicar of Winsham, 916

Hye *see* Iona

Hylle *see* Hille

Hylsylhayn *see* Kilsheelan

Hyne, Thomas, of Ely diocese, dispensed for plurality, 1267

Hyslington, John, rector of St Romuald's, [Shaftesbury] and vicar of Tisbury, 733

Hysth *see* Ash Priors

ap Hywel *cf.* Howell

I

Ialbim, Charles, vicar of Taghboy, death of, 784

Ialbim (*contd*)
......, *cf.* OFalvin

Ialstret *see* Ealdstreet

Ian' *see* Jane

Iboston' *see* Johnstone

Ichington (Ychyngton), Robert, of Worcester diocese, dispensed for plurality, 1181
......, ..., prior of the Augustinian priory of St Sepulchre, Warwick, 1181 *note*

Icklesham (Ickyllyscham') [Sussex], parish church of, 262

Idruymlehan *see* Drumlane

Idvie(s) (Idwy) [*now* Kirkden, co. Forfar], parish church of, 843

Ieriponte *see* Jerpoint

Ikerrin (Ogarryn), alias of Bourney, *q.v.*

'?Ileraunr' *see* 'Gleandbannam'

Illogan (St Illogan) [Corn], parish church of, union of, to a prebend in Exeter cathedral, 684

Ilongayn *see* OLongan

Imistyok *see* Inistioge

Inch (Hinche) [co. Cork], parish church of, rectory of, to be united anew to newly erected prebend of 'Ferrebiythi' in Cloyne cathedral, 1000

Inchcleraun [an island in Lough Ree, *in* Cashel, co. Longford], Augustinian monastery of B. Mary of, priorship of, 837
......, ..., priors of *see* OFarrell, Maurus and Roceus
......, ..., canon of *see* OFarrell, Maurus

Inchcolm [*in* Aberdour, co. Fife],

Inchcolm (*contd*)
    Augustinian monastery of, abbot and
    convent of, letters of protection for, 108
......, 'baptized islands' near, 108

Inchegall (Ynchgall) [*once an island in*
    Lochore (now drained) *in* Ballingry
    parish, co. Fife], chapel of St Andrew
    near, holder of, 248
......, diocese of Whithorn [*recte* St
    Andrews], 248

Inchicronan (Inisconayn, Inniscronan',
    Inyscronayn, Ynayscronayn) [co.
    Clare], [Augustinian] monastery of,
    prior of, papal mandatary, 313, 646,
    650, 948

Inchmacnerin (Insimyceryneyn *alias*
    Mitnere) [an island in Lough Key, *now*
    Church Island, *in* Boyle, co.
    Roscommon], Augustinian priory of,
    936
......, ..., priors of *see* OBanaghan, Thomas;
    OConnor, Theoderic

Inchydoney Island (Insula ?Ynmdemy) [*in*
    Island, co. Cork], parish church of,
    vicarage of, to be united to canonry of
    Ross and prebend of Curragranemore,
    256

Inell *alias* Giles (Gylis), Alexander, rector
    of Kilmington and incumbent of
    Merthyr Tydfil, 452

Ingham [Lincs], parish church of, 706

Ingham (Inghem) [Norf], Trinitarian house
    of, prior and brethren of, confirmation
    for, of house's erection and of union of
    parish church thereto, 1079

[Ingleby], John, bishop of Llandaff, death
    of, 598

[?Ingleby], Thomas, bishop of Rathlure,
    further dispensed for plurality, 1074

Inglis, Alexander, dean of Dunkeld, death
    of, 237

Inischfallayn *see* Innisfallen

Inisconayn *see* Inchicronan

Inishannon (Inisscoganayn, Ynseonnyn,
    ?Ynyseonan) [co. Cork], parish church
    of, rectory of, to be united to abbatial
    mensa of Tracton, 536
......, ..., ..., to be united to the canonry and
    prebend of Inishkenny in Cork
    cathedral, 822
......, ..., vicarage of, to be united to the
    proposed canonry and prebend of
    Ringcurran in Cork cathedral, 71
......, place in *see* ?Ballymountain

Inishcaltra (Inyschalcra) [cos. Clare and
    Galway], parish church of, vicarage of,
    to be united to canonry of Killaloe and
    prebend of Tulla, 650

Inishkenny (Ynserem) [co. Cork], prebend
    of in Cork cathedral, 822
......, ..., archdeaconry of Cork and rectory
    of Inishannon to be united to, 822

Inishlounaght (Suir) [co. Tipperary],
    Cistercian monastery of, 785, 789
......, ..., abbot of, papal mandatary, 949
......, ..., commendatory abbot of *see* Butler,
    Walter
......, ..., detainer of *see* ODonoghue,
    William
......, ..., convent and vassals of, 789

Inishmaine (Portmen', Portmen' *alias*
    Ennosmeon) [*in* Ballinchalla, cos.
    Mayo and Galway], parish church of,
    rectory of, to be erected, with Lough
    Mask, into prebend in Tuam cathedral,
    826
......, ..., ..., particle of Omey pertaining to,
    827
......, ..., rector of, assent of required for
    appropriation to another benefice of
    particle pertaining to rectory, 827

Inisscoganayn *see* Inishannon

Inistalhuhlin *see* Innisfallen

Inistioge (Imistyok, Instyog) [co. Kilkenny], [Augustinian] monastery of, prior of, papal mandatary, 545, 645

Inlymad see Tilliemaud

Innerleithen (Enerlchtan, Enerleithan, Enerlerthan, Enerlethan) [co. Peebles and Selkirk], parish church of, vicar of, 1015, 1017, 1018, 1020

Inniscronan' see Inchicronan

Innisfallen (Inischfallyn, Inistalhuhlin, Insfalben', Inyschfallyn, Isfahalen, Iusfaleyn, Ynnschfallyn) [an island in Lower Lake of Killarney, in Aghadoe, co. Kerry], [Augustinian] monastery of, prior of, papal mandatary, 250, 359, 360, 540, 939, 945, 993

Innocent III, statute of concerning abstinence, 394 [18]

Innocent VIII, Cistercian privileges confirmed by, 1020
......, consistorial provision by, 1015
......, letters of concerning notifying the camera of exchanges of benefices, 850
......, other letters of, 85, 131, 167, 215, 276, 277, 285, 318, 320, 322, 333, 424, 434, 495, 739, 862, 863, 918, 928
......, register of, exemplification from, 144

Insfalben' see Innisfallen

Insimyceryneyn alias Mitnere see Inchmacnerin

Instyog see Inistioge

Insula Vecte see Isle of Wight

Insula ?Ynmdemy see Inchydoney Island

Inver (Inwer) [co. Donegal], parish church of, rector of, 943

[Inverness, co. of], places in see Duthel; Lochaber; Petty-Brackley

Inverurie (Eurowry) [co. Aberdeen], parish church of, vicarage of, fruits of, pension on, 444
......, ..., vicar and late vicar of, 444

Inwer see Inver

Inyschalcra see Inishcaltra

Inyschfallyn see Innisfallen

Inyscronayn see Inchicronan

Inyskachy see Scattery Island

Iona (Hye) [an island in Kilfinichen and Kilvickeon, co. Argyll], Benedictine monastery of St Columba, 181
......, ..., (commendatory) abbots of see [Campbell], John; [Mackinnon], John

[ab Iorwerth], David see David [ab Iorwerth]

Ipplepen (Ipylpen') [Devon], vicarage of, union of, to the canonry and prebend of Compton Dundon of Wells cathedral, 1003

Ipswich [Suff], Augustinian priory of St Peter, 465
......, ..., canon of see Mullet, Nicholas

Ipylpen' see Ipplepen

Ireland, primate of see Armagh, archbishop of; [Spinelli (de Palatio)], Octavian
......, no studia generalia in, 511
......, places stated to be in, 22

Ireland (Irelond), William, rector of Cuxham, 858

Iseldon alias Islington, q.v.

Isertkelly (Disterkellay) [co. Galway], prebend of [in] Kilmacduagh cathedral, 983
......, parish church of, vicarage of, to be united to the canonry and prebend of

Isertkelly (*contd*)
  Isertkelly, 983

Isfahalen *see* Innisfallen

Island [co. Cork], place in *see* Inchydoney
  Island

Isle of Wight *see* Wight, Isle of

The Isles *see* Sodor

Islington (Iseldon *alias* Islington) [Midd],
  prebend of in London cathedral, union
  to, of the parish church of Great
  Langton, 873

Itahylle' *see* OCahill

Iuacbradayd *see* MacBrady

Iusfaleyn *see* Innisfallen

de Iustinis Civitatis Castelli, Paulus *see* de
  Castello, Paulus Amadei

Ivo, late bishop of Glendalough *see* [Ruffi],
  Ivo

Ivychurch (Ederose Ivychurthe) [*in*
  Alderbury, Wilts], Augustinian priory
  of, canon and prior of *see* Page, Richard

J

J *cf.* I

Jackson (Jackeson, Jakson'), John, vicar of
  Empingham, 729
......, Thomas, rector of ?Farmington, 671
......, William, rector of Crowhurst, 172

?Jacobstowe (Stove) [Devon], parish
  church of St James, rector of, 907

Jagford *alias* Jagfourth, Jagford *alias*
  Jugforth' *see* Chagford

Jakson' *see* Jackson

James [IV], king of Scots, 769
......, ..., illegitimate son of *see* Stewart,

James [IV], (*contd*)
  Alexander
......, ..., kinsman of *see* Stewart, Andrew
......, ..., licence to, to found Observant
  Franciscan house at Stirling, 1
......, ..., endowment of the chapel royal,
  Stirling, by, 765
......, ..., to have chapel royal, [Stirling],
  erected into collegiate [church], with
  union of provostship, 1214
......, ..., petition of, 64
......, ..., proposal of, to establish market at
  New Aberdeen, 64
......, ..., faculty for churchmen to study
  civil law at Aberdeen university granted
  at petition of, 1143
......, ..., conclusion to, 55, 549, 584, 588,
  620, 630, 1009, 1015, 1024, 1032
......, king of Scotland [!], conclusion to,
  637
......, ..., court of, 972
......, ..., ..., servant of *see* [de Falcutiis *or*
  Falcariis], Damianus
......, ..., chapel of, 972
......, king of Scots, chapel of, chaplain in
  see Arnot, David

James, administrator of St Andrews *see*
  [Stewart], James
......, archbishop of St Andrews *see*
  [Stewart], James
......, bishop of Clogher *see* [MacMahon],
  James
......, bishop of Dunblane *see* [Chisholm],
  James
......, late bishop of Norwich *see* [Goldwell],
  James
......, elect of St Andrews *see* [Stewart],
  James

Jane (Ian'), Thomas, archdeacon of Essex
  in the church of London, 553, 555
......, ..., canon of London cathedral, 553
......, ..., counsellor and Master of Requests
  of Henry [VII], 553
......, ..., provision of to the bishopric of
  Norwich, 553
......, ..., absolution of preliminary to
  provision, 555
......, ..., [bishop-] elect of Norwich, faculty
  for consecration of, 554

Jane (*contd*)
......, ..., bishop of Norwich, death of, 634

Jedburgh (Jedword) [co. Roxburgh], Augustinian monastery of, commendation of, 1009, 1011
......, ..., (commendatory) abbot of *see* [Blackadder], Robert; [Cranston], Thomas
......, ..., convent of, conclusion to, 1009
......, ..., vassals of, conclusion to, 1009

Jeffrey, William, rector of Withyham, 847

Jenney, Edward, rector of Kirkley, sometime portioner of Pakefield, 918

Jenynges (Jennyn), John, vicar of Queen Camel, 886

Jerpoint [*in* Jerpoint Abbey, co. Kilkenny], Cistercian monastery of, subjection to, of Cistercian monastery of Kilcooly, 574
......, ..., abbot of, confirmation of election at Kilcooly by, 574
......, ..., ..., papal mandatary, 575

Jerpoint (Ieriponte) [*now* Jerpointchurch, co. Kilkenny], parish church of, vicarage of, 545

Jersey [Channel Islands], isle of, St Helier in, *q.v.*

Jerusalem [Palestine], Hospital of St John of, master and convent of, 938
......, ..., ..., assent of required for derogation of privileges, 938
......, ..., statutes, etc. of, 938
......, ..., privileges, etc. of, 938
......, vow to visit, 374

Jeurmachan, Henry, canon of the Augustinian monastery of B. Mary *de Porto Puro*, Clonfert, 513
......, ..., ..., to have vicarage of Donanaghta and the vicarage and rectory of Kilmalinoge united thereto, 513
......, *cf.* OCormican

Johannes episcopus Mutinen. *see* [de Ferrariis], Johannes Baptista

Johannes Baptista, cardinal priest of S. Crisogono *see* [de Ferrariis], Johannes Baptista

Jo(h)annis, Gargridus, of Worcester diocese, dispensed for plurality, 1059
......, John, rector of Ockley, 678
......, *cf.* Johns

John XXII, constitution 'Execrabilis' of, detention of two incompatible benefices contrary to, 386

John XXIII, obedience of, 174
......, letters of, 174

John, late abbot of Iona *see* [Mackinnon], John
......, abbot of the Augustinian monastery of B. Mary *in Pratis*, Leicester *see* [Penny], John
......, abbot of the Cistercian monastery of Merevale, 754
......, abbot of Ramsey *see* [Huntington], John
......, bishop of Belley *see* [de Varax], John
......, late [bishop-] elect of Caithness *see* [Sinclair], John
......, [bishop-] elect of Cork and Cloyne *see* [de Geraldinis], John [Edemundi]
......, bishop of Coventry and Lichfield *see* [Arundel], John
......, bishop of Coventry and Lichfield *see* [Hales *or* Arundel], John
......, late bishop of Ely *see* [Alcock], John
......, bishop of Exeter *see* [Arundel], John
......, bishop of Lincoln *see* [Russell], John
......, bishop of Meath *see* [Payne], John
......, bishop of Salisbury *see* [Blythe], John
......, bishop of Sodor *see* [Campbell], John
......, bishop of Worcester *see* de' Gigli, John
......, cardinal priest of St Anastasia *see* [Morton], John

Johns *cf.* Johannis

Johnson (Johuson), John, rector of
     Uffington, 440
......, Thomas, of London diocese, dispensed
     for plurality, 1163

Johnstone (Iboston') [co. Dumfries], parish
     church of, incumbent of, 780

Johoill' see Youghal

Johuson see Johnson

Jones (Jonys), William, vicar of Pilton, 354

Jonys (Yonis), William, union for, of his
     parish church in Worcester diocese to
     his canonry [of St David's or Coventry
     and Lichfield?], 1230

Jordan (Jurdan'), John, canon of York,
     papal judge delegate, 8

Jordan, late bishop of Cork and Cloyne see
     [Purcell], Jordan

Josselyne, Philip, cantor in Halstead parish
     church and incumbent of Drinkstone,
     664

Joy, Edmund, detainer of rectory of Lough
     Mask, 826
......, Maurice, ostensible archdeacon of
     Tuam, 401
......, ..., detainer of canonry of Tuam and
     prebend of Kilcurnan, 401
......, ..., detainer of rectory of Inishmaine,
     826

[Joyce], William, archbishop of Tuam, 835
......, ..., ..., to have abbot deprived and
     Augustinian monastery of B. John the
     Evangelist, [Tuam] united to
     archiepiscopal mensa, 835

Juan, cardinal priest of S. Balbina see
     [Vera], Juan

Judson, John, vicar of Kensington, 910

Jugforth', an alias of Jagford, q.v.

Julius II, letter of, 1035

Jurdan' see Jordan

K

Kalyn see ?Killeen

Karsyngton' see Carsington

Kathgrell see Rathkeale

Kawall, Richard, of Ferns diocese,
     dispensed for illegitimacy, 1299

Kay (Key), Thomas, rector of Ditteridge,
     327

Kaylke' see ville Kaylke'

Kazdaglas alias Maclerystown' see
     ?Mocklerstown

Keadew or Keadue (Ched, Kede), alias of
     Urney [co. Cavan], q.v.

Kearn (Ryerin') [now Auchindoir and
     Kearn, co. Aberdeen] and Forbes [now
     Tullynessle and Forbes, co. Aberdeen],
     canonry and prebend of in Aberdeen
     cathedral, 68
......, ..., patron of, presentation by, 68

Keble, Margaret, woman of London
     diocese, litigant, 905
......, ..., ..., alleged husband of see Vernon,
     Roger
......, ..., ..., appeal of, 905

Keble (Kebull') alias Vernon (Vernon'),
     Margaret, litigant, 988
......, ..., husband of see Vernon, Roger
......, ..., appeal of, 988

Kede see Keadew or Keadue

Kellasna see Killeshin

Kells (Kellis, Kenll', Killis) [co. Kilkenny],
     [Augustinian] priory of B. Mary, prior
     of, papal mandatary, 157, 350, 545 bis

Kells (Kenlys) [co. Meath], [Augustinian] monastery of B. Mary, abbot of, papal mandatary, 537

Kelouz, John, of London diocese, dispensed for plurality, 1104

Kelso [co. Roxburgh], [Benedictine] monastery of, abbot of, papal mandatary, 642

Kelston [Som], parish church of, union of, to the canonry and prebend of Haselbere in Wells cathedral, 473

Kenll' see Kells [co. Kilkenny]

Kenlys see Kells [co. Meath]

[Kenmare, co. Kerry], place in see Killowen

Kenn (Kenne) [Devon], parish church of, union to, of the parish church of Manaton, 958

Kensington (Kensyngton) [Midd], parish church of, 910

[Kent, co. of], places in see Barham; Birling; Bishopsbourne; Burmarsh; Canterbury; Chevening; Chiddingstone; Cobham; Combwell; Cowden; Deptford; Dover; Faversham; Gravesend; Greenwich, West; Hardres, Great now Upper; Hoo; Meopham; Midley; Monkton; Norton; Plumstead; Reculver; Rochester; Smarden; Sundridge; Thanet, Isle of; Tonbridge; Wouldham

Kent, William, vicar of Box, 286

Kenton (Kenton') [Devon], parish church of, 266

Kepier (Kepyer) [in parish of St Giles, Durham, co. Durham], hospital of, foundation of, 429
......, ..., statutes and ordinances of, reform

Kepier (contd)
of, 429

Ker, George, of Glasgow diocese, dispensed for plurality, 1258
......, Thomas, of Glasgow diocese, dispensed for plurality, 1259

Kerrach see ?Curragh

[Kerry, co. of], places in see Abbeydorney; Ardfert; ?Ballingarry; Ballinskelligs; Ballyduff; Ballymacelligott; Barrow; Beara; Eaglais-na-lainne alias Ballyheige; Cahir; ?Feohanagh [in Kilquane]; Garfinny; Glennahoo; Innisfallen; Killagh; Killemlagh; ?Killinane; Killowen [in Kenmare]; Killury; Kilmalkedar; Kilmeen; 'Kylldacu(m) alias Turere'; Nohaval-Daly; Stradbally; Valentia

Keteryng see Kettering

Ketilbergh' see Kettleburgh

Ketilton, William, rector of St Peter's, Shaftesbury and incumbent of St Mary's, Wilton, 736

Kettering (Keteryng) [Northants], parish church of, incumbent of, 1035
......, ..., union of, to canonry of Lincoln and prebend of Banbury, 1035

Kettleburgh (Ktylbore alias Ketilbergh') [Suff], parish church of, 102

[Kewstoke, Som], place in see Woodspring

Key see Kay

Keymer see Kymer

Khania (Caneen.) see Agia

Kiawthtimonth see Kinnethmont

[Kidderminster], Richard, abbot of the Benedictine monastery of Winchcombe, proposed statutes of, 394

Kikonan *see* Kilronan

[Kilbarron, co. Donegal], place in *see* Assaroe

Kilbarron (Cyllbarrayn) [co. Tipperary], parish church of, vicarage of, 511

Kilbarrymeaden (Kylbarrymedyn) [co. Waterford], parish church of, vicarage of, 949

Kilbradran (Killbradarayn) [co. Limerick], parish church of, vicarage of, 820
......, ..., ..., to be united to Kilfergus, 820

Kilbride (Kylbride), alias of Callan, *q.v.*

Kilbrogan (Ryllrogan) [co. Cork], prebend of in Cork cathedral, 252
......, ..., rectory of Garrynoe and vicarage of ?Ringrone to be united to, 252

[Kilbryan, co. Roscommon], place in *see* Lough Key

Kilcarragh [*in* Kilfenora, co. Clare] *see* 'Kylthalbach'

Kilcash (Kylkassy) [co. Tipperary], parish church of, vicarage of, 790
......, ..., ..., to be erected, with Kilronan vicarage, into prebend of Lismore, 790

Kilccumpim *see* Ballenakille

[Kilcolman, co. Kerry], place in *see* Killagh

Kilcolumb (Killcolun, Kykollw') [co. Kilkenny], parish church of, vicarage of, 787
......, ..., ..., to be united to canonry and prebend of St Maul's in Ossory cathedral, 787
......, ..., vicar of, 227

?Kilcomenty (Killcomnayt) [co. Tipperary], parish church of, vicarage of, to be erected into prebend in Cashel, with vicarage of Killeenagarriff united

?Kilcomenty (*contd*)
thereto, 404

Kilcomin (Thilcorim) [co. Offaly], parish church of, vicarage of, to be united to proposed prebend of *Cenél arga* in Killaloe cathedral, 162

Kilconierin (Gyllco(n)yery(n)d) [co. Galway], chapel of, to be united to archdeaconry of Clonfert, 234

Kilcooly (An'ficampo *alias* Cilleule) [co. Tipperary], Cistercian monastery of, 574
......, ..., subjection to, of Cistercian monastery of Jerpoint, 574
......, ..., union to, of the vicarage of Clashacrow, 574
......, ..., proposed union to, of the vicarage of Odagh, 574
......, ..., abbot of *see* OMulwarden *alias* OBrophy, Donat and John
......, ..., convent of, 574
......, ..., ..., election by, 574
......, ..., monk of *see* OMulwarden *alias* OBrophy, Donat
......, ..., vassals of, 574

Kilcoona (Chilenanna) [co. Galway], parish church of, vicarage of, to be united to proposed prebend of Lackagh in Annaghdown cathedral, 163

Kilcraggan (Kiltochichan, Kyllokech'an) [*in* Ballytarsney, co. Kilkenny], parish church of, rectory of, to be united to chancellorship of Ossory, 157
......, ..., ..., union of to chancellorship of Ossory, grant of, impetration of, alleged subreption of, 545

?Kilcummin (Kylleomyn, Kyllromayn) [co. Galway], parish church of, vicarage of, to be erected with Killeroon vicarage into prebend of Annaghdown cathedral, 646
......, ..., ..., union of, to a canonry and prebend (unnamed) of Annaghdown, 845

Kilcurnan (Chilemian) [*in* Crossboyne, co. Mayo], prebend of in Tuam cathedral, 401

Kildare [co. Kildare], **[cathedral] church** of, dean of *see* Oqueronaten', Maurice
......, ..., chapter of, to be summoned over erection of canonry and prebend, *cf.* 934
......, ..., canon of, *cf.* Maclanthlaym, Peter
......, ..., prebend in *cf.* Ballyshannon

......, **bishop** of, to be summoned over erection of canonry and prebend, *cf.* 934

......, **diocese** of, persons of *see* MacKilbride, John; ONewell, Thomas
......, ..., places in *see* Ballyshannon; Greatconnell

[Kildare, co. of], places in *see* Ballyshannon; Fontstown; Greatconnell; Narraghmore; Norragh; Tippeenan

Kildorrery (Kylidariri) [co. Cork], parish church of, vicarage of, 941

Kildrumferton (Kylldrumaferthayn) [or Crosserlough, co. Cavan], parish church of, vicarage of, to be erected into prebend in Kilmore cathedral, 537

'Kilelonne' ('Kylclomee') [*unidentified*; *perhaps* Killeelaun (*in* Tuam parish, co. Galway)], parish church of, vicarage of, to be united to deanery of Tuam, 69, 75

Kilfarboy (Killnafearbay) [co. Clare], parish church of, vicarage of, 449
......, ..., ..., usurper of fruits of, 449
......, ..., ..., to be united to canonry and prebend of Kilfenora, 449
......, ..., ecclesiastical fief in, rectory of, 449
......, ..., ..., ..., to be united to canonry and prebend of Kilfenora, 449

Kilfearagh (Killsfebrach) [co. Clare], parish

Kilfearagh (*contd*)
church of, vicarage of, 818

Kilfenora [co. Clare], **[cathedral] church** of, dean of, papal mandatary, 649
......, ..., canons of *see* MacLysaght, Donald and Matthew; OBrien, Dermot, Matthew, Maurus and Thady; OCahir, Cormac; Oconenar, Cornelius; ODaly, Eugene; ONeylan, Thomas
......, ..., canonry and prebend (unnamed) of, proposed union to, of the vicarages of Kilfarboy and Killard, portion of Moanmore of the church of Scattery Island, and rectory of fief of Kilfarboy, 449
......, ..., prebend (unnamed) of, proposed union to, of the vicarage of [Killinaboy], 651
......, ..., ..., ..., of the vicarage of 'Kylthalbach', 648

......, **bishop** of *see* OBriain, Maurice
......, official of, papal mandatary, 648
......, church of, archdeacon of, papal mandatary, 649

......, **diocese** of, persons of *see* OBrien, Maurice; [OConnor], Bernard; ODea, Denis and Donald
......, ..., places in *see* Kilcarragh; Kilshanny; 'Kylthalbach'

Kilfergus (Killaressy) [co. Limerick], parish church of, vicarage of, union to, of the vicarages of Kilmoylan and Kilbradran, 820
......, place in *see* [Glin]

Kilfhyntanayn *see* Kilfintinan

[Kilfinichen and Kilvickeon, co. Argyll], place in *see* Iona

Kilfintinan (Kilfhyntanayn) [co. Clare], parish church of, vicarage of, to be united to canonry of Limerick and prebend of Donaghmore, 652

?Kilgarriff (Kylle) [co. Cork], parish church of, vicarage of, to be united to

?Kilgarriff (*contd*)
canonry of Ross and prebend of Curragranemore, 256

?Kilglass (Kyllechassy) [co. Longford], parish church of, vicarage of, 763

Kilinovan see Kilmainham

Kilkenny [co. Kilkenny], Augustinian monastery of St John the Evangelist near, priorship of, 575
......, ..., priors of *see* Cantwell, John; Comerford, Edmund
......, cathedral at *see* Ossory

[Kilkenny, co. of], places in *see* Aglish *or* Aglishmartin; Ballytarsney; Callan; Clashacrow; Coolcraheen; Dungarvan; Dunkitt; Inistioge; Jerpoint; Kells; Kilbride; Kilcolumb; Kilcraggan [*in* Ballytarsney]; Kilkenny; Kilmanagh; Odagh; Pollrone; Rosconnell; St Maul's; Thomastown

Kilkerrin (Kyltaryn) [co. Galway], parish church of, to be united to canonry and prebend of Tuam, 833

[Killabban, co. Laois], place in *see* ?Killeen

Killagh [*in* Kilcolman, co. Kerry], [Augustinian] monastery of, prior of, papal mandatary, 360, 939, 945, 993

Killagholehane (Kyllochelean) [co. Limerick], parish church of, vicarage of, to be united to proposed canonry of Limerick and prebend of Killeedy, 824

Killala [co. Mayo], [cathedral] church of, chapter of, conclusion to, 606
......, ..., canons of *see* de Burgo, Richard; Magonghail, Roger; Obruchan, Thomas

......, bishop of, to receive oath of fealty in pope's name, 591, 592
......, ..., *see* [Barrett], Thomas; Clerke, Thomas
......, church of, subjection of, to archbishop of Tuam, 607

Killala bishop (*contd*)
......, ..., archdeacon of, papal mandatary, 124
......, ..., vassals of, conclusion to, 606

......, city and diocese of, clergy of, conclusion to, 606
......, ..., people of, conclusion to, 606
......, diocese of, persons of *see* Barrett, Restardus; MacDonnell, Eugene; ODonegan, John; Oheuacham, William
......, ..., place in *see* Castleconor

Killaloe [co. Clare], [cathedral] church of, dean of, papal mandatary, 783
......, ..., precentor of, papal mandatary, 651, 652, 948
......, ..., ..., *see* OCurry, Lucanus
......, ..., chancellor of, papal mandatary, 162, 357
......, ..., treasurership of, to be united to a canonry and prebend (unnamed), 647
......, ..., treasurer of, papal mandatary, 651, 652
......, ..., ..., *see* MacNamara, Rory; *and see* MacNamara *alias* Scyda, James
......, ..., chapter of, to be summoned over erection of canonry and prebend, 16, 162, 230, 313, 403
......, ..., canons of *see* MacNamara, Cornelius *alias* Curnea / Cunca [i.e. *Cuveadh*], James, John, John Tatei /Thadei, and Thady; MacNamara *alias* Scyda, James; OBrien, Matthew and Maurice; OCarroll, Cornelius; OClery, Robert *alias* Robyn; OCormachan, William; ODuggan, William; OGrady, Thomas; Ohanle, Philip; OHedigan, Donat; OHogan, Donat; OKennedy, Donald; OMeagher, Dermot; Ychernolii, John
......, ..., canonry and prebend (unnamed) in, treasurership to be united to, 647
......, ..., prebends in *see* Ballyloughnane; *Cenél arga* ; Dorrha; Finnoe; Loughkeen; Quin; Rath; Tulla

......, bishop of, collation of vicarage by, 161
......, ..., union by, 357
......, ..., to be summoned over erection of

Killaloe **bishop** (*contd*)
canonry and prebend, 16, 162, 230, 313, 403
......, official of, papal mandatary, 511
......, church of, archdeaconry of, 984
......, ..., commendatory archdeacon of *see* OBrien, Matthew

......, **diocese** of, persons of *see* de Burgo, Richard /Ristardus and Walter; Geddac *alias* Ocoggobayn, Pilapus / Philip; Macberragoyn, David; Macbiragyn, Dermot; MacCahan, Cornelius and Thady; MacGilfoyle *alias* Ochalen, William; MacGilfoyle, William; Machego, Cornelius; Mackynracta, Dermot; MacMahon, Cornelius; MacNamara, James *alias* Syda, and Laurence; MacSheedy, Odo; OBehan, John; OBriain, Maurice; OBrien, Dermot and Thady; OFlanagan, Donat; OFlannery, Rory; Ogriffa, Donat; OHannon, David; OHehir, Matthew; OHurley, Maurus; OHynan, Marcus; Okellayll, Cornelius and John; OKelly, Rory; OKendrigan, John; OKennedy, Aulanus and William; Oknyllay, Gillasius; Okynayth, Edmund; Olaenayn', William; OLoonan, Dermot and John; Omachayn, Laurence; OMeagher, John; Omulgayn, Maurice; OQuinn, Roderick
......, ..., places in *see* Birr; Bourney; Bunratty; *Cenél arga*; Clonloghan; Clonrush; Dorrha; Finnoe; 'Gleandbannam'; Ikerrin; '?Ileraunr'; Inchicronan; Inishcaltra; Kilbarron; Kilcomin; Kilfarboy; Kilfearagh; Killard; Killeenagarriff; Killimer; [Killinaboy]; Killofin; ?Kilmaleery; Kinnitty; Lorrha; Loughkeen; 'Medohk' [*in* Loughkeen]; Modreeny; Monaincha; Nenagh; Ogonnelloe;Quin; Roscrea; Scattery Island; Stradbally *alias* 'Cloynacheke'; Terryglass; Uskane

[Killannin, co. Galway], place in *see* Killeroon

Killanummery (Kyllamemery, Kyllumomeri) [co. Leitrim], parish church of, vicarage of, to be united to Premonstratensian monastery of Lough Key, 846, 995

Killard (Killarda) [co. Clare], parish church of, vicarage of, to be united to canonry and prebend of Kilfenora, 449

Killaressy *see* Kilfergus

[Killarney, Lower Lake of, co. Kerry], island in *see* Innisfallen

Killbradarayn *see* Kilbradran

'Killcolin', diocese of Ardfert [*unidentified*], particle of, to be united to canonry of Ardfert and prebend of Stradbally, 939

Killcolun *see* Kilcolumb

Killcomnayt *see* ?Kilcomenty

Killea (Chiller) [co. Tipperary], parish church of, rectory of, usually held as prebend of Cashel, 14
......, ..., ..., ..., vicarages of Bourney *alias* Ikerrin and Roscrea to be united to, 14

Killeedy (Kyllide) [co. Limerick], parish church of, vicarage of, to be erected into prebend of Limerick with Killagholehane vicarage united thereto, 824

Killeelaun [*in* Tuam parish, co. Galway] *see* 'Kilelonne'

Killeely (Kyllyelly) [cos. Clare and Limerick], parish church of, vicarage of, to be united to canonry of Limerick and prebend of Donaghmore, 652

?Killeen (Kalyn) [*in* Killabban, co. Laois], parish church of, vicarage of, to be erected into prebend of Leighlin with the vicarages of ?Curragh and Killeshin united thereto, 982

Killeenagarriff (Kyllicuagaruan *alias* Aglaysydony) [co. Limerick], parish church of, vicarage of, to be united to proposed prebend of ?Kilcomenty in Cashel cathedral, 404

[Killemlagh, co. Kerry], place near *see* 'Kylldacu(m) *alias* Turere'

Killererin (Kylarerynd, Kylareyrud) *alias Muinter Murchada* (Monterahy, Monteray) [co. Galway], parish church of, rectory of, annexed to prebend of Tisaxon *alias* Templegaile in Tuam cathedral, 69, 75
......, ..., ..., appurtenances of *see* Aghiart

Killeroon (Kyllardun) [*in* Laghtgannon townland, Killannin parish, co. Galway], parish church of, vicarage of, to be erected with ?Kilcummin vicarage into prebend of Annaghdown cathedral, 646
......, ..., ..., union of, to a canonry and prebend (unnamed) of Annaghdown, 845

Killeroran (Chillerulan) [co. Galway], parish church of, 830

Killeshin (Kellasna) [co. Laois], parish church of, vicarage of, to be united to proposed canonry of Leighlin and prebend of ?Killeen, 982
......, place in *see* ?Curragh

Killimer (Kyllemuyr) [co. Clare], parish church of, vicarage of, 948

[Killinaboy, co. Clare], parish church of St ?Findchu, vicarage of, to be united to canonry and prebend of Kilfenora, 651

?Killinane (Rylonayn) [co. Kerry], parish church of, vicarage of, to be erected into prebend in Ardfert with the vicarage of 'Kylloeyn' united thereto, 360

Killis *see* Kells

Killmalayne *see* Kilmoylan

Killnafearbay *see* Kilfarboy

Killofin (Kyllesind) [co. Clare], parish church of, vicarage of, 948

Killoscobe (Kyllosala) [co. Galway], parish church of, vicarage of, to be united anew to the canonry and prebend of 'Ycluelin' in Clonfert cathedral, 167

Killosolan (Kyllosailam) [co. Galway], church of, vicarage of, to be erected into prebend in Elphin cathedral, 164
......, ..., rectory of, to be united to proposed prebend of Killosolan, 164

Killowen, co. Derry *see Druim tairsigh*

Killowen [*in* Kenmare, co. Kerry] *see* 'Kylloeyn'

Killsca'nyll' *see* Kilscannell

Killsfebrach *see* Kilfearagh

Kill'sgantayll' *see* Kilscannell

Killury (Kyllury) [co. Kerry], parish church of, rectory of, to be united to canonry of Ardfert and prebend of Stradbally, 939

Killymard (Cyllomaird, Cyllomardi) [co. Donegal], parish church of, to be united to the Cistercian monastery of Assaroe, 950
......, ..., rector of, 943

Kilmacdonogh   (?Chilmogonec, Chylmodonoc) [co. Cork], prebend of in Cloyne cathedral, 392, 852

Kilmacduagh [co. Galway], [**cathedral**] **church** of, chancellor of, papal mandatary, 449
......, ..., canons of *see* de Burgo, Geoffrey, Richard (Ristardus), Thomas, and Walter; OShaughnessy, Nemeas
......, ..., prebend of the small churches in,

Kilmacduagh [cathedral] church (*contd*)
proposed union to, of the rectory of
Terryglass and the vicarages of
Kinvarra and Claregalway, 935
......, ..., other prebends in *see* Isertkelly;
Kinvarra
......, ..., chantry in, to be united to canonry
of Kilmacduagh and prebend of
Kinvarra, 933

......, **bishop** of, papal mandatary, 449
......, official of, papal mandatary, 16

......, **diocese** of, persons of *see* Oberen,
Theoderic; OChayllyn, Odo; OGarvan,
Florence
......, ..., places in *see* Beagh *alias* Cliath-
Ceallayd; Isertkelly; Kinvarra

Kilmaelte adye *see* Kilmalkedar

Kilmaine [co. Mayo], barony of *see*
Ballinrobe
......, *see* 'Tilmadim'

Kilmainham (Kilinovan, Kilmanni) [co.
Dublin], [Hospitaller] priory of St John
of, near Dublin, prior of, papal judge
delegate, 694, 964, 1005

?Kilmaleery (Kylnayrhe) [co. Clare], parish
church of, vicarage of, to be united to
proposed canonry and prebend of Quin
in Killaloe cathedral, 313

Kilmalinoge (Chilmolonog, Kymiayd *alias*
Kylmolonog) [co. Galway], parish
church of, rectory of, to be united to
vicarage of Donanaghta, 513
......, ..., vicarage of, to be united to
vicarage of Donanaghta, 513

Kilmalkedar (Kilmaelte adye) [co. Kerry],
parish church of, vicarage of, to be
united to chancellorship of Ardfert, 993

Kilmanagh (Kylmanach) [co. Kilkenny],
parish church of, vicarage of, to be
united to canonry and prebend of St
Maul's in Ossory cathedral, 787

Kilmanni *see* Kilmainham

Kilmany (Kylmany) [co. Fife], parish
church of, vicarage of, 937

[Kilmartin, co. Argyll], places in *see* Ford;
Torran

Kilmeedy (Chilmide), alias of Drishane,
q.v.

Kilmeen (Chilmyny' *alias* Chiltual) [cos.
Kerry and Cork], parish church of,
vicarage of, to be erected into prebend
in Ardfert cathedral, 250

Kilmere *see* Kilmuir

[Kilmichael Glassary, co. Argyll], places in
see Fincharn; Ford; Glasvaar;
Kilneuair; Loch a' Choire; Loch
Leachd; Socach; Stroneskar

Kilmington (Culmyngtowe *alias*
Culmyngton') [Som], parish church of,
union to, of the parish church of
Merthyr Tydfil, 452

Kilmoney (Culmoneayn) [co. Cork], parish
church of, vicarage of, 825

Kilmore [co. Cavan], **[cathedral] church**
of, chapter of, to be summoned over
erection of canonry and prebend, 537,
538, 821, 834
......, ..., canons of *see* MacBrady, Patrick;
Mactalie, Odo; OFarrell, Adam;
OGowan, John; OMulmohery, Gillatius
and Odo; OSheridan, Fergal and
Gel(l)as(s)ius
......, ..., prebends in *see* Kildrumferton;
'Tolach'; Urney; Urney *alias* Keadew

......, **bishop** (or his vicar general) of,
collation by, 831, 832
......, bishop of, to be summoned over
erection of canonry and prebend, 537,
538, 821, 834
......, official of, papal mandatary, 821, 831,
832, 834

Kilmore (*contd*)

......, **diocese** of, persons of *see* MacBrady, Eugene, Gilbert and Nicholas; Magauran, Fergal; Maglocyn, Eugene; Margoryne, John; OFarrell, Odo; OGowan, Cormac and John; OSheridan, Fergal, father of

......, ..., places in *see* Annagh; Cavan; 'Cuacaynde' *alias* 'Clacerogarde'; Drumgoon; Drumlane; Kildrumferton *or* Crosserlough; Magheranure; Templeport *alias* Breaghwy Island; 'Tolach'; Urney; Urney *alias* Keadew *or* Keadue

Kilmore (Kylmor) [co. Roscommon], [Augustinian] monastery of, prior of, papal mandatary, 936

Kilmore *see* Kilmuir [co. Ross and Cromarty]

Kilmoylan (Killmalayne) [co. Limerick], parish church of, vicarage of, to be united to vicarage of Kilfergus, 820

Kilmuir (Kilmere, Kilmore, Kylmore) [*probably* Kilmuir Easter, co. Ross and Cromarty], church of, annexed to deanery of Ross, 782, 839

......, ..., fruits of, 782

......, ..., ..., pertaining to deanery of Ross, 840

Kilnamanagh (?Kyllmuna) [co. Cork], prebend of in Ross cathedral, 70

......, ..., Creagh vicarage to be united to, 70

Kilnamanagh [co. Tipperary] *see* 'Kylmemanch'

Kilneuair (Kylleneur) [*now part of* Kilmichael Glassary, co. Argyll], parish church of, rector of, 493

......, ..., patron of, 493

......, ..., parish of, places in (or in vicinity of) *see* 'Brenowc'; Fincharn; Ford; Glasvaar; 'Latyrewern''; 'Lochclea'; 'Lochquho' Socach; Stroneskar;

Kilneuair (*contd*)

'Terroner'

[Kilquane, co. Kerry], place in *see* ?Feohanagh

Kilronan (Kykonayn) [*in* Glenahiry barony, co. Waterford], parish church of, vicarage of, to be erected, with Kilcash vicarage, into prebend of Lismore, 790

......, ..., ..., annexed to prebend of Clashmore in Lismore cathedral, 159

......, ..., ..., ..., to be united to deanery of Lismore, 159

[Kilrush, co. Clare], place in *see* Moanmore; Scattery Island

Kilscannell (Killsca'nyll', Kill'sgantayll') [co. Limerick], parish church of, vicarage of, 485, 542

......, ..., ..., to be united to chancellorship of Limerick, 485

......, ..., ..., procuration payable by reason of, 542

Kilsensz, Thomas, provision of to canonry of Ross, 1289

Kilshannig (Chilsane) [co. Cork], parish church of, vicarage of, 74

Kilshanny (Kyllsenayd, Kyltanna, Kylthanna) [co. Clare], Augustinian monastery of, 649, 980

......, ..., abbot of, papal mandatary, 648

......, ..., ..., *see* OBrien, Dermot, Maurice and Maurus; [OCahir], Cormac; [OConnor], Bernard

......, ..., convent of, 649

......, ..., vassals of, 649

Kilsheelan (Hylsylhayn) [cos. Tipperary and Waterford], parish church of, vicarage of, to be erected, with Newtown Lennan vicarage, into prebend of Lismore, 785

Kilteale (Kylsnalay) [co. Laois], parish church of, vicarage of, 932

Kiltochichan *see* Kilcraggan

Kiltoraght, co. Clare *see* 'Kylthalbach'

Kiltullagh (Chyltoloch) [co. Galway], parish church of, vicarage of, 16
......, ..., ..., ?to be severed from the archdeaconry of Clonfert, 16

Kilvemnon, co. Tipperary *see* 'Kylmemanch'

[Kilvickeon, co. Argyll], place in *see* Iona

Kilvine (Kylfynaym) [co. Mayo], parish church of, vicarage of, united to canonry of Tuam, 828

Kilworth, North, alias of Kilworth Abbas (Kylworth Rabbas) [*now* North Kilworth, Leics], parish church of, 450

[Kimbolton, Hunts], place in *see* Stonely

[Kincardine *or* The Mearns, co. of], places in *see* Conveth; Garvock; Laurencekirk

Kincardine O'Neil [co. Aberdeen], prebend of in Aberdeen cathedral, fruits of, appropriation of residue of to chapel royal, Stirling, 768

Kincragy (Kyncragy) *see* Kyneragy

Kingsdon (Kyngesdon') [Som], parish church of, union of, to a canonry and prebend of Exeter cathedral, 663

Kingsley (Kyngesley), Robert, of Lincoln diocese, dispensed for plurality, 1190

Kingston (Ringeston, Ringeston') [Som], church of, 174
......, place in *see* Hestercombe

Kington (Kynton), John, OFM, 861

Kinloch (Kynloch'), Margaret, of St Andrews diocese, appeal of, 971

Kinloss (Kinlos, Ry'nlos) [co. Moray], Cistercian monastery of, 144, 155, 793, 928
......, ..., cession of, 144
......, ..., (abbots of), pension on fruits of Ellon parish church payable by, 144, 928
......, ..., ..., *mensa* of, pension on fruits of, 155
......, ..., ..., *see* Culross, William; [Wawain *alias* Chrystal], Thomas; *and see* Martin, Hugh
......, ..., convent of, election of abbot by, 144
......, ..., ..., consent of, to payment of pension, 144
......, ..., abbot and convent of, refusal of, to pay pension, 793
......, ..., ..., dispute with Hugh Martin over pension, 928
......, ..., ..., proctor of *see* Duncanson, John
......, ..., monk of *see* Culross, William
......, ..., parish church of Ellon united to, 144, 793, 928
......, ..., tithes pertaining to by reason of Ellon parish church, 928
......, ..., vill of Hatton pertaining to, assignment of, 155
......, place in *see* Hatton

[Kinnethmont, co. Aberdeen], place in *see* Rathmuriel

Kinnitty, co. Offaly *see* Cenél arga

[Kinross, co. of], place in *see* Carnbo [*in* Fossoway]

Kinsale (Vynsall) [co. Cork], parish church of, vicarage of, 362

Kintyre [a district, co. Argyll], 765

Kinvarra (Kuymara) [*in* Kinvarradoorus, co. Galway], prebend of in Kilmacduagh cathedral, 933
......, ..., proposed union to, of chantry in Kilmacduagh cathedral, chapel of St Mary, Galway, and vicarages of Beagh *alias* Cliath-Ceallayd and Clonrush, 933

Kinvarra (*contd*)

......, parish church of, vicarage of, to be united to canonry of Kilmacduagh and prebend of the small churches, 935

Kinver (Kynfar(e)) [Staffs], parish church of, united to Cistercian monastery of Bordesley, 298

......, ..., abbot and convent of Bordesley admonished by bishop of Coventry and Lichfield to present person for institution as vicar of, 298

......, ..., fruits of, sequestration of, 298

......, ..., parishioners of *see* Blokelay, Richard; Wolford, William

......, person of *see* Wolford, William

Kinwarton (Kynwarton) [Warw], parish church of, 431

Kirk-Andrews [*in* Borgue, co. Kirkcudbright], [parish church of], 781

Kirkby on Bain (Kyrkby de Bayne) [Lincs], parish church of, 194

Kirkcaldy (Kyrkcayde) [co. Fife], parish church of, vicarage of, dispute over, 407

......, ..., ..., fruits of, pension on, 407

......, ..., ..., pensioner of *see* [Turnbull], William

[Kirkcudbright, co. of], places in *see* Balmaclellan; Kirk-Andrews [*in* Borgue]; St Mary's Isle *or* Trail; Southwick [*modern* Colvend]; Sweetheart; Tongland

Kirkden, *once* Idvie(s), *q.v.*

Kirkested *see* Kirkstead

Kirkforthar (Kyrbforthyr) [*now in* Markinch, co. Fife], parish church of, 851

Kirkham (Kirkh(a)m) [Yorks], Augustinian monastery of, 451

......, ..., canon of *see* Morwyn, John

Kirkham (Kyrkh(a)m), William, canon of the Augustinian priory of Haltemprice, 299

Kirkley (Kyrkeley) [Suff], parish church of, rector of, 918

Kirknewton *see* Calder

Kirkstead (Kirkested) [Lincs], Cistercian monastery of, monk of *see* Garforth, Thomas

Kirkwall *see* Orkney

Klay *see* ?Clee

Knapton [Norf], parish church of, 544

Knight [of Glin de Geraldinis] *see* Militis

Knockmoy *see* Abbeyknockmoy

Knollis (Knowis), George, of St Andrews diocese, dispensed for plurality, 1312

Knollys, David, rector of the hospital of St John the Baptist, Shaftesbury and vicar of Melksham, 965

Knott (Knotte), Richard, official and commissary of the provost and chapter of Bridgnorth, 529

......, ..., ..., appeals of, 529

......, ..., ..., recourse of to the court of Canterbury for protection, 529

......, ..., ..., proceedings against, 529

Knox (Konx), James, commissary of David Cunningham, official of Glasgow, litigation before, 86

Knyghtley (Knygheley), Walter, canon of Wells, prebendary of Haselbere, and incumbent of Kelston, 473

Knyvett *cf.* Kuyvet

Kollston, alias of Rolleston, Richard, *q.v.*

Konx *see* Knox

Ktylbore *see* Kettleburgh

Kuodi, Robert, vicar of Lewknor, 331

Kuymara *see* Kinvarra

Kuyvet, John, rector of Boxworth, 516
......, *cf.* Knyvett

Kydonia (*Cydonien.*) *see* Agia

Kykollw' *see* Kilcolumb

Kykonayn *see* Kilronan

Kylarerynd, Kylareyrud *see* Killererin

Kylbarrymedyn *see* Kilbarrymeaden

Kylbride *see* Kilbride

'Kylclomee' *see* 'Kilelonne'

Kylfynaym *see* Kilvine

Kylidariri *see* Kildorrery

Kylkassy *see* Kilcash

Kyllamemery *see* Killanummery

Kyllardun *see* Killeroon

'Kylldacu(m) *alias* Turere', diocese of
Ardfert [*unidentified*; i*n vicinity of*
Killemlagh and Cahir, co. Kerry;
possibly Valentia], parish church of,
vicarage of, to be erected into prebend
in Ardfert cathedral, 72

Kylldrumaferthayn *see* Kildrumferton

Kylle *see* ?Kilgarriff

Kyllechassy *see* ?Kilglass

Kyllemuyr *see* Killimer

Kylleneur *see* Kilneuair

Kylleomyn *see* ?Kilcummin

Kyllesind *see* Killofin

Kyllicuagaruan *see* Killeenagarriff

Kyllide *see* Killeedy

?Kyllmuna *see* Kilnamanagh

Kyllochelean *see* Killagholehane

'Kylloeyn', diocese of Ardfert
[*unidentified*; *possibly* Killowen (*in*
Kenmare, co. Kerry)], parish church of,
vicarage of, to be united to canonry of
Ardfert and prebend of ?Killinane, 360

Kyllokech'an *see* Kilcraggan

Kyllosailam *see* Killosolan

Kyllosala *see* Killoscobe

Kyllromayn *see* ?Kilcummin

Kyllsenayd *see* Kilshanny

Kyllumomeri *see* Killanummery

Kyllury *see* Killury

Kyllyelly *see* Killeely

Kylmanach *see* Kilmanagh

Kylmany *see* Kilmany

'Kylmemanch', diocese of Cashel
[*unidentified; perhaps* Kilnamanagh
(*now* a barony), co. Tipperary; *or
possibly* Kilvemnon, co. Tipperary],
parish church of, vicarage of, to be
erected into prebend in Cashel, 350
......, ..., ..., vicar of, 350

Kylmolonog *see* Kilmalinoge

Kylmor *see* Kilmore

Kylmore *see* Kilmuir

Kylnayrhe *see* ?Kilmaleery

Kylsnalay *see* Kilteale

Kyltanna *see* Kilshanny

Kyltaryn *see* Kilkerrin

'Kylthalbach', diocese of Kilfenora [*unidentified; probably either* Kiltoraght, co. Clare *or* Kilcarragh (*in* Kilfenora), co. Clare], parish church of, vicarage of, to be united to canonry and prebend in Kilfenora, 648
......, ..., ..., vicar of, 648

Kylthanna *see* Kilshanny

Kylworth Rabbas *see* Kilworth Abbas

Kymer (Keymer), Gilbert, chantry of in Salisbury cathedral, 503
......, ..., ..., foundation of, 503
......, John, of Bath and Wells diocese, dispensed for plurality, 1171

Kymiayd *alias* Kylmolonog *see* Kilmalinoge

Kyngesley *see* Kingsley

Kynmara *see* Kinvarra

Kyncragy *see* Kincragy

Kyneragy (*or* Kyncragy), James, rector of Kirkforthar, 851

Kynfar(e) *see* Kinver

Kyngesdon' *see* Kingsdon

Kynloch' *see* Kinloch

Kynton *see* Kington

Kynwarton *see* Kinwarton

Kyrbforthyr *see* Kirkforthar

Kyrkby de Bayne *see* Kirkby on Bain

Kyrkcande, Kyrkcayde *see* Kirkcaldy

Kyrkeley *see* Kirkley

Kyrkh(a)m *see* Kirkham

Kystye *see* ?Colman

Kyte, John, rector of Wolferton, 178

?K...., Thomas, ostensible cleric of Lincoln diocese, occupier of parish church of Wootton, 405

L

Lackagh (Lechacolay) [co. Galway], church, called prebend, of, to be erected into prebend in Annaghdown cathedral, 163

Lackford (Lokeford) [Suff], parish church of, 755

Lacock (Lacok) [Wilts], parish church of, 654, 772

Lacy, Arthur, vicar of Braithwell, 316
......, John, rector of Desford, 956

[Laghtgannon townland, *in* Killannin, co. Galway] *see* Killeroon

Lamey, Walter, presentation of for chaplaincy in St Salvator's, St Andrews, 691
......, ..., institution of, 691
......, ..., litigant over chaplaincy, 691

Lamport [Northants], parish church of, union of, to the Augustinian monastery of Notley, 877

[Lanark, co. of], places in *see* Bothwell; Carmichael; Carnwath; Glasgow; ?Quothquan [*in* Libberton]

Lanburi *see* Layburne

[Lancaster, co. of], places in *see* Aldingham; Bury; Cartmel; Claughton; Walton on the Hill; Warton; Whalley; Winwick

[de Lanciarinis] de Fano, Ulixes, *magister registri*, letters signed by:
V *De Phano*, 1, 14-17, 19-24, 27-30, 41-47 (changed from *Fan*), 59, 60, 63, 65-71, 74, 75, 77-82, 85 (*V De phano*) 86, 87, 90, 91, 94, 101, 107, 108, 111-113, 116, 122-126, 132-137, 139-143, 146-150, 152, 153, 155-158, 161-166, 168, 172, 173, 175, 177, 178, 188, 189, 196- 198, 201, 203-214, 216, 222, 227, 234, 237, 239-246, 248-258 (*V de Phano*), 260-272, 274-290, 292, 295-301, 304, 306-308, 312-314, 318-327, 332, 336, 339, 342-344, 347, 348, 356-359, 363, 365, 366, 373, 381, 383, 384, 387, 388, 396, 402, 408-410, 412, 429, 433, 435-438, 441, 455, 456, 459, 460, 462-467, 469-475, 485, 488, 491, 494, 498, 510, 513, 515 (*V de phano*), 516, 518-521, 524-526, 542, 577, 578, 581-590, 594-601, 606-611, 627-629, 634-636; *and see* 159 note
......, ..., ..., correction of register ordered by regent of chancery done by, 13, 61, 134, 232, 281, 322
......, ..., ..., deletion in letter signed by another *magister* initialled by, 780

Landoris *see* Lindores

Lane, Edward, rector of Warkton, 169

Langenhoe (Languoo) [Essex], parish church of, 296

Langham [Essex], parish church of, union to, of the parish church of Ludgershall, 309

Langley [Norf], Premonstratensian monastery of, 321, 525, 668
......, ..., canons of *see* Loddon *alias* Galys, William; Tuddenham *alias* Moro, Thomas; Yermoth *alias* Ludhnn', Thomas

[Langley], Thomas, the late, bishop of Durham, statutes of Sherburn hospital reformed by, 429

Langton, Great [Yorks], parish church of, union of, to the canonry and prebend of Islington in London cathedral, 873

[Langton], Thomas, bishop of Winchester, death of, 626

Languoo *see* Langenhoe

Lanthony II by Gloucester (Lantone) [*or* Llanthony Secunda, Glos], Augustinian priory of B. or St Mary, 349
......, ..., priors (or commendatory priors) of exempt from payment to bishop of Meath, 442
......, ..., commendatory prior of *see* [Dean(e)], Henry
......, ..., commendatory prior and convent of, appeal of, 442
......, ..., parish churches and granges of Colp and Duleek united to, 442

Lanton' *see* Lauton

Lantone *see* Lanthony II by Gloucester

[Laois, co. of], places in *see* Abbeyleix; Aghmacart; Ballycoolan [*in* Timogue]; ?Curragh [*in* Killeshin]; ?Killeen [*in* Killabban]; Kilteale; Moyanna; Rathaspick; Rosconnell; Timahoe

Larbe, Thomas, rector of Foulsham, 31

Largs (Largis) [co. Ayr], church of, fruits of pertaining to Cluniac monastery of Paisley, grant of, 63

'Laronde', diocese of St Andrews [*unidentified; possibly* Restalrig (*in* South Leith), co. Midlothian], [collegiate] church of, dean of, papal mandatary, 366

Lasborough (Lashebarow) [Glos], free chapel of, union to, of the parish church of Bishopsbourne with Barham, 422

Lathes (Lathos), Richard, vicar of East Ham and incumbent of South Thoresby, 703

......, Robert, rector of Holy Trinity, Guildford, 175

'Latyrewern'', diocese of Lismore [*unidentified*; *in vicinity of head of* Loch Awe, co. Argyll], mountain of, 493

Launde [Leics], [Augustinian] priory of, prior of, papal judge delegate, 46

Laure(n)ce, John, rector of St Erme, 762

Laurencekirk, *once* Conveth, *q.v.*

Laury (Laurrey), Thomas, of Exeter diocese, dispensed for plurality, 1142

Lauton (Lanton'), John, layman of Coventry and Lichfield diocese, 556

......, ..., ..., sometime scribe in criminal causes, 556

......, ..., ..., ..., presentation of for Astbury parish church, 556

......, ..., ..., ..., intending cleric, 556

Lavage, John, of London diocese, dispensed for plurality, 1135

Lawnd, Robert, of Lincoln diocese, dispensed for plurality, 1293

......, *cf.* Lound *alias* Louude

Layburne (Lanburi, Layburii, Layburn, Layburn'), Roger, cleric of Durham diocese, 696

......, ..., of Durham diocese, dispensed for plurality, 1046

......, ..., cleric of Carlisle, 1012, 1013

......, ..., ..., chaplain of Henry [VII], 1012

......, ..., ..., ..., provision of to the bishopric of Carlisle, 1012

......, ..., ..., ..., absolution of preliminary to provision, 1013

......, ..., [bishop-] elect of Carlisle, faculty for consecration of, 1014

Laycestet *see* Leicester

Leaepadrayg *see* Leckpatrick

Leba', John, canon of Rennes, papal mandatary, 515

Lechacolay *see* Lackagh

Lechlade (Lechelade) [Glos], parish church of, 119, 732

......, ..., chantry of B. Mary in, 119

Leckpatrick (Leaepadrayg) [co. Tyrone], parish church of, rectory of, 249

......, ..., vicarage of, annexed to rectory, 249

......, ..., rectory (with annexed vicarage) of, to be erected into prebend in Derry cathedral, 249

Ledbury [Heref], parish church of, 875

......, ..., altar of B. Mary the Virgin in, 875

Lee, Edward, cleric of London diocese, 398

Legate, John, canon of the Augustinian monastery of Thornton, 997

Legh (Legh'), Thomas, vicar of ?Forcett, 976

Leicester (Laycestet) [Leics], vill of, 730

......, Augustinian monastery of B. Mary *in Pratis or* of the Meadow, abbot of, *see* [Penny], John

......, ..., canon of *see* Twyforth *alias* Colyns, John

......, church of B. Mary *novi operis* [i.e. Newark College], 17

......, ..., canon and prebendary of *see* Chapman, Thomas

......, church of St Margaret near, prebend of [in Lincoln cathedral], union to, of the vicarage of Croft, 749

[Leicester, co. of], places in *see* Billesdon; Bringhurst; Cotesbach; Croft; Croxton; Desford; Easton Magna; Houghton on the Hill; Kilworth, North; Launde;

[Leicester, co. of] (*contd*)
Leicester; Melton Mowbray; Owston; Waltham on the Wolds; Wymondham

Leicester (Leicetre, Leycetyr), John, rector of Stonham Aspall, 700
......, William, layman of Worcester diocese, litigant, 29

Leighlin [co. Carlow], **[cathedral] church** of, treasurer of, papal mandatary, 576, 981
......, ..., chapter of, to be summoned over erection of canonry and prebend, 982
......, ..., canons of *see* Doyle, Gerald; Omillayn, Edmund; *cf.* Okella, Edmund; Olerahur, Patrick
......, ..., prebends (unnamed) in, new prebend to be like, 982
......, ..., prebend in *see* ?Killeen

......, **bishop** of, to be summoned over erection of canonry and prebend, 982
......, church of, archdeacon of, papal mandatary, 932

......, **diocese** of, persons of *see* OCurran, Thady; Odulayud, Rory; Oeluana, William; OKelly, John; Olamyr, Donat; Omillayn, Henry; Omona, Rervallus; ONolan, Donat; William [*surname wanting*]
......, ..., places in *see* Abbeyleix; Ballon; Ballycoolan [*in* Timogue]; ?Curragh [*in* Killeshin]; ?Killeen [*in* Killabban]; Killeshin; Kilteale; Moyanna; Rathaspick; Timahoe

Leighmoney (Lyeamhune) [co. Cork], parish church of, rectory of, to be united to abbatial *mensa* of Tracton, 536

Leighs, Little (Lyesp(er)na [*recte* Lyes parva]) [Essex], Augustinian priory of St John the Evangelist of, canon of *see* Sponar, Simon

Leighterton *see* Boxwell

Leiston (Leyston') [Suff], Premonstratensian monastery of, abbot of *see* Doget, Thomas

[Leith, South, co. Midlothian], place in *see* Restalrig

[Leitrim, co. of], place in *see* Killanummery

Lenanach *see* Nenagh

Lenat *alias* Lenet, Henry, canon of Dublin, papal judge delegate, 989
......, *cf.* Lyvet

Leon [*in* province of Leon, Spain], church of, archdeacon of Valdemeriel in, *q.v.*
......, *see* Castile

Leonardi, Ralph, OP, to have Benedictine priory of Lihou *in commendam* anew, 817

Leowas *see* Lewis

Lere, John, rector of Clanfield, 466

Lermonth (Leomonth, Lormonth't), David, chamberlain of the Augustinian monastery of St Andrews, 971
......, George, of St Andrews diocese, dispensed for plurality, 1225

Leshugton, John, of Salisbury diocese, dispensed for plurality, 1248

Leuues *see* Lewes

Leversege, Roger, vicar of Ealing, 107

Levokenore, John, rector of Broadwater, 870

Lewes [Sussex], archdeacon of, papal judge delegate, 197

Lewes (Leuues), Josiana, woman of London, litigant, 8

Lewis (Leowas) [island in the Western Isles *or* Outer Hebrides, co. Ross and Cromarty], place in, 116

Lewknor (Lukenor) [Oxon], parish church of, 331

Lewtrenchard (Lewtreneherd) [Devon], parish church of, rector of, 324

Lexa *see* Angersleigh

Leycetyr *see* Leicester

Leynham, alias of Bysshope, William, *q.v.*

Leyston' *see* Leiston

'Li', diocese of Sodor [*unidentified*; *perhaps* Eye (now part of Stornoway) *or* Uig] in Lewis [Western Isles, co. Ross and Cromarty], parish church of, rectory of, 116
......, ..., rector of, 116

Libberton *see* ?Quothquan

Lichfield [Staffs], city of, ?conduits of, 176
......, hospital of St John the Baptist, foundation of, 176
......, ..., college for scholars and paupers in, institution of, 176
......, ..., ..., statutes and ordinances of, faculty for confirmation and approval of, 176
......, *and see* Coventry and Lichfield

Lickoran (Luoran) [co. Waterford], parish church of, vicarage of, to be erected into prebend of Lismore, with Modelligo vicarage united thereto, 946

Lidierd' *see* Lydeard St Lawrence

Liell *see* Lyell

Ligiard *see* Lydeard St Lawrence

Ligiardi *see* Lydeard

Lihou (Lyhou) [islet, *off* Guernesey, Channel Islands], Benedictine priory of, 817
......, ..., a dependency of Mont St Michel, 817
......, ..., commendatory prior of *see* Leonardi, Ralph

Limerick [co. Limerick], **city** of, mayors, bailiffs, and commonalty of, presentation by, 815
......, walls of, 815
......, ..., vicarage of St Michael's just outside, to be united to a canonry and the prebend of the parish church and of the hospital of lepers of St Laurence outside the walls, 815
......, parish church and hospital of lepers of St Laurence outside the walls of, 815
......, ..., erection of into prebend of Limerick, with union to of the vicarage of St Michael's just outside the walls, Limerick, 815

......, **[cathedral] church** of, precentorship of, 486
......, ..., ..., fruits of being taken by laymen, 486
......, ..., ..., to be united to canonry of Limerick and prebend of Tullabracky, 486
......, ..., precentor of *see* de Mivrey *alias* OHonan, William
......, ..., chancellorship of, 485
......, ..., ..., vicarage of Kilscannell to be united to, 485
......, ..., chancellor of, papal mandatary, 944
......, ..., ..., *see* OCorkery, Maurice
......, ..., treasurer of, papal mandatary, 944
......, ..., chapter of, to be summoned over erection of canonry and prebend, 824, 942
......, ..., canons of *see* Craenach, Andrew; Creagh, Andrew; de Geraldinis, Beraldus [*recte* Geraldus] Thome, James Radmundi Mauritii, and Maurice, the younger; MacNamara, Cornelius *alias* Curnea / Cunca [i.e. *Cuveadh*] and John; de Mivrey *alias* OHonan, William; OCullane, Maurice;

Limerick **[cathedral] church** (*contd*)
OFlynn, Maurice; OKennedy, Donat; ONoonan, Richard; OPhelan, Maurice; White, William

......, ..., prebends in *see Cluain Comarda*; Donaghmore; Killeedy; Tullabracky; *and see above under* Limerick, parish church and hospital of lepers of St Laurence outside the walls

......, **bishop** of, canonry and prebend erected and granted by, 815

......, ..., institution by, 815

......, ..., presence of at the Roman curia, 485

......, ..., conspiracies against, 485

......, ..., to be summoned over erection of canonry and prebend, 824, 942

......, ..., papal mandatary, 543

......, ..., vicar general of, 485

......, [church of], archdeacon of *see Militis* [i.e. of the Knight (of Glin de Geraldinis)], John

......, **diocese** of, persons of *see* Aherne, Denis; Appleyard, John; [Creagh], David; Deipatientia, William; de Geraldinis, Gerald David; MacClancy, Donald; MacKeaghan, Philip; Macraych, John; ODonegan, William; Offaeyn, Thomas; Offahym, David; Oflayterah, Thady; OLahiff, Thady; ONoonan, Donald; OPhelan, Eugene; ORonan, James; Os..ayn, Davit; ?Warnygtiu(m), Richard; Ymolierayn, Gerard

......, ..., places in *see* Adare; ?Ballycahane; *Cluain Comarda* [*now* ?Colmanswell]; Kilbradran; Kilfergus; Kilfintinan; Killagholehane; Killeedy; Killeely; Kilmoylan; Kilscannell; Monasteranenagh; Rathkeale

[Limerick, co. of], places in *see* Abington; Donaghmore; Glenbane [*in* Shanagolden]; [Glin]; Killeenagarriff; Limerick; Ludden; Stradbally *alias* 'Cloynacheke'; Tullabracky; *and all places except* Kilfintinan *listed above under* Limerick, diocese of

Limington (Lymyngton, Lymyngton') [Som], parish church of, 23, 682

Lincoln [co. Lincoln], college of B. Mary of, at Oxford, *q.v.*

......, **[cathedral] church** of, dean of, papal mandatary, 423

......, ..., ..., faculty to, to reform statutes of Tattershall church, 423

......, ..., canons of *see* Fitz Hugh, George; Hornby, Henry; Spencer, Robert; Whitstones, James; *and see* Cutler, John

......, ..., chaplain in *see* Thorpe, William

......, ..., prebends in *see* Banbury; Cropredy; Leicester St Margaret; Milton Manor; Nassington

......, **bishop** (or his vicar general) of, presentation of person for benefice to, 363, 386

......, ..., institution by, 363, 386

......, bishop of, union by, of Wootton parish church to the Augustinian provostry of Moncenisio, 405

......, ..., letters of ratifying agreement concerning Poolham chapel, 379

......, ..., to receive oath of fealty in pope's name, 581, 582

......, ..., papal judge delegate, 28, 261, 298, 405

......, ..., papal mandatary, 423

......, ..., faculty to, to reform statutes of Tattershall church, 423

......, ..., papal commissary and mandatary, 721

......, ..., *see* [Russell], John; [Smith], William

......, ..., commissary of *see* Hutton, Thomas

......, official of, papal mandatary, 386

......, church of, *sede vacante* administrator of *see* Vallos, John

......, ..., archdeacon of Huntingdon in *see* Warham, William

......, ..., archdeacon [of Lincoln] in *see* Hutton, Thomas

......, **diocese** of, rectors of parish churches of, cognizance of causes moved by

Lincoln, **diocese** (*contd*)

against their parishioners belongs to the archbishop of Canterbury, or, when the see of Canterbury is vacant, to the chapter of Canterbury, 906

......, ..., persons of *see* Alison, John; Andeleyn, Henry; Andrew, William; Aplien, John; [Attercliff], Elias; Baker, Richard; Barkeworth, Robert; de Basodonys, John Baptist; Bexwike, Thomas; Carpenter, Richard; [Caversham], Peter; Chapman, Thomas; Clarell', Thomas; Cole, John; Cook, John; Coren, Robert; Cotton, Walter; Crosley, Christopher; Davy, Thomas; Denh(a)m, John; Dey, John and Thomas; Dighton, Richard; Done, Nicholas; Donyngton', Thomas; Dotson', Laurence; Dubler, William; Duxbery, Robert; Edmond, John; Elys, William; Emley, John; Evedon, Robert; Everard, Thomas; Faulkener, John; Fox, Thomas; Franck, John; Franklin, William; Freston, William; Garford *alias* Crouulandi, Thomas; Garforth, Thomas; Gilbert, Robert; Hafter, John; Hales, Thomas; Hammond, John; Harrison, Hugh; Harrop, Thomas; Hawlay, Robert; Helmsley, Henry; Helwys, Richard; Hodgson, Patrick; [Hogeson], Thomas; Holdirnessa, Robert; Hunden', Thomas; Hunt, John; [Huntington], John; Hussey, Thomas; Ireland, William; Jackson, John; Johnson, John; Kingsley, Robert; Kuodi, Robert; ?K...., Thomas; Lacy, John; Lane, Edward; Lathes, Richard; Lawnd, Robert; Legate, John; Long, John; Lound *alias* Louude, Robert; Lowthe, Robert; Lynley, Robert; Mandeville, Edmund and John; Manfield, Thomas; Marshall, John; Mason, William; Mathews, John; Morlandi, John; Nicholl, Richard; Nicolson, Thomas; Ormeston, Thomas; [Penny], John; Peston *alias* Conell,' Gilbert; Plominer, Christopher; Ranbino, Richard; Ravyn, John; Rayens, Thomas; Robertson, Richard; Rogers, James; Rose, Joan; Ruer, Thomas; [Salley], Miles; Sandford,

Lincoln, **diocese** (*contd*)

Roger; Saunder, Andrew; Saunders, Thomas; Smyth, John, Richard, and Thurstan; Spencer, William; Spenser, Robert; Stanbank, Edmund; Sterne, Edmund; [S]vyst, Thomas; Tanfeld, Thomas; Taylard, William; Taylor, John; Thimbleby, Richard; Thomson, John; Thymylby, Thomas; Tonge, William; Tothoth', Vincent; Turton', George; Twyforth *alias* Colyns, John; Tybard, Henry; ?Ulreby, Thomas; Underhill, John; Vassar, Peter; Veysey *alias* Harman, John; Wadyluff, Robert; Wayfleot, Robert; Welles, Thomas; Wellys, John; West, Reginald; Wigston, Thomas; Wildon, John; Wilford, Edmund; Wilkes, William; Woodington, Thomas; Wyllesford, Edmund; Wytheley, John; Ynyago, John; Yonge, John; [*no surname*], Geoffrey and Robert; and *cf.* Lyttelman, Robert

......, ..., places in *see* Ashwell [Rut]; Battlesden; Billesdon; Bledlow; Boughton; Bringhurst *alias* Easton Magna; Braybrooke; Brington; Bruern; Burnham; Byfield; Chacombe; Checkendon; Clifton Reynes; Conington; Cosgrove; Cotesbach; Croxton; Cuxham; Desford; 'Dino'; Dorchester; Dunstable; Easington; Empingham; Eynsham; Farthingstone; Fawley; Ferriby; Glatton; Hamerton; Hanwell; Harrowden; Henley on Thames; Hethe; Heyford Warren; ?Holcot; Holwell; Horwood, Great; Houghton Conquest; Houghton on the Hill; Kettering; Kilworth, North; Lamport; Launde; Leicester; Lewknor; Ludgershall; Marston Moretaine; Medmenham; Melton Mowbray; Missenden; Moulton; Northampton; Northmoor; Notley; Oakley [Bucks]; Orton Longueville; Oundle; Owston; Oxford; Penn; Peterborough; Potton; Ramsey; Ravensthorpe; Ripton, Abbots; St Albans; Shillington; Stoke Talmage; Stonely; Sutton [Beds]; Thame; Tinwell; Turville; Warkton;

Lincoln, **diocese** (*contd*)
Woburn; Woodstock; Wootton; Wymondham; *and, with the exception of* Stamford *and* South Ferriby, *all the places listed below under* [Lincoln, co. of]

[Lincoln, co. of], places in *see* Bardney; Brocklesby; Broxholme; ?Clee; Corby; Croft; Deeping, West; Edlington; Evedon; Ferriby, South; Gedney; Glentham; Grantham; Grimoldby; Habrough; Ingham; Kirkby on Bain; Kirkstead; Morton (by Bourne); Nettleton; ?Newton; Ormsby, North; Partney; Poolham; Revesby; Saltfleetby; Sempringham; Skirbeck; Sleaford; Stamford; Stoke, South; Sutterton; Tattershall; Tetford; Thoresby, South; Thornholme; Thornton; Tupholme; Uffington; Utterby; Waltham; Whaplode

Lindores (Lundo[r]is, Lundotis) [*in* Abdie, co. Fife], Benedictine monastery of B. Mary, abbot and convent of, claimants to right of patronage to chaplaincy in St Salvator's, St Andrews, 691
......, ..., ..., presentation by, 691
......, ..., ..., ..., of person for vicarage of Rathmuriel and Kinnethmont, 778
......, ..., ..., litigants, 812
......, ..., fruits of, reservation of, 1260
......, ..., monk, recently abbot, of *see* [Caueris], Andrew

[Lindsay], John, earl of Crawford, patron of chaplaincy in St Salvator's, St Andrews, presentation by, 691
......, ..., ..., supplication of, 691

Linguiaila *see* Lynally

Linlithgow (Linlithquew) [co. Linlithgow], parish church of, 979

[Linlithgow *or* West Lothian, co. of], places in *see* Carriden; Linlithgow

Linlithquew *see* Linlithgow

Lismore [an island at the mouth of Loch Linnhe, co. Argyll], **[cathedral] church** of [*at* ?Clachan *on* Lismore island *in* Lismore and Appin, co. Argyll], chapter of, conclusion to, 55
......, **bishop** of, papal judge delegate, 80
......, ..., *see* [Colquhoun], Robert; Hamilton, David
......, church of, subjection of, to the archbishop of Glasgow, 57
......, ..., vassals of, conclusion to, 55

......, **city and diocese** of, clergy of, conclusion to, 55
......, ..., people of, conclusion to, 55
......, diocese of, persons of *see* Scrimgeour, James and John
......, ..., places in *see* Ardchattan; 'Brenowc'; Fincharn; Ford; Glasvaar; Kilneuair; 'Latyrewern''; 'Lochclea'; 'Lochquho'; Socach; Stroneskar; 'Terroner'

Lismore [co. Waterford], **[cathedral] church** of, deanery of, prebend of Clashmore and vicarage of Kilronan annexed to it to be united thereto, 159
......, ..., dean of, papal mandatary, 852, 941
......, ..., ..., *see* Butler *alias* Okynala, William; de Geraldinis, Gerald, James and John Philippi; OKett, Gillasius; Russell, Thomas
......, ..., precentorship of, 158
......, ..., precentor of, papal judge delegate, 221
......, ..., ..., *see* de Geraldinis, Gerald Johannis; de Mandeville, Walter
......, ..., chancellor of, papal judge delegate, 221
......, ..., ..., papal mandatary, 227, 949
......, ..., chapter of, to be summoned over erection of canonry and prebend, 785, 790, 946
......, ..., canons of *see* Butler, Walter; de Geraldinis, John Philippi; MacGrath, Thomas; OFlavin, William; [?OFlavin], William; OKett, Philip; Purcell, Edmund and Jordan; Russell, James; Stack, Philip
......, ..., prebends in *see* Clashmore; Kilronan and Kilcash; Kilsheelan and

Lismore, [cathedral] church (*contd*)
Newtown Lennan; Lickoran; Modelligo

......, **bishop** of, canonry and prebend
resigned into hands of, 381
......, ..., collation by, of canonry and
prebend, 381
......, ..., as local ordinary, simoniacal
collation by, *cf.* 946
......, ..., to be summoned over erection of
canonry and prebend, 785, 790, 946
......, ..., papal mandatary, 381
......, ..., *see* [Purcell], Thomas

......, **diocese** of, persons of *see* Butler,
Peter; Fitzgibbon, Edmund; de
Geraldinis, Gerald Johannis; Loweys,
John; MacGrath, Thomas; Machaestyn,
Maurice; Mnacarnara, Donat; Mockler,
Henry; OBogue, William; OCahill,
Maurice and Thomas; ODonoghue,
William; Oflyijd, Thady; OKinneally
alias ?MacKinneally, Thady;
OMorrissey, William; Power, Thomas;
Purcell, Thomas; White, Joan;
Yhacgeryn, John; *and see* Aplialo,
Thomas; Brydach, Philip
......, ..., places in *see* Caher; ?Colman;
Donaghmore; Inishlounaght;
Kilbarrymeaden; Kilcash; Kilronan;
Kilsheelan; Lickoran; Modelligo;
Molana; Mothel; Newtown Lennan;
Outeragh; Rossmire; *and see*
Moorstown

Little Leighs *see* Leighs, Little

Little Rissington *see* Rissington, Little

Little Whelnetham *see* Whelnetham, Little

Little Wilbraham *see* Wilbraham, Little

Litton (Lutton') [Som], parish church of,
rector of, 310

Llanbadarn Fawr (Llanbadarne Vawr) [co.
Cardigan], parish church of, vicar of,
893

Llandaff [co. Glamorgan], [cathedral]
church of, chapter of, conclusion to,
598
......, bishop of *see* [Ingleby], John; [Salley],
Miles
......, church of, subject to archbishop of
Canterbury, 599
......, ..., vassals of, conclusion to, 598
......, city and diocese of, clergy of,
conclusion to, 598
......, ..., people of, conclusion to, 598
......, diocese of, persons of *see* Inell *alias*
Giles, Alexander
......, ..., place in *see* Merthyr Tydfil

Llandeilo Vawr (Llandylovaure) [co.
Carmarthen], parish church of, vicar of,
892

[Llandysilio *or* Llantysilio co. Denbigh],
place in *see* Valle Crucis

Llan Egwestl *or* Llan Egwast
(Ryneguvesteyll', Rynegvuesteyll',
Rynegwesteyll'), alias of Valle Crucis,
q.v.

Llanfallteg (Llanvailldeg) [cos. Carmarthen
and Pembroke], parish church of, rector
of, 272

?Llanfarchell (Llanvarchell') [*near*
Denbigh, co. Denbigh], parish church
of, incumbent of, 483
......, ..., union of, to canonry of St Asaph
and prebend of ?Meifod, otherwise
cursal, 483

?Llanfechell (?Nanudechell') [co.
Anglesey], parish church of St
Machutus, rector of, 393

Llanfyrnach on Taff (Ranuernach' super
Cave) [*modern* Llanfyrnach, co.
Pembroke], parish church of, 460

[Llangan, co. Carmarthen], place in *see*
Whitland

Llanllwchaiarn (Llanllaychayarin',
Llanlloycharn') [co. Cardigan], parish
church of, rector of, 318, 739

Llanthony Secunda *see* Lanthony II by Gloucester

Llantysilio *see* Llandysilio

Llanvailldeg *see* Llanfallteg

Llanvarchell' *see* ?Llanfarchell

Lochaber [a district, co. Inverness], 765

Loch a' Choire, Loch Awe *see* 'Lochquho'

'Lochclea' [*unidentified; in vicinity of head of* Loch Awe, co. Argyll; *possibly* Loch Leachd (*in* Kilmichael Glassary, co. Argyll)], place of, 493

Loch Ke, Lochlie *see* Lough Key

Loch Leachd *see* 'Lochclea'

[Loch Linnhe, co. Argyll] *see* Lismore

Lochore *see* Inchegall

'Lochquho', diocese of Lismore [*unidentified; in vicinity of head of* Loch Awe, co. Argyll; *probably* Loch a' Choire *near* Ederline *in* Kilmichael Glassary, co. Argyll; *possibly* Loch Awe *itself*], lake of, 493

Lochwinnoch (Lotwinʒok) [co. Renfrew], church of, fruits of pertaining to Cluniac monastery of Paisley, grant of, 63
......, place in *see* Glen

[Lockeen, co. Tipperary], place in *see* Ballyloughnane

Locmask *see* Lough Mask

Locquyn *see* Loughkeen

Locrerdh, Loctriach *see* Loughrea

Loddon (Loddon') *alias* Galys, William, canon of the Premonstratensian monastery of Langley, 668

Lodien' *see* Ludden

Lodua *see* Ballyloughloe

Logie Durno (Logidurno) [*part of modern* Chapel of Garioch, co. Aberdeen], parish church of, vicarage of, 992

Lokeford *see* Lackford

Lokton, John, scholar of Canterbury diocese, 895

Lolworth (Lolleworth', Lowlworth') [Cambs], parish church of, rector of, 207, 685
......, ..., union of to Brington, 685

Lonayn *alias* Balenoe *see* Newtown Lennan

London [Midd], **city** of, streets etc.:
Bishopsgate (Bisshopsgate), 564
Bread Street, 665
Cornhill (Cornehill'), 903
East Cheap (Eschepe), 969
Lombard Street (Lombardstrete), 464
New Temple, bars of, 923
Walbrook (Walbroke), 365
......, ..., any house, hospice, or shop in, tithe payable by inhabitants of, 365
......, ..., company in:
Drapers', 903
......, ..., parish churches in:
All Hallows the Great *or* at the Hay, 559
altar of B. Mary the Virgin in, "Louergues channtre" at, 559
St Andrew Hubbard (Hubert), 969
St Clement Danes, 923
St Dionis [Backchurch], 233
[St John the Baptist], Walbrook (Walbroke), tithe payable to rector of, 365
St Mary Abchurch, union of, to the parish church of West Tilbury, 375
St Michael, Cornhill (Cornehill'), Drapers' Company in, guild of, guardians and brothers of, to exchange with Evesham abbey

London, **city** (*contd*)
      goods yielding annual pension for
      patronage of St Michael's, 903
      St Mildred, Bread Street, 665
      St Nicholas Acon, 464
......, ..., ..., tithe payable to rectors of, 365
......, ..., hospital in:
      B. Mary the Virgin without
      Bishopsgate, OSA, 564

......, [**cathedral**] **church** of, dean of, papal
    mandatary, 963
......, ..., ..., *see* Say, William
......, ..., chapter of, conclusion to, 617
......, ..., canons of *see* Eduard, William;
    Greves, Peter; Harington, William; Hill,
    John; Jane, Thomas; Underwood,
    Edward; Wyppyll, John
......, ..., prebends in *see* Ealdstreet;
    Islington
......, ..., chaplaincy in *see below under*
    crypt
......, ..., chantries in:
    of Philip and Fulk Bassett and Peter
      Newport, 748
    of Roger Holme and Adam Bury, 800
    of Roger Walden, 426
    at altar of B. Mary the Virgin near the
      tomb of John Beauchamp, 518
......, ..., chaplains in *see* Brady, Thomas;
    Curleus, Nicholas; Richardson,
    William; Tactorm', William; William,
    Peter
......, ..., altars in:
    of B. Mary the Virgin, 518
    of the Holy Spirit, 800
    of St George, 748
    and see below under crypt
......, ..., tomb of John Beauchamp, knight,
    in, 518
......, ..., crypt of, 856
......, ..., ..., altar of B. Mary in, 856
......, ..., ..., ..., chaplaincy founded at by
    the late William Say, 856

......, **bishop** of, papal judge delegate, 661,
    905
......, ..., papal mandatary, 903
......, ..., *see* [?Courtenay], William;
    [Savage], Thomas; [Warham], Thomas
......, official of *see* Vaughan, Edward

London, **bishop** (*contd*)
......, church of, subject to the archbishop of
    Canterbury, 619
......, ..., vassals of, conclusion to, 617
......, ..., ..., archdeacon of, papal judge
    delegate, 8
......, ..., ..., papal mandatary, 963
......, ..., ..., court of, official of, litigation
    before, 8
......, ..., archdeacon of Colchester in *see*
    Perott, John
......, ..., archdeacon of Essex in *see* Jane,
    Thomas

......, **city and diocese** of, clergy of,
    conclusion to, 617
......, ..., people of, conclusion to, 617
......, ..., persons of *see* Abbot, Thomas;
    Aderei, Thomas; Andrenoson, Gilbert;
    Appulby, Thomas; Arrowsmith,
    William; Aubrey, Joan; Beaumont,
    Thomas; Beaumont, viscount, William
    and his wife Elizabeth; Bew, William;
    Brady, Thomas; Bray, John and
    Reginald; Bride, Ralph; Bright, Robert;
    Chester, Alice; Clerke, Richard and
    Thomas; Cowp(er), Edmund; Crafford,
    Robert; Crosby, John; Docura, John;
    Fabell, John; Ferdinandi, Gonzalo; Fitz
    Herbert, Thomas; Forster, John;
    Gimnays, William; Gunby, Thomas;
    Hare, Thomas; Hayne, John; Hobyll,
    John; Hunt, Henry; Johnson, Thomas;
    Josselyne, Philip; Judson, John; Keble,
    Margaret; Kelouz, John; Lathes,
    Richard; Lavage, John; Lee, Edward;
    Leversege, Roger; Lewes, Josiana;
    Lubbenh(a)m, Roger; Marowte, Joan;
    Martyr, John; Mayhew, Henry;
    Narbonne, Henry Petri of; Nicolson,
    Thomas; Parker, John; Payntoure,
    Roger; Peston *alias* Conell', Gilbert;
    Picherd, Richard; Podynger, John;
    Pontesbury, Edward; Remiyan,
    William; Rutter, John; Ryther, John;
    Shrager, William; Silvester, Gabriel;
    Sponar, Simon; Stampe, John;
    Stockdale, William; Sutton, John;
    Synyer, Richard; Tarkii, Peter;
    Thornburgh, William; Tonge, William;
    Trotter, John; Trufodi, Hugh; Ungram,

London, persons of (*contd*)
John; Urswick, Nicholas; Vernon, Roger; Wetton, Thomas; Witt, John; Wylleys, Richard; ?...burg', [*Christian name wanting*]; *and cf.* Ely, Thomas; Grafton, Adam; Hatton, John
......, diocese of, places in *see* Chiswick; Ealing; Enfield; Harringay; Hendon; Hornsey; Kensington; Pelham, Furneux; Twickenham; Westminster; *and* places *listed above under* [Essex, co. of]
......, *and see* Bermondsey

Londonderry *see* Derry

Long (Longe), John, union for, of one of his parish churches to the other, Lincoln diocese, 1091
......, Thomas, scholar of Canterbury diocese, 326
......, ..., scholar of Salisbury diocese, 891

Long Crendon *see* Crendon, Long

[Longant], Andrew, abbot of the Cistercian monastery of Newbattle, 1032
......, ..., ..., consent of, to appointment of coadjutor, 1032
......, ..., ..., coadjutor of *see* Turnbull, John

Longe *see* Long

Longford (Longforth) [Derb], parish church of, 290

[Longford, barony of, co. Galway], places probably in *see* 'Arodmuneach'; 'Bearnduamlegynd'; 'Bruachtalach'; 'Glochmor'; 'Gortnuybg''; 'Gortuaglothbg''; '?Goven'; 'Syliam'

[Longford, co. of], places in *see* Abbeyderg; Abbeyshrule; Ardagh; Inchcleraun; ?Kilglass; Saints Island

Longformacus *see* Ellem

Longforth, Henry, rector of Longford, 290

Longforth *see* Longford

Lonthree *see* Lowther

Looder, John, vicar of Worth [and] Swanage, 710

Lopa, Lora *see* Lorrha

Lormonth't *see* Lermonth

Lornisen, Michael, monk of the Benedictine monastery of Dunfermline, 409

Lorrha (Lopa, Lora, Loro) [co. Tipperary], [Augustinian] monastery of, prior of, papal mandatary, 16, 162, 403, 511

Lothian, archdeacon and archdeaconry of in the church of St Andrews, *q.v.*
......, district of, external official in, litigation before, 792
......, ..., ..., appointment of by the archbishop of St Andrews, 792

[Lothian, East] *see* [Haddington, co. of]

[Lothian, West] *see* [Linlithgow, co. of]

Lotwinȝok *see* Lochwinnoch

Louer, John, of Salisbury diocese, dispensed for plurality, 1187

"Louergues channtre" in All Hallows' the Great, London, 559

Loughkeen (Bayllilocacayn, Locquyn) [co. Tipperary], parish church of, vicarage of, 162, 403
......, ..., ..., to be united to proposed prebend of *Cenél arga* in Killaloe cathedral, 162
......, ..., ..., to be erected into prebend in Killaloe with vicarage of Uskane and church, called rectory or particle, of lands of 'Medohk' united thereto, 403
......, ..., vicar of, church of 'Medohk' customarily ruled by, 403
......, ..., limits of, lands of 'Medohk' in, 403

Lough Key (Loch Ke, Lochlie) [*on* Trinity Island, *in* Kilbryan, co. Roscommon], Premonstratensian monastery of, 846, 995

......, ..., abbots of *see* [MacDonagh], Magonius; MacElheron, Malachy

......, ..., canons of *see* MacElheron, Malachy

......, ..., proposed union to, of vicarages of Coola and Killanummery, 846, 995

......, ..., simoniacal union to, of vicarage of Coola, 846

......, ..., subject to bishop of Elphin, 846

......, island in *see* Inchmacnerin

Lough Mask (Locmask) [cos. Galway and Mayo], parish church of, rectory of, to be erected, with Inishmaine, into prebend of Tuam, 826

Loughrea (Locrerdh, Loctriach) [co. Galway], parish church of, vicarage of, 16, 512

......, ..., ..., to be erected into prebend in Clonfert cathedral, 16

......, ..., ..., to be united to canonry of Clonfert and prebend of Ballynakill, 512

Lough Ree, Inchcleraun in, *q.v.*

Louis [XII], king of the Franks, conclusion to, 577

Lound (Lounde) *alias* Louude, Robert, vicar of Glentham, 2

......, *cf.* Lawnd

[Louth, co. of], places in *see* Drogheda; Mansfieldstown; Mellifont

Louude, alias of Lound, Robert, *q.v.*

Louuyn', Geoffrey, monk of the Cluniac priory of Castle Acre, 287

Loweys, John, detainer of vicarage of ?Colman, 786

Lowlworth' *see* Lolworth

Lowthe, Robert, rector of Hamerton and incumbent of Stretton on the Fosse, 282

Lowther (Lonthree), Robert, of Carlisle diocese, dispensed for plurality, 1270

Lubbenh(a)m, Roger, cantor of the "Louergues channtre" in All Hallows' the Great, London, 559

Lucca [Italy], Augustinian priory of S. Michele in Foro, rebuilding of, 441

......, ..., commendatory prior of *see* [de' Gigli], Silvester

......, [cathedral] church of, archpriest of *see* de' Gigli, Silvester

......, ..., canons of *see* de' Gigli, Silvester; Mazzarosa, Sebastiano di Bartolomeo

......, city and diocese of, persons of *see* de Ciampantibus, Hercules; da ?Civezzano, Paolo di Niccolò; Orsini, Orsino

......, diocese of, places in *see* Benabbio; Cortesora; Stazzema

Ludden (Lodien') [co. Limerick], parish church of, vicarage of, 380

......, ..., ..., proposed union to, of the vicarage of Stradbally *alias* 'Cloynacheke', 380

Ludgershall (Ludgarsall') [Bucks], parish church of, union of, to the parish church of Langham, 309

Ludhnn', alias of Yermoth, Thomas, *q.v.*

Ludie *see* Lundie

Ludovicus, bishop of Maurienne *see* [de Gorrevodo], Ludovicus

Lugwardyn (Luguuardyn'), John, canon of Wells, prebendary of Timberscombe, and incumbent of Axbridge, 295

Luirreae *see* Quarr

Lukenor *see* Lewknor

Lunbard, John, chaplain in Ledbury parish church, 875

Lundie (Ludie) [*part of* Lundie and Fowlis, cos. Forfar and Perth], parish church of, 65

Lundo[r]is, Lundotis *see* Lindores

Lundy, Andrew, of Carnbo (and of Balgonie), repeated appeal of, 971

Luoran *see* Lickoran

Lutton' *see* Litton

Ly [i.e. *le* or *lie*] *see under* main element

Lydeard (Ligiardi) [L~ St Lawrence *or* Bishop's L~, Som], land of, 174

Lydeard St Lawrence (Lidierd', Ligiard) [Som], church of, 174

Lyeamhune *see* Leighmoney

Lyell (Liell), Andrew, vicar of Logie Durno, resignation of, 992
......, ..., proctor of *see* Fabri, John
......, William, priest of Aberdeen diocese, 992
......, ..., ..., to have vicarage of Logie Durno, 992

Lyesp(er)na *see* Little Leighs

Lyhou *see* Lihou

Lympsham (Lymplesham, Lympysham) [Som], parish church of, union of, to the parish church of Mells, 293
......, ..., union of, to a canonry and prebend of Exeter, 717

Lymyngton, Lymyngton' *see* Limington

Lynally (Linguiaila) [co. Offaly], rectory of, to be united to proposed prebend of *Cenél arga* in Killaloe cathedral, 162

Lynley, Robert, rector of Easington, 223

Lynton', William, rector of Spaxton, 132

Lyon [*in dép.* of Rhône, France], archbishop of, conclusion to, 577
......, diocese of, person of *see* Bone, Philibertus
......, ..., places in *see* Ambronay; ?Monfavrey

Lyttelman, Robert, brother of the hospital of Santo Spirito in Saxia, Rome, 339

Lyvet *cf.* Lenat *alias* Lenet

M

Macaedh *see* MacKee

Macahayn *see* MacCahan

MacAllen (Macallan'), John, canon of Raphoe, papal mandatary, 249

Macaryg *see* MacCarthy

MacAuliffe (Machauli, Machaulyn, Makavlly), Donat, canon of Cloyne, papal mandatary, 250, 359, 360

Macberragoyn, David, priest of Killaloe diocese, to have vicarage of Ludden with vicarage of Stradbally *alias* 'Cloynacheke' united thereto, 380

Macbiragyn, Dermot, ostensible priest of Killaloe diocese, detainer of vicarage of Killeenagarriff, 404

Macbloshayd *see* MacCloskey

MacBrady (Iuacbradayd, Macbraday, Macbradi, Magbraday), Eugene, priest of Kilmore diocese, to have vicarage of Drumgoon otherwise called the *plebs* of Magheranure anew, 832
......, Gilbert, cleric of Kilmore diocese, to have rectory of Urney *alias* Keadew, 834
......, Nicholas, priest of Kilmore diocese, to have vicarage of Urney *alias* Keadew and the rectory of the church, called *plebs*, of 'Cuacaynde *alias* Clacerogarde' anew, 831

MacBrady (*contd*)

......, Patrick, canon of Kilmore, papal mandatary, 821, 831, 832, 834

......, ..., to have vicarage in Kilmore diocese erected into a canonry [of Kilmore?], 1280

MacBratney *cf.* MacBritany

MacBrien (Macbreyn, Machibren), Charles, canon of Emly, 52-54

......, ..., ..., provision of to the bishopric of Emly, 52

......, ..., ..., absolution of preliminary to provision, 53

......, ..., ..., dispensation of for illegitimacy preliminary to provision, 54

......, William, detainer of deanery of Emly, 838

MacBritany *cf.* Brechimay; MacBratney

MacCahan (Macahayn, Machayn), Cornelius, priest of Killaloe diocese, to have vicarage of Kilfearagh and portion of 'Gleandbannam', vulgarly '?Ileraunr', in the collegiate church of Scattery Island, 818

......, Thady, detainer of portion of Moanmore in [collegiate] church of Scattery Island, 449

...... *cf.* MacKeane

Maccamilii *see* MacCawell

MacCarthy (Macaryg, Machareyg, Macharyg, Mackaryg, Magearyg, Makaryg, Makryg, Mecharri), Cormac, cleric of Cork diocese and *de facto* vicar of ?Ringrone, to have canonry and prebend of Kilbrogan in Cork cathedral with rectory of Garrynoe and his vicarage of ?Ringrone united thereto, 252

......, ..., to have vicarage in Ardfert diocese erected into a prebend [in Ardfert cathedral], 1071

......, Donat, canon of Cork (and prebendary of Inishkenny), 816, 822, 825

......, ..., ..., to be administrator of fabric of St Finbar's church, Cork, 816

MacCarthy (*contd*)

......, ..., ..., to have archdeaconry of Cork and rectory of Inishannon united to his canonry and prebend, 822

......, ..., ..., papal mandatary, 825

......, Eugene, cleric of Ardfert diocese, to be canon of Ardfert and prebendary of Drishane *alias* Kilmeedy, 540

......, Felmicus, canon of Cloyne, papal mandatary, 125

......, Thady, canon of Cork, papal mandatary, 256

......, ..., cleric of Cork diocese, to have deanery of Cork and rectories of Burren and Rathclarin united thereto, 258

......, ..., ..., to be archdeacon of Ross and canon and prebendary of Dromdaleague in Cork cathedral, and have the rectory in the ecclesiastical fief of Schull and the vicarage of Schull united to the archdeaconry, 257

MacCawell (Maccamilii), Eugenius, to have vicarage in ?Achonry diocese, 1261

Macchomara *see* MacNamara

MacClancy (Maclanchi), Donald, detainer of vicarage of Kilmoylan, 820

MacCloskey (Macbloshayd), Bernard, canon of Derry, papal mandatary, 259

Macco'mara *see* MacNamara

Macconagaland, Patrick, detainer of rectory of Banagher, 253

......, *cf.* MacConnolly

Macconcour *see* MacConnor

Macco(n)mara, Macconmara, Macco(n)marra *see* MacNamara

MacConnolly *cf.* Macconagaland

MacConnor (Macconcour), Brendan, vicar of Ballymacelligott, to have also rectory of Ballyduff *alias* Glennahoo, 994

MacCoughlan *cf.* Mathoblayn

[MacDonagh], Magonius, abbot of the Premonstratensian monastery of Lough Key, to be deprived for alleged misdeeds, 846

MacDonnell (Macdonall), Eugene, cleric of Killala diocese, to have vicarage of Castleconor, 124

MacDowell *cf.* Doyle

Macduyl, Macduyll *see* Doyle

MacEgan (Machagan, Machrgan, Machyachayn, Macohegan), Fergal, archdeacon of Cloyne (*recte* Clonmacnois?), to be deprived, 228
......, Thady, canon of Clonfert, papal mandatary, 229, 492, 935
......, ..., ..., commendatory abbot of the Augustinian monastery of B. Mary, Clonfert, to be removed for alleged misdeeds, 229
......, *cf.* MacKeaghan

MacElheron (Macgillakyeran, Macgyllakieran), Malachy, canon of the Premonstratensian monastery of Lough Key, 846, 995
......, ..., ..., provision of as abbot, 846, 995

MacElligott (Mare'lligoid), John, to have vicarage in Ardfert diocese erected into canonry [of Ardfert], 1314

MacEvilly (Machmiloyd, Macmyloyd), Hobertus, canon of Clonfert, papal mandatary, 330, 935

Macfail (Matefaill), Donald, to have regular priory in Sodor diocese, 1115
......, *cf.* MacPhail

MacGellage (Macgyllage) *alias* OGallagher (Ogallcubayr), Patrick, detainer of Killymard parish church, 950

MacGilbride *cf.* MacKilbride

MacGilfoyle (Machclofol, Machillefoyl) (*alias* Ochalen), William, ostensible priest of Killaloe diocese, detainer of vicarage of Roscrea, 14
......, ..., priest of Killaloe diocese, to have vicarage of Roscrea anew, 161

Macgillakyeran *see* MacElheron

Macgillanach (Mackyllanaha), Thomas, canon of Tuam, papal mandatary, 234

Macgillarni, John, canon of Elphin, papal mandatary, 830
......, *cf.* MacKilroy

MacGillespy (Margillespy), Malcolm, provided anew to rectory in Sodor diocese, 1114

MacGilsenan (Mangynsenan), Bernard, to have monastery in Clogher diocese, 1215

MacGovern, MacGowran *cf.* Magauran

MacGrath (Magra), Thomas, cleric of Lismore diocese, *de facto* canon of Lismore and prebendary of Modelligo, 381
......, ..., ..., ..., to have his canonry and prebend anew, 381
......, ..., ..., ..., relations (unnamed) of, 381
......, *cf.* Macraych; Magrath

MacGuiness *cf.* Magennis

Macgyllabryde *see* MacKilbride

Macgyllage *see* MacGellage

Macgyllakieran *see* MacElheron

Macgyllysacdy *see* MacLysaght

Machaestyn, Maurice, detainer of vicarage of Kilcash, 790

Machagan *see* MacEgan

Macharembahyr *see* Magheranure

Machareyg, Macharyg *see* MacCarthy

Machauli, Machaulyn *see* MacAuliffe

Machayg, John, ostensible monk and detainer of the Cistercian monastery of Macosquin, 259

Machayn *see* MacCahan

Machclofol *see* MacGilfoyle

Machdil *see* Doyle

Machego, Cornelius, ostensible cleric of Killaloe diocese, detainer, with Laurence MacNamara, of the vicarage of Stradbally *alias* 'Cloynacheke', 380
......, *cf.* MacKeogh

Machibren *see* MacBrien

Machillefoyl *alias* Ochalen *see* MacGilfoyle

Machkyth *see* MacKeogh

Machmiloyd *see* MacEvilly

Machnayn, Maurice, canon of Clonfert, papal mandatary, 492
......, ..., *cf.* Macvaney, Maurice

Machomara *see* MacNamara

Machoskan *alias de Clarofonte see* Macosquin

Machranayn *see* MacRedmond

Machrgan *see* MacEgan

Machsyda *see* MacSheedy

Machyachayn *see* MacEgan

Mackaryg *see* MacCarthy

MacKeaghan (Makehycayn), Philip, vicar of Kilfergus, 820
......, *cf.* MacEgan

MacKeane *cf.* MacCahan

MacKee (Macaedh), Toroletus, canon of Derry, papal mandatary, 950

Mackehic *see* MacKeogh

Mackellay, Donat, detainer of rectory of Garrynoe, 252

MacKeogh (Machkyth, Mackehic), Carb(e)ricus / Cornelius, ostensible Augustinian canon, 492
......, ..., detainer of the Augustinian priory of Aughrim, 492, 512
......, *cf.* Machego

MacKilbride (Macgyllabryde, Magyllabryde, Margilabryde), John, to have monastery in Kildare diocese, 1123
......, ..., to have rectory in ?Raphoe diocese erected into a prebend [in Raphoe cathedral], 1127
......, Odo, to have vicarage in Raphoe diocese, 1196
......, *cf.* MacGilbride

MacKilpatrick (Magillapadrie), John, canon of Ossory, papal mandatary, 510

MacKilroy *cf.* Macgillarni

?MacKinneally, alias of OKinneally, Thady, *q.v.*

[Mackinnon], John, abbot of the Benedictine monastery of St Columba, Iona, death of, 181

Mackyllanaha *see* Macgillanach

Mackyneala *see* ?MacKinneally

Mackynracta, Dermot, ostensible priest of Killaloe diocese, detainer of vicarage of Killofin, 948

Maclanchi *see* MacClancy

Maclanthlaym, Peter, priest of Derry [*recte* Kildare?] diocese, 934
......, ..., ..., to be canon of Derry [*recte* Kildare?], have rectory of Ballyshannon erected into a prebend, and have vicarages of Norragh and Tippeenan united thereto, 934

MacLaughlin *cf.* Maclanthlaym

Macleod *cf.* ?Nacleobi

Maclerystown' *see* ?Mocklerstown

MacLysaght (Macgyllysacdy), Donald, canon of Kilfenora, papal mandatary, 980
......, Matthew, canon of Kilfenora, papal mandatary, 980

MacMahon (Macmabona, Magmahuna, Magniahuna), Corbanus, canon of Clogher, papal mandatary, 538, 834
......, Cornelius, ostensible priest of Killaloe diocese, detainer of portion of 'Gleandbannam', vulgarly '?Ileraunr', in the collegiate church of Scattery Island, 818
......, James, bishop of Clogher residing in the diocese of Ross [Ireland], papal judge delegate, 811

Macmyloyd *see* MacEvilly

MacNamara (Macchomara, Macco'mara, Macco(n)mara, Macconmara, Macco(n)marra, Machomara, Macomara, Maconmara, Mathanamara), Cornelius *alias* Curnea / Cunca [i.e. *Cuveadh*], cleric of Killaloe diocese, 650, 652
......, ..., to have canonry of Killaloe and prebend of Tulla with vicarages of Clonrush, Inishcaltra, and Ogonnelloe united thereto, 650
......, ..., to have canonry of Limerick and prebend of Donnaghmore with vicarages of Killeely, Kilfintinan, Quin, Clonloghan, and Bunratty united thereto, 652

MacNamara (*contd*)
......, James, canon of Killaloe, papal mandatary, 783
......, James *alias* Syda [*cf. Síoda*], detainer of the vicarage of B. Mary *alias* of the Holy Trinity, [Ogonnelloe], 650
......, ..., *and see* MacNamara *alias* Scyda; OSheedy
......, John, canon of Killaloe, papal mandatary, 651
......, ..., detainer of canonry of Killaloe and prebend of Tulla, 650
......, ..., detainer of canonry of Limerick and prebend of Donaghmore, and of vicarages of Killeely and Kilfintinan, 652
......, John Tatei / Thadei, canon of Killaloe, papal mandatary, 313, 652
......, Laurence, detainer of the vicarage of Quin, 313
......, ..., ostensible cleric of Killaloe diocese, detainer, with Cornelius Machego, of the vicarage of Stradbally *alias* 'Cloynacheke', 380
......, Rory, detainer of treasurership of Killaloe, 647
......, Thady, cleric of Killaloe diocese, to be canon of Killaloe, have vicarage of Quin erected into a prebend and vicarages of Clonloghan and ?Kilmaleery united thereto, 313
......, ..., detainer of vicarage of Quin, 652

MacNamara *alias* Scyda, James, canon of Killaloe, to have treasurership of Killaloe united to his canonry and prebend, 647
......, *cf.* MacNamara, James *alias* Syda; OSheedy

Macnaughton (Maknathan, Maknathtan), Donald, vicar (called portionary) of the parish church of Fortingall, 187, 188
......, ..., to have vicarage of Fortingall erected into a perpetual undivided vicarage and adequately endowed, 188

MacNelly (Malignyl), Nemeas, canon of Tuam, papal mandatary, 835

Macnrocnallyd, Fracha, cleric of Tuam diocese, to have vicarage of Omey, 126

Macohegan *see* MacEgan

Macomara, Maconmara *see* MacNamara

Macosquin (Machoskan *alias de Clarofonte*) [co. Derry], Cistercian monastery of, 259
......, ..., abbots of *see* Machayg, John; OCahan, Donat
......, ..., convent of, 259
......, ..., monks of *see* Machayg, John (ostensible); OCahan, Donat (prospective)
......, ..., vassals of, 259
......, ..., proposed union to, of the rectory of *Druim tairsigh*, 259

MacPhail *cf.* Macfail

MacRannall *cf.* Magragalli

Macravayn *see* MacRedmond

Macraych, John, ostensible priest of Limerick diocese, detainer of St Michael's vicarage outside the walls of Limerick, 815
......, *cf.* MacGrath

MacRedmond (Machranayn, Macravayn, Meranayn), Thomas, canon of Tuam, papal mandatary, 122, 163
......, ..., vicar of Killoscobe, 167

Macroom (Mocromuhu) [co. Cork], parish church of, vicarage of, to be erected into prebend in Cloyne cathedral, 823

MacSheedy (Machsyda), Odo, detainer of vicarage of Inishcaltra, 650

Mactalie, Odo, canon of Kilmore, papal mandatary, 834

MacTurley *cf.* Makterrelaigh

Macvaney, Maurice, canon of Clonfert, papal mandatary, 853
......, ..., *cf.* Machnayn, Maurice
......, Maurus, detainer of vicarage of Duniry, 853

Mac.ard, Cornelius, priest of Elphin diocese, to have parish church of Killeroran, 830

Mader, Richard, vicar of Pitminster, 461

Madorack, Andrew, reservation for, of pension over archdeaconry of Glasgow, 1146
......, *cf.* Makbrek

'Maedona' [*unidentified*], land of given to Taunton priory, 174

Magauran (Megauran), Fergal, priest of Kilmore diocese, to have vicarage of Templeport *alias* Breaghwy Island, 940
......, *cf.* MacGovern; MacGowran

Magbraday *see* MacBrady

Magdeugii *see* Modelligo

Magearyg *see* MacCarthy

?Mageier *see* Magner

Magennis (Magnassa, Magnyssa), Gelasius / Gellassius, commendatory [abbot] of the Cistercian monastery of St Benedict, [Newry], 235
......, ..., ..., to have prebend of Clonallan in Dromore cathedral united to Fabric of monastery, 235
......, ..., detainer of Benedictine priory of Downpatrick, 391
......, *cf.* MacGuiness

Maghera [co. Londonderry] *see* Rathlure

Magheranure (Macharembahyr), *plebs* of, alternative name to Drumgoon, *q.v.*

Magillapadrie *see* MacKilpatrick

Maginell *see* Magner

Maginn *cf.* Magxan

de Magio see Monasteranenagh

Magliano Sabina *see* Sabina

Maglocyn, Eugene, priest of Kilmore diocese, detainer of Killanummery vicarage, 995

Magmahuna *see* MacMahon

Magna Harde *see* Hardres, Great

Magna Wenlock *see* Much Wenlock

Magnassa *see* Magennis

Magnay, John, cleric of Clonfert diocese, to have vicarage of Duniry, 853

Magner (?Mageier, Maginell, Magniell'), David, cleric of Cloyne diocese, to be canon, then prior, of the Augustinian monastery of Ballybeg, 128
......, Edmund, canon of Cloyne, papal mandatary, 74, 125

Magniahuna *see* MacMahon

Magniell' *see* Magner

Magnyssa *see* Magennis

Magonghail, Roger, collation [empty?] to, of canonries of Raphoe and Killala with reservation of prebends, 115

Magonius, abbot of Lough Key *see* [MacDonagh], Magonius

Magonuayl, [Magonius], vicar of Rasharkin, to be deprived for alleged misdeeds, 361

Magra *see* MacGrath

Magragalli, Cormac, canon of Elphin, papal mandatary, 830
......, *cf.* MacRannall

Magrath *cf.* MacGrath

Magryche, John, rector of Willand, 889

Magxan [*recte* Magyan?], William, rector of [?Ardquin], 391
......, ..., ..., to be monk, then prior, of the Benedictine priory of Downpatrick, 391
......, *cf.* Maginn

Magyllabryde *see* MacKilbride

Mahbrak *see* Makbrek

Maicha, Aulanus, detainer of vicarage of Kilcoona, 163

Mains (of Auchterellon) (Ly Mains) [*in* Ellon, co. Aberdeen], tithes of, 928

de Maio see Monasteranenagh

Maio *alias* Petinveyn *see* May *alias* Pittenweem

Makaryg *see* MacCarthy

Makavlly *see* MacAuliffe

Makbrek (Mahbrak), Andrew, of Dunblane diocese, dispensed for plurality, 1254
......, *cf.* Madorack

Makehycayn *see* MacKeaghan

Maknathan, Maknathtan *see* Macnaughton

Makryg *see* MacCarthy

Makterrelaigh, John, canon of Cork, papal mandatary, 129
......, *cf.* MacTurley

Maldon (Maldon') [Essex], parish church of All Saints of, 519
......, ..., Darcy chantry in, 519

Malecomb (Malecomys) [*in* East Dean, West Sussex], fields in, tithes from, 661

Malignyl *see* MacNelly

Mallis *see* Mells

Malpas, Thomas, layman of Hereford, proceedings at instance of, 529

[Maltby, Yorks], place in *see* Roche

Malvezzi (de Malvetiis), Galeazzo, cleric of Bologna, continual commensal of the pope, 358
......, ..., provision of, to the united parish churches of St Peter and St Nicholas, Verucchio, 358

Mamudebylyston *see* Mansfieldstown

Man *see* Sodor

Manaton (Maneton') [Devon], parish church of, union of, to the parish church of Kenn, 958

(de) Mandeville (Mandevyl, Mandvell, Mandyllyll'), Edmund, vicar of Burnham, 860
......, John, rector of Orton Longueville, 45
......, Walter, detainer of precentorship of Lismore, 158

Mane *see* Many

Manesyn Rydware *see* Mavesyn Ridware

Maneton' *see* Manaton

Manfield (Manfeld), Thomas, pension paid to on fruits of Wymondham parish church, 386

Mangneri, Antonius, familiar of Fer(di)nandus Ponzettus, *q.v.*
......, ..., provision of, to the rectory of the chapel of Sts Clarus and Blasius, ?Monfavrey, 855

Mangynsenan *see* MacGilsenan

Mannering *cf.* Meynoryng

Manningford (Manyngsford) [Abbots *or* Bruce, Wilts], parish church of, rector of, 869

Mansfieldstown (Mamudebylyston) [co. Louth], parish church of, rector of, 901

Many (Mane), John, rector of St Tudy, 288, 753
......, ..., ..., vicar of Cuby, 753

Manyngsford *see* Manningford

Maqin *see* Matyn

Marasca, Giuliano, registry scribe *see* frontispiece

Marchaston *see* Merchinston

Marchyell *see* Marshall

Marcilhac [*in dép.* of Lot, France], Benedictine monastery of, 196
......, ..., abbot of *see* [Ebrard], Fiocardus
......, ..., pertains immediately to the Roman church, 196
......, ..., foundation of, by Pepin, king of the Franks, 196
......, ..., detention of, by the English, 196
......, ..., ruin and projected repair of, 196

Mare'lligoid *see* MacElligott

Margaret, countess of Richmond (and Derby) *see* [Beaufort], Margaret

Margilabryde *see* MacKilbride

Margillespy *see* MacGillespy

Margoryne, John, to have vicarage in Kilmore diocese, 1202

de' Mari (Maris), Severus, OP, 454

Mariana (*Marianen.*) [Corsica], Octavianus, bishop of *see* de Fornariis, Octavianus

Maris *see* de' Mari

[Markinch, co. Fife], places in *see* Balgonie; Kirkforthar; Milton of Balgonie

Marnhull (Maruchull) [Dors], parish church of, 276

Marowod *see* Marwood

Marowte, Joan, woman of London, appeal of, 924
......, ..., ..., executrix of the will of John Crosby, 924

Marshall (Marchyell, Marschall, Marshal), John, of Lincoln diocese, dispensed for plurality, 1140
......, Richard, of Bath and Wells diocese, dispensed for plurality, 1168
......, Thomas, monk of the Benedictine monastery of Chertsey, 914

Marston Moretaine (Marston Mortemayen') [Beds], parish church of, 275

Marteley *see* Martley

Martin (Martini), Hugh, cleric of St Andrews diocese, 144
......, ..., canon of Brechin, 793, 928
......, ..., ..., cession by, of Cistercian monastery of Kinloss, 144
......, ..., assignment to, of pension on fruits (notably tithes) of Ellon parish church, 144, 793, 928
......, ..., appeal of, over non-payment of pension, 793
......, ..., dispute with Kinloss over pension, 928
......, ..., assignment to, of pension in place of previous one, 928
......, ..., proctor of *see* Duncanson, John
......, Robert, vicar of Garvock, 986
......, *and see* Martyn

Martini *see* Martin; Martyn

Martley (Marteley) [Worcs], parish church of, 265

Martond *see* Merton

Martyn (Martini, Martyn'), Thomas, rector of Fugglestone (St Peter) and vicar of Wilsford, 702, 719
......, ..., ..., sometime vicar of North Moreton, 719
......, *and see* Martin; *cf.* Martyr

Martyr, John, union for, of his parish church to his canonry [of Hereford?], London diocese, 1139
......, *cf.* Martyn

Maruchull *see* Marnhull

Marwood (Marowod), John, of Bath and Wells diocese, dispensed for plurality, 1060

Masham (Maschin') [Yorks], church of, 142

Mason, William, rector of Tinwell, 501

Massa Marittima [*in* Grosseto province, Italy], diocese of, place in *see* Piombino

de Massaroza *see* Mazzarosa

Matefaill *see* Macfail

Mathanamara *see* MacNamara

Matheus *see* Mathews

Mathew *alias* Norwich (Norwich'), John, monk of the Benedictine monastery of Wymondham, 314

Mathews (Matheus), John, rector of West Deeping, 246

Mathoblayn, Eugene, dean of Clonmacnois [*erroneously* Cloyne], death of, 226
......, *cf.* MacCoughlan

Matyn (Maqin), [Ralph], 174

Maurienne *see* Saint-Jean-de-Maurienne

Mavesyn Ridware *see* Ridware, Mavesyn

May *alias* Pittenweem (Maio *alias* Petinveyn, Mayo *alias* Petynveyn, Mayo *alias* Petynveymen) [co. Fife], Augustinian priory of, 698
......, ..., prior of *see* Forman, Andrew
......, ..., a dependency of the Augustinian [cathedral] church of St Andrews, 632

Maydenhithe (Maydenhuth), [John de], 174

Mayhew (Mayheu), Henry, of London diocese, dispensed for plurality, 1145

Mayo [co. Mayo], parish church of St Gerald, vicarage of, to be united to deanery of Mayo, 402
......, Augustinian monastery of B. *or* St Michael, abbot of, papal mandatary, 401, 826, 827
......, ..., canon of *see* Prendergast, Miler

......, [cathedral] church of, deanery of, 402
......, ..., ..., variously called rectory or *personatus* , 402
......, ..., ..., united as a rectory to a canonry of Tuam, 402
......, ..., ..., proposed union to, of the vicarages of Balla and St Gerald, Mayo, 402
......, ..., dean of *see* Prendergast, David

......, diocese of *see* Tuam *alias* / or Mayo

[Mayo, co. of], places in *see* Annagh; Balla; Ballinrobe; Ballintober; Bohola; Cong; Inishmaine [*in* Ballinchalla]; Kilcurnan [*in* Crossboyne]; Killala; Kilmaine; Kilvine; Lough Mask; Mayo; Oughaval; Tagheen; Umall, Upper and Lower; place *probably* in *see* 'Tilmadim'

Mayo *alias* Petynveymen, Mayo *alias* Petynveyn *see* May *alias* Pittenweem

Maywel, Thomas, vicar of Rathmuriel and Kinnethmont, 778

Maywel (*contd*)
......, ..., ..., pension payable by, 778
......, ..., ..., proctor of *see* Halkerston, Thomas

Maz(z)ara del Vallo [*in* Trapani province, Sicily], diocese of, place in *see* Trapani

Mazzarosa (de Massaroza), Sebastiano di Bartolomeo, provision of, to a canonry and prebend of Lucca, 1002

Mean Stoke *see* Meonstoke

[Mearns, The] *see* [Kincardine, co. of]

Meath, bishop of, subjects of, visitation of by the archbishop of Armagh, 1005
......, ..., *mensa* of, 1005
......, ..., disputed payment to, by priors of Lanthony II by Gloucester and vicars of Duleek and Colp, 442
......, ..., *see* [Payne], John
......, official of, papal mandatary, 537
......, church of, archdeacon of, *ex officio* inquiry *sede vacante* by, 694
......, ..., ..., commissary of, 694

......, city [i.e. Newtown Trim?] and diocese of, clerics and laymen of, adherents of bishop John [Payne], intended action against, 442
......, *cf.* 1164
......, diocese of, persons of *see* Cussen, John; Durham, Martin; Plunket, Christopher and Robert; Puscon, Catherine; Troy, John; Walsh, Richard; Warde, John; Wellesley, Edward and Walter
......, places in *see* Abbeyshrule; Drogheda; Lynally; Mellifont; *and* places *listed below under* [Meath, co. of]

[Meath, co. of], places in *see* Colp; Duleek; Kells; Newtown Trim; Trim

Mecharri *see* MacCarthy

Medmenham (Medmeham) [Bucks], Cistercian monastery of, 973
......, ..., monk of *see* Franck, John

'Medohk' [*unidentified*], lands of, church called rectory or particle of, in the parish of Loughkeen, 403

......, ..., ..., customarily ruled by the vicar of Loughkeen, 403

......, ..., ..., to be united to the proposed prebend of Loughkeen in Killaloe cathedral, 403

Medrum *see* Meldrum

Megauran *see* Magauran

?Meifod (Minot) [co. Montgomery], prebend of, otherwise cursal, in St Asaph cathedral, 483

......, ..., ..., ..., union to, of the parish churches of ?Llanfarchell and ?Bodfari, 483

?Meikle (Modele) [*in* Slains, co. Aberdeen], tithes of, 928

Meldrum (Medrum), David, official of St Andrews, litigation before, 921, 971

......, William, bishop of Brechin, lessor of church property [in Brechin diocese?], to have lease confirmed, 1227

Melksham (Mylkeshme') [Wilts], vicarage of, union of, to the hospital of St John the Baptist, Shaftesbury, 965

Mellifont [*in* Tullyallen, co. Louth], Cistercian monastery of, abbot of, abbacy of Monasteranenagh in gift of, 383

......, ..., ..., *see* Troy, John

......, ..., monk of *see* Vynter *alias* Fynter, Thomas

Mells (Mallis) [Som], parish church of, union to, of the parish church of Lympsham, 293

Melrose (Melros) [co. Roxburgh], parish church of, clerkship of, 642

......, Cistercian monastery of, abbacy of, lawsuits over, 1015, 1016, 1018-1020

......, ..., abbot and convent of, licensed to lease property of the monastery, 1295

Melrose (*contd*)

......, ..., abbot of, conclusion to, 1032

......, ..., ..., *see* Bell, Bernard; Brown, David; Turnbull, William

......, ..., convent of, election of abbot by, 1015

......, ..., ..., conclusion to, 1015

......, ..., monks of *see* Bell, Bernard; Turnbull, William (prospective)

......, ..., vassals of, conclusion to, 1015

Melton Mowbray (Meltone Moubrey) [Leics], parish church of, 709

Menendez, *abbreviator de parco minori*, conclusion expedited by, 776

Menewynuyke, William, vicar of Milton Abbot, 323

Meonstoke (Mean Stoke) [Hants], parish church of, 342

Meopham (Mepham) [Kent], parish church of, 809

Meranayn *see* MacRedmond

Merchinston (Marchaston), James, [? reservation of] pension for [? on fruits of church] in Glasgow diocese, 1256

Merchiston (Merchinston) [*now represented by* Merchiston Castle in the district of Morningside, parish of St Cuthbert, Edinburgh, co. Midlothian], person of *see* Napier, John

Merevale (Miravall) [Warw], Cistercian monastery of, abbot of *see* John

Merinton (Meruiton), Hugh, chantry of in St Michael's, Coventry, 496, 715

Merioneth (Meryonyth'), archdeacon of in the church of Bangor, *q.v.*

Mersea, West (Westuuersey) [Essex], parish church of, 215

Merthyr Tydfil (Merther Tudefeld) [co. Glamorgan], parish church of, union of, to the parish church of Kilmington, 452

Merton (Martond, Merton') [Surrey], Augustinian priory of, prior of, papal judge delegate, 365
......, ..., canon of *see* Herbert *alias* Newlond, James

Meruiton *see* Merinton

Meryonyth' *see* Merioneth

Metcalfe (Metralff), Thomas, commissary of Martin Colyns, official and commissary general of Thomas [Rotherham], archbishop of York, litigation before, 94

Metz [*in* Alsace Lorraine province, Germany], diocese of, place in *see* Vinningen

Meynoryng, John, rector of Warmingham, 44
......, *cf.* Mannering

Michael, late bishop of St Asaph *see* [Deacon], Michael

Michelham (Mycchylh(a)m) [*in* Hailsham, Sussex], Augustinian priory of, canon of *see* Wode, William

Michell (Michell'), Robert, vicar of Bovey Tracy, 177
......, Thomas, rector of Heddington, 389

Mickleton (Mikilton) [Glos], parish church of, 373

Midaldona *see* Milton

Mid Calder *see* Calder; Calder, Mid

Middelton *see* Middleton

[Middlesex, co. of], places in *see* Chiswick; Ealing; Enfield; Harringay; Hendon; Hornsey; Islington; Kensington; London; Twickenham; Westminster

Middleton (Middelton), Leonard, rector of Zeal Monachorum, 218
......, William, of Lichfield diocese, dispensed for plurality, 1112

Midleton [co. Cork], [Cistercian] monastery of, abbot of, papal mandatary, 156, 573, 1000

Midley (Mydley)[Kent], parish church of, 437

[Midlothian *or* Edinburgh, co. of], places in *see* Cairns [*in* Mid Calder]; Calder; Crichton; Edinburgh; Merchiston; Newbattle; Restalrig

Mikilton *see* Mickleton

Milborne St Andrew (Milburne) and Dewlish (Dewlych') [Dors], parish church of, 920
......, *and see* Dewlish

Milde, John, chaplain in York cathedral and incumbent of Skirpenbeck, 879

Mildenhall (Mildenhal) [Wilts], parish church of, union of, to the canonry and prebend of Faringdon in Salisbury cathedral, 908

Mileham (Myleh(a)m), Henry, prior of the Augustinian priory of Coxford, 48

Miler, abbot of the Augustinian monastery of B. John the Evangelist, [Tuam] *see* [de Burgo], Miler

Miles, bishop (-elect) of Llandaff *see* [Salley], Miles

Militis [i.e. of the Knight (of Glin de Geraldinis)], John, to have archdeaconry of Limerick, 1216

Milton (Midaldona) [Som], land of, 174

Milton Abbot (Mylton Abbat') [Devon], parish church of, vicarage of, 434
....., ..., vicar of, 323

Milton Manor (Myltonmante) [*in* Great Milton, Oxon], prebend of in Lincoln cathedral, 203

Milton of Balgonie (le Mylicton' of Balgony) [*in* Markinch, co. Fife], place or vill of, tithes of belonging to the Augustinian monastery of St Andrews, 971

Milverton (Mylverton') [Som], parish church of, 561

Ministre *see* Minster

Minot *see* ?Meifod

Minster (Ministre) *alias* Talcarne (Talkaryn' or Terkaryn') [*now* Minster, Corn], parish church of, 90

Miravall *see* Merevale

Missenden (Myssenden') [*in* Great Missenden, Bucks], [Augustinian] monastery of, abbot of, papal judge delegate, 8

Mitford (Mytford'), Nicholas, cleric of Durham diocese, 1004

Mitnere *see* Inchmacnerin

de Mivrey *alias* OHonan (Hohounyn), William, detainer of precentorship of Limerick and of canonry and prebend of Tullabracky, 486

Mnacarnara, Donat, ostensible cleric of Lismore diocese, litigant over abbacy of Augustinian monastery of Molana, 573

Moanmore (Moynneor) [*in* Kilrush, co. Clare], portion of in [collegiate] church of Scattery Island, 449
......, ..., to be united to canonry and prebend of Kilfenora, 449

Mochomor *see* Muckamore

Mockler (Mocleyr), Henry, rector of ?Mocklerstown, 786
......, ..., ..., to be canon of Cashel and have his rectory erected into a prebend, with the vicarages of Moorstown, Donaghmore, and ?Colman united thereto, 786
......, *cf.* Morlier

?Mocklerstown (Kazdaglas *alias* Maclerystown') [*in* Colman, co. Tipperary], parish church of, rector of, 786
......, ..., rectory of, to be erected into prebend of Cashel, with the vicarages of Moorstown, Donaghmore, and ?Colman united thereto, 786

Mocleyr *see* Mockler

Mocromuhu *see* Macroom

Modele *see* ?Meikle

Modelligo (Magdeugii, Modelyg) [co. Waterford], prebend of in Lismore cathedral, 381
......, ..., patrons of, consent of to collation by bishop, 381
......, ..., to be collated anew, 381
......, parish church of, vicarage of, 946
......, ..., ..., to be united to canonry of Lismore and prebend of Lickoran, 946

Modena (*Mutinen.*) [Italy], bishop of, papal mandatary, 50, 147
......, Johannes, bishop of *see* [de Ferrariis], Johannes (Baptista)

Modreeny (Modrine) [co. Tipperary], parish church of, rectory and vicarage of, to be united anew to canonry of Killaloe and prebend of Ballyloughnane, 357

[Mogeely, co. Cork], place in *see* Templevalley

Mogridge *cf.* Magryche

Mohl'an, John, canon of Ossory, to have chancellorship of Ossory and vicarage of Jerpoint, 545
......, *cf.* OMolan

Molana (Mylanochv)[*in* Templemichael, co. Waterford], Augustinian monastery of, litigation over, 573
......, ..., abbot of, papal mandatary, 158, 852
......, ..., ..., *see* Fitzgibbon, Edmund; Mnacarnara, Donat; Yhacgeryn, John
......, ..., convent of, 573
......, ..., canon of *see* Yhacgeryn, John
......, ..., vassals of, 573

Molyneux, Henry, rector of Ashmore, 801

Monaincha [*in* Corbally, co. Tipperary], Augustinian monastery of, prior of, ostensible priest of Killaloe diocese, detainer of vicarage of Bourney *alias* Ikerrin, 14
......, ..., ..., papal mandatary, 16, 157, 161, 162, 545, 930

Monasteranenagh (*de Magio, de Maio*) [co. Limerick], Cistercian monastery of B. Mary, litigation over, 383
......, ..., abbacy of in gift of abbot of Mellifont, 383
......, ..., abbot of, papal mandatary, 542
......, ..., ..., *see* Deipatientia, William
......, ..., intruder into *see* de Geraldinis, Gerald David
......, ..., convent of, 383
......, ..., monk of *see* Deipatientia, William
......, ..., vassals of, 383

Moncenisio [*in* province of Turin, Italy], Augustinian provostry of B. Mary, 405
......, ..., union to, of the parish church of Wootton, called Woodstock, dissolution of, 405
......, ..., commendatory provost of *see* [de Varax], John
......, ..., provost and convent of, adherents of Felix V, 405
......, ..., ..., lease from to abbot and convent of the Cistercian monastery of Bruern of the fruits of Wootton parish church, 405

Moncenisio (*contd*)
......, ..., ..., proctor (unnamed) of, 405
......, ..., convent of, 405
......, ..., canons of, 405
......, ..., hospital of, reception in, of poor travellers crossing [the Alps], 405

Moneton' Hampsted *see* Moreton Hampstead

?Monfavrey [*in* St-Nizier-le-Désert, *dép.* of Ain, France], chapel of Sts Clarus and Blasius of, rectory of, 855

[Monivea, co. Galway], place in *see* Tisaxon

Monkland (Monklane) [Heref], parish church of, 289

Monkton (Monkton') [Kent], parish church of, 88

Monkton (Mukton', Mu'kton') [*now* Monkton and Prestwick, co. Ayr], parish church of, 61, 63
......, church of, fruits of pertaining to Cluniac monastery of Paisley, grant of, 63
......, place of, lordship or territory of, lands, mills, annual revenues, and fisheries in pertaining to Paisley, grant of, 63

Monkyston *alias* Annekeyke *see* Monxton

Monley'sayle *see* Zeal Monachorum

Monmouth (Monomuth') [co. Monmouth], Benedictine priory of, monk of *see* Brent, John

[Monmouth, co. of], place in *see* Monmouth

Monnington on Wye (Monyton' *alias* Monyngton') [Heref], parish church of, 805

Monomuth' *see* Monmouth

Monorgund (Monorgono), William, provision of to canonry, St Andrews diocese, 1200

Mons (Monten') [*in* Hainault, Belgium], church of St Germain of, dean of, papal mandatary, 144

[Montacute] [Som], Cluniac monastery of Bs Peter and Paul, monk of *see* Cherell, Thomas
......, ..., dependency of *see* St Carrok

Mont-Cenis *cf.* Moncenisio

Monten' *see* Mons

Monterahy, Monteray *see* *Muinter Murchada*

Montere Kenayd' *see* *Muinter Chineith*

[Montgomery, co. of], place in *see* ?Meifod

Montgomery (Mungmuri [*recte* Mungumri]), Alexander, of Braidstane, nobleman, 80
......, Hugh, lord of, nobleman, 80
......, John, knight, nobleman, 80
......, Robert, nobleman, 80

Montpellier [*in dép.* of Hérault, France], letter dated at, 174

Mont St Michel [*in dép.* of La Manche, France], Benedictine monastery of, priory of Lihou, Guernesey, a dependency of, 817
......, ..., abbot of, collation by, 817

Monxton (Monkyston) *alias* Annekeyke [Hants], parish church of, 344

Monyngton', Monyton' *see* Monnington on Wye

Moorstown (Ballimunora *alias* Murtown) [*in* Mora, co. Tipperary], parish church of, vicarage of, to be united to canonry of Cashel and prebend of ?Mocklerstown, 786

Mora *see* ?Westmoor

[Mora, co. Tipperary], place in *see* Moorstown

Moray, [cathedral] church of [at Elgin, co. Moray], dean of, papal mandatary, 68, 144, 643, 782, 839, 844, 992
......, ..., precentorship of, 931
......, ..., precentors of *see* Gordon, Adam and Alexander
......, ..., succentorship of, 844
......, ..., ..., foundation of, 780
......, ..., ..., succentors of *see* Halkerston, Thomas; Spens, John
......, ..., treasurer of *see* Hepburn, George
......, ..., chapter of, conclusion to, 630
......, ..., prebends in *see* Duthel; Petty-Brackley

......, **bishop** of, to receive oath of fealty in pope's name, 1009, 1011
......, ..., papal mandatary, 50, 68, 190, 552, 793
......, ..., *see* [Forman], Andrew; [Stewart], Andrew
......, official of, papal mandatary, 50, 144, 643, 840, 928, 931
......, church of, subject to archbishop of St Andrews, 631
......, ..., vassals of, conclusion to, 630

......, **city and diocese** of, clergy of, conclusion to, 630
......, ..., people of, conclusion to, 630
......, diocese of, persons of *see* Cicheton, George; Culross, William; Martin, Hugh; [Wawain *alias* Chrystal], Thomas; *and see* Thomson of Auchinhamper, Duncan
......, ..., places in *see* Auchinhamper [*in* Inverkeithny]; Kinloss

[Moray *or* Elgin and Nairn, co. of], places in *see* Duthel; Hatton; Kinloss; Petty-Brackley

More *see* Northmoor

More, John, of Worcester diocese, dispensed for plurality, 1047
......, Richard, rector of Bondleigh, 111
......, ..., of Worcester diocese, dispensed for plurality, 1049

Moreton (Moreton') [Essex], parish church of, 474

Moreton Hampstead (Moneton' Hampsted) [Devon], parish church of, 120

Moreton, North (Northmoreton) [Berks], parish church of, 719

Moris, Hugh, priest of Worcester, 644
......, ..., ..., *de facto* collation of to St Martin's, Worcester, 644
......, ..., ..., to have St Martin's anew, 644
......, *and see* Morris

Morlandi, John, canon of the Premonstratensian monastery of Tupholme, 798

Morlier, Edmund, to have church in Cashel diocese erected into prebend [in Cashel cathedral?], 1194
......, *cf.* Mockler

Morne, Robert, scholar of Worcester diocese, 378

Moro, alias of Tuddenham, Thomas, *q.v.*

[Morpeth, Northumb], place in *see* Newminster

Morris (Morys), John, rector of Telscombe, 24
......, William, rector of Porlock, 4
......, *and see* Moris

Mors, William, ostensible canon of Annaghdown, papal judge delegate, litigation before, 29

Morton (by Bourne) (Morton') [Lincs], parish church of, 303

Morton (Morton'), John, cardinal priest of St Anastasia, 8, 28, 29, 46, 197
......, ..., legate (born) of the apostolic see (in the kingdom of England / in those parts), 8, 28, 29, 46, 197, 906
......, ..., archbishop of Canterbury / president of the church of Canterbury, 28, 29, 46, 197, 906
......, ..., primate of the whole kingdom of England / primate of all England, 28, 29, 46, 197, 906
......, ..., death of, 906
......, ..., cognizance of causes moved by rectors of parish churches in Lincoln diocese against their parishioners belongs to, 906
......, ..., appeal to, commission of, 8
......, ..., case committed by, 197
......, ..., recourse to, 29, 46
......, ..., auditor of causes and matters of *see* Peynthwyn, Hugh
......, ..., commissaries of *see* Coke, Thomas; Durham, bishop of; Peynthwyn, Hugh
......, Nicholas, rector of Minster, 90
......, Robert, bishop of Worcester, the late, 29
......, ..., ..., commissary of *see* Barbour, John

Morwel, Wynninus, of Glasgow diocese, dispensed for plurality, 1095

Morwyn, John, canon of the Augustinian monastery of Kirkham, 451

Morys *see* Morris

Moschalaiy, alias of de Anglo, Henry, *q.v.*

Mothel (Motalea, Motallea) [co. Waterford], [Augustinian] monastery of, abbot of, papal commissary and mandatary, 946
......, ..., ..., papal mandatary, 785, 789, 790

Moton', Richard, vicar of St Veep, 216

Moulton (Multon') [Northants], parish church of, 693

Moville (Mubille) [*in* Newtownards, co. Down], [Augustinian] monastery of, abbot of, papal mandatary, 391

Moyanna (Muanay) [co. Laois], parish church of, vicarage of, 932

[Moycarn, barony of, co. Roscommon], places *probably in see* 'Arodmuneach'; 'Bearnduamlegynd'; 'Bruachtalach'; 'Glochmor'; 'Gortnuybg''; 'Gortuaglothbg''; '?Goven'; 'Syliam'

Moynneor *see* Moanmore

Muanay *see* Moyanna

Mubille *see* Moville

Much Wenlock *see* Wenlock, Much

Muckamore (Mochomor) [*in* Muckamore Grange, co. Antrim], [Augustinian] monastery of, prior of, papal mandatary, 236

Muinter Chineith (Montere Kenayd') [*now probably area covered by* the townlands of Coolderry, Culliaghbeg and Gortnasharvoge *in* Creagh, co. Roscommon], lands of, 146

Muinter Murchada (Monterahy, Monteray), alias of Killererin, *q.v.*

Mukton', Mu'kton' *see* Monkton

Mullet, Nicholas, canon of the Augustinian priory of St Peter, Ipswich, 465

Multon' *see* Moulton

Mungmuri *see* Montgomery

Murray, James, of noble birth, 643
......, ..., ..., collation to, of canonry of Ross, with reservation of prebend and dignity etc. of Ross, and of benefice in gift of bishop and chapter etc. of Brechin, 643
......, Patrick, treasurer of Dunblane, 390

Murtown *see* Moorstown

Musgrave [*now* Great Musgrave, Westm], parish church of, 960

Mutton (Mutton'), Robert, rector of Burmarsh, 335

Mycchylh(a)m *see* Michelham

Mydley *see* Midley

Mylanochv *see* Molana

Myleh(a)m *see* Mileham

le Mylicton' of Balgony *see* Milton of Balgonie

Mylkeshme' *see* Melksham

Myln (Myll, Mylne'), John, priest of St Andrews diocese, 691
......, ..., ..., presentation of for chaplaincy in St Salvator's, St Andrews, 691
......, ..., ..., litigant over chaplaincy, 691
......, ..., ..., appeal of, 691
......, Thomas, of St Andrews diocese, appeal of, 971

Mylton Abbat' *see* Milton Abbot

Myltonmante *see* Milton Manor

Mylverton' *see* Milverton

Myninayn, Thady, detainer, with Donat OHennessy, of vicarage of Kildorrery, 941

Myssenden' *see* Missenden

Mytford' *see* Mitford

N

Nabbos, John, rector of Warton and incumbent of Bury, 270

?Nacleobi, John, priest of Sodor diocese, to have rectory of 'Li' in Lewis anew, 116
......, *cf.* Macleod

Nafferton (Nasferton') [Yorks], parish church of, 312

[Nairn, co. of] *see* [Moray *or* Elgin and Nairn]

Nance *see* Nans

Nangle *cf.* de Anglo

Nans (Nance), John, prebendary in Exeter cathedral, incumbent of Illogan, 684
......, ..., provost of Glasney, sometime incumbent of Gwennap, 85
......, ..., vicar of St Gluvias, 85, 684
......, ..., vicar of the bishop of Exeter, 456
......, ..., ..., refusal of to institute person presented for parish church, 456
......, ..., ..., assignment to by official of metropolitical court of Canterbury of term to inquire into right of presentation, 456

?Nanudechell' *see* ?Llanfechell

Napier (Naper), Archibald, layman of St Andrews diocese, 792
......, ..., ostensible son of John Napier and executor of his will, 792
......, ..., ..., prosecutor of father's suit, 792
......, John, of Merchiston, layman of St Andrews diocese, 792
......, ..., ..., ..., and guarantee entered into with commonalty of Edinburgh, 792
......, ..., ..., ..., ..., litigant over repayment of money, 792
......, ..., ..., ostensible son of *see* Napier, Archibald
......, ..., ..., will of, ostensible executor of *see* Napier, Archibald
......, ..., ..., death of, 792

Narbonne [*in dép.* of Aude, France], Henry Petri of, cleric of London diocese, 210
......, ..., father of *see* Narbonne, Peter of
......, Peter of, barber of Henry [VII], 210
......, ..., son of *see* Narbonne, Henry Petri of

Narford (Narsforth) [Norf], parish church of, vicarage of, 336

Narnayd *alias* Ched *see* Urney

Narraghmore, *once* Norragh, *q.v.*

Narsforth *see* Narford

Nasferton' *see* Nafferton

Naso, Andreas, cleric of Palermo, provision of to chaplaincy in parish church of St Laurence, Trapani, 417

Nassington (Nassyngton') [Northants], prebend of in Lincoln cathedral, 154
......, ..., union to, of the parish church of Burton Bradstock, 154

Negropont (*Nigropontem., Nigroponten., Nigropontin.*) [titular see on island of Euboea, Greece], [bishop-] elect of *see* Hatton, John

Nelson, Thomas, the late, vicar of parish church [*name lost*], 990, 999
......, ..., ..., ..., will of, executor (named) of, 990, 999

Nenagh (Lenanach) [co. Tipperary], Augustinian monastery of St John the Baptist, priorship of, 984
......, ..., priors of *see* OBrien, Matthew; OKennedy, William

Nentoun *see* Newtown

Nepi [*in* Viterbo province, Italy], bishop of, papal mandatary, 130
......, letters dated at, 292, 899, 917, 957, 973, 974

Netteley *see* Notley

Nettellton' *see* Nettleton

Netteswell (Nettyswell) [Essex], parish church of, 467

Nettleton (Nettellton') [Lincs], parish church of, union of, to the canonry and prebend of Milton Manor in Lincoln cathedral, 203

Nettyswell *see* Netteswell

Neuay' *see* Nevay

Neuporte *see* Newport

Neuubotil *see* Newbattle

Neuuman *see* Newman

Nevay (Neuay') [*in* Eassie and Nevay, co. Forfar], parish church of, rector of, 301

[Newabbey, co. Kirkcudbright], place in *see* Sweetheart

Newbattle (Neuubotil, Newbotil, Newbotyl) [co. Midlothian], Cistercian monastery of, abbot of, to receive intending religious as monk [elsewhere], bestow habit on him, and admit his profession, 1017
......, ..., abbot of *see* [Longant], Andrew
......, ..., coadjutor of *see* Turnbull, John
......, ..., monk and cellarer of *see* Turnbull, John
......, ..., convent of, conclusion to, 1032
......, ..., vassals of, conclusion to, 1032

Newbirn *see* Newburn

Newbotil, Newbotyl *see* Newbattle

Newburn (Newbirn) [Fife], parish church of, 842

Newel *see* ONewell

Newenham (Newham) [*in* Axminster, Devon], Cistercian monastery of, monk of *see* Garlond, Richard

Newlond, alias of Herbert, James, *q.v.*

Newman (Neuuman), Thomas, of Worcester diocese, dispensed for plurality, 1134

Newminster [*in* Morpeth, Northumb], [Cistercian] monastery of, abbot of, papal judge delegate, 94

Newport (Neuporte), Peter, chantry of in London cathedral, 748
......, Richard, canon of Salisbury and prebendary of Faringdon, incumbent of Mildenhall, 908

[Newry, co. Down], Cistercian monastery of St Benedict, 235
......, ..., commendator of *see* Magennis, Gelasius
......, ..., Fabric of, proposed union to, of prebend of Clonallan in Dromore cathedral, 235

?Newton (Newton') [*in* the wapentake and deanery of Aveland, Lincs], parish church of, rector of, 131

Newton Ferrers (Newton' Fereers) [Devon], parish church of, 372

Newton Kyme (Newton' Kyme) [Yorks], parish church of, 100

Newtown (Nentoun) [*in* Auchtertool, co. Fife], lands of pertaining to episcopal *mensa* of Dunkeld, lease of, 558

[Newtownards, co. Down], place in *see* Moville

Newtown Lennan (Lonayn *alias* Balenoe) [co. Tipperary], parish church of, vicarage of, to be erected, with Kilsheelan vicarage, into prebend of Lismore, 785

Newtown Trim *see* Trim, Newtown

Nicholas, recently bishop of Elphin *see* [OFlanagan], Nicholas

Nicholl (Nicholl'), Richard, rector of ?Holcot, 114

Nicolson, Thomas, rector of Paglesham, 670
......, ..., of Lincoln diocese, dispensed for plurality, 1186

Nigropontem., Nigroponten., Nigropontin. see Negropont

Nikke *see* Nykke

Niton (Nyton) [Isle of Wight, Hants], parish church of, 959

Nocera [*either* N ~ Umbra (*in* province of Perugia, Italy) *or* N~ dei Pagani (*in* province of Salerno, Italy)], diocese of, place in *see* '*de Cassano*'

'Nodylfeld'' (i.e. 'Nether field'?) [*unidentified*; *in* East Dean, West Sussex], fields of, tithes from, 661

Nohaval-Daly (Norabal) [cos. Cork and Kerry], parish church of, vicarage of, to be united to vicarage of Cullen, 359

Norbery, Thomas, rector of Albury, 675

Norbourne, alias of Ffreuill', Robert, *q.v.*

Norbury, William, of Bath and Wells diocese, dispensed for plurality, 1105

Norchac *see* Norragh

[Norfolk, co. of], places in *see* Aldborough; Barsham, North; Blickling; Bradfield; Broomholm; Burnham Deepdale; Carleton Rode; Castle Acre; Coxford; Croxton; Fakenham; Feltwell; Fincham; Foulsham; Hardingham; Heydon; Hickling; Holkham; Ingham; Knapton; Langley; Narford; Norwich; Raynham; Saxlingham [*near* Holt]; Sparham; Stokesby; Swanton Abbot; Walsingham; Walton, West; Wendling; Whissonsett; Wickmere; Wolferton; Worsted; Wretham, West; Wymondham; Yelverton

Normandy (*Normaniam*), 174

Nornay *alias* Kede *see* Urney *alias* Keadew

Norragh (Norchac) [*now* Narraghmore, co.

Norragh (*contd*)
Kildare], parish church of, vicarage of, to be united to proposed prebend of Ballyshannon in Derry [*recte* Kildare], 934

Northampton (Northampton') [Northants], vill of, 176
......, college of St John, patron of, 176
......, ..., statutes and ordinances of, faculty for confirmation and approval of, 176
......, Moulton by, 693

[Northampton, co. of], places in *see* Boughton; Braybrooke; Brington; Byfield; Chacombe; Cosgrove; Farthingstone; Harrowden; Kettering; Lamport; Moulton; Nassington; Northampton; Oundle; Peterborough; Ravensthorpe; Stamford; Warkton; *and see* Deene

North Barsham *see* Barsham, North

Northeolynghin *see* Collingham, North

'Northfelde' (i.e. 'Northern field'?) [*unidentified*; *in* East Dean, West Sussex], fields of, tithes from, 661

North Kilworth *see* Kilworth, North

Northmoor (More) [Oxon], parish church of, 716

Northmoreton *see* Moreton, North

North Ormsby *see* Ormsby, North

North Tidworth *see* Tidworth

[Northumberland, co. of], places in *see* Alnwick; Newminster

Northuuynfeld' *see* Wingfield, North

North Walton' *see* Waltham, ?North

Northwillishrre' *see* Wiltshire

North Wingfield *see* Wingfield, North

Norton (Norton') [Kent], parish church of, 667

Norton, Henry, of Norwich diocese, dispensed for plurality, 1094

Norwich [Norf], **city** of, parish churches of, bones of dead of carried to chapel of Sts John the Baptist and John the Evangelist in the cemetery of Norwich cathedral, 777

......, ..., parish church of St Clement [at the bridge] in, 388

......, [collegiate] church of B. Mary in the Fields, canonry and prebend of, union to, of the vicarage of Twickenham, 872

......, **[cathedral] church** of, chapter of, conclusion to, 553, 634

......, ..., cemetery of, chapel of Sts John the Baptist and John the Evangelist in [i.e. Carnary College or chapel of St John at the Gates *now* part of the Grammar School], foundation of, 777

......, ..., ..., ..., master of *see* Grove, Thomas

......, ..., ..., ..., portionaries in, 777

......, ..., ..., ..., bones of the dead of the parish churches of the city of Norwich carried to, 777

......, **bishop** of, to receive oath of fealty in pope's name, 625, 626

......, ..., papal mandatary, 655

......, ..., *see* [Goldwell], James; [Jane], Thomas; [Nykke], Richard

......, church of, subject to the archbishop of Canterbury, 554, 636

......, ..., archdeacon of Norwich in *see* Honywood, Robert

......, ..., vassals of, conclusion to, 553, 634

......, **city and diocese** of, clergy of, conclusion to, 553, 634

......, ..., people of, conclusion to, 553, 634

......, **diocese** of, persons of *see* Adam, Thomas; Alenson', John; Aleyns, Edmund; Barker, David; Barney, John; Benett, William; Beverley, William; Bevys, Thomas; Bingrey, Thomas;

Norwich **diocese** (*contd*)
Bradley, Edward; Bradshaw, James; Braye, Walter; Brokesby, Richard; Burdale, Thomas; Chamberlain, Edward; Chambyr, Robert; Chappeley3, Olive; Church, Thomas; Clerk, John; Cliff, John; Cobbe, William; [Codenham *alias* Bunting], William; [Connesburgh], Edmund; Cook, Edmund; Copping, John; Corttis, Laurence; Cryppyng, Thomas; Curll, Henry; Dagget, Thomas; Dersham, William; Doget, Thomas; Dussyng, Robert; Einster, Thomas; Exsalle, Thomas; Ffoter, William; Fineham, Simon; Foster, William; Garard, Thomas; Goodnow, Roger; Gottis, Richard; Gretyngham, Laurence; Grove, Thomas; Haolt *alias* Baker, Henry; Hare, Thomas; Harrys, John; Hedge, Thomas; Jenney, Edward; Josselyne, Philip; Kyte, John; Larbe, Thomas; Leicester, John; Loddon *alias* Galys, William; Louuyn', Geoffrey; Mathew *alias* Norwich, John; Mileham, Henry; Mullet, Nicholas; Norton, Henry; Penton, John; Pinchbeck, John; Pluttinger, John; Poxwell, Robert; Quogno, Stephen; Rabett, Henry; Ravyn, John; Rede, Thomas; Re'pe, Thomas; Rokeby, William; Ruynet, John; Smyth, John; Staxeley, George; Taverner, Thomas; ?Thelau, Alan; Tuddenham *alias* Moro, Thomas; Tybenh(a)m, Thomas; Untum, John; Urswick, Christopher; Walsohayn, Thomas; Wardall, John; Wayen, John; Willoughby, Robert; Woliner, Walter; Wyatt, Richard; Yermoth *alias* Ludhnn', Thomas

......, ..., places in *see* Bradley [*probably* Great]; Burwell St Mary; Bury St Edmunds; Drinkstone; Dunwich; Euston; Eye; Ipswich; Kettleburgh; Kirkley; Lackford; Leiston; Pakefield; Preston; Shottisham; Stonham Aspall; Tannington; Westleton; Whelnetham, Little; *and* places *listed above under* [Norfolk, co. of]

Norwich, alias of Mathew, John, *q.v.*

Nothinghin' *see* Nottingham

Notley (Netteley) [*in* Long Crendon, Bucks], Augustinian monastery of, abbot of *see* [Caversham], Peter
......, ..., union to, of the parish church of Lamport, 877

Nottingham (Nothinghin') [Notts], vill of, parish church of B. Mary the Virgin in, 278

[Nottingham, co. of], places in *see* Collingham, North; Eakring; Nottingham; Tollerton

Nova Sancte Trinitatis *see* Ogonnelloe

Nullius diocesis, persons of *see* Goryng, John; Underwood, John

Nykke (Nikke), Richard, archdeacon of Wells, 634, 635
......, ..., ..., provision of to the bishopric of Norwich, 634
......, ..., ..., absolution of preliminary to provision, 635
......, ..., [bishop-] elect of Norwich, faculty for consecration of, 636

Nynehead (Nyuhede) [Som], [church of], 174

Nyton *see* Niton

Nyuhede *see* Nynehead

N. [= *nomen* ? (Cosyn?)], William, union for, of a parish church in Chichester diocese to his deanery [of Wells?], 1184

O

O *cf.* Y; H

OAherne *see* Aherne

Oakford (Okfford) [Devon], parish church of, 568

Oakley (Okeley) [Bucks], parish church of, 170

OBanaghan (Obenathayn), Thomas, prior of the Augustinian priory of Inchmacnerin, to be deprived for alleged misdeeds, 936

OBehan (Obechayn), John, ostensible priest of Killaloe diocese, detainer of portion of 'Gleandbannam', vulgarly '?Ileraunr', in the collegiate church of Scattery Island, 818

OBeirne (Oberynd), John, vicar, called stipendiary, in Tuam cathedral, death of, 123
......, *cf.* Oberyn

Obenathayn *see* OBanaghan

Obeolen', John, detainer of Carrickfergus, 236
......, *cf.* OBoylan

Oberen, Theoderic, detainer of canonry of Annaghdown and prebend of the small churches, 935
......, ..., ..., detainer of vicarage of Kinvarra, 935
......, *cf.* OBrien

OBergin (Obergyn), Cornelius, detainer of parish church of Rosconnell, 510
......, Malachy, cleric of Ossory diocese, to have parish church of Rosconnell, 510
......, Thady, rector of parish church of Rosconnell, death of, 510

Oberyn, Maurice *see* OBriain, Maurice
......, Odo, canon of Elphin, papal mandatary, 763
......, *cf.* OBeirne

Oberynd *see* OBeirne

Obingill, Obiugil *see* OBoyle

OBogue (Obuoe), William, detainer of vicarage of Donaghmore, 786

OBoylan *cf.* Obeolen'

OBoyle (Obingill, Obiugil), Bernard, canon
of Derry, papal mandatary, 950
......, Donald, monk of the Cistercian
monastery of Assaroe, formerly rector
of Inver and Killymard, 943
......, ..., election of, as abbot of Assaroe,
943
......, ..., provision of to Assaroe, 943
......, ..., abbot of Assaroe, 950
......, Tancred, canon of Derry, papal
mandatary, 950

OBrazil *cf.* Obresel

Obresel, Dermot, ostensible priest of
Cloyne (*recte* Clonmacnois) diocese,
detainer of Ballyloughloe vicarage, 226

OBriain (Oberyn), Maurice, bishop of
Kilfenora, detainer of vicarage of
Kilfearagh, 818

OBrien (Bryen, Obriel, Obryen, Obryey,
Ubryen, Ybrien, Ybryen), Dermot, the
late, canon of Kilfenora, 648
......, ..., (commendatory) abbot of the
Augustinian monastery of Kilshanny,
death of, 649, 980
......, ..., layman, usurper of fruits of
Kilfarboy vicarage, 449
......, Matthew, canon of Kilfenora, 449
......, ..., ..., papal mandatary, 815, 820
......, ..., ..., to have vicarages of Kilfarboy
and Killard, portion of Moanmore in
the [collegiate] church of Scattery
Island, and rectory of fief of Kilfarboy
united to his canonry and prebend, 449
......, ..., canon of Killaloe, 984
......, ..., ..., papal mandatary, 930, 938, 948
......, ..., ..., commendatory archdeacon of
Killaloe, 984
......, ..., ..., ..., to have, as well, the
priorship of the Augustinian monastery
of Nenagh *in commendam*, 984
......, Maurice, canon of Killaloe, papal
mandatary, 648
......, ..., canon of Killaloe and prebendary
of Rath, 649
......, ..., ..., to have Augustinian monastery

OBrien (*contd*)
of Kilshanny *in commendam*, 649
......, ..., *cf.* OBrien, Maurus
......, Maurus, canon of Kilfenora, papal
mandatary, 650
......, ..., ..., to be commendatory abbot of
the Augustinian monastery of
Kilshanny, 980
......, ..., *cf.* OBrien, Maurice
......, Thady, canon of Kilfenora, to have
vicarage of [Killinaboy] united to his
canonry and prebend, 651
......, *cf.* Oberen

de Obroch *see* OBrogy

Obrodear, Morinanus, detainer of vicarage
of Fahy, 225
......, *cf.* Broder; Broderick; Browder

OBrogy (de Obroch, Obrog, Obroghy), clan
of, 146
......, Gregory, the late, bishop of Clonfert,
146
......, ..., ..., ..., grant of mensal lands by,
146
......, James, the late, cleric of Clonfert,
grant to of Clonfert mensal lands, 146
......, ..., ..., successors of *see* OBrogy,
Odo; OBrogy, William Jacobi viventis
......, Odo, cleric of Clonfert, 146
......, ..., ..., a successor of OBrogy, James,
q.v.
......, Thady, cleric of Clonfert diocese, to
be canon of Clonfert and have prebend
of Annacalla and vicarage of Fahy, 225
......, William, detainer of archdeaconry of
Clonfert, 512
......, ..., canon of Clonfert, papal
mandatary, 819
......, ..., canon of Cloyne, papal mandatary,
227
......, William Jacobi viventis, cleric of
Clonfert, 146
......, ..., ..., a successor of OBrogy, James,
q.v.

OBrohan *cf.* Obruchan

OBrophy (Abrohe, Obrohe), alias of OMulwarden, Donat and John, *qq.v.*

OBrosnan (Obrosoacan, Obrusnakayn), Thady, canon of Ardfert, papal mandatary, 359, 994

Obruchan, Thomas, canon of Killala, papal mandatary, 124
......, *cf.* OBrohan

Obrusnakayn *see* OBrosnan

Obryen, Obryey *see* OBrien

Obuoe *see* OBogue

Ocaassay *see* OCasey

Ocaeley, Odo, cleric of Connor diocese, to have rectory of Carrickfergus, 236
......, *cf.* OKelly

Ocaeylte *see* OQuilty

OCahan (Okahan), Donat, cleric of Derry diocese, to be monk, then abbot, of Macosquin, 259

OCahill (Itahylle', Ochayll, Ykayl), Cornelius, to have vicarage united to monastery, Ossory diocese, 1287
......, Maurice, detainer of vicarage of Newtown Lennan, 785
......, Philip, bishop of Emly, death of, 52
......, ..., detainer of vicarage of Kilmanagh, 787
......, Thomas, once vicar of one or more of the following : Ballysheehan, Crumpstown, ?Erry, Railstown, 998
......, ..., Cistercian monk, detainer of vicarage of Kilsheelan, 785

OCahir (Ykyhyr), Cormac, cleric of Kilfenora diocese, to have canonry and prebend of Kilfenora, with vicarage of 'Kylthalbach' united thereto, 648
......, ..., late abbot of the Augustinian monastery of Kilshanny, 980

OCarolan (Okernalan, Oquervalan), Maurice, canon of Derry, papal mandatary, 448
......, Nellanus / Nillanus, canon of Derry, papal mandatary, 448
......, ..., ostensible priest of Derry diocese, detainer of the rectory of Leckpatrick, 249

OCarran (Okaraen'), Maurice, canon of Ferns, papal judge delegate, 192

OCarroll (Okeacboyll, Ykerwayli), Cornelius, cleric of Killaloe diocese, 357
......, ..., ..., provided anew to canonry of Killaloe and prebend of Ballyloughnane, 357
......, ..., ..., to have rectories of Birr and Modreeny and vicarage of Modreeny united anew to his canonry and prebend, 357
......, Odo, detainer of priorship of Augustinian monastery of Seirkieran, 930
......, *cf.* Okellayll

OCasey (Ocaassay), William, canon of Tuam, papal mandatary, 933

Ocayllt *see* OQuilty

Occhanassoy *see* OShaughnessy

Occullan *see* OCullane

Ocealli, Oceally, Ocell', Ocellayd *see* OKelly

Ochacheri *see* Aherne

Ochalen, alias of MacGilfoyle, William, *q.v.*

Ochavaym *see* OHonan

Ochayll *see* OCahill

Ochayllyn, Odo, to have vicarage in Kilmacduagh diocese, 1204

Ochedrscoyll *see* ODriscoll

Ochellay *see* OKelly

Ocherim, David, canon of Tuam, papal mandatary, 126

Ocherlahe *see* OHerlihy

Oche'tuyle *see* Auchtertool

Ochill', Odo, canon of Connor, papal mandatary, 235
......, *cf.* OKelly

Ochniede *see* OKennedy

Ochoncenayn *see* OConcannon

Ochonyll *see* OConnell

Ochormachan *see* OCormachan

?Ochvygh, Lewis, canon of Ross, papal mandatary, 70

Ockley (Okley) [Surrey], parish church of, 678

OClery (Oclere, Ycleri), Dermot, detainer of vicarage of Callan *alias* Kilbride, 575
......, Robert *alias* Robyn, cleric of Killaloe diocese, 403
......, ..., ..., to be canon of Killaloe, have vicarage of Loughkeen erected into a prebend, and have vicarage of Uskane and church, called rectory or particle, of the lands of 'Medohk' in Loughkeen parish united thereto, 403

Oclmuran, William, cleric of Annaghdown diocese, to have chapel of B. Mary, Galway, 829

OCloney *cf.* Oeluana

Ocogavayn, Ocoggobayn, alias of Geddac, Philip / Pilapus, *q.v.*

Ocolla *see* Coll

Ocomyll, Oconayll' *see* OConnell

OConcannon (Ochoncenayn, Oconceanind, Oconcenind, Oconcenndynd, Oconcenynd, Ocontennan, Otonconnan, Otontenynd), Cornelius, canon of Tuam, papal judge delegate, 167
......, ..., ..., subdelegate of *see* OMulkerrill, Charles
......, ..., ..., death of, 167
......, John, canon of Tuam, papal mandatary, 784, 788
......, Malachy, canon of Tuam, papal mandatary, 784, 788, 835
......, William, canon of Tuam, papal mandatary, 69, 73, 75, 164, 784, 788; *cf.* 330
......, ..., *cf.* OConcannon, Wolmus
......, Wolmus, canon of Tuam, 833
......, ..., invalid collation to of Kilkerrin parish church, 833
......, ..., to have Kilkerrin parish church united to his canonry and prebend, 833
......, ..., *cf.* OConcannon, William
......, *cf.* Yco'mimayn

Oconenar, Cornelius, canon of Kilfenora, papal mandatary, 980
......, *cf.* OConnor

OConnell (Ochonyll, Ocomyll, Oconayll', Oconnyll), Donat, canon of Ardfert, papal mandatary, 125, 128
......, ..., to have vicarage in Ardfert diocese united to his canonry [of Ardfert], 1070
......, Galfrigidus, cleric of Ardfert diocese, to be canon of Ardfert and have vicarage of 'Kylldacu(m) *alias* Turere' erected into prebend, 72

OConnor (Oconuhur, Otontuyr), Bernard, late abbot of the Augustinian abbey of Kilshanny, 980
......, Donald, detainer of vicarage of Macroom, 823
......, Theoderic, cleric of Elphin diocese, to have deanery of Elphin with provostry of Elphin and rectory of *Clann*

OConnor (*contd*)
   conchobair and vicarage of Ogulla united thereto, and to have Augustinian priory of Inchmacnerin *in commendam*, 936
......, *cf.* Oconenar

Oconnyll *see* OConnell

Oconray *see* OCurry

Ocontennan *see* OConcannon

Oconuhur *see* OConnor

OCorkery (Ymulcorcny), Maurice, chancellor of Limerick cathedral, 485
......, ..., ..., a conspirator against bishop of Limerick, 485
......, ..., ..., other excesses of, 485
......, ..., ..., to have vicarage of Kilscannell united to his chancellorship, 485

OCormachan (Ochormachan), William, canon of Killaloe, papal mandatary, 330

OCormican *cf.* Jeurmachan; Ocorra'chan

Ocorra'chan, John, detainer of rectory of Kilmalinoge, 513

OCorregan', Thomas, detainer of vicarage of Jerpoint, 545

OCorrigan *cf.* O Corregan'

OCremin *cf.* Oeromyn

OCronin (Ocronyn, Yeronyn), Donat, detainer of vicarage of Aghinagh, 825
......, William, cleric of Cork diocese, to be canon of Cork and have the church of Gortnacrusha erected into a prebend, with the rectory of Templetrine and the church of ?Ballymountain united thereto, 255
......, *cf.* Oeromyn

Octavian, archbishop of Armagh *see* [Spinelli (de Palatio)], Octavian

Ocua, William, canon of Derry, papal mandatary, 235

Oculay, John, canon of Tuam, papal mandatary, 165
......, *cf.* OCuolahan; OKelly, John

OCullane (Occullan), Maurice, canon of Limerick, papal mandatary, 401
......, *cf.* Collins

OCullen, Donat, to have parish church in Clogher diocese, 1205

OCullinane (Ocullenayn, Ocullynayn), Maurice, canon of Ross, papal mandatary, 254, 255
......, *cf.* Onilleayn

OCuolahan *cf.* Oculay

OCurran (Occurrin), Thady, detainer of vicarages of ?Killeen and ?Curragh, 982

OCurry (Oconray), Lucanus, precentor of Killaloe, papal mandatary, 512

Ocwynd *see* OQuinn

Odagh (Casleandriohc') [co. Kilkenny], parish church of, vicarage of, to be united to Cistercian monastery of Kilcooly, 574

Odal *see* ODaly

ODallaghan *cf.* ODollaghan

ODaly (Odal, Odalle), Bernard, detainer of vicarage of Nohaval-Daly, 359
......, Eugene, canon of Kilfenora, papal mandatary, 649

Odarnussihy *see* ODempsey

Oday *see* ODea

Oddomayll *see* ODonnell

Oddonis *see* Odo

Oddowelyan, Cornelius, vicar of Taghboy, death of, 784
......, *cf.* ODolan

ODea (Oday), Denis, the late, vicar of 'Kylthalbach', 648
......, Donald, detainer of vicarage of 'Kylthalbach', 648

ODempsey (Odarnussihy, ?Odimusia), William, detainer of vicarage of Loughrea, 16, 512

Odiham (Odyham) [Hants], parish church of, 495

?Odimusia *see* ODempsey

Odnyguyn *see* ODuggan

Odo (Oddonis), William, son of, property gifted to Taunton priory by, 174

Odolagan *see* ODollaghan

ODolan *cf.* Oddowelyan; Odulcayn

ODollaghan (Odolagan), John, canon of Cloyne [*recte* Clonmacnois], papal mandatary, 225
......, *cf.* ODallaghan

ODolohan *cf.* ODollaghan

Odonallan *see* ODonnellan

Odonchw *see* ODonoghue

ODonegan (Odunagayn, Odunnegan), John, detainer of vicarage of Castleconor, 124
......, William, detainer of vicarage of Kilbradran, 820

Odoni *see* [de Geraldinis?], John Odoni[s]

ODonnell (Oddomayll), Edmund, to have parish church in Raphoe diocese, 1117

ODonnellan (Odonallan), William, canon of Elphin, papal mandatary, 830

ODonoghue (Odonchw), William, ostensible Cistercian monk, detainer of Cistercian monastery of Inishlounaght, 789

ODoolan *cf.* Odulcayn

ODoonan *cf.* Odunan

ODoorley (Odurla), James, canon of Clonmacnois [*sometimes erroneously* Cloyne], papal mandatary, 225, 226, 229, 230

Odorna (Odorana, Odornay), Dermot, canon of Cloyne, papal mandatary, 392, 514, 539, 540

[ODorney, co. Kerry], place in *see* Abbeydorney

Odowna *see* Odunan

ODowney (Oduny), John, detainer of canonry of Cloyne and prebend of Cooliney, 514

ODriscoll (Ochedrscoyll, Ohederscoyll, Ohedriscoll', Ohedrscoyll, Yhedriscoll', Yhedrscoyll, Yhhederscoyll), Bernard, canon of Ross and prebendary of Kilnamanagh, 70
......, ..., collation to him of Creagh vicarage feared invalid, 70
......, ..., to have vicarage united to his canonry and prebend, 70
......, Dermot, detainer of vicarage of Clear Island, 129
......, Donald, detainer of rectory of Creagh and Gortnaclohy, 129
......, John, detainer of archdeaconry of Ross, 257
......, ..., canon of Ross, papal mandatary, 70
......, Odo, cleric of Ross diocese, to be canon of Ross, have vicarage of Clear Island erected into prebend and

ODriscoll (*contd*)
rectories of Clear Island, Creagh, and Gortnaclohy united thereto, 129
......, Thady, cleric of Ross diocese, to be canon of Ross and prebendary of Creagh and have rectory and vicarage of Tullagh united thereto, 251

ODuggan (Dugin, Odnyguyn), John, to have chancellorship of Waterford, 1155
......, William, canon of Killaloe, papal mandatary, 161

Oduir *see* ODwyer

Odulayud, Rory, ostensible priest of Leighlin diocese, detainer of vicarage of Rathaspick, 576

Odulcayn, Kynetus, ostensible canon of the Augustinian monastery of Clontuskert, detainer of vicarage of Creagh, 819
......, *cf.* ODolan; ODoolan

Odunagayn *see* ODonegan

Odunan (Odowna), John, canon of Annaghdown, papal mandatary, 234, 829
......, *cf.* ODoonan

ODunn *cf.* Odunan

Odunnegan *see* ODonegan

Oduny *see* ODowney

Odurla *see* ODoorley

Oduyll', Eugene, cleric of Derry diocese, to have vicarage of Rasharkin, 361

ODwyer (Oduir, Odwir), Philip, canon of Cashel, papal mandatary, 942
......, Redmundus, ostensible brother of the Hospital of St John of Jerusalem, detainer of preceptorship of Clonoulty, 938
......, Thomas, cleric of Cashel diocese, to have the preceptorship of the Hospitaller house of Clonoulty *in*

ODwyer (*contd*)
commendam, 938
......, ..., ..., to be a brother-knight and have preceptorship, 938

Odyham *see* Odiham

Oeluana, William, priest of Leighlin diocese, to have vicarages of Kilteale and Moyanna, 932
......, *cf.* OCloney

Oeromyn, David, priest of Cork diocese, to have vicarage of Desertserges, 231
......, Denis, detainer of vicarage of Desertserges, 231
......, *cf.* OCremin; OCronin

OFahy (Affahy, Ofathy, Yfahy), Dermot, canon of Clonfert and prebendary of Ballynakill with Duniry vicarage united thereto, 512
......, ..., ..., to have archdeaconry of Clonfert, priorship of the Augustinian monastery of Aughrim *in commendam,* and vicarage of Loughrea united to his canonry and prebend, 512
......, Eugene, detainer of chapel of Kilconierin, 234
......, Thady, canon of Clonfert, papal mandatary, 16

OFallon (Ofallwy), Charles, canon of Elphin, papal mandatary, 837

OFalvin *cf.* Ialbim

OFarrell (Hofergil, Ofergyl, Offegail, Offegayd, Offergil, Offergill, Ofirgil), Adam, cleric of Kilmore diocese, to be canon of Kilmore and have the church of 'Tolach' erected into a prebend with the vicarage of Annagh united thereto, 821
......, ..., canon of Kilmore, papal mandatary, 832
......, Donald, vicar of ?Kilglass, death of, 763
......, Fantutius, canon of the Augustinian monastery of B. Mary, Saints Island, to have priorship, 836

OFarrell (*contd*)

......, John, cleric of Ardagh diocese, to have vicarage of ?Kilglass, 763

......, Maurice, canon of Ardagh, papal mandatary, 995

....., Maurus, ostensible Augustinian canon, detainer of priorship of Inchcleraun, 837

......, Odo, the late, rector of Annagh and 'Tolach', death of, 821

......, Roceus, canon of the Augustinian monastery of B. Mary, Saints Island, to have priorship of Inchcleraun, 837

......, Thomas, ostensible Augustinian canon, detainer of priorship of the Augustinian monastery of Saints Island, 836

Ofathy *see* OFahy

OFeehan *cf.* Ffyhan'

OFeeny *cf.* Ofyne

Ofergyl *see* OFarrell

Offaellayn *see* OPhelan

Offaeyn, Thomas, ostensible priest of Limerick diocese, detainer of vicarage of *Cluain Comarda*, 942

......, *cf.* Offahym; Os..ayn

Offahym, David, canon of the Augustinian monastery of Rathkeale, to be prior, 944

......, *cf.* Offaeyn; OFlynn; Os..ayn

[Offaly, co. of], places in *see* Ballybritt; Birr; Clonmacnois; Gallen; Kilcomin; Kinnitty; Lynally; Roscrea; Seirkieran

Offanach *see* ?Feohanagh

Offegail, Offegayd *see* OFarrell

Offelathayn, Offellayn *see* OPhelan

Offergil, Offergill *see* OFarrell

Offlahud *see* OFlahy

Offlamyagayn *see* OFlanagan

Offlavin, Offlawan' *see* OFlavin

Offlayn *see* OFlynn

Offuyra, William, canon and prebendary of Clonmacnois, to have archdeaconry of Cloyne [*recte* Clonmacnois?], 228

......, *cf.* OFurey

Offyellan *see* OPhelan

Offyllyg, Donat, detainer of rectory of Templetrine and church of Gortnacrusha, 255

......, *cf.* OFlyng

Offyn *see* OFinn

Ofinchua, Nemeas, detainer of vicarage of Ogulla, 936

OFinn (Offyn), Donald, detainer of rectory of Ballyduff *alias* Glennahoo, 994

......, *cf.* Ofyne

Ofirgil *see* OFarrell

Oflacharthyd, Oflachyrdayd *see* OFlaherty

OFlahavan *cf.* OFlavin

OFlaherty (Oflacharthyd, Oflachyrdayd, Yfflaytbertay), Magonius, vicar of Killeroon and ?Kilcummin, death of, 845

......, ..., cleric of Annaghdown diocese, to be canon of Annaghdown and have vicarages of ?Kilcummin and Killeroon erected into a prebend, 646

......, Odo, canon of Annaghdown, has vicarages of ?Kilcummin and Killeroon united to his canonry and prebend, 845

......, *cf.* Oflayterah

OFlahy *cf.* Oflayterah; OLahiff

OFlanagan (Offlamyagayn, Oflandegayn), Dermot, provost of Elphin, to be

OFlanagan (*contd*)
deprived for alleged misdeeds, 936
......, ...[another?], collation to of canonry
and prebend of Elphin, 936
......, Donat, detainer of rectory of
ecclesiastical fief in Kilfarboy parish
church, 449
......, Lewis, detainer of rectory of *Clann
conchobair* [*in* Baslick], 936
......, Nicholas, bishop of Elphin, cession
by, 591
......, *cf.* Oslannagail

OFlannelly *cf.* Oslannagail

OFlannery (Oflannira, Oflanura), Rory,
detainer of vicarage of Clonrush, 650,
933

OFlavahan *cf.* OFlavin

OFlavin (Offlavin, Offlawan', Oflawan),
Maurice, commissary of Thomas
[Purcell], bishop of Lismore, 811
......, William, canon of Lismore, papal
mandatary, 944
......, ..., cleric of Lismore diocese, to be
canon of Lismore, have Lickoran
vicarage erected into prebend, with
Modelligo vicarage united thereto, 946

[?OFlavin], William, to have canonry
erected in Lismore, 1282

Oflayterah (Offlahud), Thady, (ostensible)
prior of the Augustinian monastery of
Rathkeale, 485, 542
......, ..., ..., alleged disobedience and
excommunication of, 542
......, ..., ..., to be deprived, 542
......, ..., ..., detainer of vicarage of
Kilscannell, 485
......, *and see* OLahiff; *cf.* OFlaherty;
OFlahy

Oflin *see* OFlynn

Oflyijd, Thady, cleric of Lismore diocese,
to have vicarages of Kilbarrymeaden
and Rossmire, 949

OFlyng *cf.* Offyllyg
......, *and see* OFlynn

OFlynn (Offlayn, Oflin), Donat, priest of
Cloyne diocese, to be vicar of
Kilshannig, 74
......, Maurice, canon of Limerick, papal
mandatary, 383
......, *cf.* Offahym
......, *and see* OFlyng

OFurey *cf.* Offuyra

Ofyne, alias of OHedian, Thomas, *q.v.*
......, *cf.* OFeeny; OFinn

OGallagher (Ogaleur, Ogallcubayr,
Ogalrabayr, Ogaltabayr), Arthur, abbot
of Assaroe, death of, 943
......, Laurence, to have parish church in
Raphoe diocese, 1203
......, Nigel, priest of Elphin diocese,
detainer of Cistercian monastery of
Assaroe, 943
......, alias of MacGellage, Patrick, *q.v.*

OGara *cf.* Oscara

Ogarmilegayd, Henry, cleric of Derry
diocese, to have vicarage of ?*Cell
cairill* [*now* Termonamongan], 448

Ogarryn *see* Ikerrin

OGarvan (Ogenwayn, Ogernayn,
Ogerranayn, Ogerrwayn, Ogervan,
Ogervayn, Ogerwayn, Ugerrimayn,
Ygervayn), Florence, canon of Clonfert,
papal mandatary, 16, 330, 512, 853,
932, 934-936, 984
......, ..., ..., ..., (replaced), 982 *note*
......, ..., canon of Kilmacduagh, papal
mandatary, 933
......, ..., late vicar of Isertkelly, 983

Ogiellyry, Thomas, canon of Cloyne, papal
mandatary, 824

Ogoband *see* OGowan

Ogonnelloe (Nova Sancte Trinitatis) [co. Clare], parish church of B. Mary *alias* of the Holy Trinity, vicarage of, 650
......, ..., ..., to be united to canonry of Killaloe and prebend of Tulla, 650

Ogorlakane *see* Abbeygormacan

OGowan (Ogoband), Cormac, detainer of Kildrumferton vicarage, 537
......, John, cleric of Kilmore diocese, to have canonry of Kilmore and Kildrumferton vicarage erected into prebend, 537

OGrady (Ograda), Thomas, canon of Killaloe, papal mandatary, 783

Ogriffa, Donat, detainer of Killard vicarage, 449

Ogulla (Godellw) [co. Roscommon], parish church of, vicarage of, to be united to deanery of Elphin, 936

Ogyllamyr, Maurice, canon of Connor, papal mandatary, 236

Ohadean *alias* Ofyne *see* OHedian *alias* Ofyne

OHalley *cf.* Ohanle

Ohallmarayl, William, canon of Annaghdown, papal mandatary, 647

Ohanle (Yhanllyd), Philip, cleric of Killaloe diocese, to be canon of Killaloe, have rectory of Finnoe erected into prebend, and rectory of Terryglass united thereto, 16
......, ..., detainer of rectory of Terryglass, 935
......, *cf.* OHalley; OKelly

OHanley *cf.* Ohanle

OHannon (Ohaynayn), David, detainer of vicarage of Kilcomin, 162

OHaugh *cf.* Geddac *alias* Ocoggobayn

Ohaynayn *see* OHannon

OHea (Hohe, Hohea, Horga, Oheaga, Oheaig, Ohega, Oheyga), Cormac, canon of Emly, papal mandatary, 357, 392, 403, 404, 511-513, 539
......, Maurice, canon of Ross, papal mandatary, 252, 254, 255
......, Odo, detainer of canonry of Ross and prebend of Curragranemore, and vicarages of Inchydoney Island and ?Kilgarriff, 256

OHealy (Yhily), John, to have canonry erected in Ossory, 1156

Ohederscoyll *see* ODriscoll

OHedian (Edegayn, Hedyan, Hedyan', Ohadean), Henry, canon of Cashel, papal mandatary, 787
......, James, vicar of Jerpoint, death of, 545
......, ..., collector or sub-collector of apostolic camera, 545
......, Robert, canon of Cashel, papal mandatary, 575, 645, 787
...... *alias* Ofyne, Thomas, dean of Elphin, to be deprived for alleged misdeeds, 936

OHedigan (Iharadgreyn), Donat, to have vicarage in Killaloe diocese erected into canonry [of Killaloe], 1285

Ohedriscoll', Ohedrscoyll *see* ODriscoll

Ohega *see* OHea

OHegarty (Ohegertay), Eugene, canon of Derry, papal mandatary, 253

OHehir (Ohehyr), Matthew, cleric of Killaloe diocese, to have vicarages of Killimer and Killofin, 948

Ohenahaga *see* Ohenega

Ohenassa *see* OHennessy

Ohenega (Ohenahaga), William, canon of Derry, papal mandatary, 361

......, ..., priest of Derry diocese and vicar of Banagher, 253

......, ..., ..., to have rectory of Banagher with his vicarage united thereto, 253

OHennessy (Ohenassa), Donat, detainer, with Thady Myninayn, of vicarage of Kildorrery, 941

Ohergedayn, John, canon of Elphin, papal mandatary, 947

OHerlihy (Ocherlahe, Oherlahe, Oherlay, Yherlahe), Donat, detainer of vicarage of Ballyvourney, 541

......, John, detainer, with Matthew OMahoney, of the deanery of Cork, 258

......, ..., canon of Cork, papal (commissary and) mandatary, 816, 822, 823

......, ..., the elder, priest of Cork diocese, to have vicarage of Kilmoney anew, and vicarage of Aghinagh, 825

......, ..., cleric of Cloyne diocese, to be canon of Cloyne and prebendary of Ballyvourney, 541

Oheuacham, William, to have vicarage in Killala diocese erected into prebend [in Killala?], 1072

OHevican cf. Oheuacham

Oheyga see OHea

OHiggins (Ohugynd), Malachy, detainer of vicarage, called stipend, in Tuam cathedral, 123

OHingerdell (Ohyngardayll), Donald, to have vicarage in Ardfert diocese, 1116

Óhlonmhaineáin cf. ONoonan

OHogan (Ohogayn), Donat, canon of Killaloe, papal mandatary, 14

......, ..., detainer of vicarage of Templeachally alias Callathamery, 783

OHonan (Hohenayn, Hohounyn, Ochavaym, Ohonayn, Ohoney), Maurice, canon of Ardfert, papal mandatary, 449, 815, 818, 820

......, de Mivrey alias, q.v.

OHoolahan cf. OHoulihan

OHoran (Ohuran), Donat, canon of Clonfert and prebendary of Annacalla, to be deprived, 225

OHoulihan (Ohullachayn), Edmund, detainer of 'Kylldacu(m) alias Turere', Ardfert diocese, 72

Ohugynd see OHiggins

Ohullachayn see OHoulihan

Ohunwnan see ONoonan

Ohuran see OHoran

OHurley (Ohurelly), Maurus, detainer of vicarage of Uskane, 403

......, cf. OMurilly

OHynan (Ohuynayn), Marcus, detainer of church, called rectory or particle, of lands of 'Medohk' in Loughkeen parish, 403

Ohyngardayll see OHingerdell

Ohynwayn' see ONoonan

Okaelly see OKelly

Okahan see OCahan

Okaraen' see OCarran

[Oke], Thomas, abbot of the Premonstratensian monastery of Titchfield, 707

Okeacboyll see OCarroll

OKeeffe cf. Okwym

Okeley *see* Oakley (Bucks)

Okelhyd *see* OKelly

Okella, Edmund, to have one vicarage erected into canonry and another into a prebend [of Leighlin], 1126
......, *cf.* OKelly

Okellay, Okellayd *see* OKelly

Okellayll, Cornelius, detainer, with John Okellayll, of the rectory of *Cenél arga*, 162
......, John, detainer, with Cornelius Okellayll, of the rectory of *Cenél arga*, 162
......, *cf.* OCarroll

OKelly (Ocealli, Oceally, Ocell', Ocellayd, Ochellay, Okaelly, Okelhyd, Okellay, Okellayd, Ycellard, Ycellayd, Yhelay, Ykallayd), Cornelius, canon of Elphin, to have vicarage of Taghboy, 784
......, ..., detainer of vicarage of Fohanagh, 788
......, ..., detainer of vicarage of Killosolan, 164
......, Donald, detainer of parish church of Killeroran, 830
......, Donat, canon of Elphin, to have vicarage of Fohanagh, 788
......, ..., ..., to have vicarage of Killosolan erected into prebend for his canonry and rectories of Killosolan and Ahascragh united thereto, 164, *cf.* 73
......, John, detainer of archdeaconry of Clonfert, 16
......, ..., archdeacon of Clonfert, death of, 234
......, ..., ..., ..., in England *en route* to Roman curia, 512
......, ..., canon of Tuam and prebendary of Tisaxon *alias* Templegaile, 69, 75
......, ..., ..., commendatory abbot / detainer of the Cistercian monastery of Abbeyknockmoy, 69, 75, 330
......, ..., ..., ..., to be dean of Tuam and have vicarage of 'Kilelonne' and his canonry and prebend united to deanery,

OKelly (*contd*)
69, 75
......, ..., ostensible priest of Leighlin diocese, detainer of vicarage of Ballycoolan, 576
......, ..., *cf.* Oculay, John
......, Malachy, cleric of Clonfert diocese, to be commendatory prior of the Augustinian monastery of Aughrim, 492
......, Odo, to be dean of Tuam, 330, 1124
......, ..., canon of Tuam, 166
......, ..., ..., to have chaplaincy, called stipend, in Tuam cathedral erected into prebend, 166
......, ..., ..., to be commendatory abbot of the Premonstratensian monastery of the Holy Trinity outside the walls of Tuam, 166
......, Rory, ostensible priest of Killaloe diocese, detainer of vicarage of Killimer, 948
......, Thomas, bishop of Clonfert, grant of mensal lands anew by, 146
......, *cf.* Ocaeley; Ochill'; Ohanle; Okella; Yolei

OKendrigan (Okyngrigayn), John, detainer of vicarage of Bunratty, 652

OKennedy (Ochniede, Okermada, Okynmede), Aulanus, detainer of vicarage of Kilbarron, 511
......, Donald, cleric of Killaloe diocese, to be canon of Killaloe and have rectory of Dorrha erected into prebend, 230
......, Donat, canon of Limerick, papal judge delegate, litigation before, 221
......, William, detainer of the priorship of the Augustinian monastery of Nenagh, 984
......, *cf.* Ychernolii

Okermada *see* OKennedy

Okernalan *see* OCarolan

OKett (Oketk, Ytreyth'), Gillasius, the late, dean of Lismore, 159
......, Philip, canon of Lismore, papal mandatary, 852

Okfford *see* Oakford

OKielt *cf.* OQuilty

Okinaill', Donat, cleric of Derry diocese, to be canon of Derry and prebendary of Leckpatrick, 249

OKinneally *cf.* Oknyllay; Okynala

OKinneally (Okyneala) *alias* ?MacKinneally (Mackyneala), Thady, priest of Lismore diocese, detainer of vicarages of Kilbarrymeaden and Rossmire, 949

Okley *see* Ockley

Okmayn, Maurice, cleric of Ossory diocese, reservation for, of canonry of Waterford and prebend of Corbally, 543

Oknyllay, Gillasius, detainer of Killard vicarage, 449
......, *cf.* OKinneally

Okwym, William, canon of Cloyne, papal mandatary, 514
......, *cf.* OKeeffe

Okynala, alias of Butler, William, *q.v.*
......, *cf.* OKinneally

Okynayth, Edmund, cleric of Killaloe diocese, to have vicarage of Kilbarron, 511

Okyneala *see* OKinneally

Okyngrigayn *see* OKendrigan

Okynmede *see* OKennedy

Olacgacy, Olaegarii *see* OLeary

Olaenayn', William, ostensible priest of Killaloe diocese, detainer of rectory of Dorrha, 230
......, *cf.* OLoonan

OLahiff (Ylathym), Thady, prior of the Augustinian monastery of Rathkeale, death of, 944
......, *and see* Oflayterah; *cf.* OFlahy

Olamyr, Donat, ostensible priest of Leighlin diocese, detainer of vicarage of Timahoe, 576

Olarnyn, Thomas, to be provided anew to vicarage in Tuam diocese, 1199

OLasty (Olaste), John, canon of Raphoe and commendatory abbot of Assaroe, death of, 943
......, *cf.* OLosty

Old Craig *see* Craig

Old Sodbury *see* Sodbury

Olealonyr, Maurus, detainer of rectory of Coolcraheen, 645

OLeary (Olacgacy, Olaegarii), Dermot, detainer of vicarage of Brinny, 67
......, Matthew, detainer of vicarage of Inishannon, 71

Olerahur, Patrick, to have vicarage erected into canonry and benefice into prebend, Dublin and Leighlin dioceses, 1121

Oliviero, [cardinal] bishop of Sabina *see* [Caraffa], Oliviero

Ologan' *see* OLongan

Olonayn *see* OLoonan

OLongan (Ilongayn, Ologan'), David, canon of Clonfert, papal mandatary, 492, 513
......, Maurice, rector of Aghinagh, to be canon and prebendary of Cloyne, 15

OLoonan (Olonayn), Dermot, detainer of rectory of Terryglass, 16
......, John, detainer of rectory of Finnoe, 16
......, *cf.* Olaenayn'

OLosty *cf.* OLasty

Olstoon *see* Alveston

Omachar *see* OMeagher

Omachayn, Laurence, detainer of vicarage of Clonloghan, 313, 652

OMacken *cf.* Omachayn

OMahony (Omahuna, Omothuna, Oniahuna), David, detainer of the rectory of the ecclesiastical fief of Schull, 257
......, Dermot, detainer, with Thady OMurphy, of canonry and prebend of Kilbrogan in Cork cathedral, 252
......, Matthew, detainer, with John OHerlihy, of the deanery of Cork, 258

OMalley (Amalle, Omallay, Ymaylle), Cormac, cleric of Tuam diocese, to have prebend of 'Tilmadim', Umall, Upper and Lower, and vicarage of Oughaval united thereto, 165
......, John, canon of Clonfert, papal mandatary, 819
......, Rory, canon of Tuam, papal mandatary, 165

OManahan *cf.* Homana'

Omanin *see* OMannin

Omanna', John, canon of Cork, papal mandatary, 231

OMannin (Omanin, Omanuyn, Omaynyn, Ymarryn), Donald, cleric of Clonfert diocese, to have vicarage of Creagh, 819
......, Malachy, canon of Clonfert, papal mandatary, 166
......, ..., cleric of Tuam diocese, to be provided anew to canonry of Clonfert and prebend of 'Ycluelin', 167
......, ..., ..., to have vicarage of Killoscobe united anew to his canonry and prebend, 167

OMannin (*contd*)
......, ..., ..., relatives of, 167
......, ..., canon of Tuam, papal mandatary, 123
......, *cf.* Omaytin; Omuynayn

Omaynnachan *see* OMoynihan

Omaynyn *see* OMannin

Omaytin, Malachy, scholar and prospective cleric of Clonfert diocese, to have Augustinian monastery of B. Mary, Clonfert *in commendam*, 229
......, *cf.* OMannin

OMeagher (Omachar, Omeakir, Omecayr, Ymecayr), Dermot, canon of Killaloe, papal mandatary, 161
......, John, cleric of Killaloe diocese, to have canonry of Cashel and prebend of Killea with vicarages of Bourney *alias* Ikerrin and Roscrea united thereto, 14
......, ..., father of, 14
......, Thady, vicar of 'Kylmemanch', to be canon of Cashel and have his vicarage erected into prebend, 350
......, ..., *cf.* Omuchyre, Thady
......, William, detainer of canonry of Cashel and prebend of Killea, 14

OMeehan (Onuchan), Cornelius, canon of Emly, papal mandatary, 404
......, *cf.* Ymukcan

OMelaghlin *cf.* Omilaolayn

Omey (Omy, Oue) [co. Galway], parish church of, vicarage of, 126, 827
......, ..., ..., particle of Omey to be appropriated to, 827
......, ..., ..., to be erected, with appropriated particle into prebend of Tuam, 827
......, particle of, within the parish of Omey, 827
......, ..., pertaining to rectory of Inishmaine, 827
......, ..., ..., ..., to be appropriated to vicarage of Omey, 827

Omiday, Robert, detainer of vicarage of Dungarvan, 787

Omilaolayn, Terence, cleric of Cloyne [*recte* Clonmacnois] diocese, 226
......, ..., ..., to have deanery of Cloyne [*recte* Clonmacnois] with vicarage of Ballyloughloe united thereto, 226
......, *cf.* OMelaghlin

Omilkerayn, Maurice, priest of Elphin diocese, to have vicarage of Tumna, 947

Omillayn (Omyllayn), Edmund, cleric of Leighlin diocese, to be canon of Leighlin and have the vicarage of ?Killeen erected into a prebend, with the vicarages of ?Curragh and Killeshin united thereto, 982
......, Henry, detainer of vicarage of Killeshin, 982
......, *cf.* ONolan

Omillon, Omilon *see* OMullan

Omogan, John, ostensible priest of Derry diocese, detainer of vicarage of ?*Cell cairill* [*now* Termonamongan], 448
......, *cf.* OMongan

Omogri, John, canon of Tuam, papal mandatary, 123

Omolain, Omolan *see* OMullan

OMolan *cf.* Mohl'an

Omolon *see* OMullan

Omona, Rervallus, to have vicarage and rectory in Leighlin diocese, 1125
......, *cf.* OMore

OMongan (Omongayn), Donat, detainer, with John de Courcy, of the church of ?Ballymountain, 255
......, *cf.* Omogan

Omorchu *see* OMurphy

OMore *cf.* Omona

Omori, Bernard, canon of Elphin, papal mandatary, 947, 995
......, *cf.* OMurray

Omoriele *see* OMurilly

OMorrissey (Omorisa, Omorissa, Omurgissa, Omurrysse), Willerius, to have vicarage in Waterford diocese, 1153
......, William, canon of Derry, papal mandatary, 448
......, ..., canon of Ossory, papal judge delegate, litigation before, 989
......, ..., ..., papal mandatary, 350
......, ..., detainer of vicarage of Kilcolumb, 787
......, ..., to have several vicarages in Lismore [and Ossory?] dioceses united to his canonry [of Ossory?], 1150

Omothuna *see* OMahony

OMoynihan (Omaynnachan), Rory, cleric of Ossory diocese, to be canon, then prior, of the Augustinian monastery of Seirkieran, 930

Omuchyre, Thady, canon of Cashel, papal mandatary, 787
......, ..., *cf.* OMeagher, Thady

Omukean, Matheus, ostensible priest of Cashel diocese, detainer of vicarage of ?Kilcomenty, 404

Omulcaryl, Omulcaryll *see* OMulkerrill

Omulgayn, Maurice, detainer of vicarage of ?Kilmaleery, 313

Omulinochory *see* OMulmohery

OMulkerrill (Omulcaryl, Omulcaryll, Omulkaryll', Omullcaryl), Charles, canon of Tuam, papal mandatary, 69, 73, 75, 122, 163, 164; *cf.* 330
......, ..., priest of Clonfert diocese, to have

OMulkerrill (*contd*)
vicarage, called stipend, in Tuam cathedral, 123
......, ..., ..., subdelegate of papal judge delegate, 167

OMullally (Omullalyd, Omullayd), John, canon of Clonfert, papal mandatary, 166
......, Magonius, canon of Clonfert, papal mandatary, 122, 166

OMullan (Omillon, Omilon, Omolain, Omolan, Omolon), Cristinus, canon of Clonmacnois [*sometimes erroneously* Cloyne], papal mandatary, 226, 229, 230
......, Thomas, canon of Tuam, papal mandatary, 833, 835-837

OMullanphy (Omulleampuyll), Maurice, cleric of Cashel diocese, to have vicarage of Templeachally *alias* Callathamery, 783

Omullayd *see* OMullally

Omullcaryl *see* OMulkerrill

Omulleampuyll *see* OMullanphy

OMulmohery (Omulinochory, Omulmochere, Omulmothore), Gillatius, canon of Kilmore, papal mandatary, 940
......, Odo, canon of Kilmore, papal mandatary, 821, 831, 940

OMulwarden (Omulvardayn) *alias* OBrophy (Abrohe, Obrohe), Donat, ostensible monk and detainer of the Cistercian monastery of Kilcooly, 574
......, John, cleric of Cashel diocese, sometime student, 574
......, ..., ..., ..., to be monk, then abbot, of the Cistercian monastery of Kilcooly and have vicarage of Odagh united thereto, 574

Omurcha *see* OMurphy

Omurchele *see* OMurilly

Omurchu, Omurchw, Omurckw *see* OMurphy

Omurgissa *see* OMorrissey

Omurhu *see* OMurphy

OMurilly (Omoriele, Omurrale, Omurchele), John, canon of Cork, to have vicarage of Corrsruhara united to his canonry and prebend, 254
......, Renaldus, canon of Cork, papal mandatary, 231
......, ..., detainer of canonry and prebend of Dromdaleague in Cork cathedral, 257
......, *cf.* OHurley

OMurphy (Omorchu, Omurcha, Omurchu, Omurchw, Omurckw, Omurhu, Omwrhow, Ymirechu, Ymurchu, Ymurchw, Ymurhu), Cornelius, cleric of Cork diocese, to be canon of Cloyne and have vicarage of Macroom erected into prebend, 823
......, Donald, canon of Cork, papal mandatary, 822
......, ..., to have vicarage in Cork diocese united to canonry [of Cork], 1313
......, Donat, canon of Cloyne, papal mandatary, 159, 824
......, Edmund, canon of Cork, papal mandatary, 67, 70, 71
......, ..., canon of Cloyne, papal mandatary, 128, 159, 160
......, John, late rector of Bohola, 828
......, ..., cleric of Clonfert diocese, vicar of Cullen, 359
......, ..., ..., ..., to have vicarage of Nohaval-Daly united to vicarage of Cullen, 359
......, Philip, cleric of Cloyne diocese, to be canon of Cloyne and have vicarage of Templevalley erected into prebend, 160
......, Thady, vicar of Templevalley, death of, 160
......, ..., detainer, with Dermot OMahony, of canonry and prebend of Kilbrogan in Cork cathedral, 252

OMurphy (*contd*)
......, Thomas, canon of Tuam, papal mandatary, 384
......, ..., detainer of vicarage of Kilmalkedar, 993

Omurrale *see* OMurilly

OMurray *cf.* Omori

Omurrysse *see* OMorrissey

Omuynayn, Magonius, detainer of vicarage, called stipend, of Tuam cathedral, 122
......, *cf.* OMannin

Omwrhow *see* OMurphy

Omy *see* Omey

Omyllayn *see* Omillayn

ONewell (Newel), Thomas, detainer of rectory of Ballyshannon, 934

ONeylan (Oneyllayn), Thomas, canon of Kilfenora, papal mandatary, 815, 820

Oniahuna *see* OMahony

Onilleayn, David, canon of Tuam, papal mandatary, 828
......, *cf.* OCullinane

ONolan (Ymillam), Donat, cleric of Leighlin diocese, to have possessions of the grange of Ballon belonging to the priory of Glascarrig in farm, 981
......, *cf.* Omillayn

ONoonan (Ohunwnan, Ohynwayn', Yhunwnan), Donald, detainer of vicarage of Killagholehane, 824
......, John, cleric of Cloyne diocese, to have vicarage of Tullylease, 156
......, Richard, cleric of Limerick diocese, to be canon of Limerick, have vicarage of Killeedy erected into prebend, and have Killagholehane vicarage united thereto, 824
......, Thady, detainer of vicarage of

ONoonan (*contd*)
Tullylease, 156
......, *cf.Óh Ionmhaineáin*

Onuchan *see* OMeehan

Onyrtonlongevyle *see* Orton Longueville

OPhelan (Felayn, Fellaim, Ffelayn, Flellain, Flellayn, Offaellayn, Offelathayn, Offellayn, Offyellan, Yffaclaij), Eugene, minister of the Trinitarian house of Adare, death of, 221
......, Maurice, canon of Limerick, papal mandatary, 485, 486, 542, 543, 938, 982
......, ..., detainer of vicarage of Killeedy, 824
......, ..., to have regular priory in Limerick diocese, 1284
......, ..., priest of Limerick diocese, detainer of priorship of the Augustinian monastery of Rathkeale, 944

Oqueronaten', Maurice, to have deanery of Kildare, 1213

Oquervalan *see* OCarolan

OQuilty (Ocaeylte, Ocayllt), Laurence, canon of Derry, papal mandatary, 361
......, Odo, canon of Derry, papal mandatary, 253
......, *cf.* OKielt

OQuinn (Ocwynd), Roderick, priest of Killaloe diocese, detainer of vicarage of [Killinaboy], 651

Oranmore (Surmiricor) [co. Galway], prebend of in Annaghdown cathedral, 935

Orauri, John, canon of Tuam, papal mandatary, 833
......, *cf.* ORuane

Orchard Portman (Orchod) [Som], chapel of St Michael, 174

ORegan (Orygayn), Runaldus, detainer of vicarage of Corrsruhara, 254

OReilly (Orelly), Cormac, vicar of Kilcolumb, to have Benedictine monastery of St John the Evangelist outside the walls of Waterford *in commendam*, 227

ORiordan (Ormrdayn), Cornelius, detainer of vicarage of Drishane *alias* Kilmeedy, 540

Orkney, [cathedral] church of [*at* Kirkwall, co. Orkney and Shetland], chapter of, consent of to appointment of coadjutor, 549
......, ..., ..., conclusion to, 549
......, ..., canon of *see* Stewart, Edward

......, bishop of, fruits and emoluments arising within archdeaconry of Shetland customarily received by, 552
......, ..., collation etc. of benefices within archdeaconry of Shetland pertaining to, 552
......, ..., *see* [Painter], Andrew; Stewart, Edward
......, coadjutor of *see* Stewart, Edward
......, church of, subject to the archbishop of St Andrews, 551
......, ..., vassals of, conclusion to, 549

......, city and diocese of, clergy of, conclusion to, 549
......, ..., people of, conclusion to, 549
......, diocese of, places in *see* Sanday; Shetland

[Orkney and Shetland, co. of], places in *see* Kirkwall; Sanday; Shetland

Orme, Henry, provision of to monastery in St Andrews diocese, 1318
......, ..., absolution of preliminary to provision, 1320
......, ..., faculty for consecration of, 1319

Ormeston (Urmeston', Urmyston'), Thomas, rector of Lolworth, 207

Ormeston (*contd*)
......, ..., rector of Brington and incumbent of Lolworth, 685
......, ...[*another*?], vicar of a parish church [name lost], litigant, 990
......, *cf.* Urmston

Ormrdayn *see* ORiordan

Ormsby, North [Lincs], Gilbertine priory of, prior of, presentation by, 30
......, ..., ..., ..., presentation of person for vicarage of Utterby pertains to, 30

ORodehan *cf.* Orodochan

Orodochan, Thady, canon of Ardagh, papal mandatary, 537

ORonan (Oronayn), James, ostensible cleric of Limerick diocese, detainer of vicarage of ?Ballycahane, 942

Orsini (de Orsiniis), Giovanni Battista, cardinal priest of SS Giovanni e Paolo, suit before, 1015
......, Orsino, notary of the pope, provision of to St Mary's, Stazzema, 697

Ortega de Gomiel, Johannes, letters expedited by, as *abbreviator de parco maiori*:
Jo. Ortega, 21, 23, 24, 31-40, 42, 85, 91-94, 119, 120, 148, 154, 157, 173, 174, 176, 193, 195, 209, 215-220, 222, 253, 264, 267 (*Ortega*), 268 (*Ortega*), 270, 290-292, 296, 297, 299, 302, 309, 316, 328, 329, 336, 337, 352, 382, 419, 434, 510, 524, 529, 543, 572, 575, 616, 661, 669, 681, 691, 696, 734, 764, 782, 791, 793, 811, 839
......, ..., ..., as apostolic secretary:
Jo. Ortega, 244

Orton (Ortons), Thomas, chaplain in St Michael's, Coventry, 496, 715

Orton Longueville (Onyrtonlongevyle) [*also called* Overton Longvile, Hunts], parish church of, rector of, 45

ORuane *cf.* Orauri

Oruya, Eugene, detainer of prebend of Clonallan in Dromore cathedral, 235

Oryac *alias* Suchyhyn *see* Creagh

Orygayn *see* ORegan

OScanlan (Oskanlay'), Cornelius, detainer of vicarage of Schull, 257

Oscara (Oschara), David, canon of Tuam, papal mandatary, 384, 402
......, *cf.* OGara

OScingin (Oscingyn), Peter, canon of Elphin, papal mandatary, 836, 837

Oscolayn, Dermot, priest of Ardfert diocese, detainer of vicarage of Dromtariff, 125

OScully (Yscolay), John, cleric of Cloyne diocese, to be canon of Ardfert and have Kilmeen vicarage erected into prebend, 250
......, *cf.* Oscolayn

Oscyiridan *see* OSheridan

Osega *see* OShea

Oselveston' *see* Owston

Oseyndan *see* OSheridan

OShaughnessy (Occhanassoy), Nemeas, detainer of canonry of Kilmacduagh and prebend of Kinvarra, of chantry in Kilmacduagh cathedral, and of the vicarage of Beagh *alias* Cliath-Ceallayd, 933

OShea (Osega), Cornelius, ostensible priest of Ardfert diocese, detainer of vicarage of ?Killinane, 360

OSheedy *cf.* MacNamara *alias* Scyda; MacNamara, James *alias* Syda

OSheehan (Osicham), Dermot, detainer of Kilshannig vicarage, 74
......, *cf.* Ossian

OSheridan (Oscyiridan, Oseyndan, Osidereau, Yscrydan', Ysiridan), Fergal, cleric of Kilmore diocese, to have canonry of Kilmore and rectory of Urney erected into prebend, 538
......, ..., ..., grant to of same, impetration of, alleged subreption of, 834
......, ..., father of, rector of Urney *alias* Keadew, 834
......, Gelasius / Gellassius, canon of Kilmore, papal mandatary, 538, 834
......, ..., to have regular priory in Kilmore diocese, 1201

Osicham *see* OSheehan

Osidereau *see* OSheridan

Oskanlay' *see* OScanlan

Oslannagail, Donat, to have one vicarage united to another, Clogher diocese, 1206
......, *cf.* OFlanagan; OFlannelly

Ospelan, Ospelayn, Ospellayn *see* Spelman

Ossian, William, canon of Ossory, papal mandatary, 510
......, *cf.* OSheehan

Ossory, **[cathedral] church** of [*at* Kilkenny, co. Kilkenny], deanery of, 575
......, ..., dean of, papal mandatary, 574, 576
......, ..., ..., *see* Comerford, Edmund
......, ..., chancellorship of, 157, 545
......, ..., ..., proposed union to, of vicarages of Pollrone and Dunkitt and rectory of Kilcraggan, 157
......, ..., ..., ..., of Dunkitt vicarage and Kilcraggan rectory, grant of, impetration of, alleged subreption of, 545
......, ..., chancellors of *see* Brennagh, Hoellus; Clinton, William; Mohl'an,

Ossory, **[cathedral] church** (*contd*)
John
......, ..., chapter of, to be summoned over erection of canonry and prebend, 645
......, ..., canons of *see* Comerford, William; Ffyhan', William; Grant, John; MacKilpatrick, John; Mohl'an, John; OHealy, John; OMorrissey, William; Ossian, William; Shortall, James; Tobin, John; *and see* Purcell, Richard
......, ..., prebends in *see* Coolcraheen; St Maul's

......, **bishop** of, or his vicar general, collation by, 157
......, ..., to be summoned over erection of canonry and prebend, 645
......, ..., papal judge delegate, 1005
......, ..., papal mandatary, 930
......, official of, papal mandatary, 545
......, church of, archdeacon of, papal mandatary, 786

......, **diocese** of, persons of *see* Cantwell, John; OBergin, Cornelius, Malachy and Thady; OCahill, Cornelius and Philip; OCarroll, Odo; OClery, Dermot; OCorregan', Thomas; OHedian, James; Okmayn, Maurice; Olealonyr, Maurus; Omiday, Robert; OMoynihan, Rory; OReilly, Cormac
......, ..., places in *see* Aghmacart; Aglish *or* Aglishmartin; Ballytarsney; Callan; Clashacrow; Coolcraheen; Dungarvan; Dunkitt; Inistioge; Jerpoint; Kells; Kilbride; Kilcolumb; Kilcraggan [*in* Ballytarsney]; Kilkenny; Kilmanagh; Odagh; Pollrone; Rosconnell; Seirkieran; Thomastown

Ossquean *see* Uskane

Ossullewayn *see* OSullivan

Ostia [*in* province of Rome, Italy], letters dated at, 75, 123, 127, 571

OSullivan (Ossullewayn, Osulenayn, Osuyllybayn', Vsulebayn, Ysulebayn), Dermot, canon of Ardfert, papal mandatary, 513

OSullivan (*contd*)
......, Eugene, canon of Cork, papal mandatary, 15
......, Florence, priest of Ardfert diocese, to have vicarage of Dromtariff, 125
......, John, canon of Ardfert, papal mandatary, 362
......, ..., cleric of Ardfert diocese, holder of vicarage of 'Kylloeyn', 360
......, ..., ..., ..., to be canon of Ardfert and have the vicarage of ?Killinane erected into a prebend with the vicarage of 'Kylloeyn' united thereto, 360

Os..ayn, Davit, vicar of *Cluain Comarda*, death of, 942
......, *cf.* Offaeyn; Offahym

Otonconnan, Otontenynd *see* OConcannon

Otontuyr *see* OConnor

OToole *cf.* Otuocayll'

Otterburn (Ottirburn), Gilbert, rector of Slains, death of, 50

Otto [Candidus] and Ottobuono [Fieschi], legates of the apostolic see in the kingdom of England, constitutions of [*regularly mentioned in the notwithstanding clauses of English (and Welsh) letters; only noticed by the Calendar in exceptional cases*], 22, 97, 136, 273, 274, 339, 445, 446, 454, 632, 717, 808, 817, 861, 958, 963

Ottwrby *see* Utterby

Otuocayll' (Otugayll'), Donald, canon of Derry, papal mandatary, 253, 361
......, *cf.* OToole

Oue *see* Omey

Oughaval (Vachamayll) [co. Mayo], parish church of, vicarage of, to be united to prebend of 'Tilmadim', Umall, Upper and Lower, 165

Oundle (Undyll' *alias* Oundyll') [Northants], parish church of, union of, to the Benedictine monastery of Peterborough, 425
......, ..., vicar of, portion for, 425

Outer Hebrides *see* Lewis

Outeragh (Woctherratha) [co. Tipperary], parish church of, rectory of, 385
......, ..., ..., patrons of, 385

Overton (Overton') [Hants], parish church of, 346

Overton Longville *see* Orton Longueville

Overwalop *see* Wallop, Over

Owen Ap D[avi]d, of St David's diocese, dispensed for plurality, 1065

Owen ap Rhys (Apris), union for, of one of his parish churches to the other, 1263

Owston (Oselveston') [Leics], [Augustinian] monastery of, abbot of, papal judge delegate, 46

Oxenbregge, John, vicar of Cullompton and vicar of Icklesham, 262

Oxford [Oxon], vill of, 176
......, parish church of St Ebba the Virgin, rector of, 481
......, parish church of St Martin, 957
......, Lincoln College of B. Mary at, patron of, 176
......, ..., statutes and ordinances of, faculty for confirmation and approval of, 176
......, university of, student at *see* FitzMaurice, Edmund

[Oxford, co. of], places in *see* Banbury; Bruern; Checkendon; Cropredy; Cuxham; Dorchester; Easington; Eynsham; Hanwell; Henley on Thames; Hethe; Heyford Warren; Lewknor; Milton Manor; Northmoor; Oxford; Stoke Talmage; Thame; Woodstock; Wootton

P

Page, Richard, rector of Monkland, 289
......, ..., canon and prior of the Augustinian priory of Ivychurch, 283

Paglesham (Pakelhesham) [Essex], parish church of, 670

[Painter], Andrew, bishop of Orkney, 549-552
......, ..., ..., age and infirmity of, 549
......., ..., ..., death or resignation of contemplated, 550, 551
......, ..., ..., consent of, to appointment of coadjutor, 549
......, ..., ..., ..., to assignment of fruits customarily received by, 552
......, ..., ..., ..., to assignment of collation etc. of benefices pertaining to, 552
......, ..., ..., vicar general of *see* Stewart, Edward
......., ..., ..., coadjutor of *see* Stewart, Edward
......, *cf.* Pannetter; Panter; Paynter; Payntoure

Paisley [co. Renfrew], Cluniac monastery of, 61
......, ..., cession and commend of, 63
......, ..., abbot of, papal mandatary, 767, 768
......, ..., ..., *see* Shaw, George and Robert
......, ..., monks of *see* Pannetter, Thomas; Shaw, George
......, ..., possessions of *see* Auchinleck; Craigie; ?Cumbray; Dalmilling; Dundonald; Glen; Largs; Lochwinnoch; Monkton; Prestwick; Riccarton; St Quivox

Pakefield (Pakefelde) [Suff], parish church of, portions of, 918
......, ..., rectors of, 918
......, ..., portioner of, 918

Pakelhesham *see* Paglesham

[de Palatio] *see* [Spinelli]

Palermo [*in* province of Palermo, Sicily], city of, person of *see* Naso, Andreas

[Pallavicini], Antoniotto, cardinal priest of S Prassede, suit before, 1015

Pannetter, Thomas, monk of the Cluniac monastery of Paisley, 27
......, cf. Painter; Paynter; Payntoure

Panter, Patrick, collation to, of the vicarage of Kilmany, 937
......, Richard, rector of Semley, 418
......, cf. Painter; Paynter; Payntoure

Papworth Everard (Papwortheverard) [Cambs], parish church of, 183

Parchis see Parkes

Paris [France], university of, student at see [de Falcutiis or Falcariis] de Cesena, Damianus

Parkeham see Parkham

Parker, John, vicar of South Benfleet, 727

Parkes (Parchis), Thomas, vicar of Mickleton, 373

Parkham (Parkeham) [Devon], parish church of, 890

Parkins, William, of Winchester diocese, dispensed for plurality, 1178

Parma [in province of Parma, Italy], diocese of, place in see Collécchio

de Parma, F. see [de Arianis] de Parma, Franciscus

Parson alias Wyllys, Richard, chaplain in Salisbury cathedral, 193

Partney (Pertenay) [Lincs], parish church of, 673

Parva Wylburgh(a)m see Wilbraham, Little

[Pas-de-Calais, France], places in see Guemps; Guînes

[Patexe, alias of Skevington], Thomas, q.v.

Patrick, [bishop-] elect of Cork and Cloyne see [Cant], Patrick

Pattoy see Potton

Patuorth' see Petworth

Paul II, letters Cum in omnibus judiciis ... of, 146, 366, 558, 765, 981
......, other letters of, 143, 502
......, renewal by, of sentences against simoniacs, 167, 846, 946

[Payne], John, bishop of Meath, 442, 927, 1005
......, ..., ..., assertion of, that the prior of Lanthony II by Gloucester and the vicars of Colp and Duleek were bound to pay the bishop of Meath, 442
......, ..., ..., adherents of, 442
......, ..., ..., litigation before, 927
......, ..., ..., case remitted to archbishop of Armagh by, 927
......, ..., ..., appeals from to the metropolitical court of Armagh, 1005
......, ..., ..., dispute of, with archbishop of Armagh over metropolitical jurisdiction, 1005

Paynter, John, vicar of Sodbury, 78
......, cf. Painter; Pannetter; Panter

Payntoure, Roger, rector of Chingford, 1036
......, cf. Painter; Pannetter; Panter; Peyntour

Pebmarsh (Pebemerche) [Essex], parish church of, 810

[Peebles and Selkirk, co. of], places in see Glenholm; Innerleithen; Skirling

de Pelegrinis, Johannes Baptista, abbreviator de parco minori, conclusions expedited by: Jo de Pelegrinis, 1029

Pelham, Furneux (Pelh(a)m ffurneux)

Pelham (*contd*)
[Hertford], parish church of, 93

Pemberton (Pimburton), John, of
Winchester diocese, dispensed for
plurality, 1304

Pembroke (*Penbrochia*) [co. Pembroke],
parish church of St Nicholas, 340

[Pembroke, co. of], places in *see*
Llanfallteg; Llanfyrnach; Pembroke; St
David's; Whitchurch

Pen *see* Penn

Penbrochia see Pembroke

Pendeigras *see* Prendergast

Penn (Pen) [Bucks], parish church of, vicar
of, 62

Penne [*in* province of Pescara, Italy],
bishop of, papal mandatary, 61, 63

[Penny], John, abbot of the Augustinian
monastery of B. Mary *in Pratis*,
Leicester, 904

Penryn *see* Glasney

Penton, John, of Norwich diocese,
dispensed for plurality, 1159

Penton Grafton *see* Weyhill

Pepin, king of the Franks, Benedictine
monastery of Marcilhac founded by,
196

[Peppardstown, co. Tipperary], place in *see*
Crampscastle

Percy, Nicholas, chantry of, in Holy
Trinity's, [Coventry], 506

de Pereriis, William, the late, papal
chaplain and auditor of causes of the
apostolic palace, litigation before, 928

Perott (Perot), John, rector of Wouldham
and archdeacon of Colchester, 502

Perrins (Peryns), Robert, cleric of Coventry
and Lichfield diocese, 690

Pershore (Pershoure) [Worcs], parish
church of, 978

Pertenay *see* Partney

[Perth, co. of], places in *see* Crieff;
Dunblane; Dunkeld; Fortingall; Scone;
Weem

Pertinendam *see* Pitmedden

Peryns *see* Perrins

Pesaro (*Pisauren.*) [*in* province of Pesaro e
Urbino, Italy], A[loysius bishop of] *see*
[Capra], Aloysius

Peston *alias* Conell', Gilbert, monk of the
Benedictine monastery of St Peter,
Westminster, 363
......, ..., ..., ..., to have vicarage of
Sleaford anew, 363
......, ..., ..., ..., present at Roman curia,
363

Peterborough [Northants], parish church of,
714
......, Benedictine monastery of, 425
......, ..., abbot of, indult for, to use mitre,
425
......, ..., ..., ..., to give benediction etc.,
425
......, ..., abbot and convent of, indult for, to
farm out fruits, 425
......, ..., ..., foundations by in Stamford-
Baron, of hospital of St John the Baptist
with chapel of St Thomas the Martyr,
of hospital with leper house of St Giles,
and of [Benedictine] nunnery of St
Michael, 425
......, ..., abbot and convent and sacristy of,
confirmation of right of, 425
......, ..., privileges etc. of, grants and
confirmations of, 425

Peterborough (*contd*)

......, ..., union to, of the parish churches of North Collingham, Bringhurst, and Oundle, 425

......, ..., first founders of, 425

......, ..., gift to, of dwellings in Stamford-Baron, 425

Petinveyn *see* Pittenweem

Petmedan, Petmedane *see* Pitmedden

de Petra, Galeatius, registry scribe, 8 *note*, 9 *note*

Petty [cos. Inverness and Nairn]-Brackley [*in* Petty, cos. Inverness and Nairn], prebend of in Moray cathedral, fruits of, appropriation of residue of to chapel royal, Stirling, 768

Petworth (Patuorth') [Sussex], parish church of, rector of, 33

Petynveymen, Petynveyn *see* Pittenweem

Peverell (Peverell'), John, monk of the Cluniac monastery of Bermondsey, 280

Peynthwyn (Peyntwhyn, Peyntwyn, Peyntwyn'), Hugh, archdeacon of (the church of) Canterbury, 8, 28, 29, 46, 197

......, ..., cleric, 906

......, ..., auditor of causes and matters of John [Morton], archbishop of Canterbury, etc., litigation before, 906

......, ..., auditor of causes and matters of the audience of the archbishop of Canterbury, etc., litigation before, 987

......, ..., ostensible commissary or auditor of the archbishop of Canterbury, ?proceedings by, 924

......, ..., commissary of John [Morton], archbishop of Canterbury, etc., litigation before, 8, 28, 29, 46, 197

......, ..., auditor of the chapter of Canterbury *sede vacante*, litigation before, 906

......, ..., ostensible steward or official of the

Peynthwyn (*contd*)

prior and chapter of Canterbury *sede vacante, ex officio* proceedings of, 529

Peyntour *cf.* Payntoure

Peyntwhyn, Peyntwyn, Peyntwyn' *see* Peynthwyn

De Phano, V see [de Lanciarinis] de Fano, Ulixes

Philip (Phelype), David, vicar of St Nicholas's, Pembroke, 340

......, *cf.* Philpson

Philip, late bishop of Emly *see* [OCahill], Philip

Philipson *cf.* Philpson

Philpson (Philpi), Henry, of St Andrews diocese, appeal of, 971

......, *cf.* Philip

Phympton' *see* Plympton

Pichard (Picherdi), Robert, union for, of parish church to his canonry, York diocese, 1169

Picher, William, rector of Buckland St Mary, 353

Picherd, Richard, of London diocese, dispensed for plurality, 1082

Picherdi *see* Pichard

Pickton (Picton, Pykton'), John, cleric of Canterbury diocese, 113

......, ..., of Canterbury diocese, dispensed for plurality, 1241

Piddiltouon *see* Puddletown

[Pigot], Thomas, abbot of the Benedictine monastery of Chertsey, 602, 604, 605

......, ..., ..., provision of to the bishopric of Bangor, 602

......, ..., ..., absolution of preliminary to provision, 604

[Pigot], Thomas (*contd*)
......, ..., [bishop-] elect of Bangor, faculty for consecration of, 603
......, ..., ..., to retain Chertsey *in commendam*, 605

Pikeman *see* Pykeman

Pilton (Pylton') [Som], parish church of, 354

Pimburton *see* Pemberton

Pinchbeck (Pinchibek), John, rector of Aldborough, 912

Pindagras *see* Prendergast

Pinkerton [*in* Dunbar, co. Haddington], [canonry and prebend of in the collegiate church of Dunbar], 781

Piombino [*in* province of Livorno, Italy], letters dated at, 764, 779, 829

Pipunistre *see* Pitminster

Pisauren., A see Pesaro

Pitimuster *see* Pitminster

Pitmedden (Pertinendam, Petmedan, Petmedane) [*in* Udny, co. Aberdeen], tithes of pertaining to Ellon parish church, 144, 793, 928

Pitminster (Pipunistre, Pitimuster, Pytynynstre) [Som], (parish) church of, 174, 461
......, place in *see* Blagdon

Pittemyster, alias of Hooper, Richard, *q.v.*

Pittenweem (Petinveyn, Petynveymen, Petynveyn), alias of May, *q.v.*

[Pittington, co. Durham], place in *see* Sherburn

Pittuam *see* Puttenham

Pius II, letters of, 502

de Planca, Paulus, *abbreviator de parco maiori*, letters expedited by:
P de Planca, 20, 179, 185, 190, 213, 230, 272, 643, 778, 780, 815, 818-820, 864, 872, 879, 914 (*P Planca*), 928, 933, 986, 1004

Plemen, Richard, canon of Tuam, 384, 401, 402
......, ..., ..., papal mandatary, 402
......, ..., ..., to have canonry of Tuam and prebend of Kilcurnan, 401
......, ..., ..., to have vicarage of Tagheen anew, 384
......, *cf.* Fleming

Plemyn, alias of Fleming, Richard, *q.v.*

Plominer, Christopher, rector of Skirbeck, 562

Plumbland (Plumlonde) [Cumb], parish church of, 523

Plumstead (Plumsted) [Kent], parish church of, 494

Plunket (Pluncket), Christopher, layman of Meath diocese, litigant, 927
......, ..., ..., marriage of to Catherine Puscon, 927
......, Robert, scholar of Meath diocese, 18

Pluttinger, John, of Norwich diocese, dispensed for plurality, 1198

Plympton (Phympton') [*in* Plympton St Mary, Devon], Augustinian priory of, prior and convent of, presentation of person for parish church of Exminster pertains to, 456
......, ..., ..., presentation by, 456
......, ..., ..., right of presentation of, inquiry into, 456

Podynger, John, rector of Aldham, 864

Pokyswell *see* Poxwell

Pollesholt *see* Poulshot

Pollrone (Polruan) [co. Kilkenny], parish church of, vicarage of, to be united to chancellorship of Ossory, 157

Polum *see* Poolham

Poncetus *see* Ponzettus

Pontefract [Yorks], Cluniac priory of, 92
......, ..., immediately subject to the Roman church, 397
......, ..., priors of, indult for, to use mitre etc., 397
......, ..., prior of *see* Flint, John

Pontesbury, Edward, rector of St Andrew Hubbard, London, 969
......, *cf.* Spoutesbury

[?Pontisbury], Richard, abbot of the Augustinian monastery of Haughmond, 686
......, ..., ..., faculty to, for himself and his successors, to use mitre etc. 686

Ponzettus (Poncetus, Ponzectus, Ponzetus, Ponzzettus), (master) Fer(di)nandus, cleric of the apostolic camera, 382, 996
......, ..., secretary of the pope, 382
......, ..., abbreviator [*de parco minori*] of apostolic letters, 616
......, ..., scriptor [*apostolicus*], 382, 616, 855, 996, 1001
......, ..., notary of the pope, 1001
......, ..., familiar of the pope, 382, 855, 1001
......, ..., chaplain of the pope, 382, 996
......, ..., cleric of Florence, 382, 996
......, ..., canon and prebendary of the church of the Holy Trinity, Speyer, resignation of, 1001
......, ..., to have the Camaldolese monastery of B. Mary, d'Adelmo *in commendam*, 382
......, ..., provision of to the parish church *de Cassano*, diocese of Nocera, 996
......, ..., (continual commensal) familiars of *see* Fabri, Johannes; Goler, Wolffgangus; Mangneri, Antonius

Poolham (Polum) [*in* Woodhall, Lincs], chapel of, erection of baptismal font in, 379
......, ..., chaplain in, nomination of, 379
......, ..., ..., admission of, 379
......, ..., mother church of *see* Edlington
......, field of, 379
......, temporal lord of *see* Barkeworth, Robert; Thimbleby, Richard

Porcel, Porcell *see* Purcell

Porlock (Pornoke) [Som], parish church of, rector of, 4

Porol *see* Purcell

de la Porta, Dominicus, regent of the chancery, correction of register ordered by, 972

Portell *see* Purcell

Porter, John, vicar of Tirley, 10
......, Thomas, layman of Worcester diocese, litigant, 29

Portmen' *alias* Ennosmeon *see* Inishmaine

Potter, Laurence, rector of Mavesyn Ridware, 455

Potton (Pattoy) [Beds], Sutton near, *q.v.*

Poulshot (Pollesholt) [Wilts], parish church of, 98

Power (Pwer), John, cleric of Cloyne diocese, to have anew canonry of Cloyne and prebend of 'Ferrebiythi' with rectory of Inch united thereto, 1000
......, Thomas, to have one vicarage in Lismore diocese united to another, 1120

Poxwell (Pokyswell), Robert, of Norwich diocese, dispensed for plurality, 1131

de Pral, Walter, property gifted to Taunton priory by, 174

Premichiam *see* Bermingham

Prendergast (Pendeigras, Pindagras, Prindragas, Pymd(..)gas), David, canon of Tuam, papal mandatary, 384
......, ..., ..., deanery of Mayo united as a rectory to his canonry, 402
......, ..., ..., to have deanery of Mayo and vicarages of Balla and St Gerald, Mayo, united thereto, 402
......, Miler, to have vicarage and a church without cure, Tuam diocese, 1207
......, ..., canon of the Augustinian monastery of B. Michael, Mayo, 384
......, ..., ..., ..., commendatory vicar of Tagheen, cession of, 384
......, Patrick, ostensible cleric or priest of Ferns, *de facto* collation to, of vicarage of Rathaspick, 192
......, Richard, canon of Tuam, papal mandatary, 402

Preston (Preston') [Suff], parish church of, 953

Preston, William, vicar of Newburn, 842
......, *cf.* Puscon

Prestwick (Prestwik) [*now* Monkton and Prestwick, co. Ayr], church of, fruits of pertaining to Cluniac monastery of Paisley, grant of, 63
......, *and see* Monkton

Prindragas *see* Prendergast

[Prior, co. Kerry], place in *see* Ballinskelligs

Probus [Corn], parish church of, 285

Prowse (Prons), John, prior of the Augustinian priory of Taunton, 174, 1108
......, ..., ..., indulged to retain portable altar, 1108
......, ..., ..., indulged to use pontifical *insignia*, 1109

Prud, John, rector of Parkham, 890

Puccius, Laurentius, *abbreviator de parco maiori*, letters expedited by:
L *Patius* ,2
L *Pucceus*, 654
L *Puccius*, 25, 26, 44-46, 77-79, 81, 84, 95-107, 109-111, 113, 114, 118, 130-135, 138-143, 149-153, 172, 175, 177, 178, 180, 184, 194, 197, 198, 201, 204-206, 208, 214, 223, 224, 233, 238-242, 247, 261, 266, 298, 314, 315, 318-326, 333-335, 338, 340-345, 347-349, 354, 355, 358, 365, 366, 372-374, 387-389, 394, 406, 410-412, 420, 426-428, 445, 446, 450, 451, 453-459, 461-467, 469, 470, 472-474, 476, 479-481 *note*, 482, 483, 488, 491, 494-498, 502, 503, 505, 544, 547, 548, 581-583, 591-601, 612-615, 617-619, 624-628, 642, 653, 656, 694, 701, 707, 711-713, 715, 716, 723-726, 729, 730, 732, 733, 735-741, 744-747, 750-760, 762, 766, 770-775, 777, 779, 792, 812, 814, 843, 844, 847, 854-859, 861-863, 866, 868-870, 875, 876, 880, 883-891, 894-900, 903, 905-907, 910, 916-921, 924, 927, 929, 963, 964, 971, 973, 977, 982, 985, 987-991, 1001, 1005-1008, 1012, 1014, 1029-1031; *and see* 192 (no initial), 267 (deleted), 381 (uncertain initial), 860 (entry abandoned)
L *Pucius*, 441, 511, 698, 727, 873, 881, 893, 972; *and see* 892 (deleted)
L *Pulccius*, 107
L *Puteus*, 4
L *Putius*, 1, 3, 50, 395-398, 499-501

Puddletown (Piddiltouon) [Dors], parish church of, 722

[du Puiset *or* Pudsey], Hugh, bishop of Durham, re-foundation of Kepier hospital by, 429
......, ..., ..., foundation of Sherburn hospital by, 429

Purcell (Porcel, Porcell, Porol, Portell), Edmund, canon of Lismore, papal mandatary, 227
......, Jordan, bishop of Cork and Cloyne, death of, 610
......, ..., canon of Lismore, commissary of

Purcell (*contd*)

Thomas Purcell, bishop of Lismore, litigation before, 811

......, ..., of Lismore diocese, dispensed for plurality, 1090

......, Richard, to have vicarages in Ossory diocese united to canonry [of Ossory?], 1151

......, Thomas, bishop of Lismore, 811

......, ..., ..., commissaries of *see* OFlavin, Maurice; Purcell, Jordan

......, ..., of Lismore diocese, dispensed for plurality, 1089

Puscon, Catherine, woman of Meath diocese, litigant, 927

......, ..., ..., marriage of to Christopher Plunket, 927

......, ..., ..., appeal of, 927

......, *cf.* Preston

Putford, West (Westputtfordi) [Devon], parish church of, 239

Puttenham (Pittuam) [Surrey], parish church of, 669

Pwer *see* Power

Pye, William, rector of Birdham, 247

Pykeman (Pikeman), John, union for, of parish church in Exeter diocese to his canonry [of Bath and Wells?], 1057

Pykton' *see* Pickton

Pylton' *see* Pilton

Pym(..)gas *see* Prendergast

Pytynynstre *see* Pitminster

Q

Quarr (Luirreae) [*in* Isle of Wight], Cistercian monastery of, abbot of *see* Antony

Queen Camel (Quenecauunell) [Som], parish church of, 886

Quhite *see* White

Quin (Chovehe, Cunthy) [co. Clare], parish church of, vicarage of, to be erected into prebend in Killaloe cathedral, with vicarages of Clonloghan and ?Kilmaleery united thereto, 313

......, ..., ..., to be united to canonry of Limerick and prebend of Donaghmore, 652

Quogno, Stephen, rector of Saxlingham, 922

?Quothquan (Glenguhon') [part of *modern* Libberton, co. Lanark], parish church of, rector of, 395

Quynby, Richard, rector of Puttenham, 669

R

Rabett, Henry, layman of Norwich, 655

......, ..., Helen, deceased wife of, 655

......, ..., ..., ..., godmother to child of future wife by her first husband, 655

......, ..., future wife of *see* Chappeleyȝ, Olive

Rablanich *see* Rath

Rachel, Rachȝell' *see* Rathkeale

Ractareyn *see* Rathclarin

Radcliff (Radclif), Christopher, of York diocese, dispensed for plurality, 1110

Radeliff *alias* Radeliffput *see* Redcliff

Radnaldson' *see* Ronaldson

Rageell, Ragell' *see* Rathkeale

Ragusa (*Ragusin.*) [*or* Dubrovnik, Dalmatia], archbishop of, papal mandatary, 301, 407, 643, 778, 780, 931, 937
......, ..., *see* [de Sacchis], Johannes

Rahassbuyg *see* Rathaspick

Railstown (ville Kaylke') [co. Tipperary], church of, vicarage of, union of, to the archiepiscopal *mensa* of Cashel, 998

Rainham St Mary [Norf] *see* Raynham

Ralph, [bishop-] elect of Ascalon *see* [Heylesdon], Ralph

Ramesduncrays *see* Ramsden Crays

Ramesey *see* Ramsey [Hunts]

Ramsden Crays (Ramesduncrays) [Essex], parish church of, 744

Ramsey [Essex], parish church of, 205

Ramsey (Ramesey) [Hunts], Benedictine monastery of, abbot John of, faculty for, to promote monks and appoint a cleric as notary public, 1173
......, ..., ..., indulged to exercise *pontificalia*, 1174
......, ..., abbot of *see* [Huntington], John

Ranbino, Richard, rector of 'Dino', Lincoln diocese, 334

Ranuernach' super Cave *see* Llanfyrnach on Taff

Ranulph, bishop of Durham *see* [Flambard], Ranulph

Raphoe [co. Donegal], **[cathedral] church** of, canons of *see* MacAllen, John; MacKilbride, John; Magonghail, Roger; OLasty, John

......, **diocese** of, persons of *see* MacGellage

Raphoe, **diocese** (*contd*)
alias OGallagher, Patrick; MacKilbride, Odo; OBoyle, Donald; ODonnell, Edmund; OGallagher, Arthur, Laurence and Nigel
......, ..., places in *see* Assaroe; Inver; Killymard

Rasharkin (Roscercan) [co. Antrim], parish church of, vicarage of, 361

Rath (Rablanich) [co. Clare], prebend of in Killaloe cathedral, 649

Rathaspick (Rayasbuyc) [co. Laois], parish church of, vicarage of, to be united to vicarage of Ballycoolan, 576

Rathaspick (Rahassbuyg) [co. Wexford], parish church of, vicarage of, 192
......, ..., vicar of, 192

Rathclarin (Ractareyn) [co. Cork], parish church of, rectory of, to be united to deanery of Cork, 258
......, *see* Burren

Rathkeale (Kathgrell, Rachel, Rachʒell', Rageell, Ragell', Rattgell, Raydgaylle) [co. Limerick], Augustinian monastery of, 542, 944
......, ..., prior of, papal mandatary, 306, 938, 941, 942
......, ..., ..., *see* Aherne, Denis; Offahym, David; Oflayterah, Thady; OLahiff, Thady; OPhelan, Maurice, Ymolierayn, Gerard
......, ..., canon of *see* Aherne, Denis; Offahym, David
......, ..., procuration payable by reason of, 542

Rathlure [*an ancient name for* Maghera, co. Londonderry], bishop of *see* [?Ingleby], Thomas

Rathmuriel (Rothtmariel) [*in* Kinnethmont] and Kinnethmont (Kiawthtimonth) [co. Aberdeen], parish church of, vicarage of, dispute over, 778
......, ..., ..., fruits of, pension on, 778

Rattgell *see* Rathkeale

Raven' *see* Ravyn

Ravenna [*in* province of Ravenna, Italy], Augustinian monastery of St Mary in Portico canon of *see* [de Falcutiis *or* Falcariis] de Cesena, Damianus

Ravensthorpe (Ravensthorppe) [Northants], parish church of, 656

Ravyn (Raven'), John, rector of Shillington and incumbent of Burwell St Mary,351

Rayasbuyc *see* Rathaspick

Raydgaylle *see* Rathkeale

Rayens, Thomas, rector of Marston Moretaine, 275
......, *cf.* Raynes; Reynes

Rayner (Raynar), Martin, of Canterbury diocese, dispensed for plurality, 1294

Raynes *cf.* Rayens

Raynham (Reynham) [*modern* East Raynham *also called* Rainham St Mary, Norf], parish church of St Mary, rector of, 3

Recte, Agnes, woman of Salisbury diocese, 137
......, ..., ..., future husband of *see* Weston, Richard
......, *cf.* Rest

Reculver (Reculv') [Kent], parish church of, 490

Redcliff (Radeliff *alias* Radeliffput), part of [Bristol], *q.v.*

Reddman' *see* Redman

Rede, Thomas, rector of Carleton Rode, 771

Redford [*in* Dysart, co. Fife], place probably near *see* 'Spittale'

Redinayd, Richard, of Carlisle diocese, dispensed for plurality, 1268
......, *cf.* Redmayne

Reding *cf.* Rydyng

Redman (Reddman'), Richard, bishop of Exeter, 627-629
......, ..., ..., translation of to Ely, 627-629
......, ..., ..., absolution of preliminary to translation, 629
......, ..., ..., to take oath of fealty, 627
......, ..., ..., ..., commission over, 628
......, Walter, rector of Plumbland, 523

Redmayn, Edward, cleric of Carlisle diocese,746
......, ..., *cf.* Redmayne, Ewart

Redmayne (Redmayn), Edward, 756 *note*
......, Ewart, scholar of Carlisle diocese, 756
......, ..., *cf.* Redmayn, Edward
......, John, of Exeter diocese, dispensed for plurality, 1239
......, *cf.* Redinayd

Reeper, John, chaplain in the chapel of B. Mary the Virgin, ?Hognaston, 292

Regis, Thomas, canon of Saint-Malo, papal mandatary, 190

Reigate (Reygate) [Surrey], Augustinian priory of, prior of *see* Robson, John

Remiyan, William, rector of Sible Hedingham, 189

Rendcombe (Rendecombe) [Glos], parish church of, 813

Renfrew (Renfrow), county of, places (named) stated to be in, 63

[Renfrew, co. of], places in *see* Braidstane [*in* ?Beith]; Glenhead; Lochwinnoch; Paisley

Renfrow *see* Renfrew

Rennes [*in dép.* of Ille-et-Vilaine, France], [cathedral] church of, canon of *see* Leba', John

Re'pe, Thomas, rector of North Barsham, 726

Rerysby, John, subdeacon of York diocese, 19

Rest *cf.* Recte

Resta, [?Hieronimus], registry scribe, 8 *note*, 9 *note*, 1035

Restalrig [*in* South Leith, co. Midlothian], possibly identifiable with 'Laronde', *q.v.*

Restennet [*in* Forfar, co. Forfar], [Augustinian priory of], 781

Resynden Parva *see* Rissington, Little

Revesby (Revesbi) [Lincs], Cistercian monastery of, monk of *see* Helmsley, Henry

Reygate *see* Reigate

Reynes *cf.* Rayens

Reynham *see* Raynham

Rhodes [*an island in* the Aegean], Master and Convent of, 938

Rhys *cf.* Ris

Riccarton (Ricardton') [co. Ayr], church of, fruits of pertaining to the Cluniac monastery of Paisley, grant of, 63

Richard I, king of England, confirmation by, 425

Richard [III], king of England, good estate of, divine offices to be celebrated daily for, 292

Richard [III] (*contd*)
......, ..., wife of *see* Anne, queen of England

Richard, bishop of Durham, afterwards bishop of Winchester *see* [Fox], Richard
......, bishop of Exeter, afterwards bishop of Ely *see* [Redman], Richard
......, [bishop-] elect of Norwich *see* [Nykke], Richard
......, abbot of Haughmond *see* [?Pontisbury], Richard
......, abbot of Winchcombe *see* [Kidderminster], Richard

Richard ap David, monk of the Cistercian monastery of Whitland, 319

Richardson (Richardson'), Robert, rector of Church Stretton, 242
......, William, chaplain in London cathedral, 800

Richmond (and Derby), countess of *see* [Beaufort], Margaret

Ridware, Hamstall (Rydware Hampstall') [Staffs], parish church of, 202

Ridware, Mavesyn (Manesyn Rydware) [Staffs], parish church of, 455

Rimini [*in* province of Forlì, Italy], diocese of, place in *see* Verucchio

Ringcurran (Ryncorrain) [co. Cork], parish church of, rectory of, to be erected into prebend in Cork [cathedral] with Inishannon vicarage united thereto, 71

Ringeston, Ringeston' *see* Kingston

?Ringrone (Rygne) [co. Cork], parish church of, vicarage of, to be united to canonry and prebend of Kilbrogan in Cork cathedral, 252

Rinn-bheara (Ryndweare) [*now* Beara *or* Barrow *in modern parish of* Ardfert, co.

Rinn-bheara (*contd*)

Kerry], parish church of, rectory of *see* ?Ballingarry

......, ..., vicarage of, to be united to canonry and prebend of ?Ballingarry in Ardfert cathedral, 306

......, *cf. Eaglais na lainne alias* Ballyheige

Ripley (Riplay) [Yorks], vill of, parish church of, rector of, 143

Ripon (Ripon') [Yorks], [collegiate] church of, 182

......, ..., canons of *see* Brundholm, Richard

......, ..., prebends in *see* Studley

......, place in *see* Studley

Ripton, Abbots [Hunts], parish church of, 329

Ris, alias of Chest, Henry, *q.v.*

......, *cf.* Rhys

Riscon *see* Ruishton

Rissington, Little (Resynden Parva) [Glos], parish church of, 806

Robardis Bridge *see* Robertsbridge

Robe, river *see* Ballinrobe

[Robeen, co. Mayo] place in *see* Annagh

Robert, archbishop of Glasgow and commendator of Jedburgh *see* [Blackadder], Robert

......, bishop of Lismore *see* [Colquhoun], Robert

......, the late, bishop of Worcester *see* [Morton], Robert

......, recently abbot of Holyrood *see* [Bellenden], Robert

...... [*no surname*], rector of Checkendon, litigant, 46

Robertsbridge (Robardis Bridge) [*in* Salehurst, Sussex], Cistercian monastery of, 527, 926, 962

......, ..., abbot of, papal judge delegate, 197

Robertsbridge (*contd*)

......, ..., ..., *see* Goodwyn, John

......, ..., monk of *see* Anstyn', William; Bekeryng *alias* Sandherst, Robert

Robertson (Robertson'), Richard, vicar of Gedney, 469

......, William, of St Andrews diocese, 971

Roborough (Rouaborough') [Devon], parish church of, 89

Robson (Robson'), John, prior of the Augustinian priory of Reigate, 484

Roch *see* Roscrea

Roche (*de Rupe*) [*in* Maltby, Yorks], Cistercian monastery of, 961; *cf.* 962 *note*

......, ..., monk of *see* Smales, John

Roche, George, cleric of Cork diocese, to be archdeacon of Cork, 539

......, Peter, vicar of Ballyhay, 514

......, ..., ..., to be canon of Cloyne and prebendary of Cooliney and have his vicarage of Ballyhay united thereto, 514

......, William, ostensible abbot of the Cistercian monastery of Tracton, 67

Rochester (*Roffen.*; sometimes *Rossen.* in error) [Kent], Benedictine [**cathedral priory**] **church** of, prior of *see* Bysshope *alias* Leynham, William

......, **bishop** of, papal judge delegate, 28, 261

......, ..., papal mandatary, 394

......, *and see* Rossen.

......, **diocese** of, persons of *see* Alan, John; Ba(m)buri, Thomas; Bradshaw, Peter; Perott, John; Rydyng, Henry; Saunders, Hugh; Starkey, Thomas; *and see* Copping, John; Dokett, Robert; Gardener, Richard; Grene, Thomas; Hatton, John; Watson, William

......, ..., places in *see* Cobham; Cowden; Deptford; Gravesend; Greenwich, West; Hoo; Meopham; Plumstead;

Rochester, **diocese** (*contd*)
    Tonbridge; Wouldham; *and see* Birling;
    Chevening; Chiddingstone; Sundridge;
    Tannington

Roger, Edward, cleric of St Andrews
    diocese, 243

Roger, [bishop-] elect of Carlisle *see*
    [Layburne], Roger

Rogers, James, rector of Fawley, 885

Rokeby, William, rector of Fakenham and
    incumbent of Sproatley, 797

Rolland (Rollandi), William, of Aberdeen
    diocese, dispensed for plurality, 1297
......, *cf.* Rowlandson

Rolleston (Rollescon' *alias* Kollston),
    Richard, rector of Stonegrave and
    incumbent of Weston-on-Trent, 355

Rome [Italy], titular **churches** in:
    St Anastasia, cardinal priest of *see*
        [Morton], John
    S Balbina, cardinal priest of *see* [Vera],
        Juan
    S. Crisogono, cardinal priest of *see* [de
        Ferrariis], Johannes Baptista
    SS Giovanni e Paolo, cardinal priest of
        see [Orsini], Giovanni Battista
    SS Nereo e Achilleo, cardinal priest of
        see [de Sangiorgio], Giovanni Antonio
    S Prassede, cardinal priest of *see*
        [Pallavicini], Antoniotto
    St Theodorus, cardinal deacon of *see*
        [Sanseverinas], Federicus
    S. Vitus in Macello Martirum, cardinal
        deacon of *see* [Sforza], Ascanius Maria
......, [S Paolo fuori le Mura, Basilica of],
    tomb of the Apostle Paul at, vow to
    visit, 374
......, ..., ..., ..., visit to, 416
......, ..., ..., ..., pilgrims to and from, 7
......, [S Pietro in Vaticano, Basilica of],
    tomb of the Apostle Peter at, vow to
    visit, 374
......, ..., ..., ..., visit to, 416
......, ..., ..., ..., pilgrims to and from, 7

Rome (*contd*)
......, hospital of Santo Spirito in Saxia, 339
......, ..., brother of *see* Lyttelman, Robert
......, Cistercian monastery of Tre Fontane
    outside the walls of, church of, chapel
    of Scala Coeli in, 807
......, churches and basilicas within and
    without appointed for jubilee
    indulgence, 374
......, apostolic palace, auditor of causes of,
    litigation before, 237, 687,
......, ..., ..., commission of case to, 844
......, ..., papal chaplain and auditor of
    causes of *see* de Pereriis, William

......, **popes** of *see* Alexander III; Alexander
    IV; [Alexander VI]; Benedict XII;
    Boniface VIII; Boniface IX; Boniface
    XII; Clement V; Eugenius III; Eugenius
    IV; Gregory IX; Innocent III; Innocent
    VIII; John XXII; John XXIII; Paul II;
    Pius II; Sixtus IV

......, **court** of, litigation at, 417
......, ..., ..., *and see above under* Rome,
    apostolic palace
......, ..., bishop of Limerick at, 485
......, ..., bishop of Worcester at, 363
......, ..., petitioner stated to be present in
    see Peston *alias* Conell', Gilbert
......, ..., death of Edward Cockburn at, 130
......, ..., person (named) dying *en route* to,
    234, 512
......, ..., travellers to and from, 7
......, ..., British and Irish persons at, *cf.*
    Barbour, John; Elphinstone, Adam
......, ..., curialists (bureaucrats, judges,
    officials, etc.) at: –
    camera:
    cleric of *see* Ponzettus, Fer(di)nandus
    collector or sub-collector of fruits due
        to *see* OHedian, James
    chancery:
    abbreviatores de parco maiori see [de
        Arianis] de Parma, Franciscus;
        Bregeon, Franciscus and Nicolaus;
        [de Caccialupis] de Sancto
        Severino, Antonius; de Castello,
        Nicolaus Olivius; de Castello,
        Paulus Amadei de Iustinis; de
        Castello, Saldonus de Saldis;

Rome, **court** (*contd*)

Colotius, Angelus; Ortega de Gomiel, Johannes; de Planca, Paulus; Puccius, Laurentius; de Scorciatis, Camillus

abbreviatores de parco minori see de Acre, Alfonsus; de Brinis, Antonius; Menendez; de Pelegrinis, Johannes Baptista; Ponzettus, Fer(di)nandus; de Scarsiis, Dominicus; de Turchis, Johannes Petrus

magistri registri see Bagarothus, Baptista; de Battiferro, Matheus; Bolis, Bartholomeus; Colotius, Angelus; Dulcius, Lucas; de Fornariis, Octavianus; de Galves, Johannes; [de Lanciarinis] de Fano, Ulixes; de Sanctoris, Fatius; Thomarotius, Paulus

regents see [Capra], Aloysius; [de Ferrariis], Johannes Baptista; de la Porta, Dominicus; [de Sacchis], Johannes; de Valle, Andreas

scriptores apostolici see de Bertinis, Leonard; Ponzettus, Fer(di)nandus; Tuba, Paul

scriptores registri see Boccapaduli, Evangelista; Damiani, Bernardino; Marasca, Giuliano; de Petra, Galeatius; Resta, [?Hieronimus]

solicitor *see* Fabri, John

vicechancellor *see* [Sforza], Ascanius Maria

protonotaries *see* Castellesi, Hadrian; Orsini, Orsino

rota: *see above under* Rome, apostolic palace

secretaries *see* de Gherardis de Vulterris, Jacobus; Ortega de Gomiel, Johannes

......, ..., *and see* Goler, Wolffgangus; Hermannus; *and under* [Alexander VI]

......, **as apostolic see**, quondam legates of in the kingdom of England *see* [Candidus], Otto; [Fieschi], Ottobuono

......, ..., legates born of *see* [Deane], Henry; [Morton], John; St Andrews, archbishop of

......, ..., legate of *see* [?Arundel], Thomas; [Rotherham *or* Scot], Thomas

Rome, *as* **apostolic see** (*contd*)

......, ..., nuncio of in the kingdom of England *see* Castellesi, Hadrian

......, ..., Cistercian order, monasteries, and members immediately subject to, 298

......, ..., churches immediately subject to *see* Bridgnorth; *and see below under* Rome, Holy Church of, monasteries immediately subject or pertaining to

......, ..., places under the protection of *see* 'baptized islands'; Inchcolm; *and see* Taunton

......, **Holy Church** of, cardinals of, derogation of Cistercian privileges not possible even with advice and assent of, 943

......, ..., ..., assent of to derogation of Cistercian privileges, 789

......, ..., ..., commends of Cistercian monasteries to, 121, 789

......, ..., ..., *see* [Caraffa], Oliviero; *and persons referred to above under* Rome, titular churches in

......, ..., vicechancellor of *see* [Sforza], Ascanius Maria

......, ..., monasteries immediately subject or pertaining to *see* Marcilhac; Paisley; Pontefract; *and see above under* Rome, *as* apostolic see

Ronaldson (Radnaldson'), John, of St Andrews diocese, appeal of, 971

Roode, Andrew, rector of Wistaston, 570

Rooperchiante *see under* Canterbury, [parish church of St Dunstan without Westgate of]

Ropba in Concnecule Obeara *see* Ballinrobe

Roper (Rooper), [John], chantry of in St Dunstan's, Canterbury, 195

Ros *see* Ross Carbery

Rosceran *see* Rasharkin

[Roscommon, co. of], places in *see* Athlone; Boyle; *Clann conchobair* [*in* Baslick]; [Coolderry, Culliaghbeg, and Gortnasharvoge (*all in* Creagh)]; Creagh; Elphin; Inchmacnerin; Kilmore; Lough Key; Ogulla; Taghboy; Tumna; *and see* Moycarn, barony of, places in

Rosconnell (Rosconyll) [cos. Kilkenny and Laois], parish church of, 510

Roscrea (Roch, Rostre) [co. Offaly], parish church (of St Cronan) of, vicarage of, 14, 161
......, ..., ..., to be united to canonry of Cashel and prebend of Killea, 14

Rose, Joan, woman of Lincoln diocese, litigant, 28
......, ..., ..., husband of *see* Bailey, William; *and see* Ardern', Robert

Rosemarkie (Rosmarky) [co. Ross and Cromarty], church of, tithes of, belonging to deanery of Ross, 782, 840
......, place in *see* Fortrose

Rosmyr *see* Rossmire

Ross [*in* Ireland], [**cathedral**] **church** of [*at* Ross Carbery, co. Cork], chancellor of, papal mandatary, 362
......, ..., treasurer of, papal mandatary, 258
......, ..., chapter of, to be summoned over erection of canonry and prebend, 129
......, ..., canons of *see* Condon, John; ?Ochvygh, Lewis; OCullinane, Maurice; ODriscoll, Bernard, John, Odo and Thady; OHea, Maurice and Odo; Ygonayn, Donald
......, ..., prebends in *see* Clear Island; Creagh [co. Cork]; Curragranemore; Kilnamanagh

......, **bishop** of, collation by, 70
......, ..., to be summoned over erection of canonry and prebend, 129
......, ..., papal judge delegate, 811
......, ..., papal mandatary, 536
......, official of, papal mandatary, 251

Ross [*in* Ireland], **bishop** (*contd*)
......, church of, archdeaconry of, rectory in ecclesiastical fief and vicarage of Schull to be united to, 257
......, ..., archdeacons of *see* MacCarthy, Thady; ODriscoll, John

......, **diocese** of, James [MacMahon], bishop of Clogher, residing in, 811
......, ..., persons of *see* ODriscoll, Dermot and Donald
......, ..., places in *see* Abbeymahon; Clear Island; Creagh [co. Cork]; Gortnaclohy; Inchydoney Island; ?Kilgarriff; Ross Carbery; Tullagh

Ross Carbery (Ross) [co. Cork], Benedictine monastery of B. Mary the Virgin, prior of, papal mandatary, 251, 252, 256, 257
......, ..., prior and convent of, detainers of rectory of parish church of Clear Island, 129
......, *and see above* Ross [*in* Ireland], [cathedral] church of

Ross [*in* Scotland], [**cathedral**] **church** of [*at* Fortrose *in* Rosemarkie, co. Ross and Cromarty], deanery of, 782, 839-841
......, ..., ..., church of Kilmuir annexed to, 782, 839
......, ..., ..., tithes of churches of Rosemarkie and Cromarty belonging to, 782
......, ..., ..., fruits of church of Kilmuir and tithes of churches of Rosemarkie and Cromarty pertaining to, 840
......, ..., dean of, papal mandatary, 931
......, ..., ..., *see* Fraser, Robert; Greenlaw, Hugh; Vaus, Martin
......, ..., dignity of, reservation of, 643
......, ..., chapter of, conclusion to, 637
......, ..., canons of *see* Forsyth, Thomas; Murray, James; *cf.* Kilsensz, Thomas
......, ..., prebend of, reservation of, 643

......, **bishop** of, to receive oath of fealty in pope's name, 588, 590
......, ..., papal judge delegate, 971
......, ..., papal mandatary, 780, 840

Ross [*in* Scotland], **bishop** (*contd*)
......, ..., *see* [Fraser], John; [Guthrie], John
......, official of, papal mandatary, 841
......, church of, subject to the archbishop of St Andrews, 638
......, ..., vassals of, conclusion to, 637
......, ..., archdeacon of, papal mandatary, 444, 698, 929

......, **city and diocese** of, clergy of, conclusion to, 637
......, ..., people of, conclusion to, 637
......, diocese of, person of *see* Vaus, John
......, ..., places in *see* Cromarty; Kilmuir; Rosemarkie

[Ross and Cromarty, co. of], places in *see* Cromarty; Fortrose; Kilmuir; Lewis; 'Li'; Rosemarkie

Rossen. [for Rochester?], bishop of, papal mandatary, 817
......, *recte* Rochester, q.v.

Rossmire (Rosmyr) [co. Waterford], parish church of, vicarage of, 949

Rostherne (Rotherston', Rowstorne) [Ches], parish church of, union of, to the parish church of Winwick, 475
......, ..., to be retained by [bishop] elect, 1337

Rostre *see* Roscrea

Rosynalde, Christopher, rector of Chalton, 902

[Rotherham *or* Scot], Thomas, archbishop of York, primate of England, legate of the apostolic see, 94
......, ..., ..., union by, 425
......, ..., ..., death of, 546
......, ..., ..., official and commissary general of *see* Colyns, Martin

Rotherston' *see* Rostherne

Rothtmariel *see* Rathmuriel

Rouaborugh' *see* Roborough

Rowlandson *cf.* Rolland

Rowstorne *see* Rostherne

[Roxburgh, co. of], places in *see* Jedburgh; Kelso; Melrose

Rudgwick (Ruggwyke) [Sussex], parish church or chantry of, 184

[Rudham, East, co. Norf], place in *see* Coxford

Ruer, Thomas, rector of Dodbrooke and vicar of ?Clee, 41

Ruffel *see* Russell

[Ruffi], Ivo, bishop of Glendalough, death of, 579

Ruggwyke *see* Rudgwick

Ruishton (Riscon, Russheton', Rystecheton') [Som], chapel of, 174

de Rupe see Roche

Rusell *see* Russell

Rushall (Russal) [Wilts], parish church of, 878

Russell (Ruffel, Rusell, Russel, Russell'), James, canon of Lismore and prebendary of Modelligo, simony of, 381
......, John, bishop of Lincoln, union by, 425
......, ..., cleric of Bath and Wells diocese, 795
......, Thomas, sometime dean of Lismore, 159
......, William, canon of Salisbury and prebendary of Bedminster, litigant, 987
......, ..., vicar of the chapel of ?Easton [*in* West Alvington], 413
......, ..., union for, of one of his parish churches to the other, Bath and Wells diocese, 1249

Russheton' *see* Ruishton

Ruthin (Ruthyn') [co. Denbigh], church of St Peter, 596

......, ..., commendator of *see* David [ab Iorwerth]

......, ..., to be held *in commendam*, 596

Rutland (Ruttlande) [rural deanery of?], Empingham in, 729

[Rutland, co. of], places in *see* Ashwell; Empingham; Tinwell

Rutter (Ruttur), John, of London diocese, dispensed for plurality, 1232

Ruttlande *see* Rutland

Ruttur *see* Rutter

Ruynet, John, of Norwich diocese, dispensed for plurality, 1080

Rydware Hampstall' *see* Ridware, Hamstall

Rydyng, Henry, rector of Gravesend, 522

......, *cf.* Reding

Ryerin' *see* Kearn

Rygne *see* ?Ringrone

Ryllrogan *see* Kilbrogan

Rylonayn *see* ?Killinane

Ryman (Ryman'), James, OFM, 136

Rynardus [*no surname*], rector of 'Li' in Lewis, death of, 116

Ryncorrain *see* Ringcurran

Ryndweare *see* Rinn-bheara

Ryneguvesteyll', Rynegvuesteyll', Rynegwesteyll' *see* Llan Egwestl *or* Egwast

Ry'nlos *see* Kinloss

Rystecheton' *see* Ruishton

Ryther [Yorks], parish church of, 730

Ryther, John, vicar of Halstead, 201

S

Sabina [*at* Magliano Sabina *in* province of Rieti], [cardinal] bishop of *see* [Caraffa], Oliviero

[de Sacchis], Johannes, archbishop of Ragusa, regent of the chancery, correction of register ordered by, 134, 144, 154, 175, 232, 281, 322, 396, 449, 654, 663, 717, 747, 766, 982; *and see* 626 *note*

......, ..., ..., and *cf.* Ragusa, archbishop of

Sagone [*in* Corsica], bishop of, papal mandatary, 644

St Albans [Herts], Benedictine monastery of, abbot of, papal judge delegate, 365

......, ..., monk of *see* Wytheley, John

......, ..., cell of *see* Wallingford

St Andrews [Fife], [collegiate] church of St Salvator, provost of, institution of persons presented for chaplaincy in church pertains to, 691

......, ..., ..., institution by, 691

......, ..., ..., suit before, 691

......, ..., altar in, chaplaincy at, litigation over, 691

......, ..., ..., ..., patrons of *see* Lindores, abbot and convent of; [Lindsay], John, earl of Crawford

......, ..., chaplains in *see* Esplane, Thomas; Lamey, Walter; Myln, John

......, [cathedral] church / monastery of, OSA [OSB *in error*, 921], prior of, papal judge delegate, 792

......, ..., ..., ..., papal mandatary, 782, 839, 937

......, ..., ..., prior and chapter / convent of, litigants over tithes, 921, 971

......, ..., ..., chapter of, consent of, to grant of barony and lands pertaining to archiepiscopal *mensa*, 356

......, ..., ..., chamberlain of *see* Lermonth, David

St Andrews [cathedral] church (*contd*)

......, ..., ..., tithes of Balgonie, Milton of Balgonie, and 'Spittale' belonging to, 971

......, ..., ..., dependency of *see* May *alias* Pittenweem

......, **archbishopric** of, *mensa* of, barony and lands in St Andrews diocese pertaining to, grant of, 356

......, archbishop of, primate of the whole kingdom of Scotland and legate born in, 848

......, ..., subjection to, of church of Caithness, 621

......, ..., ..., of church of Moray, 631

......, ..., ..., of church of Orkney, 551

......, ..., ..., of church of Ross, 638

......, ..., ..., of Augustinian monastery of Cambuskenneth, 1027

......, ..., superiority and jurisdiction of, Dunblane exempted from, 333

......, ..., ..., Dunblane again subjected to, 333

......, ..., appointment by, of the external official in the district of Lothian, 792

......, ..., conclusion to, 549, 584, 620, 630, 637, 1024

......, ..., court of, appeals to, 792

......, ..., ..., litigation before, 792

......, ..., commissary of *see* Fountains, Robert

......, ..., *see* [Scheves], William; Stewart, James

......, [archbishop] elect of *see* Stewart, James

......, administrator of *see* Stewart, James

......, official of, papal mandatary, 301, 366, 535, 778, 844

......, ..., *see* Meldrum, David

......, church of, archdeacon of, papal mandatary, 768

......, ..., ..., *see* Fountains, Robert

......, ..., archdeaconry of Lothian in, 371

......, ..., archdeacon of Lothian in, 768, 781

......, ..., ..., papal mandatary, 407, 765

......, ..., ..., *see* Arnot, David

......, metropolitan church of, **province** of, separation from, of church of Dunblane, 333

......, ..., ..., restoration to, of church of Dunblane, 333

St Andrews (*contd*)

......, **diocese** of, clerics (unnamed) of, 691

......, ..., persons of *see* Abirnethy, John and Walter; Aitchison, James; Anderson, John; Arnot, Henry; Ayton, John; Barbour, John; [Bellenden], Robert; Brady, John; Brown, David; [Caueris], Andrew; Cockburn, Edward, John, and Richard; Colvil, Alexander; Colȝony, Andrew; Coutts, Alan; Crawford, William; [Crichton], George; Dickson, Thomas; Dindson, Thomas; Doby, Alexander; Douglas, John, Stephen, and William; Esplane, Thomas; Forman, Andrew; Gifferd, Alexander; Halkerston, Thomas; Hepburn, John; Hoin, Elizabeth; Home, John and Ninian; Kinloch, Margaret; Knollis, George; Kyneragy, James; Lamey, Walter; Lermonth, George; [Longant], Andrew; Lornisen, Michael; Lundy, Andrew; Martin, Hugh and Robert; Monorgund, William; Myln, John and Thomas; Napier, Archibald and John; Orme, Henry; Panter, Patrick; Philpson, Henry; Preston, William; Robertson, William; Roger, Edward; Ronaldson, John; Sandeland, William; Scott, Alexander and Elizabeth; Shanwell, Robert; Sibbald, Agnes, Elizabeth and William; Spens, David; Stevenson, William; Swynton, Robert; Trechton', Patrick; Turnbull, John and William; Wallace, John; Wardlaw, William; *and see* Betonen', Robert; Wardlaw, Henry

......, ..., described as "so large and widespread", 848

......, ..., district of Lothian of, external official in, 792

......, ..., places in *see* Calder; Cambuskenneth; Carriden; Coldingham; Conveth; Cranshaws; Crichton; Dunbar; Dunfermline; Duns(e); Eccles; Edinburgh; Ellem; Falkirk; Garvock; Haddington; 'Herperseldi'; Idvie(s); Inchegall; Kelso; Kilmany; Kirkcaldy; Kirkden; Kirkforthar; 'Laronde'; Laurencekirk; Lindores; Linlithgow; Markinch; May *alias* Pittenweem; Merchiston; Nevay; Newbattle; Newburn; Pinkerton;

St Andrews **diocese** (*contd*)
Restennet; Scone; Slamannan; Stirling; Tannadice; *and see* Balgonie; Carnbo; Lundie; Milton of Balgonie; 'Spittale'

St Asaph [co. Flint], **[cathedral] church** of, chapter of, conclusion to, 594
......, ..., canon of *see* Helis, Geoffrey
......, ..., prebend in *see* ?Meifod
......, ..., cursal prebend in, 483
......, **bishops** of *see* David [ab Iorwerth]; [Deacon], Michael
......, church of, subject to archbishop of Canterbury, 595
......, ..., vassals of, conclusion to, 594

......, **city and diocese** of, clergy of, conclusion to, 594
......, ..., people of, conclusion to, 594
......, diocese of, person of *see* Salisbury, Fulk
......, ..., places in *see* ?Bodfari; ?Llanfarchell; Valle Crucis

St Benedict, Cistercian monastery of *see* [Newry]

St Botolph, priory of *see* [Colchester]

Saint-Brieuc [*in dép.* of Côtes-du-Nord, France], diocese of, person of *see* Brehault, John
......, ..., place in *see* Bosquen

St Carrok [*in* St Veep, Corn], Cluniac priory of, prior of *see* Cherell, Thomas
......, ..., a dependency of the monastery of Bs Peter and Paul, [Montacute], 267

St Catherine, monastery of *see* Waterford

St Columba, island of [*in* the Firth of Forth], monastery of *see* Inchcolm
......, ..., 'baptized islands' near, 108

St Cuby *see* Cuby

St David's, **[cathedral] church** of, canon of *see* Jonys, William
......, ..., chantry dedicated to St Nicholas

St David's, **[cathedral] church** (*contd*)
the Confessor in, 320
......, ..., chaplain in *see* David, Maurice

......, **bishop** of, papal judge delegate, 442
......, ..., vicar general of, papal mandatary, 963
......, church of, archdeacon of Brecon in *see* Walter, William
......, ..., archdeaconry of Cardigan in, *q. v*,
......, ..., archdeacon of Cardigan in *see* Howell, Thomas

......, **diocese** of, persons of *see* Adams, Maurice; Bowen, William; Cradoc, John; Eynon ap Gwalter; Gwynn, Maurice; Owen Ap D[avi]d; Owen ap Rhys; Philip, David; Richard ap David; Stoltdale, John; Wogan, Matthew
......, ..., places in *see* Abergwili; Henllan-Amgoed; Llanbadarn Fawr; Llandeilo Vawr; Llanfallteg; Llanfyrnach; Llanllwchaiarn; Pembroke; Whitchurch; Whitland

St Ebba the Virgin, parish church of *see* Oxford

St Erme [Corn], parish church of, 762

St ?Findchu *see* [Killinaboy]

St Germans [Corn], Augustinian priory of, prior of *see* Serlo, John

St Gluvias [Corn], parish church of, 85
......, ..., vicarage of, 684
......, place in *see* Glasney

St Guthlac, priory of *see* Hereford

St Helier [*on* islet of Elizabeth Castle *in* St Helier, Jersey, Channel Islands], Augustinian priory of, 515
......, ..., prior of *see* Brehault, John
......, ..., collation of pertains to kings of England, 515
......, ..., dependent on Augustinian monastery of Cherbourg, 515

St Illogan *see* Illogan

Saint-Jean-de-Maurienne [*in dép.* of Savoy, France], bishop of *see* [de Gorrevodo], Ludovicus

St John (Seynt John'), Richard, chaplain in Salisbury cathedral, 503
......, *cf.* Singen

St Kennocha *see* St Quivox

St Mala *see* St Maul's

Saint-Malo, [cathedral] church of, canon of *see* Regis, Thomas

St Mary's Isle *or* Trail [*in* Kirkcudbright, co. Kirkcudbright], Augustinian priory of, 509
......, ..., priors of *see* Crawford, John and William
......, ..., a dependency of Holyrood, 509

St Maul's (St Mala) [co. Kilkenny], prebend of in Ossory cathedral, 787
......, ..., proposed union to, of rectories of Aglishmartin and Ballytarsney and vicarages of Dungarvan, Kilcolumb, Kilmanagh, and Thomastown, 787

St Neot [Corn], parish church of, 147

St Patrick, priory, called church, of *see* Downpatrick

St Quivox (St Kennocha) [co. Ayr], church of, fruits of pertaining to the Cluniac monastery of Paisley, grant of, 63

?St Quivox [co. Ayr], place in *see* Dalmilling

St Romuald's *see* [Shaftesbury]

St Th(e)odorus, Augustinian monastery (Lateran Congregation) of, canon of *see* Grimaldi, Agostino

St Tudy [Corn], parish church of, 288
......, ..., union to, of the vicarage of Cuby, 753

St Veep (Sinepe) [Corn], parish church of, 216
......, place in *see* St Carrok

St Wolstan, priory of, diocese of Worcester [*unidentified; probably at* Worcester; *in all likelihood the Benedictine (cathedral) priory (though its dedication occurs persistently as St Mary); just possibly the Augustinian hospital of St Wulstan*], prior of, papal judge delegate, 9

Saints Island [*in* Cashel, co. Longford], Augustinian monastery of B. Mary, priorship of, 836
......, ..., priors of *see* OFarrell, Fantutius and Thomas
......, ..., canons of *see* OFarrell, Fantutius and Roceus

de Saldis Civitatis Castelli, Saldonus *see* de Castello, Saldonus de Saldis

[Salehurst, Sussex], place in *see* Robertsbridge

Salford (Salforde) [*now* Salford Priors, Warw], parish church of, 659

Saline *see* Gallen

Salisburi *see* Salisbury

Salisbury [Wilts], [cathedral] church of, dean of, licence of, 503
......, ..., ..., papal mandatary, 903
......, ..., succentorship of, 478
......, ..., succentor of *see* Toft, William
......, ..., chapter of, conclusion to, 581, 1021
......, ..., canons and prebendaries of *see* Davy, Thomas; Newport, Richard; Russell, William
......, ..., prebends in *see* Bedminster; Blewbury; Faringdon
......, ..., altar of the Annunciation of B. Mary the Virgin in, 193
......, ..., ..., chantries at, 193
......, ..., chantry of Gilbert Kymer in, 503

Salisbury, **[cathedral] church** (*contd*)
......, ..., chaplains in *see* Parson *alias* Wyllys, Richard; St John, Richard
......, ..., statutes and customs of, 503
......, ..., called "parish church of Sarum, d. Salisbury", 91

......, **bishop** of, to receive oath of fealty in pope's name, 546, 547
......, ..., papal judge delegate, 28
......, ..., papal commissary and mandatary, 137
......, ..., *see* [Audley], Edmund; Blythe, John; [Deane], Henry
......, church of, archdeaconry of Wiltshire in, 277
......, ..., archdeacon of Wiltshire in *see* Urswick, Christopher
......, ..., vassals of, conclusion to, 581, 1021

......, **city and diocese** of, clergy of, conclusion to, 581, 1021
......, ..., people of, conclusion to, 581, 1021
......, diocese of, persons of *see* Andrew, John; Aspden', John; Ayleuoard, William; Benett, Thomas; Bulkeley, John; Byrde, William; Chantrell, Nicholas; Cotell, John; Coventry, William; Cowley, Thomas; Cumberton, William; David, Philip; Dowman, John; Dunster, William; Einster, Thomas; Elys, John; Eyre, Ralph; Fishwick, Thomas; Gaunt, Richard; Goldsmith, Thomas; Grice, John; Haliday, Richard; Hallo, John; Hornby, Henry; Huntrodys, William; Hyde, John; Hyslington, John; Kay, Thomas; Kent, William; Ketilton, William; Knollys, David; Leshugton, John; Long, Thomas; Looder, John; Louer, John; Martyn, Thomas; Michell, Thomas; Molyneux, Henry; Page, Richard; Panter, Richard; Recte, Agnes; Sinclair, William; Tame, Thomas; Tayler, John; Thilde, Thomas; Trebel, John; Wekis, Robert; Weston, Richard; Wilton, William; Woarson, ?Oddowinus; Wytheley, John
......, ..., places in *see* Ashmore; Box;

Salisbury, **city and diocese** (*contd*)
Bradford-on-Avon; Broadwindsor; Burton Bradstock; Buscot; Castle Eaton; Cerne; Charlton; Dewlish; Ditteridge; Ebbesborne; Edington; Fugglestone; Hanney; Hawkchurch; Heddington; Hendred, East; Hurley; Ivychurch; Lacock; Manningford; Marnhull; Melksham; Milborne St Andrew; Mildenhall; Moreton, North; Poulshot; Puddletown; Rushall; Semley; Shaftesbury; Shottesbrooke; Silton; Stratton St Margaret; Sulhampstead Abbots; Sutton Courtenay; Sutton Mandeville; Swanage; Tidworth; Tilehurst; Tisbury; Upway; Wilsford; Wilton; Windsor; Worth; *and see* Wallingford

Salisbury (Salisburi), Fulk, cleric of St Asaph diocese, 308

[Salley], Miles, abbot of the Benedictine monastery of Eynsham, 598, 600, 601
......, ..., ..., provision of to the bishopric of Llandaff, 598
......, ..., ..., absolution of preliminary to provision, 601
......, ..., ..., to retain Eynsham *in commendam*, 600
......, ..., [bishop-] elect of Llandaff, 600
......, ..., ..., faculty for consecration of, 599
......, ..., bishop of Llandaff, 399
......, ..., ..., commendatory [abbot] of Eynsham, 399
......, ..., ..., ..., faculty for, to depute vicar to confer benefice on him, 399

Salter, Richard, ostensible keeper in spirituals of the dioceses of Coventry and Lichfield, litigation before, 991
......, ..., ostensible vicar or official of the chapter of the church of Coventry and Lichfield *sede vacante*, litigation before, 991

Saltfleetby (Saltflmbr) [Lincs], parish church of All Saints, 140

Sancti Chafudi see [?Ardquin]

Sancti Jacobi iuxta portam canonicorum see Taunton

Sancti Pauli extra Castellum see Taunton

Sancti Petri de Castello see Taunton

de Sanctona see Staunton

de Sanctoris, Fatius, *magister registri,* letters signed by:
F. *Sanctor'* , 18, 25, 26, 31-34, 48, 50, 52-54, 61, 62, 64, 72, 83, 88, 89, 92, 93, 95, 96, 102-105, 109, 110, 114, 117, 119, 120, 127-130, 151, 159, 167, 169, 170, 181-184, 187, 231-233, 235, 236, 302, 303, 305, 328, 329, 334, 335, 337, 338 (F. *Santor'*), 345, 350-355, 372, 382, 386, 403-406, 413-416, 424, 443, 476, 482, 484, 495, 527, 531, 532, 535, 536, 545, 549-552, 591-593, 602-605, 617-619, 653, 656, 695, 696, 773-775, 844, 866, 974, 1015-1020; *cf.* 106
......, ..., ..., correction of register ordered by regent of chancery done by, 91, 396

de Sancto Severino, A see [de Caccialupis] de Sancto Severino, Antonius

Sanday (Sande) [*one of the* Orkney islands, co. Orkney and Shetland], parish church of St Mary [*now* Lady], incumbent of, 552
......, ..., chapel of St Laurence united to, 552

Sandbach (Sondebach) [Ches], parish church of, vicar of, 38

Sande see Sanday

Sandeland, William, rector of Slamannan, 5

Sandford (Sondyfordy), Roger, portioner of Ferriby, 565

Sandherst, alias of Bekeryng, Robert, *q.v.*

[de Sangiorgio], Giovanni Antonio, cardinal priest of SS Nereo e Achilleo, suit before, 1015

[Sanseverinas], Federicus, cardinal deacon of St Theodorus, continual commensal (named) of, 854

Santiago de Compostela (Compostella) [*in* Corunna province, Spain], pilgrims to, 7
......, tomb of St James at, vow to visit, 374

Sanunt see Gaunt

Saprtall see Shortall

Sarum, parish church of see under Salisbury, [cathedral] church of

Sassello [*in* province of Savona, Italy], Francis of, *q.v.*

Saunder (Saun'der), Andrew, rector of Cotesbach, 497

Saunders (Sawndurs), Hugh, vicar of Meopham, 809
......, Thomas, prior of the Augustinian priory of Chacombe, 874

Savage, Thomas, (lately) bishop of London, 546, 547, 617
......, ..., ..., translation of to archbishopric of York, 546, 617
......, ..., ..., absolution of preliminary to translation, 548
......, ..., ..., to take oath of fealty, 546
......, ..., ..., ..., commission over, 547
......, ..., ..., archbishop of York, 547
......, ..., ..., ..., delivery of pallium to, 1236
......, ..., ..., ..., ..., commission over, 1237

Savoy, duke of see Amadeus

Sawndurs see Saunders

Saxlingham (Saxlyngh(a)m next the Sea) [near Holt, Norf], parish church of, 922

Say, William, the late, once dean of London cathedral, 856
......, ..., chaplaincy founded by in London cathedral, 856

Sayr *see* Seirkieran

Scarsdale (Scarysdalle) [Derb], North Wingfield in, 300

de Scarsiis, Dominicus, *abbreviator de parco minori*, conclusions expedited by: *D Scarsius*, 591

Scarysdalle *see* Scarsdale

Scattery Island (Inyskachy, Ynyskahi, Ynyskay) [*in* Kilrush, co. Clare], (secular and collegiate) church of, 818
......, ..., prior of, papal mandatary, 306
......, ..., college in, 449
......, ..., portioners in *see* MacCahan, Cornelius; MacMahon, Cornelius; OBehan, John
......, ..., portions in *see* 'Gleandbannam' vulgarly '?Ileraunr'; Moanmore

Schanwel *see* Shanwell

Schaw *see* Shaw

Scherar, Scherat *see* Shearer

Scherbone *see* Sherburn

[Scheves], William, archbishop of St Andrews, death of, 848

Schull *or* Skull (Scoll') [co. Cork], ecclesiastical fief of, rectory in, to be united to archdeaconry of Ross, 257
......, parish church of, vicarage of, to be united to archdeaconry of Ross, 257

Schw *see* Shaw

Schyllyngford *see* Shillingford St George

Schytlyngdor' *see* Shillington

Scoll' *see* Schull

Scone [co. Perth], [Augustinian] monastery of, abbot of, to receive intending religious as a canon [elsewhere],

Scone (*contd*)
bestow habit, and receive profession, 1028
......, ..., ..., papal mandatary, 371, 558

de Scorciatis, Camillus, *abbreviator de parco maiori*, letters expedited by: *C de Scorciatis*, 174, 262 (*C de Scoracti*), 269, 282, 285, 287, 301, 317, 407 (*C de S[c]ortiatis*), 468 (*S de Scorciatis*)

[Scot] *see* [Rotherham *or* Scot]

Scot *see* Scott

Scotland, king of *see* James [IV]
......, kingdom of, primate of the whole and legate born in *see* St Andrews, archbishop of
......, ..., primate of *see* [Stewart], James
......, ..., secular clerics of, custom of, of making disposition of fruits collected in year of death, 443
......, ..., pirates from, 108
......, ..., borders of, island of St Columba within, 108
......, money current in, 558

Scots, king of *see* James [IV]

Scott (Scot, Stot), Alexander, of St Andrews diocese, appeal of, 971
......, Edward, rector of Sutton Coldfield, familiar, continual commensal, and *cubicularius* of pope, 641
......, Elizabeth, of St Andrews diocese, appeal of, 971
......, John, nobleman, a supporter of John Goldsmith for the precentorship of Glasgow, 80

Scotton, John, chaplain in St John's, Beverley, 887

Scrimgeour (Scrungeour, Skeymgeour), James, rector of Kilneuair, 493
......, ..., scholar of Brechin diocese, 83
......, John, lay patron of Kilneuair, 493

Scyda, alias of MacNamara, James, *q.v.*

Scyortal, Scyortall *see* Shortall

Sedgeberrow (Segebaro) [Worcs], parish church of, union to, of the parish church of Broadwas, 294

Seirkieran (Sayr, Sir, Sire, Synr) [co. Offaly], Augustinian monastery of, priorship of, 930
......, ..., prior of, papal mandatary, 357, 403, 404
......, ..., ..., *see* OCarroll, Odo
......, ..., canon then prior *see* OMoynihan, Rory

Seleskyr *see* Selsker

[Selkirk] *see* [Peebles and Selkirk, co. of]

Selsker (Seleskyr) [*in* Wexford, co. Wexford], Augustinian monastery of Sts Peter and Paul, litigation over, 989
......, ..., prior of *see* Allen, Thomas; Baldwin, Patrick
......, ..., commendatory prior *see* Browne, Richard
......, ..., convent of, election of prior by, 989
......, ..., ..., appeal of, 989
......, ..., canon of *see* Baldwin, Patrick

Semley [Wilts], parish church of, 418

Semple (Simpill), Margaret, woman of Glasgow diocese, litigant, 86
......, ..., husband of *see* Crichton, James

Sempringham (Sempryngham) [Lincs], Gilbertine priory of, 728
......, ..., canon of *see* Edmond, John
......, order of St Gilbert of, priories of *see* Ormsby, North; Watton
......, ..., canons of, vicarage customarily held by *see* Utterby

Senhouse (Senouse), Simon, canon of the Augustinian priory of Healaugh, 742
......, ..., ..., vicar of Heversham, 742
......, *and see* [Sever *or* Senhouse]

Senior *cf.* Synyer

Senouse *see* Senhouse

Seradaualy *alias* Cloynacheke *see* Stradbally

Serin *see* Tempull na Scrine

Serlo, John, prior of the Augustinian priory of St Germans, indulged to use pontifical *insignia*, 1100

Serne *see* Cerne

Sestarffordi *see* ?Chesterfield

[Sever *or* Senhouse], William, bishop of Carlisle, 1006, 1008, 1012
......, ..., ..., translation of to Durham, 1006, 1007, 1012
......, ..., ..., absolution of preliminary to translation, 1008
......, ..., ..., to take oath of fealty, 1006
......, ..., ..., ..., commission over, 1007

Seynt John' *see* St John

[Sforza], Ascanius Maria, cardinal deacon of S Vitus in Macello Martirum, 130
......, ..., ..., vicechancellor [*SRE*], 130
......, ..., ..., ..., familiar of *see* Barbour, John

Shaftesbury [Dors], parish church of St Peter, union to, of St Mary's, Wilton, 736
......, parish church of St Romuald [*now* St Rumbold], union to, of the vicarage of Tisbury, 733
......, hospital of St John the Baptist in, union to, of the vicarage of Melksham, 965

Shamke, William, rector of Lewtrenchard and incumbent of Shillingford St George, 324

Shanwell (Schanwel), Robert, vicar of Kirkcaldy, 407
......, ..., ..., proctor of *see* Tuba, Paul
......, ..., ..., pension payable by, 407

Shap [Westm], Premonstratensian monastery of, canon of see Bedale, Robert

Shattyshm see Shottisham

Shaw (Schaw), George, monk, recently abbot, of the Cluniac monastery of Paisley, 61, 63
......, ..., cession of, 61
......, ..., to have re-entry at next vacancy, 61
......, ..., grant to, in place of annual pension, of lands, mills, annual revenues, and fisheries pertaining to Paisley in lordship or territory of places of Monkton and Dalmilling; of fruits of churches of Dundonald, Riccarton, Craigie, Monkton, St Quivox, Prestwick, Auchinleck (with its annual revenues), Largs, ?Cumbray, and Lochwinnoch; and of the lands of Glen, 63
......, Robert, vicar of Monkton, 61, 63
......, ..., ..., commend and provision to, of the Cluniac monastery of Paisley, 61
......, ..., ..., commendatory abbot of Paisley, 63
......, ..., provision of, to monastery in Glasgow diocese, 1329
......, ..., absolution of preliminary to provision, 1331
......, ..., faculty for consecration of, 1330
......, ..., derogation of statutes for, 1332
......, ..., commission over his reception as religious, 1333
......, ..., to retain vicarage, 1334

Shearer (Scherar, Scherat), Duncan, canon of Aberdeen, papal mandatary, 444
......, John, provided to canonry of Glasgow, 1257

Sherborne St John (Shirborn') [Hants], parish church of, 672

Sherburn (Scherbone) [in Pittington, co. Durham], leper hospital of, foundation of, 429
......, ..., statutes of, reform of, 429

Shetland [co. Orkney and Shetland], archdeaconry of, fruits and emoluments arising from goods within limits of customarily received by bishop of Orkney, assignment of, 552
......, ..., collation etc. of benefices within pertaining to bishop of Orkney, assignment of, 552

Shillingford St George (Schyllyngford) [Devon], parish church of, incumbent of, 324

Shillington (Schytlyngdor') [Beds], parish church of, 351

Shirborn' see Sherborne St John

Shobrooke (Shogbroke) [Devon], parish church of, 149

Shortall (Saprtall, Scyortal, Scyortall, Styortal, Styortall), James, canon of Ossory, papal mandatary, 647, 785, 786, 789, 790
......, ..., canon of Ossory and prebendary of St Maul's, 787
......, ..., ..., to have rectories of Aglishmartin and Ballytarsney and vicarages of Dungarvan, Kilcolumb, Kilmanagh, and Thomastown united to his canonry and prebend, 787

Shottesbrooke (Sthorisbroke) [Berks], parish church of, 476

Shottisham (Shattyshm) [Suff], parish church of, 660

Shrager, William, vicar of West Ham, 307

Shrewsbury [Salop], vill of, 233
......, ..., St Alkmund's in, 233

Shropshire (Shropshmc), archdeacon of [in the church of Hereford], papal judge delegate, 906

[Shropshire], places in see Bridgnorth; Burford; Church Stretton; Edgmond;

[Shropshire], (contd)
Haughmond; Much Wenlock; Shrewsbury; Upton Magna

Shyrbek see Skirbeck

Sibbald (Sibbaldi), Agnes, of St Andrews diocese, appeal of, 971
......, Elizabeth, of Balgonie, repeated appeal of, 971
......, William, of St Andrews diocese, appeal of, 971

Sible Hedingham see Hedingham, Sible

[Sidlesham, Sussex], place in see Highleigh

Siena [in province of Siena, Italy], priest of see de Bertinis, Leonard

Silton (Sylton') [Dors], parish church of, 109

Silvester (Silvestro), Gabriel, rector of Widdington, 750

Silvester, (bishop-) elect of Worcester see [de' Gigli], Silvester

Silvestro see Silvester

Simon, Richard, rector of Great Hardres, 297

Simson (Symson), Alexander, pension for, Aberdeen diocese, 1208
......, George, rector of Warmsworth, 212

Simpill see Semple

Sinclair (Synkclare), John, [bishop-] elect of Caithness, death of, 620
......, William, vicar of Milborne St Andrew and Dewlish, 920

Sinepe see St Veep

Singen cf. St John

Sir, Sire see Seirkieran

Sitzhugh see Fitz Hugh

Sixtus IV, letters of, 198, 233, 271, 277, 351, 355, 393, 434, 447, 741, 850

Skerpenbek see Skirpenbeck

[Skevington alias Patexe], Thomas, abbot of the Cistercian monastery of Waverley, 291

Skeymgeour see Scrimgeour

Skirbeck (Shyrbek) [Lincs], parish church of, 562

Skirling (Straling) [co. Peebles and Selkirk], lord of see Cockburn, Adam

Skirpenbeck (Skerpenbek) [Yorks], parish church of, 879

Skull see Schull

Slains (Slanis) [now Slains and Forvie, co. Aberdeen], parish church of, rectory of, 50
......, ..., ..., patron of, presentation by, 50
......, places in see ?Collieston; ?Meikle

Slamannan (Slamanan') [co. Stirling], parish church of, 5

Slanis see Slains

Sleaford (Slefordie) [Lincs], parish church of, vicarage of, 363
......, ..., vicar of, 363
......, ..., rector, called prebendary, of, 363

Sleford, Henry, rector of Cheriton, 966

Slefordie see Sleaford

[Sligo, co. of], places in see Achonry; Castleconor; Coola [in Ballynakill]

Smales, John, monk of the Cistercian monastery of Roche, 961

Smarden (Smardeyn) [Kent], parish church of, 489

[Smith], William, bishop of Lincoln, 176

......, ..., ..., licence and faculty for, to confirm and approve statutes and ordinances of college in hospital of St John the Baptist, Lichfield; of Lincoln College, Oxford; and of the college of St John Northampton, 176

......, ..., sometime bishop of Coventry and Lichfield, 176

......, ..., ..., foundation by, of hospital of St John the Baptist, Lichfield, 176

......, ..., ..., institution by, of college in hospital, 176

Smyth (Smyth'), John, vicar of Heckfield, 84, 96

......, ..., rector of Knapton, 544

......, ..., canon of the Gilbertine priory of Watton, 30

......, ..., ..., holder of vicarage of Utterby, 30

......, Richard, rector of Waltham, 406

......, Thurstan, vicar of Habrough, 427

......, William, rector of St Peter's, ?North Waltham, 459

Smyth (Smyth') *alias* Gogh, John, chaplain in Holy Trinity's, [Coventry], 506

Sneede *see* Sueede

Socach (Soctocha) [*in* Kilmichael Glassary, co. Argyll], place of, 493

Sodbury (Sodburi) [*now* Old Sodbury, Glos], parish church of, vicar of, 78

'Sodesaltera' [*unidentified*], land of gifted to Taunton priory, 174

Sodor [*or* The Isles], **bishopric** of, *mensa* of, fruits of, occupation of, by the English and local nobility, 181

......, bishop of, papal judge delegate, 991

......, ..., *see* [Campbell], John

......, church of, archdeacon of *see* Clerke, Thomas

......, ..., occupation of, by the English and local nobility, 181

......, **diocese** of, persons of *see* Macfail,

Sodor **diocese** (*contd*)
Donald; MacGillespy, Malcolinus; [Mackinnon], John; ?Nacleobi, John; Rynardus [*no surname*]

......, ..., places in *see* Bute; Iona; Lewis; 'Li'

[Somerset, co. of], places in *see* Compton Dundon; Haselbury Plucknett; Lydeard; Timberscombe; Wiveliscombe; *and* places *listed above under* Bath (and Wells), diocese(s) of

Sondebach *see* Sandbach

Sondyfordy *see* Sandford

Soriano, John, to have archpresbytery, Exeter diocese, 1279

South Benfleet *see* Benfleet, South

South Bradon *see* Bradon, South

South Ferriby *see* Ferriby

'Southgasten'' [*unidentified*; *in* East Dean, West Sussex], fields of, tithes from, 661

[South Leith] *see* [Leith, South]

South Stoke *see* Stoke, South

South Thoresby *see* Thoresby, South

Southwick [*modern* Colvend, co. Kirkcudbright], [parish church of], 781

Southwode *cf.* Sowthwode

Sovana [*in* Sorano commune, Grosseto province, Italy], bishop of, papal mandatary, 155, 181

Sowthwode, John, rector of Holy Trinity, Guildford, 968

......, *cf.* Southwode

Sparham (Sperham) [Norf], parish church of, 898

Spaxton (Spaxton') [Som], parish church of, 132

Speke, Christopher, rector of Moreton Hampstead, 120

Spelman (Ospelan, Ospelayn, Ospellayn), Cristinus, canon of Tuam, papal mandatary, 69, 73, 75, 123, 163, 164; cf. 330
......, ..., vicar of the parish church of the Great Gate at the [Cistercian] monastery of Abbeyknockmoy, 122
......, ..., ..., to have vicarage, called stipend, of Tuam cathedral, 122

Spencer (Spenser), Robert, canon of Lincoln, prebendary of Milton Manor, and incumbent of Nettleton, 203
......, William, vicar of Grantham (northern part), 482
......, cf. Spenser

Spenfer see Spenser

Spens, David, rector of Conveth, 792
......, ..., ..., guarantee entered into for with the commonalty of Edinburgh, 792
......, ..., ..., ..., litigant over repayment of money, 792
......, ..., ..., ..., ..., appeals of, 792
......, John, succentor of Moray cathedral, 780, 844
......, ..., ..., litigant over succentorship, 844
......, ..., ..., consent of, to payment of pension on fruits of succentorship, 844
......, ..., incumbent of Johnstone, 780
......, ..., proctor of see Bologna, Alexander of

Spenser (Spenfer), Robert, of Lincoln diocese, dispensed for plurality, 1076
......, Thomas, master of hospital of Domus Dei, called St John, Bridgwater, 1107
......, cf. Spencer

Sperham see Sparham

Speyer [in Bavaria, Germany], church of the Holy Trinity, canons and prebendaries of see Goler, Wolffgangus; Ponzettus, Fer(di)nandus

Spicer, Robert, layman of the city and diocese of Hereford, proceedings against, 9
......, William, rector of Clopton, 701

[Spinelli (de Palatio)], Octavian, archbishop of Armagh, metropolitan and primate of Ireland, litigation before, 442
......, ..., ..., in provincial council, 927
......, ..., ..., visitation of Meath by, 1005
......, ..., ..., alleged abuse of his metropolitical jurisdiction, 1005
......, ..., ..., remission of case to by bishop of Meath, 927
......, ..., ..., litigation before, 927
......, ..., ..., commission by virtue of an appeal, 1164

Spittal [in Auchterderran, co. Fife], possibly identifiable with 'Spittale', q.v.

'Spittale' [unidentified; probably place (now unnamed) on R. Ore, near Redford [in Dysart, co. Fife]; possibly Spittal (in Auchterderran, co. Fife)], place or vill of, tithes of belonging to the Augustinian monastery of St Andrews, 971

Sponar, Simon, canon of the Augustinian priory of Little Leighs, 43

Spoutesbury cf. Pontesbury

Spring (Spryngo), Richard, prior of the Augustinian monastery of Woodspring, 863
......, ..., ..., vicar of Worle, 863

Sproatley (Sprotley) [Yorks], parish church of, union of, to the parish church of Fakenham, 797

Spryngo see Spring

Squyer, Roger, rector of All Saints', Canterbury, 533

Stack (Stak), Gerald, cleric of Ardfert diocese, detainer of the archdeaconry of

Stack (*contd*)
Ardfert, 945
......, ..., detainer, with David FitzMaurice, of the chancellorship of Ardfert, 993
......, Philip, cleric of Ardfert diocese, to be canon of Lismore and have vicarages of Kilronan and Kilcash erected into a prebend, 790

Stafford [Staffs], archdeaconry and archdeacons of in the church of Coventry and Lichfield, *q.v.*

[Stafford, co. of], places in *see* Bradley; Bromley, Abbots; Croxden; Eaton, Church; Kinver; Ridware, Hamstall *and* Mavesyn; Stafford; Walsall

Stainbauke *see* Stanbank

Stak *see* Stack

Stamford [Lincs and Northants], vill or town of, part of towards Peterborough [i.e. Stamford-Baron, Northants], dwellings in, gift of to the Benedictine monastery of Peterborough, 425
......, ..., ..., hospital of St John the Baptist with chapel of St Thomas the Martyr, foundation of by abbot and convent of Peterborough, 425
......, ..., ..., hospital with leper house of St Giles, foundation of by abbot and convent of Peterborough, 425
......, ..., ..., [Benedictine] nunnery of St Michael, foundation of by abbot and convent of Peterborough, 425

Stampe, John, prior of the [Augustinian] priory of St Botolph, [Colchester], 8
......, ..., ..., ..., papal judge delegate, litigation before, 8
......, ..., ..., ..., ..., sub-delegate of *see* Hill, John

Stanbank (Stainbauke), Edmund, of Lincoln diocese, dispensed for plurality, 1245

Standerwike, John, vicar of Westbury (sub Mendip), 311

Stanford Rivers (Stan Vordrynees) [Essex], parish church of, union of, to the parish church of North Wingfield, 300

Stanley, Humphrey, cleric of Coventry and Lichfield diocese, 534
......, James, rector of Winwick and incumbent of Rostherne, 475
......, ..., union for, of one of his parish churches to the other, 1229
......, John, intended marriage of, to Ann Ardion', 76

Stanton' *see* Churchstanton

de Stantona *see* Staunton

Stan Vordrynees *see* Stanford Rivers

Stapleton (Stapulton), Patrick, to have monastery and regular priory in Cashel diocese, 1084

Stapylton, Brian, cleric of York diocese, 761

Stargrawerde *see* Stonegrave

Starkey, Thomas, canon of the Augustinian monastery of Tonbridge, 871

Staunton (de Sanctona, de Stantona), Edmund, detainer of vicarage of Balla, 402
......, Hebertus, detainer of vicarage of Omey, 827
......, ..., *cf.* Staunton, Obertus
......, Ilialmus, cleric of Tuam diocese, to be canon of Tuam and have vicarage of Omey, with particle of Omey appropriated thereto, erected into prebend, 827
......, Obertus, 126 *note*
......, ..., *cf.* Staunton, Hebertus
......, Robert, ostensible priest of Tuam diocese, detainer of vicarage of Omey, 126

Staverton (Staverton') [Devon], parish church of, 803

Staxley, George, vicar of Westleton, 708

Staynclyff, Edward, priest of York diocese, 104

Stazzema [*in* province of Lucca, Italy], parish church of St Mary, rectory of, 697

Steluart, Stenvart *see* Stewart

Stephani *see* Stevenson

Stephen, prior of the Augustinian priory of Taunton, 174

Sterne, Edmund, canon of the Augustinian monastery of St Peter, Dunstable, 563

Sternilyng *see* Stirling

Stevenson (Stephani), William, of St Andrews diocese, appeal of, 971

Stevyns, Richard, chaplain of the Roper chantry [in St Dunstan's, Canterbury], 195

Steward *see* Stewart

Stewardi, William, of Howden, priest of York diocese, litigant, 94
......, ..., ..., ..., allegedly despoiling prior and chapter of Durham of tithes of parish church of Brantingham, 94

Stewardson *cf.* Stewardi

Stewart (Steluart, Stenvart, Steward, Stowart), Alexander, scholar of Glasgow diocese, 408
......, ..., ..., illegitimate son of James [IV], 408
......, ..., cleric of Glasgow diocese, 769
......, ..., ..., illegitimate son of king of Scots, 769
......, Andrew, kinsman of James [IV], king of Scots, 620, 622, 623
......, ..., ..., canon of Glasgow, 620, 622, 623
......, ..., ..., ..., provision of to the bishopric of Caithness, 620
......, ..., ..., ..., absolution of preliminary to provision, 622

Stewart (*contd*)
......, ..., ..., ..., dispensed for minority and illegitimacy preliminary to provision, 623
......, ..., [bishop-] elect of Caithness, faculty for promotion to priesthood and consecration of, 621
......, ..., bishop of Moray, death of, 630
......, Archibald, to have parish church in Whithorn diocese, 1165
......, Edward, canon of Orkney, 549-552
......, ..., ..., vicar general of Andrew [Painter], bishop of Orkney, 549, 550
......, ..., ..., ..., appointment of as coadjutor (with subsequent provision) to the bishopric of Orkney, 549, 552
......, ..., ..., ..., absolution of preliminary to appointment and provision, 550
......, ..., ..., coadjutor and prospective bishop of Orkney, faculty for consecration of, 551
......, ..., ..., assignment to of fruits etc. and collation etc. of benefices within archdeaconry of Shetland, 552
......, ..., ..., incumbent of St Mary's, Sanday, 552
......, James, priest of Aberdeen diocese, to have rectory of Slains, 50
......, ..., ..., appeal of to the apostolic see, 50
......, ..., elect of St Andrews, 848
......, ..., ..., appointment and provision of, as administrator then archbishop of St Andrews, 848
......, ..., ..., faculty to, for reconciling churches and cemeteries by deputy, 848
......, ..., administrator of St Andrews, petition of for restoration of Dunblane to province of St Andrews, 333
......, ..., archbishop of St Andrews, primate of the whole kingdom of Scotland and legate born of the apostolic see, 356
......, ..., ..., grant by, of barony and lands in St Andrews diocese pertaining to archiepiscopal *mensa*, 356
......, ..., ..., cession by, of commend of the Augustinian monastery of Holyrood, 584
......, ..., ..., commend to of the Benedictine monastery of Dunfermline, 588

Stewart (*contd*)

......, ..., ..., ..., absolution of preliminary to commend, 589

......, ..., ..., ..., to take oath of fealty, 588

......, ..., ..., ..., ..., mandate over, 590

......, ..., ..., commendator of Dunfermline, 590

......, ..., ..., provision of to monastery in St Andrews diocese, 1321

......, ..., ..., ..., absolution of preliminary to provision, 1322

......, Walter, cleric of Glasgow diocese, 766

Sthorisbroke *see* Shottesbrooke

Stirling (Sternilyng) [co. Stirling], town of, Observant Franciscan house to be founded at, 1

......, ..., [church, called] chapel royal, [of B. Mary and St Michael within the palace of James, king of Scots], erection of into collegiate [church] with union of provostship, 765, 1214

......, ..., ..., ..., ..., ..., ..., confirmation of, 781

......, ..., ..., ..., ..., ..., ..., endowment of, 765

......, ..., ..., ..., ..., ..., ..., appropriation to of residues of fruits of canonry of Glasgow and prebend of Ayr; of canonry of Aberdeen and prebend of Kincardine O'Neil; of canonry of Dunkeld and prebend of Crieff; of canonry of Moray and prebend of Petty-Brackley; and of canonry of Moray and prebend of Duthel, 768

......, ..., ..., erection of cantorship in, 781

......, ..., ..., letters conservatory for, 767

......, place in *see* Cambuskenneth

[Stirling, co. of], places in *see* Cambuskenneth; Falkirk; Slamannan; Stirling

Stockdale (Stokdale), William, vicar of West Mersea and incumbent of St Leonard's of the New Hithe, Colchester, 215

......, *cf.* Stoltdale

Stockfish (Stokefish), William, vicar of Kenton, 266

......, *cf.* Stoliefish

Stodely *see* Studley

Stokchertte *see* Stoke Charity

Stokdale *see* Stockdale

Stoke Charity (Stokchertte) [Hants], parish church of, 866

Stoke Lacy (Stokelacy) [Heref], parish church of, 517

Stoke, South (Stoke near Granth(a)m) [Lincs], parish church of, 202

......, ..., ..., southern moiety in, 202

Stoke Talmage (Stooke Talmache) [Oxon], parish church of, 526

Stokefish *see* Stockfish

Stokes (Stokys), Robert, OESA, 151

Stokesby (Stokysby) [Norf], parish church of, rector of, 47

Stokesley, Robert, cleric of York diocese, 500

Stokys *see* Stokes

Stokysby *see* Stokesby

Stoliefish, William, of Exeter diocese, indulged for non-residence, 1238

......, *cf.* Stockfish

Stoltdale, John, of St David's diocese, dispensed for plurality, 1185

......, *cf.* Stockdale

Stonegrave (Stargrawerde) [Yorks], parish church of, rector of, 355

Stoneham Aspal *alias* Lambard *see* Stonham Aspall

Stonely (Stoneley) [*in* Kimbolton, Hunts], Augustinian priory of, canon of *see* Garford *alias* Crouulandi, Thomas

Stonham (Stoneham) Aspall (Aspal) *alias* [St] Lambert (Lambard) [*now* Stonham Aspall, Suff], parish church of, 700

Stooke Talmache *see* Stoke Talmage

Stornoway *see* 'Li'

[Story], Edward, bishop of Chichester, 179, 919
......, ..., ..., statute and ordinance of, whereby canonry of Chichester and prebend of Highleigh destined for teacher at Chichester grammar-school, confirmation of, 179
......, ..., ..., ..., ..., letters in this regard fortified with his seal, 179
......, ..., ..., notary in episcopal curia appointed by (with chapter), 919

Stot *see* Scott

Stove *see* ?Jacobstowe

Stowart *see* Stewart

Strachan (Strachakin), William, cleric of Aberdeen diocese, to have newly erected parish church of New Aberdeen, 64

Stradbally (Ardwalebeg) [co. Kerry], parish church of, rectory of, 939
......, ..., ..., to be erected into prebend of Ardfert cathedral, with rectories of *Eaglais-na-lainne alias* Ballyheige and Killury and particle of 'Killcolin' united thereto, 939

Stradbally (Seradaualy) [co. Limerick] *alias* 'Cloynacheke' [*unidentified*; *possibly* Cloon Island *or* Clounclieffe *both in* Stradbally, co. Limerick], parish church of, vicarage of, 380
......, ..., ..., to be united to vicarage of Ludden, 380

Straling *see* Skirling

Strangways (Stranguais), Edward, union for, of one of his parish churches to the other, diocese of Durham, 1081
......, George, archdeacon of Coventry and rector of Ripley, sometime incumbent of Bulmer, 143

Stratford Langthorne (Stratforde Langthorn') [*in* West Ham, Essex], [Cistercian] monastery of, abbot of, papal judge delegate, 365

Stratton (Straton) [Corn], parish church of, 900

Stratton St Margaret (Stratton' Margarete) [Wilts], parish church of, 338

Street (Strete) [Som], parish church of, 276

Stretton on the Fosse (Stretton' on Fos') [Warw], parish church of, union of, to the parish church of Hamerton, 282

Stretton, Church (Stretton super Strett) [Salop], parish church of, rector of, 242

Strickland (Strykland), Thomas, of York diocese, dispensed for plurality, 1278

Stroneskar (Strovesk) [*in* Kilmichael Glassary, co. Argyll], place of, 493

Strykland *see* Strickland

Stubbs (Stubis), John, of Coventry and Lichfield diocese, dispensed for plurality, 1276

Studley (Stodely) [*in* Ripon, Yorks], prebend of in [collegiate] church of Ripon, union to, of Little Wilbraham, 182

Styortal, Styortall *see* Shortall

Suchyhyn *see* Creagh [co. Roscommon]

Sueede (*or* Sneede), Nicholas, vicar of Salford, 659

[Suffolk, co. of], places in *see* Bradley [*probably* Great]; Bury St Edmunds; Drinkstone; Dunwich; Euston; Eye; Ipswich; Kettleburgh; Kirkley; Lackford; Leiston; Pakefield; Preston; Shottisham; Stonham Aspall; Tannington; Westleton; Whelnetham, Little

Suir *see* Inishlounaght

Sulhampstead Abbots (Sulh(a)msted) [Berks], parish church of, 224

Sundridge (Sundrich) [Kent], parish church of, 917

Surmiricor *see* Oranmore

[Surrey, co. of], places in *see* Albury; Bermondsey; Chertsey; Guildford; Merton; Ockley; Puttenham; Reigate; Waverley

Surtees *cf.* Surteys

Surteys (Surteis, de Surteys), Stephen, vicar of Ashbourne, 35, 292
......, ..., ..., consent of, to celebration of divine offices and administration of sacraments in chapel within Ashbourne parish, 292

[Sussex, co. of], places in *see* Chichester; Highleigh; Lewes; *and* places *listed above under* Chichester, diocese of

[Sutherland, co. of], place in *see* [Dornoch]

Suthyke, Richard, of Winchester diocese, dispensed for plurality, 1066

Sutterton (Sutturton') [Lincs], parish church of, 720

Sutton *see* Sutton Courtenay

Sutton (Sutton'), John, layman of London, 365
......, ..., ..., inhabitant of house in parish of [St John the Baptist], Walbrook, London, appeal of, 365

Sutton Coldfield (Sutton in Colfeld) [Warw], parish church of, rector of, 641

Sutton Courtenay (Sutton) [Berks], parish church of, 911

Sutton Mandeville (Sutton Maundevyle) [Wilts], parish church of, 472

Sutton (Sutton') near Potton (Pattoy) [*now* Sutton, Beds], parish church of, union of, to prebend of Blewbury in Salisbury cathedral, 91

Sutturton' *see* Sutterton

[S]vyst, Thomas, rector of ?Newton and incumbent of Wickersley, sometime incumbent of Brocklesby, 131

Swaffham (Swafpham) [Cambs], parish church of Sts Cyriac and Julitta, 376

Swanage *see* Worth [and] Swanage

Swanton Abbot (Swanton' Abbat') [Norf], parish church of, 952

Sweetheart [*in* Newabbey, co. Kirkcudbright], monastery of, abbot of, to receive intending religious as monk [elsewhere], bestow habit on him, and admit his profession, 1017

Swynton, Robert, monk of the Benedictine monastery of Dunfermline, 145

Sydnor (Syndmor), Richard, vicar of Ermington, 915

'Syliam' (*apud Syliam*) [*unidentified*; *perhaps obsolete* ; *probably in* the barony of Moycarn, co. Roscommon *or* the barony of Longford, co. Galway, *near* the confluence of the Suck and Shannon], gorge called 'Bruachtalach' at, 146

Sylton' *see* Silton

Symson *see* Simson

Syndmor *see* Sydnor

Synkclare *see* Sinclair

Synr *see* Seirkieran

Synyer, Richard, vicar of Furneux Pelham, 93
......, *cf.* Senior

T

Tactorm', William, chaplain in London cathedral, 856

Taff, river, Llanfyrnach on, *q.v.*

Taghboy (Teacboych) [cos. Galway and Roscommon], parish church of, vicarage of, 784

Tagheen (Thayn) [co. Mayo], parish church of, vicarage of, 384

[Taghsheenod, co. Longford], place in *see* Abbeyderg

Tailar *see* Taylor

Talcarne (Talkaryn' or Terkaryn'), alias of Minster, *q.v.*

Tame, Thomas, rector of Castle Eaton, 499

Tanadas, Tana'das *see* Tannadice

Taneto, insula de see Thanet, Isle of

Tanfeld, Thomas, prior of the Augustinian monastery of Thornholme, 859

Tannadice (Tanadas, Tana'das) [co. Forfar], parish church of, 849
......, ..., litigation over, 687
......, ..., rector of, 812
......, ..., ..., coadjutor to, 812

Tannington (Tatington') [Suff], parish church of, vicar of, 25

Tannten', Tannton', Tanntonne *see* Taunton

Tapinan *see* Tippeenan

[Tardebigg, Worcs], place in *see* Bordesley

Tarkii, Peter, guardian of the guild of the Drapers' Company in St Michael, Cornhill, London, 903

Tarlacon *see* Thurloxton

Tarquinia *see* Corneto

Tateshall *see* Tattershall

Tatington' *see* Tannington

Tattershall (Tateshall) [Lincs], church of the Holy Trinity of, chapter of, 423
......, ..., statutes and ordinances of, reform of, 423
......, ..., patroness of *see* [Beaufort], Margaret

Taunton (Tannten', Tannton', Tanntonne, Tauutonne, Tawnton') [Som], chapel of St James by the canon's gate (*Sancti Jacobi iuxta portam canonicorum*), 174
......, parish church of B. Mary Magdalene, united to the Augustinian priory of Taunton, 174
......, chapel of St Paul without the castle (*Sancti Pauli extra Castellum*), 174
......, chapel of St Peter of the castle (*Sancti Petri de Castello*), 174
......, Augustinian priory of St Peter, priors of *see* Prowse, John; Stephen
......, ..., prior and convent of, 174
......, ..., convent of, 1109
......, ..., canon of *see* Harww, John
......, ..., parish church of B. Mary Magdalene united to, 174
......, ..., rights and titles of, 174
......, ..., letter of protection etc. for, confirmation of, 174

Taverner (Thaverner), Nicholas, canon of Chichester and prebendary of Highleigh, 179
......, ..., ..., consent of, to statute and ordinance of Edward [Story], bishop of

Taverner (*contd*)
Chichester, whereby his canonry and prebend destined, on his vacating it, for teacher at Chichester grammar school, 179
......, Thomas, of Norwich diocese, dispensed for plurality, 1161

Tawnton' *see* Taunton

Taylard, William, rector of Abbots Ripton, 329

Tayler, John, rector of Shottesbrooke, 476

Taylor (Tailar), John, rector of Northmoor, 716

Teacboych *see* Taghboy

Teachsassan, Teachsasari *see* Tisaxon

Telscombe (Tetylscombe) [Sussex], parish church of, rector of, 24

Templeachally (Tempullacallay) *alias* Callathamery (Caladama'rain) [co. Tipperary], parish church of, vicarage of, 783

Templegaile (*de Templo Albo*), alias of Tisaxon, *q.v.*

[Templemichael, co. Waterford], place in *see* Molana

Templeport (Tempulpuirt) [co. Cavan] *alias* Breaghwy Island (Ynesbrachyn) [*in* ?Templeport, co. Cavan], parish church of, vicarage of, 940

Templetogher (Calioco *alias* Tempul Antoter) [co. Galway], parish church of, vicarage of, 833
......, ..., ..., [?annexed] to canonry and prebend of Tuam, 833

Templetrine (Treve) [co. Cork], parish church of, rectory of, to be united to the proposed canonry and prebend of Gortnacrusha in Cork cathedral, 255
......, place in *see* Gortnacrusha

Templevalley (Belach) [*in* Mogeely, co. Cork], parish church of, vicarage of, to be erected into prebend in Cloyne cathedral, 160

de Templo Albo see Templegaile

Tempul Antoter *see* Templetogher

Tempullacallay *see* Templeachally

Tempull na Scrine (Serin) [*in modern* Tuam parish, co. Galway], parish church of, vicarage of, *alias* the custodianship of the relics of St Jarlath outside the walls of Tuam, 163
......, ..., ..., ..., to be united to the proposed prebend of Lackagh in Annaghdown cathedral, 163

Tempulpuirt *see* Templeport

Terkaryn' *see* Talcarne

Termonamongan *see* ?Cell cairill

Terracina (*Terracinen.*) [*in* province of Latina, Italy], [bishop-] elect / bishop of *see* de Galves, Johannes

'Terroner', diocese of Lismore [*unidentified* : *in vicinity of head of* Loch Awe; *possibly* Torran (*in* Kilmartin), co. Argyll], place of, 493

Terryglass (Thyrdaglas, Tiraglas) [co. Tipperary], parish church of, rectory of, 16, 935
......, ..., ..., to have been united to proposed canonry and prebend of Finnoe in Killaloe cathedral, 16
......, ..., ..., to be united to proposed canonry and prebend of Loughrea in Clonfert cathedral, 16
......, ..., ..., to be united to canonry of Kilmacduagh and prebend of the small churches, 935

Tetford [Lincs], parish church of, 11

Tetylscombe *see* Telscombe

Tewkesbury (Tevukesbury) [Glos], [Benedictine] monastery of, abbot of, papal judge delegate, 298

Teyntyhull *see* Tintinhull

Thame [Oxon], [Cistercian (*not* Benedictine)] monastery of, abbot and convent of, litigants, 46

Thamohoc *alias* Baleuatibenda *see* Timahoe

Thanet, Isle of (*insula de Taneto*) [Kent], 88

Thatcher (Theccher), William, rector of West Dean, 657

Thaverner *see* Taverner

Thayn *see* Tagheen

Theccher *see* Thatcher

?Thelau, Alan, of Norwich diocese, dispensed for plurality, 1221

Thérouanne [France], diocese, person of *see* Chadworth, George
......, ..., places in *see* Guemps; Guînes

Thilcorim *see* Kilcomin

Thilde, Thomas, vicar of Dewlish, 82

Thimbleby (Tymylby), Richard, temporal lord of Poolham, 379
......, ..., the heir of Robert Barkeworth, 379
......, ..., confirmation at petition of, of agreement concerning chapel of Poolham, 379

Thobym, Thobyn *see* Tobin

Thomarotius, Paulus, *magister registri*, letters signed by:
  P. Thomarotius, 859, 861-863, 871, 947, 954, 968, 978, 1001, 1003, 1024-1028

Thomas, abbot of Chertsey *see* [Pigot], Thomas
......, late abbot of Jedburgh *see* [Cranston], Thomas
......, abbot of Kinloss *see* [Wawain *alias* Chrystal], Thomas
......, abbot of Titchfield *see* [Oke], Thomas
......, abbot of Torre *see* [Dyer], Thomas
......, abbot of Waverley *see* [Skevington *alias* Patexe], Thomas
......, abbot of Woburn *see* [Hogeson], Thomas
......, (the late,) archbishop of Canterbury *see* [?Arundel], Thomas
......, archbishop of York *see* [Rotherham *or* Scot], Thomas
......, ..., lately bishop of London *see* [Savage], Thomas
......, [bishop-] elect of Bangor *see* [Pigot], Thomas
......, bishop of Clonfert *see* [OKelly], Thomas
......, bishop of Durham *see* [Langley], Thomas
......, late bishop of Killala *see* [Barrett], Thomas
......, bishop / [bishop-] elect of Killala *see* [Clerke], Thomas
......, bishop of Lismore *see* [Purcell], Thomas
......, bishop of London, afterwards archbishop of York *see* [Savage], Thomas
......, late bishop / [bishop-] elect of Norwich *see* [Jane], Thomas
......, bishop of Winchester *see* [Langton], Thomas

Thomastown (Thomastown') [co. Kilkenny], parish church of, vicarage of, to be united to canonry and prebend of St Maul's in Ossory cathedral, 787

Thome, Beraldus *see* [de Geraldinis], Beraldus [*recte* Geraldus], Thome
......, John, vicar of All Saints, Bristol, 106
......, *and see* Thomson

Thomson (Thome, Tompson), Duncan, of Auchinhamper, lessee of church property in Aberdeen diocese, to have

Thomson (*contd*)
lease confirmed, 1226
......, John, of Lincoln diocese, dispensed
for plurality, 1083
......, Thomas, rector of Niton, 959

Thomuay *see* Tumna

Thoresby, South (Thorisby) [Lincs], parish
church of, union of, to the vicarage of
East Ham, 703

Thormerton' *see* ?Farmington

Thornburgh (Thorneburgh), William, of
London diocese, dispensed for plurality,
1148

Thorncombe [Dors *formerly* Devon], place
in *see* Forde

Thorneburgh *see* Thornburgh

Thornholme (*alias* Thornh(a)m) [*in*
Appleby, Lincs], Augustinian
monastery of, prior of *see* Tanfeld,
Thomas

Thornton (Thoruton) [*in* Thornton Curtis,
Lincs], Augustinian monastery of, 997
......, ..., canon of *see* Legate, John

Thorpe (Thorpe'), William, chaplain in
Lincoln cathedral, 896

Thoruton *see* Thornton

Thruleber' *see* Thurlbear

Thuinnia *alias* Thomuay *see* Tumna

Thurlbear (Thruleber') [Som], [church of],
174

Thurloxton (Tarlacon) [Som], land of, 174

Thwaytes (Thwaytis), John, vicar of
Faversham, 491

Thymylby, Thomas, rector of Tetford, 11

Thyndyn', Thomas, rector of Eakring, 751

Thyrdaglas *see* Terryglass

Tidworth (Tuduuorth') [*now* North
Tidworth, Wilts], parish church of, 420

Tilbury, West (Westtilbury) [Essex], parish
church of, union to, of St Mary
Abchurch, London, 375

Tilehurst (Tylehurst) [Berks], parish church
of, vicar of, 26

Tilliemaud (Inlymad, Tulimaod, Tulyma',
Tulymod) [*in* Udny, co. Aberdeen],
tithes of pertaining to Ellon parish
church, 144, 793, 928

'Tilmadim', diocese of Tuam [*unidentified
;probably ancient territory in vicinity of*
Clew Bay, co. Mayo; *perhaps*
Kilmaine], Umall, Upper and Lower
(Wmallyacd ac *and* Vacdachr) [*ancient
divisions of* co. Mayo *represented by
the* baronies of Murrisk and
Burrishoole], place of, church, called
prebend of, 165
......, ..., ..., ..., ..., ..., ..., proposed union
to, of vicarage of Oughaval, 165

Timahoe (Thamohoc *alias* Baleuatibenda)
[co. Laois], parish church of, vicarage
of, 576

Timberscombe (Tymberiscomb') [Som],
prebend of in Wells cathedral, union to,
of the parish church of Axbridge, 295

[Timogue, co. Laois], place in *see*
Ballycoolan

Tinos [an island in Aegean Sea, Greece],
bishop of *see* [Cornish], Thomas

?Tinos, bishop of, papal judge delegate,
987 *note*

Tintinhull (Teyntyhull) [Som], parish
church of, 723

Tinwell (Tynvuell') [Rut], parish church of, 501

Tippeenan (Tapinan) [*in* Fontstown, co. Kildare], parish church of, vicarage of, to be united to proposed prebend of Ballyshannon in Derry [*recte* Kildare], 934

[Tipperary, co. of], places in *see* Ballyloughnane; Ballysheehan; Bourney; Caher; Cashel; Clonoulty; ?Colman; Crampscastle; Donaghmore; Dorrha; Emly; ?Erry; Finnoe; Holycross; Ikerrin; Inishlounaght; Kilbarron; Kilcash; ?Kilcomenty; Kilcooly; Killea; Kilsheelan; Lorrha; Loughkeen; 'Medohk' [*in* Loughkeen]; ?Mocklerstown [*in* Colman]; Modreeny; Monaincha; Moorstown [*in* Mora]; Nenagh; Newtown Lennan; Outeragh; Railstown; Templeachally *alias* Callathamery; Terryglass; Uskane; *and see* Kilnamanagh; Kilvemnon

Tiraglas *see* Terryglass

Tirley (Trynley) [Glos], parish church of, vicar of, 10

Tisaxon (Teachsasari, Teachsassan) *alias* Templegaile (*de Templo Albo*) [*in* Monivea, co. Galway], prebend of in Tuam cathedral, 69, 75
......, ..., rectory of Killererin *alias* Muinter Murchada with appurtenances of Aghiart annexed to, 69, 75
......, ..., to be united to deanery of Tuam, 69, 75

Tisbury (Tysbury) [Wilts], vicarage of, union of, to the parish church of St Romuald, [Shaftesbury], 733

Titchfield (Tychefeld) [Hants], Premonstratensian monastery of, abbot of *see* [Oke], Thomas

Tobin (Thobym, Thobyn, Tohin), John, canon of Ossory, papal mandatary, 350, 785, 789, 790

Tocton' *see* Totnes

Toft, William, of the chapel royal, succentor of Salisbury, 478

Tohin *see* Tobin

Tolach *see* Tullagh

'Tolach', diocese of Kilmore [*unidentified*], church, called chapel, of Sts Patrick, Columba, and Canicus, to be erected into prebend in Kilmore cathedral with vicarage of Annagh united thereto, 821

Toliburnem, Toliburnen' *see* Cockburn

Tollebrache *see* Tullabracky

Tollerton (Torleston) [Notts], parish church of, 764

Tompson *see* Thomson

Tonbridge (Tunbrigge) [Kent], Augustinian monastery of, 871
......, ..., canon of *see* Starkey, Thomas

Tonge, William, rector of Langham, incumbent of Ludgershall, 309

Tongland [co. Kirkcudbright], [Premonstratensian] monastery of, abbot of, papal mandatary, 509

Tonker, alias of Chaplain, John, *q.v.*

Toppyng, John, of Winchester diocese, dispensed for plurality, 1102

Tor *see* Torre

Torci *see* Torry

Torleston *see* Tollerton

[Tormoham, Devon], place in *see* Torre

Torran [*in* Kilmartin, co. Argyll] *see* 'Terroner'

Torre (Tor) [*in* Tormoham, Devon], Premonstratensian monastery of, abbot of *see* [Dyer], Thomas

Torry (Torci) [*in* Udny, co. Aberdeen], tithes of pertaining to Ellon parish church, 144, 793, 928

Tortington [Sussex], Augustinian priory of, 758
......, ..., canon of *see* Burra, William

Tothoth', Vincent, vicar of Corby, 345
......, *cf.* Totofte

Totinczhanen *see* Cottingham

Totnes (Tocton') [Devon], archdeacon of in the church of Exeter, *q.v.*

Totofte *cf.* Tothoth'

Toulouse [*in dép.* of Haute-Garonne, France], cleric of *see* André, Bernard

Touris (Tourys), Thomas, layman of Dunkeld diocese, and his wife Elizabeth, lease to, of lands of Newtown and Craigton, 558

Tracton [co. Cork], Cistercian monastery of, 536
......, ..., abbot of, papal mandatary, 71, 254, 362
......, ..., ..., *see* Barry, James, John and Edmund; Roche, William
......, ..., convent of, 67, 536
......, ..., monk of *see* Barry, James
......, ..., vassals of, 67, 536
......, ..., proposed union to, of Brinny vicarage, 67
......, ..., abbatial *mensa* of, rectories of Inishannon and Leighmoney to be united to, 536
......, ..., founder of, progeny of, 67
......, ..., subject to the bishop of Cork, 536

Traig *see* Craig

Trail *see* St Mary's Isle

Trant (Trawt), Davit, canon of Ardfert, papal mandatary, 994

Trapani [*in* province of Trapani, Sicily], parish church of St Laurence, 417

Trappe, John, canon of the Augustinian monastery of Heryngham, 438

Trawt *see* Trant

Trebel, John, monk of the Benedictine monastery of Cerne, 139

Trechton', Patrick, scholar of St Andrews diocese, 370
......, *cf.* Crichton

Treglio [*in* province of Chieti, Italy], parish church of, provision to, 854

Tregony *see* Cuby

Tregulan, John, of Exeter diocese, dispensed for plurality, 1266

Trehed *see* ?Craigheid

Treminet (*de Tribus Menetis* [i.e. from Les Trois Minettes *in dép.* of Calvados, France]), William, property gifted to Taunton priory by, 174

Tremlett *cf.* Treminet

Trendell' *see* Trull

Tresh(a)m, Richard, rector of Rendcombe, 813

Treve *see* Templetrine

de Tribus Menetis see Treminet

Trier [*in* Rhine province, Germany], diocese of, person of *see* Fabri, Johannes

Trim (Tryme) [co. Meath], parish church of St Patrick, rectors of, 694
......, ..., grant of, impetation of, alleged

Trim (*contd*)
    obreption and subreption of, 694
......, Augustinian priory of St Peter *see* [Newtown] Trim
......, place in *see* Trim, Newtown

Trim, Newtown (Trixin, Trym') [*in* Trim, co. Meath], priory of St John near Trim, OCrucif, prior of, commissary of archdeacon of the church of Meath, proceedings by, 694
......, ..., Augustinian hospital of the *Cruciferi Sancti Johannis cum stella*, prior of, alleged dishonesty of, 416
......, ..., ..., brother of *see* Cussen, John
......, ..., reduced income of, 416
......, ..., Augustinian priory of St Peter, canon of *see* Durham, Martin
......, ..., *and see under* Meath

Trinity Island *see* Lough Key

Trinla *see* Trull

Trixin *see* Trim

Troie *see* Troy

Trompostan' *see* Crumpstown

Trotter, John, scholar of London diocese, 740

Troy (Troie), John, abbot of the Cistercian monastery of Mellifont, 383

Trufodi, Hugh, of London diocese, dispensed for plurality, 1310

Trull (Trendell', Trinla) [Som], chapel of, 174

Trym', Tryme *see* Trim

Trynley *see* Tirley

Tuam [co. Galway], Augustinian monastery of B. John the Evangelist, abbot of *see* [de Burgo], Miler
......, ..., misrule and disrepair of, 835
......, ..., to be united to archiepiscopal

Tuam (*contd*)
    mensa of Tuam, 835
......, Premonstratensian monastery of the Holy Trinity outside the walls of, 166
......, ..., (commendatory) abbots of *see* Bermingham, William; OKelly, Odo
......, ..., chapel of B. Mary, *Templi Collis*, at Galway annexed to, 166
......, walls of, 163, 166
......, ..., place just outside *see* Tempull na Scrine

......, [cathedral] church of, deanery of, 69, 75, 330
......, ..., dean of, customarily elected by the chapter, 330
......, ..., ..., papal commissary and mandatary, 167
......, ..., ..., *see* Bermingham, Walter; de Burgo, Thomas; OKelly, John and Odo
......, ..., chapter of, dean customarily elected by, 330
......, ..., ..., to be summoned over erection of (canonry and) prebend, 166, 826, 827
......, ..., canons of *see* Bermingham, Thomas; de Burgo, John, Richard, Theobald and William; Cussen, Walter; Macgillanach, Thomas; MacNelly, Nemeas; MacRedmond, Thomas; OCasey, William; Ocherim, David; OConcannon, Cornelius, John, Malachy, William, and Wolmus; Oculay, John; OKelly, John and Odo; OMalley, Rory; OMannin, Malachy; Omogri, John; OMulkerrill, Charles; OMullan, Thomas; OMurphy, Thomas; Onilleayn, David; Orauri, John; Oscara, David; Plemen, Richard; Prendergast, David and Richard; Spelman, Cristinus; Staunton, Ilialmus; *and see* Joy, Maurice
......, ..., canonry [unspecified] of, vicarage of Kilvine united to, 828
......, ..., canonry and prebend [unnamed] of, vicarages of Clonbern and Templetogher [?annexed] to, 833
......, ..., ..., Kilkerrin parish church to be united to, 833
......, ..., prebends in *see* Inishmaine and Lough Mask; Kilcurnan; Omey; Tisaxon *alias* Templegaile; *cf.*

Tuam, **[cathedral] church** (*contd*)
'Tilmadim', Umall, Upper and Lower;
and see below under Tuam, [cathedral]
church of, chaplaincy, called stipend, in
......, ..., vicarage, called stipend, in, 122,
123
......, ..., vicars, called stipendiaries, in *see*
OBeirne, John; OHiggins, Malachy;
OMulkerrill, Charles; Omuynayn,
Magonius; Spelman, Cristinus
......, ..., chaplaincy, called stipend, in, to be
erected into prebend, 166

......, **archbishopric** of, *mensa* of, demesne
tax and possessions of, 835
......, ..., ..., ..., detention of by laymen,
835
......, ..., ..., proposed union to, of the
Augustinian monastery of B. John the
Evangelist, [Tuam], 835
......, archbishop of, cession of commend
into hands of, 384
......, ..., *de facto* collation and provision of
vicarage by, 384
......, ..., as local ordinary, admission of
resignation of vicarage by, *cf.* 167
......, ..., ..., *de facto* union by, *cf.* 167
......, ..., or his vicar general, parish church
resigned into hands of, 833
......, ..., ..., collation and provision of
parish church by, 833
......, ..., to be summoned over erection of
(canonry and) prebend, 166, 826, 827
......, ..., conclusion to, 591, 606
......, ..., subjection to, of the church of
Killala, 607
......, ..., ..., of the Augustinian monastery
of Cong, 127
......, ..., *see* [Joyce], William
......, church of, archdeacon of, papal
mandatary, 126
......, ..., ..., *see* Bermingham, William;
Joy, Maurice

......, **diocese** of, persons of *see* de Burgo,
Miler and Thomas; Joy, Edmund and
Maurice; Macnrocnallyd, Fracha;
Olarnyn, Thomas; OMalley, Cormac;
Prendergast, Miler; Staunton, Hebertus,
Obertus, and Robert; Tyichironus
......, ..., places in *see* Abbeyknockmoy;

Tuam, **diocese** (*contd*)
Aghiart; Annagh; Ballinrobe;
Ballintober; Clonbern; Cong;
Inishmaine [*in* Ballinchalla];
'Kilelonne'; Kilkerrin; Killererin *alias
Muinter Murchada*; Killoscobe;
Kilvine; Lough Mask; Mayo; Omey;
Oughaval; Templetogher; *Tempull na
Scrine*; 'Tilmadim'; Umall, Upper and
Lower
......, ..., *and see* Tuam *alias* / or Mayo

Tuam *alias* / or Mayo, diocese of, persons
of *see* Cussen, Walter; Prendergast,
Miler; Staunton, Edmund; *and see*
Prendergast, David
......, ..., places in *see* Balla; Mayo;
Tagheen

Tuba, master Paul, papal scriptor and
familiar, 407
......, ..., ..., proctor of Robert Shanwell,
407

Tuddenham (Tudenh(a)m) *alias* Moro,
Thomas,   canon   of   the
Premonstratensian   monastery   of
Langley, 321

Tuduuorth' *see* Tidworth

Tuliburnen' *see* Cockburn

Tulimaod *see* Tilliemaud

Tulla (Tullachannasbach) [co. Clare],
prebend of in Killaloe cathedral, 650

Tullabracky (Tollebrache) [co. Limerick],
prebend of in Limerick cathedral, 486
......, ..., proposed union to, of
precentorship of Limerick, 486

Tullachannasbach *see* Tulla

Tullagh (Tolach) [co. Cork], parish church
of, vicarage of, 251
......, ..., ..., to be united to prebend of
Creagh in Ross cathedral, 251
......, ..., rectory of, in ecclesiastical fief,
251

Tullagh (*contd*)
......, ..., ..., ..., to be united to prebend of Creagh in Ross cathedral, 251

Tullales *see* Tullylease

[Tullyallen, co. Louth], place in *see* Mellifont

Tullylease (Tullales) [co. Cork], parish church of, vicarage of, 156

Tullynessle *see* Kearn

Tulyma', Tulymod *see* Tilliemaud

Tumna (Thuinnia *alias* Thomuay) [co. Roscommon], parish church of, vicarage of, 947

Tunbrigge *see* Tonbridge

Tunstall (Turistall), Cuthbert, rector of Claughton, 521

Tupholme [Lincs], Premonstratensian monastery of, 798
......, ..., canon of *see* Morlandi, John

de Turchis, Johannes Petrus, *abbreviator de parco minori*, conclusions expedited by: *Jo de Turchis*, 637

Turen. [Tinos?], bishop of, papal judge delegate, 987

'Turere', alias of 'Kylldacu(m)', *q.v.*

Turin [*in* province of Turin, Italy], diocese of, place in *see* Moncenisio

Turistall *see* Tunstall

Turnbull (Turnbal, Turnbul), John, (monk and) cellarer of the Cistercian monastery of Newbattle, 1032-1034
......, ..., ..., appointment and provision of, as coadjutor and abbot, 1032
......, ..., ..., absolution of preliminary to appointment and provision, 1034

Turnbull (*contd*)
......, ..., ..., coadjutor, prospectively abbot, of Newbattle, 1033
......, ..., ..., ..., ..., ..., faculty for benediction of in event of his becoming abbot, 1033
......, ..., ..., ..., ..., ..., to take oath of fealty to pope, 1033
......, William, cleric of Glasgow diocese, proctor of Gilbert Cranston, 444
......, ..., late rector of Annan, 929
......, ..., cleric of Glasgow diocese, vicarage of Kirkcaldy disputed by, 407
......, ..., ..., ..., assignment to, of pension on fruits of vicarage, 407
......, ..., vicar of Innerleithen, 1015, 1017, 1018, 1020
......, ..., ..., surrogation and provision of to the abbacy of Melrose, 1015, 1016, 1019, 1020
......, ..., ..., absolution of, preliminary to surrogation and provision, 1018
......, ..., ..., to take habit and make profession, 1015
......, ..., ..., reception as monk at Melrose, bestowal of habit on him, and admission of his profession, mandate over, 1017, 1019
......, ..., ..., surrogation and appointment as abbot of Melrose without taking habit and making profession, dispensation for, 1020
......, ..., abbot of the Cistercian monastery of Melrose, faculty for benediction of, 1016
......, ..., pensioner of Kirkcaldy and of Aberlady, to retain pensions with abbacy of Melrose, 1019

Turtom', George, rector of Broxholme, 110

Turville (Tyrfeldi) [Bucks], parish church of, 470

Tusculum [*at* Frascati, *in* province of Rome], [cardinal] bishop of *see* [Zeno], Battista

Twickenham (Twykenh(a)m) [Midd], vicarage of, union of, to a canonry and prebend of the [collegiate] church of B. Mary in the Fields, Norwich, 872

Twyforth *alias* Colyns, John, canon of the Augustinian monastery of B. Mary the Virgin of the Meadow, Leicester, 730

......, ..., ..., ..., incumbent of Ryther, 730

Twykenh(a)m *see* Twickenham

[?Twynyng], John, [abbot of Winchcombe] *cf.* 394 [12] *and note* 14

Tyake (Tyak), John, rector of Kenn and incumbent of Manaton, 958

Tybard (Tybardi), Henry, vicar of Bledlow, 135

Tybenh(a)m, Thomas, rector of Preston, 953

Tychefeld *see* Titchfield

Tyichironus, brother of the third order of B. Francis, called *de Penitentia*, and incumbent of Kilkerrin, 833

Tylehurst *see* Tilehurst

Tymberiscomb' *see* Timberscombe

Tymylby *see* Thimbleby

Tynvuell' *see* Tinwell

Tyrfeldi *see* Turville

[Tyrone, co. of], places in *see* Clogher; Leckpatrick; Termonamongan

Tysbury *see* Tisbury

U

Ubryen *see* OBrien

?Udny (Wetno') [co. Aberdeen], tithes of, 928

[Udny, co. Aberdeen], places in *see* Allathan; Ardmore; Craig; Dumbreck; Housieside; Pitmedden; Tilliemaud; Torry; Woodland

Uffington (Uffyngton') [Lincs], parish church of, 440

Ugerrimayn *see* OGarvan

Uig *see* 'Li'

?Ulreby, Thomas, of Lincoln diocese, dispensed for plurality, 1160

Ulverton *see* Dulverton

Umall, Upper and Lower (Wmallyacd ac *and* Vacdachr), associated with 'Tilmadim', *q.v.*

Underdown (Underdowne), Richard, layman of Chichester diocese, litigant, 197

Underhill (Undrchill'), John, portioner of Houghton Conquest, 279

Underwood (Underwode, Undyrwod), Edward, canon of London, papal judge delegate, 991

......, John, *nullius diocesis*, dispensed for plurality, 1052

Undrchill' *see* Underhill

Undyll' *alias* Oundyll' *see* Oundle

Undyrwod *see* Underwood

Ungram, John, vicar of Horndon on the Hill, 913

Unichecomba *see* Winchcombe

Untum, John, of Norwich diocese, dispensed for plurality, 1242

?Upcott (Uppeccota) [Som], land of, 174

Upinam, John, of Dublin diocese, dispensed for plurality, 1078

Upminster (Upmynster) [Essex], parish church of, 897

Uppeccota *see* ?Upcott

Upper Hardres *see* Hardres, Upper

Upton Magna (Upton) [Salop], parish church of, 233

Upton Warren (Upton' Waren') [Worcs], parish church of, 304

Upway (Upuoay) [Dors], parish church of, 734

Urmeston', Urmyston' *see* Ormeston

Urmston *cf.* Ormeston

Urney (Narnayd, Nornay, Vornay) [co. Cavan] *alias* Keadew (Ched, Kede) [*or* Keadue, *in* Urney, co. Cavan], parish church of, rectory of, 538, 834
......, ..., ..., to be erected into prebend in Kilmore cathedral, 538
......, ..., ..., erection of into prebend in Kilmore cathedral, grant of, impetration of, alleged subreption of, 834
......, parish church of St Bridget, vicarage of, 831

Urney [co. Cavan], places in *see* Cavan; Keadew

Urswick (Ursewik, Urswyke), Christopher, archdeacon of Wiltshire, 277
......, ..., sometime incumbent of Croxton and of Chedzoy, 277
......, ..., counsellor to Henry [VII], 277
......, Nicholas, rector of St Nicholas Acon, London, 464

Uskane (Ossquean) [co. Tipperary], parish church of, vicarage of, to be united to proposed prebend of Loughkeen in Killaloe cathedral, 403

Utherellon, Uthtirelone *see* Auchterellon

Utterby (Ottwrby) [Lincs], parish church of, vicarage of, customarily held by Gilbertine canons, 30

Utterby (*contd*)
......, ..., ..., presentation of person for pertains to prior of Gilbertine priory of North Ormsby, 30

V

Vacdachr *see* Umall, Upper and Lower

Vachamayll *see* Oughaval

Vaghan, Vaghii *see* Vaughan

Valastz, William, [reservation for], of pension [on fruits of benefice in] Glasgow diocese, 1288
......, *cf.* Wallace

Valdemeriel, archdeacon of in the church of Leon, papal mandatary, 791

[Valentia, co. Kerry] *possibly identifiable with* 'Kylldacu(m)' *alias* 'Turere', *q.v.*

[de Valle], A[ndreas], bishop of Cotrone, regent of the chancery, correction of register ordered by, 862

Valle, John, vicar in Masham church, 142

Valle Crucis *alias* Llan Egwestl or Llan Egwast (Ryneguvesteyll', Rynegvuesteyll', Rynegwesteyll') [*in* Llandysilio or Llantysilio, co. Denbigh], Cistercian monastery of, to be held *in commendam*, 596
......, ..., (commendatory) abbot of *see* David [ab Iorwerth]

Vallos, John, administrator of the church of Lincoln *sede vacante*, 46
......, ..., ..., commissary of *see* Veysey *alias* Harman, John
......, *cf.* Walles

Valtertoun *see* Waterton

Vanghan *see* Vaughan

Vaplod *see* Whaplode

[de Varax], John, bishop of Belley and commendatory provost of the Augustinian provostry of B. Mary, Moncenisio, 405

Vardelano *see* Wardlaw

Varter, Richard, rector of Boxwell [with] Leighterton, 153
......, *cf.* Warter

Vassar (Vasor), Peter, rector of Henley on Thames, appeal of, 906

Vatirtone, Vattytonn' *see* Waterton

Vaughan (Vaghan, Vaghii, Vanghan, Vaughn), Edward, official of London, litigation before, 365
......, ..., ..., refusal of, to administer justice, 261
......, John, vicar of Bedminster, appeal of, 987
......, ..., of Bath and Wells diocese, dispensed for plurality, 1068

Vaus (Wans), John, of Ross diocese, dispensed for plurality, 1298
......, Martin, cleric of Ross diocese, 840
......, ..., priest of Aberdeen, 782
......, ..., resignation of deanery of Ross of, 782, 839-841
......, ..., assignment to, in place of pension, of fruits of church of Kilmuir and (part of) tithes of churches of Rosemarkie and Cromarty, 782, 840
......, ..., proctor of *see* de Bertinis, Leonard
......, ..., proctor (unnamed) of, 782, 840

Vawan *see* Wawain

[Vera], Juan, cardinal priest of S Balbina, suit before, 1015

Vernon (Vernen', Vernon'), Roger, of Westminster, layman of London diocese, litigant, 905
......, ..., layman of Coventry and Lichfield diocese, appeal of, 988
......, ..., (alleged) wife of *see* Keble *(alias* Vernon), Margaret

Vernon (*contd*)
......, ..., blood relations of, 988
......, alias of Keble, Margaret, *q.v.*

Verucchio [*in* province of Forlì, Italy], united parish churches of St Peter and St Nicholas, 358

Veysey *alias* Harman (Vesy, Veysey, Veysy, Veysye *alias* Harmon, Weysi *alias* Harmon), John, rector of Clifton Reynes, 569
......, ..., sometime incumbent of Clifton Reynes, 191
......, ..., rector of St Mary's on the Hill, Chester, 191
......, ..., incumbent of Edgmond, 191, 1038
......, ..., canon and prebendary of Darlington, 1038
......, ..., official or commissary of John [Arundel], bishop of Coventry and Lichfield, proceedings by, 298
......, ..., commissary of John Vallos, administrator of the church of Lincoln, *sede vacante,* proceedings by, 46

Vhytt *see* White

Vienne [*in dép.* of Isère, France], council of, constitution of Clement V concerning hospitals published in, 130

Vildelanda *see* Willand

ville Kaylke' *see* Railstown

Vilton *see* Wilton

Vincent, provision of to bishopric of ?Clogher, 1338; *cf.* 1339

Vinningen [*in* Bavaria, Germany], parish church of, 616

Vodesol *see* Woodstock

Vodland, Vodlande *see* Woodland

Volateranus, Ja see [de Gherardis de Vulterris], Jacobus

Volchoppe *see* Woolhope

Volcke *see* Duleek

?Voolni *see* Wolvey

Vornay *see* Urney [co. Cavan]

Vororono *see* Wootton

Voudland *see* Woodland

Vronon, George, of Lichfield diocese, dispensed for plurality, 1192

Vsulebayn *see* OSullivan

Vuolfordi *see* Wolford

Vuolsauve, Humphrey, chaplain in the parish church of Ashbourne, 292
......, *cf.* Wolshawe

Vurlle *see* Worle

Vynsall *see* Kinsale

Vynter *alias* Fynter, Thomas, monk of the Cistercian monastery of Mellifont, 368
......, *cf.* Wynter

W

W *cf.* V

Wadyluff, Robert, vicar of Ravensthorpe, 656

Walbrond, Hugh, rector of Cromhall, 433

Walden (Walden'), Roger, chantry of, in London cathedral, 426

Wales, prince of *see* Arthur

Walkington (Walkynton) [Yorks], parish church of, 200

Wallace (Wallas'), John, vicar of Linlithgow, 979
......, *cf.* Valastz

Walles *cf.* Vallos

Walley *see* Whalley

Wallingford (Walyngfordi) [Berks], [Benedictine priory of], a cell of St Albans, 49
......, ..., monk living in *see* Wytheley, John

Wallop, Over (Overwalop) [Hants], parish church of, 713

Walsall [Staffs], parish church of, 348
......, ..., altar of St John the Baptist in, chantry at, 348

Walsh (Walshe), Richard, the late, rector of St Patrick's, Trim, crimes of, 694
......, ..., deprivation and appeal of, 694
......, ..., death of, 694
......, ..., appeal of prosecuted by John Warde, *q.v.*

Walsingham (Walsyngh(a)m) [Norf], Augustinian priory of, canon of *see* Gottis, Richard

Walsohayn, Thomas, of Norwich diocese, dispensed for plurality, 1244

Walsyngh(a)m *see* Walsingham

Walter, William, vicar of Odiham and archdeacon of Brecon, 495

Walter, archbishop of Dublin *see* [FitzSimons], Walter

Waltham [Lincs *or* W~ on the Wolds, Leics], parish church of, rector of, 406

Waltham, ?North (North Walton') [Hants], parish church of St Peter, rector of, 459

Walton (Waltun) [*either* W~ on the Hill, Lancs *or* W~ upon Trent, Derb], parish church of, rector of, 724

Walton, West (Westwalton) [Norf], parish church of, 241

Waltun *see* Walton

Walyngfordi *see* Wallingford

Wans *see* Vaus

Wardall, John, rector of Sparham, 898

Warde, Christopher, cleric of York diocese, 240
......, John, rector of St Patrick's, Trim, 694
......, ..., prosecutor of appeal of the late Richard Walsh over St Patrick's, 694
......, ..., monk of the Benedictine monastery of St Mary, Coventry, 867

Wardlaw (Vardelano), Henry, knight, of St Andrews or another diocese, appeal of, 921
......, William, vicar of Carriden and holder of the chapel of St Andrew, Inchegall, 248
......, ..., sometime vicar of Carnwath, 248

Wardroper, John, archdeacon of Stafford, 692
......, ..., of Lichfield diocese, dispensed for plurality, 1292

Waren, Thomas, of Armagh diocese, commission by virtue of an appeal, 1050

Warham (Warh(a)m), William, archdeacon of Huntingdon, Master of the Rolls, 617
......, ..., ..., ..., provision of to the bishopric of London, 617
......, ..., ..., absolution of preliminary to provision, 618
......, ..., [bishop-] elect of London, faculty for consecration of, 619
......, ..., ..., to retain the parish church of Sherborne St John, 672

Warkton (Werketon) [Northants], parish church of, 169

Warmingham (Wermyngeham) [Ches], parish church of, rector of, 44

Warmsworth (Warmy Worth) [Yorks], parish church of, 212

?Warnygtiu(m), Richard, late rector of the parish church and leper hospital of St Laurence outside the walls of Limerick, 815

Warter *cf.* Varter

Warton [Lancs], parish church of, union to, of the parish church of Bury, 270

Warwick [Warw], Augustinian priory of St Sepulchre, prior of *see* Ichington, Robert

[Warwick, co. of], places in *see* Alveston; Barcheston; Churchover; Coventry; Kinwarton; Merevale; Salford Priors; Stretton on the Fosse; Sutton Coldfield; Wolvey

Water, Waterer *cf.* Watrer

Waterford [co. Waterford], [Augustinian] monastery of St Catherine, prior of, papal mandatary, 157, 545
......, Benedictine monastery of St John the Evangelist outside the walls of, priorship of, 227
......, ..., commendatory prior of *see* OReilly, Cormac
......, ..., monk and detainer of *see* Derrus, John

......, **[cathedral] church** of, deanery of, 543
......, ..., ..., canonry and prebend united to, 543
......, ..., dean of, papal mandatary, 645
......, ..., ..., *see* Brown, Rupert; White, Nicholas
......, ..., chancellor of *see* ODuggan, John
......, ..., chapter of, inhibition of, 543
......, ..., canons of *see* White, Nicholas; *and see* Okmayn, Maurice
......, ..., canonry and prebend united to deanery, 543
......, ..., prebend in *see* Corbally

Waterford (*contd*)
......, **bishop** of, inhibition of, 543

......, **diocese** of, person of *see* OMorrissey, Willerius

[Waterford, co. of], places in *see* Clashmore; Corbally; Kilbarrymeaden; Kilronan; Kilsheelan; Lickoran; Lismore; Modelligo; Molana; Mothel; Rossmire; Waterford

Waterton (Valtertoun, Vatirtone, Vattytonn', Wattirtonn') [*in* Ellon, co. Aberdeen], annex of, tithes of pertaining to Ellon parish church, 928
......, tithes of, 144, 793
......, *and see* Bannerman, Alexander

Watithon' *see* Watton

Watrer, Thomas, master of the hospital of poor priests, Canterbury, 101
......, *cf.* Water; Waterer

Watson, William, vicar of Birling, 487

Wattirtonn' *see* Waterton

Watton (Watithon')[Yorks], Gilbertine priory of, canon of *see* Smyth, John

Wauvri, William, canon of Aberdeen, papal judge delegate, 80
......, *cf.* Wawane

Waverley [*in* Farnham, Surrey], Cistercian monastery of, abbot of *see* [Skevington *alias* Patexe], Thomas

Wawain (Vawan) [*alias* Chrystal], Thomas, provision of to monastery in Moray diocese, 1340
......, ..., absolution of preliminary to provision, 1342
......, ..., faculty for consecration of, 1341
......, ..., provision of to the Cistercian monastery of Kinloss, 155
......, ..., abbot of Kinloss, 793, 928

Wawane (Wawan'), William, canon of Aberdeen, papal mandatary, 155
......, *cf.* Wauvri

Wayen, John, of Norwich diocese, dispensed for plurality, 1308
......, *cf.* Wayne

Wayfleot, Robert, of Lincoln diocese, dispensed for plurality, 1149
......, *cf.* Waynflete

Wayne *cf.* Wayen

Waynflete *cf.* Wayfleot

Wedyngton *see* Widdington

Weeks *cf.* Wekis

Weem (Weyme') [co. Perth], parish church of, 791

Wekis (Wykes), Robert, vicar of Lacock, 654, 772
......, *cf.* Weeks

Welles (Wellis), Thomas, rector of Heyford Warren, 955

Wellesley (Welsley), Edward, cleric of Meath diocese, 694
......, ..., collation to, of St Patrick's, Trim, 694
......, ..., death of, 694
......, Walter, provision of to St Patrick's, Trim, grant of, impetration of, alleged obreption and subreption of, 694

Wellis *see* Welles

Wells [Som], [cathedral] church of *see* [Bath and] Wells

Wellys, John, rector of Barcheston, 202
......, ..., sometime incumbent of Hamstall Ridware, 202
......, ..., holder of the southern moiety in South Stoke, 202

Welsley *see* Wellesley

Wendling (Wendlyng) [Norf], Premonstratensian monastery of, 337

Wendling (*contd*)
......, ..., canon of *see* Haolt *alias* Baker, Henry

Wenlock, Much (Magna Wenlok, Wenloke) [Salop], parish church of, 1037
......, ..., [Cluniac] priory of, prior of, papal judge delegate, 9

Werketon *see* Warkton

Wermyngeham *see* Warmingham

Weseden' *see* West Dean [West Sussex]

'Wesefelde' (i.e. 'Western field'?) [*unidentified* ; *in* East Dean, West Sussex], fields of, tithes from, 661

West, Reginald, rector of St Ebba's, [Oxford], 481

West Alvington *see* Alvington, West

Westbury [*or* Westbury sub Mendip, Som], parish church of, 311

West Calder *see* Calder

Westcoker *see* Coker, West

West Craig *see* Craig

West Dean [East *and* West Sussex] *see* Dean, West

West Deeping *see* Deeping, West

Westden' *see* Dean, West

West Deping *see* Deeping, West

Western Isles *see* Lewis

Westgoynewich' *see* Greenwich, West

Westhan' *see* Ham, West

West Hanney *see* Hanney

Westleton [Suff], parish church of, 708

West Lothian *see* Lothian, West

[Westmeath, co. of], place in *see* Ballyloughloe

West Mersea *see* Mersea, West

Westminster [Midd], Benedictine monastery of St Peter, abbot of, 363
......, ..., ..., papal judge delegate, 661, 924
......, ..., chapter of, 363
......, ..., monk of *see* Peston *alias* Conell', Gilbert; *cf.* Ely, Thomas
......, ..., jurisdiction of, archdeaconry within the limits of, 905
......, ..., archdeacon of *see* Ely, Thomas
......, ..., statutes and customs of, 363
......, ..., church of, high altar of, 363
......, ..., choir of, 363
......, parish church of St Margaret, litigant to appear before archdeacon of Westminster abbey in, 905
......, person of *see* Vernon, Roger

?Westmoor (Mora) [*in* Curry Rivel, Som], land of, 174

[Westmorland, co. of], places in *see* Asby; Heversham; Musgrave, Great; Shap

Weston (Weston'), Ambrose, monk of the Benedictine monastery of St Peter, Gloucester, 505
......, Richard, layman of Salisbury diocese, 137
......, ..., ..., future wife of *see* Recte, Agnes

Weston-on-Trent (Weston super Trent) [Derb], parish church of, incumbent of, 355

Westputtfordi *see* Putford, West

Westtilbury *see* Tilbury, West

Westuuersey *see* West Mersea

Westwalton *see* Walton, West

Westwrethin' *see* Wretham, West

Wetno' *see* ?Udny

Wetton, Edward, vicar of Lechlade, 732
......, Thomas, vicar of Chiswick, 99

Wexford (Weysford) [co. Wexford],
Selsker near, *q.v.*
......, place in *see* Selsker

[Wexford, co. of], places in *see* Ferns;
Glascarrig; Rathaspick; Selsker;
Wexford

Weyhill (Wey) [*also called* Penton Grafton,
Hants], parish church of, 680

Weyme' *see* Weem

Weysford *see* Wexford

Weysi *alias* Harmon *see* Veysey *alias*
Harman

de Wglas *see* Douglas

Whalley (Walley) [Lancs], [Cistercian]
monastery of, abbot of, papal judge
delegate, 990, 999

Whaplode (Vaplod) [Lincs], parish church
of, 731

Whelnetham, Little (Whelmeth(a)m Parva)
[Suff], parish church of, 488

Wherre *alias* Excester, William, monk of
the Cistercian monastery of Forde, 32

Whimple (Wymple) [Devon], parish church
of, union of, to a canonry and prebend
of Exeter cathedral, 909

Whissonsett (Wissyngsette) [Norf], parish
church of, 419

Whitchurch (Whitechurche, *Album
Monasterium*) [co. Pembroke], parish
church of, 320

White (Fuye, Fwin, Quhite, Vhytt, Whyte),
Henry, official of Dunblane, litigation
before, 435
......, Joan, woman of Lismore diocese, 811
......, ..., alleged husband of *see* Bennett,
John
......, ..., blood relations of, 811
......, Nicholas, canon of Waterford, papal
mandatary, 575
......, ..., ..., prebendary of Corbally, 543
......, ..., ..., ..., dean of Waterford, 543
......, Philip, cleric of Cloyne diocese, to be
canon of Cloyne and prebendary of
Kilmacdonogh, 852
......, Thomas, of Bath and Wells diocese,
dispensed for plurality, 1182
......, William, canon of Limerick, papal
mandatary, 647

Whitelegg (Whitleg), Robert, of Hereford
diocese, dispensed for plurality, 1220

Whithorn [co. Wigtown],
[Premonstratensian cathedral] church /
priory of, prior of, papal mandatary, 61,
63
......, bishop of, to receive oath of fealty in
pope's name, 1006, 1007
......, diocese of, persons of *see* Crawford,
John and William; Stewart, Archibald;
and see Wardlaw, William
......, ..., places in *see* Balmaclellan; Kirk-
Andrews [*in* Borgue]; St Mary's Isle *or*
Trail; Tongland; *and see* Inchegall

Whitland [*in* Llangan, co. Carmarthen],
Cistercian monastery of, 319
......, ..., monk of *see* Richard ap David

Whitleg *see* Whitelegg

Whitrow (Whytraw), Stephen, rector of
East Worlington, 881

Whitstones (Whitston', Withston'), James,
canon of Lincoln and prebendary of
Banbury, incumbent of Kettering, 1035
......, ..., canon of Lincoln, papal
mandatary, 423
......, ..., ..., faculty to, to reform statutes of
[collegiate] church of Tattershall, 423

Whynby, Thomas, rector of Carsington, 463

Whyte see White

Whytraw see Whitrow

Wich' see Wyche

Wickersley (Wikerslere) [Yorks], parish church of, incumbent of, 131

[Wicklow, co. of], place in see Glendalough

Wickmere (Wykmer) [Norf], parish church of, 269

Widdington (Wedyngton) [Essex], parish church of, 750

Wight, Isle of (*Insula Vecte*), places in see Carisbrooke; Quarr

Wigston (Wygston'), Thomas, rector of Houghton on the Hill, 152

[Wigtown, co. of], place in see Whithorn

Wikerslere see Wickersley

Wilbraham, Little (Parva Wylburgh(a)m) [Cambs], parish church of, union of, to the canonry and prebend of Studley in the [collegiate] church of Ripon, 182

Wilcock (Wilcok), John, of Canterbury diocese, papal letters in the form *Provisionis nostre* [i.e. exemplification from the register] for, 1097

Wilçon' see Wilton [Som]

Wildon (Wildon'), John, vicar of Turville, 470

Wilford (Wylford), Edmund, of Lincoln diocese, dispensed for plurality, 1040
......, cf. Wyllesford

Wilkes, William, canon of the Augustinian

Wilkes (*contd*)
monastery of Peter and Paul the Apostles, Dorchester, 888

Willand (Vildelanda, Wylbond) [Devon], land of, 174
......, vill of, church of, 174
......, parish church of, 889

Willeys see Wylleys

William (Willyam), Peter, chaplain in London cathedral, 748

William, abbot of Bury St Edmunds see [Codenham *alias* Bunting], William
......, abbot of Kinloss see [Culross], William
......, abbot of Melrose see [Turnbull], William
......, late archbishop of St Andrews see [Scheves], William
......, archbishop of Tuam see [Joyce], William
......, bishop of Aberdeen see [Elphinstone], William
......, bishop of Carlisle, afterwards bishop of Durham see [Sever or Senhouse], William
......, bishop of Lincoln see [Smith], William
......, [bishop-] elect of London see [Warham], William
......, the late, bishop of London see [?Courtenay], William
......, bishop of Winchester see [Giffard], William
......, prospective canon of Lismore see [?OFlavin], William
......, [surname wanting], to have vicarages of Ballycoolan and Timahoe and vicarage of Rathaspick united to that of Ballycoolan, 576

Willoughby (Willughby, Willu'ghby, Wylloghby), Edward, dean of Exeter, archdeacon of Stafford, and incumbent of Chagford, 434
......, ..., ..., canon of Wells and prebendary of Wiveliscombe, and incumbent of Chagford, 683

Willoughby (*contd*)

......, ..., sometime vicar of Milton Abbot, 434

......, ..., Robert, cleric of Norwich diocese, 457

Willyam *see* William

Wilsford (Wyluesfordi) [Wilts], parish church of, 719

......, ..., vicarage of, union of, to the parish church of Fugglestone, 702

Wilson (Wilson'), Richard, canon of the Augustinian monastery of Drax, incumbent of Walkington, 200

Wiltan, William, ostensible cleric living in the kingdom of England, proceedings by, 9

......, ..., *cf.* Wilton, William

Wilton (*de Fonte*, Wilcon') [Som], church of St George, 174

......, [chapel of], 174

Wilton (Vilton) [Wilts], parish church of St Mary in Breadstreet (Bredstret), union of, to St Peter's, Shaftesbury, 736

......, Breadstreet in, 736

Wilton (Wylton'), William, rector of Street and incumbent of Marnhull, 276

......, ..., ostensible commissary or auditor of the archbishop of Canterbury, proceedings by, 924

......, ..., *cf.* Wiltan, William

Wiltshire (Northwillishrre'), archdeaconry and archdeacon of in the church of Salisbury, *q.v.*

[Wiltshire], places in *see* Box; Bradford-on-Avon; Castle Eaton; Charlton; Ditteridge; Ebbesborne; Edington; Fugglestone St Peter; Heddington; Ivychurch; Lacock; Manningford; Melksham; Mildenhall; Poulshot; Rushall; Salisbury; Semley; Stratton St Margaret; Sutton Mandeville; Tidworth; Tisbury; Wilsford; Wilton

Winchcombe (Unichecomba) [Glos], Benedictine monastery of, statutes of, 394

......, ..., abbot of *see* [Kidderminster], Richard; *and see* [?Twynyng], John

......, ..., church, oratory, or chapel of, 394 [14], [17]

......, ..., manor of *see* Corndean

Winchelsea (Wynchelsee) [Sussex], parish church of St Thomas, 674

Winchester [Hants], Benedictine monastery of Hyde, monk of *see* Buttler *alias* Berkeley, Thomas

......, [Benedictine **cathedral priory**] **church** of, chapter of, conclusion to, 626

......, **bishop** of, to receive oath of fealty in pope's name, 1021, 1023

......, ..., papal judge delegate, 661, 905, 924

......, ..., papal mandatary, 394, 903

......, ..., *mensa* of *cf.* 1311

......, ..., *see* [de Blois], Henry; [Fox], Richard; [Giffard], William; [Langton], Thomas

......, official of, papal mandatary, 515

......, church of, vassals of, conclusion to, 626

......, **city and diocese** of, clergy of, conclusion to, 626

......, ..., people of, conclusion to, 626

......, **diocese** of, persons of *see* Antony, abbot of Quarr; Bailey, William; Bangchier', Clement; Bernardi, Robert; Beyto, John; Blenkinsop, Robert; Bradbridge, Nicholas; Brime, John; Brownesmyth, John; Bukarawl, Henry; Bury, John; Buttler *alias* Berkeley, Thomas; Chaundler, John; Combe, Humphrey; Dunche, William; Dyneley, John; Edward, [bishop-] elect of Gallipoli; Elesmere, Robert; Grigg, John; Hedygton', William; Herbert *alias* Newlond, James; Hungersord' *alias* Doderoffe, Thomas; Johannis, John; Lathes, Robert; Leonardi, Ralph; Lere,

Winchester **city and diocese** (*contd*)
John; Marshall, Thomas; Norbery,
Thomas; [Oke], Thomas; Parkins,
William; Pemberton, John; Peverell,
John; [Pigot], Thomas; Quynby,
Richard; Robson, John; Rosynalde,
Christopher; [Skevington *alias* Patexe],
Thomas; Sleford, Henry; Smyth, John
and William; Sowthwode, John;
Suthyke, Richard; Thomson, Thomas;
Toppyng, John; Walter, William;
[Warham], William
......, ..., places in *see* Albury; Andover;
Ashe; Bermondsey; Breamore;
Burghclere; Carisbrooke castle;
Chalton; Cheriton; Chertsey; Clanfield;
Guildford; Heckfield; Hyde [*at*
Winchester]; Lihou, Guernesey;
Meonstoke; Merton; Monxton; Niton;
Ockley; Odiham; Overton; Puttenham;
Quarr; Reigate; St Helier, Jersey;
Sherborne St John; Stoke Charity;
Titchfield; Wallop, Over; Waltham,
?North; Waverley; Weyhill

Windsor (Windesore) [Berks], town of,
proposed chapel of Margaret [Beaufort]
in, 807

Wineswyk *see* Winwick

Wingfield, North (?Hallewynsm' *alias*
Northuuynfeld') [Derb], parish church
of, union to, of the parish church of
Stanford Rivers, 300

Winsham (Wynsh(a)m) [Som], parish
church of, 916

Winter *see* Wynter

Winwick (Wineswyk) [Lancs], parish
church of, union to, of the parish church
of Rostherne, 475

Wischaston *see* Wistaston

Wissyngsette *see* Whissonsett

Wistaston (Wischaston) [Ches], parish
church of, 570

Withiel Florey (Wythoell') [Som], [church
of], 174

Withston' *see* Whitstones

Withyham (Withyam) [Sussex], parish
church of, 847

Witt (Wytt), John, chaplain in Danbury
parish church, 387

Witthens, John, of Worcester diocese,
dispensed for plurality, 1138

Wiveliscombe (Wyvelestom') [Som],
prebend of in Wells cathedral, union to,
of the parish church of Chagford, 683

Wmallyacd ac *and* Vacdachr *see* Umall,
Upper and Lower

Woarson, ?Oddowinus, of Salisbury
diocese, dispensed for plurality, 1180

Woburn (Woburma) [Beds], Cistercian
monastery of, abbot of *see* [Hogeson],
Thomas

Woctherratha *see* Outeragh

Wod *see* Wood

Wode, William, canon of the Augustinian
monastery of Michelham, 268
......, *cf.* Wood

Wodyngton *see* Woodington

Wogan (Hugan), Matthew, of St David's
diocese, dispensed for plurality, 1223

Woldham *see* Wouldham

Wolferton (Wolverton') [Norf], parish
church of, 178

Wolford (Vuolfordi), William, of Kinver,
layman, parishioner of Kinver, 298

Woliner, Walter, rector of Blickling, 471

Wollmer *cf.* Woliner

Wolsey (Wuley), Thomas, rector of Limington, 682

Wolshawe *cf.* Vuolsauve

Wolverton' *see* Wolferton

Wolvey (? Voolni) [Warw], prebend of in Lichfield cathedral, union to, of the parish church of Byfield, 428

Wood (Wod), Henry, [provision of], to precentorship of Dunkeld, [vacant] by exchange, 1157
......, *cf.* Wode

Woodburn (Hudburryn) [*in* Carrickfergus, co. Antrim], [Premonstratensian] monastery of, abbot of, papal mandatary, 391

[Woodhall, Lincs], place in *see* Poolham

Woodington (Wodyngton), Thomas, rector of St Helen's, Worcester and incumbent of Great Horwood, 424

Woodland (Vodland, Vodlande, Voudland) [*in* Udny, co. Aberdeen], tithes of pertaining to Ellon parish church, 144, 793, 928

Woodspring *or* Worspring (Woyspiynge) [*in* Kewstoke, Som], Augustinian monastery of, prior of *see* Spring, Richard

Woodstock (Vodesol) [*in* Wootton, Oxon] *see* Wootton

Woolhope (Volchoppe) [Heref], parish church of, 517

Wootton (Vororono) [Oxon], called Woodstock (Vodesol) [*in* Wootton, Oxon], parish church of B. Mary, union of, to the Augustinian provostry of B. Mary, Moncenisio, 405

Wootton (*contd*)
......, ..., ..., patron of *see* Edward [I]
......, ..., ..., fruits of, lease of, by provost and convent of Moncenisio to abbot and convent of the Cistercian monastery of Bruern, 405
......, ..., ..., union of, to Bruern, 405
......, ..., ..., occupant of, 405
......, ..., ..., fruits of, usurpation of, 405

Worcester [Worcs], parish churches in:
All Saints, 39
St Clement, rector of, 432
St Helen, 424
St Martin, 644
......, collation of, 644
......, ..., pertains to the prior of the Benedictine cathedral church of Worcester, 644
......, Augustinian hospital of St Wulstan *see* St Wolstan

......, [Benedictine **cathedral priory**] church, prior of, papal judge delegate, 29, 529; *cf.* 9
......, ..., ..., collation of St Martin's, Worcester, pertains to, 644
......, ..., ..., collation by, 644
......, ..., chapter of, conclusion to, 59
......, Benedictine monastery of B. Mary the Virgin, 325
......, ..., monk of *see* Chest *alias* Ris, Henry
......, ..., *cf.* St Wolstan

......, **bishop** of, cognizance of defamation cases between lay persons of Worcester diocese pertains to, 29
......, ..., to receive oath of fealty in pope's name, 581, 582
......, ..., impliedly present at Roman curia, 363
......, ..., papal (commissary and) mandatary, 174, 363, 416, 515, 817
......, ..., papal mandatary (foreign business), 358, 382, 417, 616, 697, 854, 855, 996, 1001
......, ..., *mensa* of, assignment of pension on fruits of, 963; *cf.* 1311
......, ..., vicar general of, papal mandatary, 644

Worcester, **bishop** (*contd*)
......, ..., *see* [de' Gigli], John and Silvester; [Morton], Robert
......, [bishop-] elect of *see* [de' Gigli], John
......, official of, papal mandatary, 118, 386
......, church of, archdeacon of, papal mandatary, 644
......, ..., vassals of, conclusion to, 59

......, **city and diocese** of, clergy of, conclusion to, 59
......, ..., people of, conclusion to, 59
......, **diocese** of, persons of *see* Barbour, Thomas; Barton, William; Beaumont, Thomas; Bilmer, Richard; Blount, Walter; Brown, John; Butler, James; Churche, Roger; Cowper, William; Darby, Edward; [Deane], Henry; Edward, [bishop-] elect of Gallipoli; Farley, Nicholas; Fovonys, Nicholas; Gay, Richard; Griffith, John; Hancock, William; Harrald, John; Haseley, Edward; Hebran, William; Ichington, Robert; Jackson, Thomas; Jo(h)annis, Gargridus; Jonys, William; [Kidderminster], Richard; Leicester, William; Lowthe, Robert; More, John and Richard; Moris, Hugh; Morne, Robert; Newman, Thomas; Parkes, Thomas; Paynter, John; Porter, John and Thomas; Sueede (*or* Sneede), Nicholas; Thome, John; Tresh(a)m, Richard; [?Twynyng], John; Varter, Richard; Walbrond, Hugh; Wellys, John; Weston, Ambrose; Wetton, Edward; Witthens, John; Woodington, Thomas
......, ..., places in *see* Alveston; Barcheston; Boxwell; Bristol; Cromhall; ?Farmington; Gloucester; Hartpury; Haselton; Kinwarton; Lanthony II by Gloucester; Lasborough; Lechlade; Leighterton; Mickleton; Rendcombe; Rissington, Little; Salford; Sodbury; Stretton on the Fosse; Tewkesbury; Tirley; Warwick; *and* places *listed below under* [Worcester, co. of]

[Worcester, co. of], places in *see* Bordesley; Broadwas; Droitwich; Evesham; Martley; Pershore; Sedgeberrow; Upton Warren; Winchcombe; Worcester

Wordysted', alias of Worsted', *q.v.*

Worle (Vurlle) [Som], parish church of, vicarage of, 863

Worlington, East (Estvokyngton) [Devon], parish church of, 881

Worspring *see* Woodspring

Worsted (Worsted' *alias* Wordysted') [Norf], parish church of, 388

Worth [and] Swanage (Wurthswanewych') [*the former now* Worth Matravers, Dors], parish church of, 710

Wouldham (Woldham) [Kent], parish church of, 502

Wretham, West (Westwrethin') [Norf], parish church of, 737

Wright, John, of Coventry and Lichfield diocese, dispensed for plurality, 1191

Wthertllon *see* Auchterellon

Wuley *see* Wolsey

Wurthswanewych' *see* Worth [and] Swanage

Wyatt (Wyart), Richard, rector of Hardingham, 532
......, ..., of Ely diocese, dispensed for plurality, 1246

Wyche (Wich'), John, rector of Tintinhull, 723

Wygston' *see* Wigston

Wyke *see* Droitwich

Wykes *see* Wekis

Wykmer *see* Wickmere

Wylbond *see* Willand

Wylford *see* Wilford

Wyllesford (Wylfordi), Edmund, canon of
Lichfield and prebendary of Wolvey,
incumbent of Byfield, 428
......, *cf.* Wilford

Wylleys (Willeys), Richard, rector of
Ramsden Crays, 744

Wylloghby *see* Willoughby

Wyllys, alias of Parson, Richard, *q.v.*

Wylton' *see* Wilton

Wyluesfordi *see* Wilsford

Wymondham (Wymondahm') [Leics],
parish church of, 386
......, ..., incumbent of, 386
......, ..., patron of, 386

Wymondham (Wymondh(a)m) [Norf],
Benedictine monastery of, 314
......, ..., monk of *see* Mathew *alias*
Norwich, John

Wymple *see* Whimple

Wynchelsee *see* Winchelsea

Wyngho, Christopher, canon of Exeter and
incumbent of Kingsdon, 663

Wynsh(a)m *see* Winsham

Wynter *cf.* Vynter *alias* Fynter

Wyppyll, John, canon of London and
prebendary of Ealdstreet, rector of
Harringay (*now* Hornsey), 281

Wyses chantry, in Danbury parish church,
528

Wytheley, John, monk of the Benedictine
monastery of St Albans living in the
cell of Wallingford, 49

Wythoell' *see* Withiel Florey

Wytt *see* Witt

Wyvelestom' *see* Wiveliscombe

Y

Yates (Yatis), Simon, vicar of B V Mary's,
Nottingham, 278

Ybrien, Ybryen *see* OBrien

Ycellard, Ycellayd *see* OKelly

Ychernolii, John, [?cleric of Killaloe
diocese], 162
......, ..., to be canon of Killaloe, have
rectory of *Cenél arga* erected into
prebend, and the rectory of Lynally and
the vicarages of Kilcomin and
Loughkeen united thereto, 162
......, *cf.* OKennedy

Ychyngton, Ychyngton' *see* Ichington

Ycleri *see* OClery

'Ycluelin', diocese of Clonfert [
unidentified], tithes of belonging to
capitular *mensa* of Clonfert, 167
......, ..., ..., to be erected anew into
prebend in Clonfert cathedral, with
vicarage of Killoscobe united thereto,
likewise anew, 167

Yco'mimayn, Roger, incumbent of
vicarages of ?Kilcummin and Killeroon,
death of, 646

Ydona *see* Hidona

Yelverton [Norf], parish church of, 770

Yeo, Leonard, rector of Huish, 954

Yermoth *alias* Ludhnn', Thomas, canon of
the Premonstratensian monastery of
Langley, 525

Yeronyn *see* OCronin

Yfahy *see* OFahy

Yffaclaij *see* OPhelan

Yfflaytbertay *see* OFlaherty

Ygervayn *see* OGarvan

Ygonayn, Donald, cleric of Ross diocese, to
have canonry of Ross and prebend of
Curragranemore, with vicarages of
Inchydoney Island and ?Kilgarriff
united thereto, 256

Yhacgeryn, John, canon of the Augustinian
monastery of Molana, 573
......, ..., ..., provision of as commendatory
abbot of Molana, disputed, 573
......, ..., ..., to be provided anew, 573

Yhanllyd *see* Ohanle

Yhedriscoll', Yhedrscoyll *see* ODriscoll

Yhelay *see* OKelly

Yherlahe *see* OHerlihy

Yhhederscoyll *see* ODriscoll

Yhily *see* OHealy

Yhunwnan *see* ONoonan

Ykallayd *see* OKelly

Ykayl *see* OCahill

Ykayllis, Nicholas, cleric of Cork diocese,
to be canon of Cork and have
Ringcurran rectory erected into
prebend, with vicarage of Inishannon
united thereto, 71

Ykerwayli *see* OCarroll

Ykyhyr *see* OCahir

Ylathym *see* OLahiff

Ylla *see* Bishop's Hull

Ymarryn *see* OMannin

Ymaylle *see* OMalley

Ymecayr *see* OMeagher

Ymillam *see* ONolan

Ymirechu *see* OMurphy

Ymolierayn, Gerard, prior of the
Augustinian monastery of Rathkeale,
death of, 944

Ymorrij, Donald, formerly vicar of
?Kilglass, 763

Ymukcan, Odo, ?cleric of Cashel diocese,
to be canon of Cashel, have
?Kilcomenty vicarage erected into a
prebend and Killeenagarriff vicarage
united thereto, 404
......, *cf.* OMeehan

Ymulcorcny *see* OCorkery

Ymurchu, Ymurchw, Ymurhu *see*
OMurphy

Ynayscronayn *see* Inchicronan

Ynchgall *see* Inchegall

Ynesbrachyn *see* Breaghwy Island

Ynnschfallyn *see* Innisfallen

Ynseonnyn *see* Inishannon

Ynserem *see* Inishkenny

Ynyago, John, of Lincoln diocese,
dispensed for plurality, 1042

?Ynyseonan *see* Inishannon

Ynyskahi, Ynyskay *see* Scattery Island

Yolei, John, prior of the Augustinian monastery of Aughrim, death of, 492 ......, *cf.* OKelly

Yonder Auchterellon (ʒotidest Utherellon) [*now* Yonderton, *in* Ellon, co. Aberdeen], tithes of, 928

Yonge (Yong), John, rector of St Martin's, [Oxford], 957

York [Yorks], **[cathedral] church** of, dean of, *see* [Blythe], Geoffrey
......, ..., chapter of, conclusion to, 546
......, ..., canon of *see* Jordan, John
......, ..., chaplains in *see* Burdelewer, William; Milde, John
......, ..., altar of All Saints in, 879
......, ..., altar of Sts Andrew and Cuthbert in, 415

......, **archbishop** of, conclusion to, 1006, 1012
......, ..., *see* [Rotherham *or* Scot], Thomas; [Savage], Thomas
......, church of, suffragans of, conclusion to, 546
......, ..., vassals of, conclusion to, 546

......, **city and diocese** of, clergy of, conclusion to, 546
......, ..., people of, conclusion to, 546
......, diocese of, persons of *see* Aleshe, John; Atkyngson, John; Baker, William; Barker, Thomas; Blythe, Thomas; Boude, Robert; Bound, Henry; Brundholm, Richard; Bulmer, Ralph; Butterworth, Ralph; Calverley, Nicholas; Colyns, Martin; Constable, Thomas; Cook, Richard; Cooke, Robert; Dalton, William; Fitz Hugh, George; Flint, John; [Forman], Andrew; Gascoigne, Humphrey; Grymston, Henry; Harington, James and William; Hasting, John; Kirkham, William; Lacy, Arthur; Legh, Thomas; Morwyn, John; Nabbos, John; Pichard, Robert; Radcliff, Christopher; Rerysby, John;

York [Yorks], **city and diocese** (*contd*)
Rokeby, William; Rolleston, Richard; Scotton, John; Senhouse, Simon; Simson, George; Smales, John; Smyth, John; Stapylton, Brian; Staynclyff, Edward; Stewardi, William; Stokesley, Robert; Strangways, George; Strickland, Thomas; [S]vyst, Thomas; Thyndyn', Thomas; Tunstall, Cuthbert; Twyforth *alias* Colyns, John; Valle, John; Warde, Christopher; Wilson, Richard; Yates, Simon; *and see* Metcalfe, Thomas
......, ..., places in *see* Aldingham; Cartmel; Claughton; Collingham, North; Eakring; Heversham; Nottingham; Tollerton; Warton; *and* places *listed below under* [York, co. of]

[York, co. of], places in *see* Adlingfleet; Badsworth; Batley; Beverley; Blacktoft; Braithwell; Brantingham; Bulmer; Cottingham; Drax; Ellerker; ?Forcett; Goodmanham; Guisborough; Haltemprice; Healaugh; Kirkham; Langton, Great; Masham; Nafferton; Newton Kyme; Pontefract; Ripley; Ripon; Roche; Ryther; Skirpenbeck; Sproatley; Stonegrave; Studley; Walkington; Warmsworth; Watton; Wickersley

Youghal (Johoill') [co. Cork], new college of clerics of B. Mary, warden of *see* Bennett, John

Young (ʒung), Alexander, once canon of Aberdeen and prebendary of Kearn and Forbes, 68

Yscolay *see* OScully

Yscrydan', Ysiridan *see* OSheridan

Ysulebayn *see* OSullivan

Ytharture *see* Annagh

Ytreyth' *see* OKett

ȝ

Ȝotidest Utherellon *see* Yonder Auchterellon

Ȝung *see* Young

Z

Zeal Monachorum (Monley'sayle) [Devon], parish church of, rector of, 218

[Zeno], Battista, the late, [cardinal] bishop of Tusculum, suit before, 1015

INDEX OF SUBJECTS

Unless preceded by p. (page) or note, references are to the serial number of calendar entries. Cross references to proper names of persons and places are to the INDEX OF PERSONS AND PLACES.

A

Abbots, election of, by convent, 144, 1015
......, ..., ..., confirmed by superior abbot, 574, 943
......, grants to, for benediction by any catholic bishop, 67, 127, 259, 536, 574, 846, 943, 1016, 1027, 1033
......, grant to, to use benediction, 573
......, indult etc., to exercise *pontificalia*, 1174
......, ..., to farm fruits of benefices, use mitre etc., give benediction, consecrate churches etc. and vestments etc. and reconcile polluted churches, 425
......, ..., to use mitre etc., give benediction, confer minor orders, bless ecclesiastical ornaments (including images) and reconcile polluted churches etc., 686
......, surrogation as, 1015, 1020
......, *see also* Provision, *and under individual religious orders*

Abbreviatores see under Rome, court of, curialists at

Absolution, as preliminary to promotion etc. to archbishopric, bishopric or headship of religious house, 53, 56, 60, 548, 550, 555, 580, 583, 586, 589, 593, 597, 601, 604, 609, 611, 615, 618, 622, 624, 629, 633, 635, 639, 1008, 1010, 1013, 1018, 1022, 1026, 1030, 1034, 1210, 1317, 1320, 1322, 1327, 1331, 1336, 1342
......, by metropolitan, from sentences of excommunication passed by suffragan bishop, 1005
......, conditional, from sentence of excommunication, 9, 28, 29, 80, 192, 529, 661, 691, 792, 812, 905, 987; *and cf.* 199
......, ..., from suspension, 529
......, for violence towards cleric, 14
......, for perjury, 129, 574

Absolution (*contd*)
......, for simony, 167, 946
......, for unfulfilled vows, 374
......, *see also under* Excommunication; Irregularity; Simony

Abstinence, 394 [18]

Accusation *see under* Deprivation; Litigation

Acolyte, papal *see under* Households

Administrationem, grant of archbishopric *in*, by papal authority, to person below lawful age, with subsequent appointment as archbishop, 848

Affinity *see under* Illegitimacy; Marriage

Age, defect of, dispensations and indults in respect of, to persons of the following age:-
    6, to hold — on completing seventh year — canonries and prebends of cathedral churches, 688, 689
    6, to hold — at age 9 — any cathedral canonries and prebends, 370
    7, below, to be marked — at age 7 — with clerical character and receive any benefices without cure, and — at age 17 — one, and — at age 19 — two incompatible benefices, and — at lawful age — to be promoted to all orders and receive any compatible benefices with and without cure, 332
    7, to hold a benefice, even canonry etc. and— until age 13 — have it served by a suitable cleric, 572
    7, to be promoted — at lawful age — to all orders; to hold — at age 11 — a dignity etc., and — hence-

Age (*contd*)

forth —any number of benefices without cure and — at lawful age — with and without cure compatible mutually, 408 *and cf.* 769

8, henceforth to hold a dignity etc. (not major or principal), 769

8, to hold a canonry and prebend, 72

10, to hold a canonry and prebend, 646

11, henceforth to hold any canonries and prebends and — at age 16 — a benefice with cure etc., 210

13, to hold a benefice with cure at age 15, 173

13, to receive a conventual priory *in commendam,* 492

13, to receive a precentorship and hold it *in commendam* until age 17 and thereafter *in titulum,* 158

14, already to be promoted to all orders and hold two compatible benefices, but now dispensed to hold — at age 17 — one incompatible and — at lawful age — two incompatible benefices; and —henceforth — to hold any number of benefices without cure and — at lawful age — with and without cure compatible mutually and with the two incompatibles, 66

14, henceforth to hold chaplaincies and altars requiring orders and — at age 17— a benefice with cure, 369

14, henceforth to be provided to the canonry and prebend he had — at age 9— acquired *de facto,* 381

14, to hold a benefice with cure, 180, 711

14, to hold — at age 15 — one incompatible benefice, 868

14, to hold one benefice henceforth and — at age 19 — any two benefices with cure, 220

15, below, to hold — at age 15 — a benefice with cure and — at age 19 — two, 891

15, to hold a benefice with cure, 113

16, to hold a benefice with cure, 761

Age (*contd*)

16, to hold a deanery, 258

17, below, to hold — at age 17 — a benefice with cure etc., 458

17, to hold an archdeaconry, 539

17, to hold a deanery, 838

17, to hold a benefice with cure, 308, 690

17, to hold one incompatible benefice and —at age 19 — two, 326

17, to hold a benefice with cure and — at age 20 — two, 740

18, below, to hold a benefice with cure at age 18, 18

18, recently dispensed to be promoted to the subdiaconate and diaconate and — at age 22 — priesthood and —at lawful age —a benefice with cure; now dispensed to hold a benefice with cure, 756

18, to be appointed administrator, with provision as archbishop at lawful age, 848

18, to hold a benefice with cure, 209, 240, 378, 534, 662, 746, 1004

18, to hold two incompatible benefices, 868

18, to hold a benefice with cure and — at age 21 — to be promoted to the priesthood, 245

unstated, to hold a benefice with cure at age 19, 19

19, to hold a benefice with cure, 795

19, to hold a benefice with cure and — at age 21 — to be promoted to all orders, 398

19, to hold a benefice with cure and — at age 21 — to be promoted to the priesthood, 479

19, to hold a deanery, 75

19, to hold a priory, 410

19, to hold a sacerdotal canonry and prebend of any cathedral, 412

19, to rule a monastery, 259

19, to hold two benefices, 808

19, to hold two benefices with cure, 516

19, to hold two benefices on completing twentieth year, 351

Age (*contd*))
    20, to hold a benefice with cure, 975
    20, to hold a deanery, 402
    20, to hold a third benefice, 808
    22, to hold a deanery, 226
    22, to hold a monastery, 574
    23, to hold a deanery, 936
    23, to hold — at lawful age — three incompatible benefices, 308
    24, to preside over etc. a bishopric and receive consecration, 623
    25, to preside over etc. a bishopric and receive consecration, 58
    27, to preside over etc. a bishopric and receive consecration, 614
    60, to choose a confessor, 244
    septuagenarian, to be absolved from unfulfilled vows of pilgrimages; to choose a confessor and to receive Jubilee indulgence without visiting Rome, 374
    below lawful age, archbishop-elect to reconcile churches by deputy, 848
Age, given:-
    79, unable to fulfil episcopal duties, 549

Alienation, of ecclesiastical property, faculty granted to Augustinian canon for, 443
......, of property of perpetual chaplaincy, confirmation of, 366
......, *see also under* Farm; Lease; Legislation; Pension *and references to dilapidations under* Deprivation

Alms, in food, drink and clothes, 394 [12]
......, 394 [14]

Altars, portable, indult for, 1108
......, statute enabling prior to bless in priory church and dependencies, 400

Ambassador, of Ferdinand [V], king of Castile and Leon, to Henry [VII], king of England, son of *see* Ferdinandi, Gonzalo

Annexation *see* Unions

Anniversary, in perpetual chaplaincy, 292

Apostasy, incurred by Augustinian canon

Apostasy (*contd*)
    wearing secular dress and participating in secular affairs in king's service, absolution for, 972
......, incurred by brother of Augustinian hospital wearing secular dress and serving in parish churches, absolution for, 416
......, incurred by Benedictine monk leaving monastery and participating in secular affairs, absolution for, 363
......, *cf.* 394 [3]

Apostolos, 987

Appeals, to apostolic see, (*rubricellae* of), 1050, 1051, 1073, 1103, 1162, 1164, 1224, 1306, 1307
......, ..., against bishop's admonitions etc., 298
......, ..., against sentence of excommunication etc., 9
......, ..., by archbishop over precentorship, 80
......, ..., contempt of, 29, 529, 661, 792, 811, 812
......, ..., from deprivation of vicarage and *de facto* collation of it to detractor, 192
......, ..., from definitive sentence, 28, 29, 46, 86, 94, 197, 221, 365, 435, 442, 661, 694, 792, 812, 906, 921, 927, 987, 989, 990, 1015
......, ..., from sentence(s), 573, 971
......, ..., from exactions etc. relating to two parish churches, 442
......, ..., from grievances inflicted, 8
......, ..., from insufficient injury, 988
......, ..., from suspension and excommunication, 529
......, ..., in defamation case, 29
......, ..., in marriage case, 28, 261, 811, 905, 927, 988; *see also* 86
......, ..., in tithes case, 94, 921
......, ..., not prosecuted within proper time, 192, 197, 365, 573, 691, 694, 812, 906
......, ..., over archbishop's visitation of two hospitals, 964
......, ..., over infringements of exemption and jurisdiction, 529
......, ..., over metropolitical jurisdiction, 1005
......, ..., over monastery, 573, 1015

Appeals (*contd*)
......, ..., over parish church, 991
......, ..., over patronage of perpetual chaplaincy, 691
......, ..., over payments due to parish church, 365
......, ..., over non-payment of money, 435
......, ..., over priory, 989
......, ..., over rectory, 694
......, ..., over refusal to pay pension, 793
......, ..., over refusal by bishop to institute etc., 50, 456
......, ..., in testamentary case, 924, 990; *cf.* 999
......, ..., in tithes case, 971
......, ..., extra-judicial, *cf.* 844, 1005
......, to apostolic legate, from definitive sentence of archdeacon's court, 8
......, ..., *cf.* 29
......, to archbishop of Canterbury, for tuitorial protection, 298
......, to archbishop of Dublin, for tuitorial protection, 192
......, to court of archbishop of Canterbury, over infringements of exemption and jurisdiction, 529
......, to court of archbishop of St Andrews, over repayment of money, 792
......, to local metropolitical court, concerning bishop's refusal to institute, 456
......, ..., suit respecting, 1005

Application, of particle to vicarage, 827

Appropriation *see* Fruits; Unions

Archbishops *see under* Bishops and Archbishops *and under individual sees*

Archdeacons, court of, suit before, 8
......, indults to, to choose confessor, 377
......, ..., to visit by deputy and receive procurations in ready money, 371, 1098, 1309

Arroasian Congregation, OSA, religious house designated of, 989

Arts, student of, 72
......, *for graduates in see under* Degrees

Auditor of causes of the apostolic palace *see*

Auditor of causes (*contd*)
    under Rome, apostolic palace

Auditors of court of audience of archbishop of Canterbury *see* Barocis, William; Peynthwyn, Hugh; Wilton, William

Augustinian Hermits, Order of:-
    privileges of, prohibiting professors having voice in chapter while holding benefice, *ad hoc* derogation of, 138
    ...., concerning obedience to apostolic letters granted to professors, 151
    professors of, dispensed to hold a secular benefice, 274, 741
    ...., dispensed to hold a secular benefice *in commendam* with vicarage, 741
    ...., dispensed to hold a secular benefice *in titulum* or a regular *in commendam* and enjoy all privileges etc. and have voice etc., 138
    ...., dispensed and indulged to hold a secular benefice and enjoy privileges and have voice etc., 151

Augustinian Order:-
    statutes of, prohibiting canons holding property, *ad hoc* derogation of, 356
    privileges granted to monastery, approved and confirmed, 174
    abbots of, child of, 543
    ...., dispensed to be appointed to and preside over monastery for eight months without taking the habit or making profession, 1024, 1025
    ...., dispensed to hold a regular or secular benefice *in commendam* with house, 904
    ...., dispensed to retain two perpetual vicarages *in commendam* with house, 127
    ...., granted indult and faculty to use mitre etc., give benediction, promote to minor orders, bless images etc. and reconcile churches etc., 686
    brothers of hospitals of, dispensed to hold a secular benefice, 339, 416 453, 564
    brother of house of Bonshommes of, dispensed to hold a secular benefice, 186

Augustinian Order (*contd*)

canons of, children of, 225, 248, 332

...., collation of priorship to, with translation and admission thereto, 837

...., dispensed to hold a regular benefice *in titulum* and a regular or secular benefice *in commendam*, 43

...., dispensed to hold a regular or secular benefice *in commendam* with vicarage, 742

...., dispensed to hold a regular benefice *in titulum* and a secular or regular *in commendam* and indulged for non-residence, 336

...., dispensed to hold a secular benefice, 6, 12, 22, 87, 200, 268, 299, 438, 451, 465, 563, 571, 712, 730, 735, 742, 758, 802, 857, 871, 888, 899, 972, 997

...., dispensed to hold two secular benefices, 730

...., dispensed to hold two secular benefices, or one secular and one regular, or two regular (if dependencies of the same monastery), 200

...., dispensed to receive a canonical portion while holding a secular benefice, 730

...., dispensed to serve in king's chapel, 972

...., dispensed to wear secular dress over habit, 972

...., granted faculty to alienate ecclesiastical property for funeral expenses etc., 443

...., practising medicine at king's court, absolved for apostasy, 972

...., to be admitted by papal authority, 1028

...., ..., with subsequent collation of headship of house, 128, 930

masters of hospital of, dispensed to hold a secular benefice *in commendam* with hospital, 7

priors of, assignment of property to, papal confirmation of and dispensation concerning, 356

...., dispensed to hold a regular or secular benefice *in commendam* with house, 48, 260, 283, 484, 524, 859, 874, 904

...., dispensed to hold a secular benefice

Augustinian Order (*contd*)

in commendam with house, 863

...., dispensed to hold three regular benefices or two regular and one secular; one regular *in titulum*, the other benefices *in commendam*, 863

...., dispensed to retain priory and rectory after provision as bishop and acquisition of see, 632

...., excommunicated by father abbot for disobedience and refusal to pay procurations etc., 542

rector of hospital of, dispensed to hold a regular or secular benefice *in commendam* with hospital and indulged to wear cross under his robe, 396

houses of, abbot and convent of, granted letters of protection against pirates, 108

...., in litigation with group of laymen and women over tithes, 971

...., secular cleric dispensed to hold headship of, for six months without taking the habit or making profession, 930

houses and hospitals of, in England *see* Barnwell; Breamore; Bridgwater; Bristol (Redcliff); Bruton; Cartmel; Chacombe; Colchester; Combwell; Coxford; Dorchester; Dover; Drax; Dunstable; Guisborough; Haltemprice; Hardham (*see under* Heryngham); Haughmond; Healaugh; Heryngham or Hardham; Hickling; Ipswich; Ivychurch; Kirkham; Lanthony II by Gloucester;Launde; Leeds; Leicester; Leighs, Little; London (BVM without Bishopsgate); Merton; Michelham; Missenden; Notley; Owston; Plympton; Reigate; St Germans; Stonely; Taunton; Thornholme; Thornton; Tonbridge; Tortington; Walsingham; Warwick; Woodspring

house of Bonshommes of, in England *see* Edington

house of, in France *see* Cherbourg

houses and hospitals of, in Ireland *see* Abbeyderg; Abbeygormacan; Aghmacart; Annaghdown; Aughrim; Ballinskelligs; Ballintober;

Augustinian Order (*contd*)

Ballybeg; Bangor; Bridgetown; Caher; Clonfert; Clontuskert; Cong; Cork; Drumlane; Dublin; Dungiven; Gallen; Greatconnell; Inchcleraun; Inchicronan; Inchmacnerin; Inistioge; Innisfallen; Kells [co. Kilkenny]; Kells [co. Meath]; Kilkenny; Killagh; Kilmore; Kilshanny; Lorrha; Mayo; Molana; Monaincha; Monasteranenagh; Mothel; Moville; Muckamore; Nenagh; Rathkeale; Saints Island; Seirkieran; Selsker; Trim, Newtown; Tuam; Waterford

houses and hospitals of, in Italy *see* Lucca; Moncenisio; Ravenna; Rome; St Theodorus

houses of, in Scotland *see* Cambuskenneth; Holyrood; Inchcolm; Jedburgh; May *alias* Pittenweem; Restennet; St Andrews; St Mary's Isle; Scone

...., in the Channel Islands *see* St Helier, Jersey

......, *see also under* Apostasy

B

Baptism, 292

Baptismal font, to be erected in chapel, 379
......, 64

Barber *see* Narbonne, Peter of

Bells, indult etc. to abbot to bless, 686
......, 64

Bell-tower, 64

Benedictine Order:-
chapter of, 394 [29]
constitution of, *cf.* 394 [6]
presidents of, visitation by contemplated in house's proposed statutes, 394 [6]
privileges, indulgences, graces of monastery, 394 [25]
province of, presidents of, 394 [29]
monastery of, statutes etc. concerning

Benedictine Order (*contd*)
profession of, 363
monastery of, statutes etc. proposed:-
touching organization:-
abbot, letters [?commendatory] of, for monk students at university, 394 [29]
...., to render account and financial statement (*statum*), 394 [6]
...., prodigality of, to be denounced at visitation, 394 [6]
...., *and passim*
accounts and audit, 394 [1], [2], [4], [5], [6]
almsgiving, 394 [12], [14]
boundary (*limites*) of monastery, 394 [3], [10], [22]
cantors, secular, 394 [14]
cellarer, 394 [2], [3], [4], [5], [6], [7], [18]
sub-cellarer, 394 [3], [4], [5]
chapel, 394 [14], [17]
chapter, 394 [6], [25]
chapter house, 394
chest, common, all incoming money to be deposited in, 394 [1]
...., ..., keys of, number and custody of, 394 [1]
church, cemeteries of, 394 [15], [17]
...., lighting, ornaments and repairs in, 394 [14]
...., sacristy, 394 [2]
cloister, 394 [15], [23]
...., boundary (*limites*) of, 394 [15], [25]
congregation, 394 [25]
convent, 394 [18], [25]
...., majority of, consent of, a requisite for establishing reformed statutes, 394
dormitory, 394 [24]
enclosure (*clausura*), 394 [3], [16], [17], [21]
entrance(s), 394 [16], [17], [23]
guardians, 394 [24]
guest-house, 394 [16]
guests, 394 [2], [8], [16]
hospitality, 394 [14] *and see above under* guest-house and guests
income, to be received in common, 394 [1]

Benedictine Order (*contd*)

infirmary, 394 [2], [8], [15], [18]

kitchen, 394 [26]

kitchener, 394 [4]

?lay brothers (*laicos commissos*), 394 [25]

laymen, 394 [26]

manor, 394 [18], [22], [23]

misericord, [place for meat-eating], 394 [8], [18]

money, incoming, to be deposited in common chest, 394 [1]

...., 394 passim

officials, assignment to of specified income, to be revoked, 394 [1]

...., 394 [3], [4]

oratory, 394 [14]

parlour, 394 [17]

precinct, 394 [19]

precentor, 394 [1]

prior, 394 (in particular [1], [5], [6], [13], [17])

properties, to be visited by abbot, 394 [9]

...., *cf.* 394 [6]

refectory, 394 [8], [15], [18], [19]

senior monks, 394 (in particular [2], [5], [6])

servants, 394 [22]

teacher, 394 [29]

treasurer, 394 [1]

vestry, 394 [2]

touching regular life:-

abstinence, 394 [18]

...., *and see* fasting

austerities, custom of taking days off from, 394 [21]

...., 394 [25]

choir, custom of taking days off from, 394 [21]

...., *and see below under* office

clothing, 394 [2], [10], [12], [14], [24]

...., *and see below under* habit

eating and drinking, 394 [8], [10], [12], [14], [16], [18], [19], [22]

exeats, 394 [20]

fasting, 394 [19]

habit, 394 [24], [25]

letters, not to be given to or by monks without abbot's licence, 394 [13]

Benedictine Order (*contd*)

money, to be handed over, 394 [11]

...., retention of, punishment of as *proprietarius*, 394 [11]

office, divine, 394 [7]; *cf.* [28] *and see above under* choir

presents, (*enxenia*), to be handed over, 394 [13]

probation, of ?lay brothers (*laicos commissos*), 394 [25]

property, private ownership of, prohibited, 394 (in particular [13] *and see above under* money)

punishment, 394 *cf.* [6], *and see above under* money

recreation etc., 394 [10], [21], [22]

"reform(s)", 394 [14], [25]

relatives, 394 [16]

sickness and debility, mitigations on account of, 394 [18], [19], [24], [28], [29]

silence, observance of, 394 [21]

sleeping, 394 [24]

study, claustral, 394 [15]

...., elsewhere, 394 [29]

talking, with guests, 394 [16]

...., with seculars, 394 [22]

...., with women, 394 [15], [17]

tokens (*munuscula*), not to be given to or by monks without abbot's licence, 394 [13]

vow(s), three principal or essential, 394 (in particular [25])

...., of chastity, 394 [15], [25]

...., of obedience, 394 [25]

...., of poverty, 394 (in particular [25])

walks, 394 [22]

wandering, prevention of, 394 [3]

women, to be barred from specified places, 394 [15], [17], [23]

...., royal etc., may pernoctate, 394 [17]

...., *and see above under* talking

abbots of, dispensed to hold with house formerly two and now three benefices, 196

...., dispensed to retain monastery *in commendam* after provision as bishop and acquisition of see, 600, 605

monks of, absolved from apostasy and

Benedictine Order (*contd*)

dispensed to hold a secular benefice, live outside monastery and wear habit under secular dress, 363

...., dispensed to hold a secular benefice, 49, 133, 145, 305, 322, 409, 867, 914; *and cf.*745

...., dispensed to hold a secular benefice and indulged to wear habit under secular dress, 264, 314

...., dispensed to hold a secular benefice with monacal portion, 505

...., dispensed to hold a secular benefice with monacal portion and have stall in choir and voice in chapter, 20, 133, 139, 325, 743

...., dispensed to hold two secular benefices: one *in titulum*, the other *in commendam*, 322

...., dispensed to wear habit under secular dress, 322

...., to be admitted by papal authority, with subsequent collation of headship of house, 391

priors of, dispensed to hold a regular or secular benefice *in commendam* with place, monacal portion and claustral priorship, and have stall, place and voice while holding a secular benefice, 341

...., dispensed to hold a secular benefice *in commendam* with house, 882

...., dispensed to hold a secular benefice *in commendam* with house, or *in titulum* without it, 967

...., dispensed to retain rectory with house, 391

...., indulged to have re-entry, 535

cell of, in England *see* Wallingford

houses of, in England *see* Bardney; Battle; Birkenhead; Bury St Edmunds; Canterbury; Cerne; Chertsey; Coventry; Dover; Evesham; Eye; Eynsham; Glastonbury; Gloucester; Hereford; Hurley; Hyde; Monmouth; Peterborough; Ramsey; Rochester; St Albans; Westminster; Winchcombe; Winchester; Worcester; Wymondham; *and cf.* Bermondsey and Thame (so styled)

Benedictine Order (*contd*)

...., in France *see* Ambronay; Marcilhac; Mont St Michel

...., in Ireland *see* Athlone; Downpatrick; Glascarrig; Ross Carbery; Waterford

...., in Scotland *see* Coldingham; Dunfermline; Iona; Kelso; Lindores; *and cf.* St Andrews (so styled)

...., in the Channel Islands *see* Lihou, Guernsey

......, *see also under* Apostasy; Residence

Benedictine Rule, cited 394 (in particular [8], [12], [14], [18], [20], [21])

Benediction, indult etc. to abbot to bestow, 425, 686

...., indult etc. to prior to bestow, 397

...., *see also under* Abbots

Benefices, incompatible, dispensations for, (*rubricellae* of), 1040-1047, 1049, 1052, 1054-1056, 1058-1069, 1074, 1076-1078, 1080, 1082, 1083, 1085-1090, 1093-1096, 1099, 1101, 1102, 1104-1106, 1110, 1112, 1113, 1129-1136, 1138, 1140-1142, 1145, 1147-1149, 1159-1161, 1163, 1166-1168, 1170, 1171, 1177-1183, 1185-1187, 1189-1192, 1198, 1218-1223, 1225, 1228, 1231-1235, 1239-1248, 1251-1254, 1258, 1259, 1262, 1264-1278, 1291-1294, 1297, 1298, 1302-1304, 1308, 1310, 1312

Benefices, secular clerics (and prospective clerics), dispensed by papal authority, to hold for life, resign and exchange, two incompatible, 2-5, 10, 11, 21, 23-26, 31, 33, 34, 36, 38, 40, 44, 45, 47, 62, 65, 77-79, 81, 82, 84, 85, 88-90, 93, 95, 96, 98-107, 109-112, 114, 119, 120, 131, 132, 135, 140-143, 147, 149, 150, 152, 153, 168-170, 172, 175, 177, 178, 183-185, 187, 189, 191, 193-195, 198, 201, 202, 204-208, 211-216, 218, 222-224, 232, 233, 237-239, 241, 242, 246, 247, 262, 263, 265, 266, 269, 271, 272, 275-279, 284-286, 288, 289, 296, 297, 303, 304, 307, 310-312, 315-318, 320, 327-329, 331, 334, 335, 338, 340, 342, 344-348,

Benefices (*contd*)

351, 352, 354, 355, 367, 372, 373, 376, 385-387, 389, 390, 395, 406, 414, 415, 418-421, 424, 426, 427, 430, 432-434, 436, 437, 439, 440, 450, 455, 459-464, 466, 467, 469-472, 474, 476-478, 481, 482, 487-491, 494-502, 506-508, 516-523, 526, 528, 530-533, 544, 545, 557, 559-562, 565-570, 575, 653, 654, 656, 657, 659, 660, 665-667, 669-671, 673-682, 687, 692, 693, 695, 699-701, 705, 706, 708-710, 713-716, 718-720, 722-727, 729, 731, 732, 734, 737-740, 744, 748, 750, 751, 755, 757, 759, 760, 762, 764, 770-775, 794, 796, 799-801, 803-806, 808-810, 813, 814, 825, 842, 843, 847, 849, 851, 856, 858, 860, 862, 864-866, 868-870, 875, 876, 878-881, 883-887, 889-894, 896-898, 900, 907, 910-913, 915-918, 920, 922, 923, 948, 949, 952-956, 959, 960, 966, 968-970, 976-979, 985, 986, 994, 1036, 1037; *and see* 347, 388, 671, 901, 902

......, ..., ..., to hold for life, resign and exchange, two incompatible, (including one canonry and prebend etc.), 393
......, ..., ..., to hold for life, resign and exchange, two incompatible, not major and principal dignities, 35, 248, 290
......, ..., ..., to hold for life, resign and exchange two perpetual vicarages, 122
......, ..., ..., to hold for life, two (vicarages), (without clauses providing for resignation and exchange), 932
......, ..., ..., to hold for life, resign and exchange, two incompatible, not parish churches and perpetual vicarages or major and principal dignities, 237
......, ..., ..., to hold for life, resign and exchange, two incompatible and any number of compatible, 766
......, ..., ..., to hold for life, resign and exchange, three incompatible, 17, 39, 117, 308, 431, 457, 480, 503, 641, 704, 957
......, ..., ..., to hold for life, resign and exchange, a third incompatible, 11, 85, 131, 143, 191, 198, 202, 215, 232, 233, 262, 271, 276, 285, 318, 320, 351, 355, 393, 424, 434, 495, 502, 508, 517, 719,

Benefices (*contd*)

739, 808, 849, 862, 879, 911, 923; *and cf.* 277
......, ..., ..., to hold, resign and exchange, a third incompatible, for ten-year period, prorogued for life, 277
......, ..., ..., to hold, resign and exchange, a fourth incompatible, 277, 434
......, ..., ..., to hold, resign and exchange once, two compatible, 893
......, ..., ..., to hold any number of compatible, 623, 895
......, ..., ..., to hold, resign and exchange any number of compatible, 530
......, ..., ..., to hold any benefices, even canonries and prebends etc. (despite homicide), 650
......, ..., ..., to hold, resign and exchange, one, 556
......, ..., dispensed by nuncio, to hold two compatible, 644
......, ..., licensed etc. by papal authority, to resign precentorship simply or in exchange for another benefice etc. to local ordinary etc., 850
......, religious orders, members of, dispensed by papal authority, to hold one secular, 6, 12, 13, 22, 32, 37, 49, 87, 133, 136, 145, 171, 186, 219, 264, 267, 268, 273, 274, 280, 299, 302, 305, 314, 319, 321, 322, 337, 339, 363, 409, 416, 438, 445-447, 451, 453, 454, 465, 468, 525, 563, 564, 571, 658, 668, 712, 728, 730, 735, 741, 742, 745, 758, 798, 802, 857, 861, 867, 871, 888, 899, 914, 926, 961-963, 973, 997; *and cf.* 30
......, ..., ..., to hold with canonical portion one secular, 730
......, ..., ..., to hold for life with monacal portion one secular, 505, 743
......, ..., ..., to hold for life with priory one secular, 92
......, ..., ..., ..., to have stall in choir and voice in chapter etc. while holding (with place and monacal portion) one secular, 133, 139, 325
......, ..., ..., ..., to have stall in choir and voice in monastery and chapters in other congregations of order while holding one secular, 743
...., ..., ..., ..., to have voice in capitular acts

Benefices (*contd*)

while holding one secular, 97

......, ..., ..., ..., to hold for life two secular, 730

......, ..., ..., ..., to hold two secular benefices, or one secular and one regular or two regular etc., 200

......, ..., ..., ..., to hold with monastery two and then (by a further dispensation), three other, 196

......, ..., ..., ..., to hold one regular of order (with or without cure) or one secular (with cure) in gift of house, 27

......, ..., ..., ..., to hold one or more secular or regular benefices *see also under Commendam*

......, dispensation from obligation to proceed to orders, imposed by *see under* Orders

......, dispensation for retention with bishopric *see under* Bishops and Archbishops

......, dispensation for retention with monastery, 1334

......, ordinance enabling holders of named chapel and chaplaincies to hold any number of compatible benefices, 777

......, *see also under* Age; Collations and provisions; *Commendam*; Illegitimacy; Simony

Birth, illegitimate *see* Illegitimacy

......, noble, grants etc. to persons of, 11, 67, 75, 143, 157, 159, 162, 164, 166, 173, 196, 226, 229, 232, 234, 257, 258, 306, 313, 330, 369-371, 402, 410, 434, 435, 475, 481, 492, 494, 508, 572, 610, 630, 643, 646, 649, 652, 683, 711, 746, 752, 785, 789, 838, 868, 933, 936, 939, 945, 980, 1000, 1024

......, baronial, grant etc. to person of, 410, 1024

......, comital, grant etc. to person of, 127, 933

......, comital and baronial, grants etc. to persons of, 785, 789

......, knightly, grants etc. to persons of, 143, 369

......, knightly and baronial, grant etc. to person of, 196

......, noble, validation of grant etc. to person claiming incorrectly, 502

......, other references to nobility, 16, 58, 75,

Birth (*contd*)

80, 86, 158, 259, 332, 357, 366, 423, 435, 449, 691, 925, 938, 984

Bishopric *in partibus infidelium* provision to, 963, 1324,

Bishops and Archbishops, appointment of coadjutor for, 549

......, collation of cathedral precentorship by, challenged by lay nobles, 80

......, commanded to act personally in the erection and endowment of a new parish church, 64

......, conspiracies against while at Roman curia, 485

......, dispensed to be provided as, despite defects of age (and birth), 58, 614, 623

......, dispensed to retain (or hold) the following benefices together with see:-

Augustinian priory, 349

Augustinian priory and rectory, 632; *and cf.* 698

Benedictine monastery, 600, 605

Cistercian monastery, 121

regular or secular benefice (in addition to Benedictine monastery), 399

any number of secular (compatible) and regular benefices, 608

church (called custodianship or guardianship) and Cistercian monastery, 596

life pension and two regular or secular benefices, 963

parish church and basilica or chapel, 552

rectory, 672

cf. 1311, 1323, 1326, 1337

......, establishing that a canonry and prebend be collated to a teacher for the local grammar school, 179

......, faculties for consecration of, by any catholic bishop, 57, 551, 554, 595, 599, 603, 607, 613, 619, 621, 631, 636, 638, 1014, 1031

......, faculty for promotion to orders, by any catholic bishop outside lawful times, 613

......, faculty (or indult) to reconcile polluted churches etc. by deputy, 411, 848

......, foundation of college by; thereafter

Bishops and Archbishops (*contd*)
granted faculty to confirm and reform its statutes and those of other named colleges, 176
......, instrument of, defining right to tithes in city and diocese, 118
......, licence and faculty to to bestow orders on three Sundays or feastdays even outside lawful times and successively, 398
......, licensed to reform statutes etc. of two hospitals, 429
......, jurisdiction of, over Cistercian house, disputed, 298
......, ..., over collegiate church, disputed, 529
......, ..., over separated cathedral church etc., restored, 333
......, ..., over subjects of suffragans, disputed, 1005
......, visitation of two hospitals of the poor and extortion of procurations by, 964
......, *see also under Administrationem*; Collations and provisions; Holy-water; Institution; Letters, episcopal; *Mensa*; Orders; Provision; Reconciliation; Translation *and under individual sees*

Blessing, of altars etc. and vestments etc., statute enabling prior to perform, 400
......, of ecclesiastical ornaments, indult for, 686
......, of vestments etc., indult for, 397
......, *see also under* Holy-water

Bonshommes *see under* Augustinian Order

Books, chapel to be furnished with, 807
......, of perpetual chaplaincy, 292
......, provision of, for monks' teacher, 394 [29]

Bureaucracy, papal *see under* Rome

Burial, in college chapel without diocesan's licence, 343
......, of parishioners, 188
......, rights of, to remain with the mother church, 379
......, *cf.* 777, 807
......, *cf.* Funeral expenses

C

Camaldolese Order, houses of, in Italy *see* d'Adelmo

Camera, apostolic, to be notified of exchanges of benefices, 850
......, ..., *see also under* Rome, court of, curialists at

Canonries *see under* Cathedral churches

Cantorship *see* Stirling

Capital punishment *see under* Irregularity
......, *cf.* also 80

Capons *see under* Rent

Cardinals *see under* Rome, titular churches in

Carmelite Order, professor of, dispensed to hold a secular benefice, 273

Castles *see* Carisbrooke; Fincharn

Cathedral churches, canonries and prebends of, papal decree invalidating provisions to persons who have not completed their fourteenth year, 72, 210, 332, 572
......, in England, prebends in, erection of rectory into, *cf.* 987
......, in Ireland, canonries, new, in, erection of, by papal authority, 15, 16, 71, 129, 162, 163, 167, 230, 249, 250, 255, 306, 313, 350, 360, 403, 404, 512, 537, 540, 541, 645, 646, 785, 786, 789, 790, 821, 823, 824, 826, 827, 934, 939, 942, 946, 982, 1121, 1126, 1152, 1156, 1280, 1285, 1314; *and cf.* 1282
......, in Scotland, canonries, new, in, erection of, by papal authority, *cf.* 1282
......, ..., canonry and prebend, reservation of, 543
......, ..., prebends in, erection of parish churches into, by ordinary authority, 815, 1000
......, ..., prebends in, erection of rectories

Cathedral churches (*contd*)
and vicarages etc. into, by papal authority, 15, 16, 71, 72, 129, 160, 162-164, 166, 230, 249, 250, 255, 306, 313, 350, 360, 403, 404, 512, 537, 538, 540, 541, 645, 646, 785, 786, 789, 790, 821, 823, 824, 826, 827, 834, 934, 939, 942, 946, 982, 1000, 1071, 1072, 1121, 1126, 1127, 1194; *and cf.* 987
......, ..., prebends in, erection of tithes belonging to capitular *mensa* into, 167
......, in Scotland, appropriation (to chapel royal) of fruits of named canonries and prebends in, 768
......, ..., sacrilegiously occupied by lay nobles in support of claimant to precentorship, 80
......, for chantries and chaplaincies in *see under* Chantries; Chaplaincies
......, *see also under individual cathedrals*

Cemeteries, chantry (charnel house) in, 777
......, 394 [15], [17]
......, *cf.* 64
......, *and see under* Burial; Reconciliation

Cession *see* Resignation

Chalices, 807

Chancery, papal *see under* Rome, court of, curialists at
......, royal, Keeper of the Rolls of *see* Warham, William

Chantries, foundation of, requiring celebration of mass, matins, vespers etc. and offices of the dead, 193
......, ..., requiring daily celebration of requiem mass, *ad hoc* derogation of, 348
......, foundation of, derogation of, 426, 503, 518, 777; *and cf.* 800
......, foundation and endowment of by lay patrons, (in detail), 292
......, founded as a charnel house, 777
......, ruled by three perpetual chaplains, 800
......, to be served by capable substitute, indult for, 348
......, *see* Canterbury (St Dunstan's without Westgate); Coventry; Danbury; Halstead; Kilmacduagh; Lechlade;

Chantries (*contd*)
London (cathedral church of; and city of); Maldon; Norwich; Rudgwick; St David's; Salisbury; Walsall; York; *cf.* Beverley; Ledbury; 856
......, *cf.* Chaplaincies

Chapels, (chosen by Countess Margaret [Beaufort] for her tomb), endowment etc. of and indulgences for, 807
......, composition over, confirmation of, 379
......, indulgence for, 413
......, of college, celebration of mass etc. in, 343
......, foundation of perpetual chaplaincy relating to, 292
......, *see* Aston; Barham; Blacktoft; Cambridge; Ellerker; Galway; ?Hognaston; Kilconierin; Lasborough; Poolham; Ruishton; *and cf.* Windsor

Chapel royal, (Stirling), appropriation of certain fruits of named canonries and prebends for, 768
......, ..., confirmation of erection into collegiate church and erection of cantorship in, 781
......, ..., endowment of chapel royal (newly erected into collegiate church), 765
......, ..., erection into collegiate church, with union to provostship, 1214
......, ..., letters conservatory in favour of, 767

Chaplaincies, perpetual, foundation of, prohibiting holding another benefice and requiring residence, 800
......, ..., foundation and endowment of by lay patrons, 292
......, ..., lease of land for, 366
......, ..., *see* Beverley; Canterbury; Coventry; Danbury; Hastings; Lechlade; Ledbury; Lincoln; London; Norwich; St Andrews; Salisbury; Trapani; Tuam; York
......, *cf.* Chantries

Chaplains, in chapel, composition over, 379
......, ..., of James, king of Scots, 371
......, in hospital, to perform divine offices and care for lepers, 429

Chaplains (*contd*)
......, of perpetual chaplaincy, functions etc. of, 292

Charnel house *see under* Chantries

Cistercian Order:-
    licence to build monastery for professed nuns of, 779
    privilege of exemption from jurisdiction etc. disputed by bishop, 298
    privileges etc. of, forbidding appointment as abbot of persons not professed, *ad hoc* derogation of, 943
    privileges etc. of, forbidding appointment as abbot of persons not proved and professed, *ad hoc* derogation of, 1020
    privileges of, *ad hoc* derogation of, 121, 789, 928, 943
    abbots of, dispensed to be surrogated and be appointed without taking the habit or making profession, 1015
    ...., dispensed to be appointed without taking the habit or making profession, 1019
    ...., dispensed to exercise care of monastery despite defects of age and birth, 259
    ...., dispensed to hold existing pensions with house, 1019
    ...., dispensed to hold a regular or secular benefice *in commendam* with house, 754
    ...., dispensed to hold a secular benefice *in commendam* with house, 291, 527
    ...., dispensed to retain house *in commendam* after provision as bishop and acquisition of see, 121, 596
    ...., indulged to preside over monastery for one month after acquisition without taking the habit or making profession, 67
    cellarer of, designated coadjutor for ageing abbot, with provision as abbot, 1032
    monks of, child of, 165
    ...., dispensed to hold a secular benefice, 13, 32, 37, 171, 319, 447, 468, 515, 926, 961, 962, 973
    ...., dispensed to hold a secular benefice

Cistercian Order (*contd*)
    with annual pension on fruits of monastery (of which he was formerly abbot), 148
    ...., dispensed to hold a benefice with or without cure of his order, 368
    ...., dispensed to be translated to OCist (from OFM), 383
    ...., indulged to wear habit under secular dress and live like a secular priest, 447
    ...., promoted to all orders by superior's licence, despite illegitimacy, 368
    ...., to be admitted by papal authority, 1017
    ...., ..., with subsequent collation of headship of house, 259, 574
    ...., translated from house in Germany to England, 973
    nun of, dispensed to hold priory despite defect of age, 410
    houses of, in England, *see* Bordesley; Bruern; Croxden; Dunkeswell; Forde; Kirkstead; Medmenham; Merevale; Newenham; Newminster; Quarr; Revesby; Robertsbridge; Roche; Thame; Waverley; Whalley; Woburn
    ...., in France, *see* Bosquen; Cîteaux
    ...., in Germany, *see* Fürstenfeld
    ...., in Ireland, *see* Abbeydorney; Abbeyknockmoy; Abbeyleix; Abbeymahon; Abbeyshrule; Abington; Assaroe; Boyle; Buckland; Dublin; Fermoy; Holycross; Inishlounaght; Jerpoint; Kilcooly; Killymard; Kinloss; Macosquin; Mellifont; Midleton; Monasteranenagh; Newry; Suir; Tracton
    ...., in Scotland, *see* Eccles; Kinloss; Melrose; Newbattle
    ...., in Spain *see* Cordova
    ...., in Wales, *see* Valle Crucis; Whitland

Citation *see under* Judicial Procedure

Clerical character, child under 7 to be marked with (despite illegitimacy) by bishop of his choice, 332
......, conferral of, by ordinary authority, 938,

Clerical character (*contd*)
941
......, licence and faculty to be marked with by any catholic bishop, 229

Cluniac Order:-
   privileges of, *ad hoc* derogation of, 27
   privileges of, restricting grants *in commendam*, *ad hoc* derogation of, 138, 399
   abbots of, to have re-entry, 61
   ...., to receive house *in commendam* for six months and be provided on becoming a monk, 61, 63
   monks of, dispensed to hold a secular benefice, 280, 658; *and cf.* 745
   ...., dispensed to hold a secular benefice and indulged to wear habit under secular dress, 287
   ...., dispensed (despite illegitimacy) to hold OClun benefice or a secular benefice in gift of house and be abbot; and indulged to enjoy privileges etc. in event of non-residence, 27
   ...., dispensed to hold a secular benefice and indulged to have stall and voice etc., while holding it, 267
   priors of, dispensed to hold a secular benefice with house, 92
   ...., indulged to use pontifical *insignia*, give benediction and bless vestments etc., 397
   houses of, in England *see* Bermondsey; Broomholm; Castle Acre; Chertsey; Montacute; Pontefract; St Carrok; Wenlock, Much
   ...., in France *see* Cluny
   ...., in Scotland *see* Paisley

Coadjutorship, consistorial appointment to, 549
......, of monastery, granted to cellarer with consent of ageing abbot, 1032; *and cf.* 1033, 1034
......, *and cf.* 812

Collations and provisions, by abbot, of regular benefice, vacant *certo modo*, 383
......, by alleged papal judge delegate, of religious house, 221

Collations etc. (*contd*)
......, by alleged sub-delegate of deceased papal judge delegate, of secular benefices, *de facto*, 167
......, by archdeacon, of secular benefice, *de facto*, 694
......, by bishop, of secular benefice, *de facto*, 192
......, by king of England, of priory in the Channel Islands, *de facto*, 515
......, by ordinary authority, of regular benefice, received *in commendam*, 817
......, ..., of secular benefices, 70, 80, 157, 161, 301, 384, 444, 644, 825, 831-833, 1000
......, ..., ..., vacant *certo modo*, 407, 687, 849
......, ..., ..., invalidated by simoniacal agreement, 381, 946
......, by someone without faculty, 545
......, by papal authority, of regular benefices, in Ireland, conditional on deprivation of incumbent, 127, 542, 835, 846
......, ..., ..., ..., *motu proprio*, *cf.* 115
......, ..., ..., ..., their collation having devolved on the apostolic see by statutes of the Third Lateran Council (with mandates for removal of intruders), 128, 930, 944
......, ..., ..., ..., in form "Si neutri", 573
......, ..., ..., ..., vacant by canonical sanctions, 67, 574; *and cf.* 259
......, ..., ..., ..., vacant by death, 1123
......, ..., ..., ..., vacant by death outside the Roman curia, 536, 944
......, ..., ..., ..., vacant by deprivation, 1215
......, ..., ..., ..., vacant by dissolution of union, 1283
......, ..., ..., ..., vacant *certo modo*, 259, 306, 383, 536, 573, 836, 837, 943, 1084, 1118, 1201; *and cf.* 938
......, ..., ..., ..., vacant by resignation, 1284
......, ..., ..., in Scotland, conditional on deprivation of incumbent, 509
......, ..., ..., ..., in form "Si neutri", 1018-1020
......, ..., ..., ..., vacant by death, 1115
......, ..., ..., ..., vacant *certo modo*, 144, 928
......, ..., ..., ..., vacant by resignation, 1217
......, ..., ..., ..., vacant by resignation to pope, 61, 63, 155, 535, 584

Collations etc., papal (*contd*)

......, ..., of secular benefices, in England, vacant by acquisition of a second benefice without dispensation, 386

......, ..., ..., ..., vacant by constitution "Execrabilis", 386

......, ..., ..., ..., vacant *certo modo*, 363, 644

......, ..., ..., ..., vacant by death, *cf.* 1279

......, ..., ..., in Ireland, 'new', 1199

......, ..., ..., ..., conditional on deprivation of incumbent, 225, 228, 361, 936

......, ..., ..., ..., conditional on voidance of previous collation etc., 834

......, ..., ..., ..., their collation having devolved on the apostolic see by statutes of the Third Lateran Council (with mandates for the removal of intruders), 14, 16, 69, 71, 72, 74, 75, 122, 124-126, 129, 156-159, 162-166, 225, 226, 230, 234, 236, 249-253, 255-258, 306, 313, 330, 359, 360, 362, 380, 392, 401-404, 448, 486, 511-514, 540, 541, 545, 574-576, 645, 646, 650, 652, 783-786, 788, 790, 818, 819, 823-830, 838, 852, 853, 933-936, 939-941, 945, 947-949, 982, 993, 994; *and cf.* 67

......, ..., ..., ..., vacant by death, 1124

......, ..., ..., ..., vacant by death outside the Roman curia (with mandates for the removal of intruders), 123, 142, 160, 226, 330, 510, 512, 543, 545, 648, 763, 784, 821; *and cf.* 234, 845

......, ..., ..., ..., vacant by deprivation, 1117, 1213

......, ..., ..., ..., vacant by devolution, 1195

......, ..., ..., ..., vacant by non-promotion to priesthood, 252, 359, 939

......, ..., ..., ..., vacant by resignation, 1155; *and cf.* 1289

......, ..., ..., ..., vacant by resignation outside the Roman curia, 381,

......, ..., ..., ..., vacant by unjust detention of another benefice, 385

......, ..., ..., ..., vacant *certo modo*, 157, 161, 231, 234, 306, 330, 385, 512, 536-539, 823, 831, 832, 834, 932, 942, 946, 984, 994, 1000, 1116, 1118, 1125, 1153, 1196, 1197, 1202-1205, 1207, 1216; *and cf.* 1154

......, ..., ..., ..., vacant *certo modo*, 'new', 357

Collations etc., papal (*contd*)

......, ..., ..., ..., *cf. also* 167, 384, 485, 545, 789

......, ..., ..., in Scotland, 'new', 1114, 1128

......, ..., ..., ..., on erection of new parish church, 64

......, ..., ..., ..., their collation having devolved on the apostolic see by statutes of the Third Lateran Council (with mandates for the removal of intruders), 642, 791

......, ..., ..., ..., vacant by acquisition, 1200

......, ..., ..., ..., vacant being newly erected into an undivided vicarage, 188

......, ..., ..., ..., vacant by death at the apostolic see, 190

......, ..., ..., ..., vacant by death outside the Roman curia, 50, 68, 116, 237

......, ..., ..., ..., vacant by deprivation, 1188

......, ..., ..., ..., vacant by resignation, 1296; *and cf.* 1289

......, ..., ..., ..., vacant by resignation at the apostolic see, 190

......, ..., ..., ..., vacant by resignation to pope, 782, 839-841, 929, 931, 937, 992

......, ..., ..., ..., vacant *certo modo*, 116, 301, 407, 844, 1165, *and cf.* 1154

......, ..., *cf. also* 358, 364, 417, 616, 697, 854, 855, 951, 996, 1001, 1002

......, *see also under* Expectation; Provision; Reservation; *cf. also* Unions

Collector *see under* Rome, court of, curialists at: camera

Colleges, foundation of and publication of statutes etc. by bishop and faculty for him to confirm and reform the said statutes and those of other named colleges, 176

......, warden and scholars of, licensed to celebrate etc. in chapel of, 343

......, *see* Cambridge; Cobham; Lichfield; Northampton; Oxford; Youghal

......, *cf.* Collegiate churches

Collegiate churches, canonries and prebends of, impetration by person under ten, 332

......, erection of chapel royal into, 781, 1214; *and cf.* 765

......, in England *see* Beverley; Bridgnorth;

Collegiate churches (*contd*)
Darlington; Glasney; Ripon; Tattershall
......, in Ireland *see* Galway; Scattery Island; Youghal
......, in Scotland *see* Bothwell; Crichton; Dumbarton; Dunbar; 'Laronde'; St Andrews; Stirling; *and cf.* Restalrig
......, in Wales *see* Abergwili
......, *cf.* Colleges

Commendam:-
benefices held *in*, 127, 384, 596, 632; *and cf.* 877, 1003
religious houses held *in*, 69, 75, 229,235, 349, 399, 405, 441, 442, 943
bishop dispensed to hold with his see an Augustinian house *in*, 349
bishop dispensed to hold with his see an Augustinian house and rectory *in*, 632
bishop dispensed to hold with his see a Benedictine house *in*, 600, 605
bishop dispensed to hold with his see a Cistercian house *in*, 121
bishop dispensed to hold with his see a church (called custodianship or guardianship) and Cistercian house *in*, 596
bishop dispensed to hold with his see (in addition to a Benedictine house *in*) a regular or secular benefice *in*, 399
bishop dispensed to hold with his see any number of secular and regular benefices *in*, 608
bishop dispensed to hold with his see two secular or regular benefices *in*, 963
dispensation to hold a regular benefice *in*, 817
dispensation to hold a regular or secular benefice *in*, with a regular or secular benefice, 742
dispensation to hold a regular or secular benefice *in*, with Augustinian house, 48, 260, 283, 484, 524, 859, 874, 904
dispensation to hold a regular or secular benefice *in*, with Augustinian hospital, 396
dispensation to hold a regular or secular benefice *in*, with Benedictine house, 341
dispensation to hold a regular or secular

Commendam (*contd*)
benefice *in*, with Cistercian house, 754
dispensation to hold a regular or secular benefice *in*, with Premonstratensian house, 707, 747
dispensation to hold a regular or secular benefice *in*, with a regular benefice *in titulum*, 43
dispensation to hold two regular benefices or one regular and one secular *in*, with Augustinian house, 863
dispensation to hold a secular benefice *in*, with Augustinian house, 283, 863
dispensation to hold a secular benefice *in*, with Benedictine house, 882, 967
dispensation to hold a secular benefice *in*, with Cistercian house, 291, 527
dispensation to hold a secular benefice *in*, with Premonstratensian house, 42, 974
dispensation to hold a secular benefice *in*, with another secular benefice, 741
dispensation to retain a regular benefice *in*, with a secular or regular benefice, 336
dispensation to retain two perpetual vicarages *in*, with Augustinian house, 127
dispensation to Benedictine monk to hold a secular benefice *in*, with another secular benefice, 322
dispensation to masters of hospital to hold a secular benefice *in*, with hospital, 7
dispensation to professor OESA to hold a regular benefice *in*, 138
grants made *in*, by papal authority, of religious houses in France, 196, 577
...., ..., of religious houses in Ireland, 221
...., ..., ..., vacant *certo modo*, 789
...., ..., ..., conditional on deprivation of incumbent, 229, 936
...., ..., ..., their provision having lawfully devolved on the apostolic see by canonical sanctions, 163, 166, 330
...., ..., ..., their collation having devolved on the apostolic see by statutes of the Third Lateran Council, 227, 575, 984; *and cf.* 989
...., ..., ..., vacant *certo modo*, 512, 573, 785

Commendam (*contd*)

...., ..., ..., vacant by death outside the Roman curia, 492, 649, 980

...., ..., ..., vacant by provision of incumbent, 588

...., ..., of house of Hospitallers in Ireland, for six months, 938

...., ..., of precentorship until age 17, 158

...., ..., of religious house in Italy, 382

...., ..., of religious houses in Scotland, 181, 584, 588, 1009

..., consistorial, of religious houses in Scotland, for six months, 61, 63

...., by papal authority, of religious houses in the Channel Islands, vacant *certo modo*, 515, 817

...., ..., of secular benefices in Ireland, their collation having devolved on the apostolic see by statutes of the Third Lateran Council, until grantee reaches age 17, 158

...., ..., ..., vacant *certo modo*, 984

...., ..., of secular benefices in Italy, 364

Commission, on papal authority, by virtue of an appeal, relating to England, 1051

......, ..., ..., relating to Ireland, 1050, 1073, 1162, 1164, 1306

......, ..., ..., relating to Scotland, 1103, 1224, 1307

Composition, between parties in dispute, 118

Concubinage, clerical *see under* Deprivation

Confession, *cf.* 1 *and* 394 [15], [28]

Confessor, indults to choose, 244, 374, 377

Confirmation, papal, of archiepiscopal grant of mensal lands, 356

......, ..., of episcopal constitution etc. concerning tithes in Bangor city and diocese, 118

......, ..., of episcopal grant of mensal lands, 146

......, ..., of composition over chapel, 379

......, ..., of public instrument and episcopal letters concerning lay patrons' foundation of chaplaincy, 292

Confraternity, in priory church, indulgence for members of, 400

......, *see* Drapers' Company

Consanguinity *see under* Illegitimacy; Marriage

......, *and cf.* 620, 622, 811

Consecration, faculties for, (*rubricellae* of), 1211, 1319, 1325, 1330, 1341

......, of bishops etc., faculties for, *see under* Bishops and Archbishops

......, of churches etc. and vestments etc., indult for, confirmation of, and faculty for, 425

Contumacy, in non-appearance before dean, excommunication for, 9

......, *cf.* 28, 298

Courts, ecclesiastical *see under* Canterbury; Dublin; Rome; *and also under* Judges delegate; Judicial Procedure; Litigation

Crime, examination of persons accused of, 556, 895

......, jurisdiction over punishment etc. of, 9, 529

......, *see also under* Homicide(s); Pirates

Cruciferi cum Stella, Order of, hospital of *see* Trim, Newtown

Cure of souls, of parishioners, 188

D

Dedications[1] of churches, etc.:-

All Saints *see* Batley; Battlesden; Braybrooke; Bristol; Canterbury; ?Chesterfield; Chingford; Goodmanham; Maldon; Monxton; Netteswell; Ripley; Saltfleetby; Shillington; Worcester; York; *and see under* London, city of (All Hallows' at the Hay)

Annunciation of BVM *see* Cambridge; Salisbury

Christchurch *see* Canterbury

Holy Cross *see* (?)Ardkeen; Cuxham;

[1] Place-names which may derive from a dedication are also included.

Dedications (*contd*)

Heryngham or Hardham; Holycross; Kilcooly; Reigate

Holy Spirit *see* London; Rome

Holy Trinity *see* Ballintober; Coventry; Dublin; Edinburgh; Exeter; Guildford; Kirkham; Michelham; Orton Longueville; Speyer; Tattershall; Tuam; Wenlock, Much

Holy Trinity *see under* B. Mary *alias* Holy Trinity

[Holy] Trinity, B.Mary, St Oswald and all other saints *see* Ashbourne; (?)Hognaston

Maison Dieu *see* Dover

Nativity of BVM *see* Conington

St Alban *see* St Albans

St Alkmund *see* Shrewsbury

St Andrew *see* Blickling; Broomholm; Eakring; Heddington; Inchegall; Ipplepen; Kenn; London; Milborne St Andrew; Pershore; Pitminster; Rushall; St Andrews; Stokesby; Thoresby, South; Utterby

St Andrew the Apostle *see* Cromhall

Sts Andrew and Cuthbert *see* York

St Bartholomew *see* 'Cassano'

St Bartholomew the Apostle *see* Sulhampstead Abbots

St Benedict *see* Newry

St Blasius *see under* Sts Clarus and Blasius

St Botulph *see* Colchester

St Bridget *see* Urney *alias* Keadew

St Brogan *see under* Sts Coan and Brogan

St Canicus *see under* Sts Patrick, Columba and Canicus

St Carrok *cf.* St Carrok

St Catherine *see* Aughrim; Beverley; Waterford

St Cedd (or St Chad) *see* Bromley, Abbots

S. Chafudi *see* (?)Ardquin

St Ciaran *see* Seirkieran

Sts Clarus and Blasius *see* (?)Monfavrey

St Clement *see* Hastings; Norwich; Worcester; *and cf.* London

Sts Coan and Brogan *see* Mothel

St Columba *see* Inchcolm; Iona

...., *and see under* Sts Patrick, Columba

Dedications (*contd*)

and Canicus

St Cronan *see* Roscrea

St Cuby *see* Cuby

St Cuthbert *see under* Sts Andrew and Cuthbert

St Cyriac *see* Lacock

Sts Cyriac and Julitta *see* Swaffham

St Dionis *see* London

St Dubritius *see* Porlock

St Dunstan *see* Canterbury

St Ebba the Virgin *see* Oxford

St Edmund *see* Bury St Edmunds

St Erkenwald *see* Chertsey

St Erme *cf.* 762

St Finbar *see* Cork

St Findchu *see* Killinaboy

St Fintan *see* Tippeenan

St George *see* Georgeham; Hethe; London; Manaton; Wilton

St George the Martyr *see* Crowhurst

St Gerald *see* Mayo

St Germain *see* Mons

St Gilbert *see* Sempringham

St Giles *see* Stamford

St Gluvias *cf.* St Gluvias

St Guthlac *see* Hereford

St Helen *see* Edlington; Wingfield, North; Worcester

St Helier *cf.* St Helier

St Illogan *see* Illogan

St James *see* Adare; Ballyshannon; Clanfield; Santiago de Compostela; Jacobstowe; Taunton

St James the Apostle *see* Birdham; Horwood, Great

St Jarlath *see* Tempull na Scrine

St John *see* Beverley; Bridgwater; Kilmainham; Tisbury; Trim, Newtown

St John the Apostle *see* Croxton

St John the Baptist *see* Axbridge; Bath; Boughton; Bridgwater; Bristol (Redcliff); Broadwindsor; Danbury; Ditteridge; Dunwich; Lichfield; Nenagh; Nettleton; Northampton; Norwich; Notley; Pilton; Shaftesbury; Stamford; Walsall

St John the Apostle and Evangelist *see* Haughmond; Pontefract

B. John the Evangelist *see* Tuam

Dedications (*contd*)

St John the Evangelist *see* Healaugh;
Kilkenny; Leighs, Little; Norwich;
Pontefract; Waterford

.... *see under* B. Mary and St John the
Evangelist

St Julitta *see under* Sts Cyriac and Julitta

St Kenelm *see under* B. Mary and St
Kenelm, King and Martyr

St Kieran *see* Clashacrow; Seirkieran

St Lambert *see* Stonham Aspall

St Laurence *see* Lackford; Lechlade;
Limerick; Lydeard St Lawrence;
Sanday; Stretton, Church; Trapani

St Laurence the Martyr *see* Drogheda

St Leonard *see* Colchester

St Machar *see* Aberdeen

St Machutus *see* Llanfechell

St Margaret *see* Leicester; Shottisham;
Tintinhull; Westminster; *and cf.*
Stratton St Margaret

St Martha *cf.* 111 note

St Martin *see* Coker, West; Dover;
Hereford; Oxford; Worcester

B. Mary *see* Abbeydorney;
Abbeyknockmoy; Abbeyleix;
Abbeymahon; Abington; d'Adelmo;
Aghmacart; Ambronay;
Annaghdown; Ashwell; Assaroe;
Bayham; Benfleet, South; Bosquen;
Boyle; Broadwater; Bruton; Callan;
Cambuskenneth; Chevening;
(?)Clee; Clonfert; Combwell; Cong;
Cork (Gill Abbey); Coventry;
Coxford; Croxden; Drumlane;
Dublin; Edinburgh; Feltwell;
Fermoy; Forde; Gallen; Galway;
Glascarrig; Greatconnell;
Guisborough; Hickling; Hurley;
Inchcleraun; Innisfallen; Ivychurch;
Jedburgh; Kells [co. Kilkenny];
Kells [co. Meath]; Kensington;
Killagh; Kilshanny; Kinloss;
Kirkstead; Langham; Langley;
Lanthony II by Gloucester;
Lechlade; Leicester; Lindores;
London; Ludgershall; Lyhou; Mayo;
Medmenham; Mellifont; Melrose;
Merevale; Merton; Midleton;
Monaincha; Monasteranenagh;
Moncenisio; Monmouth;

Dedications (*contd*)

Muckamore; Norwich; Notley;
Oxford; Puddletown; Rathkeale;
Revesby; Robertsbridge; Roche;
Saints Island; Sparham; Suir;
Thornholme; Tortington; Tracton;
Twickenham; Winsham; Wootton;
Worlington, East; Worth [and]
Swanage; Youghal

B. Mary *alias* Holy Trinity *see*
Ogonnelloe

B. Mary *see under* [Holy] Trinity,
B.Mary, St Oswald and all other
saints

B. Mary and St John the Baptist *see*
Notley

B. Mary and St John the Evangelist *see*
Titchfield

B. Mary and St Kenelm, King and
Martyr *see* Winchcombe

B. Mary and St Nicholas *see* Leeds

BVM *see* Burford; Chester; Croxden;
Dunkeswell; Fürstenfeld; Gedney;
Gravesend; Haddington;
?Hognaston; Ledbury; Leicester;
Leiston; London; Mansfieldstown;
Mellifont; Nottingham; Overton;
Ramsden Crays; Rathkeale; Ross
Carbery; Stonely; Wendling;
Whitland; Worcester

.... *and see under* Annunciation of BVM

BVM and St Egwin *see* Evesham

St Mary *see* Banbury; Bondleigh;
Burwell St Mary; Coventry;
Drogheda; Galway; Kingston;
Lanthony II by Gloucester;
Muckamore; Norton; Rathkeale;
Ravenna; Raynham; Reculver; St
Mary's Isle; Sanday; Stanford
Rivers; Stazzema; Suir; Treglio;
Watton; Waverley; Willand; Wilton

St Mary *de populo see* Cordova

Sts Mary and Michael *see* Benabbio

B. Mary Magdalen *see* Shap; Taunton;
Tortington

St Mary Magdalen *see* Bermondsey;
Ham, East

B. Michael *see* Mayo

St Michael *see* Ballinskelligs; Cortesora;
Coventry; Limerick; Lucca; Mayo;
Melksham; Orchard Portman;

Dedications (*contd*)

  Smarden; Stamford; Weyhill; Wilsford

  St Michael *see under* Sts Mary and Michael

  St Michael the Archangel *see* Breamore; London; Milverton

  St Mildred *see* London

  B. Mirren *see* Paisley

  Sts Molanus and Queranus *see* Annagh

  St Neot *cf.* St Neot

  St Nicholas *see* Carisbrooke; Combe St Nicholas; Drax; Galway; Glatton; Greenwich, West *alias* Deptford; Guildford; Odagh; Pembroke; Plumstead; Stretton on the Fosse; Upton Magna; Verucchio

  St Nicholas *see under* B. Mary and St Nicholas; St Peter and St Nicholas

  St Nicholas the Confessor *see* St David's

  St Nicholas (Acon) *see* London

  St Oswald *see* Ashbourne

  St Oswald *see under* [Holy] Trinity, B. Mary, St Oswald and all other saints

  St Patrick *see* Downpatrick; Drumgoon; Kildrumferton; Norragh; Trim

  Sts Patrick, Columba and Canicus *see* 'Tolach'

  B. Paul *see under* Bs. Peter and Paul (the Apostles)

  St Paul *see* Taunton

  St Paul *see under* Sts Peter and Paul

  B. Peter *see* Westminster

  Bs. Peter and Paul *see* Mersea, West; Montacute; Westleton

  (Bs.) Peter and Paul the Apostles *see* Athlone; Dorchester; Horndon on the Hill; Plympton

  St Peter *see* Chertsey; Dunstable; Edgmond; Fakenham; Fugglestone St Peter; Gloucester; Hedingham, Sible; Hereford; Heydon; Ipswich; Marcilhac; Ruthin; Shaftesbury; Shobrooke; Taunton; Trim, Newtown; Waltham, ?North; Westminster

  St Peter and St Nicholas *see* Verruchio

  Sts Peter and Paul *see* Chacombe; Kettering; Selsker; Taunton

  St Petroc *see* Bodmin

Dedications (*contd*)

  St Probus *cf.* Probus

  St Prosper *see* Collécchio

  St Queranus *see under* Sts Molanus and Queranus

  St Romuald *see* Shaftesbury

  St Salvator *see* St Andrews

  St Saviour *see* Bermondsey; Torre

  St Senan *see* Helland

  St Sepulchre *see* Warwick

  St Swithin *see* Sproatley

  St Theodorus *see* St Theodorus

  St Thomas *see* Winchelsea

  St Thomas the Martyr *see* Ballybeg; Dodbrooke; Glasney; Stamford

  St Tudy *cf.* 288

  St Tydfil *see* Merthyr Tydfil

  St Wennapa (or St Wenep or Veep) *cf.* Gwennap

  St Werburgh *see* Hoo

  St Withburga *see* Holkham

  St Wulfram *see* Grantham

  St Wulstan *see* St Wolstan

  Sanctus (?)Sunanus 676

...., corrected by order of the Regent of the Chancery, 747

Defamation, litigation over, 29, 197, 811

Defects, of age *see* Age

......, of birth *see* Illegitimacy

Deformity, of eye, dispensation to be promoted to all orders and hold a canonry and prebend despite, 14

......, ..., dispensation to be promoted to all orders, minister at altar and hold a benefice with cure despite, 721

Degrees[1]:-

  Arts, bachelor of *see* Baker, Richard; Cook, Robert; Dotson', Laurence; Kuodi, Robert; Lacy, Arthur; Molyneux, Henry; Payntoure, Roger; St John, Richard; Thymylby, Thomas; Willoughby, Robert; *and see* Perott, John

  ...., licentiate in *see* Forman, Andrew

---

1 Though not so treated by the chancery the BA and LicA are, for convenience, here included among the degrees.

Degrees, Arts (*contd*)

...., master of *see* Adam, Thomas; Bacheler, John; Barker, David; Beaumont, Thomas; Bernardi, Robert; Betonen', Robert; Beyto, John; Borgh, Thomas; Bowen, William; Brown, John; Byford, David; Chapman, Thomas; Chubbe, William; Dampeyr, Richard; Darby, Edward; Dickson, Thomas; Dubler, William; Dunche, William; Dussyng, Robert; Eduard, William; Eglifeld, Leonard; Ffoter, William; Gaunt, Richard; Gilbert, Robert; Gwynn, Maurice; Gybbons, William; Hafter, John; Hamilton, David; Harrald, John; Harrop, Thomas; Hawlay, Robert; Hicks, John; Holt, John; Hunden', Thomas; Ketilton, William; Lynley, Robert; Many, John; Michell, Thomas; Murray, James; Ormeston, Thomas; Preston, William; Quynby, Richard; Rede, Thomas; Ruer, Thomas; Smyth *alias* Gogh, John; Stewart, Edward; Stewart, Walter; Strangways, George; Sydnor, Richard; Thorpe, William; Tybard, Henry; Tybenh(a)m, Thomas; Urmeston, Thomas; Vaughan, John; Wekis, Robert; Welles, Thomas; Whitrow, Stephen; Wigston, Thomas; Willoughby, Edward; Wolsey, Thomas; Wykes, Robert; *cf.* Taylor, John

Law, canon, bachelor of (BDec) *see* Adams, Maurice; Barton, William; Bradshaw, Peter; Bromuoych, James; Chadworth, George; Chapman, Thomas; Clayton, Nicholas; Cocke, John; Colyns, Martin; Cook, John; Crosley, Christopher; David, Maurice; Dedworth, Robert; Docura, John; Dyllon, John; Edwardes, Thomas; Everard, Thomas; Fishwick, Thomas; Garard, Thomas; Gottis, Richard; Hedge, Thomas; Hyde, John; Inell *alias* Giles, Alexander; Josselyne, Philip; Knollys, David; Kyte, John; Lathes, Richard;

Degrees, Law, canon (*contd*)

Leicester, John; Lugwardyn, John; Orton, Thomas; Paynter, John; Re'pe, Thomas; Smyth, John; Spicer, William; Standerwike, John; Stewart, Edward; Thatcher, William; Thome, John; Tyake, John; Valle, John; Yates, Simon; *and see* Perott, John

Law, canon, licentiate in (Lic Dec) *see* Taylard, William

...., ..., doctor of (DDec) Boket, William; Brundholm, Richard; Churche, Roger; Colyns, Martin; Cutfolde, Thomas; Ebrard, Fiocardus; Fitz Herbert, Thomas; Gilbert, Thomas; Jane, Thomas; Martyn, Thomas; Ravyn, John; Rokeby, William; Russell, William; Veysey *alias* Harman, John; Urswick, Christopher; Warde, John; Whitstones, James; Wilton, William

Laws, bachelor of *see* Adam, James; Barbour, Thomas; Blount, Walter; Brownesmyth, John; Bulkeley, Richard; Bunt, Thomas; Cotton, Walter; Dalison, Thomas; Eynon ap Gwalter; Gascoigne, Humphrey; Gimnays, William; Grene, Hugh; Grene, Thomas; Howell, Thomas ap; Kay, Thomas; Lane, Edward; Newport, Richard; Oxenbregge, John; Parker, John; Podynger, John; Rogers, James; Simon, Richard; Smyth, John; Speke, Christopher; Vassar, Peter

...., doctor of *see* Bright, Robert; Dowman, John; Draper, Richard; Hare, Thomas; Harington, William; Jenynges, John; Morris, William; Peynthwyn, Hugh; Scot, Edward; Veysey *alias* Harman, John; Warham, William; Yonge, John

...., both (*utriusque iuris*), bachelor of *see* Barbour, John; Grafton, Adam; Sandford, Roger; Wardroper, John; Wyche, John; Wylleys, Richard

...., ..., licentiate in *see* Mason, William

...., ..., doctor of *see* de Bone, Philibertus; Malvezzi, Galeazzo; Nans, John; Walter, William;

Degrees, Laws, both (*contd*)
  Woodington, Thomas
  Medicine, master of *see* Knyghtley, Walter
  Theology, bachelor of *see* Andrenoson, Gilbert; Andrew, John; Beledhey, John; Bevys, Thomas; Cobaldi, Thomas; Denh(a)m, John; Dokett, Robert; Edimundi, John; Ellbardi, Thomas; Hafter, John; Lathes, Robert; Layburne, Roger; Legh, Thomas; Panter, Richard; Prud, John; Redman, Walter; Sowthwode, John; de Surteys, Stephen; Thomson, Thomas; Wardall, John; Watrer, Thomas
  ...., master of *see* Barbour, Robert; Blythe, Geoffrey; Chaundler, Thomas; Hobyll, John; Hornby, Henry; Mandeville, Edmund; Ponzettus, Fer(di)nandus; Saunders, Hugh; Stockdale, William; Wyllesford, Edmund
  ...., doctor of *see* [?FitzJohn], Francis *and see* Taylor, John

Deprivation, by archdeacon of vicar, 192
......, by clerics and laymen of vicar, 192
......, by prior of rector, litigation over, 694
......, by papal authority, if following allegations are proved:-
  of heads of religious houses, alienation (dilapidation and dissipation) of property, 127, 509, 835, 846, 936
  ...., appropriation and with-holding of canons' portions, 229
  ...., celebration of mass and participation in divine offices while excommunicate, 542
  ...., destruction of private property, 229
  ...., disobedience to monastic superior, 542
  ...., failure to remain in monastery, despite oath, 229
  ...., failure to reside continuously, 835
  ...., keeping concubine, 936
  ...., neglect of monastic buildings, 835
  ...., neglect of religion and conventual life, 229
  ...., presence at and involvement in homicides, 127, 229

Deprivation (*contd*)
  ...., refusal to pay procuration, 542
  ...., simony, 835
  of regular clergy, celebration of divine offices while excommunicate, 542
  of secular clergy, celebration of mass etc. while excommunicate, 361, 936
  ...., celebration of mass in place under interdict, 361
  ...., dissipation of church property, 816
  ...., failure to be promoted to required orders, 228
  ...., involvement in secular affairs, 228
  ...., keeping concubine, 228, 936
  ...., misuse of church property, 228
  ...., participation in divine offices in contempt of the keys, 361
  ...., participation in divine offices while excommunicate, 936
  ...., perjury, 361, 936
  ...., presence at homicide, 127
  ...., presence at and involvement in homicide, 225
  ...., simony, 936

Dilapidation of ecclesiastical property *see under* Deprivation

Disability, rehabilitation for, 416
......, ..., incurred by acquiring benefice without dispensation, 386
......, ..., incurred by detaining benefice by pretext of *de facto* collation and provision and receiving fruits *de facto*, 161, 515, 644
......, ..., incurred by detaining benefice unjustly, 385
......, ..., incurred by conspiracy against bishop, 485
......, ..., incurred by violence etc. towards cleric, 14, 167
......, ..., incurred by perjury, 129
......, ..., incurred by presence at homicides etc., 127, 573, 982, 984
......, ..., incurred by presence at homicides, pillaging, sacrilege etc., 485
......, ..., incurred by simoniacal agreement, 846 (*and cf.* 995), 946
......, ..., incurred by taking fruits of benefices *de facto*, 363
......, ..., incurred by taking fruits of

Disability (*contd*)
    benefices while lacking required orders, 252, 359, 939, 943
......, ..., incurred by theft and false denial, 574
......, *see also* Irregularity; Simony

Dispensation *see under* Age; Benefices; Habit; Illegitimacy; Marriage; Orders; Residence; *and cf.* Indult

Dominican Order, professors of, dispensed to hold a secular benefice, 454
......, ..., dispensed to hold a secular benefice *in titulum* or a regular *in commendam*, 817
......, ..., provision of as bishop, 579

Drapers' Company, confraternity of, in St Michael's Cornhill, petitioning to acquire (by exchange) right of presentation, 903

Drunkenness, of laymen during sacrilegious occupation of cathedral church, 80

Duke, of Savoy, Amadeus *see under* Felix V

Duress, plea of, 936

E

Education:-
    college for scholars, institution of, in hospital, 176
    confirmation of arrangement whereby a certain canonry and prebend is collated to a teacher for the local grammar school, 179
    monastic, statutes of Benedict XII cited, 394 [29]
    monks accustomed to study in cloister, 394 [15]
    teacher, monks', salary of, 394 [28]
    ...., ..., books for, 394 [29]
    see also under Books; Language; *Studia generalia*; Universities

Election *see under* Abbots; Priors

Eucharist, to be kept in college chapel with-

Eucharist (*contd*)
    out diocesan's licence, 343

"Evidences", 29

Examination, stipulated as prerequisite for collation, 116, 158, 258, 509, 841, 992
......, of deformity, 14
......, *cf. under* Crime

Exchange of benefices, *cf.* 1157, 1158
......, *see also under* Resignation

Excommunication, absolution conditional, from *q.v.*
......, as disincentive to commit homicides etc. in named locality, 493
......, for violence towards cleric, 14
......, sentence of, faculty granted to abbot to aggravate and re-aggravate, 108
......, ..., imposed by archbishop on laymen for occupying cathedral church in support of claimant to precentorship, defied, 80
......, ..., imposed by archbishop's commissary during litigation over money, 812
......, ..., imposed by bishop on vicar despite his having letters of protection from archbishop, 192
......, ..., imposed by dean against laymen and by cleric (at their instance) against him, 9
......, ..., imposed by legate's commissary on couple for contact despite inhibition, 28
......, ..., imposed by vicar general, for conspiracy against absent bishop, 485
......, ..., imposed by papal judge delegate for non-payment of costs of litigation, 29
......, ..., imposed on Augustinian prior by his father abbot for disobedience and refusal to pay procuration etc., 542
......, ..., incurred by non-payment of annual pension and deprivation of rights etc., 987
......, sentence of greater, in Canterbury constitution, 197

Exemplification *see under* Letters, papal, exemplification of

Exemption *see under* Jurisdiction

Expectation, grant of, to benefice, with or without cure, 643
......, ..., to prebend in cathedral church, with provision of a canonry, 643
......, *cf.* 543

Expectative grace, letters of, 80; *and cf.* 115 *and* 1137

Extortion, to be discouraged in named locality by automatic excommunication, 493
......, of money from suffragan bishops' subjects, by metropolitan on visitation, 1005
......, of procurations from two hospitals of the poor, by archbishop on visitation, 964

F

Fabric, administratorship of, appointment to, conditional on deprivation of incumbent, 816
......, of monastery in disrepair, union of prebend to, 235

Fabric fund, required for monastery in France formerly detained by the English etc., 196

Falsification *see* Forgery

Familiars *see under* Households

Farm, of fruits of benefices, indult for, 425
......, (or rent), possessions of priory granted in, 981

Fasting, time of, 394 [19]

Fealty, oath of, to mother church, required from incoming chaplain, 379
......, ..., to pope and Roman church, required from certain heads of religious houses, dignitaries, and bishops and archbishops, 57, 181, 258, 509, 546, 547, 551, 554, 577, 578, 581, 582, 584, 587, 588, 590-592, 595, 599, 603, 607, 613, 619, 621, 625-628, 631, 636, 638, 841, 1006, 1007, 1009, 1011, 1021, 1023, 1027, 1031, 1033; *and cf.* 1212, 1316

Fealty (*contd*)
......, ..., to archbishop by bishop, relaxed on change of superiority and jurisdiction, 333

Fear, of adversary, a plea in litigation, 28, 199, 261, 988

Feast days, as legal *termini*, Nativity of Jesus Christ, 155, 407, 444, 778, 931, 963
......, ..., Nativity of B. John the Baptist, 155, 356, 407, 444, 778, 931, 963
......, ..., Pentecost, 144, 301, 366, 379, 782, 844
......, ..., St Martin in November, 144, 301, 366, 379, 782, 844
......, ..., St Michael the Archangel, 118
......, as visiting days, Annunciation of BVM, 413, 807
......, ..., Assumption of BVM, 413, 807
......, ..., Conception of BVM, 807
......, ..., Nativity of BVM, 413, 807
......, ..., Purification of BVM, 413, 807
......, ..., Visitation of BVM, 807
......, Ascension, vigil of, procession on, 394 [23]
......, Palm Sunday, vigil of, sacrilegious occupation of cathedral church on, 80
......, (specified), accounts to be rendered by, 394 [5], [6]
......, *see also* 292, 394 [19]

Food, 394 [12], [18], [19]

Forgery, of "evidences", 29
......, 197

Fornication *see under* Deprivation; Illegitimacy

Foundation, of religious house, licence for, 1
......, *see under* Chantries; Chaplaincies; Colleges; Hospitals *and cf. under* Legislation; Residence

Franciscan Order:-
    privileges etc. of, granted to proposed new house and its personnel, 1
    ...., prohibiting professors having voice in capitular acts while holding a secular benefice, *ad hoc* derogation of, 97

Franciscan Order (*contd*)
  brother of third order of, resigning secular benefice, 833
  child of tertiary of, 123
  professors of, dispensed to be translated to OCist, 383
  ...., dispensed to hold a secular benefice, 136, 302, 446, 861, 963
  ...., dispensed to have voice in chapters etc., be elected to prelacies etc. and use privileges, while holding a secular benefice, 445
  ...., dispensed and indulged to have voice in capitular acts, while holding a secular benefice, 97
  ...., provided to bishopric *in partibus infidelium*, pension assigned to, 963
  houses of, in Ireland *see* Cavan; Galway
  ...., in Scotland *see* Stirling

Friars *see under* Augustinian Hermits; Dominican; Franciscan

Fruits, indult to take despite absence, 780
...., of canonries and prebends in cathedral churches, to be partially appropriated to chapel royal, 768
......, of parish churches, to be appropriated to newly erected undivided vicarage, 188
......, ..., sequestration of, 298, 991
......, of perpetual chaplaincy, to be used — during vacancy — for repair of books etc., 292
......, *see also under* Farm; Pension; Tithes

Funeral expenses etc. (in Scotland), faculty to alienate ecclesiastical property for, 443

G

Gift of churches, to hospital, confirmation of, 1107

Gilbertine Order, canons of, dispensed to hold a secular benefice, 30, 728
......, houses of, in England *see* Ormsby, North; Sempringham; Watton

Graduates *see under* Degrees

Grammar school *see under* Education

Guild *see* Drapers' Company

H

Habit, religious, dispensations or indults for wearing under secular dress, 264, 287, 314, 322, 363, 447
......, ..., indult for wearing cross under outer robe, 396
......, ..., Augustinian canon at king's court, dispensed to wear secular dress over, 972
......, ..., laid aside repeatedly by brother of Augustinian hospital, 416
......, ..., 394 [24], [25]

Harvest, citation during, 971

Holy-water, blessing of, by bishop, 411, 425, 848; *and cf.* 686

Homicide, accidental, dispensation of clergy on account of, by papal authority, for promotion to all orders and tenure of benefices, 650
......, clerics involved in, 225, 573, 650, 982

Homicides etc., in named locality to be discouraged by automatic excommunication, 493

Hospitality, for pilgrims, at religious house, 7
......, for poor travellers crossing the Alps and others, at provostry, 405
......, in religious house, to be undiminished, 394 [14]

Hospitallers, of St John of Jerusalem:-
  privileges etc. of, forbidding provision to preceptorships etc. of persons not proved and professed etc., *ad hoc* derogation of, 938
  houses of, preceptorship of, to be commended for up to six months and then (after reception as brother) collated, 938
  ...., in Ireland *see* Clonoulty; Dublin; Kilmainham

Hospitallers (*contd*)
...., in Palestine *see* Jerusalem

Hospitals, appointments to pertaining to the
    mayor etc., yet visited by archbishop,
    964
......, commission of to governor, 130
......, foundation of and reformation of
    statutes of, 429
......, in England *see* Bath; Bridgwater;
    Bristol (Redcliff); Canterbury; Dover;
    Kepier; Lichfield; London (BVM with-
    out Bishopsgate); Northampton; Oxford;
    Shaftesbury; Sherburn; Stamford; *and
    see under* Peterborough
......, in Ireland *see* Drogheda; Kilkenny;
    Limerick
......, in Italy *see* Cortesora; Moncenisio;
    Rome
......, in Scotland *see* Duns

Households, of pope, acolyte of *see* Lyell,
    Andrew
......, ..., chaplain of *see* Lyell, Andrew; de
    Pereriis, William; Ponzettus, Fer(di)nan-
    dus
......, ..., continual commensal of *see*
    Forman, Robert; Malvezzi, Galeazzo;
    Scot, Edward
......, ..., *cubicularius* of *see* Scot, Edward
......, ..., familiar of *see* de Bertinis, Leonard;
    Forman, Robert; Ponzettus, Fer(di)nan-
    dus; Scot, Edward; Tuba, Paul
......, ..., notary of *see* Ponzettus, Fer(di)nan-
    dus
......, ..., secretary of *see* Ponzettus
    Fer(di)nandus
......, of Cardinal Ascanius Maria [Sforza],
    continual commensal of *see* Barbour,
    John
......, of Cardinal Federicus [Sanseverinas],
    continual commensal of *see* Grimaldi,
    Agostino
......, of [de Ferrariis], Johannes Baptista, *cf.*
    Forman, Robert
......, of [de' Gigli], Silvester, continual com-
    mensal familiar of *see* da ?Civezzano,
    Paolo di Niccolò
......, of Ponzettus, Fer(di)nandus, continual
    commensal familiar of *see* Fabri, John;
    Goler, Wolffgangus; Mangneri,

Households (*contd*)
    Antonius
......, of Henry [VII], king of England, barber
    of *see* Narbonne, Peter of
......, ..., ..., chaplains of *see* [Blythe],
    Geoffrey; Layburne, Roger
......, ..., ..., counsellors of *see* [Blythe],
    Geoffrey; Colyns, Martin; [Jane],
    Thomas; Urswick, Christopher

I

Illegitimacy:-
    children of laymen, married man and
        married woman, 383
    ...., married man and unmarried woman,
        892
    ...., unmarried king and unmarried
        woman, 408, 769
    ...., unmarried man and unmarried
        woman, 27, 35, 54, 66, 83, 124, 243,
        290, 495, 513, 574, 644, 756, 821,
        933, 994; *and cf.* 648
    ...., unmarried man of noble birth and
        married woman, 16
    ...., unmarried man of noble birth and
        unmarried woman, 58, 357, 449, 486
    ...., unmarried man and unmarried
        woman of noble birth, 158
    ...., unmarried man and unmarried
        woman, related by consanguinity
        and affinity, 127
    children of regular clergy, Augustinian
        abbot and unmarried woman, 543
    ...., Augustinian canon (in priest's
        orders) and unmarried woman, 225,
        248
    ...., Augustinian canon and unmarried
        woman of noble birth, 332
    ...., Cistercian monk (in priest's orders)
        and an unmarried woman, related by
        consanguinity, 165
    ...., Premonstratensian canon (in priest's
        orders) and an unmarried woman,
        846
    ...., priest professed of third order of
        minors and married woman, 123
    children of secular clergy (including
        cathedral canons), bishop and
        unmarried woman, 940
    ...., cleric and unmarried woman, 14, 71,

Illegitimacy (*contd*)
160, 648, 790, 944
...., cleric and unmarried woman of noble birth, related by consanguinity and affinity, 652
...., cleric of noble birth and unmarried woman, 259, 984
...., simple, unmarried cleric and unmarried woman, 537
...., unmarried cleric and unmarried woman, 231, 510, 930, 941
...., unmarried, noble cleric and unmarried noblewoman, 938
...., dean (then a chaplain) and unmarried woman, 645
...., priest and married woman, 853
...., priest (then an unmarried man) and married woman, 640
...., priest and unmarried woman, 116, 134, 236, 250, 255, 361, 368, 393, 416, 511, 512, 576, 766, 783, 833, 893, 932, 934, 982; *and cf.* 35
...., priest of illustrious birth and unmarried woman, 623
......, conferral of clerical character, by ordinary authority, despite, 231, 486, 938, 941
......, dispensation, by ordinary authority, for being marked with clerical character, despite, 124, 225, 449, 486
......, ..., ..., for promotion to minor orders, despite, 644
......, ..., by papal authority, for being marked with clerical character, despite, 332
......, ..., ..., for ministering in orders taken, despite, 644
......, ..., ..., for presiding over bishopric and receiving consecration, despite, 54, 58, 640
......, ..., ..., for promotion to orders and/or tenure of benefices, despite, 14, 16, 27, 35, 54, 58, 66, 71, 83, 116, 123, 124, 134, 158, 160, 165, 225, 231, 236, 243, 248, 250, 255, 259, 290, 332, 357, 361, 368, 383, 393, 408, 416, 449, 486, 495, 510-513, 537, 543, 574, 576, 623, 640, 644, 645, 648, 652, 756, 766, 769, 783, 790, 821, 833, 846, 853, 892, 893, 932-934, 938, 940, 941, 944, 984,

Illegitimacy (*contd*)
994
......, ..., ..., for provision to a monastery and receiving benediction, despite, 846
......, dispensation for, 1299
......, promotion of Cistercian monk to all orders by superior's licence, despite, 368

Images etc., indult etc. to abbot, to bless, 686

Imprisonment, of woman in marriage case, 28

Indulgences, grants of, by papal authority, for visits to:-
altars of church of choice instead of church appointed for Jubilee, 374
altars of priory church or other church (for prior and members of convent and confraternity), 400
chapel, 413, 807
church and chapel (where chantry established), 292

Indulgences, translation of grants of, from the chapel Countess Margaret [Beaufort] had proposed to found etc. to another of her choice, 807

Indult *see under* Age; Altars; Benediction; Blessing; Confessor; Habit; Images; Mitre; Ornaments ecclesiastical; *and cf.* Dispensation

Infamy *cf.* Disability

Inheritance, cleric dispensed (by count palatine) to receive, 644

Institution, by bishop (or vicar general or local ordinary), to secular benefices, in England, (*de facto*), 30, 363, 386
......, ..., to secular benefices, in Ireland, 815
......, ..., to secular benefices, in Scotland, *de facto*, 116
......, ..., to secular benefices, in Scotland, refused, 50, 68
......, by provost, to secular benefice, in Scotland, disputed, 691

Institution (*contd*)

......, refused by bishop, litigation over, 456

......, *cf. also* 298

Instrument, concerning foundation of chantry, to be published annually, 292

Interdict, public, celebration of mass in place under, 361

Interest payments, 529

Intruders in benefices *see* Collations and provisions ..., with mandates for removal of intruders

Irregularity, incurred by acting as scribe in criminal causes and consequent involvement in torture etc. and capital punishment, 556

......, incurred by acting as scribe of trial or temporal justice and consequent involvement in capital punishment etc., 895

......, incurred by celebration of (or participation in) divine offices while under sentence of excommunication, 167, 363, 416, 485

......, incurred by involvement in secular affairs, 972

......, incurred by presence at homicides (etc.), 127, 573, 982, 984

......, incurred by promotion to orders before lawful age, ministering in them and participation in divine offices, and thereafter acquiring vicarage (without rehabilitation), 892

......, incurred by promotion to sacred orders without proper dispensation, 644

......, incurred by simoniacal agreement, 846 (*and cf.* 995)

......, *see also* Deprivation; *cf.* Disability

J

Jubilee, year of, indulgence of, 374

Judges delegate, papal, cases committed to, over archbishop's visitation of two hospitals and extortion of procuration, 964

......, ..., ..., over bishop's refusal to institute etc., 456

Judges delegate (*contd*)

......, ..., ..., over Cistercian monastery's exemption from jurisdiction (concerning obligation to present perpetual vicar for parish church), 298

......, ..., ..., over collegiate church's exemption from jurisdiction, 529

......, ..., ..., over defamation, 197

......, ..., ..., over defamation concerning forgery of "evidences", 29

......, ..., ..., over deprivation of vicarage, 192

......, ..., ..., over dispute between religious house and rector, 46

......, ..., ..., over dispute between two women, 8

......, ..., ..., over failure of inhabitant of city of London to pay tithes on property, 365

......, ..., ..., over injuries to cleric investigating crimes of laymen, 9

......, ..., ..., over late father's marriage and ownership of property, 86

......, ..., ..., over marriage, 28, 261, 905, 927, 988

......, ..., ..., over metropolitical jurisdiction, 1005

......, ..., ..., over ministership of religious house, 221

......, ..., ..., over non-payment of money, 435, 812

......, ..., ..., over non-payment of pension, 793, 987

......, ..., ..., over parish church, 991

......, ..., ..., over parish church in England formerly united to provostry in Italy, 405

......, ..., ..., over parishioner's failure to pay tithes etc., 906

......, ..., ..., over patronage of perpetual chaplaincy, 691

......, ..., ..., over precentorship of cathedral church, 80

......, ..., ..., over priory, 989

......, ..., ..., over rectory, 694

......, ..., ..., over repayment of money, 792

......, ..., ..., over tithes, 94, 661, 921, 971

......, ..., ..., testamentary, 924, 990

......, ..., alleged sub-delegate of, 167

......, ..., *see also under* Litigation

Judicial Procedure, defects or alleged defects in:-

Judicial Procedure (*contd*)

admission of unsuitable witnesses, 924

admonishing etc. without jurisdiction, 298

assignment of excessively long term for inquiry, 456

citation at harvest or vintage festival time, 971

citation *de facto*, 991

citation within insufficient term, 298

citation to unsafe place, 694

defendant required to reply and appear personally having already done so, 905

failure to enable defendant to speak freely, 988

failure to follow usual legal procedure, 987

false witness, 197

imposition of excessive costs, 29

non-citation of defendants, 28, 924; *and cf.* 811

refusal to admit lawful exceptions, 8, 971

refusal to admit relevant exceptions and lawful allegations etc., 792

refusal to allow defendant to prove title etc., 661

refusal to assign competent term for defence, 991,

refusal to defer to appeal to the apostolic see, 435, 921

refusal to examine witnesses, 8

refusal to give the *Apostolos*, 987

refusal to proceed summarily, 28

refusal to see plaintiff and administer justice, 261

rejection of exceptions and relevant defences, 927

......, *see also* Citation; Litigation

Jurisdiction, Cistercian privilege of exemption from, disputed, 298

......, metropolitical, over cases pending between subjects of suffragans, 1005

......, ordinary, collegiate church's exemption from, infringed, 529

......, over a cathedral church, assigned from one metropolitan church to another and later restored, 333

......, *cf.* 905, 906, 1176

Justice, temporal *see under* Scribe of trial or temporal justice

K

Kings, of Castile and Leon *see* Ferdinand [V]

......, of England *see* Edward [I]; Henry [VII]; Richard I; Richard [III]

......, of the English *see* Henry I

......, of Franks *see* Louis [XII]; Pepin

......, of Scots *see* James [IV]

......, *see also under* Patronage

Knights *see* Hospitallers

L

Lambs *see under* Tithes

Language, Latin, exercises in, 394 [29]

......, ..., preaching in, 394 [30]

......, ..., *cf.* 179

......, vernacular, preaching in, 394 [30]

......, ..., to be used during divine service, 292

Law, canon, grants etc. to students of, 257, 258

......, civil, faculty and licence to study in Aberdeen university, 1143

......, *for graduates in see under* Degrees

Laws, both, grants etc. to student of, 646

Laymen, detaining property of archiepiscopal *mensa*, 835

......, (earl), in dispute with monastery over patronage of perpetual chaplaincy, 691

......, foundation and endowment of perpetual chaplaincy by, 292

......, foundation of perpetual chaplaincy and lease of land by, 366

......, involved in *de facto* acquisition of priory, 989

......, involved in deprivation of vicar, 192

......, (king and local residents) wanting parish church for new vill, 64

......, leasing property of episcopal *mensa*, 558

......, married, exercising office of notary of

Laymen (*contd*)
episcopal curia, 919
......, occupying property of episcopal *mensa*, 181
......, (nobles and their followers) sacrilegiously occupying cathedral church in support of claimant to precentorship, 80
......, previously secretary and scribe in secular courts, wishing to become a cleric, 556
......, refusing to appear before dean over crimes, 9
......, taking fruits of precentorship, 486
......, wanting a perpetual vicar presented for parish church, 298
......, *see also under* Confessor; Marriage; Patronage *and references to disputes and litigation over marriage, money, testaments and tithes under* Appeals; Litigation; Tithes

Lease, of fruits, of parish church, subsequently challenged, 405
......, of land, (belonging to episcopal *mensa*), confirmation of, 558
......, ..., (belonging to perpetual chaplaincy), confirmation of, 366
......, of monastery's property, abbot and convent licensed to grant, 1295
......, *cf. also* 365, 1226, 1227

Lectures, in Winchcombe abbey, attendance at, 394 [29]

Legates *see under* Rome *as* apostolic see

Legislation, legatine, constitutions of Otto and Ottobuono *see under* Otto [Candidus] and Ottobuono [Fieschi]
......, local, England, episcopal constitution requiring residents of city of London to pay tithes on property to parish church, 365
......, ..., ..., episcopal statutes etc. concerning college; with faculty to the bishop to confirm and reform them and those of other named colleges, 176
......, ..., ..., provincial constitution of Canterbury against deprivers (of annual pension and rights), 987
......, ..., ..., provincial constitution of

Legislation (*contd*)
Canterbury containing sentence of greater excommunication, 197
......, ..., ..., provincial and synodal constitutions or constitutions of episcopal curia, prohibiting exercise of office of notary after marriage, *ad hoc* derogation of, 919
......, ..., ..., concerning punishment of offenders in secular courts, 556
......, ..., ..., ordinance enabling holders of chapel and its chaplaincies to hold compatible benefices, 777
......, ..., ..., statutes of cathedral church prohibiting holding another benefice and requiring residence, *ad hoc* derogation of, 503
......, ..., ..., statutes etc. of church, correction of, 423
......, ..., ..., statutes etc. of two hospitals, reformation of, 429
......, ..., ..., statutes etc. of monastery concerning profession, 363
......, ..., ..., statutes etc. (recited) for Benedictine monastery, 394
......, ..., Ireland, concerning foundation of two hospitals of the poor, 964
......, ..., Wales, concerning tithes in Bangor city and diocese, 118
......, general or special constitutions prohibiting holding parish church or perpetual vicarage unless in order of diaconate, *ad hoc* derogation of, 479
......, papal, prohibiting holding of cathedral canonries and prebends by persons who have not completed their fourteenth year, 72, 210, 332, 370, 408, 572, 646, 688, 689
......, ..., on impetration of collegiate canonries and prebends by persons under ten, 332, 408
......, ..., ordinance concerning Cambridge college, 343
......, ..., privilege exempting collegiate church etc. from jurisdiction, 529
......, ..., statute whereby persons committing crimes in a certain locality in Scotland incur automatic excommunication, 493
......, ..., (Alexander IV), constitution "Abbates" of, 397, 425, 686
......, ..., (Boniface VIII), constitution *Pastoralis* of, 549, 1032

Legislation (*contd*)

......, ..., (Boniface VIII), constitution prohibiting mendicants from receiving new places of, 1

......, ..., (Boniface VIII), constitution(s) prohibiting indults *de fructibus percipiendis in absentia* of, 147, 780

......, ..., (Boniface XII), statute concerning abstinence of, 394 [18]

......, ..., (Clement V), constitution concerning hospitals published at Council of Vienne of, 130

......, ..., (Gregory IX), constitution concerning reconciliation of polluted churches of, 411; *and cf.* 848

......, ..., (Innocent III), statute concerning abstinence of, 394 [18]

......, ..., (John XXII), constitution "Execrabilis" of, 386

......, ..., (Paul II), on alienation, 146, 366, 558, 981

......, of military orders *see under* Hospitallers

......, of religious orders *see under* Augustinian Hermits, Order of; Augustinian Order; Benedictine Order; Cistercian Order; Cluniac Order; Franciscan Order

Lepers, houses or hospitals of, in England *see* Sherburn; Stamford

......, ..., in Ireland *see* Limerick

Letters [?commendatory], of abbot for monk students at university, 394 [29]

Letters conservatory, in favour of chapel royal, 767

Letters, archiepiscopal, 356, 964

......, episcopal, 146, 176, 179, 292, 298, 357, 379

......, of archdeacon, *cf.* 905

......, of official of Canterbury court, 456

......, of tuitorial protection, impetrated from archbishop of Dublin, 192

Letters patent, of kings of England, 425

Letters, papal, drawn in the name of Alexander VI, but dated in pontificate of

Letters, papal (*contd*)
Julius II, 1035

......, ..., exemplification of, 144, 1097

......, ..., given at places other than St Peters, Rome *see* Civita Castellana; Civitavecchia; Constance; Corneto; Gallese; Montpellier; Nepi; Ostia; Piombino

......, ..., incomplete or abortive enregistrations of, 51, 73, 76, 96, 115, 504, 508, 860, 901, 902, 999, 1038

......, ..., lost, 248

......, ..., of protection, 108, 174

......, ..., publication of, in locality concerned, 493

......, ..., subreption and/or obreption alleged of, 16, 69, 221, 330, 405, 426, 512, 545, 694, 793, 834, 927, 989

......, ..., transumpt(s) of, to have same trustworthiness as original, 686

......, ..., ..., 394

......, ..., validation of, 69, 330, 426, 502, 739, 918, 1290

Letters, papal, expedition of:-
expedited *Gratis de mandato*, 641
expedited *Gratis pro deo*, 123, 124, 126, 358, 384, 401, 417, 616, 855, 947
expedited *Gratis pro deo pro familiari Scriptoris*, 1001
expedited *Gratis pro familiari Reverendissimi domini Vicecancellarii*, 130
expedited *Gratis pro Scriptore*, 996
expedited *Gratis pro sotio*, 382

Letters, papal, incipits of proems of:-
Ad cumulum, 52, 55, 59, 549, 553, 579, 581, 591, 594, 598, 602, 606, 610, 612, 617, 620, 626, 627, 630, 634, 637, 1006, 1012, 1029; *and cf.* 1021
Ad ea ex iniuncto, 768
Ad futuram rei [or *rey*] *memoriam* (Proems to which this is prefixed are indexed separately.) 91, 144, 154, 182, 203, 217, 270, 281, 282, 293-295, 300, 309, 356, 375, 422, 428, 452, 473, 475, 483, 585, 663, 664, 683-685, 702, 703, 717, 733, 736, 749, 752, 753, 797, 845, 872, 873, 877, 908, 909, 958, 965, 998, 1003,

Letters, papal, incipits (*contd*)
    1035, 1038; *and cf.* 174
    Ad perpetuam rei memoriam, 108, 174,
       179, 292, 333, 343, 379, 400, 425,
       493, 768, 777, 781, 807; *and cf.* 146,
       366, 558, 981
    Ad singula que, 292
    Admonet nos suscepti, 166
    Apostolatus officium, 52, 55, 59, 553,
       579, 594, 598, 602, 606, 610, 612,
       620, 630, 634, 637
    Apostolice nobis desuper meritis, 781
    Apostolice sedis circumspecta benigni-
       tas ad ea, 56, 541
    Apostolice sedis circumspecta benigni-
       tas cupientibus vitam ducere regu-
       larem, 128, 259; *and cf.* 67
    Apostolice sedis circumspecta benigni-
       tas de statu personarum, 597, 601,
       615, 618, 635, 1013, 1030
    Apostolice sedis circumspecta benigni-
       tas regularem vitam ducere cupien-
       tibus, 930
    Apostolice sedis circumspecta clementia
       ne dispositiones, 624, 629
    Apostolice sedis circumspecta providen-
       tia ad ea, 350
    Apostolice sedis circumspecta providen-
       tia votis fidelium, 72
    Apostolice sedis consueta clementia ad
       ea, 589, 1010, 1034
    Apostolice sedis consueta clementia ne
       dispositiones, 548, 550, 604, 611,
       622, 624, 633, 635, 1008, 1018,
       1022, 1026
    Apostolice sedis indefessa clementia ad
       ea, 53, 60, 555, 580
    Apostolice sedis indefessa clementia lap-
       sis, 14
    Apostolice sedis indefessa clementia
       recurrentibus, 129, 161, 359, 573,
       574
    Apostolice sedis providentia circum-
       specta ad ea, 15, 16, 69, 71, 73, 164,
       226, 249, 253, 257, 403, 486, 537,
       538, 540, 650, 820, 821, 823, 934,
       1000
    Apostolice sedis providentia circum-
       specta cupientibus, 938
    Apostolice sedis providentia circum-
       specta vota, 230

Letters, papal, incipits (*contd*)
    Apostolice sedis providentia circum-
       specta votis illis, 648
    Apostolice servitutis nobis iniunctum
       desuper, 356
    Ascensurus in celum Christus, 807
    Commissum nobis desuper, 493
    Cum hodie, 1007
    Cum hodie dilectus filius, 1016
    Cum igitur, 1024
    Cum in omnibus iudiciis, cf. 146, 366,
       558, 981
    Cum nos hodie, 547, 578, 582, 587, 590,
       592, 625, 628, 1009, 1011, 1023,
       1027, 1033
    Cum nos pridem, 57, 551, 554, 595, 599,
       603, 607, 613, 619, 621, 631, 636,
       638, 1014, 1031
    Cupientibus vitam ducere regularem,
       391, 1017, 1028
    Decet ex benignitate, 936
    Decet Romanum pontificem votis, 154,
       182, 203, 234, 251, 254, 256, 293,
       295, 357, 380, 512-514, 576, 647,
       822, 845
    Digna exauditione vota, cf. 174
    Digna reddimur attentione, 410
    Dignum (arbitramur) et cetera, 116,
       158, 381, 509, 841, 992
    Divina disponente clementia, 617, 1012,
       1029
    Divina propitiatione disponente, 425
    Divina supereminens largitas, 54, 623,
       640
    Divina superveniens largitas, 58
    Dum inter cetera, 1 *note* 2
    Dum inter nostre mentis archana, 1
    Ea que pro ecclesiarum omnium, 118
    Ex apostolico nobis desuper, 300
    Ex debito ministerii pastoralis, 558
    Ex debito pastoralis officii circa eccle-
       siarum, 1032
    Ex debito pastoralis officii meritis licet
       insufficientibus, 777
    Ex debito pastoralis officii nobis licet
       inmeritis superna, 645, 646, 785, 790
    Ex debito pastoralis officii nobis licet
       insufficientibus, 827
    Ex debito pastoralis officii nobis meritis
       licet insufficientibus, 400, 786
    Ex debito pastoralis officii quamquam

Letters, papal, incipits (*contd*)

insufficientibus nobis, 826

Ex iniuncto nobis desuper, 75, 91, 159, 188, 217, 235, 258, 270, 282, 306, 366, 441, 449, 765, 815, 824, 872, 877, 903, 908, 942, 950, 965, 981

Exigentibus meritis tue devotionis, 429

Exigit tue devotionis sinceritas, 1020, 1025

Eximie devotionis affectus, 423, 925

Exposcit tue devotionis sinceritas, 397

Exposcit vestre devotionis sinceritas, 686

Gerentes in desideriis cordis, 130

Grata devotionis et familiaritatis obsequia, 996

Grata devotionis obsequia, 697

Grata familiaritatis obsequia, 358, 641, 850

Gratie divine, 55, 59, 546, 549, 553, 591, 594, 598, 602, 606, 617, 620, 626, 627, 630, 634, 637, 776, 1006, 1012, 1021, 1029

Gratie et cetera, 581

Hiis que pro divini cultus, 379

Hiis que pro ecclesiarum, 146

Hiis que pro statu, cf. 174

Hodie cum dilectus filius, 61, 63, 144, 535, 1015

Hodie cum ecclesie, 698

Hodie dilecto filio, 155, 190, 301, 364, 371, 407, 444, 552, 643, 697, 778, 780, 839, 840, 844, 854, 855, 928, 931, 937, 963, 1001, 1002, 1032

Hodie dilectum filium, 549

Hodie dilectus filius, 782

Hodie ecclesie, 52, 55, 59, 553, 579, 594, 598, 602, 606, 617, 620, 630, 634, 637, 1012

Hodie (...) ecclesiis, 610, 612, 1029

Hodie et cetera, 52, 546, 553, 577, 579, 581, 584, 588, 591, 594, 598, 602, 606, 610, 617, 626, 630, 634, 637, 1009, 1012, 1021, 1024, 1029, 1032

Hodie et cetera. Ad cumulum et cetera, 626

Hodie ex certis causis, 768

Hodie monasterio vestro, 584, 1024

Hodie monasterium vestrum, 577, 588, 1009

Hodie venerabilem et cetera, 627

Letters, papal, incipits (*contd*)

Hodie venerabilem fratrem nostrum, 546, 581, 591, 626, 627, 1006, 1021

Honestis petentium presertim, 64

Humilibus et cetera, 8, 9, 28, 29, 46, 80, 86, 94, 192, 197, 199, 221, 261, 298, 365, 405, 435, 442, 456, 529, 661, 691, 694, 792, 793, 811, 812, 905, 906, 921, 924, 927, 964, 971, 987-991, 1005; *and cf.* 999

In apostolice dignitatis culmine, 174

In suprema militantis ecclesie specula, 160

Iniunctum nobis desuper apostolice servitutis officium, 108, 165, 179

Inter cetera nostri desideria cordis, 816

Inter curas multiplices, 779

Laudabilia dilecti filii, 951

Laudabilia probitatis et virtutum merita, 919

Laudabilia tue infantilis, 332

Laudabilia tue puerilis, 210, 408, 769

Licet is de cuius munere, 413

Litterarum scientia [occasionally spelt *sientia*], *vite ac morum honestas,* 4, 17, 26, 35, 39-41, 47, 65, 78, 81, 84 (*avite*), 85, 88, 96, 100, 101, 106, 112, 117, 119, 120, 135, 140, 152, 169, 175, 178, 191, 194, 207, 213-215, 223, 233, 262, 269, 272, 276-278, 284, 288, 296, 311, 317, 318, 320, 327, 329, 344, 346, 351, 352, 367, 372, 388, 389, 418, 421, 424, 436, 439, 450, 460, 477, 480, 488-490, 495, 496, 501, 502, 506, 517, 523, 526, 531, 544, 557, 560, 561, 565, 568, 569, 653, 654, 657, 666, 667, 669, 681, 682, 692, 696, 699-701, 704, 713, 715, 716, 719, 720, 723, 726, 727, 731, 734, 737, 739, 744, 760, 766, 771, 772, 774, 794, 803, 806, 809, 842, 843, 860, 862, 864-866, 880, 881, 885, 886, 890, 892, 893, 896-898, 911, 915, 917, 923, 953, 955, 957, 959, 968, 976, 1036 (errs?), 1037; *and see* 33 *note,* 35, 142 *note,* 211 *note,* 297 *note*

Meruit tue devotionis sinceritas, 371

Militanti ecclesie, 767

Nobilitas generis ac laudabilia tue pueri[li]s etatis, 370, 572

Letters, papal, incipits (*contd*)

Nobilitas generis, litterarum scientia, vite ac morum honestas, 143, 434, 643; and *cf.* 494 *note*

Nobilitas generis, vite ac morum honestas, 11, 157, 173, 232, 369, 481, 492, 494, 508, 711, 746, 838, 868, 945

Oblate nobis nuper pro parte, 76, 655

Oblate nobis pro parte, 137

Pastoralis officii debitum, 835

Personam tuam, 42, 121, 196, 291, 349, 399, 527, 552, 596, 600, 605, 608, 632, 672, 707, 747, 754, 904, 963, 974, 1019

Piis fidelium votis, 162, 250, 255, 313, 343, 360

Provisionis nostre, 144; and *cf.* 1097

Quam sit onusta dispendiis, 581, 591, 626, 627, 1006

Quia presentis vite conditio, 443

Quo circa, 617

Regiminis[!] universalis ecclesie presidentes, 402

Religionis zelus, litterarum scientia, vite ac morum honestas, 97, 138, 151, 302, 336, 445, 743, 817

Religionis zelus, vite ac morum honestas, 6, 7, 12, 13, 20, 22, 27, 30, 32, 43, 48, 49, 61, 63, 87, 92, 133, 136, 139, 145, 148, 155, 171, 186, 200, 219, 260, 264, 267, 268, 273, 274, 280, 283, 287, 299, 305, 314, 319, 321, 322, 325, 337, 339, 341, 368, 396, 409, 438, 446, 447, 451, 453, 454, 465, 468, 484, 505, 524, 525, 535, 542, 563, 564, 571, 658, 668, 712, 728, 730, 735, 741, 742, 745, 758, 798, 802, 836, 837, 854, 857, 859, 861, 863, 867, 871, 874, 882, 888, 899, 914, 926, 944, 961, 962, 967, 973, 997; and *cf.* 37

Romani pontificis circumspecta benignitas, 583, 593

Romani pontificis copiosa benignitas, 609

Romani pontificis gratiosa benignitas, 586

Romani pontificis providentia circumspecta, 163, 181, 229, 330, 382, 536, 577, 588, 649, 789, 980, 1009

Romani pontificis quem pastor, 546, 1021

Letters, papal, incipits (*contd*)

Romanum decet pontificem votis, 70, 281, 294, 309, 333, 375, 422, 428, 452, 473, 475, 651, 663, 664, 683-685, 702, 703, 717, 733, 736, 749, 752, 753, 787, 797, 833, 873, 909, 958, 995, 998, 1003, 1035, 1038

Romanus pontifex ad quem, 585

Romanus pontifex in potestatis, 549 *note*

Sedes apostolica, pia mater, ad ea, 939, 946

Sedes apostolica, pia mater, recurrentibus, 127, 252, 385, 386, 416, 485, 515, 644, 846, 943, 972, 982, 984

Sincera fervensque, 244, 374, 377

Solet apostolice sedis exuberans, 363

Solet sedis apostolice indefessa, 167

Spes future probitatis, 688, 689

Summi dispositione rectoris, 584, 1015, 1024

Supereminens divina largitas, 614

Suscepti cura regiminis, 383

Tue devotionis precibus, 176, 848

Tue devotionis sinceritas, 411

Universis Christifidelibus, 413

Vite ac morum honestas, 2, 3, 5, 10, 18, 19, 21, 23-25, 31, 33 (despite BTheol), 34, 36, 38, 44, 45, 50, 62, 66, 68, 74, 77, 79, 82, 83, 89, 90, 93, 95, 98, 99, 102-105, 107, 109-111, 113-115, 122-126, 131, 132, 134, 141, 142 (errs), 144, 147, 149, 150, 153 (*Vita*), 156, 168, 170, 172, 177, 180, 183-185, 187, 189, 190, 193, 195, 198, 201, 202, 204-206, 208, 209, 211 (errs), 212, 216, 218, 220, 222, 224, 225, 227, 228, 231, 236-243, 245-248, 263, 265, 266, 271, 275, 279, 285, 286, 289, 290, 297(errs?), 301, 303, 304, 307, 308, 310, 312, 315, 316, 323, 324, 326, 328, 331, 334, 335, 338, 340, 342, 345, 347, 348, 353-355, 361, 362, 364, 373, 376, 378, 384, 387, 390, 392, 393, 395, 398, 401, 406, 407, 412, 414, 415, 417, 419, 420, 426, 427, 430-433, 437, 440, 444, 448, 455, 457-459, 461-464, 466, 467, 469-472, 474, 476, 478, 479, 482, 487, 491, 497-500, 503, 504, 507, 510, 511, 516, 518-522, 528, 530,

Letters, papal, incipits (*contd*)
532-534, 539, 543, 545, 556, 559,
562, 566, 567, 570, 575, 616, 642,
652, 656, 659, 660, 662, 665, 670,
671, 673-680, 687, 690, 693, 695,
705, 706, 708-710, 714, 718, 721,
722, 724, 725, 729, 732, 738, 740,
748, 750, 751, 755-757, 759, 761-
764, 770, 773, 775, 778, 780, 782-
784, 788, 791, 795, 796, 799-801,
804, 805, 808, 810, 813, 814, 818,
819, 825, 828-832, 834, 839, 840,
844, 847, 849, 851-853, 855, 856,
858, 869, 870, 875, 876, 878, 879,
883, 884, 887, 889, 891, 894, 895,
900, 901, 907, 910, 912, 913, 916,
918, 920, 922, 928, 929, 931-933,
935, 937, 940, 941, 947-949, 952,
954, 956, 960, 966, 969, 970, 975,
977-979, 983, 985, 986, 993, 994,
1001, 1002, 1004; *and cf.* 902
Votis fidelium omnium, 483
......, *see also under Motu proprio*

Libel, exhibited in marriage case, 28

Liberties *see* Exemption

Licence, papal, concerning celebration of
mass etc. in college chapel, 343
......, ..., to be marked with clerical character,
229
......, ..., to bishop to bestow orders etc., 398
......, ..., to build house for nuns, 779
......, ..., to confirm (or reform) statutes etc.
of colleges, 176
......, ..., to exchange right of presentation for
goods, 903
......, ..., to found religious house and enable
the friars to receive it, 1
......, ..., to rebuild religious house, 441
......, ..., to reform statutes etc. of two hospitals, 429
......, ..., to resign and exchange benefice
(not major and principal dignities), 850

Litigation, costs of, 29, 46, 86, 94, 197, 365,
661, 927, 987
......, ..., allegedly fixed at excessive sum, 29
......, ..., excommunication for non-payment
of, 29

Litigation (*contd*)
......, before judge (ordinary or delegate),
abbot and convent's plea of inability to
pursue robbers and pirates by means of,
108
......, beneficiary, before papal judges delegate (or deputies of), 199, 221, 383, 573,
694, 989, 1015, 1016, 1018-1020
......, ..., in Roman curia, 237, 417, 687, 849,
1018-1020
......, ..., over pension, 928
......, ..., other references to, 14, 301, 407,
778
......, between bishop and Cistercian house
over the latter's failure to present perpetual vicar for parish church, 298
......, between rector and layman, over non-
payment of tithes on property in the city
of London, before official, 365
......, between religious house and rector,
before bishop's commissary and administrator's commissary and then before
archbishop of Canterbury's commissary,
46
......, over bishop's refusal to institute, before
official of local metropolitical court, 456
......, over defamation, before bishop's commissary and then before archbishop of
Canterbury's (and legate's) commissary,
29
......, ..., before archbishop of Canterbury's
(and legate's) commissary, 197
......, over defamation and marriage bond,
before bishop's commissaries, 811
......, over execution of late vicar's will,
before local ecclesiastical judge, 990; *cf.*
999
......, over injuries, before official of archdeacon of London's court, then before
legate's commissary and then before
papal judges delegate, 8
......, over late father's marriage and ownership of property, before official's commissary and then before papal judges
delegate, 86
......, marriage, before legate's commissary
and then before papal judges delegate, 28
......, ..., before archdeacon, 905, 988
......, ..., before bishop's commissaries, 811
......, ..., before local bishop, then before
archbishop of Armagh and then before

Litigation (*contd*)
    papal judge delegate, 927
......, ..., *and cf.* 261
......, over ministership of Trinitarian house, before papal judge delegate, 221
......, over money, before archbishop's commissary, 812
......, over non-payment of annual pension and deprivation of rights, before auditor of archbishop of Canterbury's court, 987
......, over non-payment of money, before official, 435
......, over parish church, 199, 991
......, over patronage of perpetual chaplaincy before provost, 691
......, over repayment of money, before external official and then before archbishop's court, 792
......, over rule of Cistercian monastery, in Roman curia, 1020
......, testamentary, before auditor of archbishop's court, 924
......, ..., before a local ecclesiastical judge, 990; *cf.* 999
......, tithes, before official (or his commissary), 94, 661, 921, 971
......, ..., before auditor of archbishop of Canterbury's court, 906
......, suit called to pope, 928

M

Magistri registri see under Rome, court of, curialists at

Market, proposed by king of Scots for Aberdeen, 64

Marriage, an impediment to exercising office of notary of episcopal curia, 919
......, dispensation for, notwithstanding affinity, 76
......, ..., notwithstanding consanguinity, 137
......, ..., ..., disputed, 927
......, ..., notwithstanding spiritual relationship, 655
......, disputed by son after father's death despite dispensation notwithstanding consanguinity or affinity, 86
......, solemnization of, 292
......, *see also under* Appeals; Litigation; *and*

Marriage (*contd*)
    cf. Illegitimacy

Mass, to be celebrated (with music) in college chapel by persons not in sacred orders, without diocesan's licence, 343
......, celebration of (with musical notation) in perpetual chaplaincy, 292
......, celebration of, 193, 394 [28]
......, *cf.* 1175

Matins *see under* Office, Divine

Medicine, expert in, at king's court *see* [de Falcutiis *or* Falcariis] de Cesena, Damianus
......, *for graduates in see under* Degrees

Mendicant Orders *see under individual orders*

Mensa, abbatial, pension assigned on fruits of, 155
......, ..., rectories to be united to, 536
......, archiepiscopal, barony and lands of, assigned to prior in part-payment, 356
......, ..., demesne tax and possessions of, detained by laymen, 835
......, ..., unions of benefices to, 835, 998
......, capitular, fruits hitherto received from a parish church by, to be appropriated to undivided perpetual vicarage, 188
......, ..., right to tithes of, disputed by priest, 94
......, ..., ..., disputed by rector, 661
......, ..., tithes belonging to, to be erected into prebend, 167
......, episcopal, lands of, granted in perpetual tenancy to laymen, 146
......, ..., pension assigned on fruits of, 963; *cf.* 1311
......, ..., property of, leased to laymen, 558
......, ..., rights and jurisdiction of infringed and property of damaged, by metropolitan, 1005
......, ..., tithes belonging to, grant of, 1039
......, ..., in Scotland, property of occupied by the English and by local nobles, 181

Metropolitan church, erection of cathedral church into, 333

Metropolitan church (*contd*)
......, restoration of superiority etc. over cathedral church, to, 333

Military Orders *see under* Religious Orders etc.

Mitre etc., indult etc. to abbot to use, 425, 686
......, indult etc. to prior to use, 397

Money:-
  carlini, theft of, 574
  ducats, gold, of the camera, 196, 252, 309, 363, 428, 443, 452, 475, 515, 672, 685, 702, 703, 752, 753, 817, 872, 951, 963, 1002, 1038
  ducats, gold, of the camera, with equivalent in English marks, 684, 717, 733, 736, 749, 908
  ducats, gold, of the camera, with equivalent in marks of "those parts" [England], 473, 877
  ducats, gold, of the camera, with equivalent in marks of "those parts" [Wales], 483
  ducats, gold, of the camera, with equivalent in marks sterling [England], 154, 182, 203, 217, 282, 293, 295, 349, 375, 422, 644, 663, 664, 797, 909, 958, 965, 1003
  ducats, gold, of the camera, with equivalent in English pounds, 683
  ducats, gold, of the camera, with equivalent in pounds of "those parts" [England], 300
  ducats, gold, of the camera, with equivalent in pounds sterling, 91
  ducats, gold, of the camera, with equivalent in English marks, 684, 717, 733, 736, 749, 908
  ducats, in Ireland, *cf.* 385
  florins, gold, of the camera, 364, 386, 605, 608, 850, 873
  florins, gold, of the camera, with equivalent in marks sterling [England], 270
  florins, gold, of the camera, with equivalent in marks sterling [Ireland], 946
  florins, gold, of Florence, with equivalent in silver tournois, 371
  marks, English, with equivalent in gold

Money (*contd*)
  ducats of the camera, 684, 717, 733, 736, 749, 908
  marks, of "those parts" [England], with equivalent in gold ducats of the camera, 473, 877
  marks, of "those parts" [Scotland], 793
  marks, of "those parts" [Wales], with equivalent in gold ducats of the camera, 483
  marks, in England, 596, 600
  marks, in Ireland, *cf.* 385
  marks Scots, 144, 188, 356, 928, 1019
  marks Scots, with equivalent in pounds sterling, 301, 444, 778, 844
  marks sterling, in England, 281
  marks sterling, in England, with equivalent in gold ducats of the camera, 154, 182, 203, 217, 270, 282, 293, 295, 349, 375, 422, 644, 663, 664, 797, 909, 958, 965, 1003
  marks sterling, in England, with equivalent in gold florins of the camera, 270
  marks sterling, in Ireland, 14-16, 67, 70-72, 74, 75, 121-129, 146, 156-167, 225-231, 234-236, 249-259, 306, 313, 330, 350, 357, 359-362, 380, 381, 383, 384, 391, 392, 401-404, 448, 449, 485, 486, 492, 510-514, 536-543, 545, 573-576, 645-652, 763, 783-790, 815, 818-838, 845, 846, 852, 853, 930, 932-936, 938-950, 980, 982-984, 993-995, 998, 1000
  marks sterling, in Ireland, with equivalent in gold florins of the camera, 946
  marks sterling in Scotland, 643
  nobles, gold, of "those parts" [England], 365
  pounds, in England, 596
  pounds, English, with equivalent in gold ducats of the camera, 683
  pounds, of "those parts" [England], with equivalent in gold ducats of the camera, 300
  pounds (etc.) Scots, 144, 366, 558, 928, 1019
  pounds Scots, with equivalent in pounds sterling, 407
  pounds, of "those parts" [Scotland], 155, 792

Money (*contd*)

pounds (etc.) sterling, in England, 365, 1035; *and cf.* 903

pounds sterling, in England, with equivalent in gold ducats of the camera, 91

pounds sterling, with equivalent in marks Scots, 301, 444, 778, 844

pounds sterling, in Scotland, 50, 64, 68, 116, 130, 181, 188, 190, 509, 552, 632, 642, 791, 839-841, 929, 931, 937, 992, 1019

pounds sterling, with equivalent in pounds Scots, 407

shillings etc., in England, 379

tournois, silver, with equivalent in gold florins of Florence, 371

...., coming into monastery to be deposited in common chest, 394 [1]

...., *cf. also* 292

...., *see also under* Litigation; Rent

Mortuary dues, composition over, 379

Mother church, rights of, in composition over chapel, 379

Motu proprio, papal grants etc., so made, 54, 58, 63, 121, 144, 155, 349, 552, 585, 596, 600, 605, 608, 614, 623, 632, 640, 643, 672, 963, 1019, 1020, 1024, 1025; *and cf.* 115

Music, in college chapel, 343

......, *and cf.* 292

N

Nobility *see under* Birth

Notary, of episcopal curia, indult to layman to exercise office of, despite marriage, 919

......, papal *see* Castellesi, Hadrian; Forman, Andrew; Orsini, Orsino; Ponzettus, Fer(di)nandus

......, public, publication of statutes etc. by, 394

Nuncio, of the apostolic see, in England *see* Castellesi, Hadrian

Nuns, house of, 425

......, (OCist), licence to build house for, 779

O

Oaths, confessor enabled to relax, 374

......, of suffragan to archbishop, relaxation of, 333

......, (on image) falsely denying theft, 574

......, to observe constitutions and not to impetrate apostolic letters contrary to them, 147, 641, 957

......, to observe ordinances of perpetual chaplaincy required from chaplains on appointment, 292

......, to observe statutes etc., relaxation of, 491, 503

......, to remain in monastery, broken, 229

......, to reside in benefice, relaxation of, 439, 559

......, not to impetrate benefice, 129; *and cf.* 780

......, not to impetrate benefice, relaxation of, 936

......, relaxation of, 199

......, *see also* Fealty; Perjury

Oblations etc. belonging to parish church and chapels, litigation over, 94

Obreption *see under* Letters, papal

Observance, regular, incomplete, 429

......, *and see under* Franciscan Order

Office, Divine, celebration of in college chapel, 343

......, ..., obligation to celebrate (mass, matins, vespers etc.) at chantry, 193

......, ..., obligation to celebrate (requiem mass) at chantry, 348

Orders, dispensation from obligation to be promoted to, by reason of benefice, 530

......, dispensation (or indult) from obligation to proceed beyond subdiaconate by reason of benefice, for three years, 402

......, ..., for five years, 943

......, ..., for seven years, 159, 385, 485, 512, 556, 567, 576, 641

Orders (*contd*)

......, ..., (time scale wanting), 536

......, dispensation from obligation to proceed beyond subdiaconate, while at a *studium generale vel particulare*, for seven years, 511

......, dispensation to be promoted — at age 21 — to priest's, 245, 479

......, dispensation to be promoted — at age 21 — to all by any catholic bishop outside lawful times, with licence etc., 398

......, dispensation to be promoted to all by any catholic bishop, 225

......, dispensation to be promoted to and minister in, (after irregularity), 556, 895

......, dispensation to minister in, (after irregularity), 363, 644

......, ..., despite deformity of eye, 721

......, dispensation to proceed to all, despite homicide, 650

......, dispensation to use those taken and be promoted to and minister in all, 127

......, dispensation to local ordinary to confer all on an illegitimate cleric, 250

......, dispensation granted by count palatine for promotion to all, 644

......, faculty to be promoted to by any catholic bishop outside lawful times, 613, 621

......, failure to be promoted to, 228

......, foundations requiring, *ad hoc* derogation of, 66, 369

......, impediments to *see under* Age; Illegitimacy

......, minor, indult etc. enabling abbot to promote canons etc. to, 686

......, minor (all), statute enabling prior to confer on canons of priory, 400

......, monk (OCist) promoted to all by his superior despite illegitimacy, 368

......, non-promotion to, plea of failure by the ordinary to advise against, 485

......, promotion to and ministering in before lawful age, incurring irregularity, 892

......, scholars resident in college hostel and fellows etc. enabled to celebrate in college chapel without being promoted to sacred, 343

......, voidance of benefices by non-promotion of incumbent to, 252, 359, 939, 943

Ornaments, ecclesiastical, for chapel, to be provided by layman, 379

......, ..., chapel to be adorned with, 807

......, ..., indult to abbot to bless, 425

......, ..., of chapel, to be kept in repair, 292

......, ..., statute enabling prior to bless for priory church and dependencies, 400

......, ..., 394 [14]

......, *and cf.* Images

P

Palls, blessing of, 400

Pallium, delivery of, 1236, 1250

......, ..., commission over, 1237

Parish churches, rectories and vicarages of:-
    called a chapel, perpetual simple benefice in, 642
    called a portion, 188
    called *plebs*, 831, 832
    chantry established in, 292
    entitled under episcopal constitution to annual payments on property from local residents, 365
    erection, endowment and provision of, 64
    erection and endowment of perpetual undivided vicarage, 188
    failure to present perpetual vicar for, litigation over, 298
    perpetual benefice in, 202, 528
    perpetual benefice, called a prebend, in, 91
    perpetual simple benefice, called a rectory of an ecclesiastical fief, in, 449
    perpetual simple benefice, called a clerkship, in, 642
    perpetual chantry in, 664
    perpetual vicarage, called a stipend, in cathedral church, 123
    ruled by two rectors, 141, 241, 279, 414, 417, 565, 738, 918
    tithes and oblations of, litigation over, 94
    tithes for the support of, 118
    union to provostry disputed, 405
    (united to religious house), celebration of divine offices and administration of sacraments for parishioners of, 174

Parish churches etc. (*contd*)
......, *see also references to disputes and litigation concerning under* Litigation

Parishioners, cure of souls of, administration of sacraments to and burial of, 188

Patronage, clerical, of college etc., 176
......, ..., 691
......, lay, benefices in or partially in, 15, 16, 50, 67, 69, 71, 75, 116, 130, 157, 162, 230, 236, 251, 252, 255, 258, 306, 366, 381, 385, 386, 403, 423, 493, 513, 536, 545, 556, 645, 691, 787, 791, 815, 822, 823, 825, 826, 828, 833, 934, 939 950, 994, 1000
......, ..., of hospital of the poor, derogation of, 130
......, of king of England, benefice in, 405
......, of princes, clause specifying, 487, 489, 490
......, of temporal lord, benefice in, 68
......, of perpetual chaplaincy, litigation over, 691
......, right of, over perpetual chaplaincy to belong forever to the lay founders and their heirs, 292

Patrons, presentation for benefices by, 50, 68, 116, 386, 556, 815

Penance, relaxation of, 413, 807
......, ..., at chapel, 292

Pension, annual, possessions of priory farmed or rented for, 981
......, ..., non-payment of, litigation over, 987
......, appeal to apostolic see over refusal to pay, 793
......, assigned on (fruits of) benefices, by papal authority, 144, 155, 301, 407, 444, 778, 793, 844, 928, 931, 963, 1019, 1146; *see also* 425, 1208, 1256, 1288, 1301
......, ..., (authority not specified), 386
......, assigned to monk on fruits of monastery, by papal authority, 148
......, litigation over, 928
......, fruits etc. and tithes assigned (by papal authority) in place of, 535
......, lands etc. assigned (by papal authority)

Pension (*contd*)
in place of, 63
......, tithes of corn and fruits etc. assigned (by papal authority) in place of, 782, 840; *and cf.* 793
......, vill assigned (by papal authority) in place of, 155
......, *cf.* 394 [1], 903
......, *see also* Reservation of fruits

Perjury *see under* Absolution; Deprivation; Oaths

Pilgrimages, to Rome, by brother of Augustinian hospital, 416
......, to Jerusalem, Rome and Santiago de Compostela, vow of, unfulfilled, 374
......, *cf.* Travel

Pilgrims, to be accomodated in monastery guest-house, 394 [16]
......, travelling abroad receiving hospitality at religious house at Dover, 7

Pirates, harassing monastery on island, 108

Pluralism *see* Benefices

Poet laureate *see* André, Bernard

Pontifical *insignia*, indults for, 397, 425, 1100, 1109

Poor, alms for the, 394 [12]
......, hospitals of the, 964

Popes *see under* Rome, popes of

Portions, assigned to perpetual vicar during dispute over jurisdiction, 298
......, for monks at university, 394 [29]
......, to be erected into perpetual undivided vicarage, 188
......, 141, 241, 279, 414, 417, 425, 449, 565, 738, 800, 918
......, sacerdotal, 817

Preaching, in Latin and the vernacular, 394 [30]
......, licence for, 530
......, *cf.* 1

Prebends, erection of benefices into *see under* Cathedral churches

Premonstratensian Order:-
abbots of, dispensed to hold a regular or secular benefice *in commendam* with house, 707, 747
....., dispensed to hold (for life) a secular benefice *in commendam* with house, 42, 974
canons of, child of, 846
....., dispensed to hold a secular benefice, 219, 321, 337, 525, 668, 798
houses of, in England *see* Alnwick; Bayham; Croxton; Langley; Leiston; Shap; Titchfield; Torre; Tupholme; Wendling; Woodburn
....., in Ireland *see* Lough Key; Tuam, Holy Trinity
....., in Scotland *see* Whithorn

Presentation, for benefices, 30, 68, 116, 363, 386, 456, 556, 691, 778, 815
......, of perpetual vicar for parish church, obligation concerning, disputed, 298
......, of suitable persons for perpetual chaplaincy, obligatory within time-limits, 292
......, right of, licensed to be exchanged for goods, 903
......, ..., to belong forever to the lay founders and their heirs, 292
......, *see also* Patronage; Patrons

Prince of Wales, Arthur, preceptor and poet laureate of *see* André, Bernard

Priors, election of, by convent, 989
......, indult for portable altar, 1108
......, indult to use mitre, bestow benediction and bless ecclesiastical ornaments, 397
......, indults to use pontifical *insignia*, 1100, 1109
......, *see also under* Provision

Privileges (etc.), papal, exempting collegiate church from jurisdiction, 529
......, ..., to Augustinian monastery, approval and confirmation of, 174
......, ..., granted to Cistercian monastery and

Privileges (*contd*)
order, derogation of, 928
......, of monastery, confirmation of, 425
......, ..., 394

Probate *cf.* 529

Procedure, Judicial, *q.v.*

Procession, on vigil of Ascension, 394 [23]

Proctors *see* de Bertinis, Leonard; Bologna, Alexander of; Brown, David; Duncanson, John; Fabri, John; Halkerston, Thomas; Tuba, Paul; Turnbul, William

Procuration *see under* Archbishops; Archdeacons

Profession, statutes etc. of Benedictine monastery concerning, 363

Property, residential and commercial in the city of London, tithe due on, 365

Protection, archiepiscopal, letters of, 192
......, papal, letters of, 108, 174

Protonotaries *see under* Rome, court of, curialists at

Provision, of abbots and priors, 67, 383, 574, 1015, 1016, 1018-1020, 1024, 1032, 1318, 1321, 1329; *and cf.* 1033, 1034
......, of archbishop at lawful age, 848
......, of bishops and archbishops, 52, 55, 59, 549, 553, 579, 594, 598, 602, 606, 610, 612, 617, 620, 630, 634, 637, 776, 963, 1012, 1029, 1209, 1324, 1335; *and cf.* 155
......, *cf.* Translation
......, *see also* Collations and provisions

Publication, annual, of instrument concerning foundation of chantry, 292
......, initial and at times of visitation, of statutes etc. of monastery, 394
......, of papal letters and processes over them during dispute, 80
......, of papal letters imposing automatic

Publication (*contd*)
  excommunication for homicide etc. in
    locality, 493
......, of statutes etc. of college, 176

Purification of women, 292

Q

Queen, of England *see* Anne

R

Reconciliation of polluted churches and
  cemeteries, indults and faculties granted
  for:-
    to abbots, 425, 686
    to [archbishop-] elect to perform by
      deputy, 848
    to bishop to perform by deputy, 411

Rectories *see* Parish churches, rectories and
  vicarages

Re-entry, abbots and priors indulged for, 61,
  535

Registers, papal, official corrections of
  ordered by the Regent of the Chancery,
  13, 35, 61, 91, 97, 111, 134, 144, 154,
  175, 232, 281, 322, 396, 449, 626, 654,
  663, 717, 747, 766, 862, 972, 982

Rehabilitation *see* Disability

Relaxation *see under* Oaths

Relics, of St Jarlath, custodianship of, 163
......, showing of, 394 [15]

Religious Houses *see under individual religious orders*

Religious Orders etc. *see* Augustinian
  Hermits;   Augustinian   Order;
  Benedictine Order; Camaldolese Order;
  Cistercian   Order;   Cluniac   Order;
  Cruciferi cum Stella; Dominican Order;
  Franciscan Order; Gilbertine Order;
  Hospitallers; Premonstratensian Order;
  Trinitarian Order; Valliscaulian Order

Religious Orders, enclosed, parlour of, 394
  [17]
......, unspecified, reception in, commission
  for, 1333

Rent, of barony and land, (belonging to
  archiepiscopal *mensa*), of a red rose
  payable on request, 356
...., of land, (belonging to episcopal *mensa*),
  of money, sheep and capons payable
  annually, 558
....(or farm), possessions of priory granted
  in, 981

Requests, Master of, of Henry king of
  England *see* Jane, Thomas

Reservation, of collations etc. to pope:-
  general, of benefices vacated at the apos-
    tolic see, 190, 306, 584, 588, 839-
    841, 929, 937, 983, 992
  ...., of bishoprics vacated at the apostolic
    see, 59, 591, 612, 617, 1006, 1012,
    1021, 1029
  ...., of bishopric vacated by translation, 602
  ...., of conventual priories, 391, 492, 535
  ...., of major and principal dignities, 226,
    237, 330, 385, 782, 840, 931
  special, of bishoprics, 52, 55, 546, 553,
    579, 581, 594, 598, 606, 610, 620,
    626, 627, 630, 634, 637
...., of monasteries, 1009, 1024
......, of fruits etc. levied by bishop and collations etc. of benefices, in coadjutor's
  favour, 552
......, of canonry and prebend, 543
......, of fruits of monastery, 1260
......, of tithes of monastery, 1255
......, *see also under* Collations and provisions; Expectation; Pension

Residence (in benefices), indult not to be
  compelled to maintain, 530, 1111, 1172,
  1238, 1328
......, ..., while at a *studium generale*, 262,
  375, 378, 556
......, ..., while resident in other benefice
  held, 193
......, ..., while resident in other benefice held
  or at a *studium generale*, 331

Residence (*contd*)

......, ..., while resident in Roman curia or other benefice held or at a *studium generale*, 21, 23, 39, 41, 135, 184, 189, 204, 207, 222, 238, 247, 307, 309, 312, 323, 324, 331, 336, 345, 348, 351, 353, 388, 422, 430, 436, 437, 439, 457, 461, 469, 470, 488, 491, 496, 503, 506, 531, 532, 559-561, 567, 641, 654, 659, 669, 670, 681, 682, 696, 700, 716, 727, 740, 748, 750, 755, 760, 772-775, 794, 800, 801, 806, 814, 847, 856, 864-866, 870, 879-881, 884, 885, 890, 892, 893, 900, 910, 916, 917, 920, 952, 955-957, 966, 969, 970

......, ..., while serving as chaplains to Countess Margaret [Beaufort], 925

......, indult to take fruits without, while resident in Roman curia or other benefice held or at *studium generale*, 147, 780

......, foundation of perpetual chaplaincy requiring, 292

......, foundation of chantry requiring, *ad hoc* derogation of, 559

......, statutes of cathedral church requiring, *ad hoc* derogation of, 503

......, statutes of churches etc. requiring, *ad hoc* derogation of, 491

Residence (in religious houses), dispensation to Benedictine monk to live outside monastery, 363

......, indult to Cluniac monk not to loose privileges etc. if non-resident, 27

Resignation, of bishopric, to pope, 591, 612

......, of regular benefices or rights in, to pope, 61, 63, 144, 155, 535, 584, 1015, 1016, 1018-1020

......, of secular benefices or rights in, to archbishop (or his vicar), 384, 833

......, ..., to ordinary, 167, 381, 444, 778

......, ..., to pope, 306, 364, 782, 839-841, 844, 929, 931, 937, 951, 983, 992, 1002; *and cf.* 1001

......, ..., outside Roman curia before notary public and witnesses, 301

......, ..., payment to procure, 167, 381

......, of precentorship, simply or for exchange, to local ordinary, licence etc. for, 850

Resignation (*contd*)

......, of religious house, may be deemed evasive of future deprivation, 509

Robbery etc. in named locality, to be discouraged by automatic excommunication, 493

Rolls, Keeper of the, of the Chancery of Henry, king of England *see* Warham, William

Rose, red *see under* Rent

Rota *see under* Rome, apostolic palace

Royalty, references to kinship to, 620, 622, 623

S

Sacraments, administration of, appointment by college warden and fellows of chaplain or priest for, without diocesan's licence, 343

......, ..., in chaplaincy, 292, 379

......, ..., to parishioners, 188

Sacrilege, committed by laymen in cathedral church, 80

......, 485

Sacristy, 64, 394 [2]

St John of Jerusalem, Hospital of *see* Hospitallers

Scribe, in secular courts, incurring irregularity by his functions, 556

......, of trial or temporal justice, incurring irregularity by his functions, 895

Scriptores see under Rome, court of, curialists at

Scripture (*sacrarum litterarum*), knowledge and learning of at Winchcombe abbey, advancement of, 394 [29]

Secular authority, limitations of, in named locality, 493

Sempringham, Order of *see* Gilbertine Order

Sequestration *see under* Fruits

Sheep *see under* Rent; Tithes

Silence, observance of, 394 [21]

Simony, payment for reception of canons, 835
......, payment to ordinary, for collation, 946
......, ..., for union, 846 (*and cf*. 995)
......, payment to procure resignation of benefices, 167, 381
......, *see also under* Deprivation; Disability

Solicitor *see under* Rome, court of, curialists at

"Sorning", 493

Statutes and ordinances *see under* Legislation

Studia generalia, for privileges to those attending see under Orders; Residence
......, colleges of Black Monks at, 394 [29]
......, none in Ireland, 511
......, *see* Universities

Subreption *see under* Letters, papal

Surrogation, consistorial, as abbot of monastery, 1015, 1018-1020

Suspension, from divine service, of collegiate church's official and commissary, 529
......, ..., of perpetual vicar, 192

Synod, general, in 1497 at Bangor, 118

T

Teacher *see under* Education

Tenure of land, (of episcopal *mensa*), confirmation of grant of, 146

Testaments *see under* Appeals; Litigation

Testaments (*contd*)
......, *and cf*. 529

Theft *see under* Disability

Theology, professors of, 97, 151, 445, 817, 861
......, *for graduates in see under* Degrees
......, *cf*. Scripture

Tithes, bishop's grant of, 1039
......, due at altar of chapel, composition over, 379
......, of corn assigned in place of or for pension, 144, 782, 793, 840, 928
......, of fruits and of sheeps' wool and lambs, litigation over, 94
......, to be erected into prebend, 167
......, reservation of, 1255
......, various, in Bangor city and diocese, constitution etc. concerning, 118
......, 394 [1]
......, disputes over *see under* Appeals; Litigation

Torture *see under* Irregularity

Towns and vills, new, public market and parish church for, 64
......, in England *see* Ash Priors; Bromley, Abbots; Hatton; Leicester; Northampton; Nottingham; Oxford; Ripley; Shrewsbury; Stamford; Willand; Windsor
......, in Ireland *see* Drogheda; Trim, Newtown
......, in Scotland *see* Balgonie; Edinburgh; Milton of Balgonie; 'Spittale'; Stirling; *and for new vill see under* Aberdeen

Translation, consistorial, of bishops and archbishops, 546, 581, 591, 626, 627, 1006, 1012, 1021, 1029, 1315, 1338; *and cf*. 617
......, of indulgences, 807

Travel:-
...., union of parish church in England to provostry in Italy for support of poor travellers crossing the Alps, 405
...., 394 [1]

Travel (*contd*)
...., *see also under* Pilgrimages; Pilgrims

Trinitarian Order, houses of, confirmation of erection of house and union of parish church thereto, 1079
......, ..., ministership of house of, litigation over, 221
......, ..., in England *see* Inghem
......, ..., in Ireland *see* Adare

U

Unions of benefices, by archbishop and bishop, permanent, confirmation of, 425
......, by ordinary authority, permanent, (of parish church in England to provostry in Italy), 405
......, ..., temporary, 357, 1000
......, ..., ..., *de facto*, 167,
......, ..., 402, 828
......, ..., simoniacal, 846
......, by papal authority, temporary, of benefices already held, 91, 154, 182, 203, 217, 270, 281, 282, 293-295, 300, 309, 375, 422, 428, 452, 473, 475, 483, 663, 664, 683-685, 702, 703, 717, 733, 736, 749, 752, 753, 797, 872, 873, 877, 908, 909, 958, 965, 1003, 1038; *cf. also* 1035
......, ..., ..., of benefices not already held, 14, 16, 67, 69-71, 75, 129, 157, 159, 162-165, 167, 226, 234, 235, 251-259, 306, 313, 357, 359, 360, 380, 402-404, 449, 485, 486, 512-514, 536, 545, 574, 576, 647, 648, 650-652, 786, 787, 815, 820-822, 824, 833, 835, 845, 846, 933-936, 939, 942, 946, 950, 982, 983, 993, 995, 998
......, ..., ..., ..., renewal of, 1000
......, permanent, (*rubricellae* of), 1079, 1214
......, temporary, (*rubricellae* of), 1048, 1057, 1070, 1075, 1081, 1091, 1092, 1119, 1120, 1122, 1139, 1150, 1151, 1169, 1184, 1193, 1206, 1229, 1230, 1249, 1263, 1286, 1287, 1305, 1313; *cf. also* 1300
......, other references to, 94, 144, 174, 188, 249, 298, 391, 442, 478, 512, 543, 552, 793, 928
......, dissolution of, by papal authority, 405;

Unions (*contd*)
cf. also 16, 1283

Universities, college of, divine services in chapel of, 343
......, faculty and licence to study civil law in, 1143
......, monks at , to observe local custom as to meat-eating, 394 [18]
......, ..., portion for, 394 [29]
......, students at *see* [de Falcutiis or Falcariis] de Cesena, Damianus; Fitzmaurice, Edmund
......, *for privileges to those attending see under* Orders; Residence
......, *cf. Studia generalia*

V

Vacancy, at apostolic see, decree of, concerning Benedictine house, 585

Validation *see under* Letters, papal, validation of

Valliscaulian Order, houses of, in Scotland *see* Ardchattan

Vespers *see under* Office, Divine

Vicarages *see* Parish churches, rectories and vicarages

Visitation, monastery not bound to show its rights and titles when undergoing, 174
......, monastery to show its letters when undergoing, 394
......, of monastery, by ordinary or the order, 394 [6]
......, of suffragan bishop's subjects, by metropolitan, 1005
......, of two hospitals of the poor, by archbishop, dispute over, 964
......, *see also* Archdeacons

Vows, monastic, 394 (in particular [15], [25])
......, unfulfilled, absolution for, 374

W

War, income of hospital diminished by, 416

Women, as threat to observance of vow of
    chastity, 394 [15]
......, *see under* Marriage; Nuns; Purification
    of; *and for involvement in disputes see
    under* Litigation

Wool, sheeps' *see under* Tithes

The Irish Manuscripts Commission has limited stocks of earlier volumes in this series :-

Papal Letters :

Vol. I (1893)	1198 - 1304
Vol. II (1895)	1305 - 1342
Vol. III (1897)	1342 - 1362
Vol. IV (1902)	1362 - 1404
Vol. V (1904)	1396 - 1404
Vol. VI (1904)	1404 - 1415
Vol. VII (1906)	1417 - 1431
Vol. VIII (1909)	1427 - 1447
Vol. IX (1912)	1431 - 1447
Vol. X (1915)	1447 - 1455
Vol XI (1921)	1455 - 1464
Vol. XII (1933)	1458 - 1471
Vol. XIII, part I (1955)	1471 - 1484
Vol. XIII, part II (1955)	1471 - 1484
Vol. XIV (1960)	1484 - 1492
Vol. XV (1978)	1484 - 1492
Vol. XVI (1986)	1492 - 1498
Vol. XVIII (1989)	1503 - 1513

Petitions to the Pope :

Vol I (1896)	1342 - 1419

Note. (1) The volume of *Petitions to the Pope* is an essential companion to volumes III and IV of *Papal Letters* which refer repeatedly to it. (2) The date in parentheses is that on the title page. Though proximate, it is not always that of publication.

A price list is obtainable from :
The Secretary,
Irish Manuscripts Commission,
73 Merrion Square,
Dublin 2,
Republic of Ireland.